IMPORTANT:

HERE IS YOUR REGISTRATION CODE TO ACCESS
YOUR PREMIUM McGRAW-HILL ONLINE RESOURCES.

D0149026

For key premium online resources you need THIS CODE to gain access. Once the code is entered, you will be able to use the Web resources for the length of your course.

If your course is using **WebCT** or **Blackboard**, you'll be able to use this code to access the McGraw-Hill content within your instructor's online course.

Access is provided if you have purchased a new book. If the registration code is missing from this book, the registration screen on our Website, and within your WebCT or Blackboard course, will tell you how to obtain your new code.

Registering for McGraw-Hill Online Resources

TO gain access to your MCGraw-Hill web resources simply follow the steps below:

1. USE YOUR WEB BROWSER TO GO TO: **http://www.mhhe.com/santrockep2**

2. CLICK ON **FIRST TIME USER**.

3. ENTER THE REGISTRATION CODE* PRINTED ON THE TEAR-OFF BOOKMARK ON THE RIGHT.

4. AFTER YOU HAVE ENTERED YOUR REGISTRATION CODE, CLICK **REGISTER**.

5. FOLLOW THE INSTRUCTIONS TO SET-UP YOUR PERSONAL UserID AND PASSWORD.

6. WRITE YOUR UserID AND PASSWORD DOWN FOR FUTURE REFERENCE. KEEP IT IN A SAFE PLACE.

TO GAIN ACCESS to the McGraw-Hill content in your instructor's **WebCT** or **Blackboard** course simply log in to the course with the UserID and Password provided by your instructor. Enter the registration code exactly as it appears in the box to the right when prompted by the system. You will only need to use the code the first time you click on McGraw-Hill content.

Thank you, and welcome to your MCGraw-Hill online Resources!

0-07-297674-8 T/A SANTROCK, PSYCHOLOGY: ESSENTIALS UPDATED 2/E

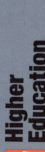

REGISTRATION CODE

6RKJ-YVY0-6FB3-4ULS-HEL1

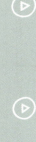

Psychology: Essentials

UPDATED SECOND EDITION

John W. Santrock

University of Texas at Dallas

Boston   Burr Ridge, IL   Dubuque, IA   Madison, WI   New York   San Francisco   St. Louis
Bangkok   Bogotá   Caracas   Kuala Lumpur   Lisbon   London   Madrid   Mexico City
Milan   Montreal   New Delhi   Santiago   Seoul   Singapore   Sydney   Taipei   Toronto

Higher Education

PSYCHOLOGY: ESSENTIALS, UPDATED SECOND EDITION

Published by McGraw-Hill, a business unit of The McGraw-Hill Companies, Inc., 1221 Avenue of the Americas, New York, NY 10020. Copyright © 2005 by The McGraw-Hill Companies, Inc. All rights reserved. Previous edition(s) 2003, 2000. All rights reserved. No part of this publication may be reproduced or distributed in any form or by any means, or stored in a database or retrieval system, without the prior written consent of The McGraw-Hill Companies, Inc., including, but not limited to, in any network or other electronic storage or transmission, or broadcast for distance learning.

Some ancillaries, including electronic and print components, may not be available to customers outside the United States.

This book is printed on recycled, acid-free paper containing 10% postconsumer waste.

1 2 3 4 5 6 7 8 9 0 VNH/VNH 0 9 8 7 6 5 4

ISBN 0-07-293762-9

Vice president and editor-in-chief: *Thalia Dorwick*
Publisher: *Stephen D. Rutter*
Senior developmental editor: *Judith Kromm*
Developmental editor: *Sienne Patch*
Marketing manager: *Melissa Caughlin*
Project manager: *Richard H. Hecker*
Production supervisor: *Carol Bielski*
Senior media technology producer: *Sean Crowley*
Designer: *Preston Thomas*
Illustrators: *John & Judy Waller and EPS, Inc.*
Cover image: *© Moonrunner Design*
Manager, Art: *Robin Mouat*
Photo research coordinator: *Alexandra Ambrose*
Lead supplement producer: *Marc Mattson*
Compositor: *The GTS Companies*
Typeface: *9.5/12 Meridian Roman*
Printer: *Von Hoffmann Press*

The credits section for this book begins on page C-1and is considered an extension of the copyright page.

Library of Congress Cataloging-in-Publication Data

Santrock, John W.
    Psychology: Essentials / John W. Santrock.—Updated 2nd ed.
     p. cm.
    Includes bibliographical references and index.
    ISBN 0-07-293762-9
    1. Psychology—Textbooks. I. Title.
    BF121.S2642 2005
    150—dc22

                                 2003070616

The Internet addresses listed in the text were accurate at the time of publication. The inclusion of a website does not indicate an endorsement by the authors or McGraw-Hill, and McGraw-Hill does not guarantee the accuracy of the information presented at these sites.

www.mhhe.com

Find Balance!

Balance scientific research with real-world applications.

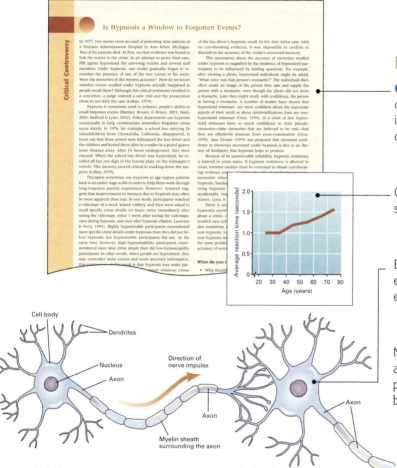

Is Hypnosis a Window to Forgotten Events?

Research

Critical Controversy boxes in each chapter highlight current debates in psychology and pose thought-provoking questions to encourage students to examine the evidence on both sides of an issue.

Clearly labeled graphs and explanatory captions help students become familiar with visual data presentation.

Expanded and updated coverage of neuroscience and evolutionary psychology reflects psychology's increasing emphasis on the biological bases of behavior.

New coverage of gender and cross-cultural research, as well as positive psychology and evolutionary psychology, is indexed inside the back cover of the book.

Cell body

Dendrites

Nucleus

Axon

Direction of nerve impulse

Axon

Axon

Myelin sheath surrounding the axon

Sending Neuron

Receiving Neuron

Applications

Are You Depressed?

In each chapter of the text, a **Psychology and Life** feature invites students to apply what they've learned to daily life.

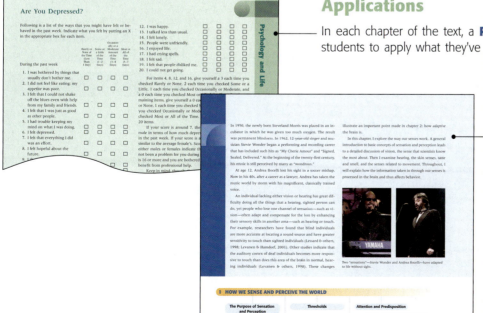

Introductory vignettes relate to each chapter's application of psychology with real-life examples.

I HOW WE SENSE AND PERCEIVE THE WORLD

| The Purpose of Sensation and Perception | Thresholds | Attention and Predisposition |

Sensory Receptors

Stay Focused and Learn!

Students need help finding the key ideas in introductory psychology. Santrock's unique **learning system** keeps students **focused** on these ideas so they learn and remember fundamental psychological concepts.

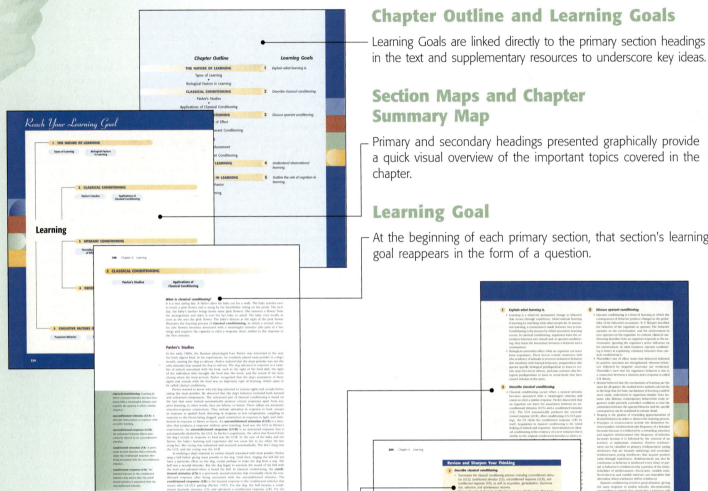

Chapter Outline and Learning Goals

Learning Goals are linked directly to the primary section headings in the text and supplementary resources to underscore key ideas.

Section Maps and Chapter Summary Map

Primary and secondary headings presented graphically provide a quick visual overview of the important topics covered in the chapter.

Learning Goal

At the beginning of each primary section, that section's learning goal reappears in the form of a question.

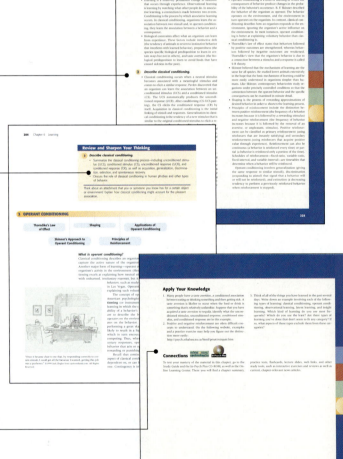

Reach Your Learning Goals

The chapter summary restates the Learning Goals and provides a bulleted review that matches up in a one-to-one fashion with the bulleted review statements in the section reviews.

Review and Sharpen Your Thinking

Learning Goals frame the section reviews, which end with an exercise designed to hone critical thinking skills.

Connections

References to review quizzes, crossword puzzles, and additional resources remind students of the text-specific materials available for content review and enrichment.

Make Connections and Succeed!

Supplementary print and media resources include a variety of review and assessment tools that carry through the text's emphasis on key ideas, reinforcing learning and enhancing student **success.**

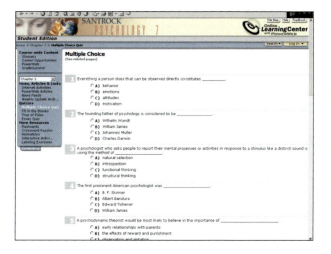

Online Learning Center

www.mhhe.com/santrockep2u

Student Resources Chapter outlines and practice quizzes are keyed to the text Learning Goals. The student section of the website also contains flashcards, interactive review exercises, and access, via **PowerWeb,** to current news about psychology, research tools, and many other valuable study tools.

Instructor Resources Teaching resources on this password-protected site include the Instructor's Course Planner, Image Bank, PowerPoint files, and Web links to additional resources.

Student Study Guide

A guided review of the chapter is organized by text section and Learning Goals, as are the three practice tests provided for each chapter. As in the text, **Connections** direct students to other text-correlated resources for additional help in mastering key ideas and concepts.

Instructor's Course Planner

The same Learning Goals that reinforce the key ideas in the text and Study Guide frame the teaching suggestions in this valuable manual. Chapter overviews, lecture/discussion suggestions, and goal reinforcement activities are a few of the resources provided in the Instructor's Course Planner.

New! In-Psych Plus CD-ROM

In-Psych Plus features video clips and interactivities that are referenced within the main text. The video clips, chosen for interest and relevance, expand on significant concepts and theories discussed in the text and are accompanied by summaries and quizzes. The CD-ROMs also include practice self-tests with feedback and a learning styles assessment, as well as other valuable features.

Chapter 1—What Is Psychology?

Learning Goals

1. Explain what psychology is and how it developed.
2. Describe six contemporary approaches to psychology.
3. Describe two movements that reflect a positive approach to psychology.
4. Evaluate careers and areas of specialization in psychology.
5. Apply some strategies that will help you succeed in psychology.

The Big Picture: Chapter Overview

Psychology is a science dedicated to the study of behavior and mental processes. In this chapter you are introduced to the history of this science, a variety of contemporary perspectives in psychology, the positive psychology movement, and an overview of psychology-related careers. At the end of the chapter, the reader learns about the most effective methods of studying and learning.

There are three concepts important to the definition of psychology: science, behavior and mental processes. Psychologists use scientific methods to observe, describe, predict, and explain behaviors and mental processes. Behaviors are actions that can be directly observed, while mental processes are experiences that cannot be observed directly, such as thoughts and feelings.

The history of psychology is rooted in philosophy, biology, and physiology. Rene Descartes and Charles Darwin strongly influenced the origins of psychology. Descartes contributed with his view of a separate mind and body, thus opening the door for studies focusing exclusively on the mind. Darwin proposed that humans are part of an evolutionary process he termed *natural selection*. This view led psychologists to consider the role of the environment and adaptation in psychology.

In 1879, Wilhelm Wundt developed the first psychology laboratory. Wundt's approach, which emphasized the importance of conscious thought and classification of the mind's structures, was called *structuralism*. While structuralism focused inside the mind, William James emphasized the functions of the mind in adapting to the environment. James's approach was called *functionalism*.

Structuralism and functionalism were the first two schools of thought in psychology; however,

Chapter One: What Is Psychology?
- **Chapter Overview**
- **Teaching Objectives**
- **Teaching the Chapter**
  - Lecture Outlines by Section
  - Lecture/Discussion Suggestions by Section
  - **Explorations in Psychology**
  - Critical Thinking Questions
  - **Thinking About Psychology in Everyday Life**
  - **Goal Reinforcement Activities**
  - **Activity Handouts**
- **Resources for Psychology and Life**
  - Suggested Articles from Annual Editions
  - Suggested Articles from Sources: Notable Selections in Psychology
  - Film Suggestions
  - Suggestions for Additional Reading
  - Organizations
  - **Connections**

Chapter Overview

Study: Tiger Woods: By opening the chapter with this feature, Santrock illustrates one of hology's most important constructs: The psychology of any human being is a complex system of ghts and behaviors constructed from and influenced by multiple determinants. Because multiple erminants require multiple approaches, psychology studies the complexity of human nature from a ultitude of perspectives—each designed to address very different aspects of what makes us human. The Tiger Woods theme is revisited for each psychological approach.

Defining Psychology: Psychology is defined as the science seeks to observe, describe

Brief Contents

Contents

Preface

Since I started teaching introductory psychology in 1967, my motivation and love for introducing students to this relevant science have not wavered. This commitment to relevance and to science has been not only a foundation of my teaching but also the heart of this book. This second edition of *Psychology: Essentials* still uses the theme of psychology as a relevant science and, in line with current trends in the discipline, has increased the emphasis on the biological aspects of psychology and on the positive changes psychology can help us achieve in our lives. These themes, together with a stronger focus on the key ideas in psychology, are the main features of this update of **Psychology: Essentials.**

New! Media Integration

References to video clips and interactivities, all drawn from various McGraw-Hill media resources and chosen for their interest and relevancy to the main content, appear within the main text. The *In-Psych Plus* CD-ROM marginal icon provides an additional, visual reference to the media. Each video and interactivity that is mentioned in the text appears on the *In-Psych Plus* CD-ROM, which is packaged free with the text. In addition, pedagogy, activities, test questions, and other features have been created to complement these video clips and reinforce students' grasp of the key concepts they illustrate. These materials are found on the *In-Psych Plus* CD-ROM, in the *Study Guide*, in the *Instructor's Course Planner*, and in the *Test Item Files*.

Psychology: The Relevant Science

Many students go into an introductory psychology class asking why they should study psychology when their major is physics, computer science, or French. To a psychologist, the answer is obvious: It will help you to understand yourself and others better. Psychology is relevant to almost every aspect of daily life. What psychologists have learned from memory research, for example, can be used to study more effectively, no matter what the subject is. Principles of learning can be applied to change undesirable behavior in children. Knowledge of sensation and perception can be used to design computers more effectively. Psychology teaches us about the roots of aggression and the influence of groups on individual behavior, highly relevant topics in light of recent terrorist activities. Research on stress, coping, and health can help people to live fuller, happier lives, regardless of their circumstances.

In addition to relevance, this edition continues to stress the scientific nature of the discipline. A hallmark of the book has always been its focus on research, the foundation of all sciences. Here the latest research findings are discussed, along with the classic studies that established psychology as an objective science. There are more than 900 citations from the twenty-first century, including many from 2002 through 2004. Also, numerous new graphs show students how scientific data can be presented visually.

To make the second edition an up-to-date reflection of the discipline of psychology, I have interwoven a couple of new themes into the chapters:

- **Biological influences on behavior.** Psychologists are increasingly relying on neuroscience and genetics research to understand the effects of biology on behavior. Evolutionary psychology, which examines the survival value of human behaviors, is another area of increasing interest. Knowing that students often have difficulty understanding why it is important to learn biology in a course on psychology, I've taken particular care to present these topics in a psychological context and to underscore the complex relationship among biology, environment, and behavior wherever appropriate. Neuroscientist Lawrence Cauller provided outstanding guidance for incorporating stronger biological neuroscience in this edition.
- **Positive psychology.** Currently, there is a movement in psychology to focus attention on the positive contributions psychology can make to everyday life. Proponents of positive psychology, notably Mihaly Csikszentmihalyi, share the belief that, for much of the twentieth century, psychology concentrated on the negative aspects of life and that it's time to emphasize the positive aspects. Positive psychology offers us the opportunity to take control of and find balance in our lives. With Csikszentmihalyi's expert guidance, I have incorporated material on positive psychology throughout the book.

Focus on Key Ideas

Mastering the core content of the introductory psychology course is a significant challenge. Students today are often overwhelmed by information from lectures, textbooks, the

Internet, and other media and have more trouble than ever finding the main ideas in their courses. To address these challenges and help students achieve the best possible outcome, I have developed a learning system for this edition that emphasizes basic concepts and ideas, encourages review, and promotes critical thinking. This system frames the presentation in the textbook and the supplements, providing a truly integrated package that facilitates and reinforces learning.

The learning system has several components, all centered on three to six key ideas per chapter. These ideas are encapsulated in learning goals, which correspond with the chapter's main headings, as shown at the opening of each chapter. The learning goals reappear at several places in the chapter: as a question at the beginning of the main section, in a guided review at the end of the section (titled Review and Sharpen Your Thinking), and again in a summary at the end of the chapter. Each main section also begins with a content map of the section and subsection headings. A complete chapter map at the end of the chapter shows how all the sections work together to illuminate the topic. Thus the content maps provide a visual guide to the core concepts that support the learning goals.

To encourage application of the core concepts and increase the likelihood that they will be remembered, the learning system includes critical thinking questions keyed to the learning goals in the Review and Sharpen Your Thinking sections. Additionally, What do you think? exercises accompany the Critical Controversy boxes, and three or more critical thinking exercises follow the review section at the end of each chapter in the Apply Your Knowledge section. For students who have access to the Web, the end-of-chapter exercises include at least one Web-based activity.

To help students make the best use of the student supplements, an additional reminder appears in the Connections section at the very end of each chapter. Repeating the learning goals and maps in the student supplements reinforces the lessons from the book and eliminates the confusion many students have about how to use the supplements to boost performance in a course.

Changes in Coverage

In addition to increased emphasis on neuroscience, evolutionary psychology, and positive psychology, the second edition of this book contains increased coverage of human diversity and controversies in psychology. This material is presented where appropriate throughout the book.

The second edition of *Psychology: Essentials* has much the same table of contents and chapter sequence as the first edition, with two major exceptions. First, the chapter on human development now falls closer to the beginning of the book (chapter 3). Second, a chapter on health and well-being has been added (chapter 13).

The substance and presentation in each chapter have been thoroughly revised. Some of the detail that is less relevant today than it once was has been pruned to make room for cutting-edge research, and some of the presentation was reconceptualized to focus on the key ideas reflected in the learning goals. Although there isn't enough space here to list all of the changes in this edition, here are the highlights:

CHAPTER 1 The Science of Psychology

- New discussion of attitudes central to the scientific approach
- Reorganized section on research methods, focusing on descriptive, correlational, and experimental research and including new coverage of positive and negative correlations and their interpretation
- Expanded, updated coverage of the evolutionary psychology approach and a new section on positive approaches to psychology, including the humanistic movement and the positive psychology movement
- New section on how to get the most out of psychology, focusing on study habits and skills

CHAPTER 2 The Brain and Behavior

- New opening discussion of the characteristics of the nervous system, focusing on complexity, integration, adaptability, and electrochemical transmission
- Revised presentation of neuron structure and function, including new material on neurotransmitters and neural networks
- Updated coverage of functioning in the left and right hemispheres of the brain and many new drawings of the brain
- Separate section on the endocrine system
- New section on genetics and evolution

CHAPTER 3 Human Development

- Added coverage on the brain and how it changes from infancy to adulthood
- Revised discussion of socioemotional development in childhood, including the effects of parenting style and gender development
- New sections on positive psychology and development in childhood, adolescence, and adulthood
- Expanded discussion of biological aspects of aging, including updated information on Alzheimer's disease
- Updated coverage of cognitive changes and aging, including new figures on age-related changes in intellectual abilities and reaction time
- Discussion of research on what makes a successful marriage and research on emotion, social networks, and aging

CHAPTER 4 Sensation and Perception

- Completely revised discussion of how we sense and perceive the world
- New coverage on parallel processing in the visual cortex
- New information on sound localization in the discussion of the auditory system
- Expanded coverage of pain, including new discussions of the "fast" and "slow" pain pathways and pain control and treatment

CHAPTER 5 States of Consciousness

- Neuroscience coverage incorporated in sections on consciousness, stages of sleep, dreams, and psychoactive drugs
- Greater coverage of circadian rhythms
- New coverage of the role of sleep in the storage and maintenance of long-term memory
- Addition of recent research on sleep deprivation in adolescents and older adults
- Inclusion of new research on dream content across cultures
- Most recent data on trends in adolescent drug use

CHAPTER 6 Learning

- Expanded and clarified discussion of classical conditioning, including the role of classical conditioning in health problems and applications to consumer psychology
- Easier-to-understand examples of positive and negative reinforcement
- Improved comparison of punishment and negative reinforcement
- Expanded discussion of applications of operant conditioning, including the use of shaping and behavior modification in the classroom

CHAPTER 7 Memory

- Revised coverage of memory encoding, including the effects of divided attention
- Revised coverage of memory storage with a new section on connectionist networks
- Revised discussion of forgetting, including the forgetting curve, decay and transience, and motivated forgetting
- Complete reorganization of memory and study strategy section to correspond to the organization of the preceding discussion of memory

CHAPTER 8 Thinking, Language, and Intelligence

- Earlier discussion of the link between cognition and language
- Revised section on language acquisition and development, including material on the effects of maternal speech on vocabulary development in infants and a new figure showing language milestones
- Added sections on theories of multiple intelligences and emotional intelligence
- New section on the influence of heredity and environment on intelligence, including gender and cultural comparisons

CHAPTER 9 Motivation and Emotion

- Improved section on motivation theory, including additional information on the evolutionary approach to motivation, arousal and sensation seeking, and intrinsic and extrinsic motivation
- Expanded and updated discussion of blood chemistry and obesity, neurotransmitters and hunger, obesity in the U.S., and anorexia nervosa and bulimia nervosa
- New discussion of the importance of self-generated goals in achievement, along with a cross-cultural comparison of math achievement in the United States, Japan, and Taiwan
- New discussion of the roles of neural circuits and neurotransmitters, including the links between emotion and the brain's hemispheres
- New focus on positive emotions and how they might enhance people's well-being

CHAPTER 10 Personality

- Revision of social cognitive theory section to include discussions of personal control, perceptions of control, and optimism
- Expansion of section on personality assessment to include assessment of the big five factors and locus of control

CHAPTER 11 Psychological Disorders

- Greater coverage of the multiaxial system in *DSM-IV*, including a new figure on the major categories of psychological disorders, organized according to Axis I and Axis II
- Introduction of the concept of etiology, new discussion of the etiology of anxiety disorders, and expanded discussion of post-traumatic stress disorder
- Updated discussion of mood disorders, including new coverage on neurobiological abnormalities and new material on the depressive realism view of depression
- New section on suicide, including comparison of suicide rates across cultures
- Expanded discussion of schizophrenia, including recent information about heredity and neurobiological factors

CHAPTER 12 Therapies

- Substantial reorganization to place biological therapies at the beginning of the chapter
- Updated discussion on the effects of drug therapies, including Prozac and Risperdal
- New sections on cognitive-behavior therapy and the use of cognitive therapy to treat psychological disorders
- New section on sociocultural approaches, including coverage of the community mental health movement
- New discussion of the relationship between the effectiveness of psychotherapy and ethnicity and gender

CHAPTER 13 Health and Well-Being

- Discussion of stress that focuses on sources—including the workplace—and physical, sociocultural, and cognitive responses
- Section on stress and illness that covers the link between positive emotions and health
- Section on coping strategies that covers problem-focused and emotion-focused coping, optimism and positive thinking, and the role of religion in helping people cope with stress
- Section on healthful living, with coverage of the effectiveness of the antidepressant Zyban, nicotine patches, and other methods in helping people to quit smoking

CHAPTER 14 Social Psychology

- Expanded discussion of the symptoms of groupthink and strategies for avoiding groupthink
- Discussion of leadership styles in women and men
- Expanded, updated discussion of prejudice, focusing on the reasons people develop prejudice
- Updated section on social interaction, including discussion of neurotransmitters and recent information on children's TV viewing habits and possible links to aggression
- Addition of recent research on gender and relationships

Print and Media Supplements

For the Student

Online Learning Center for Students The official website for *Psychology: Essentials* contains chapter outlines, practice quizzes that can be emailed to the professor, key term flashcards, interactive exercises, Internet activities, Web links to relevant psychology sites, drag-and-drop labeling exercises, Internet primer, career appendix, and a statistics primer. New and exclusive to this edition of the Online Learning Center is a collection of brief "FYI" enrichment articles about selected topics tied to each chapter at www.mhhe.com/santrockep2u.

PowerWeb This unique online tool, accessed through the Online Learning Center, provides current articles, curriculum-based materials, weekly updates with assessment, informative and timely world news, refereed Web links, research tools, study tools, and interactive exercises. A PowerWeb access card is packaged FREE with each new copy of *Psychology: Essentials.*

New! *In-Psych Plus* **Student CD-ROM** *In-Psych Plus* sets a new standard for introductory psychology multimedia. Packaged FREE with the book, *In-Psych Plus* is organized according to the textbook's chapter outlines and features video clips, audio clips, and interactivities chosen to illustrate especially difficult core concepts in introductory psychology. *In-Psych Plus* also includes a pre-test, follow-up assignments, Web resources, chapter quizzes, a student research guide, and an interactive timeline that puts events, key figures, and research in psychology in historical perspective.

GradeSummit This Internet service is a diagnostic self-assessment and exam-preparation tool designed to focus student attention on the key material and to make study time more efficient. *GradeSummit* reveals student strengths and weaknesses in comprehension and provides feedback and direction for increasing understanding. *GradeSummit* contains thousands of unique examlike questions written by professors and peer-reviewed for quality and accuracy. For more information, visit www.gradesummit.com.

Study Guide

Ruth Hallongren, Triton College

Designed to reinforce the key ideas in *Psychology: Essentials,* the *Study Guide* contains the following features for each chapter: content overview, learning objectives, guided review for each section, three practice tests, essay questions, crossword puzzle, learning goal checklist, and diagram labeling exercises.

Psych On-Line This supplement points the way to the Internet for psychology research and provides general resource locations. Psychology sites are grouped by topic with a brief explanation of each site.

For the Instructor

Instructor's Course Planner

Susan Weldon, Eastern Michigan University

This manual provides many useful tools to enhance teaching. For each chapter, the manual provides teaching objectives, chapter overviews, key terms, Teaching the Chapter, lecture/discussion suggestions, goal reinforcement classroom activities, an Experiencing Psychology boxed feature, critical thinking questions, video/media suggestions, and references and sources of bibliographical information.

Test Item Files

Test Item File I: Ron Mulson, Hudson Valley Community College

Test Item File II: Susan E. Swithers, Purdue University

Two sets of test items provide a wide variety of questions, enough to last the life of this edition. The questions in the *Test Item Files* are available in computerized format, as well as in Word and Rich Text formats, on the *Instructor's Resource CD-ROM*. With the computerized version, instructors can easily select questions and print tests and answer keys. Instructors can also customize questions, headings, and instructions; add or import their own questions; and print tests in a choice of printer-supported fonts.

PowerPoint Lectures

Available on the Internet and on the *Instructor's Resource CD-ROM*, these presentations cover the key points of the chapter and include charts and graphs from the text. Helpful lecture guidelines are provided in the Notes section for each slide. They can be used as they are or modified to meet instructional needs.

Overhead Transparencies

More than 70 key images from the text are available to the instructor upon adoption. A separate package, the *Introductory Psychology Transparency Set,* provides more than 100 additional images illustrating key concepts in general psychology.

Online Learning Center for Instructors

The password-protected instructor side of the text website contains the *Instructor's Course Planner,* a sample chapter from the textbook, PowerPoint presentations, Web links, and other teaching resources at www.mhhe.com/Santrockep2u.

PageOut™

This exclusive McGraw-Hill product allows even the most inexperienced computer user to quickly and easily create a professional-looking course website. The instructor simply fills in templates with course-specific information and with content provided by McGraw-Hill and then chooses a design. Best of all, it's FREE! www.pageout.net

Instructor's Resource CD-ROM

This comprehensive CD-ROM includes the contents of the *Instructor's Course Planner; Test Item Files* in computerized, Word, and Rich Text Versions; an image gallery; and PowerPoint slides. The Presentation Manager provides an easy-to-use interface for the design and delivery of multimedia classroom presentations.

Acknowledgments

Many people guided this update of *Psychology: Essentials*. The McGraw-Hill team of Steve DeBow, president; Thalia Dorwick, editor in chief; Stephen Rutter, publisher; Melissa Caughlin, marketing manager; Judith Kromm, director of development; and Sienne Patch, developmental editor, all played key roles and spent long hours in the planning, revision, and publication process for this update.

Reviewers for the Second Edition

Psychology: Essentials has benefited considerably from advice and analysis provided by the reviewers of the seventh edition of the comprehensive book, *Psychology,* on which this volume is based. The following individuals deserve special thanks for their in-depth input:

Tamara L. Brown, University of Kentucky
Larry Cauller, University of Texas at Dallas
Peter B. Crabb, Pennsylvania State University–Abington
Mihaly Csikszentmihalyi, Claremont Graduate University
William Fabricius, Arizona State University
Linda E. Flickinger, St. Clair County Community College
Edwin E. Gantt, Brigham Young University
Debra L. Hollister, Valencia Community College
Richard Kandus, Mt. San Jacinto College
Saera Khan, Western Washington University
Maria LeBaron, Randolph Community College
Brennis Lucero-Wagoner, California State University–Northridge
Wendy Mills, San Jacinto College North
John Mitterer, Brock University
Doug Peterson, The University of South Dakota
James S. Previte, Victor Valley College
Steven V. Rouse, Pepperdine University
John Ruys, University of California–Davis
H.R. Schiffman, Rutgers University
Susan Spencer, Eastern Oklahoma State College
Meredith Stanford-Pollack, University of Massachusetts at Lowell
Susie Swithers, Purdue University
Katharine Webb, Maria College
Fred Whitford, Montana State University

In addition, I would like to thank the following expert reviewers, who provided in-depth comments on neuroscience and cognitive psychology:

James C. Bartlett, University of Texas at Dallas
Mike Kilgard, University of Texas at Dallas

The following psychologists directly helped to make the second edition of *Psychology: Essentials* a much better book through their thoughtful reviews of the first edition:

Lisa Ansara, University of Massachusetts at Lowell
John Biondo, Community College of Allegheny County
Heather Frasier Chabot, New England College
Marcella Desrochers, College of Charleston
John Foust, Parkland College
Peggy F. Malone, St. Gregory's University
Paul J. Mullen, North Central College
Doris Van Auken, Holy Cross College

Reviewers for and contributors to both the previous edition of *Psychology: Essentials* and all seven editions of *Psychology* have also helped in ways too numerous to mention: Valerie Ahl, University of Wisconsin–Madison; Susan Amato, Boise State University; Richard Anderson, Bowling Green State University; Jim Backlund, Kirtland Community College; Stella B. Baldwin, Wake Technical Community College; James Bartlett, University of Texas at Dallas; Jackson Beatty, UCLA; Ludy Benjamin, Texas A&M; Pearl Berman, Indiana University of Pennsylvania; Joy L. Berrenberg, University of Colorado at Denver; John Best, Eastern Illinois University; Michelle Boyer-Pennington, Middle Tennessee State University; Charles Brewer, Clemson University; Richard Brislin, University of Hawaii; Frederick M. Brown, Penn State University; David Buss, University of Texas at Austin; James Calhoun, University of Georgia; Richard Cavasina, California University of Pennsylvania; George A. Cicala, University of Delaware; Lillian Comas-Diaz, Transcultural Mental Health Institute; Pamela Costa, Tacoma Commmunity College; Mihaly Csikszentmihalyi, Claremont Graduate University; Donna Dahlgren, Indiana University Southeast; Florence Denmark, Pace University; Ellen Dennehy, University of Texas at Dallas; Kim Dielmann, University of Central Arkansas; G. William Domhoff, University of California, Santa Cruz; Leta Fenell, Chesapeake College; Roseanne L. Flores, Hunter College; James Francis, San Jacinto College; Bety Jane Fratzke, Indiana Wesleyan University; Stanley Gaines, Pomona College; Robert Gallen, Indiana University of Pennsylvania; J. P. Garofalo, University of Pittsburgh; Michael Kaye Garza, Brookhaven College; Robert Gifford, University of Victoria; Roderick C. Gillis, University of Miami; Jean Berko Gleason, Boston University; James Greer, Louisiana State University; Leslie Grout, Hudson Valley Community College; Arthur Gutman, Florida Institute of Technology; Richard Halgin, University of Massachusetts–Amherst; Christine Harness, University of Wisconsin, Milwaukee; John Harvey, University of Iowa; James R. Heard, Antelope Valley College; Paul Hernandez, South Texas Community College; N. C. Higgins, University of North British Columbia; James J. Johnson, Illinois State University; James Jones, University of Delaware; Karen Jordan, University of Illinois at Chicago; Seth Kalichman, Georgia State University; Kevin Keating, Broward Community College; Saera Khan, Western Washington University; Brian Kim, University of Maryland College Park; Laura King, Southern Methodist University; Paul R. Kleinginna, Georgia Southern University; Linda Kline, California State University, Chico; Karen Kopera-Frye, University of Akron; Phil Kraemer, University of Kentucky; Eric Landrum, Boise State University; Gary D. Laver, California Polytechnic State University, San Luis Obispo; Michele K. Lewis, Northern Virginia Community College, Annandale; Marta Losonczy, Salisbury State University; Karen E. Luh, University of Wisconsin–Madison; Jerry Marshall, University of Central Florida; Diane Martichuski, University of Colorado at Boulder; Vicki Mays, University of California, Los Angeles; Wanda McCarthy, Northern Kentucky University; Glenn E. Meyer, Trinity University; Fred Miller, Oregon Health Sciences University, Portland Community College; Richard Miller, Western Kentucky University; Ann Miner, Indiana University of Pennsylvania; David Mostofsky, Boston University; Carol Nemeroff, Arizona State University; David Neufeldt, Hutchinson Community College; Illene Noppe, University of Wisconsin–Green Bay; Cindy Nordstrom, Illinois State University; Arthur G. Olguin, Santa Barbara City College; Alice O'Toole, University of Texas at Dallas; Raymond Paloutzian, Westmont College; David Penn, Louisiana State University; James Pennebaker, University of Texas at Austin; Jeffrey Pedroza, Lansing Community College; Lawrence A. Pervin, Rutgers University; Michelle Perry, University of Illinois at Urbana, Champaign; Vincent Punzo, Earlham College; Barbara Radigan, Community College of Allegheny County, Allegheny Campus; Ed Raymaker, Eastern Main Technical College; Pamela Regan, California State University, Los Angeles; Bob Riesenberg, Whatcom Community College; Daniel Schacter, Harvard University; Susan J. Shapiro, Indiana University East; Judith A. Sheiman, Kutztown University; Paula Shear, University of Cincinnati; Cynthia Sifonis, University of Illinois; Charles M. Slem, California Polytechnic State University, San Luis Obispo; Steven Smith, Texas A&M; John E. Sparrow, University of New Hampshire, Manchester; Meredith Stanford-Pollock, University of Massachusetts–Lowell; Keith E. Stanovich, University of Toronto; Barry Stein, Tennessee Technological University; Jutta M. Street, Wake Technical Community College; Susan Swithers, Purdue University; Roger M. Tarpy, Jr., Bucknell University; Christopher Taylor, University of Arizona; Jeremy Turner, University of Tennessee at Martin; David Wasieleski, Valdosta State University; Leonard Williams, Rowan University; Marek Wosinski, Arizona State University; Michael Zickar, Bowling Green State University.

The Science of Psychology

The chapter themes and corresponding learning goals listed here preview the most important ideas in the chapter. The chapter themes are the primary section titles in the outline. The learning goals will help you to review each of the main ideas, and, at the end of the chapter, they will help you to make sure you know the key points in each section. The maps at the beginning of each primary section provide a visual guide to the section themes. Use the complete chapter map at the end of the chapter as a visual guide to help you recall the material covered in the chapter.

Chapter Outline

Learning Goals

WHAT MAKES PSYCHOLOGY A SCIENCE? **1**

Questions About the Mind and Behavior
▼
The Beginnings of Psychology as a Science
▼
A Scientific Way of Thinking
▼
The Scientific Method

Explain what makes psychology a science.

TYPES OF PSYCHOLOGICAL RESEARCH **2**

Descriptive Research
▼
Correlational Research
▼
Experimental Research

Discuss the three types of research that are used in psychology.

CONTEMPORARY APPROACHES TO PSYCHOLOGY **3**

Behavioral Approach
▼
Psychodynamic Approach
▼
Cognitive Approach
▼
Behavioral Neuroscience
▼
Evolutionary Psychology
▼
Sociocultural Approach
▼
Humanistic Movement and Positive Psychology

Describe seven contemporary approaches to psychology.

HOW TO BENEFIT FROM STUDYING PSYCHOLOGY **4**

Being a Wise Consumer of Information About Psychology
▼
Developing Good Study Habits
▼
Using the Book's Learning Tools to Succeed in This Course

Explain how studying psychology will benefit you in your studies and other aspects of your life.

Who could have predicted the startling success of golfer Eldrick—better known as Tiger—Woods? In 2000, at the age of 24, Woods became the youngest person ever to win golf's four major championships: the Master's, the U.S. Open, the PGA, and the British Open.

At the age of 6 months, Tiger Woods sat in his high chair, watching his father hit golf balls into a net in the garage. At 18 months of age, he played his first hole of golf (410 yards, par four) and finished in 11 shots (8 to reach the green)! When Tiger was 2 years old, a sports announcer predicted, "This young boy is going to be to golf what Jimmy Connors and Chris Evert are to tennis" (Strege, 1997).

Tiger's triumphs raise an interesting question for psychologists: What factors enable some children to achieve greatness? Is it possible for parents, coaches, and others to shape a child's life and turn him or her into a champion? Did Tiger's parents play an important role in his development as a great golfer? The only child of doting parents, Tiger was coached and encouraged to excel. He won his first major tournament at the age of 8.

Some parents, though, try to get their children to become champions in a particular sport, using similar strategies to those of Tiger's parents, and the children end up being miserable and the parents frustrated. What other factors could be involved in Tiger's success as a golf champion beyond supportive parenting and excellent coaching? Might Tiger have a special mix of genes and athletic skills that most others don't have?

In this chapter, we explore ways of answering questions like these. In the process, you will discover why psychological science is a trustworthy method for seeking answers to questions about the human mind and behavior. First, we survey the scientific roots of psychology and the different research methods available for studying human behavior. Second, we explore the variety of approaches that psychologists use to understand human beings. And, third, we discuss some ways to think critically, both in class and in everyday life, that will help you understand psychology more clearly, and some study strategies that will benefit you throughout your college career.

Tiger Woods, one of the world's leading golfers. Psychology helps us understand what makes him so successful.

1 WHAT MAKES PSYCHOLOGY A SCIENCE?

Questions About the Mind and Behavior

A Scientific Way of Thinking

The Scientific Method

The Beginnings of Psychology as a Science

What makes psychology a science?

Imagine that you are seated at a dinner table next to someone who says she is a psychologist. Many people would say that she analyzes people's problems. When my wife is asked what her husband does for a living, she commonly hears another question: "Does he psychoanalyze you all of the time?" When people find out I am a psychologist, I can see by their reaction that they are thinking, "Uh, oh, I'd better be on my guard or he will find out what I am really like."

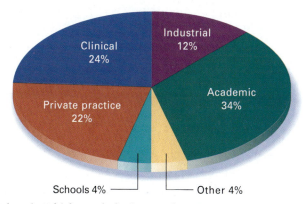

FIGURE 1.1 Settings in Which Psychologists Work More psychologists work in academic settings (34%), such as colleges and universities, than any other. However, clinical (24%) and private practice (22%) settings, in which many psychologists in the mental health professions work, combined make up almost half of the total.

Many psychologists do analyze people's problems and try to help them cope more effectively. However, many psychologists are researchers, not therapists (see figure 1.1). No single image captures psychologists' varied activities. Consider the following descriptions of some contemporary psychologists at work:

- A research psychologist trained in cognitive psychology painstakingly constructs the thousands of steps in a computer program that, presented with hundreds of sentences, will learn language as an infant does.
- Another research psychologist trained in physiological psychology and neuroscience injects epinephrine into a rat that has learned a maze to determine how the hormone affects the rat's memory.
- A clinical psychologist probes a depressed client's thoughts for clues about the cause of the depression and thinks about ways to help the client become psychologically healthier.
- A psychologist interested in gender and women's issues teaches at a community college and works with her college and the community to eliminate sexual harassment.
- An organizational psychologist has a consulting firm that advises corporations on ways to improve communication and work productivity.
- A sport psychologist works closely with an Olympic track team to improve members' perfomance and their ability to take challenges and disappointments in stride.
- A researcher works at Educational Testing Service to ferret out possible cultural bias in psychological tests.
- A forensic psychologist is a trial consultant who prepares witnesses to testify and teaches attorneys how to present themselves to jurors.

PEANUTS reprinted by permission of United Feature Syndicate, Inc.

Is Psychology in Your Future?

Instructions

Students who are successful as psychology majors tend to have a certain profile. Answer true or false to each item below to see how well you fit the profile.

	True	*False*
1. I often think about what makes people do what they do.	____	____
2. I like reading about new findings that scientists have discovered doing behavioral research.	____	____
3. I am often skeptical when someone tries to persuade me about behavioral claims, unless there is evidence to back up the claim.	____	____
4. I like the prospect of measuring behavior and doing statistics to determine meaningful differences.	____	____
5. I can usually come up with multiple explanations to account for behavior.	____	____
6. I think I could come up with ideas to research to help explain behaviors I am curious about.	____	____
7. I am often approached by others who want me to listen to their problems and share my ideas about what to do.	____	____
8. I don't get especially frustrated if I can't get answers to my questions.	____	____
9. I am usually careful with details.	____	____
10. I enjoy writing and speaking about things I am learning.	____	____
11. I like to solve puzzles.	____	____
12. I feel comfortable that psychology can provide me with an education that will lead to a good job.	____	____

Scoring and Interpretation

If you answered true to a majority of the items, psychology is a major that likely matches up well with your interests. Although the items are not a perfect predictor of whether you will enjoy majoring in and pursuing a career in psychology, they can give you an indication of whether you might benefit from finding out more about what psychologists do and what is involved in becoming a psychologist. Your psychology professor or a career counselor at your college likely can inform you about the best way to pursue a career in psychology.

These are but a few of the many different portraits of psychologists. As you read further, you will become even more aware that psychology is a diverse field and that psychologists have wide-ranging interests.

To reflect on whether a career in psychology might be in your future, see the Psychology and Life box.

Questions About the Mind and Behavior

Psychology may strike you as being simple common sense, but researchers often turn up the unexpected in human behavior. For example, it may seem obvious that couples who live together (cohabit) before marriage have a better chance of making the marriage last. After all, practice makes perfect, doesn't it? But researchers have actually found a higher rate of success for couples who marry before living together (National Center for Health Statistics, 2002). It also might seem obvious that we would experience more stress and be less happy if we had to function in many different roles than if we functioned in only one role. However, women who engage in multiple roles (such as wife, mother, and career woman) report more satisfaction with their lives than women who engage in a single role or fewer roles (such as wife or wife and mother) (Watkins & Subich, 1995). As you can see, psychology doesn't accept assumptions at face value, however reasonable they sound. Psychology is a rigorous discipline that tests assumptions (Stangor, 2004).

Formally defined, **psychology** is the scientific study of behavior and mental processes. There are three key terms in this definition: *science, behavior,* and *mental processes.* To understand what psychology is, you need to know what each of these terms means.

As a **science,** psychology uses systematic methods to observe, describe, predict, and explain human behavior and mental processes. Scientific methods are not casual. Researchers carefully and precisely plan and conduct their studies and try to *observe* the results without influencing them in any way. In psychology, it is also desirable to obtain results that *describe* the behavior of many different people. For example, researchers might construct a questionnaire on sexual attitudes and give it to 500 individuals. They might spend considerable time devising the questions and determining the backgrounds of the people chosen to participate in the survey. The researchers may try to *predict* the sexual activity of college students based on their liberal or conservative attitudes or on their sexual knowledge, for example. After the psychologists have analyzed their data, they also will want to *explain* why any change in behavior occurred. They might ask, "Is the reason an increased fear of sexually transmitted diseases?" Because psychologists use the same research methods as physicists, biologists, and other scientists, psychology is a *scientific* discipline.

Let's now examine what behavior and mental processes are. **Behavior** is everything we do that can be directly observed—two people kissing, a baby crying, a college student riding a motorcycle.

Mental processes are trickier to define than behavior; they are the thoughts, feelings, and motives that each of us experiences privately but that cannot be observed directly. Though we cannot directly see thoughts and feelings, they are nonetheless real. They include *thinking* about kissing someone, a baby's *feelings* when its mother leaves the room, and a college student's *memory* of the motorcycle ride.

The Beginnings of Psychology as a Science

Psychology seeks to answer questions that people have been asking for thousands of years:

How do our senses perceive the world?
What is the connection between thinking and behavior?
How do we learn? What is memory?
Are we in conscious control of our lives, or is behavior determined by unconscious forces?
Why does one person grow and flourish, whereas another person struggles in life?
What makes some people smarter than others?
Do dreams matter?
Why do some children so strongly resemble their parents in how they think and act? How do some children turn out so differently?
Can people learn to be happier and more optimistic?

From the time human language included the word *why* and became rich enough to let people talk about the past, we have been creating myths to explain why things are the way they are. Ancient myths attributed most important events to the pleasure or displeasure of the gods: When a volcano erupted, the gods were angry; if two people fell in love, they had been hit by Cupid's arrows. Gradually, myths gave way to philosophy, the rational investigation of the underlying principles of being and knowledge. People attempted to explain events in terms of natural rather than supernatural causes (Viney & King, 2003). Psychology grew out of the philosophical tradition of thinking about the mind and body.

psychology The scientific study of behavior and mental processes.

science In psychology, the use of systematic methods to observe, describe, predict, and explain behavior.

behavior Everything we do that can be directly observed.

mental processes Thoughts, feelings, and motives experienced privately and that cannot be observed directly.

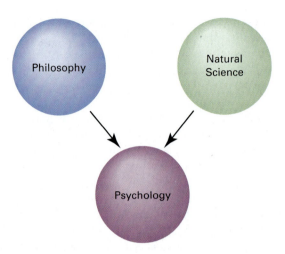

FIGURE 1.2 Psychology's Beginnings Psychology's seeds were sown in the nineteenth century by merging ideas from philosophy and from natural sciences, such as biology and physiology.

Philosophy was not the only discipline from which psychology emerged. Psychology also has roots in the natural sciences of biology and physiology (Benjamin, 1999). The intellectual atmosphere when psychology emerged as a science in the late nineteenth century was dominated by the work of the British naturalist Charles Darwin (1809–1882). In 1859, Darwin published his ideas in *On the Origin of Species*. He proposed the principle of **natural selection,** an evolutionary process that favors organisms' traits or characteristics that are best adapted to reproduce and survive. Nineteenth-century physiologists also gave the new field of psychology a boost. The German physiologist Johannes Müller (1801–1858) and others proposed that an important role of the brain is to associate incoming sensory information with appropriate motor responses.

Thus, by the late nineteenth century, conditions were ripe for psychology to emerge as a scientific discipline, a hybrid offspring of philosophy and natural science (see figure 1.2). Indeed, it was a philosopher-physician who put the pieces of the philosophy–natural science puzzle together to create the academic discipline of psychology.

Some historians like to say that modern psychology was born in December 1879 at the University of Leipzig, when German physiologist Wilhelm Wundt (1832–1920) and two young students performed an experiment to measure the time lag between the instant at which a person heard a sound and the instant at which that person actually pressed a telegraph key to signal that he had heard. At the heart of this experiment was the idea that mental processes had a particular structure and could be studied quantitatively—that is, that mental processes could be measured. This focus ushered in the new science of psychology.

Meanwhile, the American William James (1842–1910) and another group of psychologists were studying the functions of mind and behavior in adapting to the environment. In a way, Wundt and his adherents were looking *inside* the mind, searching for its structures, whereas James and his adherents were looking at what was going on in the person's interaction with the *outside* world. James saw the mind as flexible and fluid, characterized by constant change and adaptation in response to a flow of information.

A Scientific Way of Thinking

natural selection An evolutionary process that favors organisms' traits or characteristics that are best adapted to reproduce and survive.

Although psychologists have different interests and different ways of looking at their discipline, they all use a scientific approach. Science is not defined by *what* it investigates but by *how* it investigates. Central to the scientific approach are four attitudes: curiosity, skepticism, objectivity, and a willingness to think critically.

- *Being curious.* Mary Whiton Calkins (1863–1930), the first woman president of the American Psychological Association, was enormously curious, with broad-ranging interests. Curiosity leads to asking questions. Among the questions Calkins asked were "Do people remember numbers better when they are paired with vivid colors than with more neutral colors?" and "What is the most accurate description of the self?"
- *Being skeptical.* Skeptical people question things that other people take for granted. They wonder whether a supposed fact is really true. Calkins and other female psychologists began to doubt that information collected by males from male participants would be the same as information collected by females from female participants. Skeptical people ask what evidence there is for an idea and question whether the evidence is really strong enough to be accepted as accurate and factual.
- *Being objective.* Scientists believe that one of the best ways to be objective is to conduct research studies (Pittenger, 2003). For example, Mary Calkins (1896) conducted an experiment and found that people did, indeed, remember numbers better when they were associated with vivid colors. She also discovered in her study that the most important determinant of remembering numbers was not the association but simply how frequently the participants were exposed to the number/color pairs. It is sometimes said that experience is the most important teacher. We do generalize from what we observe and frequently turn memorable encounters into lifetime "truths." But how valid are these conclusions? As individuals, we often misinterpret what we see and hear. Our personal judgments are often based on a need to protect our egos and self-esteem (McMillan, 2000; McMillan & Wergin, 2002). Being objective means trying to see things as they really are, not just as we would like them to be. It means using methods of decision making that keep us in touch with the real world.
- *Thinking critically.* Critical thinkers question what some people say are "facts." They test the "facts." They examine research to see how sound its support of an idea really is.

MARY WHITON CALKINS (1863–1930). *What important role did she play in the early history of psychology?*

These four attitudes are all ideals. No scientist possesses them all at every moment in life. But the closer we embrace these attitudes, the better we are able to use the basic tools of scientific theory and objective observation. They reduce the likelihood that information will be based on unreliable personal beliefs, opinions, and emotions. As you go through this book, practice using these scientific attitudes. You also would do well to call on these attitudes whenever you hear people discussing "facts" and arguing about issues.

The Scientific Method

One of the hallmarks of taking a scientific approach involves adopting the scientific method in studying topics in psychology (Langston, 2002; Salkind, 2003; Stanovich, 2004). The scientific method is essentially a four-step process:

1. Conceptualize a problem.
2. Collect research information (data).
3. Analyze data.
4. Draw conclusions.

Two key concepts in the scientific approach, especially in conceptualizing a problem are theory and hypothesis. A **theory** is a broad idea or set of closely related ideas that attempts to explain certain observations. Theories try to explain why certain things have happened. They can also be used to make predictions about future observations. If your friend's new car stops dead in the street, you might have a theory to explain why it happened. Your theory probably includes the idea that there is an engine somewhere inside the car that is supposed to make it go. Your theory might also include the ideas that engines run on gasoline and that other parts of the car, such as the brakes, are designed to prevent the car from moving. This theory gives you a

theory A broad idea or set of closely related ideas that attempts to explain certain observations. Theories try to explain why certain things have happened. Thus they also can be used to make predictions about future observations.

framework for trying to figure out why your friend's car isn't running and what you can do to make it run in the future.

In psychology, theories serve a similar purpose. They help to organize and connect observations and research. The overall meaning of the large numbers of research studies that are always being conducted in psychology would be difficult to grasp if theories did not provide a structure for summarizing and understanding them and putting them in a context with other research studies. In addition, good, testable theories generate interesting research questions and allow researchers to make observations that might answer those questions.

The second key idea underlying the scientific method is central to the process of testing a theory. A **hypothesis** is an idea that is arrived at logically from a theory. It is a prediction that can be tested. For example, if your theory about the car includes the idea of gasoline, you can test the hypothesis that a lack of gasoline caused the car to stop. You would simply add gas to the tank. If you observe that the car runs again after you add the fuel, you might conclude that your hypothesis is correct.

The relationship between theories and hypotheses is not necessarily as straightforward as this simple example indicates. A theory can generate many hypotheses. If more and more hypotheses related to a theory turn out to be true, the theory gains in credibility. One reason that so many scientists hold the theory of evolution in high esteem is that it has been able to predict many observations.

On the other hand, if some of the hypotheses derived from a theory are not supported by observation, the theory will have to be revised. In fact, entirely new theories have arisen when researchers have found that no existing theory explains the facts that they have observed. Sigmund Freud's theory that no significant psychological changes take place in adulthood is an example of a theory that has been revised. For example, Erik Erikson (1968) observed that changes take place throughout the adult years, beginning with an increased motivation for intimacy during the 20s and 30s.

In-Psych Plus

Keep in mind that a revision of theory usually occurs only after a number of studies produce similar results. Before we change a theory, we want to be sure that the research is reliable. *Reliability* is the extent to which research yields a consistent, reproducible result. Go to the interactivity "Reliability, Validity, & Variance" to explore the special challenges of measuring psychological variables.

Essentially, then, the scientific method is a process of developing and testing theories. Scientists do not regard theories as being exactly, entirely, and permanently correct. A theory is judged by its ability to generate hypotheses that predict important events and behaviors. Depending on how well it predicts, a theory gains or loses support. Some theories sound great at first, but testing shows them to be worthless. Other theories start out sounding less useful but are shaped and improved in the course of testing.

The following review should help you to reach your learning goals related to this initial exploration of the science of psychology.

hypothesis An idea that is a testable prediction, often arrived at logically from a theory.

Review and Sharpen Your Thinking

1 *Explain what makes psychology a science.*

- Define psychology, and explain the three terms contained in the definition.
- Describe the contributions of philosophy and natural science to psychology and the two main ways that early psychologists conceptualized the mind.
- Discuss the four attributes of a scientific attitude.
- Explain the role of theory and hypothesis in the scientific method.

Do you have some questions about mind and behavior that a deeper understanding of psychology might help you answer?

| Descriptive Research | Correlational Research | Experimental Research |

How do psychologists collect research data?

As you have seen, research is an important part of the scientific method. The collection of data is the fundamental means of testing hypotheses. This section describes the major ways that data about behavior and mental processes can be gathered. There are three basic types of research used in psychology: descriptive, correlational, and experimental. Each has strengths and weaknesses.

Descriptive Research

Some important psychological theories have grown out of descriptive research, which serves the purpose of observing and recording behavior and mental states. For example, a psychologist might observe the extent to which people are altruistic or aggressive toward each other. By itself, descriptive research cannot prove what causes some phenomenon, but it can reveal important information about people's behaviors and attitudes. Descriptive research methods include observation, surveys and interviews, standardized tests, and case studies.

Observation   For observations to be effective, they have to be systematic (Leary, 2001). We have to have some idea of what we are looking for. We have to know whom we are observing, when and where we will observe, and how the observations will be made. And in what form will they be recorded (Billmann, 2003)? In writing? Tape recording? Video?

And if we are going to make observations, where should we make them? We have two choices: the laboratory and the everyday world. Much of psychology's research is conducted in a laboratory, a controlled setting with many of the complex factors of the "real world" removed. Laboratory-based observation is useful when psychologists need to control certain factors that determine behavior but are not the focus of the inquiry (Crano & Brewer, 2002; Hoyle & Judd, 2002).

A famous experiment, in which children behaved more aggressively after observing a model being rewarded for aggression, was conducted by Albert Bandura (1965) in a laboratory. Thus he controlled when each child witnessed aggression, how much aggression the child saw, and what form the aggression took. Bandura conducted this study with adults the child participants did not know. Bandura would not have had as much control over the experiment or as much confidence in the results if the study had been conducted in the children's homes and if familiar people had been present, such as the child's parents, siblings, or friends.

Laboratory research does have some drawbacks:

- It is almost impossible to conduct research without the participants' knowing they are being studied.
- The laboratory setting is unnatural and therefore can cause the participants to behave unnaturally.

THE FAR SIDE® By GARY LARSON

"For crying out loud, gentlemen! That's us! Someone's installed the one-way mirror in backward!"

A researcher codes the behavior of children in a play group as part of a research study. *What are some advantages and disadvantages of laboratory research?*

Jane Goodall was a young woman when she made her first trip to the Gombe Research Center in Tanzania, Africa. Fascinated by chimpanzees, she embarked on a career in the bush that involved long and solitary hours of careful, patient naturalistic observation. Due to her efforts, our understanding of chimpanzees in natural settings dramatically improved. *What are some other aspects of behavior that could be studied by using naturalistic observation?*

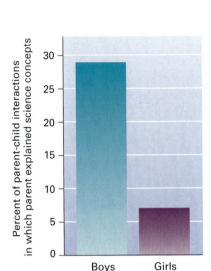

FIGURE 1.3 Parents' Explanations of Science to Sons and Daughters at a Science Museum In a naturalistic observation study at a children's science museum, parents were three times more likely to explain science to boys than to girls (Crowley & others, 2001). The gender difference occurred regardless of whether the father, the mother, or both parents were with the child, although the gender difference was greatest for fathers' science explanations to sons and daughters.

naturalistic observation Observation of behavior in a real-world setting with no effort made to manipulate or control the situation.

standardized test A test that requires people to answer a series of written and/ or oral questions. Standardized tests have two distinct features: (1) An individual's score is totaled to yield a single score or set of scores; and (2) the individual's score can be compared with the scores of a large group of similar people to determine how the individual responded relative to others.

- People who are willing to go to a university laboratory may not fairly represent groups from diverse cultural backgrounds. Those who are unfamiliar with university settings and with the idea of "helping science" may be intimidated by the setting.
- Some aspects of mind and behavior are difficult if not impossible to examine in the laboratory. Laboratory studies of certain types of stress, for example, may even be unethical.

Naturalistic observation provides the insight that sometimes cannot be achieved in the laboratory (Langston, 2002). **Naturalistic observation** is observing behavior in real-world settings, making no effort to manipulate or control the situation. Psychologists conduct naturalistic observations at sporting events, day-care centers, work settings, malls, and other places people live in and frequent. Suppose that you wanted to study the level of civility on your campus. Most likely, you would want to include some naturalistic observation of how people treat one another in places such as the cafeteria or the library reading room.

Naturalistic observation was used in one study focused on conversations in a children's science museum (Crowley & others, 2001). Parents were three times as likely to engage boys than girls in explanatory talk while visiting different exhibits at the science museum, suggesting a gender bias that encourages boys more than girls in science (see figure 1.3). In another study, Mexican American parents who had completed high school used more explanations with their children when visiting a science museum than Mexican American parents who had not completed high school (Tenenbaum & others, 2002).

Naturalistic observation was used in another study that focused on the relationship between caregiving behavior and the positive development of toddlers from 18 to 30 months of age (Wachs & others, 1993). The study was conducted in Egypt. Twice a month, researchers observed children and the caregivers in the children's homes for a period of 30 minutes, noting such behaviors as how frequently the caregivers talked with the children and guided their play. They also observed the number of vocalizations made by the children and the amount of time they spent playing with objects. As had been found in studies of Western families, the more the Egyptian caregivers talked with and guided young children's play, the more alert, vocal, and actively involved in play the children were (Bukatko & Daehler, 2001). Studying the children under these circumstances made it more likely that their behavior would be natural, although the lack of controls made it harder to guarantee that the nature of their interaction with adults affected the nature of their play.

Surveys and Interviews   Sometimes the best and quickest way to get information about people is to ask them for it. One technique is to interview them directly. A related method that is especially useful when information from many people is needed is the survey, sometimes referred to as a questionnaire. A standard set of questions is used to obtain people's self-reported attitudes or beliefs about a particular topic. In a good survey, the questions are clear and unbiased, allowing respondents to answer unambiguously.

Surveys and interviews can be used to study a wide range of topics, from religious beliefs to sexual habits to attitudes about gun control (Cozby, 2004). Surveys and interviews can be conducted in person or over the telephone or Internet. Large-scale surveys, such as like the Gallup poll, are often featured in news reports and shape marketing decisions as well as public policy.

"Would you say Attila is doing an excellent job, a good job, a fair job, or a poor job?" Drawing by Chas Addams; ©1982 The New Yorker Magazine, Inc.

Some survey and interview questions are unstructured and open-ended, such as "Could you elaborate on your optimistic tendencies?" or "How fulfilling would you say your marriage is?" They allow for unique responses from each person surveyed. Other survey and interview questions are more structured and ask about more specific things. For example, a structured survey or interview question might ask, "How many times have you talked with your partner about a personal problem in the past month: 0, 1–2, 3–5, 6–10, 10–30, every day?"

One problem with surveys and interviews is the tendency of participants to answer questions in a way that they think is socially acceptable or desirable rather than telling what they truly think or feel (Nardi, 2003). Go to the interactivity "Self-Report Bias in Surveys" to learn more about the challenges of using self-reports in psychological research. For example, a person might exaggerate the amount of communication that goes on in a relationship in order to impress the interviewer.

Standardized Tests   A **standardized test** requires people to answer a series of written or oral questions or sometimes both (Gregory, 2004). A standardized test has two distinct features: (1) An individual's answers are tallied to yield a single score, or set of scores, that reflects something about that individual, and (2) the individual's

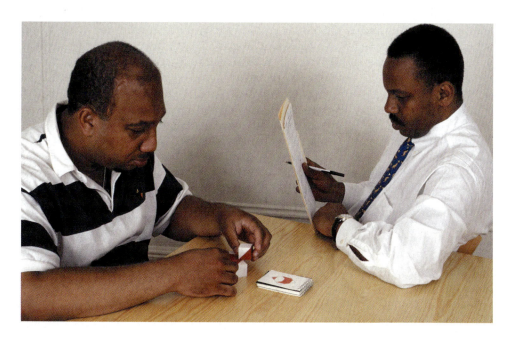

Standardized tests require individuals to answer a series of written or oral questions. The individual on the left is being given a standardized test of intelligence. *What is a limitation of standardized tests?*

Mahatma Gandhi was the spiritual leader of India in the middle of the twentieth century. Erik Erikson conducted an extensive case study of Gandhi's life to determine what contributed to his identity development. *What are some limitations of the case study approach?*

score is compared with the scores of a large group of similar people to determine how the individual responded relative to others (Cohen & Swerdlik, 2002). One widely used standardized test is the Scholastic Assessment Test (SAT).

Scores on standardized tests are often stated in percentiles. Suppose you scored in the 92nd percentile on the SAT. This score would mean that 91 percent of a large group of individuals who previously took the test received scores lower than yours.

The main advantage of standardized tests is that they provide information about individual differences among people (Aiken, 2003; Walsh & Betz, 2001). One problem with standardized tests is that they do not always predict behavior in nontest situations. Another problem is that standardized tests are based on the belief that a person's behavior is consistent and stable, yet personality and intelligence—two primary targets of standardized testing—can vary with the situation. For example, a person may perform poorly on a standardized intelligence test in an office setting but score much higher at home, where he or she is less anxious.

This criticism is especially relevant for members of minority groups, some of whom have been inaccurately classified as mentally retarded on the basis of their scores on intelligence tests (Valencia & Suzuki, 2001). In addition, cross-cultural psychologists caution that many psychological tests developed in Western cultures might not be appropriate in other cultures (Cushner & Brislin, 1995). People in other cultures may have had experiences that cause them to interpret and respond to questions much differently from the people on whom the test was standardized.

Case Studies A **case study,** or case history, is an in-depth look at a single individual. Case studies are performed mainly by clinical psychologists when, for either practical or ethical reasons, the unique aspects of an individual's life cannot be duplicated and tested in other individuals (Dattilio, 2001). A case study provides information about one person's fears, hopes, fantasies, traumatic experiences, upbringing, family relationships, health, or anything else that helps the psychologist understand the person's mind and behavior.

Traumatic experiences have produced some truly fascinating case studies in psychology. Consider the following: A 26-year-old schoolteacher met a woman with whom he fell intensely in love. But several months after their love affair began, the schoolteacher became depressed, drank heavily, and talked about suicide. The suicidal ideas progressed to images of murder and suicide. Only 8 months after meeting his beloved, the teacher fatally shot her while he was a passenger in the car that she was driving. Soon after the act, he ran to a telephone booth to call his priest (Revitch & Schlesinger, 1978). This case reveals how depressive moods and bizarre thinking can precede violent acts, such as murder. It doesn't indicate how everyone will react in similar circumstances, but it gives us an idea of the range of possibilities in human behavior and some of the effects of different experiences.

Another, more positive example of a case study is the analysis of India's spiritual leader Mahatma Gandhi by psychodynamic theorist Erik Erikson (1969). Erikson studied Gandhi's life in great depth to discover insights into how his positive spiritual identity developed, especially during his youth. In putting the pieces of Gandhi's identity development together, Erikson described the contributions of culture, history, family, and various other factors that might affect the way other people develop an identity.

Case histories provide dramatic, in-depth portrayals of people's lives, but remember that we must be cautious when generalizing from this information. The subject of a case study is unique, with a genetic makeup and personal history that no one else shares. In addition, case studies involve judgments of unknown reliability. Psychologists who conduct case studies rarely check to see whether other psychologists agree with their observations.

case study An in-depth look at a single individual.

correlational research Research with the goal of describing the strength of the relationship between two or more events or characteristics.

Correlational Research

In **correlational research,** the goal is to describe the strength of the relationship between two or more events or characteristics. The more strongly the two events are correlated (or related, or associated), the more effectively we can predict one event from the other (Vernoy & Kyle, 2003). This form of research is a key method of data analysis, which, you may recall, is the third step in the scientific method.

Positive and Negative Correlations   The degree of relationship between two variables is expressed as a numerical value called a *correlational coefficient.* Let's assume that we have data on the relationship between how long your instructor lectures (the *X* variable) and the number of times students yawn (the *Y* variable). The closer the number is to 1.00, the stronger the correlation; conversely, the closer the number is to .00, the weaker the correlation. Figure 1.4 offers guidelines for interpreting correlational numbers.

The numeric value of a correlation coefficient always falls within the range from $+1.00$ to -1.00, but the negative numbers do not indicate a lower value than positive numbers. A correlation of $-.70$ is just as strong as a correlation of $+.70$. What the plus or minus sign does tell you is the *direction* of the relationship between the two variables. A *positive correlation* is a relationship in which the two factors vary in the same direction. Both factors tend to increase together, or both factors tend to decrease together. Either relationship represents a positive correlation. A *negative* correlation, in contrast, is a relationship in which the two factors vary in opposite directions. As one factor increases, the other factor decreases. Thus a correlation of $+.15$ indicates a weak positive correlation, and a $-.74$ indicates a strong negative correlation. Examples of charts showing positive and negative correlations appear in figure 1.5.

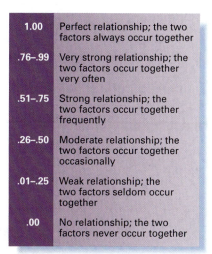

1.00	Perfect relationship; the two factors always occur together
.76–.99	Very strong relationship; the two factors occur together very often
.51–.75	Strong relationship; the two factors occur together frequently
.26–.50	Moderate relationship; the two factors occur together occasionally
.01–.25	Weak relationship; the two factors seldom occur together
.00	No relationship; the two factors never occur together

FIGURE 1.4 Guidelines for Interpreting Correlational Numbers

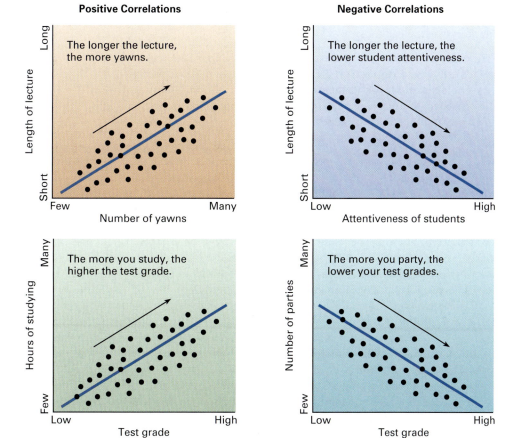

FIGURE 1.5 Charts Showing Positive and Negative Correlations A positive correlation is a relationship in which two factors vary in the same direction, as shown in the two charts (scatter plots) on the left. A negative correlation is a relationship in which two factors vary in opposite directions, as shown in the two scatter plots on the right.

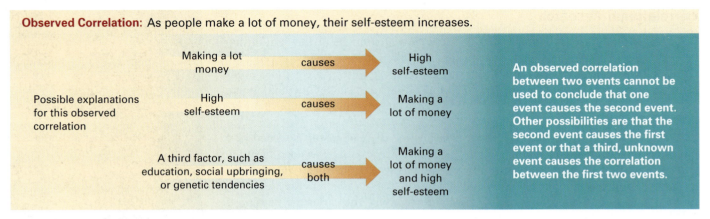

Observed Correlation: As people make a lot of money, their self-esteem increases.

Possible explanations for this observed correlation

Making a lot money →causes→ High self-esteem

High self-esteem →causes→ Making a lot of money

A third factor, such as education, social upbringing, or genetic tendencies →causes both→ Making a lot of money and high self-esteem

An observed correlation between two events cannot be used to conclude that one event causes the second event. Other possibilities are that the second event causes the first event or that a third, unknown event causes the correlation between the first two events.

FIGURE 1.6 **Possible Explanations for Correlational Data**

As you can see, a correlation coefficient has two parts: the number and the sign. Let's return to the example about the +.70 correlation between how long your professor lectures and the number of times students yawn to see how the two elements work together. What does the number .70 tell us? These two factors happen together frequently. And what does the plus sign indicate? The two factors vary in the same direction. As the amount of time your professor lectures increases, so does the number of yawns.

An example of a negative correlation is the relationship between how long your instructor lectures and the level of student attentiveness. As the length of time your instructor lectures increases, the level of student attentiveness decreases. These two factors vary in opposite directions and thus have a negative correlation.

Correlation and Causation In trying to make sense of the world, people often make a big mistake about correlation. Look at the terms in bold type in the following newspaper headlines:

Researchers **Link** Coffee Consumption to Cancer of Pancreas
Scientists Find **Connection** Between Ear Hair and Heart Attacks
Psychologists Discover **Relationship** Between Marital Status and Health
Researchers Identify **Association** Between Loneliness and Social Skills
Parental Discipline **Tied** to Personality Disorders in Children

Reading these headlines, the public might conclude that coffee causes cancer, ear hair causes heart attacks, and so on. But all of the words in bold type are synonymous only with correlation, not with causality. *Correlation does not equal causation.*

As you read about the findings of psychological studies, or findings in other sciences, guard against making the same mistake. Remember, correlation means only that two factors seem to occur together. Being able to predict one event based on the occurrence of another event does not necessarily tell us anything about the cause of either event (Sprinthall, 2003). The interactivity "Correlational Research" offers both an overview of correlational research and an opportunity to learn more about the meaning of correlations by engaging in a correlational study.

In-Psych Plus

To ensure that you understand the difference between correlation and causation, imagine a study that finds people who make a lot of money to have higher self-esteem than their counterparts who make less money. We could interpret this correlation to mean that making a lot of money causes high self-esteem. But we need to consider two other interpretations (see figure 1.6). One is that developing high self-esteem causes people to make a lot of money. Another interpretation is that a third factor—such as education, social upbringing, or genetic tendencies—causes the correlation between making a lot of money and high self-esteem.

If correlational studies are so limited, why do researchers even bother doing them? Why don't they simply conduct experiments, which provide the most compelling evidence of causality? There are several reasons. One is that some experiments would be unethical to carry out—for instance, asking expectant mothers to smoke varying numbers of cigarettes to see how cigarette smoke affects birth weight and fetal activity level. Also, the issue under investigation may be post hoc (after the fact) or historical, such as studying the childhood backgrounds of people who are abusive parents. Further, sometimes the factors simply cannot be manipulated experimentally, such as the effects of the September 11, 2001, attack on the World Trade Center on the residents of New York City.

Throughout this book, you will read about numerous correlational research studies. Keep in mind how easy it is to assume causality when two events or characteristics are merely correlated.

Experimental Research

Many research psychologists who are interested in determining causes of behavior—that is, why people do what they do—use experimental research (Beins, 2004; Myers & Hansen, 2002). An **experiment** is a carefully regulated procedure in which one or more factors believed to influence the behavior being studied are manipulated while all other factors are held constant.

If the behavior under study changes when a factor is manipulated, we say that the manipulated factor has caused the behavior to change. In other words, the experiment has demonstrated cause and effect. The cause is the factor that was manipulated, and the effect is the behavior that changed because of the manipulation. Nonexperimental research methods (descriptive and correlational research) cannot establish cause and effect because they do not involve manipulating factors in a controlled way.

Independent and Dependent Variables
Experiments have two types of changeable factors, or variables: independent and dependent. An **independent variable** is a manipulated, influential, experimental factor. It is a potential cause. The label *independent* is used because this variable can be manipulated independently of other factors to determine its effect. Researchers have a vast array of options open to them in selecting independent variables, and one experiment may include several independent variables (McBurney & White, 2004; Shaughnessy, Zeichmeister, & Zeichmeister, 2003).

In an experiment studying the effects on college students' health of their writing about emotional experiences, conducted by James Pennebaker and Sandra Beall (1986), the independent variable was writing about emotions. Pennebaker and Beall manipulated this variable by asking different participants to write about their problems in different ways. For example, they asked some participants to write about an emotional situation and how they felt about it. They asked other participants to write about a topic that was unrelated to emotional events.

A **dependent variable** is a factor that can change in an experiment in response to changes in the independent variable. As researchers manipulate the independent variable, they measure the dependent variable for any resulting effect. In Pennebaker and Beall's experiment, the dependent variable was the number of visits that the student made to the health center during the several months after beginning to write about an emotional or nonemotional experience. They found that the number of visits depended on the sort of writing that the student was asked to do (see figure 1.7).

Experimental and Control Groups
Experiments can involve one or more experimental groups and one or more control groups. An **experimental group** is a group whose experience is manipulated. A **control group** is a comparison group that is as much like the experimental group as possible and that is treated in every way like the experimental group except for the manipulated factor. The control group serves as a baseline against which the effects of the manipulated condition can be compared.

In Pennebaker and Beall's study, the experimental group was asked to write about their emotions. The control group was asked to write about some other, nonemotional topic.

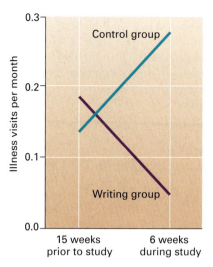

FIGURE 1.7 **Health-Center Visits Before and After Writing About Emotional Experiences**

experiment A carefully regulated procedure in which one or more factors believed to influence the behavior being studied are manipulated and all other factors are held constant.

independent variable The manipulated, influential, experimental factor in an experiment.

dependent variable The factor that can change in an experiment in response to changes in the independent variable.

experimental group A group in a research study whose experience is manipulated.

control group A comparison group that is treated in every way like the experimental group except for the manipulated factor.

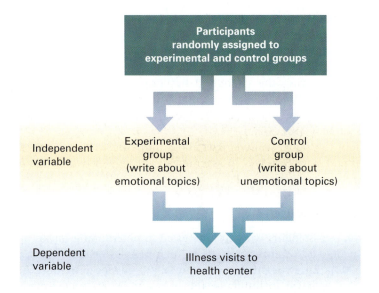

FIGURE 1.8 Random Assignment and Experimental Design

Random assignment is an important principle in deciding whether each participant will be placed in the experimental group or in the control group. **Random assignment** means that researchers assign participants to experimental and control groups by chance. It reduces the likelihood that the experiment's results the experiment's will be due to any preexisting differences between groups (Martin, 2004).

In Pennebaker and Beall's experiment, suppose the participants had not been randomly assigned but had been allowed to choose which group they would join—either the group that would write about emotions or the group that would write about something else. In that situation, people who were comfortable expressing their emotions might choose to join the first group, and people who were not comfortable expressing their emotions might choose to be in the second. As a result, any difference between the groups in terms of health at the end of the experiment might owe nothing to the effects of writing but simply reflect the effects of a person's comfort in expressing emotions. Go to the interactivity "Samples and Populations" to participate in an exercise that demonstrates the costs and benefits of random samples.

Pennebaker and Beall randomly assigned each participant to one of two groups: (1) the experimental group that wrote about emotional experiences or (2) a control group that wrote about a nonemotional topic. The independent variable (which is always the manipulated variable) was the type of writing the students did (about the emotional situation or about something else). The dependent variable was the number of illness visits that students paid to the health center after the writing. The design of this experiment allowed Pennebaker and Beall to argue that the emotional writing caused better health. Figure 1.8 depicts the design of their experiment.

In-Psych Plus

random assignment The assignment of participants to experimental and control groups by chance.

experimenter bias The influence of the experimenter's own expectations on the outcome of the research.

research participant bias The influence of research participants' expectations on their behavior within an experiment.

double-blind experiment An experiment that is conducted so that neither the experimenter nor the participants are aware of which participants are in the experimental group and which are in the control group until after the results are calculated.

Double-Blind Experiments Experimenters may subtly (and unknowingly) influence research participants. **Experimenter bias** occurs when an experimenter's expectations influence the outcome of research. Like experimenters, research participants may have expectations that affect the results of experiments (Christiansen, 2001). **Research participant bias** occurs when the behavior of participants during the experiment is influenced by how they think they are supposed to behave. A way to make sure that neither the experimenter's nor the participants' expectations affect the outcome is to design a **double-blind experiment.** In this design, neither the experimenter nor the participants know which participants are in the experimental group and which are in the control group until the results are calculated.

A study of drug treatment for social phobia is an example of a double-blind experiment (Van Ameringen & others, 2001). Both the experimenter, who administered the drug, and the participants were kept in the dark about which individuals were receiving the drug and which were receiving a placebo that merely looked like the drug. Thus the experimenter could not make subtle gestures signaling who was receiving the drug and who was not. A double-blind study allows researchers to tease apart the actual effects of the independent variable from the possible effects of the experimenter's and the participants' expectations about it. Go to the interactivity "Independent and Dependent Variables" to learn more about manipulating independent variables and measuring dependent variables. In this interactivity you get to be a track coach and use the experimental method to find performance tips.

At this point, you have read about several different types of research in psychology. For another look how these methodologies differ, see figure 1.9.

"Well, you don't look like an experimental psychologist to *me*."

Ethics in Research   You may never become a researcher in psychology, but you may carry out experimental projects in psychology courses. Remember to consider the rights of those who serve in the experiments. A student might think, "I volunteer in a home for the mentally retarded. I can use the residents of the home in my study to see if a particular treatment helps improve their memory for everyday tasks." But without proper permissions, the most well-meaning, kind, and considerate studies still violate the rights of the participants.

Safeguarding the rights of research participants is a challenge because the potential harm is not always obvious. At first glance, you might not imagine that a questionnaire on dating relationships would have any substantial impact or that an experiment involving treatment of memory loss would be anything but beneficial. But lasting harm might come to the participants in any psychological study.

Today, colleges and universities have review boards that evaluate the ethical nature of research conducted at their institutions. Proposed research plans must pass the scrutiny of a research ethics committee before the research can be initiated.

In addition, the American Psychological Association (APA) has developed ethics guidelines for its members. The code of ethics instructs psychologists to protect their

In-Psych Plus

FIGURE 1.9 **Psychology's Research Methods Applied to Dreaming** Methods used in descriptive research are shown at top; correlational and experimental research may also be used.

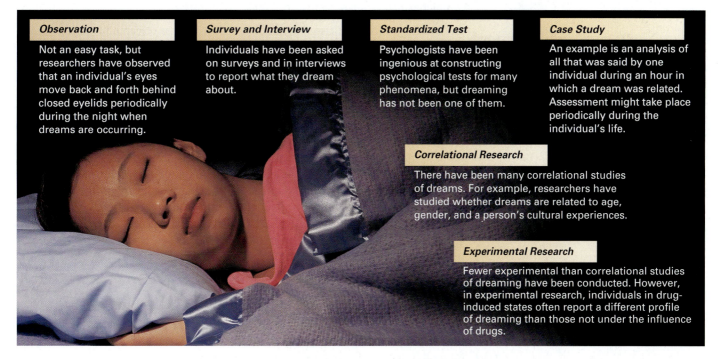

Observation
Not an easy task, but researchers have observed that an individual's eyes move back and forth behind closed eyelids periodically during the night when dreams are occurring.

Survey and Interview
Individuals have been asked on surveys and in interviews to report what they dream about.

Standardized Test
Psychologists have been ingenious at constructing psychological tests for many phenomena, but dreaming has not been one of them.

Case Study
An example is an analysis of all that was said by one individual during an hour in which a dream was related. Assessment might take place periodically during the individual's life.

Correlational Research
There have been many correlational studies of dreams. For example, researchers have studied whether dreams are related to age, gender, and a person's cultural experiences.

Experimental Research
Fewer experimental than correlational studies of dreaming have been conducted. However, in experimental research, individuals in drug-induced states often report a different profile of dreaming than those not under the influence of drugs.

participants from mental and physical harm. The participants' best interests need to be kept foremost in the researcher's mind (Fisher, 2003; Rosnow, 1995). APA's guidelines address four important issues:

- *Informed consent.* All participants must know what their participation will involve and what risks might develop. For example, participants in a study on dating should be told beforehand that a questionnaire might stimulate thoughts about issues in their relationships that they have not considered. Participants also should be informed that in some instances a discussion of the issues might improve their relationships but that in others it might worsen the relationships and even end them. Even after informed consent is given, participants must retain the right to withdraw from the study at any time and for any reason.
- *Confidentiality.* Researchers are responsible for keeping all of the data they gather on individuals completely confidential and, when possible, completely anonymous.
- *Debriefing.* After the study has been completed, participants should be informed of its purpose and the methods that were used. In most cases, the experimenter also can inform participants in a general manner beforehand about the purpose of the research without leading participants to behave in a way that they think the experimenter is expecting. When preliminary information about the study is likely to affect the results, participants can at least be debriefed after the study has been completed.
- *Deception.* This is an ethical issue that psychologists debate extensively (Hoyle & Judd, 2002). In some circumstances, telling the participants beforehand what the research study is about substantially alters the participants' behavior and invalidates the researcher's data. For example, suppose a psychologist wants to know whether bystanders will report a theft. A mock theft is staged, and the psychologist observes which bystanders report it. Had the psychologist informed the participants beforehand that the study intended to discover the percentage of bystanders who will report a theft, the whole study would have been undermined. Thus the researcher deceives participants about the purpose of the study, perhaps leading them to believe that it has some other purpose. In all cases of deception, however, the psychologist must ensure that the deception will not harm the participants and that the participants will be told the complete nature of the study (will be debriefed) as soon as possible after the study is completed (Chastain & Landrum, 1999).

The federal government also takes a role in ensuring that research involving human participants is conducted ethically. It has an office devoted to ensuring the well-being of participants in research studies. Over the years, the Federal Office for Protection from Research Risks has been faced with many challenging and controversial decisions—among them informed consent rules for research on mental disorders, regulations governing research on pregnant women and fetuses, ethical issues regarding AIDS vaccine research, and the ramifications of surreptitious egg and embryo swapping by nationally recognized fertility researchers (now convicted on felony charges).

The question of research ethics also extends to animal studies. For generations, animal studies have provided a better understanding of and solutions for many human problems (Leavitt, 2000). Neal Miller, who has made important discoveries about the effects of biofeedback on health, listed the following areas in which animal research has benefited humans (Miller, 1985):

- Psychotherapy techniques and behavioral medicine
- Rehabilitation of neuromuscular disorders
- Alleviation of the effects of stress and pain
- Drugs to treat anxiety and severe mental illness
- Methods for avoiding drug addiction and relapse
- Treatments to help premature infants gain weight so they can leave the hospital sooner
- Methods used to alleviate memory deficits in old age

Only about 5 percent of APA members use animals in their research; rats and mice account for 90 percent of all psychological research with animals. Animal welfare and rights activists would have you believe that abuse to these animals is extensive. It is true that researchers sometimes use procedures that would be unethical with humans, but they are guided by a set of standards for housing, feeding, and maintaining the psychological and physical well-being of their animal subjects. Researchers are required to weigh potential benefits of the research against possible harm to the animal and to avoid inflicting unnecessary pain. Animal abuse simply is not as common as animal activist groups charge. Stringent ethical guidelines must be followed, whether animals or humans are the subjects in psychological research (Herzog, 1995).

Review and Sharpen Your Thinking

2   *Discuss the three types of research that are used in psychology.*

- Name and describe four kinds of descriptive research and identify at least one advantage of each kind of study.
- State the goal of correlational research and explain the significance of the correlation coefficient.
- Discuss the experimental method, including its components and potential pitfalls.

You have learned that correlation does not equal causation. Develop an example of two variables (two sets of observations) that are correlated but that you believe almost certainly have no causal tie between them.

CONTEMPORARY APPROACHES TO PSYCHOLOGY 3

Behavioral Approach   **Cognitive Approach**   **Evolutionary Psychology**   **Humanistic Movement and Positive Psychology**

Psychodynamic Approach   **Behavioral Neuroscience**   **Sociocultural Approach**

How do contemporary psychologists approach the study of behavior?

Efforts to understand the complexity of mental processes and behavior have given rise to a number of broad approaches in psychology. The following sections will introduce seven contemporary approaches: behavioral, psychodynamic, cognitive, behavioral neuroscience, evolutionary psychology, sociocultural, and humanistic or positivist. Knowing about these approaches is important because many of the debates and controversies in psychology reflect differences in researchers' perspectives. In addition, much of the research discussed throughout the book can be understood more clearly against the background of one or more of these approaches.

As you consider how these approaches might illuminate human thought and behavior, keep three ideas in mind:

- Although psychology may often seem to focus on the individual, human beings are profoundly social. They need other people to satisfy their wants and needs. Parents, teachers, peers, friends, and partners in close relationships play important roles in our socially connected lives (Bornstein & Bradley, 2003; Day, 2003). How we treat others and they us, whether caring or hurting, stirs our thoughts and emotions (Clark & Brisette, 2003).
- Theories can help us to understand human behavior in general, but there is still enormous individual variation (Ewen, 2003). No two lives play out in the

B. F. Skinner was a tinkerer who liked to make new gadgets. The younger of his two daughters, Deborah, was raised in Skinner's enclosed Air-Crib. Some critics accused Skinner of monstrous experimentation with his children; however, the early controlled environment has not had any noticeable harmful effects. Debbie, shown here as a child with her parents, is currently a successful artist, is married, and lives in London. *Do you think it was unethical and wrong for Skinner to use his infant daughter in his research?*

same way. Roommates, parents and children, teachers and students, friends and lovers soon discover their differences. One task of psychology is to chart not only our commonalities but also what makes us unique (Stanovich, 2004). Your mixture of genes and experiences cannot be duplicated. Even in these days of animal cloning and the potential for human cloning, experience uniquely imprints each person's life (Gottlieb, 2002; D. Moore, 2001).

- One approach is not necessarily better than the other. Individual psychologists may become invested in a particular approach, but all of them provide valid ways of looking at human behavior. Some approaches are simply more useful in some situations and at certain times in the development of the field. Just as blueprints, floor plans, and photographs are all valid ways of looking at a house, some approaches are better for some purposes than others. For instance, a floor plan is more useful than a photograph for deciding how much lumber to buy. Similarly, the behavioral neuroscience approach is more useful than the sociocultural approach for explaining the fundamental aspects of perception. At the same time, the sociocultural approach is more useful than the behavioral neuroscience approach for understanding how to reduce prejudice and discrimination.

To increase your understanding of these approaches, in the following discussion we will ask what each approach might tell us about Tiger Woods.

Behavioral Approach

The **behavioral approach** emphasizes the scientific study of observable behavioral responses and their environmental determinants. In other words, the behavioral approach focuses on human interactions with the environment that can be seen and measured. The principles of the behavioral approach also have been widely applied to help people change their behavior for the better. The psychologists who adopt this approach are called *behaviorists.* Under the intellectual leadership of John B. Watson

behavioral approach Emphasizes the scientific study of behavior and asserts that behavior is shaped by the environment.

(1878–1958) and B. F. Skinner (1904–1990), behaviorism dominated psychological research during the first half of the twentieth century.

Many studies with a behavioral approach take place in experimental laboratories under carefully controlled conditions. When behaviorism was in its infancy, virtually all behavioral studies were conducted in the laboratory, although today many take place outside the laboratory in natural settings, such as schools and homes.

Skinner emphasized that what we *do* is the ultimate test of who we are. He believed that rewards and punishments determine our behavior. For example, a child might behave in a well-mannered fashion because her parents have rewarded this behavior. An adult might work hard at a job because of the money he gets for his effort. We do these things, say behaviorists, not because of an inborn motivation to be competent people but rather because of the environmental conditions we have experienced and continue to experience (Skinner, 1938).

Contemporary behaviorists still emphasize the importance of observing behavior to understand an individual and continue to use the rigorous sorts of experimental methods advocated by Watson and Skinner (Martin & Pear, 2003; Miltenberger, 2004; Watson & Tharp, 2003). They also continue to stress the importance of environmental determinants of behavior (Baldwin & Baldwin, 2001; Spiegler & Guevremont, 2003). However, not every behaviorist accepts the earlier behaviorists' rejection of thought processes (often called cognition) (Mischel, 2004; Schunk, 2004).

Social cognitive theory, as proposed by Albert Bandura (1925–), stresses that behavior is determined not only by environmental conditions but also by how thoughts modify the effects of environment on behavior (Bandura, 1986, 2001). Bandura believes that imitation is one of the main ways in which we learn about our world. To reproduce a model's behavior, we must enter and store the information in memory, which is a mental (cognitive) process. Thus social cognitive theorists have broadened the scope of behaviorism to include not only observed behavior but also the ways in which the mind processes information about the environment.

What can the behavioral approach tell us about Tiger Woods? Behaviorists would tell us not to look inside Tiger to try to find out what makes him a great golfer. According to behaviorists, motives and feelings cannot be directly observed, so they won't help us understand his behavior. Behaviorists would examine Tiger's learning history. If Tiger was praised for his practice and achievements, he might have worked even harder on his golf game. Social cognitive theorists such as Bandura would stress that Tiger developed his golf skills through extensive observational learning. They also would suggest that Tiger developed positive expectations and the self-confidence to become a great golfer through interactions with others.

SIGMUND FREUD (1856–1939)
How does Freud's psychoanalytic method differ from the psychodynamic approach that grew out of it?

Psychodynamic Approach

The **psychodynamic approach** emphasizes unconscious thought, the conflict between biological instincts and society's demands, and early family experiences. This approach argues that unlearned biological instincts, especially sexual and aggressive impulses, influence the way people think, feel, and behave. These instincts, buried deep within the unconscious mind, are often at odds with society's demands. Although Sigmund Freud (1856–1939), the founding father of the psychodynamic approach, saw much of psychological development as instinctual, he believed that early relationships with parents are the chief forces that shape an individual's personality. Freud's (1917) theory was the basis for the therapeutic technique that he termed *psychoanalysis.* His approach was controversial when he introduced it in Vienna at the beginning of the twentieth century. However, his ideas flourished, and many clinicians still find value in his insights. (See the video clip "Freud's Contribution to Psychology" to learn more about Freud's role in the history of psychology.) Today's psychodynamic theories tend to place less emphasis on sexual instincts, however, and more on cultural experiences as determinants of behavior.

In-Psych Plus

social cognitive theory Stresses that behavior is determined not only by environmental conditions but also by how thoughts modify the impact of environment on behavior.

psychodynamic approach Emphasizes the unconscious aspects of the mind, conflict between biological instincts and society's demands, and early family experiences.

Neuroscientists have studied the memory of the sea slug, a tiny snail with only about 10,000 nerve cells. *How did they investigate the sea slug's memory?*

Unlike the behavioral approach, the psychodynamic approach focuses almost exclusively on clinical applications rather than on experimental research. For this reason, psychodynamic theories always have been controversial and difficult to validate. Nonetheless, they are an important part of psychology.

What can the psychodynamic approach tell us about Tiger Woods? The psychodynamic approach suggests that Tiger is likely to be unaware of why he became a great golfer and why he behaves the way he does. It also suggests that his early experiences with his parents likely formed his outgoing personality and ability to get along with others.

Cognitive Approach

According to cognitive psychologists, your brain hosts or embodies a "mind," whose mental processes allow you to remember, make decisions, plan, set goals, and be creative (Hunt & Ellis, 2004; Sternberg, 2003). The **cognitive approach,** then, emphasizes the mental processes involved in knowing: how we direct our attention, how we perceive, how we remember, and how we think and solve problems. For example, cognitive psychologists want to know how we solve algebraic equations, why we remember some things for only a short time but remember others for a lifetime, and how we use imagery to plan for the future.

Cognitive psychologists view the mind as an active and aware problem-solving system (Baddeley, 1998; Simon, 1996). This positive view contrasts with the behavioral view, which portrays behavior as controlled by external environmental forces. The cognitive view also contrasts with pessimistic views (such as those of Freud) that see human behavior as being controlled by instincts or other unconscious forces. In the cognitive view, an individual's mental processes are in control of behavior through memories, perceptions, images, and thinking (Medin, Ross, & Markham, 2001; Reed, 2004).

What can the cognitive approach tell us about Tiger Woods? Cognitive psychologists would be impressed with Tiger's ability to process information, especially his ability to concentrate and focus his attention. They also would be interested in his ability to remember how to swing a golf club so accurately time after time. Cognitive psychologists might be intrigued by Tiger's ability to solve problems and make decisions, not only while playing in a golf tournament but also in his daily life.

Behavioral Neuroscience

The **behavioral neuroscience approach** emphasizes that the brain and nervous system are central to understanding behavior, thought, and emotion. Neuroscientists believe that thoughts and emotions have a physical basis. Electrical impulses zoom throughout the brain's cells, releasing chemical substances that enable us to think, feel, and behave. Our remarkable human capabilities would not be possible without the brain and nervous system, which constitute the most complex, intricate, and elegant system imaginable.

Enormous strides have been made in understanding the brain and its role in psychological matters in recent years (Kolb & Whishaw, 2001; Zillmer & Spiers, 2001). Much of what we know about the brain comes from research on animals that have simpler brains with far fewer nerve cells than humans (Changeux & Chavillion, 1995). Consider the memory of the sea slug, a tiny snail with only about 10,000 nerve cells. The sea slug is a slow creature, but if given an electric shock to its tail it withdraws the tail quickly—and even more quickly if the tail was previously shocked. In a primitive way, the sea slug remembers. Shocking the sea slug's tail releases a chemical that basically reminds the organism that the tail was previously shocked. This memory informs the nerve cells to send out chemical commands to retract the tail (Kandel & Schwartz, 1982). As nature builds complexity out of simplicity, so the mechanism used by the sea slug may work in the human brain as well. In humans, the memory might come from the sight of a close friend, a dog's bark, or the sound of a car horn. Chemicals are the ink with which these memories are written.

cognitive approach Focuses on the mental processes involved in knowing: how we direct our attention, perceive, remember, think, and solve problems.

behavioral neuroscience approach Views understanding the brain and nervous system as central to understanding behavior, thought, and emotion.

What can the behavioral neuroscience approach tell us about Tiger Woods? Neuroscientists are intrigued by the neural circuitry that underlies virtually all behaviors. They would be interested in the brain processes that underlie Tiger's amazing athletic skills. They would attempt to explain how Tiger's brain coordinates so many things so quickly to allow him to strike a golf ball smoothly and powerfully.

Evolutionary Psychology

Although Darwin introduced the theory of evolution by natural selection in the middle of the nineteenth century, his ideas about evolution only recently became a popular framework for explaining behavior. One of psychology's newest approaches, the **evolutionary psychology approach,** emphasizes the importance of adaptation, reproduction, and "survival of the fittest" in explaining behavior. In this view, natural selection favors behaviors that increase the organism's reproductive success and ability to pass its genes on to the next generation.

David Buss (1995, 2000, 2004) argues that, just as evolution shapes our physical features, such as body shape and height, it also pervasively influences our decision-making methods, our level of aggressiveness, our fears, and our mating patterns. The way we adapt in our world today can be traced to problems that animals and early humans faced in adapting to their evolutionary environments (Crawford & Salmon, 2004).

Steven Pinker (1999) also believes that evolutionary psychology is an important approach to understanding behavior. According to Pinker, the way the mind works can be summarized by three points: (1) The mind computes, (2) the mind was designed to compute by evolution, and (3) these computations are performed by specialized brain systems that natural selection has designed to achieve specific kinds of goals, such as survival. The mind analyzes sensory input in ways that would have benefited prehistoric humans. People with minds that understood causes and effects—who could build tools, set traps, and avoid poisonous mushrooms—had the best chance of surviving and having offspring.

Evolutionary psychologists believe that their approach unifies the diverse fields of psychology. Not all psychologists agree. Some argue that no single approach is likely to explain the complex field of psychology (Graziano, 1995). Others stress that the evolutionary approach does not adequately account for cultural diversity (Paludi, 2002). But evolutionary psychology is young, and its future may be fruitful (Cosmides & others, 2003; Janicki, 2004). For an example of the application of the evolutionary perspective, go to the audio clip "Evolutionary Psychology."

What can evolutionary psychology tell us about Tiger Woods? The evolutionary approach would stress that Tiger's golfing abilities are the result of a long evolutionary process in which genes involving excellent hand-eye motor coordination survived and were passed down from generation to generation. This approach also would call attention to the adaptive behavior that allows Tiger to function competently in his world.

Sociocultural Approach

The **sociocultural approach** examines the ways in which the social and cultural environments influence behavior. The sociocultural approach argues that a full understanding of a person's behavior requires knowing about the cultural context in which the behavior occurs (Azuma, 2004; Berry, 2004). For instance, in some cultures, such as in the United States, it may be entirely acceptable for a woman to be assertive, but in another culture, such as in Iran, female assertiveness may be considered inappropriate.

The tapestry of American culture has changed dramatically in recent years. Ethnic minority groups—African American, Latino, Native American, and Asian, for example—made up approximately one-third of individuals under the age of 17 in the United States in the year 2000. Two of psychology's challenges are to become more sensitive to race and ethnic origin and to provide improved services to ethnic minority individuals. *What might these communication strategies be like?*

In-Psych Plus

evolutionary psychology approach Emphasizes the importance of functional purpose and adaptation in explaining why behaviors are formed, are modified, and survive.

sociocultural approach Emphasizes social and cultural influences on behavior.

Humanists believe that we have a natural tendency to be loving toward each other and that each of us has the capacity to be a loving person if we would recognize it. *How does that approach differ from other psychological approaches?*

In-Psych Plus

Mihaly Csikszentmihalyi is one of the main architects of the current positive psychology movement. *What prompted Csikszentmihalyi and others to start the movement?*

humanistic movement Emphasizes a person's capacity for personal growth, freedom to choose a destiny, and positive qualities.

positive psychology movement Emphasizes the experiences that people value subjectively (such as happiness), positive individual traits (such as the capacity for love), and positive group and civic values (such as responsibility).

The sociocultural approach focuses not only on comparisons of behavior across countries but also on the behavior of people from different ethnic and cultural groups within a country (Matsumoto & Juang, 2004). Thus there is increasing interest in the behavior of African Americans, Latinos, and Asian Americans, especially in terms of the factors that have restricted or enhanced their ability to adapt to and cope with living in a predominantly White society (Banks, 2002, 2003).

What can the sociocultural approach tell us about Tiger Woods? The sociocultural approach would be especially interested in Tiger's multiethnic background and how it might have hindered or helped the development of his skills and behavior. In an interview with Oprah Winfrey, Woods said that he made up the term *Cablinasian* when he was a young boy so that he could respond to frequent inquiries about his ethnicity. He chose this unusual term because he did not want to ignore any aspect of his heritage (his mother's ethnic heritage is Thai and Chinese; his father's is Native American, African American, and White).

The sociocultural approach can provide insights into behavior that other approaches, such as the evolutionary psychology approach, do not adequately explain. See the Critical Controversy box for a discussion of altruism, which is one of these behaviors. To contrast the sociocultural and evolutionary approaches to another topic—mating preferences—see the video clip "Attraction."

Humanistic Movement and Positive Psychology

If you are like most people, you probably associate psychology with problems, such as depression and eating disorders. Psychologists sometimes think that their field focuses too much on problems and not enough on the positive aspects of behavior. Two movements have emerged that focus on positive characteristics: The humanistic movement appeared in the middle of the twentieth century; positive psychology began gaining momentum at the beginning of the twenty-first century.

The **humanistic movement** emphasizes a person's positive qualities, the capacity for positive growth, and the freedom to choose any destiny. Humanistic psychologists stress that people have the ability to control their lives and avoid being manipulated by the environment (Maslow, 1971; Rogers, 1961). They believe that, rather than being driven by unconscious impulses, as the psychodynamic approach dictates, or by external rewards, as the behavioral approach emphasizes, people can choose to live by higher values, such as altruism. See the video clip "Self-Actualization" to learn more about how the humanistic perspective views human choices and motivations. Humanistic psychologists also think that people have a tremendous potential for self-understanding and that the way to help others achieve self-understanding is by being warm, nurturant, and supportive. Many aspects of this optimistic approach to defining human nature appear in clinical practice today.

In 2000, two influential American psychologists, Mihaly Csikszentmihalyi and Martin Seligman, edited a special issue of the journal *American Psychologist* in which they introduced positive psychology (Seligman & Csikszentmihalyi, 2000). Their analysis of psychology in the twentieth century was that it had become far too negative, focusing on what can go wrong in people's lives rather than on what they can do competently. Too often, they said, psychology has characterized people as passive and victimized. Seligman, Csikszentmihalyi, and others hope to usher in a new focus (Diener, 2000; Nakamura & Csikszentmihalyi, 2002; Seligman, 2002). They describe the **positive psychology movement** as giving a stronger emphasis to and conducting more research on three general topics (Seligman & Csikszentmihalyi, 2000):

- Experiences that people value subjectively, such as hope, optimism, and happiness. Go to the audio clip "Positive Psychology" to learn about research on happiness from the positive psychology perspective.
- Positive individual traits, such as the capacity for love, work, creativity, talent, and interpersonal skills
- Positive group and civic values, such as responsibility, nurturance, and tolerance

Can Humans Really Be Altruistic?

If there was a silver lining in the dark cloud of September 11, 2001, it was that firefighters, police officers, emergency medical personnel, and many ordinary individuals altruistically risked their own lives to help other people caught in the collapse of the twin towers of the World Trade Center in New York City. Altruistic behavior is often defined as voluntary behavior that is intended to benefit others and is not motivated by any expectation of personal gain. The most extreme form of altruism is giving one's life to save someone else, as many of those who responded to the September 11th attack did.

Altruism poses an important problem for the evolutionary psychology approach (Caporael, 2001). According to Charles Darwin's theory of evolution, only the behaviors that favor an organism's reproductive success are likely to be passed on to future generations. Over many generations, selfish behavior, ensuring the propagation of their own genes, should be favored. Altruistic behavior should die out.

Referring to altruistic behavior among social insects, Darwin (1859/1979) wrote about one circumstance that is difficult for evolutionary theory to explain. Worker bees, born without the ability to reproduce, spend their lives caring for the offspring of the queen bee in their hive. Natural selection predicts that sterile worker bees should become extinct over time. But, in fact, they always outnumber the queen bees.

The concept of *kin selection* provides one way to reconcile altruism with evolutionary theory. According to this concept, our genes survive not just when we reproduce but also when our relatives reproduce. The worker bees in a hive turn out to be genetically related to the queen bee and, hence, to all of the other bees in the hive, including any eggs the queen bee lays. Thus, even though a worker bee has no direct offspring, its genes survive when the hive thrives. The theory of kin selection can explain why some people forgo having their own children and choose instead to care for relatives and relatives' children. What this theory cannot explain is altruism directed toward people outside the family and especially toward strangers.

In contrast to the evolutionary psychology approach, the sociocultural approach attempts to explain altruistic behavior as being the result of social and cultural experiences (Dovidio & Penner, 2001; Gergen, 1994). According to this approach, each of us is a product of many culturally and socially derived relationships, which continually unfold over time. Because our relationships within our culture are open-ended and adaptable rather than rigidly determined by our genes, genuine acts of altruism are possible. Simply put, if our culture teaches us to be kind without regard for our own gain, then we can become true altruists.

The evolutionary psychology approach forces us to look at our capacity for selfishness and to refine our notions of kindness

Many firefighters, police officers, and others lost their lives on September 11, 2001, while trying to rescue victims of the terrorist attack on the World Trade Center. *Is their altruism better explained as an attempt to perpetuate their own genes or as an outgrowth of their social and cultural experiences?*

and altruism (Belk & Ruse, 2000), yet the sociocultural approach is attractive because it stresses that people can be genuinely altruistic. In the end, this contrast in views helps to sharpen our understanding of what it is to be fully human.

What do you think?

- Are people ever truly altruistic? Or are they acting on selfish motives?
- Have you ever acted in a truly altruistic fashion? Or could your behavior be explained by the theory of kin selection?
- What kind of research might settle the question of whether humans are capable of genuine altruism?

Behavioral

Why has Woods found golf so rewarding ever since the first year of his life?

Psychodynamic

How much of Woods' ambition stems from his mother's and father's differing early influences on him?

Cognitive

How does Woods' memory store information about the contours of a green?

Behavioral Neuroscience

How does Woods' brain allow him to calmly focus attention on a crucial stroke?

Evolutionary

How has the evolution of the brain made possible such fine coordination between visual perception and movement of a golfer's limbs?

Sociocultural

Does Woods' multiethnic background matter in his life and golfing career?

FIGURE 1.10 Questions About Tiger Woods Derived from Seven Psychological Approaches

In-Psych Plus

What can the humanistic movement and positive psychology tell us about Tiger Woods? Humanistic and positive psychologists might look beyond the mechanics of Tiger's brain and nervous system, beyond the way he processes information and translates it into action, and focus on the strength he draws from his spiritual beliefs and inner drive. They might study the way that he has overcome setbacks to continue winning golf championships. They would be interested in the way that his parents nurtured the confidence, patience, persistence, and skills that make him a success. They would also focus on the positive values that Tiger embodies, such as responsibility, civility, and tolerance.

Figure 1.10 provides exemplary questions from the seven psychological approaches to help you remember how each might consider Tiger Woods and, therefore, how each approach's perspective varies. Use the interactivity "Identifying Psychological Perspectives" to test your understanding of these approaches.

Review and Sharpen Your Thinking

3   *Describe seven contemporary approaches to psychology.*

- Define each of the seven approaches in your own words.
- Classify the approaches according to whether they emphasize what is going on inside the person or focus on interactions with the outside environment.

Suppose you could talk with a psychologist from each of these approaches. Think about the members of your family and other people you know. Write down at least one question you might want to ask about the thoughts and behaviors of these people.

4   HOW TO BENEFIT FROM STUDYING PSYCHOLOGY

| Being a Wise Consumer of Information About Psychology | Developing Good Study Habits | Using the Book's Learning Tools to Succeed in This Course |

What life skills and study habits can I develop in this course?

Students take the introductory psychology course for several reasons. First and foremost, psychology is an interesting topic because it helps to explain why people do what they do. Certainly, the behavior of people around us affects us constantly, and hardly a day goes by that we do not encounter puzzling human behavior in the news and entertainment media. In addition, many psychological findings relate to the learning and thinking skills that students need to succeed in all their college courses and their later life. Obviously, the introductory psychology course is important to many students because they need the credits for their general studies or a psychology major.

For all these reasons, you are probably interested in getting the maximum results from the time you spend in this course. This section offers some practical tips for doing so. First, it explains how to think critically about information regarding psychology, whether you encounter it in class or out. Then, it recommends some skills that will help you study more effectively and points out the learning tools in this book that will make your study of introductory psychology easier and more effective.

Being a Wise Consumer of Information About Psychology

Television, radio, newspapers, and magazines frequently report on psychological research that is likely to be of interest to the general public. Much of the information has been published in professional journals or presented at national meetings, and most major colleges and universities have a media relations department that contacts the press about current research by their faculty.

You should be aware, however, that not all psychological information that is presented for public consumption comes from professionals with excellent credentials and reputations at colleges or universities or in applied mental health settings (Stanovich, 2004). Because journalists, television reporters, and other media personnel are not usually trained in psychological research, they often have trouble sorting through the widely varying material they find and making sound decisions about the best information to present to the public.

In addition, the media often focus on sensationalistic and dramatic psychological findings to capture your attention. They tend to go beyond what actual research articles and clinical findings really say.

Even when the media present the results of excellent research, they have trouble adequately informing people about what has been found and the implications for people's lives. For example, this entire book is designed to carry out the task of carefully introducing, defining, and elaborating on key concepts and issues, research, and clinical findings. The media, however, do not have the luxury of so much time and space to specify the limitations and qualifications of research. They often have only a few minutes or a few lines to summarize as best they can the complex findings of a study or a psychological concept.

In the end, you have to take responsibility for evaluating the reports on psychological research that you encounter in the media. To put it another way, you have to consume psychological information wisely. Six guidelines follow.

Think Critically   Understanding the complex nature of mind and behavior requires **critical thinking,** the process of thinking reflectively and productively and then evaluating the evidence. The ability to evaluate information critically is essential to all academic disciplines as well as to all areas of daily life (Halpern, 2002, 2003). For example, if you were planning to buy a car, you would want to collect information about different makes and models and evaluate their features and costs before deciding which one to test-drive. This would be an exercise in critical thinking. You need to practice your critical thinking skills regularly on a wide variety of problems to keep your skills sharp.

Thinking critically means asking yourself how you know something. Too often we have a tendency to recite, define, describe, state, and list rather than analyze, infer, connect, synthesize, criticize, create, evaluate, think, and rethink (Brooks & Brooks, 2001). Following is a brief sampling of some thinking strategies that can stimulate you to think reflectively and productively:

- *Be open-minded.* Explore options and avoid narrow thinking.
- *Be intellectually curious.* Wonder, probe, question, and inquire. Also be alert for problems and inconsistencies.

critical thinking The process of thinking reflectively and productively, as well as evaluating evidence.

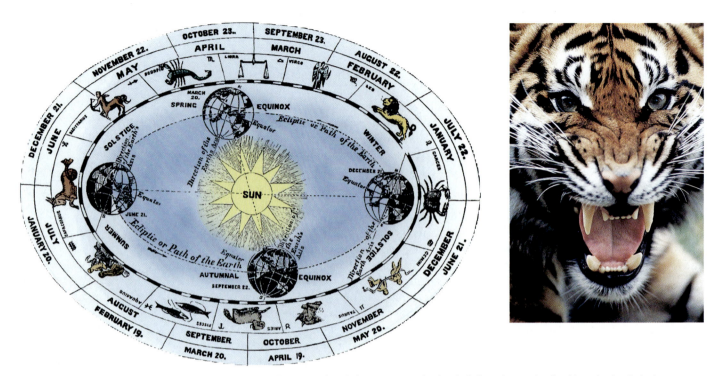

Why does the science of psychology urge you to be skeptical of astrology? Why should you be skeptical when you hear that eating a ground-up penis of a tiger will increase the human male's sexual potency?

- *Be intellectually careful.* Check for inaccuracies and errors, be precise, and be organized.
- *Look for multiple explanations.* People have a tendency to explain things as having a single cause. That's a lot easier than having to analyze the complexity of, say, mind and behavior and come up with multiple explanations. However, one of psychology's important lessons is that mind and behavior have multiple determinants. For example, having an open mind is one of critical thinking's multiple dimensions, but it does not *cause* critical thinking. Other dimensions are involved, too, such as practice or a supportive environment.
- *Think like a scientist.* Scientific thinkers examine the available evidence, evaluate how strongly the data (information) support their hunches, analyze disconfirming evidence, and carefully consider whether they have explored all of the possible factors and explanations. Scientific thinkers always look for biases in the way people think and behave. For example, a person who is wildly enthusiastic about the remarkable effects of exercise on health when responding to survey questions about health awareness might sell exercise videos on the side and thus have a strong bias toward that one aspect of health. Thinking like a scientist means taking that kind of potential bias into account.

Examples of the failure to think critically range from taking advice based on horoscopes to believing that eating a ground-up potion of a tiger's sexual organ will increase the human male's sexual potency. If you believe in phenomena such as these, psychologists urge you to be more skeptical. Remember that thinking like a scientist means that you demand to see the evidence for such phenomena as channeling, crystal power, and plant consciousness. There is no scientific evidence for the existence of any of them, only personal anecdotes and coincidences—and those do not meet science's criteria of objectivity and public verifiability.

If you still aren't convinced that these phenomena do not exist, at least critically examine the vague language that is often used. For example, astrologers' predictions are successful only because they are so vague that they are virtually guaranteed to be applicable (for example, "Money is likely to be a concern for you this month" or "A tragic plane crash will occur in the southern United States this winter"). Astrologers' more specific predictions (such as "An unidentified flying object will land on the field during the halftime of the *ABC Monday Night Football* game on October 11, 2004") never hold up.

When you think like a scientist, you will be skeptical of anything that claims wondrous powers and access to supernatural forces (Ward & Grashial, 1995). If something sounds too good to be true, think through the claims logically and demand to see the evidence. The same cautions apply when a psychologist is making claims. Carefully consider the evidence.

Distinguish Between Group Results and Individual Needs   People who learn about psychological research through the media are likely to apply the results to their individual circumstances, yet most research focuses on groups, and individual variations in participants' responses are seldom emphasized. As a result, the ill-informed consumer of psychological research may get the wrong idea about the "normality" of his or her circumstances. For example, researchers might conduct a study of 50 divorced women and 50 married women and conclude that the divorced women, as a group, cope more poorly with stress than the married women in the study do. In this particular study, however, some of the divorced women are likely to be coping better than some of the married women. Indeed, of the 100 women in the study, the 2 or 3 women who are coping the best with stress may be the divorced women. It would be accurate to report the findings as showing that divorced women (as a group) cope less effectively with stress than married women (as a group) do. But it would not be sensible to conclude, after reading a summary of the results of the study, that your divorced sister may not be coping with stress as well as she thinks and recommend that she see a therapist. The only conclusion you can reasonably draw is that the study's married women tended to cope better than the divorced women did.

The failure of the media to distinguish adequately between research on groups and the individual needs of consumers is not entirely their fault. Researchers have not made the difference clear, either. They often fail to examine the overlap in the data on the groups they are comparing and look for only the differences. And then too often they highlight only these differences in their reports.

Avoid Overgeneralizing from a Small Sample   Media presentations of psychological information often don't have the space or time to go into details about the nature of the sample used in the study. Sometimes you will get basic information about the sample's size—whether it is based on 10 participants, 50 participants, or 200 participants, for example. If you can't learn anything else about the sample, at least pay attention to the number of people studied.

Small or very small samples require caution in generalizing to a larger population of individuals. For example, a sample of only 10 or 20 divorced women may have some unique characteristics that would make the study's finding inapplicable to many women. The women in the sample might all have high incomes, be Anglo American, be childless, live in a small southern town, and be undergoing psychotherapy. Divorced women who have moderate to low incomes, are from other ethnic backgrounds, have children, are living in different contexts, and are not undergoing psychotherapy might have given very different responses.

Look for Answers Beyond a Single Study   The media might identify an interesting piece of research or a clinical finding and claim that it is something phenomenal with far-reaching implications. Although such pivotal studies do occur, they are rare. It is safer to assume that no single study will provide conclusive answers to an important question, especially answers that apply to all people. In fact, in most psychological domains that prompt many investigations, conflicting results are common.

Answers to questions in research usually emerge after many scientists have conducted similar investigations that yield similar conclusions.

If one study reports that a particular therapy conducted by a particular therapist has been especially effective with divorced adults, you should not conclude that the therapy will work as effectively with all divorced adults and with other therapists until more studies are conducted. Remember that you should not take a report of one research study as the absolute, final answer to a problem.

Avoid Attributing Causes Where None Have Been Found   Drawing causal conclusions from correlational studies is one of the most common mistakes made by the media. When a true experiment has not been conducted—that is, when participants have not been randomly assigned to treatments or experiences—two variables or factors might have only a noncausal relationship to each other (Leavitt, 2000). Remember from the discussion of correlation earlier in the chapter that causal interpretations cannot be made when two or more factors are simply correlated. We cannot say that one causes the other.

In the case of divorce, imagine that you read this headline: "Low income causes divorced women to have a high degree of stress." You can instantly conclude that the story is about a correlational study, not an experimental study, and that the word *causes* is used in error. Why? For ethical and practical reasons, participants cannot be randomly assigned to become divorced or stay married, and divorced women cannot be randomly assigned to be poor or rich. A more accurate headline would probably be "Low-income divorced women have a high degree of stress," meaning that the researchers found a correlation between being divorced, having a low income, and having a lot of stress. Be skeptical of words indicating causation until you know more about the research they are describing.

Consider the Source of Psychological Information   Studies conducted by psychologists are not automatically accepted by the rest of the research community. The researchers usually must submit their findings to a journal for review by their colleagues, who make a decision about whether to publish the paper or not, depending on the care taken in conducting the research. Although the quality of research and findings is not uniform among all psychology journals, in most cases journals submit the findings to far greater scrutiny than the popular media do (Stanovich, 2004).

Within the media, though, you can usually draw a distinction. The reports of psychological research in respected newspapers, such as the *New York Times* and *Washington Post*, as well as in credible magazines, such as *Time* and *Newsweek*, are far more trustworthy than reports in tabloids, such as the *National Inquirer* and *Star*. But regardless of the source—serious publication, tabloid, or even academic journal—you are responsible for reading the details of the research behind the findings that are presented and analyzing the credibility of the source yourself.

Developing Good Study Habits

Very likely, you are taking other courses besides psychology. You will have a lot of reading and studying to do, and you probably will have to take a number of tests. What are some good strategies for succeeding in this and other courses? Here we focus on five important strategies for success: time management, choice of study environment, reading effectiveness, attentiveness in class, and test preparation.

Plan and Manage Your Time Effectively   Learning takes time. You will benefit enormously in this course and others if you become a great time manager. If you waste too much time, for instance, you will find yourself poorly prepared the night before an important exam. If you manage time well, you will have time to relax before exams and other deadlines. Time management can help you to be more productive and less stressed, with a better balance between work and play.

FIGURE 1.11 Example of a Student's To-Do List

To Do

The Most Important:

1. Study for Psychology Test

Next Two:

2. Go to English and History classes

3. Make appointment to see advisor

Task	Time	Done
Study for psychology test	Early morn., night	
Call home	Morning	
Go to English class	Morning	
Buy test book	Morning	
Call Ann about test	Morning	
Make advisor appt.	Afternoon	
Go to history class	Afternoon	
Do exercise workout	Afternoon	

One week has 168 hours. Students vary in how they invest those hours. A typical full-time college student sleeps 50 hours, attends class between 12 and 20 hours, and spends 11 hours a week eating. Students divide the remaining hours between study, work, family obligations, and leisure pursuits.

You might find it helpful to fill out a term calendar with dates for the tests in this and your other courses. Many students also benefit from keeping a weekly calendar to see how they are allocating their time. Students who consistently get *A*s in courses often report that they study 2 to 3 hours outside class for every hour they are in class (Santrock & Halonen, 2002). Thus, if you are in class 15 hours a week and you want to get *A*s, a rule of thumb is to study 30 to 45 hours a week outside of class.

A good strategy for managing your time is to space out your study in a particular course rather than cramming it all into one or two study sessions just before the test. On a weekly schedule, block out at least 1 hour a day for 6 days to read this book and study your notes for this course. Then you will be better prepared when the time comes for each test, and you won't have to cram.

It is a good idea to plan not only for the term and the week but also for tomorrow. Great time managers identify the most important things to do each day and allocate enough time to get them done. Figuring out what is most important involves setting priorities. An effective way to set priorities is to create a manageable to-do list. Set a goal of making a to-do list for the next day every night or, at the latest, early in the morning. Figure 1.11 shows one student's to-do list.

"Doctor, have you any advice to offer a young man who would love to be a physician but whose crowded schedule simply doesn't permit time for medical school?" © The New Yorker Collection 1990, Robert Weber, from cartoonbank.com. All Rights Reserved.

Choose the Most Effective Study Environment   Too many distractions can keep you from studying or remembering what you have studied. Select your place of study carefully, paying close attention to the features of the environment that will let you do your best work.

Some students do best when they always study in the same place. Ideally, the area should be well lighted, without glare, and at a comfortable temperature. A quiet location will let you concentrate much better than a noisy one. Noise is a major distraction to effective study. Turn off the stereo, radio, or TV while you are studying to minimize distraction.

Maximize Your Reading Effectiveness   Many students approach the challenge of reading a textbook as just so many pages to plow through. There is a difference between *reading to read* (to complete the required number of pages) and *reading to learn*. Reading to learn from a textbook improves if you approach the book as a conversation the author is having with you about the discipline's concepts. As in any effective conversation, you must pay attention, figure out how the parts of the conversation fit together, and make some judgments as you go about understanding the author's intent.

The following reading strategy can help you to maximize your ability to understand and retain what you read:

1. *Preview and plan.* Look at the number of pages you have to read and plan how to read the assignment. If the task is very long, determine at what points it would be appropriate to take breaks. For example, I have divided each chapter into three to six main sections, so a good time to take a break in your reading might be after you have read one or two main sections.
2. *Skim.* Look at the reading assignment and determine what main ideas will be covered. Look at the main headings. Read the paragraphs that introduce new sections. Examine the chapter reviews and summary. When you skim, you begin to build a foundation for the main ideas of the chapter.
3. *Read to comprehend.* There is no way around the effort and hard work involved in learning the material in a textbook. However, you can do several things to increase your understanding of what you read:
   - Pay attention to the sections of the reading assignment as meaningful units. Take one section at a time. Read each one until you are satisfied that you know the ideas.
   - Don't skip over what you don't understand. Find a classmate who is willing to discuss the ideas that are challenging.
   - Work on your reading speed. Practice taking in more words as your eyes sweep the line of print. Mouthing the words as you read only slows you down.
4. *Read to retain.* Most students need to read assignments more than once if they are going to learn the material. Periodically ask yourself the meaning of what you have been reading. Thinking about personal examples that illustrate concepts is another good memory aid.
5. *Review.* After you have used the aforementioned strategies, you will need to review the material you have read at least several times before you take a test. Just because you have read a chapter once, don't think that you will be able to remember everything in it that is important.

Be a Good Listener and Concentrate in Class   You need to do more than just memorize or passively absorb new information in class. To do well in most classes, including this one, you need to treat each and every class hour as an important learning experience. To carry out this strategy, you obviously have to be there. It also helps to prepare for the class by reading in advance about the topic(s) that will be covered in class.

In preparing for a lecture, motivate yourself by telling yourself that it is important for you to stay alert and listen carefully. Make sure you get sufficient sleep the night before so that you will be able to maximize your learning in class the next day. Many students find that a regular exercise program increases their alertness and ability to concentrate in class and when they are studying.

Take notes in class, but don't try to write down everything the instructor says. As you listen to a lecture, focus on the main ideas and take notes about them. If you miss an idea, get together later with one or more students in the class to find out what the idea was. Many students find it helpful to review their notes right after class, because the material in the lecture will be fresher in their minds than if they wait several days or more to review.

Prepare Effectively for the Test   In most cases, your grade in a course will depend on how well you do on the exams given periodically during the term. At the beginning of the term, find out what kinds of tests your instructor will be giving. Will they be all multiple-choice items? Will there be essay questions? Will the exams be a mixture of these or include other types of items, such as true-false?

A good strategy is to complete all of your textbook reading several days before the exam. All of your classroom notes should be in order so you can easily review them. If you have been studying on a regular basis, you should be in a good position to consolidate what you have learned for the test.

Some students find it helpful to develop their own questions and practice answering them. You may also find it helpful to study in a small group with other students in the class, who may be able to contribute information that you might have missed or did not adequately understand.

When you take a test, you will have to remember information. If you have practiced good study skills day after day and week after week leading up to the test, your ability to remember information will be enhanced when you take the test. In chapter 7, I discuss a number of strategies for remembering effectively. The interactivity "Chunking in Memory" and the video clip "Mnemonic Strategies in Memory" present two of these strategies for improving your memory.

In-Psych Plus

Using the Book's Learning Tools to Succeed in This Course

This book provides important study tools to help you learn about psychology more effectively. I describe these study tools in the student preface; reviewing it will give you an understanding of how to improve your learning skills. Here I briefly mention the book's most important study tools.

Learning Goals and Chapter Maps   Each chapter has a system of linked features designed to help you preview, skim, read, and review (see figure 1.12). At the beginning of each chapter, you will see three to six main headings and learning goals that preview the chapter's main themes and underscore its most important ideas.

At the beginning of each major section, you will see a map that includes the main heading and subheadings for that section. It provides a visual preview of what you will be reading in the section. Then, following each main heading, you will come across the relevant learning goal, rephrased as a question. At the end of each major section, you will come to the heading Review and Sharpen Your Thinking. The first part restates the section's learning goal and asks you to review each of the main topics in the section. The bulleted review statements are correlated with the map at the beginning of the section.

Finally, at the end of each chapter is a section called Reach Your Learning Goals. It includes a map of the chapter to give you a visual reminder of the main topics. It also restates the chapter's learning goals and verbally summarizes the material related to each one. This information is provided in bulleted form and matches up in a one-to-one fashion with the bulleted statements in the chapter's Review sections.

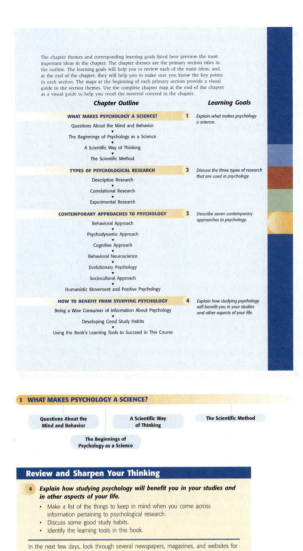

The learning goals and chapter maps are integrated in each chapter from beginning to end. One review strategy that makes use of this system is to look at a bulleted item in Review and Sharpen Your Thinking within a chapter, try to answer the item, and then turn to the corresponding bulleted item in the Reach Your Learning Goals section at the end of the chapter to see if your answer is on track.

Keep in mind that, although the Reach Your Learning Goals section is an organized, systematic review of the entire chapter, it is *not* a substitute for reading and studying the chapter. It leaves out a lot of details and thus cannot give you a flexible understanding of the material. Use it only as a guide to help organize your study of the chapter.

Thinking Exercises As you read through each chapter, you will be asked questions designed to encourage you to think more deeply and reflect on the topic at hand. Also in each chapter, the second part of Review and Sharpen Your Thinking at the end of each major section includes one or more questions to stimulate your thinking about a topic in the section you have just read. In many cases, these thought questions are personalized so that you will be able to relate them to your own life or to people you know.

In each chapter, you will find a box titled Psychology and Life, which is intended to stimulate you to think about applications of a psychology topic to the real world. Many of these features ask you to think about how you can apply what you have learned to your own life.

In addition, in each chapter you will read an in-depth Critical Controversy highlighting an important contemporary topic in psychology about which there is spirited debate. Psychology has advanced as a field because it does not accept simple explanations and because psychologists do not always agree with each other about why mind and behavior work the way they do. We have reached a more accurate understanding of mind and behavior *because* psychology fosters controversies and *because* psychologists think deeply and reflectively and

FIGURE 1.12 Chapter Learning Goal and Map System

FIGURE 1.13 Key Terms and Glossary

psychology The scientific study of behavior and mental processes.

Key Terms

psychology, p. 7
science, p. 7
behavior, p. 7
mental processes, p. 7
natural selection, p. 8
theory, p. 9
hypothesis, p. 10
naturalistic observation, p. 12
case study, p. 14
correlational research, p. 14
experiment, p. 17
independed variable, p. 17
dependent variable, p. 17
experimental group, p. 17
control group, p. 17
random assignment, p. 18
experimenter bias, p. 18
double-blind experiment, p. 18
behavioral approach, p. 22
social cognitive theory, p. 23
psychodynamic approach, p. 23
cognitive approach, p. 24
behavioral neuroscience
evolutionary psychology approach, p. 25
sociocultural approach, p. 25
humanistic movement, p. 26
positive psychology movement, p. 26
critical thinking, p. 29

Glossary

A

abnormal behavior Behavior that is deviant, maladaptive, or personally distressful. p. 20

absolute threshold The minimum amount of stimulus energy that people can detect. p. 180

accommodation Occurs when individuals adjust their schemas to new information. p. 128

acculturative stress The negative consequences that result from contact between two distinctive cultural groups. p. 610

achievement tests Tests that measure what a person has learned or the skills that a person has mastered. p. 393

acquired immunodeficiency syndrome (AIDS) Caused by the human immunodeficiency virus (HIV), a sexually transmitted disease that destroys the body's immune system. p. 638

acquisition (in classical conditioning) The initial learning of the stimulus-response link, which involves a neutral stimulus being associated with a UCS and becoming a conditioned stimulus (CS) that elicits the CR. p. 272

action potential The term used to describe the brief wave of electrical charge that sweeps down the axon during the transmission of a nerve impulse. p. 84

activation-synthesis theory States that dreaming occurs when the cerebral cortex synthesizes neural signals emanating from activity in the lower part of the brain. p. 245

addiction A pattern of behavior characterized by an overwhelming need to use the drug and to secure its supply. p. 261

adrenal glands Important endocrine glands that are instrumental in regulating moods, energy level, and the ability to cope with stress. p. 103

affectionate love Also called *companionate love*; the type of love that occurs when individuals desire to have the other person near and have a deep, caring affection for the person. p. 688

afferent nerves Sensory nerves that transport information to the brain. p. 80

agonist A drug that mimics or increases a neurotransmitter's effects. p. 88

agoraphobia A cluster of fears centered around public places and being unable to escape or to find help should one become incapacitated. p. 528

alcoholism A disorder that involves long-term, repeated, uncontrolled, compulsive, and excessive use of alcoholic beverages and that impairs the drinker's health and work and social relationships. p. 254

algorithms Strategies that guarantee a solution to a problem. p. 357

all-or-none principle Once an electrical impulse reaches a certain level of intensity, it fires and moves all the way down the axon without losing any of its intensity. p. 83

altruism An unselfish interest in helping someone else. p. 18

amnesia The loss of memory. p. 338

androgens The main class of male sex hormones. p. 145

anorexia nervosa An eating disorder that involves the relentless pursuit of thinness through starvation. p. 436

antagonist A drug that blocks a neurotransmitter's effects. p. 88

anterograde amnesia A memory disorder that affects the retention of new information or events p. 338

antianxiety drugs Commonly known as *tranquilizers*, they reduce anxiety by making people calmer and less excitable. p. 563

antidepressant drugs Drugs that regulate mood. p. 563

antipsychotic drugs Powerful drugs that diminish agitated behavior, reduce tension, decrease hallucinations, improve social behavior, and produce better sleep patterns in people who have a severe psychological disorder, such as schizophrenia. p. 565

anxiety disorders Psychological disorders that include these features: motor tension, hyperactivity, and apprehensive expectations and thoughts. p. 527

apparent movement The perception that a stationary object is moving. p. 201

applied behavior analysis (behavior modification) The application of operant conditioning principles to change human behavior. p. 288

approach/approach conflict A conflict in which the individual must choose between two attractive stimuli or circumstances. p. 698

approach/avoidance conflict A conflict involving a single stimulus or circumstance that has both positive and negative characteristics. p. 608

aptitude tests Tests that predict an individual's ability to learn. p. 393

archetypes The name Jung gave to the emotionally laden ideas and images in the collective unconscious that have rich and symbolic meaning. p. 483

artificial intelligence (AI) The science of creating machines capable of performing activities that require intelligence when they are done by people. p. 352

assimilation Occurs when individuals incorporate new information into existing knowledge. p. 128

association cortex Region of the cerebral cortex in which the highest intellectual functions, including thinking and problem solving, occur (also called association areas). p. 98

associative learning In which a connection is made between two events. p. 269

Atkinson-Shiffrin theory The view that memory involves a sequence of three stages: sensory memory, short-term memory, and long-term memory. p. 311

attachment The close emotional bond between an infant and its caregiver. p. 136

attitudes Beliefs or opinions about people, objects, and ideas. p. 653

attribution theory Views people as motivated to discover the underlying causes of behavior as part of their effort to make sense of the behavior. p. 447

G-1

examine the evidence on both sides. I call your attention to a number of controversies in this book. You will be asked a number of questions to encourage you to think critically about each of them.

Key Terms An important aspect of your study should be to understand a number of key terms in each chapter. To help you accomplish this task, key terms are boldfaced, defined in the margins, and listed and page referenced at the end of the chapter. In the Glossary at the end of the book, you will find definitions for the key terms, along with, again, a reference to the page on which the term is introduced (see figure 1.13).

Review and Sharpen Your Thinking

4 ***Explain how studying psychology will benefit you in your studies and in other aspects of your life.***

- Make a list of the things to keep in mind when you come across information pertaining to psychological research.
- Discuss some good study habits.
- Identify the learning tools in this book.

In the next few days, look through several newspapers, magazines, and websites for information about psychological research. Also, notice what you see and hear on television about psychology. Try applying the guidelines for being a wise consumer of psychological information to these media reports.

The Science of Psychology

1 WHAT MAKES PSYCHOLOGY A SCIENCE?

Questions About the Mind and Behavior

A Scientific Way of Thinking

The Beginnings of Psychology as a Science

The Scientific Method

2 TYPES OF PSYCHOLOGICAL RESEARCH

Descriptive Research

Correlational Research

Experimental Research

3 CONTEMPORARY APPROACHES TO PSYCHOLOGY

Behavioral Approach

Cognitive Approach

Evolutionary Psychology

Humanistic Movement and Positive Psychology

Psychodynamic Approach

Behavioral Neuroscience

Sociocultural Approach

4 HOW TO BENEFIT FROM STUDYING PSYCHOLOGY

Being a Wise Consumer of Information About Psychology

Developing Good Study Habits

Using the Book's Learning Tools to Succeed in This Course

At the beginning of this chapter, four learning goals were listed, and you were encouraged to review material related to these goals throughout the chapter. The following summary can be used to guide your study of the chapter and firm up your understanding of its main themes.

1 Explain what makes psychology a science.

- Psychology is the scientific study of behavior and mental processes. Science uses systematic methods to observe, describe, predict, and explain. Behavior includes everything organisms do that can be observed. Mental processes are thoughts, feelings, and motives.
- The idea that the mind is not a physical entity came from philosophy. The natural sciences of biology and physiology contributed the suggestion that the brain has an important role in behavior. Wilhelm Wundt founded the first laboratory in psychology in 1879, searching for the mind's elemental structures. William James focused on the functions of the mind in adapting to the environment.
- A scientific attitude involves being curious, being skeptical, being objective, and thinking critically.
- The scientific method is essentially a four-step process: (1) Conceptualize a problem, (2) collect research information (data), (3) analyze the data, and (4) draw conclusions. Step 1 often involves a theory, which is a possible explanation for past observations that also can be used to predict future observations. Using a theory to generate a hypothesis, or testable assumption, a researcher can collect and analyze data and then draw conclusions about the validity of the hypothesis.

2 Discuss the three types of research that are used in psychology.

- Descriptive research has the purpose of systematically observing and recording behavior. Four types of descriptive research are observations (in a laboratory or a naturalistic setting), surveys based on questionnaires and interviews, standardized tests, and case studies.
- In correlational research, the goal is to describe the strength of the relationship between two or more events or characteristics. A correlation coefficient is the numerical value that expresses the degree of relationship between two variables. A positive correlation indicates that the two factors tend to increase or decrease together. A negative correlation indicates that they tend to vary in opposite directions. It is important to remember that correlation does not equal causation.
- Experimental research involves a systematic, controlled study in which one or more factors believed to influence the behavior being studied are manipulated while all other factors are held constant. An experiment can determine cause and effect. An independent variable in an experiment is the manipulated factor. A dependent variable is the factor that can change in response to changes in the independent variable. An experimental group is the group whose experience is being manipulated. The control group is a comparison group that is treated in every way like the experimental group except for the factor that is being manipulated. In random assignment, researchers assign participants to experimental and control groups by chance. Experimenter bias and research participant bias are potential pitfalls in experimental research. In a double-blind experiment, neither the experimenter nor the participant is aware of which participants are in the experimental or the control group until the results are analyzed—thus reducing the effects of bias. Researchers have ethical responsibilities to protect both human participants and animal subjects.

3 Describe seven contemporary approaches to psychology.

- Contemporary approaches to psychology are the behavioral, psychodynamic, cognitive, behavioral neuroscience, evolutionary psychology, sociocultural, and humanistic and positive psychology approaches. The behavioral approach emphasizes the scientific study of observable behavioral responses and their environmental determinants; social cognitive theory is a contemporary behavioral approach. The psychodynamic approach emphasizes unconscious thought, the conflict between biological instincts and society's demands, and early family experiences. The cognitive approach emphasizes the mental processes involved in knowing. The behavioral neuroscience approach emphasizes that the brain and nervous system are central to understanding behavior. The evolutionary psychology approach stresses the importance of adaptation, reproduction, and "survival of the fittest." The sociocultural approach focuses on the social and cultural determinants of behavior. The humanistic and positive psychology approach focuses on the positive aspects of behavior and human competence.
- Psychodynamic, cognitive, behavioral neuroscience, evolutionary psychology, and humanistic and positive psychology approaches emphasize what is going on inside the person. Behavioral and sociocultural approaches focus on interactions with the outside environment.

4 *Explain how studying psychology will benefit you in your studies and in other aspects of your life.*

- Being a wise consumer of information about psychology means thinking critically; distinguishing between group results and individual needs; not overgeneralizing based on a small sample; understanding that a single study usually is not the defining word about an issue or a problem; not making causal conclusions from correlational studies; and evaluating the source of the information and its credibility.

- Good study habits include planning and managing study time, choosing a conducive study environment, maximizing reading effectiveness, being a good listener and concentrating in class, and preparing effectively for tests.

- This book's learning tools include a learning goal and chapter map system, critical thinking exercises, key terms, and connections for learning more about a topic.

Key Terms

psychology, p. 7
science, p. 7
behavior, p. 7
mental processes, p. 7
natural selection, p. 8
theory, p. 9
hypothesis, p. 10
naturalistic observation, p. 12
standardized test, p. 12

case study, p. 14
correlational research, p. 14
experiment, p. 17
independed variable, p. 17
dependent variable, p. 17
experimental group, p. 17
control group, p. 17
random assignment, p. 18
experimenter bias, p. 18
research participant bias, p. 18

double-blind experiment, p. 18
behavioral approach, p. 22
social cognitive theory, p. 23
psychodynamic approach, p. 23
cognitive approach, p. 24
behavioral neuroscience approach, p. 24

evolutionary psychology approach, p. 25
sociocultural approach, p. 25
humanistic movement, p. 26
positive psychology movement, p. 26
critical thinking, p. 29

Apply Your Knowledge

1. Visit the website of a major book retailer and enter *psychology* as a search term. Examine descriptions of the five to seven most popular psychology books listed. How well do the themes covered represent your perceptions of what psychology is? How well do they represent the approaches to psychology discussed in this chapter? Are any perspectives overrepresented or underrepresented? Why do you think that is?

2. Find a website dedicated to astrology, psychic phenomena, UFOs, or ghosts. Using the four attributes of a scientific attitude, critically examine the claims made on the website. Describe the theory, the hypothesis, the data, and the analysis. Can you find all of this information on the website? If not, how would a scientist respond to the website?

3. Visit the library at your school and find an article in a psychology journal. Describe what kind of study was done. Was it descriptive, correlational, or experimental? If it was an ex-

periment, what were the independent and dependent variables? How did the experimenter match the experimental and control groups? Can you tell if the double-blind method was used?

4. Much of the experimental research in psychology has been conducted using undergraduate students. How might this choice influence the extension of the results to other groups, such as children or older adults? Describe some of the special ethical issues that might be involved in using children and older adults in psychological experiments.

5. Ask three of your friends to describe how they prepared for the last exam they took. Using what you have learned about study strategies in this chapter, analyze your friends' study habits, including things that they're doing well and things that they might improve on. Do the same for yourself. Are there some tasks that everyone has trouble with, or are study habits highly individual?

Connections

To test your mastery of the material in this chapter, go to the Study Guide and the In-Psych Plus CD-ROM, as well as the Online Learning Center. There you will find a chapter summary, practice tests, flashcards, lecture slides, web links, and other study tools, such as interactive exercises and reviews as well as current, chapter-relevant news articles. Another special feature of the Online Learning Center is an interactive Statistics Primer.

2 The Brain and Behavior

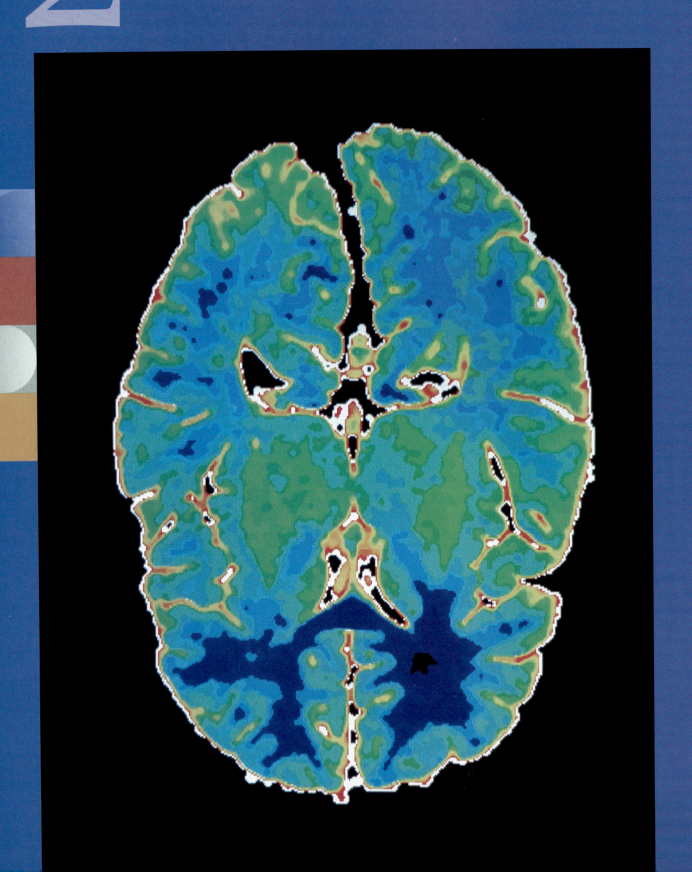

Chapter Outline

THE NERVOUS SYSTEM **1**

Key Characteristics of the Nervous System
▼
Pathways in the Nervous System
▼
Divisions of the Nervous System

NEURONS **2**

Specialized Cell Structure
▼
The Neural Impulse
▼
Synapses and Neurotransmitters
▼
Neural Networks

STRUCTURES OF THE BRAIN AND THEIR FUNCTIONS **3**

Levels of Organization in the Brain
▼
The Cerebral Cortex
▼
The Cerebral Hemispheres and Split-Brain Research
▼
Integration of Function in the Brain

THE ENDOCRINE SYSTEM **4**

GENETIC AND EVOLUTIONARY BLUEPRINTS OF BEHAVIOR **5**

Chromosomes, Genes, and DNA
▼
The Study of Genetics
▼
Genetics and Evolution

Learning Goals

1 Discuss the nature and basic functions of the nervous system.

2 Explain what neurons are and how they process information.

3 Identify the brain's levels and structures, and summarize the functions of its structures.

4 State what the endocrine system is and how it affects behavior.

5 Explain how genetics and evolutionary psychology increase our understanding of behavior.

When Brandi Binder was just 6 years old, surgeons at the University of California at Los Angeles removed the right side of her cerebral cortex (the outermost part and highest level of the brain) in an effort to subdue frequent seizures caused by very severe and uncontrollable epilepsy.

Epileptic seizures like the ones experienced by Brandi are the result of electrical "brainstorms" that flash uncontrollably from one side of the brain to the other. Nerve cells on one side become overactive and stimulate overactivity in nerve cells on the other side. The excess stimulation produces a seizure in which the individual loses consciousness and goes into convulsions. In severe cases, seizures can occur numerous times during the day. Physicians have discovered that, by severing the connection between the two sides of the brain or by removing the side of the brain in which the overactivity originates, they can eliminate the seizures or at least reduce their severity. Although not without risks and disadvantages, such surgery may greatly improve an individual's quality of life.

After her surgery, Brandi Binder had almost no control over the muscles on the left side of her body, the side controlled

Brandi Binder is evidence of the brain's great power, flexibility, and resilience. Despite having had the right side of her cortex removed, Brandi engages in many activities often portrayed as right-brain activities. She loves music, math, and art; she is shown here working on one of her paintings.

by the right side of her brain. She needed years of therapy to regain abilities that she lost with the right side of her brain. At age 13, however, Brandi was an *A* student. She also loved music, math, and art, all of which are commonly associated with the brain's right side.

It is not by coincidence that the human brain is so versatile. It has evolved over millions of years from a small, fairly primitive organ into a very complex network capable of coordinating our body functions, thoughts, emotions, and behavior. Evolutionary psychologists believe that the complex human brain has evolved because individuals with more complex brains were able to behave in ways that gave them and their descendants a better chance of survival—for example, by being able to anticipate adversity and plan ways to avoid it or cope with it.

This chapter examines the important biological foundations of human behavior. The main focus is the nervous system and its command center—the brain. But it also explores the genetic and evolutionary processes that have a significant influence on who we are as individuals and how we behave.

1 THE NERVOUS SYSTEM

| Key Characteristics of the Nervous System | Pathways in the Nervous System | Divisions of the Nervous System |

What is the nervous system and what does it do?

The **nervous system** is the body's electrochemical communication circuitry. The field that studies the nervous system is called *neuroscience,* and the people who study it are *neuroscientists.*

The human nervous system is made up of billions of interconnected cells, and it is likely the most intricately organized aggregate of matter on Earth. A single cubic centimeter of the human brain consists of well over 50 million nerve cells, each of which communicates with many other nerve cells in information processing networks that make the most elaborate computer seem primitive.

nervous system The body's electrochemical communication circuitry, made up of billions of neurons.

Key Characteristics of the Nervous System

The brain and nervous system guide our interaction with the world around us, move the body through the world, and direct our adaptation to our environment (Wilson, 2003). Four extraordinary characteristics allow the nervous system to direct our behavior:

- *Complexity.* The brain and nervous system are enormously complex. The brain itself is composed of billions of nerve cells. The orchestration of all of these cells to allow people to sing, dance, write, talk, and think is an awe-inspiring task. As Brandi Binder paints a piece of art, her brain is carrying out a huge number of tasks—breathing, seeing, thinking, moving—in which extensive assemblies of nerve cells are participating.

- *Integration.* Neuroscientist Steven Hyman (2001) calls the brain the great integrator. The brain does a wonderful job of pulling information together: sounds, sights, touch, taste, genes, environment. Brain activity is integrated across different levels and many different parts through countless interconnections of brain cells and extensive pathways. Each nerve cell communicates, on average, with 10,000 others, making up miles and miles of connections (Bloom, Nelson, & Lazerson, 2001; Johnson, 2003). Interconnected nerve cells relay information through the nervous system in a very orderly fashion to the highest level of the brain (Blair, 2002). Brandi Binder's painting does not occur because of what is going on in a single brain cell or a single part of her brain but rather because of the coordinated, integrated effort of many different nerve cells and parts of her brain.

- *Adaptability.* The world around us is constantly changing. To survive, we must adapt to new conditions (Bloom, Nelson, & Lazerson, 2001). Our brain and nervous system together serve as our agent in adapting to the world. Although nerve cells reside in certain brain regions, they are not fixed and immutable structures. They have a hereditary, biological foundation, but they are constantly adapting to changes in the body and the environment. The term **plasticity** denotes the brain's special capacity for change. The experiences that we have contribute to the wiring or rewiring of the brain (Jay, 2003; Ward & Frankowiak, 2004). The brain's plasticity is nowhere more evident than in Brandi Binder's case. After she lost much of the right side of her brain, the left side took over many functions that often are thought to reside only in the right side. (For another example, follow the case of Jodi Miller in the video clip "Brain Plasticity.")

In-Psych Plus

- *Electrochemical transmission.* The brain and the nervous system function essentially as an information processing system, powered by electrical impulses and chemical messengers. When people speak to each other, they use words. When neurons communicate with each other, they use chemicals. The electrochemical communication system works effectively in most people to allow us to think and act. However, when the electrochemical system is short-circuited, as in the case of Brandi's epilepsy, the flow of information is disrupted, the brain is unable to channel information accurately, and the person cannot effectively engage in mental processing and behavior. Just as an electrical surge during a lightning storm can disrupt the circuits in a computer, the electrical surge that produces an epileptic seizure disrupts the brain's information processing circuits. The brains of individuals with epilepsy work effectively to process information between seizures, unless the seizures occur with such regularity that they cause brain damage. In about 75 percent of epilepsy cases, seizures do not cause structural damage to the brain.

Pathways in the Nervous System

As we interact with and adapt to the world, the brain and the nervous system receive and transmit sensory input, integrate the information received from the environment, and direct the body's motor activities. Information flows into the brain through sensory

plasticity The brain's special capacity for change.

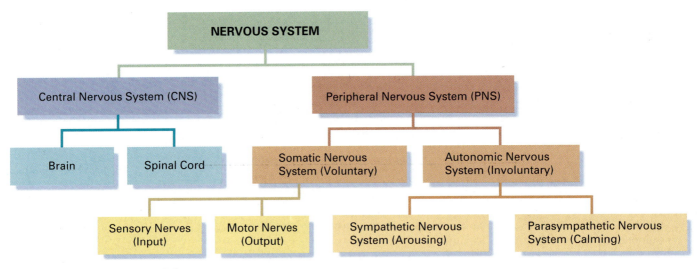

FIGURE 2.1 **Major Divisions of the Human Nervous System**

neural networks Clusters of nerve cells that are interconnected to process sensory and motor information.

central nervous system (CNS) The brain and spinal cord.

peripheral nervous system (PNS) The network of nerves that connects the brain and spinal cord to other parts of the body. It is divided into the somatic nervous system and the autonomic nervous system.

somatic nervous system The division of the PNS consisting of sensory nerves, whose function is to convey information to the CNS, and motor nerves, whose function is to transmit information to the muscles.

autonomic nervous system The division of the PNS that communicates with the body's internal organs. It consists of the sympathetic and parasympathetic nervous systems.

sympathetic nervous system The division of the autonomic nervous system that arouses the body.

parasympathetic nervous system The division of the autonomic nervous system that calms the body.

input, becomes integrated within the brain, and then moves out of the brain to be connected with motor output (Enger & Ross, 2003).

Decision making in the nervous system occurs in specialized pathways and networks that are adapted for different functions:

- *Sensory nerves* carry information to the brain. These sensory pathways communicate information about external and bodily environments from sensory receptors into and throughout the brain.
- *Motor nerves* carry the brain's output. These motor pathways communicate information from the brain to the hands, feet, and other areas of the body that allow a person to engage in motor behavior.
- **Neural networks** in the central nervous system are networks of nerve cells that integrate sensory input and motor output (Kimoto & Okada, 2004; Mingolla, 2002). Most information processing occurs when information moves through neural networks. For example, as you read your class notes, the sensory input from your eye is transmitted to your brain, then passed through many neural networks, which translate (process) your black pen scratches into neural codes for letters, words, associations, and meaning. Some of the information is stored in the neural networks for future associations. If you read aloud, some is passed on as motor messages to your lips and tongue. Neural networks make up most of the brain. (See the animations and images in the video clip "Neurons and How They Work" to learn more about nerve cells and neural networks.)

Divisions of the Nervous System

When the nineteenth-century American poet and essayist Ralph Waldo Emerson said, "The world was built in order and the atoms march in tune," he must have had the human nervous system in mind. This truly elegant system is highly ordered and organized for effective function. Figure 2.1 shows its two primary divisions:

- The **central nervous system (CNS)** is made up of the brain and spinal cord. More than 99 percent of all nerve cells in the body are located in the CNS.
- The **peripheral nervous system (PNS)** is the network of nerves that connects the brain and spinal cord to other parts of the body. The functions of the peripheral nervous system are to take information to and from the brain and spinal cord and to carry out the commands of the CNS to execute various muscular and glandular activities.

The peripheral nervous system itself has two major divisions:

- The **somatic nervous system** consists of sensory nerves, which convey information from the skin and muscles to the CNS about conditions such as pain and temperature, and motor nerves, which tell muscles what to do.

- The **autonomic nervous system** takes messages to and from the body's internal organs, monitoring such processes as breathing, heart rate, and digestion. The autonomic nervous system also is divided into two parts: the **sympathetic nervous system** arouses the body, and the **parasympathetic nervous system** calms the body.

To better understand the various divisions of the nervous system, let's see what they do in a particular situation. Imagine that you are preparing to ask a judge to dismiss a parking ticket. As you are about to enter the courtroom, you scan a note card one last time to remember what you plan to say. Your *peripheral nervous system* carries the written marks from the note card to your central nervous system. Your *central nervous system* processes the marks, interpreting them as words, while you memorize key points and plan ways to keep the judge friendly. After studying your notes several minutes longer, you jot down an additional point that you hope will convince her. Again your *peripheral nervous system* is at work, conveying to the muscles in your arm and hand the information from your brain that enables you to make the marks on the paper. The information that is being transmitted from your eyes to your brain and to your hand is handled by the *somatic nervous system.* This is your first ticket hearing, so you are a little anxious. Your stomach feels queasy, and your heart begins to thump. This is the *sympathetic* division of the *autonomic nervous system* functioning as you become aroused. You regain your confidence after reminding yourself that you were parked in a legal spot. As you relax, the *parasympathetic* division of the *autonomic nervous system* is working.

Review and Sharpen Your Thinking

1 *Discuss the nature and basic functions of the nervous system.*
- Identify the key characteristics of the brain and nervous system.
- Name and describe the pathways that allow the nervous system to carry out its three basic functions.
- Outline the divisions of the nervous system and explain their roles.

Try this exercise without looking at figure 2.1. Suppose you (1) saw a person coming toward you, (2) realized it was someone famous, (3) got excited, (4) waved and shouted, (5) suddenly realized it was not a famous person, and (6) became suddenly calm again. Which part of your nervous system would have been heavily involved at each of these six points?

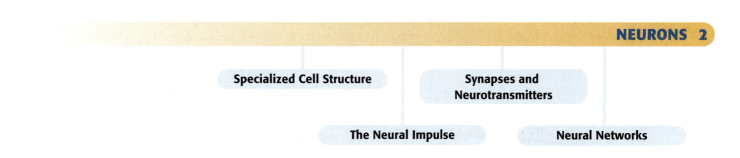

NEURONS **2**

Specialized Cell Structure   Synapses and Neurotransmitters

The Neural Impulse   Neural Networks

What are neurons and how do they communicate?

Within each division of the nervous system, much is happening at the cellular level. Nerve cells, chemicals, and electrical impulses work together to transmit information at speeds of up to 330 miles per hour. As a result, information can travel from your brain to your hands (or vice versa) in a matter of milliseconds (Krogh, 2000; Martini, 2001). Let's take a closer look at the mechanisms that allow such speedy processing.

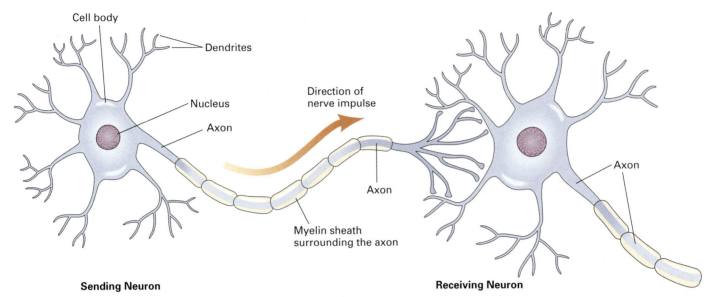

Sending Neuron   **Receiving Neuron**

FIGURE 2.2 **The Neuron** The drawing shows the parts of a neuron and the connection between one neuron and another. Note the cell body, the branching of dendrites, and the axon with a myelin sheath.

Specialized Cell Structure

There are two types of cells in the nervous system: neurons and glial cells. **Neurons** are the nerve cells that actually process information. **Glial cells** provide support and nutritional benefits to neurons (Lemke, 2001; Raabe & others, 2004). Glial cells are not specialized to process information in the way that neurons are, although there are many more of them in the nervous system than there are neurons.

The human brain contains about 100 billion neurons. The average neuron is as complex as a small computer and has as many as 10,000 physical connections with other cells. To have even the merest thought requires millions of neurons acting simultaneously (Carter, 1998). Most neurons are created very early in life, but their shape, size, and connections can change throughout the life span. Thus the way neurons function reflects the major characteristic of the nervous system described at the beginning of the chapter: plasticity.

Not all neurons are alike. They are specialized to handle different information processing functions. However, all neurons do have some common characteristics. Every neuron has three main parts (see figure 2.2):

- The **cell body** contains the *nucleus*, which directs the manufacture of substances that the neuron needs for growth and maintenance.
- **Dendrites** receive and orient information toward the cell body. One of the most distinctive features of neurons is the treelike branching of their numerous dendrites. Dendrites increase the neuron's surface area, allowing each neuron to receive input from many other neurons.
- The **axon** is the part of the neuron that carries information away from the cell body toward other cells. Although very thin (1/10,000th of an inch), axons can be very long, with many branches. In fact, some extend more than 3 feet—all the way from the top of the brain to the base of the spinal cord.

Covering all surfaces of the neurons, including the dendrites and axons, are very thin cellular membranes that are much like the surface of a bubble. The neuronal membranes are semipermeable, meaning that they contain tiny holes, or *channels,* that allow only certain substances to pass into and out of the neurons.

In addition, a **myelin sheath,** a layer of fat cells, encases and insulates most axons. By insulating axons, myelin sheaths speed up the transmission of nerve impulses (Mattson, 2002; Paus & others, 2001). Multiple sclerosis, a degenerative disease of the nervous system in which a hardening of myelin tissue occurs, disrupts neuronal communication.

neurons Nerve cells specialized for processing information. Neurons are the basic units of the nervous system.

glial cells Nerve cells that provide support and nutritional benefits to the nervous system.

cell body Part of the neuron that contains the nucleus, which directs the manufacture of substances that the neuron needs for growth and maintenance.

dendrites Branches of neurons that receive and orient information toward the cell body. Most neurons have numerous dendrites.

axon The part of the neuron that carries information away from the cell body to other cells; each neuron has only one axon.

myelin sheath A layer of fat cells that encases and insulates most axons, thus speeding up the transmission of nerve impulses.

The myelin sheath developed as the brain evolved. As brain size increased, it became necessary for information to travel over longer distances in the nervous system. Axons without myelin sheaths are not very good conductors of electricity. With the insulation of myelin sheaths, axons transmit electrical impulses and convey information much more rapidly. We can compare the myelin sheath's development to the evolution of freeways as cities grew. A freeway is a shielded road. It keeps fast-moving, long-distance traffic from getting snarled by slow local traffic.

The Neural Impulse

A neuron sends information through its axon in the form of brief impulses, or waves, of electricity. In old movies, you might have seen telegraph operators tapping out messages one click at a time over a telegraph wire to the next telegraph station. That is what neurons do. To transmit information to other neurons, a neuron sends impulses ("clicks") through its axon to the next neuron. As you reach to turn this page, hundreds of such impulses will stream down the axons in your arm to tell your muscles just when to flex and how vigorously. By changing the rate and timing of the signals, or "clicks," the neuron can vary its message.

The term **action potential** is used to describe the brief wave of positive electrical charge that sweeps down the axon. An action potential lasts only about 1/1,000th of a second. When a neuron sends an action potential, it is commonly said to be "firing."

The action potential abides by the *all-or-none principle:* Once the electrical impulse reaches a certain intensity, it fires and moves all the way down the axon without losing any of its intensity. The impulse traveling down an axon can be compared to the burning fuse of a firecracker. Whether a match or blowtorch is used to light the fuse, once the fuse has been lit, the spark travels quickly and with the same intensity down the fuse. To learn more about the action potential, see the animation in the interactivity "Neural Functioning."

In-Psych Plus

Synapses and Neurotransmitters

What happens when a neural impulse reaches the end of the axon? Neurons do not touch each other directly, but they manage to communicate. The story of the connection between one neuron and another is one of the most intriguing and highly researched areas of contemporary neuroscience (Bi & Poo, 2001; Steriade, 2004).

Synaptic Transmission **Synapses** are tiny junctions between neurons; the gap between neurons is referred to as a *synaptic gap*. Most synapses lie between the axon of one neuron and the dendrites or cell body of another neuron. Before the electrical impulse can cross the synaptic gap, it must be converted into a chemical signal.

Each axon branches out into numerous fibers that store substances called **neurotransmitters** within minute synaptic vesicles (sacs). As their name suggests, neurotransmitters transmit, or carry, information across the synaptic gap to the next neuron. When a nerve impulse reaches the end of an axon, it triggers the release of neurotransmitters, which flood the synaptic gap. The movements of the neurotransmitters are random, but some of them bump into receptor sites in the next neuron. If the shape of the receptor site corresponds to the shape of the neurotransmitter molecule, the neurotransmitter acts like a key to open the receptor site, so that the neuron can receive the signals from the previous neuron. After delivering its message, the neurotransmitter is reabsorbed by the axon that released it.

Think of the synapse as a river that blocks a road. A grocery truck (the action potential) arrives at one bank of the river, crosses by ferry, and continues its journey to market. Similarly, a message in the brain is "ferried" across the synapse by a neurotransmitter (Engelmann & MacDermott, 2004). Figure 2.3 gives an overview of how this connection between neurons takes place.

action potential The brief wave of electrical charge that sweeps down the axon during the transmission of a nerve impulse.

synapses Tiny junctions between two neurons, generally where the axon of one neuron meets the dendrites or the cell body of another neuron.

neurotransmitters Chemicals that carry information across the synaptic gap from one neuron to the next.

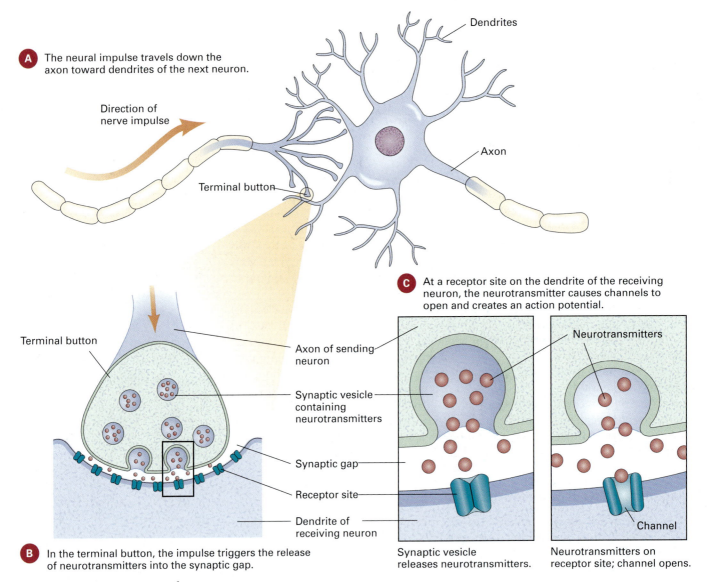

A The neural impulse travels down the axon toward dendrites of the next neuron.

Dendrites

Direction of nerve impulse

Axon

Terminal button

C At a receptor site on the dendrite of the receiving neuron, the neurotransmitter causes channels to open and creates an action potential.

Terminal button

Axon of sending neuron

Synaptic vesicle containing neurotransmitters

Synaptic gap

Receptor site

Dendrite of receiving neuron

Neurotransmitters

Channel

Synaptic vesicle releases neurotransmitters.

Neurotransmitters on receptor site; channel opens.

B In the terminal button, the impulse triggers the release of neurotransmitters into the synaptic gap.

FIGURE 2.3 How Synapses and Neurotransmitters Work *(a)* The axon of the sending neuron meets dendrites of the receiving neuron. *(b)* This is an enlargement of one synapse, showing the synaptic gap between the two neurons and the synaptic vesicles containing a neurotransmitter. *(c)* This enlargement of the receptor site shows how the neurotransmitter opens the channel, triggering the neuron to fire.

In-Psych Plus

Neurochemical Messengers   There are many neurotransmitters. Each plays a specific role and functions in a specific pathway. Whereas some neurotransmitters stimulate, or excite, neurons to fire, others can inhibit neurons from firing (Bloom, Nelson, & Lazerson, 2001). Some neurotransmitters are both excitatory and inhibitory. See the video clip "Functions of Neurotransmitters" for animations of the activity in the synaptic gap.

Most neurons secrete only one type of neurotransmitter, but often many different neurons are simultaneously secreting different neurotransmitters into the synaptic gaps of a single receiving neuron. At any given time, a neuron is receiving a mixture of messages from the neurotransmitters. So far, researchers have identified more than 50 neurotransmitters, each with a unique chemical makeup. The rapidly growing list likely will increase to more than 100 (Johnson, 2003). To get a better sense of what neurotransmitters do, let's consider just six that have major effects on our behavior:

• *Acetylcholine (ACh)* usually stimulates the firing of neurons and is involved in the action of muscles, learning, and memory (McIntyre & others, 2002; Savage, Chang, & Gold, 2003). ACh is found throughout the central and peripheral nervous systems. The venom of the black widow spider causes ACh to gush out of the synapses between the spinal cord and skeletal muscles, producing violent spasms. The drug curare, which some South American Indians apply to the tips of poison darts, blocks receptors for ACh, paralyzing muscles. In contrast, nicotine stimulates acetylcholine receptors. Individuals with Alzheimer's disease, a degenerative brain disorder that involves a decline in memory, have an acetylcholine deficiency (Herholtz 2003). Some of the drugs that alleviate the symptoms of Alzheimer's disease do so by compensating for the loss of the brain's supply of acetylcholine.

- *GABA (gamma aminobutyric acid)* is believed to be the neurotransmitter in as many as one-third of the brain's synapses and is found throughout the central nervous system. GABA is important in the brain because it keeps neurons from firing (Brambilla & others, 2003; Ryan, 2001). In this way, it helps to control the preciseness of the signal being carried from one neuron to the next. Low levels of GABA are linked with anxiety. Valium and other antianxiety drugs increase the inhibiting effects of GABA.

- *Norepinephrine* usually inhibits the firing of neurons in the central nervous system, but it excites the heart muscle, intestines, and urogenital tract. Stress stimulates the release of norepinephrine (Zaimovic & others, 2000). This neurotransmitter also helps to control alertness. Too little norepinephrine is associated with depression, too much with agitated, manic states. For example, amphetamines and cocaine cause hyperactive, manic states of behavior by rapidly increasing brain levels of norepinephrine (Arai & others, 2003). Recall from the beginning of the chapter that one of the most important characteristics of the brain and nervous system is integration. In the case of neurotransmitters, they may work in teams of two or more. For example, norepinephrine works with acetylcholine to regulate sleep and wakefulness.

- *Dopamine* mainly inhibits. It helps to control voluntary movement. Dopamine also affects sleep, mood, attention, and learning (Razmy, Lang, & Shapiro, 2004). Stimulant drugs, such as cocaine and amphetamines, produce excitement, alertness, elevated mood, decreased fatigue, and sometimes increased motor activity mainly by activating dopamine receptors. Low levels of dopamine are associated with Parkinson's disease, in which physical movements deteriorate (Wang & others, 2004). Although the actor Michael J. Fox contracted Parkinson's disease in his late 20s, the disease is uncommon before the age of 30 and becomes more common as people age (Cantuti-Castevetri, Shukitt-Hale, & Joseph, 2003). High levels of dopamine are associated with schizophrenia, a severe mental disorder that is discussed in chapter 11.

- *Serotonin* also primarily inhibits. Serotonin is involved in the regulation of sleep, mood, attention, and learning. In regulating states of sleep and wakefulness, it teams with acetylcholine and norepinephrine. Lowered levels of serotonin are associated with depression (Kanner & Balabanov, 2002; Wagner & Ambrosini, 2001). The antidepressant drug Prozac works by increasing brain levels of serotonin (Tissot, 2003).

- *Endorphins* are natural opiates that mainly stimulate the firing of neurons (Spetea & others, 2002). Endorphins shield the body from pain and elevate feelings of pleasure. A long-distance runner, a woman giving birth, and a person in shock after a car wreck all have elevated levels of endorphins (Jamurtas & others, 2000; Ortega, 2003). As early as the fourth century B.C., the Greeks used wild poppies to induce euphoria and minimize pain. More than 2,000 years later, the magical formula behind opium's addictive action was finally discovered. In the early 1970s, scientists found that some opiates mimic the action of endorphins by stimulating receptors in the brain involved with pleasure and pain (Appleyard & others, 2003; Pert, 1999; Pert & Snyder, 1973).

Like many of the drugs mentioned here, most drugs that influence behavior do so mainly by interfering with the work of neurotransmitters (Beatty, 2001; Mader, 2002). For example, alcohol blocks serotonin activity (Kelai & others, 2003). However,

How might jogging change your brain chemistry?

drugs can mimic or increase the effects of a neurotransmitter. For example, the drug morphine (the most important opiate) mimics the actions of endorphins by stimulating the receptors in the brain associated with pleasure and pain.

Neural Networks

So far in the coverage of neurons, I have focused mainly on how a single neuron functions and on how a nerve impulse travels from one neuron to another. Now let's look at how clusters of interconnected neurons, or neural networks, work together to integrate incoming information and coordinate outgoing information. Figure 2.4 shows a simplified drawing of a neural network (McIntosh, 2000). By looking at this diagram, you can get an idea of how the activity of one neuron is linked with that of many others.

Some neurons have short axons and communicate with nearby neurons. Other neurons have long axons and communicate with neurons some distance away. How are neural networks created? These networks are not static (Carlson, 2000). They can be altered through changes in the strength of synaptic connections. See the video clip "Brain Development" to learn about the relationship between biology and the environment in the creation of neural networks.

In-Psych Plus

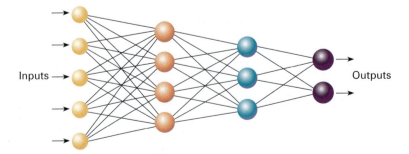

Inputs →   Outputs

FIGURE 2.4 An Example of a Neural Network Inputs (information from the environment and sensory receptors, such as the sight of a person's face) become embedded in extensive connections among neurons in the brain, which leads to outputs (such as remembering the person's face).

Any piece of information, such as a name, might be embedded in hundreds or even thousands of connections among neurons (Lee & Farhat, 2001). In this way, such human activities as being attentive, memorizing, and thinking are distributed over a wide range of connected neurons (Del-Moral-Hernandez, 2003). The strength of these connections among neurons determines how well you remember the information (Golden, 2002; Krause & others, 2000; McClelland & Rumelhart, 1986).

Let's see how the neural network concept might explain a typical memory, such as the name of a new acquaintance. Initially, the processing of the person's face might activate a small number of weak neuronal connections that make you remember a general category ("interesting woman" or "attractive man"). However, repeated experience with that person will increase the strength and possibly the number of those connections. Thus you may come to remember the person's name as the neurons activated by the name become connected with the neurons that are activated by the face. Chapter 7 explores the nature of memory at greater length.

Review and Sharpen Your Thinking

2 *Explain what neurons are and how they process information.*
- Differentiate between neurons and glial cells, and describe the functions of the parts of a neuron.
- Explain what a neural impulse is and how it is generated.
- Discuss how a neural impulse is transmitted from one neuron to another.
- Describe the function of neural networks.

Why is it important to have so many neural connections and to have integration between neurons?

STRUCTURES OF THE BRAIN AND THEIR FUNCTIONS 3

Levels of Organization in the Brain

The Cerebral Hemispheres and Split-Brain Research

The Cerebral Cortex

Integration of Function in the Brain

How is the brain organized?

The extensive and intricate networks of neurons that we have just studied are not visible to the naked eye. Fortunately, technology is available to help neuroscientists form pictures of neurons and the larger structures they make up without harming the organism being studied. (To learn more about research using this technology, see the video clip "Brain Structure and Imaging Methods.") This section explores some research findings regarding the structures and functions of the brain.

In-Psych Plus

Levels of Organization in the Brain

As a human embryo develops inside its mother's womb, the nervous system begins forming as a long, hollow tube in the embryo's back. At 3 weeks or so after conception, cells making up the tube differentiate into a mass of neurons, most of which then develop into three major regions of the brain: the hindbrain, which is adjacent

FIGURE 2.5 **Embryological Development of the Nervous System**
The photograph shows the primitive, tubular appearance of the nervous system in the human embryo at 6 weeks. The drawing shows the major brain regions and spinal cord as they appear early in embryonic development.

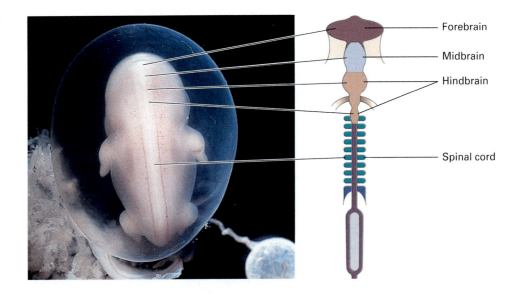

Forebrain

Midbrain

Hindbrain

Spinal cord

to the top part of the spinal cord; the midbrain, which rises above the hindbrain; and the forebrain, which is the uppermost region of the brain (see figure 2.5).

Hindbrain   The **hindbrain,** located at the skull's rear, is the lowest portion of the brain. The three main parts of the hindbrain are the medulla, cerebellum, and pons. Figure 2.6 shows the location of these brain structures (along with the main structures of the midbrain and forebrain).

The *medulla* begins where the spinal cord enters the skull. It helps to control our breathing and regulates reflexes that allow us to maintain an upright posture.

The *cerebellum* extends from the rear of the hindbrain, just above the medulla. It consists of two rounded structures thought to play important roles in motor coordination (Middleton & Strick, 2001). For example, when we play golf, practice the piano, or learn a new dance, the cerebellum is hard at work. If a higher portion of the brain commands us to write the number 7, it is the cerebellum that integrates the muscular activities required to do so. When the cerebellum is damaged, movements become uncoordinated and jerky. Extensive damage to the cerebellum even makes it impossible to stand up.

The *pons* is a bridge in the hindbrain. It contains several clusters of fibers involved in sleep and arousal (Kolb & Whishaw, 2003; Terao & others, 2004).

Midbrain   The **midbrain,** located between the hindbrain and forebrain, is an area in which many nerve-fiber systems ascend and descend to connect the higher and lower portions of the brain. In particular, the midbrain relays information between the brain and the eyes and ears. The ability to attend to an object visually, for example, is linked to one bundle of neurons in the midbrain. Parkinson's disease, a deterioration of movement that produces rigidity and tremors, damages a section near the bottom of the midbrain.

Two systems in the midbrain are of special interest. One is the **reticular formation** (refer to figure 2.6), a diffuse collection of neurons involved in stereotyped patterns of behavior, such as walking, sleeping, or turning to attend to a sudden noise (Sasaki, Yoshimura, & Naito, 2004; Soja & others, 2001). The other system consists of small groups of neurons that use the neurotransmitters serotonin, dopamine, and norepinephrine. Although these groups contain relatively few cells, they send their axons to a remarkable variety of brain regions, perhaps explaining their involvement in high-level, integrative functions (Shier, Butler, & Lewis, 1999).

A region called the **brain stem** includes much of the hindbrain (it does not include the cerebellum) and the midbrain and is so-called because it looks like a stem

hindbrain The lowest level of the brain, consisting of the medulla, cerebellum, and pons.

midbrain The region located between the hindbrain and forebrain, in which many nerve-fiber systems ascend and descend to connect the higher and lower portions of the brain.

reticular formation The midbrain system that consists of a diffuse collection of neurons involved in stereotypical behaviors, such as walking, sleeping, or turning to attend to a sudden noise.

brain stem The region of the brain that includes most of the hindbrain (excluding the cerebellum) and the midbrain.

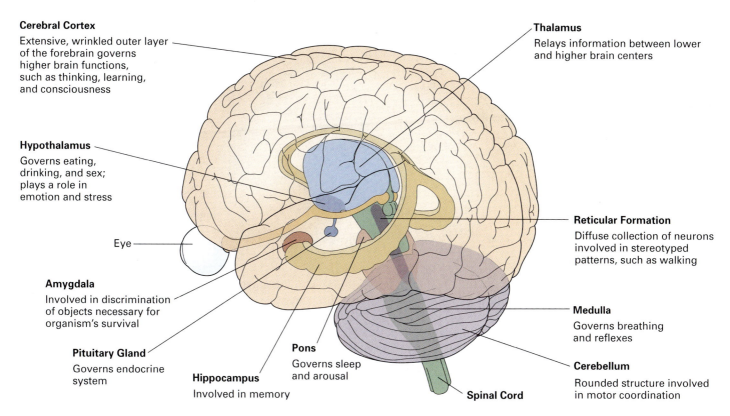

Cerebral Cortex
Extensive, wrinkled outer layer of the forebrain governs higher brain functions, such as thinking, learning, and consciousness

Hypothalamus
Governs eating, drinking, and sex; plays a role in emotion and stress

Eye

Amygdala
Involved in discrimination of objects necessary for organism's survival

Pituitary Gland
Governs endocrine system

Hippocampus
Involved in memory

Pons
Governs sleep and arousal

Spinal Cord

Thalamus
Relays information between lower and higher brain centers

Reticular Formation
Diffuse collection of neurons involved in stereotyped patterns, such as walking

Medulla
Governs breathing and reflexes

Cerebellum
Rounded structure involved in motor coordination

FIGURE 2.6 Structure and Regions of the Human Brain

(Carlson, 2001). Embedded deep within the brain, the brain stem connects with the spinal cord at its lower end and then extends upward to encase the reticular formation in the midbrain. The most ancient part of the brain, the brain stem evolved more than 500 million years ago (Carter, 1998). Clumps of cells in the brain stem determine alertness and regulate basic survival functions, such as breathing, heartbeat, and blood pressure.

Forebrain   You try to understand what all of these terms and parts of the brain mean. You talk with friends and plan a party for this weekend. You remember that it has been 6 months since you went to the dentist. You are confident you will do well on the next exam in this course. All of these experiences and millions more would not be possible without the **forebrain,** the highest level of the human brain. Go to the interactivity "Parts of the Brain" for a 3D tour of the brain.

Before we explore the structures and function of the forebrain, let's examine how the brain evolved. The brains of the earliest vertebrates were smaller and simpler than those of later animals. Genetic changes during the evolutionary process were responsible for the development of more complex brains with more parts and more interconnections (Carlson, 2001). Figure 2.7 compares the brains of a rat, cat, chimpanzee, and human. In the chimpanzee's brain, and especially the human's brain, the hindbrain and midbrain structures are covered by a forebrain structure called the cerebral cortex (Goldsmith & Zimmerman, 2001). The human hindbrain and midbrain are similar to those of other animals, so it is the forebrain structures that mainly differentiate the human brain. The human forebrain's most important structures are the limbic system, thalamus, basal ganglia, hypothalamus, and cerebral cortex.

Limbic System   The **limbic system,** a loosely connected network of structures under the cerebral cortex, is important in both memory and emotion. Its two principal structures are the amygdala and hippocampus (refer to figure 2.6).

The *amygdala* (from the Latin for "almond" shape) is involved in the discrimination of objects that are necessary for the organism's survival, such as appropriate food,

In-Psych Plus

forebrain The highest level of the brain. Key structures in the forebrain are the limbic system, thalamus, basal ganglia, hypothalamus, and cerebral cortex.

limbic system Loosely connected network of structures—including the amygdala and hippocampus—that play important roles in memory and emotion.

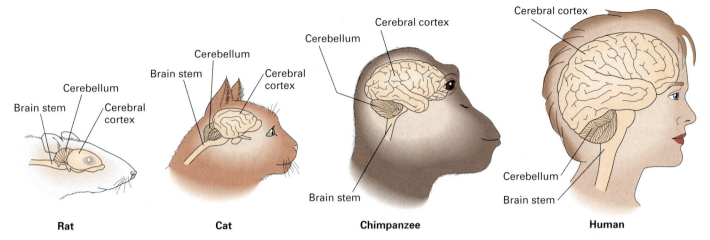

Rat   **Cat**   **Chimpanzee**   **Human**

FIGURE 2.7 Brain Structure in Different Species Note how much larger the cerebral cortex becomes, from the brain of a rat to the brain of a human, with evolutionary specialization.

mates, and social rivals. Neurons in the amygdala often fire selectively at the sight of such stimuli, and lesions in the amygdala can cause animals to attempt to eat, fight, or mate with inappropriate objects, such as chairs. The amygdala also is involved in emotional awareness and expression through its many connections with higher and lower regions of the brain (Davidson, 2000).

The *hippocampus* has a special role in the storage of memories (Bannerman & others, 2002; Ryan & Cohen, 2004). Individuals who suffer extensive hippocampal damage cannot retain any new conscious memories after the damage. However, memories probably are not stored "in" the limbic system. Instead, the limbic system seems to determine what parts of the information passing through the cortex should be "printed" into durable, lasting neural traces in the cortex.

Thalamus   The **thalamus** is a forebrain structure that sits at the top of the brain stem in the central core of the brain (refer to figure 2.6). It serves as a very important relay station, functioning much like a server in a computer network. That is, the thalamus sorts information and sends it to the appropriate places in the forebrain for further integration and interpretation (Montaqnese & others, 2004). For example, one area of the thalamus receives information from the cerebellum and projects it to the motor area of the cerebral cortex. Indeed, most neural input to the cerebral cortex goes through the thalamus. While one area of the thalamus works to orient information from the sense receptors (hearing, seeing, and so on), another region seems to be involved in sleep and wakefulness, having ties with the reticular formation.

Basal Ganglia   Above the thalamus and under the cerebral cortex lie large clusters, or *ganglia,* of neurons called basal ganglia. The **basal ganglia** work with the cerebellum and the cerebral cortex to control and coordinate voluntary movements. Basal ganglia enable people to engage in habitual behaviors, such as riding a bicycle. Individuals with damage to basal ganglia suffer from either unwanted movement, such as constant writhing or jerking of limbs, or too little movement, such as the slow and deliberate movements of those with Parkinson's disease.

Hypothalamus   The **hypothalamus,** a small forebrain structure, located just below the thalamus (refer to figure 2.6), monitors three pleasurable activities—eating, drinking, and sex—as well as emotion, stress, and reward. As is discussed later, the hypothalamus also helps direct the endocrine system. Perhaps the best way to describe the function of the hypothalamus is as a regulator of the body's internal state. It is sensitive to changes in the blood and neural input, and it responds by influencing the secretion of hormones and neural outputs. For example, if the temperature of circulating blood near the hypothalamus is increased by just 1 or 2 degrees, certain cells in the hypothalamus start increasing their rate of firing. Increased circulation through the skin and sweat glands occurs immediately to release this heat from the body. The

thalamus Forebrain structure that functions as a relay station to sort input and direct it to different areas of the cerebral cortex. It also has ties to the reticular formation.

basal ganglia Large clusters of neurons, located above the thalamus and under the cerebral cortex, that control and coordinate voluntary movements.

hypothalamus Forebrain structure involved in regulating eating, drinking, and sex; directing the endocrine system through the pituitary gland; and monitoring emotion, stress, and reward.

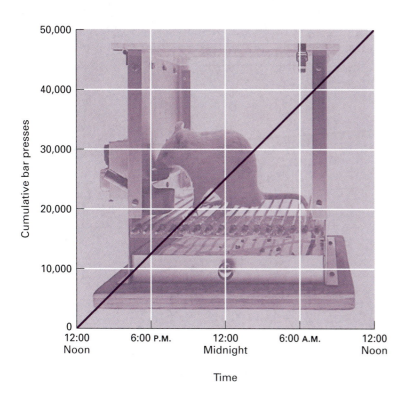

The graphed results for one rat in an experiment by Olds (1958) show that it pressed the bar more than 2,000 times an hour for a period of 24 hours to receive stimulation to its hypothalamus. One of the rats in the experiments is shown pressing the bar.

cooled blood circulating to the hypothalamus slows down the activity of some of the neurons there, stopping the process when the temperature is just right—37.1° Celsius. These temperature-sensitive neurons function like a finely tuned thermostat in maintaining the body in a balanced state.

The hypothalamus also is involved in emotional states and stress, playing an important role as an integrative location for handling stress (Hayashi & others, 2004). Much of this integration is accomplished through the hypothalamus's action on the *pituitary gland,* an important endocrine gland located just below it.

If certain areas of the hypothalamus are electrically stimulated, a feeling of pleasure results. In a classic experiment, James Olds and Peter Milner (1954) implanted an electrode in the hypothalamus of a rat's brain. When the rat ran to a corner of an enclosed area, a mild electric current was delivered to its hypothalamus. The researchers thought the electric current would cause the rat to avoid the corner. Much to their surprise, the rat kept returning to the corner. Olds and Milner believed they had discovered a pleasure center in the hypothalamus. Olds (1958) conducted further experiments and found that rats would press bars until they dropped over from exhaustion just to continue to receive a mild electric shock to their hypothalamus. One rat pressed a bar more than 2,000 times an hour for a period of 24 hours to receive the stimulation to its hypothalamus (see figure 2.8). Today researchers agree that the hypothalamus is involved in pleasurable feelings but that other areas of the brain, such as the limbic system and a bundle of fibers in the forebrain, are also important in the link between the brain and pleasure.

The Olds studies have implications for drug addiction. In the Olds studies, the rat pressed the bar mainly because doing so produced a positive, rewarding effect (pleasure), not because it wanted to avoid or escape a negative effect (pain). Cocaine users talk about the drug's ability to heighten pleasure in food, in sex, and in a variety of activities, highlighting the reward aspects of the drug (Restak, 1988).

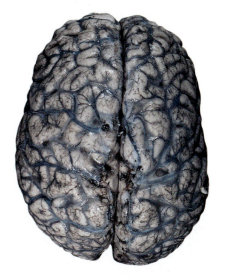

The two halves (hemispheres) of the human brain can be seen clearly in this photograph. *What is the structure that allows the two halves to work together?*

The Cerebral Cortex

The **cerebral cortex,** which is divided into two halves (hemispheres), is the highest region of the forebrain and is the most recently developed part of the brain in the evolutionary scheme. It is in the cerebral cortex that the highest mental functions, such as

cerebral cortex Highest level of the forebrain, where the highest mental functions, such as thinking and planning, take place.

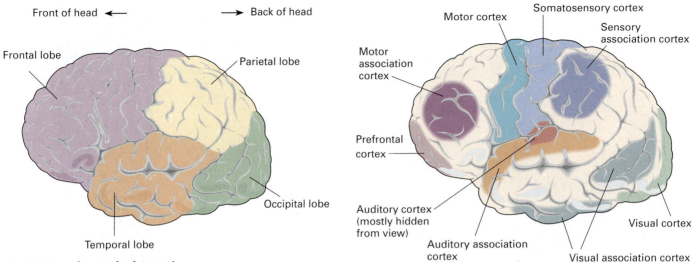

Front of head ◄——   ——► Back of head

Frontal lobe

Parietal lobe

Occipital lobe

Temporal lobe

Motor cortex

Somatosensory cortex

Sensory association cortex

Motor association cortex

Prefrontal cortex

Auditory cortex (mostly hidden from view)

Auditory association cortex

Visual association cortex

Visual cortex

FIGURE 2.9 The Cerebral Cortex's Lobes and Association Areas The cerebral cortex is roughly divided into four lobes: occipital, temporal, frontal, and parietal. The cerebral cortex also consists of the motor cortex and somatosensory cortex, as well as the association cortex. The association areas include the visual association cortex, auditory association cortex, and sensory association cortex.

A computerized reconstruction of Phineas T. Gage's accident, based on measurements taken of his skull. *Can you determine which parts of his brain were damaged?*

thinking and planning, take place. The neural tissue that makes up the cerebral cortex covers the lower portions of the brain like a large cap. In humans, the cerebral cortex is greatly convoluted with lots of grooves and bulges, which considerably enlarge its surface area (compared with a brain with a smooth surface). The cerebral cortex is highly connected with other parts of the brain. Literally millions of axons connect the neurons of the cerebral cortex with those located elsewhere in the brain. The cerebral cortex comprises the lobes, somatosensory cortex, motor cortex, and association cortex.

Lobes Each hemisphere of the cerebral cortex is subdivided into four regions—the frontal lobe, the parietal lobe, the temporal lobe, and the occipital lobe (see figure 2.9).

The **occipital lobe,** at the back of the head, responds to visual stimuli. Different areas of the two occipital lobes are connected to process such information as color, shape, and motion. A stroke or wound in the occipital lobe can cause blindness or, at a minimum, wipe out a portion of the person's visual field.

The **temporal lobe,** the portion of the cerebral cortex just above the ears, is involved in hearing, language processing, and memory. The temporal lobes have a number of connections to the limbic system. For this reason, people with damage to the temporal lobes cannot file experiences into long-term memory.

The **frontal lobe,** the portion of the cerebral cortex behind the forehead, is involved in the control of voluntary muscles, intelligence, and personality. One fascinating case study illustrates how damage to the frontal lobes can significantly alter personality. Phineas T. Gage, a 25-year-old foreman who worked for the Rutland and Burlington Railroad, met with an accident on September 13, 1848. Phineas and several co-workers were using blasting powder to construct a roadbed. The crew drilled holes in the rock and gravel, poured in the blasting powder, and then tamped down the powder with an iron rod. While Phineas was still tamping it down, the powder blew up, driving the iron rod up through the left side of his face and out through the top of his head. Though the wound in his skull healed in a matter of weeks, Phineas became a different person. He had been a mild-mannered, hardworking, emotionally calm individual prior to the accident, well liked by all who knew him. Afterward, he became obstinate, moody, irresponsible, selfish, and incapable of participating in any planned activities. Damage to the frontal lobe of his brain had dramatically altered Phineas' personality.

Without intact frontal lobes, humans are emotionally shallow, distractible, listless, and so insensitive to social contexts that they may belch with abandon at dinner parties (Hooper & Teresi, 1992). Individuals with frontal lobe damage become so distracted by irrelevant stimuli that they often cannot carry out some basic directions. One such individual, when asked to light a candle, struck a match, put the candle in his mouth, and acted as if he were smoking it (Luria, 1973).

The frontal lobes of humans are especially large when compared with those of other animals. For example, the frontal cortex of rats barely exists; in cats, it occu-

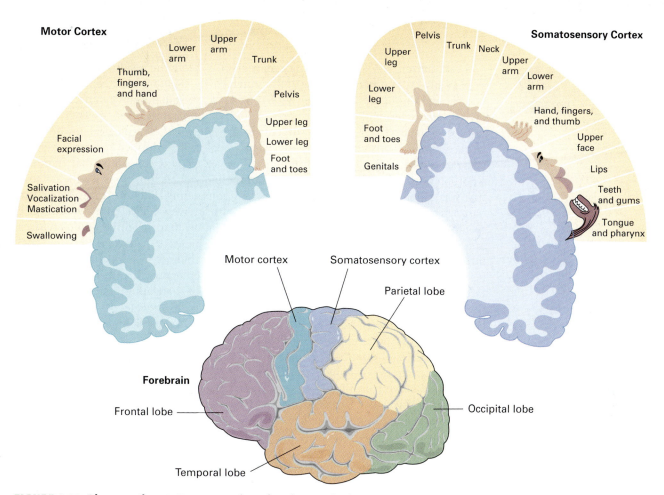

Motor Cortex

Lower arm · Upper arm · Trunk · Thumb, fingers, and hand · Pelvis · Upper leg · Lower leg · Foot and toes · Facial expression · Salivation Vocalization Mastication · Swallowing

Somatosensory Cortex

Pelvis · Trunk · Neck · Upper leg · Lower leg · Foot and toes · Genitals · Upper arm · Lower arm · Hand, fingers, and thumb · Upper face · Lips · Teeth and gums · Tongue and pharynx

Motor cortex · Somatosensory cortex · Parietal lobe

Forebrain

Frontal lobe · Occipital lobe · Temporal lobe

FIGURE 2.10 **Disproportionate Representation of Body Parts in the Motor and Somatosensory Areas of the Cortex** The amount of cortex allotted to a body part is not proportionate to the body part's size. Instead, the brain has more space for body parts that require precision and control. For example, the thumb, fingers, and hand require more brain tissue than does the arm.

pies a paltry 3½ percent of the cerebral cortex; in chimpanzees, 17 percent; and in humans, approximately 30 percent. Some neuroscientists maintain that the frontal cortex is an important index of evolutionary advancement (Hooper & Teresi, 1992).

An important part of the frontal lobes is the *prefrontal cortex,* which is at the front of the motor cortex (refer to figure 2.9). The prefrontal cortex is believed to be involved in higher cognitive functions, such as planning and reasoning (Manes & others, 2002). Some neuroscientists refer to the prefrontal cortex as an executive control system because of its role in monitoring and organizing thinking (Owen, 1997).

The **parietal lobe,** located at the top and toward the rear of each hemisphere, is involved in registering spatial location, attention, and motor control. Thus the parietal lobes are at work when you are judging how far you have to throw a ball to get it to someone else, when you shift your attention from one activity to another (turn your attention away from the TV to a noise outside), and when you turn the pages of this book. The brilliant physicist Albert Einstein said that his reasoning often was best when he imagined objects in space. It turns out that his parietal lobes were 15 percent larger than average (Witelson, Kigar, & Harvey, 1999).

A word of caution is in order about going too far in localizing function within a particular lobe. Although I have attributed specific functions to a particular lobe (such as vision in the occipital lobe), there is considerable integration and connection among the lobes and between lobes and other parts of the brain.

Somatosensory Cortex and Motor Cortex Two other important regions of the cerebral cortex are the somatosensory cortex and the motor cortex (refer to figure 2.9). The **somatosensory cortex** processes information about body sensations. It is located at the front of the parietal lobes. The **motor cortex,** just behind the frontal lobes,

occipital lobe The part of the cerebral cortex at the back of the head that is involved in vision.

temporal lobe The portion of the cerebral cortex just above the ears that is involved in hearing, language processing, and memory.

frontal lobe The part of the cerebral cortex just behind the forehead that is involved in the control of voluntary muscles, intelligence, and personality.

parietal lobe The area of the cerebral cortex at the top of the head that is involved in registering spatial location, attention, and motor control.

somatosensory cortex The area of the cerebral cortex that processes information about body sensations.

motor cortex The area of the cerebral cortex that processes information about voluntary movement.

processes information about voluntary movement. Explore the relationship between the somatosensory and motor cortexes in the interactivity "Sensorimotor Neural Circuits."

The map in figure 2.10 shows which parts of the somatosensory and motor cortex are associated with different parts of the body. It is based on research done by Wilder Penfield (1947), a neurosurgeon at the Montreal Neurological Institute. He worked with patients who had severe epilepsy and often performed surgery to remove portions of the epileptic patients' brains. However, he was concerned that removing a portion of the brain might impair some of the individuals' functions. Penfield's solution was to map the cortex during surgery by stimulating different cortical areas and observing the responses of the patients, who were given a local anesthetic so they would remain awake during the operation. He found that, when he stimulated certain somatosensory and motor areas of the brain, different parts of a patient's body moved. For both somatosensory and motor areas, there is a point-to-point relation between a part of the body and a location on the cerebral cortex. In figure 2.10, the face and hands are given proportionately more space than other body parts because the face and hands are capable of finer perceptions and movements than are other body areas and, therefore, need more cerebral cortex representation.

The point-to-point mapping of sensory fields onto the cortex's surface is the basis of our orderly and accurate perception of the world (Fox, 1996). When something touches your lip, for example, your brain knows what body part has been touched because the nerve pathways from your lip are the only pathways that project to the lip region of the sensory cortex.

One familiar example of what happens when these neural pathways get connected the wrong way is seen in Siamese cats. Many Siamese cats have a genetic defect that causes the pathways from the eyes to connect to the wrong parts of the visual cortex during development. The result is that these cats spend their lives looking at things cross-eyed in an effort to "straighten out" the visual image of their visual cortex.

Association Cortex   Embedded in the brain's lobes, the association cortex makes up 75 percent of the cerebral cortex. Processing information about sensory input and motor output is not all that is taking place in the cerebral cortex. The **association cortex** (sometimes called *association areas*) comprises the regions of the cerebral cortex that integrate this information. The highest intellectual functions, such as thinking and problem solving, occur in the association cortex. Refer back to figure 2.9 to see how the association areas relate to the locations of the lobes. By observing brain-damaged individuals and using a mapping technique, scientists have found that the association cortex is involved mainly in language and perception.

Interestingly, damage to a specific part of the association cortex often does not result in a specific loss of function. With the exception of language areas (which are localized), loss of function seems to depend more on the extent of damage to the association cortex than on the specific location of the damage. For example, the largest portion of the association cortex, the motor association cortex, is located in the frontal lobe, directly under the forehead. Damage to this area does not lead to motor loss. Indeed, it is this area that may be most directly related to thinking and problem solving.

Early studies referred to the frontal lobe as the center of intelligence, but research suggests that frontal lobe damage may not result in a lowering of intelligence. Planning and judgment are often associated with the frontal lobe. Personality also may be linked to the frontal lobe. Recall the misfortune of Phineas Gage, whose personality radically changed after he experienced frontal lobe damage.

The Cerebral Hemispheres and Split-Brain Research

At the beginning of the discussion of the cerebral cortex, I indicated that it is divided into two halves—left and right. Do these hemispheres have different functions? For many years, scientists speculated that the **corpus callosum,** a thick bundle of about

association cortex Regions of the cerebral cortex in which the highest intellectual functions, including thinking and problem solving, occur (also called *association areas*).

corpus callosum The large bundle of axons that connects the brain's two hemispheres.

80 million axons that connects the brain's two hemispheres, had something to do with relaying information between the two sides.

Roger Sperry (1974) confirmed this hypothesis in an experiment in which he cut the corpus callosum in cats. After the operation, Sperry trained the cats to solve a series of visual problems with one eye blindfolded. After a cat learned the task—say, with only its left eye covered—its other eye was blindfolded and the animal was tested again. The split-brain cat behaved as if it had never learned the task. It seems that the memory was stored only in the left hemisphere, which could no longer directly communicate with the right hemisphere.

Further evidence of the corpus callosum's function has come from studies of patients who, like Brandi Binder, have severe, even life-threatening, forms of epilepsy. Epilepsy is caused by electrical "brain-storms" that flash uncontrollably across the corpus callosum. In one famous case, neurosurgeons severed the corpus callosum of an epileptic patient now known as W. J. in a final attempt to reduce his unbearable seizures. Sperry (1968) examined W. J. and found that the corpus callosum functions the same in humans as in animals—cutting the corpus callosum seemed to leave the patient with "two separate minds," which learned and operated independently of each other.

The right hemisphere, split-brain research indicates, receives information only from the left side of the body, and the left hemisphere receives information only from the right side of the body. When you place your left hand on a surface, for example, only the right hemisphere of your brain detects the surface. When you hold an object in your right hand, only the left hemisphere of the brain detects the object. Figure 2.11 illustrates how the two hemispheres of the brain process information differently. Keep in mind, however, that, because you have a normal corpus callosum, both hemispheres receive this information.

In people with intact brains, specialization of function does occur in some areas (Corballis, 2004; Springer & Deutsch, 1998):

- *Verbal processing.* The most extensive research on the brain's two hemispheres has focused on language. Speech and grammar are localized to the left hemisphere (Gelfand & Bookheimer, 2003). A common misconception, though, is that *all* language processing is carried out in the brain's left hemisphere (Loddenkemper & others, 2004). Such aspects of language as appropriate use of language in different contexts, use of metaphor, and much of our sense of humor reside in the right hemisphere (Berman & others, 2003).
- *Nonverbal processing.* The right hemisphere is more dominant in processing non-verbal information, such as spatial perception, visual recognition, and emotion (Corballis, Funnell, & Gazzaniga, 2002). For example, the right hemisphere is mainly at work when we are processing information about people's faces (O'Toole, 2003). The right hemisphere also may be more involved in processing information about emotions, both when we express emotions ourselves and when we recognize others' emotions (Heller & others, 1997).

Because differences in the functioning of the brain's two hemispheres are known to exist, people commonly use the terms *left-brained* and *right-brained* as a way of categorizing themselves and others. Such generalizations have little scientific basis. The most common myth about hemispheric specialization is that the left brain is logical and the right brain is creative. After the publication of Roger Sperry's classic split-brain studies, his findings became oversimplified in the media and people were usually labeled either right-brained (artistic) or left-brained (logical).

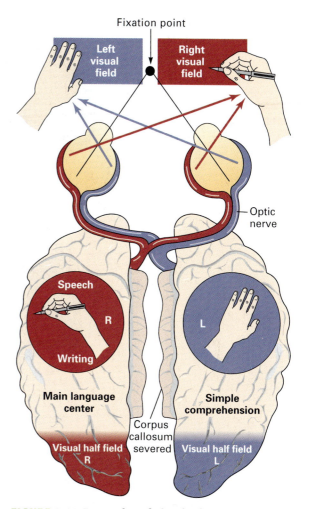

FIGURE 2.11 Processing of Visual Information in the Brain's Hemispheres Information from the visual field's left side projects to the right hemisphere. Information from the visual field's right side projects to the left hemisphere. In a split-brain patient, whose corpus callosum has been severed, these stimuli are processed only in the hemisphere to which they are projected. Normally, however, both hemispheres are involved in processing the information.

FIGURE 2.12 Integration of Language Activity This scan of the left half of the brain contrasts the different areas used in several aspects of language activity: generating words, hearing words, seeing words, and speaking words. A normal brain seamlessly integrates activity in these different areas.

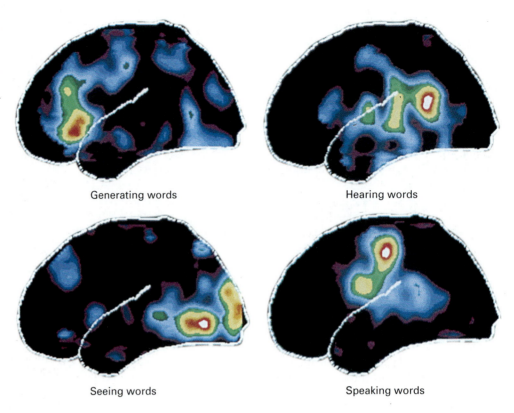

Generating words

Hearing words

Seeing words

Speaking words

Sperry did discover that the *left* hemisphere is superior in the kind of logic used to prove geometric theorems. But in everyday life, our logic problems involve integrating information and drawing conclusions. In these instances, the *right* hemisphere is crucial. In most complex activities in which people engage, the brain's two hemispheres interact (Hoptman & Davidson, 1994). For example, the right hemisphere is better at some musical skills, such as recognizing chords. But the left hemisphere is better at others, such as distinguishing which of two sounds came first. Enjoying or creating music requires the use of both hemispheres.

One positive result of the left-brain, right-brain myth is a perception that more right-brain activities should be incorporated into school programs (Edwards, 1979). In schools that rely heavily on rote learning, children probably would benefit from exercises in intuitive thought and holistic thinking. But a deficiency in school curricula has nothing at all to do with left-brain, right-brain specialization.

In sum, some specialization of functions exists in both the left hemisphere (processing of certain verbal information) and the right hemisphere (processing of certain nonverbal information) of the brain. However, in many complex tasks in which humans engage in their everyday lives, integration across the hemispheres is common.

Where do you process emotions? Most people process emotions in their right brain. Use the interactivity "Brain Lateralization" to learn more about your own brain. To learn more about the hemispheres, see the Critical Controversy box, which explores similarities and differences between men's and women's brains.

In-Psych Plus

Integration of Function in the Brain

How do all of the regions of the brain cooperate to produce the wondrous complexity of thought and behavior that characterizes humans? Neuroscience still doesn't have answers to such questions as how the brain solves a murder mystery or writes a poem or essay. However, considerable integration of function does take place in the brain (Gevins, 1999; Miller & Cohen, 2001). Neuroscientists have found, for example, that different parts of the left hemisphere are activated in a task such as meeting in a study group. Looking at your notes or textbook, discussing concepts with other students, or putting your thoughts into words each activates a particular area (see figure 2.12).

Are There "His" and "Her" Brains?

Does gender matter when it comes to brain structure and function? Human brains are very much alike, whether the brain belongs to a man or to a woman. However, researchers have found some differences between the male brain and the female brain (Blum, 1998; Goldstein & others, 2001; Kimura, 2000; Raz & others, 2001; Ryan, Atkinson, & Dunham, 2004). Among the differences that have been discovered so far are these:

- One part of the hypothalamus responsible for sexual behavior is larger in men than in women (Swaab & others, 2001, 2003).
- Portions of the corpus callosum—the band of tissues through which the brain's two hemispheres communicate—are larger in women than in men (de Lacoste-Utamsing & Holloway, 1982; Le Vay, 1994). Might this difference mean that men and women process information differently? In one study, women were more likely to use both brain hemispheres to process language, whereas men were more likely to use only the left hemisphere (Shaywitz & others, 1995). Despite these differences, the two sexes performed equally well on the task, which involved sounding out words. The researchers concluded that nature has given the brain different routes to the same ability.
- Men lose brain tissue earlier in the aging process than women do, and overall they lose more of it (Carter, 1998). Further reports suggest that men are especially prone to tissue loss in the frontal (thinking, reasoning) and temporal (hearing) lobes, but women are prone to tissue loss in the parietal lobe (spatial location) and hippocampus (memory) (Nystrand, 1996).

Differences in the ways that men's and women's brains function likely evolved over time. Some of the differences appear to be the result of a division of labor dating to early hunter-gatherer civilizations. For example, men are better than women at spatial-navigational skills, such as reading maps, judging distances, and throwing darts (Kimura, 2000; Majeres, 1999). However, some psychologists point out that in many cases such differences are small and that the differences do not mean that all men are better than all women at such tasks (Hyde & Mezulis, 2002).

In one recent neuroimaging study, an area of the parietal lobe that functions in visuospatial skills was found to be larger in men than in women (Frederikse & others, 2000). Women, on the other hand, have a better memory for words and objects and are better at fine motor skills (Halpern, 2001). These abilities, some speculate, may have evolved through making clothes and gathering and preparing food.

Are these brain differences truly innate, driven by nature through evolution, genetic programming, and hormones? Or might they be more a consequence of environment, the result of societal influences that stereotypically define sex-specific roles and characteristics, in effect shaping our brains in accordance with these roles? Some psychologists argue that the latter explanation accounts for male/female differences in math and verbal achievement (Eagly, 2002). However, many questions regarding men's and women's brains are exceedingly complex and likely cannot be answered by strictly biological or environmental arguments.

Also, as psychologist Diane Halpern (2001) points out, the fact that the brains of women and men are different does not mean that one sex's brain is better, any more than one sex's genitals are better. *Different* does not mean deficient. People can be different without being unequal in ability.

Research and speculation regarding sex differences and similarities in human brains require further study before being fully accepted as reliable and valid by the scientific community. Meanwhile, debate about whether gender differences exist and about how big or small the differences are will continue to flourish (Aartsen & others, 2004).

What do you think?

- Could sex differences in the brain be the result rather than the cause of behavioral differences? Explain.
- Have differences in women's and men's brains been exaggerated in light of the substantial similarities in their brains? Might the media be involved in any exaggerations? Explain.
- Given the differences that have been found in the brains of males and females, should males and females be educated differently? Explain.

For a more complex example of integrative brain function, consider the act of escaping from a burning building. Imagine you are sitting at your desk, writing letters, when fire breaks out behind you. The sound of crackling flames is relayed from your ear, through the thalamus, to the auditory cortex, and on to the auditory association cortex. At each stage, the stimulus is processed to extract information, and at some stage, probably at the association cortex level, the sounds are finally matched with something like a neural memory representing sounds of fires you have heard previously. The association "fire" sets new machinery in motion. Your attention (guided in part by the reticular formation) shifts to the auditory signal being held in your association cortex and then to your auditory association cortex, and simultaneously (again guided by reticular systems) your head turns toward the noise. Now your visual association cortex reports in: "Objects matching flames are present." In other regions of the association cortex, the visual and auditory reports are synthesized ("We have things that look and sound like fire"), and neural associations representing potential actions ("flee") are activated. However, firing the neurons that code the plan to flee will not get you out of the room. The basal ganglia must become engaged, and from there the commands will arise to set the brain stem, motor cortex, and cerebellum to the task of actually transporting you out of the room.

In-Psych Plus

Which part of your brain did you use to escape? Virtually all systems had a role. (To visualize how the sensory information is brought together, see the video clip "Sensory Processes and Brain Integration.") By the way, you will probably remember this event because your limbic circuitry would likely have started memory formation when the association "fire" was triggered. The next time the sounds of crackling flames reach your association cortex, the associations triggered will include this escape.

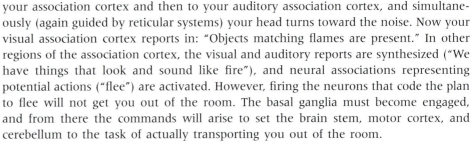

Review and Sharpen Your Thinking

3 *Identify the brain's levels and structures, and summarize the functions of its structures.*

- Outline the levels of organization in the human brain.
- Discuss the areas of the cerebral cortex and their functions.
- Explain how split-brain research has increased our understanding of the way the cerebral hemispheres function.
- Describe the integration of function in the brain.

In your experience, does human behavior differ in important ways from the behavior of other animals? What tasks are human brains able to accomplish that other animals may not be able to?

4 THE ENDOCRINE SYSTEM

What is the endocrine system and how does it affect behavior?

The **endocrine system** is a set of glands that regulate the activities of certain organs by releasing their chemical products into the bloodstream. In the past, the endocrine system was considered separate from the nervous system. However, today neuroscientists know that these two systems are often interconnected.

Hormones are the chemical messengers that are manufactured by the endocrine glands. Hormones travel more slowly than nerve impulses. The bloodstream conveys hormones to all parts of the body, and the membrane of every cell has receptors for one or more hormones.

The endocrine glands consist of the pituitary gland, the thyroid and parathyroid glands, the adrenal glands, the pancreas, and the ovaries in women and the testes in men (see figure 2.13). In much the same way that the brain's control of muscular activity is constantly monitored and altered to suit the information received by the brain, the action of the endocrine glands is continuously monitored and changed by nervous, hormonal, and chemical signals (Mader, 2002). Recall from earlier in the chapter that the autonomic nervous system regulates processes such as respiration, heart rate, and digestion. The autonomic nervous system acts on the endocrine glands to produce a number of important physiological reactions to strong emotions, such as rage and fear.

The **pituitary gland,** a pea-sized gland deep within the skull (refer to figure 2.13; also refer to figure 2.6), controls growth and regulates other glands. The front

endocrine system A set of glands that regulate the activities of certain organs by releasing hormones into the bloodstream.

hormones Chemical messengers manufactured by the endocrine glands.

pituitary gland The endocrine gland at the base of the skull that controls growth and regulates other glands.

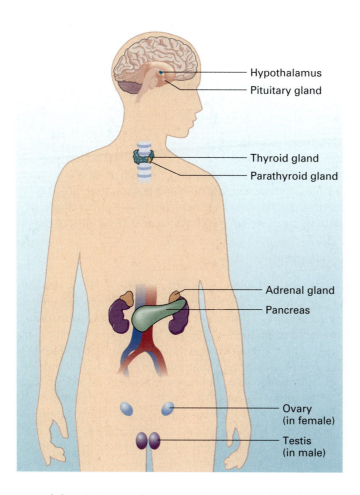

Hypothalamus
Pituitary gland
Thyroid gland
Parathyroid gland
Adrenal gland
Pancreas
Ovary
(in female)
Testis
(in male)

FIGURE 2.13 **The Major Endocrine Glands** The pituitary gland releases hormones that regulate the hormone secretions of the other glands. The pituitary gland itself is regulated by the hypothalamus.

part of the pituitary is known as the master gland, because almost all of its hormones direct the activity of target glands elsewhere in the body. In turn, the pituitary gland is controlled by the hypothalamus.

The **adrenal glands** are instrumental in regulating moods, energy level, and the ability to cope with stress. Each adrenal gland secretes epinephrine (also called adrenaline) and norepinephrine (also called noradrenaline). Unlike most hormones, epinephrine and norepinephrine act quickly. Epinephrine helps a person get ready for an emergency by acting on smooth muscles, heart, stomach, intestines, and sweat glands. In addition, epinephrine stimulates the reticular formation, which in turn arouses the sympathetic nervous system, and this system subsequently excites the adrenal glands to produce more epinephrine. Norepinephrine also alerts the individual to emergency situations by interacting with the pituitary and the liver. You may remember that norepinephrine functions as a neurotransmitter when it is released by neurons. In the adrenal glands, norepinephrine is released as a hormone. In both instances, norepinephrine conveys information (Raven & Johnson, 2002).

Review and Sharpen Your Thinking

 State what the endocrine system is and how it affects behavior.

- Describe the endocrine system, its glands, and their functions.

Is the behavior of animals such as rats, rabbits, and bulls likely to be more strongly controlled by hormones than that of humans? In answering this question, think about the differences in the brain structures of humans and lower animals, which were described earlier in the chapter.

adrenal glands Endocrine glands instrumental in regulating moods, energy level, and ability to cope with stress.

5 GENETIC AND EVOLUTIONARY BLUEPRINTS OF BEHAVIOR

Chromosomes, Genes, and DNA   The Study of Genetics   Genetics and Evolution

How do genetics and evolutionary psychology increase our understanding of behavior?

As you saw at the beginning of this chapter, genetic and evolutionary processes favor organisms that have adapted for survival. Successful adaptations can be physical, as in the case of the brain's increasing complexity, or behavioral, as in the choice of a suitable mate for raising a family. Here we take a closer look at these processes.

Chromosomes, Genes, and DNA

You began life as a single cell, a fertilized human egg, weighing about one 20-millionth of an ounce. From this single cell, you developed into a human being made up of trillions of cells. The nucleus of each human cell contains 46 **chromosomes,** which are threadlike structures that come in 23 pairs, one member of each pair coming from each parent. Chromosomes contain the remarkable substance **deoxyribonucleic acid,** or **DNA,** a complex molecule that contains genetic information. **Genes,** the units of hereditary information, are short segments of chromosomes composed of DNA. Genes act like blueprints for cells. They enable cells to reproduce and manufacture the proteins that are necessary for maintaining life. The relationship among cells, chromosomes, genes, and DNA is illustrated in figure 2.14.

When the approximately 30,000 genes from one parent combine at conception with the same number of genes from the other parent, the number of possibilities is staggering. Although scientists are still a long way from unraveling all the mysteries about the way genes work, some aspects of the process are well understood, starting with the fact that multiple genes interact to give rise to observable characteristics (Lewis, 2003; Lewis & others, 2002).

In some gene pairs, one gene is dominant over the other. If one gene of a pair is dominant and one is recessive, according to the *dominant-recessive genes principle*, the dominant gene overrides the recessive gene. In the world of dominant-recessive genes, brown eyes, farsightedness, and dimples rule over blue eyes, nearsightedness, and freckles. A recessive gene exerts its influence only if both genes of a pair are

FIGURE 2.14 Cells, Chromosomes, Genes, and DNA *(Left)* The body contains trillions of cells, which are the basic structural units of life. Each cell contains a central structure, the nucleus. *(Middle)* Chromosomes and genes are located in the nucleus of the cell. Chromosomes are made up of threadlike structures composed mainly of DNA molecules. *(Right)* A gene is a segment of DNA that contains the hereditary code for an individual. The structure of DNA resembles a spiral ladder.

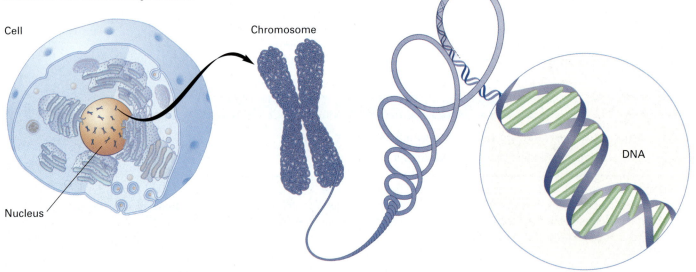

Cell

Nucleus

Chromosome

DNA

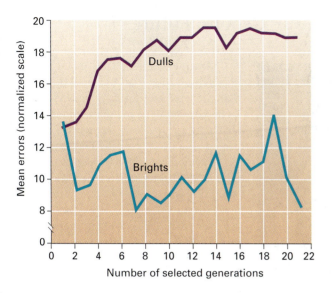

FIGURE 2.15 **Results of Selective Breeding Experiment with Maze-Bright and Maze-Dull Rats** After 21 generations of selective breeding, rats selected for their ability to navigate mazes dramatically outperformed rats selected for their lack of ability.

Calvin and Hobbes by Bill Watterson

recessive. Two brown-eyed parents can have a blue-eyed child only if each parent has a dominant gene for brown eyes and a recessive gene for blue eyes. Because dominant genes override recessive genes, the parents have brown eyes. However, the child can inherit a recessive gene for blue eyes from each parent. With no dominant genes to override the recessive genes, the child will have blue eyes.

Unlike eye color, complex human characteristics, such as personality and intelligence, are likely to be influenced by many different genes. The term *polygenic inheritance* is used to describe the influences of multiple genes on behavior.

The Study of Genetics

Historically speaking, genetics is a relatively young science. Its origins go back to the mid-nineteenth century, when an Austrian monk named Gregor Mendel studied heredity in generations of pea plants. By cross-breeding plants with different characteristics and noting the characteristics of the offspring, Mendel discovered predictable patterns of heredity. Today researchers continue to apply Mendel's methods, as well as modern technology, in their quest to expand our knowledge of genetics. This section discusses three ways to study genetics: molecular genetics, selective breeding, and behavior genetics.

Molecular Genetics The field of *molecular genetics* involves the actual manipulation of genes using technology to determine their effect on behavior. There is currently a great deal of enthusiasm about the use of molecular genetics to discover the specific locations on genes that determine an individual's susceptibility to many diseases and other aspects of health and well-being (Dolphin, 2002; Klug & Cummings, 2003; Mader, 2003, 2004).

A *genome* is the complete set of instructions for making an organism. It contains the master blueprint for all cellular structures and activities for the life span of the organism. To read about the Human Genome Project and its possible applications, see the Psychology and Life box.

Selective Breeding *Selective breeding* is a genetic method in which organisms are chosen for reproduction based on how much of a particular trait they display. Mendel developed this technique in his studies of pea plants. An example involving behavior is the classic selective breeding study conducted by Robert Tryon (1940). He chose to study maze-running ability in rats. After training a large number of rats to run a complex maze, he mated the rats that were best at maze running ("maze-bright") with each other and those that were worst ("maze-dull") with each other. He continued this process with 21 generations of rats. As can be seen in figure 2.15, the maze-bright rats significantly outperformed the maze-dull rats.

chromosomes Threadlike structures that contain genes and DNA. Humans have 23 chromosome pairs in the nucleus of every cell. Each parent contributes one chromosome to each pair.

deoxyribonucleic acid (DNA) A complex molecule, located on chromosomes, that contains information.

genes The basic units of hereditary information; short segments of chromosome composed of DNA.

The Human Genome Project and Your Genetic Future

The Human Genome Project, begun in the 1970s, has made stunning progress in mapping the human genome. Among the surprise discoveries is that humans have only about 30,000 genes—it was previously thought that we had 50,000 to 100,000. The project also has revealed that human DNA is about 98 percent identical to chimpanzee DNA (U.S. Department of Energy, 2001).

Every individual carries a number of DNA variations that might predispose that person to a serious physical disease or mental disorder. The Human Genome Project has already linked specific DNA variations with increased risk for a number of diseases and conditions, including Huntington's disease (in which the central nervous system deteriorates), some forms of cancer, asthma, diabetes, hypertension, and Alzheimer's disease (Davies, 2001). Other documented DNA variations affect the way people react to certain drugs.

The Human Genome Project is already having practical benefits. Shortly after Andrew Gobea was born, his cells were genetically altered to prevent his immune system from failing. *What are some other potential benefits—and risks—of knowing more about variations in the human genetic code?*

Identifying these flaws could enable doctors to estimate an individual's disease risks, recommend healthy lifestyle regimens, and prescribe the safest and most effective drugs. A decade or two from now, parents of a newborn baby may be able to leave the hospital with a full genome analysis of their offspring that reveals various disease risks.

However, mining DNA variations to discover health risks might increasingly threaten an individual's ability to obtain and hold jobs, obtain insurance, and keep personal information private. For example, should an aspiring airline pilot or neurosurgeon who one day may develop a disorder that makes the hands shake be allowed to pursue the chosen career?

Answering the following questions should encourage you to think further about some of the issues involved in genetic analysis of individuals (NOVA, 2001):

1. Would you want yourself (or a loved one) to be tested for a gene that increases your risk for a disease but does not determine whether you will actually develop the disease? Yes No Undecided
2. Would you want yourself and your mate tested before having offspring to determine your risk for having a child who is likely to contract various diseases? Yes No Undecided
3. Should testing of fetuses be restricted to traits that are commonly considered to have negative outcomes, such as Huntington's disease? Yes No Undecided
4. Should parents be allowed to alter a newly conceived embryo's genes to improve qualities such as intelligence, appearance, and strength? Yes No Undecided
5. Should employers be permitted access to your genetic information? Yes No Undecided
6. Should life insurance companies have access to your genetic information? Yes No Undecided

Selective breeding studies have demonstrated that genes are an important influence on behavior, but experience is still important (Pinel, 2003). For example, in another study, maze-bright and maze-dull rats were reared in one of two environments: (1) an impoverished environment that consisted of a barren wire-mesh group cage or (2) an enriched environment that contained tunnels, ramps, visual displays, and other stimulating objects (Cooper & Zubeck, 1958). When they reached maturity, the maze-dull rats that had been reared in an enriched environment made about the same number of maze-learning errors as the maze-bright rats.

Selective breeding of human beings is the principle behind the Repository for Germinal Choice in Escondido, California, which was founded by Dr. Robert Graham as a sperm bank for Nobel Prize winners and other bright individuals. The sperm is available to women whose husbands are infertile. What are the odds that the sperm bank will yield that special combination of factors required to produce a creative genius? Twentieth-century Irish-born playwright George Bernard Shaw once told a story about a beautiful woman who wrote to him, saying that, with her body and his mind, they could produce wonderful offspring. Shaw responded by saying that, unfortunately, the offspring might get his body and her mind!

What do you think about this sperm bank? Is it right to breed for intelligence? Does it raise visions of the German genetics program of the 1930s and 1940s, which was based on the Nazis' belief that certain traits were superior? The Nazis tried to produce children with such traits and killed people without them. Or does the sperm bank merely provide a social service for couples who cannot conceive a child, couples who want to maximize the probability that their offspring will have good genes?

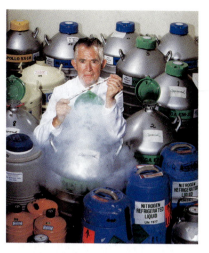

Dr. Graham holds the frozen sperm of a Nobel Prize–winning donor. *What are the moral implications of the selective breeding of human beings?*

Behavior Genetics   *Behavior genetics* is the study of the degree and nature of heredity's influence on behavior. Behavior genetics is less invasive than molecular genetics and selective breeding. Using methods such as *twin studies,* behavior geneticists examine the extent to which individuals are shaped by their heredity and their environmental experiences (Wahlsten, 2000).

In the most common type of twin study, the behavioral similarity of identical twins is compared with the behavioral similarity of fraternal twins. *Identical twins* develop from a single fertilized egg that splits into two genetically identical embryos, each of which becomes a person. *Fraternal twins* develop from separate eggs and separate sperm, making them genetically no more similar than nontwin siblings. They may even be of different sexes. In one twin study, 7,000 pairs of Finnish identical and fraternal twins were compared on the personality traits of extraversion (being outgoing) and neuroticism (being psychologically unstable) (Rose & others, 1988). The identical twins were much more alike than the fraternal twins on both of these personality traits, suggesting that genes influence both traits.

One problem with twin studies is that adults who influenced the children as they grew up might have stressed the similarities of identical twins more than those of fraternal twins. Also, identical twins might perceive themselves as a "set" and play together more than fraternal twins do. If so, observed similarities in identical twins might be more strongly influenced by environmental factors than usually thought.

In another type of twin study, researchers evaluate identical twins who have been reared in separate environments. If their behavior is similar, the assumption is that heredity has played an important role in shaping their behavior. This strategy is the basis for the Minnesota Study of Twins Reared Apart, directed by Thomas Bouchard and his colleagues (1996). They bring identical twins who have been reared apart to Minneapolis from all over the world to study their behavior. They ask thousands of questions about their family and childhood environment, personal interests, vocational orientation, and values. Detailed medical histories are obtained, including information about their diet, smoking, and exercise habits.

One pair of twins in the Minnesota study, Jim Springer and Jim Lewis, were separated at 4 weeks of age and did not see each other again until they were 39 years old. They had an uncanny number of similarities, even though they had lived apart. For example, they both worked as part-time deputy sheriffs, had vacationed in Florida, had owned Chevrolets, had dogs named Toy, and had married and divorced women named Betty. Both liked math but not spelling. Both were good at mechanical drawing. Both put on 10 pounds at about the same time in their lives, and both started suffering headaches at 18 years of age. They did have a few differences. For example, one expressed himself better orally, and the other was more proficient at writing. One parted his hair over his forehead; the other wore his hair slicked back with sideburns.

Critics argue that some of the separated twins in the Minnesota study had been together several months prior to their adoption, that some had been reunited prior to their testing (in some cases, for a number of years), that adoption agencies often put identical twins in similar homes, and that even strangers who spend several hours

The Jim twins: Jim Springer *(right)* and Jim Lewis were unaware of each other for 39 years but share an identical genetic heritage. *How coincidental are their psychological and behavioral similarities?*

together are likely to come up with some coincidental similarities (Adler, 1991). Still, it seems unlikely that all of the similarities found in identical twins reared apart could be due to experience alone. See the video clip "Nature and Nurture: The Study of Twins" to learn more about the use of twin studies for understanding the roots of physical and psychological characteristics.

Behavior geneticists also use *adoption studies* to try to determine whether the behavior of adopted children is more like that of their biological parents or their adopted parents. Another type of adoption study compares biological and adopted siblings. In one study, the educational levels attained by biological parents were better predictors of the adopted children's IQ scores than were the IQs of the children's adoptive parents (Scarr & Weinberg, 1983). Because of the stronger genetic link between the adopted children and their biological parents, the implication is that heredity plays an important role in intelligence. However, numerous studies document the critical role of environment in intelligence as well (Sternberg & Grigorenko, 2001).

Genetics and behavior, especially the way heredity and environment interact, are discussed further in chapter 3.

Genetics and Evolution

Often we can see the effects of genetics by observing family resemblances (Cummings, 2003). For example, you might have your mother's dark hair and your father's long legs. But evolutionary influences are not so easy to see, because we share physical and psychological characteristics with every other human—such as a cerebral cortex in our brain that allows us to think and plan. We also share certain problems that we have to solve and adapt to, such as how to protect ourselves from harm, how to nourish our bodies, how to find a compatible mate, and how to rear our children. In the evolutionary scheme, some individuals are more successful at solving these problems and adapting effectively than others (Crawford & Salmon, 2004; Goldsmith & Zimmerman, 2001). Those who are successful pass on their genes to the next generation. Those who are less successful do not.

In this evolutionary psychology view, psychological functions have become more specialized over human history (Buss, 2000, 2004; Cosmides & others, 2003). Among the specialized psychological functions that evolutionary psychologists study are

- Development of a fear of strangers between 3 and 24 months of age, as well as very common fears of snakes, spiders, heights, open spaces, and darkness (Marks, 1987)
- Perceptual adaptations for tracking motion (Ashida, Seiffert, & Osaka, 2001)
- Children's imitation of high-status rather than low-status models (Bandura, 1977)
- Worldwide preference for mates who are kind, intelligent, and dependable (Buss & others, 1990)

Evolutionary psychologists believe that these specialized functions developed because they helped humans adapt and solve problems in past environments (Gaulin & McBurney, 2004). In later chapters, I examine what evolutionary psychologists have to say about other psychological topics.

Much of this chapter has focused on the brain, and earlier I described how the human brain is much larger than the brains of other animals (refer to figure 2.7). In evolutionary theory, an extended "juvenile" period evolved because humans need time to develop this large brain and to learn the complexities of human social communities (Bjorklund & Pellegrini, 2002). Humans take longer to become reproductively mature than any other animal, and during this time they develop a large brain that helps them to master the complexities of human society (see figure 2.16).

In evolutionary theory, what matters is that individuals live long enough to reproduce and pass on their characteristics, so why do humans live so long after reproduction? Perhaps evolution favored a longer life because having older adults around improves the survival of more babies. For example, an evolutionary advantage may have occurred because grandparents cared for the young while parents were out hunting and gathering food. In chapter 3, we will more extensively examine development through the human life span.

Some critics caution that evolutionary psychology places too much emphasis on the biological foundations of behavior. For example, Albert Bandura (1998), whose social cognitive theory was described in chapter 1, acknowledges the importance of human adaptation and change. However, he rejects what he calls "one-sided evolutionism," in which social behavior is considered to be solely the product of evolved biology. Bandura recommends a bidirectional view: Evolutionary pressures created changes in biological structures facilitating the use of tools, which enabled organisms to manipulate, alter, and construct new environmental conditions. Environmental innovations of increasing complexity, in turn, produced new pressures for the evolution of specialized biological systems facilitating consciousness, thought, and language.

Scientists such as Steven Jay Gould (1981) agree that human evolution gave us body structures and biological potentialities, not behavioral dictates. The advanced biological capacities that evolved can be instrumental in producing diverse cultures—aggressive or peaceful, for example. Russian American scientist Theodore Dobzhansky (1977) reminds us that the human species has evolved the capacity for learnability and plasticity, which allows us to adapt to diverse contexts.

Most, if not all, psychologists would agree that the interaction of biology and environment is the basis for our own development as human beings (Coll, Bearer & Lerner, 2004). Chapter 3 further explores the influence of biology and environment on human development.

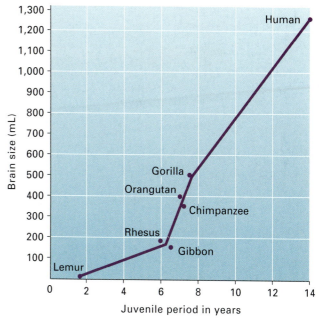

FIGURE 2.16 The Brain Sizes of Various Primates and Humans in Relation to the Length of the Juvenile Period.

Review and Sharpen Your Thinking

5 **_Explain how genetics and evolutionary psychology increase our understanding of behavior._**

- Discuss the structures and functions of chromosomes, genes, and DNA.
- Describe three methods for studying genetics.
- Explain how evolution might influence human behavior.

What ethical issues regarding genetics and behavior might arise in the future?

The Brain and Behavior

1 THE NERVOUS SYSTEM

Key Characteristics of the Nervous System

Pathways in the Nervous System

Divisions of the Nervous System

2 NEURONS

Specialized Cell Structure

Synapses and Neurotransmitters

The Neural Impulse

Neural Networks

3 STRUCTURES OF THE BRAIN AND THEIR FUNCTIONS

Levels of Organization in the Brain

The Cerebral Hemispheres and Split-Brain Research

The Cerebral Cortex

Integration of Function in the Brain

4 THE ENDOCRINE SYSTEM

5 GENETIC AND EVOLUTIONARY BLUEPRINTS OF BEHAVIOR

Chromosomes, Genes, and DNA

The Study of Genetics

Genetics and Evolution

1 Discuss the nature and basic functions of the nervous system.

- The nervous system is the body's electrochemical communication circuitry. Four important characteristics of the brain and nervous system are complexity, integration, adaptability, and electrochemical transmission. The brain's special ability to adapt and change is called plasticity.
- Decision making in the nervous system occurs in specialized pathways of nerve cells—one pathway for sensory input and one for motor output—and neural networks that integrate them.
- The nervous system is divided into two main parts: central (CNS) and peripheral (PNS). The CNS consists of the brain and spinal cord. The PNS has two major divisions: somatic and autonomic. The autonomic nervous system consists of two main divisions: sympathetic and parasympathetic.

2 Explain what neurons are and how they process information.

- Neurons are cells that specialize in processing information. They make up the communication network of the nervous system. Glial cells perform supportive and nutritive functions for neurons. The three main parts of the neuron are the cell body, dendrite (receiving part), and axon (sending part). A myelin sheath encases and insulates most axons and speeds up transmission of neural impulses.
- A neuron sends information along its axon in the form of brief electric impulses. This brief electrical wave is called the action potential. The action potential abides by the all-or-none principle: It is either on or off; its strength does not change during transmission.
- To go from one neuron to another, information must be converted from an electrical impulse to a chemical messenger called a neurotransmitter. At the synapse where neurons meet, neurotransmitters are released into the narrow gap that separates them. There, some neurotransmitter molecules attach to receptor sites on the receiving neuron, where they stimulate another electrical impulse. Most drugs that influence behavior do so by interfering with neurotransmitters' activity, but some drugs mimic or increase their activity.
- Neural networks are clusters of neurons that are interconnected to process information.

3 Identify the brain's levels and structures, and summarize the functions of its structures.

- The three major levels of the brain are the hindbrain, midbrain, and forebrain. The hindbrain is the lowest portion of the brain; it is involved in the control of breathing and posture, motor coordination, and sleep and arousal. The midbrain contains the reticular formation, which is involved in stereotypical patterns of behavior (such as walking, sleeping, or turning toward a sudden noise), and small groups of neurons that communicate with many other areas in the brain. The brain stem consists of much of the hindbrain (excluding the cerebellum) and the midbrain. The forebrain, the highest level of the brain, has several key structures. The limbic system is involved in memory and emotion. The thalamus is an important relay station for processing information. The basal ganglia help to control and coordinate voluntary movements. The hypothalamus monitors eating, drinking, and sex; directs the endocrine system through the pituitary gland; and is involved in emotion, stress, and reward. The cerebral cortex, which makes up most of the outer layer of the brain, is the site of higher mental functions, such as thinking and planning.
- The wrinkled surface of the cerebral cortex is divided into hemispheres. Each hemisphere is divided into four lobes—occipital, temporal, frontal, and parietal—which are connected and highly integrated. The cerebral cortex can also be subdivided into three areas: The somatosensory cortex processes information about body sensations. The motor cortex processes information about voluntary movement. The association cortex, which makes up 75 percent of the cerebral cortex, is instrumental in integrating information, especially for the highest intellectual functions.
- Researchers have studied what happens when the corpus callosum, a large bundle of fibers that connects the two hemispheres, has to be severed, as in some cases of severe epilepsy. Research suggests that the left hemisphere is more dominant in processing verbal information (such as language) and the right hemisphere in processing nonverbal information (such as spatial perception, visual recognition, and emotion). Nonetheless, in a normal individual whose corpus callosum is intact, both hemispheres of the cerebral cortex are involved in most complex human functioning.

- Generally, brain function is integrated and involves connections between different parts of the brain. Pathways of neurons involved in a particular function, such as memory, are integrated across different parts and levels of the brain.

4. State what the endocrine system is and how it affects behavior.

- The endocrine glands release hormones directly into the bloodstream for distribution throughout the body. The pituitary gland is the master endocrine gland. The adrenal glands play important roles in moods, energy level, and ability to cope with stress.

5. Explain how genetics and evolutionary psychology increase our understanding of behavior.

- Chromosomes are threadlike structures that come in 23 pairs, one member of each pair coming from each parent. Chromosomes contain the genetic substance deoxyribo-

nucleic acid (DNA). Genes, the units of hereditary information, are short segments of chromosomes composed of DNA. If one gene of a pair is dominant and one is recessive, the dominant gene overrides the recessive.

- Three methods used to study heredity's influence are molecular genetics (using technology to manipulate genes), selective breeding (breeding organisms to express a certain trait), and behavior genetics (studying heredity's influence on behavior). Two methods used by behavior geneticists are twin studies and adoption studies.

- Evolutionary psychologists believe that, just as parts of the brain have become specialized in function through evolution, so have mental processes and behavior. Critics stress that evolutionary advances allow humans to select their environments. Humans are not completely under the control of their evolutionary past.

Key Terms

nervous system, p. 44
plasticity, p. 45
neural networks, p. 46
central nervous system (CNS), p. 46
peripheral nervous system (PNS), p. 46
somatic nervous system, p. 46
autonomic nervous system, p. 46
sympathetic nervous system, p. 46

parasympathetic nervous system, p. 46
neurons, p. 48
glial cells, p. 48
cell body, p. 48
dendrites, p. 48
axon, p. 48
myelin sheath, p. 48
action potential, p. 49
synapses, p. 49
neurotransmitters, p. 49
hindbrain, p. 54
midbrain, p. 54

reticular formation, p. 54
brain stem, p. 54
forebrain, p. 55
limbic system, p. 55
thalamus, p. 56
basal ganglian, p. 56
hypothalamus, p. 56
cerebral cortex, p. 57
occipital lobe, p. 59
temporal lobe, p. 59
frontal lobe, p. 59
parietal lobe, p. 59
somatosensory cortex, p. 59

motor cortex, p. 59
association cortex, p. 60
corpus callosum, p. 60
endocrine system, p. 64
hormones, p. 64
pituitary gland, p. 64
adrenal glands, p. 65
chromosomes, p. 67
deoxyribonucleic acid (DNA), p. 67
genes, p. 67

Apply Your Knowledge

1. Consider the four key characteristics of the nervous system. Suppose you had to do without one of them. Which would you choose? What would be the consequences for your behavior?

2. Do a search on the World Wide Web for "nutrition" and "the brain." Examine the claims made on one or more websites. Based on what you learned in the chapter about how the nervous system works, how could nutrition affect brain function? Based on what you know about being a scientist, how believable are the claims on the website?

3. Imagine that you could make one part of your brain twice as big as it is right now. Which part would it be, and how do you think your behavior would change as a result? What if you had to make another part of your brain half its current size? Which part would you choose to shrink, and what would be the effects be?

4. It's not unusual to read headlines announcing that genes are responsible for a troublesome behavior (for example, "Next time you pig out, blame it on the genes," *Los Angeles Times,* October 19, 2000, or "Men are born fighters," *Times* [London], October 19, 2001). How would you interpret statements such as these in light of the material discussed in the chapter?

Connections

To test your mastery of the material in this chapter, go to the Study Guide and the In-Psych Plus CD-ROM, as well as the Online Learning Center. There you will find a chapter summary, practice tests, flashcards, lecture slides, web links, and other study tools, such as interactive exercises and reviews as well as current, chapter-relevant news articles.

3 Human Development

Chapter Outline

Learning Goals

KEY QUESTIONS ABOUT DEVELOPMENT **1**

What Is Development?
▼
Do Early Experiences Rule Us for Life?
▼
How Do Nature and Nurture Influence Development?

Explain how psychologists think about development.

CHILD DEVELOPMENT **2**

Prenatal Development
▼
Physical Development in Childhood
▼
Cognitive Development in Childhood
▼
Socioemotional Development in Childhood
▼
Positive Psychology and Children's Development

Describe children's development from conception to adolescence.

ADOLESCENCE **3**

Positive Psychology and Adolescents
▼
Physical Development in Adolescence
▼
Cognitive Development in Adolescence
▼
Socioemotional Development in Adolescence

Identify the most important changes that occur in adolescence.

ADULT DEVELOPMENT AND AGING **4**

Physical Development in Adulthood
▼
Cognitive Development in Adulthood
▼
Socioemotional Development in Adulthood
▼
Positive Psychology and Aging

Discuss adult development and the positive dimensions of aging.

Zhang Liyin was playing in a kindergarten class in Beijing, China, when a coach from a sports school spotted her and invited her to attend the school. Zhang was selected because of her broad shoulders, narrow hips, straight legs, symmetrical limbs, open-minded attitude, vivaciousness, and outgoing personality. Zhang's parents accepted the invitation, and now she attends the sports school in the afternoon.

Attending the sports school is a privilege given to only 260,000 of China's 200 million students from elementary school to college age. China spends lavishly on the schools, which are the only road to Olympic stardom in China.

Today, at age 6, Zhang is standing on the balance beam, stretching her arms outward as she gets ready to perform a back flip. She wears the bright red gymnastic suit of the elite—a suit given to only the 10 best girls in her class of 6- to 8-year-olds. But her face wears a fearful expression. She can't drum up enough confidence to do the flip. Maybe it is because she has had a rough week. A purple bruise decorates one leg; a nasty gash disfigures the other.

Because of her young age, Zhang stays at home during the mornings and goes to sports school from noon until 6 P.M. If she continues to perform well, next year, at age 7, she will live and study at the sports school, like many of its other students. The development of these children is closely monitored. If at any point a child shows a decline in potential, the child is asked to leave the sports school.

The skills in three areas of development—physical, cognitive, and socioemotional—that won Zhang Liyin her place at the sports school is the topic of this chapter. Like Zhang Liyin, each of us develops physically, cognitively, and socioemotionally. In this chapter, development is divided into three main time frames: childhood, adolescence, and adulthood. As you read each section, pay attention to how each aspect of development (physical, cognitive, and socioemotional) typically changes from one phase of life to another. And keep in mind that some people may develop more slowly or more quickly and to a different degree in one of these areas than other people do.

Six-year-old Zhang Liyin *(third from the left)* hopes someday to become an Olympic gymnastics champion. Attending the sports school is considered an outstanding privilege; only 260,000 of China's 200 million students are given this opportunity.

What Is Development?   **Do Early Experiences Rule Us for Life?**   **How Do Nature and Nurture Influence Development?**

How do psychologists think about development?

Not every child is as physically skilled as Zhang Liyin, but, as children, we all traveled some common paths. For example, whether you are likely to become a famous person or simply a good one, most likely you walked at about the age of 1, talked at about the age of 2, engaged in fantasy play as a young child, and began to think more logically as an older child. However, each of us also is unique. No one else in the world has the same fingerprints as you, for example. Let's explore the key questions that psychologists have addressed in their search for reasons for these differences.

What Is Development?

Development refers to the pattern of change in human capabilities that begins at conception and continues throughout the life span. Most development involves growth, although it also consists of decline (for example, processing information becomes less quick for older adults). Researchers who study development are intrigued by its universal characteristics and by its individual variations. The pattern of development is complex because it is the product of several processes:

- *Physical processes* involve changes in an individual's biological nature. Genes inherited from parents, the hormonal changes of puberty and menopause, and changes throughout life in the brain, height and weight, and motor skills all reflect the developmental role of biological processes. Psychologists refer to such biological growth processes as *maturation*. Zhang Liyin has the body build and exceptional motor skills that allow her to perform well in gymnastics.

- *Cognitive processes* involve changes in an individual's thought, intelligence, and language. Observing a colorful mobile as it swings above a crib, constructing a sentence about the future, imagining oneself as a movie star, memorizing a new telephone number—all these activities reflect the role of cognitive processes in development. The sports school helps to develop Zhang Liyin's cognitive skills by requiring her to take academic classes for part of the day.

- *Socioemotional processes* involve changes in an individual's relationships with other people, changes in emotions, and changes in personality. An infant's smile in response to her mother's touch, a girl's development of assertiveness, an adolescent's joy at the senior prom, a young man's aggressiveness in sport, and an older couple's affection for each other all reflect the role of socioemotional processes. Among the reasons that Zhang Liyin was chosen to attend the sports school were her vivaciousness and outgoing attitude, socioemotional characteristics thought to help her succeed as an Olympic athlete.

Remember as you read about physical, cognitive, and socioemotional processes that they are intricately interwoven, as figure 3.1 shows. For example, socioemotional processes shape cognitive processes, cognitive processes promote or restrict socioemotional processes, and physical processes influence cognitive processes. Although the three processes of development are discussed in separate sections of the chapter, keep in mind that you are studying the development of an integrated human being in whom body, mind, and emotion are interdependent.

In the case of Zhang Liyin, the combination of physical, cognitive, and socioemotional skills is what led her to being chosen to attend a sports school in China. As she grows up, an important issue will be whether her cognitive and socioemotional skills suffer because she spends so much time developing her physical skills.

development The pattern of change in human capabilities that begins at conception and continues throughout the life span.

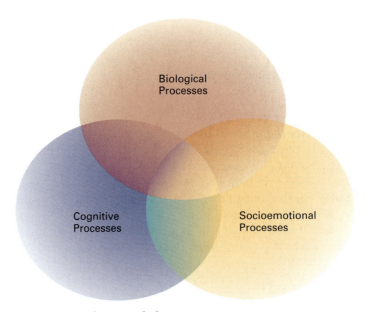

FIGURE 3.1 Factors in Developmental Change Development is the result of biological, cognitive, and socioemotional processes. These processes are interwoven as individuals develop.

Do Early Experiences Rule Us for Life?

As psychologists study development, they debate whether early experiences or later experiences are more important (Santrock, 2004). Some psychologists believe that, unless infants experience warm, nurturant caregiving in the first year or so of life, they will not develop to their full potential (Berlin & Cassidy, 2000; Bowlby, 1989). This *early-experience* doctrine suggests that, after a period of early development, we become relatively fixed and permanent in our makeup. It rests on the belief that each life is an unbroken trail on which a psychological quality can be traced back to its origin (Kagan, 1992, 2000, 2003).

In contrast, some psychologists emphasize the power of later experience and liken development in later years to the ebb and flow of a river. The *later-experience* advocates argue that children are malleable and that sensitive caregiving is just as important later as it is earlier (Lewis, 1997). A number of life-span developmentalists, who focus on both children and adults, stress that too little attention has been given to adult development (Baltes, 2000; Birren & Schaie, 2001; Lachman, 2004). They argue that, although early experiences are important contributors to development, they are not necessarily more important than later experiences. The world is full of people who have overcome difficult childhoods to become successful adults.

Research indicates that both early and later experiences are indeed important to human development (Thompson, Easterbrooks, & Walker, 2003). One correlational study examined the link between parents' relationships with their young daughters between the ages of 3 and 5 and the daughters' depression in adolescence (Gjerde, Block, & Block, 1991). It found that the adolescent girls were more likely to be depressed when the parents had been overly controlling, had demanded high achievement, and had not adequately nurtured the girls when they were 3 to 5 years of age. These results demonstrate the importance of early experience. But other research studies show that stressful experiences in adolescence—such as making low grades, breaking up with a boyfriend, or dealing with a parent's death—are also related to depression in adolescent girls (Compas & others, 2001). Thus depression in adolescent girls appears to be linked to both early and later experiences.

Most developmentalists do not take extreme positions on the issue of early versus later experience (Lerner, 2000, 2002; Santrock, 2004). They believe that, although

Alice Walker won the Pulitzer Prize for her book *The Color Purple*. Like many of the characters in her book (especially the women), Walker overcame early experiences with poverty and pain to become a very competent adult. *What does her case suggest about the effects of early experiences?*

early experience can create a foundation for later experience, both make important contributions to development.

How Do Nature and Nurture Influence Development?

The term **nature** is often used to refer to an organism's biological inheritance. The term **nurture** is often used to refer to an organism's environmental experiences, the effects of all the surrounding physical and social conditions. The interaction of nature and nurture, of genes and environment, influences every aspect of mind and behavior to a degree. Neither factor operates alone (Mader, 2003). In chapter 2, I examined the important role that genes play in human behavior, but genes exist within the context of an environment just as complex as the mixture of genes we inherit.

Throughout the life span, in many different environments, genes may or may not produce the proteins that affect experience and human development, depending on how harsh or nourishing those environments are. Psychologists are starting to agree that many complex behaviors have some genetic loading that makes people likely to develop in a particular way. But our actual development also depends on what we experience in our environment (Gottlieb, 2004). Environmental influences range from the things we lump together under nurture (such as parenting, family dynamics, peer relations, schooling, and neighborhood quality) to biological encounters (such as viruses, birth complications, and even cellular activities).

As with the question on the role of early experience, most developmentalists do not take an extreme position on nature versus nurture. Development is not all one or the other (Coll, Bearer, & Lerner, 2004; Lerner, 2002): It is an interaction of the two. Heredity and environment operate together to produce temperament, height, weight, ability to pitch a baseball, reading ability, and so on (Gottlieb, 2001; Lewis, 2003). If Zhang Liyin becomes an Olympic champion in gymnastics, will it be because of her heredity or her environment? The answer is both. According to William Greenough (2001), who studies these issues, "The interaction of heredity and environment is so extensive that to ask which is more important, nature or nurture, is like asking which is more important to a rectangle, height or width?"

Some psychologists believe, however, that we can develop beyond what our genetic inheritance and our environment give us. They argue that a key aspect of development involves seeking optimal experiences in life (Massimini & Delle Fave, 2000). They cite examples of people who go beyond simple biological adaptation to actively choose from the environment the things that serve their purposes. These individuals build and construct their own lives, authoring a unique developmental path. People who are more successful at constructing optimal life experiences than others are the ones who looked for and found meaningful life themes as they developed. Their lives were not restricted to simple biological survival or passive acceptance of environmental dictates.

Review and Sharpen Your Thinking

1 *Explain how psychologists think about development.*

- Name and describe the three main developmental processes.
- Discuss the influence of early and later experiences on human development.
- Evaluate the influences of nature and nurture on development.

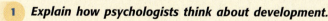

Your development as a human being is determined by multiple factors. Think about what you are like as a person today and reflect on the processes in your development that made you who you are.

nature An organism's biological inheritance.

nurture An organism's environmental experiences.

2 CHILD DEVELOPMENT

Prenatal Development

Cognitive Development
in Childhood

Positive Psychology and
Children's Development

Physical Development
in Childhood

Socioemotional Development
in Childhood

How do children develop from conception to adolescence?
How children develop has special importance because children are the future of any society. In addition, a great deal of human development takes place during childhood. Our investigation of childhood development follows the three fundamental developmental processes—physical, cognitive, and socioemotional.

Prenatal Development

Many special things have taken place in your life since you were born. But imagine—at one time you were a microscopic organism floating in a sea of fluid in your mother's womb. As the nineteenth-century American poet-essayist Samuel Taylor remarked, "The history of man for nine months preceding his birth is probably far more interesting and contains more stunning events than all the years that follow."

Prenatal development is divided into three periods:

- *Germinal period: weeks 1 and 2.* The germinal period begins with conception. The fertilized egg, a zygote, is a single cell with 23 chromosomes from the mother and 23 from the father. After 1 week and many cell divisions, the zygote is made up of 100 to 150 cells. By the end of 2 weeks, the mass of cells has attached to the uterine wall.
- *Embryonic period: weeks 3 through 8.* Before most women even know they are pregnant, the rate of cell differentiation intensifies, support systems for the cells form, and the beginnings of organs appear. In the third week, the neural tube, which eventually becomes the spinal cord, starts to form. At about 21 days, eyes begin to appear, and by 24 days the cells of the heart have begun to differentiate. During the fourth week, arm and leg buds emerge (see figure 3.2a). At 5 to 8 weeks, the heart begins to beat, arms and legs become more differentiated, the face starts to form, and the intestinal tract appears (see figure 3.2b).
- *Fetal period: months 2 through 9.* Organs mature to the point at which life can be sustained outside the womb, and muscles begin their first exercises. The mother feels the fetus move for the first time. At 6 months after conception, the eyes and eyelids are completely formed, a fine layer of hair covers the fetus, the grasping reflex appears, and irregular breathing begins. By 7 to 9 months, the fetus is much longer and weighs considerably more. In addition, the functioning of various organs steps up.

In 9 short months, a single cell has developed the capacity to live and function as a human being, with the potential for further physical, cognitive, and socioemotional changes.

Sometimes, however, normal development is disrupted (McDade & others, 2004; Tang & others, 2004). A *teratogen* (from the Greek word *tera*, meaning "monster") is any agent that causes a birth defect. The drug heroin is an example of a teratogen. Babies born to users of heroin are at risk for many problems, including premature birth, low birth weight, physical defects, breathing problems, and death.

Heavy drinking by pregnant women can also have devastating effects on their offspring (Bookstein & others, 2002; May & Gossage, 2001). *Fetal alcohol syndrome (FAS)*

a.

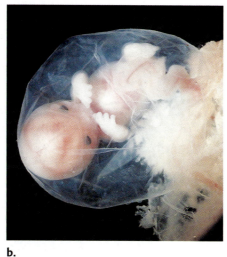

b.

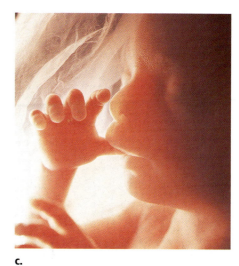

c.

FIGURE 3.2 From Embryo to Fetus
(a) At 4 weeks, an embryo is about 0.2 inches (less than 1 centimeter) long. The head, eyes, and ears begin to show; the head and neck are half the length of the body; the shoulders will be located where the whitish arm buds are attached.

(b) At 8 weeks, the developing individual is about 1.6 inches (4 centimeters) long and has reached the end of its embryonic phase. It has become a fetus. Everything that will be found in the fully developed human being has now begun to form. The fetal stage is a period of growth and perfection of detail. The heart has been beating for a month, and the muscles have just begun their first exercises.

(c) At 4½ months, the fetus is just over 7 inches (about 18 centimeters) long. When the thumb comes close to the mouth, the head may turn, and lips and tongue begin their sucking motions—a reflex for survival.

In-Psych Plus

is a cluster of abnormalities that occurs in children born to mothers who are heavy drinkers. These abnormalities include a small head and defective limbs, face, and heart (O'Leary, 2004). Most FAS children are also below average in intelligence. Concern has increased about the well-being of the fetus when pregnant women drink even small amounts of alcohol. The best advice is that a woman who is pregnant or anticipates becoming pregnant should not drink any alcohol (Streissguth, 1997).

A variety of other problems may short-circuit prenatal development. Full-term infants, who have grown in the womb for 38 to 42 weeks between conception and delivery, have the best chances of normal development in childhood. A *preterm infant*, who is born prior to 38 weeks after conception, is at greater risk. (The audio clip "Premature Babies" describes the behavioral, social, and cognitive challenges that preterm infants face during childhood.) Whether a preterm infant will have developmental problems is a complex issue, however. Very small preterm infants are more likely than their larger counterparts to have developmental problems. Also, preterm infants who grow up in poverty are more likely to have problems than are those in better socioeconomic conditions. Indeed, many larger preterm infants from middle- and high-income families do not have developmental problems. Nonetheless, more preterm infants than full-term infants have learning disorders (Kopp, 1984).

Prenatal and newborn development sets the stage for development in childhood. The changes in every realm of childhood—physical, cognitive, and social—set the foundation for our development as adults.

Physical Development in Childhood

People grow and develop physically throughout life, but at no other time will so many physical changes occur as fast as during infancy (the developmental period from birth to about 18 to 24 months of age) (Fogel, 2001). During infancy, children change from virtually immobile beings to creatures who toddle as fast as their legs can carry them.

Reflexes   Newborns are not empty-headed. They come into the world equipped with several genetically "wired" reflexes. For example, they have no fear of water, but they naturally hold their breath and contract their throats to keep water out.

Some reflexes persist throughout life—coughing, blinking, and yawning, for example. Others disappear in the months following birth as higher brain functions mature and infants develop voluntary control over many behaviors.

These are some reflexes that weaken or disappear by 6 or 7 months of age:

- *Grasping.* When the infant's palms are touched, the infant grasps tightly with its fingers (although not the thumb).

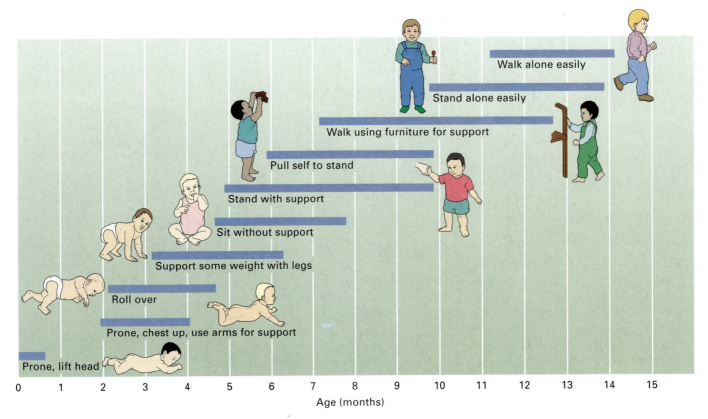

FIGURE 3.3 Developmental Accomplishments in Gross Motor Skills During the First 15 Months of Life

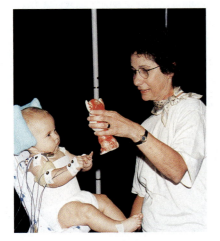

Esther Thelen is shown conducting a research study on infant motor and perceptual development. The focus of this study was to discover how infants coordinate their motor and perceptual skills to reach for and grasp an object. A computer device is used to monitor the infants's arm movements and to track muscle patterns.

- *Sucking.* When an object touches the infant's mouth, the infant automatically begins sucking.
- *Stepping.* When the infant is held above a surface with its feet lowered to touch the surface, the infant moves its feet as if to walk.
- *Startle.* When sudden stimulation occurs, such as hearing a loud noise or being dropped, the infant startles, arches its back, throws back its head, and flings out its arms and legs and then rapidly closes them to the center of its body.

Motor and Perceptual Skills At birth, the newborn has a gigantic head, relative to the rest of the body, that flops around uncontrollably. Within 12 months, the infant is capable of sitting upright, standing, stooping, climbing, and often walking. During the second year, growth decelerates, but rapid gains occur in such activities as running and climbing. Historically, researchers, such as Arnold Gesell (1934), assumed that motor milestones were like the ones shown in figure 3.3, occurring at certain ages as part of a genetic plan.

However, psychologists now recognize that motor development is not the consequence of nature alone. When infants are motivated to do something, they may create a new motor behavior (Thelen, 2000). That new behavior is the result of many converging factors: the developing nervous system, the body's physical properties and its movement possibilities, the goal the infant is motivated to reach, and environmental support for the skill. Thus both nature and nurture are involved.

Psychologists also believe that motor skills and perceptual skills are vitally linked. Babies are continually coordinating their movements with information they perceive through their senses to learn how to maintain their balance, reach for objects in space, and move across various surfaces and terrains (Thelen & Smith, 1998). Action also educates perception. For example, looking at an object while holding and touching it helps infants to learn about its texture, size, and hardness. Moving from place to place in the environment teaches babies how objects and people look from different perspectives and whether surfaces will support their weight (Gibson, 2001).

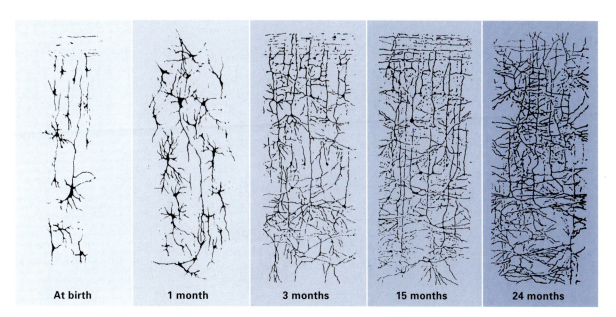

| At birth | 1 month | 3 months | 15 months | 24 months |

FIGURE 3.4 Dendritic Spreading
Note the increase in connections among neurons over the course of the first 2 years of life.

The Brain   As an infant walks, talks, runs, shakes a rattle, smiles, and frowns, his or her brain is changing dramatically. At birth and in early infancy, the brain's 100 billion neurons have only minimal connections. But, as the infant ages from birth to 2 years, the dendrites of the neurons branch out, and the neurons become far more interconnected (see figure 3.4). The infant's brain literally is ready and waiting for the experiences that will create these connections (Eliot, 2001; Greenough, 2001; Johnson, 2002).

Another important aspect of the brain's development in childhood is the dramatic increase in *synaptic connections* (Ramey & Ramey, 2000). Recall from chapter 2 that a synapse is a gap between neurons that is bridged by chemical neurotransmitters. Researchers have discovered that nearly twice as many synapses are available as will ever be used (Huttenlocher & Dabholkar, 1997). The connections that are made become stronger and will survive; the unused ones will be replaced by other neural pathways or disappear. In the language of neuroscience, these unused connections will be "pruned." Figure 3.5 vividly illustrates the dramatic growth and pruning of synapses in specific areas of the brain.

Using brain scanning techniques, such as MRI and CT, scientists recently have discovered that children's brains undergo dramatic anatomical changes between the ages of 3 and 15 (Thompson & others, 2000). The amount of brain material in some areas can nearly double within as little as a year, followed by a drastic loss of tissue as unneeded cells are purged and the brain continues to reorganize itself. The overall size of the brain does not show dramatic growth, but local patterns within the brain do change dramatically. From 3 to 6 years of age, the most rapid growth takes place in the frontal lobe areas, which are involved in planning and organizing new actions and in maintaining attention to tasks (Thompson & others, 2000).

Of course, if the dendrites and synapses are not being stimulated by a wealth of new experiences, children's brains are less likely to develop normally (Nelson, 2003). Thus, as in other areas of development, nature and nurture operate together. See the video clip "Brain Development" to learn more about the relationship between biology and environment in the development of the brain.

In-Psych Plus

Cognitive Development in Childhood

As amazing as physical development is in childhood, it is easily matched by cognitive development. As you read earlier in the chapter, cognitive processes involve thought, intelligence, and language. Until the mid-1900s, American psychologists had

FIGURE 3.5 Synaptic Density in the Human Brain from Infancy to Adulthood The graph shows the dramatic increase in synaptic density, and then pruning, in three regions of the brain: visual cortex, auditory cortex, and prefrontal cortex. Synaptic density is believed to be an important indication of the extent of connectivity among neurons.

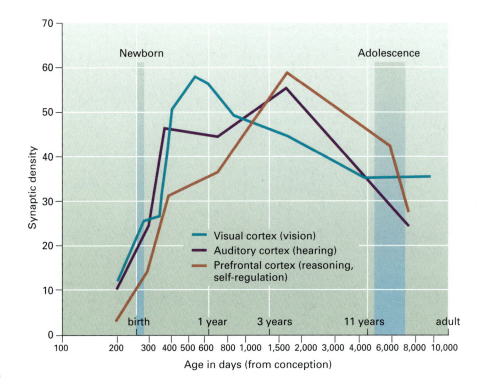

schema A concept or framework that already exists at a given moment in a person's mind and that organizes and interprets information.

assimilation Occurs when individuals incorporate new information into existing knowledge.

accommodation Occurs when individuals adjust their schemas to take new information into account.

no useful theory for explaining how children's minds change as they age. Psychologists who were interested in the topic had to view it through the lens of behaviorism, which emphasizes that children merely receive information from the environment, or through the lens of the IQ testing approach, which emphasizes individual differences in children's intelligence. But then Jean Piaget (1896–1980), the famous Swiss developmental psychologist, changed the way we think about children's minds.

Piaget's Theory of Cognitive Development   In Piaget's view, children *actively construct* their cognitive world, using schemas to make sense of what they experience. A **schema** is a concept or framework that already exists at a given moment in a person's mind and that organizes information and provides a structure for interpreting it. Schemas are expressed as various behaviors and skills that the child can exercise in relation to objects or situations. For example, sucking is an early, simple schema. Later, more complex schemas include licking, blowing, crawling, hiding, and so forth. Piaget's interest in schemas had to do with how they help in organizing and making sense out of current experience. In chapter 7, you will see how schemas also help us to understand why people don't remember the past in an exact way but reconstruct it instead.

Piaget (1952) said that the active construction of schemas involves two processes, which occur over time and after many repetitions of experience:

- **Assimilation** occurs when individuals incorporate new information into existing knowledge. That is, people *assimilate* the environment into a schema. For example, a schema in the child's mind might provide the information that some objects can be picked up. The first time a child realizes that she can pick up a set of keys, she is assimilating the category "keys" into the schema of "picking up."
- **Accommodation** occurs when individuals adjust their schemas to new information. That is, people *accommodate* their schemas to the environment. For example, a child might possess the schema of "picking up." With experience, the child might learn that some things can be picked up easily between two fingers, that other things require both hands and strong use of the arms, and

Sensorimotor Stage	Preoperational Stage	Concrete Operational Stage	Formal Operational Stage
The infant constructs an understanding of the world by coordinating sensory experiences with physical actions. An infant progresses from reflexive, instinctual action at birth to the beginning of symbolic thought toward the end of the stage.	The child begins to represent the world with words and images. These words and images reflect increased symbolic thinking and go beyond the connection of sensory information and physical action.	The child can now reason logically about concrete events and classify objects into different sets.	The adolescent reasons in more abstract, idealistic, and logical ways.
Birth to 2 Years of Age	*2 to 7 Years of Age*	*7 to 11 Years of Age*	*11 Years of Age Through Adulthood*

FIGURE 3.6 Piaget's Four Stages of Cognitive Development

that still other things cannot be picked up at all because they are too hot, for example, or too heavy. Thus the schema "picking up" becomes modified into different schemas that accommodate the realities of different types of objects.

Another important element of Piaget's theory is his observation that we go through four stages in understanding the world (see figure 3.6). Each of the stages is age-related and consists of distinct ways of thinking. In Piaget's view, it is not simply knowing more information that makes a child's thinking more advanced with each stage. Rather, the child's cognition is qualitatively different from one stage to the next.

1. *Sensorimotor stage: from birth to about 2 years of age.* In this stage, infants construct an understanding of the world by coordinating sensory experiences (such as seeing and hearing) with motor (physical) actions—hence the term *sensorimotor*. Imagine how you might experience the world if you were a 5-month-old infant. One of your toys, a monkey, falls out of your grasp and rolls behind a larger toy, a hippopotamus. Would you know the monkey is behind the hippopotamus, or would you think it is completely gone? Piaget believed that "out of sight" literally was "out of mind" for young infants. At 5 months of age, you would not have reached for the monkey when it fell behind the hippopotamus. By 8 months of age, though, infants begin to understand that out of sight is not out of mind. At this point, you probably would have reached behind the hippopotamus to search for the monkey, coordinating your senses with your movements. **Object permanence** is Piaget's term for this crucial accomplishment: understanding that objects and events continue to exist even when they cannot directly be seen, heard, or touched. The most common way to study object permanence is to show an infant an interesting toy and then block the infant's view of the toy (see figure 3.7). If infants understand that the toy still exists, they will search for it. Object permanence continues to develop throughout the sensorimotor period. For example, when infants initially understand that objects exist even when out of sight, they look only briefly for them. At the end of the sensorimotor stage, infants will engage in a prolonged and sophisticated search for an object.

2. *Preoperational stage: from approximately 2 to 7 years of age.* In preschool years, children begin to represent their world with words, images, and drawings. The type of symbolic thinking that children are able to accomplish during this stage has some limitations, however. They still cannot perform **operations**, by which Piaget meant mental representations that are "reversible." A well-known test of

sensorimotor stage The first Piagetian stage of cognitive development (birth to about 2 years of age), in which infants construct an understanding of the world by coordinating sensory experiences (such as seeing and hearing) with motor (physical) actions.

object permanence Piaget's term for the cognitive ability to understand that objects and events continue to exist even when they cannot be directly seen, heard, or touched.

preoperational stage The second Piagetian stage of cognitive development (approximately 2 to 7 years of age), in which thought becomes more symbolic, egocentric, and intuitive rather than logical; but the child cannot yet perform operations.

operations Piaget's term for mental representations that are "reversible."

FIGURE 3.7 Object Permanence
Piaget thought that object permanence was one of infancy's landmark cognitive accomplishments. For this 5-month-old boy, out of sight is literally out of mind. When his view of a toy dog is blocked, he does not search for it. In a few more months, he will search for hidden toys, reflecting the presence of object permanence.

FIGURE 3.8 Piaget's Conservation Task The beaker test determines whether a child can think operationally—that is, can mentally reverse actions and understand conservation of a substance. *(a)* Two identical beakers are presented to the child, each containing the same amount of liquid. The child pours the liquid from B into C, which is taller and thinner than A and B. *(b)* The experimenter then asks the child whether beakers A and C have the same amount of liquid. The preoperational child says no. When asked to point to the beaker that has more liquid, the child points to the tall, thin beaker.

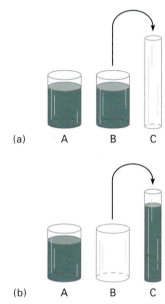

conservation Piaget's term for belief in the permanence of certain attributes of objects or situations despite superficial changes.

whether a child can think operationally is to present a child with two identical beakers, A and B, filled with liquid to the same height. Next to them is a third beaker, C, that is taller and thinner. The liquid is poured from B into C (see figure 3.8), and the child is asked whether the amounts in A and C are the same. The 4-year-old child invariably says that the amount of liquid in the tall, thin beaker (C) is greater than that in the short, wide beaker (A), because she cannot mentally reverse the pouring action; that is, she cannot imagine the liquid going back from container C to container B. Piaget said that such a child has not grasped the concept of **conservation**, a belief in the permanence of certain attributes of objects or situations in spite of superficial changes. A second limitation of the child's thought in the preoperational stage is that it is *egocentric,* meaning the child cannot distinguish between her own perspective and someone else's perspective. In the three-mountains task (see figure 3.9), the child walks around the model of the mountains and becomes familiar with what the mountains look like from different perspectives (Piaget & Inhelder, 1969). The child is then seated on one side of the table on which the mountains are placed. The experimenter takes a doll and moves it to different locations around the table, at each location asking the child to select one photo from a series of photos that most accurately reflects the view the doll is seeing. Children in the preoperational stage often pick the photo that shows the view they have rather than the view the doll has. A third limitation of preoperational

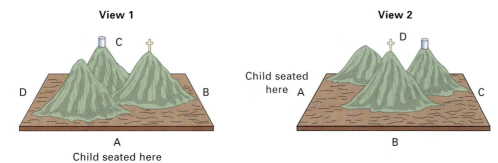

FIGURE 3.9 The Three-Mountains Test of Egocentrism View 1 shows a model from the child's perspective. View 2 shows the same model, from the perspective of a doll. The experimenter asks the child to identify a picture in which the view of the mountains looks as it would look to the doll. To correctly identify the picture, the child has to take the perspective of the doll. Invariably, a child who thinks in a preoperational way cannot perform this task and instead selects a picture showing his or her own view.

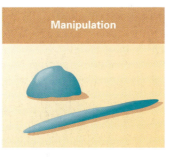

Two identical balls of clay are shown to the child. The child agrees that they are equal.

The experimenter changes the shape of one of the balls and asks the child whether they still contain equal amounts of clay.

No, the longer one has more.

Yes, they still have equal amounts.

FIGURE 3.10 The Clay Test of Operational Thinking

thought is that it is *intuitive*. When Piaget asked children why they knew something, they often did not give logical answers but offered personal insights or guesses instead. Preoperational children do not seem to be bothered by the absence of logic in their thinking. As Piaget observed, they often seem very sure that they know something, even though they do not use logical reasoning to arrive at the answer. Overall, then, preoperational thought is more symbolic than is sensorimotor thought, but it is egocentric and intuitive rather than logical, and it does not include the ability to perform operations.

3. *Concrete operational stage: from approximately 7 to 11 years of age.* Concrete operational thought involves using operations and replacing intuitive reasoning with logical reasoning in concrete situations. Classification skills are present, but abstract thinking is not yet developed. A well-known task for demonstrating operational thinking involves two identical balls of clay (see figure 3.10). As the child watches, the experimenter rolls one ball into a long, thin rod and leaves the other ball in its original spherical shape. Then the child is asked if more clay is in the ball or in the long, thin rod. By the time children reach 7 to 8 years of age, most answer that the amount of clay is the same. To solve this problem correctly, children have to recall that the ball was rolled into the shape of a rod and imagine the rod being returned to its original round shape—imagination that involves a reversible mental action. In this experiment, and in the beaker experiment mentioned earlier, the preoperational child is likely to focus on a single dimension, either height or width. The child who has reached the stage of concrete operational thought coordinates information about dimensions or characteristics. Many of the concrete operations identified by Piaget are related to properties of objects. Thus one important skill at this stage of

concrete operational stage The third Piagetian stage of cognitive development (approximately 7 to 11 years of age), in which thought becomes operational, replacing intuitive thought with logical reasoning in concrete situations.

FIGURE 3.11 Classification Task Involving a Family Tree One way to determine if children possess classification skills is to see if they can understand a family tree of four generations (Furth & Wachs, 1975). This family tree suggests that the grandfather (A) has three sons (B, C, and D), each of whom has two sons (E through J), and that one of these grandsons (J) has three sons (K, L, and M). A child who comprehends this classification system can move up and down a level (vertically), across a level (horizontally), and up and down and across a level (obliquely) within the system. A child who thinks in a concrete operational way understands that person J can, at the same time, be father, brother, and grandson. A preoperational child cannot perform this classification task and says that J cannot be a father, for example, and fulfill his other roles.

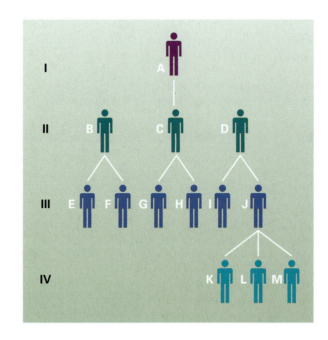

reasoning is the ability to classify or divide things into different sets or subsets and to consider their interrelations. Figure 3.11 shows an example of a classification task that concrete operational children can perform. In sum, concrete operational thought involves operational thinking, classification skills, and logical reasoning in concrete, but not abstract, contexts.

4. *Formal operational stage: beginning at 11 to 15 years of age and continuing through the adult years.* Formal operational thought is more abstract, idealistic, and logical than concrete operational thought. Unlike elementary school children, adolescents are no longer limited to actual concrete experience as the anchor of thought. They can conceive of hypothetical possibilities, which are purely abstract. Thought also becomes more idealistic. Adolescents often compare themselves and others with ideal standards. And they think about what an ideal world would be like, wondering if they couldn't carve out a better world than the one the adult generation has handed to them. At the same time, adolescents begin to think more like scientists, devising plans to solve problems and systematically testing solutions. Piaget gave this type of logical problem solving an imposing title: **hypothetical-deductive reasoning**. The term denotes adolescents' ability to develop hypotheses, or best hunches, about ways to solve problems, such as an algebraic equation. It also denotes their ability to systematically deduce, or conclude, the best path to follow to solve the problem. In contrast, prior to adolescence, children are more likely to solve problems in a trial-and-error fashion.

Piaget based his stages on careful observation of children's behavior and opened up a new way of looking at how children's minds develop. We owe him for a long list of masterful concepts that have enduring power and fascination (Scholnick, 1999): schemas, assimilation, accommodation, cognitive stages, object permanence, egocentrism, and conservation. We also owe Piaget for the currently accepted vision of children as active, constructive thinkers who manufacture (in part) their own development.

But, just as other psychological theories have been criticized and amended, so have Piaget's (Bjorklund, 2000; Brynes, 2001; Smith, 2002). For example, researchers have found that some cognitive abilities emerge earlier in some children than Piaget thought (Mandler, 2003). Renee Baillargeon (1997) has documented that infants as young as 4 months of age know that objects continue to exist even when hidden

formal operational stage The fourth and final Piagetian stage of cognitive development (emerging at about 11 to 15 years of age), in which thinking becomes more abstract, idealistic, and logical.

hypothetical-deductive reasoning Piaget's term for the ability to develop hypotheses about ways to solve a problem and to systematically deduce the best solution.

(which Piaget did not think was possible until 8 months of age). Also, memory and other forms of symbolic activity occur by at least the first half of the first year (much earlier than Piaget thought possible) (Mandler, 1998). Nor does formal operational thought emerge as consistently in early adolescence as Piaget envisioned. Many adolescents and even adults do not reason as logically as Piaget proposed. Thus infants are more cognitively competent than Piaget thought, and adolescents and adults are less competent.

Piaget has also been criticized on broader grounds. He was interested in examining the human species and general ways in which all people go through cognitive stages at particular ages. Not surprisingly, he has been criticized for ignoring individual differences.

In another broad criticism, information processing psychologists argue that Piaget's view places too much emphasis on grand stages and not enough on small, precise steps. Information processing psychologists believe that children's minds can be best understood by focusing more on their thinking strategies and skills, as well as on their speed and efficiency in processing information (Siegler, 1998). Use the interactivity "Formal Operational Thought" to test your level of cognitive development and to learn more about the information processing perspective.

The sociocultural perspective gives us yet another view of the shortcomings of Piaget's work (Rogoff, 2003). Piaget did not believe that culture and education play important roles in children's cognitive development. However, researchers have found that the age at which children acquire conservation skills is related to some extent to whether or not their culture provides relevant practice (Cole, 1999; Cole & Cole, 2003). In the view of Russian psychologist Lev Vygotsky (1962), the goal of cognitive development is to learn the skills that will allow you to be competent in your culture. Thus it is important to be guided and assisted by skilled members of the culture, much like being a cognitive apprentice (Rogoff, 1998). Vygotsky's view has become increasingly popular in educational psychology because of its emphasis on collaborative learning through interaction with skilled others (Rowe & Wertsch, 2002).

Today, children's cognitive development is approached from several perspectives (Flavell, Miller, & Miller, 2002; Thomas, 2001), yet Piaget still stands head and shoulders above all others in this field. His great work let us see that children's minds change and develop in orderly, sequential ways (Scholnick & others, 1999).

Socioemotional Development in Childhood

As children grow and develop, they are socialized by and socialize others, such as parents, siblings, peers, and teachers. Their small world widens as they grow older. In this section, you will learn about several aspects of children's socioemotional development.

Erikson's Theory of Socioemotional Development   Erik Erikson (1902–1994) spent his early life in Europe. After working as a psychoanalyst under Sigmund Freud's direction, he came to the United States and taught at Harvard University. Although he accepted some of Freud's beliefs, he disagreed with others. For example, Freud argued that *psychosexual* stages are the key to understanding development; Erikson said that eight *psychosocial* stages are the key (1968). In addition, Freud stressed that personality is shaped mainly in the first 5 years of life. In contrast, although Erikson's first four stages take place in childhood, the last four occur in adolescence and adulthood (see figure 3.12).

Each of Erikson's stages represents a developmental task, or crisis, that a person must negotiate. Each stage also marks a potential turning point toward greater personal competence or greater weakness and vulnerability. The more successfully people resolve the issues at each stage, the more competent they are likely to become. Erikson's adolescent and adult stages are examined later in the chapter, but his four childhood stages are as follows:

Jean Piaget, the famous Swiss developmental psychologist, changed the way we think about the development of children's minds. *What were his main contributions?*

In-Psych Plus

Erik Erikson (here with his wife, Joan, an artist). Erikson generated one of the most important developmental theories of the twentieth century. *What does Erickson's theory say about the process of socioemotional development?*

Erikson's Stages	Developmental Period	Characteristics
Trust versus mistrust	Infancy (Birth to 1 ½ years)	A sense of trust requires a feeling of physical comfort and minimal amount of fear about the future. Infants' basic needs are met by responsive, sensitive caregivers.
Autonomy versus shame and doubt	Toddlerhood (1 ½ to 3 years)	After gaining trust in their caregivers, infants start to discover that they have a will of their own. They assert their sense of autonomy, or independence. They realize their will. If infants are restrained too much or punished too harshly, they are likely to develop a sense of shame and doubt.
Initiative versus guilt	Early childhood (preschool years, ages 3–5)	As preschool children encounter a widening social world, they are challenged more and need to develop more purposeful behavior to cope with these challenges. Children are now asked to assume more responsibility. Uncomfortable guilt feelings may arise, though, if the children are irresponsible and are made to feel too anxious.
Industry versus inferiority	Middle and late childhood (elementary school years, 6 years–puberty)	At no other time are children more enthusiastic than at the end of early childhood's period of expansive imagination. As children move into the elementary school years, they direct their energy toward mastering knowledge and intellectual skills. The danger at this stage involves feeling incompetent and unproductive.
Identity versus identity confusion	Adolescence (10–20 years)	Individuals are faced with finding out who they are, what they are all about, and where they are going in life. An important dimension is the exploration of alternative solutions to roles. Career exploration is important.
Intimacy versus isolation	Eary adulthood (20s, 30s)	Individuals face the developmental task of forming intimate relationships with others. Erikson described intimacy as finding oneself yet losing oneself in another person.
Generativity versus stagnation	Middle adulthood (40s, 50s)	A chief concern is to assist the younger generation in developing and leading useful lives.
Integrity versus despair	Late adulthood (60s–)	Individuals look back and evaluate what they have done with their lives. The retrospective glances can either be positive (integrity) or negative (despair).

FIGURE 3.12 Erikson's Eight Stages of Socioemotional Development

1. *Trust versus mistrust: approximately the first 1½ years of life.* Trust is built when a baby's basic needs—such as comfort, food, and warmth—are met. If infants' needs are not met by responsive, sensitive caregivers, the result is mistrust. Trust in infancy sets the stage for a lifelong expectation that the world will be a good and pleasant place to live.

2. *Autonomy versus shame and doubt: from about 1½ through 3 years of age.* In this stage, children can develop either a positive sense of independence and autonomy

or negative feelings of shame and doubt. In seeking autonomy, they are likely to develop a strong sense of independence.

3. *Initiative versus guilt: from 3 to 5 years of age, the preschool years.* During these years, children's social worlds are widening, and they are being challenged to develop purposeful behavior to cope with the challenges. When asked to assume more responsibility for themselves, children can develop initiative. When allowed to be irresponsible or made to feel anxious, they can develop too much guilt. But Erikson believed that young children are resilient. He said that a sense of accomplishment quickly compensates for most guilt feelings.

4. *Industry versus inferiority: from about age 6 until puberty.* Children can achieve industry by mastering knowledge and intellectual skills. When they do not, they can feel inferior. For example, Erikson believed that, at the end of the period of expansive imagination that occurs in early childhood, children are ready to turn their energy to learning academic skills. If they do not, they can develop a sense of being incompetent and unproductive.

Erikson did not believe that the proper resolution to a stage is always completely positive. For example, developing trust is good, but one cannot trust all people under all circumstances and survive. For optimal development to take place, however, positive resolutions should dominate.

At a time when people believed that most development takes place in childhood, Erikson charted development as a lifelong challenge. His insights also helped to move us away from Freud's focus on sexuality and toward an understanding of the importance of successfully resolving different socioemotional tasks at different points in our lives. Erikson's ideas changed the way we think about some periods of development (Marcia, 2001). For example, Erikson encouraged us to look at adolescents not just as hormone-driven beings but as individuals trying to find out who they are and where their place in the world is.

But, like Piaget's theory, Erikson's also has been criticized. As I mentioned in chapter 1, Erikson practiced mainly case study research. Critics argue that a firmer research base for Erikson's entire theory has not been developed. However, research on specific stages of the theory reveal that there are important developmental tasks at certain points in our lives.

Critics also say that Erikson's attempt to capture each stage with a single concept sometimes leaves out other important developmental tasks. For example, Erikson said that the main task for young adults is to resolve the conflict between intimacy and isolation. However, another important developmental task in early adulthood involves careers and work.

Such criticisms do not tarnish Erikson's monumental contributions, however. He, like Piaget, is a giant in developmental psychology.

Attachment in Infancy In the language of developmental psychology, **attachment** is the close emotional bond between an infant and its caregiver. Theories about infant attachment abound. Freud believed that the infant becomes attached to the person or object that feeds the infant and thus provides oral satisfaction. For most infants, this is the mother.

But researchers have questioned the importance of feeding in infant attachment. Harry Harlow (1958) separated infant monkeys from their mothers at birth and placed them in cages in which they had access to two artificial "mothers." One of the mothers was made of wire, the other of cloth. Each mother could be outfitted with a feeding mechanism. Half the infant monkeys were fed by the wire mother, half by the cloth mother. The infant monkeys nestled close to the cloth mother and spent little time on the wire one, even if the wire mother was the one that gave them milk (see figure 3.13). This study clearly demonstrates that what the researchers described as "contact comfort," not feeding, is the crucial element in the attachment process.

attachment The close emotional bond between an infant and its caregiver.

FIGURE 3.13 Contact Time with Wire and Cloth Surrogate Mothers Regardless of whether the infant monkeys were fed by a wire or a cloth mother, they overwhelmingly preferred to spend contact time with the cloth mother.

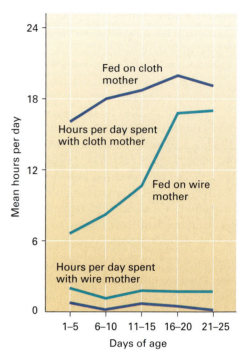

Konrad Lorenz, a pioneering student of animal behavior, is followed through the water by three imprinted greylag geese. Lorenz described imprinting as rapid, innate learning within a critical period that involves attachment to the first moving object seen. For goslings, the critical period is the first 36 hours after birth. *How does the concept of imprinting apply to human development?*

Another famous study grew out of the field of *ethology,* which examines the function and evolution of behavior. One of ethology's founders, the European zoologist Konrad Lorenz (1903–1989), examined attachment behavior in geese (1965). He separated the eggs laid by one goose into two groups. He returned one group of eggs to the goose to be hatched; the other group was hatched in an incubator. The goslings in the first group performed as predicted; they followed their mother as soon as they hatched. But those in the second group, who saw Lorenz first after hatching, followed him everywhere as if he were their mother. Lorenz marked the goslings and then placed both groups under a box. Mother goose and "mother" Lorenz stood nearby as the box was lifted. Each group of goslings went directly to its "mother." Lorenz called this process **imprinting,** the tendency of an infant animal to form an attachment to the first moving object it sees or hears.

imprinting The tendency of an infant animal to form an attachment to the first moving object it sees or hears.

For goslings, the critical period for imprinting is the first 36 hours after birth. Human infants appear to have a longer, more flexible "sensitive period" for attachment. For instance, research on attachment supports John Bowlby's view (1969, 1989) that the infant's attachment to its caregiver intensifies at about 6 to 7 months (Schaffer & Emerson, 1964). A number of developmental psychologists believe that attachment to the caregiver during the first year provides an important foundation for later development.

Some babies have more positive attachment experiences than others (Levy, 1999). Mary Ainsworth (1979) believes that the difference depends on how sensitive the caregiver is to the infant's signals. She uses the term **secure attachment** to describe how infants use the caregiver, usually the mother, as a secure base from which to explore the environment. Infants who are securely attached are more likely to have mothers who are responsive and accepting and who express affection toward them than are infants who are insecurely attached (Waters & others, 1995). The securely attached infant moves freely away from the mother but also keeps tabs on her by periodically glancing at her. The securely attached infant responds positively to being picked up by others and, when put back down, happily moves away to play. An insecurely attached infant, in contrast, avoids the mother or is ambivalent toward her. The insecurely attached infant fears strangers and is upset by minor sensations. To learn more about attachment, see the video clip "Secure Attachment."

Not all developmentalists believe that a secure attachment in infancy is the only path to competence in life. Jerome Kagan (1998, 2000), for example, believes that infants are highly resilient and can adapt to wide variations in parenting style. Kagan and others stress that genetics and temperament play more important roles in a child's social competence. For example, inheriting a low tolerance for stress, rather than having an insecure attachment bond, might be responsible for the inability of a child to get along with peers.

Another criticism of attachment theory is that it ignores the evidence that in some cultures infants show strong attachments to many people, not just their primary caregiver (Thompson, 2000). In the African Hausa culture, for instance, both grandmothers and siblings provide a significant amount of care to infants (Harkness & Super, 2002). Infants in agricultural societies tend to form attachments to older siblings who are assigned a major responsibility for younger siblings' care. The attachments formed by infants in group care in Israeli kibbutzim provide another variation.

Psychologists accept the importance of competent, nurturant caregivers in an infant's development (Bradley & Corwyn, 2004). At issue, though, is whether secure attachment, especially to a single caregiver, is critical (Rosen & Burke, 1999).

Temperament   One of the factors that some psychologists believe is a key to understanding child development is **temperament,** which is an individual's behavioral style and characteristic way of responding. Psychiatrists Alexander Chess and Stella Thomas (1977) identify three basic types or clusters of temperament in children:

- The *easy child,* who generally is in a positive mood, quickly establishes regular routines in infancy, and adapts easily to new experiences
- The *difficult child,* who tends to react negatively and cry frequently, engages in irregular daily routines, and is slow to accept new experiences
- The *slow-to-warm-up child,* who has a low activity level, is somewhat negative, shows low adaptability, and displays a low intensity of mood

Other researchers propose different dimensions as the core of temperament, such as *emotionality* (tendency to be distressed), *sociability* (tendency to prefer the company of others to being alone), and *activity level* (tempo and vigor of movement) (Buss & Plomin, 1987). Thus agreement about the core dimensions of temperament has not been reached (Sanson, Smart, & Hemphill, 2002; Wachs & Bates, 2002; Wachs & Kohnstamm, 2001).

Many parents don't believe in the importance of temperament until they have their second child (Putnam, Sanson, & Rothbart, 2002). Parents typically view the

In the Hausa culture, siblings and grandmothers provide a significant amount of care for infants. *How might this practice affect attachment?*

In-Psych Plus

secure attachment An important aspect of socioemotional development in which infants use the caregiver, usually the mother, as a secure base from which to explore the environment.

temperament An individual's behavioral style and characteristic way of responding.

firstborn child's behavior as a result of the way they have raised the child. However, management strategies that worked with the first child might be frustratingly ineffective with the second child. Such differences in children's temperament, which appear very early in their lives, support the belief that both nature and nurture influence development.

Parenting Ideas about the best way to rear children have gone through a lot of changes over the years and may vary across cultures. At one time, and in some cultures still, parents were advised to impose strict discipline along the lines of such adages as "Spare the rod and spoil the child" and "Children should be seen and not heard." But attitudes toward children—and ideas about how best to parent them—have changed to encompass more nurturing and caring.

Diana Baumrind (1971, 1991) believes parents interact with their children in one of four basic ways:

- **Authoritarian parenting** is a restrictive, punitive style in which the parent exhorts the child to follow the parent's directions and to respect work and effort. The authoritarian parent firmly limits and controls the child with little verbal exchange. In a difference of opinion about how to do something, for example, the authoritarian parent might say, "You do it my way or else. No backtalk." Authoritarian parenting is associated with children's social incompetence. Children of authoritarian parents often fail to initiate activity, have poor communication skills, and compare themselves with others.
- **Authoritative parenting** encourages children to be independent but still places limits and controls on their behavior. Extensive verbal give-and-take is allowed, and parents are warm and nurturant toward the child. An authoritative parent might put his arm around the child in a comforting way and say, "You know you should not have done that; let's talk about how you can handle the situation better next time." Children whose parents are authoritative tend to be socially competent, self-reliant, and socially responsible.
- **Neglectful parenting** is a style in which parents are uninvolved in their child's life. Ask such parents, "It's 10 P.M. Do you know where your child is?" and they are likely to answer, "No." However, children have a strong need for their parents to care about them. Children whose parents are neglectful might develop a sense that other aspects of the parents' lives are more important than they are. Children whose parents are neglectful tend to be less competent socially, to not handle independence well, and, especially, to show poor self-control.
- **Indulgent parenting** is a style in which parents are involved with their children but place few limits on them. Such parents let their children do what they want. Some parents deliberately rear their children in this way because they believe the combination of warm involvement with few restraints will produce a creative, confident child. But children whose parents are indulgent often rate poorly in social competence. They often fail to learn respect for others, expect to get their own way, and have difficulty controlling their behavior. One boy whose parents deliberately reared him in an indulgent manner moved his parents out of their bedroom suite and took it over for himself. At nearly 18 years old, he had still not learned to control his behavior; when he couldn't get something he wanted, he still threw temper tantrums. As you might expect, he wasn't popular with his peers.

Although Baumrind's theory is useful, it leaves many questions about parenting unanswered, and there is more to understanding parent-child relationships than parenting style (Lamb & others, 1999; Parke, 2004). One key issue is whether parenting style is really a product of the parents alone. For years, the socialization of children was viewed as a straightforward, one-way matter of indoctrination. However, children socialize their parents just as parents socialize their children. For example, children's smiles usually elicit positive overtures by parents. When children are difficult

authoritarian parenting A restrictive, punitive parenting style in which the parent exhorts the child to follow the parent's directions and respect work and effort.

authoritative parenting A parenting style that encourages children's independence but still places limits and controls on their behavior and that features extensive verbal give-and-take and warm and nurturant interactions with the child.

neglectful parenting A parenting style in which parents are uninvolved in their child's life.

indulgent parenting A parenting style in which parents are involved with their children but place few limits on them.

and aggressive, their parents are likely to punish them. In other words, parenting styles may be influenced by children's behavior.

Parents' circumstances also play a role. Many children are highly vulnerable to stress during the experience of divorce, for example (Kitzmann & Gaylord, 2002). Research shows that children from divorced families are more poorly adjusted (are more likely to have psychological problems, such as being overly aggressive or depressed) than their counterparts from nondivorced families (Amato & Keith, 1991). What percentage of children from divorced families have adjustment problems? The consensus is approximately 25 percent, compared with only 10 percent of children in nondivorced families (Hetherington, 2000; Hetherington & Stanley-Hagan, 2002). Remember, however, that approximately 75 percent of children in divorced families do not have adjustment problems. Among the factors that predict better adjustment for children in divorced families are harmony between the divorced parents, authoritative parenting, good schools, and the child's possession of an easy rather than a difficult temperament (Harvey & Fine, 2004; Hetherington & Kelly, 2002).

Some advocate *positive parenting* as an antidote to risk factors such as divorce, poverty, and other difficulties in the childhood environment. "Emotion-coaching parents" monitor their children's emotions, view their children's negative emotions as opportunities for teaching about emotion, and provide guidance in effectively dealing with emotions (Katz, 1999). In research, emotion-coaching parents have been observed to reject their children less, praise them more, and be more nurturant toward them than "emotion-dismissing parents" (Gottman, Katz, & Hooven, 1997). The children of the emotion-coaching parents in this research were better at toning down the intensity of their negative emotions and at focusing their attention and had fewer behavior problems than the children of emotion-dismissing parents.

Another aspect of positive parenting focuses on raising a moral child, one who is considerate of others, understands the difference between right and wrong, and is less likely to lie, cheat, or steal. Following are the positive parenting strategies that have most often been found to be helpful in raising a moral child (Eisenberg & Murphy, 1995; Eisenberg & Valiente, 2002):

- Parents are warm and supportive rather than punitive.
- Parents use reasoning the child can understand when disciplining.
- Parents provide opportunities for the child to learn about others' perspectives and feelings.
- Parents involve children in family decision making and thinking about moral decisions.
- Parents model moral behaviors and thinking themselves and provide their children with opportunities to engage in such moral behaviors and thinking.

Despite all the ways that parents have been found to influence their children's development, some psychologists argue that parenting may be less important in children's socioemotional development than we think, a controversy related to the nature versus nurture issue. For more on this issue, see the Critical Controversy box.

The Wider Social World   The family is one social context in which children's development occurs. But the broader culture, the child's peer relations, school influences, and the quality of the neighborhood in which the child lives also are important (Bronfenbrenner, 2000; Harkness & Super, 2002; Leventhal & Brooks-Gunn, 2004).

Today, psychologists are especially interested in improving the lives of children who live in impoverished neighborhoods and attend ineffective schools (Blyth, 2000; Booth & Crouter, 2000). They also are increasingly interested in studying children from ethnic minority groups. Although many ethnic minority families are not poor, poverty contributes to the stressful life experiences of many minority children, creating a double disadvantage for them (McLoyd, 1999, 2000): prejudice, discrimination, and bias because of their ethnic minority background are compounded by the stressful effects of poverty.

Parents Bring Up Their Children, Don't They?

In a provocative book, *The Nurture Assumption*, Judith Harris (1998) argues that what parents do does not make a difference in their children's behavior. Spank them. Hug them. Read to them. Ignore them. Harris says it won't influence how they turn out. She argues that children's genes and their peers are far more important than parents in children's development.

Harris (1998) explores the factors that influence an adult's personality, such as being shy or outgoing. Citing a number of twin studies (how these are conducted was discussed in chapter 2), she presents evidence that heredity explains about 50 percent of an adult's personality. In other words, she believes that 50 percent of your personality is due to the genes you inherited from your parents.

Harris, though, does not claim that the environment in which children grow up is unimportant in the development of personality. After all, children's genes, or their nature, account for only half of adult personality, in her view. Rather, she argues that children learn from many sources and that their learning is specific to certain contexts. Although children imitate their parents to learn how to behave at home, they imitate other people to learn how to behave outside the home. Harris singles out children's peer relations as an especially important aspect of the nurture part of the nature-nurture equation. Harris even believes that children would develop into the same types of adults if we left them in their homes, schools, neighborhoods, peer groups, and culture but switched their parents around.

How far-fetched is Harris' view? Some psychologists believe that it is more plausible than it first appears. One argument is that humans evolved to learn from any source, not just parents (Rowe, 1994). Such a general learning mechanism means that children might learn cultural innovations even if their parents do not. For example, the children of immigrants learn a second language faster and more completely than do their parents. They likely would not learn a second language at different rates if children learned only from their parents.

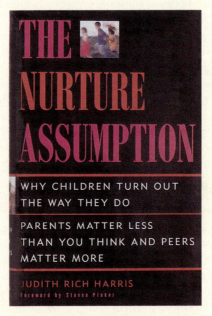

What is the theme of Judith Harris' controversial book The Assumption *(1998)? What is the nature of the controversy?*

As you might imagine, not everyone agrees with Harris' view (Vandell, 2000). Critics say Harris is right that genes matter, that she is right that peers matter, but that she is wrong in saying that parents do not matter. They argue that, in arriving at her view, Harris ignored research studies documenting the importance of parents in children's development (Maccoby, 2000). For example, many studies reveal that, when parents abuse their children, the children have problems in regulating their emotions, becoming securely attached to others, developing competent peer relations, and adapting to school. Such children also develop anxiety and depression disorders (Azar, 2002; Cicchetti & Toth, 1998; Rogosch & others, 1995).

Studies of positive intervention with parents could demonstrate whether parenting plays an important role in children's development (Bornstein & Bradley, 2003; Dunifon, Duncan, & Brooks-Gunn, 2004). In one study, training low-income mothers to respond sensitively to their infants both changed the negative responses of mothers when their infants became irritable and reduced the likelihood that distressed infants would avoid their mothers (Van den Boom, 1994). In another study, parents' participation in 16-week discussion groups on effective parenting just prior to their children's entry into kindergarten resulted in better school adjustment and higher academic achievement for their children than for children whose parents attended discussion groups without the effective parenting emphasis (Cowan & Cowan, 2001).

What do you think?

- Do you think that your personality was formed more by nature or by nurture? In other words, was your personality shaped more by your genes or by your life experiences?
- Do you believe that your personality has been influenced more by your parents or by your peers and other social influences?

Developmental psychologists also are intrigued by cultural comparisons of children in the United States and other countries. For example, parents in the United States tend to rear their children to be more independent than do their counterparts in Japan and other Asian countries (Matsumoto, 2000). Such cross-cultural variations reflect the nurture part of the nature versus nurture issue.

Kohlberg's Theory of Moral Development Moral development involves changes with age in thoughts, feelings, and behaviors regarding the principles and values that

Children's development is influenced not only by their family experiences but also by their experiences with peers, in the neighborhood, at school, and in the culture. A special concern is the effects of poverty on children's development. Poverty is especially high in ethnic minority families. *How might poverty affect socioemotional development?*

guide what people should do. Moral development has both an intrapersonal dimension (a person's basic values and sense of self) and an interpersonal dimension (what people should do in their interactions with other people) (Nucci, 2001; Turiel, 1983; Walker & Pitts, 1998).

Psychologists studying moral reasoning and thinking have based much of their work on Lawrence Kohlberg's theory of moral development. Kohlberg (1958) began his study of moral thinking by creating 11 stories and asking children, adolescents, and adults questions about the stories. One of the stories (set in Europe) goes like this:

> A woman was near death from a special kind of cancer. There was one drug that the doctors thought might save her. It was a form of radium that a druggist in the same town had recently discovered. The drug was expensive to make, but the druggist was charging ten times what the drug cost him to make. He paid $200 for the radium and charged $2,000 for a small dose of the drug. The sick woman's husband, Heinz, went to everyone he knew to borrow the money, but he could get together only $1,000. He told the druggist that his wife was dying and asked him to sell it cheaper or let him pay later. But the druggist said, "No. I discovered the drug, and I am going to make money from it." Desperate, Heinz broke into the man's store to steal the drug for his wife. (Kohlberg, 1969)

After reading the story, the interviewee was asked a series of questions about the moral dilemma. Should Heinz have stolen the drug? Was stealing it right or wrong? Why? Is it a husband's duty to steal a lifesaving drug for his wife if he can get it in no other way? Would a good husband do it? Did the druggist have the right to charge so much in the absence of a law setting a limit on the price? Why or why not? Based on the answers that people gave to the questions about this and other moral dilemmas, Kohlberg constructed his theory.

Kohlberg (1986) proposed that moral development consists of three levels, with two stages at each level (see figure 3.14):

1. The *preconventional level* is based primarily on punishments (stage 1) or rewards (stage 2) that come from the external world. In regard to the Heinz story, at stage 1 an individual might say that Heinz should not steal the drug because he might get caught and sent to jail. At stage 2, the person might say he should not steal the drug because the druggist needs to make a profit on the drug.
2. At the *conventional level,* the individual abides by standards, such as those learned from parents (stage 3) or society's laws (stage 4). At stage 3, an individual might say that Heinz should steal the drug for his wife because that is

Lawrence Kohlberg created a provocative theory of moral development. In his view, "Moral development consists of a sequence of qualitative changes in the way an individual thinks." *Why is his theory provocative?*

LEVEL 1 Preconventional Level No Internalization	LEVEL 2 Conventional Level Intermediate Internalization	LEVEL 3 Postconventional Level Full Internalization
Stage 1 Heteronomous Morality *Individuals pursue their own interests but let others do the same. What is right involves equal exchange.*	**Stage 3** Mutual Interpersonal Expectations, Relationships, and Interpersonal Conformity *Individuals value trust, caring, and loyalty to others as a basis for moral judgments.*	**Stage 5** Social Contract or Utility and Individual Rights *Individuals reason that values, rights, and principles undergird or transcend the law.*
Stage 2 Individualism, Purpose, and Exchange *Children obey because adults tell them to obey. People base their moral decisions on fear of punishment.*	**Stage 4** Social System Morality *Moral judgments are based on understanding and the social order, law, justice, and duty.*	**Stage 6** Universal Ethical Principles *The person has developed moral judgments that are based on universal human rights. When faced with a dilemma between law and conscience, a personal, individualized conscience is followed.*

FIGURE 3.14 Kohlberg's Three Levels of Moral Development Each level of development consists of two stages.

what people expect a good husband would do. At stage 4, the person might say that it is natural for Heinz to want to save his wife but that the law says it still is always wrong to steal.

3. At the *postconventional level,* the individual recognizes alternative moral courses, explores the options, and then develops a personal moral code. The code reflects the principles generally accepted by the community (stage 5), or it reflects more abstract principles for all of humanity (stage 6). At stage 5, a person might say that the law was not set up for these circumstances, so Heinz can steal the drug. Stealing is not really right, but he is justified in doing it. At stage 6, the individual evaluates alternatives but recognizes that Heinz's wife's life is more important than a law.

Kohlberg believed that these levels and stages develop in a sequence and are age-related. Some evidence for the sequence of Kohlberg's stages has been found, although few people reach stage 6 (Colby & others, 1983). Children are often in stages 1 and 2, although in the later elementary school years they may be in stage 3. Most adolescents are at stage 3 or 4. Kohlberg also believed that advances in moral development take place because of the maturation of thought (especially in concert with Piaget's stages), opportunities for role taking, and opportunities to discuss moral issues with a person who reasons at a stage just above one's own. In Kohlberg's view, parents contribute little to children's moral thinking because parent-child relationships are often too power-oriented.

Kohlberg's ideas stimulated considerable interest in the field of moral development. His provocative view continues to promote considerable research about how people think about moral issues (Lapsley & Narváez, 2004).

At the same time, his theory has numerous critics. One criticism is that moral *reasoning* does not necessarily mean moral *behavior.* When people are asked about their moral reasoning, what they say might fit into Kohlberg's advanced stages, but their actual behavior might be filled with cheating, lying, and stealing. Cheaters, liars, and thieves might know what is right and what is wrong but still do what is wrong.

A second major criticism is that Kohlberg's view does not adequately reflect interpersonal relationships and concerns for others, that it focuses too much on the intrapersonal dimension of moral development. Kohlberg's theory is thus a *justice perspective* concerned with the rights of "the individual," who stands alone and independently makes moral decisions. Carol Gilligan (1982) faults Kohlberg for greatly underplaying the *care perspective* in moral development, which views people in terms of their connectedness with others and focuses on interpersonal communication, relationships, and concern for others. She believes he may have done so because he is a male, because most of his research was with males, and because he used male responses as a model for his theory. However, not everyone adopts Gilligan's view, either, and even she argues that at the highest level of moral development the individual and relationship aspects of moral reasoning are likely to be integrated.

Gender Development Carol Gilligan's view of moral development points up another important aspect of socioemotional development in childhood: **gender,** or the social and psychological aspects of being female or male. Gilligan's view of moral development provides some good examples of the differences between girls' and boys' experiences as they grow up and the potential lasting effects of those experiences. For instance, Gilligan (1996, 1998) says that at the edge of adolescence—at about 11 to 12 years of age—girls become aware that their intense interest in intimacy is not prized by the male-dominated culture, even though society values females as caring and altruistic. The dilemma, says Gilligan, is that girls are presented with a choice that makes them appear either selfish (if they become independent and self-sufficient) or selfless (if they remain responsive to others), neither of which may be desirable. As young adolescent girls experience this dilemma, Gilligan says, they increasingly "silence" their distinctive voices. They become less confident and more tentative in offering their opinions, behavior that may persist into adulthood.

Gilligan's work is only one aspect of psychology's intense interest in gender development (Galambos, 2004; Stewart & McDermott, 2004). Other avenues of research include how strongly social experiences with parents and others influence the way girls and boys behave and how gender and cognition are linked.

An important focus of research has been the question of how strongly biology shapes gender. For instance, in rare instances, an imbalance in the secretion of hormones occurs during prenatal development, creating a hermaphrodite: an individual with both male and female sex organs. When infants genetically coded as female are born with masculine-looking genitals, surgery can achieve a genital-genetic match. But prior to puberty these females often behave in more aggressive, tomboyish ways than most girls (Berenbaum & Hines, 1992; Ehrhardt, 1987). Is the gender behavior of these surgically corrected girls due to their prenatal hormones, or is it the result of their social experience? Perhaps because these girls looked more masculine, they were treated more like boys and so adopted boyish ways. Thus, as with other aspects of development, in gender behavior both biology and experience likely are at work.

Evolutionary psychologists also take considerable interest in gender. In the evolutionary psychology view, which emphasizes the role of nature, differences in gender behavior are seen as the product of gradual genetic adaptations (Buss, 1995, 2000, 2004). In this view, male competition led to a reproductive advantage for dominant males (Wilson & Daley, 2004). Men adopted short-term mating practices because they allowed men to father more children and thus increase their reproductive advantage. In contrast, women devoted more effort to parenting and chose mates who could provide their offspring with resources for protection. Because men competed with other men for access to women, men have evolved dispositions that favor violence and risk taking. Women have developed a preference for long-term mates who can support a family. Men strive to acquire more resources than other men in order to attract more women, and women seek to attract successful, ambitious men who can provide these resources.

Critics of evolutionary psychology argue that humans have the decision-making ability to change their gender behavior and thus are not locked into their evolutionary past. They cite extensive cross-cultural variation in gender behavior and mate preference as proof that social experience affects gender behavior (J. T. Wood, 2001). For instance, Alice Eagly (1997, 2000, 2002) stresses that, as women were forced to

Carol Gilligan argues that Kohlberg's view of moral development does not give adequate attention to relationships. In Gilligan's view, "Many girls seem to fear, most of all, being alone—without friends, family, and relationships." *How would a greater concern for relationships affect moral decision making?*

gender The social and psychological aspects of being female or male.

cathy® by Cathy Guisewite

adapt to roles with less power and less status in society, they showed more cooperative and less dominant profiles than men.

We must also consider the influence of social experience. Some cultures want children to be reared to adopt traditional **gender roles** (Best, 2002), expectations for how females and males should think, act, and feel. Boys are reared to be "masculine" (powerful, aggressive, and independent, for example) and girls brought up to be "feminine" (sensitive to others, good at relationships, and less assertive, for example). Other cultures, especially in recent times, favor rearing boys and girls to be more similar—girls just as assertive as boys and boys just as caring toward others as girls, for example. The United States is moving toward more diversity in gender roles. Still, much socialization in our culture is gender-based (Lott & Maluso, 2002). Boys are dressed in blue, girls in pink. Boys are given trucks to play with; girls are given dolls. Parents let boys be more aggressive and require girls to be more reserved. Listen to the audio clip "Gender and Risk Taking" to learn about research on the relationship between parents' behavior and risk taking in boys and girls.

Peers also play an important role in gender development. Especially beginning in middle and late childhood (6 to 10 or 11 years of age or until puberty begins), peer groups are often highly segregated into boy groups and girl groups (Maccoby, 1998, 2002) (see figure 3.15). After observing children on many playgrounds, two gender researchers described the observations as like "going to gender school" (Luria & Herzog, 1985). Peers are stricter than most parents in rewarding gender-appropriate behavior in the culture and punishing gender-inappropriate behavior.

Interestingly, tolerance of gender-inappropriate behavior is itself gendered. Americans tend to disapprove more of boys engaging in feminine behavior (playing with dolls and crying, for example) than of girls displaying masculine behavior (being a tomboy and being competitive, for example). In other words, female gender roles are somewhat more flexible than male gender roles.

How do children learn what girls and boys are supposed to be like? And do girls and boys actually think differently? Both of these questions link cognitive development to gender development.

Recall from our discussion of Piaget's theory earlier in the chapter that a schema is a mental framework that organizes and guides an individual's thoughts. A recent theory proposes that children develop a gender schema based on what is considered appropriate behavior for females and males in their culture (Martin & Dinella, 2001). Their gender schema then serves as a cognitive framework for interpreting further experiences related to gender. As their gender schema develops, children knit together all sorts of things with gender, such as "Girls should be nurturant" and "Boys should be independent."

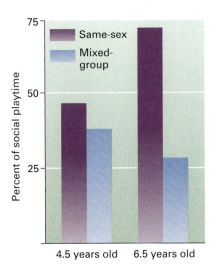

FIGURE 3.15 Developmental Changes in Percentage of Time Spent in Same-Sex and Mixed-Group Settings Observations of children show that they are more likely to play in same-sex than mixed-sex groups. This tendency increases between 4 and 6 years of age.

gender role Expectations for how females and males should think, act, and feel.

The research that has focused on how similar or different the cognitive skills of boys and girls are has mainly examined math skills, visuospatial skills, and verbal skills (Halpern, 2002). In math and visuospatial skills—the kinds of skills an architect needs to design a building's angles and dimensions—boys tend to perform better than girls, although the differences are usually small (Hyde & Plant, 1995). In the National Assessment of Educational Progress (1997), boys were better at math than girls in the fourth grade, but, in the eighth and twelfth grades, boys and girls achieved essentially equal scores. Researchers found 20 years ago that girls often had better verbal ability (such as a better vocabulary) than boys, but in most verbal areas that difference has not held up over the years (Hyde & Mezulis, 2002; National Assessment of Educational Progress, 2001). However, girls do have better reading skills than boys, and this gap actually widened from 1998 to 2000 (National Assessment of Educational Progress, 2001).

In other parts of this book, you will learn more about gender. It is one of the most frequently examined factors in psychological research. For example, chapter 14 examines gender in relationships, gender in aggression, and gender in altruism.

Source	Characteristic
Individual	Good intellectual functioning Appealing, sociable, easygoing disposition Self-confidence, high self-esteem Talents Faith
Family	Close relationship to caring parent figure Authoritative parenting: warmth, structure, high expectations Socioeconomic advantages Connections to extended supportive family networks
Extrafamilial Context	Bonds to caring adults outside the family Connections to positive organizations Attending effective schools

FIGURE 3.16 **Characteristics of Resilient Children and Their Contexts** Resilience helps children overcome hardships and setbacks.

Positive Psychology and Children's Development

Despite the hardships some children face, many grow up to be capable adults. But why does one person who is subjected to poverty, racism, or the divorce of parents remain mired in lifelong misfortune, whereas another rises above those obstacles to succeed in business, the community, or family life?

The concept of *resilient children* highlights competence and adaptability. Researchers have found that resilient children have one or more advantages that help them to overcome their disadvantages (Masten, 2001; Masten & Coatsworth, 1998). These advantages include individual factors (such as good intellectual functioning), family factors (such as a close, caring relationship with at least one parent), and extrafamilial factors (such as bonds to supportive, competent adults outside the family) (see figure 3.16). Not all of these factors need to be positive to help a child develop successfully. If a child does not have responsible, caring parents, then high self-esteem and a bond to a caring adult outside the home can make the child resilient enough to overcome negative family factors.

Unfortunately, however, many children living in at-risk circumstances—characterized by such factors as poverty, lack of quality parenting, inadequate schools, and high-crime neighborhoods—are not resilient. (Go to the audio clip "Neighborhood Violence" to learn about the impact of growing up in a violent neighborhood.) There are a lot of children at risk: Almost 20 percent of all children and more than 50 percent of ethnic minority children in the United States live in poverty today (Children's Defense Fund, 2000). These children desperately need prevention and intervention programs that give them an opportunity to become competent—for example, health education and help in developing both cognitive and socioemotional skills, including self-control, stress management, and communication (Compas & others, 2001; Kalil & DeLeire, 2004; Powell, 2001). Competence enhancement programs for children living in poverty are increasingly two-generational: They help parents find good jobs and obtain quality health care, in addition to helping the child (McLoyd, 2000; Weissberg & Greenberg, 1998).

At the beginning of the twenty-first century, the well-being of children is one of America's foremost challenges. Children who do not reach their potential, who are unable to contribute to society, and who do not take their place as productive adults diminish the vitality of society's future.

In-Psych Plus

Children learn to love when they are loved

Review and Sharpen Your Thinking

2 *Describe children's development from conception to adolescence.*

- Identify the stages of prenatal development and describe the risks associated with this period.
- Summarize the physical changes after birth that make possible rapid cognitive and socioemotional growth in childhood.
- Explain Piaget's theory of cognitive development and the key criticisms of it.
- Discuss Erikson's theory of psychosocial development and other key research on specific factors believed to have an influence on children's socioemotional development.
- Describe the contributions of positive psychology to our understanding of children's development.

Is there a best way to parent? Explain.

---

3 ADOLESCENCE

Positive Psychology and Adolescents

Cognitive Development in Adolescence

Socioemotional Development in Adolescence

Physical Development in Adolescence

What are the most important physical, cognitive, and socioemotional changes in adolescence?

Adolescence is the developmental period of transition from childhood to adulthood. It begins around 10 to 12 years of age and ends at 18 to 21 years of age. In exploring adolescence, remember that adolescents are not a homogeneous group (Santrock, 2001). Ethnic, cultural, historical, gender, socioeconomic, and lifestyle variations characterize their actual life trajectories. Our image of adolescents should take into account the particular adolescent or group of adolescents we are considering (Hirsch & others, 2000).

Positive Psychology and Adolescents

Too often, adolescents have been stereotyped as abnormal and deviant. For example, Freud described adolescents as sexually driven and conflicted. Young people of every generation have seemed radical, unnerving, and different to adults—different in how they look, how they behave, and even what music they enjoy.

However, thinking of adolescence as a time of rebellion, crisis, pathology, and deviation does little good and can do considerable disservice to adolescents. It is far more accurate to view adolescence as a time of evaluation, a time of decision making, and a time of commitment as young people carve out their place in the world (Santrock, 2003). It is an enormous error to confuse the adolescent's enthusiasm for trying on new identities and enjoying moderate amounts of outrageous behavior with hostility toward parents and society. Searching for an identity is a time-honored way in which adolescents move toward accepting, rather than rejecting, parental and societal values.

How competent adolescents will eventually become often depends on their access to legitimate opportunities for growth, such as a quality education, community and societal support for achievement and involvement, and access to good jobs. Especially

From *Penguin Dreams and Stranger Things* by Berke Breathed. Copyright © 1985 by The Washington Post Company. By permission of Little, Brown and Company.

important in adolescents' development is long-term support from adults who deeply care about them (Hamilton & Hamilton, 2004).

As evidence that the majority of adolescents develop more positively than is commonly believed, consider the research study conducted by Daniel Offer and his colleagues (1988). They sampled the self-images of adolescents around the world—in the United States, Australia, Bangladesh, Hungary, Israel, Italy, Japan, Taiwan, Turkey, and West Germany. About three of every four of these adolescents had healthy self-images. Most were happy, enjoyed life, and believed they had the ability to cope effectively with stress. They valued school and work.

But what about the one in four adolescents who did not have positive self-images? What might be done to help them negotiate adolescence? Reed Larson (2000; Larson & Wilson, 2004) argues that adolescents need more opportunities to develop the capacity for initiative, which he defined as becoming self-motivated and expending effort to reach challenging goals. Too often, adolescents find themselves bored with life. To counter this boredom and help adolescents develop more initiative, Larson recommends structured voluntary activities, such as sports, the arts, and participation in organizations.

Physical Development in Adolescence

The signature physical change in adolescence is **puberty,** a period of rapid skeletal and sexual maturation that occurs mainly in early adolescence. In general, we know when an individual is going through puberty, but we have a hard time pinpointing its beginning and its end. Except for menarche (girls' first menstrual cycle, which occurs on average at about 12½ years of age), no single marker defines it. For boys, the first whisker or first wet dream could mark its appearance, but both may go unnoticed.

In addition, a spurt in height and weight characterize pubertal change. This growth spurt occurs about 2 years earlier for girls than for boys (see figure 3.17). Today, in the United States, the mean beginning of the growth spurt is 9 years of age for girls and 11 years of age for boys. The peak of pubertal change occurs at an average age of 11½ for girls and 13½ for boys.

Hormonal changes lie at the core of pubertal development (Sarigiani & Petersen, 2000). The concentrations of certain hormones increase dramatically during puberty (Susman & Rogol, 2004). *Testosterone,* a male sex hormone, is associated in boys with the development of genitals, an increase in height, and voice change. *Estrogens,* female sex hormones, are associated in girls with breast, uterine, and skeletal development. Developmental psychologists believe that hormonal changes account for at least some of the emotional ups and downs of adolescence (Archibald, Graber, & Brooks-Gunn, 2003). Researchers have found that higher levels of male sex hormones, such as testosterone, are associated with violence and other problems in boys (van Goozen &

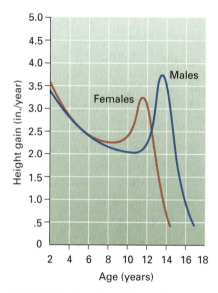

FIGURE 3.17 Pubertal Growth Spurt
On average, the pubertal growth spurt begins and peaks about 2 years earlier for girls than for boys.

puberty A period of rapid skeletal and sexual maturation that occurs mainly in early adolescence.

others, 1998). There also is some indication that increased levels of estrogens are linked with depression in adolescent girls (Angold, Costello, & Worthman, 1998).

But hormones alone are not responsible for adolescent behavior. For example, in one study, social factors (such as stress, bad grades, and relationship problems) accounted for two to four times as much variance as hormonal factors in young girls' depression and anger (Brooks-Gunn & Warren, 1989). Keep in mind, too, that stress, eating patterns, sexual activity, and depression can either activate or suppress hormones (Alan Guttmacher Institute, 2000). Also, some difficulties in adolescent decision making may be linked to the fact that the brain is still maturing. See the video clip "Adolescent Brain" to learn about the similarities and differences between the brains of adults and adolescents.

In-Psych Plus

Cognitive Development in Adolescence

Adolescents undergo some significant cognitive changes (Keating, 2004). One is the advance to Piaget's fourth, most advanced stage of cognitive development, formal operational thinking—at about 11 to 15 years of age. It is characterized by abstract, idealistic, and logical thought.

The concrete operational thinker would need to see the concrete elements A, B, and C to be able to make the logical inference that, if A = B = C, then A = C. But the formal operational thinker can solve this problem merely through verbal presentation. Another indication of the abstract quality of adolescents' thought is their increased tendency to think about thought itself. One adolescent commented, "I began thinking about why I was thinking what I was. Then I began thinking about why I was thinking about why I was thinking about what I was." Formal operational thought is also full of idealism and possibilities. Adolescents begin to engage in extended speculation about the qualities they desire in themselves and in others. In search of the ideal, their thoughts may take fantasy flights into future possibilities.

In actuality, not all adolescents engage in formal operational thought, especially in hypothetical-deductive reasoning (Flavell, Miller, & Miller, 2002). Some adolescents and adults remain at Piaget's concrete operational stage. Others may be overwhelmed at times by their idealistic thinking and may not reason very logically. It is not unusual for adolescents to become perplexed over which of many ideal standards to adopt.

Another important aspect of adolescent cognitive development, especially in early adolescence, is that adolescent thought is egocentric. *Adolescent egocentrism* involves the belief that others are as preoccupied with the adolescent as he or she is, the belief that one is unique, and the belief that one is invincible (Elkind, 1978). Adolescent egocentrism means that adolescents perceive others to be noticing and watching them more than actually is the case. Imagine the eighth-grade boy who senses that everyone else has noticed the small pimple on his face or the adolescent girl who says, "My mother has no idea about how much pain I'm going through. She has never been hurt like I have." Notice that adolescent egocentrism does not mean necessarily feeling superior to others.

The aspect of adolescent egocentrism that can produce the most harm is a sense of invincibility, which may lead to drag racing down a city street, to drug use, to suicide attempts, or to sexually transmitted diseases or adolescent pregnancy. Imagine that an adolescent girl hears that a friend of hers has become pregnant. She may exclaim, "I won't ever let that happen to me," and then go out and have unprotected sex the next week. Her sense of invincibility causes her to behave in a high-risk manner. On a positive note, the adolescent's sense of invincibility may also lead to courageous efforts to save people's lives in hazardous circumstances.

Socioemotional Development in Adolescence

The increase in abstract and idealistic thought during adolescence serves as a foundation for exploring one's identity. Many aspects of socioemotional development—such

FIGURE 3.18 **Marcia's Four Statuses of Identity**

		Has the person made a commitment?	
		Yes	**No**
Has the person explored meaningful alternatives regarding some identity question?	**Yes**	Identity Achievement	Identity Moratorium
	No	Identity Foreclosure	Identity Diffusion

as relationships with parents, peer interaction and friendships, and cultural and ethnic values—contribute to an adolescent's identity development (Santrock, 2003).

As you learned in the section on socioemotional development in children, Erik Erikson's life-span theory states that people go through eight psychosocial stages of development. Within the eight stages that Erikson (1968) proposed, his ideas about the formation of identity during adolescence are among his most important contributions to psychology. They changed the way we think about adolescence (Marcia, 2001). Erikson encouraged us to look at adolescents, in stage 5, as individuals finding out who they are and searching for their niche in the world:

5. *Identity versus identity confusion: during adolescence.* In seeking an *identity*, adolescents face the challenges of finding out who they are, what they are all about, and where they are going in life. Adolescents are confronted with many new roles and adult statuses—from the vocational to the romantic. If they do not adequately explore their identities during this stage, they emerge with a sense of confusion about who they are. What Erikson calls *identity confusion* is expressed in one of two ways: Either individuals withdraw, isolating themselves from peers and family, or they lose themselves in the crowd. Erikson argues that parents should allow adolescents to explore many different roles and paths within a particular role and not push an identity on them.

Erikson also noted that, in the American culture, adolescents want to decide freely for themselves such matters as what careers they will pursue, whether they will go to college, and whether they will marry. In other words, they want to free themselves from the control of their parents and other adults and make their own choices. At the same time, many deeply fear making the wrong decisions and failing. In some cases, the problem may be simply that adolescents have not yet realized their own growing cognitive abilities. One strength that equips them to pursue their identities effectively is that their thoughts have become more abstract and logical, and they are able to reason in increasingly sophisticated ways.

Building on Erikson's ideas, James Marcia (1980) proposed the concept of *identity status* to describe a person's position in the development of an identity. In his view, two dimensions of identity are important. *Exploration* refers to a person's investigating various options for a career and for personal values. *Commitment* involves making a decision about which identity path to follow and making a personal investment in attaining that identity. Various combinations of exploration and commitment give rise to one of four identity statuses (see figure 3.18):

• *Identity diffusion.* A person has not yet explored meaningful alternatives and has not made a commitment. Many young adolescents have a diffuse identity status. They have not yet begun to explore different career options and personal values.

"Do you have any idea who I am?"

Developing a Positive Identity

Psychology and Life

Following are some helpful attitudes for developing a positive identity:

- *Be aware that your identity is complex and will take a long time to develop.* Your identity has many components. One of your main identity tasks is to integrate all of these parts into a meaningful whole. Your identity does not spring forth in a sudden burst of insight. It is achieved in bits and pieces over your lifetime. What are some of the bits and pieces of your identity development?
- *Make the most of your college years.* For many people, the college years are an important time for identity development. College by its very nature encourages exploration and exposure to a wide variety of ideas and values. Your views likely will be challenged by instructors and classmates. In the process, you may be motivated to change some aspects of your identity.
- *Examine whether your identity is your own or your parents'.* Some college students have foreclosed on an identity

without adequately considering alternatives. Identity foreclosure occurs especially when individuals accept their parents' views without deeply questioning whether they want to be just like their parents. Individuals might eventually return to an identity similar to those of their parents; however, while evaluating different paths, a more suitable identity may be discovered. Have you adequately developed an identity that is your own?

- *Expect your identity to change.* Even people who think they have achieved the identity they want might find it changing in the future. Your world will change and you will change, especially if you explore new opportunities and face new challenges. What do you expect your identity to be like after you finish college? Different from what it is now? The same?

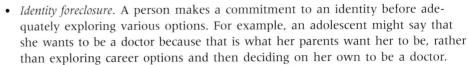

- *Identity foreclosure.* A person makes a commitment to an identity before adequately exploring various options. For example, an adolescent might say that she wants to be a doctor because that is what her parents want her to be, rather than exploring career options and then deciding on her own to be a doctor.
- *Identity moratorium.* A person is exploring alternative paths but has not yet made a commitment. Many college students are in a moratorium status with regard to a major field of study or a career.
- *Identity achievement.* A person has explored alternative paths and made a commitment. For example, an individual might have examined a number of careers over an extended period and finally decided to pursue one wholeheartedly.

Developing an identity in adolescence can be especially challenging for individuals from ethnic minority groups (Phinney, 2000, 2003; Spencer, 2000). As they mature cognitively, many adolescents become acutely aware of the evaluation of their ethnic group by the majority culture. In addition, an increasing number of minority adolescents face the challenge of biculturalism—identifying in some ways with their ethnic minority group, in other ways with the majority culture.

In one study, a researcher examined the development of ethnic identity in Asian American, African American, Latino, and White tenth-grade students in Los Angeles (Phinney, 1989). Adolescents from each of the three ethnic minority groups faced a similar need to deal with their ethnic-group identity in a predominately White culture. But the three groups faced different challenges. For Asian American adolescents, the pressure to achieve academically was an important identity concern. Female African American adolescents were concerned that White standards of beauty (especially hair and skin color) did not apply to them; male African American adolescents were concerned with possible job discrimination and the need to distinguish themselves from a negative societal image. For Latino adolescents, prejudice was a recurrent theme, as was the conflict in values between their cultural heritage and the majority culture.

For both minority and majority adolescents, developing a positive identity is an important life theme (Van Buren & Graham, 2003). To further explore your development of a positive identity, see the Psychology and Life box.

School psychologist Armando Ronquillo counsels a Latina high school student about coping with problems and pursuing a college education. *How do these concerns reflect the challenge of developing an identity for this student?*

Review and Sharpen Your Thinking

3 *Identify the most important changes that occur in adolescence.*

- Explore the contribution of positive psychology to our thinking about adolescent development.
- Discuss the nature of puberty.
- Describe the key aspects of cognitive development during adolescence.
- Explain the role of identity during adolescent socioemotional development.

Are Marcia's identity statuses useful to you in thinking about your own identity development? To explore this question, return to figure 3.18 and evaluate your levels of exploration and commitment in regard to career and personal values. Into which identity status would you place yourself?

ADULT DEVELOPMENT AND AGING 4

Physical Development in Adulthood

Socioemotional Development in Adulthood

Positive Psychology and Aging

Cognitive Development in Adulthood

What are the main physical, cognitive, and socioemotional changes in adults?

Development does not end with adolescence. It continues throughout the roughly 50 (and often more) years of adulthood. Developmental psychologists identify three approximate periods in adult development: early adulthood (20s and 30s), middle adulthood (40s and 50s), and late adulthood (60s until death). Each phase features some distinctive physical, cognitive, and socioemotional changes.

Physical Development in Adulthood

Most people reach their peak physical development during their 20s and are the healthiest then. For athletes—not only at the Olympic level but also the average athlete—performance peaks in the 20s, especially for strength and speed events, such as weight lifting and the 100-meter dash (Schultz & Curnow, 1988). The main exceptions are swimmers and female gymnasts (like Zhang Liyin, whose story started this chapter), who often peak in adolescence, and marathon runners, who tend to peak in their late 30s. Unfortunately, early adulthood also is when many skills begin to decline. The decline in strength and speed often is noticeable in the 30s.

Perhaps because of their robust physical skills and overall health, young adults rarely recognize that bad eating habits, heavy drinking, and smoking in early adulthood can impair their physical condition as they age. Despite warnings on packages and in advertisements that cigarettes are hazardous to health, individuals actually increase their use of cigarettes as they enter early adulthood (Johnston, Bachman, & O'Malley, 1989). They also increase their use of alcohol, marijuana, amphetamines, barbiturates, and hallucinogens.

The bad habits of youth begin to show up in the physical changes of middle adulthood. By the 40s or 50s, the skin begins to wrinkle and sag because of a loss of fat and collagen in underlying tissues. Small, localized areas of pigmentation in the skin produce age spots, especially in areas exposed to sunlight, such as the hands and face. Hair becomes thinner and grayer due to a lower replacement rate and a decline in melanin production.

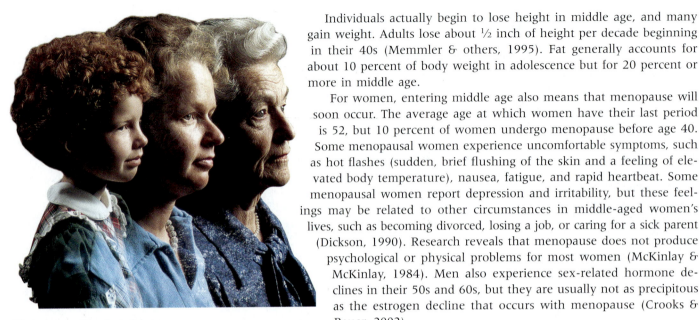

What are some of the physical changes that people go through as they age?

Individuals actually begin to lose height in middle age, and many gain weight. Adults lose about ½ inch of height per decade beginning in their 40s (Memmler & others, 1995). Fat generally accounts for about 10 percent of body weight in adolescence but for 20 percent or more in middle age.

For women, entering middle age also means that menopause will soon occur. The average age at which women have their last period is 52, but 10 percent of women undergo menopause before age 40. Some menopausal women experience uncomfortable symptoms, such as hot flashes (sudden, brief flushing of the skin and a feeling of elevated body temperature), nausea, fatigue, and rapid heartbeat. Some menopausal women report depression and irritability, but these feelings may be related to other circumstances in middle-aged women's lives, such as becoming divorced, losing a job, or caring for a sick parent (Dickson, 1990). Research reveals that menopause does not produce psychological or physical problems for most women (McKinlay & McKinlay, 1984). Men also experience sex-related hormone declines in their 50s and 60s, but they are usually not as precipitous as the estrogen decline that occurs with menopause (Crooks & Bauer, 2002).

Perhaps because the signs of aging are all too visible, we become more acutely concerned about our health in our 40s. In fact, we do experience a general decline in physical fitness throughout middle adulthood and some deterioration in health. The three greatest health concerns at this age are heart disease, cancer, and weight. Cancer related to smoking often surfaces in middle adulthood.

Physical changes become more pronounced in older adults, including cosmetic changes, such as wrinkles and age spots. Whereas weight often increases in middle age, it frequently declines after 60 because of muscle loss. Blood pressure often rises in older adults but can be treated by exercise and/or drugs.

Normal aging involves some bone tissue loss from the skeleton, and in some instances the loss can be severe, as in osteoporosis (Whitbourne, 2000). Almost two-thirds of women over 60 are affected to some degree by osteoporosis. Estrogen replacement therapy can reduce bone loss for women, and a program of weight lifting can help (Nelson & others, 1994).

Chronic diseases—characterized by a slow onset and long duration—are rare in early adulthood, increase in middle adulthood, and become more common in late adulthood. The most common chronic disorder in late adulthood is arthritis; the second most common is hypertension (high blood pressure).

Eighty-five-year-old Sadie Halperin doubled her strength after just 11 months of regular exercise. Now she says she feels wonderful. *What does her experience suggest about physical aging?*

This list of physical deteriorations may sound rather dismal. However, a substantial portion of older individuals are still robust and active. Consider 85-year-old Sadie Halperin, who has been working out for 11 months at a rehabilitation center for the aged in Boston. She lifts weights and rides a stationary bicycle. She says that, before she started working out, almost everything she did—shopping, cooking, walking—was a major struggle. She felt wobbly and had to hold on to a wall when she walked. Now she walks down the center of the hallways and reports that she feels great. Sadie's exercise routine has increased her muscle strength and helped her to battle osteoporosis by slowing the calcium loss in her bones (Ubell, 1992). Researchers continue to document how effective exercise is in slowing the aging process and helping older adults function in society (Burke & others, 2001).

Just as the aging body has been found to have a greater capacity for renewal than previously believed, so has the aging brain (Taub, 2001). For decades, scientists believed that no new brain cells are generated past the early childhood years. However, researchers recently discovered that adults can grow new brain cells throughout their lives (Gould & others, 1999). In one study, the growth of dendrites (the receiving, branching part of the neuron or nerve cell) continued through the 70s, although no new dendritic growth was discovered in people in their 90s (Coleman, 1986).

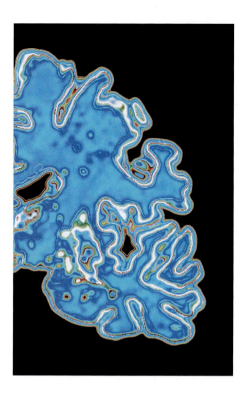 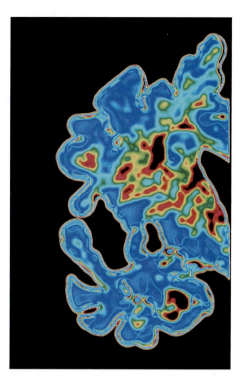

FIGURE 3.19 Two Brains: Normal Aging and Alzheimer's Disease
(Left) A slice of a normally aging brain. *(Right)* A slice of a brain ravaged by Alzheimer's disease. Notice the deterioration and shrinking in the diseased brain.

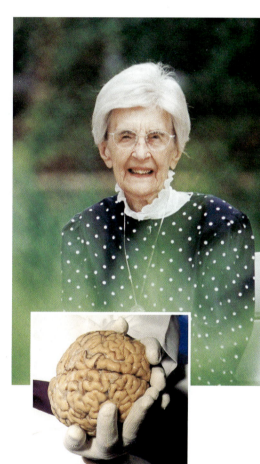

An ongoing study of the brains of a group of nuns in Mankato, Minnesota, suggests that aging does not have to mean severe losses in cognitive functioning. At 90 years old, nun study participant Sister Rosella Kreuzer, SSND, remains an active, contributing member of her community of sisters. Sister Rosella designed the nun study logo, "That You May Have Life to the Full." *(Inset)* A neuroscientist holds a brain donated by one of the nun study participants. *What possible practical lessons can we take from the Mankato nuns?*

In-Psych Plus

Even in late adulthood, the brain has remarkable repair capability. Stanley Rapaport (1994), chief of the neurosciences laboratory at the National Institute of Aging, compared the brains of younger and older adults when they were engaged in the same tasks. The older adults' brains literally rewired themselves to compensate for losses. If one neuron was not up to the job, neighboring neurons helped to pick up the slack. Rapaport concluded that, as brains age, they can actually shift responsibilities for a given task from one region to another.

Alzheimer's disease—a progressive, irreversible brain disorder that is characterized by gradual deterioration of memory, reasoning, language, and eventually physical functioning—does not present such encouraging prospects (Santacruz & Swagerty, 2001). Approximately 2.5 million people over the age of 65 in the United States have Alzheimer's disease; the percentage of people who have it doubles for every 5 years beyond age 65. See the video clip "Alzheimer's Disease" to learn more about the effects of this disease on the memory and personality of a woman. As Alzheimer's disease progresses, the brain deteriorates and shrinks (Salmon, 2000). Figure 3.19 contrasts the brain of an individual aging normally with the brain of an individual who has Alzheimer's disease. Among the main characteristics of Alzheimer's disease are the increasing number of tangles (tied bundles of proteins that impair the function of neurons) and plaques (deposits that accumulate in the brain's blood vessels). The formation of tangles and plaques is a normal part of aging, but it is far more pronounced in Alzheimer's disease. Alzheimer's disease also involves a deficiency in the neurotransmitter acetylcholine, which plays an important role in memory (Hodges, 2000; Sayer & others, 2004).

Research on the aging brain does give cause for hope. One ongoing study involves nearly 700 nuns in a convent in Mankato, Minnesota (Snowden, 1997, 2001, 2003). By examining the nuns' donated brains, as well as others, neuroscientists have documented the remarkable ability of the aging brain to grow and change. Even the oldest Mankato nuns lead intellectually challenging lives, and neuroscientists believe that stimulating mental activities increase dendritic branching. The nuns are showing almost no signs of Alzheimer's disease. Indeed, researchers have consistently found support for the "use it or lose it" concept: The cognitive skills of older adults benefit considerably when they engage in challenging intellectual activities (Schaie & Willis, 2001).

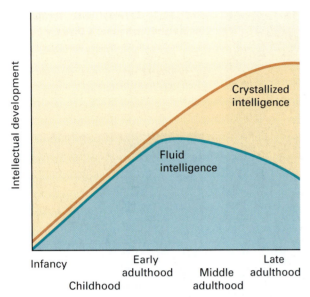

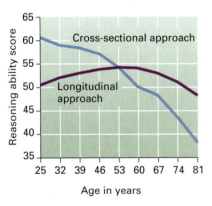

FIGURE 3.20 Fluid and Crystallized Cognitive Development Across the Life Span According to Horn, crystallized intelligence (based on cumulative learning experiences) increases throughout the life span. But fluid intelligence (the ability to perceive and manipulate information) steadily declines from middle adulthood on.

FIGURE 3.21 Cross-Sectional and Longitudinal Comparisons of Reasoning Ability Throughout Adulthood A cross-sectional approach revealed declining scores with age, whereas a longitudinal approach showed a slight rise in scores in middle adulthood and only a slight decline beginning in the early part of late adulthood.

crystallized intelligence An individual's accumulated information and verbal skills.

fluid intelligence One's ability to reason abstractly.

Cognitive Development in Adulthood

Piaget believed that formal operational thought is the highest level of thinking, and he argued that no new qualitative changes in cognition take place in adulthood. He didn't believe that a person with a Ph.D. in physics thinks any differently than does a young adolescent who has reached the stage of formal operational thought. The only difference is that the physicist has more knowledge in a specific scientific domain. The physicist and the young adolescent both use logical thought to develop alternatives for solving a problem and to deduce a solution from the options.

Remember, however, that some adolescents are not formal operational thinkers, and many adults never reach that stage, either. In addition, some experts on cognitive development argue that the typical idealism of Piaget's formal operational stage in adolescence is replaced in young adulthood by more realistic, pragmatic thinking (Labouvie-Vief, 1986). Adolescents also tend to think in absolute terms—things are either all this way or that way. As they go through the college years, individuals often begin to think in more relative and reflective ways (Kitchener & King, 1981). In sum, for the most part, intellectual skills are stronger than ever in early adulthood (Berg, 2000).

Do they begin to decline in middle age? John Horn's view is that **crystallized intelligence,** an individual's accumulated information and verbal skills, does increase in middle adulthood (Horn & Donaldson, 1980). In contrast, **fluid intelligence,** one's ability to reason abstractly, begins to decline (see figure 3.20). Horn's view is based on data he collected in a *cross-sectional study,* which assesses a number of people all at one point in time. For example, a cross-sectional study might assess the intelligence of six hundred 40-, 50-, and 60-year-olds in a single evaluation in September 2004. Thus Horn's findings may reflect the effects of living through a certain historical time in a certain culture, rather than age alone. The 40-year-olds and the 60-year-olds were born in different eras, which offered different economic, educational, and health opportunities. These differences may influence their performance on intelligence tests.

Whether data on intelligence are collected cross-sectionally or longitudinally can make a difference in the results. A *longitudinal study* assesses the participants over a lengthy period. A longitudinal study of intelligence in middle adulthood might consist of giving the same intelligence test to the same individuals over a 20-year time span, when they are 40, 50, and 60 years of age. K. Warner Schaie (1983, 1996) is conducting an extensive longitudinal study of intellectual abilities in adulthood. Five hundred individuals initially were tested in 1956. New waves of participants are added periodically. The highest level of functioning for four of the six intellectual abilities tested by Schaie and his colleagues—vocabulary, verbal memory, inductive reasoning, and spatial orientation—occur in middle adulthood (Schaie & Willis, 2001; Willis & Schaie, 1999). Only two of the six abilities—numerical ability and perceptual speed—decline in middle age. Perceptual speed shows the earliest decline, beginning in early adulthood. Schaie concluded, based on the longitudinal data he has collected so far, that middle adulthood, not early adulthood, is when many people reach their peak for many intellectual skills. However, a cross-sectional analysis Schaie has conducted shows more decline throughout middle age (see figure 3.21).

Claims about intellectual functioning through the late adult years are also provocative. Many contemporary psychologists believe that, as with middle adulthood, some dimensions of intelligence decline in late adulthood, whereas others are maintained or may even increase.

One of the most consistent findings is that, when speed of processing information is involved, older adults do more poorly than their younger counterparts (Craik & Salthouse, 2000; Madden, 2001). Figure 3.22 shows a noticeable decline in speed of processing in middle-aged adults, which becomes more pronounced in older adults. Older adults also tend to do more poorly than younger adults in most areas of memory (Backman, Small, & Wahlin, 2001; Light, 2000). Older adults do not remember the "where" and "when" of life's happenings as well as younger adults (Tulving, 2000). For example, older adults don't remember their high school classmates or the names of their teachers as well as younger adults do. In the area of memory involving knowledge of the world (for instance, the capital of Peru or the chemical formula for water), older adults usually take longer than younger adults to retrieve the information, but they often are able to retrieve it. And in the important area of memory in which individuals manipulate and assemble information to solve problems and make decisions, decline occurs in older adults (Light, 2000; Salthouse, 2000).

However, some aspects of cognition might actually improve with age. One candidate is **wisdom,** expert knowledge about the practical aspects of life. Wisdom may increase with age because of the buildup of life experiences we have. However, not every older person has wisdom (Baltes, Lindenberger, & Staudinger, 1998). Individual variations characterize all aspects of our cognitive lives (Belsky, 1999).

Do we all face the prospect of gradually becoming less competent intellectually? Not necessarily, as the study of the Mankato nuns suggests. See the video clip "Cognitive Functioning in Centenarians" to learn more about life-long practices that contribute to cognitive skills in older age. Even for those aspects of cognition that decline with age, training older adults can improve their skills (Luszcz & Bryan, 1999; Park, Nisbett, & Hedden, 1999; Schaie & Willis, 2001). Training older adults to use certain strategies can even improve their memories (Baltes, 1993; Willis & Schaie, 1994). The audio clip "Aging and Memory" describes improvements in memory that seniors experienced after a seven-session workshop. However, many experts believe that older adults are less able to adapt than younger adults and thus are limited in how much they can improve their cognitive skills (Baltes, 2000).

Socioemotional Development in Adulthood

Psychologists have proposed various theories about adult socioemotional development. Most theories address themes of work and love, career and intimacy. But before examining what psychologists have learned about these themes, let's look at the last three stages of Erikson's (1968) eight-stage theory of life-span development:

6. *Intimacy versus isolation: early adulthood.* At this time, people face the developmental task of either forming intimate relationships with others or becoming socially isolated. Erikson describes *intimacy* as both finding oneself and losing oneself in another. If the young adult develops healthy friendships and an intimate close relationship with a partner, intimacy will likely be achieved.

7. *Generativity versus stagnation: middle adulthood.* A main concern is to assist and guide the younger generation in developing and leading useful lives—this is what Erikson means by *generativity* (Pratt & others, 2001). The feeling of having done nothing to help the next generation is *stagnation.*

8. *Integrity versus despair: late adulthood.* The older adult looks back and evaluates a lifetime. If the older adult has resolved many of the earlier stages negatively, looking back likely will produce doubt or gloom—the *despair* Erikson speaks of. But if the older adult has successfully negotiated most or all of the previous stages, the looking back will reveal a picture of a life well spent, and the person will feel a sense of satisfaction—*integrity* will be attained.

These developmental tasks unfold in several contexts during adulthood. For instance, establishing oneself in a job and then a career is one of the central concerns of people in their 20s and 30s. Career interests continue to be an important dimension of life for many middle-aged adults. During midlife, many people examine what they have accomplished in their careers and become concerned about the limited time remaining. However, many reach the highest satisfaction in their careers during middle age, and only about 10 percent of Americans change careers at midlife.

Older adults might not be as quick with their thoughts as younger adults, but wisdom may be an entirely different matter. This woman shares the wisdom of her experiences with a classroom of children. *To what extent can wisdom compensate for age-related losses in other cognitive skills?*

In-Psych Plus

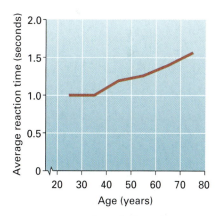

FIGURE 3.22 The Relation of Age to Reaction Time In one study of cognitive functioning, individuals of various ages were asked to match numbers with symbols on a computer screen (Salthouse, 1994). The average reaction time began to slow in the 40s, and this decline accelerated in the 60s and 70s.

wisdom Expert knowledge about the practical aspects of life.

Marriage, or any commitment to other individuals, is another arena for socioemotional development. Until about 1930, a stable marriage was accepted as a legitimate end point of adult development. In the past 70 years, however, we have seen the desire for personal fulfillment—both inside and outside a marriage—become an equally legitimate goal. As a result, in the 1990s, adults were remaining single longer than was the case a few decades ago. In addition, the quest for personal fulfillment may destabilize a marriage. The divorce rate, although it has started to slow down in recent years, increased astronomically in the 1970s and remains high. The average duration of a marriage in the United States currently is just over 9 years. Even so, Americans still show a strong preference for marriage. For example, the proportion of women who never marry remained at about 7 percent throughout the twentieth century (U.S. Bureau of the Census, 2000).

What makes a marriage work? John Gottman (1994; Gottman & Silver, 1999; Gottman & others, 1998, 2002) has been studying married couples' lives since the early 1970s. He interviews couples about the history of their marriage, their philosophy about marriage, and their views of their parents' marriages. He videotapes them talking with each other about how their day went and evaluates what they say about the good and bad times of their marriages. He uses physiological measures to assess their heart rates, blood flow, blood pressure, and immune functioning moment by moment while they discuss these topics. He also checks back with the couples every year to see how their marriages are faring. Currently, he and his colleagues are following 700 couples in seven different studies.

In his exceptionally thorough research, Gottman has found these four principles at work in successful marriages:

- *Nurturing fondness and admiration.* In successful marriages, partners sing each other's praises. When couples put a positive spin on their talk with and about each other, the marriage tends to work.
- *Turning toward each other as friends.* In good marriages, partners see each other as friends and turn toward each other for support in times of stress and difficulty.
- *Giving up some power.* Bad marriages often involve one partner who is a power monger. This is more common in husbands, but some wives have the problem as well.
- *Solving conflicts together.* In successful marriages, couples work to solve problems, regulate their emotion during times of conflict, and compromise to accommodate each other.

Personal identity and meaning in life also are an arena for socioemotional development. Research on middle-aged adults reveals that individuals vary extensively in how they cope with and perceive midlife (Vaillant, 1977). However, in a recent large-scale study of 3,032 Americans 25 to 74 years of age, the portrait of midlife was mainly positive (Brim, 1999). Only about 10 percent of individuals described themselves as experiencing a midlife crisis. In fact, middle-aged individuals (40–65 years old) had lower anxiety levels and worried less than people under 40.

Middle-aged individuals did report more negative life events than people under 40, but they showed considerable resiliency and good coping skills in facing these stresses. The midlife individuals generally had few illnesses but poor physical fitness.

More accurate than the phrase "midlife crisis" might be the phrase "midlife consciousness" (Santrock, 2004). That is, during middle age, people do become aware of the gap between being young and being old and the shrinking time left in their lives. They do think about their role in contributing to the next generation. Many individuals think more deeply about what life is all about and what they want the rest of their lives to be like. Some people who have spent much of their adult lives trying to make a lot of money

"Goodbye, Alice, I've got to get this California thing out of my system." Leo Cullum © 1984 from The New Yorker Collection. All Rights Reserved.

and succeed in a career turn their attention in middle age to more selfless pursuits. They devote more energy to helping others by volunteering or to spending more time with young people in their effort to contribute something meaningful to the next generation. These efforts can shepherd people into a positive and meaningful old age.

Researchers have also found that, the more active and involved people are in late adulthood, the more satisfied they are and the more likely they are to stay healthy (Antonucci, 2001). Older people who go to church, attend meetings, take trips, and exercise are happier than those who sit at home (George, 2001). However, older adults may become more selective about their social networks, according to one theory (Carstensen, 1995, 1998). Because they place a high value on emotional satisfaction, older adults often are motivated to spend more time with familiar individuals—close friends and family members—with whom they have had rewarding relationships. They may deliberately withdraw from social contact with individuals on the fringes of their lives. This narrowing of social interaction maximizes positive emotional experiences and minimizes emotional risks (Lang & Carstensen, 1994; Lee & Markides, 1990).

Positive Psychology and Aging

Until fairly recently, middle-aged and older adults were perceived as enduring a long decline in physical, cognitive, and socioemotional functioning, and the positive dimensions of aging were ignored (Antonucci, Vandewater, & Lansford, 2000; Rowe & Kahn, 1997). Throughout this section, however, you have seen examples and evidence of successful aging. The earlier stereotypes of aging are being overturned as researchers discover that being a middle-aged or older adult has many positive aspects.

Is there anything you can do now to prevent dementia in late adulthood? Go to the audio clip "Dementia and Intelligence" for tips on the activities and psychological characteristics associated with keeping dementia at bay.

Once developmentalists began focusing on the positive aspects of aging, they discovered that far more robust, healthy middle-aged and older adults are among us than they previously envisioned. A longitudinal study of aging documented some of the ways that positive aging can be attained (Vaillant, 2002). Individuals were assessed at age 50 and then again at 75 to 80 years of age. As shown in figure 3.23, when individuals at 50 were not heavy smokers, did not abuse alcohol, had a stable marriage, engaged in exercise, maintained a normal weight, and had good coping skills, they were more likely to be alive and happy at 75 to 80. They show all of us the effect we can have on our own well-being throughout life.

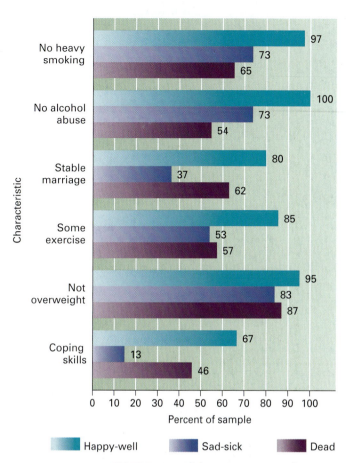

FIGURE 3.23 Linkage Between Positive Characteristics in Middle Age and Health and Happiness in Old Age
In a longitudinal study, individuals who were happy and well, sad and sick, or dead at age 75 to 80 were linked to their reported characteristics at age 50. The best predictor of health and happiness in this study was responsible use of alcohol (100%). The best predictor of sadness and sickness was a lack of coping skills (13%).

In-Psych Plus

Review and Sharpen Your Thinking

4 *Discuss adult development and the positive dimensions of aging.*

• Describe physical development throughout adulthood.
• Identify major changes in cognitive development in adulthood.
• Discuss the main aspects of socioemotional development in adulthood.
• Summarize the positive view of aging that now exists.

Suppose that you wanted to construct a test for wisdom that would be fair to adults of all ages. Write down two or three questions or items that you would want to include in your test.

1 KEY QUESTIONS ABOUT DEVELOPMENT

What Is Development?

Do Early Experiences Rule Us for Life?

How Do Nature and Nurture Influence Development?

2 CHILD DEVELOPMENT

Prenatal Development

Cognitive Development in Childhood

Positive Psychology and Children's Development

Physical Development in Childhood

Socioemotional Development in Childhood

Human Development

3 ADOLESCENCE

Positive Psychology and Adolescents

Cognitive Development in Adolescence

Physical Development in Adolescence

Socioemotional Development in Adolescence

4 ADULT DEVELOPMENT AND AGING

Physical Development in Adulthood

Socioemotional Development in Adulthood

Cognitive Development in Adulthood

Positive Psychology and Aging

1 Explain how psychologists think about development.

- *Development* refers to the pattern of changes in human capabilities that begins at conception and continues throughout the life span. Three important developmental processes are physical (the person's biological nature), cognitive (thought, intelligence, and language), and socioemotional (relationships, emotion, and personality).
- Developmental psychologists debate the extent to which early experience (as in infancy or early childhood) is more important than later experience in development. Most agree that both early and later experiences influence development.
- Both nature (biological inheritance) and nurture (environmental experience) influence development extensively. However, people are at the mercy of neither their genes nor their environment; they can actively construct optimal experiences.

2 Describe children's development from conception to adolescence.

- Prenatal development progresses through the germinal, embryonic, and fetal periods. Certain drugs, such as alcohol, can have an adverse effect on the fetus. Preterm birth is another potential problem, especially if the infant is very small or grows up in an adverse environment.
- The newborn comes into the world with several genetically "wired" reflexes, including grasping and sucking. The infant's physical development is dramatic in the first year. Motor behaviors are assembled for perceiving and acting, drawing on the infant's physical abilities, perceptual skills, and factors in the environment. Extensive changes in the brain, including denser connections between synapses, take place in infancy and childhood.
- In Piaget's view, children use schemas to actively construct their world, either assimilating new information into existing schemas or adjusting schemas to accommodate it. Piaget also said that people go through four stages of cognitive development: (1) the sensorimotor stage (birth to 2 years of age), (2) the preoperational stage (2 to 7 years of age, (3) the concrete operational stage (7 to 11 years of age), and (4) the formal operational stage (11 to 15 years of age through adulthood). Piaget opened up new ways of looking at how children's minds develop, and he gave us the model of a child as an active, constructivist thinker. However, critics believe that Piaget's stages are too rigid and do not adequately take into account the influence of culture and education on cognitive development.
- Erikson presented a major, eight-stage psychosocial view of life-span development; its first four stages occur in childhood. In each stage, the individual seeks to resolve a particular socioemotional conflict. Other researchers have focused on specific aspects of socioemotional development in childhood. For instance, Bowlby and Ainsworth theorized that the first year of life is crucial for the formation of a secure attachment between infant and caregiver. Development also depends on temperament, an individual's behavioral style or characteristic way of responding, and on parenting style and family circumstances. The family is an important context for children's development, as are peers, schools, neighborhood, and culture. Kohlberg proposed a major cognitive-developmental theory of moral development with three levels (preconventional, conventional, and postconventional) and two stages at each level. Gilligan presented an alternative view of moral development that emphasizes interpersonal relationships more heavily than Kohlberg's theory does. Gender development includes biology, social experience, and cognitive factors.
- Positive psychology emphasizes children's resiliency and focuses on improving children's lives.

3 Identify the most important changes that occur in adolescence.

- Positive psychology views adolescence as a time of evaluation, decision making, and commitment. Adolescents are not all alike, but the majority of them develop competently.
- Puberty is a period of rapid skeletal and sexual maturation that occurs mainly in early adolescence. It occurs about 2 years earlier in girls than in boys. Hormonal changes lie at the core of pubertal development.
- According to Piaget, cognitive development in adolescence is characterized by the appearance of formal operational thought, the final stage in his theory. He believed that children enter this stage between 11 and 15 years of age. This stage involves abstract, idealistic, and logical thought. Another key feature of cognitive development, especially in early adolescence, is egocentric thought.
- One of the most important aspects of socioemotional development in adolescence is identity. Erikson's fifth stage of psychosocial development involves identity versus identity confusion, for example. Marcia proposed four statuses of identity based on crisis and commitment. A special concern is the development of ethnic identity.

4 Discuss adult development and the positive dimensions of aging.

- Most adults reach their peak physical performance during their 20s and are the healthiest then. However, physical skills begin to decline during the 30s. Changes in physical appearance are among the most visible signs of aging in middle adulthood. Menopause, which also takes place during middle adulthood, has been stereo-typed as more negative than it actually is. Alzheimer's disease is a special concern during late adulthood, but the normal brain has remarkable repair capacity and plasticity until late in life.

- Piaget argued that no new cognitive changes occur in adulthood. However, some psychologists have proposed that the idealistic thinking of adolescents is replaced by the more realistic, pragmatic thinking of young adults. Horn argued that crystallized intelligence increases in middle age, whereas fluid intelligence declines. Schaie conducted a longitudinal study of intelligence and found that many cognitive skills reach their peak in middle age. Overall, older adults do not do as well on memory and other cognitive tasks and are slower to process informa-tion than younger adults. But older adults may have greater wisdom than younger adults.

- Erikson's three stages of socioemotional development in adulthood are intimacy versus isolation (early adult-hood), generativity versus stagnation (middle adulthood), and integrity versus despair (late adulthood). Career and work become central themes in the life of young adults. Lifestyles, marriage, and commitment also become im-portant aspects of adult life for most people. In middle adulthood, people begin to realize the limits of their ideals and dreams, but researchers have found that only a small percentage of middle-aged adults experience a "midlife crisis." Nevertheless, a special concern begin-ning in the 50s is understanding the meaning of life. Re-searchers have found that remaining active increases the likelihood that older adults will be happier and healthier. Older adults also often reduce their general social affilia-tions and spend more time with close friends and family members.

- The positive dimensions of aging were largely ignored until recently. Developmentalists now recognize that many adults can sustain or even improve their function-ing as they age.

Key Terms

development, p. 79
nature, p. 81
nurture, p. 81
schema, p. 86
assimilation, p. 86
accommodation, p. 86
sensorimotor stage, p. 87
object permanence, p. 87
preoperational stage, p. 87

operations, p. 87
conservation, p. 88
concrete operational stage, p. 89
formal operational stage, p. 90
hypothetical-deductive reasoning, p. 90
attachment, p. 93

imprinting, p. 94
secure attachment, p. 95
temperament, p. 95
authoritarian parenting, p. 96
authoritative parenting, p. 96
neglectful parenting, p. 96
indulgent parenting, p. 96

gender, p. 101
gender role, p. 102
puberty, p. 105
crystallized intelligence, p. 112
fluid intelligence, p. 112
wisdom, p. 113

Apply Your Knowledge

1. The possibility of human cloning has received extensive media coverage. If you could clone yourself, your clone would have the same genetic makeup as you have. Take a quick survey of some of your friends to ask whether they would clone themselves if they were given the opportunity. Ask them to explain their answers and critically examine their reasons, keeping in mind the lessons on nature and nurture in this chapter. Do you think your clone would most resemble you physically, cognitively, or socioemotionally?

2. Find a copy of a popular child-rearing book. Read a few pages and comment on how the perspective on children's development in that book relates to the scientific perspectives on children's development in this chapter. Are all perspectives represented, or does one view dominate?

3. The chapter discusses development during childhood, adolescence, and adulthood. How are the boundaries between these periods defined, and how would you decide which phase of development best describes you?

4. Visit the website of the National Center for Health Statistics maintained by the Centers for Disease Control and Prevention (http://www.cdc.gov/nchs/about/otheract/aging/trendsoverview.htm) and examine one or more of the aging trends described. How well do these trends correspond to your perception of what happens as we age?

5. Recent genetic advances have offered the possibility of expanding the human life span. Consider the physical, cognitive, and socioemotional changes of adulthood described in the chapter, and discuss what might happen to these psychological functions if the human life span increases significantly.

Connections

To test your mastery of the material in this chapter, go to the Study Guide and the In-Psych Plus CD-ROM, as well as the Online Learning Center. There you will find a chapter summary, practice tests, flashcards, lecture slides, web links, and other study tools, such as interactive exercises and reviews as well as current, chapter-relevant news articles.

4 Sensation and Perception

Chapter Outline

Learning Goals

Discuss the basic principles of sensation and perception.

Explain how the visual system enables us to see and, by communicating with the brain, to perceive the world.

Understand how the auditory system registers sound and how it connects with the brain to perceive sound.

Know how the skin, chemical, kinesthetic, and vestibular senses work.

In 1950, the newly born Steveland Morris was placed in an incubator in which he was given too much oxygen. The result was permanent blindness. In 1962, 12-year-old singer and musician Stevie Wonder began a performing and recording career that has included such hits as "My Cherie Amour" and "Signed, Sealed, Delivered." At the beginning of the twenty-first century, his music is still perceived by many as "wondrous."

At age 12, Andrea Bocelli lost his sight in a soccer mishap. Now in his 40s, after a career as a lawyer, Andrea has taken the music world by storm with his magnificent, classically trained voice.

An individual lacking either vision or hearing has great difficulty doing all the things that a hearing, sighted person can do, yet people who lose one channel of sensation—such as vision—often adapt and compensate for the loss by enhancing their sensory skills in another area—such as hearing or touch. For example, researchers have found that blind individuals are more accurate at locating a sound source and have greater sensitivity to touch than sighted individuals (Lessard & others, 1998; Levanen & Hamdorf, 2001). Other studies indicate that the auditory cortex of deaf individuals becomes more responsive to touch than does this area of the brain in normal, hearing individuals (Levanen & others, 1998). These changes illustrate an important point made in chapter 2: how *adaptive* the brain is.

In this chapter, I explore the way our senses work. A general introduction to basic concepts of sensation and perception leads to a detailed discussion of vision, the sense that scientists know the most about. Then I examine hearing, the skin senses, taste and smell, and the senses related to movement. Throughout, I will explain how the information taken in through our senses is processed in the brain and thus affects behavior.

Two "sensations"—Stevie Wonder and Andrea Bocelli—have adapted to life without sight.

1 HOW WE SENSE AND PERCEIVE THE WORLD

- The Purpose of Sensation and Perception
- Thresholds
- Attention and Predisposition
- Sensory Receptors and the Brain
- Sensory Adaptation

How do we detect and perceive the world around us?

When Stevie Wonder's hands touch the keys of a piano, his brain recognizes the sensation and directs his fingers to press one or more of the keys, and he begins to play. The brain automatically interprets the information it receives from the fingers as they feel the piano keys and respond to the sensation. What may seem like the simple act of playing one note on the piano, however, is really the outcome of two complex, virtually inseparable processes: sensation and perception.

The Purpose of Sensation and Perception

sensation The process of receiving stimulus energies from the environment.

Sensation is the process of receiving stimulus energies from the external environment. Stimuli consist of physical energy—light, sound, and heat, for example. A stimulus is

Anableps microlepis, a fish with four eyes. Two eyes allow it to observe the world above water, two the world below water, as it swims just at the surface of the water. *Why was this evolutionary adaptation developed?*

detected by specialized receptor cells in the sense organs—eyes, ears, skin, nose, and tongue. When the receptor cells have registered a stimulus, the energy is converted to an electrochemical impulse. The electrochemical energy produces an action potential, which relays information about the stimulus through the nervous system to the brain (Viana, del Pena, & Belmonte, 2002). When it reaches the brain, the information travels to the appropriate area of the cerebral cortex (Sekular & Blake, 2002).

The brain gives meaning to sensation through perception. **Perception** is the process of organizing and interpreting sensory information to give it meaning. Receptor cells in our eyes record a silver object in the sky, but they do not "see" a jet plane; receptor cells in the ear vibrate in a particular way, but they do not "hear" a symphony. Finding meaningful patterns in sensory information is the job of perception.

In everyday life, the two processes of sensation and perception are virtually inseparable. The brain automatically perceives the information it receives from the sense organs. For this reason, most psychologists refer to sensation and perception as a unified information processing system (Goldstein, 2002).

Important insights into perception can be gained by asking the simple question "What is its purpose?" According to a leading expert in this field, David Marr (1982), the purpose of perception is to represent information from the outside world internally. For example, the purpose of vision is to create a three-dimensional representation, or map, of the world in the brain.

From an evolutionary perspective, the purpose of sensation and perception is to improve a species' chances for survival. An organism must be able to sense and respond quickly and accurately to events in the immediate environment, such as the approach of a predator, the presence of prey, or the appearance of a potential mate. Thus it is not surprising that most animals—from goldfish to elephants to humans—have eyes and ears, as well as sensitivities to touch and chemicals (smell and taste).

A close comparison of sensory systems in animals reveals that each species is exquisitely adapted to the habitat in which it evolved. Consider the species of fish called *Anableps microlepis,* which has four eyes. To survive, *Anableps microlepis* swims just at the surface of the water, with two aerial eyes monitoring the visual field above the water and two aquatic eyes monitoring the visual field underwater. This remarkable adaptation enables *Anableps microlepis* to search for food while watching for predators.

perception The brain's process of organizing and interpreting sensory information to give it meaning.

FIGURE 4.1 **Sensory Receptor Cells**
These cells are specialized to detect particular stimuli.

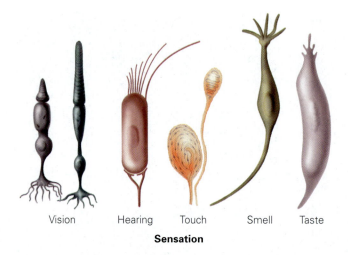

| Vision | Hearing | Touch | Smell | Taste |

Sensation

Sensory Receptors and the Brain

All sensation begins with sensory receptors. **Sensory receptors** are specialized cells that detect and transmit stimulus information to sensory nerves and the brain (Lewis & others, 2002). Sensory receptors are the openings through which the brain and nervous system experience the world. Figure 4.1 shows the types of sensory receptors for each of the five senses in humans.

The sensory receptors of every animal species have evolved to fit their environments. For example, the sensory receptors that a bat uses to find food are very different from those that an eagle uses. Bats use sound to locate prey at night, whereas eagles hunt with their eyes from great heights to avoid detection from potential prey.

Humans have multiple receptors that provide a rich tapestry of sensations (Lewis & others, 2004). Your skin, for example, contains 4 million pain receptors, 500,000 pressure receptors, 150,000 receptors for cold, and 16,000 receptors for heat. Specialized receptors in the joints, ligaments, and muscles produce information that is combined with information from other sensory receptors, such as those in the eyes and ears, to give us a sense of where certain body parts are in relation to other body parts. Thus—although vision, hearing, touch, taste, and smell are the five most commonly described senses—the nervous system blends these into a wider spectrum of sensations.

The sense organs and sensory receptors fall into several main classes based on the type of energy that is transmitted:

- *Photoreception:* detection of light, perceived as sight
- *Mechanoreception:* detection of pressure, vibration, and movement, perceived as touch, hearing, and balance
- *Chemoreception:* detection of chemical stimuli, perceived as smell and taste

Figure 4.2 depicts the general flow of information from the environment to the brain. Sensory receptors trigger action potentials in sensory neurons, which carry that information to the central nervous system. Recall from chapter 2 that an action potential is the brief wave of electrical charge that sweeps down the axon of a neuron for possible transmission to another neuron.

The action potentials of all sensory nerves are alike, which raises an intriguing question: How can an animal distinguish among sight, sound, odor, taste, and touch? The answer is that sensory receptors are selective and have different neural pathways. They are specialized to absorb a particular type of energy—light energy or mechanical energy (such as sound vibrations) for example—and convert it into the electrochemical energy of an action potential. Thus, when Andrea Bocelli hears the audience applauding sensory receptors in his ears pick up the sound in the form of mechanical energy and convert it into electrochemical energy, which the brain perceives as applause. Go to the video clip "Perceptual Integration" to see how sensory stimuli are integrated into one nuified perceptual experience.

In-Psych Plus

sensory receptors Specialized cells that detect and transmit stimulus information to sensory neurons and the brain.

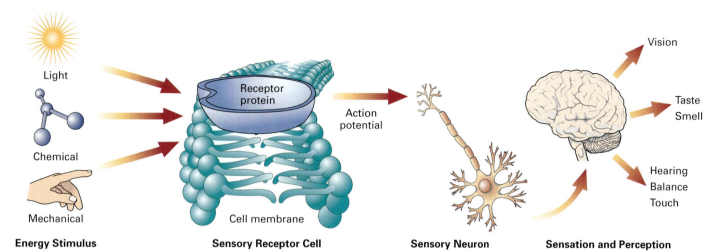

| Energy Stimulus | Sensory Receptor Cell | Sensory Neuron | Sensation and Perception |

FIGURE 4.2 **Sensory Information Flow** The diagram shows a general flow of sensory information from stimulus to sensation and perception.

In the brain, nearly all sensory signals go through the thalamus. Recall from chapter 2 that the thalamus is the brain's great relay station. From the thalamus, the signals go to the sensory areas of the cerebral cortex, where they are modified and distributed throughout a vast network of neurons. Also recall from chapter 2 that certain areas of the cerebral cortex are specialized to handle different sensory functions. Visual information is processed mainly in the occipital lobes, hearing in the temporal lobes, and pain, touch, and temperature in the parietal lobes.

Keep in mind, however, that the interactions and pathways of sensory information are complex, and the brain often must coordinate and interpret extensive information (Sejnowski, 2001). The senses evolved to help animals solve important problems, such as knowing when to flee and how to build a shelter. Large numbers of sensory neurons allow us to perceive the world in a unified way and thus make these behaviors possible. See the video clip "Sensory Processes and Brain Integration" to learn more about how the brain coordinates sensory information.

An important part of perception is figuring out what the sensory messages mean (Pines, 2001). Many factors shape this meaning, including signals from different parts of the brain, prior learning, the person's goals, and the person's level of arousal. Sensory messages also influence the process of interpretation; for example, signals from a sensory area may help other parts of the brain maintain arousal.

In-Psych Plus

Thresholds

Any sensory system must have the ability to detect varying degrees of energy in the environment. This energy can take the form of light, sound, chemical, or mechanical stimulation. How much of a stimulus is necessary for you to see, hear, taste, smell, or feel something? How close does an approaching bumblebee have to be before you can hear its buzzing? How far away from a brewing coffeepot can you be and still detect the smell of coffee? How different does the percentage of fat in the "low-fat" and "regular" versions of your favorite ice cream have to be for you to taste a difference?

Questions such as these are answered by researchers studying the links between the physical properties of stimuli and a person's experience of them. For example, an experiment might examine the relation between the rate at which a light flashes and a participant's ability to see individual flashes.

Absolute Threshold   One way to study thresholds is to assume that there is an **absolute threshold,** or minimum amount of energy that a person can detect. When the energy of a stimulus falls below this absolute threshold, we cannot detect its presence; when the energy of the stimulus rises above the absolute threshold, we can detect the stimulus.

absolute threshold The minimum amount of stimulus energy that an individual can detect.

FIGURE 4.3 Measuring Absolute Threshold Absolute threshold is the minimum amount of energy we can detect. To measure absolute threshold, psychologists have arbitrarily decided to use the criterion of detecting the stimulus 50 percent of the time. In this graph, the person's absolute threshold for detecting the ticking clock is at a distance of 20 feet.

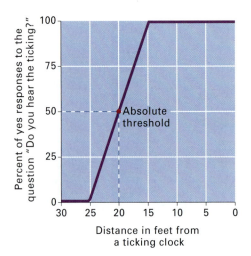

An experiment with a clock that ticks will help you understand the principle of absolute threshold. Put the clock on a table and walk far enough across the room so that you no longer hear it ticking. Then gradually move toward the clock. At some point, you will begin to hear it ticking. Hold your position and notice that occasionally the ticking fades, and you may have to move forward to reach the threshold; at other times, it may become loud, and you can move backward. In addition, if you measure your absolute threshold several times, you likely will record several different distances for detecting the stimulus.

People have different thresholds, because some people have better hearing than others and some people have better vision than others. Figure 4.3 shows one person's measured absolute threshold for detecting a clock's ticking sound. Using the same clock, another person might have a measured absolute threshold of 26 feet, and yet another, 18 feet.

Psychologists have arbitrarily decided that absolute threshold is the point at which an individual detects a stimulus 50 percent of the time. The approximate absolute thresholds for five different senses in humans are listed in figure 4.4.

Under ideal circumstances, our senses have very low absolute thresholds, so we can be remarkably good at detecting small amounts of stimulus energy. Try using a sharp pencil point to carefully lift a single hair on your forearm. Most people can easily detect this tiny bit of pressure on the skin. You might be surprised to learn that the human eye can see a candle flame at 30 miles on a dark, clear night. But our environment seldom gives us ideal conditions to detect stimuli. If the night were cloudy or the air polluted, for example, you would have to be much closer to see the flicker of a candle flame. And other lights on the horizon—car or house lights—would hinder your ability to detect the candle's flame.

Noise is the term given to irrelevant and competing stimuli. We usually think of noise as being auditory, such the TV being turned up too loud while we're trying to talk on the phone. But the psychological meaning of *noise* also involves other senses. Air pollution, cloudiness, car lights, and house lights are forms of visual noise that hamper the ability to see a candle flame from a great distance.

Subliminal Perception Can we experience sensations at levels below our absolute threshold without being aware of them? To what extent does **subliminal perception**—the ability to detect information below the level of conscious awareness—influence our behavior? In one of the bizarre moments in the 2000 presidential campaign, someone took a close look at a Republican TV commercial criticizing then Vice President Al Gore's Medicare proposal. The word *RATS* flashed for ¹/₃₀ of a second across the phrase "The Gore prescription plan: Bureaucrats decide." Presidential candidate George W. Bush's campaign team did its best to make light of the situation, but clearly

noise Irrelevant and competing stimuli.

subliminal perception The ability to detect information below the level of conscious awareness.

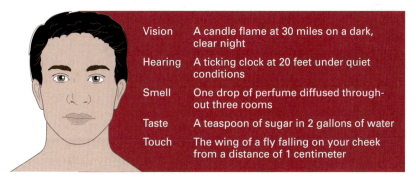

Vision	A candle flame at 30 miles on a dark, clear night
Hearing	A ticking clock at 20 feet under quiet conditions
Smell	One drop of perfume diffused throughout three rooms
Taste	A teaspoon of sugar in 2 gallons of water
Touch	The wing of a fly falling on your cheek from a distance of 1 centimeter

FIGURE 4.4 **Approximate Absolute Thresholds for Five Senses**

someone in the Bush campaign had intended to broadcast an unflattering subliminal label for the Democratic candidate. Also, when Tiger Woods was a young boy, he played subliminal motivational tapes while he was asleep at night in the hope that they would improve his golf game. Just how effective are such strategies?

An experiment by Carol Fowler and her colleagues (1981) provides some evidence that people can process information beneath their awareness. In this study, a word was shown on a screen so rapidly that the participants could not tell what they were seeing. Subsequently, they were shown two words (such as *hotel* and *book*) and asked which was most like the subliminally presented word *lodge*. The participants answered most questions correctly. More recent research has verified that people's performance is affected by stimuli that are too faint to be recognized at a conscious level (Allen, Kraus, & Bradlow, 2000; Greenwald, Draine, & Abrams, 1996; Monahan, Murphy, & Zajonc, 2000).

A controversial example of subliminal perception involves the claim that recordings of some rock groups, when played backward, contain messages from Satan. In theory, when the record is played normally (forward), the messages cannot be consciously perceived, but they influence our behavior in a subliminal way. Researchers have been unable to find any evidence whatsoever that such messages exist or, if they do, that they influence our behavior (McIver, 1988). Even if we were to take a

Mötley Crüe's *Shout at the Devil* album has been a target of groups who believe that backward messages are embedded in songs. The protesters say that this album has the phrase "Backward mask where are you, oh. Lost in error, Satan." However, researchers have been unable to find any evidence whatsoever that these and other satanic messages are encoded in the music or that, if they are, they can influence behavior. *What accounts for the belief that such messages are hidden in songs?*

very clearly recorded sentence and play it backward, no one could tell what it said. Investigators have found that people's perceptions of these messages is largely a function of what they expect to hear. In one experiment, when told beforehand that a message of a satanic nature would influence them, participants were likely to hear the message. With no such expectation, participants did not hear the message (Vokey & Read, 1985). In another study, individuals failed to perceive any information in subliminal self-help auditory tapes (Moore, 1995).

What can we learn from the research conducted by experimental psychologists? First, weak sensory stimuli can be registered by sensory receptors and is possibly encoded in the brain at a level beneath conscious awareness. Second, no evidence supports the claims of advertisers and rock music critics that such sensory registry and neural encoding have any influence on our thoughts and behavior. Rather, evidence suggests that we are most influenced by those sounds and views we are consciously aware of and can attend to efficiently (Smith & Rogers, 1994).

Extrasensory perception is another perceptual oddity that fascinates people. But proof has been just as elusive as proof of subliminal perception, as the Critical Controversy box indicates.

Difference Threshold In addition to studying how much energy is required for a stimulus to be detected, psychologists investigate the degree of difference that must exist between two stimuli before the difference is detected. This **difference threshold,** or *just noticeable difference,* is the smallest difference in stimulation required to discriminate one stimulus from another. Just as the absolute threshold is determined by a 50 percent detection rate, the difference threshold is the smallest difference in stimulation required to discriminate one stimulus from another 50 percent of the time.

An important aspect of difference thresholds is that the threshold increases with the magnitude of the stimulus. When music is playing softly, you may notice when your roommate increases the volume by even a small amount. But if he or she turns the volume up an equal amount when the music is playing very loudly, you may not notice. More than 150 years ago, E. H. Weber, a German physiologist, noticed that, regardless of their magnitude, two stimuli must differ by a constant proportion to be detected. For example, we add 1 candle to 60 candles and notice a difference in the brightness of the candles; we add 1 candle to 120 candles and do not notice a difference. However, adding 2 candles to 120 candles does produce a difference in brightness. Note that adding 2 candles to 120 candles is equivalent to 1 candle to 60 candles. The proportion of difference varies with the stimulus involved. For example, the difference threshold for a change in a tone's pitch is 3 percent, but a 20 percent change is required for a person to detect a difference in taste, and a 25 percent change in smell. Go to the interactivity "Weber's Law" to see how this law applies to you.

In-Psych Plus

Sensory Adaptation

Turning out the lights in your bedroom at night, you stumble across the room to your bed, completely blind to the objects around you. Gradually, the objects in your room become clearer. The ability of the visual system to adjust to a darkened room is an example of **sensory adaptation**—a change in the responsiveness of the sensory system based on the average level of surrounding stimulation (Durgin, 2000; Lyall & others, 2002). You have experienced sensory adaptation countless times in your life—adapting to the temperature of a shower, to the water in an initially "freezing" swimming pool, or to the smell of the Thanksgiving dinner that is wonderful to the arriving guests but almost undetectable to the cook who spent all day over it.

Although all senses adapt to prolonged stimulation, I use vision as an example to illustrate this topic. When you turn out the lights, everything is black. Conversely, when you step out into the bright sunshine after spending some time in a dark basement, your eyes are flooded and everything appears light. However, an important function of the eye is to get a good picture of the world. Good pictures have sharp

difference threshold The smallest difference in stimulation required to discriminate one stimulus from another 50 percent of the time; also called *just noticeable difference.*

sensory adaptation A change in the responsiveness of the sensory system based on the average level of surrounding stimulation.

Should We Believe the Claims of Psychics?

A woman reports that she has power over the goldfish in a 50-gallon tank. She claims that she can will them to swim to either end of the tank: As soon as she wills it, the fish take off.

Under the careful scrutiny of James Randi, this woman's account turned out to be just another fish story. The woman had written Randi, a professional magician who has a standing offer of $1 million to anyone whose psychic claims withstand his analysis. In the case of the woman and her goldfish, Randi also received a letter from her priest validating her extraordinary power. Randi talked with the priest, who told him that the woman would put her hands in front of her body and then run to one end of the tank. The fish soon followed. Because the fish could see out of the tank just as we could see into it, Randi suggested that the woman put opaque brown wrapping paper over one end of the tank and then try her powers. The woman did and called Randi to tell him that she had discovered something new about her powers: Her mind could not penetrate brown paper. The woman still believed that she had magical powers and completely misunderstood why Randi had asked her to place the brown paper over the fish tank.

To date, no one has met Randi's $1 million challenge, but he has investigated hundreds of reports of supernatural and occult powers. Recently he has evaluated cold-reading, a popular technique among psychics. When cold-reading, the psychic tells the person nothing but makes guesses, puts out suggestions, and asks questions. For example, if the "reader" says, "I am visualizing an older woman," the person usually has some reaction. It may be just a nod, somebody's name, or even an identification of a sister, an aunt, a mother, or a grandmother. But this information is supplied by the person, not the reader. Of course, almost everyone will show some reaction to such a general statement, giving the reader new information to incorporate into subsequent comments or questions.

Alternatively, the reader may say, "Mary? Do you recognize this person?" If there is a Mary, the person will give more helpful information to the reader. If no Mary is immediately recognized, the reader moves on. If "Mary" is remembered later, she is incorporated into the reader's comments. The reader can try many names, confident that the person will likely remember only suggested names that are meaningful to him or her. In this way, the person may well end up volunteering what he or she wants to hear.

According to Randi, cold-readers on television often interview people while they are waiting to get into the show. Then, when the show begins, the readers can choose to work with people they have already talked to. Suppose a person approaches the reader before the show and says he has a question about his deceased wife. That person can later be selected during the show and be asked, "Is your question about your dead wife?" To other people who are not aware of the previous conversation, the reader's comments can seem miraculous.

According to Randi, when cold-readers are not allowed to speak to anyone in advance or to be asked or told anything in advance, and people are allowed to answer only "yes" or "no" when asked direct questions, cold-readers fail miserably. In general, according to Randi, cold-readers have a way of leading people to believe that they knew something they didn't.

Randi (1997) makes a distinction between the tricks of magicians like him and the work of psychics and others who claim extraordinary powers. He says that magic is done for entertainment, the other for swindling. Read more about the Amazing Randi's skeptical approach to supernatural phenomena at his website, http://www.randi.org.

What do you think?

- Do you think the Amazing Randi's $1 million prize will ever be claimed? Why or why not?
- Why do you think people continue to believe in psychic phenomena when confronted with contradictory evidence produced by Randi and others?
- What kind of research would be necessary to establish that a particular psychic phenomenon is genuine?

contrasts between dark and light parts. The pupil of the eye adjusts the amount of light that gets into the eye and therefore helps to preserve the contrast between dark and light areas in your "picture." You may have noticed that the change in the size of the pupil as you dim or brighten the lights happens very quickly. You also may have noticed that, when you turn out the lights in your bedroom, the contrast between dark and light continues to improve for nearly 45 minutes. The reason is that the sensory receptors in your visual system also adapt their response rates. This adaptation, based on the average light level of the surrounding room, takes longer than it does for the pupil to adjust. All of these mechanisms allow the visual system to preserve contrast over an extremely large range of background illumination conditions. The price we pay for our ability to adapt to the average light level is *time.* Driving out of a dark tunnel under a mountain into the glistening and blinding reflection of the sun off the snow reminds us of this trade-off.

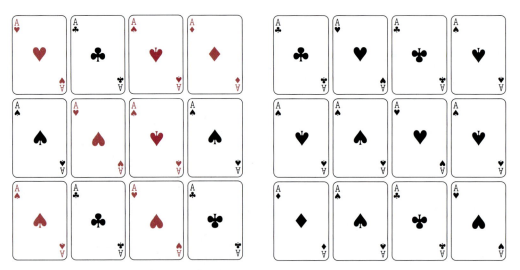

FIGURE 4.5 A Perception Experiment Place your hand over the playing cards on the right. As quickly as you can, count how many aces of spades you see on the left. Then place your hand over the cards on the left and count the number of aces of spades among the cards on the right.

Attention and Predisposition

An important part of perception is figuring out what the sensory messages mean (Pines, 2001). *Bottom-up* signals, from sensory receptors to the brain, help the brain maintain arousal, form an image of where the body is in space, or regulate movement. However, many *top-down* factors help the brain to determine what the sensory signals mean. They include signals from different parts of the brain, prior learning, and the person's goals and level of arousal.

One important top-down factor is attention. The world holds a lot of information. Right now, you are perceiving the letters and words that make up this sentence. Now look around and pick something other than this book to look at. Then curl up the toes on your right foot. In each of these circumstances, you engaged in **selective attention,** which involves focusing on a specific aspect of experience while ignoring others (Johnson & Proctor, 2004; MacLeod & others, 2002). You also demonstrated that attention is *shiftable*. The fact that you can attend selectively to one thing and shift attention readily indicates that you must be monitoring many things at once.

Why do we pay attention to some aspects of our experience and block out others? What you attend to is influenced by your motivation and interests. Art is one of my interests, so I will be more likely to attend to an advertisement for an art show than someone who has no interest in art. A person who is interested in sports is more likely to attend to an announcement that a basketball game will be on TV tonight than someone who is not interested in sports. Certain features of stimuli also cause people to attend to them. Novel stimuli (those that are new, different, or unusual) often attract our attention. If a Ferrari convertible whizzes by, you are more likely to notice it than you would a Ford. Size, color, and movement also influence our attention. Objects that are large, vividly colored, or moving are more likely to grab our attention than objects that are small, dull-colored, or stationary (Baldo & others, 2002).

See figure 4.5 for a perception experiment. Follow the instructions in the caption. Most people report that they see two or three aces of spades in the set of 12 cards on the left. However, if you look closely, you'll see that there are five. Two of the aces of spades are black and three are red. When people look at the 12 cards on the right, they are likely to count five aces of spades. Why do we perceive the two sets differently? We expect the ace of spades to be black because it is always black in a regular deck of cards. We don't expect it to be red, so we skip right over the red ones. Our expectations influence our perceptions. Go to the interactivity "Stroop Effect" to participate in a study of how predispositions influence perception.

In-Psych Plus

selective attention Focusing on a specific aspect of experience while ignoring others.

Psychologists refer to a predisposition or readiness to perceive something in a particular way as a **perceptual set.** Perceptual sets act as "psychological filters" in processing information about the environment and influence our interpretation of sensory signals. Interpretation can occur even before a stimulus or signal appears, as in the case of a runner who leaps into action before hearing the starting signal. Interestingly, young children are more accurate at the task involving the ace of spades than adults are. They have not built up the perceptual set that aces of spades are black. Perceptual sets are an example of top-down processing.

Review and Sharpen Your Thinking

 Discuss the basic principles of sensation and perception.

- Explain the purpose that sensation and perception serve.
- Outline the sensory reception process, and define three types of sensory reception.
- Distinguish between absolute threshold and difference threshold, and evaluate subliminal perception.
- Describe sensory adaptation.
- Discuss the role of attention and perceptual set in perception.

Try the absolute threshold experiment described on p. 126. Discuss your results with others in your class who tried the experiment.

VISUAL SYSTEM 2

Visual Stimuli and the Eye   **Color Vision**

Visual Processing in the Brain   **Visual Perceptions of Dimension**

How do we see the world and know what we are seeing?

Dr. P. was a distinguished musician who also taught music. However, he began having difficulty in visually perceiving his world. Sometimes he would fail to recognize his students, whom he had taught for many years, until they spoke. Dr. P. knew who they were by their voices. Aware that there was something wrong with the way he was seeing his world, Dr. P. went to see an ophthalmologist. Dr. P. was told that there was nothing wrong with his eyes but that he should see a neurologist. Dr. P. was referred to neurologist Oliver Sacks (1985), who wrote about him in *The Man Who Mistook His Wife for a Hat.* By the time he saw Sacks, nothing was familiar to Dr. P. When shown a glove, Dr. P. said it was a container of some sort, maybe a change purse. Visually, he was lost in a world of abstractions. Dr. P.'s eyes detected visual information, but his brain failed to interpret it accurately. Dr. P's case illustrates the fact that only when we consider what the eyes see and the brain interprets can we fully understand how we visually perceive the world.

Visual Stimuli and the Eye

Our ability to detect visual stimuli depends on the sensitivity of our eyes to differences in light. *Light* is a form of electromagnetic energy that, like ocean waves moving toward the beach, travels through space in waves. The *wavelength* of light is the

perceptual set A predisposition or readiness to perceive something in a particular way.

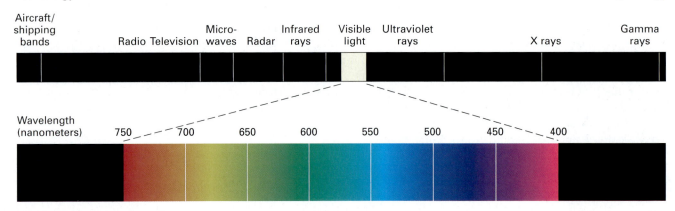

FIGURE 4.6 The Electromagnetic Spectrum and Visible Light Visible light is only a narrow band in the electromagnetic spectrum. Visible light wavelengths range from about 400 to 700 nm. X rays are much shorter, radio waves much longer.

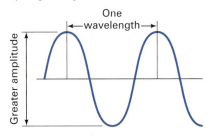

Light waves of greater amplitude make up brighter light.

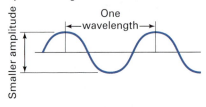

Light waves of smaller amplitude make up dimmer light.

FIGURE 4.7 Light Waves Varying in Amplitude The two graphs show how light waves vary in amplitude. Taller wavelengths are brighter; shorter wavelengths are dimmer.

distance from the peak of one wave to the peak of the next. Wavelengths of visible light range from about 400 to 700 nanometers (a nanometer is 1-billionth of a meter and is abbreviated nm). Outside the range of visible light are longer radio and infrared radiation waves and shorter ultraviolet and X rays (see figure 4.6). These other forms of electromagnetic energy continually bombard us, but we do not see them.

Light has three properties that are important to human vision. The wavelength of light that is reflected by a visual stimulus determines its *hue*, or color. *Amplitude*, which refers to the height of a wave, is linked with the brightness of a visual stimulus (see figure 4.7). *Purity*, the mixture of wavelengths in light, is related to the perceived saturation, or richness, of a visual stimulus. The color tree shown in figure 4.8 can help you to understand saturation. Colors that are very pure are located on the outside of the color tree. The closer we get to the center, the more white light has been added to the single wavelength of a particular color. In other words, the deep colors at the edge fade into pastel colors toward the center.

As I mentioned before, the eye, not unlike a camera, is constructed to get the best possible picture of the world. A good picture is in focus, is not too dark or too light, and has good contrast between the dark and light parts. Each of several structures in the eye plays an important role in this process (see figure 4.9):

- *Sclera:* the white outer part of the eye that helps to maintain the shape of the eye and to protect it from injury
- *Iris:* the colored part of the eye, which might be light blue in one individual and dark brown in another
- *Pupil:* the opening in the center of the iris

The iris contains muscles that control the size of the pupil and, hence, the amount of light that gets into the eye: The pupil acts like the aperture of a camera, opening to let in more light when it is needed and closing to let in less light when there is too much. You can demonstrate changes in the size of the pupil by looking at your eyes in the mirror and turning the room lights up and down. (You need to try this experiment in a room with sufficient light to be able to see your eyes even when the lights are turned all the way down.) As you dim the light, your pupils will begin to enlarge to let in more light; as you turn the room lights back up, your pupils will shrink to let in less light.

If the eye acts like a camera, then, in addition to having the right amount of light, the image has to be in focus at the back of the eye. Two structures serve this purpose:

- *Cornea:* a clear membrane just in front of the eye
- *Lens:* a transparent and somewhat flexible disklike entity filled with a gelatinous material

The function of both of these structures is to bend the light falling on the surface of the eye just enough to focus it at the back of the eye. The curved surface of the cornea does most of this bending, while the lens fine-tunes the focus. When you are looking at faraway objects, the lens has a relatively flat shape, because the light reaching the eye from faraway objects is parallel and the bending power of the cornea is sufficient to keep things in focus. However, the light reaching the eye from objects that are close is more scattered, so more bending of the light is required to achieve focus. As we get older, the lens of our eye begins to lose its flexibility and, hence, its ability to change from its normal flattened shape to the rounder shape needed to bring close objects into focus. This is the reason that many people whose vision is normal throughout their young adult lives will require reading glasses when they get older.

The parts of the eye that have been discussed so far work together to get the best possible picture of the world. All of this effort, however, would be for naught without a method for keeping, or "recording," the images we take of the world (De Valois, 2000)—as film or digital memory does in a camera. At the back of the eye, the multilayered **retina** is the light-sensitive surface that records what we see and converts it to neural impulses for processing in the brain. The retina is the primary mechanism of sight, but, even after decades of intense study, the full marvel of this structure is far from understood (Hood & others, 2002; Masland & Raviola, 2000).

The human retina has approximately 126 million receptor cells. They turn the electromagnetic energy of light into a form of energy that can be processed by the nervous system. There are two kinds of visual receptor cells: rods and cones. Rods and cones are involved in different aspects of vision, and they differ both in how they respond to light and in their patterns of distribution on the surface of the retina (Blake, 2000; Rex & others, 2002):

- *Rods:* the receptors in the retina that are sensitive to light but are not very useful for color vision. They function well under low illumination; as you might expect, they are hard at work at night. Humans have about 120 million rods.
- *Cones:* the receptors that we use for color perception. Like the rods, cones are light-sensitive. However, they require a larger amount of light than the rods do to respond, so they operate best in daylight or under high illumination. There are about 6 million cone cells in human eyes.

Figure 4.10 shows what rods and cones look like and summarizes their characteristics.

The most important part of the retina is the *fovea,* a minute area in the center of the retina at which vision is at its best (refer back to figure 4.9). The fovea contains only cones and is vitally important to many visual tasks (try reading out of the corner of your eye). Rods are found almost everywhere on the retina except in the fovea. Because rods require little light, we can detect fainter spots of light on the peripheral

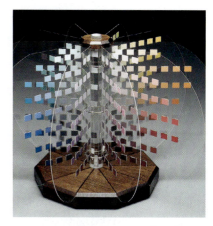

FIGURE 4.8 A Color Tree Showing Color's Three Dimensions: Hue, Saturation, and Brightness Hue is represented around the color tree, saturation horizontally, and brightness vertically.

retina The light-sensitive surface in the back of the eye that houses light receptors called rods and cones.

rods Receptors in the retina that are sensitive to light but are not very useful in color vision.

cones Receptors in the retina that process information about color.

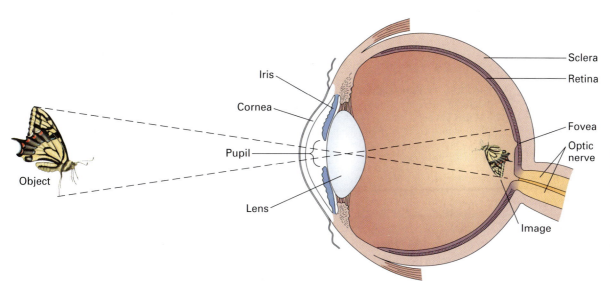

FIGURE 4.9

Parts of the Eye
Note that the image of the butterfly on the retina is upside down. The brain processes the image so we perceive it to be right side up.

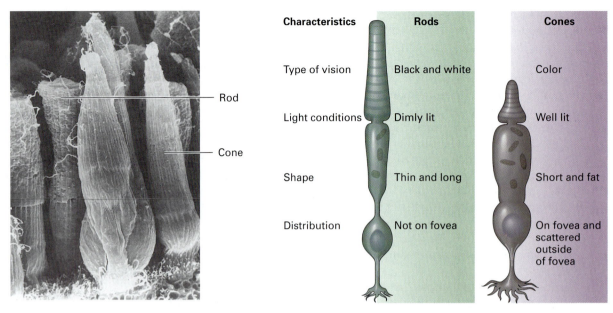

FIGURE 4.10 Rods and Cones A highly magnified image of rods and cones is accompanied by a diagram with a description of their characteristics.

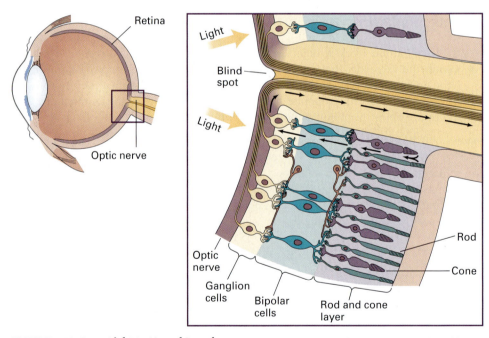

FIGURE 4.11 From Light to Neural Impulses After light passes through the cornea, pupil, and lens, it falls on the retina. Three layers of specialized cells in the retina convert the image into a neural signal that can be transmitted to the brain. First, light triggers a reaction in the rods and cones at the back of the retina, creating electrochemical impulses. Then these neural impulses activate the bipolar cells, which in turn activate the ganglion cells. These cells transmit the impulses to the optic nerve and hence to the brain.

parallel processing The simultaneous distribution of information across different neural pathways.

retina than at the fovea. Thus, if you want to see a very faint star, you should gaze slightly away from the star.

Figure 4.11 shows how the rods and cones at the back of the retina transform light into electrochemical impulses (Sandell, 2000). The signal is transmitted to the *bipolar cells* and then moves to another layer of specialized cells called *ganglion cells*. The axons

FIGURE 4.12 **The Eye's Blind Spot**
There is a normal blind spot in your eye, a small area where the optic nerve leads to the brain. To find your blind spot, hold this book at arm's length, cover your left eye, and stare at the red pepper on the left with your right eye. Move the book slowly toward you until the yellow pepper disappears. To find the blind spot in your left eye, cover your right eye, stare at the yellow pepper, and adjust the book until the red pepper disappears.

of the ganglion cells make up the optic nerve, which carries the visual information to the brain for further processing. The video clip "Vision" shows an animation of the parts of the eye.

There is one place on the retina that contains neither rods nor cones. Not surprisingly, this area is called the *blind spot;* it is the place on the retina where the optic nerve leaves the eye on its way to the brain. We cannot see anything that reaches only this part of the retina. To prove to yourself that you have a blind spot, see figure 4.12.

Visual Processing in the Brain

The eyes are just the beginning of visual perception. The next step occurs when neural impulses generated in the retina are dispatched to the brain for analysis and integration. For a reminder of the importance of this process, recall the difficulties of Dr. P., who lost the ability to recognize familiar people and objects on sight.

The optic nerve leaves the eye, carrying information about light toward the brain. Stimuli in the left visual field are registered in the right half of the retina in both eyes, and stimuli in the right visual field are registered in the left half of the retina in both eyes (see figure 4.13). In the brain, at a point called the *optic chiasm,* the optic nerve fibers divide. Approximately half of the nerve fibers cross over the midline of the brain. As a result, the visual information originating in the right halves of the two retinas is transmitted to the left side of the occipital lobe in the cerebral cortex, and the visual information coming from the left halves of the retinas is transmitted to the right side of the occipital lobe. What these crossings mean is that what we see in the left side of our visual field is registered in the right side of the brain, and what we see in the right visual field is registered in the left side of the brain.

Then this information is processed and combined into a recognizable object or scene in the *visual cortex,* located in the occipital lobe of the brain, before moving to other visual areas for further analysis (Zeki, 2001). Like the cells in the retina, many cells in the primary visual cortex are highly specialized. One neuron might show a sudden burst of activity when stimulated by lines of a particular angle; another neuron might fire only when moving stimuli appear; yet another neuron might be stimulated when an object has a combination of certain angles and sizes.

Sensory information travels rapidly through the brain because of **parallel processing,** the simultaneous distribution of information across different neural pathways (Beauchamp & others, 2002). A sensory system designed to process information about sensory qualities one at a time (such as the shapes of images, their colors, their movements, their locations, and so on) would be too slow to keep us current with a rapidly changing world. Some evidence suggests that parallel processing also occurs for the sensations of touch and hearing, not just vision (Bloom, Nelson, & Lazerson, 2001; Holting, Kosler, & Roder, 2003).

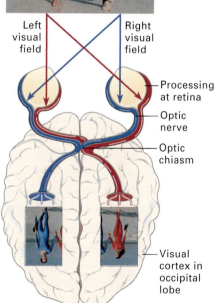

Left visual field — Right visual field

Processing at retina

Optic nerve

Optic chiasm

Visual cortex in occipital lobe

FIGURE 4.13 **Visual Pathways to and Through the Brain** Light from each side of the visual field falls on the opposite side of each eye's retina. Visual information then travels along the optic nerve to the optic chiasm, where most of the visual information crosses over to the other side of the brain. From there, visual information goes to the occipital lobe at the rear of the brain. All these crossings mean that what we see in the left side of our visual field (here, the woman) is registered in the right side of our brain, and what we see in the right visual field (the man) is registered in the left side of our brain.

FIGURE 4.14 **Examples of Stimuli Used to Test for Color Blindness**
People with normal vision see the number 16 in the left circle and the number 8 in the right circle. People with red-green color blindness may see just the 16, just the 8, or neither. A complete color blindness assessment involves the use of 15 stimuli.

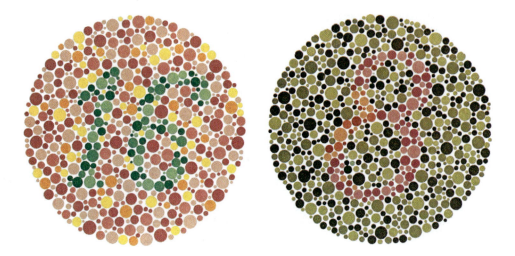

Despite parallel processing, connections between neural pathways unify sensory information into a complete picture of all we see (Humphreys, 2003; Robertson, 2003). For instance, if you look at a parrot, visual information about the parrot registers as a complete object. However, as you have seen, the sensory system breaks down this visual information and transmits it in distributed pathways to specific neurons. Seeing the whole parrot requires reassembling the information through a process called binding, in the cerebral cortex (Crick & Koch, 1998). Go to the video clip "Visual Information Processing" to see an animation of visual perception and to learn about how incoming information is compared with information in memory.

Color Vision

Imagine how dull a world without color would be. Our art museums are filled with paintings that are remarkable for their use of color, and flowers would lose much of their beauty for us if we could not see their rich colors. The ability to see color evolved because it provides many advantages to animals, including the ability to detect and discriminate among various objects (Sekuler & Blake, 2002). For example, the edibility of foods depends on ripeness, which is reflected in color. Not all animals have the same need to see color, however. Thus dogs' color vision is much more primitive than ours, whereas birds can readily detect the bright colors of flowers.

The study of human color vision using psychological methods has a long and distinguished history. A full century before the methods existed to study the anatomical and neurophysiological bases of color perception, psychological studies had discovered many of the basic principles of our color vision system. For instance, color is a pattern of neural responses, not the wavelengths of light themselves (Gegenfurtner & Kiper, 2003; Shevell, 2000). These studies also produced two main theories: trichromatic theory and opponent-process theory. Both turned out to be correct.

The *trichromatic theory* states that color perception is produced by three types of receptors (cone cells in the retina) that are particularly sensitive to different, but overlapping, ranges of wavelengths—green, red, and blue. The trichromatic theory was proposed by Thomas Young in 1802 and extended by Hermann von Helmholtz in 1852. The theory is based on experiments on color-matching abilities. Individuals are given a light of a single wavelength and asked to combine three single-wavelength lights to match the first light by changing the relative intensities of the three lights. Young and Helmholtz reasoned that, if the combination of any three wavelengths of different intensities is indistinguishable from any single pure wavelength, the visual system must base its perception of color on the relative responses of three receptor systems.

Further support for the trichromatic theory is found in the study of defective color vision, or what is commonly referred to as color blindness (Deeb & Kohl, 2003). The term *color blind* is somewhat misleading because it suggests that a color-blind

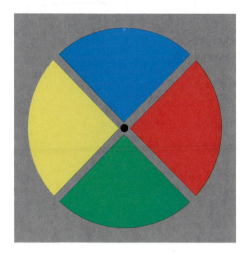 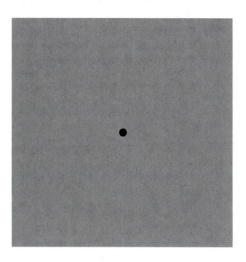

FIGURE 4.15 **Negative Afterimage: Complementary Colors** If you gaze steadily at the dot in the colored panel on the left for a few moments, then shift your gaze to the dot in the gray box on the right, you will see the original hues change into their complementary colors. The blue appears as yellow, the red as green, the green as red, and the yellow as blue. This pairing of colors has to do with the fact that color receptors in the eye are apparently sensitive as pairs: When one color is turned off (when you stop staring at the panel), the other color in the receptor is briefly turned on. The afterimage effect is especially noticeable with bright colors.

person cannot see color at all. Complete color blindness is rare; most people who are color blind, the vast majority of whom are men, can see some colors but not others. The nature of color blindness depends on which of the three kinds of cones is inoperative (Shevell, 2000). In the most common form of color blindness, the green cone system malfunctions in some way, rendering green indistinguishable from certain combinations of blue and red (see figure 4.14).

In 1878, the German physiologist Ewald Hering observed that some colors cannot exist together, whereas others can. For example, it is easy to imagine a greenish blue or a reddish yellow but nearly impossible to imagine a reddish green or a bluish yellow. Hering also noticed that trichromatic theory cannot adequately explain *afterimages,* sensations that remain after a stimulus is removed (see figure 4.15 to experience an afterimage). Color afterimages are common and involve complementary colors: If you look at red long enough, eventually a green afterimage will appear; if you look at yellow long enough, eventually a blue afterimage will appear.

Hering's observations led him to propose that the visual system treats colors as complementary pairs: red-green and blue-yellow. His *opponent-process theory* states that cells in the visual system respond to either red-green or blue-yellow colors; a given cell might be excited by red and inhibited by green, whereas another cell might be excited by yellow and inhibited by blue. Researchers have found that opponent-process theory does, indeed, explain afterimages (Hurvich & Jameson, 1969; Jameson & Hurvich, 1989). If you stare at red, for instance, your red-green system seems to "tire," and when you look away, it rebounds and gives you a green afterimage.

If the trichromatic theory of color perception is correct and we do, in fact, have three kinds of cone receptors like those predicted by Young and Helmholtz, then how can the opponent-process theory also be correct? The answer is that the red, blue, and green cones in the retina immediately translate the three-color code into the opponent-process code (see figure 4.16). For example, a green cone might inhibit and a red cone might excite a particular part of the optic nerve. Thus, *both* the trichromatic and opponent-process theories are correct—the eye and the brain use both methods to code colors.

This discussion of theories of color vision illustrates an important feature of psychology, described in chapter 1: Science often progresses when conflicting ideas are posed and investigated. In many instances, as with color vision, seemingly conflicting ideas or systems may actually work, and even work together to explain facts.

Visual Perceptions of Dimension

Perceiving visual stimuli means organizing and interpreting the fragments of information that the eye sends to the visual cortex. Information about the dimensions of

FIGURE 4.16 Trichromatic and Opponent-Process Theories: Transmission of Color Information in the Retina Cones responsive to green, blue, or red light form a trichromatic receptor system in the retina. As information is transmitted toward the optic nerve, opponent-process cells are activated. As shown here, a receptor cell is inhibited by a green cone (−) and excited by a red cone (+), producing red-green color information.

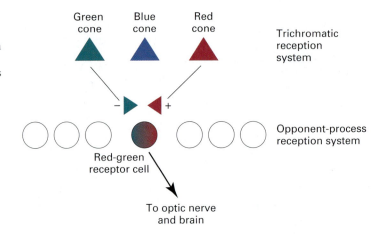

FIGURE 4.17 Reversible Figure-Ground Pattern Some figure-ground relationships are highly ambiguous, and it may be hard to tell what is figure and what is ground. Consider this well-known example. *Do you see the silhouette of a goblet or a pair of faces in profile?*

FIGURE 4.18 Gestalt Principles of Closure, Proximity, and Similarity *(a) Closure:* When we see disconnected or incomplete figures, we fill in the spaces and see them as complete figures. *(b) Proximity:* When we see objects that are near each other, they tend to be seen as a unit. You are likely to perceive the grouping as 4 columns of 4 squares each, not 1 set of 16 squares. *(c) Similarity:* When we see objects that are similar to each other, they tend to be seen as alike. Here, you are likely to see the two boxes as the same until you look closely. Then you will see vertical columns of circles and squares in the left box but horizontal rows of circles and squares in the right box.

what we are seeing is critical to this process. Among these dimensions are shape, depth, motion, and constancy.

Shape Perception Think about the visible world and its shapes—buildings against the sky, boats on the horizon, letters on this page. We see these shapes because they are marked off from the rest of what we see by a sudden change of brightness. The **figure-ground relationship** is the principle by which we organize the perceptual field into stimuli that stand out *(figure)* and those that are left over *(background),* as shown in figure 4.17.

The figure-ground relationship is a gestalt principle. (Figure 4.18 shows three others.) According to **gestalt psychology,** people naturally organize their perceptions according to certain patterns (*gestalt* is German for "configuration" or "form"). One of gestalt psychology's main principles is that the whole is different from the sum of its parts. For example, when you watch a movie, the "motion" you see in the film cannot be found in the film itself; if you examine it, you see only separate frames. When you watch the film, the frames move past a light source at a rate of many per second, and you perceive a whole that is very different from the separate frames that are the film's parts. Similarly, thousands of tiny dots (parts) make up an image (whole) in print or on a computer screen.

Depth Perception Images appear on our retinas in two-dimensional form, yet remarkably we see a three-dimensional world. Depth perception is the ability to perceive objects three-dimensionally. The scenes and objects we look at have depth. To see a world of depth, we use two kinds of information, or cues—binocular and monocular.

Because we have two eyes, we get two views of the world, one from each eye. **Binocular cues** are depth cues that depend on the combination of the images in the left and right retinas and on the way the two eyes work together. The pictures are slightly different because the eyes are in slightly different positions. Try holding your hand about 10 inches from your face. Alternately close and open your left and right eyes, so that only one eye is open at a time. The image of your hand will appear to jump back and forth because the image of your hand is in a slightly

(a)

(b)

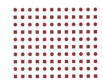

(c)

FIGURE 4.19 **Monocular Cue of Linear Perspective** Famous landscape artist J. M. W. Turner used linear perspective to give the perception of depth to his painting *Rain, Steam, and Speed.*

different place on the left and right retinas. The difference between the images in the two eyes is the binocular cue the brain uses to determine the depth or distance of an object. The two images are combined in the brain.

In addition to using binocular cues to get an idea of the depth of objects, we use a number of **monocular cues** available from the image in one eye, either right or left. These are powerful cues and under normal circumstances can provide a very compelling impression of depth. Try closing one eye—your perception of the world still retains many of its three-dimensional qualities.

Some examples of monocular cues are as follows:

- *Familiar size.* Our perceptions of the depth and distance of objects are based on what we have learned from experience about the standard sizes of objects. We know how large oranges tend to be, so we can tell something about how far away an orange is likely to be by the size of its image on the retina.
- *Height in the field of view.* All other things being equal, objects positioned higher in a picture are seen as farther away.
- *Linear perspective.* Objects that are farther away take up less space on the retina. As shown in figure 4.19, as an object recedes into the distance, parallel lines in the scene appear to converge.

figure-ground relationship The organization of the perceptual field into stimuli that stand out (figure) and those that are left over (background).

gestalt psychology The study of how people naturally organize their perceptions according to certain patterns.

binocular cues Depth cues based on the combination of the images on the left and right retinas and on the way the two eyes work together.

monocular cues Depth cues that can be extracted from the image in either eye.

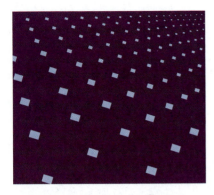

FIGURE 4.20 Texture Gradient The gradients of texture create an impression of depth on a flat surface.

In-Psych Plus

FIGURE 4.21 Size Constancy Even though our retinal images of the hot air balloons vary, we still realize the balloons are approximately the same size.

In-Psych Plus

perceptual constancy Recognition that objects are unchanging even though sensory input about them is changing.

- *Overlap.* An object that partially conceals or overlaps another object is perceived as closer.
- *Shading.* The position of the light and the position of the viewer affect depth perception. Consider an egg under a desk lamp. If you walk around the desk, you will see different shading patterns on the egg.
- *Texture gradient.* Texture becomes denser and finer the farther away it is from the viewer (see figure 4.20).

Depth perception is especially intriguing to artists, who have to paint a three-dimensional world on a two-dimensional canvas. Artists often use monocular cues to give the feeling of depth to their paintings.

Motion Perception Motion perception plays an important role in the lives of many species (Derrington, Allen, & Delicato, 2004; Pines, 2001). Both predators and their prey depend for survival on being able to detect motion quickly. Frogs and some other simple vertebrates may not even see an object unless it is moving. For example, the "bug-detecting" cells in the frog's retinas are wired to sense only movement.

In contrast, the retinas of humans and other primates cannot detect movement. According to one neuroscientist, "the dumber the animal, the 'smarter' the retina" (Baylor, 2001). In humans, the brain takes over the job of analyzing motion through highly specialized neural pathways; in fact, individual neurons are specialized to detect motion. Feedback from our body also tells us whether we are moving or whether someone or something else is moving. For example, we move our eye muscles as we watch a ball coming toward us. Further, the environment we see is rich in cues that give us information about movement. For example, when we run, what's around us appears to be moving. Go to the interactivity "Phi Phenomenon" to participate in a study of apparent motion.

Perceptual Constancy Retinal images are constantly changing, yet, even though the stimuli that fall on our retinas change as we move closer to or farther away from objects or look at objects from different orientations and in light or dark settings, our perception of them remains stable. **Perceptual constancy** is the recognition that objects are unchanging even though sensory input about them is changing.

We experience three types of perceptual constancy:

- *Size constancy* is the recognition that an object remains the same size even though the retinal image of the object changes (see figure 4.21).
- *Shape constancy* is the recognition that an object retains the same shape even though its orientation to us changes. Look around. You probably see objects of various shapes—chairs and tables, for example. If you walk around the room, you will see these objects from different sides and angles. Even though the retinal image of the objects changes as you walk, you still perceive the objects as having the same shape (see figure 4.22).
- *Brightness constancy* is the recognition that an object retains the same degree of brightness even though different amounts of light fall on it. For example, whether you are reading this book indoors or out, the whiteness and blackness of its white pages and black print do not change. Go to the interactivity "Brightness Perception" to test how the source and brightness of light affect your perception.

How are we able to resolve the discrepancy between a retinal image of an object and its actual size, shape, and brightness? Experience is important. For example, no matter how far away you are from your car, you know how large it is. In size constancy, binocular and monocular distance cues also help, even if we have never seen an object before.

FIGURE 4.22 Shape Constancy The various images of an opening door are quite different, yet you consistently perceive a rectangular door.

Review and Sharpen Your Thinking

2 *Explain how the visual system enables us to see and, by communicating with the brain, to perceive the world.*

- Explain the nature of light and how it is processed in the human eye.
- Describe how visual information is processed in the brain and reassembled into a single image.
- Discuss the trichromatic and opponent-process theories of color vision.
- State how shape, depth, motion, and perceptual constancy enable us to transform flat images into three-dimensional objects and scenes.

If you were designing safety signs and signals, what would you do to make them visually meaningful to as many people as possible? Think of what you have learned in this section about visual stimuli, visual processing, and color vision.

AUDITORY SYSTEM 3

How We Experience Sound

Auditory Processing in the Brain

Structures and Functions of the Ear

Auditory Perceptions of Location

What is the auditory system and how does it process sound so that the brain can hear it?

Just as light provides us with information about the environment, so does sound. What would life be like without music, the rushing sound of ocean waves or the wind, or the voices of family and friends? Sounds tell us about the approach of a person behind us, an oncoming car, or the mischief of a 2-year-old; perhaps most important, sounds enable us to communicate through language and song.

Luis Weiss is more conscious of what sound adds to life than most of us are (Arana-Ward, 1997). At age 3, Luis had a cochlear implant inserted into his ear. Before the procedure, Luis was deaf. When he received the cochlear implant, he experienced a rush of sound that took time for him to sort through and understand. But, by age 17, he was a senior honor student in high school; could speak English, French, and Spanish; had scored 700 on the math SAT; and wanted to be an aeronautical engineer. Although Luis would probably have done well without the implant, being able to hear made many things easier for him.

FIGURE 4.23 Physical Differences in Sound Waves and the Qualities of Sound They Produce

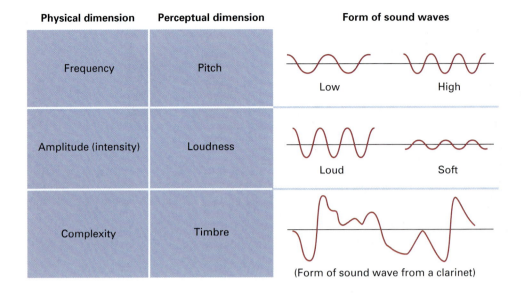

Physical dimension	Perceptual dimension	Form of sound waves
Frequency	Pitch	Low / High
Amplitude (intensity)	Loudness	Loud / Soft
Complexity	Timbre	(Form of sound wave from a clarinet)

How We Experience Sound

Many deaf people are aware that sound exists, but they experience it differently than do hearing individuals. At a rock concert, you may have felt the throbbing pulse of the music or sensed that the air around you was vibrating. Bass instruments are especially effective at creating mechanical pulsations, even causing the floor to vibrate. These are the sensations that many deaf people experience. But are they sound?

Sounds, or sound waves, are vibrations in the air that are processed by the auditory (or hearing) system. Remember that I described light waves as being much like the waves in the ocean moving toward the beach. Sound waves, too, vary in wavelength, which determines the three characteristics of sound:

- *Frequency:* number of cycles (full wavelengths) that pass through a point in a given time. *Pitch* is the perceptual interpretation of the frequency of a sound. High-frequency sounds are perceived as having a high pitch, low-frequency sounds as having a low pitch. A soprano voice sounds high-pitched, a bass voice low-pitched. As with the wavelengths of light, human sensitivity is limited to a range of sound frequencies. Other animals—dogs, for example—can hear higher frequencies than can humans, and some animals can hear lower frequencies.
- *Amplitude:* amount of pressure produced by a sound wave relative to a standard, measured in decibels (dB). Zero decibels is the weakest sound the human ear can detect. *Loudness* is the perception of the sound wave's amplitude. In general, the higher the amplitude of the sound wave, or the higher the decibel level, the louder the sound is perceived to be. The air is pressing more forcibly against you and your ears during loud sounds and more gently during quiet sounds.
- *Complexity:* number of frequencies of sound that are blended together. A single sound wave is similar to a single wavelength of pure colored light. Most sounds, including those of speech and music, are complex sounds. *Timbre* is the perceptual complexity, or the tone saturation, of a sound. Timbre is responsible for the perceptual difference between a trumpet and a trombone playing the same note and for the quality differences we hear in human voices.

Figure 4.23 illustrates the physical differences in the sound waves that produce these different qualities of sounds.

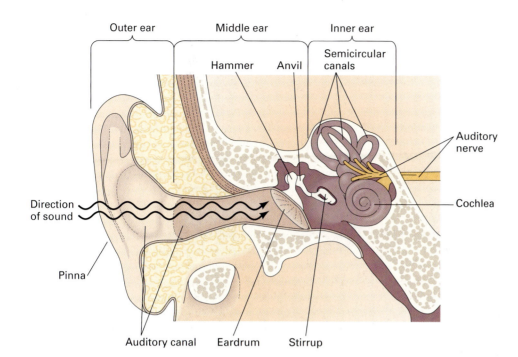

FIGURE 4.24 **Outer, Middle, and Inner Ear** On entering the outer ear, sound waves travel through the auditory canal, where they generate vibrations in the eardrum. These vibrations are transferred via the hammer, anvil, and stirrup to the fluid-filled cochlea in the inner ear. There the mechanical vibrations are converted to an electrochemical signal that the brain will recognize as sound.

Structures and Functions of the Ear

What happens to sound waves once they reach your ear? How do various structures of the ear transform sound waves into signals that the brain will recognize as sound? Functionally, the ear is analogous to the eye. The ear serves the purpose of transmitting a high-fidelity version of sounds in the world to the brain for analysis and interpretation. Just as an image needs to be in focus and sufficiently bright for the brain to interpret it, a sound needs to be transmitted in a way that preserves information about its location, its amplitude, its frequency (which helps us distinguish the voice of a child from that of an adult), and its timbre (which allows us to identify the voice of a friend on the telephone). Go to the video clip "Hearing" for an animation of the effect of sound waves on your auditory system.

In-Psych Plus

The ear is divided into three parts (see figure 4.24):

- *Outer ear:* The outer ear consists of the *pinna* and the external *auditory canal.* The funnel-shaped pinna is the visible part of the ear. (Elephants have very large pinnae.) The pinna collects sounds and channels them into the interior of the ear. The pinnae of many animals are movable and serve a more important role in locating sound than do the pinnae of humans. For example, cats turn their ears in the direction of a faint and interesting sound.
- *Middle ear:* After passing the pinna, sound waves move through the auditory canal to the middle ear. The middle ear channels the sound to the inner ear. The first structure that sound touches in the middle ear is the *eardrum,* a membrane that vibrates in response to sound. The *hammer, anvil,* and *stirrup* of the middle ear are a connected chain of the three smallest bones in the human body. When they vibrate, they transmit sound waves to the fluid-filled inner ear. Sound travels far more easily in air than in water. Sound waves entering the ear travel in air until they reach the inner ear. The hammer, anvil, and stirrup act as a lever to amplify the sound waves before they reach the fluid-filled inner ear.
- *Inner ear:* The function of the inner ear is to translate sound waves into neural impulses and send them on to the brain (Zwislocki, 2002). The stirrup of the middle ear is connected to the inner ear's membranous *oval window,* which transmits sound waves to the *cochlea,* a tubular, fluid-filled structure that is coiled up like a snail (see figure 4.25). The *basilar membrane* lines the inner

outer ear Consists of the pinna and the external auditory canal.

middle ear Consists of the eardrum, hammer, anvil, and stirrup.

inner ear Consists of the oval window, cochlea, and basilar membrane.

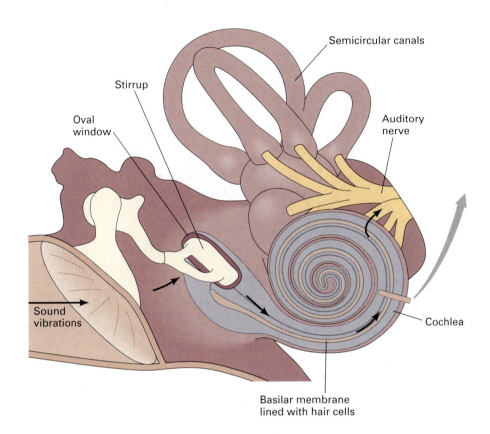

wall of the cochlea. It is narrow and rigid at the base of the cochlea but widens and becomes flexible at the top. This variation in width and flexibility allows different areas of the basilar membrane to vibrate more intensely when exposed to different sound frequencies. For example, the high-pitched tinkle of a bell stimulates the narrow region of the basilar membrane at the base of the cochlea, whereas the low-pitched tones of a tugboat whistle stimulate the wide end. In humans and other mammals, *hair cells* line the basilar membrane. These *hair cells* are the sensory receptors of the ear. They are called hair cells because of the tufts of fine bristles, or cilia, that sprout from the top of them. The movement of the hair cells generates impulses that are interpreted as sound by the brain.

One of the auditory system's mysteries is how the inner ear registers the frequency of sound. Two theories have been proposed to explain this mystery: place theory and frequency theory. *Place theory* states that each frequency produces vibrations at a particular spot on the basilar membrane (Békésy, 1960). Place theory adequately explains high-frequency sounds but not low-frequency sounds. A high-frequency sound stimulates a very precise area on the basilar membrane. In contrast, a low-frequency sound causes a large part of the basilar membrane to be displaced. Because humans can hear low-frequency sounds better than can be predicted by the basilar membrane's response to these sounds, some other factors must be involved. *Frequency theory* addresses this by stating that the perception of a sound's frequency depends on how often the auditory nerve fires: Higher-frequency sounds cause the auditory nerve to fire more often than do lower-frequency sounds.

One limitation of frequency theory is that a single neuron has a maximum firing rate of about 1,000 times per second. Therefore, frequency theory cannot be applied to tones with frequencies that would require a neuron to fire more rapidly. To deal with this limitation, a modification of frequency theory was developed, called the *volley principle*. It states that, although individual neurons cannot fire faster than 1,000 times per second, the neurons can team up and alternate their firing to attain a combined frequency above that rate, creating a volley of impulses. Thus frequency theory better explains the perception of sounds below 1,000 times per second, whereas a combination of frequency and place theory is needed to explain those above 1,000 times per second.

The hearing mechanism is more complex than it may seem and consists of many sensitive and finely calibrated parts. To find out how well you protect your hearing mechanism, see the Psychology and Life box.

Auditory Processing in the Brain

As you saw in the discussion of the visual system, once energy from the environment is picked up by our receptors, it must be transmitted to the brain for processing and interpretation. An image on the retina does not a Picasso make—likewise, a pattern of receptor responses in the cochlea does not a symphony make. In the retina, the responses of the rod and cone receptors leave the eye via the optic nerve. In the auditory system, information about sound moves from the hair cells of the inner ear to the **auditory nerve,** which carries neural impulses to the brain's auditory areas. Remember that it is the movement of the hair cells that transforms the physical stimulation of sound waves into the action potential of neural impulses.

Auditory information moves up the auditory pathway via electrochemical transmission in a more complex manner than does visual information in the visual pathway. The auditory pathway has many synapses. Most fibers cross over the midline between the hemispheres of the cerebral cortex, although some proceed directly to the hemisphere on the same side as the ear of reception. Thus most of the auditory information from the left ear goes to the right side of the brain, but some also goes to the left side of the brain. The auditory nerve extends from the cochlea to the brain stem. The cortical destination of most of these fibers is the temporal lobes of the brain. As in the case of visual information, researchers have found that various features are extracted from auditory information and transmitted along parallel pathways in the brain (Feng & Ratnam, 2000; Rubel & Fritzsch, 2002).

Auditory Perceptions of Location

When you hear the siren of a fire engine or the bark of a dog, how do you know where the sound is coming from? The basilar membrane tells us about the frequency and complexity of a sound, but it doesn't tell us where a sound is located.

Having two ears helps us to localize a sound. Imagine that a dog is barking to your left. Your left ear receives the sound sooner than your right ear. Also, your left ear receives a slightly more intense sound than your right ear in this case, for two reasons: (1) The sound has traveled less distance and (2) the other ear is in what is called the *sound shadow* of the listener's head, which provides a barrier that reduces the sound's intensity (see figure 4.26).

Thus differences in both the *timing* of the sound and the *intensity* of the sound help us to localize it. (Similarly, because our two eyes see slightly different images,

Love Your Ears

Auditory noise has little effect on us when it is at low volume or when we are doing simple, routine tasks. However, under some conditions noise can annoy us and disrupt our behavior (Passchier & others, 2001; Razdin & Sidhu, 2001).

Noise rated at 80 decibels or higher, if heard for prolonged periods of time, can cause permanent hearing loss. The damage begins with the hair cells in the inner ear, which develop blisterlike bulges, which eventually pop. The tissue beneath the hair cells swells and softens until the hair cells, and sometimes the neurons leaving the cochlea, become scarred and degenerate (Lewis, 2001).

H.E.A.R. (Hearing Education and Awareness for Rockers) was founded by rock musicians whose hearing had been damaged by their exposure to high volumes of rock music. Such hearing loss is common among rock musicians and limits what they are able to do later in their lives. The symptoms of possible hearing loss from loud noise or music include ringing or buzzing in the ears; slight muffling of sounds; difficulty in understanding speech (hearing the words but not understanding them); and problems hearing conversations in groups of people when there is background noise or in rooms with poor acoustics.

To determine how well you protect your hearing, answer the following questions:

- Do you work in a noisy environment? If so, ask your employer to inform you about the level of noise and company policy on protecting your hearing.
- If you use power equipment, are you using earmuffs or earplugs to protect your ears?
- Do you listen to music on headphones? If you listen to loud music often, go to a hearing specialist, get your hearing tested, and listen to the specialist's advice.
- Do you go to rock concerts? According to H.E.A.R., the sound levels at a rock concert can be as high as 140 dB in front of the speakers, which can damage hearing, and above 100 dB behind the speakers, still very loud and potentially dangerous.

auditory nerve Carries neural impulses to the brain's auditory areas.

145

FIGURE 4.26 **Sound Shadow** The sound shadow is caused by the listener's head, which forms a barrier that reduces the sound's intensity. Here the sound is to the person's left, so the sound shadow will delay and reduce the intensity of the sound that reaches the right ear.

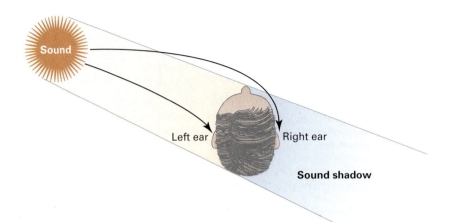

Bats navigate through their environment using echolocation. *Why do bats require this specialized auditory sense?*

we can determine visually how near or far away an object is.) Humans often have difficulty localizing a sound that is coming from a source directly in front of them because it reaches both ears simultaneously. The same is true for sounds directly above your head or directly behind you.

Compared with some animals, humans aren't very accurate at locating sounds. For example, bats are able to hunt insects at night because of their exquisitely developed sensitivity to their own echoes. They emit sounds and then listen to the echoes coming back. Using this system—called *echolocation*—bats can fly through their environment at high speeds, avoid predators, and find prey. Evolution has provided bats with such exquisite hearing because bats are nocturnal animals. Vision requires light, so any method of building internal representations of the environment that requires light would not be an effective perceptual system for the bat. Humans do not need the bat's echolocation ability because we do not hunt bugs at night. Rather, we use our eyes to pursue food by day.

Review and Sharpen Your Thinking

3 *Understand how the auditory system registers sound and how it connects with the brain to perceive sound.*

- Describe the nature of sound and how it is experienced.
- Identify the structures of the ear and their functions.
- Explain how auditory signals are transmitted to the brain for processing.
- Describe sound localization.

Suppose you were in an accident and, in order to survive, had to sacrifice either your vision or your hearing. Which sense would you preserve? Why?

4 OTHER SENSES

| Skin Senses | Chemical Senses | Kinesthetic and Vestibular Senses |

How do the skin, chemical, kinesthetic, and vestibular senses work?

Now that the visual and auditory systems have been described in some detail, let's take a look at our other sensory systems. You are familiar with the skin senses and the chemical senses, smell and taste. The lesser known kinesthetic and vestibular senses enable us to stay upright and to coordinate our movements.

Skin Senses

You know when someone has a fever by putting your hand to her head; you know how to find your way to the light switch in a darkened room by groping along the wall; and you know whether or not a pair of shoes is too tight by the way the shoes touch different parts of your feet when you walk. The skin is our largest sensory system, draped over the body with receptors for touch, temperature, and pain. A large variety of important information comes to us through our skin.

Touch   Touch is one of the senses that we most often take for granted, yet our ability to respond to touch is astounding.

In vision, we detect light energy. In audition, we detect the vibrations of air or sound waves pressing against our eardrums. In touch, we detect mechanical energy, or pressure against the skin. This kind of energy is not so different from the kind of energy we detect in vision or audition. Sometimes the only difference is intensity—the sound of a rock band playing softly is an auditory stimulus, but at the high volumes that make a concert hall reverberate, this auditory stimulus is also felt as mechanical energy pressing against your skin.

How does information about touch travel from the skin through the nervous system? Sensory fibers arising from receptors in the skin enter the spinal cord. From there, the information travels to the brain stem, at which point most fibers from each side of the body cross over to the opposite side of the brain. Then the information about touch moves on to the thalamus, which serves as a relay station. The thalamus then projects the map of the body's surface onto the somatosensory areas of the parietal lobes in the cerebral cortex (Anderson, 2002).

As in the visual and auditory systems, some cells in the somatosensory cortex respond to specific aspects of touch, such as movement across the skin. Also, such features of touch as pressure, temperature, and movement may be subject to parallel processing and recombined in the somatosensory cortex (Bloom, Nelson, & Lazerson, 2001).

Just as the visual system is more sensitive to images on the fovea than to images in the peripheral retina, our sensitivity to touch is not equally good across all areas of the skin. As you might expect of a toolmaking species, we need excellent touch discrimination in our hands but much less in other parts of the body, such as the torso or legs. The human brain thus devotes more space to analyzing touch signals coming from the hands than from the legs. See the video clip "Tactile Information Processing" to learn more about the role of the brain in the skin senses. This video also explores the effect of experience on the map of the body in the brain.

In-Psych Plus

Newborns can feel touch better than they can see, hear, or taste (Eliot, 2001). Newborn girls are more sensitive to touch than their male counterparts, a difference that remains throughout life. The sense of touch is especially helpful to infants because it helps them explore the world and is also important for health and emotional well-being. As was shown in chapter 3, touch is a key aspect of attachment.

How do the sensation and the preception of touch work in tasks such as opening a jar of pickels? Go to the interactivity "Sensorimotor Neural Circuit" to learn more about how sensory and motor information travels through the nervous system.

In-Psych Plus

Temperature   Even in the absence of direct contact with the skin, we need to detect temperature. **Thermoreceptors,** which are located under the skin, respond to changes in temperature at or near the skin and provide input needed to keep the body's temperature at 98.6° Fahrenheit.

There are two types of thermoreceptors: warm thermoreceptors respond to the warming of the skin, and cold thermoreceptors respond to the cooling of the skin.

thermoreceptors Receptors under the skin that respond to increases and decreases in temperature.

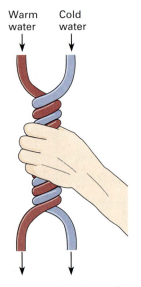

Warm water   Cold water

FIGURE 4.27 A "Hot" Experience
When two pipes, one containing cold water and the other warm water, are braided together, a person touching the pipes feels a sensation of "hot." The perceived heat coming from the pipes is so intense that a person cannot touch them for longer than a couple of seconds.

Somewhat surprisingly, when warm and cold receptors that are close to each other in the skin are stimulated simultaneously, we experience the sensation of hotness. Figure 4.27 illustrates this "hot" experience.

Pain When contact with the skin takes the form of a sharp pinch, our sensation of mechanical pressure changes from touch to pain. When a pot handle is so hot that it burns your hand, your sensation of temperature becomes one of pain. Indeed, intense stimulation of any one of the senses can produce pain—too much light, very loud sounds, or very spicy food, for example. **Pain** is the sensation that warns us of damage to our bodies. Our ability to sense pain is vital for our survival as a species. It functions as a quick-acting system that tells the motor systems of the brain that they must act to minimize or eliminate this damage. A hand touching a hot stove must be pulled away; ears should be covered up when one walks by a loud jackhammer; chili should be buffered with some crackers.

Pain receptors are dispersed widely throughout the body—in the skin, in the sheath tissue surrounding muscles, in internal organs, and in the membranes around bone (Beatty, 1995). Although all pain receptors are anatomically similar, they differ in the type of physical stimuli to which they most readily respond. Mechanical pain receptors respond mainly to pressure, as when a sharp object is encountered. Heat pain receptors respond primarily to strong heat that is capable of burning the tissue in which the receptors are embedded. Other pain receptors have a mixed function, responding to both types of painful stimuli. Many pain receptors are chemically sensitive and respond to a range of pain-producing substances.

Pain receptors have a much higher threshold for firing than receptors for temperature and touch (Bloom & others, 2001). Pain receptors react mainly to physical stimuli that distort them or to chemical stimuli that "irritate" them into action. Inflamed joints or sore, torn muscles produce *prostaglandins,* which stimulate the receptors and cause the experience of pain. Drugs such as aspirin likely reduce the feeling of pain by reducing the body's production of prostaglandins.

Two different neural pathways transmit pain messages to the brain: a fast pathway and a slow pathway (Bloom & others, 2001). In the *fast pathway,* fibers connect directly with the thalamus, then to the motor and somatosensory areas of the cerebral cortex. This pathway transmits information about sharp, localized pain, as when you cut your skin. It takes less than a second for the information in this pathway to reach the cerebral cortex. In the *slow pathway,* pain information travels through the limbic system, a detour that delays the arrival of information at the cerebral cortex by seconds. The unpleasant, nagging pain that characterizes the slow pathway may function to remind the brain that an injury has occurred, normal activity needs to be restricted, and the pain needs to be monitored.

Currently, some neuroscientists believe that the brain generates the experience of pain. There is evidence that a chemical process involving *endorphins,* which were discussed in chapter 2, turns pain signals on and turns them off. Recall that endorphins are neurotransmitters that function as natural opiates in producing pleasure and pain. Endorphins are believed to be released mainly in the synapses of the slow pathway (Bloom & others, 2001).

Perception of pain is complex and often varies from one person to the next. Some people rarely feel pain; others seem to be in great pain if they experience a minor bump or bruise. To some degree, these individual variations may be physiological. A person who experiences considerable pain even with a minor injury may have a neurotransmitter system that is deficient in endorphin production.

However, perception of pain goes beyond physiology. Although all sensations are affected by factors such as motivation and expectation, the perception of pain is especially susceptible to these factors (Philips & Rachman, 1996). Cultural and ethnic contexts can also greatly determine the degree to which an individual experiences pain. For example, one pain researcher described a ritual performed in India in which a

pain The sensation that warns us that damage to our bodies is occurring.

chosen person travels from town to town delivering blessings to the children and the crops while suspended from metal hooks embedded in his back (Melzak, 1973). The chosen person apparently reports no sensation of pain and appears to be in ecstasy.

Nowhere is cultural variation more pronounced than in the perception of pain in childbirth. In some cultures, women do not expect childbirth to be painful. They may have their babies and in a matter of hours go back to performing their normal daily activities. However, in the United States and most other Western cultures, women expect childbirth to involve considerable pain. The Lamaze method of childbirth (natural childbirth) seeks to reduce this fear of pain by training women's muscle tone and breathing patterns. Women who use the Lamaze method experience reduced perception of pain in childbirth.

Most acute pain decreases over time with avoidance of activity or with analgesic medication. Other strategies for reducing acute pain include the following:

- *Distraction.* When you get an injection, do you focus on the needle as it is about to plunge into your flesh, or do you avert your eyes and concentrate on something else? Distraction is usually the best way to reduce pain, because attention to the sensation can magnify it. You might focus your attention on something pleasant that you plan to do this weekend, for example.
- *Focused breathing.* The next time you stub your toe, try panting—short, fast breaths (similar to the breathing practiced in Lamaze childbirth). Focused breathing may successfully diminish your agony.
- *Counterstimulation.* Pinching your cheek in the aftermath of a bad cut likely will mute your pain. Applying ice to a sprained or swollen area not only reduces the pain but also can keep the swelling down.

Treatment of chronic pain is often more complex. The most successful treatment of chronic pain usually involves a combination of physical and psychological techniques (Person & Taylor, 2002; Watkins & Maier, 2000). A pain clinic may select one or more of the following techniques to treat an individual's pain: surgery, drugs, acupuncture, electrical stimulation, massage, exercise, hypnosis, relaxation, or thought distraction (Ezzo & others, 2001; Haythronthwaite, Lawrence, & Fauerbach, 2001).

Chemical Senses

The information impinging on our senses comes in diverse forms: electromagnetic energy in vision, sound waves in audition, and mechanical pressure and temperature in the skin senses. The two senses presented in this section are responsible for processing chemicals in our environment (Doty, 2001). With the sense of smell, we detect airborne chemicals, and with taste we detect chemicals that have been dissolved in saliva.

Taste and smell are frequently stimulated simultaneously. We sometimes realize the strong links between the two senses only when a nasty cold and nasal congestion take the pleasure out of eating. Our favorite foods become "tasteless" without the smells that characterize them. Despite this link, taste and smell are, indeed, two distinct systems.

Taste   We use our sense of taste to select food and to regulate food intake. Although mold on a blueberry may be hard to see or smell, a small taste is enough to sense that the fruit is no longer fit for consumption. Beyond fitness, the thought of giving up a favorite taste, such as chocolate or butter, can be very depressing. But the pleasure associated with the taste of food depends on our body's need for a particular food at a particular time (Bartoshuk & Beauchamp, 1994). The taste of devil's food cake can be very pleasurable when we are hungry but downright revolting after eating a banana split.

Many animals have a stronger sense of smell than humans do. Dogs especially have a powerful olfactory sense. Watson, a Labrador retriever, reliably paws his owner 45 minutes before her epileptic seizures begin, giving her time to move to a safe place. How does Watson do this? The best hypothesis is that the dog smells the chemical changes known to precede epileptic seizures. *Why might dogs have developed such a strong sense of smell?*

It is not a pretty sight, but try this anyway: Take a drink of milk and allow it to coat your tongue. Then go to a mirror, stick out your tongue, and look carefully at its surface. You should be able to see rounded bumps. Those bumps, called **papillae,** contain taste buds, which are the receptors for taste. About 10,000 of these taste buds are located on your tongue. As with all of the other sensory systems discussed in this chapter, the information picked up by these receptors is transmitted to the brain for analysis and, when necessary, response (spitting something out, for example).

The taste qualities we respond to can be categorized as sweet, sour, bitter, and salty (Scott, 2000). Though all areas of the tongue can detect each of the four tastes, different regions of the tongue are more sensitive to some tastes than others (Temple & others, 2002). The tip of the tongue is the most sensitive to sweet and salty substances, the sides to sour, and the rear to bitter (see figure 4.28) (Bloom & others, 2001).

Today, many neuroscientists believe that the breakdown of taste into four independent, elementary categories is oversimplified (Cauller, 2001). The taste fibers leading from a taste bud to the brain often respond strongly to a range of chemicals that span multiple taste elements, such as salty and sour (Smith & Margolskee, 2001). The brain processes these somewhat ambiguous incoming signals and integrates them into a perception of taste. Go to the interactivity "Taste" to see an animation of the sensory and perceptual processes involved in taste.

Although people still often categorize taste sensations along the four dimensions of sweet, bitter, salty, and sour, our tasting ability goes far beyond them. Wine lovers frequently use terms—such as "grassy" or "smoky"—that do not fall neatly into these categories, for example, and most of us pride ourselves on being able to distinguish among different brands of ice cream or sodas. Think of the remarkable range of tastes you encounter that are not clearly sweet, sour, bitter, or salty.

Smell   To understand the importance of smell, think about animals with more sophisticated senses of smell than our own. A dog, for example, can use its sense of smell to find its way back from a lone stroll, to distinguish friend from foe, or even (with practice) to detect illegal drugs concealed in a suitcase. In fact, dogs can detect odors in concentrations 100 times lower than those detectable by humans.

Given the nasal feats of the average dog, we might be tempted to believe that the sense of smell has outlived its usefulness in humans. What do we use smell for? For

In-Psych Plus

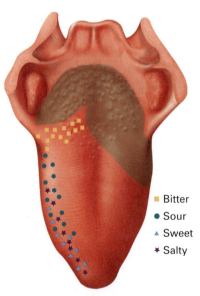

■ Bitter
● Sour
▲ Sweet
✶ Salty

FIGURE 4.28 Locations on the Tongue of Sensitivity to Sweet, Salty, Sour, and Bitter Substances

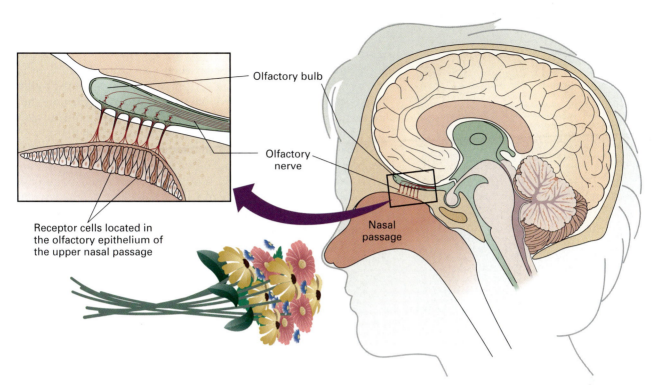

Olfactory bulb

Olfactory nerve

Receptor cells located in the olfactory epithelium of the upper nasal passage

Nasal passage

FIGURE 4.29 Olfactory Sense
Airborne molecules of an odor reach tiny receptor cells in the roof of the nasal cavity. The receptor cells form a mucus-covered membrane called the olfactory epithelium. Then the olfactory nerve carries information about the odor to the brain for further processing.

one thing, humans need the sense of smell to decide what to eat. We can distinguish rotten food from fresh food, and the smell of a food that has previously made us ill is often, by itself, enough to make us feel nauseated. Second, humans are competent odor trackers. We can follow the smell of gas to a leak, the smell of smoke to a fire, or the smell of a hot apple pie to a kitchen counter.

Just as the eyes scan the visual field for objects of interest and the pinnae prick up to direct attention to sounds of interest, the nose actively participates in smelling. The **olfactory epithelium,** lining the roof of the nasal cavity, contains a sheet of receptor cells for smell (see figure 4.29), so sniffing has the effect of maximizing the chances of detecting an odor. The receptor cells are covered with millions of minute, hairlike antennae that project through the mucus in the top of the nasal cavity and make contact with air on its way to the throat and lungs (Laurent & others, 2001; Yau, 2002). Interestingly, unlike the neurons of most sensory systems, the neurons in the olfactory epithelium tend to replace themselves after injury (Doty, 2001).

Although all other sensory pathways pass through the thalamus, the pathway for smell does not. In smell, the neural pathway first goes to the olfactory areas of the cerebral cortex in the temporal lobes. Then it projects to various brain regions, especially the limbic system, which is involved in emotion and memory. Indeed, for many people, smells have a way of generating memories—often emotion-laden ones—undoubtedly because of these neural pathways (Bloom & others, 2001). See the interactivity "Olfaction" for an animation of how the olfactory sense works.

Kinesthetic and Vestibular Senses

To perform even the simplest acts of motor coordination, such as reaching out to take a book off a shelf or getting up out of a chair, the brain must be constantly receiving and coordinating information from every part of the body. Your body has two kinds of senses that provide information about movement: The **kinesthetic senses** provide information about movement, posture, and orientation. The **vestibular sense** provides information about balance and movement.

In-Psych Plus

papillae Bumps on the tongue that contain taste buds, the receptors for taste.

olfactory epithelium A sheet of receptor cells for smell, located in the roof of the nasal cavity.

kinesthetic senses Provide information about movement, posture, and orientation.

vestibular sense Provides information about balance and movement.

FIGURE 4.30 Semicircular Canals and Vestibular Sense The semicircular canals provide feedback to this gymnast's brain as her body and head tilt in different directions. *(Inset)* The semicircular canals of the inner ear. The three canals are roughly perpendicular to each other in the three planes of space. Any angle of head rotation is registered by hair cells in one or more canals in both ears.

semicircular canals Channels containing sensory receptors that detect head position and motion, located in the inner ear.

No specific organ contains the *kinesthetic senses;* they are embedded in muscle fibers and joints. As we stretch and move, these receptors signal the state of the muscle. Kinesthesia is a sense that you often do not even notice until it is gone. Try walking when your leg is "asleep," or smiling (never mind talking) when you've just come from a dentist's office and you are still under the effects of anesthesia. Most information about the kinesthetic sense is transmitted from the joints and muscles along the same pathways to the brain as information about touch.

Perhaps the sophistication of kinesthesis can be best appreciated when we think in terms of memory. Even a mediocre typist can bang out 20 words per minute—but how many of us could write down the order of the letters on a keyboard without looking? Typing is a skill that relies on very coordinated sensitivity to the orientation, position, and movements of our fingers. We say that our fingers remember the positions of the keys. Likewise, the complicated movements a pitcher uses to throw a ball cannot be written down or communicated easily using language. They involve nearly every muscle and joint in the body.

The *vestibular sense* tells us whether our head (and, hence, usually our body) is tilted, moving, slowing down, or speeding up. It works in concert with the kinesthetic senses to coordinate feedback about the position of our limbs and body parts in relation to other body parts. Consider the combination of sensory abilities involved in the motion of an ice hockey player skating down the ice, cradling the puck and pushing it forward with the hockey stick. The hockey player is responding simultaneously to a multitude of sensations, including those produced by the slickness of the ice, the position of the puck, the speed and momentum of the forward progression, and the requirements of the play to turn and to track the other players on the ice.

The **semicircular canals,** located in the inner ear, contain the sensory receptors that detect head motion caused when we tilt or move our heads or bodies (see figure 4.30). These canals consist of three fluid-filled, circular tubes that lie in the three planes of the body—right-left, front-back, and up-down. We can picture these as three intersecting hula hoops. As you move your head, the fluid of the semicircular canals flows in different directions and, depending on the force of the head movement, at different speeds. Our perception of head movement and position is determined by the movements of these receptor cells. This ingenious system of using the motion of fluid in tubes to sense head position is not unlike the auditory system found in the inner ear. However, the fluid in the cochlea responds to the pressure that sound exerts on the oval window, whereas the movements in the semicircular canals reflect physical movements of the head and body. And just as the hair cells in the cochlea trigger hearing impulses in the brain, the hair cells in the semicircular canals are involved in transmitting information about balance and movement.

The brain pathways for the vestibular sense begin in the auditory nerve, which contains both the cochlear nerve (with information about sound) and the vestibular nerve (which has information about balance and movement). Most of the axons of the vestibular nerve connect with the medulla, although some go directly to the cerebellum. There also appear to be vestibular projections to the temporal cortex, although their specific pathways have not been fully charted. Most neuroscientists believe that the projections to the cerebral cortex are responsible for dizziness, whereas the connections to the lower brain stem produce the nausea and vomiting that accompany motion sickness (Carlson, 2001).

Information from the kinesthetic and vestibular senses is supplemented by information from vision. This simple principle has made many an amusement park and large-screen movie theater profitable. When films are shown on screens that are large enough to fill our visual field, such as those found in many theme parks, the

© King Features. Reprinted with special permission of King Features Syndicate.

motion you perceive on the screen can make you feel like you are moving. This is the same principle that causes a motorist to slam on the brakes in his tiny sports car when the big truck next to him starts to move forward. Experience has led us to expect that, when everything in our visual field appears to be moving, it is because we are moving.

Review and Sharpen Your Thinking

4 *Know how the skin, chemical, kinesthetic, and vestibular senses work.*

- Explain how the skin monitors touch, temperature, and pain.
- Discuss the chemical senses of taste and smell.
- Describe how the kinesthetic and vestibular senses function.

Why can some individuals stand more pain than others?

1 HOW WE SENSE AND PERCEIVE THE WORLD

The Purpose of Sensation and Perception

Thresholds

Attention and Predisposition

Sensory Receptors and the Brain

Sensory Adaptation

2 VISUAL SYSTEM

Visual Stimuli and the Eye

Color Vision

Visual Processing in the Brain

Visual Perceptions of Dimension

Sensation and Perception

3 AUDITORY SYSTEM

How We Experience Sound

Auditory Processing in the Brain

Structures and Functions of the Ear

Auditory Perceptions of Location

4 OTHER SENSES

Skin Senses

Chemical Senses

Kinesthetic and Vestibular Senses

Discuss the basic principles of sensation and perception.

- Sensation is the process of receiving stimulus energies from the environment. Perception is the process of organizing and interpreting sensory information to give it meaning. Together sensation and perception give an organism a representation of the outside world and help it adapt to its habitat.
- All sensation begins with sensory receptors, which are specialized cells that detect and transmit information about a stimulus to sensory neurons and the brain. Sensory receptors are selective and have different neural pathways. The three main classes of sense organs and receptors are photoreception, mechanoreception, and chemoreception.
- Absolute threshold is the minimum amount of energy that an individual can detect. The difference threshold, or just noticeable difference, is the smallest difference in stimulation required to discriminate one stimulus from another 50 percent of the time. There is no evidence that subliminal perception—the ability to detect information below the level of conscious awareness—has any substantial influence on our thoughts and behavior.
- Sensory adaptation is a change in the responsiveness of the sensory system based on the average level of surrounding stimulation.
- What we perceive depends in part on which stimuli engage our attention and on a tendency to perceive things according to our beliefs and expectations. Selective attention involves focusing on a specific aspect of experience while ignoring others. A perceptual set is a collection of experiences and expectations that influence perception.

2 Explain how the visual system enables us to see and, by communicating with the brain, to perceive the world.

- Light is a form of electromagnetic energy that can be described in terms of wavelengths. Three characteristics of light are hue, amplitude, and purity. The eye responds to light within a narrow range of wavelengths (400–700 nm). Light passes through the cornea and lens to the retina, a light-sensitive surface in the back of the eye that houses light receptors called rods (which function in low illumination) and cones (which react to color). The fovea of the retina contains only cones and sharpens detail in an image. Incoming visual information is converted to neural impulses and sent to the brain.
- The optic nerve transmits neural impulses to the brain. What we see in the left visual field is registered in the right side of the brain and vice versa. In the occipital

lobes of the cerebral cortex, the information is integrated. Visual information processing involves feature detection, parallel processing, and binding.
- The trichromatic theory of color perception stipulates that three types of color receptors in the retina allow us to perceive three colors (green, red, and blue). The opponent-process theory states that cells in the visual system respond to red-green and blue-yellow colors. Both theories seem to be correct—the eye and the brain use both methods to code colors.
- Shape perception is the ability to distinguish objects from their background. This figure-ground relationship is a principle of gestalt psychology, which emphasizes that people naturally organize their perceptions according to patterns. Depth perception is the ability to perceive objects three-dimensionally; it depends on both binocular cues and monocular cues. Motion perception by humans depends on specialized neurons, feedback from the body, and environmental cues. Perceptual constancy is the recognition that objects are stable despite changes in the way we see them. Three types of perceptual constancy are size constancy, shape constancy, and brightness constancy.

3 Understand how the auditory system registers sound and how it connects with the brain to perceive sound.

- Sounds, or sound waves, are vibrations in the air that are processed by the auditory system. Sound waves vary in wavelength. Wavelength determines frequency. Pitch is the perceptual interpretation of frequency. Loudness, measured in decibels, is the perceptual interpretation of amplitude. Complexity is the blending of frequencies in a sound. Timbre is the perceptual complexity, or tone saturation, of a sound.
- The outer ear, consisting of the pinna and external auditory canal, funnels sound to the middle ear. In the middle ear, the eardrum, hammer, anvil, and stirrup vibrate in response to sound and transfer the vibrations to the inner ear. Important parts of the fluid-filled inner ear are the oval window, cochlea, and basilar membrane. The movement of hair cells lining the basilar membrane generates nerve impulses. The inner ear registers high-frequency sounds through their stimulation of precise areas on the basilar membrane and their causing the auditory nerve to fire often. Registration of low-frequency sounds, which stimulate a large area of the basilar membrane and cause the auditory nerve to fire less often, depends on combined neurons firing in a rapid volley.
- Information about sound moves from the hair cells of the basilar membrane to the auditory nerve, which carries information to the brain's auditory areas. The cortical

destination of most fibers is the temporal lobes of the cerebral cortex.

- Localizing sound involves both the timing of the sound and the intensity of the sound arriving at each ear.

4 ***Know how the skin, chemical, kinesthetic, and vestibular senses work.***

- Touch is the detection of mechanical energy, or pressure, against the skin. Touch information travels through the spinal cord, brain stem, and thalamus and on to the somatosensory areas of the parietal lobes. Thermoreceptors under the skin respond to increases and decreases in temperature. Pain is the sensation that warns us about damage to our bodies. Two different neural pathways transmit information about pain: a fast pathway and a slow pathway. Neurotransmitters called endorphins appear to be involved in turning pain signals on and off, mainly in the synapses of the slow pathway.

- Taste and smell enable us to detect and process chemicals in the environment. Papillae are bumps on the tongue that contain taste buds, the receptors for taste. The taste qualities we respond to are categorized as sweet, sour, bitter, and salty, although our tasting ability goes beyond these four qualities. The olfactory epithelium in the roof of the nose contains a sheet of receptor cells for smell.

- The kinesthetic senses provide information about movement, posture, and orientation. The vestibular sense provides information about balance and movement. Receptors for the kinesthetic senses are embedded in muscle fibers and joints. The semicircular canals in the inner ear contain the sensory receptors that detect head, and accompanying body, position and motion.

Key Terms

Apply Your Knowledge

1. Test partner's absolute threshold for sugar. On your own, set up the following sugar-and-water mixtures. Mix 2 teaspoons of sugar in 4 cups of water; label this solution ("solution X," for example). Take 2 cups of "solution X," add 2 cups of water, and give this solution a second label ("solution D," for example). Then, take 2 cups of "solution D," add 2 cups of water, and give this a third label ("solution Q"). Continue taking 2 cups from each successive solution until there is a total of 8 solutions, making sure to keep track of which solution is which. When you're done, the concentration of the solutions should be equivalent to 1 teaspoon in each of the following amounts of water: 1 pint (2 cups), 1 quart, 1 half-gallon, 1 gallon, 2 gallons, 4 gallons, and 8 gallons. Place a sample of one of the solutions in a cup and a sample of plain water in another, identical cup. Your partner's job is to taste the solution in each cup and decide which one is the sugar solution. Do this with all the solutions until your partner can pinpoint an absolute threshold according to the definition in the chapter. Do you think the absolute threshold will vary, depending on what your partner has recently eaten? Why or why not?

2. Imagine that you have two sets of dominoes. Each set contains 100 dominoes. With the first set, you make a straight line of 100. With the second set, you make an arrangement in which tipping a single domino causes five separate lines of dominoes to fall down simultaneously. Which set of dominoes will fall the fastest? How is the action of the second set of dominoes similar to the way we process visual information?

3. Compare and contrast the consequences of losing vision in one eye versus losing hearing in one ear.

4. You smell a delicious aroma coming from the kitchen, so you head that way. But you manage to stub your toe on your roommate's backpack and then hit your head on the table as you bend down to rub your toe. Your roommate hands you what looks like a brownie; it smells pretty good, so you take a big bite. First it tastes good; then suddenly your mouth feels as if it is on fire. You grab the glass of ice water sitting on the table and take a big gulp of it. Describe the different kinds of sensory signals that your brain has processed during this episode and the different kinds of receptors you have used to make sense of what's happened.

Connections

To test your mastery of the material in this chapter, go to the Study Guide and the In-Psych Plus CD-ROM, as well as the Online Learning Center. There you will find a chapter summary, practice tests, flashcards, lecture slides, web links, and other study tools, such as interactive exercises and reviews as well as current, chapter-relevant news articles.

5
States of Consciousness

Chapter Outline

Learning Goals

THE NATURE OF CONSCIOUSNESS

1 *Discuss the nature of consciousness.*

Levels of Awareness

▼

Consciousness and the Brain

SLEEP AND DREAMS

2 *Explain the nature of sleep and dreams.*

Biological Rhythms and Sleep

▼

The Need for Sleep

▼

Sleep Stages

▼

Sleep Disorders

▼

Dreams

HYPNOSIS

3 *Describe hypnosis.*

The Nature of Hypnosis

▼

Explanations of Hypnosis

▼

Applications of Hypnosis

PSYCHOACTIVE DRUGS

4 *Evaluate the uses and types of psychoactive drugs.*

Uses of Psychoactive Drugs

▼

Depressants

▼

Stimulants

▼

Hallucinogens

Frank Offner was a twentieth-century American electrical engineer and inventor. A highly creative individual, he developed electrical controls that eventually made jet planes possible. He also invented numerous medical devices. His invention of medical instrumentation made possible the electrocardiogram (ECG) for measuring cardiovascular functioning and the electroencephalogram (EEG) for measuring brain activity.

Offner said that unique ideas for inventions often came to him in the middle of the night. When Offner was trying to figure out the topic for his Ph.D. dissertation, a new formula for explaining how nerve excitation works came to him while he was taking a shower. Many creative ideas emerge while people are relaxed and are not focusing attention on a particular problem or project. In other words, taking a break from consciously trying to generate ideas may allow ideas to develop spontaneously (Csikszentmihalyi, 1995).

Sleep and relaxation represent different levels of awareness, or consciousness. In this chapter, I discuss several states of consciousness that differ from the waking state. First, I explore the nature of consciousness itself, one of modern psychology's most intriguing topics. Second, I delve into the realm of sleep and dreams, in which most of us spend a great deal of time, and, third, into the mysterious and controversial topic of hypnosis. Fourth, I discuss the altered state of consciousness produced by psychoactive drugs and some of the reasons that people become addicted to them.

1 THE NATURE OF CONSCIOUSNESS

Levels of Awareness   **Consciousness and the Brain**

What is consciousness?

In the late nineteenth and early twentieth centuries, psychology pioneers such as Sigmund Freud and William James took great interest in the study of the conscious and unconscious mind. However, for much of the twentieth century, psychologists shunned the slippery, subjective trappings of consciousness and unconsciousness. Instead, they focused on behaviors and the rewards and punishments that determined those behaviors (Skinner, 1938; Watson, 1913). In the past decade, though, the study of consciousness has gained widespread respectability in psychology (Baars, 1999). And, for the first time in many decades, psychologists from many different fields are interested in consciousness, including its relation to subconsciousness (Blakemore, 2004; Hebb, 2002; Lehar, 2002; Schacter, 1999).

Although psychologists still disagree about how consciousness should be defined, here I define **consciousness** as awareness of external events and internal sensations, including awareness of the self and thoughts about your experiences. Externally, you might be aware that your best friend just cracked a joke about his latest body piercing, that the car in front of you just swerved to miss a dog, and that your sunglasses fell off your nose as you leapt back to the curb. Internally, you might be aware that your headache just returned, that you are breathing too fast, that your stomach is rumbling because you missed breakfast, and that you are relieved the weekend is almost here.

The contents of our awareness change from moment to moment. Information moves rapidly in and out of consciousness. William James (1890/1950) described the mind as a **stream of consciousness**—a continuous flow of changing sensations, images, thoughts, and feelings. Our minds can race from one topic to the next—from thinking about who is approaching us to how well we feel to what we are going to do tomorrow to where we are going to lunch and so on.

consciousness Awareness of external events and internal sensations, including awareness of the self and thoughts about one's experiences.

stream of consciousness James' concept that the mind is a continuous flow of sensations, images, thoughts, and feelings.

Level of Awareness	Description		
Higher-Level Consciousness	Involves controlled processing, in which individuals actively focus their efforts on attaining a goal; the most alert state of consciousness		This student is using controlled processes that require focused concentration.
Lower-Level Awareness	Includes automatic processing that requires little attention, as well as daydreaming		This woman is an experienced computer operator. Her maneuvers with the keyboard are automatic, requiring minimal awareness.
Altered States of Consciousness	Can be produced by drugs, trauma, fatigue, possibly hypnosis, and sensory deprivation		These people, who are drinking alcohol, are in an altered state of consciousness.
Subconscious Awareness	Can occur when people are awake, as well as when they are sleeping and dreaming		All of us dream while we sleep, but some of us dream more than others.
No Awareness	Freud's belief that some unconscious thoughts are too laden with anxiety and other negative emotions for consciousness to admit them		The woman on the couch is undergoing psychoanalytic therapy to reveal her unconscious thoughts.

FIGURE 5.1 Levels of Awareness

Levels of Awareness

The flow of sensations, images, thoughts, and feelings that James spoke of can occur at different levels of awareness. I discuss five levels of awareness here: higher-level consciousness, lower-level awareness, altered states of consciousness, subconscious awareness, and no awareness (see figure 5.1).

Higher-Level Consciousness **Controlled processes** represent the most alert states of human consciousness, in which individuals actively focus their efforts toward a goal (Cooper & others, 2002; Monsell & Driver, 2000). Watch Maria as she struggles to master the unfamiliar buttons on her new 10-function cell phone. She doesn't hear you humming to yourself or notice the intriguing shadow on the wall. Her state of focused awareness is what is meant by *controlled processes*. Controlled processes require *selective attention,* the ability to focus on a specific aspect of experience while ignoring others.

Lower-Level Awareness A few weeks after acquiring her cell phone, Maria flips it open and, in the middle of a conversation with you, places a call. Her fingers fly almost automatically across the buttons. She doesn't have to concentrate on dialing now and hardly seems aware of the gadget against her cheek as she continues to talk on it while finishing her lunch. For her, cell phone dialing has become automatic.

Automatic processes are states of consciousness that require minimal attention and do not interfere with other ongoing activities. Automatic processes require less conscious effort than controlled processes (Trainor, McDonald, & Alain, 2002). When we are awake, our automatic behaviors occur at a lower level of awareness than controlled processes, but they are still conscious behaviors. Maria pushed the right buttons, so she was aware of what she was doing at some level.

controlled processes Cognitive activity at the most alert state of consciousness.

automatic processes States of consciousness that require little attention and do not interfere with other ongoing activities.

"If you ask me, all three of us are in different states of awareness."

Another state of lower-level awareness is *daydreaming*, which lies somewhere between active consciousness and dreaming while asleep. Daydreams usually begin spontaneously when we are doing something that requires less than our full attention. When we daydream, we often drift into a world of fantasy. We imagine ourselves on dates, at parties, on television, in faraway places, at another time in our lives, and so on. Sometimes our daydreams are about ordinary, everyday events, such as paying the rent, getting our hair done, or dealing with somebody at work. The semiautomatic flow of daydreaming can be useful: While we are doing something else, we can make plans, solve a problem, or come up with a creative idea. Daydreams can remind us of important things ahead. Daydreaming keeps our minds active while helping us to cope, create, and fantasize (Klinger, 2000).

Altered States of Consciousness *Altered states of consciousness* are mental states that are noticeably different from normal awareness. They can be produced by drugs, trauma, fatigue, possibly hypnosis, and sensory deprivation. In some cases, drug use may create a higher level of awareness. The popularity of coffee and other beverages that contain caffeine, a stimulant drug, provides evidence of the widespread belief that caffeine increases alertness. Awareness also may be altered to a lower level. Alcohol has this effect. Later in the chapter, I discuss drugs as well as hypnosis.

Subconscious Awareness Psychologists are increasingly interested in the subconscious processing of information, which can take place while we are awake or while we are asleep (Damasio, 2001). According to creativity expert Mihaly Csikszentmihalyi (1995), insights such as those developed by inventor Frank Offner likely occur when a subconscious connection between ideas is so strong that it is forced to "pop out" into awareness, somewhat the way a cork held underwater bobs to the surface as soon as it is released. Csikszentmihalyi believes that creative ideas often "incubate" for some time below the threshold of conscious awareness before they emerge. When an idea is incubating, our minds may be processing information even though we are not aware of it.

Evidence that we are not always aware of the processing of information in our brains, even while awake, comes from studies of individuals with certain neurological disorders. In one case, a woman who suffered neurological damage was unable to describe or report the shape or size of objects in her visual field, although she was capable of describing other physical perceptions that she had (Milner & Goodale, 1995). And when she reached for an object, she could accurately adjust the size of her grip to allow her to grasp the object. Thus she did possess some subconscious knowledge of the size and shape of objects, even though she had no awareness of this knowledge.

Subconscious information processing can occur simultaneously along many parallel tracks. (Recall the discussion of parallel processing of sensory information in chapter 4.) For example, when you look at a dog running down the street, you are consciously aware of the event but not of the subconscious processing of the object's identity (a dog), its color (black), its movement (fast), and so on. In contrast, conscious processing is *serial*. That is, it occurs in sequence and is slower than much subconscious processing.

Sleep and dreams should also be viewed as low levels of consciousness, even though our level of awareness is lower than when we daydream (Schredl & Hofman, 2003). Consider the German chemist August Kekule, who in 1865 developed the insight that the benzene molecule might be shaped like a ring after he fell asleep while watching sparks in the fireplace make circles in the air. If he had remained awake, Kekule might have rejected the idea that the sparks and the shape of the benzene molecule could be linked. However, in his subconscious mind, rational thought could not censor the connection, so when Kekule woke up he did not ignore its possibility (Csikszentmihalyi, 1995).

Researchers have also found that when people are asleep they remain aware of external stimuli to some degree. For example, in sleep laboratories, when people are clearly asleep (as determined by physiological monitoring devices), they are able to respond to faint tones by pressing a handheld button (Ogilvie & Wilkinson, 1988). In another study, the presentation of pure auditory tones to sleeping individuals activated auditory processing regions of the brain, whereas participants' names activated language areas, the amygdala, and the prefrontal cortex (Stickgold, 2001). Sleep and dreams are covered more thoroughly in the next section.

No Awareness   The term *unconscious* is generally applied to someone who has been knocked out by a blow, has been anesthetized, or has fallen into a deep, prolonged unconscious state. However, Sigmund Freud (1917) used the term *unconscious* in a very different way. **Unconscious thought,** said Freud, is a reservoir of unacceptable wishes, feelings, and thoughts that are beyond conscious awareness.

According to Freud, unconscious thoughts are too laden with anxiety and other negative emotions for consciousness to admit them. For example, if a young man breaks into a cold sweat when a woman approaches him, he might be unconscious that his fear of women springs from the punitive way his mother treated him. Freud believed that one of psychotherapy's main goals was to bring unconscious thoughts into conscious awareness so they could be addressed.

Freud's concept of the unconscious mind, especially its pervasiveness, is controversial. Whether or not we accept his view of the unconscious mind, we owe a debt to Freud for recognizing the complexity of consciousness.

Consciousness and the Brain

One of the great unanswered questions about consciousness involves its location. Does consciousness stand alone (located in what might be called the *mind*), separate in some way from the brain, or is it an intrinsic aspect of the brain's functioning? If consciousness is in the brain, is a particular location the seat of consciousness, or is consciousness distributed across different areas of the brain?

Most neuroscientists do not believe that a specific location in the brain takes incoming information and converts it into the conscious world that we can report on. Rather, it seems likely that a number of separate processing systems connect to produce consciousness. Depending on what a person is aware of at a particular time, different areas of the brain are activated (Alkire, Haier, & James, 1998; Kosslyn, 1994). It may be that the integration of information from the senses, along with information about emotions and memories in the association areas of the cerebral cortex, creates consciousness (Bloom, Nelson, & Lazerson, 2001). See the video clip "Sensory Processes and Brain Integration" for an explanation of how the brain brings together incoming information and produces conscious experience.

Among those who practice altered states of consciousness for religious reasons are *(top)* Zen monks, who explore the Buddha-nature at the center of their beings, and *(bottom)* Muslims in Pakistan, who fast from dawn to dusk during the month of Ramadan. *What are some other ways in which altered states of consciousness might be involved in religion?*

In-Psych Plus

Review and Sharpen Your Thinking

1   *Discuss the nature of consciousness.*
   - Define consciousness and describe five levels of awareness.
   - Explain the brain's role in consciousness.

How many different states of awareness have you experienced? In one or two sentences, describe the nature of your experience in each state.

unconscious thought Freud's concept of a reservoir of unacceptable wishes, feelings, and thoughts that are beyond conscious awareness.

2 SLEEP AND DREAMS

Biological Rhythms and Sleep	Sleep Stages	Dreams

The Need For Sleep	Sleep Disorders

What is the nature of sleep and dreams?

Sleep claims about one-third of the time in our lives, more than any other pursuit. But many of us are not getting enough sleep to function optimally. What is sleep and why is it so important? This section explores the answers to these questions, as well as the fascinating world of dreams.

Biological Rhythms and Sleep

Biological rhythms are periodic physiological fluctuations in the body. We are unaware of most biological rhythms, such as the rise and fall of hormones in the bloodstream, accelerated and decelerated cycles of brain activity, and highs and lows in body temperature, but they can influence our behavior. These rhythms are controlled by *biological clocks,* which include the following:

- *Annual or seasonal cycles,* such the migration of birds, the hibernation of bears, and the seasonal fluctuations of humans' eating habits
- *Twenty-eight-day cycles,* such as the female menstrual cycle
- *Twenty-four-hour cycles,* including the sleep/wake cycle and changes in body temperature, blood pressure, and blood sugar level

The 24-hour cycles are referred to as **circadian rhythms,** daily behavioral or physiological cycles (Homma & others, 2003; Van Gelder & others, 2003). The term *circadian* comes from the Latin words *circa,* meaning "about," and *dies,* meaning "day." For example, body temperature fluctuates about 3° Fahrenheit in a 24-hour day, peaking in the afternoon and reaching its lowest point between 2 A.M. and 5 A.M.

Researchers have discovered that the change from day to night is monitored by a small structure in the brain that synchronizes its own rhythm with the daily cycle of light and dark, based on input from the retina (Zisapel, 2001). Many individuals who are totally blind experience lifelong sleeping problems because their retinas are unable to detect light (National Institute of Neurological Disorders and Stroke, 2001).

Desynchronizing the Biological Clock Biological clocks can become desynchronized, or thrown off their regular schedules (Jensen & others, 2003). For instance, if you fly from Los Angeles to New York and then go to bed at 11 P.M. Eastern Standard Time, you may have trouble falling asleep because your body is still on Pacific Time. Even if you sleep for 8 hours that night, you may have a hard time waking up at 7 A.M. Eastern Time, because your body thinks it is 4 A.M. If you stay in New York for several days, your body will adjust to this new schedule.

The jet lag you experienced when you flew from Los Angeles to New York occurred because two or more body rhythms were out of sync. You usually go to bed when your body temperature begins to drop, but, in your new location, you might be trying to go to sleep when it is rising. In the morning, your adrenal glands release large doses of the hormone *cortisol* to help you wake up. In your new geographical time zone, the glands may be releasing this chemical just as you are getting ready for bed at night.

Circadian rhythms may also become desynchronized when shift workers change their work hours (Ahasan & others, 2001). A number of near accidents in air travel

biological rhythms Periodic physiological fluctuations in the body.

circadian rhythms Daily behavioral or physiological cycles, such as the sleep/wake cycle.

have been associated with pilots who have not yet become synchronized to their new shifts and are not working as efficiently as usual. Shift rotation also may have been one of the causes of the nuclear accident at Three Mile Island in 1979 (Moore-Ede, Sulzman, & Fuller, 1982). The team of workers monitoring the nuclear plant when the accident took place had been placed on the night shift just after a 6-week period of constant shift rotation.

Shift-work problems most often affect night-shift workers who never fully adjust to sleeping in the daytime. They may fall asleep at work and are at increased risk for heart disease and gastrointestinal disorders (Quinlin, Mayhew, & Bohle, 2001). Not all shift workers are affected equally, though (Garbarino & others, 2002; Monk, 1993). A small portion actually prefer shift work. Individuals older than 50, those who require more than 9 hours of sleep a night, or those with a tendency to be "morning types" (get up early, go to bed early) are the most adversely affected by shift work.

Resetting the Biological Clock If your biological clock for sleeping and waking becomes desynchronized, how can you reset it? With regard to jet lag, if you arrive at your destination during the day, it is a good idea to spend as much time outside in the daylight as possible. Bright light during the day, especially in the morning, increases wakefulness, whereas bright light at night delays sleep (Oren & Terman, 1998).

Melatonin, a hormone that increases at night in humans, also is being studied for its possible effects in reducing jet lag (Sharkey & Eastman, 2002). A number of recent studies have shown that a small dosage of melatonin can reduce jet lag by advancing the circadian clock, which makes it useful for eastward jet lag but not westward jet lag (Herxheimer & Petrie, 2001; Suhner & others, 2001). Note, however, that, although melatonin is available over the counter, the quality of the drug may vary. Further, the potential side effects of melatonin are still largely unknown, and negative long-term effects have not yet been adequately studied (National Institute of Neurological Disorders and Stroke, 2001).

Strategies for shift workers who need to reset their biological clocks include splitting sleep between after-work morning naps and before-work late-afternoon naps to increase the number of hours of sleep, increasing the amount of light in the workplace, and going to sleep in complete darkness. Sedatives do not affect circadian realignment, and their long-term use is inadvisable for shift workers.

The Need for Sleep

Everyone sleeps, and when we do not get enough sleep, we often do not function well, physically or mentally. Sleep has four important benefits:

- *Restoration.* Because all animals require sleep, it seems that sleep is a fundamental mechanism for survival. Examining the evolutionary basis for sleep, scientists have proposed that sleep restores, replenishes, and rebuilds our brains and bodies, which can feel depleted by the day's waking activities. This idea fits with the feeling of being "worn out" before we go to sleep and feeling "restored" when we wake up. Many of the body's cells do, indeed, show increased production and reduced breakdown of proteins during deep sleep (National Institute of Neurological Disorders and Stroke, 2001). Protein molecules are the building blocks needed for cell growth and for repair of damages from factors such as stress. Also, some neuroscientists believe that sleep gives neurons that are used while we are awake a chance to shut down and repair themselves (National Institute of Neurological Disorders and Stroke, 2001).

- *Adaptation.* Sleep may also have developed because animals need to protect themselves. For example, for some animals the search for food and water

A person's biological clock is typically desynchronized by abrupt changes in the sleep/wake cycle, as occur during major changes in work shifts and long-distance air travel. *How can the biological clock be reset to minimize the ill effects of too little sleep?*

is easier in the day, when the sun is out. When it is dark, it is adaptive for these animals to save energy, avoid getting eaten, and avoid falling off a cliff that they cannot see. In general, animals that serve as food for other animals sleep the least. Figure 5.2 portrays the average amount of sleep per day of several animals.

- *Growth.* Sleep may be beneficial to physical growth and brain development in infants and children. For example, deep sleep coincides with the release of growth hormone in children (National Institute of Neurological Disorders and Stroke, 2001).
- *Memory.* Sleep is now thought to play an important role in the storage and maintenance of long-term memory. REM ("active") sleep has been linked with the formation of emotional memories in humans (Wagner, Gais, & Born, 2001). One possible explanation is that during sleep the cerebral cortex is not busy with processing sensory input, active awareness, and motor functions. Therefore, it is free to integrate memories formed during recent waking hours into long-term memory storage. Thus, if you are thinking about studying all night for the next test in one of your classes, you might want to think again. In one study, a good night's sleep helped the brain to store the memory of what had been learned during the day (Stickgold & Hobson, 2000). The individuals who stayed up all night on one of the nights during the study could not remember as well as the individuals who got a good night's sleep every night during the study. Lost sleep often results in lost memories.

Effects of Chronic Sleep Deprivation In a national survey of more than 1,000 American adults, conducted by the National Sleep Foundation (2001), 63 percent said that they get less than 8 hours of sleep a night, and 31 percent said that they get less than 7 hours of sleep a night. Many said they try to catch up on their sleep on the weekend, but they still reported getting less than 8 hours on weekend nights. Forty percent of those surveyed said that they become so sleepy during the day that their work suffers at least a few days per month, and 22 percent said their work suffers a few days each week. Seven percent said sleepiness on the job is a daily problem for them.

Testing the limits of his capacity to function without sleep, one 17-year-old high school student, Randy Gardner, went without sleep for 264 hours (about 11 days), the longest observed period of total sleep deprivation. He did it as part of a science fair project (Dement, 1978). Randy, who was carefully monitored by sleep researchers, did suffer some hallucinations, as well as speech and movement problems. However, on the last night, Gardner played arcade games with sleep researcher William Dement and consistently beat him. Randy recovered fully, as well as could be detected, after a 14-hour, 40-minute restorative sleep. Randy's story is exceptional in that he was able to maintain a high level of physical activity and in that he received

FIGURE 5.2 Sleep in Animals

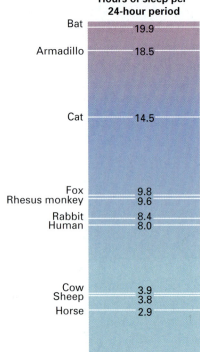

	Hours of sleep per 24-hour period
Bat	19.9
Armadillo	18.5
Cat	14.5
Fox	9.8
Rhesus monkey	9.6
Rabbit	8.4
Human	8.0
Cow	3.9
Sheep	3.8
Horse	2.9

national TV coverage, which helped him to stay awake. Even so, he almost fell asleep several times, but his observers would not let him close his eyes. In more normal circumstances, individuals have far more difficulty staying awake all night, especially between 3 A.M. and 6 A.M.

Although Randy Gardner was able to go about 11 days without sleep, the following discussion should convince you that even getting 60 to 90 minutes less sleep than you need at night can harm your ability to stay fully functional and perform optimally the next day (Dement, 1999).

Sleep expert James Maas (1998) argues that the quality of our lives, if not life itself, is jeopardized by sleep deprivation. A sleep debt can build quickly, not unlike finance charges on an unpaid credit card balance, when you are burning the candle at both ends. Consider a medical technician who tried to get by on 4 hours of sleep a night—ironically, while working at a sleep-disorders center—so she could take care of her infant daughter during the day. Before long, she developed heart palpitations, dizziness, a fear of driving, and wide mood swings.

An increasing number of research studies underscore that optimal performance is enhanced by sleeping more than 8 hours a night and reduced by sleeping less. At one sleep-disorders research center, the alertness of 8-hour sleepers who claimed to be well rested increased when they added 2 hours to their nightly sleep total (Roehrs & Roth, 1998). In another study, brain scans revealed that sleep deprivation decreased brain activity in the thalamus and the prefrontal cortex (Thomas & others, 2001). Alertness and cognitive performance also declined. In another study, sleep deprivation was linked with an inability to sustain attention (Doran, Van Dongen, & Dinges, 2001). In yet another study, brain scans of individuals who experienced total sleep deprivation for 24 hours revealed a decline in the complexity of brain activity (Jeong & others, 2001).

Sleep deprivation also can affect decision making. A review of studies concluded that sleep deprivation adversely affects aspects of decision making, such as being able to deal with the unexpected, innovate, revise plans, and communicate (Harrison & Horne, 2000).

Why are Americans getting too little sleep? Work pressures, school pressures, family obligations, and social obligations often lead to long hours of wakefulness and irregular sleep/wake schedules. Not having enough hours to do all we want to do in a day, we cheat on our sleep. Most people need to get 60 to 90 minutes more sleep each night than they presently get.

For an idea of whether a lack of sleep is causing you problems—and some suggestions for improving your ability to sleep—see the Psychology and Life box.

Sleep Deprivation in Adolescents and Older Adults Interest in adolescent sleep patterns has surged recently. Many adolescents seem to get too little sleep. Are there physiological underpinnings to adolescents' desires to stay up later at night and sleep longer in the morning? The answer has implications for understanding when adolescents learn most effectively in school (Eliasson & others, 2002).

Mary Carskadon and her colleagues (Carskadon, Acebo, & Seifer, 2001; Carskadon & others, 1998, 1999) have conducted a number of research studies on adolescent sleep patterns. They have found that adolescents sleep an average of 9 hours and 25 minutes when given the opportunity to sleep as long as they like. Most adolescents get considerably less sleep, however, especially during the week. The result is a sleep debt, which adolescents often try to make up for on the weekend.

The researchers found that older adolescents (16–18 years old) are often sleepier during the day than younger adolescents (13–15 years old) are. Carskadon believes this difference is not due to factors such as academic work and social pressures. Rather, her research suggests that adolescents' biological clocks undergo a hormonal shift as they get older, which pushes the time of wakefulness to an hour later than when they were younger adolescents. In her research, Carskadon found that this shift was caused by a delay in the nightly release of melatonin. Melatonin is secreted at

Sleep researchers recorded Randy Gardner's behavior (including these push-ups) during his 264-hour marathon of sleep deprivation. Most people have difficulty staying awake even one night. *Why shouldn't you follow Gardner's sleep deprivation example?*

Typical sleep patterns appear to change during adolescence. *How might this developmental change influence alertness at school?*

Do You Get Enough Sleep?

Many college students do not get enough sleep. In a survey of more than 200,000 first-year students, more than 80 percent said they stayed up all night at least once during the year (Sax & others, 1995). To evaluate whether you are sleep deprived, agree or disagree with the following statements:

Yes	No	
_____	_____	I need an alarm clock to wake up at the appropriate time.
_____	_____	It's a struggle for me to get out of bed in the morning.
_____	_____	I feel tired, irritable, and stressed out during the week.
_____	_____	I have trouble concentrating.
_____	_____	I have trouble remembering.
_____	_____	I feel slow with critical thinking, problem solving, and creativity.
_____	_____	I often fall asleep watching TV.
_____	_____	I often fall asleep in boring meetings or lectures in warm rooms.
_____	_____	I often fall asleep after heavy meals or after low doses of alcohol.
_____	_____	I often fall asleep within 5 minutes of getting into bed.
_____	_____	I often feel drowsy while driving.
_____	_____	I often sleep extra hours on weekend mornings.
_____	_____	I often need a nap to get through the day.
_____	_____	I have dark circles around my eyes.

According to sleep expert James Maas (1998), who developed this quiz, if you responded "yes" to three or more of these items, you probably are not getting enough sleep.

If you are not getting enough sleep, the following behavioral strategies might help you:

1. Reduce stress as much as possible.
2. Exercise regularly, but not just before you go to bed.
3. Keep mentally stimulated during the day.
4. Become a good time manager.
5. Eat a proper diet.
6. Stop smoking.
7. Reduce caffeine intake.
8. Avoid alcohol, especially near bedtime.
9. Take a warm bath before bed.
10. Maintain a relaxing atmosphere in the bedroom.
11. Clear your mind at bedtime.
12. Before going to bed, engage in a relaxation technique, such as listening to a tape designed for relaxation.
13. Learn to value sleep.
14. If necessary, contact the health service at your college or university for advice about your sleeping problem.

about 9:30 P.M. in younger adolescents, but it is secreted about 10:30 P.M. in older adolescents, delaying the onset of sleep.

Carskadon determined that early school starting times can result in grogginess and lack of attention in class and poor performance on tests. Based on this research, in 1997 schools in Edina, Minnesota, made the decision to start classes at 8:40 A.M. instead of the former starting time of 7:15 A.M. Since this decision, illnesses and referrals for discipline problems have decreased. Test scores have improved among high school students but not middle school students, an outcome that supports Carskadon's conclusion that early school starting times are more of a problem for older adolescents than younger adolescents.

Sleep patterns also change as people age through the middle-adult (40s, 50s) and late-adult (60s and older) years. Many aging adults go to bed earlier at night and wake up earlier in the morning than they once did. Thus by middle age a clear reversal occurs in the time at which individuals go to bed—later to bed as adolescents, earlier to bed in middle age. Beginning in the 40s, individuals also report that they are less likely to sleep through the entire night than when they were younger (Katchadourian, 1987). Middle-aged adults also spend less time in the deepest sleep stage than when they were younger. And almost one-half of individuals in late adulthood report that they experience some degree of insomnia.

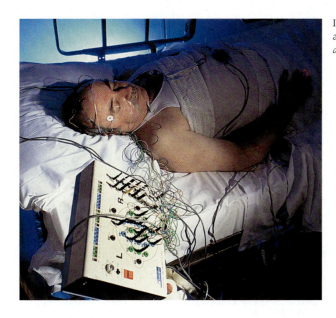

In sleep experiments, individuals are monitored by an EEG. *What does an EEG measure?*

"My problem has always been an over-abundance of alpha waves."
© 1990 by Sidney Harris.

In-Psych Plus

Sleep Stages

Have you ever been awakened from your sleep and been totally disoriented? Have you ever awakened in the middle of a dream and gone right back into the dream as if it were a movie running just under the surface of your consciousness? These two circumstances reflect two distinct stages in the sleep cycle. Using the electroencephalograph (EEG) to monitor the brain's electrical activity during waking and sleep states, scientists have discovered five distinct stages of sleep and two stages of wakefulness.

When people are awake, their EEG patterns exhibit two types of waves. *Beta waves* are the highest in frequency and lowest in amplitude, and they do not form a very consistent pattern. Inconsistent patterning makes sense, given the extensive variation in sensory input and activities we experience when we are awake. When we are relaxed but still awake, our brain waves slow down, increase in amplitude, and become more regular. These are *alpha waves.*

The five stages of sleep are differentiated by the depth of sleep and the wave patterns detected with an EEG, as you can see in the animations in the interactivity "Stages of Sleep" and in figure 5.3:

- *Stage 1 sleep.* This stage is characterized by *theta waves,* which are even slower in frequency and greater in amplitude than alpha waves. The transition from just being relaxed to entering stage 1 sleep is gradual.
- *Stage 2 sleep.* Theta waves continue but are interspersed with a defining characteristic of stage 2 sleep: *sleep spindles,* or sudden increases in wave frequency (Gottselig, Bassetti, & Ackermann, 2002). Stages 1 and 2 are both relatively light stages of sleep, and if people awaken during one of these stages, they often report not having been asleep at all.
- *Stage 3 and stage 4 sleep.* These stages are characterized by delta waves, the slowest and highest-amplitude brain waves during sleep. These two stages are often referred to as *delta sleep.* Distinguishing between stage 3 and stage 4 is difficult. Typically, stage 3 is characterized by delta waves occurring less than 50 percent of the time and stage 4 by delta waves occurring more than 50 percent of the time. Delta sleep is our deepest sleep, the time when brain waves are least like waking brain waves. Sleepers are most difficult to wake during delta sleep. If awakened during this stage, they usually are disoriented.
- *REM sleep.* After going through stages 1 through 4, sleepers drift up through the sleep stages toward wakefulness. But, instead of reentering stage 1, they enter stage 5, a different form of sleep called **REM sleep** (rapid-eye-movement

REM sleep Rapid-eye-movement sleep (stage 5), during which most dreaming occurs.

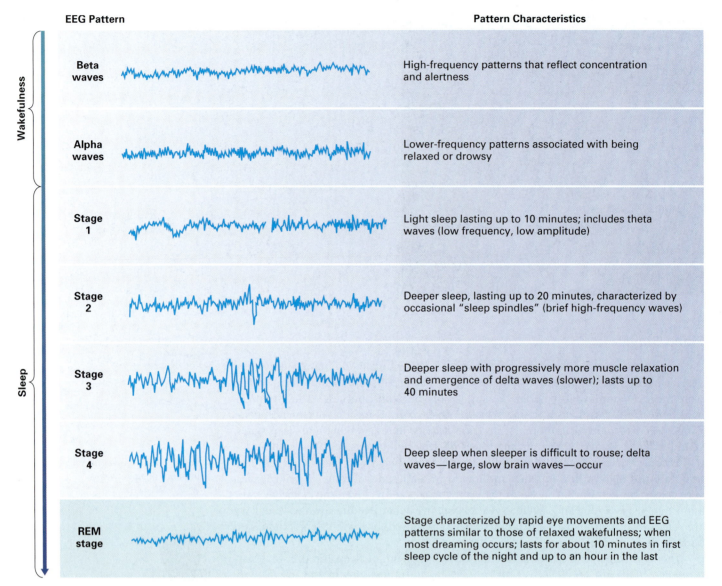

	EEG Pattern		Pattern Characteristics
Wakefulness	Beta waves		High-frequency patterns that reflect concentration and alertness
	Alpha waves		Lower-frequency patterns associated with being relaxed or drowsy
Sleep	Stage 1		Light sleep lasting up to 10 minutes; includes theta waves (low frequency, low amplitude)
	Stage 2		Deeper sleep, lasting up to 20 minutes, characterized by occasional "sleep spindles" (brief high-frequency waves)
	Stage 3		Deeper sleep with progressively more muscle relaxation and emergence of delta waves (slower); lasts up to 40 minutes
	Stage 4		Deep sleep when sleeper is difficult to rouse; delta waves—large, slow brain waves—occur
	REM stage		Stage characterized by rapid eye movements and EEG patterns similar to those of relaxed wakefulness; when most dreaming occurs; lasts for about 10 minutes in first sleep cycle of the night and up to an hour in the last

FIGURE 5.3 EEG Recordings During Stages of Wakefulness and Sleep

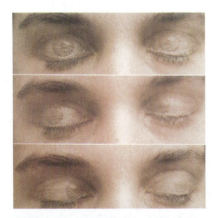

FIGURE 5.4 REM Sleep During REM sleep, your eyes move rapidly, as if you were observing the images moving in your dreams.

sleep). REM sleep is an active stage of sleep, during which dreaming occurs. During REM sleep, the EEG pattern shows fast waves similar to those of relaxed wakefulness, and the sleeper's eyeballs move rapidly up and down and from left to right (see figure 5.4). The longer the period of REM sleep, the more likely it is that the person will report dreaming. Dreams also occur during slow-wave or non-REM sleep, but the frequency of dreams in these stages is relatively low (Takeuchi & others, 2001). Reports of dreaming by individuals awakened from REM sleep are typically longer, more vivid, more animated, more emotionally charged, and less related to waking life than reports by those awakened from non-REM sleep (Hobson, Pace-Schott, & Stickgold, 2000). REM sleep also likely contributes to memory. Researchers have presented individuals with unique phrases before they go to bed (Empson & Clarke, 1970). When they are awakened just before they begin REM sleep, they remember less the next morning than when they are awakened during the other sleep stages.

The five stages of sleep described here make up a normal cycle of sleep. As shown in figure 5.5, a cycle lasts about 90 to 100 minutes and recurs several times during the night. The amount of deep sleep (stages 3 and 4) is much greater in the first half of a night's sleep than in the second half. Most REM sleep takes place toward the end of a night's sleep, when the REM stage becomes progressively longer. The night's first REM stage might last for only 10 minutes, and the final REM stage might continue for as long as an hour. During a normal night of sleep, individuals will spend about 60 percent of sleep in the light sleep stages (1 and 2), 20 percent in delta or deep sleep, and 20 percent in REM sleep (Webb, 2000).

The amount of time we spend in REM and non-REM sleep changes over the life span, however. As shown in figure 5.6, the percentage of total sleep during a 24-hour period that consists of REM sleep is especially large during early infancy (almost 8 hours). Older adults have less than 1 hour of REM sleep per 24-hour period. These dramatic developmental changes in sleep, especially REM sleep, raise questions about the function of sleep. For young infants, REM sleep may play a role in stimulating the brain and contributing to its growth. See the video clip "REM Sleep" for more information on the effects of REM sleep and how these relate to Freud's ideas about dreams.

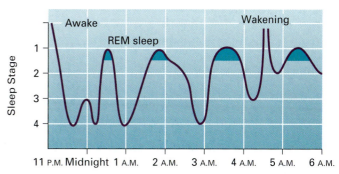

FIGURE 5.5 Cycles in a Night's Sleep During a night, we go through several cycles. Depth of sleep decreases and REM sleep (shown in dark turquoise) increases as the night progresses. In this graph, the person is depicted as awakening at about 5 A.M. and then going back to sleep for another hour.

Sleep Disorders

Each year, at least 40 million Americans suffer from chronic, long-term sleep disorders, and an additional 20 million experience occasional sleep problems (National Institute of Neurological Disorders and Stroke, 2001). Many people suffer from undiagnosed and untreated sleep disorders (National Commission on Sleep Disorders Research, 1993). Here are some of the major sleep problems:

- *Insomnia,* the inability to sleep, can involve having trouble falling asleep, waking up during the night, or waking up too early (Harvey, 2001; Mahendran, 2001). As many as one in five Americans has insomnia. It is more common among women and older adults, as well as people who are thin, stressed, or depressed (Devries, 1998). For short-term insomnia, most physicians prescribe sleeping pills (Ramesh & Roberts, 2002). However, most sleeping pills stop working after several weeks of nightly use, and their long-term use can actually interfere with good sleep. Mild insomnia often can be reduced by simply practicing good sleep habits. In more serious cases of insomnia, researchers are experimenting with light therapy, melatonin supplements, and other ways to alter

FIGURE 5.6 Sleep Across the Human Life Span

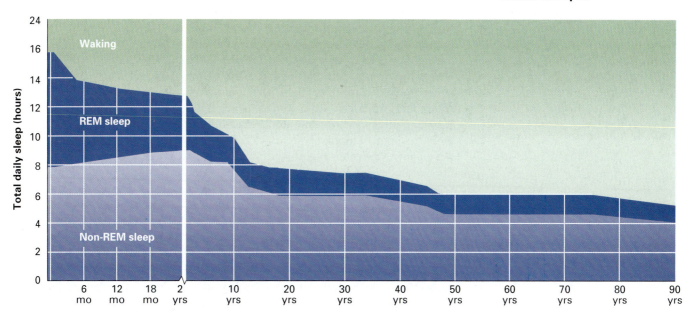

circadian cycles (Cohen, 2002; Kennaway & Wright, 2002). Behavioral changes can also help insomniacs to increase their sleep time, as well as to awaken less frequently in the night. In one study, insomniacs were restricted from taking a nap during the day, and they were required to set an alarm and to get out of bed in the morning (Edinger & others, 2001). The longer the insomniacs stayed awake during the day, the better they were able to sleep at night.

In-Psych Plus

- *Sleepwalking,* or *somnambulism,* occurs during the deepest stages of sleep. For many years, experts believed that somnambulists were just acting out their dreams. But somnambulism occurs during stages 3 and 4, usually early in the night, at the time when a person is unlikely to be dreaming (Stein & Ferber, 2001). There is nothing really abnormal about sleepwalking. Despite superstition, it is safe to awaken sleepwalkers; in fact, they probably should be awakened, as they may harm themselves, wandering around in the dark (Swanson, 1999). Go to the interactivity "Sleep Stages" to explore the stages of sleep and think critically about somnambulism.

- *Sleep talking* is another quirky night behavior (Hublin & others, 2001). Although sleep talkers will talk with you and make fairly coherent statements, they are soundly asleep.

- *Nightmares* are frightening dreams that awaken a dreamer from REM sleep. The nightmare's content invariably involves danger—the dreamer is chased, robbed, raped, murdered, or thrown off a cliff. Most of us have had nightmares, especially when we were young children. Nightmares peak at 3 to 6 years of age and then decline, although the average college student experiences four to eight nightmares a year (Hartmann, 1993). Reported increases in nightmares or worsening nightmares are often associated with an increase in stress in people's lives.

- *Night terrors* are characterized by sudden arousal from sleep and intense fear. Night terrors are accompanied by a number of physiological reactions, such as rapid heart rate and breathing, loud screams, heavy perspiration, and movement (Thiedke, 2001). Night terrors are less common than nightmares. Unlike nightmares, night terrors occur during slow-wave, non-REM sleep. Night terrors peak at 5 to 7 years of age and decline thereafter.

- *Narcolepsy* is the overpowering urge to sleep. The urge is so strong that the person may fall asleep while talking or standing up. Narcoleptics immediately enter REM sleep rather than progressing through the first four sleep stages (Mignot, 2001; Mignot & Thorsby, 2001). Researchers suspect that narcolepsy is inherited. Treatment usually involves counseling to discover potential causes of the excessive sleepiness.

- *Sleep apnea* is a sleep disorder in which individuals stop breathing because the windpipe fails to open or because brain processes involved in respiration fail to work properly. People with sleep apnea experience numerous brief awakenings during the night so that they can breathe, although they usually are not aware of the awakenings. During the day, these people may feel sleepy because they were deprived of sleep at night. Sleep apnea affects approximately 12 million Americans (American Sleep Apnea Association, 2001). Sleep apnea is most common among infants and adults over the age of 65. Sleep apnea also occurs more frequently among obese individuals (Davidson & Callery, 2001). Untreated, sleep apnea can cause high blood pressure, strokes, and impotence. In addition, the daytime sleepiness it causes can result in accidents, lost productivity, and relationship problems (Billmann & Ware, 2002).

Dreams

Ever since the dawn of language, dreams have had historical, personal, and religious significance. Many people in modern societies, such as in the United States, view dreams as separate from reality and usually as having little importance to their waking lives. However, in primitive societies dreams are often thought of as an extension of reality.

Through the centuries, artists have been adept at capturing the enchanting or nightmarish characteristics of our dreams. *(Left)* Dutch painter Hieronymus Bosch (1450–1516) captured both the enchanting and frightening nature of dreams in *Garden of Earthly Delights. (Right)* Marc Chagall (1887–1985) painted a world of dreams in *I and the Village. Do you believe any of the images in these paintings are symbolic? What might they symbolize?*

For example, in one account, an African chief dreamed that he had visited England. On awakening, he ordered a wardrobe of European clothes. As he walked through the village in his new wardrobe, he was congratulated for having made the trip. Similarly, Cherokee Indians who dreamed of being bitten by snakes were treated for the snakebite. The Inuit people who live in the Arctic region of North America believe that dreams provide a vehicle for entering the spiritual world. In the Colombian village of Arimatima, many dreams are thought to symbolize the deaths of relatives (Paquin, 2000).

The Senoi people of Malaysia were reported to be able to control their dreams and have extraordinary mental health (Stewart, 1954). However, this view was debunked when scientists found that it was promoted by an American adventurer who did not know their language and spent only a few weeks with them (Domhoff, 2003). Nonetheless, in terms of dream content, small traditional societies show a higher percentage of animal characters in their dreams, and variations exist from culture to culture in the percentage of aggressive actions in dreams (Domhoff, 1999).

The dreams of men and women also seem to be different (Kolchakian & Hill, 2002). Men are more likely than women to dream about aggression, torso anatomy, sexuality, and their own success (Domhoff & Schneider, 1998). The dream content of women is more likely to include friends and victimization.

Why do we dream? Many theorists and researchers have attempted to explain dreaming. But because dreams are written in the mind with little or no conscious participation, it is difficult to unravel their mysteries (Loden, 2003).

One of the most prominent theories of dreams is Sigmund Freud's (1900/1953). He thought that the reason we dream is **wish fulfillment,** an unconscious attempt to fulfill needs (especially for sex and aggression) that cannot be expressed or that go ungratified during waking hours. In this view, for example, people who had strong aggressive tendencies but suppressed anger while awake would be inclined to have dreams filled with violence and hostility.

Freud also stressed that dreams often contain memories of infant and child experiences, especially events associated with parents. He distinguished between a dream's manifest content and its latent content. **Manifest content** is the dream's surface content, which contains dream symbols that distort and disguise the dream's true meaning. **Latent content** is the dream's hidden content, its unconscious meaning. For

wish fulfillment Freud's concept of dreaming as an unconscious attempt to fulfill needs (especially for sex and aggression) that cannot be expressed, or that go ungratified, while awake.

manifest content In Freud's view, a dream's surface content, which contains symbols that distort and disguise the dream's true meaning.

latent content In Freud's view, a dream's hidden content; its unconscious meaning.

In-Psych Plus

example, if a person had a dream about a king or a president, Freud believed that these authority figures would symbolize a father or the therapist and thus reveal the underlying latent content. Freud thought that, once a therapist understood a client's symbolism, the dream could be interpreted. A final point about Freud's dream theory involves its scientific merit. Researchers have found it very difficult to devise methods to verify the theory. See the video clip "Freudian Interpretation of Dreams" to explore the psychodynamic analysis of dreams.

Freud's theory has largely given way to newer theories of dreams, such as the *cognitive theory of dreaming.* It proposes that dreaming can be understood by relying on the same cognitive concepts that are used in studying the waking mind. That is, dreaming involves information processing, memory, and problem solving. The cognitive theory of dreaming involves little or no search for the hidden, symbolic content of dreams that Freud sought (Foulkes, 1993, 1999). Rather, dreams are considered to be a mental realm in which we can solve problems and think creatively. For example, Elias Howe, attempting to invent a machine that sewed, reportedly dreamed that he was captured by savages carrying spears with holes in their tips. On waking, he realized that he should place the hole for the thread at the end of the needle, not in the middle. Dreams may spark such gifts of inspiration because, in unique and creative ways, they weave together current experiences with the past. Criticisms of the cognitive theory of dreaming focus on skepticism about the ability to resolve problems during sleep and the lack of attention to the roles of brain structures and activity in dreaming.

Neuroscientists address this shortcoming with the view that dreams reflect the brain's efforts to make sense out of neural activity that takes place during sleep (Hobson, 1999). When we are awake and alert, the contents of our conscious experience tend to be driven by external stimuli that result in specific motor behavior. During sleep, however, conscious experience is driven by internally generated stimuli that have no apparent behavioral consequence. A key source of this internal stimulation is spontaneous neural activity in the reticular formation of the limbic system, at the base of the brain (Hobson, 2000). Recently, some have suggested that neural networks in the forebrain also play a specific role in dreaming (Hobson & others, 2000). For instance, they believe that the primary motor and somatosensory areas of the forebrain are activated in the sensorimotor aspects of the dream. They explain the fact that dreams tend to end, dissolve, or shift suddenly in midstream as a result of normal cycles of neural activation (Hobson, 2000). As levels of neurotransmitters rise and fall during the stages of sleep, some neural networks are activated, and others shut down. Like all dream theories, this theory has its critics. They question whether the brain stem is the only starting point for neural activity in dreaming and point out that experiences stimulate and shape dreaming more than the neuroscientific theory acknowledges (Domhoff, 2001; Solms, 1997).

Review and Sharpen Your Thinking

2 *Explain the nature of sleep and dreams.*

- Describe the relationship between biological rhythms and sleep.
- Summarize the benefits of sleep and the effects of sleep deprivation.
- Describe the five stages of sleep and changes in the level of activity in the brain during sleep.
- Name and describe seven types of sleep disorders, and explain why they are problematic.
- Summarize three theories of why people dream.

Do you know someone who might have a sleep disorder? What might he or she be able to do about it?

The Nature of Hypnosis   **Explanations of Hypnosis**   **Applications of Hypnosis**

Is hypnosis an altered state of consciousness?

A young cancer patient is about to undergo a painful bone marrow transplant. His doctor directs the boy's attention, asking him to breathe and listen carefully. Soon the boy is absorbed in a pleasant fantasy in which he is riding a motorcycle over a huge pizza, dodging anchovies, and maneuvering around blobs of melted mozzarella. Minutes later, the procedure is over. The boy is relaxed and feels good about his self-control. The doctor has successfully used hypnosis to help the patient control pain by reducing his perception of it.

Hypnosis is a psychological state, or possibly a state of altered attention and awareness, in which the individual is unusually receptive to suggestions. Basic hypnotic techniques have been used since the beginning of recorded history in association with various religious ceremonies, magic, the supernatural, and many erroneous psychological theories.

In the late nineteenth century, the Austrian physician Friedrich Anton Mesmer cured patients of various problems by passing magnets over their bodies. Mesmer said the problems were cured by "animal magnetism," an intangible force that passes from therapist to patient. In reality, the cures were due to some form of hypnotic suggestion. A committee was appointed by the French Academy of Science to investigate Mesmer's claims. The committee agreed that his treatment was effective. However, they disputed his theory about animal magnetism and prohibited him from practicing in Paris. Mesmer's theory was called "mesmerism," and even today we use the term *mesmerized* to mean hypnotized or enthralled.

Today, hypnosis is recognized as a legitimate process in psychology and medicine, although we still have much to learn about how it works. In addition, as is discussed shortly, there still is debate about whether hypnosis truly is an altered state of consciousness (Chaves, 2000).

The Nature of Hypnosis

A common misconception is that the hypnotic state is much like a sleep state. Unlike sleepers, hypnotized individuals are aware of what is happening and remember the experience later unless they are instructed to forget what happened. EEG studies document that individuals in a hypnotic state show a predominance of alpha and beta waves, characteristic of persons in a relaxed waking state (De Benedittis & Sironi, 1985; Graffin, Ray, & Lundy, 1995; Williams & Gruzelier, 2001). However, during hypnosis individuals show different patterns of brain activity than they do when they are not under hypnosis (Isotani & others, 2001; Jensen & others, 2001).

Successful hypnosis involves four steps:

1. The hypnotist minimizes distractions and makes the person to be hypnotized comfortable.
2. The hypnotist tells the person to concentrate on something specific, such as an imagined scene or the ticking of a watch.
3. The hypnotist tells the person what to expect in the hypnotic state, such as relaxation or a pleasant floating sensation.
4. The hypnotist suggests certain events or feelings that he or she knows will occur or observes occurring, such as "Your eyes are getting tired." When the suggested effects occur, the person interprets them as being caused by the hypnotist's suggestions. The person's expectations that the hypnotist will make things happen in the future increase further and make the person even more suggestible.

The brain activity of a hypnotized individual is being monitored. *How is hypnosis different from sleep?*

hypnosis A psychological state, or possibly a state of altered attention and awareness, in which the individual is unusually responsive to suggestions.

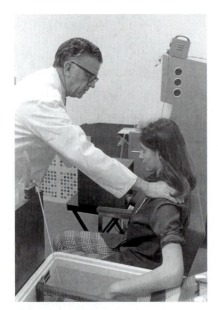

FIGURE 5.7 Divided Consciousness
Ernest Hilgard *(left)* tests a participant in the study in which he had individuals place one arm in ice-cold water. *Why did he believe this study demonstrated the presence of divided consciousness?*

Do you think that you can be hypnotized? For as long as hypnosis has been studied (about 200 years), some people have been found to be more easily hypnotized than others. About 10 to 20 percent of the population is very susceptible to hypnosis, 10 percent or less cannot be hypnotized at all, and the remainder fall somewhere in between (Hilgard, 1965). There is no simple way to tell beforehand who can be hypnotized. But if you have the capacity to immerse yourself in imaginative activities—listening to a favorite piece of music or reading a novel, for example—you are a likely candidate. People susceptible to hypnosis become completely absorbed in what they are doing, removing the boundaries between themselves and what they are experiencing in their environment. Nonetheless, such absorption is best described as a weak rather than a strong predictor of a person's likelihood of being hypnotized (Nash, 2001; Nash & Nadon, 1997).

If you are in a hypnotic state, can the hypnotist make you do something against your will? Individuals being hypnotized abdicate their responsibility to the hypnotist and follow the hypnotist's suggestions. However, they are unlikely to do anything in a hypnotic state that violates their morals or that is dangerous.

Explanations of Hypnosis

Ever since Anton Mesmer proposed his theory of animal magnetism, psychologists have been trying to figure out why hypnosis works. Contemporary theorists are divided on their answers to the question "Is hypnosis a divided state of consciousness, or is it simply a form of learned social behavior?"

Ernest Hilgard (1977, 1992) proposed that hypnosis involves a special divided state of consciousness, a sort of splitting of consciousness into separate components. One component follows the hypnotist's commands, while another component acts as a "hidden observer." In one situation, Hilgard placed one arm of hypnotized individuals in a bucket of ice-cold water and told them that they would not feel any pain but that another part of their minds—the hidden part that is aware of what is going on—could signal any true pain by pressing a key with the hand that was not submerged (see figure 5.7). The individuals under hypnosis reported afterward that they did not experience any pain, but, while their arms were submerged in the ice-cold water, they had, indeed, pressed the key with their nonsubmerged hands. And they pressed it more frequently the longer their arms were in the cold water. Thus, in Hilgard's view, consciousness has a hidden part that stays in contact with reality during hypnosis and that feels pain while another part of consciousness feels no pain.

Some experts are skeptical that hypnosis is truly an altered state of consciousness (Chaves, 2000). They believe that hypnosis is a normal state in which the hypnotized person behaves the way he or she believes a hypnotized person should behave. In this view, the important questions about hypnosis focus on cognitive factors—the attitudes, expectations, and beliefs of good hypnotic participants—and on the social context in which hypnosis occurs (Barber, 1969; Spanos & Chaves, 1989).

Applications of Hypnosis

Hypnosis is widely used in medicine and dentistry, in criminal investigations, and in sports. Hypnosis has also been used in psychotherapy to treat alcoholism, somnambulism, suicidal tendencies, overeating, and smoking (Eimer, 2000; Yapko, 2001). Among the least effective, but most common, applications of hypnosis are those intended to help people stop overeating or quit smoking. Hypnotists direct individuals to stop these behaviors, but dramatic results rarely are achieved unless the individuals are already motivated to change. Hypnosis is most effective when combined with psychotherapy (Borckardt, 2002).

A long history of research and practice clearly has demonstrated that hypnosis can reduce the experience of pain (Crasilneck, 1995; Langenfeld, Cipani, & Borckardt, 2002; Patterson & Jensen, 2003). However, not everyone is hypnotizable enough to

Etzel Cardena, a professor of psychology and a hypnotherapist, is shown here hypnotizing an adolescent. Etzel is especially interested in hypnosis as a dissociated state of consciousness and its use in helping people who have experienced trauma and various mental disorders. *What does hypnosis seem best suited to do? What may be beyond its capabilities?*

benefit from this effect. Moreover, hypnosis has not been shown to increase muscular strength, endurance, or sensory thresholds (Druckman & Bjork, 1994).

Hypnosis has sometimes been used in attempts to enhance people's ability to accurately recall forgotten events (Coleman, Stevens, & Reeder, 2001). For example, police departments sometimes arrange to have eyewitnesses to crimes hypnotized in the hope that their recall of the crime will significantly improve.

To read about the research on this topic and the issues involved, see the Critical Controversy box on the next page.

Review and Sharpen Your Thinking

3 **Describe hypnosis.**

- Explain what hypnosis is.
- Discuss two theoretical explanations of hypnosis.
- Identify some applications of hypnosis.

Do you think you are a good candidate for hypnosis? Why or why not?

PSYCHOACTIVE DRUGS 4

Depressants   Hallucinogens

Uses of Psychoactive Drugs   Stimulants

What are psychoactive drugs, and how do they affect behavior?

During one phase of his career, Sigmund Freud experimented with therapeutic uses of cocaine. He was searching for possible medical applications, such as a painkiller for eye surgery. He soon found that the drug induced ecstasy. Writing to his fiancée, he told her how just a small dose of cocaine produced wonderful, lofty sensations. As it became apparent that cocaine also produced considerable risk to its users, and after

Is Hypnosis a Window to Forgotten Events?

In 1977, two nurses were accused of poisoning nine patients at a Veterans Administration Hospital in Ann Arbor, Michigan. Two of the patients died. At first, no clear evidence was found to link the nurses to the crime. In an attempt to prove their case, FBI agents hypnotized the surviving victims and several staff members. Under hypnosis, one victim gradually began to remember the presence of one of the two nurses in his room. Were the memories of this witness accurate? How do we know whether events recalled under hypnosis actually happened as people recall them? Although this critical testimony resulted in a conviction, a judge ordered a new trial and the prosecution chose to not retry the case (Loftus, 1979).

Hypnosis is sometimes used to enhance people's ability to recall forgotten events (Barnier, Bryant, & Brisco, 2001; Nash, 2001; Stafford & Lynn, 2002). Police departments use hypnosis occasionally to help eyewitnesses remember forgotten crime scene details. In 1976, for example, a school bus carrying 26 schoolchildren from Chowchilla, California, disappeared. It turns out that three armed men kidnapped the bus driver and the children and buried them alive in a trailer in a gravel quarry some distance away. After 16 hours underground, they were rescued. When the school bus driver was hypnotized, he recalled all but one digit of the license plate on the kidnapper's vehicle. This memory proved critical in tracking down the suspects (Loftus, 1979).

Therapists sometimes use hypnosis to age-regress patients back to an earlier stage in life in order to help them work through long-forgotten painful experiences. However, research suggests that improvements in memory due to hypnosis may often be more apparent than real. In one study, participants watched a videotape of a mock armed robbery and then were asked to recall specific crime details six times: twice immediately after seeing the videotape, twice 1 week after seeing the videotape, once during hypnosis, and once after hypnosis (Nadon, Laurence & Perry, 1991). Highly hypnotizable participants remembered more specific crime details under hypnosis than they did just before hypnosis; less hypnotizable participants did not. At the same time, however, high-hypnotizability participants misremembered more false crime details than did low-hypnotizability participants. In other words, when people are hypnotized, they may remember more correct and more incorrect information. One explanation of this result is that hypnosis may make participants more willing than normal to report whatever comes into their minds (Klatzky & Erdelyi, 1985).

Unfortunately for police and therapists, in most real-life circumstances it may be impossible to discriminate between correct and incorrect memories. In the Chowchilla case mentioned previously, corroborating evidence confirmed the accuracy of the bus driver's hypnotic recall. In the Ann Arbor case, with no corroborating evidence, it was impossible to confirm or disconfirm the accuracy of the victim's recovered memory.

This uncertainty about the accuracy of memories recalled under hypnosis is magnified by the tendency of hypnotized participants to be influenced by leading questions. For example, after viewing a photo, hypnotized individuals might be asked, "What color was that person's mustache?" The individuals then often create an image of the person they saw and supply the person with a mustache, even though the photo did not show a mustache. Later they might recall, with confidence, the person as having a mustache. A number of studies have shown that hypnotized witnesses are more confident about the inaccurate aspects of their recall or about misidentifications than are non-hypnotized witnesses (Orne, 1959). In a court of law, hypnotized witnesses have so much confidence in their pseudo-memories—false memories that are believed to be real—that they are effectively immune from cross-examination (Orne, 1959). Jane Dywan (1995) has proposed that increased confidence in memories recovered under hypnosis is due to an illusion of familiarity that hypnosis helps to produce.

Because of its questionable reliability, hypnotic testimony is banned in some states. If hypnotic testimony is allowed in court, extreme caution must be exercised to obtain corroborating evidence and to minimize the risk of implanting pseudomemories when questioning victims and witnesses under hypnosis. Similarly, clinical psychologists must be careful when using hypnosis with their clients to minimize the risk of accidentally implanting highly emotional pseudomemories (Green, Lynn, & Malinoski, 1998).

There is some evidence that it may not be necessary to hypnotize eyewitnesses to help them remember more details about a crime. In one study, although individuals sometimes recalled new information following a hypnotic interview, they also sometimes recalled new information when motivated by non-hypnotic instructions (Frischoltz, 1995). However, even non-hypnotic methods of improving memory are vulnerable to the same problems, leading to the general concerns about the accuracy of recovered memories (Loftus, 1979).

What do you think?

- Why should extreme caution be exercised when evaluating memories generated by hypnotic testimony?
- Might age regression be a valuable therapeutic technique regardless of the risk of generating pseudomemories?
- Why might hypnosis cause someone to report recalled events inaccurately?

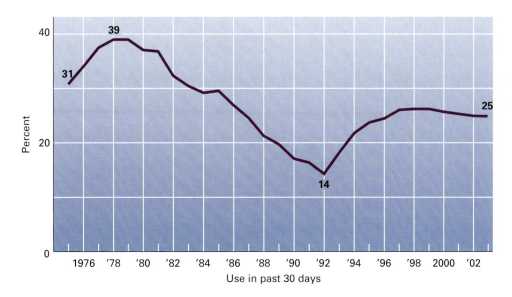

several died from overdoses, Freud quit using the drug. Cocaine is just one of many drugs taken to alter consciousness.

Illicit drug use is a global problem. More than 200 million people worldwide abuse drugs (UNDCP, 2001). Images of drug abusers span all segments of society: the urban professional snorting cocaine in a downtown nightclub, the farmer addicted to the opium poppy he grows, the teenage Ecstasy user in a comfortable suburban home.

Overall drug use among U.S. adolescents, as shown in figure 5.8, decreased in the 1980s but rose once again in the 1990s (Johnston, O'Malley, & Bachman, 2003). I describe trends in adolescents' use of specific drugs throughout this section.

Uses of Psychoactive Drugs

Psychoactive drugs are substances that act on the nervous system to alter states of consciousness, modify perceptions, and change moods. Psychoactive substances are attractive because they can help people adapt to an ever-changing environment. Drinking, smoking, and taking drugs reduce tension, relieve boredom and fatigue, and in some cases help people to escape from the harsh realities of the world. Some people take drugs because they are curious about their effects. Others may take drugs for social reasons—for example, to feel more at ease and happier in interacting with others.

The use of psychoactive drugs for personal gratification and temporary adaptation can carry a high price tag: drug dependence, personal disarray, and a predisposition to serious, sometimes fatal, diseases (Goldberg, 2003). What was initially intended to be pleasurable and adaptive can eventually turn unpleasant and maladaptive. For example, drinking alcohol may initially help people relax and forget about their worries. But if they turn more and more to alcohol to escape reality, they may develop a dependence that can destroy relationships, careers, and their bodies.

Continued use of psychoactive drugs leads to **tolerance,** which is the need to take increasing amounts of a drug to get the same effect. For example, the first time someone takes 5 milligrams of the tranquilizer Valium, the drug will make him or her feel very relaxed. However, after taking the pill every day for 6 months, the person may need to take 10 milligrams to achieve the same calming effect.

Continuing drug use can also result in **physical dependence,** the physiological need for a drug, which causes unpleasant *withdrawal* symptoms, such as physical pain and a craving for the drug, when it is discontinued. **Psychological dependence** is the strong desire to repeat the use of a drug for emotional reasons, such as a feeling of well-being and reduction of stress. Experts on drug abuse use the term **addiction** to describe an overwhelming need to use the drug and to secure its supply. Addiction can describe physical or psychological dependence

psychoactive drugs Drugs that act on the nervous system to alter consciousness, modify perceptions, and change moods.

tolerance The need to take increasing amounts of a drug to produce the same effect.

physical dependence The physical need for a drug, which creates unpleasant withdrawal symptoms when the drug is discontinued.

psychological dependence The strong desire and craving to repeat the use of a drug for emotional reasons.

addiction An overwhelming need to use a drug and to secure its supply.

FIGURE 5.9 Brain's Reward Pathway for Psychoactive Drugs The neurotransmitter dopamine, which affects sleep, mood, and attention, travels the reward pathway in greater abundance when psychoactive drugs are used. However, dopamine directly affects only the limbic and prefrontal areas.

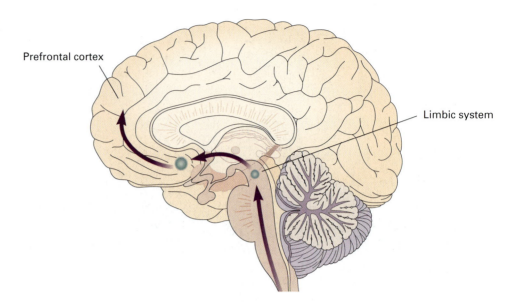

Prefrontal cortex

Limbic system

In-Psych Plus

(Carroll, 2003). See the video clip "Substance Abuse" to learn about the experience of addiction and recovery.

Can the brain become addicted? See the video clip "Neurochemical Basis of Addiction" to learn about the effect of psychoactive drugs on the brain. Psychoactive drugs increase dopamine levels in the brain's reward pathway (see figure 5.9) (National Institute on Drug Abuse [NIDA], 2001). Only the limbic and prefrontal areas of the brain are directly activated by dopamine (Kandel, Schwartz, & Jessell, 2003). Although different drugs have different mechanisms of action, each drug increases the activity of the reward pathway by increasing dopamine transmission.

Psychoactive drugs fall into three main categories: depressants, stimulants, and hallucinogens. All of them have the potential to cause health or behavior problems, or both. To evaluate whether you abuse drugs, see figure 5.10.

Depressants

Depressants are psychoactive drugs that slow down mental and physical activity. Among the most widely used depressants are alcohol, barbiturates, tranquilizers, and opiates.

In-Psych Plus

Alcohol Alcohol is a powerful drug. It acts on the body primarily as a depressant and slows down the brain's activities. People often "loosen up" after a few drinks because the areas of the brain involved in inhibition and judgment slow down. As people drink more, their inhibitions become further reduced, and their judgment becomes increasingly impaired. (Listen to the audio clip "Effects of Alcohol" to learn about the relationship between alcohol intoxication and risky sexual behaviors.) Activities that require intellectual functioning and motor skills, such as driving, become increasingly impaired as more alcohol is consumed. Eventually the drinker becomes drowsy and falls asleep. With extreme intoxication, a person may lapse into a coma and die. Each of these effects varies with how the person's body metabolizes alcohol, how much the body weighs, how much alcohol has been consumed, and whether previous drinking has led to tolerance (Gotz & others, 2001).

Like other psychoactive drugs, alcohol goes to the brain's reward pathway (NIDA, 2001). Alcohol also increases the concentration of the neurotransmitter GABA, which is widely distributed in many areas of the brain (Melis & others, 2002). Researchers believe that the frontal cortex, which is involved in decision making and memory, holds a memory of the pleasure involved in prior alcohol use (relaxation, lowered stress, less inhibition) and contributes to continued drinking. Alcohol use also may affect the areas of the frontal cortex involved in judgment and impulse control (Mantere & others, 2002). The basal ganglia, which are involved in compulsive

depressants Psychoactive drugs that slow down mental and physical activity.

FIGURE 5.10 Do You Abuse Drugs?

Respond yes or no to the following items:

Yes	No	
_____	_____	I have gotten into problems because of using drugs.
_____	_____	Using alcohol or other drugs has made my life unhappy at times.
_____	_____	Drinking alcohol or taking other drugs has been a factor in my losing a job.
_____	_____	Drinking alcohol or taking other drugs has interfered with my studying for exams.
_____	_____	Drinking alcohol or taking drugs has jeopardized my academic performance.
_____	_____	My ambition is not as strong since I've been drinking a lot or taking drugs.
_____	_____	Drinking or taking drugs has caused me to have difficulty sleeping.
_____	_____	I have felt remorse after drinking or taking drugs.
_____	_____	I crave a drink or other drugs at a definite time of the day.
_____	_____	I want a drink or other drug in the morning.
_____	_____	I have had a complete or partial loss of memory as a result of drinking or using other drugs.
_____	_____	Drinking or using other drugs is affecting my reputation.
_____	_____	I have been in the hospital or another institution because of my drinking or taking drugs.

College students who responded yes to items similar to these on the Rutgers Collegiate Abuse Screening Test were more likely to be substance abusers than those who answered no. If you responded yes to just 1 of the 13 items on this screening test, consider going to your college health or counseling center for further screening.

behaviors, may activate a greater demand for alcohol, regardless of reason and consequences (Brink, 2001).

After caffeine, alcohol is the most widely used drug in America. Surveys indicate that as many as two-thirds of American adults drink beer, wine, or liquor at least occasionally, and in one recent survey approximately 10 percent reported that they drink excessively (National Center for Health Statistics, 2001b). Drinking excessively in this survey was defined as consuming five or more drinks on one occasion at least 12 times in the past year.

Around the world, there are differences in alcohol use by gender, religion, and culture (Koenig, 2001; Lieber, 1997; Melinder & Andersson, 2001). Males drink alcohol more than females. Catholics, Reform Jews, and liberal Protestants all consume alcohol at a fairly high level. In some religions, such as Islam, the use of alcohol is forbidden. Europeans, especially the French, drink alcohol at high rates. Estimates are that about 30 percent of French adults have health problems related to high alcohol consumption. Alcohol use also is high in Russia; its use in China is low.

Alcohol abuse has a high social and personal cost. Approximately 20,000 people are killed and 1.5 million injured by drunk drivers each year. More than 60 percent of homicides involve the use of alcohol by either the offender or the victim, and 65 percent of aggressive sexual acts against women involve the use of alcohol by the offender.

A special concern is the high rate of alcohol use by high school and college students in the United States. In a recent national survey of more than 17,000 high school seniors, 78 percent had tried alcohol, and about half had done so by the eighth grade (Johnston, O'Malley, & Bachman, 2003). In this survey, 62 percent of the twelfth graders and 23 percent of the eighth graders reported having been drunk at least once in their lives. Binge drinking (defined as having five or more drinks in a row at least once in the previous 2 weeks) had been engaged in by 28 percent of the high school seniors in the previous month.

FIGURE 5.11 Consequences of Binge Drinking

The Troubles Frequent Binge Drinkers Create For . . .

Themselves[1]		And Others[2]	
(% of those surveyed who admitted having had the problem)		(% of those surveyed who had been affected)	
Missed class	61	Had study or sleep interrupted	68
Forgot where they were or what they did	54	Had to care for drunken student	54
Engaged in unplanned sex	41	Were insulted or humiliated	34
Got hurt	23	Experienced unwanted sexual advances	26
Had unprotected sex	22	Had serious argument	20
Damaged property	22	Had property damaged	15
Got into trouble with campus or local police	11	Were pushed or assaulted	13
Had five or more alcohol-related problems in school year	47	Had at least one of the above problems	87

[1] Frequent binge drinkers were defined as those who had at least four or five drinks at one time on at least three occasions in the previous 2 weeks.
[2] These figures are from colleges where at least 50 percent of students are binge drinkers.

Binge drinking often increases during the first 2 years of college (Schulenberg, 1999). Chronic binge drinking is more common among male college students than among females and among students living away from home, especially males living in fraternity houses (Schulenberg & others, 2000). In one national survey of drinking patterns on college campuses, almost half the binge drinkers reported problems that included missed classes, injuries, trouble with police, and unprotected sex (Wechsler & others, 2000) (see figure 5.11). Binge-drinking college students were 11 times more likely to fall behind in school, 10 times more likely to drive after drinking, and twice as likely to have unprotected sex as college students who did not binge drink. Many young people decrease their use of alcohol as they move into adult roles, such as a permanent job, marriage or cohabitation, and parenthood.

Alcoholism is a disorder involving long-term, repeated, uncontrolled, compulsive, and excessive use of alcoholic beverages that impairs the drinker's health and social relationships. Approximately 14 million people in the United States are alcoholics (Brink, 2001); alcoholism is the third leading killer in the United States. However, only one in nine individuals who drink continues on the path to alcoholism.

Those who do become alcoholics are disproportionately first-degree relatives of alcoholics (Hannigan & others, 1999). Indeed, researchers have found that heredity likely plays a role in alcoholism, although the precise mechanism has not been found (Crabbe, 2001, 2002; Wall & others, 2001). An estimated 50 to 60 percent of those who become alcoholics are believed to have a genetic predisposition for it. One possible explanation is that the brains of people genetically predisposed to alcoholism may be unable to produce adequate dopamine, a neurotransmitter that can make us feel pleasure. For these individuals, alcohol may increase dopamine concentration and resulting pleasure to the point at which it leads to addiction. Although studies reveal a genetic influence on alcoholism, they also show that environmental factors play a role (Heath & others, 2002). For example, family studies indicate that many alcoholics do not have close relatives who are alcoholics (Sher, 1993). The large cultural variations in alcohol use mentioned earlier also underscore the environment's role in alcoholism.

About one-third of alcoholics recover, whether they are in a treatment program or not. This finding came from a long-term study of 700 individuals over 50 years (Vaillant, 1983, 1992) and has consistently been found by other researchers as well. George Vaillant formulated the one-third rule for alcoholism: By age 65, one-third are dead or in terrible shape; one-third are still trying to beat their addiction; and one-third are abstinent or drinking only socially. Vaillant found that recovery from alcoholism was predicted by several factors: a strong negative experience with drinking, such as a serious medical emergency or condition; a substitute dependency, such

alcoholism A disorder that involves long-term, repeated, uncontrolled, compulsive, and excessive use of alcoholic beverages and that impairs the drinker's health and work and social relationships.

as meditation, exercise, or overeating; new, positive relationships (such as a helpful employer or a new marriage); and participation in a support group, such as a religious organization or Alcoholics Anonymous. See the video clip "Alcohol Addiction" to learn about detoxification and the benefits of psychotherapy.

Other Depressant Drugs   I have presented an extensive discussion of alcohol use and its effects because it is so widely used and abused. But several other depressant drugs also have great potential for abuse:

- **Barbiturates,** such as Nembutal and Seconal, are depressant drugs that are used to decrease central nervous system activity. They were once widely prescribed as sleep aids. In heavy dosages, they can lead to impaired memory and decision making. When combined with alcohol (for example, sleeping pills taken after a night of binge drinking), barbiturates can be lethal. Heavy doses of barbiturates by themselves can cause death. For this reason, barbiturates are the drugs most often used in suicide attempts. Abrupt withdrawal from barbiturates can produce seizures. Because of the addictive potential and relative ease of toxic overdose, barbiturates have been largely replaced by tranquilizers in the treatment of insomnia.
- **Tranquilizers,** such as Valium and Xanax, are depressant drugs that reduce anxiety and induce relaxation. Unlike barbiturates, which are often given to induce sleep, tranquilizers are usually given to calm an anxious, nervous individual (Rosenbloom, 2002). Tranquilizers are among the most widely prescribed drugs in the United States. They can produce withdrawal symptoms when use is stopped.
- **Opiates,** or narcotics, consisting of opium and its derivatives, depress the central nervous system's activity. The most common opiate drugs—morphine and heroin—affect synapses in the brain that use endorphins as their neurotransmitter. For several hours after taking an opiate, the person feels euphoric and pain free and has an increased appetite for food and sex. But when these drugs leave the brain, the affected synapses become understimulated. The opiates are thus highly addictive drugs, leading to craving and painful withdrawal when the drug becomes unavailable. Another hazardous consequence of opiate addiction is the risk of exposure to the virus that causes acquired immune deficiency syndrome (AIDS): Most heroin addicts inject the drug intravenously. When they share needles without sterilizing them, infected addicts can transmit the virus to others.

Stimulants

Stimulants are psychoactive drugs that increase the central nervous system's activity. The most widely used stimulants are amphetamines, cocaine, MDMA (Ecstasy), caffeine, and nicotine.

- *Amphetamines* are stimulant drugs that are used to boost energy, stay awake, or lose weight. They sometimes are called "pep pills" or "uppers." Amphetamines often are prescribed in the form of diet pills. These drugs increase the release of dopamine, which enhances the user's activity level and pleasurable feelings.
- *Cocaine* is an illegal drug that comes from the coca plant, native to Bolivia and Peru. For centuries, Bolivians and Peruvians have chewed the leaves of the plant to increase their stamina. Generally, however, cocaine is either snorted or injected in the form of crystals or powder. Used this way, cocaine can trigger a heart attack, stroke, or brain seizure. When coca leaves are chewed, small amounts of cocaine gradually enter the bloodstream, without any apparent adverse effects. However, when extracted cocaine is sniffed or injected, it enters the bloodstream very rapidly, producing a rush of euphoric feelings that lasts for about 15 to 30 minutes. Because the rush depletes the supply of the neurotransmitters dopamine, serotonin, and norepinephrine in the brain, an agitated, depressed mood usually follows as the drug's effects decline. Figure 5.12

barbiturates Depressant drugs that decrease the activity of the central nervous system.

tranquilizers Depressant drugs that reduce anxiety and induce relaxation.

opiates Opium or its derivatives; they depress central nervous system activity.

stimulants Psychoactive drugs that increase central nervous system activity.

FIGURE 5.12 Cocaine and Dopamine
Cocaine concentrates in areas of the brain that are rich in dopamine synapses. *(Top)* What happens in normal communication. The transmitting neuron releases dopamine, which stimulates the receiving neuron by binding to its receptor sites. After binding occurs, some dopamine is carried back into the transmitting neuron for later release. *(Bottom)* When cocaine (purple) is present in the synapse, it binds to the uptake pumps and prevents them from removing dopamine from the synapse. As a result, more dopamine is present in the synapse, and more dopamine receptors are activated.

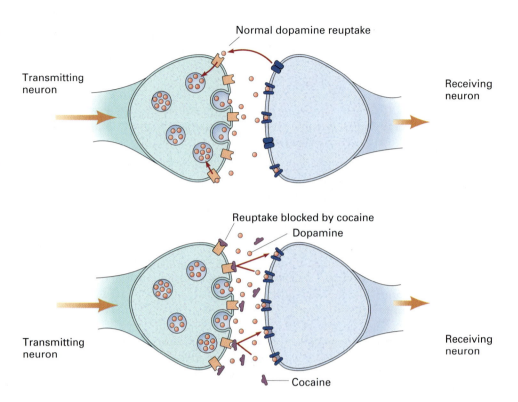

shows how cocaine affects dopamine levels in the brain. *Crack* is a potent form of cocaine, consisting of chips of pure cocaine that are usually smoked. Crack is believed to be one of the most addictive substances known, being more addictive than heroin, barbiturates, or alcohol. Cocaine's addictive properties are so strong that 6 months after treatment more than 50 percent of cocaine abusers return to the drug. Experts on drug abuse argue that prevention is the best approach to reducing cocaine use.

- *MDMA (Ecstasy)* is an illegal synthetic drug with both stimulant and hallucinogenic properties. Street names for MDMA include *Ecstasy, XTC, hug, beans,* and *love drug.* A special concern is the use of MDMA by adolescents, although its use decreased in 2002 (Johnston & others, 2003).

- *Caffeine* is the most widely used psychoactive drug in the world. Caffeine is a stimulant and a natural component of the plants that are the sources of coffee, tea, and cola drinks. Caffeine also is present in chocolate and in many nonprescribed medications. The stimulating effects of caffeine are often perceived to be beneficial for boosting energy and alertness, but some people experience unpleasant side effects. *Caffeinism* is the term given to overindulgence of caffeine. It is characterized by mood changes, anxiety, and sleep disruption. Caffeinism often develops in people who drink five or more cups of coffee each day. Common symptoms of caffeinism are insomnia, irritability, headaches, ringing in the ears, dry mouth, increased blood pressure, and digestive problems (Hogan, Hornick, & Bouchoux, 2002). Caffeine affects the brain's pleasure centers, so kicking the caffeine habit is difficult. When individuals who regularly consume caffeinated beverages remove caffeine from their diet, they typically experience headaches, lethargy, apathy, and concentration difficulties. These symptoms of withdrawal are usually mild and subside after several days.

- *Nicotine* is the main psychoactive ingredient in all forms of smoking and smokeless tobacco. Even with all the publicity given to the enormous health risks posed by tobacco, we sometimes overlook the highly addictive nature of nicotine. In the brain, nicotine stimulates the reward centers by raising dopamine levels. Behavioral effects of nicotine include improved attention and alertness, reduced anger and anxiety, and pain relief (Rezvani & Levin, 2001). Tolerance develops for nicotine both in the long run and on a daily basis, so

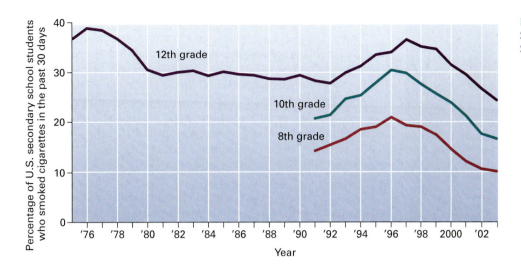

FIGURE 5.13 Trends in Cigarette Smoking by U.S. Secondary School Students

that cigarettes smoked later in the day have less effect than those smoked earlier in the day. Withdrawal from nicotine often quickly produces strong, unpleasant symptoms, such as irritability, craving, inability to focus, sleep disturbance, and increased appetite. Withdrawal symptoms can persist for months or longer. Despite the positive short-term effects of nicotine (such as increased energy and alertness), most smokers recognize the serious health risks of smoking and wish they could quit. Chapter 13 further explores the difficulty in quitting smoking and offers strategies that can be used to quit.

The good news is that cigarette smoking is decreasing among adolescents and adults. In a national survey by the Institute of Social Research, the percentage of U.S. adolescents who are current cigarette smokers continued to decline in 2002 and 2003 (Johnston, O'Malley, & Bachman, 2003). Cigarette smoking peaked in 1996 and 1997 and then declined 8 to 10 percent, depending on grade level, from 1998 to 2003 (see figure 5.13). Following peak use in 1996, smoking rates for U.S. eighth graders have fallen by 50 percent. In 2003, the following percentage of U.S. eighth, tenth, and twelfth graders said they had smoked in the last 30 days, respectively: 10.2, 16.7, 24.4. The percentage declines in upper grades have been smaller, although the picture for older adolescents should improve in the next few years as a result of the current eighth graders becoming older.

There are a number of explanations for the decline in cigarette use by U.S. youth. These include increasing prices, less tobacco advertising reaching adolescents, more antismoking advertisements, and more negative publicity about the tobacco industry. Since the mid-1990s, an increasing percentage of adolescents have reported that they perceive cigarette smoking as dangerous, that they disapprove of it, that they are less accepting of being around smokers, and that they prefer to date nonsmokers (Johnston, O'Malley, & Bachman, 2003).

The devastating effects of early smoking were brought home in a research study that found that smoking in the adolescent years causes permanent genetic changes in the lungs and forever increases the risk for lung cancer, even if the smoker quits (Weincke & others, 1999). In the study, the damage was much less likely among the smokers who had started in their 20s. One of the remarkable findings in the study was that the early age of onset of smoking was more important in predicting genetic damage than how heavily the individuals smoked.

Hallucinogens

Hallucinogens are psychoactive drugs that modify a person's perceptual experiences and produce visual images that are not real. Hallucinogens are also called psychedelic (meaning "mind-altering") drugs. Marijuana has a mild hallucinogenic effect, LSD a stronger one.

hallucinogens Psychoactive drugs that modify a person's perceptual experiences and produce visual images that are not real.

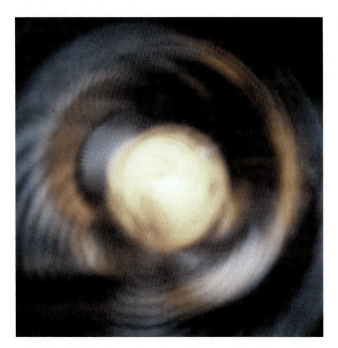

Under the influence of hallucinogenic drugs, such as LSD, several users have reported seeing tunnel-like images. *What unpleasant effects of LSD offset the dazzling images?*

- *Marijuana* is the dried leaves and flowers of the hemp plant, *Cannabis sativa,* which originated in central Asia but is now grown in most parts of the world. The plant's dried resin is known as hashish. The active ingredient in marijuana is THC (delta-9-tetrahydrocannabinol). Unlike other psychoactive drugs, THC does not affect a specific neurotransmitter. Rather, marijuana disrupts the membranes of neurons and affects the functioning of a variety of neurotransmitters and hormones. The physical effects of marijuana include increases in pulse rate and blood pressure, reddening of the eyes, coughing, and dryness of the mouth. Psychological effects include a mixture of excitation, depression, and mild hallucination, which makes it difficult to classify the drug. Marijuana can trigger spontaneous unrelated ideas; distorted perceptions of time and place; increased sensitivity to sounds, tastes, smells, and colors; and erratic verbal behavior. Marijuana can also impair attention and memory. When used daily in large amounts, marijuana also can alter sperm count and change hormonal cycles (Close, Roberts, & Berger, 1990). It may be involved in some birth defects. On a positive note, researchers have found some medical uses for marijuana, such as treating glaucoma, chemotherapy-caused vomiting, and AIDS-related weight loss. Marijuana is the illegal drug most widely used by high school students. Just over 20 percent of high school seniors in the United States say that they have used marijuana in the past year (Johnston & others, 2003).
- *LSD (lysergic acid diethylamide)* is a hallucinogen that even in low doses produces striking perceptual changes. Objects change their shapes and glow. Colors become kaleidoscopic, and images unfold. LSD can also influence a user's sense of time. Time seems to slow down dramatically, so that brief glances at objects are experienced as deep, penetrating, and lengthy examinations, and minutes seem to be hours or even days. LSD-induced images are sometimes pleasurable and sometimes grotesque. A bad LSD trip can trigger extreme anxiety, paranoia, and suicidal or homicidal impulses. LSD's effects on the body can include dizziness, nausea, and tremors. LSD acts primarily on the neurotransmitter serotonin in the brain, though it also can affect dopamine (Nichols & Sanders-Bush, 2002). Emotional and cognitive effects include rapid mood swings and impaired attention and memory. LSD is one psychoactive drug that has no beneficial effects. The use of LSD reached a peak in the 1960s and 1970s, but its popularity declined after its unpredictable effects became publicized. In the 1990s, use of LSD by high school students increased, although not to the level of use in the 1960s and 1970s (Johnston & others, 2003). A summary of the characteristics of a number of depressants, stimulants, and hallucinogens is presented in figure 5.14.

Review and Sharpen Your Thinking

4 *Evaluate the uses and types of psychoactive drugs.*

- Describe the effects of psychoactive drugs.
- Outline the characteristics of depressants, including alcohol.
- List common stimulants and describe their effects.
- Explain the effects of hallucinogens.

Do you know someone who has a drug problem? If so, describe the nature of the problem. Is he or she willing to admit to having a problem?

Drug Classification	Medical Uses	Short-Term Effects	Overdose Effects	Health Risks	Risks of Physical and Psychological Dependence
Depressants					
Alcohol	Pain relief	Relaxation, depressed brain activity, slowed behavior, reduced inhibitions	Disorientation, loss of consciousness, even death at high blood-alcohol levels	Accidents, brain damage, liver disease, heart disease, ulcers, birth defects	Moderate physical and psychological
Barbiturates	Help in sleeping	Relaxation, sleep	Breathing difficulty, coma, possible death	Accidents, coma, death	Moderate to high physical and psychological
Tranquilizers	Anxiety reduction	Relaxation, slowed behavior	Breathing difficulty, coma, possible death	Accidents, coma, possible death	Low to moderate physical, moderate to high psychological
Opiates (narcotics)	Pain relief	Euphoric feelings, drowsiness, nausea	Convulsions, coma, possible death	Accidents, infectious diseases such as AIDS	High physical, moderate to high psychological
Stimulants					
Amphetamines	Weight control	Increased alertness and excitability, decreased fatigue, irritability	Extreme irritability, feelings of persecution, convulsions	Insomnia, hypertension, malnutrition, possible death	Possible physical, moderate to high psychological
Cocaine	Local anesthesia	Increased alertness, excitability, euphoria, decreased fatigue, irritability	Extreme irritability, feelings of persecution, convulsions, cardiac arrest, possible death	Insomnia, hypertension, malnutrition, possible death	Possible physical, moderate (oral) to very high (injected or smoked) psychological
MDMA (Ecstasy)	None	Mild stimulant and hallucinogenic effects, high body temperature and dehydration, sense of well-being and social connectedness	Brain damage, especially in memory and thinking	Cardiovascular problems, death	Possible physical, moderate psychological
Caffeine	None	Alertness and sense of well-being followed by fatigue	Nervousness, anxiety, disturbed sleep	Cardiovascular problems	Moderate physical and psychological
Nicotine	None	Stimulation and stress reduction followed by fatigue and anger	Nervousness, disturbed sleep	Cancer, cardiovascular disease	High physical and psychological
Hallucinogens					
Marijuana	Treatment of the eye disorder glaucoma	Euphoric feelings, relaxation, mild hallucinations, time distortion, attention and memory impairment	Fatigue, disoriented behavior	Accidents, respiratory disease	Very low physical, moderate psychological
LSD	None	Strong hallucinations, distorted time perception	Severe mental disturbance, loss of contact with reality	Accidents	No physical, low psychological

FIGURE 5.14 **Categories of Psychoactive Drugs**

Reach Your Learning Goals

States of Consciousness

1 THE NATURE OF CONSCIOUSNESS

- Levels of Awareness
- Consciousness and the Brain

2 SLEEP AND DREAMS

- Biological Rhythms and Sleep
- The Need for Sleep
- Sleep Stages
- Sleep Disorders
- Dreams

3 HYPNOSIS

- The Nature of Hypnosis
- Explanations of Hypnosis
- Applications of Hypnosis

4 PSYCHOACTIVE DRUGS

- Uses of Psychoactive Drugs
- Depressants
- Stimulants
- Hallucinogens

1 Discuss the nature of consciousness.

- Consciousness is the awareness of external events and internal sensations, including awareness of the self and thoughts about experiences. William James described the mind as a stream of consciousness. Consciousness occurs at five different levels of awareness: higher-level consciousness (controlled processes), lower-level awareness (automatic processes and daydreaming), altered states of consciousness (produced by drugs, trauma, fatigue, and other factors), subconscious awareness (waking subconscious awareness, sleep and dreams), and no awareness (Freud's concept of unconscious thought).
- One of the great unanswered questions about consciousness is its location—in the mind or in the brain—and, if in the brain, whether there is a seat of consciousness or, rather, a distribution across different areas of the brain. Most experts agree that consciousness is likely distributed across the brain.

2 Explain the nature of sleep and dreams.

- Biological rhythms are periodic physiological fluctuations. The biological rhythm that regulates the daily sleep/wake cycle is a circadian rhythm. The part of the brain that keeps our biological clocks synchronized is a small structure in the hypothalamus that registers light. Biological clocks can become desynchronized by such things as jet travel and changing work shifts. Strategies for resetting the biological clock help to restore normal sleep patterns.
- We need sleep for physical restoration, adaptation, growth, and memory. An increasing number of research studies reveal that people do not function optimally when they are sleep-deprived. Americans generally—and adolescents and aging adults, in particular—do not seem to be getting enough sleep.
- Stages of sleep correspond to massive electrophysiological changes in the brain that can be assessed by an EEG. Humans go through four stages of non-REM sleep and one stage of REM, or rapid-eye-movement, sleep. Most dreaming occurs during REM sleep. A sleep cycle of all five stages lasts about 90 to 100 minutes and recurs several times during the night. The REM stage lasts longer toward the end of a night's sleep.
- Many Americans suffer from chronic, long-term sleep disorders, which can impair normal daily functioning. These disorders include insomnia, sleepwalking and sleep talking, nightmares and night terrors, narcolepsy, and sleep apnea.
- In Freud's view, the reason people dream is wish fulfillment. He distinguished between a dream's manifest (symbolic) and latent (unconscious) content. The cognitive theory of dreaming explains dreaming in terms of the same cognitive concepts used in studying the waking mind. In this view, dreams might be an arena for solving problems and thinking creatively. According to neuroscientists, dreaming occurs when the cerebral cortex synthesizes and tries to make sense of neural signals emanating from activity in the lower part of the brain.

3 Describe hypnosis.

- Hypnosis can be defined as a psychological state, or possibly altered attention and awareness, in which the individual is unusually receptive to suggestions. The hypnotic state is different from a sleep state, as confirmed by EEG recordings. There are substantial individual variations in people's susceptibility to hypnosis. People in a hypnotic state are unlikely to do anything that violates their morals or that involves a real danger.
- Two theories have been proposed to explain hypnosis. In Hilgard's theory, hypnosis involves a divided state of consciousness, a splitting of consciousness into separate components. One component follows the hypnotist's commands, and the other acts as a "hidden observer." The other theory is that the hypnotized individual behaves the way he or she believes a hypnotized individual is expected to behave.
- Hypnosis is widely used in psychotherapy, medicine and dentistry, criminal investigations, and sports.

4 Evaluate the uses and types of psychoactive drugs.

- Psychoactive drugs act on the nervous system to alter states of consciousness, modify perceptions, and change moods. Humans are attracted to these types of drugs because they help them adapt to change. Continued use of psychoactive drugs can lead to tolerance and physical or psychological addiction.
- Depressants slow down mental and physical activity. Among the most widely used depressants are alcohol, barbiturates, tranquilizers, and opiates. After caffeine, alcohol is the most widely used drug in America. The high rate of alcohol abuse by high school and college students is especially alarming. Alcoholism is a disorder that involves long-term, repeated, uncontrolled, compulsive, and excessive use of alcoholic beverages that impairs the drinker's health and work and social relationships.
- Stimulants increase the central nervous system's activity and include caffeine, nicotine, amphetamines, cocaine, and MDMA (Ecstasy).
- Hallucinogens modify a person's perceptual experiences and produce visual images that are not real. Marijuana has a mild hallucinogenic effect. LSD has a strong one.

Key Terms

Apply Your Knowledge

1. As noted in the chapter, we process information at many levels of consciousness. Try to bring as much sensory information into the controlled process level of consciousness as you can; pay attention to every sensation available to you. (Are your socks touching your ankles? How many sounds can you hear? What is available to your visual system? Is your stomach growling?) How long can you keep track of all this sensory information, and what would happen if something important abruptly required all your attention? What can you conclude about which levels of consciousness normally process all this information?

2. Keep a sleep journal for several nights. Compare your sleep patterns with those described in the chapter. Do you have a sleep debt? If so, which stages of sleep are you likely missing most? Keep a record of your mood and energy levels after a short night's sleep and then after you've had at least 8 hours of sleep in one night. What changes do you notice? Does a good night's sleep affect your behavior?

3. A quick web search reveals sites that offer "subliminal tapes for self-hypnosis" to help you do anything from losing weight to getting a great new job. Based on the discussion of subliminal perception in chapter 4 and on hypnosis in this chapter, explain how a scientist would regard these tapes.

4. The website of the National Institute on Drug Abuse maintains a series of reports on current scientific knowledge about many commonly abused drugs. Visit http://www.nida.nih.gov/ResearchReports/ResearchIndex.html and pick one of the listed reports. Using the report's information, compare the psychological effects and risks associated with use of this drug with the psychological effects and risks of one of the psychoactive compounds described in the chapter.

Connections

To test your mastery of the material in this chapter, go to the Study Guide and the In-Psych Plus CD-ROM, as well as the Online Learning Center. There you will find a chapter summary, practice tests, flashcards, lecture slides, web links, and other study tools, such as interactive exercises and reviews as well as current, chapter-relevant news articles.

6 Learning

Chapter Outline

Learning Goals

THE NATURE OF LEARNING

Types of Learning
▼
Biological Factors in Learning

1 *Explain what learning is.*

CLASSICAL CONDITIONING

Pavlov's Studies
▼
Applications of Classical Conditioning

2 *Describe classical conditioning.*

OPERANT CONDITIONING

Thorndike's Law of Effect
▼
Skinner's Approach to Operant Conditioning
▼
Shaping
▼
Principles of Reinforcement
▼
Applications of Operant Conditioning

3 *Discuss operant conditioning.*

OBSERVATIONAL LEARNING

4 *Understand observational learning.*

COGNITIVE FACTORS IN LEARNING

Purposive Behavior
▼
Insight Learning

5 *Outline the role of cognition in learning.*

Much of what we do results from what we have *learned*. If you had grown up in another part of the world, you would speak a different language, like different foods, and behave in ways characteristic of that culture. Why? The content of your *learning experiences* in that culture would have been different.

One way we learn is by watching what other people do and say. Television has been accused of interfering with children's learning; critics say television lures children from schoolwork and books and makes them passive learners. But television has, in fact, contributed significantly to children's learning since the mid-twentieth century, giving them a broader view of the world than before. Consider the influence of *Sesame Street*, which was specifically designed to improve children's cognitive and social skills (Wright & others, 2001). Almost half of America's 2- to 5-year-olds watch it regularly.

Highly successful at teaching kids, *Sesame Street* uses fast-paced action, sound effects, music, and humorous characters to grab the attention of its young audience. While their eyes are glued to the screen, young children learn basic academic skills, such as letter and number recognition. Researchers have found that, when regular *Sesame Street* viewers from low-income families enter the first grade, they are better prepared to learn in school than their counterparts who do not watch the program regularly (Bogatz & Ball, 1972; Cole, Richman, & Brown, 2001; Fisch & Truglio, 2001; Wright & others, 2001).

When *Sesame Street* first appeared in 1969, its creators had no idea that this "street" would lead to locations as distant as Kuwait, Israel, Latin America, and the Philippines. Since *Sesame Street* first aired in the United States, it has been televised in 84 countries, and 13 foreign-language versions have been produced. *Barrio Sesamo* is shown in 17 South and Central American

Children all over the world learn in part by observing the actions and utterances of *Sesame Street*'s characters. Here the yellow Big Bird familiar to American children is joined by his Dutch cousin, Pino.

countries, as well as in Puerto Rico. It emphasizes learning about the diversity of cultures and lifestyles in South America. *Rechov Sumsum*, shown in Israel, especially encourages children to learn how people from different ethnic and religious backgrounds can live in harmony. When children in the Netherlands watch *Sesamstraat*, they learn about the concept of school and meet a 7-foot-tall blue bird named Pino, who is always eager to learn.

Learning allows all of us to acquire new behaviors, skills, and knowledge. The focus in this chapter is on three types of learning: classical conditioning, operant conditioning, and observational learning. I also discuss the role of cognitive, or mental, processes in learning.

1   THE NATURE OF LEARNING

| Types of Learning | Biological Factors in Learning |

What is learning?

In learning the alphabet, you made some mistakes along the way, but at some point you learned all of your letters. You changed from someone who did not know the alphabet to someone who did. Learning anything new involves change. But it is also a relatively permanent influence on behavior. Once you learned the alphabet, it did not leave you. Once you learn how to drive a car, you do not have to go through the process again at a later time. You learned the alphabet through experience with the letters—you may have learned it by watching *Sesame Street.* Through experience, you may have also learned that you have to study to do well on a test, that there usually is an opening act at a rock concert, and that a field goal in American football adds 3 points to the score. Putting these pieces together, we arrive at a definition of **learning:** a relatively permanent change in behavior that occurs through experience.

Learning not only is extremely important in the lives of humans but also is vital to lower animals. To survive and function in their world, animals such as rats and rabbits have to learn and adapt just as humans do. Much learning research has been done with lower animals largely becuase of the extensive control that researchers can exercise in studies on lower animals. A century of research on learning in lower animals and in humans suggests that many of the principles generated initially in research on lower animals also apply to humans (Barker, 2001; Leahy & Harris, 2001).

Types of Learning

Psychologists explain our many experiences with a few basic learning processes (Frieman, 2002). The opening story about *Sesame Street* focused on the type of learning called *observational learning,* in which organisms learn by watching what others do. Another type of learning is **associative learning,** in which a connection, or association, is made between two events (Kazdin, 2000; Pearce & Bouton, 2001). *Conditioning* is the process of learning associations (Miller & Grace, 2003; Ormrod, 2004).

There are two types of conditioning: classical and operant. In *classical conditioning,* organisms learn the association between two stimuli. As a result of this association, organisms learn to anticipate events. For example, lightning is associated with thunder and regularly precedes it (Purdy & others, 2001). Thus, when you see lightning, you anticipate that you will hear thunder soon afterward. In *operant conditioning,* organisms learn the association between a behavior and a consequence. As a result of this association, organisms learn to increase behaviors that are followed by rewards and to decrease behaviors that are followed by punishment. For example, children whose parents reward them with candy for behaving well are likely to repeat their good manners. Also, children whose bad manners are followed by a few nasty words and glances from their parents are less likely to repeat their bad behavior.

Figure 6.1 compares classical and operant conditioning.

Biological Factors in Learning

Albert Einstein had many special talents. He combined enormous creativity with great analytic ability to develop some of the twentieth century's most important insights into the nature of matter and the universe. Einstein received an excellent, rigorous European education, and later in the United States he experienced the freedom and support believed to be important in creative exploration. Would Einstein have been able to fully develop his intellectual skills and make such brilliant insights if he had grown up in a developing country, such as Bolivia? It is unlikely. However, genes obviously endowed Einstein with extraordinary intellectual skills, which enabled him to think and reason on a very high plane.

Few of us are Einsteins, but human biology does equip us to learn certain things more readily than other animals do. Fish can't play table tennis, and cows can't solve math problems. The structure of an organism's body permits certain kinds of learning and inhibits others (Chance, 2003; Morgan, 2002). For example, chimpanzees cannot learn to speak English because they lack the necessary vocal equipment. Some of us cannot solve difficult calculus problems, others of us can, and the differences do not all seem to be the result of experiences.

learning A relatively permanent change in behavior that occurs through experience.

associative learning Learning through either classical conditioning or operant conditioning that two events are connected.

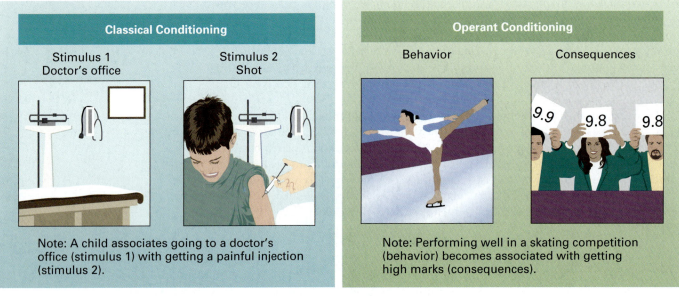

FIGURE 6.1 **Comparing Classical and Operant Conditioning** *(Left)* In classical conditioning, a child comes to associate a doctor's office with getting a painful injection. *(Right)* In operant conditioning, performing well in a skating competition becomes associated with getting high marks.

Obviously, though, learning is not unique to humans. Research with animals has demonstrated some of the biological factors that affect learning in many types of animals. An example of biological constraints on learning is **instinctive drift,** the tendency of animals to revert to instinctive behavior that interferes with learning. Consider the experience of Keller Breland and Marion Breland (1961), who used operant conditioning to train animals to perform at fairs and conventions and in television advertisements. They taught pigs to cart large wooden nickels to a piggy bank and deposit them. They also trained raccoons to pick up a coin and place it in a metal tray.

Although the pigs and raccoons, as well as chickens and other animals, performed well at most of the tasks (raccoons became adept basketball players, for example), some of the animals began acting strangely. Instead of picking up the large wooden nickels and carrying them to the piggy bank, the pigs would drop the nickels on the ground, shove them with their snouts, toss them in the air, and then repeat these actions. The raccoons began to hold on to their coins rather than dropping them into the metal tray. When two coins were introduced, the raccoons rubbed them together in a miserly fashion. Somehow these behaviors overwhelmed the strength of the training.

Why were the pigs and the raccoons misbehaving? The pigs were rooting, an instinctive movement used to uncover edible roots. The raccoons were engaged in an instinctive food-washing response. Their instinctive drift interfered with learning.

Some animals learn readily in one situation but have difficulty learning in slightly different circumstances. The difficulty might result not from some aspect of the learning situation but from the organism's biological predisposition (Seligman, 1970). **Preparedness** is the species-specific biological predisposition to learn in certain ways and not others.

Much of the evidence for preparedness comes from research on *taste aversion* (Garcia, 1989). Consider this situation: A psychologist went to dinner with his wife and ordered filet mignon with béarnaise sauce, his favorite dish. Several hours later, he became very ill with stomach pains and nausea. Several weeks later, he tried to eat béarnaise sauce but became ill again. The psychologist's experience had created a taste aversion (Yamamoto, Frequet, & Sandner, 2002). Taste aversions typically develop

instinctive drift The tendency of animals to revert to instinctive behavior that interferes with learning.

preparedness The species-specific biological predisposition to learn in certain ways and not others.

This raccoon's skill in using its hands made it an excellent basketball player. But because of instinctive drift, the raccoon had a much more difficult time dropping coins in a tray. *How does instinctive drift affect an animal's ability to learn?*

with very few learning experiences. In contrast, learning to whip up a béarnaise sauce may take much more effort.

If any organism ingests a substance that poisons but does not kill it, the organism often develops considerable distaste for that substance. Rats that experience low levels of radiation after eating, just one time, show a strong aversion to the food they were eating when the radiation made them ill. This aversion has been shown to last for as long as 32 days (Garcia, Ervin, & Koelling, 1966). Radiation and chemical treatment of cancer often produce nausea in patients, and the resulting pattern of aversions often resembles those shown by laboratory animals. The implication is that animals, including humans, have a built-in capacity to learn quickly about which ingestible substances are good for them and which are not.

Knowledge about taste aversion has been used to discourage animals from preying on certain species. For example, the livestock of ranchers may be threatened by wolves or coyotes. Instead of killing the pests or predators, the ranchers feed them poisoned meat of their prey (cattle, sheep). The wolves and coyotes, poisoned but not killed, develop a taste aversion for cattle or sheep and, hence, are less of a threat to the ranchers and their livestock. Knowing how taste aversion affects learning thus allows ranchers, cattle, sheep, wolves, and coyotes to live in a semblance of ecological balance.

Review and Sharpen Your Thinking

1   *Explain what learning is.*
  - Distinguish between observational and associative learning.
  - Discuss how biology affects learning.

How do you learn? Think of a behavior you engage in and describe how you learned it.

2 CLASSICAL CONDITIONING

| Pavlov's Studies | Applications of Classical Conditioning |

What is classical conditioning?

It is a nice spring day. A father takes his baby out for a walk. The baby reaches over to touch a pink flower and is stung by the bumblebee sitting on the petals. The next day, the baby's mother brings home some pink flowers. She removes a flower from the arrangement and takes it over for her baby to smell. The baby cries loudly as soon as she sees the pink flower. The baby's distress at the sight of the pink flower illustrates the learning process of **classical conditioning,** in which a neutral stimulus (the flower) becomes associated with a meaningful stimulus (the pain of a bee sting) and acquires the capacity to elicit a response (fear) similar to the response to the first stimulus.

Pavlov's Studies

In the early 1900s, the Russian physiologist Ivan Pavlov was interested in the way the body digests food. In his experiments, he routinely placed meat powder in a dog's mouth, causing the dog to salivate. Pavlov noticed that the meat powder was not the only stimulus that caused the dog to salivate. The dog salivated in response to a number of stimuli associated with the food, such as the sight of the food dish, the sight of the individual who brought the food into the room, and the sound of the door closing when the food arrived. Pavlov recognized that the dog's association of these sights and sounds with the food was an important type of learning, which came to be called *classical conditioning.*

Pavlov wanted to know why the dog salivated to various sights and sounds before eating the meat powder. He observed that the dog's behavior included both learned and unlearned components. The unlearned part of classical conditioning is based on the fact that some stimuli automatically produce certain responses apart from any prior learning; in other words, they are inborn, or innate. These *reflexes* are automatic stimulus-response connections. They include salivation in response to food, nausea in response to spoiled food, shivering in response to low temperature, coughing in response to the throat being clogged, pupil constriction in response to light, and withdrawal in response to blows or burns. An **unconditioned stimulus (UCS)** is a stimulus that produces a response without prior learning; food was the UCS in Pavlov's experiments. An **unconditioned response (UCR)** is an unlearned response that is automatically elicited by the UCS. In Pavlov's experiment, the saliva that flowed from the dog's mouth in response to food was the UCR. In the case of the baby and the flower, the baby's learning and experience did not cause her to cry when the bee stung her. Her crying was unlearned and occurred automatically. The bee's sting was the UCS, and the crying was the UCR.

In studying a dog's response to various stimuli associated with meat powder, Pavlov rang a bell before giving meat powder to the dog. Until then, ringing the bell did not have a particular effect on the dog, except perhaps to wake the dog from a nap. The bell was a neutral stimulus. But the dog began to associate the sound of the bell with the food and salivated when it heard the bell. In classical conditioning, the **conditioned stimulus (CS)** is a previously neutral stimulus that eventually elicits the conditioned response after being associated with the unconditioned stimulus. The **conditioned response (CR)** is the learned response to the conditioned stimulus that occurs after CS-UCS pairing (Pavlov, 1927). For the dog, the bell became a conditioned (learned) stimulus (CS) and salivation a conditioned response (CR). For the

classical conditioning Learning by which a neutral stimulus becomes associated with a meaningful stimulus and acquires the capacity to elicit a similar response.

unconditioned stimulus (UCS) A stimulus that produces a response without prior learning.

unconditioned response (UCR) An unlearned response that is automatically elicited by an unconditioned stimulus.

conditioned stimulus (CS) A previously neutral stimulus that eventually elicits the conditioned response after being associated with the unconditioned stimulus.

conditioned response (CR) The learned response to the conditioned stimulus that occurs after the conditioned stimulus is associated with the unconditioned stimulus.

unhappy baby, the flower was the "bell," or CS, and crying was the CR after the sting (UCS) and the flower (CS) were paired.

A summary of how classical conditioning works is shown in figure 6.2.

Acquisition

Acquisition in classical conditioning is the initial learning of the stimulus-response link: A neutral stimulus is associated with the UCS and becomes the conditioned stimulus (CS) that elicits the CR. Two important aspects of acquisition are timing and predictability.

The time interval between the CS and the UCS is one of the most important aspects of classical conditioning (Kotani, Kawahara, & Kirino, 2002; Weidemann, Georgilas, & Kehoe, 1999). Conditioned responses develop when the CS and UCS occur close together. Often, optimal spacing is a fraction of a second (Kimble, 1961). In Pavlov's work, if the bell had rung 20 minutes after the presentation of the food, the dog probably would not have associated the bell with the food.

Robert Rescorla (1966, 1988) believes that, for classical conditioning to take place, not only must the time interval in the CS-UCS connection be brief but also the occurrence of one stimulus must be *contingent on,* or predictable from, the presence of another. For example, as mentioned earlier, a flash of lightning usually is followed by the sound of thunder. Thus the thunder is predictable. If you see lightning, you might put your hands over your ears or lean away in anticipation of the thunder.

Generalization and Discrimination

Pavlov found that the dog salivated in response not only to the tone of the bell but also to other sounds, such as a whistle. Although Pavlov did not pair these sounds with the unconditioned stimulus of the food, he discovered that, the more similar the noise was to the original sound of the bell, the stronger was the dog's salivary flow. **Generalization** in classical conditioning is the tendency of a new stimulus that is similar to the original conditioned stimulus to elicit a response that is similar to the conditioned response (Jones, Kemenes, & Benjamin, 2001). Generalization has value in preventing learning from being tied to specific stimuli. For example, we do not have to learn how to drive all over again when we change cars or drive down a different road.

Stimulus generalization is not always beneficial. For example, a cat that generalizes from a minnow to a piranha has a major problem. **Discrimination** in classical conditioning is the process of learning to respond to certain stimuli and not to respond to others (Murphy, Baker, & Fouquet, 2001). To produce discrimination, Pavlov gave food to the dog only after ringing the bell and not after any other sounds. In this way, the dog soon learned to distinguish between the bell and other sounds.

acquisition (classical conditioning) The initial learning of the stimulus-response link, which involves a neutral stimulus being associated with an unconditioned stimulus and becoming a conditioned stimulus that elicits the conditioned response.

generalization (classical conditioning) The tendency of a new stimulus that is similar to the original stimulus to elicit a response that is similar to the conditioned response.

discrimination (classical conditioning) The process of learning to respond to certain stimuli and not to others.

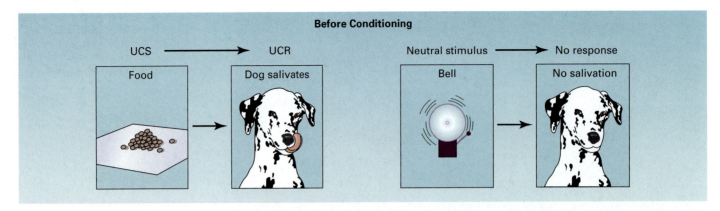

Before Conditioning

UCS ⟶ UCR

Food | Dog salivates

Neutral stimulus ⟶ No response

Bell | No salivation

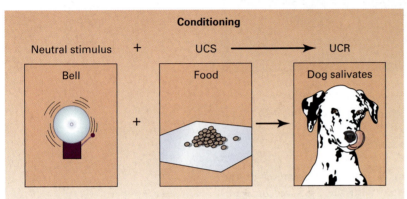

Conditioning

Neutral stimulus + UCS ⟶ UCR

Bell + Food | Dog salivates

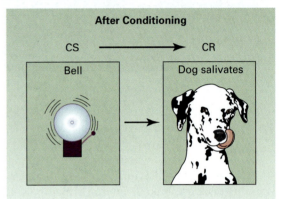

After Conditioning

CS ⟶ CR

Bell | Dog salivates

FIGURE 6.2 Pavlov's Classical Conditioning In one experiment, Pavlov presented a neutral stimulus (bell) just before an unconditioned stimulus (food). The neutral stimulus became a conditioned stimulus by being paired with the unconditioned stimulus. Subsequently, the conditioned stimulus (bell) by itself made the dog salivate.

extinction (classical conditioning) The weakening of the conditioned response in the absence of the unconditioned stimulus.

spontaneous recovery The process in classical conditioning by which a conditioned response can recur after a time delay without further conditioning.

Many multiple-choice tests place a premium on making careful discriminations among items. Professors often deliberately include similar items that require you to make fine distinctions.

Extinction and Spontaneous Recovery After conditioning the dog to salivate at the sound of a bell, Pavlov rang the bell repeatedly in a single session and did not give the dog any food. Eventually the dog stopped salivating. This result is **extinction,** which, in classical conditioning, is the weakening of the conditioned response in the absence of the unconditioned stimulus. Without continued association with the unconditioned stimulus (UCS), the conditioned stimulus (CS) loses its power to elicit the conditioned response (CR).

Extinction is not always the end of a conditioned response (Brooks, 2000). The day after Pavlov extinguished the conditioned salivation to the sound of a bell, he took the dog to the laboratory and rang the bell, still not giving the dog any meat powder. The dog salivated, indicating that an extinguished response can spontaneously recur. **Spontaneous recovery** is the process in classical conditioning by which a conditioned response recurs after a delay without further conditioning. Consider an example of spontaneous recovery you may have had: You thought that you had totally forgotten about (extinguished) an old "love." Then, all of a sudden you are in a particular context and get a mental image of the person along with an emotional reaction to him or her from the past (spontaneous recovery).

Figure 6.3 shows the sequence of acquisition, extinction, and spontaneous recovery. Spontaneous recovery can occur several times, but as long as the conditioned stimulus is presented alone, spontaneous recovery becomes weaker and eventually ceases to occur.

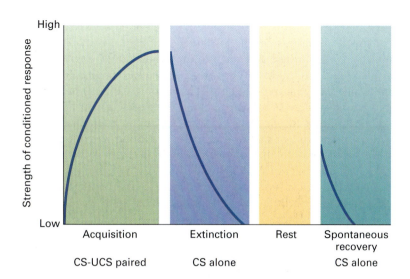

FIGURE 6.3 **Acquisition, Extinction, and Spontaneous Recovery** In classical conditioning, the conditioned stimulus and unconditioned stimulus become associated during acquisition. When acquisition occurs, the strength of the conditioned response increases. During extinction, the conditioned stimulus is presented alone, eventually resulting in a decrease of the conditioned response. After a rest period, spontaneous recovery appears, although the strength of the conditioned response is not nearly as great as it was after the CS-UCS pairings. When the CS is presented alone again, after spontaneous recovery, the response is eventually extinguished.

In-Psych Plus

Use the interactivity "Classical Conditioning 1" to review and apply the concepts of acquisition, generalization, discrimination, and extinction. Following is another example of these concepts:

- *Acquisition.* A young child learns to fear (CR) going to a dentist's office by associating it with the unlearned emotional response (UCR) to the pain of having a tooth cavity filled (UCS).
- *Generalization.* The child fears all dentists' offices and similar places, including doctors' offices and adults in them who wear white medical clothing, as well as the smells and sounds in them.
- *Discrimination.* The child goes with his mother to her doctor's office and learns that it is not associated with the pain of the UCS.
- *Extinction.* The child subsequently goes to the dentist on a number of occasions and does not have a painful experience, so the child's fear of dentists' offices goes away, at least for a while, until the child has another painful experience with a cavity being filled.

Researchers have found that the majority of dental fears originate in childhood, likely through classical conditioning, and that these fears can keep individuals from obtaining dental treatment as adults (Ost, 1991).

Interestingly, there are cultural variations in children's dental fear. Children in the United States have the most fear (20 percent have a high level of fear), and children in Norway and Sweden have the least fear (only 3 to 4 percent have a high level of fear) (Milgram, Vigehesa, & Weinstein, 1992; Neverlien & Johnsen, 1991). This cultural difference likely is due to dental care being part of a free, universal health care system in Norway and Sweden. Children there go to the dentist on a regular basis, regardless of whether they have a dental problem or not. In contrast, children in the United States often go to the dentist only when they have a problem, thus experiencing dental treatment as painful and something to be avoided. Possibly, then, differences in cultural experience influence the occurrence of conditioned emotional responses.

Applications of Classical Conditioning

Classical conditioning has a great deal of survival value (Vernoy, 1995). Because of classical conditioning, we jerk our hands away before they are burned by fire. Classical conditioning also is at work when a description of a tranquil scene, such as an empty beach with waves lapping the sand, causes a harried executive to relax as if she were actually lying on that beach. Since Pavlov conducted his experiments, individuals have been conditioned to respond to the sound of a buzzer, a glimpse of light, a puff of air, or the touch of a hand (Woodruff-Pak, 1999).

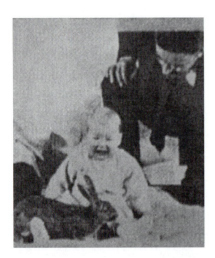

In 1920, Watson and Rayner conditioned 11-month-old Albert to fear a white rat by pairing the rat with a loud noise. When little Albert was subsequently presented with other stimuli similar to the white rat, such as the rabbit shown here, he was afraid of them, too. This experiment illustrates the principle of stimulus generalization in classical conditioning. *What are some other examples of generalization in classical conditioning?*

Mental and Physical Health Some of the behaviors we associate with health problems or mental disorders can be attributed to classical conditioning. For example, John Watson and Rosalie Rayner (1920) demonstrated classical conditioning's role in *phobias,* which are irrational fears, with an infant named Albert. They showed Albert a white laboratory rat to see if he was afraid of it. He was not. As Albert played with the rat, a loud noise was sounded behind his head. As you might imagine, the noise caused little Albert to cry. After only seven pairings of the loud noise with the white rat, Albert began to fear the rat even when the noise was not sounded. Albert's fear was generalized to a rabbit, a dog, and a sealskin coat.

Today, Watson and Rayner's (1920) study would violate the ethical guidelines of the American Psychological Association. In the early part of the twentieth century, when the experiment with little Albert was conducted, there was less concern about the ethical aspects of research.

Watson was right in concluding that many of our fears can be learned through classical conditioning. But if we can produce fears through classical conditioning, then we should be able to eliminate them using conditioning procedures. **Counterconditioning** is a classical conditioning procedure for weakening a CR by associating the fear-provoking stimulus with a new response that is incompatible with the fear. Watson and Rayner did not reverse Albert's fear of furry objects, so presumably this phobia remained with him after the experiment. However, an associate of Watson's, Mary Cover Jones (1924), did eliminate the fears of a 3-year-old boy named Peter. Peter had many of the same fears as Albert, although Peter's fears were not produced by the experimenter. Among Peter's fears were white rats, fur coats, frogs, fish, and mechanical toys. To eliminate these fears, Jones brought a rabbit into Peter's view but kept it far enough away that it would not upset him. At the same time that the rabbit was brought into view, Peter was fed crackers and milk. On each successive day, the rabbit was moved closer to Peter as he ate crackers and milk. Eventually Peter reached the point at which he would eat the food with one hand and pet the rabbit with the other. The feeling of pleasure produced by the crackers and milk was incompatible with the fear produced by the rabbit, and Peter's fear was extinguished through counterconditioning.

Classical conditioning is not restricted to unpleasant emotions, such as fear. Among the things in our lives that produce pleasure because they have become conditioned might be seeing a rainbow or hearing a favorite song. If you have a positive romantic experience, the location in which that experience took place can become a conditioned stimulus through the pairing of the place (CS) with the event (UCS). Stimuli that are often associated with sex, such as mood music, seductive clothing, and a romantic restaurant, likely become conditioned stimuli that produce sexual arousal.

Sometimes, though, classical conditioning involves an experience that is both pleasant and deviant from the norm. Consider a fetishist who becomes sexually aroused by the sight and touch of certain clothing, such as undergarments or shoes. The fetish may have developed when the fetish object (undergarment, shoe) was associated with sexual arousal, especially when the individual was young. The fetish object becomes a conditioned stimulus that can produce sexual arousal by itself (Chance, 2003).

Certain physical complaints—asthma, headaches, ulcers, and high blood pressure, for example—can also be partly the products of classical conditioning. We usually say that such health problems are caused by stress, but often what happens is that certain stimuli, such as a boss's critical attitude or a wife's threat of divorce, are conditioned stimuli for physiological responses. Over time, the frequent presence of the physiological responses may produce a health problem or disorder. A boss's persistent criticism may cause an employee to develop muscle tension, headaches, or high blood pressure. Anything associated with the boss, such as work itself, can then trigger stress in the employee (see figure 6.4).

counterconditioning A classical conditioning procedure for weakening a conditioned response by associating the fear-provoking stimulus with a new response that is incompatible with the fear.

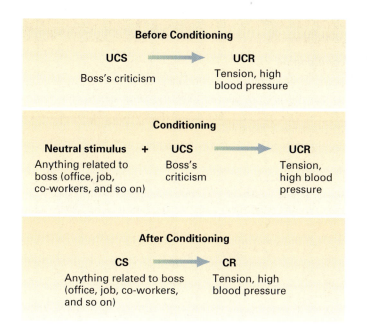

Before Conditioning

UCS ➜ UCR

Boss's criticism | Tension, high blood pressure

Conditioning

Neutral stimulus + **UCS** ➜ **UCR**

Anything related to boss (office, job, co-workers, and so on) | Boss's criticism | Tension, high blood pressure

After Conditioning

CS ➜ CR

Anything related to boss (office, job, co-workers, and so on) | Tension, high blood pressure

FIGURE 6.4 **Classical Conditioning of Health Problems**

Classical conditioning also can be involved in certain aspects of drug use. When drugs are administered in particular circumstances—at a particular time of day, in a particular location, or in a particular ritual—the body reacts in anticipation of receiving the drug. This aspect of drug use can play a role in deaths caused by drug overdoses. How might this work? A user normally takes a drug in a particular setting, such as a bathroom, and acquires a conditioned response to this location (Siegel, 1988). As soon as the drug user walks into the bathroom, his or her body begins to prepare for and anticipate the drug dose in order to lessen the effect of the insult of the drug. If the user takes the drug in an untypical location, such as at a rock concert, the effect of the drug is greater because no conditioned responses have built up in the new setting and therefore the body is not prepared for the drug. In cases in which heroin causes death, researchers often have found that the individuals took the drug at a different time or different place from that at which they usually did (Marlow, 1999).

Consumer Psychology *Consumer psychology* is the study of how consumers think, feel, reason, and select from among different brands and products. Many contemporary advertisers use classical conditioning (Perner, 2001). Consider this sequence:

- Beautiful woman (UCS) → emotional arousal (UCR) in males
- Beautiful woman (UCS) paired with an automobile (not yet a CS) many times
- Automobile (CS) → emotional arousal (CR)

Recent research has shown, however, that, if the CS is encountered outside of ads, it doesn't predict the UCS (Bettman, 2001). Thus classical conditioning may work best for infrequently encountered products and cases in which the UCS is associated with only one brand. Also, classical conditioning usually works best when the CS precedes the UCS in ads.

Not all commercials involve classical conditioning. Some just give information about the product. The next time you watch TV, observe which ads rely on classical conditioning. To review the elements of classical conditioning and its applications to human learning, go to the interactivity "Classical Conditioning 2."

In-Psych Plus

Review and Sharpen Your Thinking

2 *Describe classical conditioning.*

- Summarize the classical conditioning process—including unconditioned stimulus (UCS), conditioned stimulus (CS), unconditioned response (UCR), and conditioned response (CR), as well as acquisition, generalization, discrimination, extinction, and spontaneous recovery.
- Discuss the role of classical conditioning in human phobias and other types of behavior.

Think about an attachment that you or someone you know has for a certain object or environment. Explain how classical conditioning might account for the pleasant association.

3 OPERANT CONDITIONING

> **Thorndike's Law of Effect**
>
> **Shaping**
>
> **Applications of Operant Conditioning**
>
> **Skinner's Approach to Operant Conditioning**
>
> **Principles of Reinforcement**

What is operant conditioning?

Classical conditioning describes an organism's *response* to the environment but fails to capture the active nature of the organism and its influence on the environment. Another major form of learning—operant conditioning—places more emphasis on the organism's *activity* in the environment (Hergenhahn & Olson, 2001). Classical conditioning excels at explaining how neutral stimuli, such as a sound, become associated with unlearned, *involuntary responses,* but it is not as effective in explaining *voluntary*

"Once it became clear to me that, by responding correctly to certain stimuli, I could get all the bananas I wanted, getting this job was a pushover." ©1999 Jack Ziegler from cartoonbank.com. All Rights Reserved.

behaviors, such as studying hard for a test or playing slot machines in Las Vegas. Operant conditioning is usually much better at explaining such voluntary behaviors.

The concept of operant conditioning was developed by the American psychologist B. F. Skinner (1938). **Operant conditioning** (or instrumental conditioning) is a form of associative learning in which the consequences of behavior change the probability of a behavior's occurrence. Skinner chose the term *operant* to describe the behavior of the organism—the behavior operates on the environment, and the environment in turn operates on the behavior. As an example, in operant conditioning, performing a great skating routine in competition (behavior) is likely to result in a high score from the judges (consequences), which in turn encourages the skater to continue training and competing. Thus, whereas classical conditioning involves involuntary responses, operant conditioning consists of voluntary behavior that acts or operates on the environment and produces rewarding or punishing stimuli.

Recall that contingency, or predictability, is an important aspect of classical conditioning; the occurrence of one stimulus is dependent on, or can be predicted from, the presence of another one. Contingency is important in operant conditioning also. For

a.

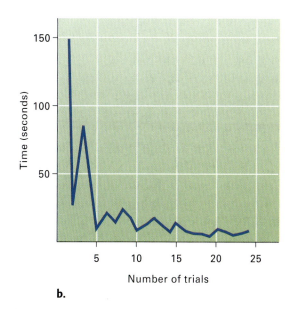

b.

FIGURE 6.5 **Thorndike's Puzzle Box and the Law of Effect** *(a)* A box typical of the puzzle boxes Thorndike used in his experiments with cats to study the law of effect. Stepping on the treadle released the door bolt; a weight attached to the door then pulled the door open and allowed the cat to escape. After accidentally pressing the treadle as it tried to get to the food, the cat learned to press the treadle to open the door. *(b)* One cat's learning curve over 24 separate trials. Notice that the cat escaped much more quickly after about 5 trials. It had learned the consequences of its behavior.

example, when a rat pushes a lever (behavior) that delivers food, the delivery of food (consequence) is contingent on that behavior.

Thorndike's Law of Effect

Although Skinner emerged as the primary figure in operant conditioning, the experiments of E. L. Thorndike (1874–1949) established the power of consequences in determining voluntary behavior. At about the same time that Pavlov was conducting classical conditioning experiments with salivating dogs, Thorndike, an American psychologist, was studying cats in puzzle boxes. Thorndike put a hungry cat inside a box and a piece of fish outside. To escape from the box and obtain the food, the cat had to learn how to open the latch inside the box.

At first, the cat made a number of ineffective responses. It clawed or bit at the bars and thrust its paw through the openings. Eventually the cat accidentally stepped on the treadle that released the door bolt. When the cat returned to the box, it went through the same random activity until it stepped on the treadle once more. On subsequent trials, the cat made fewer and fewer random movements, until finally it immediately stepped on the treadle to open the door (see figure 6.5). The **law of effect,** developed by Thorndike, states that behaviors followed by positive outcomes are strengthened, whereas behaviors followed by negative outcomes are weakened.

The key question for Thorndike was how the correct stimulus-response bond strengthens and eventually dominates incorrect stimulus-response bonds. According to Thorndike, the correct stimulus-response (S-R) association strengthens and the incorrect association weakens because of the *consequences* of the organism's actions. Thorndike's view is called *S-R theory* because the organism's behavior is due to a connection between a stimulus and a response. As the next section explains, Skinner's operant conditioning approach expanded Thorndike's basic ideas.

Skinner's Approach to Operant Conditioning

Skinner strongly believed that the mechanisms of learning are the same for all species. This conviction led him to study animals in the hope that he could discover the basic mechanisms of learning with organisms simpler than humans. During World War II, Skinner carried out an unusual study that involved a pigeon-guided missile. When the missile was in flight, a pigeon in the warhead of the missile pecked the moving

operant conditioning A form of learning in which the consequences of behavior change the probability of the behavior's occurrence; also called *instrumental conditioning.*

law of effect Thorndike's concept that behaviors followed by positive outcomes are strengthened, whereas behaviors followed by negative outcomes are weakened.

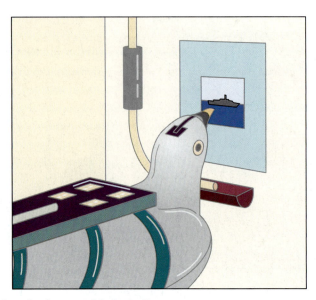

FIGURE 6.6 Skinner's Pigeon-Guided Missile Skinner wanted to help the military during World War II by using pigeons' tracking behavior. A gold electrode covered the tip of the pigeons' beaks. Contact with the screen on which the image of the target was projected sent a signal informing the missile's control mechanism of the target's location. Occasionally giving a few grains of food to the pigeons maintained their tracking behavior.

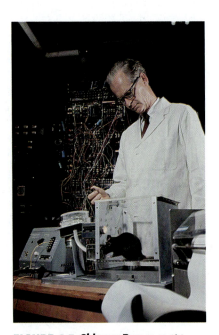

FIGURE 6.7 Skinner Box B. F. Skinner conducted operant conditioning studies in his behavioral laboratory using rats in Skinner boxes.

shaping The process of rewarding approximations of desired behavior.

image of the target on a screen. It was rewarded with food to keep the designated target in the center of the screen, in the process correcting the missile's course (see figure 6.6). The pigeons did their job well in trial runs, but top Navy officials just could not accept pigeons piloting their missiles in a war.

Following the pigeon experiment, Skinner (1948) wrote *Walden Two,* a novel in which he presented his ideas about building a scientifically managed society. Skinner envisioned a utopian society that could be engineered through operant conditioning. Skinner viewed existing societies as poorly managed because people believe in the myth of free will. He pointed out that humans are no more free than pigeons are; denying that our behavior is controlled by environmental forces is ignoring science and reality, he argued. Skinner believed that, in the long run, we would be much happier when we recognized such truths, especially his concept that operant conditioning would provide us with prosperous lives.

Skinner and other behaviorists made every effort to study organisms under precisely controlled conditions (Klein, 2002). One of Skinner's creations in the 1930s was the Skinner box (see figure 6.7). A device in the box delivered food pellets into a tray at random. After a rat became accustomed to the box, Skinner installed a lever and observed the rat's behavior. As the hungry rat explored the box, it occasionally pressed the lever, and a food pellet was dispensed. Soon the rat learned that the consequences of pressing the lever were positive: It would be fed. Additional control was achieved by soundproofing the box to ensure that the experimental manipulations were the only influence on the organism. In many of the experiments, to avoid human error, the responses were mechanically recorded and the food (the stimulus) was dispensed automatically.

Shaping

When a behavior takes time to occur, the learning process in operant conditioning can be shortened by rewarding an *approximation* of the desired behavior (Silverstein, Menditto, & Stuve, 2001). **Shaping** is the process of rewarding approximations of desired behavior. In one situation, parents used shaping to toilet train their 2-year-old son. The parents knew all too well that the grunting sound the child made signaled

Animal trainers coax some amazing behaviors from their star performers. *What type of operant conditioning is often used by animal trainers?*

he was about to fill his diaper. In the first week, they gave him candy if they heard the sound within 20 feet of the bathroom. The second week, he was given candy only if he grunted within 10 feet of the bathroom, the third week only if he was in the bathroom, and the fourth week he had to use the toilet to get the candy (Fischer & Gochros, 1975). It worked.

Shaping is extensively used in training animals. For example, shaping can be used to train a rat to press a bar to obtain food. When a rat is first placed in a Skinner box, it rarely presses the bar. Thus the experimenter may start off by giving the rat a food pellet if it is in the same half of the cage as the bar. Then the rat's behavior might be rewarded only when it is within 2 inches of the bar, then only when it touches the bar, and finally only when it presses the bar.

Shaping is also used to train animals to perform tricks. A dolphin that jumps through a hoop held high above the water has been trained to perform this behavior through shaping. You can use shaping to teach a dog tricks. For example, say that you want to teach a dog to "shake hands" with you. You first speak the command to "shake" and then wait until the dog moves one of its forepaws a little bit (operant behavior). Following this behavior, you give your dog a food treat (consequence). After requiring increasingly closer approximations to shaking your hand, the dog finally performs the desired behavior to the verbal command "shake."

Shaping can be used effectively in educational classrooms (Santrock, 2001). Suppose a teacher has a student who has never completed more than 50 percent of her math assignments. The teacher sets the target behavior at 100 percent but rewards her for successive approximations to the target. The teacher initially might provide a reward (some type of privilege, for example) when she completes 70 percent, then 80, then 90, and finally 100 percent. Shaping can be especially helpful for learning tasks that require time and persistence to complete.

Principles of Reinforcement

Reinforcement is the process by which a stimulus or an event strengthens or increases the probability of a behavior or an event that it follows. Behavioral psychologists have formulated a number of principles of reinforcement, including a distinction between positive and negative reinforcement.

reinforcement The process by which a stimulus or an event strengthens or increases the probability of a behavior or an event that it follows.

Positive Reinforcement

Behavior	Rewarding Stimulus Provided	Future Behavior
You turn in homework on time.	Teacher praises your performance.	You increasingly turn in homework on time.
You wax your skis.	The skis go faster.	You wax your skis the next time you go skiing.
You randomly press a button on the dashboard of a friend's car.	Great music begins to play.	You deliberately press the button again the next time you get into the car.

Negative Reinforcement

Behavior	Unpleasant Stimulus Removed	Future Behavior
You turn in homework on time.	Teacher stops criticizing late homework.	You increasingly turn in homework on time.
You wax your skis.	People stop zooming by you on the slope.	You wax your skis the next time.
You randomly press a button on the dashboard of a friend's car.	An annoying song shuts off.	You deliberately press the button again the next time the annoying song is on.

FIGURE 6.8 Positive and Negative Reinforcement

positive reinforcement The process that increases the frequency of a behavior by providing a rewarding stimulus.

negative reinforcement The process that increases the frequency of a behavior by removing an aversive (unpleasant) stimulus.

primary reinforcement The use of reinforcers that are innately satisfying.

secondary reinforcement The use of reinforcers that acquire their positive value through experience.

Positive and Negative Reinforcement   In **positive reinforcement,** the frequency of a behavior increases because it is followed by a rewarding stimulus. For example, if someone you meet smiles at you after you say, "Hello, how are you?" and you keep talking, the smile has reinforced your talking. The same principle of positive reinforcement is at work when you teach a dog to "shake hands" by giving it a piece of food when it lifts its paw.

Conversely, in **negative reinforcement,** the frequency of a behavior increases because it is followed by the removal of an aversive (unpleasant) stimulus. For example, if your father nagged you to clean out the garage and kept nagging until you cleaned out the garage, your response (cleaning out the garage) removed the unpleasant stimulus (nagging). Taking an aspirin when you have a headache works the same way: A reduction of pain reinforces the act of taking an aspirin for a headache.

To understand the distinction between positive and negative reinforcement, remember that "positive" and "negative" do not have anything to do with "good" and "bad." Just remember that they are processes in which something is given (positive reinforcement) or something is removed (negative reinforcement). Figure 6.8 provides some other examples to help you further to understand the distinction between positive and negative reinforcement.

Primary and Secondary Reinforcement   Positive reinforcement can be classified as primary reinforcement or secondary reinforcement, based on whether the behavior is inborn or learned. **Primary reinforcement** involves the use of reinforcers that are innately satisfying; that is, they do not take any learning on the organism's part to make them pleasurable. Food, water, and sexual satisfaction are primary reinforcers.

Secondary reinforcement acquires its positive value through experience; secondary reinforcers are learned, or conditioned, reinforcers. We encounter hundreds of secondary reinforcers in our lives, such as getting a pat on the back, praise, and eye contact. One popular story in psychology focuses on the use of eye contact as a secondary reinforcer to shape the behavior of a famous university professor, an expert on operant conditioning. Some students decided to train the professor to lecture from one corner of the classroom. They used eye contact as a reinforcer and began reinforcing successive approximations to the desired response. Each time the professor moved toward the appropriate corner, the students looked at him. If he moved in another direction, they looked away. By gradually rewarding successive approximations to the desired response, the students were able to get the professor to deliver his lecture from just one corner of the classroom. The professor denies that this shaping ever took place. Whether it did or not, the story provides an excellent example of how secondary reinforcers can be used to shape behavior (Chance, 1999).

Another example helps to illustrate the importance of secondary reinforcement in our everyday lives. When a student is given $25 for an *A* on her report card, the $25 is a secondary reinforcer. It is not innate, and it increases the likelihood that the student will work to get another *A* in the future. When an object can be exchanged for some other reinforcer, the object may have reinforcing value itself, so it is called a *token reinforcer.* Money, gift certificates, and poker chips are often referred to as token reinforcers.

Schedules of Reinforcement   Most of the examples of reinforcement we have discussed so far have involved *continuous reinforcement,* in which the behavior is reinforced every time it occurs. When continuous reinforcement occurs, organisms learn rapidly. However, when reinforcement stops, extinction also takes place quickly. If a pay telephone we often use starts "eating" our coins but not giving us a dial tone, we quickly stop putting in more coins. However, several weeks later, we might try the phone again, hoping it now works properly (this behavior illustrates spontaneous recovery).

Partial reinforcement follows a behavior only a portion of the time (Sangha & others, 2002). Most of life's experiences involve partial reinforcement. A golfer does not win every tournament she enters; a chess whiz does not win every match he plays; a student is not patted on the back each time she solves a problem. **Schedules of reinforcement** are "timetables" that determine when a behavior will be reinforced. There are four main schedules of reinforcement, two based on number of occurrences and two based on time intervals:

Slot machines are on a variable-ratio schedule of reinforcement. *Why does this schedule work so well for casinos?*

- *Fixed-ratio schedule* reinforces a behavior after a set number of behaviors. For example, if you are playing the slot machines in Atlantic City and if the machines are on a fixed-ratio schedule, you might get $5 back every 20 times you put money in the machine. It wouldn't take long to figure out that, if you watched someone else play the machine 18 or 19 times, not get any money back, and then walk away, you should step up, insert your coin, and get back $5. Fixed-ratio schedules often are used in business to increase production. For example, a salesperson might be required to sell a specific number of items to get a commission. One characteristic of fixed-ratio schedules is that performance often drops off just after reinforcement.

- *Variable-ratio schedule* rewards a behavior an average number of times but on an unpredictable basis. For example, a slot machine might pay off an average of every 20th time, but the gambler does not know when this payoff will be. The slot machine might pay off twice in a row and then not again until after 58 coins have been inserted. The average is a reward for every 20 behavioral acts, but when the reward will be given is unpredictable. Variable-ratio schedules produce high, steady rates of behavior that are more resistant to extinction than the other three schedules.

schedules of reinforcement "Timetables" that determine when a behavior will be reinforced.

FIGURE 6.9 Schedules of Reinforcement and Different Patterns of Responding In this graph, each hash mark indicates the delivery of reinforcment. Notice on the fixed-ratio schedule the dropoff in responding after each reinforcement; on the variable-ratio schedule, the high, steady rate of responding; on the fixed-interval schedule, the immediate dropoff in responding after reinforcement and the increase in responding just before reinforcement (resulting in a scallop-shaped curve); and on the variable-interval schedule, the slow, steady rate of responding.

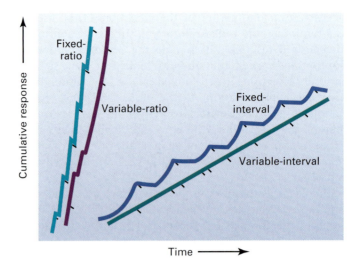

- *Fixed-interval schedule* reinforces the first appropriate behavior after a fixed amount of time has elapsed. For example, you might get a reward the first time you put money in a slot machine if it pays off every 10 minutes. The behavior of politicians campaigning for reelection often reflects a fixed-interval schedule of reinforcement. After they have been elected, they reduce their campaigning and then do not pick it up again heavily until just before the next election (which can be 2 to 4 years later). On a fixed-interval schedule, few behaviors are enacted until the time approaches when the behavior (such as campaigning to get reelected) likely will be reinforced, and at that time the rate of behavior picks up rapidly.

- *Variable-interval schedule* reinforces a behavior after a variable amount of time has elapsed (Stadden, Chelaru, & Higa, 2002). On this schedule, the slot machines might reward you after 10 minutes, then after 2 minutes, then after 18 minutes, and so on. Pop quizzes are on a variable-interval schedule. So is fishing—you don't know if the fish will bite in the next minute, in a half hour, in an hour, or at all. Because it is difficult to predict when a reward will come on a variable-interval schedule, behavior is slow and consistent.

In-Psych Plus

Figure 6.9 shows how these four schedules of reinforcement result in different rates of responding. To enhance your learning of the principles of reinforcement, go to the interactivity "Operant Conditioning."

Generalization, Discrimination, and Extinction Remember that generalization, discrimination, and extinction are important classical conditioning principles. They also are important principles in operant conditioning, but they are defined somewhat differently:

- **Generalization.** In operant conditioning, *generalization* means giving the same response to similar stimuli. For example, in one study pigeons were reinforced for pecking at a disk of a particular color (Guttman & Kalish, 1956). To assess stimulus generalization, researchers presented the pigeons with disks of varying colors. As shown in figure 6.10, the pigeons most often pecked at the disks closest in color to the original. An example from everyday life involves a student who has great success in dating people who dress neatly and not such good results with people who dress sloppily. The student subsequently seeks dates with people who dress neatly, the neater the better, and avoids dating sloppy dressers, especially the sloppiest.

generalization (operant conditioning) Giving the same response to similar stimuli.

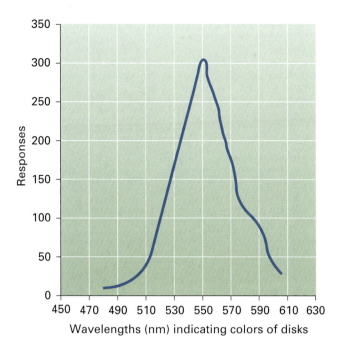

FIGURE 6.10 **Stimulus Generalization** In an experiment by Guttman and Kalish (1956), pigeons initially pecked a disk of a particular color (in this graph, a color with a wavelength of 550 nm) after they had been reinforced for this wavelength. When the pigeons were presented with disks of varying colors, they more often pecked disks of colors that were similar in wavelength to the original disk.

- **Discrimination.** In operant conditioning, *discrimination* means responding to stimuli that signal that a behavior will or will not be reinforced (Spector & Kopka, 2002). For example, you might look at two street signs, both made of metal, both the same color, and both with words on them. However, one sign says "Enter at your own risk" and the other says "Please walk this way." The words serve as discriminative stimuli because the sign that says "Please walk this way" indicates that you will be rewarded for doing so. However, the sign that says "Enter at your own risk" suggests that the consequences may not be positive. As another example, consider that football players are far more likely to tackle people in a football stadium than in a church. Further, they tackle people in a uniform with certain colors (the opposing team's rather than their own). They also don't tackle certain other people in uniforms, such as cheerleaders, referees, and police officers.

- **Extinction.** In operant conditioning, *extinction* occurs when a previously reinforced behavior is no longer reinforced and the tendency to perform the behavior decreases (Conklin & Tiffany, 2002). For example, a factory worker gets a monthly bonus for producing more than her quota. Then, as a part of economic tightening, the company decides that it can no longer afford the bonuses. When bonuses were given, the worker's productivity was above quota every month; once the bonus was removed, performance decreased. Spontaneous recovery also may follow the operant form of extinction.

Punishment   From the discussion of positive and negative reinforcement, you learned that both types of reinforcement strengthen a behavior. In contrast, the effect of punishment is usually to weaken or extinguish a behavior. In the operant conditioning context, **punishment** refers to a consequence that decreases the likelihood that a behavior will occur. For example, a child plays with an attractive matchbox and gets burned (punished) when one of the matches is lit. In the future, the child is less likely to play with matches. Or if a student interrupts the teacher and the teacher verbally reprimands the student, the student subsequently stops interrupting the teacher.

Punishment is not to be confused with negative reinforcement, in which a response increases because of its consequences. The following example should help

discrimination (operant conditioning) Responding to stimuli that signal whether a behavior will or will not be reinforced.

extinction (operant conditioning) Becoming less likely to perform a previously reinforced behavior when it is no longer reinforced.

punishment A consequence that decreases the likelihood a behavior will occur.

Punishment

Behavior	Aversive Stimulus Presented	Future Behavior
You take medication to cure a headache.	You have a bad allergic reaction.	You avoid medication in the future.
You show off to a friend by speeding past a police car.	You get a $200 speeding ticket.	You stop speeding.

Negative Reinforcement

Behavior	Aversive Stimulus Removed	Future Behavior
You take medication to cure a headache.	The headache goes away.	You take more medication in the future.
You show off to a friend by speeding past a police car.	The officer pays no attention to you, although officers have ticketed you in the past.	You continue to show off by speeding past police cars.

FIGURE 6.11 Punishment Versus Negative Reinforcement

This second-grade student has been placed in time-out for misbehaving. *Why does time-out work so well?*

you distinguish between negative reinforcement and punishment. When an alcoholic consumes liquor to alleviate uncomfortable withdrawal symptoms, the probability that the person will use alcohol in the future increases. The reduction of the withdrawal symptoms is a negative reinforcer for drinking. But if an inebriated alcoholic is seriously injured in a car wreck and subsequently drinks less, the incident served as punishment because drinking subsequently decreased. Figure 6.11 provides additional examples of the distinction between negative reinforcement and punishment.

The positive/negative distinction also can be applied to punishment, although it is not used as widely as in reinforcement. In *positive punishment,* a behavior decreases when it is followed by an unpleasant stimulus. In *negative punishment,* a behavior decreases when a positive stimulus is removed. For example, a *time-out* is a form of negative punishment in which a child is removed from a positive reinforcement. If a child is disrupting the classroom, the teacher might put the child in a chair in the corner of the room, facing away from the class, or take the child to a time-out room. Figure 6.12 on p. 214 compares positive reinforcement, negative reinforcement, positive punishment, and negative punishment.

Many people associate punishment of children with yelling at them or spanking them. All too often, though, aversive stimuli like these do not do what they are intended to do—namely, decrease an unwanted behavior (Edwards, 1999). Some people turn too quickly to aversive stimuli—perhaps because they were harshly disciplined when they were growing up and they are just repeating how their parents dealt with them; because they have developed a style of handling stress by yelling or screaming; because they feel they can effectively exercise power over their smaller charges; or because they are unaware of how positive reinforcement or other techniques, such as a time-out, can be used to improve children's behavior.

To read further about whether punishing children is an effective strategy, see the Critical Controversy box.

Timing, Reinforcement, and Punishment How does the timing of reinforcement and punishment influence behavior? And does it matter whether the reinforcement is small or large? Here are some connections between the timing and size of the reinforcement:

- *Immediate reinforcement and delayed reinforcement.* As is the case with classical conditioning, learning is more efficient in operant conditioning when the

Will Sparing the Rod Spoil the Child?

For centuries, corporal (physical) punishment, such as spanking, has been considered a necessary and even desirable method of disciplining children (Greven, 1991). Use of corporal punishment is legal in every state in America, and it is estimated that 70 to 90 percent of American parents have spanked their children (Straus, 1991). A recent cross-cultural comparison found that individuals in the United States and Canada were among the most favorable toward corporal punishment and remembered it as being used by their parents (Curran & others, 2001) (see the graph on this page).

Despite the widespread use of corporal punishment, there have been surprisingly few research studies on physical punishment, and those that have been conducted are correlational (Baumrind, Larzelere, & Cowan, 2002; Benjet & Kazdin, 2003; Kazdin & Benjet, 2003). Clearly, it would be highly unethical to assign parents randomly to either spank or not spank their children in an experimental study. Recall that cause and effect cannot be determined in a correlational study. In one correlational study, spanking by parents was linked with children's antisocial behavior, including cheating, telling lies, being mean to others, bullying, getting into fights, and being disobedient (Strauss, Sugarman, & Giles-Sims, 1997). In a recent study of White, African American, and Latino families, spanking by parents predicted an increase in children's problems over time in all three groups (McLoyd & Smith, 2002). However, when parents showed strong emotional support of the child, the link between spanking and child problems was reduced.

A recent research review concluded that corporal punishment by parents in associated with children's higher levels of immediate compliance and aggression among children, as well as lower levels of mental health (Gershoff, 2002). Some critics, though, argue that the research evidence is not yet sound enough to warrant a blanket injunction against corporal punishment, especially mild corporal punishment (Baumrind, Larzelere, & Cowan, 2002; Kazdin & Benjet, 2003). And animal studies reveal that punishment is often effective in reducing undesired behaviors (Dinsmoor, 1998).

When asked why they use corporal punishment with their children, parents often respond that their children need such strong discipline to learn how to behave. They also sometimes say that their parents punished them and they turned out okay, so there must not be that much wrong with it.

What are some reasons for avoiding spanking or similar punishments?

- When adults yell, scream, or spank, they are presenting children with out-of-control models for handling stressful situations. Children may imitate this aggressive, out-of-control behavior.
- Punishment can instill fear, rage, or avoidance. For example, spanking the child may cause the child to avoid being around the parent and fear the parent.
- Punishment tells children what not to do rather than what to do. Children should be given feedback, such as "Why don't you try this?"
- Punishment can be abusive. When parents discipline their children, they might not intend to be abusive but become so aroused when they are punishing the child that they become abusive (Baumrind, Larzelere, & Cowan, 2002).

Because of reasons such as these, Sweden passed a law in 1979 forbidding parents to physically punish (spank or slap, for example) children. Since the law was enacted, youth rates of

(Continued)

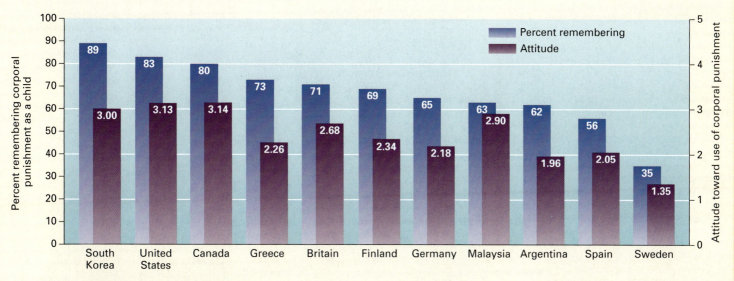

Corporal Punishment in Different Countries A 5-point scale was used to assess attitudes toward corporal punishment with scores closer to 1 indicating an attitude against its use and scores closer to 5 suggesting an attitude for its use.

Will Sparing the Rod Spoil the Child?—*Continued*

delinquency, alcohol abuse, rape, and suicide have dropped in Sweden (Durrant, 2000), although these improvements may have occurred for other reasons, such as changing attitudes and opportunities for youth. Nonetheless, the Swedish experience suggests that the physical punishment of children may be unnecessary. Other countries that have passed antispanking laws include Finland (1984), Denmark (1986), Norway (1987), Austria (1989), Cyprus (1994), Latvia (1998), Croatia (1999), Germany (2000), and Israel (2000).

What do you think?

- Should physical punishment of children be outlawed in the United States?
- Did your parents spank you when you were a child? What effect do you think it had on your behavior?
- Might negative reinforcement, such as using time-outs, be more effective than positive punishment, such as spanking? Explain.

interval between a behavior and its reinforcement is a few seconds rather than minutes or hours, especially in lower animals (Church & Kirkpatrick, 2001). If a food reward is delayed for more than 30 seconds after a rat presses a bar, it is virtually ineffective as reinforcement. However, humans have the ability to respond to delayed reinforcers (Holland, 1996). Sometimes the question is whether to obtain a small immediate reinforcer or to wait for a delayed but more highly valued reinforcer (Martin & Pear, 2003). For example, you can spend your money now on clothes, trinkets, parties, and the like, or you can save your money and buy a house and car later. Or you might play around now and enjoy yourself in return for immediate small reinforcers, or you can study hard over the long haul for delayed intermediate and long-term stronger reinforcers, such as good grades, a scholarship to graduate school, and a better job.

FIGURE 6.12 Positive Reinforcement, Negative Reinforcement, Positive Punishment, and Negative Punishment

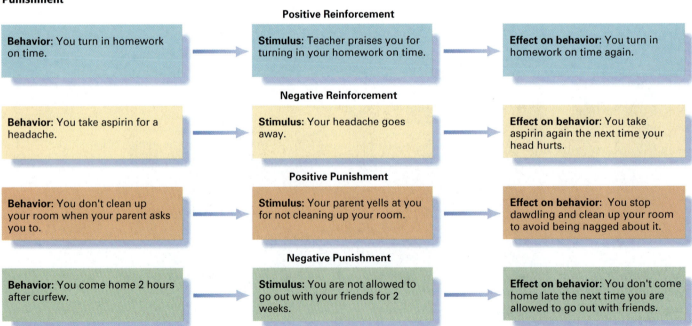

How might timing, reinforcement, and punishment be involved in overeating, drinking excessively, and smoking? How might behavior modification be able to help people change these behaviors?

- *Immediate punishment and delayed punishment.* As with reinforcement, in most instances of research with lower animals, immediate punishment is more effective than delayed punishment in decreasing the occurrence of a behavior. However, also as with reinforcement, delayed punishment can have an effect on human behavior. Why do so many of us postpone such activities as going to the dentist, scheduling minor surgery, and paying campus parking fines (Martin & Pear, 2003)? If we act immediately, we experience a weak punisher—it hurts to have our teeth drilled, it is painful to have minor surgery, and it is not pleasurable to pay a campus parking fine. However, the delayed consequences can be more punishing—our teeth might fall out, we may need major surgery, and our car might be towed away or we might be thrown in jail if we delay paying a campus parking fine.

- *Immediate and delayed reinforcement and punishment.* How does receiving immediate small reinforcement versus delayed strong punishment affect human behavior (Martin & Pear, 2002)? One reason that obesity is such a major health problem is that eating is a behavior with immediate positive consequences (food tastes great and quickly provides a pleasurable feeling) and potential delayed negative consequences (obesity and other possible health risks). When the delayed consequences of behavior are punishing and the immediate consequences are reinforcing, the immediate consequences usually win—even when the immediate consequences are minor reinforcers and the delayed consequences are major punishers. Smoking and drinking follow a similar pattern. The immediate consequences of smoking are reinforcing for most smokers: a powerful combination of positive reinforcement (tension relief, energy boost) and negative reinforcement (removal of craving). The punishing aspects of smoking are primarily long-term, such as shortness of breath, sore throat, coughing, emphysema, heart disease, and cancer. Likewise, the immediate pleasurable consequences of drinking override the delayed consequences of a hangover or even alcoholism.

    Now think about the reverse situation—when the initial consequences of a behavior are punishing and the delayed consequences are reinforcing. Why are some of us so reluctant to take up a new sport, try a new dance step, go to a social gathering, or do almost anything different? One reason is that learning new skills often involves minor punishing consequences, such as initially looking and feeling stupid, not knowing what to do, and having to put up with sarcastic comments from onlookers. In these circumstances, reinforcing consequences are often delayed. For example, it may take a long time to become a good enough golfer or a good enough dancer to enjoy these activities.

Applications of Operant Conditioning

A preschool child repeatedly throws his glasses and breaks them. A high school student and her parents have intense arguments. A college student is deeply depressed.

1. Define the problem.
2. Commit to change.
3. Collect data about yourself.
4. Design a self-control program.
5. Make the program last—maintenance.

FIGURE 6.13 Five Steps in Developing a Self-Control Program

An elderly woman is incontinent. Operant conditioning procedures have helped people such as these to adapt more successfully and cope more effectively with their problems (Sussman, 2001).

Applied behavior analysis, or **behavior modification,** is the application of operant conditioning principles to change human behavior. Consequences for behavior are established to ensure that more adaptive actions are reinforced and less adaptive ones are not (Powell & Symbaluk, 2002).

Advocates of behavior modification believe that many emotional and behavior problems are caused by inadequate, or inappropriate, response consequences (Alberto & Troutman, 1999; Petry & others, 2001). The child who throws down his glasses and breaks them may be receiving too much attention from his teacher and peers for his behavior; they unwittingly reinforce an unacceptable behavior. In this instance, the parents and teachers would be instructed to divert attention from the destructive behavior and transfer it to a more constructive behavior, such as working quietly or playing cooperatively with peers (Harris, Wolf, & Baer, 1964).

Mental and Physical Health   Barbara and her parents were on a collision course. Things got so bad that her parents decided to see a clinical psychologist. The psychologist, who had a behavioral orientation, talked with each family member, trying to get them to pinpoint the problem. The psychologist then got the family to sign a behavioral contract that spelled out what everyone needed to do to reduce the conflict. Barbara agreed to be home before 11 P.M. on weeknights; look for a part-time job so she could begin to pay for some of her activities; and refrain from calling her parents insulting names. Her parents agreed to talk to Barbara in a low tone of voice rather than yell if they were angry; refrain from criticizing teenagers, especially Barbara's friends; and give Barbara a small sum of money each week for gas, makeup, and socializing, but only until she found a job.

Sam, a 19-year-old college student, has been deeply depressed lately. His girlfriend broke off their relationship of 2 years, and his grades have been dropping. He decides to go to a psychologist who has a behavioral orientation. The psychologist enrolls him in the Coping with Depression course developed by Peter Lewinsohn (1987). Sam learns to monitor his daily moods and increase his ratio of positive-to-negative life events. The psychologist trains Sam to develop more efficient coping skills and gets Sam to agree to a behavioral contract, just as the psychologist did with Barbara and her parents.

Mary is an elderly woman who lives in a nursing home. In recent months, she has become incontinent and is increasingly dependent on the staff for help with her daily activities. The behavioral treatment designed for Mary involves teaching her to monitor her behavior and schedule going to the toilet. She is also required to do pelvic exercises. The program for decreasing Mary's dependence requires that the staff attend more to her independent behavior when it occurs and ignore dependent behavior whenever possible. Such strategies have been effective in reducing incontinence and dependence in older adults.

Behavior modification can be used to help people improve their self-control in many aspects of mental and physical health (Kazdin, 2001; Miltenberger, 2001; Watson & Tharp, 2002). Following are five steps to better self-control (Martin & Pear, 2003) (see figure 6.13):

1. *Define the behavior to be changed in specific, concrete terms.* For Al, this is easy—he is overweight and wants to lose 30 pounds. Stated even more precisely, he wants to consume about 1,000 fewer calories per day to achieve a weight loss of about 2 pounds per week. Some problems are more difficult to specify, such as "wasting time," "having a bad attitude toward school," "having a poor relationship with the boss," or "being too nervous and worrying a lot." These types of problems have been called "fuzzies" because of their abstract nature (Mager, 1972). Problems can be made manageable by writing out a goal and listing the things that would give clear evidence of having reached the goal.

applied behavior analysis (behavior modification) The use of operant conditioning principles to change human behavior.

2. *Make a commitment to change.* Both a commitment to change and a knowledge of change techniques help college students become more effective self-managers of their smoking, eating, studying, and relationship problems (Alterman, Gariti, & Mulvaney, 2001; Perkins & others, 2001). Building a commitment to change requires doing things that increase the likelihood that you will stick to your project. First, tell others about your commitment to change—they will remind you to stick to your program. Second, rearrange your environment to provide frequent reminders of your goal, making sure the reminders are associated with the positive benefits of reaching your goal. Third, put a lot of time and energy into planning your project. Make a list of statements about your project, such as "I've put a lot of time into this project; I am certainly not going to waste all of this effort now." Fourth, because you will invariably face temptations to backslide or quit your project, plan ahead for ways you can deal with temptation, tailoring these plans to your problem.

3. *Collect data about your behavior.* This step is especially important in decreasing excessive behaviors, such as overeating and frequent smoking or drinking. One of the reasons for tracking your behavior is to provide a reference point for evaluating your progress. When recording the frequency of a behavior during initial observations, you should also examine the immediate circumstances that could be maintaining the problem (Martin & Pear, 2003).

4. *Design a self-control program.* Many good self-control programs involve setting long-term and short-term goals and developing a plan for reaching the goals. Good self-control programs also usually include some type of self-talk, self-instruction, or self-reinforcement. For example, a person whose goal is to jog 30 minutes a day 5 days a week might say, "I'll never make it. It just won't work." This person can benefit by saying something like "I know it's going to be tough, but I can make it." Also, individuals can engage in self-reinforcing statements or treat themselves. They might say something like "Way to go. You are up to 30 minutes 3 days a week. You are on your way." Or they might treat themselves to something, such as a movie, a new piece of clothing, or a new CD.

5. *Make the program last—plan for maintenance.* One strategy is to establish specific dates for postchecks and to plan a course of action if your postchecks are not favorable. For instance, if your self-control program involves weight reduction, you might want to weigh yourself once a week. If your weight increases to a certain level, then you immediately go back on your self-control program. Another strategy is to establish a buddy system by finding a friend or someone with a similar problem. The two of you set mutual maintenance goals. Once a month, get together and check each other's behavior. If your goals have been maintained, get together and celebrate in an agreed-on way.

For other ideas on how to establish an effective self-control program tailored to your needs, you might want to contact the counseling center at your college or university. You also might consider consulting a good book on behavior modification or self-control, such as *Behavior Modification* (Martin & Pear, 2003).

Education Not only is behavior modification effective in improving mental and physical health, but it has also been applied in classrooms to improve the education of children (Charles, 2002; Evertson, Emmer, & Worsham, 2003; Kaufmann & others, 2002). Many of the concepts already discussed, including positive reinforcement, shaping, time-out, contracting, and self-control, have been applied to learning in the classroom.

Computers have become another tool in behavior modification. Some years ago, Skinner developed a machine to help teachers instruct students. The teaching machine engaged the student in a learning activity, paced the material at the student's rate, tested the student's knowledge of the material, and provided immediate feedback about correct and incorrect answers. Skinner hoped that the machine would revolutionize learning in schools, but that revolution never took place. Today the idea behind Skinner's teaching machine is applied through computers. Research comparisons of computer-assisted instruction with traditional teacher-based instruction suggest that, in some areas, such as drill and practice on math problems, computer-assisted instruction can produce superior results (Kulik, Kulik, & Bangert-Drowns, 1985).

The effectiveness of reinforcers may vary from child to child. For one child, the most effective reinforcer might be praise and for another it might be more time participating in a favorite activity. Natural reinforcers, such as praise and privileges, are generally recommended over material reinforcers, such as stars and candy (Hall & Hall, 1998).

Activities are some of the most common reinforcers used by teachers. Named after psychologist David Premack, the *Premack principle* states that a high-probability activity can be used to reinforce a low-probability activity. For many children, playing a game on a computer has a higher likelihood of occurrence than doing a writing assignment. Thus a teacher might tell a child, "When you complete your writing assignment, you can play a game on the computer." The Premack principle can be used with an entire classroom of children. A teacher might say, "If all of you get your homework done by Friday, we will take a field trip next week."

In-Psych Plus

Can you distinguish between behaviors learned through classical conditioning and those learned through operant conditioning? The interactivity "Classical vs. Operant Conditioning" can help sharpen your knowledge of these approaches.

Review and Sharpen Your Thinking

3   *Discuss operant conditioning.*

- Distinguish operant conditioning from classical conditioning.
- Describe Thorndike's law of effect.
- Discuss Skinner's methods of studying operant conditioning.
- Define shaping.
- Identify the principles of reinforcement, and explain how they affect behavior.
- Explain how behavior modification works.

Describe a behavior (yours or someone else's) that you would like to change through behavior modification. Outline the plan. If you enacted this plan, do you think it would work? Why or why not? Would you consider the enactment of this plan to be too manipulative? Why or why not?

4   OBSERVATIONAL LEARNING

How does observational learning occur?

Would it make sense to teach a 15-year-old boy how to drive by either classical conditioning or operant conditioning procedures? Driving a car is a voluntary behavior, so classical conditioning does not really apply. In terms of operant conditioning, we could ask him to drive down the road and then reward his positive behaviors. Not many of us would want to be on the road, though, when he made mistakes. Albert Bandura (1986, 2000) believes that, if we learned only in such a trial-and-error fashion, learning would be exceedingly tedious and at times hazardous. Instead, he says, many of our complex behaviors are the result of exposure to competent models who display appropriate behavior in solving problems and coping (Striefel, 1998). By observing other people, we can acquire knowledge, skills, rules, strategies, beliefs, and attitudes (Schunk, 2000). You initially encountered Bandura's ideas in chapter 1, in which his social cognitive theory was introduced. This section discusses his view of observational learning further.

Observational learning, also called *imitation* or *modeling,* is learning that occurs when a person observes and imitates someone's behavior. The capacity to learn behavior patterns by observation eliminates trial-and-error learning. In many instances, observational learning takes less time than operant conditioning. Bandura (1986) described four main processes that are involved in observational learning:

1. *Attention.* In order to reproduce a model's actions, you must first attend to what the model is saying or doing. You might not hear what a friend says if the stereo is blaring, or you might miss the teacher's analysis of a problem if you are admiring someone sitting in the next row. Imagine that you decide to take a class to improve your artistic skills. You need to attend to the instructor's words and hand movements. Attention to the model is influenced by a host of characteristics. For example, warm, powerful, atypical people command more attention than do cold, weak, typical people.

2. *Retention.* To reproduce a model's actions that have drawn your attention, you must code the information and keep it in memory so that it can be retrieved. A simple verbal description or a vivid image of what the model did assists retention. (Memory is such an important cognitive process that chapter 7 is devoted exclusively to it.) In the example of taking a class to improve your art skills, you will need to remember what the instructor said and did in modeling good drawing skills.

3. *Production.* The process of imitating the model's actions comes next. People might attend to a model and code in memory what they have seen, but limitations in motor development might make it difficult for them to reproduce the model's action. Thirteen-year-olds might see a professional basketball player do a reverse two-handed dunk but be unable to reproduce the pro's actions. In an art class, also, you will need good motor reproduction skills to follow the instructor's example.

4. *Reinforcement.* On many occasions, we may attend to what a model says or does, retain the information in memory, and possess the motor capabilities to perform the action, but we might fail to repeat the behavior because of inadequate reinforcement. The importance of this step was demonstrated in one of Bandura's (1965) studies in which children who had seen a model punished for aggression reproduced the model's aggression only when they were offered an incentive to do so. In art class, if the instructor chooses one of your drawings for display, the reinforcement will encourage you to keep drawing and to take another art skills class.

To think about the models and mentors in your life, see the Psychology and Life box on the next page.

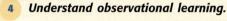

Review and Sharpen Your Thinking

4   *Understand observational learning.*

- Define observational learning and outline the four steps in Bandura's model.

Who have been the most important models in your life? What have you learned from them?

observational learning The form of learning that occurs when a person observes and imitates behavior; also called *imitation* or *modeling.*

Models and Mentors in My Life

Having positive role models and mentors to observe and learn from can play a part in whether individuals develop optimally and reach their full potential. A mentor is someone you look up to and respect, who serves as a competent model, and who is willing to work with you to help you achieve your goals.

In the Quantum Opportunities program, students from low-income backgrounds benefited significantly from having a mentor from the ninth through the twelfth grade (Carnegie Council on Adolescent Development, 1995). These mentors modeled appropriate behavior and strategies, gave sustained support, and provided guidance. Of the mentored group, 63 percent graduated from high school, but only 42 percent of a control group did; 42 percent of the mentored students enrolled in college, but only 17 percent of the control group did.

Role models and mentors can be parents, teachers, an older peer, or someone in the community. Spend a few minutes and think about the role models and mentors you have had in your life, including now. Do you remember any specific instances in which you watched them do or say something that had a lasting impact on you and that you later modeled? List the most important role models and mentors in your life and then describe what you learned from them and how they helped your learning.

A mentor can be very beneficial to students. If you currently don't have a mentor, think about the people at your college or university, or people in the community, whom you respect and look up to. Consider asking one of these people to be a mentor for you.

Or you might want to become a mentor yourself. Do you have a particular skill or knowledge that you might be able to teach children or adolescents? Mentoring a child or an adolescent and serving as a positive model in observational learning can be an extremely rewarding experience.

Role Models and Mentors	What I Learned from Them and How They Helped My Learning	Role Models and Mentors	What I Learned from Them and How They Helped My Learning
1. _____	_____ _____ _____ _____	3. _____	_____ _____ _____ _____ _____
2. _____	_____ _____ _____ _____	4. _____	_____ _____ _____ _____

5 COGNITIVE FACTORS IN LEARNING

Purposive Behavior   **Insight Learning**

What role does cognition play in learning?

In discussing learning, I have said little about cognitive processes, except as they apply in observational learning. Skinner's operant conditioning approach and Pavlov's classical conditioning approach both ignore the possibility that cognitive factors, such as memory, thinking, planning, and expectations, might be important in learning. Skinnerian behaviorists point out that they do not deny the existence of thinking processes, but, because such processes cannot be observed, they may interfere with the discovery of important environmental conditions that govern behavior.

Many contemporary psychologists, including behavioral revisionists who recognize the importance of cognition, believe learning involves more than environment-behavior connections (Bandura, 1986, 2000; Schunk, 2004). One of them is E. C. Tolman.

Purposive Behavior

E. C. Tolman (1932) emphasized the *purposiveness* of behavior. In other words, he believed that much behavior is goal-directed, not simply the result of operant conditioning. Consider high school students who are studying hard in their classes. If we focused only on their studying, we would miss the purpose of their behavior. Students don't always study hard just because they have been reinforced for studying in the past. Rather, studying is a means to intermediate goals (learning, high grades), which in turn improve their likelihood of reaching long-term goals (getting into the college or university of their choice) (Schunk, 2000).

Tolman's legacy can be seen today in the extensive interest in the role of goal setting in human behavior (Dweck, 1996; Zimmerman, 2000). Researchers are especially interested in how people engage in self-regulation and self-monitoring of their behavior to reach a goal (Pintrich, 2000; Pressley, 1995; Schunk & Ertmer, 2000; Winne & Perry, 2000). In every chapter of this book, I have set learning goals and asked you to monitor your studying so that you can reach these goals.

Expectancy, Information, and Learning   In studying the purposiveness of behavior, Tolman went beyond the stimuli and responses of Pavlov and Skinner to focus on cognitive mechanisms, such as expectancy. In classical conditioning, a young boy fears a rabbit because he expects it will hurt him. In operant conditioning, a woman works hard all week because she expects to be paid on Friday. Expectancy is acquired from experiences with the environment.

One contemporary view of classical conditioning follows this line of thought. It describes an organism as an information seeker, using relations among events, along with preconceptions, to form a representation of the world (Rescorla, 1988, 1996, 2001). A classic experiment conducted by Leon Kamin (1968) illustrates the importance of how and when information is provided in classical conditioning. A rat was conditioned by repeatedly pairing a tone (CS) and a shock (UCS), until the tone alone produced fear (CR). Then, the tone continued to be paired with the shock, but a light (a second CS) was turned on each time the tone was sounded. Even though the light (CS) and the shock (UCS) were repeatedly paired, the rat showed no conditioning to the light (the light by itself produced no CR). Conditioning to the light was blocked, almost as if the rat had not paid attention. The rat apparently used the tone as a signal to predict that a shock would be forthcoming; information about the light's pairing with the shock was redundant with the information already learned about the tone's pairing with the shock. In this experiment, conditioning was governed not by the contiguity of the CS and UCS but, rather, by the rat's history and the information it already had received. Contemporary classical conditioning researchers are exploring further the role of information in an organism's learning (Domjan, 1996; Fanselow, DeCola, & Young, 1993).

Tolman (1948) believed that an organism's expectations about which actions are needed to attain a goal take the form of cognitive maps. A *cognitive map* is an organism's mental representation of the structure of physical space. His experiments with rats in a maze led Tolman to conclude that rats developed mental awareness of physical space and the elements in it and then used these cognitive maps to find the food at the end of the maze, their goal.

Tolman's idea of cognitive maps is alive and well today. As we move around in our environment, we develop a cognitive map of where things are located. We have a cognitive map of the locations of rooms at home, and we have a cognitive map of our location in the United States. A popular exercise is to draw a cognitive map reflecting our perception of the city or state in which we live, relative to the rest of the United States. Texans, for example, usually make the state of Texas about three-fourths the size of the United States. People living in New York City often draw it to be about nine-tenths the size of the United States. Of course, such cognitive maps deliberately distort the physical world and reflect the perceivers' egocentric interest

"You will note that their ability to comprehend, assess and process information increases dramatically when Professor Podhertz throws in the cat." © Leo Cullum.

in their city or state. Thus they demonstrate that learning involves more than just a physical response to stimuli.

Latent Learning   Other evidence to support the role of cognitive maps in learning was obtained in experiments on latent learning. **Latent learning** is unreinforced learning that is not immediately reflected in behavior. In one study, two groups of hungry rats were placed in a maze and required to find their way from a starting point to an end point (Tolman & Honzik, 1930). The first group found food (a reinforcer) at the end point; the second group found nothing there. In the operant conditioning view, the first group should learn the maze better than the second group, which is exactly what happened. However, when Tolman subsequently took some of the rats from the nonreinforced group and rewarded them with food at the end point of the maze, they began to run the maze as effectively as the reinforced group. The nonreinforced rats apparently had learned a great deal about the maze as they roamed around and explored it. But their learning was *latent,* stored cognitively in their memories but not yet expressed behaviorally. When these rats were given a good reason (reinforcement with food) to run the maze speedily, they called on their latent learning to help them reach the end of the maze more quickly.

Outside of a laboratory, latent learning is evident in an animal's exploration of its surroundings. Learning the layout of its environment may bring the animal no immediate benefits, but it can prove critical in the future when fleeing a predator or searching for food. This is as true for humans as for other animals.

Insight Learning

Tolman was not the only psychologist in the first half of the twentieth century who believed that cognitive factors play an important role in learning. So did Wolfgang Köhler, a German psychologist. He spent 4 months in the Canary Islands during World War I, observing the behavior of apes. There he conducted two fascinating experiments. One is called the "stick problem," the other the "box problem." Though these two experiments are basically the same, the solutions to the problems are different. In both situations, an ape discovers that it cannot reach an alluring piece of fruit, either because the fruit is too high or because it is outside of the ape's cage and beyond reach. To solve the stick problem, the ape has to insert a small stick inside a larger stick to reach the fruit. To master the box problem, the ape must stack several boxes to reach the fruit (see figure 6.14).

According to Köhler (1925), solving these problems does not involve trial and error or simple connections between stimuli and responses. Rather, when the ape

latent learning Learning, in the absence of reinforcement, that is not immediately reflected in behavior.

FIGURE 6.14 Insight Learning Sultan, one of Köhler's brightest chimps, is faced with the problem of reaching a cluster of bananas overhead. He solves the problem by stacking boxes on top of one another to reach the bananas. Köhler called this type of problem solving insight learning.

realizes that its customary actions are not going to help it get the fruit, it often sits for a while and appears to ponder how to solve the problem. Then it quickly gets up, as if it has had a sudden flash of insight, piles the boxes on top of one another, and gets the fruit. **Insight learning** is a form of problem solving in which the organism develops a sudden insight into or understanding of a problem's solution.

Review and Sharpen Your Thinking

5 *Outline the role of cognition in learning.*

- Discuss the role of expectations, latent learning, and information and cognitive maps in learning.
- Explain insight learning.

What are your career expectations? How might these expectations influence your behavior this term?

insight learning A form of problem solving in which the organism develops a sudden insight into or understanding of the problem's solution.

1   THE NATURE OF LEARNING

Types of Learning

Biological Factors
in Learning

2   CLASSICAL CONDITIONING

Pavlov's Studies

Applications of
Classical Conditioning

Learning

3   OPERANT CONDITIONING

Thorndike's Law
of Effect

Shaping

Applications of
Operant Conditioning

Skinner's Approach to
Operant Conditioning

Principles of
Reinforcement

4   OBSERVATIONAL LEARNING

5   COGNITIVE FACTORS IN LEARNING

Purposive Behavior

Insight Learning

1 Explain what learning is.

- Learning is a relatively permanent change in behavior that occurs through experience. Observational learning is learning by watching what other people do. In associative learning, a connection is made between two events. Conditioning is the process by which associative learning occurs. In classical conditioning, organisms learn the association between two stimuli and, in operant conditioning, they learn the association between a behavior and a consequence.

- Biological constraints affect what an organism can learn from experience. These factors include instinctive drift (the tendency of animals to revert to instinctive behavior that interferes with learned behavior), preparedness (the species-specific biological predisposition to learn in certain ways but not in others), and taste aversion (the biological predisposition to learn to avoid foods that have caused sickness in the past).

2 Describe classical conditioning.

- Classical conditioning occurs when a neutral stimulus becomes associated with a meaningful stimulus and comes to elicit a similar response. Pavlov discovered that an organism can learn the association between an unconditioned stimulus (UCS) and a conditioned stimulus (CS). The UCS automatically produces the unconditioned response (UCR). After conditioning (CS-UCS pairing), the CS elicits the conditioned response (CR) by itself. Acquisition in classical conditioning is the initial linking of stimuli and responses. Generalization in classical conditioning is the tendency of a new stimulus that is similar to the original conditioned stimulus to elicit a response that is similar to the conditioned response. Discrimination in classical conditioning is the process of learning to respond to certain stimuli and not to others. Extinction in classical conditioning is the weakening of the CR in the absence of the UCS. Spontaneous recovery is the recurrence of a CR after a time delay without further conditioning.

- In humans, classical conditioning has been applied to explaining and eliminating fears. Counterconditioning weakens the CR by associating the fear-provoking stimulus with a response (a new CR) that is incompatible with the fear. Classical conditioning also can explain pleasant emotions. Some of the behaviors we associate with health problems and mental disorders, including certain aspects of drug use, can involve classical conditioning. Classical conditioning also has been used to understand consumer behavior.

3 Discuss operant conditioning.

- Operant conditioning is a form of learning in which the consequences of behavior produce changes in the probability of the behavior's occurrence. B. F. Skinner described the behavior of the organism as operant: The behavior operates on the environment, and the environment in turn operates on the organism. In contrast, classical conditioning describes how an organism responds to the environment, ignoring the organism's active influence on the environment. In most instances, operant conditioning is better at explaining voluntary behavior than classical conditioning is.

- Thorndike's law of effect states that behaviors followed by positive outcomes are strengthened, whereas behaviors followed by negative outcomes are weakened. Thorndike's view that the organism's behavior is due to a connection between a stimulus and a response is called S-R theory.

- Skinner believed that the mechanisms of learning are the same for all species. He studied lower animals extensively in the hope that the basic mechanisms of learning could be more easily understood in organisms simpler than humans. Like Skinner, contemporary behaviorists study organisms under precisely controlled conditions so that the connection between the operant behavior and the specific consequences can be examined in minute detail.

- Shaping is the process of rewarding approximations of desired behavior in order to shorten the learning process.

- Principles of reinforcement include the distinction between positive reinforcement (the frequency of a behavior increases because it is followed by a rewarding stimulus) and negative reinforcement (the frequency of behavior increases because it is followed by the removal of an aversive, or unpleasant, stimulus). Positive reinforcement can be classified as primary reinforcement (using reinforcers that are innately satisfying) and secondary reinforcement (using reinforcers that acquire positive value through experience). Reinforcement can also be continuous (a behavior is reinforced every time) or partial (a behavior is reinforced only a portion of the time). Schedules of reinforcement—fixed-ratio, variable-ratio, fixed-interval, and variable-interval—are timetables that determine when a behavior will be reinforced.

    Operant conditioning involves generalization (giving the same response to similar stimuli), discrimination (responding to stimuli that signal that a behavior will or will not be reinforced), and extinction (a decreasing tendency to perform a previously reinforced behavior when reinforcement is stopped).

Punishment is a consequence that decreases the likelihood a behavior will occur. Punishment, through which a behavior is weakened, is different from negative reinforcement, through which a behavior is strengthened. Operant conditioning is more efficient, especially in lower animals, when the interval between behavior and its reinforcement or punishment is very brief. However, in humans, delayed reinforcement and punishment can have significant effects on behavior, which has implications for understanding health problems, such as obesity and substance abuse.

- Behavior modification is the use of operant conditioning principles to change human behavior. It involves establishing consequences for behavior to reinforce desirable actions. Operant conditioning has been applied to mental and physical health, as well as to education.

4 *Understand observational learning.*

- Observational learning occurs when a person observes and imitates someone's behavior. Bandura said that observational learning includes attention, retention, production, and reinforcement.

5 *Outline the role of cognition in learning.*

- Tolman emphasized the purposiveness of behavior, meaning that much of behavior is goal-directed. In studying the purposiveness of behavior, Tolman went beyond stimuli and responses to discuss cognitive mechanisms. Tolman believed that expectancies, acquired through experiences with the environment, are an important cognitive mechanism in learning. Cognitive maps, an organism's mental representations of physical space, involve expectations about which actions are needed to reach a goal. Other evidence to support the role of cognition in learning was obtained in experiments on latent learning, which is unreinforced learning that is not immediately reflected in behavior.

- Köhler developed the concept of insight learning, a form of problem solving in which the organism develops a sudden insight into or understanding of a problem's solution.

Key Terms

learning, p. 195
associative learning, p. 195
instinctive drift, p. 196
preparedness, p. 196
classical conditioning, p. 198
unconditioned stimulus (UCS), p. 198
unconditioned response (UCR), p. 198
conditioned stimulus (CS), p. 198
conditioned response (CR), p. 198

acquisition (classical conditioning), p. 199
generalization (classical conditioning), p. 199
discrimination (classical conditioning), p. 199
extinction (classical conditioning), p. 200
spontaneous recovery, p. 200
counterconditioning, p. 202
operant conditioning, p. 205
law of effect, p. 205

shaping, p. 206
reinforcement, p. 207
positive reinforcement, p. 208
negative reinforcement, p. 208
primary reinforcement, p. 208
secondary reinforcement, p. 208
schedules of reinforcement, p. 209
generalization (operant conditioning), p. 210

discrimination (operant conditioning), p. 211
extinction (operant conditioning), p. 211
punishment, p. 211
applied behavior analysis (behavior modification), p. 216
observational learning, p. 219
latent learning, p. 222
insight learning, p. 223

Apply Your Knowledge

1. Many people have a taste aversion, a conditioned association between eating or drinking something and then getting sick. A taste aversion is likelier to occur when the food or drink is something that is relatively unfamiliar. Suppose that you have acquired a taste aversion to tequila. Identify what the unconditioned stimulus, unconditioned response, conditioned stimulus, and conditioned response are in this example.

2. Positive and negative reinforcement are often difficult concepts to understand. On the following website, examples and a practice exercise may help you figure out the distinction more easily:

   http://psych.athabascau.ca/html/prtut/reinpair.htm

3. Think of all of the things you have learned in the past several days. Write down an example involving each of the following types of learning: classical conditioning, operant conditioning, observational learning, latent learning, and insight learning. Which kind of learning do you use most frequently? Which do you use the least? Are there types of learning you've done that don't seem to fit any category? If so, what aspects of those types exclude them from these categories?

Connections

To test your mastery of the material in this chapter, go to the Study Guide and the In-Psych Plus CD-ROM, as well as the Online Learning Center. There you will find a chapter summary, practice tests, flashcards, lecture slides, web links, and other study tools, such as interactive exercises and reviews as well as current, chapter-relevant news articles.

7 Memory

Chapter Outline

Learning Goals

| THE NATURE OF MEMORY | **1** | Identify the three phases of memory. |

| MEMORY ENCODING | **2** | Explain how memories are encoded. |

Attention
▼
Levels of Processing
▼
Elaboration
▼
Imagery

| MEMORY STORAGE | **3** | Discuss how memories are stored. |

Sensory Memory
▼
Short-Term Memory
▼
Long-Term Memory
▼
How Memory Is Organized
▼
Where Memories Are Stored

| MEMORY RETRIEVAL | **4** | Summarize how memories are retrieved. |

Serial Position Effect
▼
Retrieval Cues and the Retrieval Task
▼
Accuracy in Memory Retrieval

| FORGETTING | **5** | Describe how encoding failure and retrieval failure are involved in forgetting. |

Encoding Failure
▼
Retrieval Failure

| MEMORY AND STUDY STRATEGIES | **6** | Evaluate study strategies based on an understanding of memory. |

Encoding Strategies
▼
Storage Strategies
▼
Retrieval Strategies

Unlike the other reporters, when S. listened to his editor making detailed assignments, he never took notes. Feeling exasperated by what he perceived as a lack of attention, his editor challenged S.'s professionalism. The editor was startled when S. reported not just the details of his own assignment but the details of others' assignments as well. S. was surprised himself. He thought everyone's memory operated in the same way and until this point had never thought of himself as different or special.

Psychologist Alexander Luria (1968) chronicled the life of S., whose unique visual imagination allowed him to remember an extraordinary amount of detail. Luria began with some simple research to test S.'s memory. For example, he asked S. to recall a series of words or numbers. In such tests, people usually remember at most 5 to 9 numbers. Not only could S. remember as many as 70 numbers, but he could also recall them accurately in reverse order. S. also could report the sequence flawlessly with no warning or practice even as long as 15 years after his initial exposure to the sequence. In addition, after the 15-year interval, S. could describe what Luria had been wearing and where he had been sitting when S. learned the list. Similar feats of recall included accurately reproducing passages from languages he did not know after hearing each passage only once.

How could S. manage such tasks? As long as each number or word was spoken slowly, S. could represent it as a visual image that was meaningful to him. These images were durable—S. easily remembered the image he created for each sequence long after he learned the sequence.

Although you might think it would be wonderful to possess S.'s remarkable ability to remember, S. often found that it was a serious liability. He moved from job to job, often feeling overwhelmed by the amount of detail he automatically included in his everyday work tasks. His propensity to create visual images interfered with his normal processing of information. He had trouble comprehending whole passages of a book because he became bogged down in the details. To a casual observer, S. appeared to be disorganized and rather dim-witted—a person who talked too much and derailed social conversations by reporting the images that filled his mind. Ironically, S. had a very poor memory for faces, finding them too flexible and changeable to recall.

S.'s memory, although extraordinary, helps us to understand how ordinary memory is organized and how it works, which is the subject of this chapter. As you will see, memory is a complex interaction of brain function, emotion, and individual circumstances. As psychologists learn more about this complex system and develop models to explain it, we benefit: The practical implications of psychology research are helping people overcome memory problems, and they are helping students study more effectively.

1 THE NATURE OF MEMORY

What are the three phases of memory?

Memory is the retention of information over time through encoding, storage, and retrieval. That is, for memory to work, we have to take information in, store it or represent it in some manner, and then retrieve it for some purpose later. The next three sections of the chapter focus on these three phases of memory. Although memory is very complex, thinking about it in terms of encoding, storage, and retrieval should help you to understand it better (see figure 7.1).

Except for the annoying moments when memory fails or someone we know is afflicted with memory loss, most of us don't think about how much everything we do or say depends on how smoothly our memory systems operate (Schacter, 1999, 2001). Think about how important memory is in carrying out the simple task in the following situation. You meet someone attractive at the library and would like to remember some facts about the person. To do this, you have to encode information about the person's appearance, name, major, interests, and so on. After leaving the

memory The retention of information over time through encoding, storage, and retrieval.

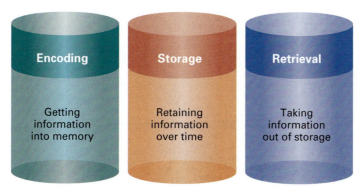

FIGURE 7.1 Processing Information in Memory As you read about the many aspects of memory in this chapter, think about the organization of memory in terms of these three main activities.

library, you don't have any way to write down the information, so you must retain it for about an hour until you get back to your room. On the way to your room, you might periodically rehearse a few of the facts about the person to help your memory. Later, you might write down the person's name to make sure you don't forget it, which involves retrieval. The next day, you see the person at the bookstore and must recognize his or her face and retrieve what you had talked about the day before to come up with something to say. Encoding, storage, and retrieval make up a kind of cycle of memory, which is repeated often as you continue to see and think about your new acquaintance.

We rely on our memory systems to carry out similar plans every day of our lives. Human memory systems truly are remarkable when you think of how much information we put into our memories and how much we must retrieve to perform all of life's activities (Willingham, 2004).

Human memory also has its imperfections, as we have all experienced. It is not unusual for two people to argue about whether something did or didn't happen or exactly how it happened, each intensely confident that his or her memory is accurate and the other person's is inaccurate. Each of us also has had the frustrating experience of trying to remember the name of someone or some place but not quite being able to retrieve it.

Clearly, people do not just coldly store and retrieve bits of data in a computer-like fashion (Schacter, 1996, 1999, 2001). Many scientists who study memory recognize its subjective nature and investigate how people reconstruct their own versions of the past. Scientists recognize that the mind can distort, invent, and forget. And they know that emotions color memories. Thus we do not store judgment-free impressions of reality. In sum, psychologists today study memory's phenomenal abilities, as well as its numerous limitations.

Review and Sharpen Your Thinking

1 **_Identify the three phases of memory._**
- Define memory and briefly profile the three phases of memory.

How important is memory in your life? What would your life be like without memory?

2 MEMORY ENCODING

| Attention | | Elaboration |
| Levels of Processing | | Imagery |

FIGURE 7.2 Encoding Memories
Look at these three pictures for a few seconds. Then look away and state what you remember about them.

How are memories encoded?

Encoding is the way in which information is processed for storage in memory. When you are listening to a lecture, watching a movie, listening to music, or talking with a friend, you are encoding information into memory. In everyday experiences, encoding has much in common with learning.

Some information gets into memory virtually automatically, whereas getting other information in takes effort. Let's examine some of the encoding processes that require effort. The issues that interest psychologists include how effectively we attend to information, how deeply we process it, how extensively we elaborate it with details, and how much we use mental imagery to encode it.

Attention

Look at the pictures of the three individuals in figure 7.2 for a few seconds. Then, before reading further, look away from them and state what you remember about the pictures. These actually are faces of famous people—George Washington, Mona Lisa, and George H. W. Bush—with Elvis Presley's hair grafted onto their images. You likely did not recognize these famous individuals at first because of the prominent hair. When we remember a face, we usually attend to only a few key features and ignore the others. Therefore, in these pictures, you may have focused more on the hair than on the facial features.

To begin the process of memory encoding, we have to attend to information (Mangels, Picton, & Craik, 2001). Recall that, in chapter 4, I discussed the role of *selective attention* in perception—that is, focusing on a specific aspect of experience while ignoring others. Attention is selective because the brain's resources are limited (O'Donnell, 2002; Reynolds & Chelazzi, 2004). Although our brains are remarkably efficient, they cannot attend to everything.

Divided attention also affects memory encoding. It occurs when a person must attend to several things simultaneously (Brouwer & others, 2002). In studies of divided attention, researchers often ask participants to remember a list of words or a story while performing an additional task that draws their attention away from the initial task (Schacter, 2001). For example, participants might be asked to monitor a series of tones and report when they hear a low- or high-pitched tone, at the same time that they are trying to memorize the list of words or story. In a number of such studies, individuals who are allowed to give their full attention to information they are asked to remember do much better on memory tests than those whose attention is divided (Pomplum, Reingold, & Shen, 2001; Reinitz, Morrissey, & Demb, 1994).

Levels of Processing

Simple attention to a stimulus does not completely explain the encoding process. For example, even if you pay attention to the word *boat*, you might process the word at three different levels. At the shallowest level, you might notice the shapes of the letters; at an intermediate level, you might think of characteristics of the word (such as that it rhymes with *coat*); and, at the deepest level, you might think about the kind of boat you would like to own and the last time you went fishing.

Depth of Processing		
Shallow Processing	Physical and perceptual features are analyzed.	The lines, angles, and contour that make up the physical appearance of an object, such as a car, are detected.
Intermediate Processing	Stimulus is recognized and labeled.	The object is recognized as a car.
Deep Processing	Semantic, meaningful, symbolic characteristics are used.	Associations connected with *car* are brought to mind—you think about the Porsche or Ferrari you hope to buy or the fun you and friends had on spring break when you drove a car to the beach.

FIGURE 7.3 Depth of Processing According to the levels of processing principle, deeper processing of stimuli produces better memory of them.

This model of the encoding process, proposed by Fergus Craik and Robert Lockhart (1972), states that encoding is on a continuum from shallow to deep, with deeper processing producing better memory (see figure 7.3):

- *Shallow processing.* The sensory or physical features of stimuli are analyzed. For instance, we might detect the lines, angles, and contours of a printed word's letters or detect a sound's frequency, duration, and loudness.
- *Intermediate processing.* The stimulus is recognized and given a label. For example, we identify a four-legged, barking object as a dog.
- *Deepest processing.* Information is processed semantically, in terms of its meaning. At this deepest level, we make associations. For example, we might associate the barking dog with a warning of danger or with good times, such as playing fetch with a pet. The more associations, the deeper the processing (Lee, Cheung, & Wurm, 2000; Otten, Henson, & Rugg, 2001).

A number of studies have shown that people's memories improve when they make associations to stimuli and use deep processing (Baddeley, 1998). For example, researchers have found that, if you encode something meaningful about a face and make associations with it, you are more likely to remember it (Harris & Kay, 1995). You might attach meaning to the face of a person in your introductory psychology class by noting that she reminds you of someone you have seen on TV, and you might associate her face with your psychology class.

Elaboration

Cognitive psychologists have recognized that, the more extensive the processing, the better the memory (Craik & Tulving, 1975). **Elaboration** is the extensiveness of processing at any given level. Thinking of examples of a concept is a good way to elaborate it. Self-reference is another effective way to elaborate information (Czienkowski & Giljohann, 2002). For example, if the word *win* is on a list of words to remember, you might think of the last time you won a bicycle race; or if the word *cook* appears, you might imagine the last time you cooked dinner. In general, deep elaboration— elaborate processing of meaningful information—is an excellent way to remember.

One reason elaboration produces good memory is that it adds to the *distinctiveness* of the "memory codes" (Ellis, 1987). To remember a piece of information, you need to search for the code that contains this information among the mass of codes contained in long-term memory. The search process is easier if the memory code is somehow unique (Hunt & Kelly, 1996). The situation is not unlike searching for a friend at a crowded airport. A friend who is 6 feet tall and has flaming red hair will

The more that you elaborate about an event, the better your memory of it will be. *If you were at an open-air rock concert, what kinds of information about the event could you encode to help you remember the concert more clearly?*

encoding How information gets into memory storage.

elaboration The extensiveness of processing at any given level of memory.

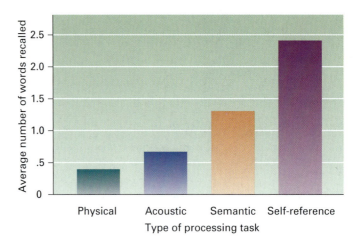

FIGURE 7.4 Efficiency of Forms of Elaboration In one study, researchers asked participants to remember lists of words according to the words' physical, acoustic (sound), semantic (meaning), or self-referent characteristics. When individuals generated self-references for the words, they remembered them better.

be easier to find in a crowd than a friend who is 5 feet, 9 inches tall with brown hair. Similarly, highly distinctive memory codes can be more easily differentiated.

As encoding becomes more elaborate, more information is stored and thus the code tends to become more distinctive—that is, easier to differentiate from other memory codes (Hunt & Ellis, 2004). Figure 7.4 compares the effectiveness of different types of elaboration.

Imagery

One of the most powerful ways to make memories distinctive is to use mental imagery. Recall from the beginning of the chapter the story of S.'s phenomenal memory. S. once was asked to remember the following formula:

$$N \cdot \sqrt{d^2 \cdot \frac{85}{VX}} \cdot 3\sqrt{\frac{276^2 \cdot 85x}{n^2 V \cdot \pi 264}} \, n^2 b$$
$$= sv \frac{1624}{32^2} \cdot r^2 s$$

S. studied the formula for 7 minutes and then reported how he memorized it. Notice in his account of this process, which follows, how he used imagery:

> Neiman *(N)* came out and jabbed at the ground with his cane (·). He looked up at a tall tree, which resembled the square-root sign ($\sqrt{\ }$), and thought to himself: "No wonder this tree has withered and begun to expose its roots. After all, it was here when I built these two houses" *(d^2)*. Once again he poked his cane (·). Then he said: "The houses are old, I'll have to get rid of them; the sale will bring in far more money." He had originally invested 85,000 in them (85). . . . (Luria, 1968)

S.'s complete story was four times this length. But the imagery in the story he created must have been powerful, because S. remembered the formula perfectly 15 years later without any advance notice.

You may not be capable of this feat, but you still are likely to use imagery to encode information. Here's a demonstration: How many windows are in your apartment or house? If you live in a dorm room with only one or two windows, this question might be too easy. If so, how many windows are in your family home? Few of us have ever set out to memorize this information, but many of us can come up with a good answer, especially if we use imagery to "reconstruct" each room. We take a mental walk through the house, counting windows as we go.

For many years, psychologists ignored the role of imagery in memory because behaviorists believed it to be too "mentalistic." But the studies of Allan Paivio (1971, 1986) documented how imagery can improve memory. Paivio argued that memory is stored in one of two ways: as a verbal code (a word or a label) or as an image code. Paivio thinks that the image code, which is highly detailed and distinctive, produces better memory than the verbal code because the memory for an image is stored both as an image code and as a verbal code. Thus we have two potential avenues by which information can be retrieved. Although imagery is widely accepted as an important aspect of memory, psychologists still debate whether we have separate codes for words and images. Nonetheless, imagery has been found helpful in many memory tasks (Kosslyn, 2004). It is especially useful in remembering associations. Imagery techniques also have helped students learn a foreign language.

Review and Sharpen Your Thinking

2 ***Explain how memories are encoded.***

- Summarize how attention is involved in memory.
- Describe the levels of processing involved in memory.
- Discuss elaboration.
- Explain the role of imagery in memory.

Think of a common object or location that you see every day (for example, your alarm clock or the place where you live) but that is not currently in your sight. Draw the object or location, or write a detailed description of it. Then compare your results with the real thing. What differences do you notice? Does what you learned about encoding help to explain the differences?

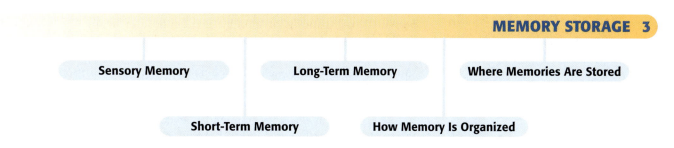

MEMORY STORAGE 3

Sensory Memory · Long-Term Memory · Where Memories Are Stored · Short-Term Memory · How Memory Is Organized

What are the three systems of memory storage, and how do they work?

The quality of encoding is not the only thing that determines the quality of memory. The memory also needs to be stored properly after it is encoded. **Storage** encompasses how information is retained over time and how it is represented in memory.

We remember some information for less than a second, some for half a minute, and some for minutes, hours, years, even a lifetime. An early popular theory that acknowledged the varying life span of memories was formulated by Richard Atkinson and Richard Shiffrin (1968). They described three separate memory systems:

- *Sensory memory:* time frames of a fraction of a second to several seconds
- *Short-term memory:* time frames up to 30 seconds
- *Long-term memory:* time frames up to a lifetime

As you read about these three memory storage systems, you will find that time frame is not the only thing that makes them different from one another. Each type of memory operates in a distinctive way and has a special purpose (see figure 7.5).

storage How information is retained over time and how it is represented in memory.

FIGURE 7.5 Atkinson and Shiffrin's Theory of Memory In this model, sensory input goes into sensory memory. Through the process of attention, information moves into short-term memory, where it remains for 30 seconds or less, unless it is rehearsed. When the information goes into long-term memory storage, it can be retrieved over the lifetime.

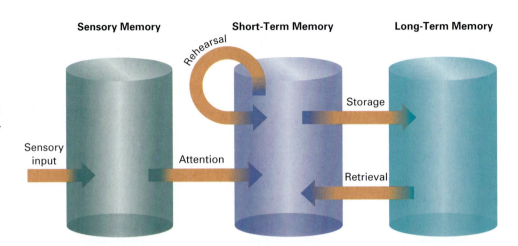

FIGURE 7.6 Sensory Memory Experiment This array of stimuli is similar to those flashed for about ¹⁄₂₀ of a second to the participants in Sperling's study of sensory memory.

In-Psych Plus

sensory memory The memory system that holds information from the world in its original form for only an instant, not much longer than the brief time it is exposed to the visual, auditory, and other senses.

short-term memory The memory system in which a limited amount of information is retained for only as long as 30 seconds unless strategies are used to retain it longer.

Sensory Memory

Sensory memory holds information from the world in its original sensory form for only an instant, not much longer than the brief time it is exposed to the visual, auditory, and other senses (Rainer & Miller, 2002). Sensory memory is very rich and detailed, but the information in it is quickly lost unless it is transferred into short-term or long-term memory.

Think about all the sights and sounds you encounter as you walk to class on a typical morning. Literally thousands of stimuli come into your fields of vision and hearing—cracks in the sidewalk, chirping birds, a noisy motorcycle, the blue sky, faces of hundreds of people. You do not process all these stimuli, but you process many more stimuli at the sensory level than you consciously notice. Sensory memory retains this information from your senses, including a large portion of what you think you ignore.

In George Sperling's (1960) classic study of sensory memory, participants were presented with patterns of stimuli, such as those in figure 7.6. Sperling flashed the letters on a screen for very brief intervals, about ¹⁄₂₀ of a second. After a pattern was flashed on the screen, the participants could report only four or five letters. With such short exposure, reporting all nine letters was impossible. But some of the participants in Sperling's study reported feeling that, for an instant, they could *see* all nine letters. One hypothesis to explain this experience is that all nine letters were initially processed as far as the sensory memory level. However, forgetting was so rapid that the participants could name only a handful of letters before the others were lost from sensory memory.

Sperling reasoned that, if all nine letters were actually processed in sensory memory, they should all be available for a brief time. To test this possibility, Sperling sounded a low, medium, or high tone just after a pattern of letters was shown. The participants were told that the tone was a signal to report only the letters from the bottom, middle, or top row. Under these conditions, the participants performed much better, suggesting a brief memory for most or all of the letters in the display. Go to the interactivity "Iconic Memory" to engage in Sperling's classic experiment.

Short-Term Memory

Much information goes no further than the stage of sensory memory of sounds and sights. However, some of the information, especially that to which we pay attention, is transferred to short-term memory. **Short-term memory** is a limited-capacity memory system in which information is usually retained for only as long as 30 seconds unless strategies are used to retain it longer.

The limited capacity of short-term memory was examined by George Miller (1956) in a classic paper, "The Magical Number Seven, Plus or Minus Two." Miller observed that on many tasks individuals are limited in how much information they can keep track of without external aids. Usually the limit is in the range of 7 ± 2 items. The most widely cited example of the 7 ± 2 phenomenon involves **memory span,** which is the number of digits an individual can report back in order after a single presentation. Most college students can remember 8 or 9 digits without making errors, but longer lists pose problems. What is the capacity of your short-term memory? Find out by engaging in the interactivity "Short-Term Memory."

Chunking and Rehearsal   Two ways to improve short-term memory are chunking and rehearsal. **Chunking** involves grouping, or "packing," information that exceeds the 7 ± 2 memory span into higher-order units that can be remembered as single units. In essence, chunking is a form of memory encoding: specifically, elaboration. It works by making large amounts of information more manageable.

For an example of how chunking works, consider this simple list of words: *hot, city, book, forget, tomorrow,* and *smile.* Try to hold these words in memory for a moment, then write them down. If you recalled the words, you succeeded in holding 34 letters, grouped into 7 chunks, in your memory.

Now try holding the following in memory and then writing it down:

O LDH ARO LDAN DYO UNGB EN

How did you do? Don't feel bad if you did poorly. This string of letters is very difficult to remember, even though it is arranged in chunks. However, if you chunk the letters to form the meaningful words *Old Harold and Young Ben,* they become much easier to remember. Recall that this sort of deep, semantic processing during encoding helps with memory tasks. Go to the interactivity "Chunking in Memory" to participate in a memory study and see how chunking enhances memory.

Another way to improve short-term memory involves **rehearsal,** the conscious repetition of information. Information stored in short-term memory lasts half a minute or less without rehearsal. However, if rehearsal is not interrupted, information can be retained indefinitely.

Rehearsal is often verbal, giving the impression of an inner voice, but it can also be visual or spatial, giving the impression of a private inner eye. One way to use your visualization skills is to maintain the image of an object or a scene for a while after you have viewed it. People who are unusually good at this task are said to have a photographic memory. All of us can do this to some degree, but a small number of individuals may be so good at maintaining an image that they "see" the appropriate page of a textbook as they try to remember information during a test. However, photographic memory is so rare that it has been difficult to study; some psychologists even doubt its existence (Gray & Gummerman, 1975).

Rehearsal works best when we need to briefly remember a list of items. When we have to remember information for longer periods, as when we are studying for a test coming up next week or even an hour from now, other strategies usually work better. A main reason rehearsal does not work well over the long term is that it often involves rotely repeating information without imparting meaning to it. Remembering information over the long term works better when we add meaning to it, which is again an example of the importance of deep, semantic processing.

Working Memory   Some contemporary experts on memory believe that Atkinson and Shiffrin's model of sensory, short-term, and long-term memory systems is too simplistic (Baddeley, 2001, 2003; Bartlett, 2001). They believe that memory does not always work in such a neatly packaged, three-stage sequence. For example, some experts believe that short-term memory involves far more than rehearsal and passive storage of information (Murdock, 1999).

memory span The number of digits an individual can repeat back in order after a single presentation of them.

chunking Grouping, or "packing," information that exceeds the 7 ± 2 memory span into higher-order units that can be remembered as single units.

rehearsal The conscious repetition of information to increase the durability of memory.

British psychologist Alan Baddeley (1998, 2000, 2001, 2003) proposed the concept of **working memory,** a system that temporarily holds information as people perform cognitive tasks. Working memory is a kind of mental "workbench" on which information is manipulated and assembled to help us comprehend language, make decisions, and solve problems. Working memory is not like a passive storehouse with shelves to store information until it moves to long-term memory. Rather, it is an active memory system (Nyberg & others, 2002). How long does your working memory last? Go to the interactivity "Working Memory" and engage in the simulation of a memory experiment.

Figure 7.7 shows Baddeley's view of the three components of working memory. Think of them as an executive (the central executive) who has two assistants (the phonological loop and visuospatial working memory) to help do the work.

- The *phonological loop* is specialized to briefly store information about the sounds of language. The phonological loop contains an acoustic code, which decays in a few seconds, and a rehearsal function, which allows individuals to repeat the words in the phonological loop.
- *Visuospatial working memory* stores visual and spatial information, including visual imagery (Logie, 1995). Visuospatial working memory also has been called the *visuospatial scratch pad.* As in the case of the phonological loop, the capacity of visuospatial working memory is limited. For example, if you try to put too many items in visuospatial working memory, you can't represent them accurately enough to retrieve them successfully. The phonological loop and visuospatial memory function independently (Reed, 2001). You could rehearse numbers in the phonological loop while making spatial arrangements of letters in visuospatial working memory (Baddeley & Hitch, 1974).
- The *central executive* integrates information not only from the phonological loop and visuospatial working memory but also from long-term memory. In Baddeley's (2001, 2003) view, the central executive plays important roles in attention, planning, and organizing. The central executive acts much like a supervisor who monitors which information deserves attention and which should be ignored. It also selects which strategies to use to process information and solve problems. As with the other two components of working memory—phonological loop and visuospatial working memory—the central executive has a limited capacity.

Working memory

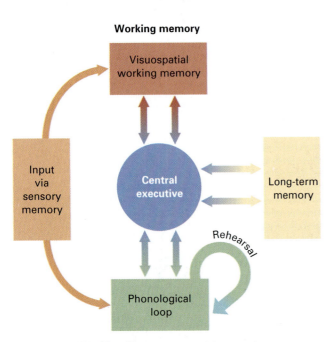

FIGURE 7.7 Working Memory In Baddeley's working memory model, working memory is like a mental workbench where a great deal of information processing is carried out. Working memory consists of three main components: The phonological loop and visuospatial working memory serve as assistants in helping the central executive do its work. Input from sensory memory goes to the phonological loop, where information about speech is stored and rehearsal takes place, and to visuospatial working memory, where visual and spatial information, including imagery, are stored. Working memory is a limited-capacity system, and information is stored there for only a brief time. Working memory interacts with long-term memory, using information from long-term memory in its work and transmitting information to long-term memory for storage.

The concept of working memory can help us understand how brain damage influences cognitive skills (LaBar & others, 2002). For example, one amnesia patient has good long-term memory despite being able to remember only two digits (Baddeley, 1992). The phonological loop is the source of this patient's memory problem. Because he cannot maintain verbal codes in the loop, his memory span suffered. He also has difficulty learning new associations between words and nonsense sounds. Working memory deficits also are involved in Alzheimer's disease—a progressive, irreversible brain disorder in older adults that was discussed in chapter 3 (Bayles, 2003). Baddeley (1998) believes the central executive of the working memory model is the culprit—Alzheimer's patients have great difficulty coordinating different mental activities, one of the central executive's functions.

Let's examine another aspect of life in which working memory is involved. In one study, verbal working memory was impaired by negative emotion (Gray, 2001). In another study, college students who wrote about a negative emotional event

working memory A three-part system that temporarily holds information as people perform tasks; a kind of mental workbench on which information is manipulated and assembled to perform other cognitive tasks.

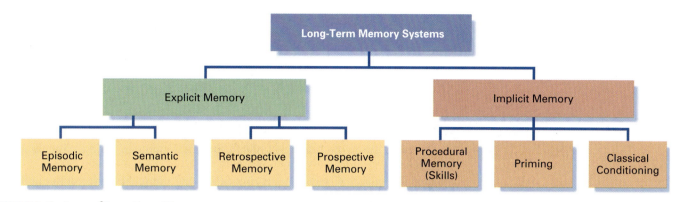

FIGURE 7.8 **Systems of Long-Term Memory**

showed sizable improvement in working memory, compared with students who wrote about a positive event and those in a control group who wrote about their daily schedules (Klein & Boals, 2001). Improvement in working memory was associated with higher grade-point averages. (Recall from chapter 1 that writing about emotionally traumatic experiences has been linked with improvement in college students' health; see Pennebaker, 1997, 2001.) An important implication of this study is its demonstration that the negative effects of emotion on working memory can be eased to some extent (Miyake, 2001). For example, students with math anxiety often have trouble with working memory when doing math problems (Ashcraft & Kirk, 2001). Writing about their math anxiety might help these students solve math problems more readily.

Long-Term Memory

Long-term memory is a relatively permanent type of memory that stores huge amounts of information for a long time. The capacity of long-term memory is, indeed, staggering. John von Neumann, a distinguished computer scientist, put the size at 2.8×10^{20} (280 quintillion) bits, which in practical terms means that our storage capacity is virtually unlimited. Von Neumann assumed that we never forget anything, but even considering that we do forget things, we can hold several billion times more information than a large computer.

Long-term memory is complex, as figure 7.8 shows. At the top level, it is divided into substructures of explicit memory and implicit memory. In simple terms, explicit memory has to do with remembering who, what, where, when, and why; implicit memory has to do with remembering how. Explicit memory can be further subdivided into episodic and semantic memory and distinguished as either retrospective or prospective memory. Implicit memory includes the systems involved in procedural memory, priming, and classical conditioning.

To explore the distinction between explicit and implicit memory, let's look at a person known as H. M. He had a severe case of epilepsy and underwent surgery in 1953 that involved removing the hippocampus and a portion of the temporal lobes of both hemispheres in his brain. (The location and functions of these areas of the brain were discussed in chapter 2.) His epilepsy improved, but something devastating happened to his memory. The most dramatic problem he developed was an inability to form new memories that outlive working memory. H. M.'s memory time frame is only a few minutes at most, so he lives, as he has done since 1953, in a perpetual present and cannot remember past events (explicit memory). In contrast, his memory of how to do things (implicit memory) was less affected. For example, he can learn new physical tasks. In one such task, H. M. was asked to trace the outline of a star-shaped figure while viewing the figure and his hand in a mirror. This is a

long-term memory The memory system in which huge amounts of information are held relatively permanently.

task that most people find difficult in the beginning. Over 3 days of training, H. M. learned this task as effectively and rapidly as normal individuals. On the second and third days, he began at the level he had achieved the previous day (a success in implicit memory), even though he was completely unaware that he had previously practiced the task (a failure in explicit memory).

Explicit Memory   **Explicit memory** is the conscious recollection of information such as specific facts or events and, at least in humans, information that can be verbally communicated (Tulving, 1989, 2000). Examples of using explicit memory include recounting the events of a movie you have seen and describing a basic principle of psychology to someone. However, you do not need to be talking to be using explicit memory. Simply sitting and consciously reflecting about Einstein's theory of relativity or the date you had last weekend involves explicit memory.

Canadian cognitive psychologist Endel Tulving (1972, 1989, 2000) has been the foremost advocate of distinguishing between two subtypes of explicit memory: episodic and semantic. **Episodic memory** is the retention of information about the where and when of life's happenings. It is autobiographical. For example, episodic memory includes the details of what it was like when your younger brother or sister was born, what happened on your first date, what you were doing when you heard of the terrorist attacks in New York City and Washington, DC, and what you had for breakfast this morning.

Semantic memory is a person's knowledge about the world. It includes your fields of expertise, general knowledge of the sort you learned in school, and everyday knowledge about meanings of words, famous individuals, important places, and common things. For example, semantic memory is involved in a person's knowledge of chess, of geometry, and of who Nelson Mandela and Mahatma Gandhi are. An important aspect of semantic memory is that it appears to be independent of an individual's personal memory of the past. You can access a fact—such as that Lima is the capital of Peru—and not have the foggiest notion of when and where you learned it.

A couple of examples may help to clarify the distinction between episodic and semantic memory. Your memory of your first day on campus involves episodic memory; in your psychology class, your memory of the information you need to know to do well on the next test involves semantic memory. Also, in a certain type of amnesia, the difference between these two types of explicit memory becomes clear. Tulving (1989) reported an especially dramatic case. A young man named K. C. suffered a motorcycle accident and lost virtually all use of his episodic memory. He was unable to consciously recollect a single thing that had ever happened to him. At the same time, K. C.'s semantic memory was sufficiently preserved that he could learn about his past as a set of facts, just as he would learn about another person's life. He could report, for example, that the saddest day of his life was when his brother died of drowning about 10 years before. But he had no conscious memory of the event. He simply knew about the drowning because he was able to recall—apparently through use of his semantic memory—what he had been told about his brother by other members of his family.

Some aspects of the episodic/semantic distinction are summarized in figure 7.9. Keep in mind, though, that many cases of explicit memory are neither purely episodic nor purely semantic but fall in between. Tulving (1983, 2000) argues that semantic and episodic systems often work together in forming new memories. In such cases, the memory that ultimately is formed might consist of an autobiographical episode *and* semantic information.

Another aspect of explicit memory, which is currently a hot topic, is the difference between **retrospective memory,** remembering the past (the main focus of this chapter), and **prospective memory,** remembering information about doing something in the future (Burgess, Quayle, & Frith, 2001; Graf, 2004; Kliegel & others, 2001; McDaniel & Einstein, 2000). Prospective memory includes memory for

explicit memory The conscious recollection of information, such as specific facts or events and, at least in humans, information that can be verbally communicated.

episodic memory The retention of information about the where and when of life's happenings.

semantic memory A person's knowledge about the world.

retrospective memory Remembering the past.

prospective memory Remembering information about doing something in the future.

Characteristic	Episodic Memory	Semantic Memory
Units	Events, episodes	Facts, ideas, concepts
Organization	Time	Concepts
Emotion	More important	Less important
Retrieval process	Deliberate (effortful)	Automatic
Retrieval report	"I remember"	"I know"
Education	Irrelevant	Relevant
Intelligence	Irrelevant	Relevant
Legal testimony	Admissible in court	Inadmissible in court

FIGURE 7.9 Some Differences Between Episodic and Semantic Memory

intentions. Many of us have had somewhat embarrassing or difficult experiences when prospective memory fails. For example, we might forget to buy a food item at the store, miss an appointment, or forget that a homework assignment is due. Prospective memory includes both *timing*—when to do something—and *content*—what it is we have to do. Older adults tend to show deficiencies in prospective memory. The audio clip "Aging and Memory" describes training that can improve the memory of seniors.

In-Psych Plus

Some failures in prospective memory are referred to as "absentmindedness." We become more absentminded when we become preoccupied with something else, are distracted by something, or are under a lot of time pressures (Matlin, 2004). Absentmindedness often involves a breakdown between attention and memory storage (Schacter, 2001). Absentmindedness may reflect the failure to elaboratively encode something we need to remember. We spend a great deal of our lives on autopilot, which helps us to perform routine tasks effectively but also makes us vulnerable to absentminded errors.

Implicit Memory   Another type of long-term memory is related to nonconsciously remembering skills and perceptions rather than consciously remembering facts. **Implicit memory** is memory in which behavior is affected by prior experience without that experience being consciously recollected. Examples of implicit memory include the skills of playing tennis and typing, as well as the repetition in your mind of a song you heard in the supermarket, even though you did not consciously attend to the music. Three subsystems of implicit memory consist of memories that you are not aware of yet predispose you to behave in certain ways (Schacter, 2000):

- **Procedural memory** involves memory for skills. For example, once you have learned to drive a car, you remember how to do it: You do not have to remember consciously how to drive the car as you put the key in the ignition, turn the steering wheel, push on the gas pedal, hit the brakes, and so on. To illustrate the distinction between explicit memory and procedural memory, imagine you are at Wimbledon. Serena Williams moves gracefully for a wide forehand, finishes her follow-through, runs quickly back to the center of the court, pushes off for a short ball, and volleys the ball for a winner. If we asked her about this rapid sequence of movements, she probably would have difficulty listing each move. In contrast, if we asked her who her toughest opponent is, she might quickly respond, "My sister." In the first instance, she would be unable to verbally describe exactly what she had done because her actions had been based on procedural memory. In the second, she would have no problem answering our question because it was based on explicit memory.

- **Priming** is the activation of information that people already have in storage to help them remember new information better and faster (Badgaiyan, Schacter, &

implicit memory Memory in which behavior is affected by prior experience without that experience being consciously recollected.

procedural memory Memory for skills.

priming A type of implicit memory; information that people already have in storage is activated to help them remember new information better and faster.

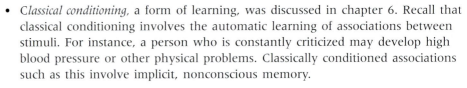

FRANK & ERNEST reprinted by permission of Newspaper Enterprise Association, Inc.

In-Psych Plus

Alpert, 2001; Huber & others, 2001). In a common demonstration of priming, individuals study a list of words (such as *hope, walk,* and *cake*). To assess explicit memory, they are asked to select all the words that appeared on the list—for example, "Did you see the word *hope?* Did you see the word *form?*" Then, to assesses implicit memory, they are shown a list of incomplete words (for example, *ho__, wa__, ca__*), called word stems, and are told to fill in the blanks with whatever word comes to mind. Individuals fill in the blanks with words they had previously studied more often than would be expected if they were filling them in randomly. For example, they are more likely to complete the stem *ho__* with *hope* than with *hole.* This is so even when individuals did not recognize the words on the earlier recognition task. Because priming occurs even when explicit memory is not required, it is assumed to be an involuntary and nonconscious process (Hauptmann & Karni, 2002). Priming can lead to false memories, however, as the video clip "When Eyes Deceive" illustrates.

- *Classical conditioning,* a form of learning, was discussed in chapter 6. Recall that classical conditioning involves the automatic learning of associations between stimuli. For instance, a person who is constantly criticized may develop high blood pressure or other physical problems. Classically conditioned associations such as this involve implicit, nonconscious memory.

How Memory Is Organized

Classifying the types of long-term memory does not address the question of how the different types of memory are organized for storage. The word *organized* is important: Memories are not haphazardly stored but are, instead, carefully sorted.

Here's a demonstration. Recall the 12 months of the year as quickly as you can. How long did it take you? What was the order of your recall? Chances are you listed them within a few seconds in "natural," chronological order (January, February, March, and so on). Now try to remember the months in alphabetical order. Did you make any errors? How long did it take you? It should be obvious that your memory for the months of the year is organized in a particular way.

One of memory's most distinctive features is its organization. Researchers have found that, if people are encouraged to organize material, their memories of the material improve, even if no warning is given that their memories will be tested (Mandler, 1980). Psychologists have four main theories of how long-term memory is organized: hierarchies, semantic networks, schemas, and connectionism.

Hierarchies In many instances, we remember facts better when we organize them hierarchically (Bruning, Schraw, & Ronning, 1999). A *hierarchy* is a system in which items are organized from general to specific classes. One common example is an organization chart showing the relationship of units in a business or a

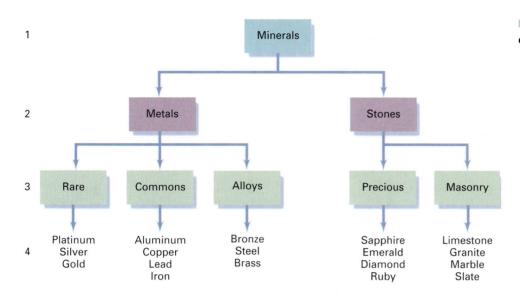

FIGURE 7.10 **Example of a Hierarchical Organization**

school, with the CEO or president at the top, the vice presidents or deans at the next level, and the managers or professors at a third level. This textbook also is organized hierarchically—with up to four levels of headings—to help you understand how the various bits of information in the book are related; the table of contents provides a visual representation of the hierarchy of the top two levels of headings.

In an early research study, Gordon Bower and his colleagues (1969) showed the importance of hierarchical organization in memory. Participants who were given words in hierarchies remembered them better than those who were given words in random groupings (see figure 7.10).

Semantic Networks   We often use semantic networks to organize material in episodic memory (a form of explicit memory). One of the first network theories claimed that memory can be envisioned as a complex network of nodes that stand for labels or concepts. The network was assumed to be hierarchically arranged, with more concrete concepts (canary, for example) nested under more abstract concepts (bird).

More recently, cognitive psychologists realized that such hierarchical networks are too simple to describe the way human cognition actually works (Shanks, 1991). For example, people take longer to answer the true-or-false statement "An ostrich is a bird" than they do to answer the statement "A canary is a bird." Memory researchers now see the semantic network as more irregular and distorted: a typical bird, such as a canary, is closer to the node, or center, of the category *bird* than is the atypical ostrich. Figure 7.11 shows an example of the revised model, which allows us to show how typical information is while illustrating how it is linked together.

We add new material to a semantic network by placing it in the middle of the appropriate region of memory. The new material is gradually tied in to related nodes in the surrounding network. This model reveals why, if you cram for a test, you will not remember the information over the long term. The new material is not woven into the long-term web. In contrast, discussing the material or incorporating it into a research paper interweaves it and connects it to other knowledge you have. These multiple connections increase the probability that you will be able to retrieve the information many months or even years later. The concept of multiple connections fits with the earlier explanation of the importance of elaboration in memory.

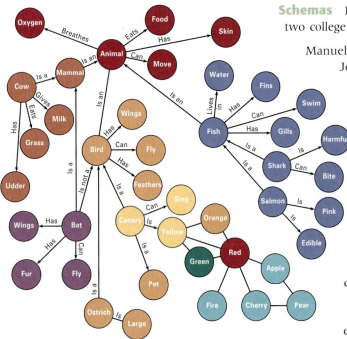

FIGURE 7.11 Revision of the Semantic Network View of Long-Term Memory Some psychologists challenged the original representation of semantic networks as too "clean" to portray the true complexity of our memory processes. This representation, they believe, is more accurate.

"Why? You cross the road because it's in the script—that's why!" © The New Yorker Collection 1986 Edward Koren from cartoonbank.com. All Rights Reserved.

schema A preexisting mental concept or framework that helps people to organize and interpret information.

script A schema for an event.

connectionism The theory that memory is stored throughout the brain in connections between neurons, several of which may work together to process a single memory.

Schemas Imagine that you overhear the following conversation between two college students living in a dorm:

Manuel: Did you order it?

Jordan: Yeah, it will be here in about 45 minutes.

Manuel: Well, I have to leave before then, but save me a couple of slices, okay?

Do you know what these two students are talking about? You likely guessed that they were talking about pizza, but how did you know? The word *pizza* was never mentioned. You knew what they were talking about because you activated your concept of "pizza" or "ordering pizza for delivery" and used that concept to comprehend the situation.

You learned in chapter 3 that, when we store information in memory, we often fit it into the collection of information that already exists. You did the same thing in comprehending the pizza delivery situation. The preexisting mental concept or framework that helps people to organize and interpret information is a **schema**. Schemas from prior encounters with the environment influence the way we encode, make inferences about, and retrieve information (Jou, Shanteau, & Harris, 1996).

Semantic network theories assume that memory involves specific facts with clear links from one to another. In contrast, schema theory claims that long-term memory is not very exact. We seldom find precisely the memory that we want, or at least not all of what we want; hence, we have to reconstruct the rest. Our schemas support the reconstruction process, helping us fill in gaps between our fragmented memories.

The schema theory of memory began with Sir Frederick Bartlett's (1932) studies of how people remember stories. He reasoned that a person's background, which is encoded in schemas, would reveal itself in the person's reconstruction (modification and distortion) of a story's content. One of Bartlett's stories was called "War of the Ghosts," an English translation of an American Indian folktale. The story tells of events that were completely foreign to Bartlett's middle- and upper-income British research participants. They read the story twice and then, after 15 minutes, wrote down the tale the best they could remember it. The participants used both their general schemas for daily experiences and their particular schemas for adventurous ghost stories to reconstruct "War of the Ghosts." Familiar details from the story that fit into the participants' schemas were successfully recalled, but details that departed from their schemas were often extensively distorted.

We have schemas for stories, for scenes or spatial layouts (a beach, a bathroom), and for common events (going to a restaurant, playing football, writing a term paper). A **script** is a schema for an event (Schank & Abelson, 1977). Scripts often have information about physical features, people, and typical occurrences. This kind of information is helpful when people need to figure out what is happening around them. For example, if you are enjoying your after-dinner coffee in a restaurant and a man in a tuxedo comes over and puts a piece of paper on the table, your script tells you that the man probably is a waiter who has just given you the check.

Connectionism Theories of hierarchies, semantic networks, and schemas have little or nothing to say about the role of the physical brain in memory. Thus a new theory based on brain research has generated a wave of excitement among psychologists. **Connectionism** is the theory that memory is stored throughout the brain in

Shown here are representative scripts from a Japanese tea ceremony, a Western dinner, and an Ethiopian meal. *With which script would you feel most comfortable? Least comfortable?*

connections among neurons, several of which may work together to process a single memory (Dehaene & Naccache, 2001; Humphreys & others, 2000; Smallwood, Obonsawin, & Heim, 2003). Recall that the concept of neural networks was initially discussed in chapter 2, the concept of parallel processing pathways in chapter 4. This section expands on those discussions and applies these concepts to memory.

In the connectionist view, memories are neither abstract concepts (as in semantic network theories) nor large knowledge structures (as in schema theories). Instead, memories are more like electrical impulses, organized only to the extent that neurons, the connections among them, and their activity are organized. Any piece of knowledge is embedded in the strengths of hundreds or thousands of connections among neurons and is not limited to a single location. Figure 7.12 compares the semantic network, schema, and connectionist theories of memories.

How does the connectionist process work? A neural activity involving memory, such as remembering the name of your dog, is distributed across a number of areas of the cerebral cortex. The locations of neural activity, called *nodes*, are interconnected.

	Theory		
	Semantic Network	**Schema**	**Connectionist**
Nature of memory units	Abstract concepts ("bird")	Large knowledge structures ("going to a restaurant")	Small units, connections among neurons
Number of units	Tens of thousands	Unknown	Tens of millions
Formation of new memories	New nodes	New schemas or modification of old ones	Increased strength of connections among neurons
Attention to brain structure	Little	Little	Extensive

FIGURE 7.12 Key Features of Semantic Network, Schema, and Connectionist Theories

When a node reaches a critical level of activation, it can affect another node across synapses. We know that the human cerebral cortex contains millions of neurons that are richly interconnected through hundreds of millions of synapses. Because of these synaptic connections, the activity of one neuron can be influenced by many other neurons. The connectionist view argues that changes in the strength of synaptic connections are the fundamental bases of memory (O'Brien & Opie, 1999).

Part of the appeal of the connectionist view is that it is consistent with what we know about the way the brain functions. Another part of its appeal is that, when programmed on a computer, the connectionist view has been successful in predicting the results of some memory experiments (Marcus, 2001; McClelland & Rumelhart, 1986). Its insights into the organization of memory also support brain research undertaken to determine where memories are stored in the brain.

Where Memories Are Stored

Karl Lashley (1950) spent a lifetime looking for a location in the brain in which memories are stored. He trained rats to discover the correct pathway in a maze and then cut out various portions of the animals' brains and retested their memory of the maze pathway. After experimenting with thousands of rats, Lashley found that the loss of various cortical areas did not affect the rats' ability to remember the pathway. Lashley concluded that memories are not stored in a specific location in the brain. Other researchers, continuing Lashley's quest, would agree that memory storage is diffuse but have developed some new insights. Canadian psychologist Donald Hebb (1949, 1980) suggested that assemblies of cells, distributed over large areas of the cerebral cortex, work together to represent information. Hebb's idea of distributed memory was farsighted.

Today, many neuroscientists believe that brain chemicals are the ink with which memories are written and that memory is located in specific sets or circuits of neurons (Squire, Stark, & Clark, 2004). Brain researcher Larry Squire (1990), for example, says that most memories are probably clustered in groups of about 1,000 neurons. Single neurons, of course, are at work in memory. Researchers who measure the electrical activity of single cells have found that some respond to faces, others to eye or hair color, for example. But for you to recognize your Uncle Albert, individual neurons that provide information about hair color, size, and other characteristics act together.

One concept that has been proposed to understand how memory functions at the neuronal level is *long-term potentiation*. In line with connectionist theory, this concept states that, if two neurons are activated at the same time, the connection between them—and thus the memory—may be strengthened (Shakesby, Anwyl, & Rowan, 2002; Squire & Kandel, 2000).

Whereas some neuroscientists are unveiling the cellular basis of memory, others are examining its broad-scale architecture. Although memory is distributed throughout the brain (Squire, 1998), a limited number of brain systems and pathways are involved, and each probably contributes in different ways (Lynch, 1990). Figure 7.13 shows the location of brain structures involved in different types of long-term memory. (Go to the interactivity "Parts of the Brain" for a 3D tour of the brain.)

In-Psych Plus

- *Explicit memory.* Neuroscientists have found that the hippocampus, the temporal lobes in the cerebral cortex, and other areas of the limbic system are involved in explicit memory (Traub, 2004; Zola & Squire, 2001). In many aspects of explicit memory, information is transmitted from the hippocampus to the frontal lobes, which are involved in both retrospective and prospective memory (Burgess & others, 2001). The left frontal lobe is especially active when we encode new information into memory; the right frontal lobe is more active when we subsequently retrieve it (Otten, Henson, & Rugg, 2001). The amygdala, part of the limbic system, is involved in emotional memories (McGaugh, 2004; Siegle & others, 2002).

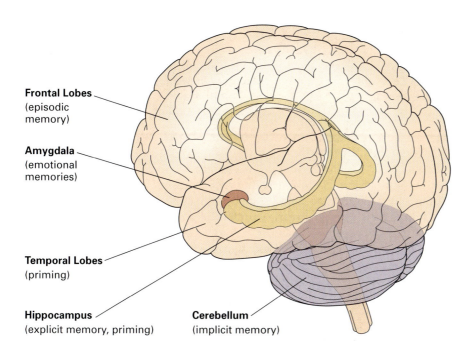

FIGURE 7.13 **Structures of the Brain Involved in Different Aspects of Long-Term Memory**

Frontal Lobes (episodic memory)

Amygdala (emotional memories)

Temporal Lobes (priming)

Hippocampus (explicit memory, priming)

Cerebellum (implicit memory)

- *Implicit memory.* The cerebellum is involved in the implicit memory required to perform skills (Krupa, Thompson, & Thompson, 1993). Various areas of the cerebral cortex, such as the temporal lobes and hippocampus, function in priming (Jernigan, Ostergaard, & Fennema-Notestine, 2001; Yasuno & others, 2000).

Neuroscientists studying memory have benefited greatly from the use of MRI scans, which allow the tracking of neural activity during cognitive tasks (Nyberg, 2004). In one research study, participants were shown color photographs of indoor and outdoor scenes while in an MRI machine (Brewer & others, 1998). They were not told that they would be given a memory test about the scenes. After the MRI scans, they were asked which pictures they remembered well, vaguely, or not at all. Their memories were compared with the brain scans. The longer that both prefrontal lobes and a particular region of the hippocampus remained lit up on the MRI scans, the better the participants remembered the scenes. Pictures paired with weak brain activity in these areas were forgotten.

As neuroscientists identify memory circuits in the brain, might the psychological study of memory become unimportant? That's unlikely. First, they are far from working out all of the complexities of the neurochemical activity underpinning human memory. And, second, even if they were successful in unraveling the neurochemical mystery of memory, each person would always have a private kingdom of memories influencing his or her thoughts and actions.

Review and Sharpen Your Thinking

3 *Discuss how memories are stored.*

- Explain sensory memory.
- Summarize how short-term memory works.
- Describe how long-term memory functions.
- Describe four theories of how memory is organized.
- Discuss the role of the brain in memory storage.

How might semantic network theory explain why cramming for a test is not a good way to acquire long-term memory?

4 MEMORY RETRIEVAL

| Serial Position Effect | Retrieval Cues and the Retrieval Task | Accuracy in Memory Retrieval |

How are memories retrieved?

Long-term memory has been compared to a library. We retrieve information in a fashion similar to the process we use to locate and check out a book. To retrieve something from our mental "data banks," we search our store of memory to find the relevant information. Memory **retrieval** takes place when information is taken out of storage.

But the process of retrieving information from long-term memory is not as precise as the library analogy suggests. When we search through our long-term memory storehouse, we don't always find the exact "book" we want. Our memories are affected by a number of things, including the pattern of facts we remember, the situations we associate with memories, and the personal or emotional context. Or we might find the book we want but discover that only several pages are intact. We have to reconstruct the rest. There has been a flurry of interest in these memory quirks and glitches.

Serial Position Effect

Understanding how retrieval works requires knowledge of the **serial position effect**—the tendency for items at the beginning and at the end of a list to be recalled more readily than items in the middle of the list (see figure 7.14) (Howard & Kahana, 1999; Surprenant, 2001). If someone gave you the directions "left on Mockingbird, right on Central, right on Stemmons, left on Balboa, and right on Parkside," you probably would remember "left on Mockingbird" and "right on Parkside" more easily than the turns and streets in the middle. The *primacy effect* refers to better recall for items at the beginning of a list. The *recency effect* refers to better recall for items at the end of the list. Go to the interactivity "Serial Position Effect" to see if you show the primacy and recency effects. One application of primacy and recency effects is the advice to job candidates to try to be the first or last candidate interviewed.

How can primacy and recency effects be explained? As for the primacy effect, the first few items in the list are easily remembered because they are rehearsed more or because they receive more elaborative processing than do words later in the list

In-Psych Plus

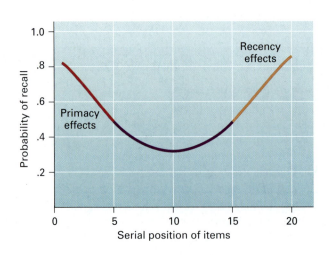

FIGURE 7.14 The Serial Position Effect When a person is asked to memorize a list of words, the words memorized last usually are recalled best, those at the beginning next best, and those in the middle least efficiently.

(Atkinson & Shiffrin, 1968; Craik & Tulving, 1975). Working memory is relatively empty when they enter, so there is little competition for rehearsal time. And, because they get more rehearsal, they stay in working memory longer and are more likely to be successfully encoded into long-term memory. In contrast, many items from the middle of the list drop out of working memory before being encoded into long-term memory.

As for the recency effect, the last several items are remembered for different reasons. First, at the time these items are recalled, they might still be in working memory. Second, even if these items are not in working memory, their relative recency, compared with other list items, makes them easier to recall. For example, if you are a sports fan, try remembering games you have seen throughout the season. You probably will find that the more recent games are easier to remember than earlier games. This example of the recency effect extends far beyond the time span of working memory.

Retrieval Cues and the Retrieval Task

Two other factors involved in retrieval are (1) the nature of the cues that can prompt your memory and (2) the retrieval task that you set for yourself. If effective cues for what you are trying to remember do not seem to be available, you need to create them—a process that takes place in working memory. For example, if you have a block about remembering a new friend's name, you might go through the alphabet, generating names that begin with each letter. If you manage to stumble across the right name, you'll probably recognize it.

We can learn to generate retrieval cues (Allan & others, 2001). One good strategy is to use different subcategories as retrieval cues. For example, write down the names of as many of your classmates from middle or junior high school as you can remember. When you run out of names, think about the activities you were involved in during those school years, such as math class, student council, eating lunch, drill team, and so on. Did this set of cues help you to remember more of your classmates?

Although cues help, your success in retrieving information also depends on the task you set for yourself. For instance, if you're simply trying to decide if something seems familiar, retrieval is probably a snap. Let's say you see a short, dark-haired woman walking toward you. You quickly decide she's someone who lives in the next dorm. But remembering her name or a precise detail, such as when you met her, can be harder. Such distinctions have implications for police investigations: A witness might be certain she has previously seen a face, yet she might have a hard time deciding if it was at the scene of the crime or in a mug shot.

Following are some task and cue considerations that affect the ability to retrieve memories:

- *Recall and recognition.* Whether the task involves recall or recognition is an important consideration (Nobel & Shiffrin, 2001). **Recall** is a memory task in which the individual has to retrieve previously learned information, as on essay tests. **Recognition** is a memory task in which the individual only has to identify (recognize) learned items when they are presented, as on multiple-choice tests. Recall tests, such as essay tests, have poor retrieval cues. You are told to try to recall a certain class of information ("Discuss the factors that caused World War II"). In recognition tests, such as multiple-choice tests, you merely judge whether a stimulus is familiar (whether it matches something you experienced in the past). Similarly, people who say that they are terrible at remembering names but that they never forget a face are probably better at recognition (realizing that they have seen a face before) than at recall (remembering a person's name in response to his or her face). Actually recalling a face is not easy, as law enforcement officers know. In some

retrieval The memory process of taking information out of storage.

serial position effect The tendency for items at the beginning and at the end of a list to be recalled more readily.

recall A memory task in which the individual must retrieve previously learned information.

recognition A memory task in which the individual only has to identify learned items when they are presented.

 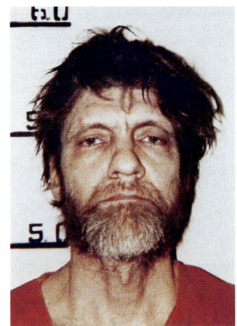

(Left) The FBI artist's sketch of Ted Kaczynski, the Unabomber. *(Right)* A photograph of Kaczynski. The FBI widely circulated the artist's sketch, which was based on bits and pieces of observations people had made, in the hope that someone would recognize the Unabomber if they saw him. *Would you have been able to recognize Kaczynski from the artist's sketch of him?*

cases, they bring in an artist to draw the suspect's face from witnesses' descriptions. But artists' sketches of suspects are frequently not detailed or accurate enough to result in apprehension.

- *Encoding specificity.* Another consideration in understanding retrieval is the amount of information present at the time of encoding or learning that can serve as a retrieval cue (Hanna & Remington, 2001; Hannon & Craik, 2001; Tulving & Thomson, 1973). Imagine that you have met someone who is a professional tennis player. If you encode that information, along with observations such as "the person looks fit and has long arms," you might remember the person's occupation when you encounter him again. Notice that this idea is compatible with the earlier discussion of elaboration. Recall that, the more elaboration you use in encoding information, the better your memory of the information will be.

- *Context and state.* An important consequence of encoding specificity is that a change between encoding and retrieval can cause memory to fail. In many instances, people remember better when they attempt to recall information in the same context in which they learned it, a process referred to as *context-dependent memory.* This is believed to occur because they have encoded features of the context in which they learned the information along with the information. Such features can later act as retrieval cues (Kimbrough, Wright, & Shea, 2001; Smith & Vela, 2001). Similarly, internal states can influence memory (Duka, Weissenborn, & Dienes, 2001; Weissenborn & Duka, 2000). People tend to remember information better when their psychological state or mood is similar at encoding and retrieval, a process referred to as *state-dependent memory.* For example, when people are in happy moods, they are inclined to remember positive experiences, such as success and acceptance (Mineka & Nugent, 1995). Unfortunately, when people who are depressed are more likely to recall negative experiences, such as failure and rejection, the memories tend to perpetuate their depression.

- *Priming.* Recall that priming means that people remember information better and faster when it is preceded by similar information (a cue). Priming is a form of implicit memory that is nonconscious (Goddard, Dritschel, & Burton,

2001). In everyday life, priming likely is involved in unintentional acts of plagiarism (Schacter, 1996). For example, you propose an idea to a friend, who seems unimpressed by it or even rejects it outright. Weeks or months later, the friend excitedly describes your idea as if she had just come up with it herself. Her memory of having the idea has been primed by your explanation of the idea. Another practical example of priming involves those times when you are wandering the grocery store, unable to remember one of the items you were supposed to buy. As you walk down an aisle, you hear two people talking about fruit, which triggers your memory that you were supposed to buy raspberries. That is, hearing *fruit* primes your memory for raspberries.

- *Tip-of-the-tongue phenomenon.* One glitch in retrieving information that we're all familiar with is the *tip-of-the-tongue phenomenon,* or *TOT state.* It occurs when people are confident that they know something but can't quite pull it out of memory (Kikyo, Ohki, & Sekihara, 2001; Schwartz, 2002). The TOT state arises because a person can retrieve some of the desired information but not all of it (Maril, Wagner, & Schacter, 2001; Schacter, 1996, 2001). For example, imagine that you spot two people standing together. You easily recall that one of them is Barbara. You know that you've seen the other person before and are sure his name begins with a *B* (a good retrieval cue). But retrieval may not be the problem. Perhaps you didn't pay enough attention to his name when you were introduced to remember more than the first letter. Your confidence in the retrieval cue can induce a strong—sometimes spurious— feeling of knowing other information (in this case, the name) that you actually haven't stored in memory. In one study of the TOT state, the researcher found that people tended to use two strategies to try to retrieve the name of a person whose photograph they recognized (Yarmey, 1973). One strategy was to pinpoint the person's profession. For example, one participant correctly identified the famous person as an artist, but the artist's name, Picasso, remained elusive. Another retrieval strategy was to repeat initial letters or syllables—such as *Monetti, Mona, Magett, Spaghetti,* and *Bogette* in an attempt to identify Liza Minnelli.

Accuracy in Memory Retrieval

By now you should realize that memory is not a perfect reflection of reality. Our memories are often wrapped in emotion, bias, and other distorting influences. The result is inaccurate encoding and storage of memories, as well as faulty retrieval (Roediger & Marsh, 2003). Several memory phenomena related to accuracy are of considerable interest to researchers and have echoes in public life:

- *Flashbulb memories* are memories of emotionally significant events that people often recall with more accuracy and vivid imagery than everyday events (Davidson & Glisky, 2002). Perhaps you can remember what you wore on your first date or where you were when you first heard of the terrorist attacks on September 11, 2001. Several decades later people often remember where they were and what was going on in their lives at the time of such an event. These memories seem to be part of an adaptive system that fixes in memory the details that accompany important events so that they can be interpreted at a later time. However, most flashbulb memories probably are not as accurately etched in our brains as we think. Many flashbulb memories deteriorate over time (Schmolck, Buffalo, & Squire, 2000). Still, flashbulb memories are far more durable and accurate than memories of day-to-day happenings (Schacter, 1996)—if only because they are often discussed and thought about in the days, weeks, and even years following an

Do you have a flashbulb memory of the terrorist attack on the World Trade Center in New York City, September 11, 2001?

event. The emotions triggered by flashbulb events also add to their durability and vividness.

- *Personal trauma* is another type of emotionally arousing experience that may create more detailed, longer-lasting memories than usual (Langer, 1991). Consider the traumatic experience of the children who were kidnapped at gunpoint on a school bus in Chowchilla, California, in 1983, then buried underground for 16 hours before escaping. The children had the classic signs of traumatic memory: detailed and vivid recollections. However, when a child psychiatrist interviewed the children 4 to 5 years after the chilling episode, she noted some striking errors and distortions in the memories of half of them (Terr, 1988). Some children might have made perceptual errors while encoding information because the episode was so shocking. Others might have distorted the information and recalled the episode as being less traumatic than it actually was in order to reduce their anxiety about what happened. Others, in discussing the traumatic event with other people, might have incorporated bits and pieces of these persons' recollections of what happened into their own version of the event. However, although memories of traumas are subject to some deterioration and distortion, the central part of the memory is almost always effectively remembered. Where distortion often arises is in the details.

In-Psych Plus

- *Eyewitness testimony,* in which people are called on to report what they saw or heard in relation to a crime, may also contain errors (Schacter, 1996, 2001). Estimates are that between 2,000 and 10,000 people are wrong-fully convicted each year in the United States because of faulty eyewitness testimony (Cutler & Penrod, 1995). (For a dramatic case of mistaken identity, see the video clip "Eye Witness Memory." Listen to the audio clip "Eye Witness Memory" to learn about the 1999 report that should change the way interrogations and suspect identifications take place.) The amount of time that has passed between an incident and a person's recollection of it is a critical factor in eyewitness testimony. In one study, people were able to identify pictures with 100 percent accuracy after a 2-hour time lapse. However, 4 months later they achieved an accuracy of only 57 percent; chance alone accounts for 50 percent accuracy (Shepard, 1967). Bias is also a factor. Studies have shown that people of one ethnic group are less likely to recognize individual differences among people of another ethnic group (Behrman & Davey, 2001). Latino eyewitnesses, for example, may have trouble distinguishing among several Asian suspects.

  Hundreds of individuals have been harmed by witnesses who made a mistake that could have been avoided (Loftus, 2003; Radelet, 2002). If you are an eyewitness to a crime and your recall is scrambled, it could send someone to prison. A recent estimate indicated that 7,500 people were arrested for serious crimes and wrongly convicted in the United States (Huff, 2002). Faulty memory is not just about accusing the wrong person. Memory persons were evident in the sniper attacks that killed 10 people in the Washington, DC, area in 2002. Witnesses reported seeing a white truck or van fleeing several of the crime scenes. It appears that the white van may have been near one of the first shootings and media repetition of this information contaminated the memories of witnesses to later attacks, making them more likely to remember the white van. When caught, the sniper suspects were driving a blue car. Before police even reached the scene of a crime, witnesses talk to each other, which can contaminate memories. In one situation, Elizabeth Loftus (2003) personally witnessed this when she entered a shop moments after a robbery had taken place and before police had arrived. In the immediate aftermath, customers and employees shared their memories. This is why, during the Washington, DC, sniper attacks in 2002, law enforcement officials advised anyone who might witness the next attack to write down immediately what

Identification of individuals from police lineups or photographs is not always reliable. Also, people from one ethnic group often have difficulty recognizing differences among people of another ethnic group. *What explains this failure of memory?*

Statements Rated as Reliable by 90 Percent or More of the Experts		
Category	**Statement**	**Percent**
Wording of questions	An eyewitness's testimony about an event can be affected by how the questions put to the witness are worded.	98
Lineup instructions	Police instructions can affect an eyewitness's willingness to make an identification.	98
Confidence malleability	An eyewitness's confidence can be influenced by factors that are unrelated to identification accuracy.	95
Mug-shot–induced bias	Exposure to mug shots of a suspect increases the likelihood that the witness will later select that suspect in the lineup.	95
Postevent information	Eyewitness testimony about an event often reflects not only what the witness saw but also information the witness obtained later on.	94
Child suggestibility	Young children are more vulnerable than adults to interviewer suggestion, peer pressures, and other social influences.	94
Attitudes and expectations	An eyewitness's perception of and memory for an event can be affected by his or her attitudes and expectations.	92
Hypnotic suggestibility	Hypnosis increases suggestibility to leading and misleading questions.	91
Alcoholic intoxication	Alcoholic intoxication impairs an eyewitness's later ability to recall persons and events.	91
Cross-race bias	Eyewitnesses are more accurate when identifying members of their own race than members of other races.	90

Statements Rated as Unreliable by 50 Percent or Less of the Experts		
Category	**Statement**	**Percent**
Elderly witness	Elderly witnesses are less accurate than are younger adults.	50
Hypnotic accuracy	Hypnosis increases the accuracy of the eyewitness's reported memory.	45
Identification speed	The more quickly a witness makes an identification upon seeing the lineup, the more accurate he or she is likely to be.	40
Trained observers	Police officers and other trained observers are no more accurate as eyewitnesses than the average person.	39
Event violence	Eyewitnesses have more difficulty remembering violent than nonviolent events.	37
Discriminability	It is possible to differentiate reliably between true and false memories.	32
Long-term repression	Traumatic experiences can be repressed for many years and then be recovered.	22

FIGURE 7.15 Experts' Judgments of Statements Regarding Eyewitness Testimony

they had seen, even using their hands if they did not have a piece of paper. To get an idea of just how much eyewitness testimony should be trusted, researchers asked 64 psychologists who had either conducted eyewitness research or testified as expert witnesses to evaluate the accuracy of 30 statements regarding eyewitness testimony (Kassin & others, 2001). Figure 7.15 lists the statements that 90 percent or more of the experts agreed with and the statements that 50 percent or less agreed with. As you can see, the experts had the most confidence in the statements related to the wording of questions and the least confidence in the statements related to the long-term repression of memories.

- *Repressed memories*, which are those pushed into some inaccessible part of the unconscious mind, may be caused by the emotional blows of personal trauma. At some later point, the memory might emerge in consciousness. Psychodynamic theory, which was initially discussed in chapter 1, contends that repression's main function is to protect the individual from threatening information.

Repression does not erase a memory, but it makes conscious remembering extremely difficult (Anderson & Green, 2001). Just how extensively repression occurs is a controversial issue. Repressed memories are further discussed in regard to psychodynamic theory in chapters 10 and 12.

For more on the accuracy of memory, particularly repressed memories, and the damage faulty memory can do to individuals, see the Critical Controversy box.

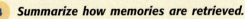

Review and Sharpen Your Thinking

4 **Summarize how memories are retrieved.**

- Describe the serial position effect.
- Explain the role of retrieval cues and the retrieval task.
- Discuss the issue of accuracy in memory retrieval.

Do you think that, on the whole, negative emotional events are likely to be more memorable than positive ones? How would you go about studying whether negative events are more memorable than positive ones?

5 FORGETTING

| Encoding Failure | Retrieval Failure |

How are encoding and retrieval involved in forgetting?

One of psychology's pioneers, Hermann Ebbinghaus (1850–1909), was the first person to conduct scientific research on forgetting. In 1885, he made up and memorized a list of 13 nonsense syllables—such as *zeq, xid, lek, vut,* and *riy*—and then assessed how many of them he could remember as time passed. Just an hour later, Ebbinghaus could recall only a few of the nonsense syllables he had memorized. Figure 7.16 shows Ebbinghaus' forgetting curve for nonsense syllables. Based on his research, Ebbinghaus concluded that the most forgetting takes place soon after we learn something.

If we forget so quickly, why put effort into learning something? Fortunately, researchers have demonstrated that forgetting is not as extensive as Ebbinghaus envisioned (Baddeley, 1992). Ebbinghaus studied meaningless nonsense syllables. But when we memorize meaningful material, such as poetry, history, or the type of material in this book, forgetting is neither so rapid nor so extensive. Following are some

HERMANN EBBINGHAUS (1850–1909)
The first psychologist to conduct scientific research on forgetting. *What was the nature of his research?*

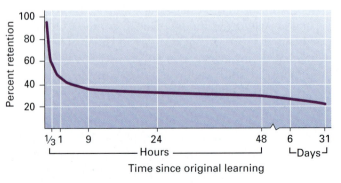

FIGURE 7.16 Ebbinghaus' Forgetting Curve

Recovered Memories or False Memories?

George Franklin, a California man, spent 6 years in prison for the 1969 murder of a young woman. His own daughter's testimony, based on her memory of the attack, was at the heart of the prosecution's case against him. What made this case unusual is that the daughter's memories were allegedly recovered in adulthood during psychotherapy (Loftus 2002, 2003). Franklin became the first person in the United States to be convicted on the basis of repressed memories. His conviction was eventually overturned when it came out that his daughter might have lied about having been hypnotized before the trial.

The idea that childhood abuse, and in particular sexual abuse, could be completely repressed yet nevertheless lead to psychological disorders in adulthood was first expressed by Sigmund Freud. Some therapists today continue to believe that adult disorders such as depression, thoughts of suicide, eating disorders, low self-esteem, sexual dysfunction, and trouble maintaining relationships may stem from sexual abuse in childhood. Treatment usually involves bringing these long-repressed childhood traumas back into consciousness, thus freeing the client from their unconscious effects. In cases in which memories have been recovered, clients have often been encouraged to confront the alleged perpetrator, usually a parent. In many cases, charges have been filed as a part of the therapeutic process (Pezdek & Banks, 1996). During the 1990s, memories allegedly recovered during therapy also served as the basis for many charges of physical and sexual abuse.

Almost all accused parents vehemently deny having ever abused their offspring in childhood. In 1992, the False Memory Syndrome (FMS) Foundation was formed as a parents' support group. The very name of this group expresses the conviction that their children's memories were not recovered but were somehow falsely implanted, perhaps as a result of the therapeutic process itself. Interestingly, almost 100 years earlier, Freud himself had come to believe that his patients' "memories" of childhood abuse were based on their own repressed sexual desires. What has complicated matters is the growing awareness that childhood sexual abuse is much more common than Freud was aware of and continues to be a serious problem today.

It was against this bitter backdrop that experimental psychology entered the fray. Led by the research of memory expert Elizabeth Loftus (2003), study after study found that it is easy to create false memories, especially by using hypnosis. All that is required is to hypnotize someone and to suggest that he or she has had an experience. After hypnosis, that person may well "remember" the experience as vividly real.

In one recent study, Loftus and Jacquie Pickrell (2001) persuaded people that they had met Bugs Bunny at Disneyland, even though Bugs is a Warner Bros. character who would never appear at a Disney theme park. Four groups of participants read ads and then answered questionnaires about a trip to Disneyland. One group saw an ad that mentioned no cartoon charac-

ters, the second read the same ad and also saw a 4-foot-tall cardboard figure of Bugs Bunny, the third read a fake ad for Disneyland with Bugs Bunny in it, and the fourth saw the same fake ad along with the cardboard Bugs. Although less than 10 percent of the first two groups later reported having actually met Bugs Bunny on a trip to Disneyland, 30 to 40 percent of the third and fourth groups reported remembering meeting Bugs at Disneyland.

Such research has led to the concern that therapists who are convinced their patients suffered sexual abuse as children may inadvertently implant false memories that are later "recovered" by the client. The end result may be false memories of abuse, which tear apart families and cause more harm than good. This research has led courts to be skeptical of recovered-memory testimony—and directly resulted in the reversal of George Franklin's murder conviction. Unfortunately, nothing can compensate him for the loss of 6 years of his life and the destruction of his family life. At the same time, rejecting all claims by adults that they were victims of childhood sexual abuse is also inappropriate.

Consensus is well represented by the American Psychological Association's (1995) interim report of the working group investigating memories of childhood abuse, which offers these tentative conclusions: (1) Controversies regarding adult recollections should not be allowed to obscure the fact that child sexual abuse is a complex and pervasive problem in America that has historically gone unacknowledged; (2) most people who were sexually abused as children remember all or part of what happened to them; (3) memories of abuse that have been forgotten for a long time may be remembered, although the mechanism by which such delayed recall occurs is not currently well understood; (4) convincing false memories for events that never occurred may be constructed, although the mechanism by which these false memories occur is not currently well understood; (5) there are gaps in our knowledge about the processes that lead to accurate and inaccurate recollections of childhood abuse.

What do you think?

- How should courts of law deal with the problem of recovered memory or false memory?
- Suppose that you meet someone who reports recovered memories of childhood abuse. How can you tell whether you should believe him or her? What should your attitude be toward that person?
- Does the likelihood that some reports of childhood sexual abuse are, in fact, false memories entitle us to conclude that childhood sexual abuse rarely, if ever, occurs? If we cannot trust the testimony of adult survivors of childhood sexual abuse, how can we determine the likelihood of its occurrence today?

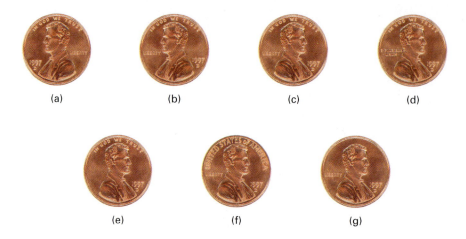

FIGURE 7.17 Which Is a Real U.S. Penny? In the original experiment, 15 versions of pennies were shown to participants, but only 1 was an actual U.S. penny. Included here are only 7 of the 15 versions, and, as you likely can tell, this still is a very difficult task. By the way, the actual U.S. penny is *(c)*.

of the factors that influence how well we can retrieve information from long-term memory.

Encoding Failure

Sometimes when people say they have forgotten something, they have not really forgotten it; they never encoded the information in the first place. *Encoding failure* occurs when the information was never entered into long-term memory.

For a demonstration of encoding failure, think about what the U.S. penny looks like. In one study, researchers showed 15 versions of the penny to participants and asked them which was correct (Nickerson & Adams, 1979). Look at the pennies in figure 7.17 (but don't look at the caption yet) and see if you can tell which one is the real penny. Most people do not do well on this task. Unless you are a coin collector, you likely have not encoded a lot of specific details about pennies. You may have encoded just enough information to distinguish them from other coins (pennies are copper-colored; dimes and nickels are silver colored; pennies fall between the sizes of dimes and quarters).

The penny exercise illustrates that we encode and enter into long-term memory only a small portion of the experiences we have in life. In a sense, then, encoding failures really are not cases of forgetting; they are cases of not remembering.

Retrieval Failure

Problems in retrieving information from memory are clearly examples of forgetting (Williams & Zacks, 2001). Psychologists have theorized that the causes of retrieval failure include the following problems:

proactive interference A disruption of memory that occurs when material learned earlier interferes with the recall of material learned later.

retroactive interference A disruption of memory that occurs when material learned later interferes with the retrieval of information learned earlier.

- *Interference*. Some psychologists propose that people forget not because memories are actually lost from storage but because other information gets in the way of what they want to remember (Altmann & Gray, 2002). **Proactive interference** occurs when material that was learned earlier disrupts the recall of material learned later (Humphreys, 2001). For example, suppose you had a good friend 10 years ago named *Prudence* and that last night you met someone named *Patience*. You might find yourself calling your new friend *Prudence* because the old information *(Prudence)* interferes with retrieval of new information *(Patience)*. **Retroactive interference,** alternatively, occurs when material learned later disrupts the retrieval of information learned earlier. Suppose you have lately become friends with *Ralph*. In sending a note to your old friend *Raul,* you might mistakenly address it to *Ralph* because the

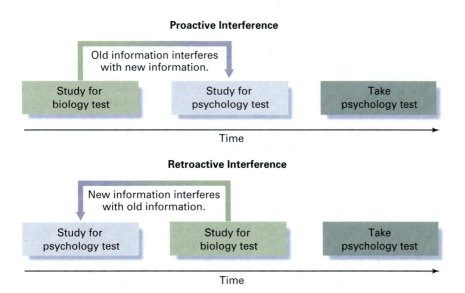

Proactive Interference

Old information interferes
with new information.

| Study for biology test | Study for psychology test | Take psychology test |

Time

Retroactive Interference

New information interferes
with old information.

| Study for psychology test | Study for biology test | Take psychology test |

Time

FIGURE 7.18 Proactive and Retroactive Interference *Pro-* means "forward"; in proactive interference, old information has a forward influence by getting in the way of new material learned. *Retro-* means "backward"; in retroactive interference, new information has a backward influence by getting in the way of material learned earlier.

new information *(Ralph)* interferes with the old information *(Raul)*. Figure 7.18 depicts another example of proactive and retroactive interference. Proactive and retroactive interference might both be explained as problems with retrieval cues. The reason *Prudence* interferes with *Patience* and *Ralph* interferes with *Raul* might be that the cue you are using to remember—perhaps "my good friend"—does not distinguish between the two memories. The result could be retrieving the wrong name. Retrieval cues (such as "friend" in our example) can also become overloaded, making us tend to forget or to retrieve incorrectly.

- *Decay and transience.* Another possible reason for forgetting is the passage of time. *Decay* is the disintegration of the neurochemical memory trace that was formed when something new was learned. Memory researcher Daniel Schacter (2001) refers to the forgetting that occurs with the passage of time as *transience*. As an example of transience, recall that on October 3, 1995, the most sensational criminal trial in recent times reached a dramatic conclusion: A jury acquitted O. J. Simpson. The Simpson verdict seemed like just the kind of flashbulb memory that most of us would remember vividly for years to come. How well can you remember finding out about it? In one research study, undergraduate students at first provided detailed accounts of how they learned about the Simpson verdict (Schmolck & others, 2000). However, 15 months later, only half remembered the details, and, nearly 3 years after the verdict, less than 30 percent of the students' memories were accurate. Memories often do fade with the passage of time, but under the right retrieval conditions, memories that seem to have been forgotten can be retrieved. You might have forgotten the face or name of someone in your high school class, but when you return to the setting in which you knew the person, you may remember these details.

- *Motivated forgetting.* People sometimes deliberately forget something because it is so painful or anxiety-laden that remembering is intolerable. This type of forgetting may be a consequence of the sort of personal emotional trauma that occurs in victims of rape or physical abuse, in war veterans, or in survivors of earthquakes, plane crashes, and other terrifying events. These emotional traumas may haunt people for many years unless they can put the details out of their minds. Even when people have not experienced trauma, they may use motivated forgetting to protect themselves from memories of painful, stressful, unpleasant circumstances. One form of motivated forgetting

Alabama businesswoman Patsy Cannon was in a car crash in 1986. Her injury was so severe that it left her with amnesia, and she had to relearn virtually everything she used to know. Patsy didn't even recognize her own daughter. The photograph on the left shows Patsy in 1986 just prior to the car crash. Today Patsy works as an advocate for individuals with brain injury. *Which type of amnesia did Patsy experience?*

is *repression,* which was described earlier in the discussion of difficulties that some people have in retrieving accurate memories. In the psychodynamic view, unpleasant memories are repressed into our unconscious minds, and we no longer are aware of them.

- *Amnesia.* Recall the case of H. M. in the discussion of explicit and implicit memory. In H. M.'s surgery, the part of his brain that was responsible for laying down new memories (the hippocampus and related structures) was damaged beyond repair, which resulted in **amnesia,** the loss of memory. Although some types of amnesia clear up over time, H. M.'s amnesia endured. The anterograde amnesia that H. M. suffered affects the retention of new information and events. What he learned before the onset of amnesia was not affected. For example, H. M. could identify his friends, recall their names, and even tell stories about them—but only if he had known them before surgery. H. M.'s postsurgical experiences were never encoded in his long-term memory. Retrograde amnesia, which involves memory loss for a segment of the past but not for new events, is much more common than the type that affected H. M. (Dutton & others, 2002). This type frequently occurs when the brain is assaulted by an electrical shock or a physical blow—such as a head injury to a football player. The key differences between the two types of amnesia are whether the forgotten information is old or new and how the amnesia affects the person's ability to acquire new memories. Sometimes, individuals with amnesia have both types.

Review and Sharpen Your Thinking

5 **Describe how encoding failure and retrieval failure are involved in forgetting.**

- Define encoding failure.
- Discuss four reasons for retrieval failure.

Think about three or four instances recently in which you were unable to remember something. What principle of forgetting do you think best explains your failure to remember in each case?

amnesia The loss of memory.

| Encoding Strategies | Storage Strategies | Retrieval Strategies |

How can you apply what you have learned about memory to your academic studies?

Most of us face memory problems far less serious than amnesia or repression. The simple memory strategies that follow can help you to encode, store, and retrieve information more effectively. Using these memory strategies to study can help you improve your academic performance.

Keep in mind that even under the best circumstances memory is not perfect. And engaging in ill-advised habits—such as not getting enough sleep, taking drugs, and not going to class regularly—may further impair the remembering that is necessary to do well on an exam.

Encoding Strategies

The first step in improving your academic performance is to make sure what you're studying is processed effectively so it can be stored in long-term memory. Although some types of information are encoded automatically, the academic learning process usually requires considerable effort (Bruning & others, 2004). Recall that encoding involves paying attention, processing information at an appropriate level, elaborating, and using imagery.

Be a Good Time Manager and Planner Managing your time effectively and planning to allow the necessary time to study will give you the hours you need to do well academically. As suggested in the discussion of study habits in chapter 1, to-do lists are an effective way of planning and managing time. To make high grades, you also need to set aside at least 2 or 3 study hours for each hour you spend in class (Santrock & Halonen, 2002). Thus, if you are in class 15 hours, you should be studying 30 to 45 hours outside of class each week.

Another aspect of good planning is having the right resources to draw on and allowing enough time for the task. When you're studying for a test, make sure you have your textbook and class notes on hand. If you are writing a paper, plan enough time to write a first draft and revise it one or more times.

Pay Attention and Minimize Distraction Once you have made a commitment to spending the time needed on your studies, you have to make sure you aren't distracted by other things during that time. If you want to remember something, you have to give it your undivided attention.

Monitor how well you are paying attention. If you find yourself getting distracted, use a cue word or phrase, such as "Focus" or "Zero in," to increase your attention.

Understand the Material Rather Than Rotely Memorize It You are more likely to remember information over the long term if you understand it rather than just rotely rehearse and memorize it. Rehearsal works well for information in short-term memory, but when you need to encode, store, and then retrieve information from long-term memory, rehearsal is much less efficient. Thus, for most information, understand it, give it meaning, elaborate on it, and personalize it.

One technique you can use to make sure you understand the material is *cognitive monitoring*, which involves taking stock of your progress in an activity such as reading or studying. For example, you might make sure that you understand the material by summarizing what you have read and restudying those parts of the material that were unclear.

Ask Yourself Questions   A self-questioning strategy can help you to remember. As you read, periodically stop and ask yourself questions, such as "What is the meaning of what I just read?" "Why is this important?" and "What is an example of the concept I just read about?" When you have made a concerted effort to ask yourself questions about what you have read or about an activity in class, you will expand the number of associations you make with the information you will need to retrieve later.

Take Good Notes   Taking good notes while listening to a lecture or reading a textbook also benefits your memory. But don't try to write down everything: It is impossible to do, and it can prevent you from getting the big picture of what the instructor or textbook author is communicating.

Good note-taking strategies include the following:

- *Summarizing.* Listen or read for a few minutes and then write down the main idea that the instructor or author is trying to get across in that time frame. Then listen or read for several more minutes and write down another idea, and so on.
- *Outlining.* Create an outline of what the instructor is saying, using a hierarchy to show which ideas are related and how general or specific they are. Model your system after the one used to organize textbook chapters, with "A"-level heads being the main topics, "B"-level heads the subtopics under the "A" heads, and "C"-level heads the subtopics under the "B" heads.
- *Concept maps.* If outlines don't seem to capture your thought processes, try drawing concept maps of what the instructor is saying or what you are reading. Concept maps may look like the diagrams at the end of each chapter in this book. Concept maps are functionally similar to outlines, but they visually display information in a chart format.
- *The Cornell method.* Divide a sheet of paper into two columns by drawing a line down the page about one-fourth to one-third of the way from the left edge. Write your notes on the right two-thirds to three-fourths of the page. When you review your notes, you can then add comments about the notes on the left side, which personalizes them for better understanding and later retrieval.
- *Note reviews.* Get into the habit of reviewing your notes periodically rather than waiting to study them at the last minute before a test. If possible, take a few minutes to review your notes just after a lecture or reading a section of the textbook. You will be able to fill in information you might have missed that is still in your memory. This strategy also helps you to consolidate your learning.

Use Mnemonic Strategies   *Mnemonics* are specific visual or verbal memory aids; the video clip "Mnemonic Strategies in Memory" shows examples. Following are three types of mnemonic devices:

- *Method of loci.* You develop an image of items to be remembered and then store them mentally in familiar locations (which is what *loci* means). Rooms of houses or stores on a street are common locations used in this memory strategy. For example, if you need to remember a list of brain structures, you can mentally place them in the rooms of a house you are familiar with, such as the entry hall, the living room, the dining room, the kitchen, and so on. Then, when you need to retrieve the information, you imagine the house, mentally go through the rooms, and retrieve the concepts.
- *Keyword method.* You attach vivid imagery to important words. For example, to remember that the limbic system consists of two main regions—amygdala and hippocampus—you might imagine two limbs or legs (limbic system) → ambling (amygdala) like a hippo (hippocampus).
- *Acronyms.* Create a word from the first letters of items to be remembered. For example, *HOMES* can be used to remember the Great Lakes: *Huron, Ontario,*

"You simply associate each number with a word, such as 'lipoprotein' and 3,467,009." © Sidney Harris.

Michigan, Erie, and *Superior.* An acronym commonly used to remember the sequence of colors in the light spectrum is the name of an imaginary man named *ROY G. BIV: R*ed, *O*range, *Y*ellow, *G*reen, *B*lue, *I*ndigo, and *V*iolet.

Many experts on memory and study skills recommend that mnemonics be used mainly when you need to memorize a list of items or specific facts. In most cases, memory techniques that promote understanding of the material are better than such rote memorization.

Storage Strategies

Perhaps the best way to promote effective memory storage is to make sure that your brain is able to function at maximum capacity. That means being well rested, well nourished, and free of mind-altering substances. In addition, you can try the following strategies.

Organize Your Memory You will remember information better if you consciously organize it while trying to absorb it. Arrange information, rework material, and give it a structure that will help you to remember it. One organizational technique is a hierarchy, like an outline. You might use a concept map, which draws on semantic network theory, or create analogies (such as the earlier comparison of retrieving a long-term memory to a finding a book in the library) that take advantage of your preexisting schemas.

Spread Out and Consolidate Your Learning To help move information from working memory to long-term memory, regularly review what you learn. You will also benefit by distributing your learning over a longer period rather than cramming for a test at the last minute. Cramming tends to produce short-term memory that is processed in a shallow rather than a deep manner. If you spread out your study sessions, you can do a final, concentrated tune-up before the test instead of struggling to learn everything at the last minute (Santrock & Halonen, 2002).

Memory and Study Strategies

Candidly respond to the following items about your own memory and study strategies. Rate yourself 1 = never, 2 = some, 3 = moderate, 4 = almost always, and 5 = always. Then total your points.

1. I'm a good time manager and planner.
2. I'm good at focusing my attention and minimizing distractions.
3. I try to understand material rather than rotely memorizing it.
4. I ask myself questions about what I have read or about class activities.
5. I take good notes in class and from textbooks.
6. I regularly review my notes.
7. I use mnemonic strategies.
8. I'm very organized in the way I encode information.
9. I spread out my studying and consolidate my learning.
10. I use good retrieval cues.
11. I use the PQ4R or a similar study system.

If you scored 50 to 55 points, you likely use good memory and study strategies. If you scored 45 to 49 points, you likely have some reasonably good memory and study strategies. If you scored below 45, spend some time working on improving your memory and study strategies. Most colleges and universities have a study skills center where specialists can help you.

Retrieval Strategies

Assuming you have encoded and stored the desired information effectively, you should have a relatively easy time retrieving it when you participate in a class discussion, take a test, or write a paper. Following are several good strategies for retrieving information more easily and making sure it is as accurate as possible.

Use Good Retrieval Cues   Tatiana Cooley was the U.S. National Memory Champion in 1999, beating out many other contestants in memorizing thousands of numbers and words, pages of faces and names, and lengthy poems (Schacter, 2001). Tatiana relied on elaborative encoding strategies, creating visual images, stories, and associations that linked new information with what she already knew.

The reason Tatiana is mentioned here, though, is that, in her everyday life she says she is incredibly absentminded. Fearing that she will forget to do many daily tasks (running errands, keeping appointments, and so on), she relies on to-do lists and notes scribbled on sticky pads as reminders. Tatiana says, "I live by Post-Its." Like Tatiana, you can help your prospective memory by using good retrieval cues, as well as focused attention and elaboration during encoding.

Use the PQ4R Method   Various systems have been developed to help students remember the information that they are studying. One of them is called *PQ4R*, which is an acronym for a six-step process (*P, Q,* and four *R*s):

1. Preview
2. Question
3. Read
4. Reflect
5. Recite
6. Review

This system can benefit you by getting you to organize information meaningfully, ask questions about it, reflect on and think about it, and review it. All of these steps together make it easier to retrieve information when you need it, as well as to encode the information effectively.

To further tune-up your study strategies, see the Psychology and Life box.

Review and Sharpen Your Thinking

6 *Evaluate study strategies based on an understanding of memory.*

- Describe some effective encoding strategies for studying.
- Summarize some good storage strategies for studying.
- Discuss some efficient retrieval strategies for studying.

Get together with three or four students in this class and compare your note-taking and study strategies for the class. How are your strategies similar to or different from those of the other students? What did you learn from the comparison, and from this chapter, about how to study more effectively?

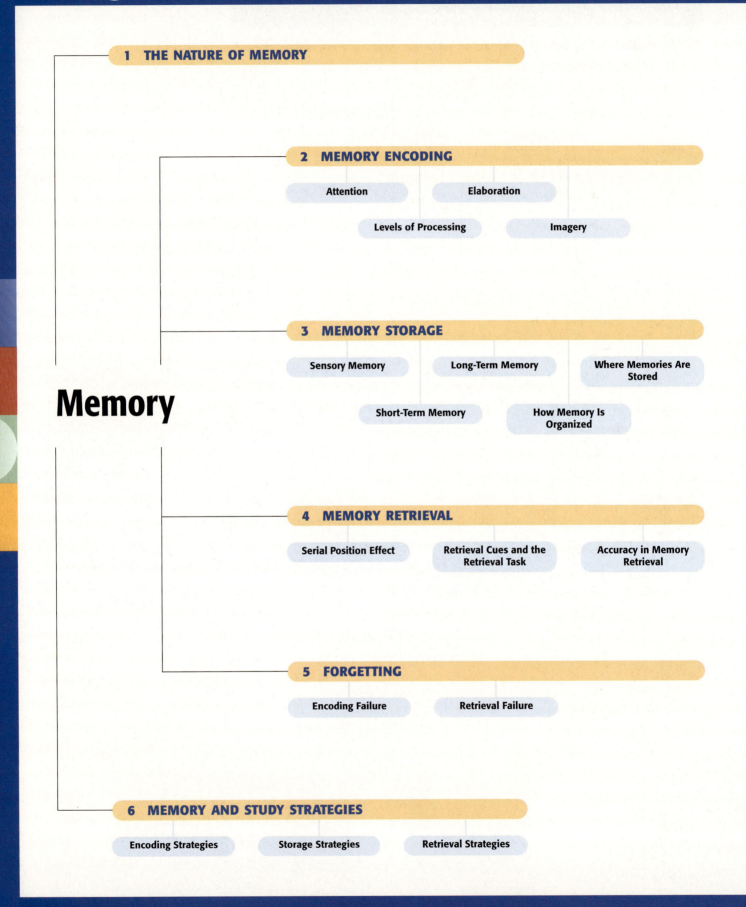

Memory

1 THE NATURE OF MEMORY

2 MEMORY ENCODING

Attention
Elaboration
Levels of Processing
Imagery

3 MEMORY STORAGE

Sensory Memory
Long-Term Memory
Where Memories Are Stored
Short-Term Memory
How Memory Is Organized

4 MEMORY RETRIEVAL

Serial Position Effect
Retrieval Cues and the Retrieval Task
Accuracy in Memory Retrieval

5 FORGETTING

Encoding Failure
Retrieval Failure

6 MEMORY AND STUDY STRATEGIES

Encoding Strategies
Storage Strategies
Retrieval Strategies

1 Identify the three phases of memory.

- Memory is the retention of information over time through encoding, storage, and retrieval—the three phases of memory. Encoding involves getting information into storage, storage consists of retaining information over time, and retrieval involves taking information out of storage.

2 Explain how memories are encoded.

- To begin the process of memory encoding, we have to attend to information. Selective attention is a necessary part of encoding. Memory is often negatively influenced by divided attention.
- Information is processed on a continuum of levels from shallow (sensory or physical features are encoded) to intermediate (labels are attached to stimuli) to deep (the meanings of stimuli and their associations with other stimuli are processed). Deeper processing produces better memory.
- Elaboration, the extensiveness of processing at any given level of memory, improves memory.
- Using imagery, or mental pictures, as a context for information can improve memory.

3 Discuss how memories are stored.

- Atkinson and Shiffrin describe memory as a three-stage process: sensory memory, short-term memory, and long-term memory. Sensory memory holds perceptions of the world for only an instant, not much longer than the brief time the person is exposed to visual, auditory, and other sensory input.
- Short-term memory is a limited-capacity memory system in which information is retained for only as long as 30 seconds. Short-term memory's limitation is 7 ± 2 bits of information. Chunking and rehearsal can benefit short-term memory. Baddeley's concept of working memory has three components: a central executive and two assistants (phonological loop and visuospatial working memory).
- Long-term memory is a relatively permanent type of memory that holds huge amounts of information for a long time. Long-term memory can be divided into two main subtypes: Explicit memory is the conscious recollection of information, such as specific facts or events. Implicit memory affects behavior through prior experiences that are not consciously recollected. Explicit memory has two dimensions: One dimension includes episodic memory and semantic memory. The other dimension includes retrospective memory and prospective memory. Implicit memory is multidimensional, too. It includes systems for procedural memory, priming, and classical conditioning.

- Several models have been developed to describe the organization of long-term memory. The simplest theory recognizes that we store information better when we represent it in an organized, hierarchical manner. Another theory recognizes that we often use semantic networks (based on labels and meaning) to organize material. Schema theory claims that long-term memory is not very exact; we construct our past by fitting new information into a preexisting mental framework. Connectionist theory states that memory is organized as a wide range of connections among neurons, many of which operate simultaneously to store memory.
- Single neurons are involved in memory, but some neuroscientists believe that many memories are stored in circuits of about 1,000 neurons. Although there is no specific memory center in the brain, some brain structures are more involved in certain aspects of memory than others. The hippocampus and nearby areas of the temporal lobes in the cerebral cortex, along with other areas of the limbic system, are involved in explicit memory. The cerebellum is involved in implicit memory.

4 Summarize how memories are retrieved.

- The serial position effect is the tendency for items at the beginning and the end of a list to be remembered better than items in the middle of a list. *The primacy effect* refers to better recall for items at the beginning of the list. *The recency effect* refers to better memory for items at the end of a list.
- Memory retrieval depends on effective cues and the nature of the retrieval task. Simple recognition of previously remembered information in the presence of cues is generally easier than recall of the information. Information present at the time of encoding or learning tends to be effective as a retrieval cue. In many instances, people's recall is better when they attempt to recall information in the same context or internal state in which they learned the information. Retrieval also benefits from priming, which activates particular connections or associations in memory. The tip-of-the-tongue phenomenon occurs when we cannot quite pull something out of memory.
- Flashbulb memories are memories of emotionally significant events that people often recall with more accuracy and vivid imagery than they do everyday events, although flashbulb memories are subject to some deterioration and change. Memory for personal trauma also is usually more accurate than memory for ordinary events, but people might distort some of the details over time. Eyewitness testimony may contain errors due to memory decay or bias. Personal trauma can cause individuals to repress emotionally laden information so that it is not

accessible to consciousness. Repression does not erase a memory; it just makes the memory far more difficult to retrieve.

5 *Describe how encoding failure and retrieval failure are involved in forgetting.*

- Encoding failure is forgetting information that was never entered into long-term memory.
- Retrieval failure can occur for at least four reasons. Sometimes we forget not because memories are lost from storage but because other information gets in the way of, or interferes with, what we want to remember. When something new is learned, a neurochemical memory trace is formed, but over time this chemical trail tends to decay, or disintegrate; the term for the fading of memories with the passage of time is *transience*. Motivated forgetting, which occurs when people want to forget something, is common when a memory becomes painful or anxiety-laden, as in the case of emotional traumas. Amnesia, the loss of memory, can affect the retention of new information or events, affect memories of the past but not new events, or affect both.

6 *Evaluate study strategies based on an understanding of memory.*

- Effective encoding strategies when studying include being a good time manager and planner, paying attention and minimizing distraction, understanding the material rather than rotely memorizing it, asking yourself questions, taking good notes, and using mnemonic strategies.
- Effective storage strategies when studying include organizing your memory and spreading out your study time and then consolidating your learning.
- Effective retrieval strategies when studying include using good retrieval cues and using the PQ4R method.

Key Terms

memory, p. 230
encoding, p. 233
elaboration, p. 233
storage, p. 235
sensory memory, p. 236
short-term memory, p. 236
memory span, p. 237
chunking, p. 237

rehearsal, p. 237
working memory, p. 238
long-term memory, p. 239
explicit memory, p. 240
episodic memory, p. 240
semantic memory, p. 240
retrospective memory,
   p. 240

prospective memory, p. 240
implicit memory, p. 241
procedural memory, p. 241
priming, p. 241
schema, p. 244
script, p. 244
connectionism, p. 244
retrieval, p. 249

serial position effect, p. 249
recall, p. 249
recognition, p. 249
proactive interference,
   p. 256
retroactive interference,
   p. 256
amnesia, p. 258

Apply Your Knowledge

1. Using a chapter of this book that you have not yet read, spend 20–30 minutes trying to learn half of the key terms in an environment filled with distractions (such as the cafeteria at lunchtime or a crowded coffeehouse). Then spend the same amount of time trying to learn the other half of the key terms in a distraction-free environment. Test yourself later on your memory for the words. Which list was easier to remember? What are the distractions in your current study environment, and how can you eliminate them?

2. Some people believe that they have memories from past lives stored in their brains. Consider each of the ways the brain may store memory. Are any of these compatible with memories from past lives?

3. It is sometimes difficult to believe that our memories are not as accurate as we think they are. To test your ability to be a good eyewitness, visit one of the following websites:

   http://www.pbs.org/wgbh/pages/frontline/shows/dna/
   http://www.vuw.ac.nz/psyc/assefiEWT/homepage.html
   http://abcnews.go.com/sections/us/dailynews/
      eyewitnesstestimony.html

   Did these exercises change your opinion of the accuracy of eyewitness testimony? What about eyewitness accounts of UFO sightings or other paranormal events? Are these likely to be more accurate than memories for other events?

4. Think about the serial position effect. What does it suggest about how you should organize your study time? When should you study information you think is most important?

5. For several days, keep a list of times when you failed to remember something. Take a look at the list and identify whether they were instances of encoding failure or one of the types of retrieval failure. Does one particular kind of forgetting seem to be most problematic for you? Can you think of any strategies to help you with this kind of forgetting?

Connections

To test your mastery of the material in this chapter, go to the Study Guide and the In-Psych Plus CD-ROM, as well as the On-line Learning Center. There you will find a chapter summary, practice tests, flashcards, lecture slides, web links, and other study tools, such as interactive exercises and reviews as well as current, chapter-relevant news articles.

8 Thinking, Language, and Intelligence

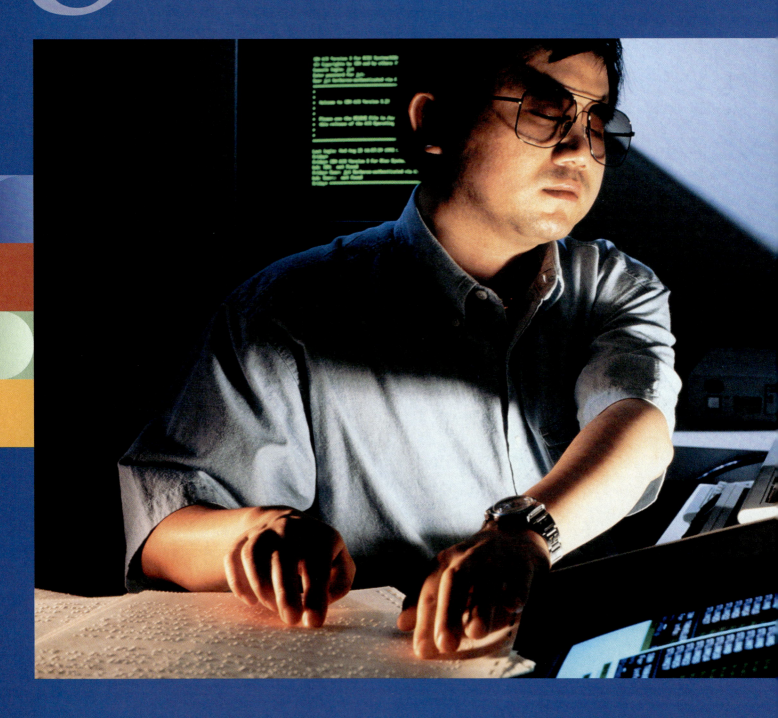

Chapter Outline

Learning Goals

THE COGNITIVE REVOLUTION IN PSYCHOLOGY　**1**

Characterize the "cognitive revolution" in psychology.

THINKING　**2**

Describe the main factors in five types of thinking.

Concept Formation
▼
Problem Solving
▼
Critical Thinking
▼
Reasoning
▼
Decision Making

LANGUAGE　**3**

Explain the importance and the development of human language.

Language and Cognition
▼
Language Acquisition and Development

INTELLIGENCE　**4**

Describe what intelligence is, and evaluate the ways that it is measured.

Intelligence Testing
▼
Multiple Intelligences
▼
Extremes of Intelligence
▼
Creativity
▼
Influences on Intelligence

When she was 18 years old, Wendy Ve-rougstraete felt that she was on the road to becoming a writer. "You are looking at a professional author," she said. "My books will be filled with drama, action, and excitement. And everyone will want to read them. I am going to write books, page after page, stack after stack."

Overhearing her remarks, you might be impressed not only by Wendy's optimism and determination but also by her expressive verbal skills. In fact, at a young age, Wendy showed a flair for writing and telling stories. And now, at age 25, Wendy has a rich vocabulary, creates lyrics for love songs, and enjoys telling stories. You probably would not be able to immediately guess that she has an IQ of only 49 and cannot tie her shoes, cross the street by herself, read or print words beyond the first-grade level, or do even simple arithmetic.

Wendy Verougstraete has *Williams syndrome*, a genetic disorder that affects about 1 in 20,000 births. The most noticeable features of the syndrome include a unique combination of expressive verbal skills, extremely low IQ, and limited spatial and motor control (Osborne & Pober, 2001; Vicari, Bellucci, & Carlesimo, 2001). Figure 8.1 shows the great disparity in the verbal and motor skills of one person with Williams syndrome. Individuals with Williams syndrome often have good musical skills and interpersonal skills (Doyle & others, 2004). The syndrome also includes a number of physical characteristics, such as heart defects and a pixielike facial appearance.

Despite having excellent verbal skills and competent interpersonal skills, most individuals with Williams syndrome can-

Wendy Verougstraete, like most individuals with Williams syndrome, has a flair for language.

not live independently (American Academy of Pediatrics, 2001). For example, Wendy Verougstraete lives in a group home for adults who are mentally retarded.

The verbal abilities of individuals with Williams syndrome are very distinct from those shown by individuals with Down syndrome, a type of mental retardation that is discussed later (Bellugi, Korenberg, & Klima, 2001; Bellugi & others, 2000). On vocabulary tests, children with Williams syndrome show a liking for unusual words. When asked to name as many animals as they can think of in 1 minute, Williams children come up with creatures such as ibex, chihuahua, saber-toothed tiger, weasel, crane, and newt. Children with Down syndrome give simple examples, such as dog, cat, and mouse. When children with Williams syndrome tell stories, their voices come alive with drama and emotion, punctuating the dialogue with attention grabbers, such as "gadzooks" or "lo and behold!" In contrast, children with Down syndrome tell very simple stories with little emotion.

Aside from being an interesting genetic disorder, Williams syndrome offers insights into the normal development of thinking, language, and intelligence. In our society, verbal ability is generally associated with high intelligence. But Williams syndrome raises the possibility that they might not be so closely related. Williams disorder is due to a defective gene that seems to protect expressive verbal ability but not reading and many other cognitive skills (Bellugi & George, 2001; Mervis, 2003). Cases such as Wendy Verougstraete's cast some doubt on the general categorization of intelligence as verbal ability and prompts the question "What is the relation between thinking and language?"

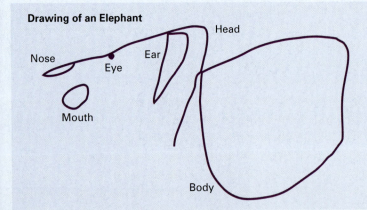

Drawing of an Elephant

Verbal Description of an Elephant

And what an elephant is, it is one of the animals. And what the elephant does, it lives in the jungle. It can also live in the zoo. And what it has, it has long gray ears, fan ears, ears that can blow in the wind. It has a long trunk that can pick up grass, or pick up hay. . . . If they're in a bad mood it can be terrible. . . . If the elephant gets mad it could stomp; it could charge. Sometimes elephants can charge. They have big long tusks. They can damage a car. . . . It could be dangerous. When they're in a pinch, when they're in a bad mood it can be terrible. You don't want an elephant as a pet. You want a cat or a dog or a bird. . . .

FIGURE 8.1 **Disparity in the Verbal and Motor Skills of an Individual with Williams Syndrome**

What is the "cognitive revolution" in psychology?

Behaviorism was a dominant force in psychology until the late 1950s and 1960s, when many psychologists began to realize that they could not understand or explain human behavior without referring to mental processes (Gardner, 1985; Reed, 2001). The term *cognitive psychology* became a label for approaches that sought to explain observable behavior by investigating mental processes and structures that cannot be directly observed (Sternberg, 2003; Willingham, 2001). Basically, cognitive psychologists study **cognition**—how information is processed and manipulated in remembering, thinking, and knowing.

Of all the factors that stimulated the growth of cognitive psychology, probably none was more important than the development of computers. The first modern computer, developed by John von Neumann in the late 1940s, showed that machines could perform logical operations. In the 1950s, researchers speculated that some mental operations might be modeled by computers, possibly telling us something about the way the human mind works (Marcus, 2001).

Cognitive psychologists also often use the computer as an analogy to help explain the relation between cognition and the brain (Levine, 2000). The physical brain is described as the computer's hardware, cognition as its software. Herbert Simon (1969) was among the pioneers in comparing the human mind to computer processing systems. In this analogy, the sensory and perceptual systems provide an "input channel," similar to the way data are entered into the computer (see figure 8.2). As input (information) goes into the mind, operations (mental processes) act on it, just as the computer's software acts on the data. The transformed input generates information that remains in memory much in the way a computer stores what it has worked on. Finally, the information is retrieved from memory and "printed out" or "displayed" (so to speak) as an overt, observable response.

Although the development of computers played an important role in psychology's cognitive revolution, inanimate computers and human brains function quite differently in some respects (Auyang, 2001; Restak, 1988). For example, each brain cell, or neuron, is alive and can respond to information, often ambiguous, transmitted

Mary Czerwinski is a a cognitive psychologist working at Microsoft. She conducts research on attention and perception in three-dimensional environments. *How does a psychology background equip a person to explore the interface between computers and humans?*

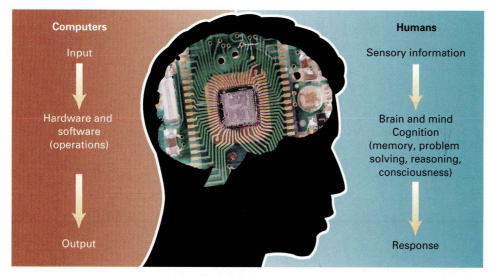

FIGURE 8.2 Computers and Human Cognition An analogy is commonly drawn between human cognition and the way computers work. The physical brain is analogous to a computer's hardware, and cognition is analogous to a computer's software.

cognition The way in which information is processed and manipulated in remembering, thinking, and knowing.

through the sensory receptors described in chapter 4, such as the eyes and ears. (The video clip "Neurons and How They Work" explores the biological foundation of cognition. Also, go to the video clip "Brain Structure and Imaging Methods" to see how brain-mapping technology shows the brain processing information.) In contrast, most computers receive information from a human who has already coded the information and removed much of the ambiguity.

Computers can do some things better than humans. Computers can perform complex numerical calculations much faster and more accurately than humans could ever hope to (Bringsjord & Ferrucci, 2000). Computers can also apply and follow rules more consistently and with fewer errors than humans and represent complex mathematical patterns better than humans can. And they can persist at a task indefinitely, without succumbing to fatigue or boredom as humans do.

But the brain's extraordinary capabilities will probably not be mimicked completely by computers any time in the near future. Attempts to use computers to process visual information or spoken language have achieved only limited success in highly specific situations. The human brain also has incredible ability to learn new rules, relationships, concepts, and patterns that it can generalize to novel situations. Computers are quite limited in their ability to learn and generalize, and they do not have the means to develop new learning goals. Furthermore, the human mind is aware of itself; the computer is not. Indeed, no computer is likely to approach the richness of human consciousness.

Review and Sharpen Your Thinking

1 **Characterize the "cognitive revolution" in psychology.**
 • Define cognition and discuss the cognitive revolution in psychology.

What can your mind do that a computer cannot do? What can a computer do that your mind cannot? Do you think you might have to answer these questions differently 40 to 50 years from now? Explain.

2 THINKING

Concept Formation

Critical Thinking

Decision Making

Problem Solving

Reasoning

What are the main factors affecting five types of thinking?

Computer systems often attempt to mimic human cognitive skills. But are their information processing capabilities the same as thinking? What exactly is thinking? **Thinking** involves manipulating information, as when we form concepts, solve problems, think critically, reason, and make decisions. Some of the processes discussed in previous chapters, such as how people perceive information (chapter 4) and how information is encoded, stored, and retrieved (chapter 7) play a part in thinking.

thinking Manipulating information, as when we form concepts, solve problems, think critically, reason, and make decisions.

concepts Mental categories used to group objects, events, and characteristics.

Concept Formation

Regardless of the kind of thinking we engage in, our thinking is fueled by concepts. **Concepts** are mental categories that are used to group objects, events, and charac-

Michelangelo's Libyan Sibyl, Sistine Chapel

Monet's *Palazzo Da Mula, Venice*

FIGURE 8.3 **Schools of Art** The concept of schools of art lets us compare paintings by different artists. How do other neoclassicist paintings compare with the one by Michelangelo? How do other impressionist paintings compare with the one by Monet? How do other expressionist paintings compare with the one by Klee?

teristics. Humans have a special ability for creating categories to help us make sense of information. We know that apples and oranges are both fruits, although they have different tastes and colors. We know that a Porsche and a Ford are both automobiles, although they differ in cost, speed, and prestige. How do we know these things? The answer lies in our ability to group them on the basis of shared features: For example, a Porsche and a Ford Focus both have an engine, four wheels, and a steering wheel, and both provide transportation. By such features, we know that they are both automobiles. In other words, we have a *concept* of what an automobile is. Go to the interactivity "Hypothesis Testing" to learn more about concept formation.

Concepts are important for several reasons:

- Concepts allow us to generalize. If we did not have concepts, each object and event in our world would be unique to us.
- Concepts allow us to associate experiences and objects. Basketball, ice hockey, and track are sports. The concept of *sport* gives us a way to compare these activities. Neoclassicism, impressionism, and expressionism are all schools of art. The concept *schools of art* lets us compare paintings by artists from these different schools (see figure 8.3).
- Concepts grease the wheels of memory, making it more efficient. For example, we don't have to relearn what the Dow Jones Industrial Average is each time we pick up a newspaper. We already have the concept.

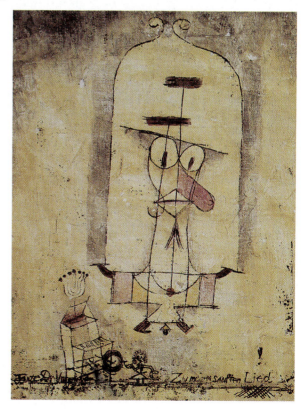

Klee's *Dance You Monster to My Soft Song*

In-Psych Plus

• Concepts provide clues about how to react to a particular object or experience. For example, if we see a bowl of pretzels, our concept of food lets us know it is okay to eat them.

Forming a concept can be a complicated learning process, involving observation, hypotheses and testing, generalization and discrimination, and experience. In general, concepts with more features and more complicated rules are more difficult to learn.

Problem Solving

Concepts are basic to another cognitive skill: problem solving. *Problem solving* is an attempt to find an appropriate way of attaining a goal when the goal is not readily available. It is impossible to solve problems without concepts. For example, William Eno, born in New York City in 1858, became concerned about the city's horrendous traffic jams. Horse-drawn vehicles were making street traffic dangerous. Eno published a paper about the urgency of street traffic reform. His proposed solutions to the problem created new concepts, such as "stop signs," "one-way streets," and "pedestrian islands," which continue to be important to traffic safety today (Bransford & Stein, 1993). Like William Eno, we face many problems in the course of our everyday lives.

Steps in Problem Solving Given the importance of solving problems in our everyday lives—and the importance of solving some extraordinarily difficult problems—psychologists have gone to great effort to specify the thinking process that individuals go through to solve problems effectively. Psychological research points to four steps in the process:

1. *Find and frame the problem.* Before a problem can be solved, it has to be recognized (Mayer, 2000). Fred Smith (founder of Federal Express) asked, "Why can't there be reliable overnight mail service?" Godfrey Hounsfield (inventor of the CT scan) asked, "Why can't we see in three dimensions what is inside the human body without cutting it open?" Many questions like these are ridiculed at first. Fred Smith proposed the idea of Federal Express during his days as a student at Yale and got a *C* on the paper; Godfrey Hounsfield was told that the CT scan was impractical. In the past, students were taught to solve problems through exercises involving well-defined problems with well-defined steps for solving them. However, many real-world problems are ill defined or vague and have no clearly defined solutions. Consider a common problem situation for students: You have to

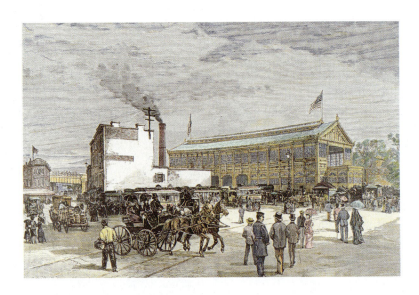

In the nineteenth century, New York City began to experience traffic jams. The horse-drawn vehicles were making street traffic dangerous. *How did William Eno solve this problem?*

write a paper for your psychology course. This is an overly general, ill-defined problem that you will have to narrow down in order to proceed. You will need to define a more specific problem, such as deciding on the area of psychology (neuroscience, cognitive psychology, abnormal psychology, and so on) you will write about. Once you have decided on the area of psychology, you will need to narrow your focus even further to find a specific problem within that area to write about. This type of exercise—finding and framing problems—is an important aspect of problem solving.

2. *Develop good problem-solving strategies.* Among the effective strategies are subgoals, algorithms, and heuristics. *Subgoals* are intermediate goals that put you in a better position for reaching the final goal or solution. Let's return to the problem of writing a paper for a psychology course. If the paper is due in 2 months, you might set a subgoal of a first draft of the paper 2 weeks before it is due, another subgoal of completing reading for the paper 1 month before it is due, and yet another subgoal of starting library research tomorrow. Often the best way to establish subgoals is to work backward from the final goal. Another useful problem-solving stategy is an **algorithm,** a strategy—such as a formula, set of instructions, or trial-and-error approach—that guarantees a solution (Allen, Pertea, & Salzberg, 2004; Crawford, 2003). We often use algorithms in cooking (by following a recipe) and driving (by following directions to an address). However, the algorithmic strategy of trying out all possible solutions should be applied only to problems with a small number of possible solutions. When the possibilities are many, a better problem-solving strategy is to use **heuristics,** guidelines that suggest a solution to a problem but do not guarantee an answer (Oaksford, Roberts, & Chater, 2000). Crossword puzzle enthusiasts know that certain combinations of letters are likelier to work than others. For example, c_nt_ _ner is likely to require a vowel between *c* and *n*, so *b, q,* and a lot of other letters won't work. We also know that only certain combinations of letters are acceptable between *t* and *n.* We might come up with "cantroner" and "contarner." Then we get it: *container.* (To see how you use heuristics in solving word puzzles, go to the interactivity "Solving Cryptograms.") In the real world, the problems we face are more likely to be solved by heuristics than by algorithms. Heuristics help us narrow down the possible solutions to find the one that works (Oppenheimer, 2003; Stanovich & West, 2000).

In-Psych Plus

3. *Evaluate solutions.* Once we think we have solved a problem, we really won't know how effective our solution is until we find out if it actually works. It helps to have in mind a clear criterion for the effectiveness of the solution. For example, what will your criterion be for judging the effectiveness of your solution to the psychology assignment, your psychology paper? Will you judge your solution effective if you simply get it completed? If you get an *A?* If the instructor says that it is one of the best papers ever turned in on the topic?

4. *Rethink and redefine problems and solutions over time.* An important final step in problem solving is to continually rethink and redefine problems (Bereiter & Scardamalia, 1993). People who are good at problem solving tend to be more motivated than the average person to improve on their past performances and to make original contributions. Thus you can examine your psychology paper after it is returned by your instructor and use the feedback to think about ways to improve it or to write a better paper the next time.

Obstacles to Solving Problems   It is easy to fall into the trap of becoming fixated on a particular strategy for solving a problem. **Fixation** involves using a prior strategy and failing to look at a problem from a fresh, new perspective. Psychologists have identified several kinds of fixation. One type is **functional fixedness,** in which individuals fail to solve a problem because they are fixated on a thing's usual functions. If you have ever used a shoe to hammer a nail, you have overcome functional

algorithm Strategy that guarantees a solution to a problem.

heuristics Guidelines that suggest, but do not guarantee, a solution to a problem.

fixation Using a prior problem-solving strategy and failing to look at a problem from a new perspective.

functional fixedness A type of fixation in which individuals fail to solve a problem because they are fixated on a thing's usual functions.

The Candle Problem
Mount a candle on a wall so that it won't drip wax on a table or a floor while it is burning.

The Nine-Dot Problem
Without lifting your pencil, connect the dots using only four straight lines.

The Six-Matchstick Problem
Arrange six matchsticks of equal length to make four equilateral triangles, the sides of which are one matchstick long.

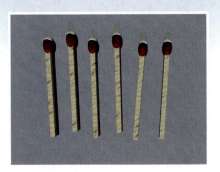

Solutions to the problems are presented at the end of the chapter on page 307.

FIGURE 8.4 Examples of How Fixation Impedes Problem Solving

In-Psych Plus

fixedness to solve a problem. Effective problem solving may also be blocked by a **mental set,** a type of fixation in which an individual tries to solve a problem in a particular way that has worked in the past. Each of us occasionally gets in the mental rut of trying to solve problems with a well-worn strategy. For a long time, I had a mental set about using a typewriter rather than a computer to write my books. Once I broke out of this mental set, the problem goal of finishing a book became much easier. You might feel the same about some aspects of technology. A good strategy is to keep an open mind and monitor whether your mental set is keeping you from trying something new. To explore how fixation might be involved in your own problem solving, see figure 8.4 and take a few minutes to do the anagrams in the interactivity "Mental Set."

Another obstacle to solving problems is not being motivated to solve them (Sternberg & Spear-Swerling, 1996). Some people give up too easily. Emotion can also facilitate or inhibit problem solving. Good problem solvers are often able to control their emotions and concentrate on a solution to a problem (Barron & Harackiewicz, 2001). Individuals who are competent at solving problems also are usually not afraid of making mistakes (Shewchuk, Johnson, & Elliott, 1999; Slavin, 2000).

Critical Thinking

In chapter 1, I defined *critical thinking* as thinking reflectively and productively and evaluating the evidence. People who think critically grasp the deeper meaning of ideas, keep an open mind about different approaches and perspectives, and decide for themselves what to believe or do (Halpern, 2002; Kamin & others, 2001). Too often, we take one side of an issue without really evaluating the issue or examining it from different perspectives. People often don't know that there even is another side to an issue or evidence contrary to what they believe (Slife & Yanchar, 2000). But, as Socrates said, knowing what it is you don't know is sometimes the first step to true wisdom.

Few schools teach students to think critically and to develop a deep understanding of concepts (Brooks & Brooks, 2001). For example, many high school students read *Hamlet* but are not asked to think about how its notions of power, greed, and conflicting relationships apply to their lives or the wider world. They rarely are stimulated to rethink their prior ideas about these matters.

Instead, schools spend too much time on getting students to give a single correct answer in an imitative way

"For God's sake, think! Why is he being so nice to you?"

rather than encouraging students to come up with new ideas (Brooks & Brooks, 2001). Too often, teachers ask students to recite, define, describe, state, and list rather than to analyze, infer, connect, synthesize, criticize, create, evaluate, think, and rethink. Too often, we are inclined to stay on the surface of problems rather than to stretch our minds (Bruning, Schraw, & Ronning, 1999).

In chapter 1, I urged you to think critically about controversies in psychology. Psychology has advanced as a field because psychologists have thought deeply about controversial issues, conducted extensive research on them, examined the evidence, and kept open minds about interpreting the results. I hope the Critical Controversy boxes that appear in each chapter challenge you to think about issues in less biased, more flexible, more reflective ways. In doing so, you will become a better critical thinker. To evaluate the extent to which you use critical thinking strategies, see the Psychology and Life box.

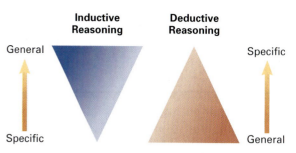

FIGURE 8.5 **Inductive and Deductive Reasoning**

Reasoning

Reasoning is the mental activity of transforming information to reach conclusions. It is a skill closely tied to critical thinking (Markman & Gentner, 2001). Reasoning can be either inductive or deductive (see figure 8.5).

Inductive reasoning is reasoning from the specific to the general (Coley & others, 2004). That is, it consists of drawing conclusions (forming concepts) about all members of a category based on observing only some members. For example, in a literature class after reading a few of Shakespeare's plays, you might draw some likely conclusions about his general ways of using language. Psychological research is often inductive as well, studying a sample of participants in order to draw conclusions about the population from which the sample is drawn. Be aware, however, that an inductive conclusion is never entirely certain—that is, it may be inconclusive. And although an inductive conclusion may be a likely possibility, there is always a chance that it is wrong, perhaps because the specific sample does not perfectly represent its general population (Johnson-Laird, 2000; Medin & others, 2003).

In contrast to inductive reasoning, **deductive reasoning** is reasoning from the general to the specific (Newstead & others, 2004). When you learn a general rule and then understand how it applies in some situations but not in others, you are engaging in deductive reasoning. When psychologists and other scientists use theories and intuitions to make predictions and then evaluate their predictions by making further observations, deductive reasoning is at work.

Deductive reasoning is always certain in the sense that, if the initial rules or assumptions are true, then the conclusion will follow directly as a matter of logic. For example, if you know the general rules that dogs bark and cats meow (and if they are always true), you can deduce whether your neighbor's strange-looking pet is a dog or a cat on the basis of the specific sound it makes. When psychologists develop a hypothesis from a theory, the hypothesis is a specific, logical extension of the general theory. And if the theory is true, then the hypothesis will be true as well.

mental set A type of fixation in which an individual tries to solve a problem in a particular way that has worked in the past.

inductive reasoning Reasoning from the specific to the general.

deductive reasoning Reasoning from the general to the specific.

Decision Making

Think of all the decisions you have to make in your life. Should I major in biology, psychology, or business? Should I go to graduate school right after college or get a job first? Should I establish myself in a career before settling down to have a family? Should I buy a house or rent? *Decision making* involves evaluating alternatives and making choices among them.

Sharpening the Saw

Critical thinkers ask good questions (Santrock & Halonen, 2002). Some college students feel discouraged about asking questions, possibly because they acquired passive learning habits in elementary and secondary school. They also may fear being embarrassed by asking a question. However, critical thinkers get their curiosity out in the open, and developing an enthusiasm for asking questions can make college more interesting and enjoyable.

Sometimes you can spot people who have studied psychology just by the questions they ask about behavior. Just as carpenters keep their tools well honed, psychological thinkers use questions as tools to help them make good judgments about behavior. Consider the following questions:

- *What exactly do you mean by that?*
  Once you have examined behavior carefully, you recognize that it is important to *describe* it precisely. Starting with precise descriptions can help you interpret behavior or make good predictions about behavior. For example, "He is a nervous person" is a fuzzy description. A more precise description is "His anxious behavior is characterized by feelings of helplessness, trembling, and sweating, which intensify when he takes tests."

- *I wonder why that happens.*
  Thinking like a psychologist involves trying to *explain* behavior. Showing curiosity about what motivates people to do what they do is a hallmark of people interested in psychology. For example, you might wonder why some people ask good questions and others don't.

- *What is the evidence to back up your claims?*
  When an explanation about the causes of behavior is at issue, personal testimony is not sufficient. When you think like a psychologist, you need to see the data that back up claims before you believe them. For example, if someone claims that the vast majority of Americans believe in vouchers for schools, ask to see the evidence: One newscaster who made this claim based the statement on a survey in which 51 percent believed in vouchers for schools, hardly an overwhelming majority.

- *Is there another way to explain the behavior?*
  When you don't have data to support an explanation, you may be able to generate other ideas. Coming up with alternative explanations for the cause of a behavior is a skill that psychologists value highly. For example, you might originally hypothesize that the reason someone is behaving in a particular way is that he or she is a firstborn child. However, further inquiry might suggest other possible explanations, such as current stressful circumstances and an impoverished childhood.

- *Is that a label or an explanation of behavior?*
  If Trudy has problems sleeping through the night, her behavior is labeled "insomnia." When asked why she has trouble sleeping, she says, "Because I have insomnia." However, insomnia is not an explanation; it is not the *cause* of her inability to sleep, it is simply the *fact* that she is unable to sleep. The *cause* of her insomnia might be drinking too much coffee at night, having too much stress in her life, or sleeping too much during the day.

In inductive reasoning, people use established rules to draw conclusions. In contrast, when we make decisions, such rules are not established, and we don't know the consequences of the decisions (Tversky & Fox, 1995). Some of the information might be missing, and we might not trust all of the information we have (Matlin, 2004). The following are some of the other mistakes we are prone to make in weighing our options (Stanovich, 1999, 2004):

- *Confirmation bias* is the tendency to search for and use information that supports our ideas rather than refutes them (Betch & others, 2001). Let's say that I have an initial hypothesis that something is going to work to solve a problem. I test the hypothesis and find that it is right some of the time. I conclude that my hypothesis was right rather than exploring possible reasons it did not work all of the time. Our decisions can also become further biased because we tend to seek out and listen to people whose views confirm our own and we tend to avoid those who have dissenting views. It is easy to detect the confirmation bias in the way that many people think. Consider politicians who ask only their supporters to serve on advisory committees. Consider also physicians who ignore symptoms that do not fit their initial diagnosis.

- *Belief perseverance* is the tendency to hold on to a belief in the face of contradictory evidence. People have a difficult time letting go of an idea or a strategy once they have embraced it. Consider the celebrity Madonna. We have a hard

"You take all the time you need, Larry–this certainly is a big decision." © The New Yorker Collection 1990, Eric Teitelbaum, from cartoonbank.com. All rights reserved.

time thinking of her in a maternal role because of the belief perseverance that she is a wild, fun-loving rock star. Another example of belief perseverance gives some students trouble in the first year of college. They may have gotten good grades in high school by using the strategy of cramming for tests the night before. Those who don't adopt a new strategy—spacing their study sessions more evenly throughout the term—often do poorly in college.

- *Overconfidence bias* is the tendency to have more confidence in judgments and decisions than we should, based on probability or past experience. People are overconfident about how long people with a fatal disease will live, which businesses will go bankrupt, which psychiatric inpatients have serious mental disorders, whether a defendant is guilty in a court trial, and which students will do well in graduate school (Kahneman & Tversky, 1995). People consistently have more faith in their judgments than predictions based on statistically objective measures indicate they should. In one study, college students were asked to make predictions about themselves in the coming academic year (Vallone & others, 1990). They were asked to predict whether they would drop any courses, vote in an election, and break up with their girlfriend or boyfriend. Then they were asked to rate how confident they were in their predictions. At the end of the year, the accuracy of their predictions was examined. The results: They were more likely to drop a class, not vote in an election, and break up with a girlfriend or a boyfriend than they had predicted.

- *Hindsight bias* is our tendency to falsely report, after the fact, that we accurately predicted an event. In other words, people tend to be overconfident about circumstances that already have happened (Louie, Curren, & Harich, 2000). As I write this chapter, baseball season is just beginning. Lots of people in different cities are predicting that their teams are going to make it to the World Series. Come October, after almost all of the teams have fallen by the wayside, many of the same people will say, "I told you our team wasn't going to have a good season."

- The *availability heuristic* is a prediction about the probability of an event based on the frequency of the event's past occurrences. Recall that heuristics are rules of thumb that suggest a solution but do not ensure that it will work; this is one heuristic that can produce flawed thinking. When an event has recently occurred, we especially tend to overestimate its future occurrence (McKelvie & Drumheller, 2001). How likely do you think you are to be a victim of a crime, for instance? The fear of crime tends to go up when the media go through a phase of highlighting murder or covering a sensational murder story. Because of the excess information about crime, we are likely to estimate that crime is more prevalent than it really is. The media contribute to this prediction error every time they expose us to a rash of vivid stories about tornadoes, murders, diseases, accidents, or terrorist attacks.

Belief perseverance is a common bias that infiltrates our judgments. *How is belief perseverance involved in thinking it improbable that Madonna would have become a mother?*

• The *representativeness heuristic* suggests that we sometimes make faulty decisions based on how well something matches a prototype—that is, the most common or representative example—rather than its relevance. Say that you are told you will meet a person who is skilled at carpentry and wrestling, owns a pet snake, knows how to repair motorcycles, and has a police record. Most likely, the description fits your prototype of a male more than a female, so you might estimate that there is a 9 in 10 chance that the person is a male. This prototype would serve you well, because far more men than women fit the description. But sometimes our prototypes do not take into account the frequency of events. For example, would you say that the person is more likely to be a member of a motorcycle gang or a salesman? If you conclude that he belongs to a motorcycle gang, you would be wrong. Although only a small percentage of the salesmen in the world fit this description, the total number of salesmen is greater than the total number of motorcycle gang members who fit the description. Let's assume that there are 10,000 members of motorcycle gangs in the world versus 100 million salesmen. Even if 1 of every 100 motorcycle gang members fits our description, there would be only 100 of them. If just 1 of every 100,000 salesmen fits our description their number would total 1,000. The probability is 10 times greater that the person is a salesman than a member of a motorcycle gang. Our lives involve many instances in which we judge probabilities based on representativeness and fail to consider frequency.

Review and Sharpen Your Thinking

2 *Discuss the main factors in five types of thinking.*

- Discuss the function of concepts.
- Identify four steps in problem solving, and evaluate some obstacles.
- Describe what critical thinking is.
- Explain the distinction between inductive and deductive reasoning.
- Summarize the biases and flawed heuristics that can develop when people make decisions.

Think of a problem that you have not been able to solve or would like to solve. How might following the steps in problem solving and avoiding obstacles in problem solving help you solve this problem? What biases and flawed heuristics might be at work? Explain.

---

3 LANGUAGE

Language and Cognition

Language Acquisition and Development

In-Psych Plus

language A form of communication, whether spoken, written, or signed, that is based on a system of symbols.

Why is language important to humans, and how does it develop?

Language is a form of communication, whether spoken, written, or signed, that is based on a system of symbols. It is not the only way we communicate, however; the video clip "Cultural Variations in Nonverbal Behavior" shows how nonverbal symbols are used around the world to convey emotions and messages. (Also, go to the video clip "Language of the Face" to learn about the nonverbal language of animals and similarities with human nonverbal language.) But think how important language is in our everyday lives. We need language to speak with others, listen to others, read, and write (de Boysson-Bardies, 2001).

Our language also enables us to describe past events in detail and to plan for the future. Without language, much of our thinking would be focused on the here and now. Language lets us pass down information from one generation to the next and create a rich cultural heritage, which in turn affects not only the language that we use but also the way that we think about the world.

Language and Cognition

We do not always think in words, but our thinking would be greatly impoverished without words. This connection between language and thought has been a topic of considerable interest to psychologists. Some psychologists have argued that we cannot think without language, a proposition that has produced heated controversy. Is thought dependent on language, or is language dependent on thought?

Language's Role in Cognition   What role does language play in important cognitive activities? For one thing, memory is stored not only in the form of sounds and images but also in words. Language helps us think, make inferences, tackle difficult decisions, and solve problems (Amsel & Byrnes, 2001). Language can be thought of as a tool for representing ideas (Gentner & Lowenstein, 2001).

Today, most psychologists would accept these points. However, linguist Benjamin Whorf (1956) went a step further. He argued that language actually determines the way we think. Whorf and his student Edward Sapir were specialists in Native American languages, and they were fascinated by the possibility that people might view the world differently as the result of the different languages they speak. The Inuit in Alaska, for instance, have a dozen or more words to describe the various textures, colors, and physical states of snow. But English has relatively few words to describe snow, and, thus, according to Whorf's view, English speakers cannot as easily talk or even think about it. The Hopi Indian language has no words for past or future, so Whorf would argue that traditional Hopis focus mainly on the present.

Critics of Whorf's view say that words merely reflect, rather than cause, the way we think. The Inuits' adaptability and livelihood in Alaska depend on their capacity to recognize various conditions of snow and ice. A skier or snowboarder, who is not Inuit, might also know numerous words for snow, far more than the average person;

Whorf's view is that our cultural experiences with a particular concept shape a catalog of names that can be either rich or poor. Consider how rich your mental library of names for camel might be if you had extensive experience with camels in a desert world and how poor your mental library of names for snow might be if you lived in a tropical world of palm trees and parrots. Despite its appeal, Whorf's view is controversial, and many psychologists do not believe it plays a pivotal role in shaping thought. *What evidence do they cite?*

and a person who doesn't know the words for the different types of snow might still be able to perceive these differences.

A study by Eleanor Rosch (1973) found that a lack of words for a concept does not reflect a lack of ability to perceive and think about it. She studied the effect of language on color perception among the Dani in New Guinea. The Dani have only two words for color—one that approximately means "white" and one that approximately means "black." If the linguistic relativity hypothesis were correct, the Dani would lack the ability to tell the difference between colors such as green, blue, red, yellow, and purple. But Rosch found that the Dani perceived colors just as we perceive them. As we know, color perception is biologically determined by receptors in the retinas in the eyes. Even though Whorf's view appears to have missed the mark— language does not determine thought—researchers agree that language can influence thought.

Cognition's Role in Language Researchers also are studying the possibility that cognition is an important foundation for language (Gupta & Dell, 1999; Albright & Hayes, 2003). If language is a reflection of cognition in general, we would expect to find a close link between language ability and general intellectual ability. In particular, we would expect to find that problems in one domain (cognition) are paralleled by problems in the other domain (language). For example, we would anticipate that general mental retardation is accompanied by impaired language abilities. That is often, but not always, the case.

Researchers have found that mental retardation is not always accompanied by poor language skills. Consider the discussion of Williams syndrome earlier in the chapter. Individuals with Williams syndrome have a general intelligence that places them in the category of mentally retarded. However, their language abilities are well within the normal range, as is their ability to use language for communicative purposes. The nature of Williams syndrome suggests a mind composed of separate, biologically prepared thinking and language abilities rather than a single, all-purpose, cognitive ability that includes language (Flavell, Miller, & Miller, 2002; Pinker, 1994).

Other evidence that cognition is separate from language comes from studies of deaf children. On a variety of thinking and problem-solving tasks, deaf children perform at the same level as children of the same age who have no hearing problems. Some of the deaf children in these studies do not even have command of written or sign language (Furth, 1971).

In sum, although thought likely can influence language, and language likely can influence thought, there is increasing evidence that language and thought are not part of a single cognitive system. Instead, they seem to have evolved as separate, modular, biologically prepared components of the mind.

Language Acquisition and Development

In 1799, a nude boy was observed running through the woods in France. The boy was captured when he was 11 years old. He was called the Wild Boy of Aveyron and was believed to have lived alone in the woods for 6 years (Lane, 1976). When found, he made no effort to communicate. Even after a number of years, he failed to learn to communicate effectively. This "wild child" case raises questions about how people acquire language. Is the ability to generate rules for language and then use them to create an infinite number of words the product of biological factors and evolution? Or is language learned and influenced by the environment? Precisely when and how does language ability develop? As you will see, the answers to these questions are complex and are still a focus of research.

Biological Influences on Language Estimates vary, but scientists believe that humans acquired language about 100,000 years ago. In evolutionary time, then,

In the wild, chimps communicate through calls, gestures, and expressions, which evolutionary psychologists believe might be the roots of true language. *Without words, how could chimp communication be considered a form of language?*

language is a very recent human ability. However, a number of experts believe biological evolution that took place long before language emerged undeniably shaped humans into linguistic creatures (Chomsky, 1975). The brain, nervous system, and vocal apparatus of our predecessors changed over hundreds of thousands of years. Physically equipped to do so, *Homo sapiens* went beyond grunting and shrieking to develop abstract speech. This sophisticated language ability gave humans an enormous edge over other animals and increased their chances of survival (Pinker, 1994).

Linguist Noam Chomsky (1975) is one of those who argues that humans are biologically prewired to learn language at a certain time and in a certain way. According to Chomsky and many other language experts, the strongest evidence for language's biological basis is the fact that children all over the world reach language milestones at about the same time developmentally and in about the same order, despite vast variations in the language input they receive from their environments. For example, in some cultures adults never talk to infants under 1 year of age, yet these infants still acquire language. Also, there is no convincing way other than biological factors to explain how quickly children learn language (Locke, 1999; Maratsos, 1999). In Chomsky's view, children also cannot possibly learn the full rules and structure of languages by only imitating what they hear. Rather, nature must provide children with a biological prewired universal grammar, allowing them to understand the basic rules of all languages and apply these rules to the speech they hear. They learn language without awareness of the underlying logic involved.

There is strong evidence to back up those who believe language has a biological foundation. Neuroscience research has shown that the brain contains particular regions predisposed to be used for language (Dick & others, 2004; Grodzinsky, 2001). As discussed in chapter 2, accumulating evidence further suggests that language processing occurs mainly in the brain's left hemisphere (Gazzaniga & others, 2001). Using brain imaging techniques, researchers have found that, when an infant is about 9 months old, the part of the brain that stores and indexes many kinds of memory becomes fully functional (Bloom, Nelson, & Lazerson, 2001). This is also the time at which infants appear to be able to attach meaning to words, suggesting a link among language, cognition, and the development of the brain.

Environmental Influences on Language   Contradicting those who believe that language is biologically determined, behaviorists have advocated the view that language is primarily determined by environmental influences. For example, the famous behaviorist B. F. Skinner (1957) said that language is just another behavior, like sitting, walking, or running. He argued that all behaviors, including language, are learned through reinforcement. Albert Bandura (1977) later emphasized that language is learned through imitation.

Roger Brown (1973) spent long hours observing parents and their young children, searching for evidence that children learn the rules of language through their parents' reinforcement (smiles, hugs, pats on the back, corrective feedback). He found that parents sometimes smiled and praised their children for sentences they liked but that they reinforced ungrammatical sentences as well. Brown concluded that no evidence exists that reinforcement is responsible for the development of children's language rule systems. Many of children's sentences are novel in the sense that the children have not previously heard them. A child might hear the sentence "The plate fell on the floor" but then be able to say, "My mirror fell on the blanket." Reinforcement and imitation simply cannot explain this utterance.

Although reinforcement and imitation are not responsible for children's development of language rule systems, it is important that children interact with language-skilled people (Snow, 1999). The Wild Boy of Aveyron was not around such people when he was a young child, and it clearly harmed his language development.

In one study of more typical language learning, researchers carefully assessed the level of maternal speech to infants (Huttenlocher & others, 1991). As indicated in

MIT linguist Noam Chomsky was one of the early architects of the view that children's language development cannot be explained solely by environmental input. In Chomsky's view, language has strong biological underpinnings, with children biologically prewired to learn language at a certain time and in a certain way. *What were some of the phenomena that convinced him of this view?*

FIGURE 8.6 Level of Maternal Speech and Infant Vocabulary The higher the level of mothers' language when communicating with their infants, the larger the children's vocabulary at age 2.

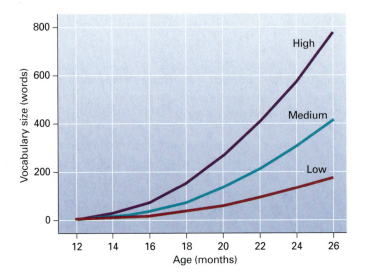

This is a wug.

Now there is another one. There are two of them. There are two _____.

FIGURE 8.7 Study of Children's Understanding of Language Rules In Jean Berko's classic study, young children were presented cards such as this one with a "wug" on it. Then the children were asked to supply the missing word and say it correctly.

figure 8.6, mothers who regularly used a higher level of language when interacting with their infants had infants with markedly larger vocabularies. By the second birthday, vocabulary differences were substantial.

What are some good strategies for parents in talking to their babies? They include the following (Baron, 1992):

- *Be an active conversational partner.* Initiate conversation with the infant. If the infant is in a day-long child-care program, ensure that he or she gets adequate language stimulation from adults.
- *Talk as if the infant understood what you are saying.* Adults can generate positive self-fulfilling prophecies by addressing their young children as if they understood what is being said. The process may take 4 to 5 years, but children gradually rise to match the language model presented to them.
- *Use a language style with which you feel comfortable.* Don't worry about how you sound to other adults when you talk with an infant. The mood and feeling you convey, not the content, are more important when talking with an infant. Use whatever type of baby talk you feel comfortable with in the first years of the child's life.

Research findings about environmental influences on language learning complicate the understanding of its foundations. In the real world of language learning, children appear to be neither exclusively biologically programmed nor exclusively socially driven (Ratner, 1993). As with all areas of psychology we have studied, we have to look at how biology and environment interact. That is, children are biologically prepared to learn language but benefit enormously from being bathed in a competent language environment from an early age (Pan & Snow, 1999; Tomasello & Slobin, 2004).

Early Development of Language One of the most interesting things about the development of language is that the child's linguistic interactions with parents and others obey certain rules (MacWhinney, 1999). Although children are learning vocabulary and concepts from an early age, they are also learning how their language is stitched together. In a classic study of this aspect of language learning, Jean Berko (1958) presented preschool and first-grade children with cards like the one shown in figure 8.7. The children were asked to look at the card while the experimenter read the words on it aloud. Then the children were asked to supply the missing word. *Wugs* is the correct response for the card shown here. Coming up with *wugs* might seem easy, but it requires an understanding of the proper word ending for plurals.

Although the children's responses were not always completely accurate, they were much better than chance. What makes Berko's study so impressive is that the words were fictional, created solely for the purpose of the study. Thus the children could not have based their answers on remembering past instances of hearing the words. Instead, they were forced to rely on rules.

In the 1960s, Eric Lenneberg (1967) proposed that there is a *critical period* between about 18 months of age and puberty during which a first language, and the rules of that language, must be acquired. Lenneberg provided support for his critical-period concept from studies of children and adults with damage in the left hemisphere of the brain, deaf children, children with mental retardation, and other people who had not been able to learn language in the typical way (Tager-Flusberg, 1994, 1999). Lenneberg found that the children he studied were able to recover their language skills, but the adults were not. Lenneberg believed that the difference was that the children's brains had plasticity and could reassign language skills to undamaged areas. Because their brain structures had matured and become more rigid, the adults no longer had the neurological capability to relearn language skills.

The stunted language development of a modern "wild child," similar to the Wild Boy of Aveyron, also supports the idea of a critical period for language acquisition. In 1970, a California social worker discovered a 13-year-old girl, Genie, who was locked away from the world. Kept in almost total isolation and severely physically restrained during her childhood, Genie could not speak or stand erect. Whenever Genie made a noise, her father beat her. He never communicated with her in words but growled and barked at her. Genie spent a number of years in extensive rehabilitation programs, such as speech and physical therapy (Curtiss, 1977; Rymer, 1993). She eventually learned to recognize many words and to speak in rudimentary sentences. Unlike normal children, however, Genie did not learn how to ask questions, and she does not understand grammar. Genie is not able to distinguish among pronouns or between passive and active verbs. As an adult, she still speaks in short, mangled sentences, such as "Father hit leg," "Big wood," and "Genie hurt." Her unfortunate story supports the idea that people have to learn language rules during childhood or miss the chance to become fully proficient.

Fortunately, most people do develop a clear understanding of their language's structure during childhood, as well as a large vocabulary. Most adults in the United States have acquired a vocabulary of nearly 50,000 words. Researchers have taken a great interest in the process by which these aspects of language develop. Through many studies, they now have an understanding of the important milestones of language development.

Before babies ever say their first words, they babble. Babbling—endlessly repeating sounds and syllables, such as *bababa or dadada*—begins at the age of 3 to 6 months and is determined by biological readiness, not by the amount of reinforcement or the ability to hear (Locke, 1993). Even deaf babies babble for a time (Lenneberg, Rebelsky, & Nichols, 1965). Babbling probably allows the baby to exercise its vocal cords and helps develop the ability to articulate different sounds.

Long before they actually begin to learn words, infants can sort through a number of spoken sounds in search of the ones that have meaning. Patricia Kuhl (1993, 2000) argues that, from birth to about 6 months of age, children are "universal linguists" who are capable of distinguishing each of the sounds that make up human speech. But, by about 6 months of age, they have started to specialize in the speech sounds of their native language (see figure 8.8).

A child's first words, uttered at the age of 10 to 13 months, name important people *(dada)*, familiar animals *(kitty)*, vehicles *(car)*, toys *(ball)*, food *(milk)*, body parts *(eye)*, clothes *(hat)*, household items *(clock)*, and greetings *(bye)*. These were babies' first words 50 years ago, and they are babies' first words today (Clark, 1983).

By the time children reach the age of 18 to 24 months, they usually utter two-word statements. They quickly grasp the importance of expressing concepts and the role

Genie's childhood was severly deprived. *What implications do Genie's experiences have for language acquisition?*

FIGURE 8.8 **From Universal Linguist to Language-Specific Listener** A baby is shown in Patricia Kuhl's researh laboratory. In this research, babies listen to tape-recorded voices that repeat syllables. When the sounds of the syllables change, the babies quickly learn to look at the bear. Using this technique, Kuhl has demonstrated that babies are universal linguists until about 6 months of age but in the next 6 months become language-specific listeners.

FIGURE 8.9 Language Milestones

Age	Milestones
0–6 Months	Cooing Discrimination of vowels Babbling by 6 months
6–12 Months	Babbling that includes sounds of spoken language Gestures used to communicate about objects First words by 10–13 months
12–18 Months	Average vocabulary of 50+ words
18–24 Months	Vocabulary of 200 words on average Two-word combinations
2 Years	Rapidly increasing vocabulary Correct use of plurals Use of past tense Use of some prepositions
3–4 Years	Mean length of utterances 3–4 words (a sentence) Use of "yes" and "no" questions, "wh-" questions Use of negatives and imperatives Increased awareness of pragmatics
5–6 Years	Vocabulary of about 10,000 words on average Coordination of simple sentences
6–8 Years	Rapidly increasing vocabulary More skilled use of language rules Improving conversational skills
9–11 Years	Word definitions that include synonyms Improving conversational strategies
11–14 Years	Vocabulary that includes more abstract words Understanding of complex grammatical forms Increased understanding of the function a word plays in a sentence Understanding of metaphor and satire
15–20 Years	Understanding of adult literary works

In-Psych Plus

Around the world, most young children learn to speak in two-word utterances at 18 to 24 months of age. *What implications does this fact have for the biological basis of language?*

that language plays in communicating with others (Schafer, 1999). To convey meaning in two-word statements, the child relies heavily on gesture, tone, and context. (Go to the interactivity "It's Not What You Say" to learn more about the nonverbal components of speech.) Still, children can communicate a wealth of meaning with two words (Slobin, 1972):

Identification: See doggie.
Location: Book there.
Repetition: More milk.
Nonexistence: Allgone thing.
Negation: Not wolf.
Possession: My candy.
Attribution: Big car.
Agent-action: Mama walk.
Action-direct-object: Hit you.
Action-indirect-object: Give papa.
Action-instrument: Cut knife.
Question: Where ball?

These examples are from children whose first languages were English, German, Russian, Finnish, Turkish, and Samoan. In every language, a child's first combination of words has this economical, telegraphic quality, omitting all unnecessary words. Of course, *telegraphic speech* is not limited to two-word phrases. As children leave the two-word stage, they move rather quickly into three-, four-, and five-word combinations, such as "Mommy give ice cream" or "Mommy give Tommy ice cream."

The early development of language skills through informal interaction with parents and other people in the family's social circle is an essential part of language acquisition. However, formal education in schools is also important. There children learn more sophisticated rules of language structure, increase their vocabularies, and apply language skills to learn about a wide variety of concepts.

Figure 8.9 highlights some of the main language milestones. Keep in mind that normal children reach these milestones earlier or later than indicated here.

Review and Sharpen Your Thinking

3 ***Explain the importance and the development of human language.***
- Summarize the possible links between language and thought.
- Discuss the relevance of a critical period in learning language and the major milestones in early language development.

Can a dog's bark or a cat's meow be considered language in the human sense? Explain.

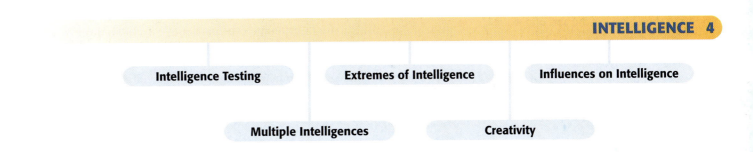

INTELLIGENCE 4

Intelligence Testing   Extremes of Intelligence   Influences on Intelligence

Multiple Intelligences   Creativity

What is intelligence, and how should it be measured?

What does the term *intelligence* mean to psychologists? Some experts describe intelligence as the ability to solve problems. Others describe it as the capacity to adapt and learn from experience. Still others argue that defining intelligence in these cognitive terms ignores other dimensions of intelligence, such as creativity and practical and interpersonal intelligence.

The problem with intelligence is that, unlike height, weight, and age, intelligence cannot be directly seen or measured. We can't peel back a person's scalp and see how much intelligence he or she has. We can evaluate intelligence only indirectly, by studying and comparing the intelligent acts that people perform (Gregory, 2004).

The main components of intelligence are similar to those of the cognitive processes of problem solving, thinking, and memory. The distinction lies in the concepts of individual differences and assessment. *Individual differences* are the stable, consistent ways in which people are different from one another. Individual differences in intelligence generally have been measured by tests designed to tell us whether a person can reason better than others who have taken the test. As you will see later in the chapter, though, the use of conventional intelligence tests to assess intelligence is controversial. However, temporarily I set aside the contentions of psychologists over the measurement of intelligence and fall back on the definition of **intelligence** as the ability to solve problems and to adapt to and learn from experience.

intelligence Problem-solving skills and the ability to adapt to and learn from everyday experiences.

THE FAR SIDE® By GARY LARSON

"The picture's pretty bleak, gentlemen. ... The world's climates are changing, the mammals are taking over, and we all have a brain about the size of a walnut."

ALFRED BINET (1857–1911)
Constructed the first intelligence test after being asked to create a measure to determine which children would not benefit from regular instruction in France's schools. *What concept did Binet develop that is at the core of today's individual intelligence tests?*

Intelligence Testing

Early psychologists completely ignored the "higher mental processes," such as thinking and problem solving, that we equate with intelligence today. They believed that simple sensory, perceptual, and motor processes were the key dimensions of intelligence. Sir Frances Galton, an English psychologist who is considered the father of mental tests, shared this point of view. In the late nineteenth century, he set out to demonstrate that there are systematic individual differences in these processes. Although his research provided few conclusive results, Galton raised many important questions about intelligence—how it should be measured, what its components are, and the degree to which it is inherited—that we continue to study today.

Binet Tests In 1904, the French Ministry of Education asked psychologist Alfred Binet to devise a method that would determine which students did not benefit from regular classroom instruction. School officials wanted to reduce overcrowding by placing those who did not benefit in special schools. Binet and his student Theophile Simon developed an intelligence test to meet this request. The test consisted of 30 items ranging from the ability to touch one's nose or ear when asked to the ability to draw designs from memory and to define abstract concepts.

Binet developed the concept of **mental age (MA),** which is an individual's level of mental development relative to others. Binet reasoned that a mentally retarded child would perform like a normal child of a younger age. He developed norms for intelligence by testing 50 nonretarded children from the ages of 3 to 11. Children suspected of mental retardation were then given the test, and their performances were compared with those of children of the same chronological age in the normal sample. Average mental age (MA) corresponds to chronological age (CA), which is age from birth. A bright child has an MA considerably above CA; a dull child has an MA considerably below CA.

The term **intelligence quotient (IQ)** was devised in 1912 by William Stern. IQ is an individual's mental age divided by chronological age and multiplied by 100:

$$IQ = \frac{MA}{CA} \times 100$$

If mental age is the same as chronological age, then the individual's IQ is 100 (average); if mental age is above chronological age, the IQ is more than 100 (above average); if mental age is below chronological age, the IQ is less than 100 (below average). For example, a 6-year-old child with a mental age of 8 has an IQ of 133, whereas a 6-year-old child with a mental age of 5 has an IQ of 83.

The Binet test has been revised many times to incorporate advances in the understanding of both intelligence and intelligence testing (Caruso, 2001; Kamphaus & Kroncke, 2004). Many of the revisions were carried out by Lewis Terman, who applied Stern's IQ concept to the test, developed extensive norms, and provided detailed, clear instructions for each problem on the test. In 1985, the test, now called the Stanford-Binet (the revisions were done at Stanford University), was revised to analyze an individual's responses in four content areas: verbal reasoning, quantitative reasoning, abstract/visual reasoning, and short-term memory. A general composite score also is obtained to reflect overall intelligence.

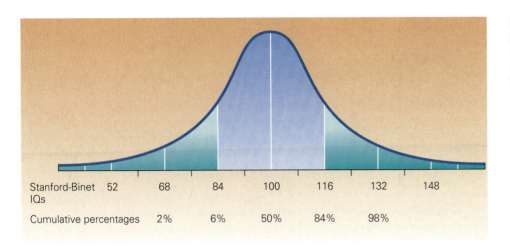

Stanford-Binet IQs	52	68	84	100	116	132	148
Cumulative percentages	2%	6%		50%	84%	98%	

FIGURE 8.10 **Normal Curve and Stanford-Binet IQ Scores** The distribution of IQ scores approximates a normal curve. Most of the population falls in the middle range of scores, between 84 and 116. Notice that extremely high and extremely low scores are rare. Only about 1 in 50 individuals has an IQ of more than 132 or less than 68.

The current Stanford-Binet is given to individuals from the age of 2 through adulthood. It includes a wide variety of items, some requiring verbal responses, others nonverbal responses. For example, items that characterize a 6-year-old's intelligence include the verbal ability to define at least six words, such as *orange* and *envelope,* and the nonverbal ability to trace a path through a maze. Items that reflect the average adult's intelligence include defining such words as *disproportionate* and *regard,* explaining a proverb, and comparing idleness and laziness.

Over the years, the Binet test has been given to thousands of children and adults of different ages selected at random from different parts of the United States. By administering the test to large numbers of individuals and recording the results, it has been found that intelligence measured by the Binet approximates a normal distribution (see figure 8.10). A **normal distribution** is a symmetrical, bell-shaped curve, with a majority of the scores falling in the middle of the possible range and few scores appearing toward the extremes of the range. The Stanford-Binet continues to be one of the most widely used individual tests of intelligence.

Wechsler Scales   The other most widely used intelligence tests are the Wechsler scales (Zhu & others, 2004). In 1939, David Wechsler introduced the first scale, designed for use with adults (Wechsler, 1939). Now the Wechsler Adult Intelligence Scale–III (WAIS-III) is in the third edition. The Wechsler Intelligence Scale for Children–III (WISC-III) is for children between the ages of 6 and 16, and the Wechsler Preschool and Primary Scale of Intelligence (WPPSI) is for children from the ages of 4 to 6½.

The Wechsler scales not only provide an overall IQ score but also yield scores on six verbal and five nonverbal measures. The examiner can separate verbal and nonverbal IQ scores to see quickly the areas of mental performance in which the individual is below average, average, or above average. The inclusion of a number of nonverbal subscales makes the Wechsler test more representative of verbal and nonverbal intelligence than the Binet test. Several of the Wechsler subscales are shown in figure 8.11.

Group Tests of Intelligence   The Stanford-Binet and Wechsler tests are individually administered intelligence tests. During testing, the psychologist observes the ease with which rapport is established, the level of energy and enthusiasm the individual expresses, and the degree of frustration tolerance and persistence the individual shows in performing difficult tasks. Each of these observations helps the psychologist understand the individual.

On some occasions, though, it is more convenient and economical to administer group intelligence tests than individual tests. For example, when World War I began, the armed services thought it would be beneficial to know the intellectual abilities of

mental age (MA) An individual's level of mental development relative to others.

intelligence quotient (IQ) An individual's mental age divided by chronological age and multiplied by 100.

normal distribution A symmetrical, bell-shaped curve, with a majority of the scores falling in the middle of the possible range and few scores appearing toward the extremes of the range.

VERBAL SUBSCALES

Similarities

An individual must think logically and abstractly to answer a number of questions about how things might be similar.

Example: "In what ways are boats and trains the same?"

Comprehension

This subscale is designed to measure an individual's judgment and common sense.

Example: "Why do individuals buy automobile insurance?"

NONVERBAL SUBSCALES

Picture Arrangement

A series of pictures out of sequence is shown to an individual, who is asked to place them in their proper order to tell an appropriate story. This subscale evaluates how individuals integrate information to make it logical and meaningful.

Example: "The pictures below need to be placed in an appropriate order to tell a story."

Block Design

An individual must assemble a set of multicolored blocks to match designs that the examiner shows. Visual-motor coordination, perceptual organization, and the ability to visualize spatially are assessed.

Example: "Use the four blocks on the left to make the pattern at the right."

FIGURE 8.11 **Sample Subscales of the Wechsler Adult Intelligence Scale—Revised** The Wechsler includes 11 subscales, 6 verbal and 5 nonverbal. Examples from four of the subscales are shown here. Wechsler Adult Intelligence Scale, Third Edition, Copyright © 1997 by the Psychological Corporation, a Harcourt Assessment Company. Reproduced by permission. All rights reserved. "Wechsler Adult Intelligence Scale" and "WAIS" are trademarks of the Psychological Corporation, a Harcourt Assessment Company, registered in the United States of America and/or other jurisdictions.

its thousands of recruits. The Army Alpha Test came out in 1917 to measure the intelligence of this large number of individuals on a group basis. In the same year, the Army Beta Test, mainly a performance test given orally, was designed for individuals who could not read the Army Alpha Test.

Though economical and convenient, group tests have some significant disadvantages. When a test is given to a large group, the examiner cannot establish rapport, determine the level of anxiety, and so on. Most testing experts recommend that, when important decisions are to be made about an individual, a group intelligence test should be supplemented by other information about the individual's abilities. For example, if a decision is to be made about placing a child in a special education class, the decision cannot legally be based on a group intelligence test. A psychologist must administer an individual intelligence test and obtain extensive additional information about the child's abilities outside the testing situation.

The Scholastic Assessment Test (SAT), a group test taken each year by more than 1 million high school seniors, measures some of the same abilities as intelligence tests.

However, it does not yield an overall IQ score; rather, the SAT provides separate scores for verbal and mathematical ability. The SAT is used widely as a predictor of success in college, but it is only one of many pieces of information that determine whether a college admits a student. High school grades, the quality of the student's high school, letters of recommendation, individual interviews with the student, and special circumstances in the student's life that might have impeded or enhanced academic ability are taken into account, along with the SAT scores.

In recent years, a debate has developed over whether private coaching can raise a student's SAT scores. Researchers have found that, on average, SAT preparation courses raise a student's scores only 15 points on the SAT's 200- to 800-point scale (Kulik, Bangert-Drowns, & Kulik, 1984). The reason may be that the student's verbal and mathematical abilities, which the SAT assesses, have been consolidated over years of experience and instruction.

Another debate focuses on possible gender bias in the SAT. In 2000, males outscored females by 42 points on average—35 points higher in the math section and 8 points in the verbal section (College Board, 2001). The publisher claims that the SAT is supposed to predict college success, especially first-year grades. However, females make better grades than males in their first year of college, so the SAT appears to underpredict the first-year success of females and overpredict that of males.

Because the SAT is used to predict college success, it has usually been referred to as an aptitude test. **Aptitude tests** predict how well an individual will be able to learn a skill or what an individual can accomplish with training. In contrast, **achievement tests** measure what an individual has learned or the skills an individual has mastered. The tests you take in this and other college courses that assess what you have learned are achievement tests. Although the SAT is used along with other information to predict college success (which makes it an aptitude test), it also examines what you have learned and the skills you have mastered, such as math and vocabulary skills (which makes it an achievement test). The name of the SAT recently was changed from Scholastic Aptitude Test to Scholastic Assessment Test to acknowledge that it measures both aptitude and achievement.

Criteria of Good Tests of Intelligence

Intelligence tests have become commonplace as psychologists have sought more precise measurement of psychology's concepts (Haladyna, 2002). But some tests are better than others. (To explore the challenges of measuring concepts such as intelligence, go to the interactivity "Reliability, Validity, and Variability.") A good test must meet three criteria:

- **Validity** is the extent to which a test measures what it is intended to measure. A test's validity can be established in a number of ways. One is making sure that the test samples a broad range of the content that is to be measured. For example, if an intelligence test purports to measure both verbal ability and problem-solving ability, the items should include a liberal sampling of items that reflect both of these domains; it should not test mostly vocabulary items. One of the most important measures of validity is the degree to which the test predicts an individual's performance when assessed by other measures. For example, a psychologist might validate an intelligence test by asking the employer of the individuals who took it how intelligent they are at work. The employer's perceptions would be another criterion for measuring intelligence. Quite often, the validation of an intelligence test is a different intelligence test.
- **Reliability** is the extent to which a test yields a consistent, reproducible measure of performance. A test that is stable and consistent should not fluctuate significantly because of chance factors, such as how much sleep the test taker gets the night before the test, who the examiner is, and what the temperature is in the room where the test is given (Aiken, 2003). Ideally, a test should

Frances Berger, a psychometrist, works for Psychometrics, Inc. She helps the company answer such questions as which staff members might be good at computer programming. Among her jobs is to get subject matter experts together to write test items on the topic at hand. She also is involved in developing tests herself and administering them. Frances has created customized tests for many large corporations and government organizations, such as AT&T, GTE, Federal Express, and the Air Force. *Where else might a specialist in psychological testing be employed?*

In-Psych Plus

aptitude tests Tests that predict how readily an individual can learn a skill or what the individual can accomplish with training.

achievement tests Tests that measure what a person has learned or the skills that a person has mastered.

validity The extent to which a test measures what it is intended to measure.

reliability The extent to which a test yields a consistent, reproducible measure of performance.

Validity

Does the test measure what it purports to measure?

Reliability

Is test performance consistent?

Standardization

Are uniform procedures for administering and scoring the test used?

FIGURE 8.12   Test Construction and Evaluation

standardization   The extent to which uniform procedures have been developed for administering and scoring a test, as well as the creation of norms for the test.

yield the same measure of performance when an individual is given the test on two different occasions. Thus, if we gave an intelligence test to a group of high school students today and then gave them the same test in 6 months, the test would be considered reliable if the same students scored high both times. However, individuals sometimes do better the second time they take the test because they are familiar with it (McMillan, 2001). Giving similar forms of a test on two different occasions is a way of dealing with this problem. This strategy eliminates the chance of individuals being familiar with the items, but it does not eliminate an individual's familiarity with the procedures and strategies involved in the testing. Also, it is difficult to create two tests in which the items are similar enough to test the same thing but not identical. Note that a test that is valid is reliable, but a test that is reliable is not necessarily valid. People can respond consistently on a test, but the test might not be measuring what it purports to measure (Carey, 2001).

- **Standardization** involves developing uniform procedures for administering and scoring a test, as well as creating *norms,* or performance standards, for the test (Impara & Plake, 2001). The test directions and the amount of time allowed to complete the test should be the same for all individuals, for example. Without standardization, it is difficult to compare individuals' scores. Standardization allows test creators to construct norms, which are created by giving the test to a large group of individuals representative of the population for whom the test is intended. Norms inform us which scores are considered high, low, or average. For example, suppose you receive a score of 120 on an intelligence test. The score takes on meaning only when we compare it with other people's scores. If only 20 percent of the standardized group scored above 120, then we can interpret your score as high rather than low or average. Tests of intelligence that are designed for individuals from diverse groups have norms for individuals of different ages, socioeconomic statuses, and ethnic groups (Popham, 2002). Figure 8.12 summarizes the criteria for test construction and evaluation.

Cultural Bias in Testing   Many of the early intelligence tests were culturally biased, favoring people who were from urban rather than rural environments, of middle socioeconomic status rather than low socioeconomic status, and White rather than African American (Miller-Jones, 1989; Nell, 2004; Provenzo, 2002; Watras, 2002). For example, a question on an early test asked what one should do if one finds a 3-year-old child in the street. The correct answer was "call the police." But children from inner-city families who perceive the police as adversaries are unlikely to choose this answer. Similarly, children from rural areas might not choose this answer if no police force is stationed nearby. Such questions clearly do not measure the knowledge necessary to adapt to one's environment or to be "intelligent" in an inner-city or rural neighborhood (Scarr, 1984). Also, members of minority groups who do not speak English or who speak nonstandard English may be at a disadvantage in trying to understand verbal questions that are framed in standard English (Banks, 2002; Gibbs & Huang, 1989; Sireci, 2004).

A specific case illustrating how cultural bias in intelligence tests can affect people is that of Gregory Ochoa. When Gregory was a high school student, he and his classmates took an IQ test. When Gregory looked at the test questions, he understood only a few words because he did not speak English very well and spoke Spanish at home. Several weeks later, Gregory was placed in a special class for mentally retarded students. Many of the students in the class, it turns out, had last names such as Ramirez and Gonzales. Gregory lost interest in school, dropped out, and eventually joined the navy, where he took high school courses and earned enough credits to attend college later. He graduated from San Jose City College as an honor student, continued his education, and became a professor of social work at the University of Washington in Seattle.

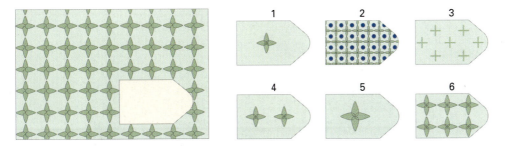

FIGURE 8.13 **Sample Item from a Culture-Fair Test** On the Raven Progressive Matrices Test, individuals are presented with an incomplete matrix arrangement of symbols and must then select the appropriate missing symbol.

As a result of such cases, researchers have tried to develop tests that accurately reflect a person's intelligence (Hambleton & others, 2004; Merenda, 2004). *Culture-fair tests* are intelligence tests that are intended to be culturally unbiased. Two types of culture-fair tests have been developed. The first includes questions that are familiar to people from all socioeconomic and ethnic backgrounds. For example, a child might be asked how a bird and a dog are different, on the assumption that virtually all children are familiar with birds and dogs. The second type of culture-fair test contains no verbal questions (see figure 8.13). Even though such tests are designed to be culture-fair, people with more education still score higher than those with less education do.

Why is it so hard to create culture-fair tests? Most tests tend to reflect what is important to the dominant culture. If tests have time limits, the test will be biased against groups not concerned with time. If languages differ, the same words might have different meanings for different language groups. Even pictures can produce bias, because some cultures have less experience with drawings and photographs (Anastasi & Urbina, 1996). Within the same culture, different groups can have different attitudes, values, and motivation, which can affect their performance on intelligence tests. Items that ask why buildings should be made of brick are biased against children who have little or no experience with brick houses. Questions about railroads, furnaces, seasons of the year, distances between cities, and so on can be biased against groups who have less experience than others with these contexts.

Multiple Intelligences

The concept of mental age and IQ is based on the idea that intelligence is a general ability. Thus, although the early Binet tests assessed some different cognitive skills (such as memory and comprehension), performance measures of these skills were combined to describe an individual's general intellectual ability. The Wechsler scales provide scores on a number of different intellectual skills, however, as well as an indication of a person's general intelligence.

Wechsler was not the first psychologist to break down intelligence into a number of abilities. Previously, Charles Spearman (1927) had proposed that intelligence has two factors: general intelligence, which he called *g*, and a number of specific abilities, or *s*. Spearman believed that these two factors accounted for a person's performance on an intelligence test. Spearman developed his theory by analyzing a number of intelligence tests. Using a similar technique, L. L. Thurstone (1938) concluded that intelligence tests measure only a number of specific factors and not general intelligence. Thurstone theorized that intelligence consists of seven primary mental abilities: verbal comprehension, number ability, word fluency, spatial visualization, associative memory, reasoning, and perceptual speed.

A number of contemporary psychologists continue to search for the specific components that make up intelligence. Unlike Wechsler and other early intelligence theorists, however, they do not rely on traditional intelligence tests in their conceptualization of intelligence. Following are several key alternative conceptions. These multiple-intelligence theories have much to offer. They have stimulated us to think

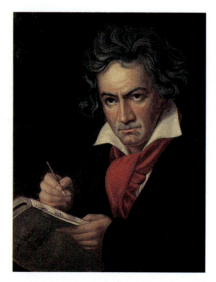

Ludwig van Beethoven, a musical genius, did not do well in math or English. *What are the implications of such capabilities for the concept of intelligence?*

Gardner	Sternberg	Salovey/Mayer/Goleman
Verbal Mathematical	Analytical	
Spatial Movement Musical		
Interpersonal Intrapersonal	Practical	Emotional
Naturalistic		
	Creative	

FIGURE 8.14 **Comparing Theories of Multiple Intelligences**

more broadly about what makes up people's intelligence and competence. Figure 8.14 provides a concise comparison of the following views.

Gardner's Eight Intelligences   Imagine someone who has great musical skills but does not do well in math or English—someone like the famous musical composer Ludwig van Beethoven. Would you call Beethoven "unintelligent"? Howard Gardner (1983, 1993, 2001, 2002) believes there are eight types of intelligence, thus accounting for genius in music and in several other domains that have not traditionally been categorized as intelligence. Gardner's eight intelligences are described in the following list, along with examples of the occupations in which they are considered strengths (Campbell, Campbell, & Dickinson, 2004):

- *Verbal skills:* The ability to think in words and to use language to express meaning. Occupations: Authors, journalists, speakers.
- *Mathematical skills:* The ability to carry out mathematical operations. Occupations: Scientists, engineers, accountants.
- *Spatial skills:* The ability to think three-dimensionally. Occupations: Architects, artists, sailors.
- *Bodily-kinesthetic skills:* The ability to manipulate objects and be physically adept. Occupations: Surgeons, craftspeople, dancers, athletes.
- *Musical skills:* A sensitivity to pitch, melody, rhythm, and tone. Occupations: Composers and musicians.
- *Interpersonal skills:* The ability to understand and interact effectively with others. Occupations: Teachers, mental health professionals.
- *Intrapersonal skills:* The ability to understand oneself. Occupations: Theologians, psychologists.
- *Naturalist skills:* The ability to observe patterns in nature and understand natural and human-made systems. Occupations: Farmers, botanists, ecologists, landscapers.

In *Rain Man*, Dustin Hoffman portrayed a man with autism and cognitive deficits who was capable of remarkable feats of counting and mathematics. Such skills are described as *savant skills. Can a person with cognitive deficits still be considered intelligent?*

Gardner believes that each of the eight intelligences can be destroyed by brain damage, that each involves unique cognitive skills, and that each shows up in exaggerated fashion both in the gifted and in individuals who have mental retardation or autism (a psychological disorder marked by deficits in social interaction and interests). The character played by Dustin Hoffman in the movie *Rain Man* dramatized one such case. Despite his autism, Hoffman's character was able to help his brother gamble successfully by keeping track of all the cards that had been played. See the video clip "Asperger Syndrome," which presents a sister and brother with a disorder associated with autism.

Some critics say that Gardner's classification of such domains as musical skills as a type of intelligence is off base. They ask whether there might not be other skills

"You're wise, but you lack tree smarts."
Donald Reilly © 1988 from the New Yorker Collection. All Rights Reserved.

domains that Gardner has left out. For example, there are outstanding chess players, prizefighters, writers, politicians, lawyers, ministers, and poets, yet we don't refer to chess intelligence, prizefighter intelligence, and so on. Other critics say that the research base to support Gardner's eight intelligences has not yet been developed.

There also are a number of psychologists who still support Spearman's concept of *g* (general intelligence), and many of them believe that Gardner's theory of multiple intelligences has taken the concept of *s* (specific intelligences) too far. For example, one expert on intelligence, Nathan Brody (2000), argues that people who excel at one type of intellectual task are likely to excel at other intellectual tasks. Thus individuals who do well at memorizing lists of digits are also likely to be good at solving verbal and spatial layout problems.

Sternberg's Triarchic Intelligence Gardner does not have a category for creativity in his intelligence theory, but Robert J. Sternberg does (2002, 2003b). He proposes that intelligence is **triarchic,** meaning that it has three main components:

- *Analytical intelligence.* Latisha scores high on traditional intelligence tests, such as the Stanford-Binet, and is a star analytical thinker. Sternberg calls Latisha's abstract reasoning ability *analytical intelligence.* It is the closest to what has traditionally been called intelligence and what is commonly assessed by intelligence tests. In Sternberg's view, analytical intelligence consists of several basic units of information processing ability, including the ability to acquire or store information; to retain or retrieve information; to transfer information; to plan, make decisions, and solve problems; and to translate thoughts into performance.
- *Creative intelligence.* Todd does not have the best test scores but has an insightful and creative mind. Sternberg calls the type of thinking at which Todd excels *creative intelligence.* According to Sternberg, creative people have the ability to solve new problems quickly, but they also learn how to solve familiar problems in an automatic, rote, way so that their minds are free to handle other problems that require insight and creativity.
- *Practical intelligence.* Emanuel is a street-smart person who learned to deal in practical ways with his world, although his scores on traditional IQ tests are low. Emanuel's street smarts and practical know-how indicate that he has what Sternberg calls *practical intelligence,* which includes the ability to get out of trouble, an aptitude for replacing a fuse, and a knack for getting along with people. Sternberg describes practical intelligence as all of the important information

triarchic In Sternberg's theory, there are three main types of intelligence: analytical, creative, and practical.

about getting along in the world that you are not taught in school. He believes practical intelligence is sometimes more important than analytical intelligence, the book knowledge that is taught in school.

Sternberg (2003b) believes that few tasks are purely analytic, creative, or practical. Most tasks require some combination of these skills. For example, when students write a book report, they might analyze the book's main themes (analytical intelligence), generate new ideas about how the book could have been written better (creative intelligence), and think about how the book's themes can be applied to people's lives (practical intelligence). Gardner (1999)—the ultimate multiple-intelligences advocate—believes that creativity, although an important aspect of human competence and functioning, is not a factor of, and should not be included in, a concept of intelligence.

Emotional Intelligence Both Gardner's and Sternberg's theories include one or more categories related to social intelligence. In Gardner's theory, the categories are interpersonal intelligence and intrapersonal intelligence; in Sternberg's theory, practical intelligence. Another theory that emphasizes interpersonal, intrapersonal, and practical aspects of intelligence is called **emotional intelligence,** which has been popularized by Daniel Goleman (1995) in his book *Emotional Intelligence.* The concept of emotional intelligence was initially developed by Peter Salovey and John Mayer (1990), who define it as the ability to perceive and express emotion accurately and adaptively (such as taking the perspective of others), to understand emotion and emotional knowledge (such as understanding the roles that emotions play in friendship and marriage), to use feelings to facilitate thought (such as being in a positive mood, which is linked to creative thinking), and to manage emotions in oneself and others (such as being able to control one's anger).

Recently, the Mayer-Salovey-Caruso Emotional Intelligence Test (MSCEIT) was developed to measure the four aspects of emotional intelligence: perceiving emotions, understanding emotions, facilitating thought, and managing emotions (Mayer, Salovey, & Caruso, 2002). The test consists of 141 items, can be given to individuals 17 years of age and older, and takes about 30–45 minutes to administer. Because the MSCEIT has been available only since 2001, few studies have been conducted to examine its ability to predict outcomes (Salovey & Pizarro, 2003). One recent study that used the MSCEIT found that youth with higher emotional intelligence were less likely to have smoked cigarettes or to have used alcohol (Trinidad & Johnson, 2002).

A number of psychologists still support Spearman's concept of *g* (general intelligence), and many of them believe that the multiple-intelligences views have taken the concept of *s* (specific intelligences) too far (Johnson & others, 2004). Some argue that people who excel at one type of intellectual task are likely to excel at other intellectual tasks. Thus individuals who do well at memorizing lists of digits are also likely to be good at solving verbal problems and spatial layout problems. To learn more about the continuing debate over general intelligence versus multiple intelligences, see the Critical Controversy box.

Extremes of Intelligence

Often, intelligence tests are used to identify exceptional individuals. Mental retardation and intellectual giftedness are the extremes of intelligence. Keeping in mind that an intelligence test should not be used as the sole basis for decisions about intelligence, let's consider these two extremes.

Mental Retardation The most distinctive feature of mental retardation is inadequate intellectual functioning. Long before formal tests were developed to assess intelligence, individuals with mental retardation were identified by a lack of age-

emotional intelligence The ability to perceive and express emotion accurately and adaptively, to understand emotion and emotional knowledge, to use feelings to express thought, and to manage emotions in oneself and others.

Do People Have a General Intelligence?

Charles Spearman (1927) believed that people have both a general intelligence *(g)* and specific intelligences *(s)*. With all of the interest in the multiple intelligences proposed by Gardner (2001) and Sternberg (1999), it might seem that the concept of a general intelligence is outdated. Contemporary experts on general intelligence disagree. They argue that individuals do have a general intelligence and that it includes abstract reasoning or thinking, the capacity to acquire knowledge, and problem-solving ability (Brody, 2000; Carroll, 1993). In addition, they maintain, it has real-world applications as a predictor of school and job success (Brody, 2000). For example, scores on tests of general intelligence are substantially correlated with academic achievement and moderately correlated with work performance (Lubinski, 2000). Individuals with higher scores on tests of general intelligence tend to get higher-paying, more prestigious jobs (Wagner, 1997).

However, general IQ tests predict only about one-fourth of the variation in job success with the majority of job success due to other factors such as motivation and education (Wagner & Sternberg, 1986). Further, the correlations between IQ and achievement decrease the longer people work at a job, presumably because as they gain more experience they perform better (Hunt, 1995).

Like Spearman, some experts on intelligence believe that people have both a general intelligence and specific intelligences. For example, in one study, John Carroll (1993) extensively assessed intellectual abilities and concluded that although all intellectual abilities are related to each other (which supports the concept of general intelligence), there are many specialized abilities as well. Beyond the broad level of general intelligence, Carroll found an intermediate level, reflected in such abilities as memory and speed of processing information to make decisions, and a narrower level, reflected in such abilities as the skill to code sounds.

There is a further wrinkle in the general intelligence issue. Researchers have found that the higher individuals' general IQ scores are, the more their scores on subtests of intellectual abilities vary (Hunt, 1995). For example, some bright individuals might score high on vocabulary and low on perceiving geometric patterns, whereas the reverse might be true for other bright individuals. However, researchers have found that individuals who score low on intelligence tests tend not to do well on any of the subtests (Hunt, 1995). These findings suggest that general intelligence might be a more appropriate concept for individuals with low intellectual ability than for individuals with high intellectual ability.

In sum, the debate about whether people have a general intelligence continues. So does the debate about what the specific intelligences are.

What do you think?

- Do you have a general intelligence? If so, how would you describe it?
- Should some specialized intellectual abilities, such as spatial abilities and mechanical abilities, be stressed more in school curriculums?
- Do you have any specialized intellectual abilities that would not be reflected in a traditional intelligence test, the kind that measures general intelligence? If so, what are they?

---

appropriate skills in learning and caring for themselves. Once intelligence tests were developed, numbers were assigned to indicate degrees of mental retardation. But it is not unusual to find that, of two individuals with mental retardation who have the same low IQ, one is married, employed, and involved in the community and the other requires constant supervision in an institution. Such differences in social competence led psychologists to include deficits in adaptive behavior in their definition of mental retardation.

Mental retardation is a condition of limited mental ability in which an individual has a low IQ, usually below 70 on a traditional intelligence test, and has difficulty adapting to everyday life; he or she first exhibited these characteristics during the so-called developmental period—by age 18. The reason for including developmental period in the definition of mental retardation is that we do not usually think of a college student who suffers massive brain damage in a car accident, resulting in an IQ of 60, as "mentally retarded." The low IQ and low adaptiveness should be evident in childhood. About 5 million Americans fit this definition of mental retardation (Hallahan & Kaufmann, 2003).

There are different ways to classifiy mental retardation (Hallahan & Kaufmann, 2003). As indicated in figure 8.15, mental retardation may be mild, moderate, severe, or profound. Note that a large majority of individuals diagnosed with mental retardation

mental retardation A condition of limited mental ability in which the individual has a low IQ, usually below 70, has difficulty adapting to everyday life, and has an onset of these characteristics in the so-called developmental period.

Type of Mental Retardation	IQ Range	Percentage of Mentally Retarded
Mild	55–70	89
Moderate	40–54	6
Severe	25–39	4
Profound	Below 25	1

FIGURE 8.15 Classification of Mental Retardation Based on IQ

fit into the mild category. Most school systems still use these classifications. However, because these categories are based on IQ ranges, they are not perfect predictors of functioning. The American Association on Mental Retardation (1992) developed a different classification scheme based on the degree of support required for a person with mental retardation to function at the highest level. As shown in figure 8.16, these categories of support are intermittent, limited, extensive, and pervasive.

Mental retardation may have an organic cause, or it may be social and cultural in origin (Martinez & others, 2004). *Organic retardation* is mental retardation caused by a genetic disorder or by brain damage. Most people who suffer from organic retardation have IQs between 0 and 50. Down syndrome, one form of organic mental retardation, occurs when an extra chromosome is present in the individual's genetic makeup. It is not known why the extra chromosome is present, but it may involve the health or age of the female ovum or male sperm. Other types of organic retardation include Williams syndrome, which was discussed at the beginning of the chapter; fragile X syndrome, caused by an abnormality in the X chromosome that is more common in males than females; prenatal malformation; metabolic disorders; and diseases that affect the brain (Das, 2000).

Cultural-familial retardation is a mental deficit in which no evidence of organic brain damage can be found. Individuals with this type of retardation have IQs between 55 and 70. Psychologists suspect that such mental deficits result at least in part from growing up in a below-average intellectual environment. As children, those who are familially retarded can be identified in school, where they often fail, need tangible rewards (candy rather than praise), and are highly sensitive to what others—

A child with Down syndrome. *What causes Down syndrome?*

Intermittent	Supports are provided "as needed." The individual may need episodic or short-term support during life-span transitions (such as job loss or acute medical crisis). Intermittent supports may be low- or high- intensity when provided.
Limited	Supports are intense and relatively consistent over time. They are time-limited but not intermittent. These supports require fewer staff members and cost less than more intense supports. They likely will be needed for adaptation to the changes involved in the school-to-adult period.
Extensive	Supports are characterized by regular involvement (e.g., daily) in at least some setting (such as home or work) and are not time-limited (for example, extended home-living support).
Pervasive	Supports are consistent, very intense, and provided across settings. They may be of a life-sustaining nature. These supports typically involve more staff members and intrusiveness than the other support categories.

FIGURE 8.16 Classification of Mental Retardation Based on Levels of Support Needed

both peers and adults—expect of them (Vaughn, Bos, & Schumm, 2003). However, as adults, the familially retarded are usually invisible, perhaps because adult settings don't tax their cognitive skills as sorely. It may also be that the familially retarded increase their intelligence as they move toward adulthood.

Giftedness   There have always been people whose abilities and accomplishments outshine those of others—the whiz kid in class, the star athlete, the natural musician. People who are **gifted** have high intelligence (an IQ of 120 or higher), superior talent for something, or both. School programs for the gifted usually select children who have intellectual superiority and academic aptitude. Children who are talented in the visual and performing arts (arts, drama, dance) or in athletics or who have other special aptitudes tend to be overlooked.

Until recently, giftedness and emotional distress were thought to go hand in hand. English novelist Virginia Woolf suffered from severe depression, for example, and eventually committed suicide. And Sir Isaac Newton, Vincent van Gogh, Anne Sexton, Socrates, and Sylvia Plath all had emotional problems. However, these individuals are the exception rather than the rule; in general, no relation between giftedness and mental disorder has been found. Lewis Terman (1925) conducted a study of 1,500 children whose Stanford-Binet IQs averaged 150. Terman found in his study that many of these gifted children went on to become successful doctors, lawyers, professors, and scientists. Recent studies also support the conclusion that gifted people tend to be more mature and have fewer emotional problems than others, and they tend to have grown up in a positive family climate (Feldhusen, 1999; Feldman, 1997).

Ellen Winner (1996) described three criteria that characterize gifted children, whether in art, music, or academic domains:

- *Precocity*. In most instances, gifted children are precocious because they have an unusually high inborn ability in a particular domain or domains. They begin to master an area earlier than their peers. Learning in their domain takes less effort for them than for ordinary children.
- *Independence*. Gifted children learn in a qualitatively different way than ordinary children do. For one thing, they need minimal help from adults to learn. In many cases, they resist any kind of explicit instruction. They also often make discoveries on their own and solve problems in unusual ways.
- *Passion to master*. Gifted children are driven to understand the domain in which they have high ability. They display an intense, obsessive interest and an ability to focus. They are not children who need to be pushed by their parents. They motivate themselves.

Art prodigy Alexandra Nechita. *What are some characteristics of gifted children?*

gifted   Individuals who have an IQ of 120 or higher, superior talent in a particular domain, or both.

Paul MacCready is one of America's most prolific inventors. His best-known invention is the Gossamer Condor, the first human-powered plane to travel a mile. MacCready's task was to design something stable and very light that would fly. It had to be different from any other airplane. MacCready's accomplishment won him $100,000 and a place in the Smithsonian Institution next to the Wright brothers' plane. *Which aspects of creativity helped MacCready win the prize?*

In-Psych Plus

Is giftedness a product of heredity or environment? Likely both. Gifted individuals often recall that they had signs of high ability in a particular area at a very young age, prior to or at the beginning of formal training (Howe & others, 1995)—suggesting innate ability. However, researchers also have found that the individuals who enjoy world-class status in the arts, mathematics, science, and sports all report strong family support and years of training and practice (Bloom, 1985). In one study, the best musicians engaged in twice as much deliberate practice over their lives as the least successful ones did (Ericsson, Krampe, & Tesch-Roemer, 1993). (For more on the possible role of heredity in giftedness, see the video clip "Beautiful Minds: An Interview with John Nash and Son.")

Although giftedness in childhood and in adulthood are linked, only a fraction of gifted children eventually become revolutionary adult creators (Winner, 2000). Those who do must make a difficult transition from child prodigy (learning rapidly and effortlessly in an established domain) to adult creator (disrupting and ultimately remaking a domain or creating a new one). One reason that some gifted children do not become gifted adults or even adult creators is that they have been pushed so hard by overzealous parents and teachers that they lose their intrinsic (internal) motivation (Winner, 1996).

Creativity

This chapter has referred to creativity a number of times. What is it? **Creativity** is the ability to think about something in novel and unusual ways and to come up with unconventional solutions to problems (Runce, 2004). Intelligence and creativity are not the same (Lubart, 2003; Michael, 1999). Sternberg (2000, 2001), who included creativity in his triarchic theory of intelligence, says that many highly intelligent people produce large numbers of products, but the products are not necessarily novel. He also believes that highly creative people defy the crowd, whereas people who are highly intelligent but not creative often try to simply please the crowd.

creativity The ability to think about something in novel and unusual ways and come up with unconventional solutions to problems.

divergent thinking Thinking that produces many answers to the same question; characteristic of creativity.

convergent thinking Thinking that produces one correct answer; characteristic of the type of thinking required on traditional intelligence tests.

In other words, creative people tend to be divergent thinkers (Guilford, 1967). **Divergent thinking** produces many answers to the same question. For example, the following question has many possible answers: What image comes to mind when you hear the phrase "sitting alone in a dark room"? In contrast, the kind of thinking required on conventional intelligence tests is **convergent thinking.** A typical item on an intelligence test is "How many quarters will you get in return for 60 dimes?" There is only one correct answer to this question.

In sum, most creative people are quite intelligent, but the reverse is not necessarily true. Many highly intelligent people (as measured by high scores on conventional tests of intelligence) are not very creative (Sternberg & O'Hara, 2000).

Steps in the Creative Process The creative process has often been described as a five-step sequence:

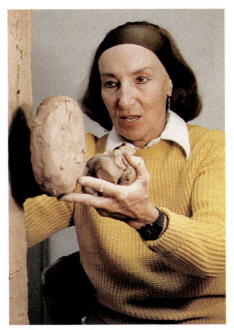

Mark Strand, former U.S. poet laureate, says that in his most creative moments he loses a sense of time and becomes absorbed in what he is doing. In this state, he feels he is dismantling meaning and remaking it. Strand comments that he can't stay in this absorbed frame of mind for an entire day. It comes and goes: His attention coils and uncoils; his focus sharpens and softens. When an idea clicks, he focuses intensely, transforming the idea into a vivid verbal image that will communicate its essence to the reader. *When do you get your most creative thoughts?*

Nina Holton, a leading contemporary sculptor, turns playfully wild germs of ideas into stunning sculptures. She says that sculpture is a combination of wonderful, unique ideas and a lot of hard work. She comments that when she is introduced to people they often say, "It must be so exciting and wonderful being a sculptor." Holton loves her work but says that most people see only its creative side, not the hard work. *At what stage of the creative process does hard work take over?*

Jonas Salk, who invented the polio vaccine, says that his best ideas come to him at night when he suddenly wakes up. After about 5 minutes of visualizing problems he had thought about the day before, he begins to see an unfolding, as if a painting or story is about to take form. Salk also believes that many creative ideas are generated through conversations with others who have open, curious minds and positive attitudes. Salk's penchant for seeing emergent possibilities often brought him into conflict with people who had orthodox opinions. *Does creativity require conflict?*

1. *Preparation.* You become immersed in a problem or an issue that interests you and arouses your curiosity.
2. *Incubation.* You churn ideas around in your head. This is the point at which you are likely to make some unusual connections in your thinking.
3. *Insight.* At this point, you experience the "Aha!" moment, when all the pieces of the puzzle seem to fit together.
4. *Evaluation.* Now you must decide whether the idea is valuable and worth pursuing. Is the idea really novel, or is it obvious?
5. *Elaboration.* This final step often covers the longest span of time and the hardest work. This is what the famous twentieth-century American inventor Thomas Edison was talking about when he said that creativity is 1 percent inspiration and 99 percent perspiration. Elaboration may require a great deal of perspiration.

Mihaly Csikszentmihalyi (1996) believes that this five-step sequence provides a helpful framework for thinking about how creative ideas are formed and developed. However, he argues that creative people don't always go through the steps in sequence. For example, elaboration is often interrupted by periods of incubation. Fresh insights also may appear during incubation, evaluation, and elaboration. And, in terms of a time frame, insight might last for years or it might take only a few hours. Sometimes the creative idea consists of one deep insight and other times a series of small ones.

"What do you mean 'What is it?' It's the spontaneous, unfettered expression of a young mind not yet bound by the restraints of narrative or pictorial representation." © Sidney Harris.

Characteristics of Creative Thinkers Creative thinkers tend to have the following characteristics (Perkins, 1994):

- *Flexibility and playful thinking.* Although creativity takes hard work, the work goes more smoothly if it is taken lightly. In a way, humor greases the wheels of creativity (Goleman, Kaufman, & Ray, 1993). When you are joking around, you are more likely to consider any possibility. Having fun helps to disarm the inner censor that can condemn your ideas as off base. *Brainstorming* is a technique in which members of a group are encouraged to come up with as many ideas as possible, play off one another's ideas, and say practically whatever comes to mind. Individuals usually avoid criticizing others' ideas until the end of the session.
- *Inner motivation.* Creative people often are motivated by the joy of creating. They tend to be less inspired by grades, money, or favorable feedback from others. Thus creative people are motivated more internally than externally. (Motivation is discussed more thoroughly in chapter 9.)
- *Willingness to risk.* Creative people make more mistakes than their less imaginative counterparts. It's not that they are less proficient but that they come up with more ideas, more possibilities. And they win some; they lose some. For example, the twentieth-century Spanish artist Pablo Picasso created more than 20,000 paintings. Not all of them were masterpieces. Creative thinkers learn to cope with unsuccessful projects and see failure as an opportunity to learn.
- *Objective evaluation of work.* Despite the stereotype that creative people are eccentric and highly subjective, most creative thinkers strive to evaluate their work objectively. They may use an established set of criteria to make judgments or rely on the judgments of respected, trusted others. In this manner, they can determine whether further creative thinking will improve their work.

Creative Living Csikszentmihalyi (1996) interviewed 90 leading figures in art, business, government, education, and science to learn how creativity works. He discovered that creative people regularly engage in challenges that absorb them. Based on his interviews with some of the most creative people in the world, he concluded that the first step toward a more creative life is to cultivate your curiosity and interest. Following are his recommendations:

- *Try to be surprised by something every day.* Maybe it is something you see, hear, or read about. Be open to what the world is telling you. Life is a stream of experiences. Swim widely and deeply in it, and your life will be richer.
- *Try to surprise at least one person every day.* In a lot of things you do, you have to be predictable and patterned. Do something different. Ask a question you normally would not ask. Invite someone to go somewhere new.
- *Write down each day what surprised you and how you surprised others.* Most creative people keep a diary, notes, or lab records to ensure that their experiences are not fleeting or forgotten. Start with this specific task: Each evening, record the most surprising event that occurred that day and your most surprising action. After a few days, reread your notes and reflect on your past experiences. After a few weeks, you might see a pattern of interest emerging in your notes, one that might suggest an area you can explore in greater depth.
- *When something sparks your interest, follow it.* Too often, we are too busy to explore something that captures our attention. Or we shy away from new experiences because we are not experts about them. However, we can't know which part of the world is best suited to our interests until we make a serious effort to learn as much about as many aspects of it as possible.
- *Wake up in the morning with a specific goal to look forward to.* Creative people wake up eager to start the day—not necessarily because they are cheerful, enthusiastic types but because they know they have something meaningful to accomplish each day, and they can't wait to get started.

- *Take charge of your schedule.* Figure out which time of the day is your most creative time. Some of us are more creative late at night, others early in the morning. Carve out time for yourself when your creative energy is at its peak.
- *Spend time in settings that stimulate your creativity.* In Csikszentmihalyi's (1996) research, he gave people an electronic pager and beeped them randomly at different times of the day. When he asked them how they felt, they reported the highest levels of creativity when walking, driving, or swimming. These activities are semiautomatic, so they leave you some time to make connections among ideas. Highly creative people also report coming up with novel ideas in the deeply relaxed state we are in when we are half-asleep, half-awake.

Influences on Intelligence

One of the hottest areas in the study of intelligence centers on the extent to which intelligence is influenced by genetics and the extent to which it is influenced by environment. In chapter 2, I indicated how difficult it is to tease apart these influences, but the difficulty has not kept psychologists from trying.

Genetic Influences on Intelligence Genes undoubtedly influence intelligence. Researchers recently have found genetic markers for intelligence on three chromosomes (Plomin, 1999; Plomin & Craig, 2001). One of these genetic markers was shown to be carried by about one-third of children with high IQs but by only one-sixth of children with average IQs (Chorney & others, 1998). As research on the human genome continues, more markers are likely to be found and identified, so the issue with respect to genetics and intelligence is the degree to which our genes make us smart (Petrill, 2003).

On one side of the debate, Arthur Jensen (1969) claims that intelligence is primarily inherited and that environment and culture play only a minimal role in intelligence. Jensen reviewed the research on intelligence, much of which involved comparisons of identical and fraternal twins. Identical twins have the same genetic makeup. If intelligence is genetically determined, Jensen reasoned, identical twins' IQs should be similar. Fraternal twins and ordinary siblings are less similar genetically, so their IQs should be less similar. Jensen found a very high positive correlation in the intelligence of identical twins and only an average correlation in the intelligence of fraternal twins, yielding a difference of .32. However in a research review, the difference was considerably less, only .15 (see figure 8.17) (Grigorenko, 2000).

Studies of adopted children have been inconclusive about the relative importance of heredity in intelligence, however. In one study, the educational levels attained by biological parents were better predictors of adopted children's IQ scores than were the IQs of the children's adoptive parents (Scarr & Weinberg, 1983). Because of the genetic link between the adopted children and their biological parents, the implication is that heredity is more important than environment. But environmental effects also have been found in such studies. For example, moving children into families with better environments than the children had in the past increased the children's IQs by an average of 12 points (Lucurto, 1990).

The concept of **heritability,** the variance in a population that can be attributed to genetics, is used to sort out the effects of heredity and environment. The *heritability index* is computed using a correlational statistical technique that measures genetic influence. The highest degree of heritability is 1.00, and correlations of .70 and above suggest a strong genetic influence.

Interestingly, researchers have found that the heritability of intelligence increases from as low as 35 percent in childhood to as high as 75 percent in adulthood (McGue & others, 1993). A committee of researchers convened by the American Psychological Association concluded that, by late adolescence, the heritability of

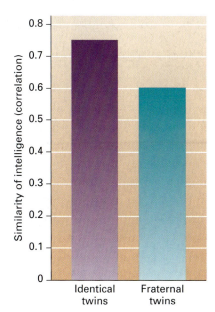

FIGURE 8.17 Correlation Between Intelligence Test Scores and Twin Status The graph summarizes research findings that compared the intelligence test scores of identical and fraternal twins. The test scores of identical twins are more similar (.75 correlation) than the test scores of fraternal twins (.60 correlation), a difference of .15.

heritability The variance in a population that is caused by genetic effects.

The intelligence of the Iatmul people of Papua, New Guinea *(left),* involves the ability to remember the names of many clans. The intelligence of the inhabitants of the Caroline Islands in the Pacific Ocean east of the Philippines *(right)* includes the ability to navigate by the stars.

intelligence is about .75, which reflects a strong role for heredity (Neisser & others, 1996). Why might hereditary influences on intelligence increase with age? Possibly as we grow older, we become more independent and thus freer to express genetic tendencies (Neisser & others, 1996). For example, sometimes children's parents push them into environments that are not compatible with their genetic inheritance (wanting them to be doctors or engineers, for example), but as adults these individuals may choose to select their own career and interests (being sculptors or hardware store owners).

An important point to keep in mind about heritability is that it applies to groups (populations), not to individuals (Okagaki, 2000). Researchers rely on the concept of heritability to describe why people differ, not to explain why a single individual has a certain level of intelligence.

The heritability index is by no means flawless (Dickens & Flynn, 2001). It is only as good as the data used and the interpretations made. One problem with the data is that they are virtually all from traditional IQ tests, which some experts believe are not always the best indicators of intelligence (Gardner, 2002; Sternberg, 2000). Also, the heritability index assumes that genetic and environmental influences are separate factors, each contributing a distinct amount of influence. Many experts believe that heredity and environment are so interconnected that any independent influence is almost impossible to determine. See the video clip "Nature and Nurture: The Study of Twins" to study one case and explore the interplay of genetic and environmental influences on intelligence.

Environmental Influences on Intelligence   Today, most researchers agree that heredity does not determine intelligence to the extent that Jensen claimed (Ceci, 1996; Coll, Bearer, & Lerner, 2004; Grigorenko, 2000). For most people, modifications in environment can change their IQ scores considerably (Campbell & Ramey, 1993). Enriching an environment can have considerable effects, improving achievement and fostering skills needed for employment. Although genetic endowment may always influence intellectual ability, environmental influences and opportunities do make a difference. For an example, listen to the audio clip "Music and Intelligence" to learn about the influence of music instruction on cognitive development.

In one study, researchers went into homes and observed how parents from welfare and middle-income professional families interacted with their young children (Hart & Risley, 1995). The middle-income professional parents were much likelier to communicate with their young children than the welfare parents were. And the more

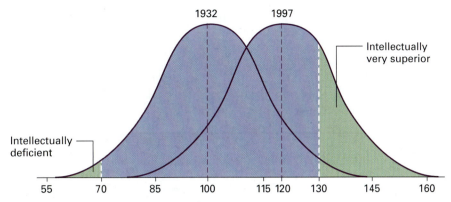

FIGURE 8.18 Increase in IQ Scores from 1932 to 1997 As measured by the Stanford-Binet intelligence test, American children seem to be getting smarter. Scores of a group tested in 1932 fell along a bell-shaped curve, with half below 100 and half above. Studies show that, if children took the same test today, using the 1932 scale, half would score above 120. Few of them would score in the "intellectually deficient" end, and about one-fourth would rank in the "very superior" range.

parents communicated with their children, the higher the children's IQs were. Others studies also have found substantial socioeconomic status differences in intelligence (Seifer, 2001).

Researchers are increasingly interested in manipulating the early environment of children who are at risk for impoverished intelligence (Blair & Ramey, 1996; Ramey, Ramey, & Lanzi, 2001; Sternberg & Grigorenko, 2001). Many low-income parents have difficulty providing an intellectually stimulating environment for their children. Programs that educate parents to be more sensitive caregivers and that train them to be better teachers can make a difference in a child's intellectual development, as can support services, such as high-quality child-care programs. Studies of schooling also reveal effects on intelligence for older children (Ceci & Gilstrap, 2000; Christian, Bachnan, & Morrison, 2001).

Another possible effect of environment on intelligence can be seen in rapidly increasing IQ scores around the world (Flynn, 1999; Mingroni, 2004; Nettelbeck & Wilson, 2004). Scores on IQ tests have been increasing so fast that a high percentage of people regarded as having average intelligence at the beginning of the twentieth century would be regarded as having below average intelligence today (Howard, 2001). If a representative sample of people today took an intelligence test used in 1932, about 25 percent would be defined as having very superior intelligence, a label accorded then to fewer than 3 percent of the population (see figure 8.18) (Horton, 2001). Because the increase has taken place in a relatively short time, it cannot be due to heredity. Rather, it may be due to increasing levels of education attained by a much greater percentage of the world's population or to other environmental factors, such as the explosion of information to which people are exposed.

Keep in mind that environmental influences are complex (Neisser & others, 1996; Sternberg, 2001). Growing up with all the advantages, for example, does not necessarily guarantee success. Children from wealthy families may have easy access to excellent schools, books, travel, and tutoring, but they may take such opportunities for granted and not be motivated to learn and to achieve. In the same way, poor or disadvantaged children may be highly motivated and successful.

Group Influences on Intelligence   Cultures vary in the way they define intelligence (Rogoff, 1990; Serpell, 2000). Most European Americans, for example, think of intelligence in terms of reasoning and thinking skills, but people in Kenya consider responsible participation in family and social life an integral part of intelligence. An intelligent person in Uganda is someone who knows what to do and

"You can't build a hut, you don't know how to find edible roots, and you know nothing about predicting the weather. In other words, you do *terribly* on our IQ test." © by Sydney Harris.

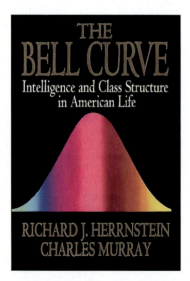

Herrnstein and Murray's *The Bell Curve* advocates a strong role for heredity in intelligence and claims that a large portion of underclass individuals, especially African Americans, are at a disadvantage because of their heredity. *What are some of the criticisms that have been leveled at Herrnstein and Murray's claims?*

In-Psych Plus

then follows through with appropriate action. Intelligence to the Iatmul people of Papua, New Guinea, involves the ability to remember the names of 10,000 to 20,000 clans. And the residents of the widely dispersed Caroline Islands incorporate the talent of navigating by the stars into their definition of intelligence. In a cross-cultural context, then, intelligence depends a great deal on environment.

Another group-related influence on intelligence is gender. The average IQ scores of males and females do not differ, but variability in their scores does (Brody, 2000). For example, males are more likely than females to have either extremely high or extremely low scores. There also are gender differences in specific intellectual abilities (Brody, 2000). Males score better than females in some nonverbal areas, such as spatial reasoning, and females score better than males in some verbal areas, such as the ability to find synonyms for words. However, as discussed in chapter 3, the scores of females and males in these areas overlap, and debate continues about how strong such differences are (Eagly, 2001; Hyde & Mezulis, 2001).

Ethnic comparisons of intelligence are also controversial. In the United States, children from African American and Latino families score below children from White families on standardized intelligence tests. On average, African American schoolchildren score 10 to 15 points lower on standardized intelligence tests than White schoolchildren do (Brody, 2000; Lynn, 1996). We are talking about average scores, though. Estimates also indicate that 15 to 25 percent of African American schoolchildren score higher than 50 percent of White schoolchildren do, and many Whites score lower than most African Americans. The reason is that the distribution of scores for African Americans and Whites overlap.

How extensively are ethnic differences in intelligence influenced by heredity and environment? Arthur Jensen (1969) claimed that genetics accounts for clear-cut differences in average intelligence between races, nationalities, and socioeconomic groups. More recently, Richard Herrnstein and Charles Murray argued in *The Bell Curve: Intelligence and Class Structure in American Life* (1994) that America is rapidly evolving a huge underclass that consists of intellectually deprived individuals. They believe that this underclass, a large proportion of which is African American, may be doomed by their shortcomings to welfare dependency, poverty, and crime. They point out that predictions about any individual based exclusively on IQ are useless, because intelligence and job success are only weakly correlated. But within large groups, say Herrnstein and Murray, the pervasive influence of IQ on human society becomes apparent.

Significant criticisms have been leveled at *The Bell Curve,* as well as at Jensen's work. Many experts raise serious questions about the ability of IQ tests to accurately measure a person's intelligence. Another criticism is that most research on heredity and environment does not include environments that differ radically. Thus it is not surprising that many studies show environment to be a fairly weak influence on intelligence (Fraser, 1995).

As African Americans have gained social, economic, and educational opportunities, the gap between African Americans and Whites on standardized intelligence tests has begun to narrow (Ogbu & Stern, 2001; Onwuegbuzi & Daley, 2001). This gap especially narrows in college, where African American and White students often experience more similar educational environments than in elementary and high school (Myerson & others, 1998). Also, when children from disadvantaged African American families are adopted into middle-socioeconomic status (SES) families, their scores on intelligence tests more closely resemble national averages for middle-SES children than for children from a lower SES (Scarr & Weinberg, 1983).

Did you know that the race gap on IQ scores is lowest at Pentagon schools? Listen to the audio clip "Intelligence and Racial Differences" to learn more about the historical trends and environmental factors involved in this issue.

One potential influence on intelligence test performance is *stereotype threat,* the anxiety that one's behavior might confirm a negative stereotype about one's group. For example, when African Americans take an intelligence test, they may experience anxiety about confirming the old stereotype that Blacks are "intellectually inferior." In one study, the verbal part of the Graduate Record Examination (GRE) was given individually to African American and White students at Stanford University (Steele & Aronson, 1995). Half the students of each ethnic group were told that the researchers were interested in assessing their intellectual ability. The other half were told that the researchers were trying to develop a test and that it might not be reliable and valid (therefore, it would not mean anything in relation to their intellectual ability). The White students did equally well on the test in both conditions. However, the African American students did more poorly when they thought the test was assessing their intellectual ability; when they thought the test was just in the development stage and might not be reliable or valid, they performed as well as the White students. Other studies have confirmed that African American students do more poorly on standardized tests if they believe they are being evaluated (Aronson, 2002; Aronson, Fried, & Good, 2002; Aronson & others, 1999). However, some critics believe that the extent to which stereotype threat explains the testing gap has been exaggerated (Sackett, 2003).

Review and Sharpen Your Thinking

4 *Describe what intelligence is, and evaluate the ways that it is measured.*

- Explain what intelligence is and what the limitations of intelligence tests are.
- Evaluate the theories of multiple intelligences.
- Describe the characteristics of mental retardation and giftedness.
- Distinguish between intelligence and creativity.
- Analyze the contributions of heredity and environment to intelligence.

Someone claims to have reached the conclusion, based on an analysis of his or her own genetic background and environmental influences, that environment has had little influence on his or her intelligence. What would you say to this person about the ability to make this determination?

The Candle Problem
The solution requires a unique perception of the function of the box in which the matches came. It can become a candleholder when tacked to the wall.

The Nine-Dot Problem
Most people have difficulty with this problem because they try to draw the lines within the boundaries of the dots. Notice that, by extending the lines beyond the dots, the problem can be solved.

The Six-Matchstick Problem
Nothing in the instructions said that the solution had to be two-dimensional.

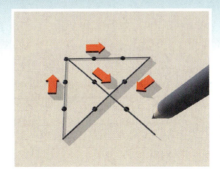
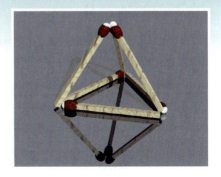

These are the solutions to the problems in figure 8.4.

Thinking, Language, and Intelligence

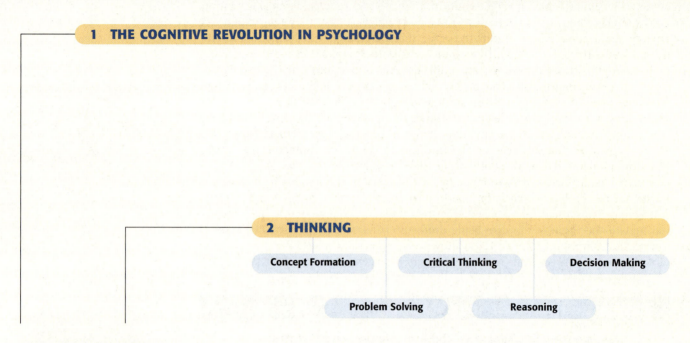

1 THE COGNITIVE REVOLUTION IN PSYCHOLOGY

2 THINKING

Concept Formation

Critical Thinking

Decision Making

Problem Solving

Reasoning

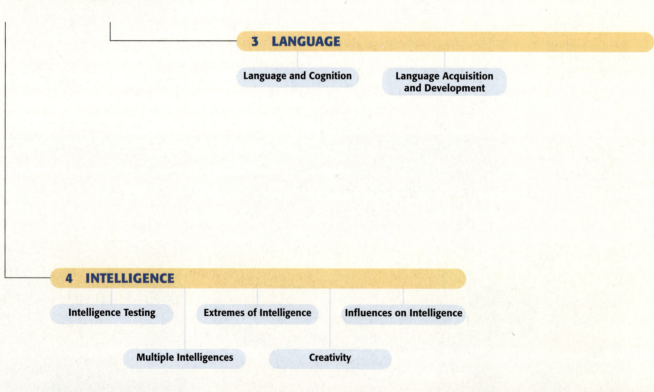

3 LANGUAGE

Language and Cognition

Language Acquisition and Development

4 INTELLIGENCE

Intelligence Testing

Extremes of Intelligence

Influences on Intelligence

Multiple Intelligences

Creativity

1. Characterize the "cognitive revolution" in psychology.

- Cognition is the way in which information is processed and manipulated in remembering, thinking, and knowing. The cognitive revolution, which has occurred over the past 50 years, is an interest in the way the mind works to process and to manipulate information. The computer has played an important role in this revolution, stimulating the model of the mind as an information processing system.

2. Discuss the main factors in five types of thinking.

- Concepts are mental categories that are used to group objects, events, and characteristics. Concepts are important because they help us to generalize, improve our memories, and keep us from constantly having to learn.
- Problem solving is an attempt to find an appropriate way of attaining a goal when the goal is not readily available. Four main steps in problem solving are (1) find and frame the problem, (2) develop good problem-solving strategies, (3) evaluate solutions, and (4) rethink and redefine problems and solutions over time. Among effective strategies for solving problems are subgoaling (setting intermediate goals that put you in a better position to reach your goal), using algorithms (strategies that guarantee a solution), and using heuristics (strategies or guidelines that suggest, but do not guarantee, a solution to a problem). Obstacles to problem solving include being fixated, as well as not being adequately motivated and not controlling emotions. Being fixated means focusing on prior strategies and failing to look at a problem from a new perspective.
- Critical thinking involves thinking reflectively and productively and evaluating the evidence. Some critics argue that schools do not do a good job of guiding students to think critically, especially in coming up with new ideas and revising earlier conclusions. Open-mindedness is a good strategy for improving critical thinking.
- Reasoning is the mental activity of transforming information to reach conclusions. Inductive reasoning is reasoning from the specific to the general. Deductive reasoning is reasoning from the general to the specific.
- Decision making involves evaluating alternatives and making choices among them. The biases and flawed heuristics that skew decisions include confirmation bias (favoring information that supports existing ideas), belief perseverance (maintaining a belief despite contradictory evidence), overconfidence bias (having unwarranted confidence about an outcome), hindsight bias (falsely reporting, after the fact, that a prediction was accurate),

the availability heuristic (predicting the probability of an event based on the past), and the representativeness heuristic (using a common or representative example to decide about a particular situation).

3. Explain the importance and the development of human language.

- Language is a form of communication, whether spoken, written, or signed, that is based on a system of symbols. Thoughts and ideas are associated with words. Language does not completely determine thought but does influence it. For instance, different languages promote different ways of thinking. Language is also important in the cognitive activities, such as memory. Cognitive activities also can influence language. Although language and thought influence each other, there is increasing evidence that they are not part of a single, automated cognitive system but, rather, evolved as separate, modular, biologically prepared components of the mind.
- Linguist Noam Chomsky said that humans are biologically prewired to learn language at a certain time and in a certain way. Behaviorists, such as B. F. Skinner and Albert Bandura, have advocated that language is primarily determined by environmental influences, especially reinforcement and imitation. The evidence suggests that children are biologically prepared to learn language but benefit enormously from being in a competent language environment from early in development. Language learning may be linked to a critical period, which is a time span in which there is learning readiness. Beyond this period, learning is difficult or impossible. However, this concept is still controversial. Far less controversial is the understanding of the milestones in early language development. Before babies say their first words, they babble. At 10 to 13 months, they utter their first word. Infants' early speech is telegraphic.

4. Describe what intelligence is, and evaluate the ways that it is measured.

- Intelligence consists of the ability to solve problems and to adapt and learn from everyday experiences. Traditionally, intelligence has been measured by tests designed to compare people's performance on cognitive tasks. The Stanford-Binet IQ test and the Wechsler scales are the main intelligence-assessment tools for individuals. The Wechsler tests provide an overall IQ, verbal and performance IQs, and information from 11 subtests. Group intelligence tests, such as the SAT, are convenient and economical, but they do not allow an examiner to monitor the testing closely. A good test of intelligence meets three criteria: validity, the extent to which a test measures what it is intended to measure; reliability, how consistently an individual performs on a test; and standardization, the uniformity of procedures for administering and scoring a test. Early intelligence tests favored White, middle socioeconomic status, urban individuals, so tests have been designed to be less culturally biased. When used by a judicious examiner, intelligence tests can be valuable tools for determining individual differences in intelligence. But test scores should be used with other types of information to evaluate an individual. IQ scores can produce unfortunate stereotypes and expectations.

• Spearman proposed two factors of intelligences, *g*, general intelligence, and *s*, a number of specific abilities. Thurstone's multiple-factor theory proposed seven primary mental abilities.

• Gardner believes there are eight types of intelligence: verbal skills, mathematical skills, spatial skills, bodily-kinesthetic skills, musical skills, interpersonal skills, intrapersonal skills, and naturalist skills. Sternberg's triarchic theory of intelligence states there are three main types of intelligence: analytical, creative, and practical. Emotional intelligence is the ability to monitor one's own and others' feelings and emotions, to discriminate among them, and to use this information to guide one's thinking and actions. The multiple-intelligences approaches have broadened the definition of intelligence, but critics maintain that the multiple-intelligences theories include factors that are not really part of intelligence, such as musical skills and creativity. Critics also say that there is not enough research to support the concept of multiple intelligences.

• Mental retardation is a condition of limited mental ability in which the individual has a low IQ, usually below 70; has difficulty adapting to everyday life; and has an onset of these characteristics during the so-called developmental period. Mental retardation can have an or-

ganic cause (organic retardation) or can be social and cultural in origin (cultural-familial retardation). People who are gifted have high intelligence (IQs of 120 or higher), superior talent for a particular domain, or both. Three characteristics of gifted children are precocity, independence, and a passion to master. Giftedness is likely a consequence of both heredity and environment.

• Creativity is the ability to think about something in novel and unusual ways and come up with unconventional solutions to problems. The difference between intelligence and creativity is the ability to produce something original or unique. Creative people tend to be divergent thinkers who can see more than one possible answer to a question. Traditional intelligence test questions have only one correct answer and thus measure convergent thinking. Characteristics of creative thinkers include flexibility and playful thinking, inner motivation, willingness to risk, and objective evaluation of their work. Csikszentmihalyi believes that cultivating curiosity and interest is the first step toward a more creative life.

• Recently, researchers have found genetic markers for intelligence on several chromosomes. Genetic similarity might explain why identical twins show stronger correlations on intelligence tests than fraternal twins do and why the IQs of adopted children are more similar to the IQs of their biological parents than to those of their adoptive parents. Environmental influences on intelligence have been demonstrated as well, though. Researchers have found that how much parents talk with their children in the first 3 years of life is correlated with the children's IQs. Intelligence test scores have risen considerably around the world in recent decades, also indicating the role of environment in intelligence. Among the ways that group influences can be linked with intelligence are comparisons of cultures, ethnic groups, and males and females.

Key Terms

cognition, p. 271
thinking, p. 272
concepts, p. 272
algorithm, p. 275
heuristics, p. 275
fixation, p. 275
functional fixedness, p. 275
mental set, p. 277

inductive reasoning, p. 277
deductive reasoning, p. 277
language, p. 280
intelligence, p. 287
mental age (MA), p. 289
intelligence
    quotient (IQ), p. 289
normal distribution, p. 289

aptitude tests, p. 291
achievement tests, p. 291
validity, p. 291
reliability, p. 291
standardization, p. 292
triarchic, p. 295
emotional intelligence,
    p. 296

mental retardation, p. 297
gifted, p. 299
creativity, p. 300
divergent thinking, p. 300
convergent thinking, p. 300
heritability, p. 303

9

Motivation and Emotion

Apply Your Knowledge

1. Due to the cognitive revolution, the computer is currently the dominant model psychologists use to think about how our brains process information. Could this model contribute to functional fixedness among psychologists? How? Can you think of a model other than the computer to describe how the brain works? Think back to how the brain actually works—in what ways might it be similar to a computer, and in what ways does it differ?

2. Think about two or three courses you are currently taking or have taken recently. Based on the definition of critical thinking discussed in this book, which courses most required or best encouraged these practices? How did they encourage critical thinking? Which was the worst course from this perspective? How might this course be improved? Should all courses encourage critical thinking, or are there some for which the development of students' critical thinking skills is not necessary?

3. Many different intelligence tests are available online. Do a web search for intelligence tests, and take one. How reliable is the test you took, and how do you know if it's reliable? How well standardized is the test, and on what evidence did you base your answer? How valid is the test, and how do you know what its validity is?

4. What is, or should be, the purpose of intelligence testing? To determine who will do well in school? To determine what career someone should pursue? To keep psychologists occupied? Given what you think the purpose should be, which definition of intelligence is most useful?

5. One controversial theory about intelligence suggests a relationship between birth order and intelligence: The IQs of children born first are higher than those of children born second, and so on. Imagine this is true. What would this tell you about the role of environment and heredity on intelligence? What does it say about large families? Now imagine it's not true. What factors might have influenced researchers to make this conclusion erroneously?

Connections

To test your mastery of the material in this chapter, go to the Study Guide and the In-Psych Plus CD-ROM, as well as the On-line Learning Center. There you will find a chapter summary, practice tests, flashcards, lecture slides, web links, and other study tools, such as interactive exercises and reviews as well as current, chapter-relevant news articles.

Chapter Outline

Learning Goals

1 Describe five psychological views of motivation.

2 Explain what motivates people to eat and to eat too much or too little.

3 Discuss the motivation for sex.

4 Explain why people are motivated to achieve.

5 Summarize the factors that influence emotion.

The 3-week, 2,000-mile-plus Tour de France, the world's premier bicycle race, is one of the great tests of human motivation in sports. American Lance Armstrong won the Tour de France cycling event not just once, but five times from 1999 through 2003. This was a remarkable accomplishment, as Lance was diagnosed with testicular cancer in 1996. Chances of his recovery were estimated at less than 50 percent.

After the cancer was diagnosed, Lance said that the first thing he thought was, "Oh, no! My career's in jeopardy! Then, they kept finding new problems and I forgot about my career—I was more worried about getting to my next birthday. I had the same emotions when I was sick as I have as a competitive athlete. At first I was angry, then I felt motivated and driven to get better. And then when I knew I was getting better, I knew I was winning."

Lance's experience with cancer motivated him to think about his priorities in life. He says that the experience ultimately made him a happier and better person. He became a spokesperson for cancer and established the Lance Armstrong Foundation, which supports cancer awareness and research. He married and became a father.

When you are motivated, you do something. The way you feel—your emotions—can either strengthen or weaken your motivation. For Lance Armstrong, motivation and emotion played a significant role in his recovery and accomplishments:

- *Motivation.* The intense motivation required to make it through grueling practices, day after day; the motivation to battle cancer and defeat it; the motivation to set a goal of winning the Tour de France and then winning it; the motivation to improve his personal life by getting married and starting a family; and the motivation to donate his time and effort to promoting cancer research and awareness
- *Emotion.* The anger that emerged when he found out that he had cancer; the fear that he would die; the happiness of getting married and starting a family; and the elation and joy of winning the Tour de France

Motives and emotions are important in all our lives. They differ not only in kind, such as an individual being motivated to eat rather than have sex or feeling happy rather than angry, but also in intensity, such as an individual as being more or less hungry or more or less happy. This chapter looks at different approaches to motivation and emotion that have sought to explain why.

Lance Armstrong, after winning the Tour de France. *How were motivation and emotion involved in his effort?*

How do psychologists think about motivation?

We are all motivated, but we are motivated to do different things at different times. Some students are motivated to hang out with friends, others to get a head start on the week's assignment. **Motivation** moves people to behave, think, and feel the way they do. Motivated behavior is energized, directed, and sustained.

There is no shortage of theories about why organisms are motivated to do what they do. The following are the main approaches:

- *Evolutionary approach.* Early in psychology's history, the evolutionary approach emphasized the role of instincts in motivation. An **instinct** is an innate (unlearned), biological pattern of behavior that is assumed to be universal throughout a species. Psychologists crafted lists of instincts, some lists running to thousands of items. However, if we say that people have an instinct for sex or for curiosity or for acquisitiveness, we are merely naming the behaviors, not explaining them. However, some motivation seems to be unlearned. As chapter 3 explains, human infants come into the world equipped with a sucking instinct. Recently, evolutionary psychology has rekindled interest in the biological basis of motivation. Evolutionary psychologists argue that sex, aggression, achievement, and other behaviors are rooted in our evolutionary past (Buss, 2000, 2004; Cosmides & others, 2003). Thus, if a species is highly competitive, it is because such competitiveness improved the chance for survival and was passed down through the genes from generation to generation.

- *Drive reduction theory.* If you do not have an instinct for sex, maybe you have a drive or a need for it. A **drive** is an aroused state that occurs because of a physiological need. A **need** is a deprivation that energizes the drive to eliminate or reduce the deprivation. The body's need for food, for example, arouses your hunger drive. Hunger motivates you to do something—to go out for a hamburger, for example—to reduce the drive and satisfy the need. From this example, you might sense that drive pertains to a psychological state; need involves a physiological state. The goal of drive reduction is **homeostasis,** the body's tendency to maintain an equilibrium, or steady state. Literally hundreds of biological states in our bodies must be maintained within a certain range: temperature, blood sugar level, potassium and sodium levels, oxygen, and so on. When you dive into an icy swimming pool, your body uses energy to maintain its normal temperature. When you walk out of an air-conditioned room into the heat of a summer day, your body releases excess heat by sweating. These physiological changes occur automatically to keep your body in an optimal state of functioning. Today, homeostasis is used to explain both physical and psychological imbalances. Most psychologists believe that drive reduction theory does not provide a comprehensive framework for understanding motivation because people often behave in ways that increase rather than reduce a drive. For example, they might skip meals in an effort to lose weight, which can increase their hunger drive rather than reduce it.

- *Optimum arousal theory.* Some people seem more motivated to seek stimulation and thrills, perhaps by sky diving or driving too fast, than to reduce a drive. But is there an optimum level of arousal that motivates behavior? Since early in the twentieth century, some psychologists have believed that performance is generally better under conditions of moderate arousal than either low or high arousal. At the low end of arousal, you might be too lethargic to perform tasks well; at the high end, you may not be able to concentrate. Think about performance in sports. A thumping heart and rapid breathing have accompanied many golfers' missed putts and basketball players' failed free-throw attempts. But if athletes' arousal is too low, they may not concentrate well on the task

motivation Gives behavior, thoughts, and feelings a purpose and makes behavior energized, directed, and sustained.

instinct An innate (unlearned), biological pattern of behavior that is assumed to be universal throughout a species.

drive An aroused state that occurs because of a physiological need.

need A deprivation that energizes the drive to eliminate or reduce the deprivation.

homeostasis The body's tendency to maintain an equilibrium, or steady state.

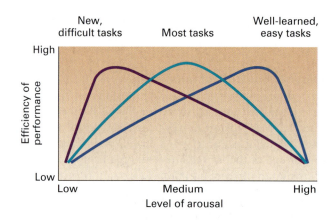

at hand. Low or high arousal sometimes produces optimal performance, however. For well-learned or simple tasks (signing your name, pushing a button on request), optimal arousal may be quite high. In contrast, when learning a task or doing something complex (solving an algebraic equation), much lower arousal is preferred. Figure 9.1 projects how arousal might influence easy, moderate, and difficult tasks. Also, some people, *sensation seekers,* crave a great deal of stimulation in their lives and enjoy the thrill of engaging in risky behavior. Zuckerman and his colleagues (Zuckerman 1994, 2000; Zuckerman & others, 1993) have found that high sensation seekers are more likely than low sensation seekers to engage in risky sports, such as mountain climbing, parachuting, hang gliding, scuba diving, car and motorcycle racing, and downhill skiing; to be attracted to vocations involving exciting experiences, such as firefighting, emergency-room work, and air traffic control; to drink heavily, smoke, and use illicit drugs; and to have a short-term hedonistic attitude toward intimate relationships and engage in more varied sexual activities with more partners.

- *Cognitive approach.* Freud's legacy to contemporary psychodynamic theory is the belief that we are largely unaware of why we behave the way we do: why we love someone, why we eat so much, why we are so aggressive, or why we are so shy. In contrast, cognitive psychologists tend to emphasize that human beings are rational and aware of their motivation. Humanistic theorists also stress our ability to examine our lives and become aware of what motivates us. Further, an important aspect of the cognitive approach to motivation is **intrinsic motivation,** which is based on internal factors, such as self-determination, curiosity, challenge, and effort. **Extrinsic motivation** is based on external incentives, such as rewards and punishments. Some students study hard because they are internally motivated to put forth considerable effort and achieve high quality in their work (intrinsic motivation). Other students study hard because they want to make good grades or avoid parental disapproval (extrinsic motivation). Research often reveals that people whose motivation is intrinsic show more interest, excitement, and confidence in what they are doing than those whose motivation is extrinsic. Intrinsic motivation often results in improved performance, persistence, creativity, and self-esteem (Deci & Ryan, 1995; Ryan & Deci, 2000, 2001; Sheldon & others, 1997). Apparently, self-determination (which is intrinsic) produces a sense of personal control that benefits the individual (deCharms, 1984; Deci & Ryan, 1994; Ryan & Deci, 2000, 2001). Researchers have found, for instance, that students' internal motivation and intrinsic interest in school tasks increase when they have some choice and some opportunities to take responsibility for their learning (Eccles, 2004; Eccles & Wigfield, 2002; Stipek, 2001). Some psychologists stress that many highly successful individuals are both intrinsically motivated (have a high personal standard of achievement and emphasize personal effort) and extrinsically

intrinsic motivation A motivation based on internal factors, such as self-determination, curiosity, challenge, and effort.

extrinsic motivation A motivation that involves external incentives, such as rewards and punishments.

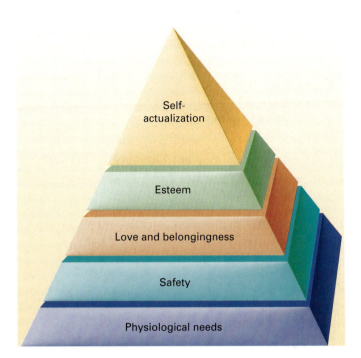

FIGURE 9.2 Maslow's Hierarchy of Needs Abraham Maslow developed the hierarchy of human needs to show that we have to satisfy basic physiological needs before we can satisfy other, higher needs.

motivated (are highly competitive). Lance Armstrong is a good example. For the most part, though, psychologists believe that intrinsic motivation is the key to achievement. Armstrong, like many other athletic champions, decided early on that he was training and racing for himself, not for his parents, his coaches, or the medals.

• *Maslow's hierarchy of human needs.* According to the humanistic theorist Abraham Maslow (1954, 1971), our basic needs must be satisfied before our higher needs can become motivating. Maslow's **hierarchy of needs** states that individuals' main needs are satisfied in the sequence shown in figure 9.2. According to this hierarchy, people are motivated to satisfy their need for food (a physiological need) first, their need for safety must be satisfied before their need for love, and so on. **Self-actualization,** the highest and most elusive of Maslow's needs, is the motivation to develop one's full potential as a human being. According to Maslow, self-actualization is possible only after the other needs in the hierarchy are met. Maslow cautions that most people stop maturing after they have developed a high level of esteem and thus do not become self-actualized. (Self-actualization is discussed further in chapter 10 and in the video clip "Self-Actualization.") The idea that human motives are hierarchically arranged is an appealing one. Maslow's theory stimulates us to think about the ordering of motives in our own lives. However, the ordering is somewhat subjective. Some people might seek advancement in a career to achieve self-esteem while putting on hold their needs for love and belongingness.

In-Psych Plus

Review and Sharpen Your Thinking

1 ***Describe five psychological views of motivation.***

• Explain the evolutionary approach to motivation, drive reduction theory, optimum arousal theory, the cognitive approach, and Maslow's hierarchy of human needs.

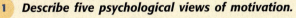

Advertisers often draw on Maslow's hierarchy of human needs to sell their products. Look through some magazine advertisements for evidence of Maslow's hierarchy.

hierarchy of needs Maslow's view that individuals' main needs are satisfied in the following sequence: physiological, safety, love and belongingness, esteem, and self-actualization.

self-actualization The highest and most elusive of Maslow's needs; the development of one's full potential as a human being.

2 HUNGER

Biology of Hunger

Obesity and Overeating

Dieting

Eating Disorders

Why do people eat, and why do they eat too much or too little?

As Maslow's hierarchy indicates, hunger is a very basic human need and a powerful motivator. Food is an important aspect of life in all cultures. Whether we have very little or large amounts of food available to us, hunger influences our behavior. We have to eat to stay alive. What mechanisms cause us to feel hungry?

Biology of Hunger

You are sitting in class and it is 2 P.M. You were so busy today that you skipped lunch. As the professor lectures, your stomach starts to growl, and you start feeling a little groggy. What role, if any, do such signals play in hunger?

Gastric Signals In 1912, Walter Cannon and A. L. Washburn conducted an experiment that revealed a close association between stomach contractions and hunger. As part of the procedure, a partially inflated balloon was passed through a tube inserted in Washburn's mouth and pushed down into his stomach (see figure 9.3). A machine that measures air pressure was connected to the balloon to monitor Washburn's stomach contractions. Every time Washburn reported hunger pangs, his stomach was also contracting. This finding, which was confirmed in subsequent experiments with other volunteers, led the two researchers to believe that gastric activity was the basis for hunger.

Stomach signals are not the only factors that affect hunger, however. People whose stomachs have been surgically removed still get hunger pangs.

The stomach can also send signals that stop hunger. We all know that a full stomach can decrease our appetite. In fact, the stomach actually tells the brain not only how full it is but also how much nutrient is present. That is why rich food stops your hunger faster than the same amount of water. A hormone, cholecystokinin, helps start the digestion of food, then travels to the brain through the bloodstream, and signals you to stop eating (Naslund, Hellstrom, & Krail, 2001).

Blood Chemistry There is a lot more involved in hunger than an empty stomach. Three important chemical substances are involved:

- *Glucose* (blood sugar) is an important factor in hunger, probably because the brain is critically dependent on sugar for energy. One set of sugar receptors, located in the brain itself, triggers hunger when sugar levels fall too low. Another set of sugar receptors is in the liver, which stores excess sugar and releases it into the blood when needed. The sugar receptors in the liver signal the brain when its sugar supply falls, and this signal can make you hungry.

- *Insulin,* a hormone, causes excess sugar in the blood to be stored in cells as fats and carbohydrates (Laboure

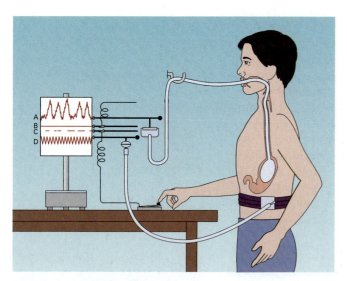

FIGURE 9.3 Cannon and Washburn's Classic Experiment on Hunger In this experiment, the researchers demonstrated that stomach contractions, which were detected by the stomach balloon, accompany a person's hunger feelings, which were indicated by pressing the key. Line A in the chart records increases and decreases in the volume of the balloon in the participant's stomach. Line B records the passage of time. Line C records the participant's manual signals of feelings of hunger. Line D records a reading from the belt wrapped around the participant's waist to detect movements of the abdominal wall and ensure that such movements are not the cause of changes in stomach volume.

FIGURE 9.4 Leptin and Obesity The genetically obese *ob* mouse on the left is untreated; the one on the right has been given injections of leptin.

& others, 2002). Insulin injections cause profound hunger because they lower blood sugar drastically. Psychologist Judith Rodin (1984) has investigated the role of insulin and glucose in hunger and eating behavior. She has pointed out that, when we eat complex carbohydrates, such as cereals, bread, and pasta, insulin levels go up and then fall off gradually. When we consume simple sugars, such as candy bars and soft drinks, insulin levels rise and then fall off sharply—the all-too-familiar "sugar low." Glucose levels in the blood are affected by complex carbohydrates and simple sugars in similar ways. The consequence is that we are more likely to feel hungry within the next several hours after eating simple sugars than after eating complex carbohydrates. And the food we eat at one meal often influences how much we will eat at our next meal. Thus, consuming doughnuts and candy bars, which provide no nutritional value, sets up an ongoing sequence of what and how much we probably will crave the next time we eat.

- *Leptin* (from the Greek word *leptos,* which means "thin") is involved in *satiety* (the sense of being full and not wanting to eat more). Leptin, a protein that is released by fat cells, decreases food intake and increases energy expenditure (Mito & others, 2004; Oberbauer & others, 2001). Leptin strongly affects metabolism and eating, acting as an antiobesity hormone (Misra & others, 2001). The role of leptin in long-term satiety was discovered in *ob mice,* a strain of genetically obese mice (Campfield & others, 1995; Carlson, 2001). The *ob* mouse has a low metabolism, overeats, and gets extremely fat. Because of a genetic mutation, the fat cells of *ob* mice cannot produce leptin. If *ob* mice are given daily injections of leptin, their metabolic rate increases, they become more active, and they eat less. Consequently, their weight falls to a normal level. Figure 9.4 shows an untreated *ob* mouse and an *ob* mouse that has received injections of leptin. In humans, leptin concentrations have been linked with weight, percentage of body fat, weight loss in a single diet episode, and cumulative percentage of weight loss in all diet episodes (Benini & others, 2001; van Dielen & others, 2002). Scientists are interested in the possibility that leptin can help obese individuals lose weight (Wauters & others, 2001).

Brain Processes   Chapter 2 described the central role of the hypothalamus in regulating important body functions, including hunger. More specifically, activity in two areas of the hypothalamus contributes to our understanding of hunger. The *lateral*

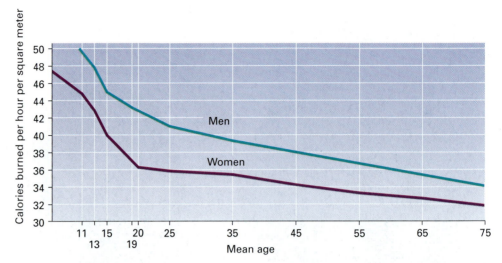

FIGURE 9.5 Changes in Basal Metabolism Rate with Age BMR varies with age and sex. Rates are usually higher for males and decline proportionately with age for both sexes.

hypothalamus is involved in stimulating eating. When it is electrically stimulated in a well-fed animal, the animal begins to eat. And if this area of the hypothalamus is destroyed, even a starving animal will show no interest in food. The *ventromedial hypothalamus* is involved in reducing hunger and restricting eating. When this area of an animal's brain is stimulated, the animal stops eating. When the area is destroyed, the animal eats profusely and quickly becomes obese.

Today, neuroscientists believe that much more of the brain helps in determining hunger than these on/off centers in the hypothalamus. They are exploring how neurotransmitters and neural circuits (clusters of neurons that often involve different parts of the brain) function in hunger.

Leptin influences eating by inhibiting the production of a neurotransmitter in the lateral hypothalamus that induces eating (Cowley & others, 2001; Sorensen & others, 2002a). The neurotransmitter serotonin is partly responsible for satiety, and drugs that block serotonin have been used to treat obesity in humans (Halford & Blundell, 2000; Thrybom, Rooth, & Lindstrom, 2001). Neural circuits involved in the action of such drugs may be in the brain stem, as well as in the hypothalamus (Carlson, 2001). The neural circuitry also extends to the cerebral cortex, where humans make decisions about whether to eat.

Obesity and Overeating

Approximately one-third of the American population is overweight enough to be at increased risk for health problems such as hypertension, cardiovascular disease, and diabetes. The health care costs linked to obesity are estimated to be $46 billion per year in the United States alone. And the rate of obesity is increasing: During the 1990s, the prevalence of obesity in the United States rose 8 percent (Friedman & Brownell, 1998). Obesity often becomes more common with increased age, especially among women (Engeland & others, 2004). Thus, as baby boomers age, the number of obese individuals is likely to increase.

Why do so many Americans overeat to the point of being obese? As is the case with much behavior, biological, cognitive, and sociocultural factors interact in diverse ways in different individuals, making it difficult to point to a specific cause. Let's look at some of the factors that are known to contribute to overeating, beginning with the biological causes.

Biology of Overeating Until recently, the genetic component of obesity was underestimated. As discussed earlier, scientists discovered an *ob* gene in mice that controls the production of leptin. In the 1990s, a similar gene was found in humans.

Some individuals do inherit a tendency to be overweight (Dancott & others, 2003; Yanovski & Yanovski, 2002). Only 10 percent of children who do not have obese parents become obese themselves, whereas 40 percent of children who have one obese parent become obese, and 70 percent of children who have two obese parents become obese. Researchers also have documented that animals can be inbred to have a propensity for obesity (Blundell, 1984). Further, identical human twins have similar weights, even when they are reared apart. Estimates of the degree to which heredity can explain obesity range from 25 to 70 percent.

Another factor in weight is **basal metabolism rate (BMR),** the minimal amount of energy an individual uses in a resting state. BMR varies with age and sex. It declines precipitously during adolescence and then more gradually in adulthood. It also is slightly higher for males than for females. Many people gradually increase their weight over many years. To some degree, this weight gain can be due to a declining basal metabolism rate (see figure 9.5).

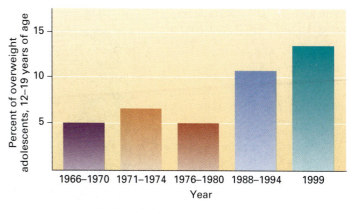

FIGURE 9.6 Increase in Adolescent Obesity in the United States

Set point, the weight maintained when no effort is made to gain or lose weight, is determined in part by the amount of stored fat in the body. Fat is stored in *adipose cells,* or fat cells. When these cells are filled, you do not get hungry. When people gain weight, the number of their fat cells increases. A normal-weight individual has 30 to 40 billion fat cells. An obese individual has 80 to 120 billion fat cells. Consequently, an obese individual has to eat more to feel satisfied. Some scientists have proposed that fat cells may shrink but might not go away.

Researchers have found that a high-fat diet may raise a person's set point for body weight (Frederich & others, 1995). They also have found that exercise can lower the body's set point for weight and contribute to weight loss (Jakicic, 2003; Rosenbaum, Leibel, & Hirsch, 1997).

Cognitive and Sociocultural Factors in Overeating Not too long ago, we believed that obesity was caused by eating in response to such factors as unhappiness or external food cues. But, according to Judith Rodin (1984), a number of biological, cognitive, and social factors are more important than emotional state and external stimuli. We already discussed some biological factors, including heredity, chemical substances, and brain processes.

In regard to cognitive and social factors, Rodin says that many people who respond to external cues also have the conscious ability to control their behavior and keep environmental food cues from controlling their eating patterns. Time and place do affect our eating, though. For example, when it is noon we are likely to feel hungry even if we have had a big breakfast and snacked at midmorning. We also associate eating with certain places. Many people link watching television with food and feel uncomfortable if they aren't eating something while they are watching TV.

Strong evidence of the environment's influence on weight is the doubling of the rate of obesity in the United States since 1900. Also, as shown in figure 9.6, obesity among adolescents in the United States has increased significantly since the late 1960s (National Center for Health Statistics, 2000b). Americans are more obese than Europeans and people in many other areas of the world.

The American culture provides substantial opportunities and encouragement for overeating. Food is everywhere you go, and it is easily accessed—in vending machines, at fast-food restaurants, at school or work. Nowhere else in the world will you find as many fast-food restaurants. Also, both portion size and the quantity of food that people eat at mealtime in the United States have grown. For example, fast-food restaurants give you the opportunity to "super-size" your meal at a relatively low additional cost. Also, a higher percentage of our food is made up of fat content than in the past. And, although we talk a lot about exercise, there is good evidence

basal metabolism rate (BMR) The minimal amount of energy an individual uses in a resting state.

set point The weight maintained when no effort is made to gain or lose weight.

Judith Rodin *(center)* has had a distinguished research and teaching career in psychology, and she became the first female president of an Ivy League university—the University of Pennsylvania—in 1993. She says that, as an undergraduate student at the University of Pennsylvania, she "fell in love with the field of psychology." In her book *Body Traps* (1993), Rodin argues that our society has constructed a number of psychological traps for women, such as the dieting rituals trap, which involves unrealistic expectations. She believes that too often women fall into the body traps of using goods and being thin as the measure of their self-worth. *What do you suppose Rodin means by "dieting rituals"?*

that Americans overall are getting less exercise than they did in the past (National Center for Health Statistics, 2000). In sum, an abundance of food in a culture that encourages food consumption, an increase in the amount of food eaten, a higher percentage of fat content in the food we eat, and a decrease in exercise add up to a population that has a serious number of overweight and obese individuals.

Dieting

Ironically, even as obesity is on the rise, dieting has become an obsession with many Americans. Many people spend their lives on one long diet, interrupted by occasional hot fudge sundaes or chocolate chip cookies. They are *restrained eaters,* individuals who chronically restrict their food intake to control their weight (Drobes & others, 2001). Restrained eaters are very conscious of what they eat and tend to feel guilty after splurging on sweets (Mulvihill, Davies, & Rogers, 2002). An interesting characteristic of restrained eaters is that, when they stop dieting, they tend to binge eat—that is, to eat large quantities of food in a short time (McFarlane, Polivy, & Herman, 1998).

The topic of dieting is of great interest to many others in the United States, including the public, health professionals, policy makers, the media, and the powerful diet and food industries. On one side are the societal norms that promote a lean body. This ideal is supported by $30 billion a year in sales of diet books, programs, videos, foods, and pills. On the other side are health professionals. Although they are alarmed by the rate of obesity, they are frustrated by high relapse rates and the widespread obsession with excessive thinness that can lead to chronic dieting and serious health risks.

Although many Americans regularly embark on diets, few are successful in keeping weight off in the long run. Whether some diet programs work better than others is still an open question. What we do know about losing weight is that the most effective programs include an exercise component (Sothern & others, 2002). Exercise not only burns calories but also continues to elevate the person's metabolic rate for several hours after the exercise. Also, exercise lowers a person's set point for weight, which makes it easier to maintain a lower weight (Bennett & Gurin, 1982).

Many people who are on diets should not be. A 10 percent reduction in body weight might produce striking benefits for an older, obese, hypertensive man yet be unhealthy for a female college student who is not overweight. The pressure to be thin, and thus to diet, is greatest among young women, yet they do not have the highest risk for obesity.

Diets may also place the dieter at risk for health problems. Listen to the audio clip "Teenage Dieting" to learn about the negative side effects of certain diets. One concern is weight cycling (commonly called "yo-yo dieting"), in which the person is in a recurring cycle of dieting and weight gain (Wadden & others, 1996). Researchers have found a link between frequent changes in weight and chronic disease (Brownell & Rodin, 1994). Also, liquid diets and other very low calorie strategies are related to gallbladder damage. But when overweight people diet and maintain their weight loss, they become less depressed and reduce their risk for a number of disorders that threaten their health and even their life (Christensen, 1996).

In-Psych Plus

Eating Disorders

This section examines two major eating problems, anorexia nervosa and bulimia nervosa. Both are more common in young women than in any other gender-age segment of the population.

Anorexia Nervosa   **Anorexia nervosa** is an eating disorder that involves the relentless pursuit of thinness through starvation. Anorexia nervosa can eventually lead to death. The main characteristics of anorexia nervosa are (Davison & Neale, 2001)

- Weighing less than 85 percent of what is considered normal for age and height
- Having an intense fear of gaining weight that does not decrease with weight loss
- Having a distorted body image (Dohm & others, 2001). Even when individuals with anorexia nervosa are extremely thin, they see themselves as fat, especially in the abdomen, buttocks, and thighs. They never think they are thin enough: They weigh themselves frequently, often take their body measurements, and gaze critically at themselves in mirrors.

Anorexia nervosa typically begins in the teenage years, often following an episode of dieting and some type of life stress (Lewinsohn, Striegel-Moore, & Seeley, 2000). About 10 times more females than males have anorexia nervosa. Although most U.S. adolescent girls go on diets at some point, less than 1 percent develop anorexia nervosa (Walters & Kendler, 1994). When anorexia nervosa does occur in males, its symptoms and other characteristics are usually similar to those reported by females who have the eating disorder (Muise, Stein, & Arbess, 2003; Olivardia & others, 1995).

Most anorexics are White adolescent or young adult females from well-educated, middle- and upper-income families that are competitive and high-achieving. Females who become anorexic often set high standards, become stressed about not being able to reach those standards, and are intensely concerned about how others perceive them (Striegel-Moore, Silberstein, & Rodin, 1993). Unable to meet their own high expectations, they turn to something they can control: their weight. The fashion slogan that "thin is beautiful" also contributes to the incidence of anorexia nervosa (Simpson, 2002).

About 70 percent of individuals with anorexia nervosa eventually recover. Recovery often takes 6 to 7 years, and relapses are common before a stable pattern of eating and weight maintenance is achieved (Kaye & others, 2000).

Bulimia Nervosa   **Bulimia nervosa** is an eating disorder in which the individual consistently follows a binge-and-purge eating pattern. The bulimic eats to excess and then purges by self-induced vomiting or using a laxative. As with anorexics, most bulimics are preoccupied with food, have a strong fear of becoming overweight, and

Might the current fashion image of "thin is beautiful" contribute to anorexia nervosa?

anorexia nervosa An eating disorder that involves the relentless pursuit of thinness through starvation.

bulimia nervosa An eating disorder in which the individual consistently follows a binge-and-purge eating pattern.

are depressed or anxious (Byrne & Mclean, 2002; Cooley & Toray, 2001). But unlike anorexia nervosa, bulimia nervosa occurs within a normal weight range, which means that it is often difficult to detect (Mizes & Miller, 2000; Speranta & others, 2003).

Bulimia nervosa typically begins in late adolescence or early adulthood (Levine, 2002). About 90 percent of bulimics are females. Approximately 1 to 2 percent of females are estimated to develop bulimia nervosa (Gotesdam & Agras, 1995). Many were somewhat overweight before the onset of the disorder, and the binge eating often begins during an episode of dieting. As with anorexia nervosa, about 70 percent of individuals with bulimia nervosa eventually recover from it (Keel & others, 1999). You can follow the case of Nancy, who had a long struggle with this disorder, in the video clip "Bulimia Nervosa."

Chapter 13 further explores eating patterns and proper nutrition.

In-Psych Plus

Review and Sharpen Your Thinking

2 *Explain what motivates people to eat and to eat too much or too little.*

- Discuss the biology of hunger.
- Describe the biological, cognitive, and sociocultural factors involved in overeating and obesity.
- Evaluate the benefits and risks of dieting.
- Distinguish between anorexia nervosa and bulimia nervosa.

The "freshman 15" refers to the approximately 15 pounds that many students gain in their first year of college. What factors might explain this weight increase?

---

3 SEXUALITY

- **Biology of Sex**
- **Psychosexual Dysfunctions**
- **Sexual Orientation**
- **Nonbiological Factors in Sexuality**
- **Sexual Attitudes and Practices**

What factors motivate our sexual behavior?

We do not need sex for everyday survival, the way we need food and water, but we do need it for the survival of the species. Like hunger, sex has a strong physiological basis, as well as cognitive and sociocultural components.

Biology of Sex

What brain areas are involved in sex? What role do hormones play in sexual motivation? What is the nature of the human sexual response?

Sex and the Brain   Motivation for sexual behavior is centered in the hypothalamus (Carter, 1998). However, like many other areas of motivation, brain functioning related to sex radiates outward to connect with a wide range of other brain areas in both the limbic system and the cerebral cortex.

The importance of the hypothalamus in sexual activity has been shown by electrically stimulating or surgically removing it. Electrical stimulation of certain hypothalamic areas increases sexual behavior; surgical removal of some hypothalamic areas

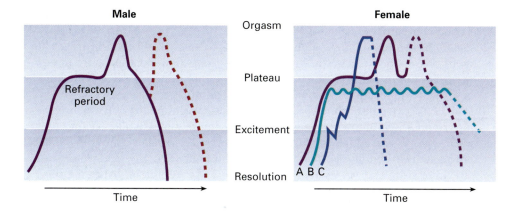

FIGURE 9.7 Male and Female Sexual Response Patterns Identified by Masters and Johnson *(Left)* Notice that males enter a refractory period, which lasts from several minutes up to a day, in which they cannot have another orgasm. *(Right)* Notice that female sexual responses follow one of three basic patterns: Pattern A somewhat resembles the male pattern, except it includes the possibility of multiple orgasms (the second peak) without falling below the plateau level. Pattern B represents nonorgasmic arousal. Pattern C represents intense female orgasm, which resembles the male pattern in its intensity and rapid resolution.

produces sexual inhibition. Electrical stimulation of the hypothalamus in a male can lead to as many as 20 ejaculations in 1 hour. The limbic system, which runs through the hypothalamus, also seems to be involved in sexual behavior. Its electrical stimulation can produce penile erection in males and orgasm in females.

In humans, the temporal lobes of the neocortex play an important role in moderating sexual arousal and directing it to an appropriate goal (Cheasty, Condren, & Cooney, 2002). And in male cats, temporal lobe damage has been shown to impair the ability to select an appropriate partner. Male cats with temporal lobe damage try to copulate with everything in sight: teddy bears, chairs, even researchers. Temporal lobe damage in humans also has been associated with changes in sexual activity (Trimble & Mendez, 1997).

The brain tissues that produce sexual feelings and behaviors are activated by various neurotransmitters in conjunction with various sex hormones. The intense reward of orgasm is caused by a massive rush of dopamine, and the deep feeling of relaxation that follows is linked with a hormone called oxytocin.

Sex Hormones Sex hormones are powerful chemicals that are controlled by the master gland in the brain, the pituitary gland. The two main classes of sex hormones are estrogens and androgens. **Estrogens,** the class of sex hormones that predominates in females, are produced mainly by the ovaries. **Androgens,** the class of sex hormones that predominates in males, are produced by the testes in males and by the adrenal glands in both males and females. Testosterone is an androgen. Estrogens and androgens can influence sexual motivation in both sexes.

The secretion of sex hormones is regulated by a feedback system. The pituitary gland monitors hormone levels and signals the testes or ovaries to manufacture sex hormones. Then the pituitary gland, through interaction with the hypothalamus, detects the point at which an optimal hormone level is reached and maintains this level.

The role of hormones in motivating human sexual behavior, especially for females, is not clear (Crooks & Bauer, 2002). For human males, higher androgen levels are associated with sexual motivation and orgasm frequency (Booth, Johnson, & Granger, 1999; Thijssen, 2002). Nonetheless, sexual behavior is so individualized in humans that it is difficult to specify the effects of hormones (Susman & Rogol, 2004).

Human Sexual Response Pattern What physiological changes do humans experience during sexual activity? To answer this question, gynecologist William Masters and his colleague Virginia Johnson (1966) carefully observed and measured the physiological responses of 382 female and 312 male volunteers as they masturbated or had sexual intercourse. The **human sexual response pattern** consists of four phases identified by Masters and Johnson (see figure 9.7).

1. *Excitement phase:* Lasts from several minutes to several hours, depending on the nature of the sex play involved. Engorgement of blood vessels and increased blood flow in genital areas and muscle tension characterize the excitement

estrogens The class of sex hormones that predominates in females.

androgens The class of sex hormones that predominates in males.

human sexual response pattern A sequence identified by Masters and Johnson; consists of four phases—excitement, plateau, orgasm, and resolution phase. The most obvious signs of response in this phase are lubrication of the vagina and partial erection of the penis.

2. *Plateau phase:* Continuation and heightening of the arousal begun in the excitement phase. The increases in breathing, pulse rate, and blood pressure that occurred during the excitement phase become more intense, penile erection and vaginal lubrication are more complete, and orgasm is closer.

3. *Orgasm:* Lasts for only about 3 to 15 seconds. Orgasm involves an explosive discharge of neuromuscular tension and an intensely pleasurable feeling. However, orgasms are not all exactly alike. For example, females show three different patterns in the orgasm phase, as shown in figure 9.7: (A) multiple orgasms, (B) no orgasm, and (C) excitement rapidly leading to orgasm, bypassing the plateau phase. The third pattern most clearly corresponds to the male pattern in intensity and resolution.

4. *Resolution phase:* Return of blood vessels to their normal state. One difference between males and females in this phase is that females may be stimulated to orgasm again without delay. Males enter a *refractory period,* lasting from several minutes to an entire day, in which they cannot have another orgasm. The length of the refractory period increases as men age.

Nonbiological Factors in Sexuality

From experience, we know that biology alone does not control human sexuality (Crooks & Bauer, 2002). Cognitive, sensory/perceptual, and cultural factors all play an important role.

Cognition and Sex   Consider the role of the mind. We might be sexually attracted to someone but understand that it is important to inhibit our sexual urges until the relationship has time to develop and we get to know the person better. We have the cognitive capacity to think about the importance of not raping or inflicting sexual harm on others. We also have the cognitive capacity to generate sexual images. For example, some individuals become sexually aroused by fantasy images of sex (Whipple, Ogden, & Komisaruk, 1992).

Sexual motivation is influenced by **sexual scripts**, stereotyped patterns of expectancies for how people should behave sexually. (Recall from the discussion of memory in chapter 7 that scripts are schemas for events.) Two sexual scripts are well known. In the *traditional religious script,* sex is accepted only within marriage. Extramarital sex is taboo, especially for women. Sex means reproduction and sometimes affection. In the *romantic script,* sex is equated with love. In this script, if we develop a relationship with someone and fall in love, it is acceptable to have sex with the person whether we are married or not. Typically, men and women have different sexual scripts. Females tend to link sexual intercourse with love more than males do, and males tend to emphasize sexual conquest. Some sexual scripts involve a double standard: For example, it is okay for male adolescents to have sex but not for females; women are generally expected to be responsible for contraception and are held solely to blame if they become pregnant.

Cognitive interpretation of sexual activity also involves our perception of the individual with whom we are having sex and his or her perception of us. We imbue our sexual acts with such perceptual questions as "Is he loyal to me?" "What is our future relationship going to be like?" "How important is sex to her?" "What if she gets pregnant?" Amid the wash of hormones in sexual activity is the cognitive ability to control, reason about, and try to make sense of the activity.

Sensation, Perception, and Sex   Along with cognitive factors, sensory/perceptual factors are involved in sexual behavior. The sensory system of touch usually predominates during sexual intimacy, but vision also plays an important role for some individuals (Brown, Steele, & Walsh-Childers, 2002). In general, women are more aroused by touch, men by what they see. This might explain why erotic magazines and movies are directed more toward males than toward females (Money, 1986).

sexual scripts Stereotyped patterns of expectancies for how people should behave sexually.

Might smell also be involved in sexual interest between women and men? **Pheromones** are scented substances that are powerful attractants in some animals (Beckman, 2002; Savic, 2002). Pheromones in the urine of ovulating female guinea pigs attract male guinea pigs. All the male cats in a neighborhood know that a female cat is in heat when they pick up the scent of pheromones. Several years ago, Jovan developed a fragrance the company claimed would attract men to women who wore it. The company advertised that the perfume contained a pheromone derived from human sweat. The fragrance was not the smashing success the perfumery anticipated, indicating that there is far more to sexual attraction in humans than smell.

Various foods and other substances also have been proposed as dramatically increasing sexual arousal. *Aphrodisiacs* are substances that supposedly arouse a person's sexual desire and increase his or her capacity for sexual activity. Recall from chapter 1 that I urged you to be skeptical about claims that eating ground-up tiger's penis will increase the male's sexual potency. Some foods, such as oysters, bananas, celery, tomatoes, and potatoes, are also touted as aphrodisiacs. Be wary of such claims. These foods do not influence sexual behavior. A substance referred to as "Spanish fly" also has been promoted as a powerful aphrodisiac. Not only is Spanish fly not an effective sexual stimulant, but it can cause genital inflammation, tissue damage, and even death.

Culture and Sex   The range of sexual values across cultures is substantial (Tolman & Diamond, 2003). Some cultures consider sexual pleasures to be "normal" or "desirable";

Sexual behavior has its magnificent moments throughout the animal kingdom. Insects mate in midair, peacocks display their plumage, and male elephant seals have prolific sex lives. Experience plays a more important role in human sexual behavior. We can talk about sex with each other, read about it in magazines, and watch it on television and the movie screen. *Which nonbiological factors make human sexual behavior different from that of other animals?*

pheromones Odorous substances released by animals that is a powerful sexual attractant.

other cultures view sexual pleasures as "weird" or "abnormal." We would consider the people who live on the small island of Ines Beag off the coast of Ireland to be among the most sexually repressed people in the world. They know nothing about tongue kissing or hand stimulation of the penis, and they detest nudity. For both females and males, premarital sex is out of the question. Men avoid most sexual experiences because they believe that sexual intercourse reduces their energy level and is bad for their health. Under these repressive conditions, sexual intercourse occurs only at night and takes place as quickly as possible as the husband opens his nightclothes under the covers and the wife raises her nightgown. As you might suspect, female orgasm is rare in this culture (Messinger, 1971).

In contrast, the Mangaian culture in the South Pacific seems promiscuous to us. In Mangaia, young boys are taught about masturbation and are encouraged to engage in it as much as they like. At age 13, the boys undergo a ritual that initiates them into sexual manhood. First, their elders instruct them about sexual strategies, including how to aid their female partner in having orgasms. Then, 2 weeks later, each boy has intercourse with an experienced woman who helps him hold back ejaculation until she can achieve orgasm with him. By the end of adolescence, Mangaians have sex pretty much every day. Mangaian women report a high frequency of orgasm.

Psychosexual Dysfunctions

Myths would have us believe that many women are uninterested in sexual pleasure and that most men can hardly get enough. Although men do think about sex more than women do, most men and women have desires for sexual pleasure, and both sexes can experience psychological problems that interfere with the attainment of sexual pleasure. (The video clip "Transvestic Fetishism" presents the example of men for whom cross-dressing is essential to sexual gratification.) **Psychosexual dysfunctions** are disorders that involve impairments in the sexual response pattern, either in the desire for gratification or in the ability to achieve it.

In-Psych Plus

In disorders associated with desire, both men and women show little or no sexual drive or interest. In disorders associated with the excitement phase, men may not be able to maintain an erection (Becker & others, 2002; McKinlay, 1999). In disorders associated with the orgasmic phase, both women and men reach orgasm either too quickly or not at all. Premature ejaculation in men occurs when the time between the beginning of sexual stimulation and ejaculation is unsatisfactorily brief. Many women do not routinely experience orgasm in sexual intercourse. Inhibited male orgasm does occur, but it is much less common than inhibited female orgasm.

The treatment of psychosexual dysfunctions has undergone a revolution in recent years. Once thought of as extremely difficult therapeutic challenges, most cases of psychosexual dysfunction now yield to techniques tailored to improve sexual functioning (Bhugra & de Silva, 1998; Crooks & Bauer, 2002). New treatments that focus directly on each sexual dysfunction have reached success rates of 90 percent or more (McConaghy, 1993). For example, the success rate of a treatment that encourages women to enjoy their bodies and engage in self-stimulation to orgasm, with a vibrator if necessary, approaches 100 percent (Anderson, 1983). Some of these women subsequently transfer their newly developed sexual responsiveness to interactions with partners.

Recently, attention has focused on Viagra, a drug designed to conquer impotence (Nehra & others, 2002; Seidman, 2002). Its success rate is in the range of 60 to 80 percent, and its prescription rate has outpaced such popular drugs as Prozac (antidepressant) and Rogaine (baldness remedy) in first-year comparisons (Padma-Nathan, 1999). However, Viagra is not an aphrodisiac; it won't work in the absence of desire. The downside of Viagra is headaches in 10 percent of men; temporary vision problems, ranging from blurred vision to a blue or green halo effect in about 3 percent of men; and blackouts due to a sudden drop in blood pressure (Steers & others, 2001). Also, scientists do not yet know the long-term effects of taking the drug, although in short-term trials it appears to be relatively safe.

psychosexual dysfunctions Disorders that involve impairments in the sexual response pattern, either in the desire for gratification or the ability to achieve it.

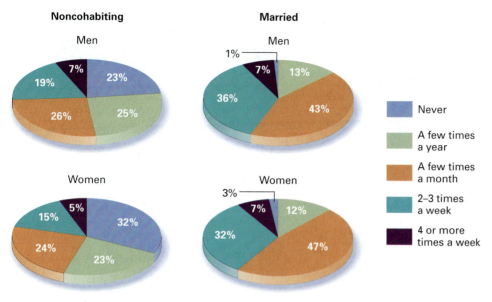

FIGURE 9.8 **1994** *Sex in America* **Survey** Percentages show noncohabiting and married males' and females' responses to the question "How often have you had sex in the past year?"

Sexual Attitudes and Practices

In the United States today, sexual behaviors and attitudes reflect a diverse, multicultural population, placing Americans somewhere in the middle of a continuum from repressive to liberal. But describing sexual practices in America has always been challenging (Dunne, 2002; Wiederman & Whitley, 2002).

In 1948, Alfred Kinsey and his colleagues shocked the nation with their report of a survey of Americans' sexual practices. It revealed that, among other observations, half of American men had engaged in extramarital affairs. However, Kinsey's results were not representative, because he recruited volunteers wherever he could find them, including hitchhikers who passed through town, fraternity men, and even mental patients. Despite the study's flaws, the Kinsey data were widely circulated, and many people felt that they must be leading more conservative sexual lives than others.

Subsequent large-scale magazine surveys confirmed a trend toward permissive sexuality (Hunt, 1974). In these surveys, Americans were portrayed as engaging in virtually unending copulation. However, most magazine polls are skewed because of the background of the readers who complete the surveys. For example, surveys in *Playboy* and *Cosmopolitan* might appeal to subscribers who want to use the survey to brag about their sexual exploits.

Not until 1994 were more accurate data obtained from a well-designed, comprehensive study of American's sexual patterns. Robert Michael and his colleagues (1994) interviewed nearly 3,500 people from 18 to 50 years of age who were randomly selected, a sharp contrast from earlier samples. Following are some of the key findings from that survey:

- Americans tend to fall into three categories: One-third have sex twice a week or more, one-third a few times a month, and one-third a few times a year or not at all.
- Married couples have sex most often and are the most likely to have orgasms when they do. Figure 9.8 portrays the frequency of sex for married and noncohabiting individuals in the year before the survey was taken.
- Most Americans do not engage in kinky sexual acts. When asked about their favorite sexual acts, the vast majority (96 percent) said that vaginal sex was "very" or "somewhat" appealing. Oral sex was in third place, after an activity that many might not even label a sexual act—watching a partner undress.

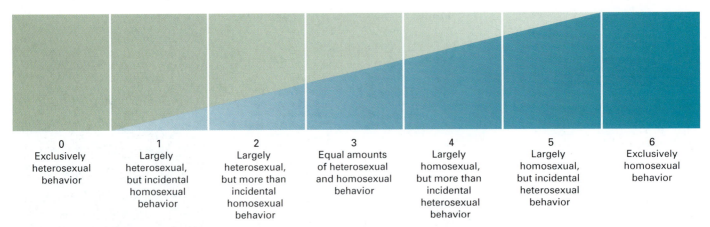

0	1	2	3	4	5	6
Exclusively heterosexual behavior	Largely heterosexual, but incidental homosexual behavior	Largely heterosexual, but more than incidental homosexual behavior	Equal amounts of heterosexual and homosexual behavior	Largely homosexual, but more than incidental heterosexual behavior	Largely homosexual, but incidental heterosexual behavior	Exclusively homosexual behavior

FIGURE 9.9 Continuum of Sexual Orientation The continuum ranges from exclusive heterosexuality, which Kinsey and associates (Kinsey, Pomeroy, & Martin, 1948) labeled 0, to exclusive homosexuality, labeled 6. People who are about equally attracted to both sexes, 2 to 4, are bisexual.

- Adultery is clearly the exception rather than the rule. Nearly 75 percent of the married men and 85 percent of the married women indicated that they have never been unfaithful.

- Men think about sex far more often than women do—54 percent of the men said they think about it every day or several times a day, whereas 67 percent of the women said they think about it only a few times a week or a few times a month.

One of the most powerful messages in the 1994 survey was that Americans' sexual lives are more conservative than previously believed. Although 17 percent of the men and 3 percent of the women said they have had sex with at least 21 partners, the overall impression from the survey was that sexual behavior is ruled by marriage and monogamy for most Americans.

We just mentioned that men think about sex more often than women do. Another gender difference is that women link sexual intercourse with love more than men do. A recent review of research also concluded that (Baumeister, Catanese, & Vohs, 2001): Men report more frequent feelings of sexual arousal, have more frequent sexual fantasies, and rate the strength of their own sex drive higher than women. Men also are more likely to masturbate, have more permissive attitudes about casual premarital sex, and have a more difficult time adhering to their vows of celibacy when they become married (Oliver & Hyde, 1993; Peplau, 2002, 2003).

According to sexuality expert Bernie Zilbergeld (1992), dramatic changes in the sexual landscape have taken place in the past several decades—from changing expectations of women to new definitions of masculinity, from the fear of disease to the renewed focus on long-term relationships. Sexuality's many myths have led to unrealistic expectations for our sexual lives. Among sexual myths, according to Zilbergeld (1992), are that men need a large penis to satisfy a woman; that male and female orgasm are absolutely necessary for sexual satisfaction; that intercourse is the only real sexual act; that good sex has to be spontaneous (without planning or talking); and that for men to have questions, doubts, or problems in sex is practically a crime.

Too often, people think of sex as a performance skill, like race car driving or swimming. However, sex is best conceptualized as a form of communication within a relationship (Hendrick, 2004). Indeed, caring couples with good communication skills can usually survive most sexual problems, whereas uncaring couples with poor communication skills often do not have lasting relationships even if their sexual experiences are adequate or even good.

Although the majority of us develop a mature sexuality, most experience some periods of vulnerability and confusion. (The video clip "Changing Genders" presents the example of Angela, who has chosen to undergo sex reassignment surgery.) Some

In-Psych Plus

worry about their sexual attractiveness, their ability to satisfy their sexual partner, and whether they will
experience their ultimate sexual
fantasy. Often our worries are fueled
by media images of sexual potency
and sexual exploits.

Sexual Orientation

Although Americans are more conservative in sexual habits than once
thought, we are somewhat more
open-minded regarding sexual orientation than a century ago. Until the
end of the nineteenth century, it was
generally believed that people were
either heterosexual or homosexual.
Today, it is more accepted to view
sexual orientation along a continuum
(Kelly, 2004). Kinsey & others,
(1948) described this continuum on a
scale ranging from 0 (exclusive heterosexuality) to 6 (exclusive homosexuality) (see figure 9.9). Also, some
individuals are *bisexual,* being sexually attracted to people of both sexes.

What determines sexual orientation?

In Kinsey's research, approximately 1 percent of individuals reported being bisexual
(1.2 percent of males and 0.7 percent of females), and about 2 to 5 percent of individuals reported being homosexual (4.7 percent of males and 1.8 percent of females). In the
1994 *Sex in America* survey, only 2.7 percent of the men and 1.3 percent of the women
reported that they had had homosexual sex in the past year (Michael & others, 1994).

Why are some individuals homosexual and others heterosexual? Speculation
about this question has been extensive, but no firm answers are available. Homosexuals and heterosexuals have similar physiological responses during sexual arousal
and seem to be aroused by the same types of touching. Investigators find no differences between homosexuals and heterosexuals in a wide range of attitudes, behaviors, and adjustments (Bell, Weinberg, & Mammersmith, 1981; Savin-Williams &
Diamond, 2004). Homosexuality once was classified as a mental disorder, but both
the American Psychiatric Association and the American Psychological Association discontinued this classification in the 1970s.

More recently, researchers have explored the possible biological basis of homosexuality (Gladue, 1994). The results of hormone studies have been inconsistent. If
male homosexuals are given male sex hormones (androgens), their sexual orientation
doesn't change; their sexual desire merely increases. But a very early prenatal critical
period might influence sexual orientation. In the second to fifth months after conception, exposure of the fetus to hormone levels characteristic of females might cause
the individual (whether male or female) to become attracted to males (Ellis & Ames,
1987). If this critical period hypothesis turns out to be correct, it would explain why
clinicians have found that sexual orientation is difficult, if not impossible, to modify.

With regard to anatomical structures, neuroscientist Simon LeVay (1991) found
that an area of the hypothalamus that governs sexual behavior is twice as large (about
the size of a grain of sand) in heterosexual males as in homosexual males. This area
was found to be about the same size in homosexual males and heterosexual females.
Critics of this research point out that many of the homosexuals in the study had AIDS
and suggest that their brains could have been altered by the disease.

An individual's sexual orientation—homosexual, heterosexual, or bisexual—is most likely determined by a combination of genetic, hormonal, cognitive, and environmental factors (Baldwin & Baldwin, 1998; Garnets, 2002). Most experts on homosexuality believe that no one factor alone causes homosexuality and that the relative weight of each factor can vary from one individual to the next. In effect, no one knows exactly why some individuals are homosexual.

Scientists have a clearer picture of what does not cause homosexuality. For example, children raised by gay or lesbian parents or couples are no more likely to be homosexual than children raised by heterosexual parents (Patterson, 2000, 2002). There also is no evidence that male homosexuality is caused by a dominant mother or a weak father or that female homosexuality is caused by girls choosing male role models.

Many gender differences that appear in heterosexual relationships also occur in homosexual relationships. Like heterosexual women (Peplau, 2002, 2003; Peplau, Fingerhut, & Beals, 2004),

- Lesbians' sexual fantasies are more likely than gay men's to be personal and romantic.
- Lesbians have fewer sex partners than gay men.
- Lesbians have less permissive attitudes about casual sex and sex outside a primary relationship than gay men.

How can gays and lesbians adapt to a world in which they are a minority? According to psychologist Laura Brown (1989), gays and lesbians experience life as a minority in a dominant majority culture. Brown believes that gays and lesbians adapt best when they don't define themselves in polarities, such as trying to live in a separate gay or lesbian world or completely accepting the majority culture. Instead, developing a bicultural identity and balancing the demands of the two cultures can often lead to more effective coping for homosexuals, says Brown.

Review and Sharpen Your Thinking

3 Discuss the motivation for sex.

- Describe the biology of sex.
- Identify cognitive, sensory/perceptual, and cultural factors that affect sexual behavior.
- Explain the nature and treatment of psychosexual dysfunctions.
- Characterize sexual behavior in the United States.
- Summarize the factors that determine sexual orientation.

A substance called "Spanish fly" has been promoted as a powerful aphrodisiac. As mentioned, it is not an effective sexual stimulant and can be dangerous. What might explain people's faith in this and other so-called aphrodisiacs?

4 NEED FOR ACHIEVEMENT

Cognitive Factors in Achievement

Sociocultural Factors in Achievement

What motivates people to achieve?

The previous discussions of hunger and sexual motivation focused to a large degree on physiological factors. Although there is a significant cognitive component to eating and sexual behavior, it does not always predominate. This section presents a motive

Calvin and Hobbes

by Bill Watterson

that has strong social cognitive foundations: the need for achievement. **Need for achievement** is the desire to accomplish something, to reach a standard of excellence, and to expend effort to excel. Some people are highly motivated to succeed and spend considerable effort striving to excel, like cyclist Lance Armstrong. But individuals differ in their achievement motivation. Others are not as motivated to succeed and don't work as hard to achieve. To explore your level of need for achievement, play a ring toss game in the interactivity "Need for Achievement."

Psychologist David McClelland (1955) assessed need for achievement by showing individuals ambiguous pictures. The individuals were asked to tell a story about the pictures, and their comments were scored according to how strongly they reflected achievement. Researchers also revealed that individuals whose stories reflected high achievement motivation had a stronger hope for success than fear of failure, were moderate rather than high or low risk takers, and persisted with effort when tasks became difficult (Atkinson & Raynor, 1974).

McClelland (1978) also wondered if increasing achievement motivation would actually encourage people to strive harder for success. To find out, he trained the businessmen in a village in India to be more achievement-oriented, encouraging them to increase their hope for success, reduce their fear of failure, take moderate risks, and try harder in the face of difficulty. Compared with businessmen in a nearby village, the men that McClelland trained started more new businesses and employed more new people in the 2 years after the training.

In-Psych Plus

Cognitive Factors in Achievement

Earlier in this chapter, I highlighted two key cognitive factors in motivation: intrinsic motivation, which is based on such internal factors as self-determination, curiosity, challenge, and effort, and extrinsic motivation, which involves external incentives, such as rewards and punishments. Intrinsic and extrinsic factors often work together to motivate achievement, as work on attribution shows. To think further about intrinsic and extrinsic motivation, see the Critical Controversy box.

Attribution   **Attribution theory** states that individuals are motivated to discover the causes of behavior in an effort to make sense of it. Like intuitive scientists, people seek the cause behind what happens. (Attribution is also discussed in chapter 14.)

The reasons individuals behave the way they do can be classified in a number of ways, but one basic distinction stands out above all others—the distinction between internal causes—such as personality traits or motives—and external causes—environmental, situational factors, such as rewards or task difficulty (Heider, 1958). If

need for achievement The desire to accomplish something, to reach a standard of excellence, and to expend effort to excel.

attribution theory The idea that individuals are motivated to discover the underlying causes of behavior as part of their effort to make sense of it.

Does Extrinsic Motivation Undermine Intrinsic Motivation?

The distinction between intrinsic and extrinsic motivation is well established in psychology (Alderman, 2004). The basic idea is that we can be motivated by internal (intrinsic) factors, such as self-generated goals, or external (extrinsic) factors, such as praise or a monetary reward. It is commonly argued that intrinsic motivation is preferable to extrinsic motivation because it leads to more positive outcomes (Deci, Koestner, & Ryan, 2001). Also extrinsic motivation is thought to reduce intrinsic motivation (Lepper, Greene, & Nisbett, 1973). A wide variety of social (extrinsic) events, such as deadlines, surveillance, and coercive rewards, can reduce the enjoyment (intrinsic motivation) associated with work, play, and study. These ideas have exerted a board influence in educational and occupational settings, where teachers and employers seek to increase the intrinsic motivation of their students and employees, respectively (Stipek, 2001; Wigfield & Eccles, 2002).

Recently, however, two reviews of studies on intrinsic and extrinsic motivation (Cameron, 2001; Deci, Koestner, & Ryan, 2001) reached opposite conclusions. Edward Deci and his colleagues (2001) analyzed more than 100 studies and concluded that the main negative effect of external rewards was to restrict self-determination and interfere with intrinsic motivation. In contrast, an analysis of more than 100 studies by Judy Cameron (2001) yielded mixed results. Cameron found that extrinsic rewards sometimes produced the expected negative effects on intrinsic motivation but that sometimes they had a positive effect or no effect at all. The true state of affairs, they suggest, is that extrinsic motivation has no overall effect on intrinsic motivation.

For example, some psychologists argue that tangible reinforces, such as money or prizes, often undermine intrinsic motivation, whereas verbal reinforcers, such as praise, can actually enhance intrinsic motivation (Lepper, Greene, & Nisbett, 2001). Thus paying a beginning reader money to read books may undermine that child's interest in reading, but praising that child for good reading may increase the child's interest. Similarly, Cameron (2001) believes that extrinsic motivation undermines intrinsic motivation when intrinsic motivation is high but can be very helpful when intrinsic motivation is low. Thus many beginning readers are motivated to read and may actually lose interest if they are reinforced for reading. In contrast, children who are not internally motiviated to read may benefit from reinforcement and encouragement until their intrinsic motivation increases.

The problem, according to Cameron (2001), lies in the rigid acceptance of general statements about motivation, such as "extrinsic motivation reduces internal motovation." In the case of beginning readers, using this statement as a guiding principle may not damage the intrinsic motivation of motivated readers, but it may also leave poorly motivated beginning readers with little reason to practice their reading. Cameron argues that people often do things that are not intrinsicially motivating (such as mowing the lawn or studying mathematics) and that, without external rewards, we may simply lose interest in doing them. In such cases, extrinsic motivation may help foster intrinsic motivation in an activity. For example, a creative mathematics teacher might use rewards, such as extra credit, math games, and verbal praise, as a way to instill a life-long love of mathematics.

Cameron (2001) suggests that we need a better understanding of extrinsic rewards and intrinsic motivation, to distinguish between the effects of verbal and material reinforcement, for example, and between weak and strong intrinsic motivation. A richer understanding of intrinsic and extrinsic motivation might make it possible to better predict when extrinsic motivation will reduce, increase, or not affect intrinsic motivation. We might then be able to help more employees and students develop the deep intrinsic motivation that most of us agree is indispensable to well-being.

What do you think?

- Can you think of examples from your own life where your intrinsic motivation was reduced by external rewards? Increased by external rewards?

- What are some other factors that might determine whether extrinsic motivation influences intrinsic motivation?

- If you were a classroom teacher and a child in your class was not motivated to learn, how would you use intrinsic and/or extrinsic motivation to help the child become more motivated to learn?

college students do not do well on a test, do they attribute their low score to the teacher's plotting against them and making the test too difficult (external cause) or to not studying hard enough (internal cause)? The answer to such a question influences how people feel about themselves. If students believe that their performance is the teacher's fault, they will not feel as bad when they do poorly as they will if they believe they did not spend enough time studying.

An extremely important aspect of internal cause for achievement is *effort*. Unlike many causes of success, effort is under a person's control and can be changed. The importance of effort in achievement is recognized even by children. In one study, third- to sixth-grade students felt that effort was the most effective strategy for good school performance (Skinner, Wellborn, & Connell, 1990).

Self-Generated Goals   One cognitive factor that helps individuals to reach their dreams, increase their self-discipline, and maintain interest is a set of goals that they determine on their own. Goal setting, planning, and self-monitoring are critical aspects of achievement (Brophy, 2004; Pintrich & Schunk, 2002) and often work in concert.

Researchers have found that individuals' achievement improves when they set goals with three qualities (Bandura, 1997; Schunk, 2000, 2004):

- *Specific*. A nonspecific goal is "I want to be successful." A concrete, specific goal is "I want to have a 3.5 average at the end of the semester."
- *Short-term*. It is okay to set long-term goals, such as "I want to be a clinical psychologist," but, if you do, make sure that you also create short-term goals as steps along the way. "I want to get an *A* on the next psychology test" or "I will do all of my studying for this class by 4 P.M. Sunday" is an example of a short-term goal.
- *Challenging*. Strong interest and eager involvement are sparked by challenges. Goals that are too easy to reach generate little interest or effort. However, unrealistically high goals can bring failure and diminish self-confidence.

Planning how to reach a goal and monitoring progress toward the goal are critical aspects of achievement (Eccles, Wigfield, & Schiefele, 1998). High-achieving individuals monitor their learning and systematically evaluate progress toward their goals more than low-achieving individuals do (Zimmerman, 2001; Zimmerman & Schunk, 2001, 2004). To evaluate how goal-directed you are, see the Psychology and Life box.

Sociocultural Factors in Achievement

Our sociocultural contexts also contribute to our motivation to achieve (Eccles, 2004; Wigfield & Eccles, 2002). This section on sociocultural factors focuses on comparisons across cultures and ethnicities. (The video clip "Culture and Self" also explores differences in motivation for achievement across cultures.)

Cross-Cultural Comparisons   One study of 104 societies revealed that, in general, parents in nonindustrialized countries placed a lower value on their children's achievement and independence and a higher value on obedience and cooperation than did parents in industrialized countries (Barry, Child, & Bacon, 1959). People in the United States are more achievement-oriented than people in many other countries. However, some cultures appear to value achievement, especially in school,

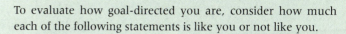
How Goal-Directed Are You?

To evaluate how goal-directed you are, consider how much each of the following statements is like you or not like you.

1. I set long-term and short-term goals.
2. I set challenging goals that are neither too easy nor beyond my reach.
3. I am good at managing my time and setting priorities to make sure I get the most important things done.
4. I regularly make "to-do" lists and successfully get most items done.
5. I set deadlines and consistently meet them.
6. I regularly monitor how well I'm progressing toward my goals and make changes in my behavior if necessary.
7. When I am under pressure, I still plan my days and weeks in a clear, logical manner.

If most of these statements characterize you, then you likely are a goal-directed individual. If these statements do not characterize you, then consider ways that you can become more goal-directed.

Asian students score considerably higher than U.S. students on math achievement tests. *What are some possible explanations for this?*

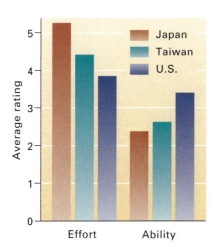

FIGURE 9.10 Mothers' Beliefs About the Factors Responsible for Children's Math Achievement in Three Countries In one study, mothers in Japan and Taiwan were more likely to believe that their children's math achievement was due to effort rather than to innate ability, whereas U.S. mothers were more likely to believe their children's math achievement was due to innate ability (Stevenson, Lee, & Stigler, 1986).

more than Americans do. In one study, American eighth-grade students fell in the average range in math and science tests comparing students from 45 countries (Atkin & Black, 1997). Students from Korea, Singapore, and Japan scored the highest.

Harold Stevenson and his colleagues (Stevenson, 1995, 2000; Stevenson & Hofer, 1999; Stevenson, Lee, & Stigler, 1986; Stevenson & others, 1990) have completed five cross-cultural studies of students in the United States, China, Taiwan, and Japan. In these studies, Asian students consistently outperform American students. And the longer they are in school, the wider the gap between Asian and American students becomes—the lowest difference is in the first grade, the highest in eleventh grade (the highest grade studied). To learn more about the reasons for these large cross-cultural differences, Stevenson and his colleagues spent thousands of hours observing in classrooms, as well as interviewing and surveying teachers, students, and parents. They found that Asian teachers spent more time teaching math than American teachers did: For example, more than one-fourth of total classroom time in the first grade was spent on math instruction in Japan, compared with only one-tenth of the time in U.S. first-grade classrooms. Also, Asian students were in school an average of 240 days a year, compared with 178 days in the United States.

Stevenson and his colleagues also found differences in Asian and American parents. American parents had much lower expectations for their children's education and achievement than Asian parents did. Also, American parents were likelier to believe that their children's math achievement is due to innate ability, whereas Asian parents were more likely to believe that their children's math achievement is the consequence of effort and training (see figure 9.10). Asian students were more likely than American students to do math homework, and Asian parents were far more likely to help their children with their math homework than American parents were (Chen & Stevenson, 1989).

In another cross-cultural comparison of math education, researchers analyzed videotapes of eighth-grade teachers' instruction in the United States, Japan, and Germany (Stigler & Hiebert, 1997). Differences included these: (1) Japanese students spent less time solving routine math problems and more time inventing, analyzing, and proving than American or German students; (2) Japanese teachers engaged in more direct lecturing than American or German teachers; and (3) Japanese teachers were more likely to emphasize math thinking, whereas American and German teachers were more likely to stress math skills (solving a specific problem or using a specific formula). Also noticeable was the emphasis on collaborative planning with other teachers in Japanese math education.

An important conclusion from these cross-cultural studies is that learning and achievement take time and effort. The more time students spend learning, the more likely they are to learn the material and achieve high standards.

Ethnic Comparisons   Until recently, researchers studying achievement focused almost exclusively on White males, and any studies of achievement in ethnic minorities measured them against standards of achievements for White males. As a result, many researchers unfortunately concluded that ethnic minorities were somehow deficient in achievement (Gibbs & Huang, 1989).

In addition, most studies on ethnic minorities have not taken into account socioeconomic status. *Socioeconomic status (SES)* is determined by a combination of occupation, education, and income. When both ethnicity and socioeconomic status are taken into account in the same study, socioeconomic status tends to be a far better predictor of achievement than is ethnicity (Graham, 1986, 2001). For example, middle SES individuals, regardless of their ethnic background, have higher aspirations and expectations than low SES individuals do. Sandra Graham (1986) has found that middle SES African American children, like middle SES White children, have high expectations for their own achievement and understand that failure is often due to lack of effort rather than to bad luck.

Psychologist Sandra Graham, from University of California, Los Angeles, talking with young boys about motivation. Dr. Graham's research shows that both African American and White middle-class children have high achievement expectations and attribute failures to lack of effort, rather than to lack of luck.

Review and Sharpen Your Thinking

4 **Explain why people are motivated to achieve.**

- Discuss the need for achievement and the factors that motivate people to excel.

Make a list of the factors that motivate you to achieve, whether at school, at work, in sports, or in some other endeavor. Which of these factors are intrinsic and which are extrinsic?

EMOTION 5

Biology of Emotion   Nonbiological Factors in Emotion   Classification of Emotions

What are the factors that influence emotion?

The terms *motivation* and *emotion* both come from the Latin word *movere,* which means "to move." Both motivation and emotion spur us into action. And just as there are different kinds and intensities of motivation, so it is with emotions. A person can be more motivated to eat than to have sex and at different times can be more or less hungry or more or less interested in having sex. Similarly, a person can be happy—ranging from pleased to ecstatic—or angry—ranging from annoyed to fuming.

Defining emotion is difficult because it is not always easy to tell when a person is in an emotional state. For our purposes, **emotion** is defined as feeling, or affect, that can involve physiological arousal (a fast heartbeat, for example), conscious experience (thinking about being in love with someone, for example), and behavioral expression (a smile or grimace, for example). Thus the body, the mind, and the face all play important roles in emotion, although psychologists debate which of these components is the most important aspect of emotion and how they mix to produce emotional experiences.

Biology of Emotion

As you drive down the highway, the fog thickens. Suddenly you see a pile of cars in front of you. Your mind temporarily freezes, your muscles tighten, your stomach becomes queasy, and your heart feels as if it is going to pound out of your chest. You immediately slam on the brakes and try to veer away from the pile of cars. Tires screech, windshield glass flies, and metal smashes. Then all is quiet. After a few short seconds, you realize that you are alive. You find that you can climb out of the car. Your fear turns to joy, as you sense your luck in not being hurt. In a couple of seconds, the joy turns to anger. You loudly ask, "Who caused this accident?" As your emotions change from fear to joy to anger, your body changes also.

emotion A feeling, or affect, that can involve physiological arousal, conscious experience, and behavioral expression.

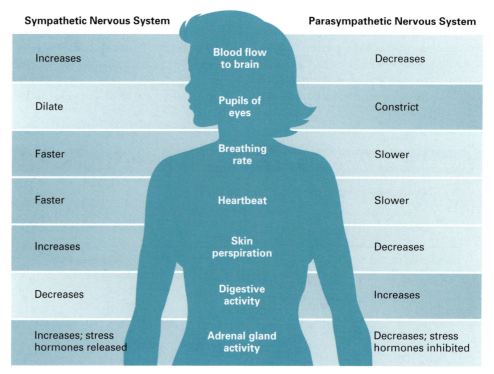

Sympathetic Nervous System		Parasympathetic Nervous System
Increases	**Blood flow to brain**	Decreases
Dilate	**Pupils of eyes**	Constrict
Faster	**Breathing rate**	Slower
Faster	**Heartbeat**	Slower
Increases	**Skin perspiration**	Decreases
Decreases	**Digestive activity**	Increases
Increases; stress hormones released	**Adrenal gland activity**	Decreases; stress hormones inhibited

FIGURE 9.11 **Autonomic Nervous System and Its Role in Arousing and Calming the Body**

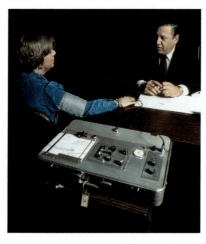

Examiners use a polygraph to determine if someone is lying. A polygraph monitors changes in the body believed to be influenced by emotional states. Controversy has swirled about the polygraph's use because it is unreliable. *What makes the polygraph unreliable?*

polygraph A machine that monitors changes in the body thought to be influenced by emotional states; it is used by examiners to try to determine if someone is lying.

Arousal Recall from chapter 2 that the *autonomic nervous system (ANS)* takes messages to and from the body's internal organs, monitoring such processes as breathing, heart rate, and digestion. The ANS is divided into the sympathetic and the parasympathetic nervous systems (see figure 9.11). The *sympathetic nervous system (SNS)* is involved in the body's arousal; it is responsible for a rapid reaction to a stressor, sometimes referred to as the fight-or-flight response. The SNS immediately causes an increase in blood pressure, a faster heart rate, more rapid breathing for greater oxygen intake, and more efficient blood flow to the brain and major muscle groups. All of these changes prepare us for action. At the same time, the body stops digesting food, which is not necessary for immediate action (this could explain why, just before an exam, students usually are not hungry). The *parasympathetic nervous system (PNS)* calms the body and promotes relaxation and healing. When the PNS is activated, heart rate and blood pressure drop, stomach activity and food digestion increase, and breathing slows.

The sympathetic and parasympathetic nervous systems evolved to improve the human species' likelihood for survival, but it does not take a life-threatening situation to activate them. Emotions, especially anger, are associated with elevated SNS activity, such as heightened blood pressure and heart rate. States of happiness and contentment also activate the SNS to a lesser extent.

Because arousal includes a physiological response, researchers have been intrigued by how to measure it accurately. One aspect of emotional arousal is *galvanic skin response (GSR)*, an increase in the skin's electrical conductivity when sweat gland activity increases. Measurement of this electrical activity provides an index of arousal that has been used in a number of studies of emotion.

Another measure of arousal is the **polygraph,** a machine used by examiners to try to determine if someone is lying; it monitors changes in the body thought to be influenced by emotional states. In a typical polygraph test, an individual is asked a number of neutral questions and several key, less neutral questions. If the individual's heart rate, breathing, and skin resistance to passage of a weak electric current

In-Psych Plus

increase substantially when the key questions are asked, the individual is assumed to be lying. (Lying has also been linked with certain facial expressions, as discussed in the video clip "Detecting Deception.")

Accurately identifying truth or deception is linked with the skill of the examiner and the skill of the individual being examined. Heart rate and breathing can increase for reasons other than lying, making it difficult to interpret these physiological indicators of arousal. Body movements and the presence of certain drugs in the person's system can interfere with the polygraph's accuracy. Experts believe that the polygraph errs just under 50 percent of the time and that it cannot distinguish between such feelings as anxiety and guilt (Iacono & Lykken, 1997). The Employee Polygraph Protection Act of 1988 restricts polygraph testing outside government agencies, and most courts do not accept the results of polygraph testing. Some psychologists defend the polygraph's use, saying that polygraph results are as sound as other, admissible forms of evidence, such as hair fiber analysis (Honts, 1998). The majority of psychologists, though, argue against the polygraph's use because of its basic inability to tell who is lying and who is not (Greenberg, 2002; Malakoff, 2003).

Psychologists are also interested in how arousal is interpreted as emotion. Imagine that you and your date are enjoying a picnic in the country. Suddenly, a bull runs across the field toward you. Why are you afraid? One well-known theory is that each emotion, from anger to rapture, arises from the perception of a distinct set of one's own physiological changes, evident in heart rate, breathing patterns, sweating, and other responses (James, 1890/1950; Lange, 1922). You see the bull scratching his hoof on the ground, and you begin to run away. Your aroused body then sends sensory messages to your brain, at which point emotion is perceived. According to this theory, you do not run away because you are afraid; rather, you are afraid because you are running away.

Another well-known theory is much the same, but it argues that different emotions cannot be associated with specific physiological changes (Bard, 1934; Cannon, 1927). Autonomic nervous system responses are too diffuse and slow to account for rapid and differentiated emotional responses. Imagine the picnic and the bull once again. Seeing the bull scratching his hoof causes the thalamus of your brain to do two things simultaneously: stimulate your autonomic nervous system to produce the physiological changes involved in emotion (increased heart rate, rapid breathing) and send messages to your cerebral cortex, where the experience of emotion is perceived. In this theory, emotion and physiological reactions occur simultaneously, and the body plays a less important role.

The question of whether or not emotions involve discrete autonomic nervous system responses continues to be debated (Christie & Friedman, 2004; Keltner & Ekman, 2000). Recent studies have documented some emotion-specific autonomic nervous system responses, though (Lang, Davis, & Ohman, 2000). For example, fear, anger, and sadness are associated with increased heart rate, but disgust is not. Also, anger is linked with increased blood flow to the hands, an effect that is not triggered by fear.

Neural Circuits and Neurotransmitters Contemporary researchers are interested in charting the neural circuitry of emotions and discovering the role of neurotransmitters. The focus of much of their work has been the amygdala, an almond-shaped structure in the limbic system (discussed in chapter 2). The amygdala houses circuits that are activated when we experience negative emotions.

Joseph LeDoux (1996, 2000, 2001, 2002; LaBar & LeDoux, 2002) has conducted a number of studies that focus on the neural circuitry of one emotion: fear. When the amygdala determines that danger is present, it shifts into high gear, marshaling the resources of the brain in an effort to protect the organism. The amygdala receives neurons from all of the senses: sight, hearing, smell, touch. If a danger is communicated by any of these neurons, the amygdala immediately sends out messages to bodily organs. This fear system was designed by evolution to detect and respond to predators and other natural dangers that threatened survival or territory.

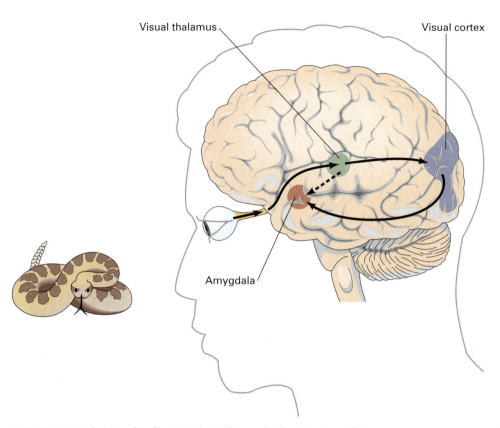

FIGURE 9.12 Direct and Indirect Brain Pathways in the Emotion of Fear Information about fear can follow two pathways in the brain. The direct pathway *(broken arrow)* conveys information rapidly from the thalamus to the amygdala. The indirect pathway *(solid arrows)* transmits information more slowly from the thalamus to the sensory cortex, then to the amygdala.

The brain circuitry that involves the emotion of fear can follow two pathways: a direct pathway from the thalamus to the amygdala or an indirect pathway from the thalamus through the sensory cortex to the amygdala (see figure 9.12). The direct pathway does not convey detailed information about the stimulus, but it has the advantage of speed. And speed clearly is important when an organism faces a threat to its survival. The indirect pathway carries nerve impulses from the sensory organs (eye or ear, for example) to the thalamus. From the thalamus, the nerve impulses travel to the sensory cortex, which then sends appropriate signals to the amygdala.

The amygdala is also linked with emotional memories. LeDoux (2000, 2001) says that the amygdala hardly ever forgets. This quality is useful because, once we learn that something is dangerous, we don't have to relearn it. However, we pay a penalty for this ability. Many people carry fears that they would like to get rid of but cannot seem to shake. Part of the reason for this dilemma is that the amygdala is well connected to the cerebral cortex, in which thinking and decision making primarily occur (McGaugh & Cahill, 2002). The amygdala is in a much better position to influence the cerebral cortex than the other way around, because it sends more connections to the cerebral cortex than it gets back. This may explain why it is so hard to control our emotions, and why, once a fear is learned, it is so hard to erase.

Researchers are also finding that the cerebral hemispheres may be involved in understanding emotion. Richard Davidson and his colleagues (Davidson 2000; Davidson, Shackman, & Pizzagalli, 2002; Reuter-Lorenz & Davidson, 1981) Davidson, have shown that *approach-related emotions,* such as happiness, are linked more strongly with left-hemisphere brain activity, whereas *withdrawal-related emotions,* such as disgust, show stronger activity in the right hemisphere. (Go to the interactivity "Brain Lateralization" to see which hemisphere you use to process information about emotions.)

In-Psych Plus

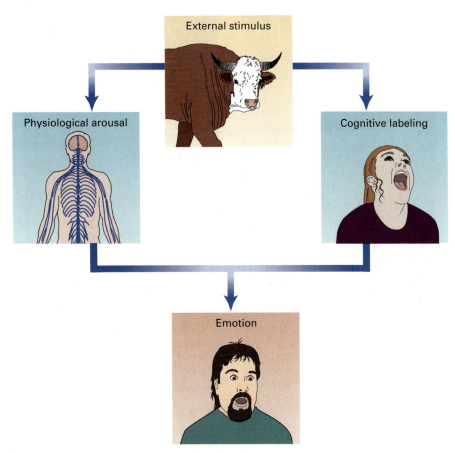

FIGURE 9.13 Two-Factor Theory of Emotion As Schachter and Singer theorize, emotion has both a physiological and an emotional component.

In addition to charting the main brain structures involved in neural pathways of emotions, researchers are intrigued by the roles that neurotransmitters play in these pathways. Endorphins and dopamine might be involved in positive emotions, such as happiness, and norepinephrine might function in regulating arousal (Berridge & O'Neil, 2001; Panskepp, 1993; Robbins, 2000).

Nonbiological Factors in Emotion

Remember that our definition of emotion includes not only a physiological component but also cognitive, behavioral, and sociocultural components. A queasy feeling, for example, may be interpreted as anxiety, love, or indigestion. What the person does in response will also vary, depending on individual factors as well as on the responses suggested by the person's culture.

Cognitive Factors in Emotion Does emotion depend on the tides of the mind? Are we happy only when we think we are happy? Cognitive theories of emotion center on the premise that emotion always has a cognitive component (Derryberry & Reed, 2002; Ellsworth, 2002). Cognitive theorists recognize the role of the brain and body in emotion, but they give cognitive processes the main credit.

According to the **two-factor theory of emotion** developed by Stanley Schachter and Jerome Singer (1962), emotion is determined by physiological arousal and cognitive labeling (see figure 9.13). They argue that we look to the external world for an explanation of why we are aroused. For example, if you feel good after someone has made a pleasant comment to you, you might label the emotion "happy." If you feel bad after you have done something wrong, you might label the feeling

two-factor theory of emotion
Schachter and Singer's theory that emotion is determined by two main factors: physiological arousal and cognitive labeling.

 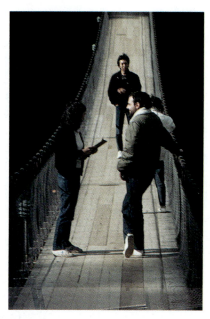

FIGURE 9.14 Capilano River Bridge Experiment *(Left)* The precarious Capilano River Bridge in British Columbia. *(Right)* The experiment is shown in progress. An attractive woman approached men while they were crossing the bridge and asked them to make up a story to help her with a creativity project. She also made the same request on a lower, much safer bridge. The men on the Capilano River Bridge told sexier stories, probably because they were aroused by the fear or excitement of being up so high on a swaying bridge and they interpreted their arousal as sexual attraction for the female interviewer.

"guilty." To test their theory, Schachter and Singer (1962) injected volunteer participants with epinephrine, a drug that produces high arousal. Then the participants observed someone else behave in either a euphoric way (shooting papers at a wastebasket) or an angry way (stomping out of the room). As predicted, the euphoric and angry behaviors influenced the participants' cognitive interpretation of their own arousal. When they were with a happy person, they said they were happy; when they were with an angry person, they said they were angry. But this effect occurred only when the participants were not told about the true effects of the injection. When they were told that the drug would increase their heart rate and make them jittery, they said the reason for their own arousal was the drug, not the other person's behavior.

Psychologists have had difficulty replicating Schachter and Singer's experiment, but, in general, research supports the belief that misinterpreted arousal intensifies emotional experiences (Leventhal & Tomarken, 1986). In one intriguing study, Dutton and Aron (1974) substantiated this conclusion. An attractive woman approached men without a female companion while they were walking across the Capilano River Bridge in British Columbia. The woman asked the men to make up a brief story for a project she was doing on creativity. The Capilano River Bridge sways precariously more than 200 feet above rapids and rocks (see figure 9.14). The female interviewer made the same request of other men crossing a lower, much safer bridge. The men on the Capilano River Bridge told more sexually oriented stories and rated the female interviewer as more attractive than did men on the lower, less frightening bridge.

Psychologists continue to debate whether cognition or emotion comes first. Richard Lazarus (1991) believes cognitive activity is a precondition for emotion. He says that we cognitively appraise ourselves and our social circumstances and develop emotions in that context. People may feel happy because they have a deep religious commitment, angry because they did not get the raise they anticipated, or fearful because they expect to fail an exam. Alternatively, Robert Zajonc (1984) says that emotions are primary and our thoughts are a result of them. Who is right? Both likely are. Some of our emotional reactions are virtually instantaneous and probably do not

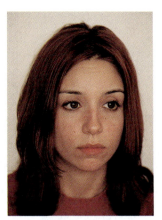

FIGURE 9.15 Recognizing Emotions in Facial Expressions Before reading further, look at the six faces and determine the emotion reflected in each face. They are *(top row across)* happiness, anger, sadness; *(bottom row across)* surprise, disgust, fear.

involve cognitive appraisal, such as shrieking on detecting a snake. Other emotional circumstances, especially those that occur over a long period, such as a depressed mood or anger toward a friend, are more likely to involve cognitive appraisal. Indeed, neuroscientific research supports the idea that some of our emotional reactions do not involve deliberate thinking, whereas others do (LeDoux, 2000, 2001).

Behavioral Factors in Emotion The behavioral component of emotion can be verbal or nonverbal. Verbally, a person might show love for someone by professing it or might display anger by saying some nasty things. Nonverbally, a person might smile, frown, show a fearful expression, look down, or slouch.

Emotion researchers have been intrigued by people's ability to detect emotion from a person's facial expression. In a typical research study, participants shown photographs like those in figure 9.15 are usually able to identify these six emotions: happiness, anger, sadness, surprise, disgust, and fear (Ekman & O'Sullivan, 1991). (See the video clip "Language of the Face" to learn more about the messages we convey with facial expressions.)

In-Psych Plus

Might our facial expressions not only reflect our emotions but also influence them? The **facial feedback hypothesis** states that facial expressions can influence emotions, as well as reflect them. Facial muscles send signals to the brain, which help individuals to recognize the emotion they are experiencing (Keillor & others, 2002). For example, we feel happier when we smile and sadder when we frown. Support for this hypothesis comes from an experiment by Ekman and his colleagues (1983). Professional actors moved their facial muscles in very precise ways, such as raising their eyebrows and pulling them together, raising their upper eyelids, and stretching their lips horizontally back to their ears. They were asked to hold each expression for 10 seconds, during which time the researchers measured their heart rate and body temperature. When they moved facial muscles as described here, they showed a rise in heart rate and a steady body temperature, physiological reactions that characterize

facial feedback hypothesis The idea that facial expressions can influence emotions, as well as reflect them.

FIGURE 9.16 Emotional Expressions in the United States and New Guinea *(Left)* Two women from the United States. *(Right)* Two men from the Fore tribe in New Guinea. Notice the similarity in their expressions of disgust and happiness. Psychologists believe that the facial expression of emotion is virtually the same in all cultures.

fear. When the actors made an angry expression with their faces (eyes have a penetrating stare, brows are drawn together and downward, and lips are pressed together or opened and pushed forward), their heart rate and body temperature both increased. The concept involved in the facial feedback hypothesis might sound familiar. It provides support for the theory that says emotional experiences can be generated by changes in and awareness of our own bodily states.

Sociocultural Factors in Emotion   In *The Expression of the Emotions in Man and Animals,* Charles Darwin (1872/1965) stated that the facial expressions of human beings are innate, not learned; are the same in all cultures around the world; and evolved from the emotions of animals. Darwin compared the similarity of human snarls of anger with the growls of dogs and the hisses of cats. He compared the giggling of chimpanzees when they are tickled under their arms with human laughter.

Today psychologists still believe that emotions, especially facial expressions of emotion, have strong biological ties (Goldsmith, 2002). For example, children who are blind from birth and have never observed the smile or frown on another person's face smile or frown in the same way that children with normal vision do.

If emotions and facial expressions that go with them are unlearned, then they should be the same the world over. The universality of facial expressions and the ability of people from different cultures to accurately label the emotion that lies behind the facial expression has been researched extensively. Psychologist Paul Ekman's (1980, 1996) careful observations reveal that the many faces of emotion do not differ significantly from one culture to another. For example, Ekman photographed people expressing emotions, such as happiness, fear, surprise, disgust, and grief. When researchers showed the photographs to people from the United States, Chile, Japan, Brazil, and Borneo (an Indonesian island in the western Pacific), all tended to label the same faces with the same emotions (Ekman & Friesen, 1968). Another study focused on the way the Fore tribe, an isolated Stone Age culture in New Guinea, matched descriptions of emotions with facial expressions (Ekman & Friesen, 1971). Before Ekman's visit, most of the Fore had never seen a Caucasian face. The similarity of facial expressions of emotions by persons in New Guinea and the United States is shown in figure 9.16. (To learn more about Ekman's research on universal expressions of emotions, listen to the audio clip "Evolutionary Psychology.")

Just as facial expressions are, some other nonverbal signals appear to be universal indicators of certain emotions. For example, when people are depressed, it shows not only in their sad facial expressions but also in their slow body movements, downturned heads, and slumped posture.

In the Middle Eastern country of Yemen, male-to-male kissing is commonplace, but in the United States it is uncommon. *What other forms of nonverbal expression vary across cultures?*

Many nonverbal signals of emotion, though, vary from one culture to another (Cohen & Borsoi, 1996; Mesquita, 2002). For example, male-to-male kissing is commonplace in Yemen but uncommon in the United States. And the "thumbs up" sign, which in most cultures either means everything is okay or signals the desire to hitch a ride, is an insult in Greece, similar to a raised third finger in the United States.

Display rules for emotion also are not culturally universal. **Display rules** are sociocultural standards that determine when, where, and how emotions should be expressed. For example, members of the Utku culture in Alaska discourage anger by cultivating acceptance and by dissociating themselves from any display of anger. If a trip is hampered by an unexpected snowstorm, the Utku do not become frustrated but accept the snowstorm and build an igloo. See the video clip "Cultural Variations in Nonverbal Behavior" for more information on cross-cultural research on nonverbal communication.

In-Psych Plus

Another sociocultural influence in emotion is gender. The stereotype that females are emotional and males are not is a powerful and pervasive image in our culture and many others (Shields, 1991). But females and males are often more alike in the way they experience emotion than the stereotype suggests. Females and males often use the same facial expressions, adopt the same language, and describe their emotional experiences similarly when they keep diaries about their experiences. Both sexes are equally likely to experience love, jealousy, and anxiety in new social situations, anger when they are insulted, grief when close relationships end, and embarrassment when they make mistakes in public (Tavris & Wade, 1984).

When we consider specific emotional experiences, contexts in which emotion is displayed, and certain beliefs about emotion, gender does matter (Shields, 1991). Consider anger. Men are more likely than women to show anger toward strangers (especially other men) when they feel they have been challenged and to turn their anger into aggressive action. Gender differences are also more likely to occur in contexts that highlight social relationships. For example, females are more likely than males to give accounts of emotion that include interpersonal relationships. And females are more likely to express fear and sadness than males are, especially when communicating with their friends and family.

Classification of Emotions

There are more than 200 words for emotions in the English language, indicating the complexity and variety of emotions. A number of psychologists have classified the emotions we experience by placing them on a wheel. One such model was

display rules Sociocultural standards that determine when, where, and how emotions should be expressed.

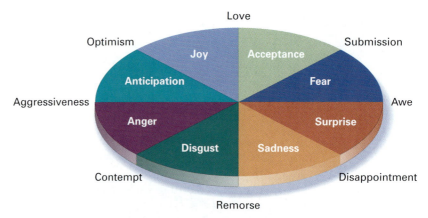

FIGURE 9.17 A Wheel Classification of Emotions Plutchik theorized that people experience the eight primary emotions represented in the colored sections of the drawing, as well as combinations of these emotions, as shown outside the wheel.

proposed by Robert Plutchik (1980). He believes emotions have four dimensions: (1) They are positive or negative, (2) they are primary or mixed, (3) many are polar opposites, and (4) they vary in intensity. For example, think about your ecstasy when you get an unexpected *A* on a test or your enthusiasm about a football game this weekend—these are positive emotions. In contrast, think about negative emotions, such as grief when someone close to you dies or anger when someone verbally attacks you. Positive emotions enhance our self-esteem; negative emotions lower our self-esteem. Positive emotions improve our relationships with others; negative emotions depress the quality of those relationships. Plutchik believes that emotions are like colors. Every color of the spectrum can be produced by mixing the primary colors. Happiness, disgust, surprise, sadness, anger, and fear are candidates for primary emotions. Combining sadness and surprise produces disappointment. Jealousy is composed of love and anger. Plutchik developed the emotion wheel in figure 9.17 to show how primary emotions adjacent to each other produce other emotions. Also note that some emotions are opposites—love and remorse, optimism and disappointment. Theorists such as Plutchik view emotions as innate reactions that require little cognitive interpretation: an evolutionary perspective.

A different approach is to classify emotions along two broad dimensions: positive and negative. **Positive affectivity (PA)** refers to positive emotions, such as joy, happiness, love, and interest. **Negative affectivity (NA)** refers to negative emotions, such as anxiety, anger, guilt, and sadness. Positive emotions facilitate approach behavior (Davidson, 1993; Watson, 2001; Watson & others, 1999). In other words, positive affect increases the likelihood that individuals will interact with their environment and engage in activities that are adaptive for the individual, its species, or both. Positive emotions can broaden people's horizons and build their personal resources. For example, joy broadens by creating the urge to play, push limits, and be creative. Interest broadens by creating the motivation to explore, absorb new information and experiences, and expand the self (Csikzentmihalyi, 1990; Ryan & Deci, 2000). Negative emotions, such as fear, facilitate withdrawal behavior and thus carry direct and immediate adaptive benefits in situations that threaten survival. However, whereas positive emotions tend to broaden a person's attention, negative emotions—such as anxiety and depression—often narrow attention even in nonthreatening situations (Basso & others, 1996).

There is increasing interest in the role that positive affectivity might play in well-being (Frederickson, 2001). For example, positive emotions appear to improve coping. In one study, individuals who experienced more positive emotions than others developed broader-based coping strategies, such as thinking about different ways to deal with a problem and stepping back from the situation and being more objective (Frederickson & Joiner, 2002). In some cases, positive emotions, such as joy, happiness, love, and interest—may override, or undo the lingering effects of, negative emotions—such as sadness, anger, and despair (Diener, 1999; Frederickson, 2001). For example,

positive affectivity (PA) Positive emotions, such as joy, happiness, love, and interest.

negative affectivity (NA) Negative emotions, such as anxiety, anger, guilt, and sadness.

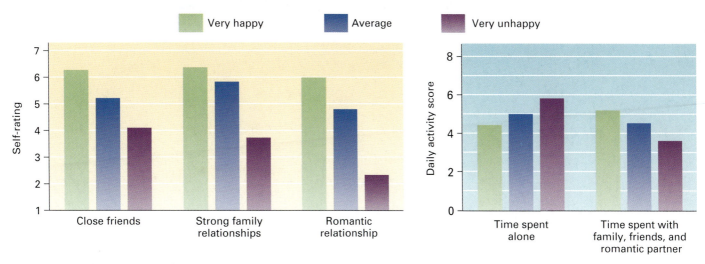

FIGURE 9.18 Characteristics of Very Happy College Students (Diener & Seligman, 2002)
Self-ratings were made on a scale of 1 to 7, with 1 being much below the average of college students on the campus studied (University of Illinois) and 7 being much above the average of college students on the campus. Daily activity scores reflect mean times, with 1 representing no time and 10 reflecting 8 hours per day.

mild joy and contentment have been found to undo the lingering cardiovascular effects of negative emotions, such as sadness (Frederickson & Levenson, 1998). In sum, positive emotions likely serve important functions in an individual's adaptation, growth, and social connection. By building personal and social resources, positive emotions improve people's well-being.

One aspect of positive emotion that is increasingly being studied is happiness. Psychologists' interest in happiness focuses on positive ways we experience life, including cognitive judgments of our well-being (Diener, Lucas, & Oishi, 2001; Locke, 2002). That is, psychologists want to know what makes you happy and how you perceive your happiness. Recent research reviews indicate that these factors are linked with happiness (Diener & Seligman, 2002; Diener & others, 1999):

- Psychological and personality characteristics: high levels of self-esteem, optimism, extraversion, and personal control
- A supportive network of close relationships
- A culture that offers positive interpretations of most daily events
- Being engaged by work and leisure
- A faith that embodies social support, purpose, hope, and religious attendance

The importance of close relationships in happiness was documented in a recent study of what makes college students happy (Diener & Seligman, 2002). College students were divided into three groups: very happy, average, and very unhappy. The very happy college students were highly social, were more extraverted, and had stronger romantic and social relationships than the less happy college students (see figure 9.18).

Review and Sharpen Your Thinking

5 *Summarize the factors that influence emotion.*

- Explain the biology of emotion in terms of arousal and neural activity.
- Discuss the roles of cognition, behavior, and sociocultural similarities and differences in the expression of emotion.
- Compare two models for classifying emotions.

Think about the last time you became angry. How did biological, cognitive, behavioral, and sociocultural factors influence your interpretation and expression of anger?

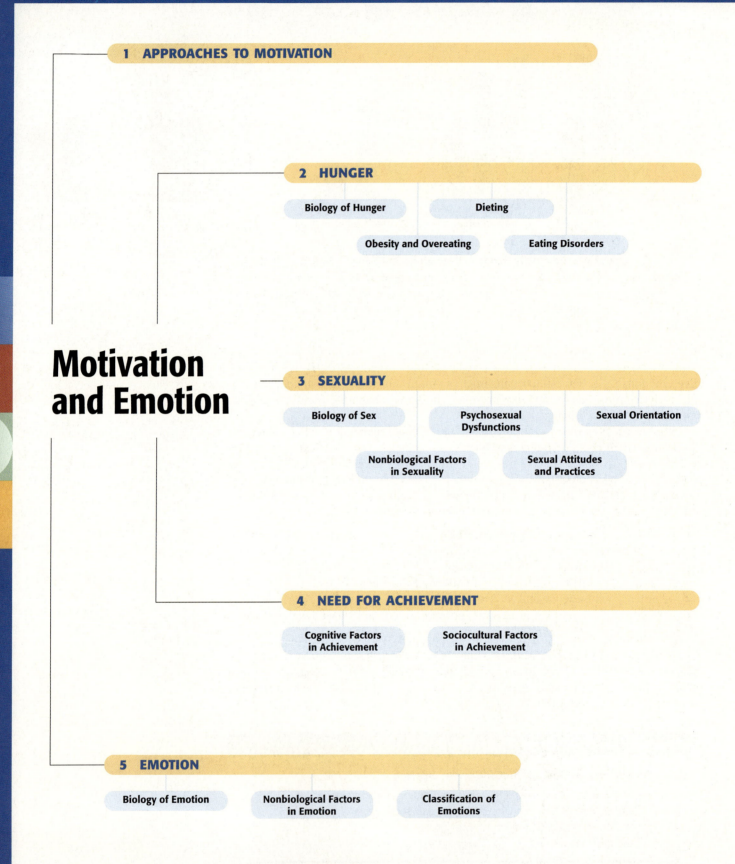

Motivation and Emotion

1 APPROACHES TO MOTIVATION

2 HUNGER

Biology of Hunger

Dieting

Obesity and Overeating

Eating Disorders

3 SEXUALITY

Biology of Sex

Psychosexual Dysfunctions

Sexual Orientation

Nonbiological Factors in Sexuality

Sexual Attitudes and Practices

4 NEED FOR ACHIEVEMENT

Cognitive Factors in Achievement

Sociocultural Factors in Achievement

5 EMOTION

Biology of Emotion

Nonbiological Factors in Emotion

Classification of Emotions

1 *Describe five psychological views of motivation.*

- Motivation gives our behavior, thoughts, and feelings a purpose. Early evolutionary theorists considered motivation to be based on instinct, the innate biological pattern of behavior that is assumed to be universal throughout a species; the idea that some of our motivation is unlearned and involves physiological factors is still present in the evolutionary approach today. Drive reduction theory relies on the concept of drive, an aroused state that occurs because of a physiological need; the goal of drive reduction is homeostasis, the body's tendency to maintain an equilibrium. Optimum arousal theory states that performance is best under conditions of moderate rather than low or high arousal, although at times low or high arousal is linked with better performance. The cognitive approach emphasizes the effect on motivation of such information processing abilities as attention, memory, and problem solving; intrinsic motivation, based on internal factors such as self-determination, curiosity, challenge, and effort, contrasts with extrinsic motivation, based on external incentives such as rewards and punishments. According to Maslow's hierarchy of needs, our main needs are satisfied in this sequence: physiological, safety, love and belongingness, esteem, and self-actualization.

2 *Explain what motivates people to eat and to eat too much or too little.*

- Stomach signals are one biological factor linked to hunger. Another is glucose (blood sugar), probably because the brain is critically dependent on sugar for energy. Leptin, a protein secreted by fat cells, decreases food intake and increases energy expenditure. The hypothalamus plays an important role in regulating hunger, one part involved in stimulating eating and another part in restricting eating. Today, neuroscientists are exploring the roles that neurotransmitters and neural circuits play in hunger.
- Obesity is a serious and pervasive problem in the United States. Heredity, basal metabolism, set point, and fat cells are biological factors involved in obesity. Obese persons are more responsive to external eating cues than normal-weight persons are, although some individuals at all weight levels respond more to external than to internal stimuli. Time and place affect eating, as does the type of food available. Self-control is an important cognitive factor in eating behavior. The dramatic increase in obesity in the late twentieth century underscores the significance of environmental factors in obesity as increasing numbers of people eat high-fat foods and lead sedentary lives.

- Dieting for weight loss and restrained eating for weight control are common in American society. Most diets don't work over time, unless they are combined with exercise. The pressure to be thin and diet can be harmful for people who are not overweight. However, when overweight people diet and maintain their weight loss, they reap health benefits.
- Anorexia nervosa is an eating disorder that involves the relentless pursuit of thinness through starvation. Bulimia nervosa is an eating disorder that consists of a binge-and-purge pattern. Both disorders are most common among adolescent and young adult females.

3 *Discuss the motivation for sex.*

- Motivation for sexual behavior involves the hypothalamus. The pituitary gland controls the secretion of two classes of sex hormones: estrogens, which predominate in females, and androgens, which predominate in males. The role of sex hormones in human sexual behavior, especially in women, is not clear. Masters and Johnson mapped out the human sexual response pattern, which consists of four physiological phases: excitement, plateau, orgasm, and resolution.
- Thoughts and images are central in the sexual lives of humans. Sexual scripts influence sexual behavior, as do sensory/perceptual factors. Females tend to be more sexually aroused by touch, males by visual stimulation. Pheromones are sexual attractants for many nonhuman animals, but their role in human sexual behavior has not been documented. Many substances allegedly act as aphrodisiacs, or sexual stimulants, but there is no clear evidence that what we eat, drink, or inject has aphrodisiac qualities. Sexual values vary extensively across cultures. These values exert significant effects on sexual behavior.
- Psychosexual dysfunctions involve impairments in the sexual response pattern. Significant advances have been made in treating these dysfunctions in recent years. Most effective are treatments of specific dysfunctions in sexual response.
- Describing sexual practices in America has always been challenging due to the difficulty of surveying a representative sample of the population. The 1994 *Sex in America* survey was a major improvement over earlier surveys. It revealed that Americans' sex lives are more conservative than earlier surveys had indicated.
- Sexual orientation—heterosexual, homosexual, or bisexual—is most likely determined by a combination of genetic, hormonal, cognitive, and environmental factors.

4 *Explain why people are motived to achieve.*

- Early interest in achievement focused on the need for achievement. Cognitive factors in achievement include intrinsic motivation, attribution, and self-generated goals. Attribution theory states that people are motivated to discover the underlying causes of behavior in an effort to make sense of it. The main emphasis in attribution theory has focused on internal causes, especially effort, and external causes. High achievers often set specific, short-term, challenging goals. Individuals in the United States are more achievement-oriented than individuals in many other countries, although recent comparisons with Asian countries indicate a higher value placed on achievement in those countries. A special concern is accurately determining effects of ethnicity on achievement. Socioeconomic status (SES) usually is a better predictor of achievement than ethnicity.

5 *Summarize the factors that influence emotion.*

- Emotion is feeling, or affect, that has three components: physiological arousal, conscious experience, and behavioral expression. The biology of emotion focuses on physiological arousal involving the autonomic nervous system and its two subsystems. The galvanic skin response and the polygraph have been used to measure emotional arousal. The polygraph is considered unreliable for use as a lie detector. One early theory states that emotion follows physiological states triggered by environmental stimuli. Another early theory states that emotion and physiological reactions occur simultaneously. However, contemporary biological views of emotion increasingly highlight neural circuitry and neurotransmitters. Positive and negative emotions appear to use different neural circuitry and neurotransmitters.

- One cognitive theory of emotion states that emotion is the result of both physiological arousal and cognitive labeling. It appears that cognition sometimes directs emotion and that emotion sometimes directs cognition. Research on the behavioral component of emotion focuses on facial expressions. The facial feedback hypothesis states that facial expressions can influence emotions, as well as reflect them. Most psychologists believe that facial expressions of basic emotions are the same across cultures. However, display rules, which involve nonverbal signals of body movement, posture, and gesture, vary across cultures. The gender stereotype that women are emotional and men are not is belied by the similarity of emotions in both genders. However, context often influences the expression of emotion by males and females.

- Classifications of emotions have included wheel models and the two-dimensional approach. Plutchik's wheel model portrays emotions in terms of four dimensions: positive or negative, primary or mixed, polar opposites, and intensity. The two-dimensional approach to classifying emotions argues that there are just two broad dimensions of emotional experiences: positive affectivity and negative affectivity.

Key Terms

motivation, p. 315
instinct, p. 315
drive, p. 315
need, p. 315
homeostasis, p. 315
intrinsic motivation, p. 316
extrinsic motivation, p. 316
hierarchy of needs, p. 317
self-actualization, p. 317

basal metabolism rate (BMR), p. 321
set point, p. 321
anorexia nervosa, p. 323
bulimia nervosa, p. 323
estrogens, p. 325
androgens, p. 325
human sexual response pattern, p. 325

sexual scripts, p. 326
pheromones, p. 327
psychosexual dysfunctions, p. 328
need for achievement, p. 333
attribution theory, p. 333
emotion, p. 337
polygraph, p. 338

two-factor theory of emotion, p. 341
facial feedback hypothesis, p. 343
display rules, p. 345
positive affectivity (PA), p. 346
negative affectivity (NA), p. 346

Apply Your Knowledge

1. Ask your friends to define the word *motivation*. Think about the way they define it and the way psychologists approach motivation. What are the similarities? What are the differences? Are your friends likelier to say they have too much motivation or not enough? Why might that be?

2. Do a web search for the word *hunger*. What kinds of sites are listed first? How do the topics that these sites cover compare with the discussion of hunger in the chapter? Do the sites give you any insight into the role of environment in hunger?

3. Imagine that someone offered you a pill that would double the size of your lateral hypothalamus but make your androgen levels go down to half their current level. How might this pill affect your eating and sexual behavior? Would you take the pill?

4. How much of our interpretation of emotions depends on verbal or nonverbal cues? Try the following exercise: Watch a movie that you're not familiar with and find a scene with a number of people in it. First, watch the scene with the sound off and try to guess what emotions are being experienced by each person; describe the nonverbal cues that led you to your conclusions. Then, find a different scene, and listen to it without watching to guess what emotions are being experienced; describe the verbal cues that you used. Then, watch both scenes with the sound on. Were verbal or nonverbal cues more useful?

Connections

To test your mastery of the material in this chapter, go to the Study Guide and the In-Pysch Plus CD-ROM, as well as the Online Learning Center. There you will find a chapter summary, practice tests, flashcards, lecture slides, web links, and other study tools, such as interactive exercises and reviews as well as current, chapter-relevant news articles.

What makes a U.S. president great? Do certain personality traits characterize successful candidates? In one research study, Steve Rubenzer and his colleagues (2000) asked more than 100 history experts to rate presidents on their personality characteristics for the 5 years before they became president. The researchers did not ask the historians to assess a president's personality while in office because the researchers believed that the pressure might alter his personality.

Rubenzer and his colleagues then correlated each president's personality traits with his degree of presidential greatness, as determined by referencing generally accepted lists of great U.S. presidents. In order, Abraham Lincoln, Franklin Roosevelt, George Washington, Thomas Jefferson, Theodore Roosevelt, Woodrow Wilson, Harry Truman, Andrew Jackson, Dwight Eisenhower, and James Madison have been ranked by expert historians as the 10 greatest U.S. presidents.

The personality trait of openness to experience showed the highest correlation with greatness as a president. The researchers speculated that individuals with higher cognitive abilities have more open minds. However, they had no available data on the cognitive ability of presidents to test this idea.

Great presidents were also rated as attentive to their emotions, willing to question traditional values and try new ways of doing things, imaginative, and more interested in art and beauty than less successful presidents. Successful presidents also have tended to be *assertive*—to be stubborn and willing to stand up for their ideas.

The researchers also found that most presidents are extraverts, although earlier presidents were less extraverted than more recent ones. The increasing extraversion of U.S. presidents has coincided with the increased exposure of presidents in the media.

The personality of presidents is interesting, but what about your own personality? Think about your own characteristics, and write down seven or eight personality traits that you think best describe you. Do people who know you well describe you as serious or wild? Shy or outgoing? Self-confident or uncertain? Friendly or hostile?

In compiling this list, you likely chose personality characteristics that you believe are an enduring part of your makeup as a person. For example, if you said that you are an outgoing person, wouldn't you also say that you were outgoing a year ago and that you will probably be an outgoing person 1 year, 5 years, and 10 years from now? The concept of personality involves the notion that we are not just a random collection of traits that change from day to day. Each of us has a more or less persistent style of thinking and behaving, a unified and enduring pattern of core characteristics. Personality theories, which are the topic of this chapter, seek to describe such patterns and their underlying causes (Carver & Scheier, 2004; Cloninger, 2004; Pervin & John, 2001).

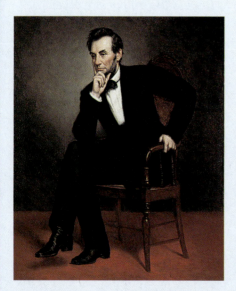 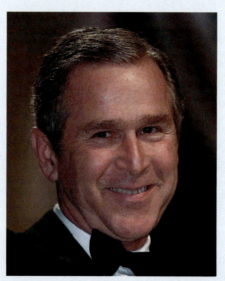 

How might the personalities of presidential candidates influence the outcome of a presidential election? Do you think the personalities of George W. Bush and Al Gore influenced the 2000 presidential election? How? How are the personalities of Bush and Gore similar to or different from those of great presidents, such as Abraham Lincoln?

What is personality, and what are the major issues in studying it?

Personality is one of those concepts that is familiar to everyone but is difficult to define. In this chapter, **personality** is defined as a pattern of enduring, distinctive thoughts, emotions, and behaviors that characterize the way an individual adapts to the world.

Personality theorists and researchers ask why individuals react to the same situation in different ways, and they come up with different answers. Some theorists believe that biological and genetic factors are responsible; others argue that life experiences are more important factors. Some theorists claim that the way we think about ourselves is the key to understanding personality, whereas others stress that the way we behave toward each other is. This chapter presents four broad theoretical perspectives on personality—psychodynamic, behavioral and social cognitive, humanistic, and trait—and you will see how different the answers can be.

As you read about these perspectives on personality, you will notice that they address three important questions:

- *Is personality innate or learned?* Is personality due more to heredity and biological factors or more to learning and environmental experiences? For example, are individuals conceited and self-centered because they inherited the tendency to be conceited and self-centered from their parents, or did they learn to be that way through experiences with other conceited, self-centered individuals? As you will see, psychodynamic perspectives have a strong biogenetic foundation, although some theorists who adopt this approach believe that environmental experiences and culture play a role in determining personality. Behavioral and social cognitive perspectives, along with humanistic perspectives, endorse environment as a powerful determinant of personality. Humanistic theorists believe that people have the innate ability to reach their full potential. Trait perspectives vary in their emphasis on heredity and environment.

- *Is personality conscious or unconscious?* How aware are individuals that they are, say, conceited and self-centered? How aware are they of the reasons they became conceited and self-centered? Most psychodynamic theorists argue that we are largely unaware of how our individual personalities developed. Behaviorists argue that neither unconscious nor conscious thought is important in determining personality. Social cognitive theorists believe that conscious thought affects the way the environment influences personality. Humanists stress the conscious aspects of personality, especially in the form of self-perception. Trait theorists pay little attention to the conscious or unconscious issue.

- *Is personality influenced by internal factors or external factors?* Is the way personality is expressed in any given situation due more to an inner disposition or to the situation itself? Are individuals conceited and self-centered because of something inside themselves, an inherent characteristic, or are they conceited and self-centered because of the situations they are in and the ways they are influenced by people around them? Psychodynamic, humanistic, and trait theorists emphasize the internal dimensions of personality. Behaviorists emphasize personality's external, situational determinants. Social cognitive theorists examine both external and internal determinants.

You will learn more about how the four theoretical perspectives address these issues in the rest of the chapter. The diversity of theories makes understanding personality a challenging undertaking. To keep from getting frustrated, remember that personality is a complex, multifaceted topic. And, remember, much of the information is complementary rather than contradictory. Each theory has contributed an important piece or pieces to the personality puzzle. Together they let us see the total landscape of personality in all its richness (Funder, 2001).

personality A pattern of enduring, distinctive thoughts, emotions, and behaviors that characterize the way an individual adapts to the world.

Review and Sharpen Your Thinking

1   *Define personality and identify the major issues in the study of personality.*

• Define the concept of personality and summarize three issues addressed by the major personality perspectives.

In the chapter introduction, you were asked to list your main personality characteristics. Go over the list and evaluate whether you think you inherited these traits or learned them, how conscious you are of these traits, and the extent to which they are internally or externally determined.

2   PSYCHODYNAMIC PERSPECTIVES

| **Freud's Psychoanalytic Theory** | **Psychodynamic Dissenters and Revisionists** | **Evaluating Psychodynamic Perspectives** |

In-Psych Plus

What are the main themes of psychodynamic perspectives?

Psychodynamic perspectives view personality as being primarily unconscious (that is, beyond awareness) and as developing in stages. Most psychodynamic perspectives emphasize that early experiences with parents play an important role in sculpting the individual's personality. Psychodynamic theorists believe that behavior is merely a surface characteristic and that to truly understand someone's personality we have to explore the symbolic meanings of behavior and the deep inner workings of the mind (Feist & Feist, 2002). These characteristics were sketched by the architect of psychoanalytic theory—Sigmund Freud. As you learned in chapter 1, some psychodynamic theorists who followed Freud diverged from his theory but still embrace his core ideas (see the video clip "Freud's Contribution to Psychology").

Freud's Psychoanalytic Theory

Sigmund Freud (1856–1939), one of the most influential thinkers of the twentieth century, was a medical doctor who specialized in neurology. He developed his ideas about psychoanalytic theory from his work with psychiatric patients. As a child, Freud was doted on by his mother, who was beautiful and some 20 years younger than Freud's father. One aspect of Freud's theory emphasizes a young boy's sexual attraction to his mother; it is possible that this aspect of his theory derived from a romantic attachment to his own mother.

For Freud, the unconscious mind holds the key to understanding behavior. Our lives are filled with tension and conflict; to reduce them, we keep troubling information locked in our unconscious mind. Freud believed that even trivial behaviors have special significance when the unconscious forces behind them are revealed. A twitch, a doodle, a joke, a smile, each may have an unconscious reason for appearing. For example, Barbara is kissing and hugging Tom, whom she is to marry in several weeks. She says, "Oh, *Jeff*, I love you so much." Tom pushes her away and says, "Why did you call me Jeff? I thought you didn't think about him anymore. We need to have a talk!" You probably can think of times when these so-called *Freudian slips* (misstatements that perhaps reveal unconscious thoughts) have tumbled out of your own mouth.

Freud also believed that dreams hold important clues to our behavior (Blum, 2001). He said dreams are unconscious representations of the conflicts and tensions

SIGMUND FREUD (1856–1939)
The architect of psychoanalytic theory.
Which of his ideas do today's psychodynamic theorists still embrace?

psychodynamic perspectives View personality as primarily unconscious (beyond awareness) and as developing in stages. Most psychodynamic perspectives emphasize early experiences' effects on personality.

in our everyday lives that are too painful to handle consciously. As chapter 5 indicated, much dream content is disguised in symbolism and requires extensive analysis to be understood.

Remember that Freud considered the unconscious mind to be the key to understanding personality (Gedo, 2002). He likened personality to an iceberg, existing mostly below the level of awareness, just as most of an iceberg is beneath the surface of the water. Figure 10.1 illustrates this analogy and how extensive the unconscious part of our mind is in Freud's view.

Personality's Structures   Notice that figure 10.1 shows the iceberg divided into three segments. Freud (1917) believed that personality has three structures: the id, the ego, and the superego.

The **id** consists of instincts and is the individual's reservoir of psychic energy. In Freud's view, the id is unconscious; it has no contact with reality. The id works according to the *pleasure principle*, the Freudian concept that the id always seeks pleasure and avoids pain.

It would be a dangerous and scary world, however, if our personalities were all id. As young children mature, they learn they cannot slug other children in the face. They also learn that they have to use the toilet instead of their diaper. As children experience the demands and constraints of reality, a new structure of personality is formed—the **ego,** the Freudian structure of personality that deals with the demands of reality. According to Freud, the ego abides by the *reality principle*. It tries to bring the individual pleasure within the norms of society. Most of us recognize that our sexual and aggressive impulses cannot all go unrestrained. The ego helps us to test reality, to see how far we can go without getting into trouble and hurting ourselves. Whereas the id is completely unconscious, the ego is partly conscious. It houses our higher mental functions—reasoning, problem solving, and decision making, for example.

The id and ego do not consider whether something is right or wrong. The **superego** is the moral branch of personality. It is what we often call our "conscience." Like the id, the superego does not consider reality; it only considers whether the id's impulses can be satisfied in moral terms.

Both the id and the superego make life rough for the ego. Your ego might say, "I will have sex only occasionally and be sure to use an effective form of birth control." But your id is saying, "I want to be satisfied; sex feels so good." And your superego says, "I feel guilty about having sex at all." (For a description of how id, ego, and superego develop and interact, see the video clip "Freudian Structures of the Mind.")

Defense Mechanisms   The ego calls on many strategies to resolve the conflict among its demands for reality, the wishes of the id, and the constraints of the superego. These **defense mechanisms** reduce anxiety by unconsciously distorting reality.

Repression is the most powerful and pervasive defense mechanism, according to Freud. It pushes unacceptable id impulses out of awareness and back into the unconscious mind. Repression is the foundation for all of the psychological defense mechanisms, the goal of which is to push, or *repress*, threatening impulses out of awareness. Freud said that our early childhood experiences, many of which he believed were sexually laden, are too threatening and stressful for us to deal with consciously, so we reduce the anxiety of childhood conflict through repression.

"Good morning beheaded—uh, I mean beloved."

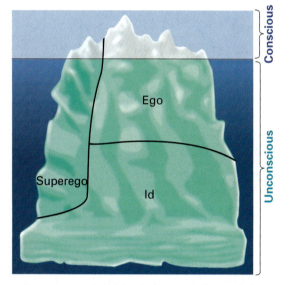

FIGURE 10.1 Conscious and Unconscious Mind
The conscious mind is the part of the iceberg above water, the unconscious mind the part below water. Notice that the id is totally unconscious, whereas the ego and superego can operate at either the conscious or the unconscious level.

id The Freudian structure of personality that consists of instincts, which are the individual's reservoir of psychic energy.

ego The Freudian structure of personality that deals with the demands of reality.

superego The Freudian structure of personality that deals with morality.

defense mechanisms The ego's protective methods for reducing anxiety by unconsciously distorting reality.

Defense Mechanism	How It Works	Example
Repression	The master defense mechanism; the ego pushes unacceptable impulses out of awareness, back into the unconscious mind.	A young girl was sexually abused by her uncle. As an adult, she can't remember anything about the traumatic experience.
Rationalization	The ego replaces a less acceptable motive with a more acceptable one.	A college student does not get into the fraternity of his choice. He says that if he had tried harder he could have gotten in.
Displacement	The ego shifts feelings toward an unacceptable object to another, more acceptable object.	A woman can't take her anger out on her boss so she goes home and takes it out on her husband.
Sublimation	The ego replaces an unacceptable impulse with a socially acceptable one.	A man with strong sexual urges becomes an artist who paints nudes.
Projection	The ego attributes personal shortcomings, problems, and faults to others.	A man who has a strong desire to have an extramarital affair accuses his wife of flirting with other men.
Reaction Formation	The ego transforms an unacceptable motive into its opposite.	A woman who fears her sexual urges becomes a religious zealot.
Denial	The ego refuses to acknowledge anxiety-producing realities.	A man won't acknowledge that he has cancer even though a team of doctors has diagnosed his cancer.
Regression	The ego seeks the security of an earlier developmental period in the face of stress.	A woman returns home to mother every time she and her husband have a big argument.

FIGURE 10.2 Defense Mechanisms
Defense mechanisms reduce anxiety in various ways, but in all instances by distorting reality.

Two final points about defense mechanisms need to be understood. First, they are unconscious; we are not aware that we are calling on them. Second, when used in moderation or on a temporary basis, defense mechanisms are not necessarily unhealthy. For example, the defense mechanism of *denial* can help a person cope with impending death. For the most part, though, it is not healthy to let defense mechanisms dominate our behavior and prevent us from facing life's demands. Figure 10.2 describes several of Freud's defense mechanisms and gives an example of each. All of them work to protect the ego and reduce anxiety.

Personality Development   As Freud listened to, probed, and analyzed his patients, he became convinced that their personalities were the result of experiences early in life. Freud believed that we go through five stages of personality development and that at each stage of development we experience pleasure in one part of the body more than in others. *Erogenous zones,* according to Freud, are parts of the body that have especially strong pleasure-giving qualities at particular stages of development. Freud thought that our adult personality is determined by the way we resolve conflicts between these early sources of pleasure—the mouth, the anus, and then the genitals—and the demands of reality during these five stages:

1. *Oral stage* (first 18 months of age). Chewing, sucking, and biting are the chief sources of pleasure that reduce tension in the infant.
2. *Anal stage* (18 to 36 months of age). The child's greatest pleasure involves the anus or the eliminative functions associated with it. In Freud's view, the exercise of anal muscles reduces tension.

Stage	Adult Extensions (Fixations)	Sublimations	Reaction Formations
Oral	Smoking, eating, kissing, oral hygiene, drinking, chewing gum	Seeking knowledge, humor, wit, sarcasm, being a food or wine expert	Speech purist, food faddist, prohibitionist, dislike of milk
Anal	Notable interest in one's bowel movements, love of bathroom humor, extreme messiness	Interest in painting or sculpture, being overly giving, great interest in statistics	Extreme disgust with feces, fear of dirt, prudishness, irritability
Phallic	Heavy reliance on masturbation, flirtatiousness, expressions of virility	Interest in poetry, love of love, interest in acting, striving for success	Puritanical attitude toward sex, excessive modesty

FIGURE 10.3 **Defense Mechanisms and Freudian Stages**

3. *Phallic stage* (3 to 6 years of age). The name of Freud's third stage comes from the Latin word *phallus,* which means "penis." Pleasure focuses on the genitals as the child discovers that self-stimulation is enjoyable. In Freud's view, the phallic stage has a special importance in personality development because it triggers the **Oedipus complex,** the young child's development of an intense desire to replace the same-sex parent and enjoy the affections of the opposite-sex parent. This name comes from Greek mythology, in which Oedipus unwittingly killed his father and married his mother. At about 5 to 6 years of age, children recognize that their same-sex parent might punish them for their incestuous wishes. To reduce this conflict, the child identifies with the same-sex parent, striving to be like him or her.

4. *Latency stage* (6 years of age to puberty). The child represses all interest in sexuality and develops social and intellectual skills. This activity channels much of the child's energy into emotionally safe areas and aids the child in forgetting the highly stressful conflicts of the phallic stage.

5. *Genital stage* (adolescence and adulthood). In a sexual reawakening, the source of sexual pleasure becomes someone outside of the family. Freud believed that unresolved conflicts with parents reemerged during adolescence. But once they are resolved, the individual becomes capable of developing a mature love relationship and functioning independently as an adult.

Freud believed that the individual may become fixated at any of these stages of development if the underlying conflict is not resolved. *Fixation* is the psychoanalytic defense mechanism that occurs when the individual remains locked in an earlier developmental stage because needs are under- or overgratified. For example, a parent might wean a child too early, be too strict in toilet training, punish the child for masturbation, or "smother" the child with too much attention. Figure 10.3 illustrates some possible links between adult personality characteristics and fixation at oral, anal, and phallic stages.

THE FAR SIDE® BY GARY LARSON

© 1982 FarWorks, Inc. All Rights Reserved/Dist. by Creators Syndicate

"So, Mr. Fenton ... let's begin with your mother."

Psychodynamic Dissenters and Revisionists

Because Freud was among the first theorists to explore personality, over time some of his ideas have needed to be updated, others revised, and some tossed out altogether (Adler, 1927; Erikson, 1968; Fromm, 1947; Horney, 1945; Jung, 1917; Kohut, 1977; Rapaport, 1967; Sullivan, 1953). His critics stress the following points:

- Sexuality is not the pervasive force behind personality that Freud believed it to be. Nor was the Oedipus complex as universal as Freud believed. Freud's

Oedipus complex In Freud's theory, the young child's development of an intense desire to replace the same-sex parent and enjoy the affections of the opposite-sex parent.

KAREN HORNEY (1885–1952)
Developed the first feminist criticism of Freud's theory. *What does Horney's view emphasize?*

Swiss theorist Carl Jung developed the concepts of the collective unconscious and archetypes. *What was the main difference between Jung's theory and Freud's?*

collective unconscious Jung's term for the impersonal, deepest layer of the unconscious mind, shared by all human beings because of their common ancestral past.

concepts were heavily influenced by the setting in which he lived and worked—turn-of-the-century Vienna, a society that was, compared with contemporary society, sexually repressed and paternalistic.

- The first 5 years of life are not as powerful in shaping adult personality as Freud thought; later experiences deserve more attention.
- The ego and conscious thought processes play more dominant roles in our personality than Freud gave them credit for; he claimed that we are forever in thrall to the instinctual, unconscious clutches of the id. Also, the ego has a separate line of development from the id, so achievement, thinking, and reasoning are not always tied to sexual impulses.
- Sociocultural factors are much more important than Freud believed. In stressing the id's dominance, Freud placed more emphasis on the biological basis of personality.

The theories of three dissenters and revisionists—Horney, Jung, and Adler—have been especially influential in the development of psychodynamic theories, the successors to Freud's psychoanalytic theory.

Horney's Sociocultural Approach Karen Horney (1885–1952) insisted that Freud's hypotheses be supported with observable data before being accepted as fact and that sociocultural influences on personality development be considered. Take Freud's concept of "penis envy": He attributed some of the behavior of his female patients to their repressed desire to have a penis. Horney pointed out that, during Freud's time, men were the ones who described women, who influenced and represented the culture, and who determined the standards for suitable growth and development. She countered the notion of penis envy with the hypothesis that both sexes envy the attributes of the other, with men coveting women's reproductive capacities. She also argued that women who feel penis envy are desirous only of the status that men have in most societies (Gilman, 2001).

Horney also believed that the need for security, not for sex or aggression, is the prime motive in human existence. She suggested that people usually develop one of three strategies in their effort to cope with anxiety. Some individuals might *move toward* people, seeking love and support. Other individuals might *move away* from people, becoming more independent. And still other individuals might *move against* people, becoming competitive and domineering. The secure individual uses all three of these ways of coping in moderation and balance, whereas the insecure individual often uses one or another of these strategies in an exaggerated fashion, becoming too dependent, too independent, or too aggressive.

Psychologists are still revamping psychoanalytic theory in the sociocultural direction that Horney pointed. Nancy Chodorow's (1978, 1989) feminist revision of psychoanalytic theory, for example, emphasizes that many more women than men define themselves in terms of their relationships and that emotions tend to be more important in women's lives. In short, personality is not simply a matter of biology; social experiences and culture also shape personality.

Jung's Analytical Theory Freud's contemporary Carl Jung (1875–1961) had a different complaint about psychoanalytic theory. Jung shared Freud's interest in the unconscious, but he believed that Freud underplayed the unconscious mind's role in personality (Solomon, 2003). In fact, Jung believed that the roots of personality go back to the dawn of human existence. The **collective unconscious** is the impersonal, deepest layer of the unconscious mind, shared by all human beings because of their common ancestral past. The experiences of a common past have made a deep, permanent impression on the human mind (Mayer, 2002).

The collective unconscious is expressed through what Jung called **archetypes,** emotionally laden ideas and images that have rich and symbolic meaning for all people. Jung believed that these archetypes emerge in art, religion, and dreams.

In *Star Wars,* Ben Kenobi *(left)* represented the archetype of good and Darth Vader the archetype of evil. *What other popular archetypes of good and evil can you think of?*

FIGURE 10.4 Mandala as an Archetype of the Self In his exploration of mythology, Carl Jung found that the self is often symbolized by a mandala, which he believed represents the self's unity.

He used archetypes to help people understand themselves (Knox, 2002; McDowell, 2001).

Two common archetypes are anima (woman) and animus (man). Jung believed each of us has a passive, "feminine" side and an assertive, "masculine" side. Another archetype is the shadow, our darker self. The shadow, which is evil and immoral, is represented by many fictional characters, such as Dracula, Mr. Hyde (of Jekyll and Hyde), and Darth Vader in the *Star Wars* films (Peterson, 1988). Another archetype, the mandala, a figure within a circle, has been used so often in art that Jung took it to represent the self (see figure 10.4).

Adler's Individual Psychology

Alfred Adler (1870–1937) was another of Freud's contemporaries. In Adler's **individual psychology,** people are motivated by purposes and goals. They are creators of their own lives. Unlike Freud, who believed in the overwhelming power of the unconscious mind, Adler argued that people have the ability to consciously monitor their lives. He also believed that social factors are more important than sexual motivation in shaping personality (Silverman & Corsini, 1984).

Adler thought that everyone strives for superiority, seeking to adapt, improve, and master the environment. Striving for superiority is our response to the uncomfortable feelings of inferiority that we all experience as infants and young children when we interact with people who are bigger and more powerful. *Compensation* is Adler's term for the individual's attempt to overcome imagined or real inferiorities or weaknesses by developing other abilities. Adler believed that compensation is normal. For example, one person may be a mediocre student but compensate by excelling in athletics.

Overcompensation is Adler's term for the individual's attempt to deny rather than acknowledge a real situation or for the exaggerated effort to conceal a weakness. Adler described two patterns of overcompensation: *Inferiority complex* is his term for exaggerated feelings of inadequacy; *superiority complex* is his term for exaggerated self-importance invoked to mask feelings of inferiority.

archetypes The name Jung gave to the emotionally laden ideas and images in the collective unconscious that have rich and symbolic meaning.

individual psychology Adler's approach, which views people as motivated by purposes and goals, being creators of their own lives.

Evaluating Psychodynamic Perspectives

Although psychodynamic theories have diverged from Freud's original psychoanalytic version, they do share some core principles:

- Personality is determined both by current experiences and, as the original psychoanalytic theory proposed, by those from early in life.
- Personality can be better understood by examining it developmentally, as a series of stages that unfold with the individual's physical, cognitive, and socioemotional development.
- We mentally transform our experiences, giving them meaning that shapes our personality.
- The mind is not all consciousness; unconscious motives lie behind some of our puzzling behavior.
- The individual's inner world often conflicts with the outer demands of reality, creating anxiety that is not easy to resolve.
- Personality and adjustment—not just the experimental laboratory topics of sensation, perception, and learning—are rightful and important topics of psychological inquiry.

One persistent criticism of the psychodynamic perspectives is that the main concepts have been difficult to test; they are largely matters of inference and interpretation. Researchers have not, for example, successfully investigated such key concepts as repression in the laboratory. Thus much of the data used to support psychodynamic theories have come from clinicians' subjective evaluations of clients; clinicians can easily see evidence of theories they hold. Other data come from patients' recollections of the distant past (especially those from early childhood) and are of unknown accuracy.

Some object that psychodynamic perspectives have too negative and pessimistic a view of the person. For example, these perspectives place too much weight on early experiences within the family and their influence on personality and do not acknowledge that we retain the capacity for adaptation throughout our lives. Some psychologists believe that Freud and Jung placed too much faith in the unconscious mind's ability to control behavior. Others object that Freud overemphasized the importance of sexuality in understanding personality; we are not born into the world with only a bundle of sexual and aggressive instincts. The demands of reality do not always conflict with our biological needs.

Finally, some critics have noted that many psychodynamic perspectives, especially Freud's, have a male, Western bias. Although Horney's theory helped to correct this bias, psychodynamic theory continues to be revised today by psychologists studying female personality development, as well as personality development in various ethnicities and cultures (Callan, 2002).

Review and Sharpen Your Thinking

2 *Summarize the psychodynamic perspectives.*

- Explain the key concepts in Freud's psychoanalytic theory.
- Discuss how the ideas of three psychodynamic dissenters and revisionists differed from Freud's.
- Identify the pros and cons of the psychodynamic perspectives.

What psychodynamic ideas may apply to all human beings? Which ones may not apply to everyone?

| Skinner's Behaviorism | Bandura's Social Cognitive Theory | Evaluating Behavioral and Social Cognitive Perspectives |

What are the main features of the behavioral and social cognitive perspectives?
Tom and Ann are engaged to be married. Both have warm, friendly personalities, and they enjoy being with each other. Psychodynamic theorists would say that their personalities derive from long-standing relationships with their parents, especially from their early childhood experiences. They also would say that the reason for their attraction is unconscious, that they are unaware of how their biological heritage and early life experiences have been carried forward to influence their adult personalities.

But behaviorists and social cognitive theorists would observe Tom and Ann and see something quite different. They would examine the two people's experiences, especially their most recent ones, to understand the reason for Tom and Ann's attraction to each another. Tom might be described as rewarding Ann's behavior, and vice versa. Behaviorists and social cognitive theorists would make no reference to unconscious thoughts, the Oedipus complex, defense mechanisms, and so on.

The **behavioral and social cognitive perspectives** emphasize the importance of environmental experiences and people's observable behavior to understand their personalities. Within that broad framework, behaviorists focus on behavior; social cognitive theorists also examine cognitive factors in personality.

Skinner's Behaviorism

Chapter 6 described B. F. Skinner's approach to learning, called operant conditioning. To him, personality is nothing more than the individual's observed, overt behavior, which is determined by the external environment; personality does not include internal traits and thoughts. Skinner believed we do not have to understand biological or cognitive processes to explain personality (behavior). Some psychologists say that including Skinner among personality theorists is like inviting a wolf to a party of lambs because he took the "person" out of personality (Phares, 1984).

Behaviorists counter that you cannot pinpoint where personality is or how it is determined; you can only observe what people do. For example, observations of Sam might reveal his shy, achievement-oriented, and caring behaviors. According to Skinner, these behaviors *are* his personality. Furthermore, Sam is this way because rewards and punishments shaped him into a shy, achievement-oriented, and caring person. Because of interactions with family, friends, and others, Sam learned to behave in this fashion. (See the video clip "Operant Conditioning" to review the principles of operant conditioning and explore how personality may be shaped.)

In-Psych Plus

Skinner stressed that our behavior always can change if we encounter new experiences. For example, shy, achievement-oriented, caring Sam may be uninhibited on Saturday night with friends at a bar, unmotivated to excel in English class, and occasionally nasty to his sister. Skinnerians believe that consistency in behavior comes only from consistency in environmental experiences: If a pattern of behavior is consistently rewarded, it likely will be consistent. The issue of consistency in personality is an important one that is discussed often throughout this chapter.

Because behaviorists believe that personality is learned and often changes according to environmental experiences and situations, it follows that, by rearranging the environment, personality can be changed. For the behaviorist, shy behavior can be changed into outgoing behavior; aggressive behavior can be changed into docile behavior; and lethargic behavior can be changed into enthusiastic behavior.

behavioral and social cognitive perspectives Emphasize the importance of environmental experiences in personality.

Albert Bandura *(above)* and Walter Mischel are the architects of contemporary social cognitive theory. *What three important concepts are part of this theory?*

Bandura's Social Cognitive Theory

Some psychologists believe the behaviorists are right when they say that personality is learned and influenced strongly by environmental experiences. But they think Skinner went too far in declaring that characteristics of the person are irrelevant in understanding personality. **Social cognitive theory** states that behavior, environment, and cognitive factors are important in understanding personality. Like the behavioral approach of Skinner, the social cognitive view relies on empirical research in studying personality. But this research has looked at both observable behavior and the cognitive factors that influence what we are like as people. Albert Bandura (1986, 1997, 2000, 2001) and Walter Mischel (1973, 1995, 2004 Idson & Mischel, 2001; Mischel & Shoda, 2001) are the main architects of social cognitive theory's contemporary version, which initially was labeled *cognitive social learning theory* by Mischel (1973). Bandura, Mischel, and others are actively developing this perspective today.

Remember from chapter 6 that Bandura believes observational learning is a key aspect of how we learn. Through observational learning, we form ideas about the behavior of others and then possibly adopt this behavior ourselves. For example, a young boy might observe his father's aggressive outbursts and hostile exchanges with people. When the boy is with his peers, he interacts in a highly aggressive way, showing the same characteristics that his father's behavior does. Social cognitive theorists believe that we acquire a wide range of behaviors, thoughts, and feelings through observing others' behavior; these observations form an important part of our personalities.

Social cognitive theorists also differ from the behaviorists by emphasizing that we can regulate and control our own behavior, despite our changing environment (Metcalfe & Mischel, 1999; Mischel & Shoda, 2001; Mischel, Shoda, & Mendoza-Denton, 2002). Imagine that someone tries to persuade you to join a particular club on campus. You consider your interests and beliefs and decide not to join. Your cognition (your thoughts) leads you to control your behavior and resist environmental influence in this instance. Bandura (2001) and other social cognitive psychologists emphasize that psychological health—being well-adjusted—can be measured by people's beliefs in their capacity to exercise some control over their own functioning and over environmental events. Those who can defer immediate satisfaction for a desirable future outcome are also demonstrating the importance of person/cognitive factors in determining their own behavior (Mischel, Cantor & Feldman, 1996; Mischel & Moore, 1980). The point is that we are capable of controlling our behavior rather than being influenced by others.

Self-Efficacy **Self-efficacy** is the belief that one can master a situation and produce positive outcomes. Bandura (1997, 2000, 2001; Bandura & Locke, 2003) and others have shown that self-efficacy is related to a number of positive developments in people's lives, including solving problems, becoming more sociable, initiating a diet or exercise program and maintaining it, and quitting smoking (Borrelli & others, 2002; Fletcher & Banasik, 2001; Warnecke & others, 2001) (see figure 10.5). Self-efficacy influences whether people even try to develop healthy habits, as well as how much effort they expend in coping with stress, how long they persist in the face of obstacles, and even how much stress they experience (Clark & Dodge, 1999). Self-efficacy is related to whether people initiate psychotherapy to deal with their problems and whether it succeeds or not (Kavanaugh & Wilson, 1989; Longo, Lent, & Brown, 1992). Researchers also have found that self-efficacy is linked with successful job performance (Judge & Bono, 2001).

Self-efficacy helps people in unsatisfactory situations by encouraging them to believe that they can succeed (Schunk, 2004). Overweight individuals will likely have more success with their diets if they believe they have the self-control to restrict their eating. Smokers who believe they will not be able to break their habit probably won't

social cognitive theory States that behavior, environment, and person/cognitive factors are important in understanding personality.

self-efficacy The belief that one can master a situation and produce positive outcomes.

even try to quit smoking, even though they know that smoking is likely to cause poor health and shorten their lives.

How can you increase your self-efficacy? The following strategies can help (Watson & Tharp, 2002):

- Make a list of the specific kinds of situations in which you expect to have the most difficulty and the least difficulty. Begin with the easier tasks and cope with the harder ones after you have developed some self-efficacy.
- Distinguish between past performance and your present project. You might come to expect from past failures that you cannot do certain things. However, remind yourself that your past failures are in the past and that you now have a new sense of confidence and accomplishment.
- Some individuals have a tendency to note their failures but not their successes. Keep written records so that you will be concretely aware of your successes. A student who sticks to a study schedule for 4 days and then fails to stick to it on the fifth day should not think, "I'm a failure. I can't do this." This statement ignores the fact that the student has been successful 80 percent of the time so far.

Locus of Control

Much of psychology's current interest in intrinsic motivation, self-determination, and self-responsibility (discussed in chapter 9) grew out of the concept of **locus of control.** This concept refers to individuals' beliefs about whether the outcomes of their actions depend on what they do (internal control) or on events outside of their personal control (external control) (Rotter, 1966). Internally controlled people assume that their own behaviors and actions are responsible for the consequences that happen to them. Externally controlled people believe that, regardless of how they behave, they are subject to the whims of fate, luck, or other people.

Locus of control has especially been studied in regard to physical and mental health (Leganger & Kraft, 2003; Wu, Tang, & Kwok, 2004). Individuals with internal locus of control know more about the conditions that lead to good physical and psychological health and are likelier to take positive steps to improve their health, such as quitting smoking, avoiding substance abuse, and exercising regularly (Lindqvist & Aberg, 2002; Powell, 1992). Individuals with external locus of control are more likely to conform and not question authority (Singh, 1984). They often use defensive strategies in problem solving and coping instead of actively pursuing solutions; thus they fail more often (Lester, 1992). A wealth of research has documented that having an internal locus of control is a personality characteristic associated with positive functioning and adjustment (Engler, 1999).

Optimism

Another factor that is often related to positive functioning and adjustment is being optimistic (Gana, Alaphilippe, & Bailly, 2004; Seligman & Pawelski, 2003). Interest in the concept of optimism in the field of psychology has especially been fueled by Martin Seligman's (1990) research. Seligman views optimists as people who explain the causes of bad events as due to external, unstable, and specific causes. Pessimists explain bad events as due to internal, stable, and global causes.

To illustrate the power of optimism, Seligman (1990) recalled a person he met when he was a consultant for an insurance company. Seligman had persuaded the company to hire salespeople who did not meet all of their qualifications but were high in optimism. One of the 130 applicants who were identified as "optimists" on a measure included in the application package was 45-year-old Bob Dell, who had a wife, two children, and a mortgage. After working 25 years in a meat-packing plant, Bob had been suddenly fired from his job. With no immediate job prospects and only a high school education, his situation looked grim. When he was approached by an insurance agent who wanted to sell him a policy, Bob informed the agent that he was unemployed. The agent told Bob that his company currently was hiring sales representatives and suggested that he apply for a position. Bob

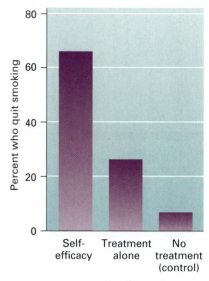

FIGURE 10.5 Self-Efficacy and Smoking Cessation In one study, smokers were randomly assigned to one of three conditions. In the self-efficacy condition, individuals were told they had been chosen for the study because they had great potential to quit smoking. Then they participated in a 14-week program on smoking cessation. In the treatment-alone condition, individuals participated in the 14-week smoking cessation program but were told that they had been randomly selected for it. In the no-treatment control condition, individuals did not participate in the smoking cessation program. At the conclusion of the 14-week program, individuals in the self-efficacy condition were more likely to have quit smoking than their counterparts in the other two groups.

locus of control Individuals' beliefs about whether the outcomes of their actions depend on what they do (internal control) or on events outside of their personal control (external control).

Martin Seligman went from pessimist to optimist and believes that you can, too. *How does Seligman's theme relate to positive psychology, which you read about in chapter 1?*

had never sold anything, but, being an optimist, he decided to give it a try. In less than 1 year, Bob went from sausage-stuffer to super-salesman, earning twice what he had at the meat-packing plant. When Bob learned from a magazine article about the experimental program that he had participated in, with characteristic optimism, he called Seligman, introduced himself, and sold him a retirement policy.

Seligman's interest in optimism stemmed from his work on *learned helplessness,* which initially focused on animals that became passive and unresponsive after they experienced uncontrollable negative events (1975). In his view, pessimism is much like learned helplessness and belief in external locus of control. Optimism is much like self-efficacy and internal locus of control.

Numerous studies reveal that optimists generally function more effectively and are healthier than pessimists:

- *Physical health.* In one study, people who were classified as optimistic at age 25 were healthier at ages 45 to 60 than those who had been classified as pessimistic (Peterson, Seligman, & Vaillant, 1988). In another study, pessimism was linked with less effective immune system functioning and poor health (Brennan & Charnetski, 2000). Optimists also have been found to have lower blood pressure than pessimists (Raikkonen & others, 1999).
- *Mental health.* In one study, optimism was a better predictor than self-efficacy of the person's ability to avoid depression over time (Shnek & others, 2001). In another study, optimism was related to better mental health in cancer patients (Cohen, de Moor, & Amato, 2001). In yet another study, optimism was linked with better mental health and lower perceptions of pain in older adults (Achat & others, 2000).

Optimism is not always good, however, especially if it encourages a person to be overly unrealistic (Clarke & others, 2000; Peterson, 2000; Schneider, 2001). But being optimistic is a good strategy when you have some chance of affecting the future through an optimistic outlook. Thinking optimistically is discussed further in chapter 13.

Evaluating Behavioral and Social Cognitive Perspectives

The behavioral and social cognitive theories both focus on the influence of environment on personality. They have fostered a scientific climate for understanding personality that highlights the observation of behavior. In addition, social cognitive theory emphasizes the influence of cognitive processes in explaining personality and suggests that people have the ability to control their environment.

Criticism of the behavioral and social cognitive perspectives includes one or more of the following points:

- The behavioral view is criticized for ignoring the importance of cognition in personality and giving too much importance to the role of environmental experiences.
- Both approaches have been described as too concerned with change and situational influences on personality and not paying adequate tribute to the enduring qualities of personality.
- Both views are said to ignore the role biology plays in personality.
- Both are labeled reductionistic, which means they try to explain the complex concept of personality in terms of one or two factors.
- Both the behavioral and social cognitive views are criticized for being too mechanical, missing the most exciting, richest dimensions of personality.

The final criticism—that the creative, spontaneous, human dimensions of personality are missing from both the behavioral and social cognitive perspectives—has been made on numerous occasions by humanists, whose perspective is considered next.

Review and Sharpen Your Thinking

3   *Explain the behavioral and social cognitive perspectives.*
- Summarize Skinner's behaviorism.
- Discuss Bandura's social cognitive theory.
- Evaluate the behavioral and social cognitive perspectives.

Are you an optimist or a pessimist? Explain how your style of thinking about bad events has helped you or hindered you as a student.

HUMANISTIC PERSPECTIVES 4

Rogers' Approach   Self-Esteem

Maslow's Approach   Evaluating Humanistic Perspectives

What are the main themes of the humanistic perspectives?

Remember the example of the engaged couple, Tom and Ann? Humanistic psychologists would say that Tom's and Ann's warm, friendly personalities are a reflection of their inner selves. They would emphasize that a key to understanding the attraction between Tom and Ann is their positive perception of each other. Tom and Ann are not trying to control each other. Rather, they have determined their own courses of action, and each has freely chosen to marry. According to the humanistic perspectives, neither raw biological instincts nor unconscious thoughts are reasons for their attraction.

The **humanistic perspectives** stress a person's capacity for personal growth, freedom to choose one's own destiny, and positive human qualities. Humanistic psychologists believe that each of us has the ability to cope with stress, to control our lives, and to achieve what we desire (Cain, 2001; Smith, 2001). Each of us has the ability to break through and understand ourselves and our world.

The humanistic perspectives provide clear contrasts to the psychodynamic perspectives, which often seem to be based on conflict, destructive drives, and a pessimistic view of human nature. The humanistic perspectives also seem to contrast with the behavioral perspective, which, at its extreme, reduces human beings to mere puppets on the strings of rewards and punishments. It does have some similarities with the social cognitive perspective, though, especially with those theories that emphasize the role of personal control and optimism in personality.

Rogers' Approach

Like Freud, Carl Rogers (1902–1987) began his inquiry about human nature with people who were troubled. In the knotted, anxious, defensive musings of his clients, Rogers (1961) noted the things that seemed to be keeping them from having positive self-concepts and reaching their full potential as human beings.

Rogers believed that most people have considerable difficulty accepting their own true, innately positive feelings. As we grow up, people who are central to our lives condition us to move away from these positive feelings. Too often, we hear our parents, siblings, teachers, and peers say things like "Don't do that," "You didn't do that right," and "How can you be so stupid?" When we don't do something right, we often get punished. Parents may even threaten to withhold their love unless we conform to their standards. The result is lower self-esteem.

humanistic perspectives Stress the person's capacity for personal growth, freedom to choose a destiny, and positive qualities.

Carl Rogers was a pioneer in the development of the humanistic perspective. *For which three concepts is he known?*

These constraints and negative feedback continue during our adult lives. The result tends to be either that our relationships carry the dark cloud of conflict or that we conform to what others want. As we struggle to live up to society's standards, we distort and devalue our true selves. And we might even completely lose our sense of self by mirroring what others want.

Rogers is known for three concepts:

- *The self.* Through the individual's experiences with the world, a self emerges— the "I" or "me" of our existence. Rogers did not believe that all aspects of the self are conscious, but he did believe they are all accessible to consciousness. The self is a whole, consisting of one's self-perceptions (how attractive I am, how well I get along with others, how good an athlete I am) and the values we attach to these perceptions (good/bad, worthy/unworthy). **Self-concept** is individuals' overall perceptions and assessments of their abilities, behavior, and personalities. In Rogers' view, a person who has an inaccurate self-concept is likely to be maladjusted. The greater the discrepancy between the real self, which is the self resulting from our experiences, and the ideal self, which is the self we would like to be, said Rogers, the more maladjusted we will be. To improve our adjustment, we can develop more positive perceptions of our real self, not worry as much about what others want, and increase our positive experiences in the world.

- *Unconditional positive regard, empathy, and genuineness.* Rogers proposed three ways to help a person develop a more positive self-concept. Rogers said we need to be accepted by others, regardless of what we do. **Unconditional positive regard** is his term for accepting, valuing, and being positive toward another person regardless of the person's behavior. He strongly believed that unconditional positive regard elevates the person's self-worth. However, Rogers (1974) distinguished between unconditional positive regard directed at the individual as a person of worth and dignity and directed at the individual's behavior. For example, a therapist who adopts Rogers' view might say, "I don't like your behavior, but I accept you, value you, and care about you as a person." Rogers also said that we can help other people develop a more positive self-concept if we are *empathic* and *genuine*. Being empathic means being a sensitive listener and understanding another's true feelings. Being genuine means being open with our feelings and dropping our pretenses and facades. For Rogers, unconditional positive regard, empathy, and genuineness are the key ingredients of human relations. They help other people feel good about themselves and help us get along better with others (Bozarth, Zimring, & Tausch, 2001).

- *The fully functioning person.* Rogers (1980) stressed the importance of becoming a fully functioning person—someone who is open to experience, is not overly defensive, is aware of and sensitive to the self and the external world, and for the most part has a harmonious relationship with others. Rogers believed that we are highly resilient and capable of being fully functioning persons—whether we experience a discrepancy between our real selves and our ideal selves, whether we encounter others who may try to control us, or whether we receive too little unconditional positive regard. He believed that a person's basic tendencies are to actualize, maintain, and enhance life. He thought that the tendency for fulfillment—toward actualizing one's essential nature and attaining potential—is inborn in every person.

self-concept A central theme in Rogers' and other humanists' views; individuals' overall perceptions of their abilities, behavior, and personality.

unconditional positive regard Rogers' term for accepting, valuing, and being positive toward another person regardless of the person's behavior.

Maslow's Approach

Abraham Maslow (1908–1970) was one of the most powerful figures in psychology's humanistic movement. He called the humanistic approach the "third force" in psychology—that is, an important alternative to the psychodynamic and behavioral forces.

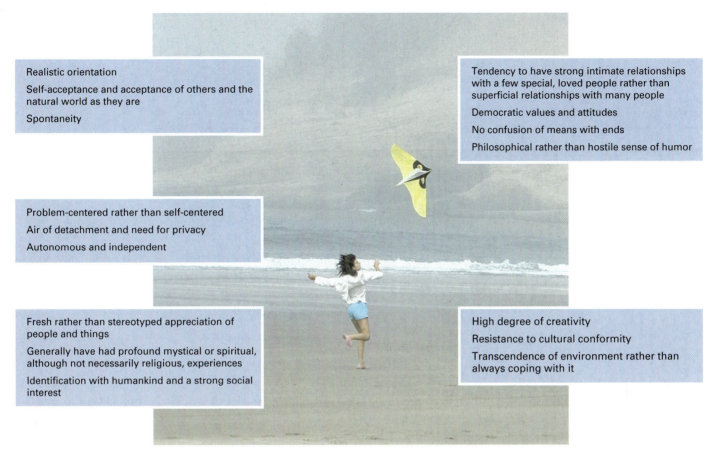

Realistic orientation

Self-acceptance and acceptance of others and the natural world as they are

Spontaneity

Tendency to have strong intimate relationships with a few special, loved people rather than superficial relationships with many people

Democratic values and attitudes

No confusion of means with ends

Philosophical rather than hostile sense of humor

Problem-centered rather than self-centered

Air of detachment and need for privacy

Autonomous and independent

Fresh rather than stereotyped appreciation of people and things

Generally have had profound mystical or spiritual, although not necessarily religious, experiences

Identification with humankind and a strong social interest

High degree of creativity

Resistance to cultural conformity

Transcendence of environment rather than always coping with it

FIGURE 10.6 **Maslow's Characteristics of Self-Actualized Individuals**

Maslow argued that psychodynamic theories place too much emphasis on disturbed individuals and their conflicts. Behaviorists ignore the person altogether, he said.

Recall from chapter 9 that Maslow believed self-actualization is the highest-level human need. The motivation to develop one's full potential as a human being was Maslow's primary focus. Figure 10.6 describes the main characteristics of a self-actualized individual. (See the video clip "Self-Actualization" for a look at the role that challenges play in the process of achieving one's full potential.)

In-Psych Plus

Maslow believed that most people have difficulty reaching this level. As examples of self-actualized people, he included Pablo Casals (cellist), Albert Einstein (physicist), Ralph Waldo Emerson (writer), William James (psychologist), Thomas Jefferson (politician), Abraham Lincoln (politician), Eleanor Roosevelt (humanitarian, diplomat), and Albert Schweitzer (humanitarian). Maslow made up his list over three decades ago. He named considerably more men than women on the complete list, and most of the individuals were from Western cultures. Keeping Maslow's description of self-actualization in mind (including the characteristics listed in figure 10.6), think of others you would add to Maslow's list of self-actualized persons. For starters, consider Mother Teresa (spiritual leader) and Martin Luther King, Jr. (clergyman, civil rights activist) (Endler, 1995).

Self-Esteem

Rogers' and Maslow's interest in the self led to the belief that self-esteem is an important aspect of personality. **Self-esteem** is a person's overall evaluation of his or her self-worth or self-image.

self-esteem A person's overall evaluation of self-worth or self-image.

FIGURE 10.7 Self-Esteem Across the Life Span One large-scale study asked more than 300,000 individuals to rate the extent to which they have high self-esteem on a 5-point scale, 5 being "strongly agree" and 1 being "strongly disagree." Self-esteem was lower in adolescence and late adulthood. Self-esteem of females was lower than self-esteem of males through most of the life span and was especially low for females during adolescence.

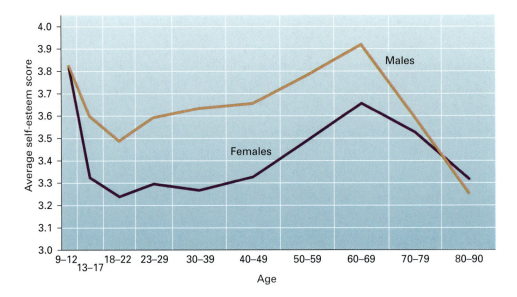

Psychologists have shown considerable interest in self-esteem and how it is developed and maintained (Baumeister & others, 2003; Hewitt, 2001; Hochschild & others, 2004). Following are some of the research issues and findings on self-esteem (Baumeister, 1997):

- *Does self-esteem fluctuate from day to day or remain stable?* Most research studies have found it to be stable at least across a month or so (Baumeister, 1991). Self-esteem can change, however, especially in response to transitions in life (such as graduating from high school or going to college) and to life events (such as getting or losing a job). One recent study found that self-esteem is high in childhood, declines in adolescence, and increases through adulthood until late adulthood, at which time it declines again (Robins & others, 2002) (See figure 10.7.) In this study, the self-esteem of males was higher than that of females through most of the life span.

- *Is self-esteem something very general, or does it consist of a number of independent self-evaluations in different areas?* That is, is it more appropriate to think of people having high or low self-esteem overall or as having high or low self-esteem in specific areas of their lives, such as high in social self-esteem and low in cognitive (academic) self-esteem? Current thinking is that people do have a general level of self-esteem but also have fluctuating levels of self-esteem in particular domains of their lives (Fleming & Courtney, 1984).

- *Does high self-esteem cause better performance, interpersonal success, happiness, or healthier lifestyles?* Based on a review of research, Roy Baumeister and his colleagues (2003) answered the four parts to this question in this way: (1) no, (2) no, (3) probably, and (4) sporadically. The modest correlations between school performance and self-esteem and occupational success and self-esteem do not indicate that high self-esteem produces good performance. Rather, it is just as likely that high self-esteem is produced by better school and vocational performance.

Researchers have not found that individuals high in self-esteem have better relationships or make better impressions on others than their counterparts with low self-esteem. Self-esteem is strongly related to happiness, and it seems likely that high self-esteem increases happiness, whereas depression lowers it. High self-esteem does not prevent children from taking drugs or engaging in early sex, although high self-esteem does reduce the incidence of bulimia nervosa. Keep in mind, though, that appraisal of the effects of high self-esteem is complicated by its heterogeneous nature. High self-esteem is a category that encompasses people who deserve their high self-esteem and are well adjusted, as well as individuals who are narcissistic, defensive, and conceited.

An important point needs to be made about much of the research on self-esteem: It is correlational rather than experimental. Remember from the discussion in chapter 1 that correlation does not equal causation. Thus, if a correlational study finds an association between low self-esteem and depression, depression might cause low self-esteem as much as low self-esteem might cause depression.

A topic of considerable interest among clinical and educational psychologists is what can be done to increase the self-esteem of individuals with low self-esteem. Researchers have found that four main strategies help to improve self-esteem (Bednar, Wells, & Peterson, 1995; Harter, 1998):

- Identifying the causes of low self-esteem
- Experiencing emotional support and approval
- Achieving goals
- Coping successfully

The strategy of experiencing emotional support and approval meshes with Carl Rogers' concept of unconditional positive regard. But some psychologists argue that the most effective ways to improve self-esteem are to improve the person's achievement and coping skills. Rogers himself believed that, when a person's achievement and coping skills improve, the individual's self-esteem is likely to follow suit. Coping skills are further discussed in chapter 13.

Evaluating Humanistic Perspectives

The humanistic perspectives made psychologists aware that the way we perceive ourselves and the world around us are key elements of personality. Humanistic psychologists also reminded us that we need to consider the whole person and the positive bent of human nature (Bohart & Greening, 2001). Their emphasis on conscious experience has given us the view that personality contains a well of potential that can be developed to its fullest (Hill, 2000).

A weakness of the humanistic perspective is that it is difficult to test. Self-actualization, for example, is not even clearly defined, much less easy to observe. Psychologists are not certain how to study this concept empirically. Complicating matters is the fact that some humanists scorn the experimental approach, preferring clinical interpretation as a database. Indeed, verification of humanistic concepts has come mainly from clinical experiences rather than from controlled experimental studies.

Some critics also believe that humanistic psychologists are too optimistic about human nature, overestimating the freedom and rationality of humans. And some critics say the humanists may encourage excessive self-love and narcissism by encouraging people to think so positively about themselves.

Review and Sharpen Your Thinking

4   *Describe the humanistic perspectives.*

- Explain the key elements in Rogers' theory.
- Summarize Maslow's theory.
- Discuss the importance of self-esteem to individuals.
- Evaluate the humanistic perspectives.

What is the level of your self-esteem? That is, on the whole, are you satisfied with yourself? Or do you wish that you could have a more positive attitude toward yourself? Is your self-esteem higher in some areas of your life than others? If so, which ones? If your self-esteem is low, what do you think it would take to get it higher?

5 TRAIT PERSPECTIVES

- Trait Theories
- Trait-Situation Interaction
- The Big Five Personality Factors
- Evaluating Trait Perspectives

What are the main ideas of the trait perspectives?

Through the ages, we have described ourselves and one another in terms of basic traits. A **trait** is an enduring personality characteristic that tends to lead to certain behaviors. Think about how you would quickly describe yourself and your friends. You might say that you're outgoing and sociable and that, in contrast, one of your friends is shy and quiet. You might refer to yourself as emotionally stable and describe one of your other friends as a bit skittish. Part of our everyday existence involves describing ourselves and others in terms of traits.

Trait Theories

Trait theories state that personality consists of broad, enduring dispositions that tend to lead to characteristic responses. In other words, people can be described in terms of the basic ways they behave, such as whether they are outgoing and friendly or dominant and assertive. People who have a strong tendency to behave in certain ways are described as high on those traits; those who have a weak tendency to behave in certain ways are described as low on those traits. Although trait theorists differ on which traits make up personality, they agree that traits are the fundamental building blocks of personality (Larson & Buss, 2002; Matthews & Dreary, 1998).

In-Psych Plus

Is the way people relate to others a trait of their personality? Assess your own response style in the interactivity "Styles of Responses."

Allport's View of Traits   Gordon Allport (1897–1967) believed that each individual has a unique set of personality traits. He argued that, if we can determine a person's traits, we can predict the individual's behavior in various circumstances.

In going through an unabridged dictionary, Allport (1937) identified more than 4,500 personality traits. To impose some organization on these many ways of describing a personality, Allport grouped traits into three main categories:

- *Cardinal traits* are the most powerful and pervasive. When they are present, they dominate an individual's personality. However, according to Allport, few people actually possess cardinal traits. We might characterize some famous individuals by their cardinal traits (Hitler's craving for power, Mother Teresa's altruism). But most people aren't characterized by just one or two traits.
- *Central traits* are limited in number. Allport believed that most people have about 6 to 12 central traits that are usually adequate to describe their personality. For an example, an individual's personality might be described as friendly, calm, kind, humorous, messy, and nostalgic.
- *Secondary traits* are limited in frequency and least important in understanding an individual's personality. They include particular attitudes and preferences, such as the type of food or music a person likes.

Eysenck's Dimensions of Personality   Hans Eysenck (1916–1997) also tackled the task of determining the basic traits of personality. He gave personality tests to large numbers of people and analyzed each person's responses. Eysenck (1967) said that three dimensions are needed to explain personality:

trait An enduring personality characteristic that tends to lead to certain behaviors.

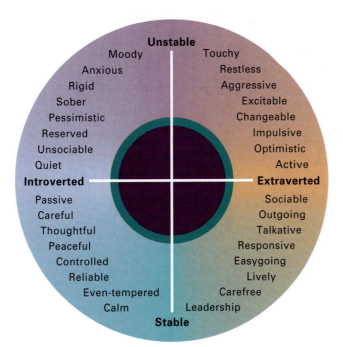

FIGURE 10.8 Eysenck's Dimensions of Personality Eysenck believed that, for people without a psychological disorder, personality consists of two basic dimensions: introverted/extraverted and stable/unstable.

- *Introverted/extraverted.* An introverted person is quiet, unsociable, passive, and careful; an extraverted person is active, optimistic, sociable, and outgoing (Thorne, 2001).
- *Stable/unstable* (known as the *neuroticism* dimension). A stable person is calm, even-tempered, carefree, and capable of leadership; an unstable person is moody, anxious, restless, and touchy.
- *Psychoticism.* This dimension reflects the degree to which people are in contact with reality, control their impulses, and are cruel or caring toward others.

Figure 10.8 shows the interaction of what Eysenck considered to be the two basic dimensions of personality: introverted/extraverted and stable/unstable. Eysenck believed that various combinations of these dimensions result in certain personality traits. For example, a person who is extraverted and unstable is likely to be impulsive. He also thought that a third dimension—psychoticism—is needed to describe the personality of individuals with a psychological disorder.

To evaluate the extent to which you are extraverted or introverted, see the Psychology and Life box.

The Big Five Personality Factors

Psychologists still take considerable interest in determining what the key factors of personality really are. A rash of research studies points toward a handful of factors as being the most important dimensions of personality (Costa & McCrae, 1995, 1998; David & Suls, 1999; Hogan, 1987; McCrae & Costa, 2001). The **big five factors of personality,** the "supertraits" that are thought to describe the main dimensions of personality, are openness, conscientiousness, extraversion, agreeableness, and neuroticism (emotional stability). Notice that, if you create an acronym from these trait names, you get the word *OCEAN.* Recall, from the beginning of the chapter, the description of the personality traits of great presidents. One trait that characterized great presidents was openness to experience. In recent years, extraversion also has characterized great presidents.

big five factors of personality Openness to experience, conscientiousness, extraversion, agreeableness, and neuroticism (emotional stability).

Are You Extraverted or Introverted?

To determine how extraverted or introverted you are, read the following questions and answer either *yes* (if it is generally true for you) or *no* (if it is not generally true for you).

	Yes	No
1. Do you often long for excitement?		
2. Are you usually carefree?		
3. Do you stop and think things over before doing anything?		
4. Would you do almost anything on a dare?		
5. Do you often do things on the spur of the moment?		
6. Generally, do you prefer reading to meeting people?		
7. Do you prefer to have few but special friends?		
8. When people shout at you, do you shout back?		
9. Do other people think of you as very lively?		
10. Are you mostly quiet when you are with people?		
11. If there is something you want to know about, would you rather look it up in a book than talk to someone about it?		
12. Do you like the kind of work that you need to pay close attention to?		
13. Do you hate being with a crowd who plays jokes on one another?		
14. Do you like doing things in which you have to act quickly?		

	Yes	No
15. Are you slow and unhurried in the way you move?		
16. Do you like talking to people so much that you never miss a chance of talking to a stranger?		
17. Would you be unhappy if you could not see lots of people most of the time?		
18. Do you find it hard to enjoy yourself at a lively party?		
19. Would you say that you are fairly self-confident?		
20. Do you like playing pranks on others?		

To arrive at your score for extraversion, give one point for each of the following items answered *yes:* 1, 2, 4, 5, 8, 9, 14, 16, 17, 19, and 20. Then give yourself one point for each of the following items answered *no:* 3, 6, 7, 10, 11, 12, 13, 15, 18. Add up all the points to arrive at a total score.

Your total score should be between 0 and 20. If your score is very high (15–20), you are the "life of the party." You clearly prefer being with others to being alone. If your score is very low (0–5), you are a loner. You find greater pleasure in solitary activities. If you are somewhere in between (6–14), you are flexible in how you prefer to spend your time. You take pleasure in the company of others (especially if your score is in the higher range) but still also appreciate solitude.

The big five factors are described in figure 10.9. The more universal, stable, and predictive they prove to be, the more confidence we can have that they truly describe a person's fundamental traits:

- *Do they show up in the assessment of personality in cultures around the world?* There is increasing evidence that they do (Ozer & Riese, 1994). Researchers have found that some version of the five factors appears in people in countries as diverse as Canada, Finland, Poland, China, and Japan (Paunonen & others, 1992).

- *Are they stable over time?* Using a five-factor personality test that they devised, Paul Costa and Robert McCrae (1995) are studying approximately 1,000 college-educated men and women ages 20 to 96, assessing the same individuals over many years. Data collection began in the 1950s to the mid-1960s. Costa and McCrae have so far concluded that openness, conscientiousness, extraversion, agreeableness, and neuroticism are all reasonably stable. For instance, individuals high on agreeableness tend to remain so throughout the years.

- *Can they help us to predict physical and mental health?* The notion that personality characteristics might influence health continues to attract widespread research

Openness	**C**onscientiousness	**E**xtraversion	**A**greeableness	**N**euroticism (emotional stability)
• Imaginative or practical	• Organized or disorganized	• Sociable or retiring	• Softhearted or ruthless	• Calm or anxious
• Interested in variety or routine	• Careful or careless	• Fun-loving or somber	• Trusting or suspicious	• Secure or insecure
• Independent or conforming	• Disciplined or impulsive	• Affectionate or reserved	• Helpful or uncooperative	• Self-satisfied or self-pitying

FIGURE 10.9 The Big Five Factors of Personality Each of the broad supertraits encompasses more narrow traits and characteristics. Use the acronym *OCEAN* to remember the big five personality factors (*o*penness, *c*onscientiousness, and so on).

attention. Much of this research, though, has been conducted using a hodge-podge of traits. The big five trait structure offers the potential of a unified, coherent framework for understanding which types of people are likely to stay healthy and to recover quickly from illness.

Research has generally supported the concept of the big five "general" traits, but some personality researchers believe this might not end up being the final list of broad supertraits and that more specific traits are better predictors of behavior (Saucier, 2001). For example, some support has been found for two additional personality dimensions: excellent/ordinary and evil/decent. The big five could become the big seven (Almagor, Tellegen, & Waller, 1995; Benet & Waller, 1995).

Trait-Situation Interaction

Today, most psychologists in the field of personality believe that both trait (person) and situation need to be taken into account to understand personality (Block, 2002; Edwards & Rothbard, 1999; Mischel & others, 2002; Roberts & Robins, 2004). They also agree that consistency in personality depends on the kind of persons, situations, and behaviors sampled (Mischel, 1995, 2004; Pervin, 2000; Swartz-Kulstad & Martin, 2000).

Suppose you want to assess the happiness of Bob, an introvert, and of Jane, an extravert. According to trait-situation interaction theory, we cannot predict who will be happier unless we know something about the situations they are in. Imagine you get the opportunity to observe them in two situations, at a party and in a library. The extravert, Jane, is likely to enjoy the party more; the introvert, Bob, is likely to enjoy the library more.

Trait-situation studies are clarifying the link between traits and situations (Martin & Swartz-Kulstad, 2000; Walsh, 1995). For example, researchers have found that (1) the narrower and more limited a trait is, the likelier it will predict behavior; (2) some people are consistent on some traits and other people are consistent on other traits; and (3) personality traits exert a stronger influence on an individual's behavior when situational influences are less powerful.

Cross-cultural psychologists go further. They believe that both the immediate setting *and* the broader cultural context are important (Kitayama, 2002; Oyserman, Coon, & Kemmelmeier, 2002). For example, if they are investigating certain aspects of personality and religion, they might observe a person's behavior in a chapel (the immediate setting) and put it in the context of conventions regarding who should be in church, when, with whom, and how the person is expected to behave (cultural characteristics). See the video clip "Culture and Self" to learn more about the profound effect of culture on the individual.

In-Psych Plus

Evaluating Trait Perspectives

Studying personality traits has practical value. Identifying a person's traits allows us to know the person better. Also, the traits that we have influence our health, the way we think, how well we do in a career, and how well we get along with others (Larson & Buss, 2002; McCrae & Costa, 2001).

However, viewing people only in terms of their traits may provide only a partial view of personality. In his landmark book *Personality and Assessment,* Walter Mischel (1968) criticized the trait perspectives. Rather than viewing personality as consisting of broad, internal traits that are consistent across situations and time, Mischel said that personality often changes according to a given situation. This view is consistent with Mischel's social cognitive perspective.

Mischel went beyond theoretical criticism, however. He reviewed an array of studies and concluded that trait measures by themselves often do a poor job of predicting actual behavior. For example, let's say Anne is described as an aggressive person. But when we observe her behavior, we find that she is aggressive with her boyfriend but almost submissive with her new boss. Mischel's view was called *situationism,* which means that personality often varies considerably from one context to another. Many trait psychologists were not willing to abandon altogether the idea of consistent, enduring personality characteristics. But Mischel's situationism helped to pave the way for viewing personality in terms of trait-situation interaction.

Review and Sharpen Your Thinking

5 **Discuss the trait perspectives.**

- Describe Allport's and Eysenck's trait theories.
- Identify the big five factors in personality.
- Explain trait-situation interaction.
- Evaluate the trait perspectives.

To what extent do you believe the big five factors capture your personality? Look at the characteristics of the five factors listed in figure 10.9 and decide how you line up on each one. Then choose one of the factors, such as extraversion or openness to experience, and give an example of how situation might influence expression of this trait in your life.

6 PERSONALITY ASSESSMENT

Projective Tests   **Self-Report Tests**   **Behavioral and Cognitive Assessment**

What are the main methods of personality assessment?

"This line running this way indicates that you are a gregarious person, someone who really enjoys being around people." These are words you might hear from a palmist. Although palmists claim to provide a complete assessment of personality through reading lines on the palm, researchers debunk palmistry as quackery. Researchers argue that palmists give no reasonable explanation for their inferences about personality and point out that the palm's characteristics can change through age and even exercise.

PERSONALITY PERSPECTIVES

	Psychodynamic Perspectives	Behavioral and Social Cognitive Perspectives	Humanistic Perspectives	Trait Perspectives
Preferred Personality Assessment Techniques	Clinical interviews, unstructured personality tests, psychohistorical analysis of clients' lives	Observation, especially laboratory observation	Self-report tests, interviews. For many humanists, clinical judgment is more important than scientific measurement.	Self-report tests, such as MMPI-2
Theoretical Issues				
Is personality innate or learned?	Freud strongly favored biological foundations. Horney, Jung, and Adler gave social experiences and culture more weight.	Skinner said personality is behavior, which is environmentally determined. Social cognitive theorists, such as Bandura, also emphasize environmental experiences.	Rogers, Maslow, and other humanistic psychologists believe personality is influenced by experience and can be changed.	Eysenck stresses personality's biological basis. Allport and other trait theorists consider both heredity and environment.
Is personality conscious or unconscious?	Psychodynamic theorists, especially Freud and Jung, place a strong emphasis on unconscious thought.	Skinner didn't think conscious or unconscious thought was important. Bandura and Mischel emphasize the cognitive process.	Humanistic psychologists stress the conscious aspects of personality, especially self-concept and self-perception.	Trait theorists pay little attention to this issue.
Is personality determined internally or externally?	Psychodynamic theorists emphasize internal determinants and internal personality structures.	Behaviorists emphasize external, situational determinants. Social cognitive theorists emphasize both internal and external determinants but especially self-control.	Humanistic theorists emphasize internal determinants such as self-concept and self-actualization.	Trait theorists stress internal, personal variables.

FIGURE 10.10 Perspectives on Personality

Even so, palmists manage to stay in business. They do so, in part, because they are keen observers—they respond to such cues as voice, general demeanor, and dress, which are more relevant signs of personality than the lines and folds on a person's palm. Palmists also are experts at offering general, trivial statements, such as "Although you usually are affectionate with others, sometimes you don't get along with people." This statement falls into the category of the *Barnum effect:* If you make your predictions broad enough, any person can fit the description. The effect was named after circus owner P. T. Barnum.

In contrast to palmists, psychologists use a number of scientifically developed methods to evaluate personality (Kraik, 2000; Walsh & Betz, 1995). And they assess personality for different reasons. Clinical and school psychologists assess personality to better understand an individual's psychological problems; they hope the assessment will improve their diagnosis and treatment of the individual. Industrial psychologists and vocational counselors assess personality to aid the individual's selection of a career. And research psychologists assess personality to investigate the theories and dimensions of personality we have discussed so far in this chapter. For example, if a psychologist wants to investigate self-concept, some measure of self-concept is needed.

Before I describe some specific personality tests, two important points need to be made about the nature of personality assessment. First, most personality tests are designed to assess stable, enduring characteristics, free of situational influence (Hy & Loevinger, 1996; Ozer, 2001). Second, the kinds of tests chosen by psychologists frequently depend on the psychologist's theoretical bent. Figure 10.10 summarizes which of the following assessment methods are advocated by different types of theorists. The figure also summarizes the positions of the main personality perspectives on the three issues mentioned earlier in the chapter: whether personality is innate or learned, whether it is conscious or unconscious, and whether it is determined internally or

FIGURE 10.11 **Type of Stimulus Used in the Rorschach Inkblot Test**

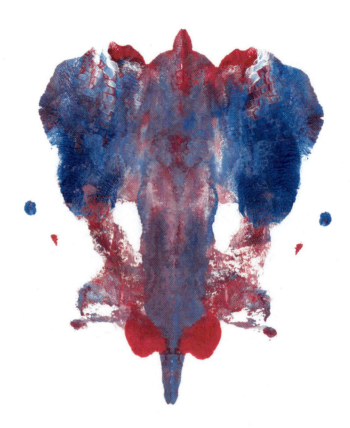

"Rorschach! What's to become of you?"
© Sidney Harris.

externally. Although the diversity of perspectives and methods may seem overwhelming, remember that together they give us a more complete picture of human complexity.

Projective Tests

A **projective test** presents individuals with an ambiguous stimulus and then asks them to describe it or tell a story about it—in other words, to *project* their own meaning onto the stimulus. Projective tests are based on the assumption that the ambiguity of the stimulus allows individuals to invest it with their feelings, desires, needs, and attitudes. The test is especially designed to elicit the individual's unconscious feelings and conflicts, providing an assessment that goes deeper than the surface of personality (Blatt, 2000; Handler, 1999; Hilsenroth, 2004; Leichtman, 2004). Projective tests attempt to get inside of your mind to discover how you really feel and think, going beyond the way you overtly present yourself. Projective tests are theoretically aligned with the psychodynamic perspectives on personality, which give more weight than the other perspectives to the unconscious.

Rorschach Inkblot Test   The **Rorschach inkblot test,** developed in 1921 by the Swiss psychiatrist Hermann Rorschach, is a widely used projective test. The test consists of 10 cards with inkblots, half in black and white and half in color, which are shown to the individual one at a time (see figure 10.11). The person taking the Rorschach test is asked to describe what he or she sees in each of the inkblots. For example, an individual may say, "That looks like two people fighting." After the individual has responded to all 10 inkblots, the examiner presents each of the inkblots again and inquires about the individual's earlier response. For example, the examiner might ask, *"Where* did you see the two people fighting?" and *"What* about the inkblot made the two people look as if they were fighting?" Besides recording the responses, the examiner notes the individual's mannerisms, gestures, and attitudes.

From a scientific perspective, researchers are skeptical about the Rorschach (Feshbach & Weiner, 1996; Garb & others, 2001; Weiner, 2004). If the Rorschach is reliable, two different scorers should agree on the personality characteristics of the individual being tested. If the Rorschach is valid, the individual's score should be able to predict behavior outside of the testing situation; that is, it should predict whether an individual will attempt suicide, become severely depressed, cope successfully with stress, or get along well with others. But research evidence suggests that the Rorschach does not meet these criteria of reliability and validity (Lilienfeld, Wood, & Garb, 2000). Thus many psychologists have serious reservations about the Rorschach's use in diagnosis and clinical practice.

However, the Rorschach continues to enjoy widespread use in clinical circles; some clinicians say the Rorschach is better than any other measure at getting at the true, underlying core of the individual's personality (Ephraim, 2000; Gronnerod, 2003; Hibbard, 2003; Meyer, 2001). They are not especially bothered by the Rorschach's low reliability and validity, pointing out that the test encourages extensive freedom of response. This freedom of response is what makes the Rorschach such a rich clinical tool, say its advocates. In one survey, Rorschach-based testimony was legally challenged in only 6 of nearly 8,000 court cases (Weiner, Exner, & Sciara, 1996).

The Citical Controversy box has more on this debate.

FIGURE 10.12 Picture from the Thematic Apperception Test (TAT)

Other Projective Tests The **Thematic Apperception Test (TAT),** which was developed by Henry Murray and Christina Morgan in the 1930s, is designed to elicit stories that reveal something about an individual's personality. The TAT consists of a series of pictures like the one in figure 10.12, each on an individual card. The person taking the TAT is asked to tell a story about each of the pictures, including events leading up to the situation described, the characters' thoughts and feelings, and the way the situation turns out (Moretti & Rossini, 2004). The tester assumes that the person projects his or her own unconscious feelings and thoughts onto the story (Herzberg, 2000). In addition to being used as a projective test in clinical practice, the TAT is used in research on people's need for achievement (Cramer, 1999; Cramer & Brilliant, 2001). Several of the TAT cards stimulate the telling of achievement-related stories (McClelland & others, 1953).

Many other projective tests are used in clinical assessment. One test asks the individual to complete a sentence (such as "I often feel . . ." or "I would like to . . ."); another test asks the individual to draw a person; and another test presents a word, such as *fear* or *happy,* and asks the individual to say the first thing that comes to mind. Like the Rorschach, these projective tests have their detractors and advocates; the detractors often criticize the tests' low reliability and validity, and the advocates describe the tests' abilities to reveal the underlying nature of the individual's personality better than more straightforward tests can (Holaday, Smith, & Sherry, 2000; Lilienfeld & others, 2000; Sherry, Dahlen, & Holaday, 2004).

Another controversial projective measure is *graphology,* the use of handwriting analysis to determine an individual's personality. Examine the writing in figure 10.13 to see the kinds of interpretations graphologists make. At one time, many firms in the United States—and even more in Israel, Japan, and Europe—used graphology as part of their employee-selection process (Levy, 1979). But the growing research literature on graphology is almost universally negative (Furnham, 1988; King & Koehler, 2000; Lindeman, 1998; Nevo, 1986).

One investigation typifies these negative results (Ben-Shakhar & others, 1986). Three professional graphologists agreed to rate handwriting samples from 52 bank employees. The graphologists were asked to assess the employees' competence at their jobs and the nature of their relationships with co-workers. The samples consisted of brief autobiographical essays and responses to a short biographical questionnaire. At the same time, the researchers used information from the samples—such as the

Thematic Apperception Test (TAT)

A projective test designed to elicit stories that will reveal something about an individual's personality.

Who Is Projecting What?

The Rorschach inkblot test has been said to be "simultaneously, the most cherished and the most reviled of all psychological assessment instruments" (Hunsley & Bailey, 1999). How can this be?

With millions of tests administered every year, the Rorschach is one of the most frequently used projective tests. According to one survey, 82 percent of clinical psychologists occasionally administer the Rorschach and 43 percent report often using the test (Watkins & others, 1995). However, the Rorschach has long been attacked as unreliable and lacking in validity (Lilenfield, Wood, & Garb, 2001).

A psychological assessment is judged to be reliable if it yields consistent results over repeated use. If different scorers can interpret the same individual's test differently, the test does not meet the reliability criterion. To understand how different clinicians might reach different conclusions about an individual from answers to a Rorschach series, consider whether a description should be scored as food-related if someone identifies the whole inkblot as a hamburger. What if the person identifies only one small portion of the inkblot as a hamburger? What if other, nonedible objects are identified in the same inkblot? What if the individual sees another person eating? What if the color of the inkblot plays, or does not play, a role in the description? And what would any of this tell you about the person's state of mind?

Some psychologists believe that many of the ways in which the Rorschach is scored are not reliable enough to be clinically useful (Lilenfield, Wood, & Garb, 2001). For example, if two clinical psychologists administered the Rorschach to the same person and came up with diametrically opposed interpretations, it could mean that the two clinicians were projecting their own personalities onto their patient's Rorschach responses. In other words, the test interpretation might depend more on the personality of the individual clinician than on any characteristic of the test taker. Because the results of a clinical assessment might well determine a course of treatment, or even the outcome of a court case, the stakes can be very high.

A psychological assessment is considered valid if it measures what it is intended to measure. One use of the Rorschach has been to diagnose psychological disorders, such as schizophrenia and depression (Weiner, 1997, 2001, 2004). Therefore, one way to test the diagnostic validity of the Rorschach would

be to administer the test to two groups, a group of normal people and a group of people diagnosed with a disorder, such as schizophrenia. If the Rorschach is valid for diagnosing schizophrenia, then the responses of the two groups should differ. Otherwise, again, a diagnosis might well depend more on the interpretation of the individual clinician than on any characteristic of the test taker. Research evidence suggests that the Rohrschach has little validity as a diagnostic tool (Lilenfield, Wood, & Garb, 2001).

Additionally, when coupled with information from structured interviews and other personality assessment tools, the results from projective tests such as the Rorschach provide extra information the insightful clinician can use to better understand an individual (Meyer & Archer, 2001). Even critics caution that projective tests such as the Rorschach should not be rejected as inherently unreliable and/or invalid (Lilenfield, Wood & Garb, 2001). Instead they urge continuing efforts to construct better projective tests.

Attempts have been made to improve reliability by standardizing scoring systems (Exner, 1974). As a result, responses are typically scored for *location* (does the person respond to the whole inkblot or specific parts?), *quality* (does the person respond to the color, shape, or perceived movement?), *content* (does the person perceive animals, humans, or objects?), and *conventionality* (how do the responses compare with average responses?). The goals of such systems include standardizing the test procedure itself as well as improving the reliability and validity of test interpretations (Gronnerod, 2003; Hibbard, 2003; Viglione & Taylor, 2003).

What do you think?

- What role should evidence based on projective tests such as the Rorschach play in courts of law?
- If you took a Rorschach test, what would you make of the results as they were explained to you by a clinical psychologist?
- Spend some time looking at the inkblot in figure 10.11. Write down everything you see there. Ask some friends to do the same. Discuss your interpretations of your responses. If you do not agree, how can you settle the matter?

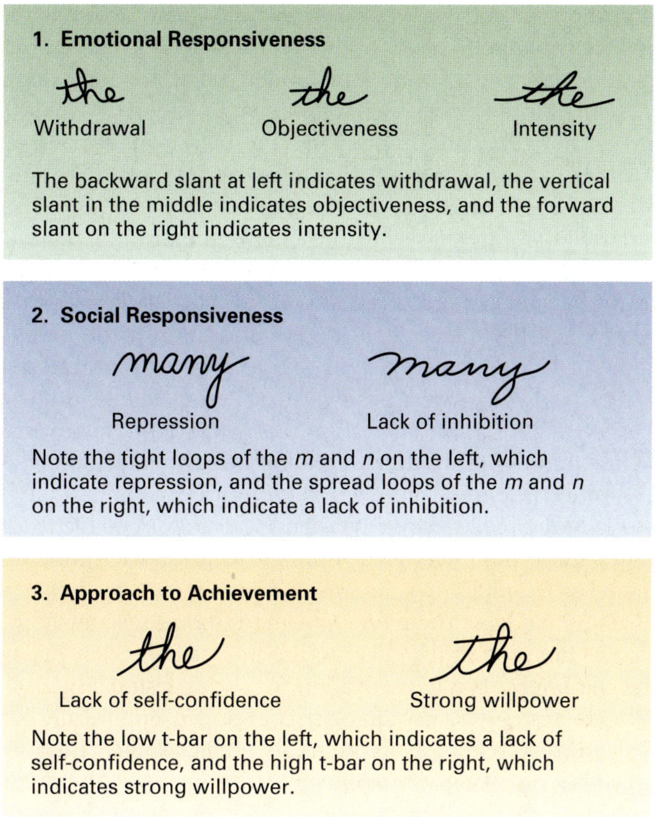

1. **Emotional Responsiveness**

the *the* *the*

Withdrawal   Objectiveness   Intensity

The backward slant at left indicates withdrawal, the vertical slant in the middle indicates objectiveness, and the forward slant on the right indicates intensity.

2. **Social Responsiveness**

many   *many*

Repression   Lack of inhibition

Note the tight loops of the *m* and *n* on the left, which indicate repression, and the spread loops of the *m* and *n* on the right, which indicate a lack of inhibition.

3. **Approach to Achievement**

the   *the*

Lack of self-confidence   Strong willpower

Note the low t-bar on the left, which indicates a lack of self-confidence, and the high t-bar on the right, which indicates strong willpower.

FIGURE 10.13 Some Graphological Interpretations Graphology is a highly controversial assessment technique, unsupported by empirical research.

employees' ages and job interests, the quality of their essays, and the attractiveness of their handwriting—to make assessments about the employees' competence. The researchers' predictions and the graphologists' ratings were compared with ratings by the employees' supervisors. The graphologists did no better than the researchers at matching the supervisors' ratings. A battery of personality tests were better at matching the supervisors' ratings. In a second study, five graphologists did no better than chance when asked to predict the occupations of 40 successful professional men based on several pages of their handwriting.

If the research results are so negative, why is graphology still used and accepted? To some degree, it is because graphologists' predictions, like those of palmists and astrologers, are usually so general they're difficult to prove or disprove. However, all projective tests are difficult to validate scientifically, which has led some to suggest that projective tests do little more than show the biases of the testers.

Self-Report Tests

Unlike projective techniques, self-report tests do not attempt to assess an individual's hidden, unconscious personality. Rather, **self-report tests,** also called *objective tests* or *inventories,* directly ask people whether items describe their personality traits or not. Self-report personality tests include items such as

- I am easily embarrassed.
- I love to go to parties.
- I like to watch cartoons on TV.

Self-report tests include a large number of statements or questions similar to these. The respondent has a limited number of answers to choose from (yes or no, true or false, agree or disagree).

self-report tests Directly ask people whether items (usually true/false or agree/disagree) describe their personality traits or not; also called *objective tests* or *inventories.*

Adherents of the trait perspectives on personality have strong faith in self-report tests. They point out that self-report tests have produced a better understanding of an individual's personality traits than can be derived from, for example, projective tests. However, some critics (especially psychodynamic theorists) believe that the self-report measures do not get at the underlying core of personality and its unconscious determinants. Other critics (especially behaviorists and social cognitive theorists) believe that the self-report measures do not adequately capture the way personality changes as the individual interacts with the environment.

Supporters of self-report tests do concede that they have room for improvement. Many of the early personality tests were based on *face validity,* which is an assumption that the content of the test items is a good indicator of the individual's personality. For example, if I develop a test item that asks you to indicate whether or not you are introverted, and you answer positively to "I enjoy being with people," I accept your response as a straightforward indication that you are not introverted. Tests based on face validity assume that you are responding honestly and nondefensively.

But not everyone is honest, and even if the individual is basically honest, he or she may give socially desirable answers. When motivated by *social desirability,* individuals say what they think the interviewer wants to hear or what they think will make them look better. For example, if I am basically a lazy person, I may try to present myself in a more positive way; therefore, I would respond negatively to the following item: "I fritter away time too much." (Go to the interactivity "Self-Report Bias in Surveys" to explore the impact of the motivation for social desirability.)

In-Psych Plus

Because of such responses, psychologists developed empirically keyed tests. An **empirically keyed test** relies on its items to predict some criterion. Unlike tests based on face validity, in which the content of the items is supposed to be a good indicator of what the individual's personality is like, empirically keyed tests make no assumptions about the nature of the items (Segal & Coolidge, 2000, 2004). Imagine that we want to develop a test that will determine whether or not applicants for a position as police officer are likely to be competent at the job. We might ask a large number of questions of police officers, some of whom have excellent job records and others who have not performed as well. We would then use the questions that differentiate between competent and incompetent police officers on our test to screen job applicants. If the item "I enjoy reading poetry" predicts success as a police officer, then we would include it on the test even though it seems unrelated to police work.

Minnesota Multiphasic Personality Inventory (MMPI)

The most widely used and researched empirically keyed self-report personality test is the **Minnesota Multiphasic Personality Inventory (MMPI).** The MMPI was initially constructed in the 1940s to assess "abnormal" personality tendencies and to improve the diagnosis of individuals with mental disorders. One thousand statements were given to both mental patients and apparently normal people. Only the items that clearly differentiated the psychiatric patients from the normal individuals were retained. For example, the statement "I sometimes tease animals" seems to have little to do with depression—that is, it has little face validity—but it might still be included on the MMPI if patients diagnosed with a depressive disorder agreed with the statement significantly more than did normal individuals.

The MMPI eventually was streamlined to 550 items, each of which can be answered "true," "false," or "cannot say." The items vary widely in content and include such statements as

- I like to read magazines.
- I never have trouble falling asleep.
- People are out to get me.

A person's answers are grouped according to 10 clinical categories, or scales, that measure depression, psychopathic deviation, schizophrenia, social introversion, and so on. Figure 10.14 shows the clinical scales of the MMPI and a sample item for each.

empirically keyed test Relies on items to predict some criterion.

Minnesota Multiphasic Personality Inventory (MMPI) The most widely used and researched self-report personality test.

Clinical Scales	Sample Items
Hypochondriasis (Hs). Abnormal concern with bodily functions.	"At times I get strong cramps in my intestines."
Depression (D). Pessimism, hopelessness, slowing of action and thought.	"I am often very tense on the job."
Conversion Hysteria (Hy). Unconscious use of physical and mental problems to avoid conflicts or responsibility.	"Sometimes there is a feeling like something is pressing in on my head."
Psychopathic Deviate (Pd). Disregard of social custom, shallow emotions, inability to profit from experience.	"I wish I could do over some of the things I have done."
Masculinity-Femininity (Mf). Items differentiating between men and women.	"I used to like to do the dances in gym class."
Paranoia (Pa). Abnormal suspiciousness, delusions of grandeur or persecution.	"It distresses me that people have the wrong ideas about me."
Psychasthenia (Pt). Obsessions, compulsiveness, fears, guilt, indecisiveness.	"The things that run through my head sometimes are horrible."
Schizophrenia (Sc). Bizarre, unusual thoughts or behavior, withdrawal, hallucinations, delusions.	"There are those out there who want to get me."
Hypomania (Ma). Emotional excitement, flight of ideas, overactivity.	"Sometimes I think so fast I can't keep up."
Social Introversion (Si). Shyness, disinterest in others, insecurity.	"I give up too easily when discussing things with others."

FIGURE 10.14 Clinical Scales of the MMPI The 10 clinical scales and a sample item for each scale. Answering each sample item "true" would reflect the direction of the scales.

The MMPI uses 4 validity scales in addition to the 10 clinical scales. The validity scales were designed to indicate whether an individual is lying, careless, defensive, or evasive when answering the test items. For example, if the individual responds "false" repeatedly to certain items, such as "I get angry sometimes," she might be trying to make herself look better-tempered than she really is. The rationale for the lie scale is that each of us gets angry at least some of the time, so the individual who responds "false" to these items may be faking her response to other items.

The MMPI was revised for the first time in 1989. The revision, called the MMPI-2, has a number of new items (for a total of 567 items), but the 10 clinical scales were retained, as were several of the validity scales (such as the lie scale). New content scales were added to the MMPI-2. These include substance abuse, eating disorders, anger, self-esteem, family problems, and inability to function in a job.

The MMPI-2 continues to be widely used around the world to assess personality and predict outcomes (Archer & others, 2001; Butcher, 1999, 2004; Dong & Church, 2003; Handel & Ben-Porath, 2000). It has been so popular that it has been translated into more than 20 languages. Not only is it used by clinical psychologists to assess a person's mental health, but it also is used to predict which individuals will make the best job candidates or which career an individual should pursue. Another important trend is the increased use of computers to score the MMPI-2 (Iverson & Barton, 1999). However, some critics argue that too often the availability of computer scoring has tempted untrained individuals to use the test in ways for which it has not been validated.

Assessments of the Big Five Factors Paul Costa and Robert McCrae (1992) constructed a test, the *Neuroticism Extraversion Openness Personality Inventory—Revised* (or *NEO-PI-R*, for short), to assess the big five factors: openness, conscientiousness, extraversion, agreeableness, and neuroticism (emotional stability). The test also evaluates six subdimensions within the five main factors. Costa and McCrae believe that the test can improve the diagnosis of personality disorders and help therapists understand how therapy might influence different types of clients. For instance, individuals who score high on the extraversion factor might prefer group over individual psychotherapy, whereas introverts might do better in individual psychotherapy.

The NEO-PI-R is used in many research studies of personality as well. For instance, it was the test used to analyze the personality traits of great presidents in the example at the beginning of the chapter.

Type of Behavior	Item
Shared activities	We sat and read together. We took a walk.
Pleasing interactive events	My spouse asked how my day was. We talked about personal feelings. My spouse showed interest in what I said by agreeing or asking relevant questions.
Displeasing interactive events	My spouse commanded me to do something. My spouse complained about something I did. My spouse interrupted me.
Pleasing affectionate behavior	We held each other. My spouse hugged and kissed me.
Displeasing affectionate behavior	My spouse rushed into intercourse without taking time for foreplay. My spouse rejected my sexual advances.
Pleasing events	My spouse did the dishes. My spouse picked up around the house.
Displeasing events	My spouse talked too much about work. My spouse yelled at the children.

FIGURE 10.15 Items from the Spouse Observation Checklist The Spouse Observation Checklist is a behavioral assessment instrument. Couples record their partner's behavior and make daily ratings of their overall satisfaction with the spouse's behavior.

Another measure that is used to assess the big five factors is the Hogan Personality Inventory (HPI), created by Robert Hogan (1986). One way in which the HPI is used, as is the NEO-PI-R, is to attempt to predict job success. Researchers have found that the HPI effectively predicts such job performance criteria as supervisor ratings and training course success (Wiggins & Trapnell, 1997).

Behavioral and Cognitive Assessment

Unlike either projective tests or self-report tests, behavioral assessment of personality is based on observing the individual's behavior directly. Instead of removing situational influence, as projective tests and self-report measures do, behavioral assessment assumes that personality cannot be evaluated apart from the environment (Heiby & Haynes, 2004).

Behavioral assessment of personality emerged from the tradition of behavior modification, which you learned about in chapter 6. The first step in the process of changing an individual's maladaptive behavior is to make baseline observations of its frequency (Hartmann, Barrios, & Wood, 2004). The therapist then modifies some aspect of the environment, such as getting the parents and the child's teacher to stop giving the child attention when he or she engages in aggressive behavior. After a specified period of time, the therapist will observe the child again to determine if the changes in the environment were effective in reducing the child's maladaptive behavior.

When direct observation is not possible, a psychologist with a behavioral orientation might ask individuals to make their own assessments of behavior, encouraging them to be sensitive to the circumstances that produced the behavior and the outcomes or consequences of the behavior (Dipboye, Wooten, & Halverson, 2004). For example, a therapist might want to know the course of marital conflict in the everyday experiences of a couple. Figure 10.15 shows a Spouse Observation Checklist that couples can use to record their partner's behavior.

The influence of social cognitive theory has increased the use of cognitive assessment in personality evaluation. The strategy is to discover what thoughts underlie the individual's behavior; that is, how do individuals think about their problems? What kinds of thoughts precede maladaptive behavior, occur while it is going on, and follow it? The psychologist assesses such cognitive processes as expectations, planning, and memory, possibly by interviewing the individual or asking him or her to complete a questionnaire. An interview might include questions that address whether the individual overexaggerates his faults and condemns himself more than is warranted. A questionnaire might ask a person what her thoughts are after an upsetting event, or it might assess the way she thinks during tension-filled moments.

Locus of control, a key concept in the social cognitive perspectives, is most often assessed with Julian Rotter's (1966) I-E Scale, in which *I* stands for *internal* and *E* for *external*. Following are examples of the types of items used on the I-E Scale:

I More Strongly Believe That	*Or That . . .*
Promotions are earned through hard work and persistence.	Making a lot of money is largely a matter of getting the right breaks.
When I am right I can convince others.	It is silly to think that one can really change another person's basic attitudes.
I believe there is a direct connection between how hard I study and the grades I get.	Many times the reactions of teachers seem haphazard to me.
I am the master of my fate.	A great deal that happens to me is probably due to chance.
The number of divorces suggests that more and more people are not trying to make their marriages work.	Marriage is largely a gamble.

If you more strongly believe that the items in the left column describe you, you likely have a stronger internal locus of control. If you more strongly believe that the items in the right column describe you, you likely have a stronger external locus of control.

The I-E Scale has been used in a wide range of research studies (Al-Mashaan, 2001; Wallston, 2001). Generally, those studies have found that individuals with an internal locus of control are more perceptive than those who have an external locus of control and are more ready to learn about their surroundings. People with an internal locus of control ask more questions and show better problem-solving skills.

Review and Sharpen Your Thinking

6   *Characterize the main methods of personality assessment.*

- Explain why psychologists use personality assessment.
- Discuss projective techniques.
- Describe self-report tests.
- Summarize behavioral and cognitive assessment.

Which of the assessment tools discussed here do you think would likely provide the most accurate picture of your personality? Explain.

Personality

1 THEORIES OF PERSONALITY

2 PSYCHODYNAMIC PERSPECTIVES

| Freud's Psychoanalytic Theory | Psychodynamic Dissenters and Revisionists | Evaluating Psychodynamic Perspectives |

3 BEHAVIORAL AND SOCIAL COGNITIVE PERSPECTIVES

| Skinner's Behaviorism | Bandura's Social Cognitive Theory | Evaluating Behavioral and Social Cognitive Perspectives |

4 HUMANISTIC PERSPECTIVES

| Rogers' Approach | Self-Esteem |
| Maslow's Approach | Evaluating Humanistic Perspectives |

5 TRAIT PERSPECTIVES

| Trait Theories | Trait-Situation Interaction |
| The Big Five Personality Factors | Evaluating Trait Perspectives |

6 PERSONALITY ASSESSMENT

| Projective Tests | Self-Report Tests | Behavioral and Cognitive Assessment |

1 **Define personality and identify the major issues in the study of personality.**

- Personality involves the enduring thoughts, emotions, and behaviors that characterize the way we adapt to the world. Different theoretical perspectives have different answers to these three key questions: Is personality innate or learned? Is personality conscious or unconscious? Is personality influenced by internal factors or external factors?

2 **Summarize the psychodynamic perspectives.**

- Freud believed that most of the mind is unconscious, and his psychoanalytic theory stated that personality has three structures: id, ego, and superego. The conflicting demands of these personality structures produce anxiety. Defense mechanisms protect the ego and reduce this anxiety. Freud was convinced that psychological problems develop because of early childhood experiences. He said that we go through five psychosexual stages: oral, anal, phallic, latency, and genital. During the phallic stage, which occurs in early childhood, the Oedipus complex is a major source of conflict.

- A number of psychodynamic theorists criticized Freud for placing too much emphasis on sexuality and the first 5 years of life. They argued that Freud gave too little credit to the ego, conscious thought, and sociocultural factors. Horney said that the need for security, not sex or aggression, is our most important need. Jung thought Freud underplayed the unconscious mind's role. He developed the concept of the collective unconscious and emphasized archetypes. Adler's theory, called individual psychology, stresses that people are striving toward a positive being and that they create their own goals. Adler placed more emphasis on social motivation than Freud did.

- The psychodynamic perspectives view personality as primarily unconscious and as occurring in stages. Most psychodynamic perspectives emphasize the importance of early experiences with parents in sculpting personality. Strengths of the psychodynamic perspectives include emphases on the individual's past experiences, on personality's developmental course, on mental representation of the environment, on the unconscious mind, and on conflict as an influence on personality. These perspectives have had a substantial influence on psychology as a discipline. Weaknesses of the psychodynamic perspectives include overreliance on reports from the past, too much emphasis on sexuality and the unconscious mind, a negative view of human nature, too much attention to early experience, and a White male, Western bias.

3 **Explain the behavioral and social cognitive perspectives.**

- Skinner's behaviorism emphasizes that cognition is unimportant in personality; personality is observable behavior, which is influenced by rewards and punishments in the environment. In the behavioral view, personality often varies according to the situation.

- Social cognitive theory states that behavior, environment, and person/cognitive factors are important in understanding personality. In Bandura's view, these factors reciprocally interact. Three important concepts in social cognitive theory are self-efficacy, locus of control, and optimism. Self-efficacy is the belief that one can master a situation and produce positive outcomes. *Locus of control* refers to individuals' beliefs about whether the outcomes of their actions depend on what they do (internal) or on events outside of their control (external). Optimists explain bad events as being caused by external, unstable, and specific circumstances. Pessimists explain bad events as being caused by internal, stable, and global causes. Optimism also involves the expectancy that good things are more likely, and bad things less likely, to occur in the future. Numerous research studies reveal that individuals characterized by self-efficacy, internal locus of control, and optimism generally show positive functioning and adjustment.

- The behavioral and social cognitive perspectives emphasize the importance of environmental experience in understanding personality. Within that broad framework, behaviorists focus on people's observable behavior; social cognitive theorists also examine cognitive factors in personality. Strengths of these perspectives include their emphases on environmental determinants and on a scientific climate for investigating personality. An additional strength of social cognitive theory is its focus on cognitive processes and self-control. The behavioral view has been criticized for taking the "person" out of personality and for ignoring cognition. These approaches also have not given adequate attention to enduring individual differences, to biological factors, and to personality as a whole.

4 **Describe the humanistic perspectives.**

- Rogers' view is that the self is typically not valued unless it meets the standards of other people. The self is the core of personality; it includes both the real and ideal selves. Rogers said that we can help others develop more positive self-concept in three ways: unconditional positive regard, empathy, and genuineness. Rogers also stressed that each of us has the innate, inner capacity to become a fully functioning person.

- Maslow called the humanistic movement the "third force" in psychology. Maslow developed the concept of the hierarchy of needs, with self-actualization being the highest human need.
- Self-esteem is the person's overall evaluation of self-worth or self-image. Four main strategies for increasing a person's self-esteem are to identify the causes of low self-esteem, provide emotional support and approval, help the person achieve valued goals, and help the person learn to cope successfully with challenges.
- The humanistic perspectives stress the person's capacity for personal growth and freedom, ability to choose a destiny, and positive qualities. These perspectives sensitize us to the importance of subjective experience, of consciousness, of self-conception, of consideration of the whole person, and of our innate, positive nature. Weaknesses are tendencies to avoid empirical research, be too optimistic, and encourage excessive self-love.

5 *Discuss the trait perspectives.*

- Allport believed that each unique set of personality traits can be grouped into three main categories: cardinal, central, and secondary. Eysenck's basic dimensions of personality are introverted/extraverted, stable/unstable (neuroticism), and psychoticism.
- There is much current interest in the big five factors in personality, which are considered to be overarching "supertraits": openness to experience, conscientiousness, extraversion, agreeableness, and neuroticism (emotional stability).
- Today, most personality psychologists believe that personality is determined by a combination of traits, or person factors, and the situation, or environmental factors.
- Trait theories emphasize that personality consists of broad, enduring dispositions that lead to characteristic responses. Trait theorists are also interested in how traits are organized within the individual. Traits are assumed to be essentially stable over time and across situations. Studying people in terms of their traits has practical value. Identifying a person's traits allows us to know the person better. Understanding a person's traits also may help us better predict the person's health, thinking, job

success, and interpersonal skills. Critics argue that personality varies across situations more than trait theorists acknowledge.

6 *Characterize the main methods of personality assessment.*

- Psychologists use a wide variety of tests and measures to assess personality. These measures often are tied to psychologists' theoretical orientations. Personality tests were designed to measure stable, enduring aspects of personality.
- A projective test presents individuals with an ambiguous stimulus and then asks them to describe it or tell a story about it. Projective tests are based on the assumption that the ambiguity of the stimuli allows individuals to project their personalities onto them. Projective tests are designed to assess the unconscious aspects of personality. The Rorschach inkblot test is a widely used projective test; its effectiveness is controversial. The Thematic Apperception Test (TAT) is another projective test.
- Self-report tests assess personality traits by asking test takers questions about their preferences and behaviors. Even though a self-report test may have face validity, it may still elicit invalid responses when people try to answer in a socially desirable way. Empirically keyed tests, which rely on items that are indirect questions about some criterion, were developed to overcome the problem of face validity. The Minnesota Multiphasic Personality Inventory (MMPI) is the most widely used and researched self-report personality test; it has 10 clinical scales to assist therapists in diagnosing psychological problems and uses validity scales. Tests also have been created to assess the big five personality factors. Two of the most popular are the Neuroticism Extraversion Openness Personality Inventory—Revised (NEO-PI-R) and the Hogan Personality Inventory (HPI).
- Behavioral assessment seeks to obtain objective information about personality through observation of behavior and its environmental ties. Cognitive assessment uses interviews and questionnaires to discover individual differences in processing and acting on information.

Key Terms

personality, p. 355

psychodynamic
    perspectives, p. 356

id, p. 357

ego, p. 357

superego, p. 357

defense mechanisms, p. 357

Oedipus complex, p. 359

collective unconscious,
    p. 360

archetypes, p. 361

individual psychology,
    p. 361

behavioral and social
    cognitive perspectives,
    p. 363

social cognitive theory,
    p. 364

self-efficacy, p. 364

locus of control, p. 365

humanistic perspectives,
    p. 367

self-concept, p. 368

unconditional positive
    regard, p. 368

self-esteem, p. 369

trait, p. 372

big five factors of
    personality, p. 373

projective test, p. 378

Rorschach inkblot test,
    p. 378

Thematic Apperception Test
    (TAT), p. 379

self-report tests, p. 381

empirically keyed test,
    p. 382

Minnesota Multiphasic
    Personality Inventory
    (MMPI), p. 382

Apply Your Knowledge

1. Consider a facet of your personality that you might want to change. From the perspective of Freud's psychoanalytic theory, could you change this aspect of your personality? How? From the perspective of the psychodynamic revisionists, would it be possible to make the desired change? How?

2. The next time you are in a situation in which the outcome is unknown (for example, you have a test coming up, or you're thinking about an upcoming date), pay attention to how you respond to the situation in terms of the three important concepts of social cognitive theory described in this chapter. Now try to approach the situation using the characteristic opposite to whatever you would normally do. How easy or hard was switching? Did it have an effect on the outcome? How would you know?

3. Think about the big five (or big seven) factors in personality and their relationship to various situations. Which factors

can be assessed in an individual and which are measures of interactions between people? Which factors would you expect to vary more depending on the situation?

4. Type *personality test* into an online search engine, and take two or more of the tests available online. Now look at the results. Which of the personality perspectives do the results seem to reflect most? How might the structure of the tests have affected the outcomes?

5. Think about the three major issues in the study of psychology described at the beginning of the chapter. In many cases, questions posed as "either/or" turn out to be best answered by "some of both." After reading about all the theories in the chapter, how could you rephrase the three major issues if you were interested in answering them scientifically?

Connections

To test your mastery of the material in this chapter, go to the Study Guide and the In-Psych Plus CD-ROM, as well as the On-line Learning Center. There you will find a chapter summary,

practice tests, flashcards, lecture slides, web links, and other study tools, such as interactive exercises and reviews as well as current, chapter-relevant news articles.

11 Psychological Disorders

Learning Goals

1 Discuss the characteristics and classifications of abnormal behavior.

2 Distinguish among the various anxiety disorders.

3 Describe the dissociative disorders.

4 Compare the mood disorders and specify the risk factors for depression and suicide.

5 Characterize schizophrenia.

6 Identify the behavior patterns typical of personality disorders.

Kay Redfield Jamison is a psychologist and a leading expert on serious mood disorders. For years, Jamison harbored a secret. She herself had a serious psychological disorder: bipolar disorder, in which moods alternate between mania (an overexcited, unrealistically optimistic state) and depression so severe she sometimes wanted to die. In her memoir, Jamison (1995) tells of her battle with the disorder:

> There is a particular kind of pain, elation, loneliness, and terror involved in this kind of madness. When you're high it's tremendous. The ideas and feelings are fast and frequent like shooting stars, and you follow them until you find better and brighter ones. Shyness goes, the right words and gestures are suddenly there, the power to captivate others a felt certainty. There are interests found in unin-

Kay Redfield Jamison, a psychologist who has waged her own personal battle with bipolar disorder.

teresting people. Sensuality is pervasive and the desire to seduce and be seduced irresistible. Feelings of ease, intensity, power, well-being, financial omnipotence, and euphoria pervade one's marrow. But, somewhere this changes. The fast ideas are too fast, and there are far too many, overwhelming confusion replaces clarity. Memory goes. Everything previously moving with the grain is now against you. . . . You are irritable, angry, frightened, uncontrollable, and submerged totally in the blackest caves of the mind.

Through strong support from friends and colleagues, excellent mental health care, medication, and her own acceptance of the disorder, Jamison has been able to dampen and control her mood swings. Today she continues to be an expert on psychological disorders as a professor at Johns Hopkins School of Medicine.

1 PERSPECTIVES ON PSYCHOLOGICAL DISORDERS

- Defining Abnormal Behavior
- Understanding Psychological Disorders
- Classifying Abnormal Behavior

What are the characteristics of abnormal behavior, and how is it categorized?
An estimated 44 million Americans each year suffer from some kind of psychological disorder (National Institute of Mental Health [NIMH], 2001b). In one study, nearly 20,000 randomly selected individuals from five different regions of the United States were asked whether they had experienced any item on a list of psychological disorders in their lifetimes and whether they currently were suffering from one (Robins & Regier, 1991). The study included individuals both in institutions and in the community. Almost one-third (32 percent) of the respondents said that they had experienced one or more psychological disorders in their lifetimes; 20 percent said they currently had an active disorder; 17 percent had a substance abuse disorder (alcohol or other drugs). Surprisingly, only one-third of the individuals in this study who said they currently had a psychological disorder had received treatment for it in the previous 6 months.

Defining Abnormal Behavior

To understand psychological disorders, we need to examine what is meant by *abnormal behavior*. It is one of those concepts that is not easy to define (Oltmanns & Emory, 2004). The definition varies across academic disciplines and across social, medical, and legal institutions. For example, the federal courts define *insanity*—a legal term, not a psychological term—as the inability to appreciate the nature and quality or wrongfulness of one's acts (Pikona-Sapir, Melamed, & Elizur, 2001). The American

Psychiatric Association (2001) defines abnormal behavior in medical terms: a mental illness that affects or is manifested in a person's brain and can affect the way a person thinks, behaves, and interacts with people.

The line between what is normal and what is abnormal is not always clear-cut. However, we can use three criteria to help distinguish normal from abnormal behavior. **Abnormal behavior** is behavior that is deviant, maladaptive, or personally distressful. Only one of the three criteria listed needs to be met for the behavior to be classified as abnormal, but two or all three may be present. Let's take a closer look at what each of the three criteria of abnormal behavior entails:

- Abnormal behavior is *deviant*—not to be confused with *atypical*. People such as Sandra Day O'Connor and Colin Powell are atypical, because of their extraordinary abilities, but we do not usually categorize them as abnormal. When atypical behavior deviates from acceptable norms in a culture, though, it is often considered abnormal. People do not normally wash their hands three or four times an hour, take seven showers a day, and clean their apartments at least twice a day.
- Abnormal behavior is *maladaptive*, meaning that it interferes with a person's ability to function effectively in the world. A person who isolated himself from society because he believed that his breath has powerful, even harmful, effects on others would not be able to function in the everyday world (Gorenstein, 1997).
- Abnormal behavior involves *personal distress*. A person might be distressed about how driven she is to stay clean and keep her immediate environment uncontaminated. So might someone who has experienced personal setbacks in every area of her life and sees her future as extremely bleak.

There are a number of myths and misconceptions about abnormal behavior. The following are some of the most common:

Myth: Abnormal behavior is always bizarre.
Fact: The behavior of many people who are diagnosed as having a mental disorder often cannot be distinguished from that of normal people. Belief in the power of your breath to harm is bizarre. However, feeling distressed about personal setbacks is not considered bizarre.

Myth: Normal and abnormal behavior are different in kind.
Fact: Few, if any, types of behavior displayed by people with a mental disorder are unique to them. Abnormal behavior consists of a poor fit between the behavior and the situation in which it is enacted.

Myth: Once people have a mental disorder, they will always have it.
Fact: Most people, such as Kay Redfield Jamison, can be successfully treated for a mental disorder.

Understanding Psychological Disorders

What causes people to develop a psychological disorder—to behave in deviant, maladaptive, and personally distressful ways? We can look to the biological, psychological, and sociocultural perspectives for theoretical explanations and can consider the possibility that a combination of factors contribute to an individual's maladaptive behavior.

Biological Approach The biological approach to psychological disorders attributes them to organic, internal causes. Scientists who adopt a biological approach to psychological disorders often focus on brain and genetic factors as the sources of abnormal behavior. In the biological approach, drug therapy is frequently used to treat abnormal behavior.

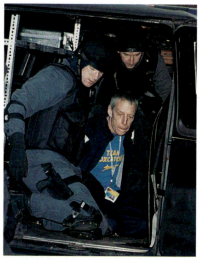

In 1996, multimillionaire John Dupont, a 58-year-old heir to the Dupont chemical fortune, pulled out a gun and killed Olympic Gold Medal wrestler David Schultz, who lived in a home on Dupont's estate and was one of several wrestlers training at Dupont's state-of-the-art wrestling facility. No one disputes that Dupont killed Schultz, but Dupont's lawyers, using the so-called insanity defense, argued that he was so incapacitated by schizophrenia that he could not be held accountable for the murder. Prosecutors claimed he was an eccentric man driven by envy and anger who knew exactly what he was doing. After a week's deliberation, the jury concluded that Dupont had a psychological disorder but found him guilty of third-degree murder. *What does "insanity" mean today?*

abnormal behavior Behavior that is deviant, maladaptive, or personally distressful.

The biological approach is evident in the **medical model,** which describes psychological disorders as medical diseases with a biological origin. From the perspective of the medical model, abnormalities are called mental *illnesses*, the individuals afflicted are *patients*, and they are treated by *doctors*.

Biological views on psychological disorders fall into three main categories (Nolen-Hoeksema, 2004):

* *Structural views*. Abnormalities in the brain's structure cause mental disorders.
* *Biochemical views*. Imbalances in neurotransmitters or hormones cause mental disorders.
* *Genetic views*. Disordered genes cause mental disorders.

These biological factors are discussed later in the chapter.

Psychological Approach   Chapter 10 described the psychodynamic, behavioral and social cognitive, and humanistic perspectives on personality. These perspectives serve as a foundation for understanding the psychological factors involved in psychological disorders:

* *Psychodynamic perspectives*. Psychological disorders arise from unconscious conflicts that produce anxiety and result in maladaptive behavior. Ineffective early relationships with parents are believed to be the origin of psychological disorders. Recall that these ideas stem from Freud's psychoanalytic theory but that some contemporary proponents of this approach place less emphasis on unconscious thought and sexuality than he did.
* *Behavioral and social cognitive perspectives*. In the behavioral perspective, the focus is on the rewards and punishments in the environment that determine abnormal behavior. Social cognitive theory accepts that environmental experiences are important determinants of psychological disorders but adds that a number of social cognitive factors also are involved. Observational learning, expectancies, self-efficacy, self-control, beliefs about oneself and the world, and many other cognitive processes are key to psychological disorders.
* *Humanistic perspectives*. These perspectives emphasize a capacity for growth, freedom to choose one's own destiny, and positive personal qualities. A psychological disorder reflects an inability to fulfill one's potential, likely arising from pressures of society to conform to others' expectations and values. A person with a psychological disorder is likely to have a weak self-concept because he or she has experienced excessive criticism and negative circumstances.

The psychological perspectives focus mainly on the individual. Chapter 12 extensively examines how these theories of personality influence the treatment of psychological disorders.

Sociocultural Approach   Although the psychological approach attributes psychological problems mainly to factors within the individual, it still gives environmental experiences a role (Nolen-Hoeksema, 2001). The sociocultural approach places more emphasis on the larger social contexts in which a person lives—including the individual's marriage or family, neighborhood, socioeconomic status, ethnicity, gender, or culture—than do the other approaches. For example, any number of psychological problems can develop because of power struggles in a family: sibling conflicts, one child being favored over another, marital conflict, and so on.

Individuals from low-income, minority neighborhoods have the highest rates of mental disorders. Studies show that socioeconomic status plays a much stronger role than does ethnicity: The living conditions of poverty often create stressful circumstances that can contribute to the development of a mental disorder (Elliott, Beattie, & Kaitfors, 2001; Schultz & others, 2000; Weich, Lewis, & Jenkins, 2001).

medical model A biological approach that describes psychological disorders as medical diseases with a biological origin.

Disorder	Culture	Description/Characteristics
Amok	Malaysia, Philippines, Africa	This disorder involves sudden, uncontrolled outbursts of anger in which the person may injure or kill someone. Amok is often found in males who are emotionally withdrawn before the onset of the disorder. After the attack on someone, the individual feels exhausted and depressed and does not remember the rage and attack.
Anorexia nervosa	Western cultures, especially the United States	This eating disorder involves a relentless pursuit of thinness through starvation and can eventually lead to death.
Windigo	Algonquin Indian hunters	This disorder involves a fear of being bewitched. The hunter becomes anxious and agitated, worrying he will be turned into a cannibal with a craving for human flesh.

FIGURE 11.1 Some Culture-Related Psychological Disorders

Gender is another sociocultural factor strongly associated with certain psychological disorders (Greenglass, 1998; Nolen-Hoeksema, 2004; Wood, 2001). Women, who are socialized to turn their feelings inward, tend to be diagnosed with internalized disorders. In particular, women are more likely than men to be diagnosed with anxiety disorders and depression, which have symptoms that are turned inward. Conversely, men, who are socialized to direct their energy toward the outside world, tend to be diagnosed with externalized disorders. In particular, men are more often diagnosed with disorders that involve aggression and substance abuse. Gender differences are discussed more fully later in the chapter.

Many psychological disorders are universal (Al-Issa, 1982). However, the frequency and intensity of psychological disorders vary and depend on social, economic, technological, and religious aspects of cultures (Cueller & Paniagua, 2000; Draguns, 1990; Lopez & Guarnaccia, 2000; Tanaka-Matsumi, 2001). And some disorders are clearly culture-related, as indicated in figure 11.1 (Marsella, 2000).

Biopsychosocial Approach   Normal and abnormal behavior alike may involve biological, psychological, and sociocultural factors alone or in combination with other factors. Abnormal behavior can be influenced by biological factors (such as brain processes and heredity), psychological factors (such as distorted thoughts or low self-esteem), and sociocultural factors (such as ineffective family functioning or poverty). These factors can interact to produce abnormal behavior. This interactionist approach is often called *biopsychosocial* (Evans, 1999).

Classifying Abnormal Behavior

Ever since human history began, people have suffered from diseases, sadness, and bizarre behavior. And, for almost as long, healers have tried to treat and cure them. (For an introduction to the history of psychological disorders, see the video clip "History of Mental Illness.") The classification of psychological disorders goes back to the ancient Egyptians and Greeks and has its roots in biology and medicine. To this day, the classification of psychological disorders follows a medical model.

In-Psych Plus

Classifying psychological disorders is a difficult undertaking and one that provokes criticism not only from mental health professionals but also from many other segments of society (Lowe & others, 2004). However, the benefits of a classification system far outweigh the disadvantages. For one thing, a classification system gives mental health professionals a common basis for communicating. For example, if one psychologist says in a case review that her client has a panic disorder and another says that his client has Asperger syndrome, the two psychologists understand that the clients exhibited certain behavior that led to their diagnoses. (The video clip "ADHD" describes the case of David, a 16-year-old with attention-deficit hyperactivity disorder. Go to the video clip "Asperger Syndrome" to learn more about this disorder, the mildest form of autism.) In addition, a classification system can help clinicians make predictions; it provides information about the likelihood that a disorder will occur, about which individuals are most susceptible to the disorder, about how the disorder will progress, and about the prognosis for treatment (Rogers, 2001).

DSM-IV Classification System   In 1952, the American Psychiatric Association published the first major classification of psychological disorders in the United States. *DSM-IV* (*Diagnostic and Statistical Manual of Mental Disorders*, 4th edition) (American Psychiatric Association [APA], 1994) is the current edition of the APA's guidelines. It contains 17 major classifications and describes more than 200 specific disorders. Continuing changes in the *DSM* reflect advances in knowledge about the classification of psychological disorders (Canino & others, 2004; First & Pincus, 2002; Widiger, 2000). On the basis of research and clinical experience, the *DSM-IV* added, dropped, or revised categories, sometimes generating controversy.

A key feature of the *DSM-IV* is its *multiaxial system*, which classifies individuals on the basis of five dimensions, or axes, which take into account the individual's history and highest level of functioning in the previous year. This system ensures that the individual is not merely assigned to a psychological disorder category but, instead, is characterized in terms of a number of clinical factors (Gelder, Mayou, & Geddes, 1999). The five axes of *DSM-IV* are

Axis I: All diagnostic categories except personality disorders and
    mental retardation
Axis II: Personality disorders and mental retardation
Axis III: General medical conditions
Axis IV: Psychosocial and environmental problems
Axis V: Current level of functioning

Axes I and II comprise the classification of psychological disorders (Davison & Neale, 2001). Figure 11.2 describes the major categories of these psychological disorders. Axes III through V may not be needed to diagnose a psychological disorder, but they are included so that the person's overall life situation is considered. Thus a person might have a heart condition (Axis III), which has important implications for treatment because some antidepressant drugs can worsen heart conditions. Axis IV includes occupational problems, economic problems, and family problems. On Axis V, the clinician makes a diagnosis about the highest level of adaptive functioning the person has attained in the preceding year in social, occupational, or school activities. This diagnosis can range from a rating of 100 (superior functioning in a wide range of activities) to 10 (persistent danger of severely hurting self or others). A rating of 50 indicates serious symptoms or impairment in social, occupational, or school functioning.

The more than 200 mental health professionals who contributed to the development of the *DSM-IV* were a much more diverse group than their predecessors, who were mainly White male psychiatrists. More women, ethnic minorities, and nonpsychiatrists, such as clinical psychologists, were involved in the construction of the *DSM-IV*, and greater attention was given to gender- and ethnicity-related diagnoses (Nathan, 1994). Also, the *DSM-IV* is accompanied by a number of sourcebooks that present the empirical base of the *DSM-IV*. In previous versions of the *DSM*, the reasons for diagnostic changes were not always explicit, so the evidence that led to their formulation was never available for public evaluation.

DSM-IV *Diagnostic and Statistical Manual of Mental Disorders*, 4th edition; the most recent major classification of psychological disorders by the American Psychiatric Association.

Major Categories of Psychological Disorders	Description
Axis I Disorders	
Disorders usually first diagnosed in infancy, childhood, or adolescence and communication disorders	Include disorders that appear before adolescence, such as attention-deficit hyperactivity disorder, autism, learning disorders (stuttering, for example).
Anxiety disorders	Characterized by motor tension, hyperactivity, and apprehensive expectations/thoughts. Includes generalized anxiety disorder, panic disorder, phobic disorder, obsessive-compulsive disorder, and post-traumatic stress disorder.
Somatoform disorders	Occur when psychological symptoms take a physical form even though no physical causes can be found. Includes hypochondriasis and conversion disorder.
Factitious disorders	The person deliberately fabricates symptoms of a medical or mental disorder, but not for external gain (such as a disability claim).
Dissociative disorders	Involve a sudden loss of memory or change of identity. Include the disorders of dissociative amnesia, dissociative fugue, and dissociative identity disorder.
Delirium, dementia, amnestic, and other cognitive disorders	Consist of mental disorders involving problems in consciousness and cognition, such as substance-induced delirium or dementia involving Alzheimer's disease.
Mood disorders	Disorders in which there is a primary disturbance in mood; include depressive disorders and bipolar disorder (which involves wide mood swings from deep depression to extreme euphoria and agitation).
Schizophrenia and other psychotic disorders	Disorders characterized by distorted thoughts and perceptions, odd communication, inappropriate emotion, and other unusual behaviors.
Substance-related disorders	Include alcohol-related disorders, cocaine-related disorders, hallucinogen-related disorders, and other drug-related disorders.
Sexual and gender-identity disorders	Consist of three main types of disorders: gender-identity disorders (person is not comfortable with biological identity as a female or male), preferences for unusual sexual acts to stimulate sexual arousal, and sexual dysfunctions (impairments in sexual functioning).
Eating disorders	Include anorexia nervosa and bulimia nervosa.
Sleep disorders	Consist of primary sleep disorders, such as insomnia and narcolepsy, and sleep disorders due to a general medical condition.
Impulse control disorders not elsewhere classified	Include kleptomania, pyromania, and compulsive gambling.
Adjustment disorders	Characterized by distressing emotional or behavioral symptoms in response to an identifiable stressor.
Axis II Disorders	
Mental retardation	Consists of low intellectual functioning and an inability to adapt to everyday life.
Personality disorders	Develop when personality traits become inflexible and maladaptive.
Other conditions that may be a focus of clinical attention	Include relational problems (with a partner, sibling, and so on), problems related to abuse or neglect (physical abuse of a child, for example), or additional conditions (such as bereavement, academic problems, religious or spiritual problems).

FIGURE 11.2 Main Categories of Psychological Disorders in the *DSM-IV*

The most controversial aspect of the *DSM-IV* is an issue that has existed since the publication of the *DSM-I* in 1952. Although more nonpsychiatrists than ever were responsible for drafting the *DSM-IV*, it still reflects a medical, or disease, model (Clark, Watson, & Reynolds, 1995; Nathan & Langenbucher, 1999, 2003; Oltmanns & Emory, 2004; Sarbin & Keen, 1998). Classifying individuals based on their symptoms and using medical terminology continue the psychiatric tradition of thinking about mental disorders in terms of illness and disease. This classification system implies an internal cause that is more or less independent of external or environmental factors (Adams & Cassidy, 1993), even though researchers have begun to shed light on the complex interaction of genetic, neurobiological, cognitive, and environmental factors in the *DSM* disorders.

Although psychologists usually go along with the *DSM-IV*, psychiatrists are more satisfied with it because of its medical approach. Even though the *DSM-IV* has its critics, it is still the most comprehensive classification system available.

A new edition of the *DSM* will not be published until 2006, but the American Psychiatric Association has revised the text of *DSM-IV* to include new research information conducted since its publication in 1994. The revision, *DSM-IV-TR* (Text Revision) (APA, 2000) includes changes in the criteria for several disorders. For example, sexual disorders such as exhibitionism and voyeurism can now be diagnosed if they are acted on, even though they may not cause the person whose behavior is in question distress or impaired functioning.

Risks of Labeling The *DSM-IV* is also controversial because it labels as psychological disorders what are often thought of as everyday problems. For example, under learning or academic skills disorders, the *DSM-IV* includes the categories of reading disorder, mathematics disorder, and disorder of written expression. Under substance-related disorders, the *DSM-IV* includes the category of caffeine-use disorders. We don't usually think of these everyday problems as mental disorders, but including them implies that these "normal" behaviors should be treated as abnormal. The developers of the *DSM* system argue that mental health providers have been treating many problems not included in earlier editions of *DSM* and that the classification system should be more comprehensive. One practical reason for including everyday problems in living in the *DSM-IV* is to help more individuals get their health insurance companies to pay for professional help. Most health insurance companies reimburse their clients only for disorders listed in the *DSM-IV* system.

Another criticism of the *DSM-IV*, and indeed of this type of classification system in general, is that the system focuses strictly on pathology and problems, with a bias toward finding something wrong with anyone who becomes the object of diagnostic study (Allen, 1998). Because labels can become self-fulfilling prophecies, emphasizing strengths as well as weaknesses might help to destigmatize labels such as *paranoid schizophrenic* or *ex-mental patient*. It would also help to provide clues to treatments that promote mental competence rather than working only to reduce mental distress.

In a classic and controversial study that illustrated the problem of labeling a person with a psychological disorder, David Rosenhan (1973) recruited eight college students, none with a psychological disorder, to see a psychiatrist at a hospital. They were instructed to act in a normal way except to complain about hearing voices that said such things as "empty" and "thud." All eight expressed an interest in leaving the hospital and behaved in a cooperative manner. Nonetheless, they were labeled with schizophrenia, a severe psychological disorder, and kept in the hospital from 3 to 52 days.

Labels can be damaging to a person when they draw attention to one aspect of a person and ignore others (Sarason & Sarason, 2002). For example, the label of "mental patient" or a label of any disorder, such as anxiety disorder, often has negative connotations, implying that the person is incompetent, dangerous, and socially

Are Psychological Disorders a Myth?

When he published *The Myth of Mental Illness* in 1961, psychiatrist Thomas Szasz set off a bitter debate, which still rages today. He made the surprising claim that there is no such thing as "mental illness." Szasz begins his argument with a distinction between diseases of the brain and diseases of the mind. Although he accepts that there are diseases of the brain, such as epilepsy, he suggests that psychological disorders are not "illnesses" and are better labeled "problems of living." Imagine someone, for example, who believes that his or her body is already dead. That person may behave in strange ways but may exhibit no physical defects or diseases. In this case, according to Szasz, the person certainly holds some maladaptive beliefs but does not have a psychological disorder.

For Szasz this is not just a question of semantics. Suppose someone's "problems of living" stem from interacting with other people. In such instances, Szasz says, it is inconsistent to refer to that person's social problems as "mental illness" and treat the problem through a medical model that prescribes drugs. If the person who believes that his or her body is already dead does nothing more than offend or frighten other people with his bizarre belief, then what right do mental health professionals have to label him "mentally ill" and administer drugs to him?

Published the following year, Ken Kesey's 1962 novel, *One Flew over the Cuckoo's Nest*, explores just such a tragedy. The antihero, McMurphy, is a social outsider who opts to go to a mental institution instead of prison. Unfortunately for him, the hospital staff do not take kindly to his unruliness. He is treated with drugs and electroshock therapy until he loses his identity. Kesey wrote his best-seller based on his experiences in working a mental hospital.

A poignant example of dealing with "problems of living" can be found in the origins of dissociative identity disorder (having two or more distinct personalities or selves) (Braun, 1985). Children whose parents have dissociative identity disorder may develop signs of the disorder as a learned behavior. This tragedy may be compounded by diagnosing such children as having a psychological disorder and treating them with drugs. For Szasz, the treatment of such children should be sociocultural (such as removing them from unhealthy environments and placing them in healthy ones) and may involve behavioral techniques.

Szasz's critique extends to suggesting that the insanity defense be abolished. He says that finding people not guilty of a crime by reason of insanity means that they have a psychological disorder, which he disputes. Rather, they are misbehaving by committing a crime, in which case they should be held responsible. Stripping them of responsibility yet depriving them of liberty for a longer period than they would have served for a criminal conviction is doing them no favor.

Szasz's critics cite sound evidence that biological factors are implicated in psychological disorders, including the mood disorders and schizophrenia. They also argue that many psychological disorders are now successfully treated using drug therapies that were unavailable when Szasz first published his arguments. When it comes to the insanity defense, critics argue that imprisoning someone suffering from a psychological disorder for a crime is much less humane than providing him or her with treatment aimed at curing the disorder.

This issue continues to attract attention, as in this commentary: "There is a heightened awareness of the dangers inherent in labeling somebody with a disease category like schizophrenia, and many people are beginning to realize that there is no such entity" (Masson, 1998, p. 2). Also, a majority of individuals with all but the most severe psychological disorders improve without benefit of systematic psychotherapy (Woods, 1986). Szasz's supporters argue that defining an individual's problems as illness only undermines his or her hope of improving.

If any resolution to this controversy is in sight, it is that everyone agrees on the need for further research to clarify what "depression" and "schizophrenia" really are. In the end, nobody wants to label inappropriately, misdiagnose, or mistreat people who are already suffering.

What do you think?

- When do you think it is appropriate to label someone as having a psychological disorder?
- When do you think medical interventions for mental disorders are appropriate?
- Under what circumstances, if any, is the insanity defense an acceptable legal alternative? Why?

unacceptable. Negative labels can reduce a person's self-esteem and cause the person to be discriminated against. People may be reluctant to seek help because they don't want to be labeled "mentally ill" or "crazy." Also, even when a person who has had a psychological disorder is successfully treated, the label may stay with the person. Listen to the audio clip "Stigma of Mental Illness" to learn about ways to reduce the negative effects of labeling.

With these shortcomings in mind, some have gone so far as to argue that psychological disorders are a myth, as detailed in the Critical Controversy box.

In-Psych Plus

2 ANXIETY DISORDERS

Generalized Anxiety Disorder

Phobic Disorder

Post-Traumatic Stress Disorder

Panic Disorder

Obsessive-Compulsive Disorder

In-Psych Plus

What are the characteristics of the various anxiety disorders?

Anxiety is a diffuse, vague, highly unpleasant feeling of fear and apprehension. How anxious are you? Go to the interactivity "Measuring Anxiety" to assess your level of anxiety. People with high levels of anxiety worry a lot, but their anxiety does not necessarily impair their ability to function in the world. **Anxiety disorders** are psychological disorders that feature motor tension (jumpiness, trembling, inability to relax), hyperactivity (dizziness, a racing heart, or possibly perspiration), and apprehensive expectations and thoughts. Approximately 19.1 million American adults from 18 to 54 years of age, or about 13.3 percent of people in this age group, are diagnosed with an anxiety disorder in any given year (NIMH, 2001a). The five types of anxiety disorders are generalized anxiety disorder, panic disorder, phobic disorders, obsessive-compulsive disorder, and post-traumatic stress disorder.

Generalized Anxiety Disorder

anxiety disorders Psychological disorders that include motor tension, hyperactivity, and apprehensive expectations and thoughts.

generalized anxiety disorder An anxiety disorder that consists of persistent anxiety for at least 1 month; the individual with this disorder cannot specify the reasons for the anxiety.

Anna, who is 27 years old, has just arrived for her visit with the psychologist. She was very nervous, wringing her hands, crossing and uncrossing her legs, and playing nervously with strands of her hair. She said her stomach felt like it was in knots, that her hands were cold, and that her neck muscles were so tight they hurt. She said that lately arguments with her husband had escalated. In recent weeks, Anna indicated that she felt more and more nervous throughout the day as if something bad were about to happen. If the doorbell sounded or the phone rang, her heart beat rapidly and her breathing quickened. When she was around people, she had a difficult time speaking. She began to isolate herself. Her husband became impatient with Anna, so she decided to see a psychologist. (Goodstein & Calhoun, 1982)

Anna has a **generalized anxiety disorder,** an anxiety disorder that consists of persistent anxiety for at least 1 month; a person with generalized anxiety disorder cannot specify the reasons for the anxiety (Coupland, 2002; Rickels & Rynn, 2001; Stanley, Diefenbach, & Hopko, 2004). People with generalized anxiety disorder are nervous most of the time. They may worry about their work, their relationships, their health. They also may worry about minor things, such as whether they will be late for an appointment or whether their clothes fit just right. Their anxiety often shifts from one target to another. Approximately 4 million Americans from 18 to 54 years of age, or about 2.8 percent of this age group, have generalized anxiety disorder in any given year (NIMH, 2001a).

What is the etiology of generalized anxiety disorder? **Etiology** means the causes or significant antecedents of a disorder. Among the biological factors involved in generalized anxiety disorder are a genetic predisposition and a deficiency in the neurotransmitter GABA (Nutt, 2001). Among the psychological and sociocultural factors are having harsh self-standards that are virtually impossible to achieve or maintain, having parents who were overly strict and critical (which can produce low self-esteem and excessive self-criticism), automatic negative thoughts in the face of stress, and a history of uncontrollable stressors or traumas, such as an abusive parent.

Panic Disorder

Panic disorder is an anxiety disorder marked by the recurrent, sudden onset of intense apprehension or terror. The individual often has a feeling of impending doom but may not feel anxious all the time. Panic attacks often strike without warning and produce severe palpitations, extreme shortness of breath, chest pains, trembling, sweating, dizziness, and a feeling of helplessness (Caldriola & others, 2004; Slaap & others, 2004). Victims are seized by fear that they will die, go crazy, or do something they cannot control. Approximately 2.4 million Americans from 18 to 54 years of age, or about 1.7 percent of the people in this age group, have panic disorder in any given year (NIMH, 2001a).

In many instances, a stressful life event occurred in the 6 months prior to the onset of panic disorder, most often a threatened or actual separation from a loved one or a change in job. Biological factors in panic disorder also have been explored (Battaglia, 2002; Otte & others, 2002). For example, a panic attack is associated with an overreaction to lactic acid (which is produced by the body when it is under stress).

In *DSM-IV*, panic disorder can be classified as with or without **agoraphobia,** a cluster of fears centered on public places and an inability either to escape or to find help, should one become incapacitated (Fava & others, 2001; Yardley & others, 2001). Being in crowded public places; traveling away from home, especially by public transportation; feeling confined; and being separated from a place or person all can produce agoraphobia. Agoraphobia causes some people to remain housebound. It usually first appears in early adulthood. Females are more likely than males to have panic disorder, with 2.5 percent of individuals in the United States classified as having the disorder. Annie, a young woman with panic attacks and agoraphobia, is described in the video clip "Agoraphobia"; the following is another example:

In-Psych Plus

> Mrs. Reiss is a 48-year-old woman who is afraid to go out alone, a fear that she has had for six years but which has intensified in the last two years. The first signs of her fear appeared after an argument with her husband. After the argument, she went to the mailbox to get the mail and began to feel very anxious and dizzy. It was a struggle for her to get back to the house. Her fear lessened for several years, but reappeared even more intensely after she learned that her sister had cancer. Her fear continued to escalate after arguments with her husband. She became increasingly apprehensive about going outside alone. When she did try to leave, her heart would pound, she would perspire, and she would begin to tremble. After being outside only briefly, she would quickly go back into her house. (Greenberg, Szmulker, & Tantum, 1986)

etiology The causes or significant antecedents of a disorder.

panic disorder An anxiety disorder marked by the recurrent, sudden onset of intense apprehension or terror.

agoraphobia A cluster of fears centered around public places and being unable to escape or to find help, should one become incapacitated.

Many experts interpret Edvard Munch's painting *The Scream* as an expression of the terror brought on by a panic attack. *What behaviors signal panic?*

What is the etiology of panic disorder? Individuals may have a biological predisposition for the disorder, which runs in families and occurs more often in identical than in fraternal twins (Goldstein & others, 1997; Torgerson, 1986). One biological view is that individuals who experience panic disorder may have an autonomic nervous system that is predisposed to be overly active (Barlow, 1988). Another biological view is that panic disorder may be caused by problems involving either or both of two neurotransmitters: norepinephrine and GABA (Sand & others, 2001; Versiani & others, 2002). In yet another biological link, panic attacks involve hyperventilation, or overbreathing (Abelson & others, 2001; Nardi & others, 2001).

One psychological view focuses on panic disorder with agoraphobia. It is called the *fear-of-fear hypothesis*, which means that agoraphobia may not represent a fear of public places but, rather, a fear of having a panic attack in public places.

In terms of sociocultural factors, U.S. women are twice as likely as men to have panic attacks with or without agoraphobia (Fodor & Epstein, 2002). However, in India, men are far likelier to have panic disorders, probably because in India and other Eastern and Middle Eastern countries women rarely leave home alone (McNally, 1994). Reasons for U.S. women having a higher incidence than men of panic disorder, with or without agoraphobia, include gender socialization (boys are encouraged to be more independent, girls are protected more) and traumatic experiences (rape and child sexual abuse occur more often in the lives of women than men) (Fodor & Epstein, 2002).

Phobic Disorder

phobic disorder Commonly called *phobia;* an anxiety disorder in which the individual has an irrational, overwhelming, persistent fear of a particular object or situation.

A **phobic disorder,** commonly called *phobia,* is an anxiety disorder in which the individual has an irrational, overwhelming, persistent fear of a particular object or situation. Individuals with generalized anxiety disorder cannot pinpoint the cause of their nervous feelings; individuals with phobias can (Barlow, 2001). A fear becomes a phobia when an object or a situation is so dreaded that an individual goes to almost any length to avoid it. Some phobias are more debilitating than others. An individual with a fear of automobiles has a more difficult time functioning in our society than a person with a fear of snakes, for example. Approximately 6.3 million Americans from 18 to 54 years of age, or about 4.4 percent of the people in this age group, have a phobic disorder in any given year (NIMH, 2001a).

Phobias come in many forms. Some of the most common phobias involve social situations, dogs, height, dirt, flying, and snakes. Figure 11.3 labels and describes a number of phobias. Let's look at one person with a phobic disorder.

Agnes is an unmarried 30-year-old who has been unable to go higher than the second floor of any building for more than a year. When she tried to overcome her fear of heights by going up to the third, fourth, and fifth floor, she became overwhelmed by anxiety. She remembers how it all began. One evening she was working alone and was seized by an urge to jump out of an eighth-story window. She was so frightened by her impulse that she hid behind a file cabinet for more than 2 hours until she calmed down enough to gather her belongings and go home. As she reached the first floor of the building, her heart was pounding and she was perspiring heavily. After several months, she gave up her position and became a lower-paid salesperson so she could work on the bottom floor of the building. (Cameron, 1963)

Another phobia is *social phobia,* an intense fear of being humiliated or embarrassed in social situations. Individuals with this phobia are afraid that they will say or do the wrong thing. As a consequence, they might avoid speaking up in a conversation, giving a speech, going out to eat, or attending a party. Their intense fear of such contexts can severely restrict their social lives and increase their loneliness (Erwin & others, 2002; McLean & Wood, 2001; Van Ameringen & others, 2004). Figure 11.4 shows the percentage of people in the United States who say they have experienced certain types of social phobia in their lifetimes (Kessler, Stein, & Berglund, 1998).

What is the etiology of phobic disorders? Biologically, identical twins reared apart sometimes develop the same phobias (Eckert, Heston, & Bouchard, 1981); about 16 percent of the parents and siblings of individuals with social phobia have an increased risk of developing the phobia, compared with only 5 percent of the relatives of people without social phobia (Kessler, Olfson, & Berglund, 1998). A neural circuit has

Acrophobia	Fear of high places
Aerophobia	Fear of flying
Ailurophobia	Fear of cats
Algophobia	Fear of pain
Amaxophobia	Fear of vehicles, driving
Arachnophobia	Fear of spiders
Astrapophobia	Fear of lightning
Cynophobia	Fear of dogs
Gamophobia	Fear of marriage
Hydrophobia	Fear of water
Melissophobia	Fear of bees
Mysophobia	Fear of dirt
Nyctophobia	Fear of darkness
Ophidiophobia	Fear of nonpoisonous snakes
Thanatophobia	Fear of death
Xenophobia	Fear of strangers

FIGURE 11.3 Phobias This is only a partial listing of the phobias that have been named.

Popular professional football announcer and former coach John Madden has a fear of flying. Because of this phobia, Madden crisscrosses the United States during football season in his "Madden-cruiser" bus. *What is the difference between anxiety and phobia?*

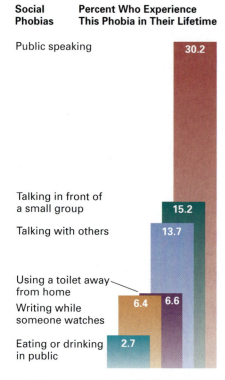

Social Phobias	Percent Who Experience This Phobia in Their Lifetime
Public speaking	30.2
Talking in front of a small group	15.2
Talking with others	13.7
Using a toilet away from home	6.6
Writing while someone watches	6.4
Eating or drinking in public	2.7

FIGURE 11.4 Social Phobias in the United States In a national survey, the most common social phobia was public speaking.

been proposed for social phobia that includes the thalamus, amygdala, and cerebral cortex (Li, Chokka, & Tibbo, 2001). Also, a number of neurotransmitters may be involved in social phobia, especially serotonin (Van Ameringen & others, 2000).

In terms of psychological factors, different theoretical perspectives provide different explanations (Coupland, 2001; Kendler, Myers, & Prescott, 2002). Psychodynamic theorists, for example, say phobias develop as defense mechanisms to ward off threatening or unacceptable impulses: Agnes hid behind a file cabinet because she feared she would jump out of an eighth-story window. Behavioral and social cognitive theorists, however, explain phobias differently; they say phobias are learned fears. In Agnes' case, she may have fallen from a high place when she was a little girl. As a result, she associates falling with pain and now fears high places (a classical conditioning explanation). Or she may have heard about or seen other people who were afraid of high places (an observational-learning explanation).

Obsessive-Compulsive Disorder

As a young adult, Bob found himself ensnared in an exacting ritual. He removes his clothes in a prearranged sequence, then scrubs every inch of his body from head to toe. He dresses himself in an order precisely the opposite to that in which he takes off his clothes. If he deviates from this order, he feels compelled to start the sequence all over again. Sometimes Bob performs the cleansing ritual four or five times a day, and even though he is aware that the ritual is absurd, he simply cannot stop performing it. (Meyer & Osborne, 1982)

Obsessive-compulsive disorder (OCD) is an anxiety disorder in which the individual has anxiety-provoking thoughts that will not go away (obsession) or has urges to perform repetitive, ritualistic behaviors to prevent or produce some future situation (compulsion). Individuals with OCD repeat and rehearse normal doubts and daily routines, sometimes hundreds of times a day (Frost & Steketee, 1998; Ricther & others, 2003). Approximately 3.3 million Americans from 18 to 54 years of age, or about 2.3 percent of the people in this age group, have obsessive-compulsive disorder in any given year (NIMH, 2001a).

The most common compulsions are excessive checking, cleansing, and counting. For example, a young man feels he has to check his apartment for gas leaks and make sure the windows are locked. His behavior is not compulsive if he does this once, but if he goes back to check five or six times and then constantly worries that he might not have checked carefully enough once he has left the house, his behavior is compulsive. Most individuals do not enjoy their ritualistic behavior but feel anxious when they do not carry it out.

What is the etiology of obsessive-compulsive disorder? There seems to be a genetic component, because OCD runs in families (Bellodi & others, 2001). Also, researchers using brain-imaging techniques have found neurological links for OCD

obsessive-compulsive disorder (OCD) An anxiety disorder; the individual has anxiety-provoking thoughts that will not go away (obsession) or urges to perform repetitive, ritualistic behaviors to prevent or produce some future situation (compulsion).

"He always times '60 Minutes.'"

Jack Nicholson portrayed an individual with obsessive-compulsive disorder in the movie *As Good As It Gets. What were the character's symptoms?*

(Cavedini & others, 2002). One interpretation of these data is that the frontal cortex or basal ganglia are so active in OCD that numerous impulses reach the thalamus, generating obsessive thoughts or compulsive actions (see figure 11.5) (Rappaport, 1989). Depletion of the neurotransmitter serotonin likely is involved in the neural circuitry linked with OCD (Jenike, 2001; Simpson & others, 2003).

In terms of psychological factors, OCD often occurs during a period of life stress, such as childbirth, a change in occupational status, or a change in marital status (Stanley, 2000). According to the cognitive perspective, what differentiates individuals with OCD from those who do not have it is the inability to turn off negative, intrusive thoughts by ignoring or dismissing them (Salkovskis & others, 1997). Onset of the disorder frequently occurs in late adolescence or early adulthood, although it can also emerge in young children. Two friends discuss their experience with OCD in the video clip "Obsessive-Compulsive Disorder."

In-Psych Plus

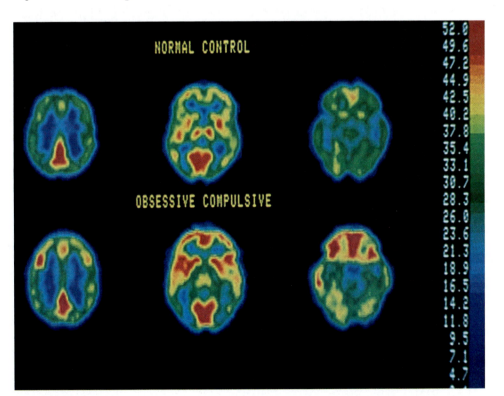

FIGURE 11.5 Brain Scans of Individuals with Obsessive-Compulsive Disorder *(Top)* Brain images of normal individuals. *(Bottom)* Brain images of individuals with obsessive-compulsive disorder (OCD). The brain images of the individuals with OCD show more activity in the frontal cortex, basal ganglia, and thalamus than do the brain images of normal individuals.

Post-Traumatic Stress Disorder

Post-traumatic stress disorder (PTSD) is a psychological disorder that overloads the individual's usual coping abilities. It develops through exposure to a traumatic event, such as war; severely oppressive situations, such as the Holocaust; severe abuse, as in rape; natural disasters, such as floods and tornadoes; and unnatural disasters, such as plane crashes (Wilson, Friedman, & Lindy, 2001). Approximately 5.2 million Americans between the ages of 18 and 54, or about 3.6 percent of people in this age group, have PTSD in any given year (NIMH, 2001c). Some experts consider sexual abuse and assault victims to be the single largest group of post-traumatic stress disorder sufferers (Koss & Boeschen, 1998).

The symptoms of PTSD vary but can include the following:

- Flashbacks, in which the individual relives the event
- Constricted ability to feel emotions, often reported as feeling numb, resulting in an inability to experience happiness, sexual desire, or enjoyable interpersonal relationships
- Excessive arousal, resulting in an exaggerated startle response or inability to sleep
- Difficulties with memory and concentration
- Feelings of apprehension, including nervous tremors
- Impulsive outbursts of behavior, such as aggressiveness, or sudden changes in lifestyle

Not every individual exposed to the same event develops post-traumatic stress disorder (Clark, 2001; Livanou & others, 2002; Norris & others, 2001). For example, it is estimated that 15 to 20 percent of Vietnam veterans experienced PTSD. Vietnam veterans who had some autonomy and decision-making authority, such as Green Berets, were less likely to develop the disorder than soldiers who had no control over where they would be sent or when and who had no option but to follow orders. Preparation for a trauma also makes a difference in whether an individual will develop the disorder. Emergency workers who are trained to cope with traumatic circumstances usually do not develop PTSD.

PTSD symptoms may immediately follow trauma or be delayed by months or even years (Berkowitz & Marans, 2003; Ford, 1999). Most people who are exposed to a traumatic, stressful event experience some anxiety symptoms in the following days and weeks (National Center for PTSD, 2001). Overall, approximately 8 percent of men and 20 percent of women go on to develop PTSD, and about 30 percent of these individuals develop a chronic form. The course of PTSD typically involves periods in which symptoms increase, followed by remission or decrease, although symptoms may be unremitting and severe.

Ordinary events can serve as reminders of the trauma and trigger flashbacks or intrusive images. A flashback can make the person lose touch with reality and re-enact the event for seconds, hours or, very rarely, days. A person having a flashback, which can come in the form of images, sounds, smells, and/or feelings, usually believes that the traumatic event is happening all over again.

Much of what is known about PTSD comes from individuals who developed the disorder because of combat and war-related traumas (Freeman & Roca, 2001; Golier & others, 2003; Hotph & others, 2003). The video clip "Post-Traumatic Stress Disorder" introduces Carl, a Vietnam War veteran experiencing PTSD. In another study, 10 percent of Vietnamese, Hmong, Laotian, and Cambodian refugees who left their war-torn countries to live in California had PTSD (Gong-Guy, 1986). A study of Bosnian refugees just after they had come to the United States indicated that 65 percent had PTSD (Weine & others, 1995). This figure may be so high because many of these Bosnian refugees had experienced numerous atrocities, organized mass rapes, and murders of relatives and neighbors.

Rather than waiting years for the stress of combat to take its toll on those who have served in the military, the U.S. armed forces now takes preventive measures in

In-Psych Plus

post-traumatic stress disorder (PTSD) An anxiety disorder that develops through exposure to a traumatic event, a severely oppressive situation, severe abuse, or a natural or an unnatural disaster.

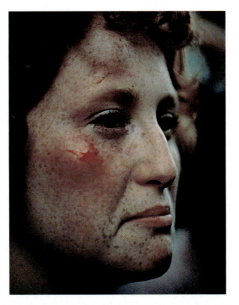

Post-traumatic stress disorder (PTSD) can be caused by a variety of traumatic events, including *(clockwise from left)* war (PTSD has been a common disorder in Vietnam veterans), abuse (such as spousal abuse or rape), unnatural disasters (such as terrorist attacks), and natural disasters (such as hurricanes). *What are the symptoms that all these people might share?*

combat zones around the world (Rabasca, 2000). The special mental health units typically have a psychologist, a social worker, and several mental health technicians. Units also might have a psychiatrist, psychiatric nurses, and occupational therapists. Treatment begins as soon as possible after a service member shows such symptoms as tremors, nightmares, or headaches. Military data indicate that 70 to 90 percent of service members return to active duty within several days when they are treated at the front (Rabasca, 2000).

Abuse is another frequent cause of PTSD. It can come in many forms, including abuse of a spouse, the sexual abuse of rape or incest, and emotional abuse (as when parents harshly criticize and belittle their children) (Hanson & others, 2001: Trowell & others, 2002). Researchers have found that approximately 95 percent of rape survivors experience PTSD symptoms in the first 2 weeks following the traumatic event. About 50 percent still have symptoms 3 months later, and as many as 25 percent have symptoms 4 to 5 years after the rape (Foa & Riggs, 1995).

Natural disasters, such as tornadoes, hurricanes, earthquakes, and fires, can also cause PTSD (Auger & others, 2000; Goenjian & others, 2001). In one study of children who lived through Hurricane Andrew in 1992, 20 percent still had PTSD 1 year later (La Greca & others, 1996). Fourteen years after a flood destroyed the community of Buffalo Creek in West Virginia, 25 percent of the survivors were still suffering from PTSD (Green & others, 1992). Similar problems arise from unnatural disasters, such as plane crashes and terrorist attacks. The September 11, 2001, terrorist attacks on New York City and Washington, DC, have produced PTSD in some of the survivors, and probably more will develop PTSD in the coming years. (Niles, Wolf, & Kutter, 2003; Norris & others, 2001).

Review and Sharpen Your Thinking

2   *Distinguish among the various anxiety disorders.*

- Characterize generalized anxiety disorder.
- State the key features of panic disorder.
- Identify the sources of anxiety in phobic disorder.
- Explain obsessive-compulsive disorder.
- Describe post-traumatic stress disorder.

Family members and friends of individuals with obsessive-compulsive disorder frequently tell them to stop their obsessions and compulsions. However, just telling someone to stop usually does not work. If you had a friend with this disorder, what would you try to do about it?

---

3   DISSOCIATIVE DISORDERS

Dissociative Amnesia and Fugue

Dissociative Identity Disorder

What are the dissociative disorders?

Dissociative disorders are psychological disorders that involve a sudden loss of memory or change in identity. Under extreme stress or shock, the individual's conscious awareness becomes dissociated (separated or split) from previous memories and thoughts (Gast & others, 2001; Simeon & others, 2002). Three kinds of dissociative disorders are dissociative amnesia, dissociative fugue, and dissociative identity disorder.

Dissociative Amnesia and Fugue

Recall from chapter 7 that amnesia is the inability to recall important events (LaBar & others, 2002). Amnesia can be caused by a blow to the head, causing trauma to the brain (Bob, 2003). But **dissociative amnesia** is a dissociative disorder characterized by extreme memory loss that is caused by extensive psychological stress. For example, imagine that an individual shows up at a hospital and says he does not know who he is. After several days in the hospital, he remembers that he was involved in an automobile accident in which a pedestrian was killed. The extreme stress of the accident and the fear that he might be held responsible have triggered amnesia.

    Dissociative fugue (*fugue* means "flight") is a dissociative disorder in which the individual not only develops amnesia but also unexpectedly wanders off for a time

dissociative disorders Psychological disorders that involve a sudden loss of memory or change in identity.

dissociative amnesia A dissociative disorder involving extreme memory loss caused by extensive psychological stress.

dissociative fugue A dissociative disorder in which the individual not only develops amnesia but also unexpectedly travels away from home and may establish a new identity.

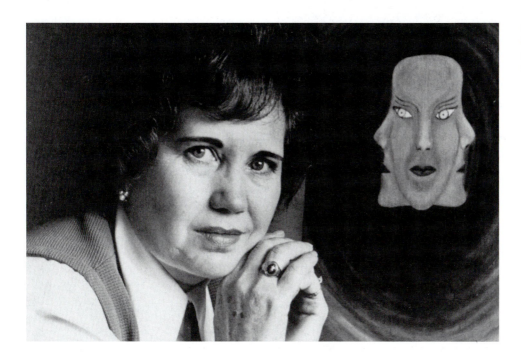

or even may travel away from home and assume a new identity. Consider the following example of this disorder:

> One day a woman named Barbara vanished without a trace. Two weeks later, looking more like a teenager—with her hair in a ponytail and wearing bobby socks—than a 31-year-old woman, Barbara was picked up by police in a nearby city. When her husband came to see her, Barbara asked, "Who are you?" She could not remember anything about the last 2 weeks of her life. During psychotherapy, she gradually began to recall her past. She had left home with enough money to buy a bus ticket to the town where she grew up as a child. She spent days walking the streets and standing near a building where her father had worked. Later she went to the motel with a man. According to the motel manager, she entertained a series of men there over a three-day period. (Goldstein & Palmer, 1975)

Dissociative Identity Disorder

Dissociative identity disorder (DID), formerly called *multiple personality disorder,* is the most dramatic but least common dissociative disorder. Individuals suffering from this disorder have two or more distinct personalities or selves, like the fictional Dr. Jekyll and Mr. Hyde of Robert Louis Stevenson's short story. Each personality has its own memories, behaviors, and relationships; one personality dominates the individual at one time, and another personality takes over at another time. The shift from one personality to the other usually occurs under distress (Dell, 2002; Gleaves, May, & Cardena, 2001; Reinder & others, 2003).

One of the most famous cases of dissociative identity disorder involves the "three faces of Eve":

> Eve White was the original dominant personality. She had no knowledge of her second personality, Eve Black, although Eve Black had been alternating with Eve White for a number of years. Eve White was bland, quiet, and serious—a rather dull personality. By contrast, Eve Black was carefree, mischievous, and uninhibited. She would "come out" at the most inappropriate times, leaving Eve White with hangovers, bills, and a reputation in local bars that she could not explain. During treatment, a third personality, Jane, emerged. More mature than the other two, Jane seemed to have developed as a result of therapy. (Thigpen & Cleckley, 1957)

dissociative identity disorder (DID)
Formerly called *multiple personality disorder,* this is the most dramatic but least common dissociative disorder; individuals suffering from this disorder have two or more distinct personalities.

In some cases, therapists have been ascribed responsibility for creating a second or third personality. At one point, Eve said that her therapist had created one of her personalities. Go to the video clip "Personality Disorder" to see how a man with dissociative identity disorder describes his various personalities.

A summary of research on dissociative identity disorder suggests a link with frequent sexual or physical abuse during early childhood (McAllister, 2000; Stafford & Lynn, 2002). Sexual abuse occurred in 56 percent of reported cases. However, the majority of individuals who have been sexually abused do not develop dissociative identity disorder. Mothers of individuals who develop this disorder tend to be rejecting and depressed; fathers distant, alcoholic, and abusive. The vast majority of individuals with dissociative identity disorder are adult females. When males develop the disorder, they show more aggression than females with the disorder (Ross & Norton, 1989). A genetic predisposition might exist, as the disorder tends to run in families (Dell & Eisenhower, 1990). Some research suggests that a person's different personalities have different EEG patterns (Allen & Movius, 2000; APA, 1994).

Fascinating as it is, dissociative identity disorder is rare. Until the 1980s, only about 300 cases had ever been reported (Suinn, 1984). In the past decade, hundreds more cases have been labeled dissociative identity disorder, although some psychologists argue this increase represents a diagnostic fad. Others believe that it is not so rare but has been frequently misdiagnosed as schizophrenia. Improved techniques for assessing physiological changes that occur when individuals change personalities increase the likelihood that more accurate rates of occurrence can be determined.

Review and Sharpen Your Thinking

3 Describe the dissociative disorders.

- Explain dissociative amnesia and fugue.
- Discuss dissociative identity disorder.

Imagine that you are on a jury in which an individual who has been accused of killing someone claims that he suffers from dissociative identity disorder and doesn't remember committing the murder. How difficult would it be for you and the other jury members to determine if he really has this disorder? What questions would you want answered before making your decision about the individual?

4 MOOD DISORDERS

Depressive Disorders

Causes of Mood Disorders

Bipolar Disorder

Suicide

What are mood disorders, and who is at risk for depression and suicide?

The **mood disorders** are psychological disorders characterized by a disturbance of mood (prolonged emotion that colors the individual's entire emotional state). The mood disturbance can include cognitive, behavioral, and physical symptoms, as well as interpersonal difficulties (Coyne, 2000). Two main types of mood disorders are the depressive disorders and bipolar disorder. Depression can occur alone, as in the depressive disorders, or it can alternate with mania (an overexcited, unrealistically

mood disorders Psychological disorders in which there is a disturbance in mood (prolonged emotion that colors the individual's entire emotional state).

optimistic state), as in bipolar disorder. Recall Kay Redfield Jamison's description of her oscillations between manic highs and terrifying depressions. Approximately 18.8 million Americans between the ages of 18 and 54, or about 9.5 percent of the people in this age group, have a mood disorder in any given year (NIMH, 2001a).

Depressive Disorders

The **depressive disorders** are mood disorders in which the individual suffers depression without ever experiencing mania. The severity of the depressive disorders varies. Some individuals experience what is classified as *major depressive disorder*, whereas others experience *dysthymic disorder* (a more chronic depression with fewer symptoms than major depression) (Beckham, 2000). Consider this case:

> Peter had been depressed for several months. Nothing cheered him up. As he reflected, "My brain is like on time out. I just can't get anything done. I feel virtually exhausted all the time. I try to study but I read the same pages over and over again and can't remember a thing I've read. I feel like the bottom is falling out of my life. It's so empty." Nothing cheered Peter up. His depression began when the girl he wanted to marry decided that marriage was not for her, at least not marriage to Peter. Peter's emotional state deteriorated to the point at which he didn't leave his room for days at a time, he kept his shades down and the room dark, and he could hardly get out of bed in the morning.

This painting by Vincent Van Gogh, *Portrait of Dr. Gachet*, reflects the extreme melancholy that characterizes the depressive disorders. *What other symptoms might Dr. Gachet exhibit if he has a depressive disorder?*

Peter was diagnosed with **major depressive disorder (MDD),** in which the individual experiences a major depressive episode and symptoms of depression, such as lethargy and hopelessness, for at least 2 weeks. The individual's daily functioning becomes impaired. (For another example, see the video clip "Major Depression"; it presents the account of Tara, who has lived with this disorder for more than 15 years.) A recent national study found that 16.2 percent of U.S. adults (about 34 million) had major depressive disorder in their lifetime and 6.2 percent had MDD in the previous 12 months (Kessler & others, 2003). The individuals with MDD were on average unable to work or do normal activities for 5 weeks out of a year. In this study, only 20 percent of individuals with MDD were getting effective treatment, although most can be successfully treated.

Nine symptoms define a major depressive episode (at least five of which must be present during a 2-week period):

- Depressed mood most of the day
- Reduced interest or pleasure in all or most activities
- Significant weight loss or gain or significant decrease or interest in appetite
- Trouble sleeping or sleeping too much
- Psychomotor agitation or retardation
- Fatigue or loss of energy
- Feeling worthless or guilty in an excessive or inappropriate manner
- Problems in thinking, concentrating, or making decisions
- Recurrent thoughts of death and suicide

Dysthymic disorder is generally more chronic and has fewer symptoms than major depressive disorder (Dunner & others, 2002). The individual is in a depressed mood for most days for at least 2 years as an adult or at least 1 year as a child or an adolescent. To be classified as having dysthymic disorder, a major depressive episode must not have occurred, and the period of depression must not have been broken by a normal mood lasting more than 2 months. Two or more of these six symptoms must be present: poor appetite or overeating, sleep problems, low energy or fatigue, low self-esteem, poor concentration or difficulty making decisions, and feelings of hopelessness (Ball & Steer, 2003; Munoz, 1998). See the case of Roberto in the video clip "Dysthymic Disorder." Approximately 10.9 million people in the United States, or about 5.4 percent of the population, will have dysthymic disorder in their lifetimes (NIMH, 2001a).

depressive disorders Mood disorders in which the individual suffers depression without ever experiencing mania.

major depressive disorder (MDD) A mood disorder indicated by a major depressive episode and depressed characteristics, such as lethargy and hopelessness, lasting at least 2 weeks.

dysthymic disorder A depressive disorder that is generally more chronic and has fewer symptoms than major depressive disorder.

Although most people do not spiral into major depression, everyone feels "blue" sometimes. In our stress-filled world, people often use the term *depression* to describe brief bouts of normal sadness or discontent over life's problems. Perhaps you haven't done well in a class or things aren't working out in your love life. You say you are depressed, but in most instances your depression won't last as long or be as intense as Peter's. After a few hours, days, or weeks, you snap out of your gloomy state and begin to cope more effectively with your problems. Nonetheless, depression is so widespread that it has been called the "common cold" of mental disorders; more than 250,000 individuals are hospitalized every year for the disorder. No one is immune to depression.

The inadequate care that results from a lack of understanding or a misunderstanding of depression is tragic. Given the psychological and pharmacological treatments available today, individuals who go untreated suffer needlessly. To evaluate whether you might be depressed, see the Psychology and Life box.

Bipolar Disorder

Although she had experienced extreme mood swings since she was a child, Mrs. M. was first admitted to a mental hospital at the age of 38. At 33, shortly before the birth of her first child, she became very depressed. One month after the baby was born, she became agitated and euphoric. Mrs. M. signed a year's lease on an apartment, bought furniture, piled up debts. Several years later other manic and depressive mood swings occurred. In one of her excitatory moods, Mrs. M. swore loudly and created a disturbance at a club where she was not a member. Several days later she began divorce proceedings. On the day prior to her admission to the mental hospital, she went on a spending spree and bought 57 hats. Several weeks later, she became despondent, saying, "I have no energy. My brain doesn't work right. I have let my family down. I don't have anything to live for." In a subsequent manic bout, Mrs. M. pursued a romantic relationship with a doctor. (Kolb, 1973)

Bipolar disorder is a mood disorder that is characterized by extreme mood swings that include one or more episodes of mania (an overexcited, unrealistically optimistic state) (Brickman, LoPiccolo, & Johnson, 2002; Dickerson & others, 2004). *Bipolar* means that the person may experience both depression and mania. Most bipolar individuals experience multiple cycles of depression interspersed with mania. Less than 10 percent of bipolar individuals tend to experience episodes of mania with no depression. Approximately 2.3 million Americans, or about 1.2 percent of the U.S. population 18 years and older, have bipolar disorder in any given year (NIMH, 2001a).

A manic episode is the flip side of a depressive episode (Miklowitz, 2002). The person feels euphoric and on top of the world. However, as the manic episode unfolds, the person can experience panic and eventually depression. Instead of feeling fatigued, as many depressed individuals do, individuals experiencing mania have tremendous energy and might sleep very little. Individuals in a manic state often act impulsively, which can get them in trouble in business and legal transactions. For example, they might spend their life savings on a foolish business venture. To see how one person describes his cycles of mania and depression, go to the video clip "Bipolar Disorder I."

In-Psych Plus

By definition in the *DSM-IV* classification, manic episodes must last at least 1 week. They average 8 to 16 weeks. Individuals with bipolar disorder can have manic and depressive episodes that occur four or more times a year, but they usually are separated by 6 months to 1 year.

Bipolar disorder is much less common than depressive disorders (MacKinnon & others, 2002). Unlike depressive disorders (which are more common in females), bipolar disorder is equally common in females and males. About 1 to 2 percent of people are estimated to experience bipolar disorder at some point in their lifetime (Kessler & others, 1994).

bipolar disorder A mood disorder characterized by extreme mood swings, including one or more episodes of mania.

Are You Depressed?

Following is a list of the ways that you might have felt or behaved in the past week. Indicate what you felt by putting an X in the appropriate box for each item.

During the past week	Rarely or None of the Time (Less Than 1 Day)	Some or a Little of the Time (1–2 Days)	Occasionally or a Moderate Amount of the Time (3–4 Days)	Most or All of the Time (5–7 Days)
1. I was bothered by things that usually don't bother me.	☐	☐	☐	☐
2. I did not feel like eating; my appetite was poor.	☐	☐	☐	☐
3. I felt that I could not shake off the blues even with help from my family and friends.	☐	☐	☐	☐
4. I felt that I was just as good as other people.	☐	☐	☐	☐
5. I had trouble keeping my mind on what I was doing.	☐	☐	☐	☐
6. I felt depressed.	☐	☐	☐	☐
7. I felt that everything I did was an effort.	☐	☐	☐	☐
8. I felt hopeful about the future.	☐	☐	☐	☐
9. I thought my life had been a failure.	☐	☐	☐	☐
10. I felt fearful.	☐	☐	☐	☐
11. My sleep was restless.	☐	☐	☐	☐
12. I was happy.	☐	☐	☐	☐
13. I talked less than usual.	☐	☐	☐	☐
14. I felt lonely.	☐	☐	☐	☐
15. People were unfriendly.	☐	☐	☐	☐
16. I enjoyed life.	☐	☐	☐	☐
17. I had crying spells.	☐	☐	☐	☐
18. I felt sad.	☐	☐	☐	☐
19. I felt that people disliked me.	☐	☐	☐	☐
20. I could not get going.	☐	☐	☐	☐

For items 4, 8, 12, and 16, give yourself a 3 each time you checked Rarely or None, 2 each time you checked Some or a Little, 1 each time you checked Occasionally or Moderate, and a 0 each time you checked Most or All of the Time. For the remaining items, give yourself a 0 each time you checked Rarely or None, 1 each time you checked Some or a Little, 2 each time you checked Occasionally or Moderate, and 3 each time you checked Most or All of the Time. Total up your score for all 20 items.

If your score is around 7, then you are like the average male in terms of how much depression you have experienced in the past week. If your score is around 8 or 9, your score is similar to the average female's. Scores less than the average for either males or females indicate that depression probably has not been a problem for you during the past week. If your score is 16 or more and you are bothered by your feelings, you might benefit from professional help.

Keep in mind, though, that self-diagnosis is not always accurate. Seek the professional judgment of a qualified clinician.

Causes of Mood Disorders

Mood disorders, such as Peter's depression and Mrs. M.'s bipolar disorder, can involve biological, psychological, and sociocultural factors. I distinguish between depressive disorders and bipolar disorder as appropriate in discussing the causes of mood disorders.

Biological Factors in Mood Disorders   The links between biology and mood disorders are well established (Hammen, 2003; Nolen-Hoeksema, 2004) (you can explore the biology of mood disorders in the video clip "Bipolar Disorder II"):

In-Psych Plus

- *Heredity.* Mood disorders tend to run in families, although the family link is stronger for bipolar disorder than for depressive disorders (Bradbury, 2001). One of the greatest risks of developing a mood disorder is having a biological parent who suffers from a mood disorder. The rate of bipolar disorder in the parents and siblings of those with bipolar disorder is 10 to 20 times higher than in the general population (MacKinnon, Jamison, & DePaulo, 1997). An individual with an identical twin who has bipolar disorder has a much greater probability of also having the disorder than an individual with a bipolar fraternal twin (see figure 11.6). Researchers are zeroing in on the specific genetic location of bipolar disorder (Kelsoe & others, 2001).

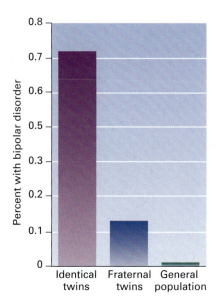

FIGURE 11.6 Risk for Bipolar Disorder Notice how much stronger the incidence of bipolar disorder is in identical twins compared with fraternal twins and the general population. These statistics suggest a strong genetic role in the disorder.

- *Neurobiological abnormalities.* One of the most consistent findings in individuals with mood disorders is altered brain-wave activity during sleep. Depressed individuals experience less slow-wave sleep (which contributes to a feeling of being rested and restored) and go into rapid-eye-movement (REM) sleep earlier in the night than nondepressed individuals (Benca, 2001). These neurobiological abnormalities correspond to the reports of depressed individuals that they have difficulty going to sleep at night or remaining asleep, that they often wake up early in the morning and can't get back to sleep, and that they do not feel rested after they sleep (Cosgrave & others, 2000). Neuroimaging studies also reveal decreased metabolic activity in the cerebral cortex of individuals with severe major depressive disorder (Buchsbaum & others, 1997). Figure 11.7 shows the decrease in metabolic activity in the brain during depression and the increase in metabolic activity during mania (Baxter & others, 1995). Although most areas of the brains of depressed individuals are underactive—for example, one section of the prefrontal cortex, which is involved in generating actions—certain brain areas are overactive, such as the amygdala (Posner & Raichle, 1998; Van Elst, Ebert, & Trimble, 2001). Some of depression's symptoms may be explained by this change in brain activity in the amygdala, which helps to store and recall emotionally charged memories. The prefrontal cortex should signal the amygdala to slow down when the source of the emotion is gone. But, in depression, the prefrontal cortex may fail to send the all-clear signal. Thus the amygdala may continue sending signals that keep triggering extended rumination about sad events. Another neurobiological abnormality in depression is neuron death or disability (Manji, 2001). Individuals with depression seem to have fewer neurons in some parts of their brain, including the prefrontal cortex (Drevets, 2001).
- *Neurotransmitter deregulation.* Abnormalities in the *monoamine neurotransmitters,* such as norepinephrine, serotonin, and dopamine, have been implicated in mood disorders (Harley, 2003; Stahl, 2002). An imbalance in the monoamine neurotransmitters in one direction is thought to be involved in depression, an imbalance in the other direction in mania. Individuals with major depressive disorder appear to have too few receptors for serotonin and norepinephrine (Wong & others, 2000). Recent studies also have revealed that changes in other neurotransmitters occur in bipolar disorder and depression (Benes & others, 2000; Pacher & others, 2001).
- *Hormones.* Depressed individuals show chronic hyperactivity in the endocrine system (including the pituitary gland and adrenal cortex) and an inability to return to normal functioning following a stressful experience (Young & Korzun, 1998). In turn, the excess hormones produced by the neuroendocrine glands may be linked to the deregulation of the monoamine neurotransmitters. Some argue that women's increased vulnerability to depression is also linked to their ovarian hormones, estrogen and progesterone. However, the evidence that women's moods are tied to their hormones is mixed (Nolen-Hoeksema, 2004). Some women do experience more depression during the postpartum period, menopause, and other times when their hormone levels are changing. Nonetheless, the extent to which hormonal changes in women account for their higher rate of depression in comparison with men is less clear.

Psychological Factors in Mood Disorders Psychodynamic, behavioral, and cognitive theories have all proposed explanations for depression. These ideas are significant for their influence on the treatment of disorders, which are discussed in chapter 12.

- *Psychodynamic explanations.* Depression stems from childhood experiences that prevent individuals from developing a strong, positive sense of self (Nolen-Hoeksema, 2004). Depressed individuals become overly dependent on the

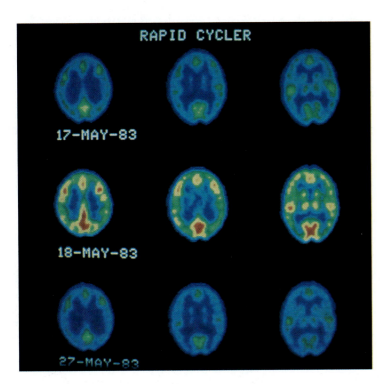

RAPID CYCLER

17-MAY-83

18-MAY-83

27-MAY-83

FIGURE 11.7 **Brain Metabolism in Mania and Depression** Brain scans of an individual with bipolar disorder, who is described as a rapid cycler because of how quickly severe mood changes occur in the individual. *(top, bottom)* The person's brain in a depressed state. *(middle)* A manic state. The brain scans reveal how the brain's energy consumption falls in depression and rises in mania. The red areas in the middle row reflect rapid consumption of glucose.

evaluations and approval of others for their self-esteem, mainly because of inadequate nurturing by parents (Blatt & Zuroff, 1992). Many modern psychodynamic theorists also still rely on Freud's (1917) theory that depression is a turning inward of aggressive instincts. Because the child cannot openly express feelings of anger or frustration toward the individual he or she loves (usually the mother), the hostility is turned inward and experienced as depression. The unresolved mixture of anger and love is carried forward to adolescence and adulthood, when any loss can bring back these early feelings.

• *Behavioral explanations.* Life's stresses can lead to depression by reducing the positive reinforcers in a person's life (Lewinsohn, Joiner, & Rohde, 2001). When people experience considerable stress in their lives, they may withdraw from the stress. The withdrawal produces a further reduction in positive reinforcers, which can lead to more withdrawal, which leads to even fewer positive reinforcers. Another behavioral view of depression focuses on **learned helplessness,** a state of apathy and unresponsiveness that occurs when individuals are exposed to prolonged stress over which they feel they have no control and that eventually leads to feelings of helplessness and depression (Seligman, 1975). Other depressed individuals may focus intently on how they feel (their sadness and hopelessness) but may not try to do anything about the feelings. In a series of research studies, Susan Nolen-Hoeksema and her colleagues (Nolen-Hoeksema, Larson, & Grayson, 1999; Nolen-Hoeksema & Morrow, 1991; Nolen-Hoeksema, Parker, & Larson, 1994) have found that individuals with depression remain depressed longer when they just ruminate about their depression rather than adopting an action-oriented coping style. Women are likelier to ruminate when they are depressed than men are (Nolen-Hoeksema & others, 1999).

• *Cognitive explanations.* The cognitive approach provides several explanations for mood disorders (Newman & others, 2002; Page & Hook, 2003; Riso & Newman, 2003). First, individuals who are depressed rarely think positive thoughts; they interpret their lives in self-defeating ways and have negative expectations about the future (Gilbert, 2001). Such negative thoughts may reflect schemas that shape the depressed individual's experiences (Beck, 1967).

learned helplessness A response to prolonged stress over which the individual has no control; apathy and helplessness may lead to depression.

All-or-nothing thinking	You see things in black-and-white categories. If your performance falls short of perfect, you see yourself as a total failure.
Overgeneralization	You see a single negative event as a never-ending pattern of defeat.
Mental filter	You pick out a single negative detail and dwell on it exclusively so that your vision of all reality becomes darkened, like the drop of ink that discolors the entire beaker of water.
Disqualifying the positive	You reject positive experiences by insisting they "don't count" for some reason. In this way, you can maintain a negative belief that is contradicted by your everyday experiences.
Jumping to conclusions	You make a negative interpretation even though there are no definite facts that convincingly support your conclusion. (a) *Mind reading*. You arbitrarily conclude that someone is reacting negatively to you, and you don't bother to check this out. (b) *The Fortune Teller Error*. You anticipate that things will turn out badly, and you feel convinced that your prediction is an already-established fact.
Magnification (catastrophizing) or minimization	You exaggerate the importance of things (such as your goof-up or someone else's achievement), or you inappropriately shrink things until they appear tiny (your own desirable qualities or other fellow's imperfections). This is also called the "binocular trick."
Emotional reasoning	You assume that your negative emotions necessarily reflect the way things really are: "I feel it; therefore, it must be true."
Should statements	You try to motivate yourself with shoulds and shouldn'ts, as if you had to be whipped and punished before you could be expected to do anything. "Musts" and "oughts" are also offenders. The emotional consequence is guilt. When you direct should statements toward others, you feel anger, frustration, and resentment.
Labeling and mislabeling	This is an extreme form of overgeneralization. Instead of describing your error, you attach a negative label to yourself: "I'm a *loser*." When someone else's behavior rubs you the wrong way, you attach a negative label to him or her: "He's a . . . louse." Mislabeling involves describing an event with language that is highly colored and emotionally loaded.
Personalization	You see yourself as the cause of some negative external event, which, in fact, you were not primarily responsible for.

FIGURE 11.8 Cognitive Distortions That Can Contribute to Depression

These habitual negative thoughts magnify and expand a depressed person's negative experiences (Teasdale & others, 1995). Also, the accumulation of cognitive distortions such as the ones in figure 11.8 can lead to depression. Second, learned helplessness may play a role (Joiner & others, 2001). Individuals who regularly explain negative events as being caused by internal ("It is my fault I failed the exam"), stable ("I'm going to fail again and again"), and global ("Failing this exam shows how I won't do well in any of my courses") factors blame themselves for negative events, expect the negative events to recur in their lives in the future, and tend to experience negative events in many areas of their lives (see figure 11.9) (Abramson, Seligman, & Teasdale, 1978). Third, being either optimistic or pessimistic can have profound effects on a person's well-being. In one study, lasting 2½ years, the researchers found that, among college students with no prior history of depression, 17 percent of the students with a pessimistic style developed major depression, whereas only 1 percent of those with an optimistic style did (Alloy, Abramson, & Francis, 1999). Also, among students with a history of depression, 27 percent of those who had a pessimistic style relapsed into depression over the 2½ years, but only 6 percent of those with an optimistic style did.

Interestingly, some people who are depressed may be seeing their world accurately and realistically (McKendree-Smith & Scogin, 2000). That is, there really are negative things going on in their lives that make them depressed. Researchers have found that, when depressed individuals are asked to make judgments about how much control they have over situations that actually cannot be controlled, they are accurate in saying that they do not have control

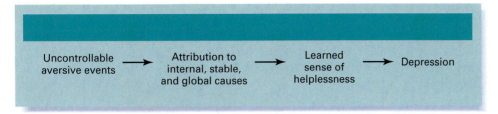

FIGURE 11.9 Attributions and Learned Helplessness

(Alloy & Abramson, 1979). In contrast, nondepressed individuals overestimate the amount of control they have in such situations.

Sociocultural Factors in Mood Disorders Among the sociocultural factors involved in depression are the following:

- *Interpersonal relationships.* One view of depression is that it may stem from problems that develop in relationships with other people (Segrin, 2001). Both recent and earlier interpersonal experiences might be involved. For example, recent marital conflict might trigger depression, or possibly inadequate early relationships with parents influence the occurrence of depression later in a person's life. Indeed, one study of college students found that those with an anxious, insecure attachment style were more likely to have depressive symptoms than those with secure attachment styles (Roberts, Gottlib, & Kassel, 1996). The British psychiatrist John Bowlby (1989) suggested that both interpersonal relationships and cognitive factors can explain the development of depression. He believes a combination of an insecure attachment to the mother, a lack of love and affection as a child, and the actual loss of a parent during childhood give rise to a negative schema. With this schema, the individual interprets later losses as yet other failures in the effort to establish enduring and close positive relationships.

- *Socioeconomic and ethnic factors.* Individuals with a low socioeconomic status (SES), especially those living in poverty, are more likely to develop depression than their higher SES counterparts. In addition, in one study, Latinos in the United States had a higher incidence of depression than Whites (Blazer & others, 1994), although the higher rate of depression among Latinos may be due to their higher incidence of poverty. Very high rates of depression also have been found in Native Americans, among whom poverty, hopelessness, and alcoholism are widespread (Manson & others, 1990).

- *Cultural variations.* Martin Seligman (1989) believes that the reason so many young American adults are prone to depression is our society's emphasis on self, independence, and individualism, coupled with an erosion of connectedness to others, family, and religion. This phenomenon, Seligman says, has spawned a widespread sense of hopelessness. Depressive disorders are found in virtually all cultures in the world, but their incidence, intensity, and components vary across cultures. The incidence of depressive disorders is lower in less industrialized, less modernized countries than in more industrialized, modernized countries (Cross-National Collaborative Group, 1992). This difference likely is due to the fast-paced, stressful lifestyles of individuals in industrialized, modernized countries and the stronger orientation toward family and community in less industrialized, less modernized countries. Also, Western cultures seem to spawn more guilt and self-deprecation than non-Western cultures do (Draguns, 1990).

- *Gender.* Bipolar disorder occurs about equally among women and men, but women are about twice as likely as men to develop depression (Nolen-Hoeksema, 2004). This gender difference occurs in many countries (see figure 11.10)

FIGURE 11.10 Gender Differences in Depression Across Cultures One study showed that women were more likely than men to have major depression in nine cultures.

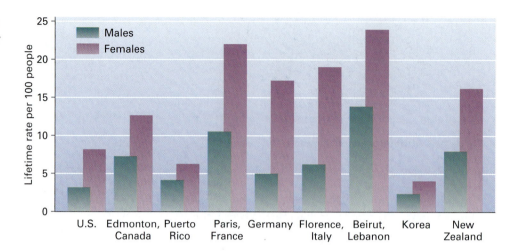

(Weissman & Olfson, 1995). Depression is especially high among single women who are the heads of households and among young married women who work at unsatisfying, dead-end jobs (Bernstein, 2001). In unhappy marriages, women are three times as likely as men to be depressed. Mothers of young children are especially vulnerable to stress and depression. Also, the more children in the household, the more depression women report. As mentioned earlier, poverty may be a pathway to depression, and three of every four people living in poverty in the United States are women and children. Minority women also are a high-risk group for depression. Careful diagnosis of depression in women is critical (Kornstein & Clayton, 2002). According to the American Psychological Association's Task Force on Women and Depression, depression is misdiagnosed at least 30 to 50 percent of the time in women (McGrath & others, 1990). Approximately 70 percent of prescriptions for antidepressants are given to women, too often with improper diagnosis and monitoring.

Suicide

Severe depression and other psychological disorders can cause individuals to want to end their lives. Although attempting suicide is abnormal behavior, it is not uncommon for individuals to contemplate suicide at some point in their lives. For example, as many as two of every three college students have thought about suicide on at least one occasion.

Approximately 29,000 individuals commit suicide every year in the United States, and the number of attempted suicides is estimated at 600,000 (NIMH, 2000). The number of actual suicides reflects a three-fold increase since 1950.

After about the age of 15, the suicide rate begins to rise rapidly (Weissman & others, 1999). Sucide is the third leading cause (after automobile accidents and homicides) of death today among adolescents 13 through 19 years of age (National Center for Health Statistics, 2001b).

Females are more likely than males to attempt suicide, but males are more likely to actually commit suicide. This difference may be due to the fact that males tend to use lethal means, such as guns, whereas females tend to cut their wrists or take overdoses of sleeping pills, which are less likely to result in death (Maris, 1998).

Suicide has a number of causes:

- *Biological factors.* Suicide tends to run in families (Fu & others, 2002). Consider the Hemingway family, five members of which, spread across generations, committed suicide. The best-known of the five Hemingways are the writer Ernest

Hemingway and his granddaughter Margaux (who committed suicide on the 35th anniversary of her father's suicide). A number of studies have also linked suicide with low levels of the neurotransmitter serotonin (Courtet & others, 2004; Mann & Arango, 1999; van Pragg, 2000). Postmortem analyses of the brains of individuals who have committed suicide show abnormally low levels of serotonin. Also, individuals who attempt suicide and who have low levels of serotonin are 10 times more likely to attempt suicide again than are those attempters who have high levels of serotonin (Roy, 1992). Poor physical health, especially when it is long-standing and chronic, is another risk factor for suicide. For example, Ernest Hemingway had been in failing health for a number of years when he committed suicide.

- *Psychological factors.* Approximately 90 percent of individuals who commit suicide are estimated to have a diagnosable mental disorder (NIMH, 2000). The most common mental disorder among individuals who commit suicide is depression (Bradvik, 2003; Fergusson & Woodward, 2002). In addition, highly stressful circumstances, such as losing a job, flunking out of school, or having an unwanted pregnancy, can lead people to threaten or commit suicide (Rudd, Joiner, & Rajab, 2001). Substance abuse is also linked with suicide more today than it was in the past.

- *Sociocultural factors.* The loss of a loved one through death, divorce, or separation can lead to a suicide attempt (Heikkinen, Aro, & Loennqvist, 1992). There also is a link between suicide and a long-standing history of family instability and unhappiness. And chronic economic hardship can be a factor in suicide (Nishimura & others, 2004). In one study, 8.5 percent of people living below the poverty line, compared with 5.4 percent living above the line, said that they had contemplated suicide (Crosby, Cheltenham, & Sacks, 1999). In the United States, Native Americans have the highest suicide rate of all demographic groups, followed by Whites (Hendin, 1995). Across cultures, Hungary, Germany, Austria, Denmark, and Japan have the highest suicide rates, and Egypt, Mexico, Greece, and Spain have the lowest rates (National Center for Health Statistics, 1994). Suicide rates for the United States and Canada fall between the rates in these countries. Among the reasons for the differences is the varying strength of cultural and religious norms against suicide. Those who have had special training are best able to prevent someone else from committing suicide, but figure 11.11 provides some good advice for anyone who knows someone who is threatening suicide.

Suicide tends to run in families. Five suicides occurred in different generations of the Hemingway family, including famous author Ernest *(top)* and his granddaughter Margaux *(bottom). What other factors might be involved in this family's history of suicide?*

What to Do

1. Ask direct, straightforward questions in a calm manner. For example: "Are you thinking about hurting yourself?"

2. Be a good listener and be supportive. Emphasize that unbearable pain can be survived.

3. Take the suicide threat very seriously. Ask questions about the person's feelings, relationships, and thoughts and about the method to be used. If a gun, pills, rope, or other means is mentioned and a specific plan has been developed, the situation is dangerous. Stay with the person until help arrives.

4. Encourage the person to get professional help and assist him or her in getting help. If the person is willing, take the person to a mental health facility or hospital.

What Not to Do

1. Don't ignore the warning signs.

2. Don't refuse to talk about suicide if the person wants to talk about it.

3. Don't react with horror, disapproval, or repulsion.

4. Don't offer false reassurances ("Everything will be all right") or make judgments ("You should be thankful for . . .").

5. Don't abandon the person after the crisis seems to have passed or after professional counseling has begun.

FIGURE 11.11 **What to Do and What Not to Do When Someone Is Threatening Suicide**

Review and Sharpen Your Thinking

4 ***Compare the mood disorders and specify the risk factors for depression and suicide.***

- Distinguish between depressive disorders and normal feelings of sadness.
- Describe the mood disturbances that characterize bipolar disorder.
- Discuss the causes of mood disorders.
- Explain the factors that can lead to suicide.

Do any of the theories about the causes of depression seem better at accounting for depression in college students than others do? Explain.

5 SCHIZOPHRENIA

Types of Schizophrenia

Causes of Schizophrenia

What is the nature of schizophrenia and its different forms?

> One day, while I was in the principal's office, suddenly the room became enormous, illuminated by a dreadful electric light that cast false shadows. Everything was exact, smooth, artificial, extremely tense; the chairs and tables seemed models placed here and there. Pupils and teachers were puppets revolving without cause, without objective. I recognized nothing, nobody. It was as though reality, attenuated, had slipped away from all these things and these people. Profound dread overwhelmed me, and as though lost, I looked around desperately for help. I heard people talking, but I did not grasp the meaning of their words. The voices were metallic, without warmth or color. From time to time, a word detached itself from the rest. It repeated itself over and over in my head, absurd, as though cut off by a knife. (Sechehaye, 1951, p. 22)

In-Psych Plus

This passage was written by a person with **schizophrenia,** a severe psychological disorder characterized by highly disordered thought processes. (For an introduction to schizophrenia, see the video clip "History of Mental Illness.") Individuals with schizophrenia may show odd communication, inappropriate emotion, abnormal movements, and social withdrawal (Heinrichs, 2001). The term *schizophrenia* comes from the Latin words *schizo,* meaning "split," and *phrenia,* meaning "mind." Schizophrenia is not the same as multiple personality, which sometimes is called "split personality." Schizophrenia involves the split of an individual's personality from reality, not the coexistence of several personalities within one individual. Approximately 2.2 million adults in the United States, or about 1.1 percent of the population 18 years and older, have schizophrenia in any given year (NIMH, 2001a).

Schizophrenia is a serious, debilitating mental disorder (Fowles, 2003). About one-half of the patients in mental hospitals are individuals with schizophrenia. However, more often now than in the past, individuals with schizophrenia live in society and return to mental hospitals periodically for treatment. Drug therapy is the main reason for fewer individuals with schizophrenia being hospitalized. The "rule of fourths" characterizes outcomes for individuals with schizophrenia: one-fourth get well and stay well; one-fourth go on medication, do relatively well, and are able to live independently; another one-fourth are well enough to live in a group home; and one-fourth do poorly and are usually institutionalized.

Schizophrenia produces a bizarre set of symptoms and wreaks havoc on the individual's personality (VandenBos, 2000). For example, individuals with schizophrenia

schizophrenia A severe psychological disorder characterized by highly disordered thought processes.

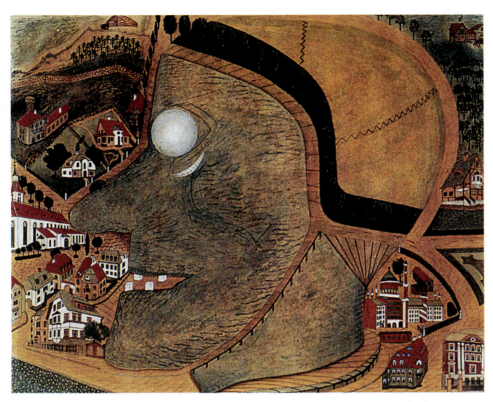

Landscape, by August Neter, who was a successful electrical engineer until he became schizophrenic in 1907. He lost interest in his work as his mind became disorganized. *What does the painting suggest about the schizophrenic mind?*

have *delusions*, or false beliefs. One individual might think he is Jesus Christ or Napoléon. One individual might think her thoughts are being broadcast over the radio or that a double agent is controlling her every move. Individuals with schizophrenia also might hear, see, feel, smell, and taste things that are not there. These *hallucinations* often take the form of voices. An individual with schizophrenia might think that he hears two people talking about him. Or he might say, "Hear that rumbling noise in the pipe? That is one of my men watching out for me."

Often individuals with schizophrenia do not make sense when they talk or write. For example, an individual with schizophrenia might say, "Well, Rocky, babe, help is out, happening, but where, when, up, top, side, over, you know, out of the way, that's it. Sign off." Such speech has no meaning. These incoherent, loose word associations are called *word salad.*

The motor behavior of the individual with schizophrenia can be bizarre, sometimes taking the form of an odd appearance, pacing, statuelike postures, or strange mannerisms. Some individuals with schizophrenia withdraw from their social world, totally absorbed in their own thoughts.

Types of Schizophrenia

There are four main types of schizophrenia. Their outward behavior patterns vary, but they have in common the characteristics of disordered thought processes.

- **Disorganized schizophrenia** is a type of schizophrenia in which an individual has delusions and hallucinations that have little or no recognizable meaning—hence, the label "disorganized." An individual with disorganized schizophrenia may withdraw from human contact and may regress to silly, childlike gestures and behavior. Many of these individuals were isolated or maladjusted during adolescence.

disorganized schizophrenia A type of schizophrenia in which an individual has delusions and hallucinations with little or no recognizable meaning.

Unusual motor behaviors are prominent symptoms in catatonic schizophrenia. Individuals may cease to move altogether, sometimes holding bizarre postures. *Is this person conscious or unconscious?*

In-Psych Plus

- **Catatonic schizophrenia** is characterized by bizarre motor behavior, which sometimes takes the form of a completely immobile stupor. Even in this stupor, individuals with catatonic schizophrenia are completely conscious of what is happening around them. In a catatonic state, the individual sometimes shows *waxy flexibility*; for example, if the person's arm is raised and then let go of, the arm stays in the new position.
- **Paranoid schizophrenia** is characterized by delusions of reference, grandeur, and persecution. The delusions usually form an elaborate system based on a complete misinterpretation of events. Individuals with paranoid schizophrenia often develop all three types of delusions in a specific order. First, they sense that they have been singled out for attention. Individuals with delusions of reference misinterpret chance events as being directly relevant to their own lives—a thunderstorm, for example, might be perceived as a personal message from God. Second, they believe that this special attention is the result of their special characteristics (delusions of grandeur). Individuals with delusions of grandeur think of themselves as exalted beings—the pope or the president, for example. Third, they think that others are so jealous and threatened by these characteristics that they spy and plot against them (delusions of persecution). Individuals with delusions of persecution often feel that they are the target of a conspiracy. A woman describes the onset of paranoid schizophrenia and its symptoms in the video clip "Paranoid Schizophrenia."
- **Undifferentiated schizophrenia** is characterized by disorganized behavior, hallucinations, delusions, and incoherence. This diagnosis is used when an individual's symptoms either do not meet the criteria for one of the other types or meet the criteria for more than one of the other types. Go to the video clip "Schizophrenia" to see interviews with two individuals, one experiencing the undifferentiated type and the other the disorganized type.

Causes of Schizophrenia

Like the mood disorders, schizophrenia may have biological, psychological, and sociocultural causes. Schizophrenia is a heavily researched mental disorder, with recent research especially focusing on biological factors (Walker & others, 2004).

Biological Factors in Schizophrenia   There is strong research support for biological explanations of schizophrenia. Particularly compelling is the evidence for a genetic predisposition, but structural abnormalities and neurotransmitters also seem to be linked to this devastating disorder.

- *Heredity.* If you have a relative with schizophrenia, what are the chances you will develop schizophrenia? It depends on how closely you are related (Tsuang, Stone, & Faraone, 2001). Figure 11.12 shows the risk of schizophrenia for identical twins, fraternal twins, siblings, nephews and nieces, and the general population (Gottesman & Shields, 1982). The role of heredity in schizophrenia may be illustrated through the story of the Genain quadruplets, who have been extensively studied at the National Institute of Mental Health (NIMH). Serious mental problems emerged by the time the quadruplets reached high school. By the time they were in their 20s, each had been diagnosed with schizophrenia. A research team at NIMH, led by David Rosenthal (1963), began extensive evaluation of the schizophrenic quadruplets. About 20 years later, psychologist Alan Mirksy invited the quadruplets back to NIMH. Brain scans revealed an unusually high rate of energy use in the rear portion of the quadruplets' brains (see figure 11.13), as well as an unusually low rate of alpha-wave activity. Remember that alpha-wave activity appears in individuals in a relaxed state; scientists speculate that the onset of hallucinations

catatonic schizophrenia A type of schizophrenia characterized by bizarre motor behavior, which sometimes takes the form of a completely immobile stupor.

paranoid schizophrenia A type of schizophrenia characterized by delusions of reference, grandeur, and persecution.

undifferentiated schizophrenia A type of schizophrenia characterized by disorganized behavior, hallucinations, delusions, and incoherence.

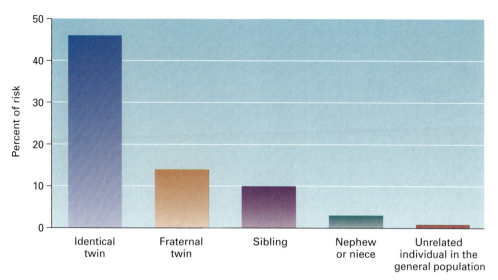

FIGURE 11.12 **Lifetime Risk of Developing Schizophrenia, According to Genetic Relatedness**
As genetic relatedness to an individual with schizophrenia increases, so does the risk of developing schizophrenia.

might possibly block alpha-wave activity. Environmental experiences may have contributed to the Genain quadruplets' schizophrenia as well. Their father placed strict demands on his daughters, delighted in watching them undress, and would not let them participate in social activities, even as adults. In a follow-up of the Genain quadruplets when they were 66 years of age, significant variations in their lives were apparent (Mirsky & others, 2000). Myra worked, married, and raised a family. Hester never completed high school and has never been able to function independently outside a group home or an institution. Nora and Iris have never married or had substantial careers. But the Genain quadruplets' thought processes remained stable or even improved somewhat as they got older, indicating that schizophrenia is not a degenerative disorder. See the video clip "Beautiful Minds: An Interview with John Nash and Son" to explore the role of heredity in schizophrenia.

- *Brain abnormalities.* Structural abnormalities in the brain have been found in individuals with schizophrenia. Imaging techniques clearly show enlarged ventricles in the brains of these people (Puri & others, 1999, 2001). Ventricles are fluid-filled spaces in the brain, and enlargement of the ventricles indicates atrophy or deterioration in other brain tissue. Individuals with schizophrenia also have a small frontal cortex (the area in which thinking, planning, and decision

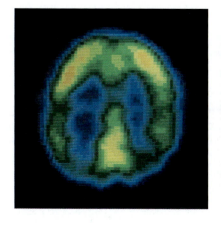
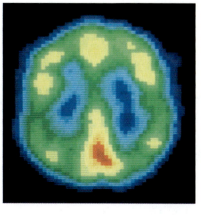

FIGURE 11.13 **Brain Scans of Two of the Genain Quadruplets** In a normal brain *(left)*, the areas of high energy use are at the top, in the frontal lobes. The quadruplets all showed abnormal energy use in the visual areas at the bottom *(right, red area). Are these hallucinations?*

The Genain quadruplets as children and as middle-aged adults. All four had been diagnosed with schizophrenia by the time they were in their 20s. *What might account for the differences in their life trajectories?*

making take place) and show less activity than is seen in individuals who do not have schizophrenia (Allen, Goldstein, & Weiner, 2001; Cotter & others, 2002). Do these deficits cause the disorder? Or are they simply symptoms of a disorder whose true origin lies deeper in the brain, in the genes, or in the environment?

- *Neurotransmitter deregulation.* An early biological explanation for schizophrenia stated that individuals with schizophrenia produce higher than normal levels of the neurotransmitter dopamine and that the excess dopamine causes schizophrenia. That theory is probably too simple, although there is good evidence that dopamine does play a role in schizophrenia (Bressan & others, 2001).

Psychological Factors in Schizophrenia   Although contemporary theorists do not propose psychological factors as stand-alone causes of schizophrenia, stress may be a contributing factor. One model argues that a combination of biogenetic predisposition and stress causes schizophrenia (Meehl, 1962). A defective genetic makeup might produce schizophrenia only when the individual lives in a stressful environment. Advocates of this view emphasize the importance of stress reduction and family support in treating schizophrenia.

Sociocultural Factors in Schizophrenia   Disorders of thought and emotion are common to schizophrenia in all cultures, but the type and incidence of schizophrenic disorders may vary from culture to culture. Individuals living in poverty are likelier to have schizophrenia than people at higher socioeconomic levels. The link between schizophrenia and poverty is correlational, and contemporary theorists do not believe that poverty causes schizophrenia (Schiffman & Walker, 1998).

Review and Sharpen Your Thinking

5   *Characterize schizophrenia.*

- Describe the different types of schizophrenia.
- Explain the causes of schizophrenia.

Imagine that you are a clinical psychologist who has been given the opportunity to interview the Genain quadruplets. What questions would you want to ask them in an effort to understand why the paths of their schizophrenia varied through their adult years?

Odd/Eccentric Cluster	Dramatic/Emotionally Problematic Cluster	Chronic-Fearfulness/ Avoidant Cluster

What behavior patterns are typical of personality disorders?

Personality disorders are chronic, maladaptive cognitive-behavioral patterns that are thoroughly integrated into the individual's personality. They may be troublesome to others, harmful to the individual who has one, or illegal (Livesly, 2001). The patterns are often recognizable by adolescence or earlier. However, personality disorders usually are not as bizarre as schizophrenia, and they do not have the intense, diffuse feelings of fear and apprehension that characterize the anxiety disorders (Evans & others, 2002; Trull & Widiger, 2003).

In the *DSM-IV*, the personality disorders are grouped into three clusters: odd/eccentric, dramatic/emotionally problematic, and chronic-fearfulness/avoidant.

Odd/Eccentric Cluster

The odd/eccentric cluster includes three personality disorders:

- *Paranoid*. These individuals have a lack of trust in others and are suspicious. They see themselves as morally correct yet vulnerable and envied.
- *Schizoid*. They do not form adequate social relationships. They are shy, show withdrawn behavior, and have difficulty expressing anger. Most are considered to be "cold" people.
- *Schizotypal*. They show odd thinking patterns that reflect eccentric beliefs, overt suspicion, and overt hostility. The following case describes an individual with schizotypal personality disorder.

> Mr. S. was a 35-year-old chronically unemployed man who was thought to have a vitamin deficiency. This was believed to have occurred because Mr. S. avoided any foods that could have been contaminated by a machine. He had started to develop alternative ideas about food and diet in his 20s. He left his family to study an eastern religion. As he said, "It opened my third eye, corruption is all about." Later, Mr. S. moved to live by himself on a small farm, attempting to grow his own food. He spent his days and evenings researching the mechanisms of food contamination. (Quality Assurance Project, 1990, p. 344)

As you can see, some personality disorders have names that are similar to other disorders described earlier in the chapter, such as schizophrenic disorders. However, individuals with schizotypal disorder are not as clearly bizarre in their thinking and behavior as those with schizophrenia.

Individuals with paranoid personality disorder show chronic and pervasive mistrust and suspicion of other people that is not warranted. *How does this disorder differ from schizoid and schizotypal personality disorders?*

Dramatic/Emotionally Problematic Cluster

The dramatic and emotionally problematic cluster consists of four personality disorders:

- *Histrionic*. These individuals seek a lot of attention and tend to overreact. They respond more dramatically and intensely than is required by the situation, hence the term *histrionic*. The disorder is more common in women than men.
- *Narcissistic*. They have an unrealistic sense of self-importance, can't take criticism, manipulate people, and lack empathy. These characteristics lead to substantial problems in relationships.
- *Borderline*. These individuals are often emotionally unstable, impulsive, unpredictable, irritable, and anxious. They also are prone to boredom. Their behavior is similar to that of individuals with schizotypal personality disorder, but they

personality disorders Chronic, maladaptive cognitive-behavioral patterns that are thoroughly integrated into the individual's personality.

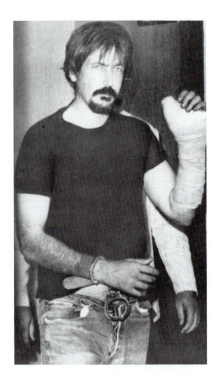

Gary Gilmore was a classic case of antisocial personality disorder. As a young adolescent, Gilmore had low grades, was often truant, and stole from classmates. At 14, he was placed in a juvenile detention center for stealing a car. He was arrested on numerous occasions in high school and at 20 was sent to the state penitentiary for burglary and robbery. Several years later, Gilmore was released, but it didn't take long for him to be put back in the penitentiary for other armed robberies. Released again, he moved in with a woman, but his drinking, carousing, and fighting caused her to kick him out. Later that year, he pulled into a gas station in Utah and ordered the attendant to hand over the cash, which the attendant did. Gilmore shot him twice in the head, anyway, killing him. The next morning, Gilmore walked into a hotel and shot the manager. Gilmore was caught and convicted of the two murders. He was executed in 1977. *Why might he have developed antisocial personality disorder?*

are not as consistently withdrawn and bizarre. The video clip "Borderline Personality Disorder" presents the example of Becky, who has engaged in self-mutilation and shows uncontrollable anger.

- *Antisocial*. They are guiltless, law-breaking, exploitive, self-indulgent, irresponsible, and intrusive. They often resort to a life of crime and violence. This disorder is far more common in men than in women.

In a national study of the prevalence of psychological disorders, 2.6 percent of the individuals reported that they had at some time experienced an antisocial personality disorder (Robins & Regier, 1991). The following individual is an example:

Mark, 22 years old, is awaiting trial for car theft and armed robbery. He has a long history of arrests beginning at 9 years of age, when he was arrested for vandalism. He was expelled from high school for truancy and disruptive behavior. He ran away from home on numerous occasions. He has not held a job for more than two days at a time, even though his charming manner enables him to obtain work rather easily. Mark is a loner with few friends and, although initially charming, he soon antagonizes the people he meets with his aggressive, self-oriented behavior. While Mark was awaiting trial, he skipped bail and left town. (Carson, Butcher, & Mineka, 2000)

People with antisocial personality disorder used to be called psychopaths or sociopaths. They regularly violate other people's rights. The disorder begins before the age of 15 and continues into adulthood. These individuals represent a small percentage of the population but commit a disproportionately large percentage of crimes (Meyer, Wolverton, & Deitsch, 1998). The disorder is very difficult to treat. Most health maintenance organizations will not authorize the treatment of this or any of the other personality disorders.

Explanations for the causes of antisocial personality disorder include biological, psychological, and sociocultural factors. In terms of biological factors, a genetic predisposition for the disorder may be present (Goldstein, Prescott, & Kendler, 2001). For example, the disorder is likelier to appear in identical twins than in fraternal twins (Gottesman & Goldsmith, 1994). In terms of psychological factors, the impulsive and aggressive behavior that characterizes individuals with antisocial personality disorders suggests that they have not adequately learned how to delay gratification. In terms of sociocultural factors, inadequate socialization regularly appears in the history of individuals who develop antisocial personality disorder (Sutker & Allain, 1993). Parents of these children may be neglectful or inconsistent and punitive in their discipline. Individuals with this disorder are more likely to have at least one parent with antisocial personality traits than are those without the disorder. Thus children growing up in these families presumably have many opportunities to observe and imitate parents who behave in exploitive, immoral ways.

Chronic-Fearfulness/Avoidant Cluster

The chronic-fearfulness/avoidant cluster includes four personality disorders:

- *Avoidant*. These individuals are shy and inhibited yet desire interpersonal relationships, which distinguishes them from those with the schizoid and schizotypal disorders. They often have low self-esteem and are extremely sensitive to rejection. This disorder is close to being an anxiety disorder but is not characterized by as much personal distress.
- *Dependent*. They lack self-confidence, do not express their own personalities, and have a pervasive need to cling to stronger personalities, whom they allow to make decisions for them. The disorder is far more common in women than in men.
- *Passive-aggressive*. These individuals often pout and procrastinate; they are stubborn or are intentionally inefficient in an effort to frustrate others.

- *Obsessive-compulsive.* This personality disorder is often confused with obsessive-compulsive anxiety disorder. However, an individual with obsessive-compulsive personality disorder rarely becomes obsessed about issues. In the personality disorder, the individual engages in a specific behavior, such as persistent hand washing. And in the personality disorder, the person does not become upset or distressed about his or her lifestyle. These individuals are obsessed with rules, are emotionally insensitive, and are oriented toward a lifestyle of productivity and efficiency.

Review and Sharpen Your Thinking

6 *Identify the behavior patterns typical of personality disorders.*

- Discuss the odd/eccentric cluster.
- Explain the dramatic/emotionally problematic cluster.
- Describe the chronic-fearfulness/avoidant cluster.

This section described a possible psychological cause for antisocial personality disorder. Try to come up with psychological explanations of the other personality disorders.

Psychological Disorders

1 PERSPECTIVES ON PSYCHOLOGICAL DISORDERS

Defining Abnormal Behavior

Understanding Psychological Disorders

Classifying Abnormal Behavior

2 ANXIETY DISORDERS

Generalized Anxiety Disorder

Phobic Disorder

Post-Traumatic Stress Disorder

Panic Disorder

Obsessive-Compulsive Disorder

3 DISSOCIATIVE DISORDERS

Dissociative Amnesia and Fugue

Dissociative Identity Disorder

4 MOOD DISORDERS

Depressive Disorders

Causes of Mood Disorders

Bipolar Disorder

Suicide

5 SCHIZOPHRENIA

Types of Schizophrenia

Causes of Schizophrenia

6 PERSONALITY DISORDERS

Odd/Eccentric Cluster

Dramatic/Emotionally Problematic Cluster

Chronic-Fearfulness/ Avoidant Cluster

1 Discuss the characteristics and classifications of abnormal behavior.

- Psychologists define abnormal behavior as behavior that is deviant, maladaptive, or personally distressful. Only one of these criteria is necessary for the classification of abnormal behavior, but two or three may be present. The line between normal and abnormal behavior is often thin.
- The biological approach to psychological disorders is a medical model, which describes psychological disorders as diseases with a biological origin. Structural, biochemical, and genetic views also have been proposed. Psychological approaches include the psychodynamic perspective, the behavioral and social cognitive perspectives, and the humanistic perspective. The sociocultural approach places more emphasis on the larger social context in which a person lives than on psychological factors. Sociocultural contexts include the individual's marriage or family, neighborhood, socioeconomic status, ethnicity, gender, and culture. The biopsychosocial approach considers the interaction of biological, psychological, and sociocultural factors in psychological disorders.
- The classification of mental disorders gives mental health professionals a shorthand to use in communicating with one another and allows clinicians to make predictions about disorders and determine what kind of treatment is appropriate. The *Diagnostic and Statistical Manual of Mental Disorders (DSM)*, published by the American Psychiatric Association, is the classification system used by clinicians to diagnose and treat psychological disorders. *DSM-IV* features a multiaxial diagnostic system that enables clinicians to characterize an individual on five dimensions. Some psychologists contend that *DSM-IV* perpetuates the medical model of psychological disorders and labels some everyday problems that are not deviant or maladaptive as psychological disorders.

2 Distinguish among the various anxiety disorders.

- Anxiety is a diffuse, vague, highly unpleasant feeling of fear and apprehension. The main features of anxiety disorders are motor tension, hyperactivity, and apprehensive expectations and thoughts. Generalized anxiety disorder is defined as anxiety that persists for at least 1 month with no specific reason for the anxiety. Biological, psychological, and sociocultural factors may be involved.
- Recurrent panic attacks marked by the sudden onset of intense apprehension or terror characterize panic disorder. Panic disorder can occur with or without agoraphobia. Biological and psychological factors may contribute to the development of panic disorder.

- Phobic disorders involve an irrational, overwhelming fear of a particular object, such as snakes, or situation, such as flying. Biological and psychological factors have been proposed as causes of phobias.
- Obsessive-compulsive disorder (OCD) is an anxiety disorder in which the individual has anxiety-provoking thoughts that will not go away (obsession) or urges to perform repetitive, ritualistic behaviors to prevent or produce some future situation (compulsion). Biological and psychological factors are likely involved in OCD.
- Post-traumatic stress disorder (PTSD) is an anxiety disorder that develops through exposure to traumatic events, such as war; severely oppressive situations, such as the Holocaust; severe abuse, as in rape; natural disasters, such as floods and tornadoes; and unnatural disasters, such as plane crashes and terrorist attacks. Symptoms, which include flashbacks, may appear immediately after the trauma or may be delayed.

3 Describe the dissociative disorders.

- Dissociative disorders are characterized by a sudden loss of memory or change in identity. Under extreme stress, conscious awareness becomes dissociated (separated or split) from previous memories and thoughts. Dissociative amnesia involves memory loss caused by extensive psychological stress. Dissociative fugue also involves a loss of memory, but individuals with this disorder also unexpectedly wander off for a time or even travel away from home and assume a new identity.
- Dissociative identity disorder, formerly called multiple personality disorder, involves the presence of two or more distinct personalities in the same individual. This disorder is rare.

4 Compare the mood disorders and specify the risk factors for depression and suicide.

- Mood disorders are psychological disorders in which there is a disturbance of mood. The mood disturbance can include cognitive, behavioral, and physical symptoms, as well as interpersonal difficulties. Two main types of mood disorders are depressive disorders and bipolar disorder. In the depressive disorders, the individual suffers depression without ever experiencing mania. In major depressive disorder (MDD), the individual experiences a major depressive episode and depressed characteristics, such as lethargy and hopelessness. Dysthymic disorder is generally more chronic and has fewer symptoms than major depressive disorder. In contrast, normal feelings of gloom and sadness do not last as long or feel as intense as depressive disorders do.

- Bipolar disorder is characterized by extreme mood swings that include both depression and one or more episodes of mania (an overexcited, unrealistic, optimistic state). Less than 10 percent of bipolar individuals experience mania without depression.
- Biological explanations of mood disorders focus on heredity, neurophysiological abnormalities, neurotransmitter deregulation, and hormonal factors. Psychological explanations include psychodynamic, behavioral, and cognitive concepts. Sociocultural explanations emphasize interpersonal relationships, socioeconomic and ethnic factors, cultural variations, and gender.
- Severe depression and other psychological disorders can cause individuals to want to end their lives. Biological, psychological, and sociocultural explanations of suicide have been proposed.

5 *Characterize schizophrenia.*

- Schizophrenia is a severe psychological disorder that is characterized by highly disordered thought processes. Individuals with schizophrenia may show odd communication, inappropriate emotion, abnormal motor behavior, and social withdrawal. There are four main types of schizophrenia. In disorganized schizophrenia, an individual has delusions and hallucinations with little or no recognizable meaning. Catatonic schizophrenia is characterized by bizarre motor behavior, which may take the form of a completely immobile stupor. Paranoid schizophrenia is characterized by delusions of reference, grandeur, and persecution. Undifferentiated schizophrenia is characterized by disorganized behavior, hallucinations, delusions, and incoherence.
- Biological factors (heredity, structural brain abnormalities, and neurotransmitter deregulation), psychological factors (a combination of biogenetic predisposition and environmental stress), and sociocultural factors may be involved in schizophrenia. Psychological and sociocultural factors do not cause schizophrenia by themselves.

6 *Identify the behavior patterns typical of personality disorders.*

- Personality disorders are chronic, maladaptive cognitive-behavioral patterns that are thoroughly integrated into the individual's personality. The odd/eccentric cluster of personality disorders includes the paranoid, schizoid, and schizotypal personality disorders.
- The dramatic/emotionally problematic cluster consists of the histrionic, narcissistic, borderline, and antisocial personality disorders. Biological, psychological, and sociocultural explanations of antisocial personality disorder have been proposed.
- The chronic-fearfulness/avoidant cluster includes the avoidant, dependent, passive-aggressive, and obsessive-compulsive personality disorders.

Key Terms

abnormal behavior, p. 393
medical model, p. 394
DSM-IV, p. 396
anxiety disorders, p. 400
generalized anxiety
   disorder, p. 400
etiology, p. 401
panic disorder, p. 401
agoraphobia, p. 401
phobic disorder, p. 402

obsessive-compulsive
   disorder (OCD), p. 404
post-traumatic stress
   disorder (PTSD), p. 406
dissociative disorders, p. 408
dissociative amnesia, p. 408
dissociative fugue, p. 408
dissociative identity
   disorder (DID), p. 409
mood disorders, p. 410

depressive disorders, p. 411
major depressive disorder,
   (MDD), p. 411
dysthymic disorder, p. 411
bipolar disorder, p. 412
learned helplessness, p. 415
schizophrenia, p. 420
disorganized schizophrenia,
   p. 421

catatonic schizophrenia,
   p. 422
paranoid schizophrenia,
   p. 422
undifferentiated
   schizophrenia, p. 422
personality disorders, p. 425

Apply Your Knowledge

1. Spend 15 to 20 minutes observing in an area with a large number of people (a mall, the cafeteria, or the like), and identify behaviors that you would classify as abnormal. How does your list of behaviors compare with the definition of abnormal in the chapter? What would change on the list if you were in a different setting (a church, a bar, a library)? What does this tell you about defining abnormal behavior?

2. Imagine the following events. For each event, describe the kind of anxiety or dissociative disorder that might be most likely to develop. Is it more likely that the person would or would not develop the disorder?
   a. Marcy was bitten by a dog as a young child.
   b. On September 11, 2001, Alex, a firefighter in New York City, was called to the World Trade Center to aid in the rescue efforts.
   c. Andy was involved in a serious automobile accident.
   d. Sam's parents were always critical about her behavior and sometimes locked her in a room for several days at a time when she was growing up.

3. Take a quick survey of your friends and acquaintances and ask them whether they've ever experienced the symptoms of a common cold (runny nose, coughing, stuffy head). Then ask them if they've ever experienced symptoms of the "common cold" of mental disorders, as described in the chapter. How many indicate they've had colds, and how many indicate they've had a mood disorder? Are the numbers consistent with the numbers suggested in the book? Why might your numbers be different from those in the book?

4. The Internet provides a wealth of mental health information. Find a site (such as mentalhealth.com) that gives more information about personality disorders or schizophrenia. What information can you find that is not discussed in the chapter? Does it change your view of either disorder?

Connections

To test your mastery of the material in this chapter, go to the Study Guide and the In-Psych Plus CD-ROM, as well as the On-line Learning Center. There you will find a chapter summary, practice tests, flashcards, lecture slides, web links, and other study tools, such as interactive exercises and reviews as well as current, chapter-relevant news articles.

12

Therapies

Learning Goals

1 *Describe the biological therapies.*

2 *Characterize four types of psychotherapies.*

3 *Explain the sociocultural approaches to treatment.*

4 *Evaluate the effectiveness of psychotherapy.*

Steve M. has paranoid schizophrenia, which you read about in chapter 11. He hears voices all the time, telling him he has done something wrong, and feels that he is being constantly monitored by people he doesn't know. He is convinced that a transmitter has been placed in his head and someone is transmitting messages to it.

Medications from the psychiatrist he sees on a regular basis have significantly reduced the frequency of the voices Steve hears. Whenever he stops taking the medication, Steve has to be hospitalized for treatment. In between hospitalizations, he goes to a day treatment program and has taken some college classes.

In the clinic at the day program Steve attends, he has developed a long-term relationship with a psychologist he sees once a week. The psychotherapist is helping Steve to set some short-term goals and improve his outlook on life. The day treatment program, including his sessions with the psychotherapist, is providing him with practice in coping with stress, interacting more effectively with people, and living an independent life. His mother and stepfather have joined a support group, which is helping them to better understand Steve's psychological disorder and what needs to be done to help him (Bernheim, 1997). Steve still struggles with what is real and not real in his life. However, through psychotherapy, he has learned to trust certain people, especially his mother, brother, and stepfather.

Steve has benefited from several types of therapy—biological therapy, the use of medications to reduce the frequency of the voices he hears and his fear that people he does not know are monitoring him; psychotherapy, to help him cope more effectively and adjust to daily living; and sociocultural therapy, support groups to help his parents understand his disorder better and help him with his adjustment to the disorder.

The discussion of personality and psychological disorders in chapters 10 and 11 provides a foundation for understanding the modes of treatment that are used to help people with their psychological problems. Like those chapters, this one focuses on biological, psychological, and sociocultural factors and on how they are used in therapy to improve the lives of people with psychological disorders.

1 BIOLOGICAL THERAPIES

| Drug Therapy | Electroconvulsive Therapy | Psychosurgery |

What are the biological therapies?

Biological therapies are treatments to reduce or eliminate the symptoms of psychological disorders by altering the way an individual's body functions. Drug therapy is the most common form of biological therapy. Much less widely used biological therapies are electroconvulsive therapy and psychosurgery. Psychiatrists, who are medical doctors, can administer drugs as part of therapy. However, psychologists are not trained as medical doctors and cannot administer drugs as part of therapy. Instead, psychologists and other mental health professionals may provide **psychotherapy** to help individuals recognize and overcome their problems in conjunction with the biological therapy administered by psychiatrists and other medical doctors. A combination of psychotherapy and medication is often a desirable course of treatment (Kay, 2002).

Drug Therapy

Although medicine and herbs have long been used to alleviate symptoms of emotional distress, it was not until the twentieth century that drug treatments began to revolutionize mental health care. Psychotherapeutic drugs are used mainly in three diagnostic categories: anxiety disorders, mood disorders, and schizophrenia.

Antianxiety Drugs **Antianxiety drugs** are commonly known as *tranquilizers*. These drugs reduce anxiety by making individuals calmer and less excitable. Benzodiazepines are the antianxiety drugs that most often offer relief for anxiety symptoms.

biological therapies A class of treatment that reduces or eliminates the symptoms of psychological disorders by altering the way an individual's body functions.

psychotherapy The process used by mental health professionals to help individuals recognize, define, and overcome their psychological and interpersonal difficulties.

antianxiety drugs Commonly known as tranquilizers; reduce anxiety by making people calmer and less excitable.

They work by binding to the receptor sites of neurotransmitters that become overactive during anxiety. The most frequently prescribed benzodiazepines include Xanax, Valium, and Librium. A nonbenzodiazepine—buspirone, or BuSpar—is commonly used to treat generalized anxiety disorder.

Benzodiazepines are relatively fast-acting medications, taking effect within hours. Buspirone must be taken daily for 2 to 3 weeks before it takes effect.

Benzodiazepines, like all drugs, have some side effects (Roy-Byrne & Cowley, 2002, Stein, 2003). They can be addicting. Also, drowsiness, loss of coordination, fatigue, and mental slowing can accompany their use. These effects can be hazardous when driving or operating machinery, especially when the person first starts taking benzodiazepines. Benzodiazepines also have been linked to abnormalities in babies born to mothers who took them during pregnancy (Perault & others, 2000). When combined with alcohol, anesthetics, antihistamines, sedatives, muscle relaxants, and some prescription pain medications, benzodiazepines can cause depression (Dalfen & Stewart, 2001; Gutierrez-Lobos & others, 2001).

Many individuals experience stress or anxiety, so family physicians and psychiatrists widely prescribe these drugs. The relaxed feelings brought on by antianxiety drugs bring welcome relief from anxiety and stress and improve people's ability to cope with their problems. Antianxiety medications are best used only temporarily, however. As mentioned earlier, they can become addictive.

Antidepressant Drugs   **Antidepressant drugs** regulate mood. There are three main classes of antidepressant drugs:

- *Tricyclics,* named for their three-ringed molecular structure, are believed to work by increasing the level of certain neurotransmitters, especially norepinephrine and serotonin (Evans, 1999; Feighner, 1999). (To explore the relationship between neurochemical balance and mood disorders, see the video clip "Functions of Neurotransmitters.") The tricyclics (such as Elavil) reduce symptoms of depression in approximately 60 to 70 percent of cases. They usually take 2 to 4 weeks to improve mood. They sometimes have adverse side effects, such as restlessness, faintness, trembling, sleepiness, and difficulty remembering.

In-Psych Plus

- *MAO (monoamine oxidase) inhibitors* are not as widely used as the tricyclics because they are more toxic. However, some individuals who do not respond to the tricyclics do respond to the MAO inhibitors (such as Nardil). The MAO inhibitors may be especially risky because of their potential interactions with certain foods and drugs. Cheese and other fermented foods, as well as some alcoholic beverages such as red wine, can interact with the MAO inhibitors to increase blood pressure and eventually cause a stroke.

- *Selective serotonin reuptake inhibitors (SSRIs)* work mainly by interfering with the reabsorption of serotonin in the brain (Green, 2003). Three widely prescribed SSRI antidepressants are Prozac (fluoxetine), Paxil (paroxetine), and Zoloft (sertraline). Their popularity is based on their effectiveness in reducing the symptoms of depression with fewer side effects than other antidepressants (Metzel & Angel, 2004; Nemeroff & Schatzberg, 2002; Polsky & others, 2002). Nonetheless, they can have negative effects, including insomnia, anxiety, headache, and diarrhea. They also can impair sexual functioning and produce severe withdrawal symptoms if their use is ended too abruptly (Clayton & others, 2001).

Lithium is widely used to treat the mood swings of bipolar disorder; see the video clip "Bipolar Disorder II" to learn about one man's experience with the drug. The amount of lithium that circulates in the bloodstream must be carefully monitored because the effective dosage is precariously close to toxic levels. Kidney and thyroid gland complications can arise as a consequence of lithium therapy (Sachs, 2003).

Antidepressant drugs not only are used to treat mood disorders but also are often effective for a number of anxiety disorders, including generalized anxiety disorder, panic disorder, obsessive-compulsive disorder, social phobia, and post-traumatic stress

In-Psych Plus

antidepressant drugs Drugs that regulate mood.

Should Depression Be Treated with Drugs?

The 1993 publication of Peter Kramer's *Listening to Prozac* led to a fierce controversy over the way drugs are used to treat depression. The argument started when Kramer reported that Prozac (fluoxetine), an SSRI (selective serotonin reuptake inhibitor), did more than alleviate depression. Apparently, patients' personalities became instantly altered, and they believed Prozac gave them insight into their own psychological fragilities. In the end, they felt that Prozac allowed them to overcome their problems and limitations and become better adjusted. Kramer called this phenomenon "listening to Prozac." Partly as a result of the publication of the book, Prozac became one of the most widely prescribed drugs in history. People asked their doctors for Prozac for everything from poor appetites to a lack of competitiveness. Some even wanted to try Prozac just to find out what the fuss was all about.

In 1995, Peter Breggin and Ginger Ross Breggin published *Talking to Prozac: What Doctors Aren't Telling You About Today's Most Controversial Drug,* which criticized the then-rampant overprescription of Prozac. They raised the interesting question of how research on antidepressants establishes the usefulness of a particular drug. In a *clinical double-blind study,* the most common approach, the drug is administered to one group and a placebo to another, and both groups and the data collection team are kept in the dark about who is actually taking the medication. Under these conditions, if the drug produces better results than the placebo, it can be said to show promise. According to Breggin and Breggin (1995), some of the original studies of Prozac found that people taking a placebo improved more than those in the treatment group who were taking Prozac.

The general question of the effectiveness of Prozac and other depressants, as compared with placebos, has since been a focus of ongoing investigation. One meta-analysis included 19 clinical double-blind trials involving 2,318 patients randomly assigned to antidepressant or placebo conditions (Kirsch & Sapperstein, 1998). The results revealed that placebos produced 75 percent of the effectiveness of actual drugs and that drug and placebo effects were very highly correlated (+.90). Further,

active drugs that were not antidepressants also produced strong effects. The conclusion of the researchers was that the effects of antidepressant drugs may be due to an active placebo effect (Kirsch & Sapperstein, 1998).

Although this conclusion is open to argument (Rehm, 1998), it does raise the questions of how a placebo might alleviate depression and just what depression is. Feeling down now and then is part of living and may be psychologically healthy in some cases. Immediately using drugs to treat despondent moods as a "disorder" may interrupt normal processes of grieving or self-evaluation, possibly blocking healthy development. Also, a diet rich in refined carbohydrates and alcohol may produce some depression. The choice, then, may not be between Prozac and other antidepressant medications but between drugs and "natural" interventions, such as dietary improvements and exercise. Another benefit is that such natural interventions do not have the side effects that antidepressants do, such as a tendency toward increased violence in some people.

In the end, this controversy will likely lessen as researchers discover more about how different antidepressants exert their influence and, more important, learn more about depression itself. As mental health professionals develop better diagnostic techniques and learn to avoid overprescription, they may more confidently deliver antidepressant medication to people with otherwise untreatable biochemical imbalances while learning how to help many others cope naturally with the inevitable cases of the blues (Yidiz, Pauler, & Sachs, 2003).

What do you think?

- Have antidepressants helped anyone you know? Were you aware of any negative side effects? Any positive side effects?
- What do you think of the tendency to treat depression first with medication?
- Do you think occasional bouts of depression might play a normal role in psychological development?

disorder (Shelton & Hollon, 2000). In addition, eating disorders, especially bulimia nervosa, may be treatable with antidepressant drugs (Devlin & others, 2000).

Although antidepressant drugs, especially the SSRI drugs, have been effective in treating many cases of depression, at least 25 percent of individuals with major depressive disorder do not respond to any antidepressant drug (Shelton & Hollon, 2000). People with a personality disorder or psychotic symptoms also may not respond (Sharma, 2003).

The use of antidepressant drugs to treat depression is not without controversy, as the Critical Controversy box explains.

antipsychotic drugs Powerful drugs that diminish agitated behavior, reduce tension, decrease hallucinations, improve social behavior, and produce better sleep patterns in people who have a severe psychological disorder, such as schizophrenia.

Antipsychotic Drugs **Antipsychotic drugs** are powerful drugs that diminish agitated behavior, reduce tension, decrease hallucinations, improve social behavior, and produce better sleep patterns in individuals who have a severe psychological disorder,

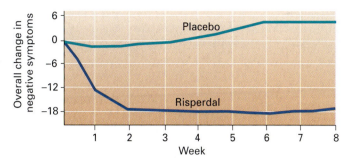

FIGURE 12.1 **Effects of Risperdal on Schizophrenics' Negative Symptoms** In one study, researchers found that just 1 week after starting treatment with Risperdal, negative symptoms (such as disorganized thought and uncontrolled hostility or excitement) were substantially reduced in schizophrenics. Negative symptoms in the placebo group actually increased slightly over the 8 weeks of the study.

especially schizophrenia (Pelak & Liu, 2004). Before antipsychotic drugs were developed in the 1950s, few, if any, interventions brought relief from the torment of psychotic symptoms. Once the effectiveness of these medications was apparent, the medical community significantly reduced more intrusive interventions, such as brain surgery, for schizophrenia (Grunberg, Klein, & Brown, 1998).

The *neuroleptics* are the most widely used class of antipsychotic drugs (Bradford, Stroup, & Lieberman, 2002). Numerous well-controlled investigations reveal that, when used in sufficient doses, the neuroleptics reduce a variety of schizophrenic symptoms, at least in the short term (Friedman, Temporini, & Davis, 1999; Holcomb & others, 1996). The most widely accepted explanation for their effectiveness is their ability to block the dopamine system's action in the brain (Rebec, 1996). Schizophrenics have too much of the neurochemical messenger dopamine.

The neuroleptics treat the symptoms of schizophrenia, not its causes. If an individual with schizophrenia stops taking the drug, the symptoms return. Neuroleptic drugs have substantially reduced the length of hospital stays for individuals with schizophrenia and allow them to return to the community. However, most of these individuals have difficulty coping with the demands of society, and most are chronically unemployed. Also, the neuroleptics can have severe side effects (Naidu, Singh, & Kulkarni, 2004).

A major side effect of neuroleptics is a neurological disorder characterized by grotesque, involuntary movements of the facial muscles and mouth, as well as extensive twitching of the neck, arms, and legs (Janno & others, 2004). As many as 20 percent of individuals with schizophrenia who take neuroleptics develop this disorder. Older women are especially vulnerable. Long-term neuroleptic therapy also is associated with increased depression and anxiety. Nonetheless, for the majority of schizophrenics, the benefits of neuroleptic treatment outweigh the risk and discomforts.

A group of medications called *atypical antipsychotic medications* was introduced in the 1990s. Like the SSRI drugs, atypical antipsychotic medications block the reuptake of the neurotransmitter serotonin. The two most widely used drugs in this group are Clozaril and Risperdal, which show promise for reducing schizophrenia's symptoms without the side effects of neuroleptics (Buckley & others, 2001). Figure 12.1 shows the substantial reduction in negative symptoms when schizophrenics take Risperdal (Marder, Davis, & Chouinard, 1997).

Strategies to increase the effectiveness of the antipsychotic drugs involve administering small dosages over time, rather than a large initial dose, and combining drug therapy with psychotherapy. The fact that only a small percentage of schizophrenics are able to hold jobs suggests that drugs alone will not help them be contributing members of society. They also need training in vocational, family, and social skills.

A summary of the drugs used to treat various psychological disorders is shown in figure 12.2. Notice that, for some types of anxiety disorders, such as agoraphobia, MAO inhibitors (antidepressant drugs) might be used, rather than antianxiety drugs.

Psychological Disorder	Drug	Effectiveness	Side Effects
Everyday Anxiety and Anxiety Disorders			
Everyday anxiety	Antianxiety drugs; antidepressant drugs	Substantial improvement short-term	Antianxiety drugs: less powerful the longer people take them; may be addictive Antidepressant drugs: see under depressive disorders
Generalized anxiety disorder	Antianxiety drugs	Not very effective	Less powerful the longer people take them; may be addictive
Panic disorder	Antianxiety drugs	About half show improvement	Less powerful the longer people take them; may be addictive
Agoraphobia	Tricyclic drugs and MAO inhibitors	Majority show improvement	Tricyclics: restlessness, fainting, and trembling MAO inhibitors: toxicity
Specific phobias	Antianxiety drugs	Not very effective	Less powerful the longer people take them; may be addictive
Mood Disorders			
Depressive disorders	Tricyclic drugs, MAO inhibitors, and SSRI drugs	Majority show moderate improvement	Tricylics: cardiac problems, mania, confusion, memory loss, fatigue MAO inhibitors: toxicity SSRI drugs: nausea, nervousness, insomnia, and in a few cases suicidal thoughts
Bipolar disorder	Lithium	Large majority show substantial improvement	Toxicity
Schizophrenic Disorders			
Schizophrenia	Neuroleptics; atypical antipsychotic medications	Majority show partial improvement	Neuroleptics: irregular heartbeat, low blood pressure, uncontrolled fidgeting, grotesque facial movements, twitching, and immobility of face Atypical antipsychotic medications: Less extensive side effects than with neuroleptics; can have a toxic effect on white blood cells

FIGURE 12.2 Drug Therapy for Psychological Disorders

Electroconvulsive Therapy

Electroconvulsive therapy (ECT), commonly called *shock therapy,* is used mainly to treat severely depressed individuals. The goal is to cause a seizure in the brain much like what happens in some forms of epilepsy. A small electric current lasting for 1 second or less passes through two electrodes placed on the individual's head. The current stimulates a seizure, which lasts for approximately 1 minute. ECT has been used for more than 40 years. In earlier years, it was used indiscriminately, sometimes to punish patients. ECT is still used with as many as 60,000 individuals a year, mainly individuals who have not responded to drug therapy or psychotherapy.

The manner in which ECT is administered today involves little discomfort. The patient is given anesthesia and muscle relaxants before the current is applied, which allows the individual to sleep through the procedure, minimizes convulsions, and reduces the risk for physical injury. The individual awakens shortly afterward with no conscious memory of the treatment. See the video clip "Major Depression" for a description of a patient's experience with ECT.

One analysis of studies of the use of electroconvulsive therapy compared its effectiveness in treating depression with cognitive therapy and antidepressant drugs (Seligman, 1994). ECT was as effective as cognitive therapy or drug therapy, with about four of five individuals showing marked improvement in all three therapies. However, as with the other therapies, the relapse rate for ECT is moderate to high.

Adverse side effects, such as memory loss and other cognitive impairments, are more severe than most drug side effects (Andrade, Shah, & Tharyan, 2003). Cognitive

In-Psych Plus

electroconvulsive therapy (ECT)
Commonly called *shock therapy;* a treatment for severely depressed individuals that causes a seizure in the brain.

therapy shows no side effects. A positive aspect of ECT is that its beneficial effects appear in a matter of days, whereas the beneficial effects of antidepressant drugs can take weeks, and those of cognitive therapy months, to appear (Dannon & others, 2002). Listen to the audio clip "Electroconvulsive Therapy" for a discussion of the benefits and risks of this therapy.

Psychosurgery

Psychosurgery is a biological therapy that involves removal or destruction of brain tissue. The effects of psychosurgery are irreversible.

In the 1930s, Portuguese physician Egas Moniz developed a procedure known as a *prefrontal lobotomy*. In this procedure, a surgical instrument is inserted into the brain and rotated, severing fibers that connect the frontal lobe, which is important in higher thought processes, and the thalamus, important in emotion. Moniz theorized that, by severing the connections between these brain structures, the symptoms of severe mental disorders could be alleviated. Prefrontal lobotomies were conducted on thousands of patients from the 1930s through the 1950s. Moniz was awarded the Nobel Prize for his work. However, whereas some patients may have benefited from the lobotomies, many were left in a vegetable-like state because of the massive assaults on their brains.

These crude lobotomies are no longer performed. Since the 1960s, psychosurgery has become more precise. When psychosurgery is now performed, a small lesion is made in the amygdala or another part of the limbic system. Today, only several hundred patients who have severely debilitating conditions undergo psychosurgery each year. It is used only as a last resort and with extreme caution (Ruck, 2003).

Electroconvulsive therapy (ECT), commonly called "shock therapy," causes a seizure in the brain. ECT is still given to as many as 60,000 people a year, mainly to treat major depressive disorder. *What are the pros and cons of ECT?*

Review and Sharpen Your Thinking

1 ***Describe the biological therapies.***

- Identify the types of drugs used to treat psychological disorders.
- Explain what electroconvulsive therapy is and when it is used.
- Discuss psychosurgery.

Before prescribing drug therapy for an individual, what might be some important factors for a psychiatrist or another medical doctor (such as a general practitioner) to consider?

PSYCHOTHERAPIES 2

Psychodynamic Therapies   Behavior Therapies

Humanistic Therapies   Cognitive Therapies

What are the four main types of psychotherapy?

Psychotherapy is the process used by mental health professionals to help individuals recognize, define, and overcome their psychological and interpersonal difficulties and improve their adjustment. Psychotherapists use a number of strategies to accomplish these goals: talking, interpreting, listening, rewarding, and modeling, for example. Both psychologists and psychiatrists use psychotherapy.

This section focuses on four main approaches to psychotherapy: psychodynamic, humanistic, behavior, and cognitive. The term **insight therapy** characterizes both

psychosurgery A biological therapy that involves removal or destruction of brain tissue to improve an individual's adjustment.

insight therapy The psychodynamic and humanistic therapies, which share the goal of encouraging insight and self-awareness.

psychodynamic and humanistic therapies, because they encourage insight and self-awareness. The psychodynamic therapies are the oldest of these approaches.

Psychodynamic Therapies

The **psychodynamic therapies** stress the importance of the unconscious mind, extensive interpretation by the therapist, and the role of early-childhood experiences in the development of an individual's problems. Psychodynamic therapies aim to help individuals recognize the maladaptive ways in which they have been coping and the sources of their unconscious conflicts (Nolen-Hoeksema, 2004). Many psychodynamic approaches grew out of Freud's psychoanalytic theory. Some therapists with a psychodynamic perspective still practice Freudian techniques (Chiesa, Fonagy, & Holmes, 2003).

"Looking good!" © The New Yorker Collection 1994. Gahan Wilson from cartoonbank.com. All Rights Reserved.

Freud's Psychoanalysis Freud believed that the therapist acts as a psychological detective, sometimes taking the smallest clue and using it as a springboard for understanding the individual's major problems. The following shows how one analyst approached an individual's problems:

A 50-year-old business executive came to therapy because he felt depressed and anxious and these feelings would not go away. Although he was perceived as being very successful by his family and business associates, he perceived himself to be weak and incompetent. Through many sessions, the psychoanalyst had begun to suspect that the man's feelings of failure stemmed from his childhood experiences with a critical and punitive father. The father never seemed satisfied with the son's efforts. Following is an exchange between the analyst and the businessman that occurred one year into therapy:

Client: "I don't really feel like talking today."
Analyst: Remains silent for several minutes, then says, "Perhaps you would like to talk about why you don't feel like talking."
Client: "There you go again, making demands on me, insisting I do what I just don't feel up to doing. (Pause) Do I always have to talk here, when I don't feel like it? (Voice becomes angry and petulant) Can't you just get off my back? You don't really care how I feel."
Analyst: "I wonder why you feel I don't care?"
Client: "Because you're always pressuring me to do what I feel I can't do."

This exchange was interpreted by the analyst as an expression of resentment by the client of his father's pressures that were put on him and had little to do with the analyst himself. The transfer of the client's feelings from the father to the analyst was regarded as significant by the analyst and was used in subsequent sessions to help the client overcome his fear of expressing anger toward his father. (Davison & Neale, 1994)

Psychoanalysis is Freud's therapeutic technique for analyzing an individual's unconscious thoughts. Freud believed that clients' problems could be traced to childhood experiences, many of which involved conflicts about sexuality but that early experiences were not readily available to the conscious mind. Only through extensive questioning, probing, and analyzing was Freud able to help the individual become aware of how these early experiences were affecting adult behavior. (See the video clip "Freud's Contribution to Psychology" for a description of a typical patient of Freud and a review of the psychodynamic perspective.)

To reach the shadowy world of the unconscious, psychoanalytic therapists often use the following therapeutic techniques:

- **Free association** consists of encouraging individuals to say aloud whatever comes to mind, no matter how trivial or embarrassing (Hartocollis, 2003; Kris, 2002). When Freud detected a person resisting the spontaneous flow of thoughts, he probed further. He believed that the crux of the person's emotional

psychodynamic therapies A class of treatment that stresses the importance of the unconscious mind, extensive interpretation by the therapist, and the role of experiences in the early-childhood years. The goal is to help individuals recognize the maladaptive ways they have been coping and the sources of their unconscious conflicts.

psychoanalysis Freud's psychotherapeutic technique for analyzing an individual's unconscious thoughts. Freud believed that clients' problems could be traced to childhood experiences, many of which involved conflicts about sexuality.

free association The psychoanalytic technique of having individuals say aloud whatever comes into their minds.

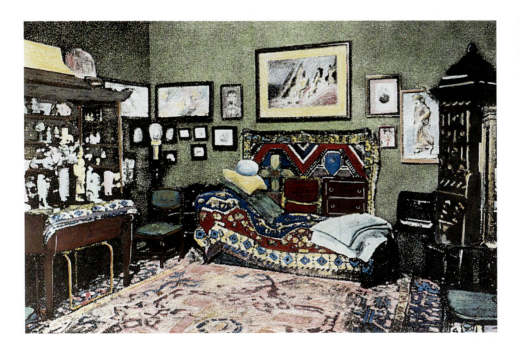

To encourage his patients to relax, Freud had them recline on the couch while he sat in the chair on the left, out of their view. *Why do you think Freud remained out of sight?*

problem probably lurked below this point of resistance. Encouraging people to talk freely, Freud thought, would help emotional feelings to emerge.

- **Catharsis** is the release of emotional tension that a person experiences when reliving an emotionally charged and conflicted experience.
- *Interpretation* plays an important role in psychoanalysis. To understand what is truly causing the person's conflicts, the therapist constantly searches for symbolic, hidden meanings in what the individual says and does. From time to time, the therapist suggests possible meanings of the person's statements and behavior.
- *Dream analysis* is important to psychoanalysts because they believe dreams contain information about the individual's unconscious thoughts and conflicts. As chapter 5 mentioned, Freud distinguished between the dream's *manifest content,* the conscious, remembered aspects of a dream, and its *latent content,* the unconscious, unremembered, symbolic aspects. The psychoanalyst interprets the dream by analyzing the manifest content for disguised unconscious wishes and needs, especially those that are sexual and aggressive. For some examples of the sexual symbols psychoanalysts use to interpret dreams, see figure 12.3. But even Freud cautioned against overinterpreting. As he once quipped, "Sometimes a cigar is just a cigar." See the video clip "Freudian Interpretation of Dreams" to learn more about dream analysis.

In-Psych Plus

- **Transference** is the person's relating to the analyst in ways that reproduce or relive important relationships in the individual's life. A person might interact with an analyst as if the analyst were a parent or lover, for example. When transference dominates therapy, the person's comments may become directed toward the analyst's personal life. Transference is often difficult to overcome in psychotherapy. However, Freud believed transference was an inevitable and essential aspect of the analyst-patient relationship. It can be used therapeutically as a model of how individuals relate to important people in their lives (Holm-Hadulla, 2003; Marcus, 2002).
- **Resistance** is the person's unconscious defense strategies that prevent the analyst from understanding the person's problems. Breakdown of resistance is a major goal of the analyst (Strean, 1996). Resistance occurs because it is painful to bring conflicts into conscious awareness. By resisting therapy, individuals do not have to face their problems. Showing up late or missing sessions, arguing with the

catharsis The release of emotional tension a person experiences when reliving an emotionally charged and conflicted experience.

transference The client's relating to the analyst in ways that reproduce or relive important relationships in the individual's life.

resistance The client's unconscious defense strategies that prevent the analyst from understanding the person's problems.

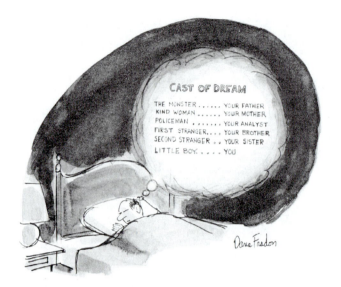

psychoanalyst, or faking free associations are examples of resistance. Some people go on endlessly about trivial matters to avoid facing their conflicts.

Contemporary Psychodynamic Therapies   Only a small percentage of contemporary therapists rigorously practice Freudian psychoanalysis. Nevertheless, many contemporary psychodynamic therapists still probe a person's unconscious thoughts about early childhood experiences to obtain clues to the person's current problems (Giannoni, 2003; Guimaraes, 2003; Marcus, 2002; Sugarman & DePottel, 2002). Many contemporary psychodynamic therapists also try to help individuals gain insight into their emotionally laden, repressed conflicts (Horowitz, 1998; Sonnenberg & Ursano, 2002). But they also accord more power to the conscious mind and to a person's current relationships than Freud did (Orfanos, 2002). Today individuals rarely lie on a couch or see their therapist several times a week. Instead, weekly appointments are typical, and people sit in a comfortable chair, facing the therapist. Some contemporary psychodynamic therapies can be intensive and extensive, lasting for years. However, in some cases, contemporary psychodynamic therapy lasts only a few months.

Contemporary psychodynamic approaches emphasize the development of the self in social contexts (Erikson, 1968; Horowitz, 1998). For example, in Heinz Kohut's (1977) view, early relationships with attachment figures, such as one's parents, are critical. As we develop, we do not relinquish these attachments; we continue to need them. Kohut's prescription for therapy involves getting the person to identify and seek out appropriate relationships with others. He also wants individuals to develop more realistic appraisals of relationships. Kohut believes therapists need to interact with individuals in ways that are empathic and understanding.

Humanistic Therapies

Empathy and understanding are absolute cornerstones for humanistic therapists, who encourage individuals to further their sense of self. The underlying philosophy of humanistic therapies is captured by the

Sexual Theme	Objects or Activities in Dreams That Symbolize Sexual Themes
Male genitals, especially penis	Umbrellas, knives, poles, swords, airplanes, guns, serpents, neckties, tree trunks, hoses
Female genitals, especially vagina	Boxes, caves, pockets, pouches, the mouth, jewel cases, ovens, closets
Sexual intercourse	Climbing, swimming, flying, riding (a horse, an elevator, a roller coaster)
Parents	Kings, queens, emperors, empresses
Siblings	Little animals

FIGURE 12.3 Freudian Interpretation of Sexual Symbolism in Dreams

metaphor of how an acorn, if provided with appropriate conditions, will grow in positive ways, pushing naturally toward its actualization as an oak (Corey, 1996; Schneider, 2002). In the **humanistic therapies,** people are encouraged to understand themselves and to grow personally. The humanistic therapies are unique in their emphasis on the person's self-healing capacities (Bohart, 1995). In contrast to the psychodynamic therapies, the humanistic therapies emphasize conscious rather than unconscious thoughts, the present rather than the past, and growth and self-fulfillment rather than illness.

Client-Centered Therapy

> Therapist: Everything's lousy, huh? You feel lousy. [Silence of 39 seconds] Want to come in Friday at 12 at the usual time?
>
> Client: [Yawns and mutters something unintelligible. Silence of 48 seconds]
>
> Therapist: Just kind of feel sunk way down deep in those lousy, lousy feelings, hm? Is that something like it?
>
> Client: No.
>
> Therapist: No? [Silence of 20 seconds]
>
> Client: No. I'm just no good to anybody, never was, and never will be.
>
> Therapist: Feeling that now, hm? That you're no good to yourself, no good to anybody. Just that you're completely worthless, huh? Those are really lousy feelings. Just feel that you're no good at all, hm?

This is an excerpt from a therapy session conducted by a client-centered therapist with a young man who was depressed. The therapist was Carl Rogers (Meador & Rogers, 1979). Notice how Rogers unconditionally accepted the client's feelings. **Client-centered therapy** is a form of humanistic therapy, developed by Carl Rogers (1961, 1980), in which the therapist provides a warm, supportive atmosphere to improve the client's self-concept and encourage the client to gain insight into problems. Compared with psychodynamic therapies, which emphasize analysis and interpretation by the therapist, client-centered therapy places far more emphasis on the client's self-reflection (Hill, 2000).

The relationship between the therapist and the client is an important aspect of Rogers' therapy. The therapist must enter into an intensely personal relationship with the client, not as a physician diagnosing a disease but as one human being to another.

You might recall from chapter 10 that Rogers believed each of us grows up in a world filled with *conditional positive regard.* We usually do not receive love and praise unless we conform to the standards and demands of others. Rarely do we feel that we measure up to such standards or that we are as good as others expect us to be, and thus we have low self-esteem.

To free a person from worry about society's demands, the therapist conveys *unconditional positive regard,* never disapproving of the client. Rogers believed this unconditional positive regard improves the person's self-esteem. The therapist's role is nondirective; that is, he or she does not lead the client to any particular revelation. The therapist is there to listen sympathetically to the client's problems and to encourage positive self-regard, independent self-appraisal, and independent decision making. Though client-centered therapists give approval of the person, they do not always approve of the person's behavior.

In addition to unconditional positive regard, Rogers advocated the use of the following two techniques in client-centered therapy:

- *Genuineness* (also called *congruence*), which involves letting a client know the therapist's feelings and not hiding behind a facade
- *Active listening,* which consists of giving total attention to what the person says and means; one way therapists improve active listening is to restate and support what the client has said and done

humanistic therapies A class of treatment that encourages people to understand themselves and to grow personally; the humanistic therapies are unique in their emphasis on self-healing capacities.

client-centered therapy Rogers' humanistic therapy, in which the therapist provides a warm, supportive atmosphere to improve the client's self-concept and encourage the client to gain insight into problems.

Frederick (Fritz) Perls was the founder of gestalt therapy. *What style of interaction with clients did he advocate?*

Gestalt Therapy **Gestalt therapy** is a humanistic therapy, developed by Fritz Perls (1893–1970), in which the therapist challenges clients to help them become more aware of their feelings and face their problems. Perls was trained in Europe as a Freudian psychoanalyst, but he developed his own ideas and eventually parted from some of Freud's teachings.

Perls (1969) agreed with Freud that psychological problems originate in unresolved past conflicts and that these conflicts need to be acknowledged and worked through. Also like Freud, Perls stressed that interpretation of dreams is an important aspect of therapy. But, in other ways, Perls and Freud were miles apart. Perls believed that unresolved conflicts should be brought to bear on the here and now of the individual's life. The therapist pushes clients into deciding whether they will continue to allow the past to control their future or whether they will choose right now what they want to be in the future. To this end, Perls encouraged individuals to actively control their lives and to be open about their feelings (Garza, 1999).

To stimulate change, the therapist often openly confronts the client. To demonstrate an important point to a client, the gestalt therapist might exaggerate a client's characteristics. In the following excerpt from a gestalt therapy session, the therapist (in this case, Perls himself) exaggerates a phrase the client uses:

> Perls: Now talk to your Top Dog! Stop nagging.
>
> Jane: [Loud, pained] Leave me alone.
>
> Perls: Yah, again.
>
> Jane: Leave me alone.
>
> Perls: Again.
>
> Jane: [Screaming it and crying] Leave me alone!
>
> Perls: Again.
>
> Jane: [She screams it, a real blast.] Leave me alone! I don't have to do what you say! [Still crying] I don't have to be in this chair! I don't have to. You make me. You make me come here! [Screams] Aarhh. You make me pick my face [crying], that's what you do. [Screams and cries] Aarhh! I'd like to kill you.
>
> Perls: Say this again.
>
> Jane: I'd like to kill you.
>
> Perls: Again.
>
> Jane: I'd like to kill you.

Another technique used in gestalt therapy is role playing by the client, the therapist, or both. For example, if an individual is bothered by conflict with her mother, the therapist might play the role of the mother and reopen the quarrel. The therapist might encourage the individual to act out her hostile feelings toward her mother by yelling, swearing, or kicking the couch. In this way, gestalt therapists hope to help individuals better manage their feelings instead of letting their feelings control them.

As you probably noticed, the gestalt therapist is much more directive than the client-centered therapist and provides more interpretation and feedback (Zahm & Gold, 2002). Nonetheless, both of these humanistic therapies encourage individuals to take responsibility for their feelings and actions, to truly be themselves, to understand themselves, to develop a sense of freedom, and to look at what they are doing with their lives.

Behavior Therapies

Having explored the insight therapies—the psychodynamic and humanistic approaches—we turn to therapies that take a very different approach to reducing people's problems and improving their adjustment: the behavior therapies, which offer action-oriented strategies to help people change what they are doing (Kazdin, 2002; Spiegler & Guevremont, 2003).

Behavior therapies use principles of learning to reduce or eliminate maladaptive behavior. Behavior therapists do not search for unconscious conflicts, as psychodynamic therapists do, or encourage individuals to develop accurate perceptions of their feelings

gestalt therapy Perls' humanistic therapy, in which the therapist challenges clients to help them become more aware of their feelings and face their problems.

behavior therapies A class of treatment that uses principles of learning to reduce or eliminate maladaptive behavior.

1. A month before an examination
2. Two weeks before an examination
3. A week before an examination
4. Five days before an examination
5. Four days before an examination
6. Three days before an examination
7. Two days before an examination
8. One day before an examination
9. The night before an examination
10. On the way to the university on the day of an examination
11. Before the unopened doors of the examination room
12. Awaiting distribution of examination papers
13. The examination paper lies facedown before her
14. In the process of answering the exam questions

FIGURE 12.4 A Desensitization Hierarchy Involving Test Anxiety In the hierarchy, the individual begins with the least feared circumstance (a month before the exam) and moves through each circumstance until reaching the most feared circumstance (the exam paper face down in front of her). At each step, the person replaces fear with deep relaxation and successful visualizations.

and selves, as humanistic therapists do. Instead, behavior therapists assume that the overt maladaptive symptoms are the problem (Sloan & Mizes, 1999). Individuals can become aware of why they are depressed and still be depressed, say the behavior therapists. The behavior therapist tries to eliminate the depressed symptoms or behaviors themselves, rather than trying to get individuals to gain insight into or awareness of why they are depressed (Forsyth & Savsevitz, 2002; Lazarus, 1996).

The behavior therapies were initially based almost exclusively on the learning principles of classical and operant conditioning, but they have become more diverse in recent years (McKay & Tryon, 2002). As social cognitive theory grew in popularity, behavior therapists increasingly included observational learning, cognitive factors, and self-instruction in their efforts to help people with their problems (Maultsby & Wirga, 1998; Tracy, Sherry, & Albright, 1999).

Techniques Based on Classical Conditioning   Some behaviors, especially fears, can be acquired through classical conditioning. (To review the elements of classical conditioning, go to the interactivity "Classical Conditioning II.") If fears can be learned through classical conditioning, perhaps they can be unlearned through counterconditioning (Taylor, 2002). The following are two types of counterconditioning:

- **Systematic desensitization** is a method of behavior therapy, based on classical conditioning, that treats anxiety by getting the person to associate deep relaxation with increasingly intense anxiety-producing situations (Wolpe, 1963). Consider the common fear of taking an exam. Using systematic desensitization, the behavior therapist first asks the person which aspects of the feared situation are the most and least frightening. Then the behavior therapist arranges these circumstances in a desensitization hierarchy like the one in figure 12.4. The next step is to teach clients to recognize muscular contractions or tensions in various parts of their bodies and then to contract and relax different muscles. Once individuals are relaxed, the therapist asks them to imagine the least feared stimulus in the hierarchy. The therapist moves up the list of items, from least to most feared, while clients remain relaxed. Eventually, individuals are able to imagine the most fearsome circumstance without being afraid—in our example, the exam paper face down on the desk. Individuals learn to relax while thinking about the exam instead of feeling anxious. (For another example, go to the video clip "Tourette's Syndrome," in which a young man explains how he uses relaxation techniques to relieve some symptoms.)

systematic desensitization A method of behavior therapy, based on classical conditioning, that treats anxiety by getting the person to associate deep relaxation with increasingly intense anxiety-producing situations.

Systematic desensitization has a new format. Virtual reality technology is being used by some therapists to expose individuals to more vivid situations than their imagination might generate. Here, an individual with a fear of spiders is wearing a virtual reality headset and has become immersed in a vivid, three-dimensional world in which spiders appear very real. *How might such a treatment help the client overcome a fear of spiders?*

• **Aversive conditioning** consists of repeated pairings of the undesirable behavior with aversive stimuli to decrease the behavior's rewards. Aversive conditioning is used to teach people to avoid such behaviors as smoking, eating, and drinking. Electric shocks, nausea-inducing substances, and verbal insults are some of the noxious stimuli used in aversive conditioning. How could aversive conditioning be used to reduce a person's alcohol consumption? Every time a person drank an alcoholic beverage, he or she also would consume a mixture that induced nausea. In classical conditioning terminology, the alcoholic beverage is the conditioned stimulus and the nausea-inducing agent is the unconditioned stimulus. By repeatedly pairing alcohol with the nausea-inducing agent, alcohol becomes the conditioned stimulus that elicits nausea, the conditioned response. As a consequence, alcohol no longer is associated with something pleasant but, rather, with something highly unpleasant. Figure 12.5 illustrates how classical conditioning is the backbone of aversive conditioning.

Operant Conditioning Approaches The basic philosophy behind using operant conditioning as a therapy approach is that, because maladaptive behavior patterns are learned, they can be unlearned. Therapy involves conducting a careful analysis of the person's environment to determine what factors need to be modified. Especially important is changing the consequences of the person's behavior to ensure that behavioral responses are followed by positive reinforcement.

Operant therapy's best-known technique is **behavior modification,** the application of operant conditioning principles to changing human behavior. Consequences for behavior are established to ensure that acceptable actions are reinforced and unacceptable ones are not (Kearney & Vecchio, 2002; Poling & Carr, 2002). Advocates of behavior modification believe that many emotional and behavior problems are caused by inadequate (or inappropriate) consequences (Stanley & Turner, 1995).

A behavior modification system in which acceptable behaviors are reinforced with tokens (such as poker chips) that later can be exchanged for desired rewards (such as candy, money, or going to a movie) is called a *token economy.* Gradually, the rate at which tokens are rewarded declines, and the positive behavior remains. Token economies have been established in classrooms, institutions for the mentally retarded, homes for delinquents, and mental hospitals.

Behavior modification does not always work. One person may become so wedded to the tokens that, when they are no longer given, the positive behavior associated with them may disappear. Some critics also object to behavior modification because they believe such extensive control of another person's behavior is unethical.

However, behavior modification has often succeeded in helping an individual to replace maladaptive responses with more adaptive ones, as in the following case:

Henry Greene is a 36-year-old lawyer who wrestled with depression for months before finally seeking psychotherapy. His initial complaints were physical—fitful sleep, often ending at 3 A.M., lack of appetite, weight loss of 15 pounds, and a disinterest in sex. Henry began to move more slowly and his voice became monotonous. He reached the point where he could hardly bear to cope with life. Henry finally let his guard down and confessed that, although he looked successful on the outside, he felt like a failure on the inside. He said that he actually was a third-rate lawyer, husband, lover, and father. He felt that he was bound to remain that way. . . .

Henry Greene was first given the assignment of monitoring his moods. This task forced him to pay attention to his daily mood changes, and the information was used to determine which events are associated with which moods. Relaxation training followed, because relaxation skills improve an individual's sense of well-being.

The next step for Henry Greene was to determine how his moods are associated with pleasant and unpleasant events in his life. Henry was asked to fill out a "Pleasant Events Schedule" and an "Unpleasant Events Schedule." Each week, Henry completed a graph showing the number of pleasant and unpleasant events, as well as his mood, for each day. Henry was able to see a close relation between pleasant events and pleasant moods and between

aversive conditioning A classical conditioning treatment that consists of repeated pairings of the undesirable behavior with aversive stimuli to decrease the behavior's rewards.

behavior modification The application of operant conditioning principles to changing human behavior, with the goal of replacing unacceptable, maladaptive behaviors with acceptable, adaptive behaviors.

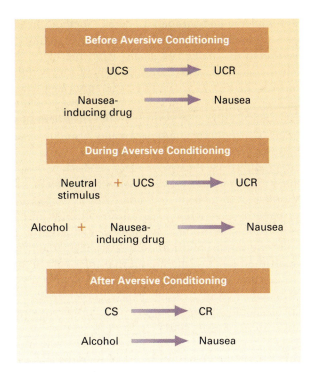

FIGURE 12.5 Aversive Conditioning Classical conditioning can provide a conditional aversion to alcohol. After the association of the drug with alcohol, the alcohol becomes a conditioned stimulus for nausea. Recall these abbreviations from chapter 6: UCS (unconditioned stimulus), UCR (unconditioned response), CS (conditioned stimulus), and CR (conditioned response).

unpleasant events and unpleasant moods. The therapist then encouraged Henry to increase the amount of time he spends in pleasant activities with the hope that more positive moods would follow. The positive outcome was that Henry was able to gain control over his moods.

The final stage for Henry was maintenance planning. Henry was asked to identify the components of behavior therapy that were the most successful in changing his maladaptive behavior. Once Henry identified these, he was encouraged to continue their use. He also was required to develop emergency plans for those times when stress might overwhelm him. Henry continued to go to follow-up sessions for 6 months after his initial treatment. (Rosenfeld, 1985)

Cognitive Therapies

D., a 21-year-old single undergraduate student, perceives himself as a failure in school and a failure to his parents. He is preoccupied with negative thoughts, dwells on his problems, and exaggerates his faults. **Cognitive therapies** emphasize that such cognitions, or thoughts, are the main source of psychological problems, and they attempt to change the individual's feelings and behaviors by changing cognitions. *Cognitive restructuring*, a general concept for changing a pattern of thought that is presumed to be causing maladaptive behavior or emotion, is central to cognitive therapies.

Cognitive therapies differ from psychodynamic therapies by focusing more on overt symptoms than on deep-seated unconscious thoughts, by providing more structure to the individual's thoughts, and by being less concerned about the origin of the problem. Unlike humanistic therapies, cognitive therapies provide more structure, more analysis, and more specific cognitive techniques.

Cognitive therapists guide individuals in identifying their irrational and self-defeating thoughts. Then they use various techniques to get clients to challenge these thoughts and consider different, more positive ways of thinking. These cognitive

cognitive therapies A class of treatment emphasizing that individuals' cognitions, or thoughts, are the main source of abnormal behavior and psychological problems.

techniques often are implemented through a Socratic method of asking questions to help clients gain self-understanding about their negative thinking. As part of this process, a cognitive therapist usually asks clients what the worst thing is that could happen to them. Then clients are asked to propose how they would cope with their ultimate worst situation. In this way, cognitive therapists help clients see that they will be able to cope even if the worst possible thing happens to them.

Cognitive therapy has been used effectively in the treatment of some anxiety disorders, mood disorders, schizophrenia, and personality disorders (Barlow, 2001; Beck, 2002; Borkovec & Ruscio, 2001; Wells & Papageorgiou, 2001). In many instances, cognitive therapy used with drug therapy is effective (Barlow & others, 2000).

Among the anxiety disorders to which cognitive therapy has been successfully applied is panic disorder (Stuart, Treat, & Wade, 2000). The central concept in the cognitive model of panic is that individuals catastrophically misinterpret relatively benign physical or psychological events. In cognitive therapy, the therapist encourages individuals to test the catastrophic misinterpretations by inducing an actual panic attack. The individuals then can test the notion that they will die or go crazy, which they find out is not the case. In one recent study, a combination of an SSRI drug and cognitive therapy was effective in treating panic disorder (Azhar, 2001). Cognitive therapy has shown considerable promise in the treatment of post-traumatic stress disorder (Cohen, Mannarino, & Rogal, 2001).

One of the earliest applications of cognitive therapy was in the treatment of depression. A number of studies have shown that cognitive therapy can be just as successful as drug therapy (Dunner, 2001). Some studies also have shown that individuals treated with cognitive therapy are less likely to relapse into depression than individuals treated with drug therapy (Jarrett & others, 2001).

Considerable strides have been made in recent years in applying cognitive therapy to the treatment of schizophrenia. Although not a substitute for drug therapy, cognitive therapy has been effective in reducing the schizophrenic's belief in delusions and lowering the probability that the schizophrenic will act out in an impulsive fashion (Rector & Beck, 2001).

Cognitive therapy also has been used effectively in treating personality disorders. The focus is on using cognitive therapy to change individuals' core beliefs and to reduce their automatic negative thoughts.

The two main forms of cognitive therapy are Albert Ellis' rational-emotive behavior therapy and Aaron Beck's cognitive therapy. A third approach, cognitive-behavior therapy, uses a combination of cognitive and behavorial techniques.

Rational-Emotive Behavior Therapy

Rational-emotive behavior therapy (REBT) is based on Albert Ellis' assertion that individuals develop a psychological disorder because of their beliefs, especially irrational and self-defeating beliefs. Ellis (1962, 1996, 2002) says that we usually talk to ourselves when we experience stress; too often, the statements are irrational, making them more harmful than helpful.

Ellis (2002) believes that many individuals with psychological disorders construct three basic demands:

- I *absolutely must* perform well and win the approval of other people.
- Other people *have to* treat me kindly and fairly.
- My life conditions *should not be* frustrating but, rather, *should be* enjoyable.

Once people convert their important desires into these demands, they often develop dysfunctional, exaggerated beliefs, such as "Because I'm not performing well, as I *absolutely must,* I'm an inadequate person."

The goal of REBT is to get the person to eliminate self-defeating beliefs by rationally examining them. Clients are shown how to dispute their dysfunctional beliefs—especially their absolute musts—and change them to realistic and logical thoughts. Homework assignments provide them with opportunities to engage in the new self-talk and experience the positive results of not viewing life in a castastrophic way.

rational-emotive behavior therapy (REBT) A cognitive therapy based on Ellis' assertion that individuals develop a psychological disorder because of their beliefs, especially those that are irrational and self-defeating.

Beck's Cognitive Therapy   Aaron Beck (1976, 1993) developed a somewhat different form of cognitive therapy to treat psychological problems, especially depression. A basic assumption Beck makes is that psychological problems result when people think illogically about themselves, the world they live in, and the future. Beck's approach shares with Ellis' the idea that the goal of therapy should be to help people to recognize and discard self-defeating cognitions.

In the initial phases of therapy, individuals are taught to make connections between their patterns of thinking and their emotional responses. With the therapist's assistance, they learn about logical errors in their thinking and learn to challenge the accuracy of these automatic thoughts. Figure 12.6 describes some of the most widely used cognitive therapy techniques.

Logical errors in thinking can lead an individual to the following types of erroneous beliefs (Carson, Butcher, & Mineka, 2003):

- Perceiving the world as harmful while ignoring evidence to the contrary—for example, feeling worthless even though a friend has just told her how much other people like her
- Overgeneralizing on the basis of limited examples, such as seeing himself as worthless because one individual stopped dating him
- Magnifying the importance of undesirable events, such as seeing the loss of a dating partner as the end of the world
- Engaging in absolutist thinking, such as exaggerating the importance of someone's mildly critical comment and perceiving it as proof of total inadequacy

The following case study involves a cognitive therapist guiding a depressed 26-year-old graduate student to understand the connection between how she interprets her experiences and the way she feels and to begin seeing the inaccuracy of her interpretations:

Student: I agree with the description of me but I guess I don't agree that the way I think makes me depressed.

Therapist: How do you understand it?

Student: I get depressed when things go wrong. Like when I fail a test.

Therapist: How can failing a test make you depressed?

Student: Well, if I fail I'll never get into law school.

Therapist: So failing the test means a lot to you. But if failing a test could drive people into clinical depression, wouldn't you expect everyone who failed the test to have depression? Did everyone who failed the test get depressed enough to require treatment?

Student: No, but it depends on how important the test was to the person.

Therapist: Right, and who decides the importance?

Student: I do.

Therapist: And so, what we have to examine is your way of viewing the test or the way that you think about the test and how it affects your chances of getting into law school. Do you agree?

Student: Right . . .

Therapist: Now what did failing mean?

Student: (Tearful) That I couldn't get into law school.

Therapist: And what does that mean to you?

Student: That I'm just not smart enough.

Therapist: Anything else?

Student: That I can never be happy.

Therapist: And how do these thoughts make you feel?

Student: Very unhappy.

Therapist: So it is the meaning of failing a test that makes you very unhappy. In fact, believing that you can never be happy is a powerful factor in producing unhappiness. So, you get yourself into a trap—by definition, failure to get into law school equals, "I can never be happy." (Beck & others, 1979, pp. 145–146)

Cognitive Therapy Technique	Description	Example
Challenge idiosyncratic meanings	Explore personal meaning attached to the client's words and ask the client to consider alternatives.	When a client says he will be "devastated" by his spouse's leaving, ask just how he would be devastated and ways he could avoid being devastated.
Question the evidence	Systematically examine the evidence for the client's beliefs or assertions.	When a client says she can't live without her spouse, explore how she lived without the spouse before she was married.
Reattribute responsibility	Help the client distribute responsibility for events appropriately.	When a client says that his son's failure in school must be his fault, explore other possibilities, such as the quality of the school.
Examine options and alternatives	Help the client generate alternative actions to maladaptive ones.	If a client considers leaving school, explore whether tutoring or going part-time to school are good alternatives.
Decatastrophize	Help the client evaluate whether she is overestimating the nature of a situation.	If a client states that failure in a course means she must give up the dream of medical school, question whether this is a necessary conclusion.
Fantasize consequences	Explore fantasies of a feared situation: if realistic, work on effective coping strategies.	Help a client who fantasizes "falling apart" when asking the boss for a raise to role-play the situation and develop effective skills for making the request.
Examine advantages and disadvantages	Examine advantages and disadvantages of issue, to instill a broader perspective.	If a client says he "was just born depressed and will always be that way," explore the advantages and disadvantages of holding that perspective versus other perspectives.
Turn adversity to advantage	Explore ways that difficult situations can be transformed to opportunities.	If a client has just been laid off, explore whether this is an opportunity for her to return to school.
Conduct guided association	Help the client see connections between thoughts or ideas.	Draw the connections between a client's anger at his wife for going on a business trip and his fear of being alone.
Scale	Ask the client to rate her emotions or thoughts on scales to help gain perspective.	If a client says she was overwhelmed by an emotion, ask her to rate it on a scale from 0 (not at all present) to 100 (I fell down in a faint).
Stop negative thoughts	Provide the client with ways of stopping a cascade of negative thoughts.	Teach an anxious client to picture a stop sign or hear a bell when anxious thoughts begin to snowball.
Distract	Help the client find benign or positive distractions to take attention away from negative thoughts or emotions temporarily.	Have a client count to 200 by 13s when he feels himself becoming anxious.
Label distortions	Provide labels for specific types of distorted thinking to help the client gain more distance and perspective.	Have a client keep a record of the number of times a day she engages in all-or-nothing thinking—seeing things as all bad or all good.

FIGURE 12.6 Cognitive Therapy Techniques

Although Beck's and Ellis' cognitive therapies have some similarities, there also are some differences: Rational-emotive behavior therapy is very directive, persuasive, and confrontational. In contrast, Beck's cognitive therapy involves more of an open-ended dialogue between the therapist and the individual. The aim of this dialogue is to get individuals to reflect on personal issues and discover their own misconceptions. Beck's approach also encourages individuals to gather information about themselves and to try out unbiased experiments that reveal the inaccuracies of their beliefs.

Cognitive-Behavior Therapy   **Cognitive-behavior therapy** consists of a combination of cognitive therapy, with an emphasis on reducing self-defeating thoughts,

cognitive-behavior therapy A treatment combining cognitive therapy and behavior therapy.

and behavior therapy, with an emphasis on changing behavior (Epstein & Baucom, 2002; Roth, Eng, & Heimberg, 2002; Stanley & others, 2004). An important aspect of cognitive-behavior therapy is *self-efficacy*, Albert Bandura's (1997, 2001) concept that one can master a situation and produce positive outcomes. At each step of the therapy process, people bolster their confidence by telling themselves, "I'm going to master my problem," "I can do it," "I'm improving," "I'm getting better," and so on. As people gain confidence and engage in adaptive behavior, the successes become intrinsically motivating. Before long, individuals persist with considerable effort in their attempts to solve personal problems because of the positive outcomes that were set in motion by self-efficacy.

Self-instructional methods are cognitive-behavior techniques aimed at teaching individuals to modify their own behavior (Dowd, 2002; Eisenman, 2004; Meichenbaum, 1977). The therapist gives the client examples of constructive statements, known as "reinforcing self-statements," that the client can repeat in order to take positive steps to cope with stress or meet a goal. The therapist also will encourage the client to practice the statements through role playing and will strengthen the client's newly acquired skills through reinforcement. Following is a series of examples of self-instructional methods individuals can use to cope with stressful situations (Meichenbaum, Turk, & Burstein, 1975):

Preparing for anxiety or stress:
   What do I have to do?
   I'm going to map out a plan to deal with it.
   I'll just think about what I have to do.
   I won't worry. Worry doesn't help anything.
   I have a lot of different strategies I can call on.
Confronting and handling anxiety or stress:
   I can meet the challenge.
   I'll keep on taking one step at a time.
   I can handle it. I'll just relax, breathe deeply, and use one of the strategies.
   I won't think about the pain. I will think about what I have to do.
Coping with feelings at critical moments:
   What is it I have to do?
   I was supposed to expect the pain to increase. I just have to keep myself in control.
   When the pain comes, I will just pause and keep focusing on what I have to do.
Reinforcing self-statements:
   Good, I did it.
   I handled it well.
   I knew I could do it.
   Wait until I tell other people how I did it!

In one study, cognitive-behavior therapy was given to children (as well as their parents) who were highly anxious about going to school (Dadds & others, 1999). As shown in figure 12.7, the therapy, provided over a 10-week period, was considerably more effective in reducing anxiety than no therapy at all, and the positive effects of the therapy were still present 2 years later.

A comparison of the four psychotherapies—psychodynamic, humanistic, behavior, and cognitive—is presented in figure 12.8.

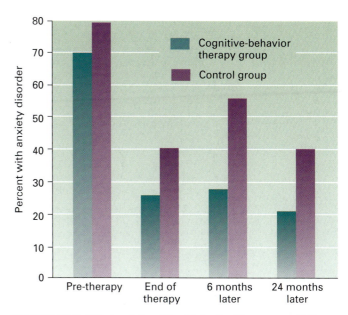

FIGURE 12.7 Effects of Cognitive-Behavior Therapy on Children's Anxiety About School Children and their parents participated in a 10-week cognitive-behavior therapy program. Compared with a control group of children, the children in the therapy program were less likely to have an anxiety disorder 24 months after the therapy.

	Cause of Problem	Therapy Emphasis	Nature of Therapy and Techniques
Psychodynamic Therapies	Client's problems are symptoms of deep-seated, unresolved, unconscious conflicts.	Discover underlying, unconscious conflicts and work with client to develop insight.	Psychoanalysis, including free association, dream analysis, resistance, and transference: therapist interprets heavily.
Humanistic Therapies	Client is not functioning at an optimal level of development.	Develop awareness of inherent potential for growth.	Person-centered therapy, including unconditional positive regard, genuineness, accurate empathy, and active listening; gestalt therapy, including confrontation to encourage honest expression of feelings; self-appreciation emphasized.
Behavior Therapies	Client has learned maladaptive behavior patterns.	Learn adaptive behavior patterns through changes in the environment or cognitive processes.	Observation of behavior and its controlling conditions; specific advice given about what should be done; therapies based on classical conditioning or operant conditioning.
Cognitive Therapies	Client has developed inappropriate thoughts.	Change feelings and behaviors by changing cognitions.	Conversation with client designed to get him or her to change irrational and self-defeating beliefs.

FIGURE 12.8 Therapy Comparisons

Review and Sharpen Your Thinking

2 *Characterize four types of psychotherapies.*
- Describe the psychodynamic therapies.
- Discuss the humanistic therapies.
- Summarize the classical conditioning and operant conditioning approaches to behavior therapies.
- Distinguish among three cognitive therapies.

Imagine that you are a psychotherapist and that you diagnose an individual as having a depressive disorder. Which of the psychotherapies would you use to treat the individual? Explain your choice.

3 SOCIOCULTURAL APPROACHES

Group Therapy   **Self-Help Support Groups**

Family and Couples Therapy   **Community Mental Health**

What treatment needs do the sociocultural approaches address?

In the treatment of psychological disorders, biological therapies change the person's body, behavior therapies modify the person's behavior, and cognitive therapies alter the person's thinking. This section focuses on sociocultural approaches to the treatment of psychological disorders. These approaches view the individual as part of a

Because many psychological problems develop in the context of interpersonal relationships and group experiences—within family, marriage, work or social group—group therapy can be an important context for learning how to cope more effectively with these problems. *What do therapy group members provide to one another?*

social system of relationships, influenced by various social and cultural factors, that must be dealt with in the treatment of psychological disorders (Nolen-Hoeksema, 2004; Yonkers, 2003). The sociocultural approaches include group therapy, family and couples therapy, self-help support groups, and community mental health.

Group Therapy

A major issue in therapy is how to structure it to reach more people at less cost. One way to address this problem is for the therapist to see clients in a group (Corey, 2004; MacKenzie, 2002). Advocates of group therapy point out that, unlike individual therapy, it takes place in the normal context of relationships (Gladding, 1999; Kline, 2003). Many psychological problems develop in the context of one's family, marriage, or peer group, for example. By taking into account the dynamics of groups such as these, group therapy may be more effective than individual therapy in some cases (Capuzzi, 2003; Gazda, Horne, & Ginter, 2001).

Psychodynamic, humanistic, behavior, and cognitive therapies are all used in group therapy, in addition to approaches that are not based on these major psychotherapeutic perspectives. Six features make group therapy attractive (Yalom, 1995):

- *Information.* Individuals receive information about their problems from either the group leader or other group members.
- *Universality.* Many individuals develop the sense that no one else has frightening and unacceptable impulses. In the group, individuals observe that others feel anguish and suffering as well.
- *Altruism.* Group members support one another with advice and sympathy and learn that they have something to offer others.
- *Resemblance to the family group.* A therapy group often resembles a family (in family therapy, the group *is* a family), with the leaders representing parents and the other members siblings. In this "new" family, old wounds may be healed and new, more positive "family" ties made.
- *Development of social skills.* Corrective feedback from peers may correct flaws in the individual's interpersonal skills. A self-centered man may see that he is self-centered if five other group members give him examples of his self-centeredness; in individual therapy, he might not believe the therapist.
- *Interpersonal learning.* The group can serve as a training ground for practicing new behaviors and relationships. A hostile woman may learn that she can get along better with others by behaving less aggressively, for example.

Family therapy has become increasingly popular in recent years. In family therapy, the assumption is that psychological adjustment is related to patterns of interaction within the family unit. *Which ethnic groups might prefer family therapy over individual therapy?*

Family and Couples Therapy

"A friend loves you for your intelligence, a mistress for your charm, but your family's love is unreasoning; you were born into it and are of its flesh and blood. Nevertheless, it can irritate you more than any group of people in the world," commented the French biographer André Maurois. As his statement suggests, the family may be the source of an individual's problems.

Family therapy is group therapy with family members. **Couples therapy** is group therapy with married or unmarried couples whose major problem is within their relationship. These approaches stress that, although one person may have some abnormal symptoms, the symptoms are a function of the family or couple relationship (Capuzzi & Gross, 1999; Griffin, 2002; Kumpfer, Alvarado, & Whiteside, 2003; Nichols & Schwartz, 2004). Psychodynamic, humanistic, and behavior therapies may be used in family and couples therapy.

Four of the most widely used family therapy techniques are

- *Validation.* The therapist expresses an understanding and acceptance of each family member's feelings and beliefs and thus validates each person. When the therapist talks with each family member, she finds something positive to say.
- *Reframing.* The therapist teaches families to reframe problems; a problem is cast as a family problem, not an individual's problem. A delinquent adolescent boy's problems may be reframed to include such causes as the father's lack of attention to his son and marital conflict, for example.
- *Structural change.* The family therapist tries to restructure the coalitions in a family. For example, the therapist might suggest that the father take a stronger disciplinarian role to relieve some of the burden from the mother. Restructuring might be as simple as suggesting that parents explore satisfying ways to be together; the therapist may recommend that once a week the parents go out for a quiet dinner together.
- *Detriangulation.* In some families, one member is the scapegoat for two other members who are in conflict but pretend not to be. For example, two parents may insist that their marriage is fine but find themselves in subtle conflict over how to handle their child (the third person in the triangle). The therapist tries to disentangle, or detriangulate, this situation by shifting attention away from the child to the conflict between the parents.

Couples therapy proceeds in much the same way as family therapy. Conflict in marriages and in relationships between unmarried individuals frequently involves poor communication. In some cases, the therapist focuses on communication that has broken down entirely. In other cases, the therapist focuses on the roles partners play: one may be "strong," the other "weak"; one may be "responsible," the other "spoiled," for example. Couples therapy addresses diverse problems, such as jealousy, sexual messages, delayed childbearing, infidelity, gender roles, two-career families, divorce, and remarriage (Hewison, 2003; Kuenzler & Beutler, 2003; Sullivan & Christensen, 1998).

Self-Help Support Groups

Self-help support groups are voluntary organizations of individuals who get together on a regular basis to discuss problems of common interest. The groups are not conducted by a professional therapist but, rather, by a member of the common interest group or by a **paraprofessional,** someone who has been taught by a professional to provide some mental health services but who does not have formal mental health training.

Self-help support groups play an important role in our nation's mental health, with as many as 10 million people participating in such groups each year. These groups are relatively inexpensive. Thus they serve people who are less likely to receive help otherwise, such as less educated adults, individuals living in low-income circumstances, and homemakers.

family therapy Group therapy with family members.

couples therapy Therapy with married or unmarried couples whose major problem is within their relationship.

paraprofessional A person who has been taught by a professional to provide some mental health services but who does not have formal mental health training.

Self-help support groups provide members with a sympathetic audience (Burlingame & Davies, 2002; Floyd, McKendree-Smith, & Scogin, 2004). The social support, role modeling, and sharing of concrete strategies for solving problems that unfold in self-help groups add to their effectiveness. A woman who has been raped might not believe a male therapist who tells her that, with time, she will be able to work through much of the psychological pain. But the same message from another rape survivor—someone who has had to work through the same feelings of rage, fear, and violation—might be more believable.

Alcoholics Anonymous (AA), founded in 1935 by a doctor and reformed alcoholic, is one of the best-known self-help groups. Mental health professionals often recommend AA for their alcoholic clients. A self-help organization called Compeer matches community volunteers with children and adults receiving mental health treatment. In some cases, both partners in a Compeer relationship have psychological disorders. There are myriad other self-help groups, such as Parents Without Partners, lesbian and gay support groups, cocaine abuse support groups, Weight Watchers, and child abuse support groups. See the video clip "Bipolar Disorder II" to learn about the positive effect of self-help groups for people coping with this disorder.

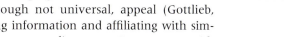

In-Psych Plus

Self-help support groups have broad, though not universal, appeal (Gottlieb, 1998). For people who tend to cope by seeking information and affiliating with similar peers, such groups can reduce stress and promote adjustment. However, as with any group therapy, negative emotions may spread through the group, especially if the members face circumstances that deteriorate over time, such as terminal cancer patients. Group leaders who are sensitive to the spread of negative emotions can minimize such effects.

Community Mental Health

The community mental health movement was born in the 1960s when it became apparent that the mental health care system was not reaching the poor and when the care of large numbers of individuals with psychological disorders was transferred from mental institutions to community-based facilities. This transfer (called *deinstitutionalization*) came about largely because of the development of new drugs for treating individuals with psychological disorders, especially schizophrenia.

The community mental health approach is to train teachers, ministers, family physicians, and others who directly interact with community members to offer lay counseling and workshops on such topics as coping with stress, reducing drug use, and being more assertive (Duffy & Wong, 2003). The underlying principle is that the best way to treat a psychological disorder is to prevent it from happening in the first place (Birkel & others, 2003). Prevention takes one of three courses:

- *Primary prevention.* The goal is to reduce the number of new cases of psychological disorders. In some instances, high-risk populations are targeted for prevention, such as children of alcoholics, children with chronic illnesses, and children in poverty.
- *Secondary prevention.* Screening for early detection of problems and early intervention may take place. Secondary prevention programs seek to reach large numbers of people. One way they do this is by educating paraprofessionals about preventing psychological problems and by having them work with psychologists. One type of early intervention involves screening schoolchildren to find those who show early signs of problems and provide them with psychological services.
- *Tertiary prevention.* Psychological disorders that were not prevented or arrested early in the course of the disorders are treated. Tertiary programs are often geared toward people who once required hospitalization but now are living in the community. An example of a tertiary program is *halfway houses* (community residences for individuals who no longer require institutionalization but who still need support in readjusting to the community) for schizophrenics.

An explicit goal of community mental health is to help people who are disenfranchised from society, such as those living in poverty, to lead happier, more productive lives. A key concept involved in this effort is *empowerment,* assisting individuals to develop the skills they need to control their own lives.

Review and Sharpen Your Thinking

 3 **Explain the sociocultural approaches to treatment.**

- Define group therapy.
- Describe family and couples therapy.
- Discuss the features of self-help support groups.
- Explain the community mental health approach.

Which therapy setting do you think you would benefit from the most—individual or group? Why?

4 EFFECTIVENESS OF PSYCHOTHERAPY

| Research on the Effectiveness of Psychotherapy | Common Themes in Psychotherapy | Cultural Issues in Treatment | Therapy Integrations |

How effective is psychotherapy?

Do individuals who go through therapy get better? Are some approaches more effective than others? How would we evaluate the effectiveness of psychotherapy? Would we take the client's word? The therapist's word? What would be our criteria for effectiveness? Would they be based on the mainstream values of Western culture or take other perspectives into account? How objectively can therapeutic results be judged?

Research on the Effectiveness of Psychotherapy

About five decades ago, Hans Eysenck (1952) analyzed 24 studies of psychotherapy and found that approximately two-thirds of the individuals with neurotic symptoms improved. Eysenck also found that a similar percentage of neurotic individuals on waiting lists to see a psychotherapist showed marked improvement, even though they were not given any psychotherapy at all. Eysenck's findings prompted a flurry of research on psychotherapy's effectiveness (Orlinsky & Howard, 2000; Pilkonis, 1999; Pilkonis & Krause, 1999). Hundreds of studies on the outcome of psychotherapy have now been conducted.

One strategy for analyzing these diverse studies is **meta-analysis,** in which the researcher statistically combines the results of many different studies (Rosenthal & DiMatteo, 2001). In one meta-analysis of psychotherapy research, 475 studies were statistically combined (Smith, Glass, & Miller, 1980). Only those studies in which a therapy group had been compared with an untreated control group were used. The results showed greater psychotherapy effectiveness than Eysenck's earlier results: On 88 percent of the measures, individuals who received therapy improved more than those who did not. This meta-analysis and others (Lipsey & Wilson, 1993) document that psychotherapy is effective in general, but they do not inform us about the specific ways in which different therapies might be effective.

meta-analysis Statistical analysis that combines the results of many different studies.

Figure 12.9 summarizes a meta-analysis of numerous studies and reviews of research in which clients were randomly assigned to a no-treatment control group, a placebo control group, or a psychotherapy treatment (Lambert, 2001; Lambert & Ogles, 2002). Some of the individuals who did not get treatment improved, probably because they sought help from friends, family, the clergy, or others. Individuals who were in a placebo control group fared better than nontreated individuals, probably because of their contact with a therapist, expectations of being helped, or the reassurance and support that they were given during the study. However, by far the best outcomes were for individuals who were given psychotherapy.

People who are thinking about seeing a psychotherapist want to know not only whether psychotherapy in general is effective but also especially which form of psychotherapy is most effective for their particular problem. Mary Lee Smith and her colleagues (1980) conducted a meta-analysis to compare types of psychotherapy. They found that both behavior therapies and insight therapies (psychodynamic and humanistic) were superior to no treatment at all, but these therapies did not differ in effectiveness.

However, some therapies have been found to be more effective than others in treating some disorders (DeRubeis & Crits-Cristoph, 1998; Nathan & Gorman, 2002; Nathan, Stuart, & Dolan, 2000):

- Cognitive therapies and behavior therapies have been successful in treating anxiety disorders (Barlow, 2001; Bowers & Clum, 1988; Sanderson, 1995).
- Cognitive therapies and behavior therapies have been successful in treating depressive disorders (Butler & others, 1991; Clark & others, 1994; Craighead & Craighead, 2001).
- Relaxation therapy also has been successful in treating anxiety disorders (Hidalgo & Davidson, 2001).

Individuals who see a therapist also want to know how long it will take them to get better. In one study, individuals showed substantial improvement in therapy over the course of the first 6 months, with diminishing returns after that (Howard & others, 1996). In another study, individuals rated their symptoms, interpersonal relations, and quality of life on a weekly basis before each treatment session (Anderson & Lambert, 2001). Figure 12.10 shows that 33 percent of the individuals had improved by the 10th session, 50 percent by the 20th session, and 70 percent by the 45th session. In sum, therapy benefits most individuals with psychological problems at least through the first 6 months of therapy and possibly longer.

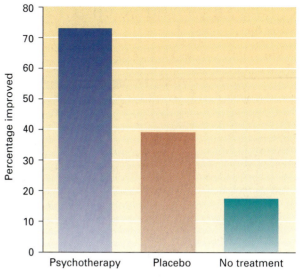

FIGURE 12.9 Effects of Psychotherapy A recent review of studies found that more than 70 percent of individuals who saw a therapist improved, whereas less than 40 percent who received a placebo and less than 20 percent who received no treatment improved (Lambert, 2001; Lambert & Ogles, 2002).

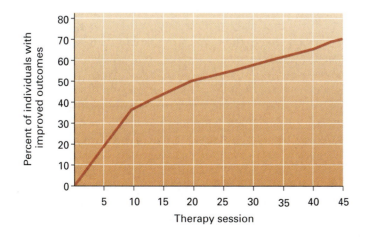

FIGURE 12.10 Number of Therapy Sessions and Improvement In one study, a large number of people undergoing therapy rated their well-being (based on symptoms, interpersonal relations, and quality of life) before each treatment session (Anderson & Lambert, 2001). About 33 percent of the individuals recovered by the 10th session, 50 percent by the 20th session, and 70 percent by the 45th session.

Do You Need a Therapist?

There are no hard-and-fast rules about when people should go to a psychotherapist for help with their personal problems. However, to get a sense of whether you should see a psychotherapist, evaluate whether you have recently experienced the following:

- I feel sad or blue a lot.
- My self-esteem is really low.
- I feel like other people are always out to get me.
- I feel so anxious that it is hard for me to function.
- I have trouble concentrating on my work.
- I don't do anything social and spend much of my spare time alone.
- I have a tendency to alienate people when I don't really want to.
- I'm frightened by things that I know should not be fear-provoking.
- I hear voices that tell me what I should do.
- I know I have problems, but I just don't feel I can talk with anyone about them.

If any of these statements describe your life, consider talking over your concerns with a qualified therapist. Most colleges and universities have counseling or mental health services that are covered by your student fees. This is a good place to start in seeking mental health consultation.

People who aren't sure whether psychotherapy will help them may wish to consult the checklist in the Psychology and Life box.

Common Themes in Psychotherapy

After carefully studying the nature of psychotherapy for more than 25 years, Jerome Frank (1982) concluded that effective psychotherapies have three common elements:

- *Expectations.* By inspiring expectations of help, the therapist motivates the client to continue going to therapy (Jennings & Skovholt, 1999). These expectations are powerful morale builders and symptom relievers in themselves (Arnkoff, Glass, & Shapiro, 2002).
- *Mastery.* The therapist also increases the client's sense of mastery and competence (Brammer & MacDonald, 1999; Hill & O'Brien, 1999). For example, clients begin to feel that they can cope effectively with their world.
- *Emotional arousal.* Therapy also arouses the individual's emotions, an essential motivator for behavior change, according to Frank.

The *therapeutic relationship* is another important element of successful psychotherapy (Norcross, 2002; Strupp, 1995). A relationship in which the client has confidence and trust in the therapist is essential. In one study, the most common ingredient in the success of different psychotherapies was the therapist's supportiveness of the client (Wallerstein, 1989). The client and therapist engage in a "healing ritual," which requires the active participation of both. As part of this ritual, the client gains hope and becomes less alienated.

Cultural Issues in Treatment

Most of the psychotherapies discussed in this chapter focus mainly on the individual. This approach is compatible with the needs of many people in Western cultures, such as in the United States, where the focus is on the individual rather than on the family, community, or ethnic group. However, individualistic psychotherapies may not be as effective with people who live in *collectivist* cultures that place more importance on the group. For example, some psychologists argue that people in cultures that place a high value on the family, such as Latino and Asian cultures, are more likely to benefit from family therapy than individual therapy (Tharp, 1991).

Ethnicity   Researchers have found that many ethnic minority individuals prefer discussing problems with parents, friends, and relatives rather than mental health professionals (Atkinson, 2004; Canino & Spurlock, 2000; Sue, 2003). Researchers have also found that, when the therapist and the client are from the same ethnic group and when ethnic-specific services are provided, clients are less likely to drop out of therapy early and in many cases have better results (Jackson & Greene, 2000; Orlinksy, Grawe, & Parks, 1994; Sue, 2003). Ethnic-specific services include culturally appropriate greetings and arrangements (for example, serving tea rather than coffee to Chinese American clients), flexible hours for treatment, and a bicultural/bilingual staff (Nystul, 1999).

Therapy can be effective when the therapist and client are from different ethnic backgrounds if the therapist has excellent clinical skills and is culturally sensitive (Gibson & Mitchell, 2003; Pedersen & Carey, 2003; Sue, 2003). Culturally skilled psychotherapists have good knowledge of the cultural groups they work with, understand sociopolitical influences, and have skills in working with culturally diverse groups (Foulks, 2002; Jenkins, 2002).

Gender Traditionally, the goal of psychotherapy has been autonomy and self-determination for the client. However, autonomy and self-determination are often more central to men's lives than to women's lives. Women generally are more motivated by relatedness and connection with others than men are. Thus some psychologists believe that therapy should emphasize more relatedness and connection with others, especially for women (Notman & Nadelson, 2002).

Several nontraditional therapeutic approaches have arisen to address the specific concerns of women. Their goal is to help people break free from traditional gender roles and stereotypes. Feminist therapists believe that traditional psychotherapy continues to carry considerable gender bias. The goals of feminist therapists are no different from other therapists' goals, and feminist therapists make no effort to turn clients into feminists. However, they do want clients to be fully aware of how the traditional female role in American society can contribute to the development of a psychological disorder.

Therapy Integrations

In the single-therapy approach, the therapist believes that one kind of therapy works best. However, approximately 30 to 50 percent of practicing therapists do not identify themselves as adhering to one particular approach but, rather, refer to themselves as "integrative" or "eclectic" (Castonguay & others, 2003; Gold, 2002; Norcross & Kobayshi, 2000; Norcross & Prochaska, 1983, 1988). **Integrative therapy** is a combination of techniques from different therapies based on the therapist's judgment of which techniques will provide the greatest benefit for the client.

Integrative therapy is characterized by an openness to various ways of integrating diverse therapies. For example, a therapist might use a behavioral approach to treat an individual with panic disorder and a cognitive therapy approach to treat an individual with major depressive disorder. There is no single, well-defined integrative therapy that ties all of the therapy approaches together. For that reason, the term *therapy integrations* probably best captures what is taking place in this field (Arkowitz, 1997).

At its best, integrative therapy is an effective, systematic use of a variety of therapy approaches (Corey, 2001; Prochaska & Norcross, 2003). However, one worry about integrative therapy is that its increased use will result in an unsystematic, haphazard eclecticism, which some therapists say would be no better than a narrow, dogmatic approach to therapy (Lazarus, Beutler, & Norcross, 1992).

Stanley Sue is a professor at the University of California at Davis. Unlike psychologists who specialize in a technique or a theory, he specializes in a population. Much of his work focuses on Asian American clients with special needs, especially immigrants. When he was thinking about a career, Sue told his father, who was a Chinese immigrant to the United States, that he wanted to be a clinical psychologist. His father told Sue that he didn't understand what a psychologist does and didn't think Sue could make a living at it. But Sue persisted and obtained a Ph.D. in clinical psychology. His three brothers are psychologists, and one married a psychologist. In his research, Dr. Sue has found that Asian Americans underuse mental health services and that those who do use them often have very serious psychological problems. Thus many Asian Americans with more moderate psychological problems are not getting adequate therapy (Sue, 2000). *Why might people in this population with moderate problems not be using mental health services?*

Review and Sharpen Your Thinking

4 *Evaluate the effectiveness of psychotherapy.*

- Discuss research on psychotherapy effectiveness.
- Describe common themes in psychotherapy.
- Identify cultural perspectives that can affect the success of treatment.
- Characterize therapy integrations.

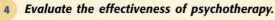

Explain why meta-analysis is important in research on psychotherapy effectiveness.

integrative therapy A combination of techniques from different therapies based on the therapist's judgment of which techniques will provide the greatest benefit for the client.

Reach Your Learning Goals

Therapies

1 BIOLOGICAL THERAPIES
- Drug Therapy
- Electroconvulsive Therapy
- Psychosurgery

2 PSYCHOTHERAPIES
- Psychodynamic Therapies
- Behavior Therapies
- Humanistic Therapies
- Cognitive Therapies

3 SOCIOCULTURAL APPROACHES
- Group Therapy
- Self-Help Support Groups
- Family and Couples Therapy
- Community Mental Health

4 EFFECTIVENESS OF PSYCHOTHERAPY
- Research on the Effectiveness of Psychotherapy
- Common Themes in Psychotherapy
- Cultural Issues in Treatment
- Therapy Integrations

1 Describe the biological therapies.

- Psychotherapeutic drugs that are used to treat psychological disorders fall into three main categories: antianxiety drugs, antidepressant drugs, and antipsychotic drugs. Antianxiety drugs are commonly known as tranquilizers. Benzodiazepines are the most commonly used antianxiety drugs. Antidepressant drugs regulate mood; the three main classes are tricyclics, MAO inhibitors, and SSRI drugs. Lithium often is successful in treating bipolar disorder. The antidepressant drugs are increasingly being used to treat some anxiety disorders as well. Antipsychotic drugs are powerful drugs that are used to treat people with severe psychological disorders, especially schizophrenia.
- Electroconvulsive therapy, commonly called "shock therapy," is used to treat severe depression when other strategies have not worked.
- Psychosurgery is an irreversible procedure in which brain tissue is destroyed in an attempt to improve adjustment. Today, psychosurgery is rarely used but is more precise than the early prefrontal lobotomies.

2 Characterize four types of psychotherapies.

- Psychotherapy is the process used by mental health professionals to help individuals recognize, define, and overcome their psychological and interpersonal difficulties and improve their adjustment. The insight therapies consist of the psychodynamic therapies and the humanistic therapies. Psychodynamic therapies stress the importance of the unconscious mind, early family experiences, and extensive interpretation by therapists. As in Freudian psychoanalysis, many contemporary psychodynamic therapists still probe the unconscious mind for early family experiences that might provide clues to clients' current problems. In Kohut's contemporary approach, however, the development of the self in social contexts is an important theme.
- In humanistic therapies, clients are encouraged to understand themselves and to grow personally. The humanistic therapies emphasize conscious thoughts, the present, and growth and fulfillment. In Carl Rogers' client-centered therapy, the therapist provides unconditional positive regard, genuineness, empathy, and active listening to raise the client's self-esteem. Fritz Perls developed gestalt therapy, in which therapists use role playing and challenge clients to help them become more aware of their feelings and face their problems.
- Behavior therapies use principles of learning to reduce or eliminate maladaptive behavior. They seek to eliminate the symptoms of behaviors rather than to help individuals gain insight into their problems. The two main therapy techniques based on classical conditioning are systematic desensitization and aversive conditioning. In systematic desensitization, anxiety is treated by getting the individual to associate deep relaxation with increasingly intense anxiety-producing situations. In aversive conditioning, the undesirable behavior is repeatedly paired with aversive stimuli to decrease the behavior's rewards. In operant conditioning approaches to therapy, behavior modification is used to decrease the frequency of unacceptable, maladaptive behaviors and increase the frequency of acceptable, adaptive ones. In a token economy, for example, behaviors are reinforced with tokens that later can be exchanged for desired rewards.
- Cognitive therapies emphasize that the individual's cognitions, or thoughts, are the main source of abnormal behavior. Cognitive therapies attempt to change the person's feelings and behaviors by changing cognitions. There are three main forms of cognitive therapy. Ellis' rational-emotive behavior therapy is based on the assertion that individuals develop psychological disorders because of their beliefs, especially those that are irrational and self-defeating. Beck's cognitive therapy has been especially effective in treating depression. In Beck's therapy, the therapist assists the client in learning about logical errors in thinking and then guides the client in challenging these thinking errors. Ellis' approach is more directive, persuasive, and confrontational than Beck's. Cognitive-behavior therapy, combining cognitive therapy and behavior therapy techniques, uses self-efficacy and self-instructional methods. Cognitive therapy has been demonstrated to be effective in treating a number of psychological problems.

3 Explain the sociocultural approaches to treatment.

- Group therapy emphasizes that relationships can hold the key to successful therapy. Psychodynamic, humanistic, behavior, and cognitive therapies, as well as various group approaches, are used in group therapy.
- Family therapy is group therapy with family members. Four widely used family therapy techniques are validation, reframing, structural change, and detriangulation. Couples therapy is group therapy with married or unmarried couples whose major problem is within their relationship.
- Self-help support groups are voluntary organizations of individuals who get together on a regular basis to discuss problems of common interest. They are conducted without a professional therapist.

- The community mental health movement was born out of the belief that the mental health care system was not adequately reaching people in poverty and people who had been deinstitutionalized. Community mental health emphasizes prevention. Empowerment is often a goal of community mental health.

4 *Evaluate the effectiveness of psychotherapy.*

- Psychotherapy is generally effective. Researchers have found, using meta-analysis, that the cognitive and behavior therapies are successful in treating anxiety and depressive disorders. Relaxation therapy also has been effective in treating anxiety disorders.
- Common themes in successful psychotherapy include the client's positive expectations of help, sense of mastery, emotional arousal, and confidence and trust in the therapist.
- Psychotherapies have focused mainly on the individual, which may work well in individualized cultures, such as in the United States. However, these psychotherapies may not work as well in collectivist cultures. Many ethnic minority individuals prefer to discuss problems with parents, friends, and relatives rather than mental health professionals. Therapy is often more effective when there is an ethnic match between the therapist and the client, although culturally sensitive therapy can be provided by a therapist who is from a different ethnic background. In addition, the emphasis on autonomy in psychotherapies may produce a problem for many women, who place a strong emphasis on connectedness in relationships. Some feminist-based therapies have emerged.
- Approximately 30 to 50 percent of practicing therapists refer to themselves as "integrative" or "eclectic." Integrative therapy uses a combination of techniques from different therapies based on the therapist's judgment of which techniques will provide the greatest benefit for the client.

Key Terms

biological therapies, p. 434
psychotherapy, p. 434
antianxiety drugs, p. 434
antidepressant drugs, p. 435
antipsychotic drugs, p. 436
electroconvulsive therapy (ECT), p. 438
psychosurgery, p. 439
insight therapy, p. 439
psychodynamic therapies, p. 440

psychoanalysis, p. 440
free association, p. 440
catharsis, p. 441
transference, p. 441
resistance, p. 441
humanistic therapies, p. 443
client-centered therapy, p. 443
gestalt therapy, p. 444
behavior therapies, p. 444

systematic desensitization, p. 445
aversive conditioning, p. 446
behavior modification, p. 446
cognitive therapies, p. 447
rational-emotive behavior therapy (REBT), p. 448

cognitive-behavior therapy, p. 450
family therapy, p. 451
couples therapy, p. 454
paraprofessional, p. 454
meta-analysis, p. 456
integrative therapy, p. 459

Apply Your Knowledge

1. The chapter describes some types of psychosurgery previously performed on patients. Use the Internet to research the kinds of problems currently treated with psychosurgery. Do you think psychosurgery should still be used?

2. Think critically about the use of antidepressant and antipsychotic drugs. Using your library, do some research for evidence that drug therapy works. If you were diagnosed with a psychological disorder, would you take a drug? Why or why not?

3. Behavioral and cognitive approaches may be helpful to change behaviors that wouldn't be considered abnormal but that you might want to change (for example, procrastinating, eating unhealthy food, or watching too much TV). Think about a behavior that you would like to do more, or less, frequently; then think like a behavior or cognitive therapist and describe the kinds of recommendations you might hear during a therapy session.

4. For which kinds of problems would you be likely to choose a sociocultural approach to therapy? Which approach would you choose? Do some research and see whether you can find a local group or therapist who would be helpful to someone with this kind of problem. What would you do if none were available in your area?

5. Imagine that a good friend confesses that he or she has been having some difficulties coping with some aspects of his or her life and asks you for advice in finding a psychotherapist. Based on the therapies discussed in this chapter, what kind of advice would you give your friend?

Connections

To test your mastery of the material in this chapter, go to the Study Guide and the In-Psych Plus CD-ROM, as well as the Online Learning Center. There you will find a chapter summary, practice tests, flashcards, lecture slides, web links, and other study tools, such as interactive exercises and reviews as well as current, chapter-relevant news articles.

13
Health and Well-Being

Learning Goals

Describe the scope of health psychology and behavioral medicine.

Define stress and identify its sources.

Explain how people respond to stress.

Discuss the links between stress and illness.

Outline strategies for coping with stress.

Summarize how to promote your health.

Mort, age 52, has worked as an air traffic controller for the past 15 years. An excitable person, he compares the job to being in a cage. During peak air traffic, the tension is almost unbearable. In these frenzied moments, Mort's emotions are a mixture of rage, fear, and anxiety. Unfortunately, the tension also spills over into his family life. In his own words, "When I go home, my nerves are still hopping. I tend to take it out on the nearest person." Two years ago, Mort's wife, Sally, told him that, if he could not learn to calm his emotions and handle stress more effectively, she would leave him. She suggested that he change to a less-tension-filled job, but he ignored her advice, and she filed for divorce.

Last Sunday evening, the computer that monitors air traffic temporarily went down, and Mort had a heart attack. Quadruple bypass surgery saved his life.

Yesterday Mort's doctor talked with him about the stress in his life and what could be done to reduce it. Mort rarely gets enough sleep, weighs too much but frequently skips meals, never exercises, smokes two packs of cigarettes a day, and drinks two or three scotches every evening (more on weekends). He professes no religious interests. He rarely dates since his divorce and has no relatives living within 50 miles. He has only one friend and does not feel very close to him. Mort says that he never has enough time to do the things he wants to do and rarely has quiet time to himself during the day. He does something fun only about once every 2 weeks.

The doctor gave Mort a test, shown in figure 13.1, to highlight his vulnerability to stress. Mort scored 68, indicating he is seriously vulnerable to stress and close to the extremely vulnerable range. How do *you* fare on the stress test?

Rate yourself on each item, using a scale of 1–5:

1 = almost always	2 = often	3 = sometimes	4 = seldom	5 = never

_____ 1. I eat at least one hot, balanced meal a day.

_____ 2. I get 7 to 8 hours of sleep at least four nights a week.

_____ 3. I give and receive affection regularly.

_____ 4. I have at least one relative within 50 miles whom I can rely on.

_____ 5. I exercise to the point of perspiration at least twice a week.

_____ 6. I smoke less than half a pack of cigarettes a day.

_____ 7. I have fewer than five alcoholic drinks a week.

_____ 8. I am the appropriate weight for my height.

_____ 9. I have an income adequate to meet my basic expenses.

_____ 10. I get strength from my religious beliefs.

_____ 11. I regularly attend church.

_____ 12. I have a network of friends and acquaintances.

_____ 13. I have one or more friends to confide in about personal matters.

_____ 14. I am in good health (including eyesight, hearing, teeth).

_____ 15. I am able to speak openly about my feelings when angry or worried.

_____ 16. I have regular conversations with the people I live with about domestic problems (e.g., chores, money, and daily living issues).

_____ 17. I do something for fun at least once a week.

_____ 18. I am able to organize my time effectively.

_____ 19. I drink fewer than three cups of coffee (or tea or cola drinks) a day.

_____ 20. I take quiet time for myself during the day.

Total: _____

To get your total score, add your answers and subtract 20. Any number over 30 indicates a vulnerability to stress. You are seriously vulnerable if your score is between 50 and 75, extremely vulnerable if it is over 75.

FIGURE 13.1 **How Stressed Are You?**

What is the scope of health psychology and behavioral medicine?

Stress is inevitable in human lives, given the conflict between our needs and desires and the realities of our environment and relationships. Sometimes stress is useful, but extreme stress often leads to serious health problems, like Mort's. However, throughout most of history, physical illness has been viewed purely in biological terms. That is, health has been thought to involve only bodily factors, not mental factors. Today, we are returning to an ancient view: that body *and* mind can exert important influences on health (Marks, Sykes, & McKinley, 2003). Indeed, a combination of biological, psychological, and social factors may be causes of health or illness. The *biopsychosocial model* discussed in chapter 11 thus applies to health psychology as well.

Two relatively new fields of study—health psychology and behavioral medicine—reflect the belief that lifestyles and psychological states can play important roles in health (Fogel, 2003; Murphy & Bennett, 2004). **Health psychology** emphasizes psychology's role in promoting and maintaining health and preventing and treating illness. **Behavioral medicine** is an interdisciplinary field that focuses on developing and integrating behavioral and biomedical knowledge to promote health and reduce illness. Behavioral medicine and health psychology are overlapping, and sometimes indistinguishable, fields. But when distinctions are made, behavioral medicine is viewed as a broader field that focuses on behavioral and biomedical factors, whereas health psychology tends to focus on behavioral and cognitive factors.

The interests of health psychologists and behavioral medicine researchers are extensive (Anderson, 2004; Baum, Revenson, & Singer, 2001; Boll & others, 2002; Kok & others, 2004; Lewis & Vitulano, 2003). They include examining how stress affects an individual's immune functioning, why we do or do not comply with medical advice, how effective media campaigns are in reducing smoking, what psychological factors play a part in losing weight, and how exercise helps in reducing stress (Stowell & others, 2003; Wood, 2001).

Changing patterns of illness in developed countries have fueled the increased interest in health psychology and behavioral medicine. Just a century ago, the leading causes of death were infectious diseases, such as influenza, tuberculosis, polio, typhoid fever, rubella, and smallpox. Today, none of these diseases are among the major causes of death in developed countries. Rather, 7 of the 10 leading causes of death in the United States today are related to personal habits and lifestyles. The major causes of death now are heart disease (36 percent), cancer (22 percent), and stroke (17 percent). Other chronic diseases, such as diabetes, are also major contributors to disability and death. Health behaviors often play key roles in these diseases, as they did in the heart attack suffered by Mort, the air traffic controller (Taylor, 2003).

Because of the increase in chronic disease, America's annual health care costs are soaring toward the $1 trillion mark. Health experts hope to make a dent in these costs by encouraging people to live healthier lives. Many corporations now recognize that health promotion for their employees is cost-effective. They increasingly are creating smoke-free work environments, on-site exercise programs, bonuses for quitting smoking and losing weight, and company-sponsored athletic events.

Health experts are also acknowledging that psychological and social factors are involved in many chronic diseases (Forshaw, 2002). In fact, the fields of health psychology and behavioral medicine evolved partly to examine these factors and to find ways to help people cope more effectively (Baum & Posluszny, 1999). One of the main areas of research in health psychology and behavioral medicine today is the link between stress and illness (Dougall & Baum, 2001).

Members of the Masai tribe in Kenya, Africa (*top*), can stay on a treadmill for a long time because of their active lives. Heart disease is extremely low in the Masai tribe, also attributable to their energetic lifestyle. Americans are increasingly recognizing the health benefits of exercise and an active lifestyle (*bottom*). *Why are psychologists interested in the role of exercise in health?*

health psychology A discipline that emphasizes psychology's role in promoting and maintaining health and preventing and treating illness.

behavioral medicine An interdisciplinary field that focuses on developing and integrating behavioral and biomedical knowledge to promote health and reduce illness.

Review and Sharpen Your Thinking

1 *Describe the scope of health psychology and behavioral medicine.*

- Define health psychology and behavioral medicine and describe how they seek to promote health and reduce illness.

How high would you estimate your stress level to be? Do you think stress affects your health? What are the signs that it does?

2 STRESS AND ITS SOURCES

| Personality Factors | Environmental Factors | Sociocultural Factors |

"I think we can rule out stress."
© Sidney Harris.

stress The response of individuals to the circumstances and events, called stressors, that threaten and tax their coping abilities.

Type A behavior pattern A cluster of characteristics—being excessively competitive, hard-driven, and hostile—thought to be related to the incidence of heart disease.

Type B behavior pattern Being relaxed and easygoing.

hardiness A personality style characterized by a sense of commitment (rather than alienation), control (rather than powerlessness), and a perception of problems as challenges (rather than threats).

What causes stress?

According to the American Academy of Family Physicians, two-thirds of office visits to family doctors these days are for stress-related symptoms. Stress is believed to be a major contributor to coronary heart disease, cancer, lung problems, accidental injuries, cirrhosis of the liver, and suicide—the six leading causes of death in the United States. Antianxiety drugs and ulcer medications are among the best-selling prescription drugs in the United States today. No one really knows whether we experience more stress than our parents or grandparents did, but it seems as if we do.

Initially, the word *stress* was loosely borrowed from physics. Humans, it was thought, are in some ways similar to physical objects, such as metals, which resist moderate outside forces but lose their resiliency under greater pressure. But, unlike metals, human beings can think and reason, and they experience a myriad of social and environmental circumstances that make defining stress more complex in psychology than in physics (Hobfoll, 1989). Thus, in psychological terms, we can define **stress** as the response of individuals to the circumstances and events, called stressors, that threaten them and tax their coping abilities.

Personality Factors

Certain personality characteristics seem to help some people cope more effectively with stress than others do and make them less vulnerable to illness. Three aspects of personality that have been studied extensively in relation to stress are Type A and Type B behavior patterns, hardiness, and personal control.

Type A/Type B Behavior Patterns In the late 1950s, a secretary for two California cardiologists, Meyer Friedman and Ray Rosenman, observed that the chairs in their waiting rooms were tattered and worn, but only on the front edges. The cardiologists had also noticed the impatience of their cardiac patients, who often arrived exactly on time for an appointment and were in a great hurry to leave. Intrigued by this consistency, they conducted a study of 3,000 healthy men between the ages of 35 and 59 over a period of 8 years to find out whether people with certain behavioral characteristics might be prone to heart problems (Friedman & Rosenman, 1974). During the 8 years, one group of men had twice as many heart attacks or other forms of heart disease as the other men.

Friedman and Rosenman described the common personality characteristics of the men who developed coronary disease as the **Type A behavior pattern.** They theorized that being excessively competitive, hard-driven, impatient, and hostile is related to the incidence of heart disease. Rosenman and Friedman labeled the behavior of the healthier group, who were commonly relaxed and easygoing, the **Type B behavior pattern.** Go to the interactivity "Type A Behavior" to find out if you are Type A.

Further research on the link between Type A behavior and coronary disease indicates that the association is not as strong as Friedman and Rosenman believed (Suls & Swain, 1998; Williams, 2002). However, researchers have found that certain components of Type A behavior are more precisely linked with coronary risk.

The Type A behavior component most consistently associated with coronary problems is hostility (Markovitz, Jonas, & Davidson, 2001; Niaura & others, 2002; Pickering, 2001). People who are hostile outwardly or who turn anger inward are more likely to develop heart disease than their less angry counterparts (Eng & others, 2003; Matthews & others, 2004). Such people have been called "hot reactors" because of their intense physiological reactions to stress: Their hearts race, their breathing quickens, and their muscles tense up. One recent study found that hostility was a better predictor of coronary heart disease in older men than smoking, drinking, high caloric intake, or high levels of LDL cholesterol (Niaura & others, 2003).

Type **Z** behavior

Hardiness   **Hardiness** is a personality style characterized by a sense of commitment (rather than alienation) and of control (rather than powerlessness) and a perception of problems as challenges (rather than threats). The links among hardiness, stress, and illness were the focus of the Chicago Stress Project (Kobasa, Maddi, & Kahn, 1982; Maddi, 1998). It studied male business managers 32 to 65 years of age over a 5-year period. During the 5 years, most of the managers experienced stressful events, such as divorce, job transfers, or the death of a close friend. Managers who developed an illness (ranging from the flu to a heart attack) were compared with those who did not (Kobasa & others, 1982). Those who did not were likelier to have hardy personalities. The study also investigated whether or not hardiness, along with exercise and social support, buffered stress and reduced illness (Kobasa & others, 1986). When all three buffers—hardiness, exercise, and social support—were present, the level of illness dropped dramatically (see figure 13.2).

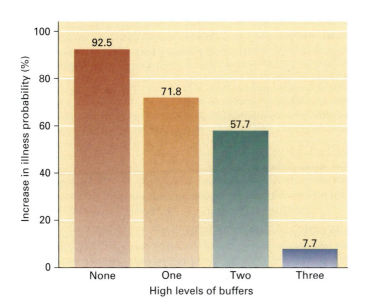

FIGURE 13.2 Illness in High-Stress Business Executives In one study of high-stress business executives (who were selected for this analysis because they were above the average stress level for the entire year of the study), a low level of all three buffers—hardiness, exercise, and social support—involved a high probability of at least one serious illness in that year. However, high levels of one, two, or all three buffers decreased the likelihood of at least one serious illness occurring.

Other researchers also have found support for the role of hardiness in illness and health (Waysman, Schwarzwald, & Solomon, 2001). The results of hardiness research suggest the power of multiple factors, rather than any single factor, in buffering stress and maintaining health (Maddi, 1998; Ouelette & DiPlacido, 2001).

Personal Control   An important aspect of stress is the extent to which people can do something to control or reduce the stress, as well as their *perception* of a sense of control (Taylor, 2003; Thompson, 2001; Wallston, 2001). As discussed in chapter 11, perceived lack of control in the face of stress can produce learned helplessness (Seligman, 1975), which can lead to depression.

In contrast, having a general sense of control reduces stress and can lead to the development of problem-solving strategies to cope with the stress. A person with a good sense of personal control might say, "If I stop smoking now, I will not develop lung cancer," or "If I exercise regularly, I won't develop cardiovascular disease." A sense of control may be especially important for people who are vulnerable to health problems, such as people with cancer and older adults.

A sense of personal control may also help people avoid a risky lifestyle. Consider a study of East German migrants to West Germany who found themselves unemployed (Mittag & Schwarzer, 1993). They often turned to heavy drinking for solace unless they had a sense of personal control (as measured by such survey items as "When I'm in trouble, I can rely on my ability to deal with the problem effectively"). Across a wide range of studies, a sense of personal control over stressful events has been related to emotional well-being, successful coping with a stressful event, behavior change that can promote good health, and good health (Decruyenaere & others, 2000; Pickering, 2001; Taylor, 2003; Thompson & Spacapan, 1991).

Environmental Factors

Many circumstances, large and small, can produce stress in our lives. Cataclysmic events, such as war, an automobile accident, a fire, or the death of a loved one, obviously produce stress. But often the everyday pounding of being overloaded with work, dealing with a difficult situation, or being frustrated in an unhappy relationship produces equally damaging stress.

Life Events and Daily Hassles   Some health psychologists have proposed that significant *life events* are the main environmental source of stress. Some of them have studied the effects of individual life events; others have evaluated the effects of multiple events. Thomas Holmes and Richard Rahe (1967) devised the Social Readjustment Rating Scale to measure the possible cumulative effect of clusters of life events. The events range from the death of a spouse (100 stress points) to minor violations of the law (11 stress points). Figure 13.3 provides an opportunity for you to evaluate the stressfulness of life events you have experienced in the past year.

People who experience clusters of stressful life events are more likely to become ill than they normally would be (Maddi, 1996). However, the ability to predict illness from life events alone is modest. Total scores of life-events scales are frequently ineffective at predicting future health problems. A life-events checklist tells us nothing about a person's physiological makeup, constitutional strengths and weaknesses, ability to cope with stressful circumstances, or support systems or the nature of the social relationships involved—all of which are important in understanding how stress is related to illness. A divorce, for example, might be less stressful than a marriage filled with day-to-day tension. And the changes related to positive events in the Social Readjustment Scale, such as reconciling with a spouse or gaining a new family member, are not as difficult to cope with as the changes that result from negative events. Go to the interactivity "Stress and Life Events" to learn more about the relationship

In-Psych Plus   between stress and illness.

The events listed below commonly occur in the lives of college students. Check the space provided for the events that have occurred in your life during the past 12 months. When you have checked off all the events that have happened in the past 12 months, total the point values in parentheses for each checked item.

(100)	_____	Death of a close family member	(25)	_____	Problems with your boss or professor
(80)	_____	Jail term	(25)	_____	Outstanding personal achievement
(63)	_____	Final year or first year in college	(25)	_____	Failure in some course
(60)	_____	Pregnancy (yours or caused by you)	(20)	_____	Final exams
(53)	_____	Severe personal illness or injury	(20)	_____	Increased or decreased dating
(50)	_____	Marriage	(20)	_____	Change in working conditions
(45)	_____	Any interpersonal problems	(20)	_____	Change in your major
(40)	_____	Financial difficulties	(18)	_____	Change in your sleeping habits
(40)	_____	Death of a close friend	(15)	_____	Several-day vacation
(40)	_____	Arguments with your roommate	(15)	_____	Change in eating habits
		(more than every other day)	(15)	_____	Family reunion
(40)	_____	Major disagreements with your family	(15)	_____	Change in recreational activities
(30)	_____	Major change in personal habits	(15)	_____	Minor illness or injury
(30)	_____	Change of living environment	(11)	_____	Minor violations of the law
(30)	_____	Beginning or ending a job			

Total Life Events Score _____

Your total may predict the frequency of serious illness you will experience in the coming year. If your life events score totals 300 points or more, you have an 80 percent chance of having a significant illness in the coming year. If your total score is 299 to 150, you have a 50 percent chance of having a significant illness. If your total score is 149 points or less, your risk of significant illness decreases to 30 percent.

Keep in mind, in interpreting your life events total score, that such events checklists don't take into account how you cope with such events. Some people who experience stressful life events cope and adjust well to them, and others do not.

FIGURE 13.3 **Impact of Life Events: Social Readjustment Rating Scale**

Because of these limitations, some health psychologists believe information about daily hassles and daily uplifts provides better clues than life events about the effects of stress (Crowther & others, 2001; D'Angelo & Wierzbick, 2003). Enduring a boring and tense job or living in poverty do not show up on scales of major life events, yet the everyday tension involved in these living conditions creates a highly stressful life and, in some cases, psychological disorder or illness. In one study, people who experienced the most daily hassles had the most negative self-images (Tolan, Miller, & Thomas, 1988).

What are the biggest hassles for college students? One study showed that the most frequent daily hassles of college students were wasting time, being lonely, and worrying about meeting high achievement standards (Kanner & others, 1981). In fact, the fear of failing in our success-oriented world often plays a role in college students' depression. College students also found that the small things in life—having fun, laughing, going to movies, getting along well with friends, and completing a task—were their main sources of daily uplifts.

Critics of the daily-hassles approach argue that it has some of the same limitations as life-events scales (Dohrenwend & Shrout, 1985). For example, knowing about a person's daily irritations and problems tell us nothing about the person's physiological resilience to stress, coping ability or strategies, or perceptions of stress. Further, the daily-hassles and -uplifts scale has not been consistently related to objective measures of health and illness. Yet another criticism is that daily hassles can be conceived of as dependent measures rather than as causes. People who complain about things, who report being anxious and unhappy, and who see the bad side of everything are likely to see more problems in their daily lives than are people with an optimistic outlook. From this perspective, problems do not predict bad moods; bad moods predict problems. But supporters of the daily-hassles and -uplifts concept reply that information about daily events can be used with information about a person's physiological reactions, coping, and perceptions of stress to provide a more complete picture of the causes and consequences of stress.

Conflict   Stress researchers who are interested in the effects of daily environmental experiences have studied a number of types of environmental stimuli. One such stimulus is conflict, which occurs when we must decide between two or more incompatible options. Neal Miller investigated (1959) three major types of conflict:

- **Approach/approach conflict:** Conflict in which the individual must choose between two attractive stimuli or circumstances. Should you go out with the attractive music lover or with the attractive sports lover? Do you buy a Mustang or a Celica? The approach/approach conflict is the least stressful of the three types of conflict because either choice leads to a positive result.
- **Avoidance/avoidance conflict:** Conflict in which the individual must choose between two unattractive stimuli or circumstances. Do you go through the stress of giving an oral presentation in class or not show up and get a zero? You want to avoid both, but you must choose one or the other. Obviously, this conflict is more stressful than having two enticing choices. In many instances, we delay our decision about the avoidance/avoidance conflict until the last possible moment.
- **Approach/avoidance conflict:** Conflict involving a single stimulus or circumstance that has both positive and negative characteristics. Let's say you really like the person you are going with and are thinking about getting married. On the one hand, you are attracted by the steady affection and love that marriage might bring, but, on the other hand, marriage is a commitment you might not feel ready to make. On a more mundane level, you might look at a menu and think the double chocolate delight would be sumptuous, but is it worth the extra pound of weight? Our world is full of such approach/avoidance conflicts, and they can be highly stressful. In these circumstances, we often waver before deciding.

Overload   Daily hassles can also result in a stress reaction called *overload*. Sometimes stimuli become so intense that we can no longer cope with them. For example, persistent high levels of noise overload our adaptability to other stimuli. Overload can occur with work as well. How often have you said to yourself, "There are not enough hours in the day to do all I have to do." In today's computer age, we are especially faced with information overload. It is easy to develop the uncomfortable feeling that we don't know as much about a topic as we should, even if we are a so-called expert.

Overload can lead to **burnout,** a state of physical and emotional exhaustion that includes a hopeless feeling, chronic fatigue, and low energy (Leiter & Maslach, 2001). Burnout usually occurs not because of one or two traumatic events but because of a gradual accumulation of everyday stresses (Demerouti & others, 2001). Burnout is most likely to occur among individuals who deal with others in highly emotional situations (such as nurses and social workers) but who have only limited control over the behavior of others or the results (Alexander & Klein, 2001; DiGiacomo & Adamson, 2001).

Burnout affects a quarter of the students at some colleges. On a number of college campuses, it is the most frequent reason students leave school before earning their degrees. Dropping out of college for a term or two used to be considered a sign of weakness. Now it is more accepted, and counselors may actually encourage some students who feel overwhelmed with stress to take a break from college. Before recommending "stopping out," though, most counselors first suggest that the student examine ways to reduce overload and explore possible coping strategies that would allow the student to remain in school. The simple strategy of taking a reduced or better-balanced course load sometimes works.

approach/approach conflict A conflict in which the individual must choose between two attractive stimuli or circumstances.

avoidance/avoidance conflict A conflict in which the individual must choose between two unattractive stimuli or circumstances.

approach/avoidance conflict A conflict involving a single stimulus or circumstance that has both negative and positive characteristics.

burnout A feeling of overload, including mental and physical exhaustion, that usually results from a gradual accumulation of everyday stresses.

Work-Related Stress American workers are working harder and longer than they have in past decades just to maintain their standard of living. In one generation, the number of hours Americans work each week has increased by 8 percent to a current average of 47. Twenty percent of Americans are working 49 hours or more per week (National Institute for Occupational Safety and Health [NIOSH], 2001). The predictable result is greater work-related stress and increased risk for psychological and physical health problems (Jones, Tanigwa, & Weiss, 2003; Hartvigsen & others, 2004; Nelson, Quick, & Simmons, 2001). Researchers have found that at least one-fourth to one-third of American workers have high job stress and are emotionally drained at the end of a work day (NIOSH, 2001).

American workers' stress levels have increased because economic dips and downsizing trends among corporations have made their jobs less secure. The stress level of workers also increases when their jobs do not meet their expectations (Rabasca, 1999). Americans want jobs that are secure, offer advancement, offer a sense of community among co-workers, and allow them to use creative and problem-solving skills. Workers also want some control over the work they do. Work-related stress usually increases when job demands are high and the individual has little choice in deciding how to meet the demands (low autonomy, high external control).

One study found that a combination of personal and job factors placed individuals at risk of getting sick (Schaubroeck, Jones, & Xie, 2001). Employees who perceived they had control over their job responsibilities but did not have confidence in their problem-solving abilities or who blamed themselves for bad outcomes were the most likely to experience stress. These types of job situations placed these employees at risk of getting infections.

Recall from the beginning of the chapter that Mort, the air traffic controller, often took the stress of his job home with him. Psychologists and policy makers worry that work-related stress can carry over to influence well-being in other areas of a person's life, especially the family (European Agency for Safety and Health at Work, 2000). In one survey, 56 percent of workers said that they felt "some" or "a great deal" of interference between their jobs and their home lives (Canadian Mental Health Association, 1984). The interference affected family routines and events, child-rearing and household responsibilities, leisure activities, and social life.

What creates stress for workers?

Sociocultural Factors

The personality and environmental factors described so far are not the only sources of stress. Sociocultural factors help to determine which stressors individuals are likely to encounter, whether they are likely to perceive events as stressful or not, and how they believe stressors should be confronted (Kawachi & Kennedy, 2001).

Acculturative Stress Moving to a new place is a stressful experience in the best of circumstances. It is even more stressful when a person from one culture moves into a different culture. **Acculturative stress** refers to the negative consequences that result from contact between two distinctive cultural groups. Many individuals who have immigrated to the United States have experienced acculturative stress (Hovey, 2000; Uppaluri, Schumm, & Lauderdale, 2001).

Canadian cross-cultural psychologist John Berry (1980) believes that, when people experience cultural change, they can adapt in one of four main ways:

- *Assimilation* occurs when individuals relinquish their native cultural identity and adopt an identity that helps them blend into the larger society. If enough individuals follow this path, the nondominant group is absorbed into the established mainstream society. Sometimes assimilation occurs when many groups merge to form a new society (what is often called a "melting pot").
- *Integration* implies that people move into the larger culture but, in contrast to assimilation, maintain many aspects of their distinctive cultural identity. In this

acculturative stress The negative consequences of contact between two distinctive cultural groups.

This Chinese American association has helped its members cope with acculturative stress. *What are some strategies for coping with acculturative stress?*

circumstance, a number of ethnic groups all cooperate within a large social system (a "mosaic").

- *Separation* refers to self-imposed withdrawal from the larger culture. If imposed by the larger society, however, separation becomes *segregation*. People might maintain their traditional way of life because they desire an independent existence (as in separatist movements), or the dominant culture may exercise its power to exclude the other culture (as in slavery and apartheid).
- *Marginalization* refers to the process by which nondominant groups lose cultural and social contact with both their traditional society and the larger, dominant society. The essential features of one's culture are lost, but they are not replaced by those of the larger society. Thus marginalization involves feelings of alienation and a loss of identity.

Marginalization is the least adaptive response to acculturation. Although separation can have benefits under certain circumstances, it may be stressful for individuals who seek separation while most members of their group seek assimilation. Integration and assimilation are healthier adaptations to acculturative pressures. But assimilation means some cultural loss, so it may be more stressful than integration. For the most part, the person who can choose the most useful features of the two cultural systems may cope best with the stresses of acculturation.

Poverty   Poverty can cause considerable stress for individuals and families (Chen & others, 2003; Landrine & Klonoff, 2001; McLoyd, 2000). Chronic conditions such as inadequate housing, dangerous neighborhoods, burdensome responsibilities, and economic uncertainties are potent stressors in the lives of the poor (Adler, 2001; Hobfoll & others, 2003; Latkin & Curry, 2003).

Ethnic minority families are disproportionately among the poor, as are female-headed families. For example, Puerto Rican families headed by women are 15 times more likely to live in poverty than are families headed by White men, and families headed by African American women are 10 times more likely to live in poverty than are families headed by White men (National Advisory Council on Economic Opportunity, 1980). Many people who become poor during their lives remain so for only 1 or 2 years. However, African Americans and female heads of household are especially at risk for persistent poverty.

Vonnie McLoyd *(right)* has conducted a number of important investigations of the roles of poverty, ethnicity, and unemployment in children's and adolescents' development. She has found that economic stressors often diminish children's and adolescents' belief in the utility of education and their achievement strivings. *What specific stressors do the poor face?*

Poverty is also related to threatening and uncontrollable life events (Russo, 1990). For example, women living in poverty are more likely to experience crime and violence than are women with higher incomes. And poverty undermines sources of social support that help to buffer the effects of stress. Poverty is related to marital unhappiness and to spouses who are unlikely to serve as confidants (Brown, Bhrolchain, & Harris, 1975). Further, poverty means having to depend on many overburdened and unresponsive bureaucratic systems for financial, housing, and health assistance, which may contribute to a poor person's perception of powerlessness—itself a factor in stress.

Review and Sharpen Your Thinking

2 *Define stress and identify its sources.*

- Explain the role of personality factors in stress.
- Identify environmental factors in stress.
- Evaluate the effects of sociocultural factors on stress.

What are the main sources of stress in your life? Would you classify them as personality factors, environmental factors, or sociocultural factors?

STRESS RESPONSES 3

| General Adaptation Syndrome | Fight or Flight, Tend and Befriend | Cognitive Appraisal |

How do people respond to stress?

When we experience stress, we may respond physiologically and cognitively. Physiological responses to stress are discussed first.

FIGURE 13.4 Selye's General Adaptation Syndrome The general adaptation syndrome (GAS) describes three stages in an individual's general response to stress: alarm, in which the body mobilizes its resources; resistance, in which resistance levels off; and exhaustion, in which resistance becomes depleted.

General Adaptation Syndrome

When we experience stress, our body readies itself to handle the assault. The physiological changes that take place were the main interest of Hans Selye (1974, 1983), the Austrian-born founder of stress research. He defined stress as wear and tear on the body due to the demands placed on it. After observing patients with different problems—the death of someone close, loss of income, arrest for embezzlement—Selye concluded that any number of environmental events or stimuli will produce the same stress response: loss of appetite, muscular weakness, and decreased interest in the world.

General adaptation syndrome (GAS) is Selye's term for the common effects on the body when demands are placed on it. The GAS consists of three stages: alarm, resistance, and exhaustion (see figure 13.4). One of the main criticisms of Selye's concept is that human beings do not always react to stress in the uniform way he proposed. There is more to understanding stress in humans than knowing their physical reactions to it. We also need to know about their personalities, their physical makeup, their perceptions, and the contexts in which the stressors occurred. Nonetheless, Selye's model is useful in helping us understand the link between stress and health.

Alarm   In trying to cope with the initial effects of stress, the body releases hormones that, in a short time, adversely affect the immune system's functioning. During this time, the individual is prone to infection and injury. Fortunately, the alarm stage passes rather quickly.

Many scientists now agree that two main biological pathways between the brain and the endocrine system, shown in figure 13.5, respond to stress in the alarm stage (B. L. Anderson, 1998, 2000; Anderson, Kiecolt-Glaser, & Glaser, 1994; Sternberg & Gold, 1996). As shown in figure 13.5, the neuroendocrine immune pathway (pathway 1) goes through the hypothalamus and pituitary gland to the adrenal glands, from which cortisol is released. Cortisol is a steroid that is good for the body over the short term because it causes cellular fuel—glucose—to move to muscles. But over the long term, high levels of cortisol can be bad for the body, suppressing the immune system and straining the brain's cellular functioning. Too much cortisol also increases appetite and can cause weight gain.

In the sympathetic nervous system pathway (pathway 2), the route is through the hypothalamus and then the sympathetic nervous system (rather than the pituitary gland). When the signal reaches the adrenal glands, epinephrine and norepinephrine (but not cortisol) are released. Recall, from chapter 9, that the sympathetic nervous system is the subsystem of the autonomic nervous system responsible for the body's arousal. It produces a quick response to a stressor (often referred to as the "fight-or-flight" response). The release of the hormones epinephrine and norepinephrine causes a number of physiological changes, including elevated blood pressure. Over time, high blood pressure can lead to increased risk for illness and disease, such as cardiovascular disease.

general adaptation syndrome (GAS) Selye's term for the common effects on the body when demands are placed on it; consists of three stages: alarm, resistance, and exhaustion.

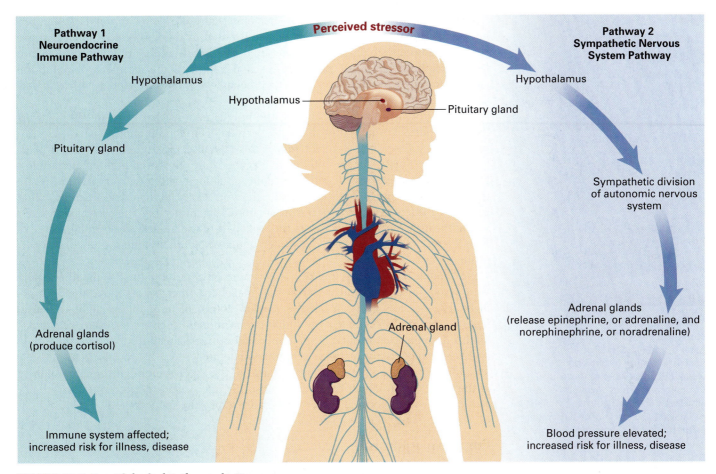

Perceived stressor

**Pathway 1
Neuroendocrine
Immune Pathway**

Hypothalamus

Pituitary gland

Adrenal glands
(produce cortisol)

Immune system affected;
increased risk for illness, disease

Hypothalamus

Pituitary gland

Adrenal gland

**Pathway 2
Sympathetic Nervous
System Pathway**

Hypothalamus

Sympathetic division
of autonomic nervous
system

Adrenal glands
(release epinephrine, or adrenaline, and
norephinephrine, or noradrenaline)

Blood pressure elevated;
increased risk for illness, disease

FIGURE 13.5 Two Biological Pathways in Stress

Resistance   In the *second* stage of Selye's general adaptation syndrome, a number of glands throughout the body begin to manufacture several hormones that protect the individual in many ways. Endocrine and sympathetic nervous system activity are not as high as in the alarm stage, although they still are elevated.

During the resistance stage, the body's immune system can fight off infection with remarkable efficiency. Similarly, hormones that reduce the inflammation normally associated with injury circulate at high levels.

Exhaustion   If the body's all-out effort to combat stress fails and the stress persists, the individual moves into the exhaustion stage. At this point, the wear and tear on the body takes its toll—the person might collapse in a state of exhaustion, and vulnerability to disease increases. Mort, the air traffic controller introduced at the beginning of the chapter, had reached this point in his life. He was so overwhelmed with stress that his body broke down and he had a heart attack. Some type of serious, possibly irreversible damage to the body, or even death, may occur in the exhaustion stage.

Fight or Flight, Tend and Befriend

Selye's concept of alarm reaction—the first stage of the general adaptation syndrome—is essentially the same as the fight-or-flight response. The central notion of both concepts is that the body's physiological resources are mobilized quickly to prepare the organism to deal with threats to survival.

Shelly Taylor and her colleagues developed the tend-and-befriend model, a reinterpretation of the fight-or-flight model, to account for the responses of females in threatening contexts. Health psychologists such as Shelly Taylor usually have a doctoral degree in psychology. At the graduate level, many doctoral programs in clinical, counseling, social, or experimental psychology have a specialized track in some area of health psychology. *What trends in medicine, psychology, and health care have combined to make health psychology so important?*

The fight-or-flight response was first observed by Walter Cannon (1929) when he studied the reaction of cats suddenly confronted by a dog. Cannon noted that the cats experienced such changes as more rapid blood circulation, muscular tension, and heavy breathing. He called the entire reaction fight or flight because it prepared the animals for engaging in one of these two behaviors when confronted with a threatening situation.

Today, threats to survival are not the only situations that generate the fight-or-flight response. Virtually any threat to personally important motives that taxes an individual's coping abilities might trigger this response.

Recently, Shelley Taylor and her colleagues (2000) proposed that females are less likely to respond to stressful and threatening situations with a fight-or-flight response than males are. They argue that females are more likely to "tend and befriend." That is, females often respond to stressful situations by protecting themselves and their young through nurturing behaviors (the *tend* part of the model) and forming alliances with a larger social group, especially one populated by other women (the *befriend* part of the model).

Although females do show the same immediate hormonal and sympathetic nervous system response to acute stress that males do, other factors make the fight-or-flight response less likely in females (Taylor, 2003). In terms of the fight response, male aggression is regulated by androgen hormones, such as testosterone, and is linked to sympathetic nervous system reactivity and hostility. In contrast, female aggression appears to be more cerebral, moderated more by social circumstances, learning, culture, and the situation. In terms of the flight response, fleeing too quickly at the first sign of danger could place offspring at risk and reduce reproductive success, which was a poor choice evolutionarily, especially for females.

Cognitive Appraisal

Although our bodies may have a similar response to stressors, not everyone perceives the same events as stressful. For example, one person may perceive an upcoming job interview as threatening, whereas another person may perceive it as challenging. To some degree, then, what is stressful depends on how people cognitively appraise and interpret events (Maier, Waldstein, & Synowski, 2003). This view has been most clearly presented by Richard Lazarus (1993, 2000). **Cognitive appraisal** is Lazarus' term for individuals' interpretation of the events in their lives as harmful, threatening, or challenging and their determination of whether they have the resources to cope effectively with the events.

In Lazarus' view, events are appraised in two steps: primary appraisal and secondary appraisal (see figure 13.6). In *primary appraisal*, individuals interpret whether an event involves *harm* or loss that has already occurred, a *threat* of some future danger, or a *challenge* to be overcome. Lazarus believes that perceiving a stressor as a challenge to be overcome, rather than as a threat, is a good strategy for reducing stress. This strategy fits with the concept of hardiness, a personality factor that improves coping with stress.

To understand Lazarus' concept of primary appraisal, consider two students, each of whom has a failing grade in their psychology class at midterm. Student A is almost frozen by the stress of the low grade and looks at the rest of the term as a threatening circumstance. In contrast, student B does not become overwhelmed by the harm already done and the threat of future failures. She looks at the low grade as a challenge that she can address and overcome.

In *secondary appraisal*, individuals evaluate their resources and determine how effectively they can be used to cope with the event. For example, student A might have some helpful resources for coping with her low midterm grade, but she views the stressful circumstance as so harmful and threatening that she doesn't use her resources. Student B would instead evaluate the resources she can call on to improve her grade during the second half of the term. These include asking the instructor for

cognitive appraisal Lazarus' term for individuals' interpretation of events in their lives as threatening, harmful, or challenging and their determination of whether they have the resources to cope effectively with the events.

suggestions about how to study better for the tests in the course, setting up a time management program to include more study hours, and asking several students who are doing well in the class about their strategies.

In many instances, viewing stress as a challenge during primary appraisal paves the way for finding effective coping resources during secondary appraisal. However, sometimes people do not have adequate resources for coping with an event they have defined as a challenge. For example, if student B is extremely shy, she might lack the courage and skills to talk to the instructor or to ask other students about their strategies for doing well in the course.

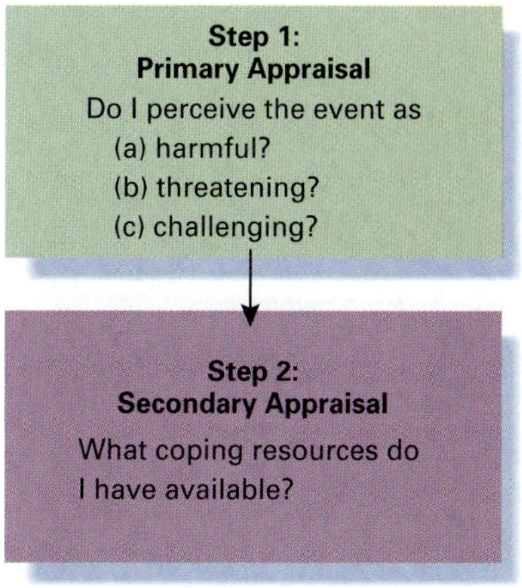

Review and Sharpen Your Thinking

3   *Explain how people respond to stress.*

- Describe the general adaptation syndrome.
- Discuss the differences between the fight-or-flight response and the tend-and-befriend response.
- Explain the nature of cognitive appraisal.

How do your body and mind react when you face a stressful experience?

Step 1:
Primary Appraisal
Do I perceive the event as
(a) harmful?
(b) threatening?
(c) challenging?

Step 2:
Secondary Appraisal
What coping resources do I have available?

FIGURE 13.6 **Lazarus' Cognitive Appraisal View of Stress** Perceiving a stressor as harmful or threatening in step 1 and having few or no coping resources available in step 2 yield high stress. Perceiving a stressor as a challenge in step 1 and having good coping resources available in step 2 reduce stress.

STRESS AND ILLNESS   4

Diseases Related to Stress   **Positive Emotions, Illness, and Health**

How are stress and illness linked?

This section examines what research has revealed about links between stress and specific types of illness. In particular, stress has been identified as a factor in weakened immune systems, cardiovascular disease, and cancer. The good news, which is also discussed in this section, is that positive emotions have been shown to help in staving off illness and maintaining health.

Diseases Related to Stress

Currently, researchers have considerable interest in links between the immune system and stress (Herberman, 2002; Glaser & others, 2003; Kiecolt-Glaser & others, 2002a, 2002b; Marsland & others, 2001). The immune system keeps us healthy by recognizing foreign materials, such as bacteria, viruses, and tumors, and then destroying them. But when a person is in the alarm or exhaustion stage of the general adaptation syndrome, the immune system functions poorly. During these stages, viruses and bacteria are more likely to multiply and cause disease (Dantzer, 2004; Greco, 2004).

A study by Sheldon Cohen and his colleagues (1998) found that adults who faced interpersonal or work-related stress for at least 1 month were more likely than people who were less stressed to catch a cold. In the study, 276 adults were exposed to viruses, then quarantined for 5 days. Individuals who reported high stress for the preceding 2 years tripled their risk of catching a cold. Those who experienced work-related stress for 1 month or longer were nearly five times more likely to develop colds than individuals without chronic stress. Those who experienced interpersonal stress for 1 month or more were twice as likely to catch a cold. Cohen concluded that stress-triggered changes in the immune system and hormones might create greater vulnerability to infection. The findings suggest that, when we know we are under stress, we need to take better care of ourselves than usual, although often we do just the opposite (Cohen, 2002; Cohen, Miller, & Rabin, 2001; Cohen & others, 2003). Cohen and his colleagues (1997) also found that positive social ties with friends and family provide a protective buffer that helps to prevent people from catching a cold.

An equally clear link between stress and cardiovascular disease has not been found, but there is evidence that major life changes and chronic emotional stress are both associated with high blood pressure, heart disease, and early death (Carroll & others, 2003; Taylor, 2003). Apparently, the surge in adrenaline caused by severe emotional stress causes the blood to clot more rapidly, and blood clotting is a major factor in heart attacks (Fogoros, 2001). One study found that a happy marriage was linked with lower blood pressure and an unhappy marriage was linked with higher blood pressure (B. Baker, 2001). People who are quick to anger or who display frequent hostility also appear to have an increased risk for cardiovascular disease (Williams, 2001). But the body's internal reactions to stress are not the only risk. People who live in a chronically stressed condition are more likely to take up smoking, start overeating, and avoid exercising. All of these stress-related behaviors are linked with the development of cardiovascular disease (O'Callahan, Andrews, & Kratz, 2003; Schneiderman & others, 2001).

The links between stress and cancer follow a similar pattern (B. L. Anderson, 2000; Anderson, Golden-Kreutz, & DiLillo, 2001):

- *Quality of life.* A number of studies have documented acute stress at the time cancer is diagnosed (McKenna & others, 1999). Lengthy cancer treatments and the disruptions the disease creates in family, social, economic, and occupational life can cause chronic stress. These stressors can suppress the body's ability to fight off many types of disease, including cancer.
- *Behavioral factors.* An increase in negative health behaviors or a decrease in positive health behaviors can accompany cancer. For instance, individuals with cancer may become depressed or anxious and may self-medicate with alcohol and other drugs or may abandon exercise. Substance abuse directly suppresses immunity and is associated with poor nutrition, which indirectly affects health (B. L. Anderson, 2000). Conversely, positive health behaviors, such as exercise, can improve both the immune and endocrine systems, even among individuals with chronic diseases (Phaneuf & Leeuwenburgh, 2001).
- *Biological pathways.* Stress sets in motion biological changes involving the autonomic, endocrine, and immune systems. But if the immune system is not compromised, it appears to help provide resistance to cancer and slow its progression (Anderson, 2000).

Positive Emotions, Illness, and Health

Researchers have focused mainly on the role of negative factors, such as emotional stress and anger, in illness. However, the recent interest in positive psychology has sparked research on the role that positive emotions might play in reducing illness and promoting health (Salovey & others, 2000; Vaillant, 2003; Vaughn & Roesch, 2003). This line of research can be controversial, as the Critical Controversy box indicates, but researchers have made several intriguing connections between positive emotions and health.

For example, positive emotions have been shown to be linked with the release of secretory immunoglobulin A (S-IgA), the antibody that is believed to be the first line of defense against the common cold (Stone & others, 1994). In one study, S-IgA levels increased after healthy college women watched a funny, happy video but dropped after watching a sad video (Labott & Martin, 1990).

Moods also can influence people's health. Researchers have found that, when people can regain and maintain positive moods, they are less likely to get sick or to use medical services when faced with a stressful life experience (Goldman, Kraemer,

Can Positive Thinking Make You Healthy?

If your best friend offered you a piece of candy when you had the flu and told you that it would make you better, would you believe it? What if the candy came from a famous medical doctor who told you the candy contained powerful medicine? If you ate the candy and your achiness and fever disappeared, the reason might simply be that the illness had run its course, and you would have felt better even if you hadn't eaten the candy. Or you might have experienced the placebo effect, a change believed to have been brought about by a medically inactive substance.

The word *placebo* stems from the Latin "I shall please" and commonly refers to a medication prescribed more for the mental or emotional relief of the patient than for any actual curative properties. The placebo effect has been known for centuries. In the second century, the Greek physician Galen noted, "He cures most successfully in whom the people have the most confidence." In the intervening centuries, doctors have been divided over whether to deliberately use the placebo effect to help their patients. Recently, the placebo effect has again become the focus of considerable controversy.

Asbjorn Hróbjartsson and Peter Gotzsche (2001) published a meta-analysis they claimed showed no support whatsoever for the use of placebos in clinical practice. In order to explore the existence of a placebo effect, they searched the medical literature to find studies that included both a placebo group and an untreated group (along, of course, with a treatment group). If the placebo effect is real, they suggested, then it should show up in comparisons of these two groups. Their meta-analysis included 114 studies, with 7,500 patients involving 40 different medical conditions. The results revealed that patients who received placebo treatment fared no better than those left untreated.

Researchers from the University of British Columbia (de la Fuente-Fernandez & others, 2001) came to the opposite conclusion. They injected patients suffering from Parkinson's disease with either a drug (apomorphine) or a placebo (an inactive salt solution). Using brain scans, they showed that the drug produced improvement by initiating the release of the neurotransmitter dopamine in the brain. Surprisingly, brain scans revealed a similar release of dopamine in patients who were given the placebo injection. These patients apparently derived real benefit from the placebo effect.

Some argue that placebos work by helping people to adopt a positive attitude about their health. For that reason alone, placebo effects are a powerful part of healing and should be used more often (Brown, 1998). In this view, placebo effects are not just inactive "sugar pills" but affect patients' attitudes toward their own health outcomes. Seeking help, getting a diagnosis, beginning treatment, and looking forward to resuming a healthful life are all part of a positive attitude toward one's own health. Thus, although the placebo itself may be inactive, the positive attitude triggered by the placebo, and other interventions, may be life-saving.

There is evidence that positive thinking is important in promoting health. In one study, older men and women who expressed a positive outlook toward life were less likely to suffer heart attacks than those who expressed a negative outlook (Ostir & others, 2001). The effect of positive thinking can even extend life. Analysis of brief autobiographies written more than 60 years ago by Catholic nuns when they were in their 20s suggests that those with a positive outlook lived longer than nuns who wrote about their lives in more neutral terms (Danner, Snowdon, & Friesen, 2001). Of course, positive attitudes may be merely a result of good health. But it is also quite possible that adopting a more positive attitude generates health benefits.

What do you think?

- Have you ever been aware of a connection between your own positive attitude and good health?
- How could you design an experiment to test whether positive thinking fosters better health or whether good health fosters positive thinking?
- A survey published in *Prevention* in February 1996 identified seven positive attitudes associated with good health: being very optimistic; having a strong belief in a higher power; thinking of the future, not the past; thinking people are good; being very trusting; thinking you control your life; and thinking you control your health. Is this list complete? What other attitudes might you add to the list? Why?

& Salovey, 1996). In another study, happy individuals were more likely to engage in health-promoting behaviors and had more confidence that these behaviors would relieve their illness than sad individuals (Salovey & Birnbaum, 1989). In yet another study, individuals who experienced more positive emotions (such as happiness) used broader coping strategies than those who experienced more negative emotions (such as sadness). For example, individuals who experienced positive emotions were more likely to think about ways to deal with the problem and to step back from the situation and be more objective than individuals who experienced negative emotions (Frederickson & Joiner, 2000).

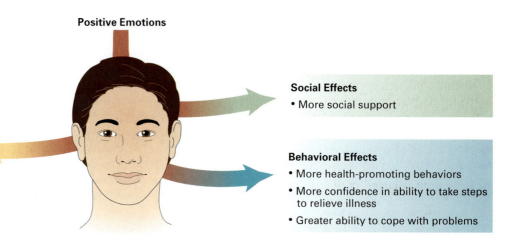

FIGURE 13.7 Some Links Between Positive Emotions and Health

Social support, such as caring family and friends, is another important factor in stress and coping that is likely linked, and linked reciprocally, with positive emotions (Salovey & others, 2000). Not only does social support improve a person's emotional state, but a person's emotional state also influences the likelihood that the support will be provided.

In sum, positive emotions do appear to be involved in helping to reduce illness and promote health (see figure 13.7). However, much more research needs to be carried out to determine the precise linkages.

Review and Sharpen Your Thinking

4 **Discuss the links between stress and illness.**

- Outline the link between stress and disease.
- Describe how positive emotions, illness, and health are related.

Think about the last several times you have been sick. Did you experience any stressful circumstances prior to getting sick? Might they have contributed to your illness?

5 COPING STRATEGIES

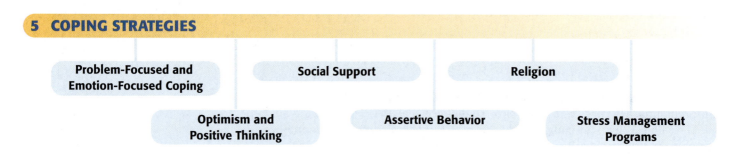

What are some good strategies for coping with stress?

A stressful circumstance is rendered considerably less stressful when a person successfully copes with it. **Coping** involves managing taxing circumstances, expending effort to solve life's problems, and seeking to master or reduce stress. Successful coping is associated with a number of factors, including a sense of personal control, a healthy immune system, personal resources, and positive emotions.

Problem-Focused and Emotion-Focused Coping

In the discussion of stress earlier in this chapter, I described Richard Lazarus' (1993, 2000) view that cognitive appraisal is critical to coping. Lazarus believes that people can make two general types of coping efforts: problem-focused coping and emotion-focused coping.

Problem-focused coping is Lazarus' term for the cognitive strategy of squarely facing our troubles and trying to solve them. For example, if you are having trouble with a class, you might go to the study skills center at your college or university and enter a training program to learn how to study more effectively. Having done so, you have faced your problem and attempted to do something about it.

Emotion-focused coping is Lazarus' term for responding to stress in an emotional manner, especially by using defensive mechanisms. In emotion-focused coping, we might avoid something, rationalize what has happened to us, deny it is occurring, laugh it off, or call on our religious faith for support. If you use emotion-focused coping, you might avoid going to a class that is a problem for you. You might say the class doesn't matter, deny that you are having a problem, laugh and joke about it with your friends, or pray that you will do better. This is not necessarily a good way to face a problem. Sometimes emotion-focused coping is adaptive and helps us deal with problems, however. For example, denial is one of the main protective psychological mechanisms for temporarily dealing with the flood of feelings that occur when the reality of death or dying becomes too great. Denial can be used to avoid or buffer the destructive impact of shock by postponing the time when you have to deal with stress.

Many individuals successfully use both problem-focused and emotion-focused coping when adjusting to a stressful circumstance. Over the long term, though, problem-focused coping rather than emotion-focused coping is what usually works best (Folkman & Moskowitz, 2004; Heppner & Lee, 2001; Park & Adler, 2003).

Optimism and Positive Thinking

Thinking positively and avoiding negative thoughts is generally a good coping strategy when trying to handle stress more effectively. A positive mood improves our ability to process information more efficiently, makes us more altruistic, and gives us higher self-esteem. In addition, in most cases, an optimistic attitude gives us a sense that we are controlling our environment. In chapter 10, I discussed the positive benefits of being optimistic. Although some individuals at times successfully use a strategy of defensive pessimism to improve their ability to cope with stress, optimism is generally better.

Cognitive Restructuring and Positive Self-Talk Martin Seligman (1990, 2001) believes the best tools for overcoming chronic pessimism lie in cognitive therapy, one of the major psychotherapies discussed in chapter 12. In cognitive therapy, the client is encouraged to think positively and talk back to negative thoughts in an optimistic style that limits self-blame and negative generalizations.

Many cognitive therapists believe the process of *cognitive restructuring*—modifying the thoughts, ideas, and beliefs that maintain an individual's problems—can also be used to get people to think more positively and optimistically. The process is often aided by changes in *self-talk* (also called *self-statements*), the soundless mental speech that we use when we think about something, plan, or solve problems. Because self-talk has a way of being self-fulfilling, uncountered negative thinking

coping Managing taxing circumstances, expending effort to solve life's problems, and seeking to master or reduce stress.

problem-focused coping Lazarus' term for the cognitive strategy of squarely facing troubles and trying to solve them.

emotion-focused coping Lazarus' term for responding to stress in an emotional manner, especially using defensive appraisals.

Situation	Negative Self-Statements	Positive Self-Statements
Having a long, difficult assignment due the next day	"I'll never get this work done by tomorrow."	"If I work real hard, I may be able to get it all done by tomorrow." "This is going to be tough, but it is still possible to do it." "Finishing this assignment by tomorrow will be a real challenge." "If I don't get it finished, I'll just have to ask the teacher for an extension."
Losing your job	"I'll never get another job."	"I'll just have to look harder for another job." "There will be rough times ahead, but I've dealt with rough times before." "Hey, maybe my next job will be a better deal altogether." "There are agencies that can probably help me get some kind of job."
Moving away from friends and family	"My whole life is left behind."	"I'll miss everyone, but it doesn't mean we can't stay in touch." "Just think of all the new people I'm going to meet." "I guess it will be kind of exciting moving to a new home." "Now I'll have two places to call home."
Breaking up with a person you love	"I have nothing to live for. He/she was all I had."	"I really thought our relationship would work, but it's not the end of the world." "Maybe we can try again in the future." "I'll just have to try to keep myself busy and not let it bother me." "If I met him (her), there is no reason why I won't meet someone else someday."
Not getting into graduate school	"I guess I'm really dumb. I don't know what I'll do."	"I'll just have to reapply next year." "There are things I can do with my life other than going to grad school." "I guess a lot of good students get turned down. It's just so unbelievably competitive." "Maybe there are a few other programs that I could apply to."
Having to participate in a class discussion	"Everyone else knows more than I do, so what's the use of saying anything?"	"I have as much to say as anyone else in the class." "My ideas may be different, but they're still valid." "It's okay to be a bit nervous; I'll relax when I start talking." "I may as well say something; how bad could it sound?"

FIGURE 13.8 Some Positive Self-Statements to Replace Negative Ones

can destroy self-confidence. Some examples of positive self-statements that might replace negative self-statements are presented in figure 13.8.

Several strategies can help you to monitor your self-talk. First, at random times during the day, ask yourself, "What am I saying to myself right now?" Then, if you can, write down your thoughts along with a few notes about the situation you are in and how you're feeling. At the beginning, record your self-talk without any censorship. Eventually make your self-talk as accurate and positive as possible.

You can also use uncomfortable emotions or moods—such as stress, depression, and anxiety—as cues for listening to your self-talk. Identify the feeling as accurately as possible. Then ask yourself, "What was I saying to myself right before I started feeling this way?" or "What have I been saying to myself since I've been feeling this way?"

Situations that you anticipate might be difficult for you also are excellent opportunities to assess your self-talk. Write down a description of the coming event. Then ask yourself, "What am I saying to myself about this event?" If your thoughts are negative, think how you can use your strengths to turn these disruptive feelings into more positive ones and help turn a potentially difficult experience into a success.

You also might compare your self-talk predictions (what you thought would or should happen in a given situation) with what actually took place. If the reality conflicts with your predictions—as it often does when your self-talk is in error—pinpoint how you can adjust your self-talk to fit reality.

You are likely to have a subjective view of your own thoughts, so you might try to enlist the assistance of a sympathetic but objective friend, partner, or therapist who is willing to listen, discuss your self-assessment with you, and help you to identify ways in which your self-talk is distorted and might be improved.

Positive Self-Illusion For a number of years, mental health professionals believed that seeing reality as accurately as possible was the best path to health. Recently, though, researchers have found increasing evidence that maintaining some positive illusions about oneself and the world is healthy. Happy people often have falsely high opinions of themselves, give self-serving explanations for events, and have exaggerated beliefs about their ability to control the world around them (Taylor, 1998; Taylor & Brown, 1994). But having too grandiose an idea of yourself can have negative consequences, just as thinking too negatively about yourself does. The ideal overall orientation may be to have either a firm grasp on reality or mildly inflated illusions (Baumeister, 1989).

Developing positive self-illusions has been shown to have dramatic effects on performance. For example, sport psychologist Jim Loehr (1989) pieced together videotaped segments of 17-year-old Michael Chang's most outstanding tennis points in the past year. Chang periodically watched the videotape and always saw himself winning, never saw himself make mistakes, and always saw himself in a positive mood. Several months later, Chang became the youngest male to win the French Open tennis championship.

What some people refer to as "just being realistic"—which can mean overstating the negative aspects of reality—can be a problem. A negative outlook can increase our chances of getting angry, feeling guilty, and magnifying our mistakes. And for some people, seeing things too accurately can lead to depression. Seeing one's suffering as meaningless and random may not help a person cope and move forward, even if the suffering is indeed random and meaningless. An absence of illusions may also thwart individuals from undertaking the risky and ambitious projects that sometimes yield the greatest rewards (Baumeister, 1993).

In some cases, though, a strategy of defensive pessimism may work best. By imagining negative outcomes, people can prepare for stressful circumstances (Norem & Cantor, 1986). Think about the honors student who is worried that she will flunk the next test or the nervous host who is afraid his lavish dinner party will fall apart. By imagining potential problems, they may develop workable strategies for dealing with or preventing the problems. One study found that negative thinking spurred several constructive responses: evaluating negative possibilities, wondering what the future would hold, psyching up for future experiences so they would be positive, feeling good about being prepared to cope with the worst, and forming positive expectations (Showers, 1986).

Self-Efficacy Earlier, I indicated that perceived control is an important factor in stress. Closely linked with the concept of perceived control is **self-efficacy,** the belief that one can master a situation and produce positive outcomes. As you read in chapter 12, self-efficacy can be an effective strategy in coping with stress and challenging circumstances.

Albert Bandura (1997, 2000, 2001) and others have shown that people's self-efficacy affects their behavior in a variety of circumstances, ranging from solving personal problems to going on diets. Self-efficacy influences whether people even try to develop healthy habits, how much effort they expend in coping with stress, how long they persist in the face of obstacles, and how much stress they experience (Clark & Dodge, 1999; Maddux, 2001).

Researchers have also found that self-efficacy can improve individuals' ability to cope and be mentally healthy (Bandura, 2001). In one study, clients' self-efficacy was strongly linked to their motivation to go to psychotherapy sessions and overcome setbacks in the course of psychotherapy (Longo & others, 1992). In another study, researchers examined a number of cognitive therapy techniques to determine their effectiveness (Kavanaugh & Wilson, 1989). Perceived self-efficacy to control dejecting thoughts was the best predictor of successful cognitive therapy.

self-efficacy The belief that one can master a situation and produce positive outcomes.

Social Support

Our crowded, polluted, noisy, and achievement-oriented world can make us feel overwhelmed and isolated. Now more than ever, we may need support systems, such as family members, friends, and co-workers, to buffer stress (Mann, 2003; Muhonen & Turkelson, 2003). **Social support** is information and feedback from others that one is loved and cared for, esteemed and valued, and included in a network of communication and mutual obligation. To learn about the effects of a lack of social ties and support, see the video clip "Social Ostracism."

Social support has three types of benefits (Taylor, 2003):

- *Tangible assistance.* Family and friends can provide actual goods and services in stressful circumstances. For example, gifts of food are often given after a death in the family occurs, so that bereaved family members won't have to cook for themselves and visiting relatives.
- *Information.* Individuals who provide support can recommend specific actions and plans to help the person under stress cope more effectively. Friends may notice that a co-worker is overloaded with work and suggest ways to manage time more efficiently or delegate tasks more effectively.
- *Emotional support.* In stressful situations, individuals often suffer emotionally and may develop depression, anxiety, and loss of self-esteem. Friends and family can reassure the person under stress that he or she is a valuable individual who is loved by others. Knowing that others care allows a person to approach stress and cope with stress with greater assurance.

Researchers consistently have found that social support may help individuals cope with stress (Albrecht & Goldsmith, 2003; Apker & Ray, 2003; Taylor, 2001). For example, in one study, depressed persons had fewer, less supportive relationships with family members, friends, and co-workers than people who were not depressed (Billings, Cronkite, & Moos, 1983). In another study, the prognosticators of cancer, mental disorders, and suicide were linked with distance from one's parents and a negative attitude toward one's family (Thomas, 1983). Widows die younger at a rate that is 3 to 13 times higher than that of married women for every known cause of death.

Having diverse social ties may be especially important in coping with stress. People who participate in more diverse social networks—for example, having a close relationship with a partner; interacting with family members, friends, neighbors, and fellow workers; and belonging to social and religious groups—live longer than people with fewer types of social relationships (Berkman & Syme, 1979; Vogt & others, 1992). One study investigated the effects of diverse social ties on susceptibility to getting a common cold (Cohen & others, 1997). Individuals reported the extent of their participation in 12 types of social ties. Then they were given nasal drops containing a cold virus and monitored for the appearance of a cold. Individuals with more diverse social ties were less likely to get a cold than their counterparts with less diverse social networks (see figure 13.9).

Keep in mind that the studies of social support are correlational. What does that mean about interpreting their results?

Assertive Behavior

Another aspect of social relationships that can affect coping is how we deal with conflict in these relationships. Assertive expression has become a communication ideal. Following are some strategies for becoming more assertive (Bourne, 1995):

- *Set up a time for discussing what you want to discuss.* Talk with the other person to establish a mutually convenient time to talk. Omit this step when you need to be assertive on the spot.
- *State the problem in terms of its consequences for you.* Outline your point of view clearly to give the other person a better sense of your position. Describe the

social support Information and feedback from others that one is loved and cared for, esteemed and valued, and included in a network of communication and mutual obligation.

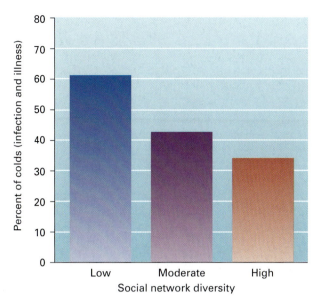

FIGURE 13.9 Diversity of Social Roles and the Common Cold In one study, the more social roles (diversity) involved in individuals' social networks, the less likely the individuals were to develop a cold after being infected by a cold virus. Note that low = one to three social roles; moderate = four to five social roles; and high = six or more social roles.

problem as objectively as you can without blaming or judging the other person. For example, you might tell a roommate or family member, "I'm having a problem with the loud music you are playing. I'm studying for a test tomorrow and the music is so loud I can't concentrate."

- *Express your feelings.* Go ahead and express your feelings openly—but noncombatively. You need to let the other person know how important the issue is to you. Suppressing your feelings prolongs the problem.
- *Make your request.* A key part of being assertive is asking for what you want in a straightforward, direct way.

Not everyone acts assertively. People deal with conflict in four main ways:

- *Acting aggressively.* People who respond aggressively to conflict run roughshod over others. They are demanding, abrasive, and hostile. Aggressive people are often insensitive to the rights of others.
- *Acting manipulatively.* Manipulative people try to get what they want by making other people feel sorry for them or feel guilty. They don't take responsibility for meeting their own needs. Instead, manipulative people play the role of the victim or martyr to get others to do things for them. They work indirectly to get their needs met.
- *Acting passively.* Passive people act in nonassertive, submissive ways. They let others run roughshod over them. Passive people don't express their feelings. They don't let others know what they want or need.
- *Acting assertively.* Assertive individuals express their feelings, ask for what they want, and say "no" to something they don't want. When individuals act assertively, they act in their own best interests and stand up for their legitimate rights. In the view of assertiveness experts Robert Alberti and Michael Emmons (1995), assertiveness builds equal relationships.

The Psychology and Life box gives you a chance to evaluate the styles that you use in various situations.

Dealing with Conflict

Think about the following situations one at a time. Check which response is most typical of the way you would behave in that situation.

	Assertive	Aggressive	Manipulative	Passive
You are being kept on the phone by a salesperson trying to sell you something you don't want.	_____	_____	_____	_____
You want to break off a relationship that is no longer working for you.	_____	_____	_____	_____
You are sitting in a movie and the people behind you are talking.	_____	_____	_____	_____
Your doctor keeps you waiting more than 20 minutes.	_____	_____	_____	_____
You are standing in line and someone cuts in front of you.	_____	_____	_____	_____
Your friend has owed you money for a long time, money that you could use.	_____	_____	_____	_____
You receive food at a restaurant that is over- or undercooked.	_____	_____	_____	_____
You want to ask a major favor of your friend, romantic partner, or roommate.	_____	_____	_____	_____
Your friends ask you to do something that you don't feel like doing.	_____	_____	_____	_____
You are in a large lecture hall. The instructor is speaking too softly and you know other students are having trouble hearing what is being said.	_____	_____	_____	_____
You want to start a conversation at a gathering, but you don't know anyone there.	_____	_____	_____	_____
You are sitting next to someone who is smoking, and the smoke bothers you.	_____	_____	_____	_____
You are talking to someone about something that is important to you, but the person doesn't seem to be listening.	_____	_____	_____	_____
You are speaking and someone interrupts you.	_____	_____	_____	_____
You receive an unjust criticism from someone.	_____	_____	_____	_____

In most circumstances, being assertive is the best strategy. However, a different style of interaction may be needed in some situations. Look at each situation again and determine if the assertive style is always the best strategy and in which circumstances the other styles might work best.

Religion

Might religion have an effect on a person's physical and mental health? Although people in some religious sects try to avoid using medical treatment or pain-relieving medications, individuals in the religious mainstream generally enjoy a positive link or neutral link between religion and physical health (Paloutzian, 2000). Researchers have found that religious commitment helps to moderate blood pressure and hypertension (Levin & Vanderpool, 1989). Also, a number of studies have confirmed that religious participation is related to a longer life (Gartner, Larson, & Allen, 1991; Hill & Pargament, 2003; McCullough & others, 2000).

How might religion promote physical health? Part of the answer may be simply that some religious organizations provide some health-related services. Another possible explanation is that religious individuals have healthier lifestyles (for example, they use fewer drugs).

In general, various dimensions of religion can also help some people cope more effectively with the stress in their lives (Butter & Pargament, 2003; Koenig & Cohen, 2002). Religious thoughts can play a role in maintaining hope and stimulating motivation for recovery (Nairn & Merluzzi, 2003). Although the evidence is not clear, it also has been argued that prayer might be associated with positive health-related

Religious interest is widespread around the world. Of the world's more than 6 billion people, approximately two-thirds either are involved in a religion or have been affected by religion in important ways. *(Center)* Worshipers at the Makka (Mecca) mosque in Saudi Arabia. *(Top left)* A Jewish rabbi reads prayer. *(Top right)* Temple of the Thousand Buddhas in Bangkok, Thailand. *(Bottom left)* Children at the San Fernando Catholic Christmas service in San Antonio, Texas. *(Bottom right)* A congregation singing at an American Protestant church. *How might religion be linked to physical and mental health?*

changes in the face of stress, such as decreased perception of pain and reduced muscle tension. A recent study found that some individuals with AIDS who lived much longer than expected had used religion as a coping strategy, participating in religious activities, such as praying and attending church services (Ironson & others, 2001).

Yet another explanation for the link between religion and good health is that religious organizations sponsor social connections; it is well documented that socially connected individuals have fewer health problems (Hill & Butter, 1995). The social connections promoted by religious activity can forestall anxiety and depression and can help to prevent isolation and loneliness (Koenig & Larson, 1998).

Meditation has been an important dimension of Asian life for centuries. *What are the health benefits of meditation?*

Stress Management Programs

Because many people have difficulty in managing stress themselves, psychologists have developed a variety of techniques that can be taught to individuals (Auerbach & Gramling, 1998; Penedo & others, 2004). **Stress management programs** teach individuals how to appraise stressful events, how to develop skills for coping with stress, and how to put these skills into use in their everyday lives. Some stress management programs are broad in scope, teaching a variety of techniques to handle stress; others teach a specific technique, such as relaxation or assertiveness training.

Do stress management programs work? In one recent study, men and women with hypertension (blood pressure greater than 140/90) were randomly assigned to one of three groups: One group received 10 hours of individual stress management training; a second group was placed in a wait-list group and eventually received the stress management training; and a third group (a control group) received no stress management training (Linden, Lenz, & Con, 2001). In the two groups that received the stress management training, blood pressure was significantly reduced. The control group experienced no reduction in blood pressure. Also, the reduced blood pressure in the first two groups was linked to a reported reduction in psychological stress and improved ability to cope with anger.

The following techniques are often used in stress management programs:

- **Meditation** is the practice and system of thought that incorporates exercises that help the individual to attain bodily and/or mental control and well-being, as well as enlightenment (Gillani & Smith, 2001; Tassi & Muzet, 2001). The strategies of meditation vary but usually take one of two forms: either cleansing the mind for new experiences or increasing concentration. Researchers have found that the practice of meditation activates neural structures involved in attention and control of the autonomic nervous system (Lazar & others, 2000). As a physiological state, meditation shows qualities of both sleep and wakefulness, yet it is distinct from either of them (Friedman, Myers, & Benson, 1998). Early research on meditation's effects on the body found that it lowers oxygen consumption, slows the heart rate, increases blood flow in the arms and forehead, and produces EEG patterns that are predominantly of the alpha variety—regular and rhythmic (Wallace & Benson, 1972). Some researchers have found support for the notion that meditation causes positive physiological changes and believe that meditation is superior to relaxation in reducing body arousal and anxiety (Eppley, Abrams, & Shear, 1989); other researchers acknowledge meditation's positive physiological effects but believe that relaxation is just as effective (Holmes, 1988). Audiotapes that induce relaxation are available in most bookstores. They usually include soothing background music along with instructions on how to meditate. These audiotapes can especially help you become more relaxed before you go to bed at night.
- **Biofeedback** is the process in which the body's activities are monitored by instruments and then the information from the instruments is given (fed back) to the individual to facilitate voluntary control of physiological activities. It is a form of operant conditioning. How does biofeedback work? Consider the problem of reducing an individual's muscle tension. A monitor tells the individual what the level of muscle tension is at that moment. Often the feedback is in the form of an audible tone (or in some cases, seeing a dot move up or down on a screen). As muscle tension rises, the tone becomes louder; as it drops, the tone becomes softer. The reinforcement in biofeedback is the raising and lowering of the tone as the individual learns to control muscle tension (Labbe, 1998). Researchers have found that biofeedback can help people reduce the intensity of migraine headaches and chronic pain (Qualls & Sheehan, 1981; Scharff, Marcus, & Masek, 2002). Whether biofeedback is more effective than less expensive, simpler methods of stress management has not been completely

stress management programs Programs that teach individuals to appraise stressful events, to develop skills for coping with stress, and to put these skills into use in their everyday lives.

meditation The practice and system of thought that incorporates exercises to attain bodily and/or mental control and well-being, as well as enlightenment.

biofeedback The process in which individuals' body activities are monitored by instruments and then the information from the instruments is fed back to the individuals, so that they can learn to voluntarily control their physiological activities.

resolved. But several large-scale studies have found no distinct advantage of biofeedback over meditation and relaxation techniques (Labbe, 1998). Indeed, relaxation is believed to be a key aspect of how biofeedback works.

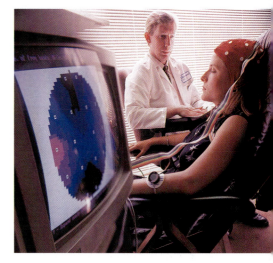

In biofeedback, instruments monitor physiological activities and give individuals information they can use to voluntarily control the activities. *Which learning theory explains the psychological mechanism at work in biofeedback?*

Review and Sharpen Your Thinking

5 **Outline strategies for coping with stress.**

- Evaluate problem-focused and emotion-focused coping.
- Understand the importance of optimism and positive thinking.
- Describe the role of social support in coping.
- Explain assertive behavior and its benefits.
- Discuss the link between religion and health.
- Summarize what stress management programs are like.

Think about a stressful circumstance that has occurred during the past year in your life. How effectively did you cope with it? Now that you have read about various coping strategies, do you think you would have been better off if you had used a different method? Explain.

HEALTHFUL LIVING **6**

Exercising Regularly

Quitting Smoking

Eating Healthily

Making Sound Sexual Decisions

What are some ways to promote your own health?

Effectively coping with stress is essential for physical and mental health. But we can do a great deal more to promote better health. Healthful living—establishing healthy habits and evaluating and changing behaviors that interfere with good health—helps avoid the damaging effects of stress (DiMatteo & Martin, 2002). Among the essential ingredients of a healthier lifestyle are regular exercise and good nutrition. Avoiding risks such as smoking and unwise sexual activity is also important.

Exercising Regularly

In 1961, President John F. Kennedy offered the following message: "We are underexercised as a nation. We look instead of play. We ride instead of walk. Our existence deprives us of the minimum of physical activity essential for healthy living." Without question, people are jogging, cycling, and taking exercise classes more today than in 1961, but we are getting far less exercise in our daily lives. Too many of us still ride instead of walk, take the elevator instead of climbing the stairs, and hire somebody else to do the little physical work that remains in our lives. Far too many of us spend most of our leisure time sitting in front of the TV or the computer screen.

One of the main reasons that health experts want us to exercise is that it helps to prevent heart disease (Billman, 2002; Williams, 2001). Although exercise designed to strengthen muscles and bones or to improve flexibility is important to fitness, many health experts stress aerobic exercise. **Aerobic exercise** is sustained activity—jogging,

aerobic exercise Sustained exercise that stimulates heart and lung activity.

FIGURE 13.10 **Moderate and Vigorous Physical Activities**

Moderate	Vigorous
Walking briskly (3–4 mph)	Walking briskly uphill or with a load
Cycling for pleasure or transportation (≤10 mph)	Cycling fast or racing (>10 mph)
Swimming, moderate effort	Swimming, fast treading crawl
Conditioning exercise, general calisthenics	Conditioning exercise, stair ergometer, ski machine
Racket sports, table tennis	Racket sports, singles tennis, racquetball
Golf, pulling cart or carrying clubs	Golf, practice at driving range
Canoeing leisurely (2.0–3.9 mph)	Canoeing rapidly (≥4 mph)
Home care, general cleaning	Moving furniture
Mowing lawn, power mower	Mowing lawn, hand mower
Home repair, painting	Fix-up projects

swimming, or cycling, for example—that stimulates heart and lung functioning. Extensive studies of 17,000 male alumni of Harvard University found that those who exercised strenuously on a regular basis had a lower risk for heart disease and were more likely to still be alive in their middle adulthood years than their more sedentary counterparts (Lee, Hsieh, & Paffenbarger, 1995; Paffenbarger & others, 1986).

People in some occupations get more vigorous exercise than those in others. (Howley, 2001). For example, longshoremen, who are on their feet all day and who lift, push, and carry heavy cargo, have about half the risk of fatal heart attacks as such co-workers as crane drivers and clerks, who have physically less demanding jobs.

Some health experts conclude that, regardless of other risk factors (smoking, high blood pressure, overweight, heredity), if you exercise enough to burn more than 2,000 calories a week, you can cut your risk for heart attack by an impressive two-thirds (Sherwood, Light, & Blumenthal, 1989). But burning up 2,000 calories a week through exercise requires a lot of effort, far more than most of us are willing to expend. To burn 300 calories a day through exercise, you would have to do one of the following: swim or run for about 25 minutes, walk for 45 minutes at about 4 miles an hour, or participate in aerobic dancing for 30 minutes.

As a more realistic goal, many health experts recommend that adults engage in 30 minutes or more of moderate physical activity on most, preferably all, days of the week. Most recommend that you should try to raise your heart rate to at least 60 percent of your maximum heart rate. Examples of the physical activities that qualify as moderate (and, for comparison, vigorous activities) are listed in figure 13.10. Only about one-fifth of adults are active at these recommended levels of physical activity.

Researchers have found that exercise benefits not only physical health but also mental health (Leith, 1998; Pennix & others, 2002; Phillips, Kiernan, & King, 2001). In particular, exercise improves self-concept and reduces anxiety and depression. In one study, 109 nonexercising volunteers were randomly assigned to one of four conditions: high-intensity aerobic training, moderate-intensity aerobic training, low-intensity nonaerobic training, and the waiting list (Moses & others, 1989). In the high-intensity aerobic group, participants engaged in a continuous walk-jog program that elevated their heart rate to between 70 and 75 percent of maximum. In the moderate-intensity aerobic group, participants engaged in walking or jogging that elevated their heart rate to 60 percent of maximum. In the low-intensity nonaerobic group, participants engaged in strength, mobility, and flexibility exercises in a slow, discontinuous manner for about 30 minutes. Those who were assigned to exercise programs worked out three to five times a week. Those who were on the waiting list did not exercise. The programs lasted for 10 weeks. As expected, the group assigned to the high-intensity aerobic program showed the greatest aerobic fitness on a 12-minute walk-run. Fitness also improved for those assigned to moderate- and low-exercise programs. However, only the people assigned to the moderate-intensity aerobic training program showed psychological benefits. These benefits appeared immediately in the form of reduced tension and anxiety and, after 3 months, in the form of improved ability to cope with stress.

Why were the psychological benefits superior in the moderate-intensity aerobic condition in this study? Perhaps the participants in the high-intensity program, who were nonexercisers prior to the study, found the training too demanding. The superiority of the moderate-intensity aerobic training program over the nonaerobic low-intensity exercise program suggests that a minimum level of aerobic conditioning may be required to obtain important psychological benefits.

Other research suggests that both moderate and intense activities may produce important physical and psychological gains (Thayer & others, 1996). Some people enjoy intense exercise; others enjoy moderate exercise. The enjoyment derived from exercise added to its aerobic benefits makes exercise one of life's most important activities. Go to the audio clip "Exercise and Mental Illness" to learn about the positive impact of exercise on efforts to overcome mental illness.

Following are some helpful strategies for building exercise into your life:

- *Reduce TV time.* Heavy TV viewing by college students is linked to their poor health (Astin, 1993). Replace some of your TV time with exercise time.
- *Chart your progress.* Systematically recording your exercise workouts will help you to chart your progress. This strategy is especially helpful in maintaining an exercise program over an extended period.
- *Get rid of excuses.* A typical excuse is "I just don't have enough time." You probably do have the time to make exercise a priority.
- *Imagine the alternative.* Ask yourself whether you are too busy to take care of your own health. What will your life be like if your lose your health?
- *Learn more about exercise.* The more you know about exercise, the more you are likely to start an exercise program and continue it.

Moderate or intense exercise benefits physical and mental health. *How might moderate exercise be more effective than intense exercise?*

In-Psych Plus

Eating Healthily

In chapter 9, I discussed many aspects of eating and weight. Obesity is a serious and pervasive health problem, with about one-third of the American population overweight enough to be at increased health risk. At the other extreme, pressure to be thin can lead

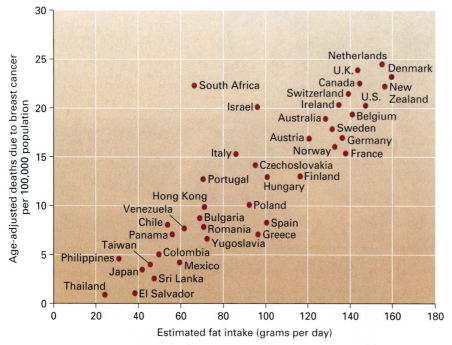

FIGURE 13.11 **Cross-Cultural Comparisons of Diet and Breast Cancer Rates** In countries in which individuals have a low daily intake of fat, the rate of breast cancer is low (in Thailand, for example). In countries in which individuals have a high daily intake of fat, the rate of breast cancer is high (the Netherlands, for example).

to harmful effects for people who are not overweight. Researchers have found that the most effective component of weight loss programs is regular exercise, not a distorted diet.

Despite the growing variety of choices Americans can make in the grocery store, many of us are unhealthy eaters. We take in too much sugar and not enough foods high in vitamins, minerals, and fiber, such as fruits, vegetables, and grains. We eat too much fast food and too few well-balanced meals, choices that increase our fat and cholesterol intake, both of which are implicated in long-term health problems (Fleshner & others, 2004).

Evidence for the negative effects of poor nutritional choices comes from both animal and cross-cultural research. For example, mice fed a high-fat diet are likelier to develop breast cancer than are mice fed on a low-fat diet. And a cross-cultural study of women found a strong positive correlation between fat consumption and death rates from breast cancer (see figure 13.11) (Cohen, 1987).

One of the most telling comparisons linking fat intake and cancer is between the United States and Japan. These countries have similar levels of industrialization and education, as well as similarly high medical standards. Although the overall cancer rates of the two countries are similar, cancers of the breast, colon, and prostate are common in the United States but rare in Japan, yet within two generations descendants of Japanese immigrants to Hawaii and California have developed breast cancer rates that are significantly higher than those in Japan and that approach those of other Americans. Many researchers believe that the high fat intake of Americans and the low fat intake of the Japanese are implicated in the different cancer rates.

American nutritional standards have changed over time, adding to our confusion about which foods we should eat. Only a few decades ago, eggs and dairy foods were promoted as ideal food sources. Now we are told that some dairy products, such as whole milk and butter, and eggs should generally be avoided.

Today, nutritionists believe that proper nutrition involves more than merely taking in an appropriate number of calories. It involves carefully selecting foods that provide appropriate nutrients along with their calories. A sound nutritional plan provides the right amounts of all the nutrients we need—fat, carbohydrates, proteins, vitamins, minerals, and water.

Several health goals can be accomplished through a sound nutritional plan. Not only does a well-balanced diet provide more energy, but it also can lower blood pressure and lessen our risk for cancer and even tooth decay (Harding & others, 2004).

Quitting Smoking

A decade after the U.S. surgeon general warned that cigarettes are responsible for major health problems, the tobacco industry was besieged with lawsuits—from consumers whose health was impaired and from states that have had to foot much of the bill for smoking-related illness. Such massive litigation prompted tobacco companies to begin negotiations with legal authorities to figure out a way to stem the tide of lawsuits and limit their liability for health-related damages.

Evidence from many studies underscores the dangers of smoking or being around smokers (Gorell & others, 2004; Millis, 1998). Smoking is linked to 30 percent of cancer deaths, 21 percent of heart disease deaths, and 82 percent of chronic pulmonary disease deaths. Secondhand smoke is implicated in as many as 9,000 lung cancer deaths a year. Children of smokers are at special risk for respiratory and middle-ear diseases.

Fewer people smoke today than in the past, and almost half of the living adults who ever smoked have quit. The prevalence of smoking in men has dropped from over 50 percent in 1965 to about 28 percent today (National Center for Health Statistics, 2000c). However, more than 50 million Americans still smoke cigarettes. And cigar smoking and tobacco chewing, which have risk levels similar to those of cigarette smoking, have increased.

Most smokers would like to quit, but their addiction to nicotine often makes quitting a challenge. Nicotine, the active drug in cigarettes, is a stimulant that increases the smoker's energy and alertness, a pleasurable and reinforcing experience (Payne & others, 1996; Seidman, Rosecan, & Role, 1999). Nicotine also stimulates neurotransmitters that have a calming or pain-reducing effect. And smoking works as a negative reinforcer by ending a smoker's painful craving for nicotine. A smoker gets relief from this aversive state simply by smoking another cigarette. The immediate gratification of smoking is hard to overcome, even for those who recognize that smoking is "suicide in slow motion."

The effort to quit is well worthwhile, however. Figure 13.12 shows that, when individuals quit smoking, over time their risk for fatal lung cancer declines.

Smokers can use five main methods to abandon their habit:

- *Using a substitute source of nicotine.* Nicotine gum, the nicotine patch, the nicotine inhaler, and nicotine spray all supply small amounts of nicotine to diminish the intensity of withdrawal (Eissenberg, Stitzer, & Henningfield, 1999). Nicotine gum, now available without a prescription, is a drug that smokers can take orally when they get the urge to smoke. The nicotine patch is a nonprescription adhesive pad that delivers a steady dose of nicotine to the individual. The dose is gradually reduced over an 8- to 12-week period. Success rates for nicotine substitutes have been encouraging. The percentage of study participants who are still not smoking after 5 months ranges from 18 percent for the nicotine patch to 30 percent for the nicotine spray (Centers for Disease Control and Prevention, 2001a).

- *Taking an antidepressant.* Bupropion SR, an antidepressant sold as Zyban, helps smokers control their cravings while they ease off nicotine. Zyban works at the neurotransmitter level in the brain by inhibiting the uptake of dopamine, serotonin, and norepinephrine. In recent research, smokers using Zyban to quit had a 30 percent average success rate after 5 months of taking the antidepressant (Centers for Disease Control and Prevention, 2001a; Gonzales & others, 2001). Some deaths have been reported as a consequence of Zyban, however, which has led to screening for the seizures that may occur in some individuals (Bhattacharjee & others, 2001).

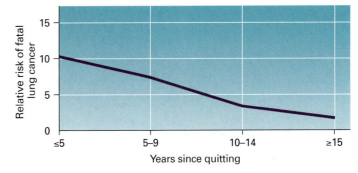

FIGURE 13.12 Fatal Lung Cancer and Years Since Quitting Smoking One study compared more than 43,000 male former smokers with almost 60,000 males who had never smoked (Enstrom, 1999). For comparison purposes, a zero level was assigned as the risk for fatal lung cancer for men who had never smoked. Over time, the relative risk for smokers who had quit declined, but even after 15 years it was still above that of nonsmokers.

- *Controlling stimuli associated with smoking.* This behavior modification technique sensitizes the smoker to social cues associated with smoking. For example, the individual might associate a morning cup of coffee or a social drink with smoking. Stimulus control strategies help the smoker to avoid these cues or learn to substitute other behaviors for smoking. This approach has met with mixed results.
- *Undergoing aversive conditioning.* Chapter 12 mentioned the behavior therapy technique of aversive conditioning, which involves repeated pairings of an undesirable behavior with aversive stimuli to decrease the behavior's rewards. Imagine smoking as many cigarettes as possible until the ashtray overflows, the smell of stale cigarettes seems permanently embedded in your fingertips, your throat is dry and scratchy, and you feel nauseated. The concept behind aversive conditioning is to make smoking so unpleasant that you won't want to smoke anymore. Sometimes this technique works; sometimes it doesn't.
- *Going cold turkey.* Some people succeed by simply stopping smoking without making any other major changes in their lifestyle. They decide they are going to quit and they do. Lighter smokers usually have more success with this approach than heavier smokers.

As you can see, no one method is foolproof for quitting smoking (Baker, Brandon, & Chassin, 2004). Often a combination of these methods is the best approach. And, often, truly quitting requires more than one try.

Making Sound Sexual Decisions

Chapter 9 discussed sexual motivations and sexual orientations. This section focuses on the importance of making healthy decisions in your sex life.

Sexual Knowledge How much do we really know about sex? According to June Reinisch (1990), director of the Kinsey Institute, the United States is a nation whose citizens know more about how their automobiles function than about how their bodies function sexually. Reinisch directed a national assessment of approximately 2,000 adults' sexual knowledge. Almost two-thirds did not know that most erection problems arise from physical, not psychological, causes. Fifty percent did not know that some oil-based lubricants can make holes in condoms or diaphragms in less than a minute.

One conclusion we can draw from Reinisch's national survey is that there is a great deal we do not know. But what might be even more problematic are the unfounded sexual myths that we believe. American adolescents especially encounter a distressing amount of misinformation about sex. There is a serious need to improve our sexual awareness and knowledge, which can help to reduce unwanted pregnancies and promote sexual self-awareness. For an assessment of your own sexual knowledge, see figure 13.13.

Contraception Most couples in the United States want to control whether and when they will conceive a child. For them, it is important to have accurate knowledge about contraception. But inadequate knowledge about contraception, coupled with inconsistent use of effective contraceptive methods, has given Americans the dubious distinction of having one of the highest adolescent pregnancy rates in the industrialized world (Alan Guttmacher Institute, 2000; Coleman, 1995; Wielandt, Bolden, & Knudsen, 2002). Adolescent pregnancy is linked with a host of problems for the mother, such as less future education and lower socioeconomic status, and for the offspring (Leadbeater & Way, 2001; Whitman & others, 2001).

Although the rate of contraceptive use among teenagers is improving, many still do not use contraception (Child Trends, 2000; Pearson, 2003). A majority of adolescents do not use contraception during their first sexual intercourse experience

Read each of the following statements and check whether you think it is true or false.

	True	False			True	False
1. There is a right way and a wrong way to have sexual intercourse.	☐	☐	7. You can tell immediately if you have a sexually transmitted disease.		☐	☐
2. It is important for couples to have simultaneous orgasms.	☐	☐	8. Gonorrhea, syphilis, and AIDS can be contracted from toilet seats.		☐	☐
3. Individuals should not have sexual intercourse at any time during pregnancy.	☐	☐	9. Masturbation can cause mental disorders.		☐	☐
4. Once individuals are sterilized, their interest in sex diminishes.	☐	☐	10. Females rarely masturbate.		☐	☐
5. You can tell the size of a man's penis by the size of his hands and feet.	☐	☐	11. Only homosexual males and intravenous drug abusers are at risk for contracting AIDS.		☐	☐
6. If you contract a sexually transmitted disease and treat it effectively, you can't get it again.	☐	☐	12. Most sexual dysfunctions are due to physical problems.		☐	☐

Most people mark one or more of the above items true. However, according to experts on human sexuality, all of the above statements are myths (Crooks & Bauer, 1999; Greenberg, Bruess, & Mullen, 1992). Although sexuality is an integral part of life, many people have misconceptions about it.

FIGURE 13.13 Sexual Myths and Realities

(Hofferth, 1990): Seventy percent of females who become sexually active before the age of 15, and about 50 percent of those who become active around the age of 18 or 19, have unprotected first intercourse.

Age also influences the choice of contraceptive method. Older adolescents and young adults are more likely to rely on the pill or diaphragm; younger adolescents are more likely to use a condom or withdrawal, both of which are less reliable than other methods (Hofferth, 1990). Even adults in stable relationships sometimes do not use adequate contraception, perhaps feeling that some contraceptives, such as condoms, interrupt the spontaneity of sex. Or they might overestimate the effectiveness of some of the more unreliable methods (Weisman & others, 2002).

No method of contraception is best for everyone (Hyde & DeLamater, 2003). When choosing a method of contraception, couples need to consider such factors as their physical and emotional concerns, the method's effectiveness, the nature of their relationship, their values and beliefs, and the method's convenience. Calculations of the effectiveness of a contraceptive method often are based on the failure rates during the first year of use. It is estimated that, if no contraceptive method were used, about 90 percent of women would become pregnant in their first year of being heterosexually active (Hatcher & others, 1988).

Sexually Transmitted Infections Sexually transmitted infections (STIs) are diseases that are contracted primarily through sex—intercourse as well as oral-genital and anal-genital sex. STIs affect about one of every six adults (National Center for Health Statistics, 2001b). The main STIs are often caused by bacterial infections, as in the case of gonorrhea and syphilis, or viruses, as in the case of genital herpes and HIV/AIDS.

No single STI has had a greater impact on sexual behavior, or created more fear, in the past couple of decades than AIDS. **Acquired immune deficiency syndrome (AIDS)** is caused by the *human immunodeficiency virus (HIV)*, a sexually transmitted virus that destroys the body's immune system. A person who has contracted HIV is thus vulnerable to germs that a normal immune system could destroy. Once an individual is infected with HIV, the prognosis is likely illness. New drug "cocktails" and a healthy lifestyle can keep HIV in check for a time, but most individuals will eventually develop AIDS and will probably die of it.

sexually transmitted infections (STIs) An infection contracted primarily through sex—intercourse as well as oral-genital and anal-genital sex.

acquired immune deficiency syndrome (AIDS) A sexually transmitted infection caused by the human immunodeficiency virus (HIV), which destroys the body's immune system.

Pat Hawkins is deputy director of the Whitman-Walker Clinic in Washington, DC, helping HIV and AIDS patients. She came to the clinic as a volunteer in 1983, just after HIV/AIDS exploded into an epidemic. Pat says that she would not do anything else but community work. "I knew I wanted to treat people clinically, but I wanted a broader impact," she says. "In private clinical work, you might see 1,000 people in a whole lifetime. I wanted to do more than that." Pat was a double major in psychology and sociology as an undergraduate and then went on to obtain her Ph.D. in community psychology.

Of the U.S. AIDS cases reported through the end of 2002, 48 percent were the result of male-to-male sexual contact, 27 percent due to injection drug use, and 15 percent a consequence of heterosexual contact (Centers for Disease Control and Prevention, 2003). Of the new U.S. HIV cases in 2000, 70 percent were male, 30 percent were female; 42 percent were the result of men having sex with men, 33 percent through heterosexual sex, and 25 percent through injection drug use. More than half of the new U.S. HIV infections in 2000 occurred among African Americans, just over one-fourth were among non-Latino Whites, and almost one-fifth were among Latinos. A concern is that HIV infections rose more than 7 percent from 2001 to 2002 and 18 percent from 1999 to 2002 in gay men after declining earlier in the 1990s (Centers for Disease Control and Prevention, 2003).

Because of education and the development of more effective drug treatments, deaths due to AIDS have begun to decline in the United States (National Center for Health Statistics, 2001b). However, the power of AIDS drugs to prolong life has increased the number of people in the United States who are living with HIV/AIDS to nearly 1 million (Fleming, 2002).

Still, the incidence of HIV/AIDS is relatively low in the United States. The disease has reached epidemic proportions in sub-Saharan Africa (World Health Organization, 2000). Adolescent girls in these countries, who are often sexually exploited by adult men, are the population most vulnerable to HIV/AIDS. In Kenya, 25 percent of 15- to 19-year-old girls are HIV-positive, compared with only 4 percent of the boys in this age group. AIDS has become the leading cause of death in adolescents and young adults in sub-Saharan Africa (Centers for Disease Control and Prevention, 2001b).

Remember that it is not who you are but what you do that puts you at risk for HIV. Experts say that HIV/AIDS can be transmitted only by (Kalichman, 1996)

- Sexual contact
- Other direct contact of cuts or mucous membranes with blood and sexual fluids
- Sharing of hypodermic needles
- Blood transfusions (which in the past few years have been tightly monitored)

Anyone who is sexually active or uses intravenous drugs is at risk. *No one* is immune. The only safe sexual behavior is abstinence, which is not perceived as an option by most individuals. Beyond abstinence, there is only safer behavior, such as sexual behavior without exchange of semen, vaginal fluids, or blood and sexual intercourse with a condom (Perloff, 2001).

Just asking a date about his or her previous sexual behavior does not guarantee protection from HIV and other sexually transmitted infections. In one investigation, 655 college students were asked to answer questions about lying and sexual behavior (Cochran & Mays, 1990). Of the 422 respondents who said they were sexually active, 34 percent of the men and 10 percent of the women said they had lied so their partner would have sex with them. Much higher percentages—47 percent of the men and 60 percent of the women—said they had been lied to by a potential sexual partner. When asked what aspects of their pasts they would be most likely to lie about, more than 40 percent of the men and women said they would understate the number of their sexual partners, and 20 percent of the men, but only 4 percent of the women, said they would lie about their results from an HIV blood test.

A 5-year study in Dallas, Denver, Long Beach, New York, and Seattle evaluated the influence of a community-level HIV prevention/intervention (CDC AIDS Community Demonstration Projects Research Group, 1999). The goal of the prevention/intervention was to promote consistent condom use among injection drug users, female sex partners of injection drug users, female commercial sex workers, at-risk youth, and nongay-identified men who have sex with men. The prevention/intervention had three key components: (1) *peer volunteer networks:* Community members distributed and promoted intervention materials with their peers; (2) *role model stories:* Media materials featured prevention/intervention messages drawn from real-life experiences of community members; and (3) *environmental facilitation:* Condoms were made readily available to community members. Based on approximately 15,000 interviews, more than 50 percent of the target population had received role model stories. Individuals in the prevention/intervention communities reported more consistent condom use and were more likely to carry condoms with them than were individuals in communities that did not receive the prevention/intervention.

What are some good strategies for protecting against HIV and other sexually transmitted diseases?

- *Know your risk status and your partner's.* Anyone who has had previous sexual activity with another person might have contracted an STI without being aware of it. Spend time getting to know a prospective partner before you have sex. Use this time to inform the other person of your STI status and inquire about your partner's. Remember that many people lie about their STI status.
- *Obtain medical examinations.* Many experts recommend that couples who want to begin a sexual relationship have a medical checkup to rule out STIs before they engage in sex. If cost is an issue, contact your campus health service or a public health clinic.
- *Have protected, not unprotected, sex.* When correctly used, latex condoms help to prevent many STIs from being transmitted. Condoms are most effective in preventing infection with gonorrhea, syphilis, chlamydia, and HIV. They are less effective against the spread of herpes.
- *Don't have sex with multiple partners.* One of the best predictors of getting STIs is having sex with multiple partners. Having more than one sex partner increases the likelihood that you will encounter one who is infected.

Review and Sharpen Your Thinking

6 **Summarize how to promote your health.**
- Explain why exercise is important to good health.
- Evaluate the role of nutrition in health.
- Describe why quitting smoking is important and how it might be accomplished.
- Discuss sound sexual decision making.

How good are you at maintaining a regular exercise program, eating nutritiously and healthily, not smoking, and engaging in sound sexual decision making? Has your lifestyle and behavior in these areas affected your health? Might they affect your health in the future? Explain.

Health and Well-Being

1 HEALTH PSYCHOLOGY AND BEHAVIORAL MEDICINE

2 STRESS AND ITS SOURCES

Personality Factors

Environmental Factors

Sociocultural Factors

3 STRESS RESPONSES

General Adaptation Syndrome

Fight or Flight, Tend and Befriend

Cognitive Appraisal

4 STRESS AND ILLNESS

Diseases Related to Stress

Positive Emotions, Illness, and Health

5 COPING STRATEGIES

Problem-Focused and Emotion-Focused Coping

Social Support

Religion

Optimism and Positive Thinking

Assertive Behavior

Stress Management Programs

6 HEALTHFUL LIVING

Exercising Regularly

Quitting Smoking

Eating Healthily

Making Sound Sexual Decisions

1 Describe the scope of health psychology and behavioral medicine.

- Health psychology is a multidimensional approach to health that emphasizes psychological factors, lifestyle, and the nature of the health care delivery system. Closely aligned with health psychology is behavioral medicine, which combines medical and behavioral knowledge to reduce illness and promote health. Both acknowledge that psychological and social factors are often involved in chronic diseases. A special interest is the link between stress and illness.

2 Define stress and identify its sources.

- Stress is the response of individuals to the circumstances and events, called stressors, that threaten them and tax their coping abilities. Personality factors involved in stress include the Type A/Type B behavior patterns, hardiness, and personal control. The Type A behavior pattern is a cluster of personality characteristics—such as being hostile, excessively competitive, impatient, and hard-driven—that seem to be related to cardiovascular disease. The dimension of the Type A cluster most consistently related to heart disease is hostility. The Type B behavior pattern includes being relaxed and easygoing. Hardiness—which involves a sense of commitment, a sense of control, and a perception of problems as challenges rather than threats—is a stress buffer and is related to reduced illness. Another important aspect of stress is the extent to which people can control or reduce the stress, as well as a related personality characteristic: their perception of control. Across a wide range of studies, a sense of personal control over stressful events has been related to emotional well-being, successful coping with stressful events, and behavior changes that can promote good health.
- Environmental factors involved in stress include life events, daily hassles, conflict, overload, and work-related stress. People who experience clusters of life events tend to become ill; daily hassles, ongoing daily annoyances, can also produce health-sapping stress. Everyday conflicts can be stressful. The three types of conflict are approach/approach (least stressful), avoidance/avoidance, and approach/avoidance. Daily hassles can result in overload, which can lead to burnout. The stress level of workers increases when their jobs do not meet their expectations, when job demands are high, and when workers have little choice in deciding how to meet the demands.
- Sociocultural sources of stress include acculturation and poverty. Acculturative stress is the negative consequences that result from contact between two distinctive cultural groups. People can adapt to cultural change in one of four ways: assimilation, integration, separation, and marginalization. The least stressful is integration. Poverty can cause considerable stress for individuals and families and is related to threatening and uncontrollable life events.

3 Explain how people respond to stress.

- Selye proposed the general adaptation syndrome as a model of how the body responds to stress. It consists of three stages: alarm, resistance, and exhaustion. Many scientists now agree that two main biological pathways can be involved in the stress response: the neuroendocrine-immune pathway and the sympathetic nervous system pathway.
- The immediate reaction to stress may be a fight-or-flight response. The central notion of this concept is that the body's physiological resources are mobilized to prepare the organism to deal with threats to survival. However, females are less likely to respond to a threatening situation with a fight-or-flight response than males are. Rather, females responding to threatening circumstances are more likely to tend (protect themselves and their young through nurturing behaviors) and befriend (form alliances with a larger social group, especially one populated by women).
- Lazarus believes that how people respond to stress depends on the way in which they cognitively appraise events. Cognitive appraisal consists of first deciding whether the stressful event is harmful, threatening, or challenging and then deciding what resources are available to cope with the stressful event.

4 Discuss the links between stress and illness.

- Researchers have found that acute stressors can produce immunological changes in healthy individuals. Chronic stressors are also associated with a downturn in immune system functioning. Emotional stress likely is an important factor contributing to cardiovascular disease as well. People who live in a chronically stressed condition are more likely to smoke, overeat, and not exercise. All of these stress-related behaviors are linked with cardiovascular disease. The link between stress and another disease, cancer, can best be understood by considering connections between stress and quality of life, behavioral factors, and biological activities.
- The recent interest in positive psychology has sparked research on the role that positive emotions might play in reducing illness and promoting health. In general, positive emotional states are thought to be associated with healthy patterns of physiological functioning in both the cardiovascular and the immune systems.

5 *Outline strategies for coping with stress.*

- Lazarus distinguished between problem-focused coping, which involves squarely facing stressors and trying to solve them, and emotion-focused coping, which consists of responding to stress in an emotional manner and usually takes the form of defensive appraisal. Problem-focused coping is usually the better coping strategy.
- Many cognitive therapists believe cognitive restructuring, including positive self-talk, can be used to get people to think more positively and optimistically. Positive self-talk is often helpful in cognitive restructuring. Individuals' ability to cope often benefits from mildly positive self-illusion, although some people cope best by facing reality. Grandiose self-illusion and negative self-illusion are generally not good coping strategies, although some people successfully use a strategy of defensive pessimism to prepare for stressful situations. Bandura has shown that self-efficacy, the belief that one can master a situation and produce positive outcomes, is an effective strategy in many domains of coping.
- Social support consists of information and feedback from others that one is loved and cared for, esteemed and valued, and included in a network of communication and mutual obligation. Three important benefits are tangible assistance, practical information, and emotional support. Researchers consistently find that social support, especially diverse social ties, helps people to cope with stress and to live healthier lives.
- People can deal with conflict aggressively, manipulatively, passively, or assertively. Assertive behavior, which is the clear expression of the individual's own needs without resort to intimidation or manipulation, has become the communication ideal.
- A positive link, or no link, has been found between religion and physical health. Various dimensions of religion can help people cope with stress in their lives, though.
- Stress management programs teach people how to appraise stressful events, develop skills for coping with stress, and put these skills into use in their everyday lives. Meditation, relaxation, and biofeedback are used in stress management. Meditation is a system of thought that incorporates exercises to attain bodily or mental control and well-being, as well as enlightenment. Researchers have found that meditation reduces body arousal and anxiety. Some researchers believe relaxation techniques may be just as effective. Biofeedback is the process in which individuals' body activities are monitored by instruments and the information from the instruments is fed back to the individuals so that they can learn to control the activities voluntarily. Biofeedback has been successful in reducing muscle tension and blood pressure.

6 *Summarize how to promote your health.*

- Both moderate and intense exercise produce important physical and/or psychological gains, such as lowered risk for heart disease and reduced anxiety.
- Too many people are unhealthy eaters, taking in too much sugar and fat and not eating balanced meals. Healthy food selections can lower blood pressure and risk for cancer and tooth decay.
- Smoking is linked to 30 percent of cancer deaths, 21 percent of heart disease deaths, and 82 percent of chronic pulmonary disease deaths. Secondhand smoke is implicated in as many as 9,000 lung cancer deaths a year. Strategies for quitting smoking include nicotine substitutes, Zyban (an antidepressant), stimulus control, aversive conditioning, and going cold turkey. Combining strategies may have the best results; quitting may require multiple tries.
- Inadequate knowledge about sex, especially contraception, and inconsistent use of effective contraceptive methods have resulted in the United States having one of the highest adolescent pregnancy rates in the industrialized world. Thus becoming knowledgeable about sex and planning contraception before having sex are both aspects of sound sexual decision making. Sexually transmitted infections (STIs) are contracted primarily through sex—intercourse as well as oral-genital and anal-genital sex. The most devastating STI is HIV/AIDS. Some good strategies for protecting against STIs are (1) know your risk status and your partner's, (2) obtain medical examinations, (3) have protected, not unprotected, sex, and (4) do not have sex with multiple partners.

Key Terms

health psychology, p. 467
behavioral medicine, p. 467
stress, p. 468
Type A behavior pattern, p. 468
Type B behavior pattern, p. 468
hardiness, p. 468
approach/approach conflict, p. 472

avoidance/avoidance conflict, p. 472
approach/avoidance conflict, p. 472
burnout, p. 472
acculturative stress, p. 473
general adaptation syndrome (GAS), p. 476
cognitive appraisal, p. 478
coping, p. 483

problem-focused coping, p. 483
emotion-focused coping, p. 483
self-efficacy, p. 485
social support, p. 486
stress management programs, p. 490
meditation, p. 490
biofeedback, p. 490

aerobic exercise, p. 491
sexually transmitted infections (STIs), p. 497
acquired immune deficiency syndrome (AIDS), p. 497

Apply Your Knowledge

1. The chapter describes personality, environment, and socio-cultural influences as three factors contributing to stress. What are the advantages and disadvantages of categorizing factors in this manner and considering them separately? Can you think of examples of stressors in which these factors clearly interact? Or in which these factors don't seem to play a role?

2. The chapter describes physiological stress responses in terms of the damage they cause to our health. If stress responses are so damaging, why do we have them? What purpose might physiological stress responses serve? Why might people (for example, men and women) differ in their physiological stress responses?

3. The links between stress and illness are currently based primarily on correlational studies. For one of the specific examples described in the chapter, explain how you would test for a causal link between stress and illness.

4. Do an Internet search on the topic of "stress management" or "coping with stress." Visit three or four sites and critically evaluate the suggestions made on the sites. How are they similar to the suggestions given in the chapter? How much information is available to evaluate any claims on the sites? Based on your critical evaluation, would you follow the suggestions or not?

5. One method that has helped to decrease unhealthy behaviors, such as smoking, is to make them more expensive. Currently, some people are calling for a tax on unhealthy foods. Would such a tax be useful? Why? Would you be in favor of such a tax or opposed to it? Why?

Connections

To test your mastery of the material in this chapter, go to the Study Guide and the In-Psych Plus CD-ROM, as well as the Online Learning Center. There you will find a chapter summary, practice tests, flashcards, lecture slides, web links, and other study tools, such as interactive exercises and reviews as well as current, chapter-relevant news articles.

14 Social Psychology

Chapter Outline

Learning Goals

SOCIAL THINKING

Attribution
▼
Social Perception
▼
Attitudes

1 Describe how people think about the social world.

SOCIAL INFLUENCE

Conformity
▼
Obedience
▼
Group Interactions
▼
Leadership

2 Identify how people are influenced in social settings.

INTERGROUP RELATIONS

Group Identity
▼
Prejudice
▼
Ways to Improve Interethnic Relations

3 Discuss intergroup relations.

SOCIAL INTERACTION

Aggression
▼
Altruism

4 Explain the roles of aggression and altruism in social interaction.

RELATIONSHIPS

Attraction
▼
Love
▼
Relationships and Gender

5 Understand the nature of relationships.

The news from Vietnam during the 1960s was troubling enough. But then in 1968 came the My Lai massacre, in which 500 women, children, babies, and old men were slaughtered by out-of-control U.S. ground troops. However, there was a ray of light in the My Lai story.

Helicopter pilot Hugh Thompson was one of the Americans who had been given orders to join a search-and-destroy mission in the area of My Lai, which was suspected to be under the control of the enemy Viet Cong and local sympathizers. The target area consisted of six different communities with a population of 10,000 people, mostly civilians. Most of the Americans who participated in the mission interpreted the orders as, quite literally, a license to kill indiscriminately.

Instead of following the search-and-destroy orders, though, Thompson and his crew set their helicopter down in the midst of the massacre and risked their lives to save nine unarmed Vietnamese civilians from certain death. Thompson also got on the airwaves, loudly protesting the massacre to other American pilots and officers. His efforts brought about a cease-fire that stopped the massacre before it worsened.

Had it not been for Thompson's resisting the impulse to conform with the commands of officers and the actions of other soldiers, many more Vietnamese civilians would have been killed. During the My Lai massacre trials that followed, despite pressure from fellow soldiers to be quiet, Thompson was a key witness for the prosecution (Angers, 1999).

Think about the times in your life when you have faced the pressure to conform to what peers or authority figures wanted

Hugh Thompson was a helicopter pilot during the Vietnam War when he defied the pressure to conform and thus saved many lives.

you to do. Did you go along to avoid conflict? Or did you have the courage of Hugh Thompson and resist their pressure? Was it easy? Probably not. What makes it so hard for human beings to follow their consciences? Later in the chapter, the factors that are related to the pressure to conform are examined.

But, more generally, this chapter is about **social psychology**—the study of how people think about, influence, and relate to other people. Social psychology differs from sociology in that social psychology focuses more on the individual as a social being, whereas sociology places more emphasis on society at large.

1 SOCIAL THINKING

Attribution	Social Perception	Attitudes

How do people think about the social world?

Among the many aspects of social life that engage psychologists, one of the most intriguing is how people think about the social world. This area of social psychology, which is often referred to as *social cognition*, involves how people select, interpret, remember, and use social information. Each person may have a unique combination of expectations, memories, and attitudes based on his or her social history. Nevertheless, certain common principles apply to the way people process information in a social situation (Bordens & Horowitz, 2002; Forgas, 2001; Higgins & Molden, 2004; Moskowitz, 2001; Wyer, 2004). The most important of these principles focus on the way people attribute causes to behavior, the way people perceive others and themselves, and the link between attitudes and behavior.

social psychology The study of how people think about, influence, and relate to other people.

Attribution

Human beings are curious, seeking answers to all sorts of questions about their social world. We might be curious about why someone is yelling at another person, why someone is in love with a particular person, or why someone joined a certain organization. Finding causal explanations for these and many other human actions is a complex task. We can observe people's behavior and listen to what they say, but to determine the underlying cause of their behavior, we often have to make inferences from these observations.

Our desire to find causal explanations is a bit of a puzzle. Why is it so important to us? Attribution theorists argue that we want to know why people do the things they do because the knowledge will enable us to cope more effectively with the situations that confront us (Alderman, 1999). Recall from chapter 9 that attribution theory views people as motivated to discover the underlying causes of behavior as part of their effort to make sense of the behavior. **Attributions** are ideas about why people behave the way they do.

Dimensions of Causality   The attributions people make vary along three dimensions (Jones, 1998):

- *Internal/external causes.* Chapter 9 explained that an important attribution people make is whether achievement is due to external causes or internal causes. *Internal attributions* include all causes internal to the person, such as personality traits, intelligence, attitudes, and health. *External attributions* include all causes external to the person, such as social pressure, aspects of the social situation, money, the weather, and luck. Fritz Heider (1958) argued that this internal/external dimension is the central issue in attribution. Consider the attributions we might make in this situation: Jason and Ashley have been dating for several months when Ashley breaks off the relationship. When we speculate about the reasons, we might observe that Ashley says she is ending the relationship because of pressure from her parents, who want her to focus on her studies (external attribution). But, we might wonder, is that the true reason she is breaking off the relationship? Possibly the vivacious Ashley is dumping Jason because she has grown tired of his introverted personality (internal attribution).
- *Stable/unstable causes.* Whether we perceive the cause to be relatively enduring and permanent or to be temporary is also involved in making attributions. If Ashley has concluded that Jason's introverted personality is not going to change, she perceives the cause of his behavior to be stable. Alternatively, if Ashley believes that Jason is quiet lately because of some personal troubles but is capable of being more outgoing, she perceives an unstable cause. These are both internal causes. If Ashley's parents never like anybody she dates, that is an external stable cause. If they don't like Jason but will approve of someone else Ashley dates, that is an external unstable cause.
- *Controllable/uncontrollable causes.* Whether a cause is perceived as controllable or uncontrollable is another dimension of causality (Weiner, 1986). This dimension can coexist with any combination of internal/external and stable/unstable dimensions. An internal unstable cause, such as effort or mood, is usually thought of as something we can control; an external unstable cause, such as luck, is generally considered beyond our control.

Bernard Weiner (1986) argues that the various types of attributions have different emotional and motivational implications. When we believe that we have succeeded because of our internal characteristics, our self-esteem is higher than it is when we believe that our success is due to external causes, such as the ease of a task or luck. Weiner believes that the attributions we make regarding controllability are of particular importance because personal responsibility is involved. Attributing to ourselves the ability to control the causes of personal failure opens us to such emotions as guilt,

attributions Ideas about why people behave the way they do.

FIGURE 14.1 Fundamental Attribution Error An observer and an actor are likely to differ in their explanations of the actor's behavior.

Actor

Tends to give external, situational explanations of own behavior

"I'm late with my report because other people keep asking me to help them with their projects."

Observer

Tends to give internal, trait explanations of actor's behavior

"He's late with his report because he can't concentrate on his own responsibilities."

shame, and humiliation. In contrast, perceiving the causes of personal failure to be uncontrollable does not lead to self-criticism. We also might hold others responsible for failures attributed to controllable causes and might even feel angry toward them. Or we might feel sympathy toward people whose failures are the result of circumstances beyond their control. For example, if a vase is accidentally knocked off a table and broken, we would feel more forgiving of a child than of a drunken adult.

Fundamental Attribution Error So far, what I have said about attribution suggests that it is a logical, rational process. However, some common errors and biases infiltrate our attributions. One of them, the fundamental attribution error, is a key to understanding how people assign causes to their own behavior and the behavior they observe. Actors, those whose actions we are observing, often explain their own behavior in terms of external causes. In contrast, observers frequently explain an actor's behavior in terms of internal causes. Thus the **fundamental attribution error** is to overestimate the importance of internal traits and underestimate the importance of external situations when seeking explanations of an actor's behavior (see figure 14.1). To learn more about the tendency to make internal attributions, go to the video clip "Fundamental Attribution Error."

In-Psych Plus

The fundamental attribution error suggests that, when we try to explain why people do repugnant or bizarre things, we tend to describe them as flawed human beings (Aronson, Wilson, & Akert, 1997). For example, in 1997, 38 people in the Heaven's Gate cult took their own lives in response to the appearance of the Hale-Bopp comet. Their leader, Marshall Herff Applewhite, is known to have believed that this mass suicide would guarantee his followers a type of immortality, taking them to the "level above human." Delusion on such a scale is hard to fathom, and it was easy to conclude that all involved were "kooks." But Applewhite was highly charismatic and exerted enormous pressure on his acolytes to go along. The public's emphasis on the traits of the actors, without considering how they may have been overpowered by the social forces of the situation, reflects the fundamental attribution error.

Self-Serving Bias Behavior is determined by a number of factors, so it is not surprising that its causes are often hard to determine (Harvey, 1995). In addition, as you have just learned, actors and observers have different ideas about what causes behavior. What accounts for these differences in attributions is often *bias* (Krull, 2001). Our personal attitudes and experiences shape our perceptions of causes.

When explaining our own actions, our bias is usually self-serving. That is, we tend to be self-enhancing in the way that we attribute the causes of our behavior, and we often exaggerate positive beliefs about ourselves (Pittman, 1998; Sedikides & others, 1998). We often believe that we are more trustworthy, moral, and physically

fundamental attribution error
The tendency to overestimate the importance of traits and underestimate the importance of situations when seeking explanations of someone else's behavior.

attractive than other people are. We tend to believe that we are above-average students, parents, and leaders. Go to the interactivity "Self-Enhancing Bias" to learn more about the self-serving bias.

Self-serving bias especially emerges when our self-esteem is threatened. We may attribute our successes to internal factors and our failures to external factors: That is, we tend to take credit for our successes and blame our failures on others or on the situation. In the case of Ashley's breaking up with Jason, Jason might find it a lot easier to accept Ashley's external attribution—that she is doing it because of her parents—than the internal attribution—that he is too introverted. Jason's bias helps to protect him from harsh self-criticism.

Social Perception

When we think about our social world and try to make sense of it, we create social perceptions: We develop impressions of other people, gain self-knowledge by comparing ourselves with others, and present ourselves in such a way as to influence the way others perceive us.

Developing Impressions of Others   As we move through the world, we develop shortcuts for evaluating which people to seek out and which to avoid. Often we use broad, polar dimensions to categorize them—good or bad, happy or sad, introvert or extravert, for example. From these broad descriptions, others can infer whether we have positive or negative impressions of people.

Our first encounter with someone contributes to the impression we form. *Primacy effect* is the term used to describe the enduring quality of initial impressions. One reason for the primacy effect is that we pay more attention to what we first learn about a person and less attention to subsequent information (Anderson, 1965). The next time you want to impress someone, a wise strategy is to make sure that you put your best foot forward in your first encounter.

As we form impressions of others, we cognitively organize the information in two important ways:

FIGURE 14.2 **Three Dimensions We Use to Categorize People**   You are likely to categorize the people you meet as good or bad and possibly as strong or weak, active or passive. These impressions are quite durable but may change with further interaction.

- *We unify our impressions.* Traits, actions, appearance, and all of the other information we have obtained about a person are closely connected in memory, even though the information may have been obtained in an interrupted or random fashion (Brown, 1986).
- *We integrate our impressions.* We reach beyond the spotty information we may have about a person—adding to, manipulating, and modifying it—to form a whole impression (Asch, 1946).

When we integrate information about people, we follow certain rules. **Implicit personality theory** is the term given to the public's or a layperson's conception of which personality traits go together (Bruner & Tagiuri, 1954). One person might have an implicit personality theory that all extraverted people are optimistic. The integration of these traits might be based on a thought process similar to this: "Because most of my friends who are extraverted also are optimistic, I assume all extraverted people are optimistic."

Recall from the discussion in chapter 7 that a *schema* is a conceptual framework that we use to organize information. We don't notice everything about what people are like and what they do, but we get the gist of their personality and behavior, and we fit the information about them into existing categories of memory.

We appear to use some evaluative dimensions more than others to categorize people. Norman Anderson (1974, 1989) thinks the most common dimension is *good/bad*. Think for a moment about the people you know. Chances are, you categorize each of them as either good or bad. Potency (*strong/weak*) and activity (*active/passive*) are two other dimensions we often use to categorize people (see figure 14.2).

implicit personality theory The layperson's conception of which personality traits go together in an individual.

"Randall, my old college nemesis, I was hoping I'd find you here." Copyright © 1996, *USA Today.* Reprinted with permission.

We also tend to simplify the task of understanding people by classifying them as members of groups or categories with which we are familiar. It takes more mental effort to consider a person's individual characteristics than it does to label her as a member of a particular group or category. Thus, when we categorize an individual, the categorization is often based on stereotypes. Imagine that you meet a sales representative. You develop an impression of him based on the "sales representative" schema in your mind. Without seeking any additional information, you might perceive that person as pushy, self-serving, and materialistic.

We do not always respond to others on the basis of categories, however. As you interact with the sales representative, you might discover that he is actually interesting, modest, bright, and altruistic. You would then have to revise your impression and perceive him differently. When we discover information that is inconsistent with a category, or when we simply become more personally involved with someone, we tend to take an individual approach rather than a category-based approach to impression formation. Go to the interactivity "Impression Formation" to participate in a simulated online chat room and explore the development of impressions of others.

Comparing Ourselves with Others How many times have you asked yourself questions such as "Am I as smart as Jill?" "Is Bob better looking than I am?" or "Is my taste as good as Carmen's?" We gain self-knowledge from our own behavior, of course, but we also gain it from others through *social comparison*, the process by which individuals evaluate their thoughts, feelings, behaviors, and abilities in relation to other people. Social comparison helps individuals to evaluate themselves, tells them what their distinctive characteristics are, and aids them in building an identity.

Some years ago, social psychologist Leon Festinger (1954) proposed a theory of social comparison. He stressed that, when no objective means is available to evaluate our opinions and abilities, we compare ourselves with others. Festinger believed that we are more likely to compare ourselves with others who are similar to us than those who are dissimilar to us. We will develop more accurate self-perceptions if we compare ourselves, for example, with people in communities similar to where we live, with people who have similar family backgrounds, and with people of the same sex or sexual orientation. Social comparison theory has been extended and modified over the years and continues to provide an important rationale for why we affiliate with others and how we come to know ourselves (Michinov & Michinov, 2001).

Festinger studied social comparison with those who are similar to us; other researchers have focused on social comparison with those whom we consider to be inferior to us. Individuals under threat (from negative feedback, low self-esteem, depression, and illness, for example) try to improve their mental well-being by comparing themselves with others who are less fortunate (Gibbons & McCoy, 1991). It can be comforting to tell ourselves, "Well, at least I'm not as bad off as that guy."

Presenting Ourselves to Others At the same time that we are forming impressions of others, others are forming impressions of us. In most cases, of course, we want others to think the best of us. We spend years and small fortunes rearranging our faces, bodies, minds, and social skills. **Impression management (self-presentation)** involves acting in a way that will present a desired image to others, which might or might not be who we really are. We use impression management especially with people we are not familiar with and with people who interest us sexually (Leary & others, 1994).

Nonverbal cues are a key element of successful impression management. Certain facial expressions, patterns of eye contact, and body postures or movements are part of the reason we are liked or disliked. Three other techniques of impression management are conforming to situational norms (for example, adopting the same form of dress and type of language and etiquette as other people), showing appreciation of others, and behavioral matching (engaging in behavior that the other person displays, such as clasping one's hands together when the other person does).

impression management (self-presentation) Acting in a way that will present a desired image of oneself as a certain type of person, which might or might not be who one really is.

These statements concern personal reactions to a number of situations. No two statements are exactly alike, so consider each statement carefully before answering. If a statement is true or mostly true as applied to you, check True. If a statement is false or not usually true as applied to you, check False.

	True	False		True	False
1. I find it hard to imitate the behavior of other people.	☐	☐	6. In different situations and with different people, I often act like very different persons.	☐	☐
2. I guess I put on a show to impress or entertain people.	☐	☐	7. I can only argue for ideas I already believe.	☐	☐
3. I would probably make a good actor.	☐	☐	8. In order to get along and be liked, I tend to be what people expect me to be.	☐	☐
4. I sometimes appear to others to be experiencing deeper emotions than I actually am.	☐	☐	9. I may deceive people by being friendly when I really dislike them.	☐	☐
5. In a group of people, I am rarely the center of attention.	☐	☐	10. I'm not always the person I appear to be.	☐	☐

Scoring: Give yourself one point for checking False in 1, 5, and 7. Give yourself one point for each of the remaining questions that you answered True. Add up your points. If you are a good judge of yourself and scored 7 or above, you are probably high in self-monitoring tendencies; 3 or below, you are probably low in self-monitoring tendencies.

FIGURE 14.3 **Self-Monitoring Checklist**

One setting in which most of us especially want to make a good impression is a job interview, and a great deal has been written about how to do it. For example, to improve the likelihood that an interviewer will have a favorable impression of you, you are advised to use the right nonverbal cues: smile often, lean forward, maintain a high degree of eye contact, and frequently nod your head in agreement with what the interviewer says. In general, researchers have found that individuals who use these impression management techniques receive more favorable ratings than individuals who do not (Riggio, 1986). Some people use nonverbal cues such as these more naturally than others. But even if you do not normally behave this way when you are interacting with someone, you can make a conscious effort to control your nonverbal behavior.

As with most forms of manipulation, impression management can become counterproductive. You overdo it if you use so many positive nonverbal cues that the other individual perceives you to be insincere. And remember that impression management goes only so far: One study found that the frequent use of nonverbal cues had favorable outcomes in a job interview only when the applicants also had the qualifications for the job (Rasmussen, 1984).

Some people are more concerned about and aware of the impressions they make than others are (Snyder & Stukas, 1999). **Self-monitoring** is paying attention to the impressions you make on others and the degree to which you fine-tune your performance to optimize the impressions you are making. Lawyers and actors are among the best self-monitors; salespeople, con artists, and politicians are not far behind.

Individuals who are very skilled at self-monitoring seek information about appropriate ways to present themselves and invest considerable time in trying to "read" and understand others (Simpson, 1995). In and of itself, such behavior is neither good nor bad. Nobody can be a successful member of a family or a community without attention to the expectations and opinions of others. The danger is that the energy spent in self-monitoring might reduce the amount of energy we can devote to trying to understand our true selves. To get an idea of your skill at self-monitoring, see figure 14.3.

self-monitoring Paying attention to the impressions one makes on others and fine-tuning one's performance accordingly.

Attitudes

Social thinking involves not only attributions and social perceptions but also attitudes. **Attitudes** are beliefs or opinions about people, objects, and ideas. We have attitudes about all sorts of things, such as "Most people are out for themselves," "Money is evil," and "Television has caused family members to talk less with one another." We also live in a world in which people try to influence others' attitudes, as when politicians try to get your vote and advertisers try to convince you that their product is the best. Social psychologists are interested not only in how attitudes are changed but also in the relationship between an individual's attitude and his or her behavior.

People sometimes say one thing but do another—for example, they might respond in a poll that they prefer one candidate and then actually vote for another. But attitudes frequently predict behavior and what people say is what they do. Studies over the course of the past half-century indicate some of the conditions under which attitudes guide actions (Eagly & Chaikin, 1998; McGuire, 2004; Smith & Fabrigar, 2000):

- *When the person's attitudes are strong* (Petty & Krosnick, 1995). For example, senators whose attitudes toward President Bush are "highly favorable" are more likely to vote for his policies than are senators who have only "moderately favorable" attitudes toward him.
- *When the person shows a strong awareness of his or her attitudes and rehearses and practices them* (Fazio & others, 1982). For example, we would expect a person who vigorously argues for a ban on snowmobiles in national parks to avoid driving one there. But a person with the same desire to protect national parks from snowmobiles who has not had to put this attitude into words or define it in public might be more likely to try riding a snowmobile in a national park.
- *When the attitudes are relevant to the behavior.* For example, one study found that general attitudes toward birth control were virtually unrelated to the use of birth control pills in the following 2 years. However, a specific attitude toward taking birth control pills showed a much higher correlation with actual use in the following 2 years (Davidson & Jacard, 1979). The more relevant the attitude is to the behavior, the better it will predict the behavior.

However, ample evidence exists that changes in behavior sometimes precede changes in attitudes (Bandura, 1989). If you go through a program to quit drinking alcohol, you may then develop a negative attitude toward drinking. If you take up an exercise program, you may then be likely to extol the benefits of cardiovascular fitness when someone asks your opinion about exercise.

Social psychologists offer two main explanations of why behavior influences attitudes. The first view is that we have a strong need for cognitive consistency; we change our attitudes to make them more consistent with our behavior (Carkenord & Bullington, 1995). The second view is that our attitudes are not completely clear even to us, so we observe our own behavior and make inferences about it to determine what our attitudes should be, as explained in the following two sections.

Cognitive Dissonance   **Cognitive dissonance**, a concept developed by social psychologist Leon Festinger (1957), is an individual's motivation to reduce the discomfort (dissonance) caused by two inconsistent thoughts. According to the theory, we are likely to feel uneasy if we cannot justify to ourselves the difference between what we believe and what we do.

We can reduce cognitive dissonance in one of two general ways: change our attitudes or change our behaviors. For example, most smokers believe that it is unhealthy to smoke, yet they can't seem to resist lighting up. This discrepancy between attitude and behavior creates discomfort. To reduce the dissonance, the smoker must either stop smoking or decide that smoking really isn't so bad. "No one has proven smoking kills people" and "I'll have to die from something" are both dissonance-reducing attitudes.

attitudes Beliefs or opinions about people, objects, and ideas.

cognitive dissonance According to Festinger, an individual's motivation to reduce the discomfort (dissonance) caused by two inconsistent thoughts.

Since Festinger's original work on cognitive dissonance, other social psychologists have refined the theory. For instance, early dissonance theory predicted that individuals will avoid information inconsistent with their views. Researchers have since found that people will avoid unpleasant information—but only if they think that they cannot refute the uncomfortable argument and if they are highly committed to their way of thinking or behaving. Perhaps you have a friend or relative who has strong political or religious opinions that are not only at odds with yours but that seem contrary to common sense. You may have tried and tried, to no avail, to introduce facts that would convince the other person to change his or her mind. These recent findings suggest that you are unlikely to succeed.

Researchers also have focused on specific reactions to dissonance. Sometimes cognitive dissonance causes us to justify things in our lives that are unpleasant (Aronson, 1995). As George Bernard Shaw said of his father's alcoholism, "If you cannot get rid of the family skeleton, you may as well make it dance." "Making the family skeleton dance" helped Shaw to reduce the tension between his attitude about his father's drinking problem and its actual occurrence.

We also try to justify the negative things we do. We need to convince ourselves that we are decent, reasonable human beings. For example, when we have had a bad argument with someone, we often develop a negative attitude toward that person, which justifies the nasty things we said.

We have a strong need to justify the effort we put forth in life. In general, goals that require considerable effort are the ones that we value most highly. If we put forth considerable effort yet still do not reach the goal, we develop dissonance. We can reduce the dissonance by convincing ourselves that we did not work as hard as we actually did, or we can say that the goal was not all that important in the first place. Think of the person who goes to a lot of trouble to get a particular job but gets passed over. The person might justify the effort by saying that she should have followed up more diligently, or she might say that the job really wasn't a good match with her skills and career goals.

Our most intense justifications of our actions take place when our self-esteem is involved (Aronson, 2000; Aronson, Cohen, & Nails, 1999). If you do something cruel, then it follows that you have to perform some mental gymnastics to keep yourself from thinking you are a cruel person. The clearest results in the hundreds of research studies on cognitive dissonance occur when self-esteem is involved, and the most dissonance results when individuals with the highest self-esteem act in cruel ways. What about individuals with low self-esteem? They probably experience less dissonance because acting in a cruel way is consistent with their attitudes toward themselves. Put another way, individuals who think of themselves as bad might do bad things because it keeps dissonance at a minimum. The emphasis on self-esteem in understanding cognitive dissonance suggests that dissonance is not produced by a discrepancy between two cognitions (as Festinger believed) but, rather, by a discrepancy between a cognition about a particular behavior and the person's self-image (Aronson, 2000).

Not all of our thoughts and behaviors are aimed at reducing dissonance. Some of us catch ourselves doing something we don't approve of, look in the mirror, and say, "You blew it. Now what can you do to prevent that from happening again?" Eliot Aronson (1995) offers three suggestions for avoiding the treadmill of dissonance reduction—simply trying to justify the bad things in our lives and the bad things we do:

- Know your defensive and dissonance-reducing tendencies. Be able to sense them before you get in over your head.
- Realize that behaving in stupid and cruel ways does not necessarily mean that you are a stupid and cruel person.
- Develop enough strengths and competencies to be able to tolerate your mistakes without having to rationalize them away.

	Cognitive Dissonance Theory	Self-Perception Theory
Theorist	Festinger	Bem
Nature of theory	We are motivated toward consistency between attitude and behavior and away from inconsistency.	We make inferences about our attitudes by perceiving and examining our behavior and the context in which it occurs, which might involve inducements to behave in certain ways.
Example	"I hate my job. I need to develop a better attitude toward it or else quit."	"I am spending all of my time thinking about how much I hate my job. I really must not like it."

FIGURE 14.4 Two Theories of the Connections Between Attitudes and Behavior

Self-Perception   Not all social psychologists believe that the theory of cognitive dissonance explains the influence of behavior on attitudes. Daryl Bem (1967), for example, believes that the cognitive dissonance view relies too heavily on internal factors, which are difficult to measure. Bem argues that we should move away from such fuzzy concepts as "cognitions" and "psychological discomfort" and replace them with more behavioral terminology.

Bem's theory stresses that individuals make inferences about their attitudes—that is, they form self-perceptions of their attitudes—by perceiving their behavior. For example, consider the remark "I am spending all of my time thinking about the test I have next week. I must be anxious" or "This is the third time I have gone to the student union in two days. I must be lonely." Bem believes we look to our own behavior when our attitudes are not completely clear.

Figure 14.4 provides a comparison of cognitive dissonance theory and self-perception theory. Which theory is right? Research on cognitive dissonance suggests that people do change their attitudes to avoid feeling cheap, stupid, or guilty about their behavior. But at the same time, Bem's self-perception theory is compelling. People who are not strongly committed to attitudes before acting on them do seem to analyze their behavior for hints about their true opinions (Aronson & others, 1997). Self-perception theory also has been more useful in explaining what happens to people's attitudes when they are offered an inducement to do something they would want to do, anyway. Cognitive dissonance theory and self-perception theory both appear to have merit in explaining the connection between attitudes and behavior.

Attitude Change   We spend many hours of our lives trying to persuade people to do certain things. You have probably tried to persuade your friends to go to a movie or to play the game that you are interested in. Professional persuaders have similar goals, but they use more polished techniques based on extensive research on attitude change. What makes people decide to give up their original attitudes and to adopt new ones instead? What makes people decide to act on an attitude that they haven't acted on before? Teachers, lawyers, and sales representatives study techniques that will help them sway their audiences (students, juries, and buyers, respectively). Politicians have arsenals of speech writers and image consultants to ensure that their words are as persuasive as possible. Perhaps most skilled of all are advertisers, who combine the full array of techniques in an effort to sell cars, insurance policies, and cornflakes.

One important factor in any effort to change attitudes is the source of the message, the communicator. Suppose you are running for president of the student body.

You tell your fellow students that you are going to make life at your college better. Would they believe you? That likely would depend on some of your characteristics. Whether or not we believe someone depends in large part on their expertise or credibility. If you have held other elective offices, students would be more likely to believe you have the expertise to be their president. Trustworthiness, power, attractiveness, likability, and similarity are all characteristics that lend credibility and help a communicator change people's attitudes or convince them to act.

Another persuasion factor is the medium or technology used to get the message across. Consider the difference between watching a presidential debate on television and reading about it in the newspaper. Television lets us see how the candidates deliver their messages, what their appearance and mannerisms are like, and so on. Because it presents live images, television is often considered to be a more powerful medium for changing attitudes. In one study, winners of various political primaries were predicted by the amount of media exposure they had (Grush, 1980).

As important a factor as the communicator is the receiver, or audience, for the message. Age and attitude strength are two audience characteristics that determine whether a message will be effective. Younger people are more likely than older ones to change their attitudes. And if the attitudes of the audience are weak, attitude change is more likely; if audience attitudes are strong, the communicator will have more difficulty changing them.

Obviously, characteristics of the message itself also affect persuasiveness. One line of research has focused on whether a rational or an emotional strategy is more effective. Is it better to use basic motivators, such as love, sex, or fear to persuade someone? Or is it better to use facts or logic?

Emotional appeals are very powerful. You may have seen the Michelin tire ad that shows a baby playing near tires or the life insurance company ad that shows a widow and her young children moving out of their home because they did not have enough insurance. Both are relying on fear to motivate buyers.

Not all emotional appeals are negative, though. Music is widely used to make us feel good about a message. Think about how few television commercials you have seen without some form of music. When we watch such commercials, we may associate the pleasant feelings of the music with the product, even though the music itself provides us with no information about the product.

The less informed we are about the topic of the message, the more likely we are to respond to an emotional appeal. However, most people are persuaded only when rational and emotional appeals are used together. The emotional appeal arouses our interest, and the facts give us a logical reason for going along with the message. Consider an ad for a new cell phone. Our emotions might be aroused by images of people using the cell phone to call for help or to keep in touch with someone attractive. But then we are given the facts that make the cell phone an appealing purchase. Perhaps the cost is reasonable, it overcomes broken connections, or it also provides an Internet connection.

One model that has been proposed to explain the relation between emotional and rational appeals is the *elaboration likelihood model*. It proposes two ways to persuade: a central route and a peripheral route (Petty & Cacioppo, 1986; Petty, Wheeler, & Bizer, 2000). The central route engages someone thoughtfully. The peripheral route involves nonmessage factors, such as the source's credibility and attractiveness or emotional appeals. The peripheral route is effective when people are not paying close attention to what the communicator is saying. As you might guess, television commercials often involve the peripheral route to persuasion on the assumption that during the commercials you are probably not paying full, critical attention to the screen. However, the central route is more persuasive when people have the ability, and are motivated, to pay attention to the facts (Lammers, 2000). See the video clip "Persuasion" to learn more about the elaboration likelihood model and its applications.

Review and Sharpen Your Thinking

1 *Describe how people think about the social world.*

- Explain attribution.
- Discuss the three main elements of social perception.
- Identify the relationship between attitudes and behavior.

Which television ads do you like the best? Have they persuaded you to buy the products that are being advertised? What is it about the ads that is persuasive?

2 SOCIAL INFLUENCE

Conformity Group Interactions

Obedience Leadership

How are people influenced in social settings?

Another topic that social psychologists are interested in is how our behavior is influenced by other people (Cialdini, 2001). The section on social thinking discussed how we present ourselves to others to influence their perceptions of us and how we can influence other people's attitudes and behavior. This section explores some other aspects of social influence: conformity, obedience, group interactions, and leadership.

Conformity

After World War II, psychologists began to seek answers to the disturbing question of how ordinary people could be influenced to allow the sort of atrocities inflicted on Jews, Gypsies, and other minorities during the Holocaust. Researchers found the answer, in part, in **conformity,** which is change in a person's behavior to coincide more closely with a group standard. Conformity comes in many forms and affects many aspects of people's lives. It is not just the force behind the Holocaust, the My Lai massacre in Vietnam, and more recent genocidal events. Conformity is at work when a person takes up mountain biking because everyone else is doing it.

Although conformity has some unpleasant or unattractive aspects, it is not entirely a negative thing. People's conformity to rules and regulations allows society to run more smoothly. Consider how chaotic life would be if most people did not conform to social norms such as driving on the correct side of the road, going to school or work regularly, and not punching others in the face. However, some of the most dramatic and insightful work on conformity has examined how we sometimes act against our better judgment in order to conform.

Asch's Conformity Experiment Imagine yourself in this situation: You are taken into a room in which you see five other people seated around a table. A person in a white lab coat enters the room and announces that you are about to participate in an experiment on perceptual accuracy. The group is shown two cards, the first having only a single vertical line on it, the second card three vertical lines of varying length. You are told that the task is to determine which of the three lines on the second card is the same length as the line on the first card. You look at the cards and think, "What a snap. It's so obvious which is the same" (see figure 14.5).

conformity A change in a person's behavior to coincide more closely with a group standard.

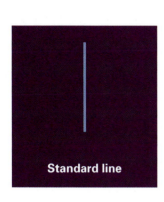

FIGURE 14.5 Asch's Conformity Experiment   The boxes on the left show the stimulus materials for the Asch conformity experiment on group influence. The photograph shows the confusion of one participant after five confederates of the experimenter chose the incorrect line.

What you do not know is that the other people in the room are actually in league with the experimenter; they've been hired to perform in ways the experimenter dictates. On the first several trials, everyone agrees about which line matches the standard. Then, on the fourth trial, each of the others picks an incorrect line. As the last person to make a choice, you have the dilemma of responding as your eyes tell you or conforming to what the others before you have said. How do you think you would answer?

Solomon Asch conducted this classic experiment on conformity in 1951. He believed few of his volunteer participants would yield to group pressure. To test his hypothesis, Asch instructed the hired accomplices to give incorrect responses on 12 of the 18 trials. To his surprise, Asch (1951) found that the volunteer participants conformed to the incorrect answers 35 percent of the time.

In a more recent test of group pressure and conformity, college students watched the third George H. W. Bush–Bill Clinton presidential debate and then rated the candidates' performances (Fein & others, 1993). Students were randomly assigned to one of three groups: (1) a 30-student group that included 10 confederates of the experimenter who openly supported Bush and criticized Clinton, (2) a 30-student group that included 10 confederates who cheered Clinton and criticized Bush, and (3) a 30-student group with no confederates of the experimenter. The group pressure exerted by the confederates was powerful; even Bush supporters rated Clinton's performance more favorably when their group included pro-Clinton confederates of the experimenter.

Many similar studies have shown the strength of the pressure to conform (Pines & Maslach, 2002). Even when faced with clear-cut information, such as the lines in the Asch experiment, we often conform to what others say and do. We do not want to be laughed at or make others angry at us.

Factors That Contribute to Conformity   Many factors influence whether an individual will conform or not (Cialdini & Trost, 1998). But in general people conform because of either normative social influence or informational social influence. **Normative social influence** is the influence to conform that other people have on us because we seek their approval or seek to avoid their disapproval. **Informational social influence** is the influence that other people have on us because we want to be right. The tendency to conform based on informational social influence depends especially on two factors: how confident we are in our own independent judgment and how well informed we perceive the other people to be.

normative social influence   The influence that other people have on us because we seek their approval or avoid their disapproval.

informational social influence   The influence that other people have on us because we want to be right.

Researchers have found some other factors that are involved in conforming or not conforming:

- *Unanimity of the group.* In Asch's study with lines on cards, the group's opinion was unanimous. When the group's opinion is divided, individuals feel less pressure to conform.
- *Prior commitment.* If you do not have a prior commitment to an idea or action, you are more likely to be influenced by others. But if you have publicly committed to an idea or action, conformity to another idea or action is less likely.
- *Personal characteristics.* People with low self-esteem and doubts about their abilities are more likely to conform (Campbell, Tesser, & Fairey, 1986).
- *Group members' characteristics.* You are more likely to conform if the group members are experts, attractive to you, or similar to you in any way.
- *Cultural values.* In experiments conducted in 14 countries, conformity rates were lower in individualistic cultures (such as in the United States), in which people tend to pursue their own interests, and higher in collectivistic cultures (such as in China), in which people typically seek to contribute to the group's success (Bond & Smith, 1994). See the video clip "Culture and Self" to learn more about the influence of culture on conformity.

In-Psych Plus

Obedience

In conformity, people change their thinking or behavior so that it will be more like that of others. There is no explicit demand to conform. In contrast, **obedience** is behavior that complies with the explicit demands of the individual in authority. That is, we are obedient when an authority figure demands that we do something and we do it. The Nazi crimes against Jews and others in World War II and the massacre of Vietnamese civilians at My Lai are examples of cruel obedience. Acts like these seem obviously wrong, yet millions of people throughout history have obeyed commands to commit them.

A classic experiment by Stanley Milgram (1965, 1974) provides insight into such obedience. Imagine that you agree to participate in a study designed to determine the effects of punishment on memory. Your role is to be the "teacher" and punish the mistakes made by the "learner" with increasingly painful electric shocks. You are given a 75-volt shock to see how it feels.

Then you are introduced to the learner, a nice 50-year-old man strapped to a chair who mumbles something about having a heart condition. You go into the next room, which has an intercom for communicating with the learner and an apparatus with 30 switches, labeled from 15 volts (light) to 450 volts (dangerous, "severe shock XXX").

As the trials proceed, the learner quickly runs into trouble and is unable to give the correct answers. At 150 volts, the learner says he's in pain and demands to have the experiment stopped. At 180 volts, he cries out that he can't stand it anymore. At 300 volts, he yells about his heart condition and pleads to be released. But if you hesitate in shocking the learner, the experimenter tells you that you have no choice; the experiment must continue.

By the way, the 50-year-old man is in league with the experimenter. He is not being shocked at all. Of course, the teachers are completely unaware that the learner is pretending to be shocked.

As you might imagine, the teachers in this experiment were uneasy about shocking the learner. At 240 volts, one teacher responded, "240 volts delivered; aw, no. You mean I've got to keep going with that scale? No sir, I'm not going to kill that man—I'm not going to give him 450 volts!" (Milgram, 1965). At the very strong voltage, the learner quit responding. When the teacher asked the experimenter what to do, the experimenter told him that it was his obligation to complete the job.

Forty psychiatrists were asked how they thought individuals would respond to this situation. The psychiatrists predicted that most teachers would go no further than

obedience Behavior that complies with the explicit demands of an individual in authority.

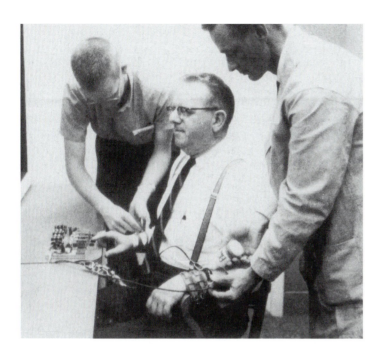

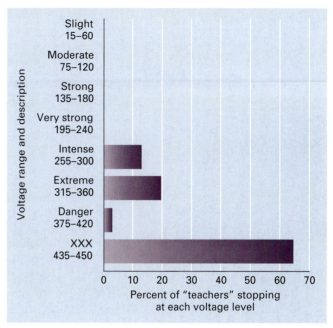

FIGURE 14.6 **Milgram Obedience**

Study   A 50-year-old man, the "learner," is strapped into a chair. The experimenter makes it look as if a shock generator is being connected to his body through several electrodes. The chart shows the percentage of "teachers" (study participants) who stopped shocking the learner at each voltage level.

150 volts, that fewer than 1 in 25 would go as far as 300 volts, and that only 1 in 1,000 would deliver the full 450 volts. The psychiatrists, it turns out, were way off the mark. The majority of the teachers obeyed the experimenter. In fact, almost two-thirds delivered the full 450 volts. Figure 14.6 shows the results of the Milgram study.

In subsequent studies, Milgram set up a storefront in Bridgeport, Connecticut, and recruited volunteers through newspaper ads. Milgram wanted to create a more natural environment for the experiment and to use a wider cross section of volunteers. In these additional studies, close to two-thirds of the individuals still selected the highest level of shock for the learner.

In variations of the experiment, Milgram discovered that more people would disobey in certain circumstances. Disobedience was more common when participants could see others disobey, when the authority figure was not perceived to be legitimate and was not close by, and when the victim was made to seem more human.

An important point has been raised about the Milgram experiments: How *ethical* were they? The volunteer teachers in Milgram's experiment clearly felt anguish, and some were very disturbed about "harming" another individual. After the experiment was completed, they were told that the learner was not actually shocked. Milgram argued that we have learned a great deal about human nature from the experiments: how far individuals will go in their obedience. The volunteers were interviewed later, and more than four-fifths said that they were glad they had participated in the study; none said that they were sorry they participated.

Nevertheless, the current ethical guidelines of the American Psychological Association stress that researchers should deceive volunteers only for very important purposes. Individuals are supposed to feel as good about themselves when the experiment is over as they did when it began. Under today's guidelines, the Milgram experiment likely would not be conducted.

The Milgram studies raise a broader question as well. If you believe that someone in a position of authority is making an unjust request or ordering you to do something wrong, what choice of action do you have?

- You can comply.
- You can give the appearance of complying but secretly do otherwise.
- You can publicly dissent by showing doubts and disenchantment but still follow directives.

In 1989, Chinese students led a massive demonstration against the government in Beijing. The students resisted the government's authority. However, the government eventually ended the protests by massacring hundreds. *In such circumstances, how might individuals continue to resist authority?*

- You can openly disregard the order and refuse to comply.
- You can challenge or confront the authority.
- You can get higher authorities to intervene or organize a group of people who agree with you to show the strength of your view.

Resistance to authority can be difficult, but living with the knowledge that you compromised your moral integrity may be more difficult in the long run. The video clip "Conformity and Obedience" presents a comprehensive introduction to the topic of social influence, including video of the original Milgram obedience study.

Group Interactions

A student joining a campus organization, a jury making a decision about a criminal case, a president of a company delegating authority to a vice president, a prejudiced remark against a minority group, conflict among nations, and attempts to reach peace—all of these circumstances reflect our lives as members of groups. They range in size from *dyads*, which consist of two people, to immense groups of all the people linked by national identity, religion, ethnicity, or gender. Some groups we choose; others we do not. We choose to belong to a club, but we are all born into a particular family, for example.

Regardless of their size, groups serve a useful human purpose. They satisfy our personal needs, reward us, provide information, raise our self-esteem, and give us an identity. We might join a group because we think it will be enjoyable and exciting and satisfy our need for affiliation and companionship. We might join a group because we will receive rewards, either material or psychological. For example, by taking a job with a company, we not only get paid to work as part of a group but we also reap a portion of the company's prestige and recognition. Groups are also an important source of information. For example, as we listen to other members talk in a Weight Watchers group we learn about their strategies for losing weight. Further, many groups—family, college, company, ethnicity—also provide identities; when asked who we are, we often answer in terms of which groups we belong to.

Structure of Groups   Any group to which you belong has certain things in common with all other groups. One is the existence of *norms*, or rules that are specific to that group and apply to all of its members. Norms can be formal or informal. An example of a formal norm is an employer's requirement that all of its workers wear socks. Informal norms are such things as the subtle pressure you face to sit in the same seat or the same area of a lecture hall every time you attend a certain class.

Another characteristic that all groups have in common is a set of *roles*, or expectations that govern certain positions in the group. Roles define how different people in the group behave. In a family, parent is one role, sibling is another role, and grandparent is yet another role. A parent isn't expected to behave the same way toward the children in a family that siblings or grandparents are expected to behave. Each member of the family has a different role to play to accomplish the group's goals.

Group Performance   The very first experiment in social psychology examined the question of whether individuals perform better in a group or when alone. Norman Triplett (1898) found that bicyclists performed better when they raced against each other than when they raced alone against the clock. Triplett also built a "competition machine" made out of fishing reels. The machine allowed two individuals to turn the reels side by side. Observing 40 children, he discovered that those who reeled next to another child worked faster than those who reeled alone.

Since Triplett's work over a century ago, many investigations of group versus individual performance have been conducted. Some studies reveal that we do better in groups, others that we are more productive when we work alone (Paulus, 1989). We can make sense out of these contradictory findings by looking more closely at three effects of working in groups:

Do you perform better as a member of a group or as an individual? Would the situation change your answer?

social loafing   The tendency for an individual to exert less effort in a group because of reduced accountability for individual effort.

- **Social facilitation** is what occurs when an individual's performance improves because of the presence of others. Robert Zajonc (1965) argued that the presence of other individuals arouses us. If our arousal is too high, however, we won't be able to learn new or difficult tasks efficiently. Social facilitation, then, improves our performance on well-learned tasks. For new or difficult tasks, we might be best advised to work things out on our own before trying them in a group.

- **Social loafing** is each person's tendency to exert less effort in a group because of reduced accountability for individual effort. The effect of social loafing is lowered group performance (Latané, 1981). Social loafing is common when a group of students is assigned a school project. Also, the larger the group, the more likely it is that a person can loaf without being detected. Among the ways to decrease social loafing are to increase the identifiability and uniqueness of individual contributions, to make it easier to evaluate these contributions and to make the task more attractive (Karau & Williams, 1993). Under certain conditions, however, working with others can increase, rather than decrease, individual effort (J. M. Levine, 2000). For example, a person who views the group's task as important and who does not expect other group members to contribute adequately to the group's performance is likely to work harder than usual. The tendency to socially loaf is also linked to gender and culture. Men are more likely to loaf than women (Karau & Williams, 1993). Why might this be the case? Women are more likely to care about the welfare of others in the group and the group's collective performance. In contrast, men tend to be more individualistic, focusing more on their own needs and performances (Wood, 1987). The tendency to socially loaf is stronger in individualistic Western cultures, such as in the United States, than in collectivistic Eastern cultures, such as in China and Japan (Karau & Williams, 1993).

- **Deindividuation** occurs when being part of a group reduces personal identity and erodes the sense of personal responsibility (Dodd, 1995). As early as 1895, Gustav LeBon observed that being in a group can foster uninhibited behavior, ranging from wild celebrations to mob activity. Ku Klux Klan violence, Mardi Gras excesses, and spring break riots might be due to deindividuated behavior. One explanation of deindividuation is that groups give us anonymity: We may act in a disinhibited way because we believe that authority figures and victims are unlikely to identify us as the culprits.

Risky Shift and Group Polarization

What happens when people make a decision as a group? How do they decide whether a criminal is guilty, whether a country should attack another, whether a family should stay home or go on vacation, or whether sex education should be part of a school curriculum? Do they take risks and stick their necks out, or do they compromise their opinions and move toward the center? The evidence is mixed.

Some research indicates that many times group decisions are riskier than individual decisions. The **risky shift** is the tendency for a group decision to be riskier than the average decision made by the individual group members. In one investigation, fictitious dilemmas were presented, and participants were asked how much risk the characters in the dilemmas were willing to take (Stoner, 1961). When the individuals discussed the dilemmas as a group, they were more willing to respond that the characters would make risky decisions than when they were queried alone. Many studies have been conducted on this topic, with similar results (Goethals & Demorest, 1995).

We do not always make riskier decisions in a group than when alone, however; hundreds of research studies show that being in a group moves us even more strongly in the direction of the position we initially held (Moscovici, 1985). The **group polarization effect** is the solidification and further strengthening of a position as a consequence of a group discussion. For instance, imagine a "hawk" and a "dove" in the U.S. Senate who listen to the same endless hours of committee discussion about

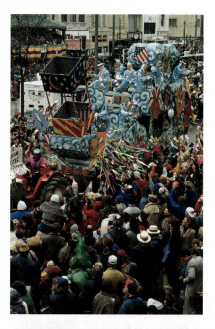

People may become deindividuated in groups. People can lose their individual identities in situations as diverse as Mardi Gras and patriotic events. *Can you think of others?*

social facilitation The tendency for an individual's performance to improve because of the presence of others.

deindividuation The tendency for an individual in a group to experience a reduced sense of personal identity and personal responsibility.

risky shift The tendency for a group decision to be riskier than the average decision made by individual group members.

group polarization effect The solidification and further strengthening of a position as a consequence of a group discussion.

nuclear disarmament. Research indicates that neither is likely to be converted to a different point of view. After 2 years on the committee, each will be even more strongly committed to his or her position than before the deliberation began. Initially held views often become more polarized because of group discussion.

Group polarization may occur because we hear other group members' new, more persuasive arguments that strengthen our original position, and we tend to dismiss the arguments that do not support our position. Group polarization also might occur because of social comparison. We may find that our opinion is not as extreme as others' opinions and be influenced to take a stand at least as strong as the most extreme advocate's position.

"All those in favor say 'Aye'."
                    "Aye."   "Aye."   "Aye."
            "Aye."   "Aye."

Groupthink In 1961, when John F. Kennedy was president, the United States sent a group of Cuban exiles into Cuba on a mission to overthrow communist dictator Fidel Castro. The plan failed miserably: The exiles were either captured or killed, Castro remained in power, and the United States looked rather foolish. How could the very intelligent men in the Kennedy administration have agreed to go through with such a fiasco as the Bay of Pigs?

According to social psychologist Irving Janis (1972), the answer is **groupthink,** group members' impaired decision making and avoidance of realistic appraisal in order to maintain group harmony. Groupthink evolves because members are motivated to boost each other's egos and promote conformity, especially in the face of stress. This motivation for harmony and unanimity can result in disastrous decisions.

Following are some of the symptoms of groupthink and how they worked in the Kennedy administration's Bay of Pigs decision (Stolley, 2001):

- *Overestimation of the power and morality of the group.* The Kennedy decision makers believed that they could keep news of their involvement secret and that the world would think the Cuban dissidents were acting on their own. Although at least two group members had misgivings about the plan's morality, these were either not voiced or not evaluated in meetings, which reflects a symptom of groupthink: ignoring moral consequences.
- *Closed-mindedness.* After a group has selected a course of action, it cannot easily change its decision, even when the course of action is going badly. Group members collectively rationalize what they have decided to do, discounting warnings and other negative indications that might call previous policy decisions into question. The Kennedy group believed that Castro's forces would be easy to overcome, an example of such discounting. However, the Cuban Air Force shot down half of the U.S. planes sent to protect the invading exiles and bombed the invaders arriving on Cuban shores.
- *Pressures toward uniformity.* Members pressure those who momentarily express misgivings to conform with the plan supported by the majority. President Kennedy did not provide adequate time for discussion of dissidents' concerns and played down the criticisms of the one group member who had serious doubts about the Bay of Pigs invasion. Some members may act as "mindguards" to suppress dissenting views or information that conflicts with the group's decision. For instance, the Secretary of State kept the group from learning about the concerns raised by the director of the United States Information Agency. Group members also tend to suppress their own doubts.

groupthink Impaired decision making within a group and avoidance of realistic appraisal by its members in order to maintain group harmony.

Groupthink has been behind many disasters. Other examples in U.S. history are the failure to prepare for the Japanese bombing of Pearl Harbor during World

War II, the escalation of the Vietnam War in the 1960s, the Watergate cover-up that led to President Richard Nixon's resignation in 1974, and the explosion of the space shuttle *Challenger* in 1986.

Following are some helpful strategies for avoiding groupthink:

- *Reduce isolation.* Invite people who are not part of the decision-making group to attend meetings. Encourage them to give their opinions and criticize plans without any retribution.
- *Make leadership impartial.* To encourage a wide range of options, leaders should not state their own preferences and expectations up front.
- *Use outside experts.* They may have a different perspective on the issues at hand and can challenge core beliefs of the group.
- *Discuss with trusted subordinates.* Before final consensus, each member should report to the group what their own associates outside of the group have to say about the topic under consideration.
- *Hold second-chance meetings and review sessions.* After the "final" decision has been made, meet again to provide a second chance to object to the group decision before it is implemented.

Majority and Minority Influence In most groups—even when groupthink is not involved—the majority of the members tend to hold sway over the minority. Think about the groups in which you have been a member. The majority sets the group's norm; those who do not go along may be ignored or even given the boot. The majority also has a greater opportunity to provide information that will influence decision making.

Although in most cases the majority wins, sometimes the minority has its day (Latané, 1996). The minority cannot win through normative pressure because it is outnumbered, so it must do its work through informational pressure. If the minority presents its view consistently and confidently, then the majority is more likely to listen to the minority's views.

Certain individuals within the minority may play a crucial role. For instance, those who can command the attention of others have a better opportunity to shape and direct the group's decision making. To achieve such influence, individuals have to distinguish themselves in various ways from the rest of the group. They have to make themselves noticed by the opinions they express, the jokes they tell, or their nonverbal style. They might be the first ones to raise a new idea, to disagree with a prevailing point of view, or to propose a creative alternative solution to a problem. People who have a strong social influence often are willing to be different.

Individuals with a history of taking minority stands also have influence. They may trigger others to dissent by showing them that disagreement is possible and may indeed be the best course. Such is the basis of some of history's greatest moments. When Abraham Lincoln spoke out against slavery, racism dominated and tore at the country; when Corazon Aquino became a candidate for president of the Philippines, few people thought Ferdinand Marcos could be beaten.

Certain individuals in the minority have played important roles in history. *(Top)* Martin Luther King, Jr., helped African Americans gain important rights. *(Bottom)* Corazon Aquino, who became president of the Philippines after defeating Ferdinand Marcos, toppled a corrupt political regime and reduced the suffering of many Philippine citizens. *What other examples of minority influence can you think of?*

The influence of the minority has been studied in jury room deliberations (Hastie, 2001). Researchers have found that the people on a jury with a minority view often convince the majority to change their minds. Is that a good thing or a bad thing? Although trials would proceed faster if the jury's initial majority vote determined the defendant's innocence or guilt, a number of social psychologists believe that the minority opinion is useful in the deliberation process (Aronson & others, 1997). First, forcing juries to reach a unanimous verdict with both majority and minority coming to an agreement makes everyone consider the evidence more carefully (Hastie, Penrod, & Pennington, 1983). Second, even if the minority seldom succeed in convincing the majority to change their opinion about guilt or innocence, the minority often does change opinions about the degree of guilt. In criminal trials, juries often have some discretion about the type of guilty verdict, such as first-degree murder, second-degree murder, or manslaughter.

Leadership

What makes some people so influential within a group that others willingly follow them into difficult or even dangerous endeavors? Is it a set of personality traits, the situations in which leaders emerge, or a combination of the two?

The *great-person theory* states that some individuals have certain traits that are best suited for leadership positions. Leaders are commonly thought to be assertive, cooperative, decisive, dominant, energetic, self-confident, tolerant of stress, willing to assume responsibility, diplomatic and tactful, and persuasive. "I am certainly not one of those who needs to be prodded," British Prime Minister Winston Churchill once said of himself. "In fact, if anything, I am the prod." This is a classic statement of the great-person theory. However, although we can list traits and skills possessed by leaders, a large number of research studies conclude that we cannot predict who will become a leader solely from the individual's personality characteristics (Wilson, 2002).

Is it the situation, then, that produces leaders? The *situational view* of leadership argues that the needs of a group change from time to time. The individual who emerges as the leader in one circumstance will not necessarily be the leader in another circumstance. But what determines who emerges as leader in a particular situation? The *contingency model* of leadership states that personality characteristics and situational influences combine to determine leadership and proposes an interactional relationship between leaders and followers. These leaders have two basic styles: They direct their efforts either toward getting a task completed or toward helping group members get along (Fielder, 1978). If working conditions are very favorable or unfavorable, a task-oriented leader is better, but if working conditions are moderate, a relationship-oriented leader is better. These ideas have not been fully researched, but the concept that leadership is a function of both personality characteristics and situational influences is an important one (Lord & Brown, 2003).

The idea of different leadership styles has been useful to social psychologists studying gender and leadership. Men appear to be more directive and task-oriented leaders, whereas women are more democratic and relationship-oriented (O'Leary & Flanagan, 2001). A man might just tell people what to do, whereas a woman might "invite discussion and solicit opinions." By adopting a participative and collaborative style, female leaders may be able to overcome others' resistance to their leadership, win their acceptance, gain self-confidence, and be effective (Lips, 2003).

And, indeed, some women have proved to be effective leaders. In a recent study, ratings of 9,000 female and male managers by subordinates and peers indicated that women were perceived as more effective leaders than men were (Center for Leadership Studies, 2000). This outcome may reflect more than just preference for relationship-oriented leadership or the influence of gender roles. It may also reflect the tendency for women to have to meet a higher standard than men to win leadership positions.

Review and Sharpen Your Thinking

2 *Identify how people are influenced in social settings.*

- Describe the factors that affect conformity.
- List some factors affecting obedience.
- Discuss group performance.
- Summarize the factors that influence leadership.

How do you think you would have responded in the Asch conformity and Milgram obedience experiments? What makes you say so? Have you ever been in a situation in which social circumstances seemed to pressure you to do something against your values?

Ethnic and cultural conflict may be more intense than any other type of conflict between groups. Examples are rampant throughout history and in today's world. Among recent interethnic conflicts are Israeli-Palestinian violence in the Middle East *(left)* and Catholic-Protestant conflict in Northern Ireland *(right)*. *Why might ethnic and cultural rivalries be so intense? How might they be reduced?*

INTERGROUP RELATIONS 3

Group Identity   **Prejudice**   **Ways to Improve Interethnic Relations**

What affects relations between groups?

Conflicts between groups, especially ethnic and cultural groups, are rampant around the world today (Chirot & Seligman, 2001). Groups such as al-Qaida attack countries, such as the United States, that they perceive to be too secular and materialistic. And the United States retaliates. Israelis and Palestinians fight over territory in the Middle East. In countries across Africa, tribal chiefs try to craft a new social order favorable to their own rule. In Northern Ireland, clashes between Catholics and Protestants still break out. Prejudice, stereotyping, ethnocentrism, and other concepts introduced by social psychologists can help us understand the intensity of such cultural and ethnic conflicts and how to reduce the conflicts (Ellemers, Spears, & Doosje, 2002; Hewstone, Rubin, & Willis, 2002).

Group Identity

When someone asks you to identify yourself, how often do you respond by mentioning your group memberships—possibly social organizations, your ethnicity, your religion, your nationality? And how much does it matter to you whether the people you associate with are members of the same groups? **Social identity** is the way we define ourselves in terms of our group membership (Deaux, 2001). In contrast to personal identity, which can be highly individualized, social identity assumes that we have some commonalities with others. To identify with a group does not necessarily mean that we know or interact with every other member of the group. However, it does mean that we believe that we share numerous features with other members of the group.

social identity A definition of ourselves in terms of our group membership.

Ethnicities and Religions

Asian American
Jewish
Southern Baptist
West Indian

Political Affiliations

Feminist
Republican
Environmentalist

Vocations and Avocations

Psychologist
Artist
Athlete
Military veteran

Relationships

Mother
Parent
Teenager
Widow

Stigmatized Identities

Person with AIDS
Homeless person
Obese person
Alcoholic

FIGURE 14.7 Types of Social Identity, with Examples

ethnocentrism The tendency to favor one's own ethnic group over other groups.

prejudice An unjustified negative attitude toward an individual based on the individual's membership in a group.

Many forms of social identity exist, reflecting the many ways in which people connect to other groups and social categories (Abrams & Hogg, 2004; Bodenhausen, McCrae, & Hugenberg, 2004). Social psychologist Kay Deaux (2001) identified five distinct types of social identity: ethnic and religious, political, vocations and avocations, personal relationships, and stigmatized groups. Some examples of each type appear in figure 14.7.

According to social identity theory, we are continually comparing our groups (in-groups) with other groups (out-groups). In the process, we often focus more on the differences between the two groups than on their similarities. Imagine two fans of professional basketball teams, one a Los Angeles Lakers fan, the other a Philadelphia 76ers fan. As these two fans talk, they are less likely to discuss how much they both like basketball than to argue about the virtues of their teams. As they strive to promote their social identities, they soon lapse into self-congratulatory remarks about their own team and nasty comments about the opposing team. In short, the theme of the conversation has become "My team is good and I am good. Your team is bad and you are bad." And so it goes with the sexes, ethnic groups, nations, socioeconomic groups, religions, sororities, fraternities, and countless other groups. These comparisons often lead to competition and even discrimination against other groups.

Social psychologist Henry Tajfel (1978) showed how easy it is to lead people to think in terms of "we" and "they." In one experiment, he assigned those who overestimated the number of dots on a screen to one group and those who underestimated the number to another group. Once assigned to the two groups, the participants were asked to award money to the other participants. Invariably, individuals awarded money only to members of their own group. If we favor our own group on such trivial criteria, it is no wonder that we show intense in-group favoritism when differences are not so trivial (Jussim, Ashmore, & Wilder, 2001).

The tendency to favor one's own cultural or ethnic group over other groups is called **ethnocentrism.** Ethnocentrism's positive side is that it fosters a sense of pride in the group that fulfills the human desire for a positive self-image. Of course, the negative side of ethnocentrism is that it encourages in-group/out-group, we/they thinking. Most members of an ethnic group attest that in celebrating their own heritage and culture they do not discriminate against others. As African American activist Stokely Carmichael said in 1966, "I'm for the Negro. I'm not against anything." In reality, however, members of ethnic groups often stress differences with others rather than solely emphasizing pride in their own group. In-group pride does not always reflect ethnocentrism, however. Members of some minority groups—such as African Americans, Latinos, and gays and lesbians—often assert in-group pride to counter the negative messages about their group transmitted by society (Crocker, Major, & Steele, 1998).

Prejudice

Like most people, you probably do not consider yourself to be prejudiced. But, in fact, each of us has prejudices. **Prejudice** is an unjustified negative attitude toward an individual based on the individual's membership in a group. The group can be made up of people of a particular race, sex, sexual orientation, age, religion, or nationality or can share some other detectable difference from the prejudiced individual (Dion, 2003; Jones, 1997, 2002; Lambert, Chasteen, & Payne, 2004; Nelson, 2002).

Prejudice is a worldwide phenomenon (Baker, 2001). It has sparked many eruptions of hatred. Serbs were so prejudiced against Bosnians that they pursued a policy of "ethnic cleansing." Hutus in Rwanda were so prejudiced against Tutsis that they went on a murderous rampage, hacking off arms and legs with machetes. (Learn about the factors that contribute to extreme aggression between groups in the video clip "Genocide.") European Americans were so prejudiced against Native Americans that they systematically robbed them of their property and self-respect, killed them, and herded survivors like animals onto reservations. The most blatant instance of

Group members often show considerable pride in their ethnic identity. *(Top)* Mexican Americans' celebration of Cinco de Mayo, Native Americans' celebration of their heritage, and Polish Americans' celebration of their cultural background. *(Bottom)* African Americans' celebration of Martin Luther King Day. *Why are such displays of ethnocentrism considered positive, whereas others are not?*

destructive prejudice in U.S. history is racial prejudice against African Americans. When Africans were brought to America as slaves, they were considered property and treated inhumanely. Lynchings of African Americans, and other acts of violence, continued well into the twentieth century. Nor are Blacks the only ones to have suffered from the prejudices of fellow Americans.

Why do people develop prejudice? Among the reasons given by social psychologists are the following (Monteith, 2000):

- *Individual personality.* Some years ago, social psychologist Theodor Adorno and his colleagues (1950) described the *authoritarian personality:* strict adherence to conventional ways of behaving, aggression against people who violate conventional norms, rigid thinking, and exaggerated submission to authority. He believed that individuals with an authoritarian personality are likely to be prejudiced. However, not all individuals who harbor prejudice have an authoritarian personality.

- *Competition between groups over scarce resources.* Feelings of hostility and prejudice can develop when a society does not have enough jobs, land, power, or status—or any of a number of other material and social resources—to go around. Certain groups may regularly be involved in competing with each other and thus be more likely to develop prejudice toward each other. For instance, immigrants often compete with established low-income members of a society for jobs, leading to persistent conflict between the two groups.

- *Motivation to enhance self-esteem.* According to Henry Tajfel (1978), individuals derive a sense of self-esteem through their identification as members of a particular group, and their self-esteem will be further enhanced to the extent that their group is viewed more favorably than other groups.

- *Cognitive processes that contribute to a tendency to categorize and stereotype others.* Human beings are limited in their capacity for careful and thorough thought (Allport, 1954). The social environment is extremely complex and makes many demands on our limited information processing capacity, which can produce simplification of the social environment through categorization and stereotyping. Once stereotypes are in place, prejudice is often not far behind.

- *Cultural learning.* Families, friends, traditional norms, and institutionalized patterns of discrimination provide plenty of opportunities for individuals to be exposed to the prejudice of others. In this manner, others' prejudiced belief systems can be incorporated into one's own system. Children often show prejudice before they even have the cognitive abilities or social opportunities to develop their own attitudes. Listen to the audio clip "Learning Prejudice" to learn about research on prejudice in preschool.

Stereotyping   At the very root of prejudice is a **stereotype,** a generalization about a group's characteristics that does not consider any variations from one individual to the next (Kite, 2001). (The video clip "Stereotype Threat" discusses the influence that stereotypes can exert on the targets of these generalizations.) Researchers have found that we are less likely to detect variations among individuals who belong to "other" groups than among individuals who belong to "our" group. For example, studies of eyewitness identification have found that Whites tend to stereotype African Americans more than other Whites during eyewitness identification (Brigham, 1986). What might be occurring is the tendency to view members of one's own group as having heterogeneous and desirable qualities and to view the members of other groups as having homogeneous and undesirable qualities.

All people stereotype. As was discussed in chapter 8, people use categories, or schemas, when thinking about groups and individuals from these groups (Fiske, 1998; Steele, 1996). Thus we might engage in stereotyping without being aware of it (Greenwald & Banaji, 1995). The main problem is not that we use these categories but that we limit our perceptions of others to the rough outlines of the schema; we do not add specific information about an individual's characteristics. In addition, we may develop biases against whole groups of people.

Emotion also can be involved in stereotyping (Bodenhausen & others, 2001). Anger especially can intensify stereotyping by producing irrational and biased judgments about people.

Discrimination   Having a stereotype does not mean that you have to act on it. But if you do act on your prejudices, you may be guilty of **discrimination,** an unjustified negative or harmful action toward a member of a group simply because the person belongs to that group. Discrimination results when negative emotional reactions combine with prejudiced beliefs and are translated into behavior.

Early research on discrimination focused on overt forms of discrimination in which the target (person or group), the action, and the intention of the actor were clear and identifiable. Overt discrimination is the outcome of old-fashioned racism or sexism. The actor tries to maintain self-esteem by using the power of being a member of a particular group to treat women or individuals from ethnic minority groups unfairly.

stereotype A generalization about a group's characteristics that does not consider any variations from one individual to another.

discrimination An unjustified negative or harmful action toward a person simply because he or she is a member of a particular group.

Overt discrimination is no longer acceptable in mainstream American society, however. Civil rights legislation and changing attitudes expressed widely in popular media have made it "politically incorrect" to discriminate publicly. But subtler forms of racism have appeared, described by such terms as *symbolic racism, aversive racism, ambivalent racism,* and *modern racism* (Blair, 2001). They involve negative feelings about minority groups, but not traditional stereotypes. Symbolic racism assumes that, because discrimination is no longer acceptable, it must not exist; any difficulties that individuals in minority groups might face are their own fault. It encompasses the ideas that African Americans, for example, are pushing too hard and too fast for equality, are making unfair demands, and are getting undeserved special attention, such as favoritism in job hiring and college admissions (Taylor, Peplau, & Sears, 2003). This subtler form of racism is based on discrimination that is covert rather than overt, unconscious rather than conscious, and denied rather than acknowledged (Monteith & Voils, 2001).

Ways to Improve Interethnic Relations

Decades ago, social psychologist Muzafer Sherif and his colleagues (1961) fueled "we/they" competition between two groups of 11-year-old boys at a summer camp called Robbers Cave in Oklahoma. One group became known as the Rattlers (a tough, cursing group whose shirts were emblazoned with a snake insignia), and the other was known as the Eagles. Sherif, who disguised himself as a janitor so he could unobtrusively observe the Rattlers and Eagles, arranged for the two groups to compete in baseball, touch football, and tug-of-war. Counselors manipulated and judged events so the teams were close. Each team perceived the other to be competing unfairly. Raiding the other group's area, burning the other group's flag, and fighting resulted. The Rattlers and Eagles further derided one another, holding their noses in the air as they passed each other. Rattlers described all Rattlers as brave, tough, and friendly and called all Eagles sneaky and smart alecks. The Eagles reciprocated by calling the Rattlers crybabies.

After "we/they" conflict transformed the Rattlers and Eagles into opposing "armies," Sherif tried several ways to reduce hatred between the groups. Only when both groups were required to work cooperatively to solve a problem did the Rattlers and Eagles develop a positive relationship. Sherif created tasks that required the efforts of both groups: working together to repair the only water supply to the camp, pooling their money to rent a movie, and cooperating to pull the camp truck out of a ditch. Figure 14.8 shows how competitive activities and cooperative activities changed perceptions of the out-group.

Might Sherif's idea—creating *cooperation* between groups rather than competition—be applied to ethnic groups? When the schools in Austin, Texas, were desegregated through extensive busing, increased racial tension among African Americans, Mexican Americans, and Whites resulted in violence in the schools. The superintendent consulted Eliot Aronson, a prominent social psychologist, who was at the University of Texas at Austin at the time. Aronson (1986) thought it was more important to prevent ethnic hostility than to control it. He stressed that the reward structure of the classrooms needed to be changed from a setting of unequal competition to one of cooperation among equals, without making any curriculum changes. To accomplish this, he recommended that each student, in small, ethnically mixed groups, be assigned different pieces of a learning project. Each student had an allotted time to study his or her part. Then the group met, and each member tried to teach his or her part to the group. After an hour or so, each student was tested on the whole project. Thus learning depended on the

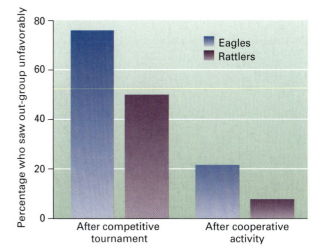

FIGURE 14.8 Attitudes Toward the Out-Group Following Competitive and Cooperative Activities In Sherif's research, hostility peaked after an athletic tournament, as reflected in the high percentage of Eagles and Rattlers who perceived the other group unfavorably following this competitive event. However, after the groups worked together to reach a goal, their unfavorable attitudes toward each other dropped considerably.

In-Psych Plus

cooperation and effort of other members. This strategy has since been widely used in the United States (Johnson & Johnson, 2003). A number of studies reveal that this type of cooperative learning is associated with increased self-esteem, better academic performance, friendships among classmates, and improved interethnic perceptions (Slavin, 1989). Go to the video clip "Social Ostracism" to see Aronson discussing his cooperative classrooms. (Also, to learn more about situations that encourage cooperation or competition, go to the interactivity "Prisoner's Dilemma.")

Another possible stategy for breaking down barriers based on prejudice is *intimate contact*—sharing personal worries, successes, failures, ambitions, and coping strategies (Brislin, 1993). Contact—attending the same school, working at the same company, living in the same neighborhood—does not by itself improve interethnic relations. But when people reveal personal information they are more likely to be perceived as individuals than as members of a category. And the sharing of personal information often produces the discovery that others have many of the same feelings, hopes, and concerns that we have, which can help to break down "we/they" barriers. Intimate contact may be more effective, however, when the individuals involved are of relatively equal status (Devine, Evett, & Vasquez-Suson, 1996).

One of the initial investigations of interethnic contact focused on African American and White residents in an integrated housing project (Deutsch & Collins, 1951). The residents lived in small apartments and shared facilities, such as laundry rooms and playgrounds. The residents discovered that it was more enjoyable to talk with each other than to stare at the walls while doing their laundry, and African American and White parents began to converse with each other as they watched their children play with each other, without regard to skin color. Initially the conversations focused on such nonintimate matters as the quality of the washing machines, but eventually they moved on to more personal matters. Whites and African Americans discovered that they shared a number of similar concerns, such as jobs, schools, and taxes. Sharing intimate information and becoming friendly with someone from another ethnic group helped to make people more tolerant and less prejudiced toward the other ethnic group (Brewer & Gaertner, 2001; Pettigrew & Tropp, 2000).

Review and Sharpen Your Thinking

3 **Discuss intergroup relations.**

- Explain how social identity leads to "we/they" thinking.
- Discuss the relationships among prejudice, stereotyping, and discrimination.
- Describe two effective strategies for improving interethnic relations.

What personal experiences have you had with prejudice, stereotyping, and discrimination? Explain why you think these occurred.

4 SOCIAL INTERACTION

Aggression   **Altruism**

What roles do aggression and altruism play in social interaction?

Our social interactions can bring us experiences we would rather forget, moments that are charged with conflict and threat. They also can bring warm and cherished acts of kindness. Let's explore these two faces of social interaction: aggression and altruism.

Aggression

The danger of aggression was captured vividly by the wise Yoda in the movie *The Empire Strikes Back:* "Beware of the dark side. Anger, fear, aggression. Easily they flow. Once you start down the dark path, it will forever dominate your destiny and consume your will." Is this dark side biologically based, or is it learned?

Biological Influences on Aggression   There is nothing new about human aggression. The primate ancestors of human beings and the earliest humans are thought to have committed aggressive acts against others of their own kind. History and literature are full of stories of aggression. In our own time, murders in the United States take place at the rate of 20,000 per year, assaults at the rate of 700,000 per year; there are at least 200,000 reports of rape per year in the United States. Should we conclude that aggression is an inborn characteristic of the human species? As Shakespeare asked, "Is there any cause in nature that makes these hard hearts?"

Ethologists say that aggression is indeed biologically based; certain stimuli release *innate* aggressive responses (Lorenz, 1965; Tinbergen, 1969). For example, a male robin will attack another male when it sees the red patch on the other bird's breast. When the patch is removed, however, no attack takes place.

Vigorous fighting does occur in the animal kingdom, but most hostile encounters do not escalate to killing or even severe harm. Much of the fighting is ritualistic and involves threat displays. For example, elephant seals show approximately 65 threat displays for every fight that actually takes place (LeBoeuf & Peterson, 1969). The type of threat display varies from one species to the next: A cat arches its back, bares its teeth, and hisses; a chimpanzee stares, stomps the ground, and screams.

Evolutionary theorists believe that human beings are not much different from other animals. A basic theme of their theory is the survival of the fittest. Thus they conclude that, early in human evolution, the survivors were probably aggressive individuals. Hunters and food gatherers not only had to kill animals to eat but also had to compete for the best food territories if they were to survive.

Genes are important in understanding the biological basis of aggression. The selective breeding of animals provides the evidence. After a number of breedings among only aggressive animals and among only docile animals, vicious and timid strains of animals emerge. The vicious strains attack nearly anything in sight; the timid strains rarely fight, even when attacked. The genetic basis for aggression is more difficult to demonstrate with humans (Brennan, Mednick, & Kandel, 1991). Nonetheless, in one investigation of 573 sets of adult twins, identical twins had more similar aggressive tendencies than did fraternal twins (Rushton & others, 1986).

Sigmund Freud (1917) also argued that aggression is biologically based. He said we have a self-destructive urge he called the *death instinct.* Because the death instinct comes in conflict with our self-preserving life instinct, the death instinct is redirected toward others in the form of aggression. Most psychologists feel uneasy about the concept of instinct when discussing human behavior. But instinct theorists often support their belief that humans have an instinct for aggression by pointing out examples of how common aggression is. However, simply calling aggression an instinct does not prove that it is one.

Rather than an instinct for aggression, what may have evolved is an aggressive capacity wired into the human neuromuscular system. Researchers point to the behavior of children born deaf and blind who still show aggressive patterns—foot stomping, teeth clenching, and fist making—even though they have had no opportunity to observe these behaviors (Eibl-Eibesfeldt, 1977).

Studies by neuroscientists indicate how the brain is involved in the biological processes of aggression (Niehoff, 1999). We do not appear to have a specific aggression center in the brain, but when the lower, more primitive areas of the brain (such as the limbic system) are stimulated by electric currents, aggressive behavior often results (Herbert, 1988). Neurotransmitters have also been linked to highly aggressive

Aggression has been pervasive throughout our history. *(Top)* Russian czar Ivan the Terrible killed his own son and destroyed the second largest city in his empire, Novgorod, in the sixteenth century. *(Bottom)* In the 1970s, 4 million Cambodians were killed by fellow Cambodians. *What does the prevalence of such events in human history tell us about aggression?*

behavior (Filley & others, 2001). Individuals with depressive disorders who commit suicide by violent means (such as using a gun) have been found to have lower levels of the neurotransmitter serotonin than most people do (Van Winkle, 2000). In one study, young men whose serotonin levels were low relative to those of other men their age were far more likely to have committed a violent crime (Moffitt & others, 1998). Also, children who show high rates of aggression have lower levels of serotonin than children who display low rates of aggression (Mitisis, Halperin, & Newcorn, 2000).

Alcohol, which acts on the brain to stifle our inhibitions, has been strongly linked to violence and aggression. Individuals under the influence of alcohol are more easily provoked than they would be when they are sober to unleash harsh words, throw a punch, or pull the trigger of a gun (Dougherty, Cherek, & Bennett, 1996; Fals-Stewart, Golden, & Schumacher, 2003). People under the influence of alcohol commit almost one-half of rapes and other violent crimes (Abbey, Ross, & McDuffie, 1993; Abbie & others, 2003). Unfortunately, the people who are already prone to aggression are also the ones who are likely to drink and then become violent when they become intoxicated (Seto & Barbaree, 1995).

Psychological Factors in Aggression   Numerous psychological factors appear to be involved in aggression. Some years ago, John Dollard and his colleagues (1939) proposed that *frustration*, the blocking of an individual's attempts to reach a goal, triggers aggression. Not much later, however, psychologists found that aggression is not the only possible response to frustration. Some individuals who experience frustration become passive, for example (Miller, 1941). Psychologists also later recognized that a broad range of aversive experiences besides frustration can cause aggression. They include physical pain, personal insults, and unpleasant events, such as divorce. Environmental psychologists have demonstrated how such factors as noise, weather, and crowding can stimulate aggression. Murder, rape, and assault increase when temperatures are the hottest (during the third quarter of the year), as well as in the hottest years and in the hottest cities (Anderson, 1989; Anderson & Bushman, 2002). Our everyday encounters with other people also produce aversive experiences that can trigger aggressive responses (Schwartz, 1999). For example, when someone cuts into a line in front of us (such as at a ticket booth), we may respond aggressively toward that person (Milgram & others, 1986).

Whether we respond aggressively to aversive situations appears to be determined by our interpretation of the event (Baumeister, 1999; Berkowitz, 1990):

- *Expectations*. You expect to be jostled on a crowded bus, but you don't expect someone to run into you when there are only five or six people on the bus. Thus you might respond more aggressively when you are bumped on a relatively empty bus than on a crowded one.
- *Equity*. If you perceive that an aversive experience is not fair, or justified, you might respond aggressively. For example, if you deserve a *D* in a class, you are less likely to say nasty things about the professor than if you perceive the grade to be unfair.
- *Intentions*. If you think someone has intentionally tripped you, you are more likely to respond aggressively than if you think the individual's feet accidentally became tangled with yours.
- *Responsibility*. When you perceive that other people are responsible for frustrating or aversive actions, you are more likely to behave aggressively toward them. For example, are you more likely to respond aggressively when an 8-year-old child runs into you with a shopping cart in a store or when her assertive, healthy 30-year-old mother does the same thing? You are likely to perceive that the mother is more responsible for her own behavior than the child is, so you would probably respond more aggressively toward the mother.

Behavioral and social cognitive theorists point out that individuals may or may not learn to behave aggressively through the processes of reinforcement and observational

Calvin and Hobbes   by Bill Watterson

learning (Englander, 2003). Aggression is reinforced when it helps people attain money, attention, sex, power, or status. For example, a young adolescent who succeeds in getting the seat he wants by glowering at the schoolmate who is occupying it may try the same sort of aggressive tactic again. If he gets no such response, he begins to learn that aggression is not the key to success. Aggression can also be learned by watching others behave aggressively (Bandura, 1989). One of the most frequent opportunities people have to observe aggression in our culture is on television.

Sociocultural Factors in Aggression   Aggression not only involves biological and cognitive factors but is also linked with factors in the wider social world. The incidence of aggression and violence has varied throughout human history, and aggression and violence are more common in some cultures than others (Bel{esiles, 1999). The risk of being murdered in the United States is much higher than in many other countries—about three times as high as in Canada and six times as high as in Europe (United Nations, 1999; U.S. Bureau of Justice Statistics, 2001). However, South Africa, Colombia, Mexico, and the Philippines have much higher homicide rates than the United States. Crime rates tend to be higher in countries with a considerable gap between the rich and the poor (Triandis, 1994).

Cultural differences in aggression and violence are related to the circumstances that people in a culture face. Famine, crowding, drought, and conflict lead to tremendous upheaval in families and moral values and make aggressive action to obtain food and water a survival measure.

Another possible cultural factor is the emphasis on violence in popular media: on the news and on television shows, in movies, in video games, and in song lyrics. Evildoers kill and get killed; police and detectives violently uphold or even break society's laws; sports announcers glorify aggressive players, whether their behavior is sportsmanlike or contributes to their team's success. It is easy to get the message that aggression and violence are the norm—in fact, are the preferred mode of behavior—in American society.

The amount of aggression on television is a special problem for children. In the 1990s, children watched an average of 26 hours of television each week (National Center for Children Exposed to Violence, 2001). Almost every day of their lives, children watch someone being stabbed, maimed, or slaughtered. In one early study of the effects of TV violence, children were randomly assigned to one of two groups: One watched violent Saturday morning cartoon shows on 11 different days; the second group watched the same cartoon shows with the violence removed (Steur, Applefield, & Smith, 1971). The children were then observed during play at their preschool. The children who saw the TV cartoon shows with violence were more likely to kick, choke, and push their playmates than were the children who saw the cartoon shows

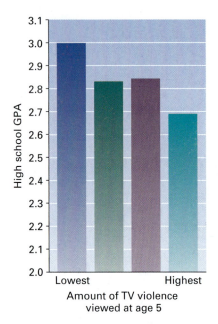

FIGURE 14.9 Viewing TV Violence and Girls' Academic Achievement

Girls who watched the least TV violence at age 5 had a higher grade-point average in high school than girls who watched more TV violence at age 5. The bar on the left represents the 25 percent of girls who watched the least violence at age 5, the second bar the next 25 percent of girls, and so on.

with the violence removed. Many experts insist that most of the evidence to date shows TV violence can cause aggressive or antisocial behavior in children (Bushman & Huesmann, 2001; Perse, 2001; Singer & Singer, 1998).

What children watch on TV is related not only to their aggression but also to their cognitive skills and achievement. In one longitudinal study, viewing educational programs as preschoolers was associated with a host of desirable characteristics in adolescence: getting higher grades, reading more books, placing a higher value on achievement, being more creative, and acting less aggressively (D.R. Anderson, & others, 2001). These associations were more consistent for boys than girls. However, girls who were more frequent viewers of violent TV programs in the preschool years had lower grades in adolescence than girls who infrequently watched violent TV programs in the preschool years (see figure 14.9).

Of course, television violence is not the only cause of aggression. Aggression, like all other social behaviors, has multiple determinants (Donnerstein, 2002). Television violence does not affect adults in isolation from such other factors as aggressive tendencies, marital problems, and job stress. Likewise, the link between TV violence and aggression in children is influenced by children's aggressive tendencies, by their attitudes toward violence, and by the monitoring of children's exposure to it.

Another aspect of media violence that interests researchers is whether watching pornography leads to violence against women (Salmon, 2004). To read further about this topic, see the Critical Controversy box.

Aggression and Gender Our stereotypes clearly tag boys and men as more aggressive than girls and women. In general, research has supported this view. As children, boys are more likely to engage in rough-and-tumble play and to get in more fights in which they are physically aggressive toward each other. As adolescents, males are more likely to be members of gangs and to commit violent acts. Children and adolescents who are diagnosed with conduct disorder (a pattern of offensive behavior that violates the basic rights of others) are three times more likely to be boys than girls (Cohen & others, 1993). As adults, men are more likely to be chronically hostile and to murder or rape than women are (Barefoot & others, 1987).

A classic analysis of research studies reached the following conclusions about aggression and gender (Maccoby & Jacklin, 1974):

- Males are more aggressive than females in all cultures.
- Males are more aggressive than females from early in life, with differences consistently appearing as early as 2 years of age.
- Aggression is more common among males than among females, in animals as well as humans.

These findings often have been interpreted as supporting the view that gender differences in aggression are biologically based.

However, environment and culture also contribute to gender differences in aggression (White, 2001). In one study, individuals in 12 countries were asked to write stories in response to conflicts presented to them (Archer & McDaniel, 1995). In all 12 countries, males wrote stories with more violent themes than females did, suggesting a biological interpretation of gender differences in aggression. However, the degree of violence used in the descriptions varied considerably across the cultures, suggesting an environmental or cultural interpretation.

Despite the strong evidence that gender is a factor in aggression, we need to remind ourselves of an important point about the conclusions drawn from psychological research. When we say that males are more aggressive than females, we cannot jump to the conclusion that all males are more aggressive than all females (Hyde, 2004). In any given culture, some females will be more aggressive than some males.

In addition, we need to consider the type of aggression. Researchers have found stronger gender differences in physical aggression than in verbal aggression (Eagly &

Does Pornography Lead to Violence Against Women?

In 1999, there were 383,000 rapes, attempted rapes, and sexual assaults in the United States, according to the Justice Department's annual National Crime Victimization Survey. Statistics such as these fuel concerns that pornography contributes to a climate in which some men feel that sexual violence toward women is acceptable. Critics of pornography have repeatedly called for laws restricting access to pornography. Defenders, often citing the First Amendment guarantee of freedom of expression, argue against such laws on the grounds that no clear link has been demonstrated between pornography and sexual violence against women (Hawkins & Zimring, 1988). Psychologists have entered the fray to attempt to evaluate scientifically whether the consumption of pornography, in fact, can lead to violence against women.

The most widely accepted explanation of how pornography may affect men's behavior toward women comes from social cognitive theory (Bandura, 1977, 2000). Studies suggest that children who regularly watch violence on television may learn to become more violent, so perhaps men who watch pornography learn to become sexually violent toward women or at least become desensitized to sexual violence.

Based on several meta-analyses and on research of their own, Neil Malamuth and his colleagues (Malamuth, Addison, & Koss, 2000) concluded that pornography consumption does have a small effect on male sexual aggression. But they caution that it is only one of a number of factors that may lead to sexual violence against women. The nature of pornographic material, the characteristics of the men viewing it, and the surrounding culture all combine to produce an effect. In other words, no one factor (such as pornography) is likely to control a complex behavior (such as men's violence against women).

Adding to the complexity of the controversy over pornography is the absence of agreement on a definition of pornography. To some people, pornography means all sexually explicit materials. In contrast, the report of the Attorney General's Commission on Pornography (1986) distinguished between erotica and pornography: Erotica depicts nudity and explicit consensual sex, whereas pornography depicts the domination and humiliation of women, as well as explicit sexual violence toward women. The consumption of erotica, and even nonviolent pornography, is not associated with increases in sexual violence toward women (Malamuth & others, 2000). Apparently, the most problematic materials are those that depict women enjoying being the victims of male sexual violence. Such violent pornography reinforces the rape myth, the false belief that women actually desire coercive sex.

Further, most men are not prone to sexual violence against women (Malamuth & others, 2000). Only men who score higher than average on self-report measures of attraction to sexual aggression, hostile masculinity, or low intelligence appear to be prone to sexual violence against women (Bogaert, Woodard, & Hafer, 1999). In addition, they tend to come from backgrounds that discount gender equality and limit education about sexuality. Such men are vulnerable to believing in the rape myth. When these at-risk men are exposed to violent pornography, they are even more prone to become perpetrators of sexual violence against women (Donnerstein, 2001).

Cultural variables may also be important (Lips, 2003). For example, research conducted after the legalization of pornography in Denmark failed to find evidence of increased criminal sexual acts as a function of the wider availability of pornography (Kutchinsky, 1991). But the Danes generally enjoy a relaxed approach to sex. Public nudity, for example, is more common and more accepted in Denmark than in the United States. Perhaps their more relaxed attitudes make the Danes less vulnerable to the effects of pornography.

One of the most difficult aspects of interpreting research on the effects of pornography on sexual violence against women is distinguishing between correlation and causality. Consider the Danish experience. The relationship between the wider availability of pornography and a lower rate of reported sexual violence probably is not a causal relationship. More likely, broader changes in Danish society underlie both variables. Similarly, it may be that high-risk men need greater stimulation, which is not satisfied even by heavy exposure to pornography. If so, pornography use may be a symptom of an underlying compulsion. Alternatively, it may be that the use of pornography increases an already high level of sexual aggressiveness above a threshold necessary to elicit actual behavior. In this case, pornography would be a contributing cause. Further research is needed to determine whether one or both of these explanations is correct.

What do you think?

- Do you think the distinction among erotica, nonviolent pornography, and violent pornography is a helpful one?
- Do you think that the availability of sexually explicit materials should be restricted?
- How could you use experimental methods to investigate whether sexually explicit materials contribute to sexual violence against women?

Steffen, 1986; Galambos, 2004). One longitudinal study found no gender differences in verbal aggression among 8-year-old children (Björkqvist, Österman, & Lagerspetz, 1994). And at age 18, females displayed more verbal aggression than males.

Ways to Reduce Aggression   You might recall that chapter 9 mentioned the powerful, negative emotion of anger, which can generate aggression. Several strategies for reducing anger apply to this discussion of aggression. Among them is *catharsis,* here the release of anger by directly engaging in anger or aggression. According to psychodynamic and ethological theories, behaving angrily or watching others behave angrily reduces subsequent anger or aggression. But social cognitive theorists disagree strongly. They believe that people who act aggressively often are rewarded for their aggression and that people who watch others behave aggressively learn to be aggressive themselves. Researchers have found more support for the social cognitive view than for the psychodynamic and ethological views on reducing aggression (Bandura, 1986, 1997). Thus good candidates for strategies that will reduce aggression are decreasing rewards for aggression and encouraging people to observe fewer incidences of aggression.

Parents have been specially targeted to help children to reduce aggression. Because of their importance in children's lives, they often have considerable influence. Recommended parenting strategies include encouraging young children to develop empathy toward others and monitoring adolescents' activities (Ceballo & others, 2003; Collins & Laursen, 2004). Gerald Patterson and his colleagues (1989) consistently have found that a lack of parental monitoring is related to juvenile delinquency.

Altruism

We know from experience that social interaction is not all a matter of aggression. We often hear or read about acts of generosity and courage, such as the police, firefighters, and others who risked their lives to save the people in the World Trade Center towers, the volunteers who rushed to the various scenes of the disaster to offer their services to victims and rescuers, and the rock concerts and fundraisers to help the victims of the terrorist attacks on September 11, 2001 (Oliner, 2001). On a more mundane level, you may have placed some of your hard-earned cash in the palm of a homeless person or perhaps cared for a wounded cat. What all of these acts have in common is **altruism,** an unselfish interest in helping someone else.

One recent study of 423 older adult couples who were followed for 5 years revealed the benefits of altruism (Brown & others, 2003). At the beginning of the study, the couples were asked about the extent to which they had given or received emotional or practical help in the past year. Five years later, those who said they had helped others were half as likely to have died. One possible reason for this finding is that helping others may reduce the output of stress hormones, which improves cardiovascular health and strengthens the immune system (Cacioppo, Hawkley, & Bernston, 2003).

Psychological and Sociocultural Foundations of Altruism
How do psychologists account for acts of human altruism? One key aspect is the concept of *reciprocity*, which encourages us to do unto others as we would have them do unto us. It is present in every widely practiced religion in the world—Judaism, Christianity, Buddhism, and Islam, for example. Complex human sentiments are involved in reciprocity: Trust in the people with whom we are interacting is probably the most important principle over the long run. But reciprocity can involve more negative sentiments, such as guilt, if we do not reciprocate a favor, and anger, if someone else does not reciprocate. One study found that college students were more likely to pledge to the charity of someone who had previously

"All I'm saying is, giving a little something to the arts might help our image." © The New Yorker Collection 1989 Peter Steiner from cartoonbank.com. All Rights Reserved.

(Left) Animals may behave altruistically, as when baboons pluck bugs from other baboons. Most acts of animal altruism involve kin. *(Right)* A young woman assists a child with a disability. *How can we explain altruism that does not benefit kin?*

bought them candy (Webster & others, 1999). Altruistic reciprocity was more likely and more generous when the donor's name was made known to the recipient.

Not all altruism is motivated by reciprocity, and not all seemingly altruistic behavior is unselfish. Some psychologists argue that truly selfless altruism has never been demonstrated. Others argue that a distinction between altruism and egoism in giving can be made (Cialdini & others, 1987). **Egoism** involves giving to another person to ensure reciprocity; to gain self-esteem; to appear powerful, competent, or caring; or to avoid social and self-censure for failing to live up to society's expectations. In contrast, altruism is giving to another person with the ultimate goal of benefiting that other person; any benefits that come to the giver are unintended.

Altruistic behavior is determined by the nature of both the person and the situation (Post & others, 2002; Sober, 2001). Describing individuals as having altruistic or egoistic motives implies that psychological variables—a person's ability to empathize with the needy or to feel a sense of responsibility for another person's welfare—are important in understanding altruistic behavior. The stronger these personality dispositions are, the less we would expect situational variables to influence whether giving, kindness, or helping occurs. But as with any human behavior, characteristics of the situation influence the strength of altruistic motivation. Some of these characteristics include the degree of need shown by the other individual, the needy person's responsibility for his or her plight, the cost of assisting the needy person, and the extent to which reciprocity is expected (Batson, 1998, 2002, 2003).

Biological Foundations of Altruism   Evolutionary psychologists believe that tremendous benefits can accrue to individuals who form cooperative, reciprocal relationships (Trivers, 1971). By being good to someone now, individuals increase the likelihood that they will receive a benefit from the other person in the future. Through this reciprocal process, both gain something beyond what they could have by acting alone.

Evolutionary psychologists also emphasize that some types of altruism help to perpetuate our genes (Janicki, 2004; Ruse, 2002; Simpson & Gangestad, 2001). A parent feeding its young is performing a biologically altruistic act because the offspring's chance of survival is increased. So is a mother bird that tries to lure predators away from the fledglings in her nest. She is willing to sacrifice herself so that some of her young offspring will have the chance to survive, thus preserving her genes.

Human beings also often show more empathy toward relatives, who share their genes or have the potential to perpetuate their genes. In natural disasters, people's uppermost concern is their family. In one study involving a hypothetical decision to help in life-or-death situations, college students chose to aid close kin over distant kin (Burnstein, Crandall, & Kitayama, 1994). They also chose to help the young over the old, the healthy over the sick, the wealthy over the poor, and premenopausal women over postmenopausal woman. In the same study, when an everyday favor rather than a life-or-death situation was involved, the college students gave less weight to kinship

altruism An unselfish interest in helping someone else.

egoism The motivation to give to another person to ensure reciprocity; to gain self-esteem; to appear powerful, competent, or caring; or to avoid social and self-censure for failing to live up to expectations.

and chose to help either the very young or the very old over those of intermediate age, the sick over the healthy, and the poor over the wealthy.

Bystander Effect One of the most widely studied aspects of altruism is why one person will help a stranger in distress, whereas another won't lift a finger (Abelson, Frey, & Gregg, 2004). Social psychologists have found that it often depends on the circumstances.

More than 30 years ago, a young woman named Kitty Genovese was brutally murdered on the street in a respectable area of New York City. The murderer left and returned three times; it took the slayer about 30 minutes to kill Kitty. Thirty-eight neighbors watched the gory scene and heard Kitty Genovese's screams. No one helped or even called the police. This incident prompted social psychologists to study the **bystander effect,** the tendency for individuals who observe an emergency to help less when other people are present than when the observers are alone.

Social psychologists John Darley and Bibb Latané (1968) documented the bystander effect in a number of criminal and medical emergencies. When alone, a person will help 75 percent of the time, but when another bystander is present, the figure drops to 50 percent. Apparently the difference is due to the diffusion of responsibility among witnesses and the tendency to look to the behavior of others for clues about what to do. We may think that someone else will call the police or that, because no one else is helping, possibly the person does not need help. (See the video clip "Bystander Effect" for an interview with John Darley and an introduction to the bystander effect and diffusion of responsibility.)

In-Psych Plus

Many other aspects of the situation influence whether the individual will intervene and come to the aid of the person in distress. Bystander intervention is less likely to occur in the following situations (Shotland, 1985):

- The situation is not clear.
- The individuals struggling or fighting appear to be married or related.
- The victim is perceived to be intoxicated.
- The victim is thought to be from a different ethnic group.
- Intervention might lead to personal harm or retaliation by the criminal.
- Helping requires considerable time, such as days in court testifying.
- Bystanders have no history of victimization themselves, have seen few crimes and intervention efforts, or have not had training in first aid, rescue, or police tactics.

Altruism and Gender Who are more helping and caring, males or females? The stereotype is that females are. However, as in most domains, it is a good idea to think about gender in context (Eisenberg & Morris, 2004).

Researchers have found that females are more likely than males to help when the context involves nurturing, such as volunteering time to help a child. However, males are more likely to help in situations in which a perceived danger is present and they feel competent to help (Eagly & Crowley, 1986). For example, males are more likely than females to help a person who is stranded by the roadside with a flat tire. Males also are more likely than females to give a ride to a hitchhiker, probably because of the greater dangers for women in this situation.

Review and Sharpen Your Thinking

4 *Explain the roles of aggression and altruism in social interaction.*

- Discuss the influences on aggressive behavior.
- Describe what social psychologists know about altruism.

Analyze the acts of altruism surrounding the September 11, 2001, terrorist attacks. Can you determine which acts likely were altruistic and which acts likely were egoistic?

bystander effect The tendency for individuals who observe an emergency to help less when someone else is present than when they are alone.

| Attraction | Love | Relationships and Gender |

What is the nature of relationships?

Our close relationships are among the most important aspects of our lives. In some cases, these relationships are extremely positive; in others, they are highly conflicted (Harvey, 2001). Social psychologists have explored several aspects of social relationships. Attraction, love, and intimacy are key dimensions (Baumeister & Bratslavsky, 1999). (For a discussion of evolutionary and sociocultural factors that may influence attraction and mating patterns, see the video clip "Attraction.")

In-Psych Plus

Attraction

What attracts us to others and motivates us to spend more time with them? Does just being around someone increase the likelihood a relationship will develop? Or are we more likely to seek out and associate with those who are similar to us? And how important is physical attraction in the initial stages of a relationship?

Familiarity and Similarity   Social psychologists have found that familiarity is a necessary condition for a close relationship to develop. For the most part, friends and lovers are people who have been around each other for a long time; they may have grown up together, gone to high school or college together, worked together, or gone to the same social events (Brehm, 2002).

But once we have been exposed to someone for a while, what is it that creates friendship and even love? One of the most powerful lessons generated by the study of close relationships is that we like to associate with people who are similar to us (Berscheid, 2000). Our friends and lovers are much more like us than unlike us. We have similar attitudes, behavior patterns, and personal characteristics, as well as similar taste in clothes, intelligence, personality, other friends, values, lifestyle, physical attractiveness, and so on. In some limited cases and on some isolated characteristics, opposites may attract. An introvert may wish to be with an extravert, or someone with little money may wish to associate with someone who has a lot of money, for example. But overall we are attracted to individuals with similar rather than opposite characteristics.

The concept of *consensual validation* explains why people are attracted to others who are similar to them. Our own attitudes and behavior are supported when someone else's attitudes and behavior are similar to ours—their attitudes and behavior validate ours. In addition, people tend to shy away from the unknown. We often prefer to be around people whose attitudes and behavior we can predict. And similarity implies that we will enjoy doing things with another person who likes the same things and has similar attitudes. In one study, this sort of similarity was shown to be especially important in successful marriages (Swann, De La Ronde, & Hixon, 1994).

Physical Attraction   As important as familiarity and similarity may be, they do not explain the spark that often ignites a romantic relationship: physical attraction. Many advertising agencies would have us believe it is the most important factor in establishing and maintaining a relationship. Psychologists do not consider the link between physical beauty and attraction to be so clear-cut, however. For example, they have determined that heterosexual men and women differ on the importance of good looks when they seek an intimate partner. Women tend to rate as most important such traits as considerateness, honesty, dependability, kindness, and understanding; men prefer good looks, cooking skills, and frugality (Buss & Barnes, 1986). The criteria for beauty also differ across cultures and over time within cultures.

DILBERT reprinted by permission of United Feature Syndicate, Inc.

Social psychologists have found that the force of similarity also operates at a physical level. We usually seek out someone at our own level of attractiveness in both physical characteristics and social attributes. Although we may prefer a more attractive person in the abstract, in the real world we end up choosing someone who is close to our own level (Kalick & Hamilton, 1986).

We should take some of these findings with a grain of salt. Much of the research on physical attraction has focused on initial or short-term encounters; researchers have not often evaluated attraction over the course of months and years. As relationships endure, physical attraction probably assumes less importance. Familiarity can overcome even negative initial reactions to a person.

Love

Some relationships never progress much beyond the attraction stage. But some relationships deepen to friendship and from there perhaps to love in one of its guises (Harvey & Weber, 2002; Rusbult & others, 2004). Three types of love have been described by social psychologists.

- **Romantic love,** also called *passionate love,* has strong components of sexuality and infatuation and often predominates in the early part of a love relationship (Hendrick & Hendrick, 2004; Metts, 2004). Well-known love researcher Ellen Berscheid (1988) says that it is romantic love we mean when we say that we are "in love" with someone. Berscheid believes that sexual desire is the most important ingredient of romantic love. In our culture, romantic love is the main reason we get married. More than half of American men and women say that not being in love is sufficient reason to dissolve a marriage (Berscheid, Snyder, & Omoto, 1989). Romantic love comprises a complex intermingling of emotions—fear, anger, sexual desire, joy, and jealousy, for example. Obviously, some of these emotions are a source of anguish. One study found that romantic lovers were more likely than friends to be the cause of depression (Berscheid & Fei, 1977).

- **Affectionate love,** also called *companionate love,* is the type of love that occurs when someone desires to have the other person near and has a deep, caring affection for the person. There is a growing belief that the early stages of love have more romantic ingredients but that, as love matures, passion tends to give way to affection (Berscheid & Reis, 1998). Phillip Shaver (1986) describes the initial phase of romantic love as a time that is fueled by a mixture of sexual attraction and gratification, a reduced sense of loneliness, uncertainty about the security of developing an attachment, and excitement from exploring the novelty of another human being. With time, he says, sexual attraction wanes, attachment anxieties either lessen or produce conflict and withdrawal, novelty is replaced with familiarity, and lovers either find

romantic love Also called *passionate love;* the type of love that has strong components of sexuality and infatuation and that often predominates in the early part of a love relationship.

affectionate love Also called *companionate love;* the type of love that occurs when individuals desire to have the other person near and have a deep, caring affection for the person.

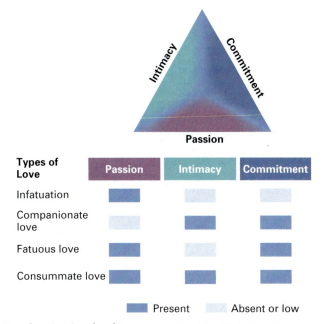

FIGURE 14.10 **Sternberg's Triangle of Love**   Sternberg identified three dimensions that shape the experience we call love: passion, intimacy, and commitment. Various combinations of the three dimensions produce particular types of love. The highest form of love is what Sternberg calls consummate love.

themselves securely attached in a deeply caring relationship or distressed—feeling bored, disappointed, lonely, or hostile, for example. In the last case, one or both partners may eventually seek a different close relationship (Duncombe & others, 2004).

• **Consummate love,** according to Robert J. Sternberg (1988), is the strongest, fullest type of love. Sternberg proposed that consummate love can be thought of as a triangle with three main dimensions—passion, intimacy, and commitment (see figure 14.10). Passion is physical and sexual attraction to another. Intimacy is emotional feelings of warmth, closeness, and sharing in a relationship (Prager & Roberts, 2004). Commitment is our cognitive appraisal of the relationship and our intent to maintain the relationship even in the face of problems (Rusbult & others, 2001). If passion is the only ingredient in a relationship (with intimacy and commitment low or absent), we are merely *infatuated*. An affair or a fling in which there is little intimacy and even less commitment is an example. A relationship marked by intimacy and commitment but low or lacking in passion is *companionate love*, a pattern often found among couples who have been married for many years. If passion and commitment are present but intimacy is not, Sternberg calls the relationship *fatuous love*, as when one person worships another from a distance. But if couples share all three dimensions—passion, intimacy, and commitment—they will experience *consummate love.*

The Psychology and Life box will help you determine what kind of relationship you have with a particular person in your life.

Relationships and Gender

Do women and men hold different views of love? One recent study found that men conceptualize love in terms of passion, whereas women think of love more in terms of friendship (Fehr & Broughton, 2001). However, both women and men associate love and affection.

consummate love The strongest, fullest type of love, comprising passion, intimacy, and commitment.

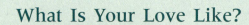
What Is Your Love Like?

Imagine the blank spaces filled in with the name of one person you love or care about deeply. Then rate each of the items from 1 to 9, with 1 = not at all, 5 = moderately, and 9 = extremely.

_____ 1. I actively support _____ 's well-being.

_____ 2. I have a warm relationship with _____ .

_____ 3. I can count on _____ in times of need.

_____ 4. _____ is able to count on me in times of need.

_____ 5. I am willing to share myself and my possessions with _____ .

_____ 6. I receive considerable emotional support from _____ .

_____ 7. I give considerable emotional support to _____ .

_____ 8. I communicate well with _____ .

_____ 9. I value _____ greatly in my life.

_____ 10. I feel close to _____ .

_____ 11. I have a comfortable relationship with _____ .

_____ 12. I feel that I really understand _____ .

_____ 13. I feel that _____ really understands me.

_____ 14. I feel that I can really trust _____ .

_____ 15. I share deeply personal information about myself with _____ .

_____ 16. Just seeing _____ excites me.

_____ 17. I find myself thinking about _____ frequently during the day.

_____ 18. My relationship with _____ is very romantic.

_____ 19. I find _____ to be very personally attractive.

_____ 20. I idealize _____ .

_____ 21. I cannot imagine another person making me as happy as _____ .

_____ 22. I would rather be with _____ than anyone.

_____ 23. There is nothing more important to me than my relationship with _____ .

_____ 24. I especially like physical contact with _____ .

_____ 25. There is something special about my relationship with _____ .

_____ 26. I adore _____ .

_____ 27. I cannot imagine my life without _____ .

_____ 28. My relationship with _____ is passionate.

_____ 29. When I see romantic movies and read romantic books, I think of _____ .

_____ 30. I fantasize about _____ .

_____ 31. I know that I care about _____ .

_____ 32. I am committed to maintaining my relationship with _____ .

_____ 33. Because of my commitment to _____ , I would not let other people come between us.

_____ 34. I have confidence in the stability of my relationship with _____ .

_____ 35. I could not let anything get in the way of my commitment to _____ .

_____ 36. I expect my love for _____ to last for the rest of my life.

_____ 37. I will always feel a strong responsibility for _____ .

_____ 38. I view my commitment to _____ as a solid one.

_____ 39. I cannot imagine ending my relationship with _____ .

_____ 40. I am certain of my love for _____ .

_____ 41. I view my relationship with _____ as permanent.

_____ 42. I view my relationship with _____ as a good decision.

_____ 43. I feel a sense of responsibility toward _____ .

_____ 44. I plan to continue my relationship with _____ .

_____ 45. Even when _____ is hard to deal with, I remain committed to our relationship.

Add up your score for each of the three areas of love: 1–15 (intimacy), 16–30 (passion), and 31–45 (commitment). Following are the average scores of a group of women and men (average age = 31) who were either married or in a close relationship:

Intimacy	Passion	Commitment	Percentile
93	73	85	15
102	85	96	30
111	98	108	50
120	110	120	70
129	123	131	85

The fourth column (percentile) shows the percentage of adults who scored at that level or above. Thus, if your intimacy score is 122, your intimacy is greater than 70 percent of the adults whose scores are averaged here.

One aspect of relationships that seems to be linked to gender is caring (Brannon, 2002; Stewart & McDermott, 2004). Recall the reference to Carol Gilligan's care perspective in chapter 3. Gilligan (1982) believes that social relationships are more important to females than they are to males and that females are more sensitive in social relationships. In contrast, she argues that males are more individualistic and self-oriented. Researchers have, indeed, found that adult females often are caring, supporting, and empathic, whereas adult males often are independent, self-reliant, and unexpressive (Fehr, 2004; Paludi, 2002). And, once the novelty, unpredictability, and urgency of sexual attraction in a love relationship have abated, women are more likely than men to detect deficiencies in caring that indicate the relationship has problems.

Another aspect of relationships that seems to be linked to gender is communication styles (Etaugh & Bridges, 2004; Lips, 2003). Deborah Tannen (1990) reported that a common complaint women have about their husbands is "He doesn't listen to me anymore" or "He doesn't talk to me anymore." Tannen explains the problem by distinguishing between rapport talk and report talk. *Rapport talk* is the language of conversation. It is a way of establishing connections and negotiating relationships. Women prefer to engage in rapport talk. Women enjoy private conversations more than men do, and it is men's lack of interest in rapport talk that bothers many women. *Report talk* is talk that is designed to give information, which includes public speaking. Men prefer to engage in report talk. Men hold center stage through such verbal performances as telling stories and jokes. They learn to use talk as a way of getting and keeping attention. Tannen argues that these gender differences are the result of girls and boys being socialized differently as they grow up. Mothers have participated far more in rearing children than fathers have and have modeled a stronger interest in relationships when interacting with their daughters than when interacting with their sons. She, and others, recommend that men develop a stronger interest in relationships and rapport talk and that women seek more opportunities for report talk, including speaking in public.

Many females show a stronger interest in relationships than many males do. *What has been your experience with the gender differences related to relationships? If you are a female, do you have a strong interest in relationships? If you are a male, do you have less interest in relationships than most females you know?*

Review and Sharpen Your Thinking

5 **Understand the nature of relationships.**

- Describe the factors involved in attraction.
- Identify three types of love.
- Explain how gender affects relationships.

Think about the people to whom you are attracted. What is it about them that attracts you?

You have arrived at the end of this book. You should be able to look back and say you have learned a lot about both yourself and other human beings. You should also see that, although many unanswered questions remain, psychology's quest to understand human behavior produces information we can use to make our lives more enjoyable and humane. What could be more intriguing and important to all of us than psychology's mission of describing, explaining, and predicting the behavior of the human species?

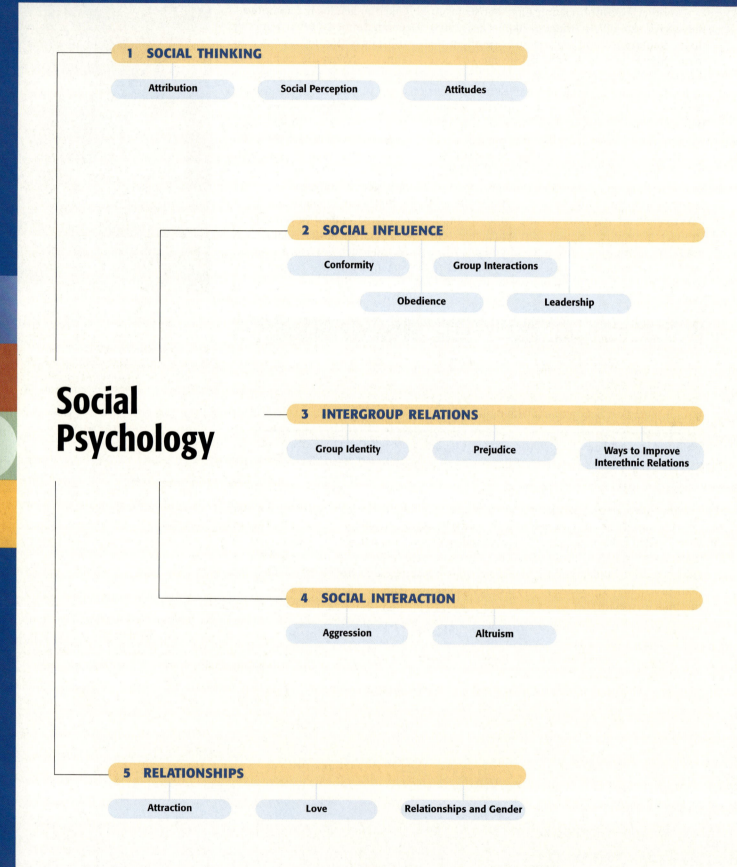

Social Psychology

1 SOCIAL THINKING

Attribution   Social Perception   Attitudes

2 SOCIAL INFLUENCE

Conformity   Group Interactions

Obedience   Leadership

3 INTERGROUP RELATIONS

Group Identity   Prejudice   Ways to Improve Interethnic Relations

4 SOCIAL INTERACTION

Aggression   Altruism

5 RELATIONSHIPS

Attraction   Love   Relationships and Gender

1 Describe how people think about the social world.

- Attributions are our thoughts about why people behave the way they do and about who or what is responsible for the outcome of events. Attribution theory views people as motivated to discover the causes of behavior as part of their effort to make sense of it. The dimensions that we use to make sense of the causes of human behavior include internal/external, stable/unstable, and controllable/uncontrollable. The fundamental attribution error states that observers overestimate the importance of traits and underestimate the importance of situations when they seek explanations of an actor's behavior. When our self-esteem is threatened, we might vary the fundamental attribution error and engage in a self-serving bias, attributing our successes to internal causes and our failures to external causes.

- Social perception involves the impressions we develop of others, comparisons of ourselves with others, and presentation of ourselves to others to influence others' perceptions. Our impressions of others are unified and integrated. An individual's conception of which traits go together is called implicit personality theory. We use social schemas, or prototypes, to simplify our impressions. First impressions are important and influence later impressions. Festinger stresses that social comparison is an important source of self-knowledge, especially when no other objective means is available. We tend to compare ourselves with similar others. Self-presentation to influence others' social perceptions includes two dimensions: impression management to present a favorable self-image and self-monitoring to fine-tune the impressions we are making.

- Attitudes are beliefs or opinions about people, objects, and ideas. We are better able to predict behavior from attitudes when the person's attitudes are strong, when the person is very aware of his or her attitudes and expresses them often, and when the attitudes are specifically relevant to the behavior. Sometimes changes in behavior precede changes in attitude. Cognitive dissonance theory, developed by Festinger, argues that we have a strong need for cognitive consistency: We change our attitudes to make them more consistent with our behavior in order to reduce dissonance. In many cases, we reduce dissonance by justifying our actions. Justification is the most intense when self-esteem is involved. Bem's more behavioral approach stresses self-perception and the importance of making inferences about our attitudes by observing our own behavior, especially when our attitudes are not clear. Success in changing someone's attitudes depends on characteristics of the communicator, the medium by which the message is transmitted, the audience for the message, and the message itself.

2 Identify how people are influenced in social settings.

- Conformity involves a change in a person's behavior to coincide more closely with a group standard. Asch's classic study on judgments of line length illustrated the power of conformity. Many factors influence whether we will conform, including normative social influence and informational social influence.

- Obedience is behavior that complies with the explicit demands of an individual in authority. Milgram's classic experiment demonstrated the power of obedience. Participants obeyed the experimenter's directions, even though they thought they were hurting someone. Disobedience is more likely when others are seen to disobey, when the authority is not considered legitimate and is not close by, and when the victim is humanized. Especially in the face of questionable commands, we have several options short of full compliance.

- Every group has norms and rules that influence its performance. Individual performance in groups is improved through social faciliation and lowered because of social loafing. In a group, we also can experience deindividuation—a loss of personal identity and a decrease in responsibility. The risky shift is the tendency for a group decision to be riskier than the average decision made by the individual group members. The group polarization effect is the solidification and further strengthening of a position as a consequence of group discussion. Groupthink involves impaired decision making and avoidance of realistic appraisal in favor of maintaining harmony in the group. The majority usually gets its way in a group, but the minority may prevail if it presents its views consistently and confidently or has a strong leader.

- Theories of group leadership include the great-person theory (leaders are born), the situational view (leaders are made), and the contingency model (leaders are people who have the ability to take charge when the situation requires it). As leaders, men tend to be more directive and task-oriented, whereas women tend to be more democratic and relationship-oriented.

3 Discuss intergroup relations.

- Social identity is how we define ourselves in terms of our group memberships. Individuals invariably think of the group to which they belong as the in-group, or "we." Identifying with the group encourages a positive self-image. Ethnocentrism is the tendency to favor one's own ethnic group over other groups. Ethnocentrism can have positive or negative outcomes.

- Prejudice is an unjustified negative attitude toward an individual based on the individual's membership in a group. Among the reasons given for why people develop prejudice are an individual's personality (authoritarian), competition between groups over scarce resources, motivation to enhance one's self-esteem, cognitive processes that contribute to a tendency to categorize and stereotype others, and cultural learning. Prejudice is based on stereotyping, a generalization about a group's characteristics that does not consider any variations from one individual to the next. The cognitive process of stereotyping can lead to discrimination, an unjustified negative or harmful action toward a member of a group simply because he or she is a member of that group. Discrimination results when negative emotional reactions combine with prejudiced beliefs and are translated into behavior.

- Contact between ethnic groups, by itself, does not decrease conflict and improve relations. Two effective strategies are to set up task-oriented cooperation and members of different ethnic groups to share intimate information.

4 **Explain the roles of aggression and altruism in social interaction.**

- Aggression may have a biological basis: Early in human evolution, the most aggressive individuals were likely to be the survivors. Freud proposed an instinct theory of aggression, but that view has not been supported. There is some evidence for a genetic basis of aggression, however. Neurobiological factors involved in aggressive behavior include the amygdala, the neurotransmitter serotonin, and alcohol's disinhibiting effects. Psychological factors in aggression include such cognitive factors as frustrating and aversive circumstances, expectations, equity, intentions, responsibility, and such behavioral and social cognitive factors as reinforcement and observational learning. Sociocultural factors include cross-cultural variations and the extensive violence on TV. Gender also is a factor: Males are consistently more physically aggressive than females, but gender differences in verbal aggression are not consistent.

- Altruism is an unselfish interest in helping someone else. Reciprocity often is involved in altruism. The motivation in helping can be altruistic or egoistic. Evolutionary psychologists stress that altruism increases the prospects of survival, as well as reproduction. Evolutionary examples involve favoritism toward kin, as well as parental care for offspring. The bystander effect is the concept that individuals who observe an emergency help less when someone else is present than when they are alone. Gender and context interact to affect altruistic behavior. Females are likelier to help in situations that are not dangerous and involve caregiving. Males are likelier to help in situations that involve danger or in which they feel competent.

5 **Understand the nature of relationships.**

- Familiarity precedes a close relationship. We also like to associate with people who are similar to us, in both social attributes and physical attractiveness. The principle of consensual validation may explain the appeal of similarity. Physical attraction is usually more important in the early part of a relationship. Criteria for physical attractiveness vary across cultures and over time.

- Romantic love (or passionate love) is involved when we say we are "in love." It includes passion, sexuality, and a mixture of emotions, not all of which are positive. Affectionate love (or companionate love) is the type of love that usually becomes more important as relationships mature. Sternberg proposed a model of love involving passion, intimacy, and commitment. Consummate love is that in which all three elements are present in relationships.

- Females have a stronger interest in relationships than males do. Tannen suggests that another important gender difference in relationships relates to communication styles: Females prefer rapport talk, and males prefer report talk.

Key Terms

social psychology, p. 506
attributions, p. 507
fundamental attribution
    error, p. 508
implicit personality theory,
    p. 509
impression management
    (self-presentation), p. 510
self-monitoring, p. 511

attitudes, p. 512
cognitive dissonance, p. 512
conformity, p. 516
normative social influence,
    p. 517
informational social
    influence, p. 517
obedience, p. 518
social facilitation, p. 521

social loafing, p. 520
deindividuation, p. 521
risky shift, p. 521
group polarization effect,
    p. 521
groupthink, p. 522
social identity, p. 525
ethnocentrism, p. 526
prejudice, p. 526

stereotype, p. 528
discrimination, p. 528
altruism, p. 537
egoism, p. 537
bystander effect, p. 538
romantic love, p. 540
affectionate love, p. 540
consummate love, p. 541

Apply Your Knowledge

1. We're often unaware of how many attributions we make about the behavior of others. Spend some time in a crowded area observing the interactions of others (or you could watch some scenes in television shows or movies). Take careful notes about the social behaviors that occur and then indicate your impression of why the people behaved the way they did. What cues did you use to make your decision about their behavior? Did your knowledge of the fundamental attribution error influence your attributions?

2. The chapter discusses stereotyping and prejudice as two factors affecting intergroup relations. Many of our stereotypes and prejudices are quite subtle, and we can be unaware of them. To help you better appreciate the effects of these subtle influences, take one of the tests at the following website:

   http://buster.cs.yale.edu/implicit/index.html. Knowing the results, how can you use the suggestions in the chapter to change your attitudes or behavior?

3. Find a movie that shows an example of aggression (or altruism). Look at the scene and assess the influences that caused the characters to behave aggressively (or altruistically). In what ways are these influences consistent with those discussed in the chapter, and in what ways do they differ?

4. Many of the conclusions about the nature of relationships are based on correlational studies. Discuss the factors that make experiments on relationships difficult, and describe an experiment that you might conduct to test one of the factors described as contributing to attraction.

Connections

To test your mastery of the material in this chapter, go to the Study Guide and the In-Psych Plus CD-ROM, as well as the Online Learning Center. There you will find a chapter summary, practice tests, flashcards, lecture slides, web links, and other study tools, such as interactive exercises and reviews as well as current, chapter-relevant news articles.

Glossary

A   **abnormal behavior** Behavior that is deviant, maladaptive, or personally distressful. p. 393

absolute threshold The minimum amount of stimulus energy that an individual can detect. p. 125

accommodation Occurs when individuals adjust their schemas to take new information into account. p. 86

acculturative stress The negative consequences of contact between two distinctive cultural groups. p. 473

achievement tests Tests that measure what a person has learned or the skills that a person has mastered. p. 291

acquired immune deficiency syndrome (AIDS) A sexually transmitted infection caused by the human immunodeficiency virus (HIV), which destroys the body's immune system. p. 497

acquisition (classical conditioning) The initial learning of the stimulus-response link, which involves a neutral stimulus being associated with an unconditioned stimulus and becoming a conditioned stimulus that elicits the conditioned response. p. 199

action potential The brief wave of electrical charge that sweeps down the axon during the transmission of a nerve impulse. p. 49

addiction An overwhelming need to use a drug and to secure its supply. p. 179

adrenal glands Endocrine glands instrumental in regulating moods, energy level, and ability to cope with stress. p. 65

aerobic exercise Sustained exercise that stimulates heart and lung activity. p. 491

affectionate love Also called *companionate love;* the type of love that occurs when individuals desire to have the other person near and have a deep, caring affection for the person. p. 540

agoraphobia A cluster of fears centered around public places and being unable to escape or to find help, should one become incapacitated. p. 401

alcoholism A disorder that involves long-term, repeated, uncontrolled, compulsive, and excessive use of alcoholic beverages and that impairs the drinker's health and work and social relationships. p. 182

algorithm Strategy that guarantees a solution to a problem. p. 275

altruism An unselfish interest in helping someone else. p. 537

amnesia The loss of memory. p. 258

androgens The class of sex hormones that predominates in males. p. 325

anorexia nervosa An eating disorder that involves the relentless pursuit of thinness through starvation. p. 323

antianxiety drugs Commonly known as tranquilizers; reduce anxiety by making people calmer and less excitable. p. 434

antidepressant drugs Drugs that regulate mood. p. 435

antipsychotic drugs Powerful drugs that diminish agitated behavior, reduce tension, decrease hallucinations, improve social behavior, and produce better sleep patterns in people who have a severe psychological disorder, such as schizophrenia. p. 436

anxiety disorders Psychological disorders that include motor tension, hyperactivity, and apprehensive expectations and thoughts. p. 400

applied behavior analysis (behavior modification) The use of operant conditioning principles to change human behavior. p. 216

approach/approach conflict A conflict in which the individual must choose between two attractive stimuli or circumstances. p. 472

approach/avoidance conflict A conflict involving a single stimulus or circumstance that has both negative and positive characteristics. p. 472

aptitude tests Tests that predict how readily an individual can learn a skill or what the individual can accomplish with training. p. 291

archetypes The name Jung gave to the emotionally laden ideas and images in the collective unconscious that have rich and symbolic meaning. p. 361

assimilation Occurs when individuals incorporate new information into existing knowledge. p. 86

association cortex Regions of the cerebral cortex in which the highest intellectual functions, including thinking and problem solving, occur (also called *association areas*). p. 60

associative learning Learning through either classical conditioning or operant conditioning that two events are connected. p. 195

attachment The close emotional bond between an infant and its caregiver. p. 93

attitudes Beliefs or opinions about people, objects, and ideas. p. 512

attribution theory The idea that individuals are motivated to discover the underlying causes of behavior as part of their effort to make sense of it. p. 333

attributions Ideas about why people behave the way they do. p. 507

auditory nerve Carries neural impulses to the brain's auditory areas. p. 145

authoritarian parenting A restrictive, punitive parenting style in which the parent exhorts the child to follow the parent's directions and respect work and effort. p. 96

authoritative parenting A parenting style that encourages children's independence but still places limits and controls on their behavior and that features extensive verbal give-and-take and warm and nurturant interactions with the child. p. 96

automatic processes States of consciousness that require little attention and do not interfere with other ongoing activities. p. 161

autonomic nervous system The division of the PNS that communicates with the body's internal organs. It consists of the sympathetic and parasympathetic nervous systems. p. 46

aversive conditioning A classical conditioning treatment that consists of repeated pairings of the undesirable behavior with aversive stimuli to decrease the behavior's rewards. p. 446

avoidance/avoidance conflict A conflict in which the individual must choose between two unattractive stimuli or circumstances. p. 472

axon The part of the neuron that carries information away from the cell body to other cells; each neuron has only one axon. p. 48

B   **barbiturates** Depressant drugs that decrease the activity of the central nervous system. p. 183

basal ganglia Large clusters of neurons, located above the thalamus and under the cerebral cortex, that control and coordinate voluntary movements. p. 56

basal metabolism rate (BMR) The minimal amount of energy an individual uses in a resting state. p. 321

behavior Everything we do that can be directly observed. p. 7

behavior modification The application of operant conditioning principles to changing human behavior, with the goal of replacing unacceptable, maladaptive behaviors with acceptable, adaptive behaviors. p. 446

behavior therapies A class of treatment that uses principles of learning to reduce or eliminate maladaptive behavior. p. 444

behavioral and social cognitive perspectives Emphasize the importance of environmental experiences in personality. p. 363

behavioral approach Emphasizes the scientific study of behavior and asserts that behavior is shaped by the environment. p. 22

behavioral medicine An interdisciplinary field that focuses on developing and integrating behavioral and biomedical knowledge to promote health and reduce illness. p. 467

behavioral neuroscience approach Views understanding the brain and nervous system as central to understanding behavior, thought, and emotion. p. 24

big five factors of personality Openness to experience, conscientiousness, extraversion, agreeableness, and neuroticism (emotional stability). p. 373

binocular cues Depth cues based on the combination of the images on the left and right retinas and on the way the two eyes work together. p. 139

biofeedback The process in which individuals' body activities are monitored by instruments and then the information from the instruments is fed back to the individuals, so that they can learn to voluntarily control their physiological activities. p. 490

biological rhythms Periodic physiological fluctuations in the body. p. 164

biological therapies A class of treatment that reduces or eliminates the symptoms of psychological disorders by altering the way an individual's body functions. p. 434

bipolar disorder A mood disorder characterized by extreme mood swings, including one or more episodes of mania. p. 412

brain stem The region of the brain that includes most of the hindbrain (excluding the cerebellum) and the midbrain. p. 54

bulimia nervosa An eating disorder in which the individual consistently follows a binge-and-purge eating pattern. p. 323

burnout A feeling of overload, including mental and physical exhaustion, that usually results from a gradual accumulation of everyday stresses. p. 472

bystander effect The tendency for individuals who observe an emergency to help less when someone else is present than when they are alone. p. 538

C case study An in-depth look at a single individual. p. 14

catatonic schizophrenia A type of schizophrenia characterized by bizarre motor behavior, which sometimes takes the form of a completely immobile stupor. p. 422

catharsis The release of emotional tension a person experiences when reliving an emotionally charged and conflicted experience. p. 441

cell body Part of the neuron that contains the nucleus, which directs the manufacture of substances that the neuron needs for growth and maintenance. p. 48

central nervous system (CNS) The brain and spinal cord. p. 46

cerebral cortex Highest level of the forebrain, where the highest mental functions, such as thinking and planning, take place. p. 57

chromosomes Threadlike structures that contain genes and DNA. Humans have 23 chromosome pairs in the nucleus of every cell. Each parent contributes one chromosome to each pair. p. 67

chunking Grouping, or "packing," information that exceeds the 7 ± 2 memory span into higher-order units that can be remembered as single units. p. 237

circadian rhythms Daily behavioral or physiological cycles, such as the sleep/wake cycle. p. 164

classical conditioning Learning by which a neutral stimulus becomes associated with a meaningful stimulus and acquires the capacity to elicit a similar response. p. 198

client-centered therapy Rogers' humanistic therapy, in which the therapist provides a warm, supportive atmosphere to improve the client's self-concept and encourage the client to gain insight into problems. p. 443

cognition The way in which information is processed and manipulated in remembering, thinking, and knowing. p. 271

cognitive appraisal Lazarus' term for individuals' interpretation of events in their lives as threatening, harmful, or challenging and

their determination of whether they have the resources to cope effectively with the events. p. 478

cognitive approach Focuses on the mental processes involved in knowing: how we direct our attention, perceive, remember, think, and solve problems. p. 24

cognitive dissonance According to Festinger, an individual's motivation to reduce the discomfort (dissonance) caused by two inconsistent thoughts. p. 512

cognitive therapies A class of treatment emphasizing that individuals' cognitions, or thoughts, are the main source of abnormal behavior and psychological problems. p. 447

cognitive-behavior therapy A treatment combining cognitive therapy and behavior therapy. p. 450

collective unconscious Jung's term for the impersonal, deepest layer of the unconscious mind, shared by all human beings because of their common ancestral past. p. 360

concepts Mental categories used to group objects, events, and characteristics. p. 272

concrete operational stage The third Piagetian stage of cognitive development (approximately 7 to 11 years of age), in which thought becomes operational, replacing intuitive thought with logical reasoning in concrete situations. p. 89

conditioned response (CR) The learned response to the conditioned stimulus that occurs after the conditioned stimulus is associated with the unconditioned stimulus. p. 198

conditioned stimulus (CS) A previously neutral stimulus that eventually elicits the conditioned response after being associated with the unconditioned stimulus. p. 198

cones Receptors in the retina that process information about color. p. 133

conformity A change in a person's behavior to coincide more closely with a group standard. p. 516

connectionism The theory that memory is stored throughout the brain in connections between neurons, several of which may work together to process a single memory. p. 244

consciousness Awareness of external events and internal sensations, including awareness of the self and thoughts about one's experiences. p. 160

conservation Piaget's term for belief in the permanence of certain attributes of objects or situations despite superficial changes. p. 88

consummate love The strongest, fullest type of love, comprising passion, intimacy, and commitment. p. 541

control group A comparison group that is treated in every way like the experimental group except for the manipulated factor. p. 17

controlled processes Cognitive activity at the most alert state of consciousness. p. 161

convergent thinking Thinking that produces one correct answer; characteristic of the type of thinking required on traditional intelligence tests. p. 300

coping Managing taxing circumstances, expending effort to solve life's problems, and seeking to master or reduce stress. p. 483

corpus callosum The large bundle of axons that connects the brain's two hemispheres. p. 60

correlational research Research with the goal of describing the strength of the relationship between two or more events or characteristics. p. 14

counterconditioning A classical conditioning procedure for weakening a conditioned response by associating the fear-provoking stimulus with a new response that is incompatible with the fear. p. 202

couples therapy Therapy with married or unmarried couples whose major problem is within their relationship. p. 454

creativity The ability to think about something in novel and unusual ways and come up with unconventional solutions to problems. p. 300

critical thinking The process of thinking reflectively and productively, as well as evaluating evidence. p. 29

crystallized intelligence An individual's accumulated information and verbal skills. p. 112

D deductive reasoning Reasoning from the general to the specific. p. 277

defense mechanisms The ego's protective methods for reducing anxiety by unconsciously distorting reality. p. 357

deindividuation The tendency for an individual in a group to experience a reduced sense of personal identity and personal responsibility. p. 521

dendrites Branches of neurons that receive and orient information toward the cell body. Most neurons have numerous dendrites. p. 48

deoxyribonucleic acid (DNA) A complex molecule, located on chromosomes, that contains information. p. 67

dependent variable The factor that can change in an experiment in response to changes in the independent variable. p. 17

depressants Psychoactive drugs that slow down mental and physical activity. p. 180

depressive disorders Mood disorders in which the individual suffers depression without ever experiencing mania. p. 411

development The pattern of change in human capabilities that begins at conception and continues throughout the life span. p. 79

difference threshold The smallest difference in stimulation required to discriminate one stimulus from another 50 percent of the time; also called *just noticeable difference.* p. 128

discrimination (classical conditioning) The process of learning to respond to certain stimuli and not to others. p. 199

discrimination (operant conditioning) Responding to stimuli that signal whether a behavior will or will not be reinforced. p. 211

discrimination An unjustified negative or harmful action toward a person simply because he or she is a member of a particular group. p. 528

disorganized schizophrenia A type of schizophrenia in which an individual has delusions and hallucinations with little or no recognizable meaning. p. 421

display rules Sociocultural standards that determine when, where, and how emotions should be expressed. p. 345

dissociative amnesia A dissociative disorder involving extreme memory loss caused by extensive psychological stress. p. 408

dissociative disorders Psychological disorders that involve a sudden loss of memory or change in identity. p. 408

dissociative fugue A dissociative disorder in which the individual not only develops amnesia but also unexpectedly travels away from home and may establish a new identity. p. 408

dissociative identity disorder (DID) Formerly called *multiple personality disorder,* this is the most dramatic but least common dissociative disorder; individuals suffering from this disorder have two or more distinct personalities. p. 409

divergent thinking Thinking that produces many answers to the same question; characteristic of creativity. p. 300

double-blind experiment An experiment that is conducted so that neither the experimenter nor the participants are aware of which participants are in the experimental group and which are in the control group until after the results are calculated. p. 18

drive An aroused state that occurs because of a physiological need. p. 315

DSM-IV *Diagnostic and Statistical Manual of Mental Disorders,* 4th edition; the most recent major classification of psychological disorders by the American Psychiatric Association. p. 396

dysthymic disorder A depressive disorder that is generally more chronic and has fewer symptoms than major depressive disorder. p. 411

E ego The Freudian structure of personality that deals with the demands of reality. p. 357

egoism The motivation to give to another person to ensure reciprocity; to gain self-esteem; to appear powerful, competent, or caring; or to avoid social and self-censure for failing to live up to expectations. p. 537

elaboration The extensiveness of processing at any given level of memory. p. 233

electroconvulsive therapy (ECT) Commonly called *shock therapy;* a treatment for severely depressed individuals that causes a seizure in the brain. p. 438

emotion A feeling, or affect, that can involve physiological arousal, conscious experience, and behavioral expression. p. 337

emotion-focused coping Lazarus' term for responding to stress in an emotional manner, especially using defensive appraisals. p. 483

emotional intelligence The ability to perceive and express emotion accurately and adaptively, to understand emotion and emotional knowledge, to use feelings to express thought, and to manage emotions in oneself and others. p. 296

empirically keyed test Relies on items to predict some criterion. p. 382

encoding How information gets into memory storage. p. 233

endocrine system A set of glands that regulate the activities of certain organs by releasing hormones into the bloodstream. p. 64

episodic memory The retention of information about the where and when of life's happenings. p. 240

estrogens The class of sex hormones that predominates in females. p. 325

ethnocentrism The tendency to favor one's own ethnic group over other groups. p. 526

etiology The causes or significant antecedents of a disorder. p. 401

evolutionary psychology approach Emphasizes the importance of functional purpose and adaptation in explaining why behaviors are formed, are modified, and survive. p. 25

experiment A carefully regulated procedure in which one or more factors believed to influence the behavior being studied are manipulated and all other factors are held constant. p. 17

experimental group A group in a research study whose experience is manipulated. p. 17

experimenter bias The influence of the experimenter's own expectations on the outcome of the research. p. 18

explicit memory The conscious recollection of information, such as specific facts or events and, at least in humans, information that can be verbally communicated. p. 240

extinction (classical conditioning) The weakening of the conditioned response in the absence of the unconditioned stimulus. p. 200

extinction (operant conditioning) Becoming less likely to perform a previously reinforced behavior when it is no longer reinforced. p. 211

extrinsic motivation A motivation that involves external incentives, such as rewards and punishments. p. 316

F **facial feedback hypothesis** The idea that facial expressions can influence emotions, as well as reflect them. p. 343

family therapy Group therapy with family members. p. 454

figure-ground relationship The organization of the perceptual field into stimuli that stand out (figure) and those that are left over (background). p. 139

fixation Using a prior problem-solving strategy and failing to look at a problem from a new perspective. p. 275

fluid intelligence One's ability to reason abstractly. p. 112

forebrain The highest level of the brain. Key structures in the forebrain are the limbic system, thalamus, basal ganglia, hypothalamus, and cerebral cortex. p. 55

formal operational stage The fourth and final Piagetian stage of cognitive development (emerging at about 11 to 15 years of age), in which thinking becomes more abstract, idealistic, and logical. p. 90

free association The psychoanalytic technique of having individuals say aloud whatever comes into their minds. p. 440

frontal lobe The part of the cerebral cortex just behind the forehead that is involved in the control of voluntary muscles, intelligence, and personality. p. 59

functional fixedness A type of fixation in which individuals fail to solve a problem because they are fixated on a thing's usual functions. p. 275

fundamental attribution error The tendency to overestimate the importance of traits and underestimate the importance of situations when seeking explanations of someone else's behavior. p. 508

G **gender** The social and psychological aspects of being female or male. p. 101

gender role Expectations for how females and males should think, act, and feel. p. 102

general adaptation syndrome (GAS) Selye's term for the common effects on the body when demands are placed on it; consists of three stages: alarm, resistance, and exhaustion. p. 476

generalization (classical conditioning) The tendency of a new stimulus that is similar to the original stimulus to elicit a response that is similar to the conditioned response. p. 199

generalization (operant conditioning) Giving the same response to similar stimuli. p. 210

generalized anxiety disorder An anxiety disorder that consists of persistent anxiety for at least 1 month; the individual with this disorder cannot specify the reasons for the anxiety. p. 400

genes The basic units of hereditary information; short segments of chromosome composed of DNA. p. 67

gestalt psychology The study of how people naturally organize their perceptions according to certain patterns. p. 139

gestalt therapy Perls' humanistic therapy, in which the therapist challenges clients to help them become more aware of their feelings and face their problems. p. 444

gifted Individuals who have an IQ of 120 or higher, superior talent in a particular domain, or both. p. 299

glial cells Nerve cells that provide support and nutritional benefits to the nervous system. p. 48

group polarization effect The solidification and further strengthening of a position as a consequence of a group discussion. p. 521

groupthink Impaired decision making within a group and avoidance of realistic appraisal by its members in order to maintain group harmony. p. 522

H **hallucinogens** Psychoactive drugs that modify a person's perceptual experiences and produce visual images that are not real. p. 185

hardiness A personality style characterized by a sense of commitment (rather than alienation), control (rather than powerlessness), and a perception of problems as challenges (rather than threats). p. 468

health psychology A discipline that emphasizes psychology's role in promoting and maintaining health and preventing and treating illness. p. 467

heritability The variance in a population that is caused by genetic effects. p. 303

heuristics Guidelines that suggest, but do not guarantee, a solution to a problem. p. 275

hierarchy of needs Maslow's view that individuals' main needs are satisfied in the following sequence: physiological, safety, love and belongingness, esteem, and self-actualization. p. 317

hindbrain The lowest level of the brain, consisting of the medulla, cerebellum, and pons. p. 54

homeostasis The body's tendency to maintain an equilibrium, or steady state. p. 315

hormones Chemical messengers manufactured by the endocrine glands. p. 64

human sexual response pattern A sequence identified by Masters and Johnson; consists of four phases—excitement, plateau, orgasm, and resolution. p. 325

humanistic movement Emphasizes a person's capacity for personal growth, freedom to choose a destiny, and positive qualities. p. 26

humanistic perspectives Stress the person's capacity for personal growth, freedom to choose a destiny, and positive qualities. p. 367

humanistic therapies A class of treatment that encourages people to understand themselves and to grow personally; the humanistic therapies are unique in their emphasis on self-healing capacities. p. 443

hypnosis A psychological state, or possibly a state of altered attention and awareness, in which the individual is unusually responsive to suggestions. p. 175

hypothalamus Forebrain structure involved in regulating eating, drinking, and sex; directing the endocrine system through the pituitary gland; and monitoring emotion, stress, and reward. p. 56

hypothesis An idea that is a testable prediction, often arrived at logically from a theory. p. 10

hypothetical-deductive reasoning Piaget's term for the ability to develop hypotheses about ways to solve a problem and to systematically deduce the best solution. p. 90

I **id** The Freudian structure of personality that consists of instincts, which are the individual's reservoir of psychic energy. p. 357

implicit memory Memory in which behavior is affected by prior experience without that experience being consciously recollected. p. 241

implicit personality theory The layperson's conception of which personality traits go together in an individual. p. 509

impression management (self-presentation) Acting in a way that will present a desired image of oneself as a certain type of person, which might or might not be who one really is. p. 510

imprinting The tendency of an infant animal to form an attachment to the first moving object it sees or hears. p. 94

independent variable The manipulated, influential, experimental factor in an experiment. p. 17

individual psychology Adler's approach, which views people as motivated by purposes and goals, being creators of their own lives. p. 361

inductive reasoning Reasoning from the specific to the general. p. 277

indulgent parenting A parenting style in which parents are involved with their children but place few limits on them. p. 96

informational social influence The influence that other people have on us because we want to be right. p. 517

inner ear Consists of the oval window, cochlea, and basilar membrane. p. 143

insight learning A form of problem solving in which the organism develops a sudden insight into or understanding of the problem's solution. p. 223

insight therapy The psychodynamic and humanistic therapies, which share the goal of encouraging insight and self-awareness. p. 439

instinct An innate (unlearned), biological pattern of behavior that is assumed to be universal throughout a species. p. 315

instinctive drift The tendency of animals to revert to instinctive behavior that interferes with learning. p. 196

integrative therapy A combination of techniques from different therapies based on the therapist's judgment of which techniques will provide the greatest benefit for the client. p. 459

intelligence Problem-solving skills and the ability to adapt to and learn from everyday experiences. p. 287

intelligence quotient (IQ) An individual's mental age divided by chronological age and multiplied by 100. p. 289

intrinsic motivation A motivation based on internal factors, such as self-determination, curiosity, challenge, and effort. p. 316

K **kinesthetic senses** Provide information about movement, posture, and orientation. p. 151

L **language** A form of communication, whether spoken, written, or signed, that is based on a system of symbols. p. 280

latent content In Freud's view, a dream's hidden content; its unconscious meaning. p. 173

latent learning Learning, in the absence of reinforcement, that is not immediately reflected in behavior. p. 222

law of effect Thorndike's concept that behaviors followed by positive outcomes are strengthened, whereas behaviors followed by negative outcomes are weakened. p. 205

learned helplessness A response to prolonged stress over which the individual has no control; apathy and helplessness may lead to depression. p. 415

learning A relatively permanent change in behavior that occurs through experience. p. 195

limbic system Loosely connected network of structures—including the amygdala and hippocampus—that play important roles in memory and emotion. p. 55

locus of control Individuals' beliefs about whether the outcomes of their actions depend on what they do (internal control) or on events outside of their personal control (external control). p. 365

long-term memory The memory system in which huge amounts of information are held relatively permanently. p. 239

M **major depressive disorder (MDD)** A mood disorder indicated by a major depressive episode and depressed characteristics, such as lethargy and hopelessness, lasting at least 2 weeks. p. 411

manifest content In Freud's view, a dream's surface content, which contains symbols that distort and disguise the dream's true meaning. p. 173

medical model A biological approach that describes psychological disorders as medical diseases with a biological origin. p. 394

meditation The practice and system of thought that incorporates exercises to attain bodily and/or mental control and well-being, as well as enlightenment. p. 490

memory The retention of information over time through encoding, storage, and retrieval. p. 230

memory span The number of digits an individual can repeat back in order after a single presentation of them. p. 237

mental age (MA) An individual's level of mental development relative to others. p. 289

mental processes Thoughts, feelings, and motives experienced privately and that cannot be observed directly. p. 7

mental retardation A condition of limited mental ability in which the individual has a low IQ, usually below 70, has difficulty adapting to everyday life, and has an onset of these characteristics in the so-called developmental period. p. 297

mental set A type of fixation in which an individual tries to solve a problem in a particular way that has worked in the past. p. 277

meta-analysis Statistical analysis that combines the results of many different studies. p. 456

midbrain The region located between the hindbrain and forebrain, in which many nerve-fiber systems ascend and descend to connect the higher and lower portions of the brain. p. 54

middle ear Consists of the eardrum, hammer, anvil, and stirrup. p. 143

Minnesota Multiphasic Personality Inventory (MMPI) The most widely used and researched self-report personality test. p. 382

monocular cues Depth cues that can be extracted from the image in either eye. p. 139

mood disorders Psychological disorders in which there is a disturbance in mood (prolonged emotion that colors the individual's entire emotional state). p. 410

motivation Gives behavior, thoughts, and feelings a purpose and makes behavior energized, directed, and sustained. p. 315

motor cortex The area of the cerebral cortex that processes information about voluntary movement. p. 59

myelin sheath A layer of fat cells that encases and insulates most axons, thus speeding up the transmission of nerve impulses. p. 48

N **natural selection** An evolutionary process that favors organisms' traits or characteristics that are best adapted to reproduce and survive. p. 8

naturalistic observation Observation of behavior in a real-world setting with no effort made to manipulate or control the situation. p. 12

nature An organism's biological inheritance. p. 81

need A deprivation that energizes the drive to eliminate or reduce the deprivation. p. 315

need for achievement The desire to accomplish something, to reach a standard of excellence, and to expend effort to excel. p. 333

negative affectivity (NA) Negative emotions, such as anxiety, anger, guilt, and sadness. p. 346

negative reinforcement The process that increases the frequency of a behavior by removing an aversive (unpleasant) stimulus. p. 208

neglectful parenting A parenting style in which parents are uninvolved in their child's life. p. 96

nervous system The body's electrochemical communication circuitry, made up of billions of neurons. p. 44

neural networks Clusters of nerve cells that are interconnected to process sensory and motor information. p. 46

neurons Nerve cells specialized for processing information. Neurons are the basic units of the nervous system. p. 48

neurotransmitters Chemicals that carry information across the synaptic gap from one neuron to the next. p. 49

noise Irrelevant and competing stimuli. p. 126

normal distribution A symmetrical, bell-shaped curve, with a majority of the scores falling in the middle of the possible range and few scores appearing toward the extremes of the range. p. 289

normative social influence The influence that other people have on us because we seek their approval or avoid their disapproval. p. 517

nurture An organism's environmental experiences. p. 81

O obedience Behavior that complies with the explicit demands of an individual in authority. p. 518

object permanence Piaget's term for the cognitive ability to understand that objects and events continue to exist even when they cannot be directly seen, heard, or touched. p. 87

observational learning The form of learning that occurs when a person observes and imitates behavior; also called *imitation* or *modeling*. p. 219

obsessive-compulsive disorder (OCD) An anxiety disorder; the individual has anxiety-provoking thoughts that will not go away (obsession) or urges to perform repetitive, ritualistic behaviors to prevent or produce some future situation (compulsion). p. 404

occipital lobe The part of the cerebral cortex at the back of the head that is involved in vision. p. 59

Oedipus complex In Freud's theory, the young child's development of an intense desire to replace the same-sex parent and enjoy the affections of the opposite-sex parent. p. 359

olfactory epithelium A sheet of receptor cells for smell, located in the roof of the nasal cavity. p. 151

operant conditioning A form of learning in which the consequences of behavior change the probability of the behavior's occurrence; also called *instrumental conditioning*. p. 205

operations Piaget's term for mental representations that are "reversible." p. 87

opiates Opium or its derivatives; they depress central nervous system activity. p. 183

outer ear Consists of the pinna and the external auditory canal. p. 143

P pain The sensation that warns us that damage to our bodies is occurring. p. 148

panic disorder An anxiety disorder marked by the recurrent, sudden onset of intense apprehension or terror. p. 401

papillae Bumps on the tongue that contain taste buds, the receptors for taste. p. 151

parallel processing The simultaneous distribution of information across different neural pathways. p. 134

paranoid schizophrenia A type of schizophrenia characterized by delusions of reference, grandeur, and persecution. p. 422

paraprofessional A person who has been taught by a professional to provide some mental health services but who does not have formal mental health training. p. 454

parasympathetic nervous system The division of the autonomic nervous system that calms the body. p. 46

parietal lobe The area of the cerebral cortex at the top of the head that is involved in registering spatial location, attention, and motor control. p. 59

perception The brain's process of organizing and interpreting sensory information to give it meaning. p. 123

perceptual constancy Recognition that objects are unchanging even though sensory input about them is changing. p. 140

perceptual set A predisposition or readiness to perceive something in a particular way. p. 131

peripheral nervous system (PNS) The network of nerves that connects the brain and spinal cord to other parts of the body. It is divided into the somatic nervous system and the autonomic nervous system. p. 46

personality A pattern of enduring, distinctive thoughts, emotions, and behaviors that characterize the way an individual adapts to the world. p. 355

personality disorders Chronic, maladaptive cognitive-behavioral patterns that are thoroughly integrated into the individual's personality. p. 425

pheromones Odorous substances released by animals that is a powerful sexual attractant. p. 327

phobic disorder Commonly called *phobia;* an anxiety disorder in which the individual has an irrational, overwhelming, persistent fear of a particular object or situation. p. 402

physical dependence The physical need for a drug, which creates unpleasant withdrawal symptoms when the drug is discontinued. p. 179

pituitary gland The endocrine gland at the base of the skull that controls growth and regulates other glands. p. 64

plasticity The brain's special capacity for change. p. 45

polygraph A machine that monitors changes in the body thought to be influenced by emotional states; it is used by examiners to try to determine if someone is lying. p. 338

positive affectivity (PA) Positive emotions, such as joy, happiness, love, and interest. p. 346

positive psychology movement Emphasizes the experiences that people value subjectively (such as happiness), positive individual traits (such as the capacity for love), and positive group and civic values (such as responsibility). p. 26

positive reinforcement The process that increases the frequency of a behavior by providing a rewarding stimulus. p. 208

post-traumatic stress disorder (PTSD) An anxiety disorder that develops through exposure to a traumatic event, a severely oppressive situation, severe abuse, or a natural or an unnatural disaster. p. 406

prejudice An unjustified negative attitude toward an individual based on the individual's membership in a group. p. 526

preoperational stage The second Piagetian stage of cognitive development (approximately 2 to 7 years of age), in which thought becomes more symbolic, egocentric, and intuitive rather than logical; but the child cannot yet perform operations. p. 87

preparedness The species-specific biological predisposition to learn in certain ways and not others. p. 196

primary reinforcement The use of reinforcers that are innately satisfying. p. 208

priming A type of implicit memory; information that people already have in storage is activated to help them remember new information better and faster. p. 241

proactive interference A disruption of memory that occurs when material learned earlier interferes with the recall of material learned later. p. 256

problem-focused coping Lazarus' term for the cognitive strategy of squarely facing troubles and trying to solve them. p. 483

procedural memory Memory for skills. p. 241

projective test Presents individuals with an ambiguous stimulus and then asks them to describe it or tell a story about it; based on the assumption that the ambiguity of the stimulus allows individuals to project their personalities onto it. p. 378

prospective memory Remembering information about doing something in the future. p. 240

psychoactive drugs Drugs that act on the nervous system to alter consciousness, modify perceptions, and change moods. p. 179

psychoanalysis Freud's psychotherapeutic technique for analyzing an individual's unconscious thoughts. Freud believed that clients' problems could be traced to childhood experiences, many of which involved conflicts about sexuality. p. 440

psychodynamic approach Emphasizes the unconscious aspects of the mind, conflict between biological instincts and society's demands, and early family experiences. p. 23

psychodynamic perspectives View personality as primarily unconscious (beyond awareness) and as developing in stages. Most psychodynamic perspectives emphasize early experiences' effects on personality. p. 356

psychodynamic therapies A class of treatment that stresses the importance of the unconscious mind, extensive interpretation by the therapist, and the role of experiences in the early-childhood years. The goal is to help individuals recognize the maladaptive ways they have been coping and the sources of their unconscious conflicts. p. 440

psychological dependence The strong desire and craving to repeat the use of a drug for emotional reasons. p. 179

psychology The scientific study of behavior and mental processes. p. 7

psychosexual dysfunctions Disorders that involve impairments in the sexual response pattern, either in the desire for gratification or the ability to achieve it. p. 328

psychosurgery A biological therapy that involves removal or destruction of brain tissue to improve an individual's adjustment. p. 439

psychotherapy The process used by mental health professionals to help individuals recognize, define, and overcome their psychological and interpersonal difficulties. p. 434

puberty A period of rapid skeletal and sexual maturation that occurs mainly in early adolescence. p. 105

punishment A consequence that decreases the likelihood a behavior will occur. p. 211

R **random assignment** The assignment of participants to experimental and control groups by chance. p. 18

rational-emotive behavior therapy (REBT) A cognitive therapy based on Ellis' assertion that individuals develop a psychological disorder because of their beliefs, especially those that are irrational and self-defeating. p. 448

recall A memory task in which the individual must retrieve previously learned information. p. 249

recognition A memory task in which the individual only has to identify learned items when they are presented. p. 249

rehearsal The conscious repetition of information to increase the durability of memory. p. 237

reinforcement The process by which a stimulus or an event strengthens or increases the probability of a behavior or an event that it follows. p. 207

reliability The extent to which a test yields a consistent, reproducible measure of performance. p. 291

REM sleep Rapid-eye-movement sleep (stage 5), during which most dreaming occurs. p. 169

research participant bias The influence of research participants' expectations on their behavior within an experiment. p. 18

resistance The client's unconscious defense strategies that prevent the analyst from understanding the person's problems. p. 441

reticular formation The midbrain system that consists of a diffuse collection of neurons involved in stereotypical behaviors, such as walking, sleeping, or turning to attend to a sudden noise. p. 54

retina The light-sensitive surface in the back of the eye that houses light receptors called rods and cones. p. 133

retrieval The memory process of taking information out of storage. p. 249

retroactive interference A disruption of memory that occurs when material learned later interferes with the retrieval of information learned earlier. p. 256

retrospective memory Remembering the past. p. 240

risky shift The tendency for a group decision to be riskier than the average decision made by individual group members. p. 521

rods Receptors in the retina that are sensitive to light but are not very useful in color vision. p. 133

romantic love Also called *passionate love;* the type of love that has strong components of sexuality and infatuation and that often predominates in the early part of a love relationship. p. 540

Rorschach inkblot test A widely used projective test that determines an individual's personality through his or her perception of inkblots. p. 378

S **schedules of reinforcement** "Timetables" that determine when a behavior will be reinforced. p. 209

schema A concept or framework that already exists at a given moment in a person's mind and that organizes and interprets information. pp. 86, 244

schizophrenia A severe psychological disorder characterized by highly disordered thought processes. p. 420

science In psychology, the use of systematic methods to observe, describe, predict, and explain behavior. p. 7

script A schema for an event. p. 244

secondary reinforcement The use of reinforcers that acquire their positive value through experience. p. 208

secure attachment An important aspect of socioemotional development in which infants use the caregiver, usually the mother, as a secure base from which to explore the environment. p. 95

selective attention Focusing on a specific aspect of experience while ignoring others. p. 130

self-actualization The highest and most elusive of Maslow's needs; the development of one's full potential as a human being. p. 317

self-concept A central theme in Rogers' and other humanists' views; individuals' overall perceptions of their abilities, behavior, and personality. p. 368

self-efficacy The belief that one can master a situation and produce positive outcomes. pp. 364, 485

self-esteem A person's overall evaluation of self-worth or self-image. p. 369

self-monitoring Paying attention to the impressions one makes on others and fine-tuning one's performance accordingly. p. 511

self-report tests Directly ask people whether items (usually true/false or agree/disagree) describe their personality traits or not; also called *objective tests* or *inventories*. p. 381

semantic memory A person's knowledge about the world. p. 240

semicircular canals Channels containing sensory receptors that detect head position and motion, located in the inner ear. p. 152

sensation The process of receiving stimulus energies from the environment. p. 122

sensorimotor stage The first Piagetian stage of cognitive development (birth to about 2 years of age), in which infants construct an understanding of the world by coordinating sensory experiences (such as seeing and hearing) with motor (physical) actions. p. 87

sensory adaptation A change in the responsiveness of the sensory system based on the average level of surrounding stimulation. p. 128

sensory memory The memory system that holds information from the world in its original form for only an instant, not much longer than the brief time it is exposed to the visual, auditory, and other senses. p. 236

sensory receptors Specialized cells that detect and transmit stimulus information to sensory neurons and the brain. p. 124

serial position effect The tendency for items at the beginning and at the end of a list to be recalled more readily. p. 249

set point The weight maintained when no effort is made to gain or lose weight. p. 321

sexual scripts Stereotyped patterns of expectancies for how people should behave sexually. p. 326

sexually transmitted infections (STIs) An infection contracted primarily through sex—intercourse as well as oral-genital and anal-genital sex. p. 497

shaping The process of rewarding approximations of desired behavior. p. 206

short-term memory The memory system in which a limited amount of information is retained for only as long as 30 seconds unless strategies are used to retain it longer. p. 236

social cognitive theory Stresses that behavior is determined not only by environmental conditions but also by how thoughts modify the impact of environment on behavior. pp. 23, 364

social facilitation The tendency for an individual's performance to improve because of the presence of others. p. 521

social identity A definition of ourselves in terms of our group membership. p. 525

social loafing The tendency for an individual to exert less effort in a group because of reduced accountability for individual effort. p. 520

social psychology The study of how people think about, influence, and relate to other people. p. 506

social support Information and feedback from others that one is loved and cared for, esteemed and valued, and included in a network of communication and mutual obligation. p. 486

sociocultural approach Emphasizes social and cultural influences on behavior. p. 25

somatic nervous system The division of the PNS consisting of sensory nerves, whose function is to convey information to the CNS, and motor nerves, whose function is to transmit information to the muscles. p. 46

somatosensory cortex The area of the cerebral cortex that processes information about body sensations. p. 59

spontaneous recovery The process in classical conditioning by which a conditioned response can recur after a time delay without further conditioning. p. 200

standardization The extent to which uniform procedures have been developed for administering and scoring a test, as well as the creation of norms for the test. p. 292

standardized test A test that requires people to answer a series of written and/or oral questions. Standardized tests have two distinct features: (1) An individual's score is totaled to yield a single score or set of scores; and (2) the individual's score can be compared with the scores of a large group of similar people to determine how the individual responded relative to others. p. 12

stereotype A generalization about a group's characteristics that does not consider any variations from one individual to another. p. 528

stimulants Psychoactive drugs that increase central nervous system activity. p. 183

storage How information is retained over time and how it is represented in memory. p. 235

stream of consciousness James' concept that the mind is a continuous flow of sensations, images, thoughts, and feelings. p. 160

stress The response of individuals to the circumstances and events, called stressors, that threaten and tax their coping abilities. p. 468

stress management programs Programs that teach individuals to appraise stressful events, to develop skills for coping with stress, and to put these skills into use in their everyday lives. p. 490

subliminal perception The ability to detect information below the level of conscious awareness. p. 126

superego The Freudian structure of personality that deals with morality. p. 357

sympathetic nervous system The division of the autonomic nervous system that arouses the body. p. 46

synapses Tiny junctions between two neurons, generally where the axon of one neuron meets the dendrites or the cell body of another neuron. p. 49

systematic desensitization A method of behavior therapy, based on classical conditioning, that treats anxiety by getting the person to associate deep relaxation with increasingly intense anxiety-producing situations. p. 445

T **temperament** An individual's behavioral style and characteristic way of responding. p. 95

temporal lobe The portion of the cerebral cortex just above the ears that is involved in hearing, language processing, and memory. p. 59

thalamus Forebrain structure that functions as a relay station to sort input and direct it to different areas of the cerebral cortex. It also has ties to the reticular formation. p. 56

Thematic Apperception Test (TAT) A projective test designed to elicit stories that will reveal something about an individual's personality. p. 379

theory A broad idea or set of closely related ideas that attempts to explain certain observations. Theories try to explain why certain things have happened. Thus they also can be used to make predictions about future observations. p. 9

thermoreceptors Receptors under the skin that respond to increases and decreases in temperature. p. 147

thinking Manipulating information, as when we form concepts, solve problems, think critically, reason, and make decisions. p. 272

tolerance The need to take increasing amounts of a drug to produce the same effect. p. 179

trait An enduring personality characteristic that tends to lead to certain behaviors. p. 372

tranquilizers Depressant drugs that reduce anxiety and induce relaxation. p. 183

transference The client's relating to the analyst in ways that reproduce or relive important relationships in the individual's life. p. 441

triarchic In Sternberg's theory, there are three main types of intelligence: analytical, creative, and practical. p. 295

two-factor theory of emotion Schachter and Singer's theory that emotion is determined by two main factors: physiological arousal and cognitive labeling. p. 341

Type A behavior pattern A cluster of characteristics—being excessively competitive, hard-driven, and hostile—thought to be related to the incidence of heart disease. p. 468

Type B behavior pattern Being relaxed and easygoing. p. 468

U **unconditional positive regard** Rogers' term for accepting, valuing, and being positive toward another person regardless of the person's behavior. p. 368

unconditioned response (UCR) An unlearned response that is automatically elicited by an unconditioned stimulus. p. 198

unconditioned stimulus (UCS) A stimulus that produces a response without prior learning. p. 198

unconscious thought Freud's concept of a reservoir of unacceptable wishes, feelings, and thoughts that are beyond conscious awareness. p. 163

undifferentiated schizophrenia A type of schizophrenia characterized by disorganized behavior, hallucinations, delusions, and incoherence. p. 422

V **validity** The extent to which a test measures what it is intended to measure. p. 291

vestibular sense Provides information about balance and movement. p. 151

 wisdom Expert knowledge about the practical aspects of life. p. 113

wish fulfillment Freud's concept of dreaming as an unconscious attempt to fulfill needs (especially for sex and aggression) that cannot be expressed, or that go ungratified, while awake. p. 173

working memory A three-part system that temporarily holds information as people perform tasks; a kind of mental workbench on which information is manipulated and assembled to perform other cognitive tasks. p. 238

References

A

Aartsen, M. J., Martin, M., Zimprich, D., & the Longitudinal Aging Study Amsterdam (2004). Gender differences in level and change in cognitive functioning: Results from the Longitudinal Aging Study Amsterdam. *Geronotology, 50,* 35–38.

Abbey, A., Clinton-Sherrod, A. M., McAuslan, P., Zawacki, T., & Buck, P. O. (2003). The relationship between quantity of alcohol consumed and the severity of sexual assaults committed by college men. *Journal of Interpersonal Violence, 18,* 813–833.

Abbey, A., Ross, L. T., & McDuffie, D. (1993). Alcohol's role in sexual assault. In R. R. Watson (Ed.), *Drug and alcohol abuse reviews. Vol. 5: Addictive behaviors in women.* Totowa, NJ: Humana Press.

Abelson, J. L., Weg, J. G., Nesse, R. M., & Curtis, G. C. (2001). Persistent respiratory irregularity in patients with panic disorder. *Biological Psychiatry, 49,* 588–595.

Abelson, R. P., Frey, K. P., & Gregg, A. P. (2004). *Experiments with people.* Mahwah, NJ: Erlbaum.

Abrams, D., & Hogg, M. A. (2004). Metatheory: Lessons from social identity research. In A. W., Kruglanski & E. T. Higgins (Eds.), *Theory construction in social-personality psychology.* Mahwah, NJ: Erlbaum.

Abramson, L. Y., Seligman, M. E. P., & Teasdale, J. (1978). Learned helplessness in humans: Critique and reformulation. *Journal of Abnormal Psychology, 87,* 49–74.

Achat, H., Kawachi, I., Spiro, A., DeMolles, D. A., & Sparrow, D. (2000). Optimism and depression as predictors of physical and mental health functioning: The Normative Aging Study. *Annals of Behavioral Medicine, 22,* 127–130.

Ackerman, P. L., Kyllonen, P. C., & Roberts, R. D. (Eds.). (1999). *Learning and individual differences: Process, trait, and content determinants.* Washington, DC: American Psychological Association.

Adams, H. E., & Cassidy, J. F. (1993). The classification of abnormal behavior: An overview. In P. B. Sutker & H. E. Adams (Eds.), *Comprehensive textbook of psychopathology* (2nd ed.). New York: Plenum Press.

Ader, R. (1974). Letter to the editor: Behaviorally conditioned immunosuppression. *Psychosomatic Medicine, 36,* 183–184.

Ader, R. (2000). On the development of psychoneuroimmunology. *European Journal of Pharmacology, 405,* 167–176.

Ader, R., & Cohen, N. (1975). Behaviorally conditioned immunosuppression. *Psychosomatic Medicine, 37,* 333–340.

Ader, R., & Cohen, N. (2000). Conditioning and immunity. In R. Ader, D. L. Felton, & N. Cohen (Eds.), *Psychoneuroimmunology,* (3rd ed.). San Diego: Academic Press.

Adler, A. (1927). *The theory and practice of individual psychology.* Fort Worth: Harcourt Brace.

Adler, N. E. (2001). A consideration of multiple pathways from socioeconomic status to health. In J.A. Auerbach & B.K. Krimgold (Eds.), *Income, socioeconomic status, and health.* Washington, DC: National Policy Association.

Adler, T. (1991, January). Seeing double? Controversial twins study is widely reported, debated. *APA Monitor, 22,* 1, 8.

Adorno, T. W., Frenkel-Brunswick, E., Levinson, D. J., & Sanford, R. N. (1950). *The authoritarian personality.* New York: Harper & Row.

Ahasan, R., Lewko, J., Campbell, D., & Slamoni, A. (2001). Adaptation to night shifts and synchronization processes of night workers. *Journal of Physiological Anthropology, 20,* 215–226.

Aiken, L. R. (2003). *Psychological testing and assessment* (11th ed.). Boston: Allyn & Bacon.

Ainsworth, M. D. S. (1979). Infant-mother attachment. *American Psychologist, 34,* 932–937.

Ajzen, I. (2001). Nature and operation of attitudes. *Annual Review of Psychology.* (Vol. 52). Palo Alto, CA: Annual Reviews.

Alan Guttmacher Institute. (2000, February 24). *United States and the Russian Federation lead the developed world in teenage pregnancy rates.* New York: The Alan Guttmacher Institute.

Alberti, R., & Emmons, M. (1995). *Your perfect right* (7th ed.). San Luis Obispo, CA: Impact.

Alberto, P., & Troutman, A. C. (1999). *Applied behavior analysis for teachers* (5th ed.). Upper Saddle River, NJ: Merrill.

Albrecht, T. L., & Goldsmith, D. J. (2003). Social support, social networks, and health. In T. L. Thompson & A. M. Dorsey (Eds.), *Handbook of health communication.* Mahwah, NJ: Erlbaum.

Albrecht, U. (2002). Invited review: Regulation of mammalian circadian clock genes. *Journal of Applied Physiology, 92,* 1348–1355.

Albright, A., & Hayes, B. (2003). Rules vs. analogy in English past tenses. *Cognition, 90,* 119–161.

Aldenkamp, A. P., & Arends, J. (2004). Effects of epileptiform EEG discharges on cognitive function: is the concept of "transient cognitive impairment" still valid? *Epilepsy and Behavior, 5, Supplement 1,* 25–34.

Alderman, M. K. (1999). *Motivation for achievement.* Mahwah, NJ: Erlbaum.

Alderman, M. K. (2004). *Motivation and achievement.* Mahwah, NJ: Erlbaum.

Alexander, D. A., & Klein, S. (2001). Caring for others can seriously damage your health. *Hospital Medicine, 62,* 264–267.

Al-Issa, I. (1982). Does culture make a difference in psychopathology? In I. Al-Issa (Ed.), *Culture and psychopathology.* Baltimore: University Park Press.

Alkire, M. T., Haier, R. J., & James, H. F. (1998). Toward the neurobiology of consciousness: Using brain imaging and anesthesia to investigate the anatomy of consciousness. In S. Hameroff, A. Kaszniak, & A. Scott (Eds.), *Toward a Science of Consciousness II.* Cambridge, MA: MIT Press.

Allan, K., Wolf, H. A., Rosenthal, C. R., & Rugg, M. D. (2001). The effects of retrieval cues on postretrieval monitoring in episodic memory: An electrophysiological study. *Brain Research, 12,* 289–299.

Allan, R., & Scheidt, S. (Eds.). (1996). *Heart and mind.* Washington, DC: American Psychological Association.

Allen, D. N., Goldstein, G., & Weiner, C. (2001). Differential neuropsychological patterns of frontal- and temporal-lobe dysfunction in patients with schizophrenia. *Schizophrenia Research, 48,* 7–15.

Allen, J., Kraus, N., & Bradlow, A. (2000). Neural representation of consciously imperceptible speech sound differences. *Perception and Psychophysics, 62,* 1383–1393.

Allen, J. E., Pertea, M., & Salzberg, S. L. (2004). Computational gene prediction using multiple sources of evidence. *Genome Research, 14,* 142–148.

Allen, J. J. (1998). DSM-IV. In H. S. Friedman (Ed.), *Encyclopedia of mental health* (Vol. 2). San Diego: Academic Press.

Allen, J. J., & Movius, H. L. (2000). The objective assessment of amnesia in dissociative identity disorder using event-related potentials. *International Journal of Psychophysiology, 38,* 21–41.

Alloy, L. B., & Abramson, L. Y. (1979). Judgment of contingency in depressed and nondepressed students: Sadder but wiser? *Journal of Experimental Psychology: General, 108,* 441–485.

Alloy, L. B., Abramson, L. Y., & Francis, E. L. (1999). Do negative cognitive styles confer vulnerability to depression? *Current Directions in Psychological Science, 8,* 128–132.

Allport, G. W. (1937). *Personality: A psychological interpretation.* New York: Holt.

Allport, G. W. (1954). *The nature of prejudice.* Reading, MA: Addison-Wesley.

Almagor, M., Tellegen, A., & Waller, N. G. (1995). The big seven model: A cross-cultural replication and further exploration of the basic dimensions of natural language trait descriptors.

Al-Mashaan, O. S. (2001). Job stress and job satisfaction in relation to neuroticism, type A behavior, and locus of control among Kuwaiti personnel. *Psychological Reports, 88,* 1145–1152.

Alterman, A. I., Gariti, P., & Mulvaney, F. (2001). Short- and long-term smoking cessation for three levels of intensity of behavioral treatment. *Psychology and Addictive Behavior, 15,* 261–264.

Altmann, E. M., & Gray, W. D. (2002). Forgetting to remember: The functional relationship of decay and interference. *Psychological Science, 13,* 27–33.

Amato, P. R., & Keith, B. (1991). Parental divorce and the well-being of children: A meta-analysis. *Psychological Bulletin, 110,* 26–46.

American Academy of Pediatrics. (2001). Health care supervision for children with Williams syndrome. *Pediatrics, 107,* 1192–1204.

American Association on Mental Retardation, Ad Hoc Committee on Terminology and Classification. (1992). *Mental retardation* (9th ed.). Washington, DC: Author.

American Psychiatric Association. (1994). *Diagnostic and statistical manual of mental disorders* (4th ed.). Washington, DC: American Psychiatric Press.

American Psychiatric Association. (2000). *Diagnostic and statistical manual of mental disorders, Fourth edition, Text revision.* Washington, DC: Author.

American Psychiatric Association. (2001). *Mental illness.* Washington, DC: Author.

American Psychological Association (1995). *Questions and answers about memories of child abuse.* Washington, DC: Author.

American Sleep Apnea Association. (2001). *Sleep apnea: General information packet.* Washington, DC: American Sleep Apnea Association.

Amsel, E., & Byrnes, J. (2001). Symbolic communication and cognitive development. In J. Byrnes & E. Amsel (Eds.), *Language, literacy, and cognitive development.* Mahwah, NJ: Erlbaum.

Anastasi, A., & Urbina, S. (1996). *Psychological testing* (7th ed.). Upper Saddle River, NJ: Prentice Hall.

Anderson, B. A., Golden-Kreutz, D. M., & DiLillo, V. (2001). Cancer. In A. Baum, T. A. Revenson, & J. E. Singer (Eds.), *Handbook of health psychology.* Mahwah, NJ: Erlbaum.

Anderson, B. L. (1983). Primary orgasmic dysfunction: Diagnostic considerations and a review of treatment. *Psychological Bulletin, 93,* 105–136.

Anderson, B. L. (1998). Cancer. In H.S. Friedman (Ed.), *Encyclopedia of mental health* (Vol. 1). San Diego: Academic Press.

Anderson, B. L. (2000). Cancer. In A. Kazdin (Ed.), *Encyclopedia of psychology*. Washington, DC, & New York: American Psychological Association and Oxford University Press.

Anderson, B. L., Kiecolt-Glaser, J. K., & Glaser. R. (1994). A biobehavioral model of cancer stress and disease course. *American Psychologist, 49,* 389–404.

Anderson, C. A. (1989). Temperature and aggression. *Journal of Personality and Social Psychology, 106,* 74–96.

Anderson, C. A., & Bushman, B. J. (2002). Human aggression. *Annual Review of Psychology* (Vol. 53). Palo Alto, CA: Annual Reviews.

Anderson, D. R., Huston, A. C., Schmitt, K., Linebarger, D., & Wright, J. C. (2001). Early television viewing and adolescent behavior: The recontact study. *Monographs of the Society for Research in Child Development, 66* (1, Serial No. 264).

Anderson, E. M., & Lambert, M. J. (2001). A survival analysis of clinically significant change in outpatient psychotherapy. *Journal of Clinical Psychology, 57,* 875–888.

Anderson, J. R. (2000). *Cognitive psychology* (5th ed.). New York: Worth.

Anderson, M. C., & Green, C. (2001, March 15). Suppressing unwanted memories by executive control. *Nature, 410,* 366–369.

Anderson, N. B. (Ed.). (2004). *Encyclopedia of health and human behavior.* Thousand Oaks, CA: Sage.

Anderson, N. H. (1965). Primacy effects in personality impression formation using a generalized order effect paradigm. *Journal of Personality and Social Psychology, 2,* 1–9.

Anderson, N. H. (1974). Cognitive algebra: Integration theory applied to social attribution. In L. Berkowitz (Ed.), *Advances in experimental social psychology* (Vol. 7). New York: Academic Press.

Anderson, N. H. (1989). Functional memory and on-line attribution. In J. N. Bassili (Ed.), *On-line cognition in person perception.* Mahwah, NJ: Erlbaum.

Anderson, R. A. (2002). Parietal lobe. *Annual Review of Neuroscience* (Vol. 25). Palo Alto, CA: Annual Reviews.

Andrade, C., Shah, N., & Tharyan, P. (2003). The dilemma of unmodified electroconvulsive therapy. *Journal of Clinical Psychiatry, 64,* 1146–1152.

Angers, T. (1999). *The forgotten hero of My Lai: The Hugh Thompson story.* Lafayette, LA: Arcadian House.

Angold, A., Costello, E. J., & Worthman, C. M. (1998). Puberty and depression: The roles of age, pubertal status, and pubertal timing. *Psychological Medicine, 28,* 51–61.

Antonucci, T. C. (2001). Social relations. In J. E. Birren & K. W. Schaie (Eds.), *Handbook of the psychology of aging* (5th ed.). San Diego: Academic Press.

Antonucci, T. C., Vandewater, E. A., & Lansford, J. E. (2000). Adult development and aging: Social processes and development. In A. Kazdin (Ed.), *Encyclopedia of psychology.* Washington, DC, & New York: American Psychological Association and Oxford University Press.

Apker, J., & Ray, E. B. (2003). Stress and social support in health care organizations. In T. L. Thompson & A. M. Dorsey (Eds.), *Handbook of health communication.* Mahwah, NJ: Erlbaum.

Appleyard, S. M., Hayward, M., Young, J. I., Butler, A. A., Cone, R. D., Rubinstein, M., & Low, M. J. (2003). A role for the endogenous opioid beta-endrophin in energy homeostasis. *Endocrinology, 144,* 1753–1760.

Arai, S., Morita, K., Kitayama, S., Kumagai, K., Kumagai, M., Kihra, K., & Dohi, T. (2003). Chronic inhibition of the norepinephrine transporter in the brain participates in seizure sensitization to cocaine and local anesthetics. *Brain Research, 964,* 83–90.

Arana-Ward, M. (1997). As technology advances, a bitter debate divides the deaf. *Washington Post,* p. A1.

Archer, D., & McDaniel, P. (1995). Violence and gender: Differences and similarities across societies. In R. B. Ruback & N. A. Weiner (Eds.), *Interpersonal violent behaviors: Social and cultural aspects.* New York: Springer.

Archer, R. P., Handel, R. W., Greene, R. L., Baer, R. A., & Elkins, D. E. (2001). An evaluation of the usefulness of the MMPI-2 F (p) sale. *Journal of Personality Assessment, 76,* 282–285.

Archibald, A. B., Graber, J. A., & Brooks-Gunn, J. (2003). Pubertal processes and physical growth in adolescence. In G. R. Adams & M. Berzonsky (Eds.), *Handbook of adolescence.* Malden, MA: Blackwell.

Arkowitz, H. (1997). Integrative theories of therapy. In P. L. Wachtel & S. B. Messer (Eds.), *Theories of psychotherapy.* Washington, DC: American Psychological Association.

Arledge, E. (Writer & Director), **& Cort, J.** (Writer). (2001). Cracking the code of life [Television series episode]. In P. S. Apsell (Executive Producer), *NOVA.* Boston: WGBH and Clear Blue Sky Productions.

Arnitz, A., & van den Hout, M. A. (1996). Psychological treatment of panic disorder without agoraphobia: Cognitive therapy versus applied relaxation. *Behaviour Research and Therapy, 34,* 113–121.

Arnkoff, D. B., Glass, C. R., & Shapiro, S. J. (2002). Expectations and preferences. In J. C. Norcross (Ed.), *Psychotherapy relationships that work.* New York: Oxford University Press.

Aron, A., & Aron, E. N. (2003). *Statistics for the behavioral and social sciences* (2nd ed.). Upper Saddle River, NJ: Prentice Hall.

Aronson, E. (1986, August). *Teaching students things they think they already know all about: The case of prejudice and desegregation.* Paper presented at the meeting of the American Psychological Association, Washington, DC.

Aronson, E. (1995). *The social animal* (7th ed.). New York: Freeman.

Aronson, E. (2000). *Nobody left to hate.* New York: Freeman.

Aronson, E., Wilson, T. D., & Akert, R. M. (1997). *Social psychology* (2nd ed.). New York: Longman.

Aronson, E., Wilson, T. D., & Akert, R. M. (2002). *Social psychology* (4th ed.). Upper Saddle River, NJ: Prentice-Hall.

Aronson, J. M. (2002). Stereotype threat: Contending and coping with unnerving expectations. In J. Arsonson (Ed.), *Improving academic achievement.* San Diego: Academic Press.

Aronson, J. M., Cohen, G., & Nails, P. R. (1999). Unwanted consequences and the self: In search of the motivation for dissonance reduction. In E. Harmon-Jones & J. Mills (Eds.), *Cognitive dissonance.* Washington, DC: American Psychological Association.

Aronson, J. M., Fried, C. B., & Good, C. (2002). Reducing the effects of stereotype threat on African American college students by shaping theories of intelligence. *Journal of Experimental Social Psychology, 38,* 113–125.

Aronson, J. M., Lustina, M. J., Good, C., Keough, K., Steele, C. M., & Brown, J. (1999). When White men can't do math: Necessary and sufficient factors in stereotype threat. *Journal of Experimental Social Psychology, 35,* 29–46.

Asch, S. E. (1946). Forming impressions of personality. *Journal of Personality and Social Psychology, 41,* 248–290.

Asch, S. E. (1951). Effects of group pressure on the modification and distortion of judgments. In H. S. Guetzkow (Ed.), *Groups, leadership, and men.* Pittsburgh: Carnegie University Press.

Ashcraft, M. H., & Kirk, E. P. (2001). The relationships among working memory, math anxiety, and performance. *Journal of Experimental Psychology: General, 130,* 224–237.

Ashcroft, D. (2003). *Personalities theories workbook* (2nd ed.). Belmont, CA: Wadsworth.

Ashida, H., Seiffert, A. E., & Osaka, N. (2001). Inefficient visual search for second-order motion. *Journal of the Optical Society of America, 18,* 2255–2266.

Astin, A. W. (1993). *What matters in college.* San Francisco: Jossey-Bass.

Atkin, J. M., & Black, P. (1997, September). Policy perils of international comparisons. *Phi Delta Kappan, 79,* 22–28.

Atkinson, D. R. (2004). *Counseling American minorities* (6th ed.). New York: McGraw-Hill.

Atkinson, J. W., & Raynor, I. O. (1974). *Motivation and achievement.* Washington, DC: Winston.

Atkinson, R. C., & Shiffrin, R. M. (1968). Human memory: A proposed system and its control processes. In K. W. Spence & J. T. Spence (Eds.), *The psychology of learning and motivation* (Vol. 2). San Diego, CA: Academic Press.

Attorney General's Commission on Pornography. (1986). *Final report.* Washington, DC: U.S. Department of Justice.

Auerbach, S. M., & Gramling, S. E. (1998). *Stress management.* Upper Saddle River, NJ: Prentice-Hall.

Auger, C., Latour, S., Trudel, M., & Fortin, M. (2000). Post-traumatic stress disorder: After the flood in Saguenay. *Canadian Family Physician, 46,* 2420–2427.

Auyang, S. Y. (2001). *Mind in everyday life and cognitive science.* Cambridge, MA: MIT Press.

Azar, S. T. (2002). Parenting and child maltreatment. In M. Bornstein (Ed.), *Handbook of parenting* (2nd ed.). Mahwah, NJ: Erlbaum.

Azhar, M. Z. (2001). Comparison of Fluvoxamine alone, Fluvoxamine and cognitive psychotherapy and psychotherapy alone in the treatment of panic disorder in Kelantan: Implications for management by family doctors. *Medical Journal of Malaysia, 55,* 402–408.

Azuma, H. (2004, August). *Conceptual issues of cultural psychology.* Paper presented at the 28th International Congress of Psychology, Beijing, China.

B

Baars, B. (1999). Psychology in a world of sentimental, self-knowing beings: A modest utopian fantasy. In R. L. Solso (Ed.), *Mind and brain sciences in the 21st century.* Cambridge, MA: MIT Press.

Backman, L., Small, B. J., & Wahlin, A. (2001). Aging and memory. In J. E. Birren & K. W. Schaie (Eds.), *Handbook of the psychology of aging* (5th ed.). San Diego: Academic Press.

Baddeley, A. (1992). Working memory. *Science, 255,* 556–560.

Baddeley, A. (1993). Working memory and conscious awareness. In A. F. Collins, S. E. Gatherhole, M. A. Conway, & P. E. Morris (Eds.), *Theories of memory.* Mahwah, NJ: Erlbaum.

Baddeley, A. (1998). *Human memory* (Rev. ed.). Boston: Allyn & Bacon.

Baddeley, A. (2000). Short-term and working memory. In E. Tulving & F. I. M. Craik (Eds.), *The Oxford handbook of memory.* New York: Oxford University Press.

Baddeley, A. (2001). *Is working memory still working?* Paper presented at the meeting of the American Psychological Association, San Francisco.

Baddeley, A. (2003). Working memory and language: An overview. *Journal of Communication Disorders, 36,* 189–208.

Baddeley, A. D., & Hitch, G. (1974). Working memory. In G. H. Bower (Eds.), *The psychology of learning and motivation* (Vol. 8). San Diego: Academic Press.

Badgaiyan, R. D., Schacter, D. L., & Alpert, N. M. (2001). Priming within and across modalities: Exploring the nature of rCBF increases and decreases. *NeuroImage, 13,* 272–282.

Baehr, E. K., Revelle, W., & Eastman, C. I. (2000). Individual differences in the phase and amplitude of the human circadian temperature rhythm with an emphasis on morningness-eveningness. *Journal of Sleep Research, 9,* 117–127.

Baillargeon, R. (1997). The object concept revisited. In C. E. Granrud (Ed.), *Visual perception and cognition in infancy.* Mahwah, NJ: Erlbaum.

Baity, M. R., & Hilsenroth, M. J. (1999). Rorschach aggression variables: A study of reliability and validity. *Journal of Personality and Assessment, 72,* 93–110.

Baker, B. (2001, March). *Marital interaction in mild hypertension.* Paper presented at the meeting of the American Psychosomatic Association, Monterey, CA.

Baker, N. L. (2001). Prejudice. In J. Worell (Ed.), *Encyclopedia of gender and women.* San Diego: Academic Press.

Baker, T. B., Brandon, T. H., & Chassin, L. (2004). The psychology of cigarette smoking. *Annual Review of Psychology, 54.* Palo Alto, CA: Annual Reviews.

Baldo, M. V., Kihra, A. H., Namba, J., & Klein, S. A. (2002). Evidence for an attentional component of the perceptual misalignment between moving and flashing stimuli. *Perception, 31,* 17–30.

Baldwin, J. D., & Baldwin, J. I. (1998). Sexual behavior. In H. S. Friedman (Ed.), *Encyclopedia of mental health* (Vol. 3). San Diego: Academic Press.

Baldwin, J. D., & Baldwin, J. I. (2001). *Behavior principles in everyday life.* Upper Saddle River, NJ: Prentice-Hall.

Ball, R., & Steer, R. A. (2003). Mean Beck Depression Inventory-II scores of outpatients with dysthymic or recurrent-episode major depressive disorders. *Psychological Reports, 93,* 507–512.

Baltes, P. B. (1993). The aging mind: Potentials and limits. *Gerontologist, 33,* 580–594.

Baltes, P. B. (2000). Life-span developmental theory. In A. Kazdin (Ed.), *Encyclopedia of psychology.* Washington, DC, & New York: American Psychological Association and Oxford University Press.

Baltes, P. B., Lindenberger, U., & Staudinger, U. M. (1998). Life-span theory in developmental psychology. In W. Damon (Ed.), *Handbook of child psychology* (5th ed., Vol. 1). New York: Wiley.

Bandura, A. (1965). Influences of models' reinforcement contingencies on the acquisition of imitative responses. *Journal of Personality and Social Psychology, 1,* 589–596.

Bandura, A. (1977). *Social learning theory.* Upper Saddle River, NJ: Prentice Hall.

Bandura, A. (1986). *Social foundations of thought and action.* Upper Saddle River, NJ: Prentice Hall.

Bandura, A. (1989). Social cognitive theory. In R. Vasta (Ed.), *Six theories of child development.* Greenwich, CT: JAI Press.

Bandura, A. (1997). *Self-efficacy: The exercise of self-control.* New York: Freeman.

Bandura, A. (1998, August). *Swimming against the mainstream: Accentuating the positive aspects of humanity.* Paper presented at the meeting of the American Psychological Association, San Francisco.

Bandura, A. (2000). Social cognitive theory. In A. Kazdin (Ed.), *Encyclopedia of psychology.* Washington, DC, and New York: American Psychological Association and Oxford University Press.

Bandura, A. (2001). Social cognitive theory. *Annual Review of Psychology* (Vol. 52). Palo Alto, CA.

Bandura, A., & Locke, E. A. (2003). Negative self-efficacy and goal effects revisited. *Journal of Applied Psychology, 88,* 87–99.

Banks, J. (2002). *Introduction to multicultural education* (5th ed.). Boston: Allyn & Bacon.

Banks, J. (2003). *Teaching strategies for ethnic studies* (7th ed.). Boston: Allyn & Bacon.

Bannerman, K., Lemaire, M., Yee, K., Iversen, D., Oswald, P., Good, A., & Rawlins, G. A. (2002). Selective cytotoxic lesions of the retrohippocampal region produce a mild deficit in social recognition memory. *Experimental Brain Research, 142,* 395–401.

Barber, T. X. (1969). *Hypnosis.* New York: Von Nostrand Reinhold.

Bard, P. (1934). Emotion. In C. Murchison (Ed.), *Handbook of general psychology.* Worcester, MA: Clark University Press.

Barefoot, J. C., Siegler, I. C., Nowlin, J. B., & Peterson, B. L. (1987). Suspiciousness, health, and mortality: A follow-up study of 500 older adults. *Psychosomatic Medicine, 49,* 450–457.

Barker, L. M. (2001). *Learning and behavior* (3rd ed.). Upper Saddle River, NJ: Prentice-Hall.

Barlow, D. H. (1988). *Anxiety and its disorders: The nature and treatment of anxiety and panic.* New York: Guilford.

Barlow, D. H. (2001). *Anxiety and its disorders* (2nd ed.). New York: Guilford.

Barlow, D. H., Gorman, J. M., Shear, M. K., & Woods, S. W. (2000). Cognitive-behavioral therapy, imipramine, or their combination for panic disorder: A randomized controlled trial. *Journal of the American Medical Association, 283,* 2229–2236.

Barnett, R. C., & James, J. (2001). *Career and family expectations of female and male freshmen.* Unpublished manuscript, Radcliffe College, Cambridge, MA.

Baron, N. (1992). *Growing up with language.* Reading, MA: Addison-Wesley.

Barron, K. E., & Harackiewicz, J. M. (2001). Achievement goals and optimal motivation: Testing multiple goal models. *Journal of Personality and Social Psychology, 80,* 706–722.

Barry, H., Child, I. L., & Bacon, M. K. (1959). Relation of child training to subsistence economy. *American Anthropologist, 61,* 51–63.

Bartlett, F. C. (1932). *Remembering.* Cambridge: Cambridge University Press.

Bartlett, J. C. (2001, June). Personal communication. Richardson, TX: University of Texas at Dallas, Program in Psychology.

Bartoshuk, L. M., & Beauchamp, G. K. (1994). Chemical senses. *Annual Review of Psychology* (Vol. 45). Palo Alto, CA: Annual Reviews.

Bassett, A. S., Cohw, E. W., Waterworth, D. M., & Brzustowicz, L. (2001). Genetic insights into schizophrenia. *Canadian Journal of Psychiatry, 46,* 121–122.

Basso, M. R., Schefft, B. K., Ris, M. D., & Dember, W. N. (1996). Mood and global-local visual processing. *Journal of the International Neuropsychological Society, 2,* 249–255.

Batson, C. D. (1998). Altruism and prosocial behavior. In D. T. Gilbert, S. T. Fiske, & G. Lindzey (Eds.), *Handbook of social psychology* (4th ed., Vol. 2). New York: McGraw-Hill.

Batson, C. D. (2002). Addressing the altruism experimentally. In S. G. Post, L. G. Underwood, J. P. Schloss, & W. B. Hurlbut (Eds.), *Altruism and altruistic love.* New York: Oxford University Press.

Batson, C. D. (2003). Altruism and prosocial behavior. In I. B. Weiner (Ed.), *Handbook of psychology* (Vol. 5). New York: Wiley.

Battaglia, M. (2002). Beyond the usual suspects: A cholingeric route for panic attacks. *Molecular Psychiatry, 7,* 239–246.

Baum, A., & Posluszny, D. M. (1999). Health Psychology. *Annual Review of Psychology, 50.* Palo Alto, CA: Annual Reviews.

Baum, A., Revenson, T. A., & Singer, J. E. (Eds.). (2001). *Handbook of health psychology.* Mahwah, NJ: Erlbaum.

Baumeister, R. F. (1989). The optimal margin of illusion. *Journal of Social and Clinical Psychology, 8,* 176–189.

Baumeister, R. F. (1991). *Meanings of life.* New York: Guilford.

Baumeister, R. F. (1993). *Self-esteem: The puzzle of low self-regard.* New York: Plenum Press.

Baumeister, R. F. (1997). Identity, self-concept, and self-esteem. In R. Hogan, J. Johnson, & S. Briggs (Eds.), *Handbook of personality psychology.* San Diego: Academic Press.

Baumeister, R. F. (1999). *Evil: Inside human violence and cruelty.* New York: Freeman.

Baumeister, R. F., & Bratslavsky, E. (1999). Passion, intimacy, and time: Passionate love as a function of change in intimacy. *Personality and Social Psychology Review, 3,* 2–22.

Baumeister, R. F., Bratslavsky, E., & Finkenauer, C. (2000). *Bad is stronger than good.* Unpublished manuscript, Case Western Reserve University.

Baumeister, R. F., Campbell, J. D., Krueger, J. I., & Vohs, K. D. (2003). Does high self-esteem cause better performance, interpersonal success, happiness, or healthier lifestyles? *Psychological Science in the Public Interest, 4,* 11–44.

Baumeister, R. F., Catanese, K. R., & Vohs, K. D. (2001). Is there a gender difference in strength of sex drive? *Personality and Social Psychology Review, 5,* 242–273.

Baumrind, D. (1971). Current patterns of parental authority. *Developmental Psychology Monographs, 4* (1, Pt. 2).

Baumrind, D. (1991). Parenting styles and adolescent development. In J. Brooks-Gunn, R. Lerner, & A. C. Petersen (Eds.), *The encyclopedia of adolescence* (Vol. 2). New York: Garland.

Baumrind, D., Larzelere, R. E., & Cowan, P. A. (2002). Ordinary physical punishment: Is it harmful? Comment on Gershoff (2002). *Psychological Bulletin, 128,* 590–595.

Baxter, L. R., Jr., Phelps, M. E., Mazziotta, J. C., Schwartz, J. M., Gerner, R. H., Selin, C. E., & Sumida, R. M. (1995). Cerebral metabolic rates for glucose in mood disorders: Studies with positron emission tomography and fluorodeoxyglucose F 18. *Archives of General Psychiatry, 42,* 441–447.

Bayles, K. A. (2003). The effects of working memory deficits on the communicative functioning of Alzheimer's dementia patients. *Journal of Communication Disorders, 36,* 209–219.

Beatty, J. (1995). *Principles of neuroscience.* New York: McGraw-Hill.

Beatty, J. (2001). *The human brain.* Thousand Oaks, CA: Sage.

Beauchamp, M. S., Less, K. E., Haxby, J. V., & Martin, A. (2002). Parallel visual motion processing streams for manipulable objects and human movements. *Neuron, 34,* 149–159.

Beck, A. T. (1967). *Depression.* New York: Harper & Row.

Beck, A. T. (1976). *Cognitive therapies and the emotional disorders.* New York: International Universities Press.

Beck, A. T. (1993). Cognitive therapy: Past, present, and future. *Journal of Consulting and Clinical Psychology, 61,* 194–198.

Beck, A. T., Rush, A. J., Shaw, B. F., & Emery, G. (1979). *Cognitive therapy of depression.* New York: Guilford.

Beck, J. (2002). Beck therapy approach. In M. Hersen & W. H. Sledge (Eds.), *Encyclopedia of psychotherapy.* San Diego: Academic Press.

Becker, A. J., Uckert, S., Stief, C. G., Scheller, F., Knapp, W. H., Hartmann, U., & Jonas, U. (2002). Cavernous and systematic plasma levels of norepinephrine and epinephrine during different penile conditions in healthy men and patients with erectile dysfunction. *Urology, 59,* 281–286.

Beckham, E. E. (2000). Depression. In A. Kazdin (Ed.), *Encyclopedia of psychology.* Washington, DC, & New York: American Psychological Association and Oxford University Press.

Beckman, M. (2002). Pheromone reception: When in doubt, mice mate rather than hate. *Science, 295,* 782.

Bednar, R. L., Wells, M. G., & Peterson, S. R. (1995). *Self-esteem* (2nd ed.). Washington, DC: American Psychological Association.

Behrman, B. W., & Davey, S. L. (2001). Eyewitness identification in actual criminal cases: an archival analysis. *Law and Human Behavior, 25,* 475–491.

Beins, B. (2004). *Research methods.* Boston: Allyn & Bacon.

Békésy, G. von (1960). Vibratory patterns of the basilar membrane. In E. G. Wever (Ed.), *Experiments in hearing.* New York: McGraw-Hill.

Belk, A., & Ruse, M. (2000). Why should evolutionary psychology be a science? *Psychological Inquiry, 11*(1), 22–23.

Bell, A. P., Weinberg, M. S., & Mammersmith, S. K. (1981). *Sexual preference.* New York: Simon & Schuster.

Bell, P., Greene, T., Fisher, J., & Baum, A. (2001). *Environmental psychology* (5th ed.). Belmont, CA: Wadsworth.

Bellesiles, M. A. (1999). *Lethal imagination.* New York: New York University Press.

Bellodi, L., Cavallini, M. C., Bertelli, S., Chiapparino, D., Riboldi, C., & Smeraldi, E. (2001). Morbidity risk for obsessive-compulsive spectrum disorders in first-degree relatives of patients with eating disorders. *American Journal of Psychiatry, 158,* 563–569.

Bellugi, U., Korenberg, J. R., & Klima, E. S. (2001). Williams syndrome: An exploration of neurocognitive and genetic features. In M. Posner (Ed.) *Journal of Clinical Neurosciences Research, 1,* 217–229.

Bellugi, U., Lichtenberger, L., Jones, W., Lai, Z., & St. George, M. (2000). The neurocognitive profile of Williams syndrome: A complex pattern of strengths and weaknesses. *Journal of Cognitive Neuroscience 12,* 1–29.

Bellugi, U., & George, M. (Eds.), *Journey from cognition to brain to gene: Perspectives from Williams syndrome.* Cambridge, MA: MIT Press.

Belsky, J. K. (1999). *The psychology of aging* (3rd ed.). Belmont, CA: Wadsworth.

Bem, D. (1967). Self-perception: An alternative explanation of cognitive dissonance phenomena. *Psychological Review, 74,* 183–200.

Benbow, C. P., & Stanley, J. C. (1983). Sex differences in mathematical reasoning ability: More facts. *Science, 222,* 1029–1031.

Benca, R. M. (2001). Consequences of insomnia and its therapies. *Journal of Clinical Psychiatry, 62* (Suppl. 10), 33–38.

Benes, F. M., Todtenkopf, M. S., Logiotatos, P., & Williams, M. (2000). Glutamite decarboxylase (65)-immunoreactive terminals in cingulate and prefrontal cortices of schizophrenic and bipolar brains. *Journal of Chemistry and Neuroanatomy, 20,* 259–269.

Benet, V., & Waller, N. G. (1995). The big seven factor model of personality description: Evidence for its cross-cultural generality in a Spanish sample.

Journal of Personality and Social Psychology, 69, 701–718.

Benini, A. L., Camilloni, M. A., Scordato, C., Lezzi, G., Savia, G., Oriani, G., Bertoli, S., Balzola, F., Liuzzi, A., & Petroni, M. L. (2001). Contribution of weight cycling to serum leptin in human obesity. *International Journal of Obesity and Related Metabolic Disorders, 25,* 721–726.

Benjamin, L. T. (1999). Psychology's portrait gallery: Part III. *Contemporary Psychology, 44,* 27–28.

Benjet, C., & Kazdin, A. E. (2003). Spanking children: The controversies, findings, and new directions. *Clinical Psychology Review, 23,* 197–224.

Bennett, W. I., & Gurin, J. (1982). *The dieter's dilemma: Eating less and weighing more.* New York: Basic Books.

Ben-Shakhar, G., Bar-Hillel, M., Yoram, B., Ben-Abba, E., & Flug, A. (1986). Can graphology predict occupational success? Two empirical studies and some methodological ruminations. *Journal of Applied Psychology, 71,* 645–653.

Bereiter, C., & Scardamalia, M. (1993). *Surpassing ourselves: An inquiry into the nature and implications of expertise.* Chicago: Open Court.

Berenbaum, S. A., & Hines, M. (1992). Early androgens are related to childhood sex-typed toy preferences. *Psychological Science, 3,* 203–206.

Berg, C. (2000). Intellectual development in adulthood. In R. J. Sternberg (Ed.), *Handbook of intelligence.* New York: Cambridge University Press.

Bergin, A. E., & Richards, P. S. (2000). Religious values and mental health. In A. Kazdin (Ed.), *Encyclopedia of psychology.* Washington, DC, & New York: American Psychological Association and Oxford University Press.

Berkman, L. F., & Syme, L. L. (1979). Social networks, host resistance, and mortality. *American Journal of Epidemiology, 109,* 186–204.

Berko, J. (1958). The child's learning of English morphology. *World, 14,* 150–157.

Berkowitz, L. (1990). On the formation and regulation of anger and aggression: A cognitive neoassociationistic analysis. *American Psychologist, 45,* 494–503.

Berkowitz, S. J., & Marans, S. (2003). The traumatized child at the emergency department. *Child and Adolescent Psychiatric Clinics of North America, 12,* 763–777.

Berlin, L., & Cassidy, J. (2000). Understanding parenting. Contributions of attachment theory and research. In J. D. Osofsky & H. E. Fitzgerald (Eds.), *WAIMH handbook of infant mental health* (Vol. 3). New York: Wiley.

Berman, S. M., Mandelkern, M. A., Phan, H., & Zaidel, E. (2003). Complementary hemispheric specialization for word and accent detection. *Neuroimage, 19,* 319–331.

Bernheim, K. F. (1997). *The Lanahan cases and readings in abnormal behavior.* Baltimore, MD: Lanahan.

Bernstein, A. B. (2001). Motherhood, health status, and health care. *Women's Health Issues, 11,* 173–184.

Berridge, C. W., & O'Neil, J. (2001). Differential sensitivity to the wake-promoting actions of norepinephrine within the medial preoptic area and the substantia innominata. *Behavioral Neuroscience, 115,* 165–174.

Berry, J. (2004, August). *Cross-cultural psychology: An ecocultural perspective.* Paper presented at the 28th International Congress of Psychology, Beijing, China.

Berry, J. W. (1980). Acculturation as varieties of adaptation. In A. Padilla (Ed.), *Acculturation: Theory, model, and some new findings.* Washington, DC: American Association for the Advancement of Science.

Berscheid, E. (1988). Some comments on love's anatomy. Or, whatever happened to an old-

fashioned lust? In R. J. Sternberg & M. L. Barnes (Eds.), *Anatomy of love.* New Haven, CT: Yale University Press.

Berscheid, E. (2000). Attraction. In A. Kazdin (Ed.), *Encyclopedia of psychology.* Washington, DC, & New York: American Psychological Association and Oxford University Press.

Berscheid, E., & Fei, J. (1977). Sexual jealousy and romantic love. In G. Clinton & G. Smith (Eds.), *Sexual jealousy.* Englewood Cliffs, NJ: Prentice-Hall.

Berscheid, E., & Reis, H. T. (1998). Attraction and close relationships. In D. T. Gilbert, S. T. Fiske, & G. Lindzey (Eds.), *Handbook of social psychology* (4th ed., Vol. 2). New York: McGraw-Hill.

Berscheid, E., Snyder, M., & Omoto, A. M. (1989). Issues in studying close relationships: Conceptualizing and measuring closeness. In C. Hendrick (Ed.), *Close relationships.* Newbury Park, CA: Sage.

Best, D. (2002). Cross-cultural gender roles. In J. Worell (Ed.), *Encyclopedia of women and gender.* New York: Oxford University Press.

Betch, T., Haberstroh, S., Glockner, A., Haar, T., & Fiedler, K. (2001). The effects of routine strength on adaptation and information search in recurrent decision making. *Organizational Behavior and Human Decision Processes, 84,* 23–53.

Bettman, J. (2001). *Learning.* Unpublished manuscript, Fuqua School of Business, Duke University, Durham, NC.

Bhattacharjee, C., Smith, M., Todd, F., & Gillepsie, M. (2001). Bupropion overdose: A potential problem with the new "miracle" antismoking drug. *International Journal of Clinical Practice, 55,* 221–222.

Bhugra, D., & de Silva, P. (1998). Sexual dysfunction therapy. In H. S. Friedman (Ed.), *Encyclopedia of mental health* (Vol. 3). San Diego: Academic Press.

Bi, G., & Poo, M. (2001). Synaptic modification by correlated activity: Hebb's postulate revisited. *Annual Review of Neuroscience, 24.* Palo Alto, CA: Annual Reviews.

Billings, A. G., Cronkite, R. C., & Moos, R. H. (1983). Social-environment factors in unipolar depression. *Journal of Abnormal Psychology, 92,* 119–133.

Billman, G. E. (2002). Aerobic exercise conditioning: A nonpharmacological antiarrhythmic intervention. *Journal of Applied Physiology, 92,* 446–454.

Billman, J. (2003). *Observation and participation in early childhood setting: A practicum guide* (2nd ed.). Boston: Allyn & Bacon.

Billmann, S. J., & Ware, J. C. (2002). Marital satisfaction of wives of untreated sleep apneic men. *Sleep Medicine, 3,* 55–59.

Birkel, R. C., Hall, L. L., Lane, T., Cohan, K., & Miller, J. (2003). Consumers and families as partners in implementing evidence-based practice. *Psychiatric Clinics of North America, 26,* 867–881.

Birren, J. E., & Schaie, K. W. (Eds.). (2001). *Handbook of the psychology of aging* (5th ed.). San Diego: Academic Press.

Bjorklund, D. F. (2000). *Children's thinking* (3rd ed.). Belmont, CA: Wadsworth.

Bjorklund, D. F., & Pelligrini, A. D. (2002). *The origins of human nature.* Washington, DC: American Psychological Association.

Björkqvist, K., Österman, K., & Lagerspetz, K. M. J. (1994). Sex differences in covert aggression among adults. *Aggressive Behavior, 20,* 27–33.

Black, I. B. (1998). Plasticity. In M. S. Gazzaniga (Ed.), *The new cognitive neurosciences* (2nd ed.). Cambridge, MA: MIT Press.

Blair, C. (2002). School readiness: Integrating cognition and emotion in a neurobiological conceptualization of children's functioning at school entry. *American Psychologist, 57,* 111–127.

Blair, C., & Ramey, C. (1996). Early intervention with low birth weight infants: The path to second generation research. In M. J. Guralnick (Ed.), *The effectiveness of early intervention.* Baltimore: Paul H. Brookes.

Blair, I. V. (2001). Implicit stereotypes and prejudice. In G. B. Moscowitz (Ed.), *Cognitive social psychology.* Mahwah, NJ: Erlbaum.

Blake, R. (2000). Vision and sight: Structure and function. In A. Kazdin (Ed.), *Encyclopedia of psychology.* Washington, DC, & New York: American Psychological Association and Oxford University Press.

Blakemore, C. (2004, August). *Consciousness: When, where, and why?* Paper presented at the 28th International Congress of Psychology, Beijing, China.

Blatt, S. J. (2000). Projective techniques. In A. Kazdin (Ed.), *Encyclopedia of psychology.* Washington; DC, & New York: American Psychological Association and Oxford University Press.

Blatt, S. J., & Zuroff, D. C. (1992). Interpersonal relatedness and self-definition: Two prototypes for depression. *Clinical Psychology Review, 12,* 527–562.

Blazer, D. G., Kessler, R. C., McGonagle, K. A., & Swartz, M. S. (1994). The prevalence and distribution of major depression in a national community sample: The National Comorbidity Study. *American Journal of Psychiatry, 151,* 979–986.

Blittner, M., Goldberg, J., & Merbaum, M. (1978). Cognitive self-control factors in the reduction of smoking behavior. *Behavior Therapy, 9,* 553–561.

Block, J. (2002). *Personality as an affect processing system.* Mahwah, NJ: Erlbaum.

Bloom, B. (1985). *Developing talent in young people.* New York: Ballantine.

Bloom, F., Nelson, C. A., & Lazerson, A. (2001). *Brain, mind, and behavior* (3rd ed.). New York: Worth.

Blum, D. (1998). *Sex on the brain: The biological differences between men and women.* New York: Penguin.

Blum, H. P. (2001). Freud's private mini-monograph on his own dreams. *International Journal of Psychoanalysis, 82,* 953–964.

Blundell, J. E. (1984). Systems and interactions: An approach to the pharmacology of feeding. In A. J. Stunkard & E. Stellar (Eds.), *Eating and its disorders.* New York: Raven Press.

Blyth, D. (2000). Community approaches to improving outcomes for urban children, youth, and families. In A. Booth & A. C. Crouter (Eds.), *Does it take a village?* Mahwah, NJ: Erlbaum.

Bob, P. (2003). Dissociation and neuroscience. *International Journal of Neuroscience, 113,* 903–914.

Bodenhausen, G. V., McCrae, K., & Hugenberg, K. (2004). Activating and inhibiting social identities. In G. V. Bodenhausen & A. J. Lambert (Eds.), *Foundations of social cognition.* Mahwah, NJ: Erlbaum.

Bodenhausen, G. V., Mussweiler, T., Gabriel, S., & Moreno, K. N. (2001). Affective influences on stereotyping and intergroup relations. In J. P. Forgas (Ed.), *Handbook of affect and cognition.* Mahwah, NJ: Erlbaum.

Bogaert, A. F., Woodard, U., & Hafer, C. L. (1999). Intellectual ability and reactions to pornography. *Journal of Sex Research, 36,* 283–291.

Bogatz, G., & Ball, S. (1972). *Reading with television: An evaluation of the Electric Company.* Princeton, NJ: Educational Testing Service.

Bohart, A. C. (1995). The person-centered psychotherapies. In A. S. Gurman (Ed.), *Essential psychotherapies: Theory and practice* (pp. 55–84). New York: Guilford Press.

Bohart, A. C., & Greening, T. (2001). Humanistic psychology and positive psychology. *American Psychologist, 56,* 81–82.

Boll, T. J., Johnon, B., Perry, N., & Rozensky, R. H. (Eds.). (2002). *Handbook of clinical health psychology, Vol. 1.* Washington, DC: American Psychological Association.

Bond, R., & Smith, P. B. (1994). Culture and conformity: A meta-analysis of studies using the Asch-type perceptual judgment task. *British Psychological Society 1994 Proceedings, 9,* 297–308.

Booth, A., & Crouter, A. C. (Eds.). (2000). *Does it take a village?* Mahwah, NJ: Erlbaum.

Booth, A., Johnson, D. R., & Granger, D. A. (1999). Testosterone and men's health. *Journal of Behavioral Medicine, 22,* 1–12.

Boraud, T., Bezard, E., Bioulac, B., & Gross, C. E. (2002). From single extracellular unit recording in experimental and human Parkinsonism to the development of a functional concept of the role played by the basal ganglia in motor control. *Progress in Neurobiology, 66,* 265–283.

Borckardt, J. J. (2002). Case study examining the efficacy of a multi-modal psychotherapeutic intervention for hypertension. *International Journal of Clinical and Experimental Hypnosis, 50,* 189–201.

Bordens, K. S., & Horowitz, I. A. (2002). *Social psychology* (2nd ed.). Mahwah, NJ: Erlbaum.

Borkovec, T. D., & Ruscio, A. M. (2001). Psychotherapy for generalized anxiety disorder. *Journal of Clinical Psychiatry, 62* (Suppl. 11), 37–42.

Bornstein, M. H., & Bradley, R. H. (Eds.). (2003). *Socioeconomic status, parenting, and child development.* Mahwah, NJ: Erlbaum.

Bornstein, M. H., & Tamis-LeMonda, C. S. (2001). Mother-infant interaction. In A. Fogel & G. Bremner (Eds.), *Blackwell handbook of infant development.* London: Blackwell.

Borrelli, B., Hogan, J. W., Bock, B., Pinto, B., Roberts, M., & Marcus, B. (2002). Predictors of quitting and dropout among women in a clinic-based smoking cessation program. *Psychology of Addictive Behaviors, 16,* 22–27.

Bouchard, T. J., Lykken, D. T., Tellegen, A., & McGue, M. (1996). Genes, drives, environment, and experience. In D. Lubinski & C. Benbow (Eds.), *Psychometrics and social issues concerning intellectual talent.* Baltimore: Johns Hopkins University Press.

Bou-Flores, C., & Berger, A. J. (2001). Gap junctions and inhibitory synapses modulate inspiratory motoneuron synchronization. *Journal of Neurophysiology, 85,* 1543–1551.

Bourne, E. J. (1995). *The anxiety and phobia workbook* (2nd ed.). Oakland, CA: New Harbinger.

Bower, G. H., Clark, M., Winzenz, D., & Lesgold, A. (1969). Hierarchical retrieval schemes in recall of categorized word lists. *Journal of Verbal Learning and Verbal Behavior, 3,* 323–343.

Bowers, T. G., & Clum, G. A. (1988). Relative contribution of specific and nonspecific treatment effects: Meta-analysis of placebo-controlled behavior therapy research. *Psychological Bulletin, 103,* 315–323.

Bowlby, J. (1969). *Attachment and loss* (Vol. 1). London: Hogarth Press.

Bowlby, J. (1989). *Secure and insecure attachment.* New York: Basic Books.

Boyer, L. B. (1999). *Countertransference and aggression.* Mahwah, NJ: Erlbaum.

Bozarth, J. D., Zimring, F. M., & Tausch, R. (2001). Client-centered therapy: The evolution of a revolution. In D. J. Cain & J. Seeman (Eds.), *Humanistic psychotherapies.* Washington, DC: American Psychological Association.

Bradbury, J. (2001). Teasing out the genetics of bipolar disorder. *Lancet, 357,* 156.

Bradford, D., Stroup, S., & Lieberman, J. (2002). Pharmacological treatments for schizophrenia. In P. Nathan & J. M. Gorman (Eds.), *A guide to treatments that work (2nd Ed.).* New York: Oxford University Press.

Bradley, R., & Corwyn, C. (2004). "Family process" investments that matter for child well being. In A. Kalil & T. DeLeire (Eds.), *Family investments in children's potential.* Mahwah, NJ: Erlbaum.

Bradvik, L. (2003). Suicide after suicide attempt in severe depression: a long-term follow-up. *Suicide and Life-Threatening Behavior, 33,* 365–372.

Brain, P. F., & Susman, E. J. (1997). Hormonal aspects of aggression and violence. In D. M. Stoff, J. Breiling, & J. D. Maser (Eds.), *Handbook of antisocial personality disorder* (pp. 314–323). New York: Wiley.

Brambilla, P., Perez, J., Barale, F., Schettini, G., & Soares, J. C. (2003). GABAeric dysfunction in mood disorders. *Molecular Psychiatry, 8,* 721–737.

Brammer, L. M., & MacDonald, G. (1999). *The helping relationship* (7th ed.). Boston: Allyn & Bacon.

Brannon, L. (2002). *Gender: Psychological perspectives.* Boston: Allyn & Bacon.

Bransford, J. D., & Stein, B. S. (1993). *The IDEAL problem solver.* New York: Freeman.

Braun, B. G. (1985). Transgenerational incidence of dissociation and multiple personality disorder: A preliminary report. In R. P. Kluft (Ed.), *Childhood antecedents of multiple personality.* Washington, DC: American Psychiatric Press.

Breggin, P. R., & Breggin, G. R. (1995). *Talking back to Prozac: What doctors aren't telling you about today's most controversial drug.* New York: St. Martin's Press.

Brehm, S. S. (2002). *Intimate relationships* (3rd ed.). New York: McGraw-Hill.

Breland, K., & Breland, M. (1961). The misbehavior of organisms. *American Psychologist, 16,* 681–684.

Brennan, F. X., & Charnetski, C. J. (2000). Explanatory style and immunglobin A (IgA). *Integration of Physiology and Behavioral Science, 35,* 251–255.

Brennan, P., Mednick, S., & Kandel, E. (1991). Congenital determinants of violent and property offencing. In D. Pepler & K. Rubin (Eds.), *The development and treatment of childhood aggression.* Mahwah, NJ: Erlbaum.

Bressan, R. A., Jones, H. M., Ell, P. J., & Pilowksy, L. S. (2001). Dopamine d (2) receptor blockade in schizophrenia. *American Journal of Psychiatry, 158,* 971–972.

Brewer, J. B., Zuo, Z., Desmond, J. E., Glover, G. H., & Gabrieli, J. D. E. (1998). Making memories: Brain activity that predicts how well visual experience will be remembered. *Science, 281,* 1185–1187.

Brewer, M. B., & Gaertner, S. L., (2001). Toward reduction of prejudice: Intergroup contact and social categorization. In R. Brown & S.L. Gaertner (Eds.), *Handbook of social psychology: Intergroup processes.* Malden, MA: Blackwell.

Brickman, A. L., LoPiccolo, C. J., & Johnson, S. L. (2002). Screening for bipolar disorder. *Psychiatric Services, 53,* 349.

Brigham, J. C. (1986). Race and eyewitness identifications. In S. Worschel & W. G. Austin (Eds.), *Psychology of intergroup relations.* Chicago: Nelson-Hall.

Brim, O. (1999). *The McArthur Foundation study of midlife development.* Vero Beach, FL: The McArthur Foundation.

Bringsjord, S., & Ferrucci, D. (2000). *Artificial intelligence and literary creativity.* Mahwah, NJ: Erlbaum.

Brink, S. (2001, May 7). Your brain on alcohol. *U.S. News & World Report, 130*(18), 50–57.

Brislin, R. (1993). *Understanding culture's influence on behavior.* Fort Worth, TX: Harcourt Brace.

Brody, N. (2000). Intelligence. In A. Kazdin (Ed.), *Encyclopedia of psychology.* Washington, DC, & New York: American Psychological Association and Oxford University Press.

Bronfenbrenner, U. (2000). Ecological systems theory. In A. Kazdin (Ed.), *Encyclopedia of psychology*. Washington, DC, and New York: American Psychological Association and Oxford University Press.

Bronfenbrenner, U., & Morris, P. (1998). The ecology of developmental processes. In W. Damon (Ed.), *Handbook of child psychology* (5th ed., Vol. 1). New York: Wiley.

Brooks, D. C. (2000). Recent and remote extinction cues reduce spontaneous recovery. *Quarterly Journal of Experimental Psychology, 3,* 25–58.

Brooks, J. G., & Brooks, M. G. (2001). *In search of understanding: The case for the constructivist classroom.* Upper Saddle River, NJ: Prentice-Hall.

Brooks-Gunn, J., & Warren, M. P. (1989). The psychological significance of secondary sexual characteristics in 9- to 11-year-old girls. *Child Development, 59,* 161–169.

Brophy, J. (2004). *Motivating students to learn* (2nd ed.). Mahwah, NJ: Erlbaum.

Brosvic, G. M., Dihoff, R. E., & Fama, J. (2002). Age-related susceptibility to the Muller-Lyer and the horizontal-vertical illusion. *Perceptual and Motor Skills, 94,* 229–234.

Brouwer, W. H., Withaar, F. K., Tant, M. L., & van Zomeren, A. H. (2002). Attention and driving in traumatic brain injury: A question of coping with time pressure. *Journal of Head and Trauma Rehabilitation, 17,* 1–15.

Brown, E., Deffenbacher, K., & Sturgill, W. (1977). Memory for faces and the circumstances of encounter. *Journal of Applied Psychology, 62,* 311–318.

Brown, G., Bhrolchain, M., & Harris, T. (1975). Social class and psychiatric disturbance among women in an urban population. *Sociology, 9,* 225–254.

Brown, J. D., Steele, J. R., & Walsh-Childers, K. (Eds.). (2002). *Sexual teens, sexual media.* Mahwah, NJ: Erlbaum.

Brown, L. S. (1989). New voices, new visions: Toward a lesbian/gay paradigm for psychology. *Psychology of Women Quarterly, 13,* 445–458.

Brown, R. (1973). *A first language: The early stages.* Cambridge, MA: Harvard University Press.

Brown, R. (1986). *Social psychology* (2nd ed.). New York: Free Press.

Brown, S. L., Nesse, R. N., Vinokur, A. D., & Smith, D. M. (2003). Providing social support may be more beneficial than receiving it: Results from a prospective study of mortality. *Psychological Science, 14,* 320–327.

Brownell, K. A., & Rodin, J. (1994). The dieting maelstrom: Is it possible to lose weight? *American Psychologist, 9,* 781–791.

Bruner, J. S., & Tagiuri, R. (1954). The perception of people. In G. Lindzey (Ed.), *Handbook of social psychology* (Vol. 2). Boston: Addison-Wesley.

Bruning, R. H., Schraw, G. J., Norby, M. M., & Ronning, R. R. (2004). *Cognitive psychology and instruction* (4th ed.). Upper Saddle River, NJ: Prentice-Hall.

Bruning, R. H., Schraw, G. J., & Ronning, R. R. (1999). *Cognitive psychology and instruction* (3rd ed.). Upper Saddle River, NJ: Erlbaum.

Brynes, J. P. (2001). *Cognitive development and learning in instructional contexts* (2nd ed.). Boston: Allyn & Bacon.

Buchsbaum, M. S., Someya, T., Wu, J. C., Tang, C. Y., & Bunney, W. E. (1997). Neuroimaging bipolar illness with positron emission tomography and magnetic resonance imaging. *Psychiatric Annals, 27,* 489–495.

Buckley, P. F., Miller, D. D., Singer, B., & Donenwirth, K. (2001). The evolving clinical profile of an atypical antipsychotic medications. *Canadian Journal of Psychiatry, 46,* 285.

Bukatko, D., & Daehler, M. W. (2001). *Child development* (4th ed.). Boston: Houghton Mifflin.

Burgess, P. W., Quayle, A., & Frith, C. D. (2001). Brain regions involved in prospective memory as determined by positron emission tomography. *Neuropsychologica, 39,* 545–555.

Burke, G. L., Arnold, A. M., Bild, D., Cushman, M., Fried, O., Newman, A., & Robbins, C. (2001). Factors associated with healthy aging. *Journal of the American Geriatric Society, 49,* 254–262.

Burlingame, G., & Davies, R. (2002). Self-help groups. In M. Hersen & W. H. Sledge (Eds.), *Encyclopedia of psychotherapy.* San Diego: Academic Press.

Burns, D. D. (1980). *Feeling good: The new mood therapy.* New York: Morrow.

Burnstein, E., Crandall, C., & Kitayama, S. (1994). Some neo-Darwinian decision rules for altruism: Weighing cues for inclusive fitness as a function of the biological importance of the decision. *Journal of Personality and Social Psychology, 67,* 773–789.

Bushman, B. J., & Huesmann, L. R. (2001). Effects of televised violence on aggression. In D. Singer & J. Singer (Eds.), *Handbook of children and the media.* Thousand Oaks, CA: Sage.

Buss, A. H., & Plomin, R. (1987). Commentary. In H. H. Goldsmith, A. H. Buss, R. Plomin, M. K. Rothbart, A. Thomas, A. Chess, R. R. Hinde, & R. B. McCall (Eds.), Roundtable: What is temperament? Four approaches. *Child Development, 58,* 505–529.

Buss, D. (2004). *Evolutionary psychology* (2nd ed.). Boston: Allyn & Bacon.

Buss, D. M. (1995). Psychological sex differences: Origins through sexual selection. *American Psychologist, 50,* 164–168.

Buss, D. M. (2000). Evolutionary psychology. In A. Kazdin (Ed.), *Encyclopedia of psychology.* Washington, DC, & New York: American Psychological Association and Oxford University Press.

Buss, D. M., & Barnes, M. (1986). Preferences in human mate selection. *Journal of Personality and Social Psychology, 50,* 559–570.

Buss, D. M., & Others. (1990). International preferences in selecting mates: A study of 37 cultures. *Journal of Cross-Cultural Psychology, 21,* 5–47.

Butcher, J. N. (1999). *A beginner's guide to the MMPI-2.* Washington, DC: American Psychological Association.

Butcher, J. N. (2004). The Minnesota Multiphasic Personality Inventory (MMPI-2). In M. Hersen (Ed.), *Comprehensive handbook of psychological assessment* (Vol. 2). New York: Wiley.

Butler, G., Fennell, M., Robson, P., & Gelder, M. (1991). Comparison of behavior therapy and cognitive behavior therapy in the treatment of generalized anxiety disorder. *Journal of Consulting and Clinical Psychology, 59,* 167–175.

Butter, E. M., & Pargament, K. I. (2003). Development of a model for assessing religious coping: Initial validation of the process evaluation model. *Mental Health, Religion, and Culture, 6,* 175–194.

Byrne, S. M., & McLean, N. J. (2002). The cognitive-behavioral model of bulimia nervosa: A direct evaluation. *International Journal of Eating Disorders, 31,* 17–31.

C

Cacioppo, J. T., Hawkley, L. C., & Bernston, G. G. (2003). The anatomy of loneliness. *Current Directions in Psychological Science, 12,* 71–74.

Cain, D. J. (2001). Defining characteristics, history, and evolution of humanistic psychotherapies. In D. J. Cain & J. Seeman (Eds.), *Humanistic psychotherapies.* Washington, DC: American Psychological Association.

Caldirola, D., Bellodi, L., Caumo, A., Migiarese, G., & Perna, G. (2004). Approximate entropy of respiratory patterns in panic disorder. *American Journal of Psychiatry, 161,* 79–87.

Calkins, M. (1896). Association. *Psychological Review, 2* (Monograph suppl.), 4–5.

Callan, J. E. (2002). Gender development: Psychoanalytic perspectives. In J. Worell (Ed.), *Encyclopedia of women and gender.* San Diego: Academic Press.

Cameron, J. R. (2001). Negative effects of reward on intrinsic motivation—a limited phenomenon. *Review of Educational Research, 71,* 29–42.

Cameron, N. (1963). *Personality development and psychopathology.* Boston: Houghton Mifflin.

Campbell, F. A., & Ramey, C. T. (1993, March). *Mid-adolescent outcomes for high risk students: An examination of the continuing effects of early intervention.* Paper presented at the biennial meeting of the Society for Research in Child Development, New Orleans.

Campbell, J. D., Tesser, A., & Fairey, P. J. (1986). Conformity and attention to the stimulus: Some temporal and contextual dynamics. *Journal of Personality and Social Psychology, 51,* 315–324.

Campbell, L., Campbell, B., & Dickinson, D. (2004). *Teaching and learning through multiple intelligences* (3rd ed.). Boston: Allyn & Bacon.

Campbell, N. A., Reece, J. B., & Mitchell, L. G. (2002). *Biology* (6th ed.). Reading, MA, & Menlo Park, CA: Benjamin/ Cummings.

Campfield, L. A., Smith, F. J., Gulsez, Y., Devos, R., & Burn, P. (1995). Mouse OB protein: Evidence for a peripheral signal linking adiposity and central neural networks. *Science, 269,* 546–549.

Canadian Mental Health Association. (1984). *Links between work and home.* Toronto: Canadian Mental Health Association.

Canino, G., & Others (2004). The DSM-IV rates of child and adolescent disorders in Puerto Rico. *Archives of General Psychiatry, 61,* 85–93. (too many authors to list)

Canino, I. A., & Spurlock, J. (2000). *Culturally diverse children and adolescents: Assessment, diagnosis, and treatment.* New York: Guilford Press.

Cannon, W. B. (1927). The James-Lange theory of emotions: A critical examination and an alternative theory. *American Journal of Psychology, 39,* 106–124.

Cannon, W. B. (1929). *Bodily changes in pain, hunger, fear, and rage* (2nd ed.). New York: Appleton-Century-Crofts.

Cannon, W. B., & Washburn, A. L. (1912). An explanation of hunger. *American Journal of Physiology, 29,* 444–454.

Cantuti-Castevetri, J. Shukitt-Hale, B., & Joseph, J. A. (2003). Dopamine neurotoxicity: Age-dependent behavioral and histological effects. *Neurobiology of Aging, 24,* 697–706.

Caporael, L. (2001). Evolutionary psychology: Toward a unifying theory and a hybrid science. *Annual Review of Psychology, 52,* 607–628.

Capuzzi, D. (2003). *Approaches to group counseling.* Upper Saddle River, NJ: Prentice-Hall.

Capuzzi, D., & Gross, D. R. (1999). *Counseling and psychotherapy* (2nd ed.). Upper Saddle River, NJ: Prentice-Hall.

Capuzzi, D., & Gross, D. R. (2003). *Counseling and psychotherapy* (3rd ed.). Upper Saddle River, NJ: Prentice-Hall.

Carey, L. M. (2001). *Measuring and evaluating school learning* (3rd ed.). Boston: Allyn & Bacon.

Carkenord, D. M., & Bullington, J. (1995). Bringing cognitive dissonance to the classroom. In M. E. Ware & D. E. Johnson (Eds.), *Demonstrations and activities in teaching of psychology* (Vol. 3). Mahwah, NJ: Erlbaum.

Carlson, N. R. (2000). Neuron. In A. Kazdin (Ed.), *Encyclopedia of psychology.* Washington, DC, & New York: American Psychological Association and Oxford University Press.

Carlson, N. R. (2001). *Physiology of behavior* (7th ed.). Boston: Allyn & Bacon.

Carnegie Council on Adolescent Development. (1995). *Great transitions.* New York: Carnegie Foundation.

Carroll, C. R. (2003). *Drugs in modern society* (6th ed.). New York: McGraw-Hill.

Carroll, D., Ring, C., Hunt, K., Ford, G., & Macintyre, S. (2003). Blood pressure reactions to stress and the prediction of future blood pressure: effects of sex, age, and socioeconomic position. *Psychosomatic Medicine, 65,* 1058–1064.

Carroll, J. (1993). *Human cognitive abilities.* Cambridge, England: Cambridge University Press.

Carskadon, M. A., Acebo, C., & Seifer, R. (2001). Extended nights, sleep loss, and recovery sleep in adolescents. *Archives of Italian Biology, 139,* 301–312.

Carskadon, M. A., Labyak, S. E., Acebo, C., & Seifer, R. (1999). Intrinsic circadian period of adolescent humans measured in conditions of forced desynchrony. *Neuroscience Letters, 260,* 129–132.

Carskadon, M. A., Wolfson, A. R., Acebo, C., Tzischinsky, O., & Seifer, R. (1998). Adolescent sleep patterns, circadian timing, and sleepiness at a transition to early school days. *Sleep, 21,* 873–884.

Carson, R. C., Butcher, J. N., & Mineka, S. (2000). *Abnormal psychology and modern life* (11th ed.). Boston: Allyn & Bacon.

Carson, R. C., Butcher, J. N., & Mineka, S. (2003). *Abnormal psychology and modern life.* (12th ed.). New York: HarperCollins.

Carstensen, L. L. (1995). Evidence for a life-span theory of socioemotional selectivity. *Current Directions in Psychological Science, 4,* 151–156.

Carstensen, L. L. (1998). A life-span approach to social motivation. In J. Heckhausen & C. Dweck (Eds.), *Motivation and self-regulation across the life span.* New York: Cambridge University Press.

Carstensen, L. L., Pasupathi, M., & Nesselroade, J. R. (2000). Emotional experience in everyday life across the life span. *Journal of Personality and Social Psychology, 79,* 644–655.

Carstensen, L. L., & Turk-Charles, S. (1994). The salience of emotion across the adult life span. *Psychology and Aging, 9,* 262. American Psychological Association.

Carter, R. (1998). *Mapping the mind.* Berkeley, CA: University of California Press.

Caruso, J. C. (2001). Reliable component analysis of the Stanford-Binet: Fourth Edition for 2- to 6-year-olds. *Psychological Assessment, 13,* 261–266.

Carver, C. S., & Scheier, M. F. (2004). *Perspectives on personality* (5th ed.). Boston: Allyn & Bacon.

Castonguay, L. G., Gottfried, M. R., Halperin, G. S., & Reid, J. J. (2003). Psychotherapy integration. In I. B. Weiner (Ed.), *Handbook of psychology* (Vol. 8). New York: Wiley.

Castro-Alamancos, M. A., & Calcagnotto, M. E. (2001). High-pass filtering of corticothalamic activity by neuromodulators released during arousal. *Journal of Neurophysiology, 85,* 1489–1497.

Cauller, L. (2001, May). *Review of Santrock, Psychology* (7th ed.). New York: McGraw-Hill.

Cavedini, P., Riboldi, G., Keller, R., D'Annucci, A., & Bellodi, K. L. (2002). Frontal lobe dysfunction in pathological gambling patients. *Biological Psychiatry, 15,* 334–341.

CDC AIDS Community Demonstration Projects Research Group. (1999). The CDC AIDS Community Demonstration Projects: A multi-site community-level intervention to promote HIV risk reduction. *American Journal of Public Health, 89, 3,* 336–345.

Ceballo, R., Ramirez, C., Hearn, K. D., & Maltese, K. L. (2004). Community violence and children's psychological well-being: does parental monitoring matter? *Journal of Clinical Child and Adolescent Psychology, 32,* 586–592.

Ceci, S. J. (1996). Unpublished review of *Child Development* (4) by J. W. Santrock. New York: McGraw-Hill.

Ceci, S. J., & Gilstrap, L. L. (2000). Determinants of intelligence: Schooling and intelligence. In A. Kazdin (Ed.), *Encyclopedia of Psychology.* Washington, DC, & New York: American Psychological Association and Oxford University Press.

Center for Leadership Studies. (2000). *Multifactor Leadership Questionnaire: Norms.* Retrieved November 24, 2001, from http://cls.binghamton.edu/mlq.htm

Center for Survey Research. (2000). *Hours on the job.* Storrs, CT: University of Connecticut, Center for Survey Research.

Centers for Disease Control and Prevention. (2001a). *AIDS.* Atlanta: Centers for Disease Control and Prevention.

Centers for Disease Control and Prevention. (2001b). *How to quit.* Atlanta: Centers for Disease Control and Prevention.

Centers for Disease Control and Prevention. (2003). *HIV/AIDS.* Atlanta: Author.

Chance, P. (2003). *Learning and behavior* (4th ed.). Belmont, CA: Wadsworth.

Changeux, J., & Chavillion, J. (1995). *Origins of the human brain.* New York: Oxford University Press.

Charles, C. M. (2002). *Building classroom discipline* (7th ed.). Boston: Allyn & Bacon.

Chastain, G., & Landrum, R. E. (1999). *Protecting human subjects.* Washington, DC: American Psychological Association.

Chaves, J. F. (2000). Hypnosis. In A. Kazdin (Ed.), *Encyclopedia of psychology.* Washington DC, and New York: American Psychological Association and Oxford University Press.

Cheasty, M., Condren, R., & Cooney, C. (2002). Altered sexual preference and behavior in a man with vascular ischemic lesions in the temporal lobe. International *Journal of Geriatric Psychiatry, 17,* 87–88.

Chen, C., & Stevenson, H. W. (1989). Homework: A cross-cultural comparison. *Child Development, 60,* 551–561.

Chen, E., Fisher, E. B., Bacharier, L. B., Strunk, R. C. (2003). Socioeconomic status, stress, and immune markers in adolescents with asthma. *Psychosomatic Medicine, 65,* 984–992.

Chess, S., & Thomas, A. (1977). Temperamental individuality from childhood to adolescence. *Journal of Child Psychiatry, 16,* 218–226.

Chiesa, M., Fonagy, P., & Holmes, J. (2003). When less is more: An exploration of psychoanalytically oriented hospital-based treatment for severe personality disorder. *International Journal of Psychoanalysis, 84,* 637–650.

Child Trends. (2000). Trends in sexual activity and contraceptives among teens. *Child Trends Research Brief.* Washington, DC: Author.

Children's Defense Fund. (2000). *The state of America's children: 2000.* Washington, DC: Children's Defense Fund.

Chirot, D., & Seligman, M. E. P. (Eds.). (2001). *Ethnopolitical warfare.* Washington, DC: American Psychological Association.

Chodorow, N. (1978). *The reproduction of mothering.* Berkeley: University of California Press.

Chodorow, N. (1989). *Feminism and psychoanalytic theory.* New Haven, CT: Yale University Press.

Chomsky, N. (1975). *Reflections on language.* New York: Pantheon.

Chorney, M. J., Chorney, K., Seese, N., Owen, M. J., Daniels, J., McGuffin, P., Thompson, L. A.,

Detterman, D. K., Benbow, C., Lubinski, D., Eley, T., & Plomin, R. (1998). A quantitative trait locus associated with cognitive ability in children. *Psychological Science, 9,* 159–166.

Christensen, L. (1996). *Diet-behavior relationships.* Washington, DC: American Psychological Association.

Christian, K., Bachnan, H. J., & Morrison, F. J. (2001). Schooling and cognitive development. In R. J. Sternberg & E. L. Grigorenko (Eds.), *Environmental effects on cognitive development.* Mahwah, NJ: Erlbaum.

Christiansen, L. B. (2001). *Experimental methodology* (8th ed.). Boston: Allyn & Bacon.

Christie, I. C., & Friedman, B. H. (2004). Autonomic specificity of discrete emotion and dimensions of affective space: a multivariate approach. *International Journal of Psychophysiology, 51,* 143–153.

Chung, K., & Chung, J. M. (2001). Sympathetic sprouting in the dorsal root ganglion after spinal nerve ligation; evidence of regenerative collateral sprouting. *Brain Research, 895,* 204–212.

Church, R. M., & Kirkpatrick, K. (2001). Theories of conditioning and timing. In R. R. Mowrer & S. B. Klein (Eds.), *Handbook of contemporary learning theories.* Mahwah, NJ: Erlbaum.

Cialdini, R. B. (2001). *Influence: Science and practice* (4th Ed.). Boston: Allyn & Bacon.

Cialdini, R. B., Schaller, M., Houlihan, D., Arps, K., Fultz, J., & Beaman, A. L. (1987). Empathy-based helping: Is it selflessly or selfishly motivated? *Journal of Personality and Social Psychology, 52,* 749–758.

Cialdini, R. B., & Trost, M. R. (1998). Social influence: Social norms, conformity, and compliance. In D. T. Gilbert, S. T. Fiske, & G. Lindzey (Eds.), *Handbook of social psychology* (4th ed., Vol. 2). New York: McGraw-Hill.

Cicchetti, D., & Toth, S. (1998). Perspectives on research and practice in developmental psychopathology. In I. E. Sigel & K. A. Renninger (Eds.), *Handbook of child psychology* (5th ed., Vol. 4). New York: Wiley.

Clark, D. M., Salkovskis, P. M., Hackmann, A., Middelton, H., Anastasiades, P., & Gelder, M. (1994). A comparison of cognitive therapy, applied relaxation, and imipramine in the treatment of panic disorder. *British Journal of Psychiatry, 164,* 759–769.

Clark, E. V. (1983). Meanings and concepts. In P. H. Mussen (Ed.), *Handbook of child psychology* (4th ed., Vol. 2). New York: Wiley.

Clark, L. A., Watson, D., & Reynolds, S. (1995). Diagnosis and classification in psychopathology. *Annual Review of Psychology, 46.* Palo Alto, CA: Annual Reviews.

Clark, M. S., & Brissette, I. (2003). Two types of relationship closeness and their influence on people's emotional lives. In R. J. Davidson, K. R. Scherer, & M. M. Goldsmith (Eds.), *Handbook of affective sciences.* New York: Oxford University Press.

Clark, N. M., & Dodge, J. A. (1999). Exploring self-efficacy as a predictor of disease management. *Health Education & Behavior, 26,* 72–89.

Clark, T. (2001). Post-traumatic stress disorder: Baby should not be thrown out with the bath water. *British Journal of Medicine, 322,* 1303–1304.

Clarke, V. A., Lovegrove, H., Williams, H., & Macpherson, M. (2000). Unrealistic optimism and the health belief model. *Journal of Behavioral Medicine, 25,* 367–376.

Clayton, A. H., McGarvey, E. L., Abouesh, A. L., & Pinkerton, R. C. (2001). Substitution of an SSRI with bupropion sustained release following SSRI-induced sexual dysfunction. *Journal of Clinical Psychiatry, 62,* 185–190.

Cloninger, S. C. (2004). *Theories of personality* (4th ed.). Upper Saddle River, NJ: Prentice-Hall.

Close, C. E., Roberts, P. L., & Berger, R. E. (1990). Cigarettes, alcohol, and marijuana are related to pyospermia in infertile men. *Journal of Urology, 144,* 900–903.

Cochran, S. D., & Mays, V. M. (1990). Sex, lies, and HIV. *New England Journal of Medicine, 322,* 774–775.

Cohen, J. A., Mannarino, A. P., & Rogal, S. (2001). Treatment practices for childhood post-traumatic stress disorder. *Child Abuse and Neglect, 25,* 123–135.

Cohen, L., De Moor, C., & Amato, R. J. (2001). The association between treatment-specific optimism and depressive symptomatology in patients enrolled in a Phase I cancer clinical trial. *Cancer, 91,* 1949–1953.

Cohen, L. A. (1987, November). Diet and cancer. *Scientific American,* pp. 128–137.

Cohen, P., Cohen, J., Kasen, S., Velez, C. N., Hartmark, C., Johnson, J., Rojas, M., Brook, J., & Streuning, E. L. (1993). An epidemiological study of disorders in late adolescence: I. Age- and gender-specific prevalence. *Journal of Child Psychology & Psychiatry, 6,* 851–867.

Cohen, R. J., & Swerdlik, M. E. (2002). *Psychological testing and assessment* (5th ed.). New York: McGraw-Hill.

Cohen, R. L., & Borsoi, D. (1996). The role of gestures in description-communication: A cross-sectional study of aging. *Journal of Nonverbal Behavior, 20,* 45–64.

Cohen, S. (2002). Psychosocial stress, social networks, and susceptibility to infection. In H. G. Koenig & H. J. Cohen (Eds.), *The link between religion and health.* New York: Oxford University Press.

Cohen, S., Doyle, W. J., Skoner, D. P., Rabin, B. S., & Gawaltney, J. M. (1997). Social ties and susceptibility to the common cold. *Journal of the American Medical Association, 277,* 1940–1944.

Cohen, S., Doyle, W. J., Turner, R. B., Alper, C. M., & Skoner, D. P. (2003). Emotional style and susceptibility to the common cold. *Psychosomatic Medicine, 65,* 652–657.

Cohen, S., Frank, E., Doyle, W., Skoner, D. P., Rabin, B. S., & Gwaltney, J. M. (1998). Types of stressors that increase susceptibility to the common cold in healthy adults. *Health Psychology, 17,* 214–223.

Cohen, S., Miller, G. E., & Rabin, B. S. (2001). Psychological stress and antibody response to immunization. *Psychosomatic Medicine, 63,* 7–18.

Cohen, S. I. (2002). Treatment of insomnia. *Lancet, 359,* 1433–1434.

Colby, A., Kohlberg, L., Gibbs, J., & Lieberman, M. (1983). A longitudinal study of moral judgment. *Monographs of the Society for Research in Child Development, 48* (21, Serial No. 201).

Cole, C. F., Richman, B. A., & Brown, S. K. (2001). The world of *Sesame Street* research. In S. M. Fisch & R. T. Truglio (Eds.), *"G" is for growing: Thirty years of research on children and Sesame Street.* Mahwah, NJ: Erlbaum.

Cole, M. (1999). Culture in development. In M. H. Bornstein & M. E. Lamb (Eds.), *Developmental psychology: An advanced textbook* (4th ed.). Mahwah, NJ: Erlbaum.

Cole, M., & Cole, S. R. (2003). *The development of children* (5th ed.). New York: Freeman.

Coleman, B. L., Stevens, M. J., & Reeder, G. G. (2001). What makes recovered-memory testimony compelling to jurors? *Law and Human Behavior, 25,* 317–338.

Coleman, J. (1995, March). *Adolescent sexual knowledge: Implications for health and health risks.* Paper presented at the meeting of the Society for Research in Child Development, Indianapolis.

Coleman, P. D. (1986, August). *Regulation of dendritic extent: Human aging brain and Alzheimer's disease.* Paper presented at the meeting of the American Psychological Association, Washington, DC.

Coley, J. D., Hayes, B., Lawson, C., & Moloney, M. (2004). Knowledge, expectations, and inductive reasoning within conceptual hierarchies. *Cognition, 90,* 217–253.

Coll, C. G., Bearer, E. L., & Lerner, R. M. (Eds.). (2004). *Nature and nurture.* Mahwah, NJ: Erlbaum.

College Board. (2001). *2001 college bound seniors are the largest, most diverse group in history.* Princeton, NJ: Educational Testing Service.

Collins, W. A., & Laursen, B. (2004). Parent-adolescent relationships and influences. In R. Lerner & L. Steinberg (Eds.), *Handbook of adolescent psychology.* New York: Wiley.

Collins, W. A., Maccoby, E. E., Steinberg, L., Hetherington , E. M., & Bornstein, M. H. (2000). Contemporary research on parenting: The case for nature and nurture. *American Psychologist, 55,* 218–232.

Comarow, D. D., & Chescheir, M. W. (1999). *Talking about therapy.* Westport, CT: Greenwood.

Compas, B. E., Connor-Smith, J. K., Saltzman, H., Thomsen, A. H., & Wadsworth, M. E. (2001). Coping with stress during childhood and adolescence: Problems, progress, and potential in theory and research. *Psychological Bulletin, 127,* 87–127.

Conklin, C. A., & Tiffany, S. T. (2002). Applying extinction research and theory to cue-exposure addiction treatments. *Addiction, 97,* 155–167.

Cooley, E., & Toray, T. (2001). Disordered eating in college freshmen women: A prospective study. *Journal of American College Health, 49,* 229–235.

Cooper, R. M., & Zubek, J. P. (1958). Effects of enriched and restricted early environments on the learning ability of bright and dull rats. *Canadian Journal of Psychology, 12,* 159–164.

Cooper, R. P., Yule, P., Fox, J., & Glasspool, D. W. (2002). *Modeling high-level cognitive processes.* Mahwah, NJ: Erlbaum.

Corballis, M. C. (2004, August). *The divided brain.* Paper presented at the 28th International Congress of Psychology, Beijing, China.

Corballis, P. M., Funnell, M. G., & Gazzaniga, M. S. (2002). Hemispheric asymmetries for simple visual judgments in the split brain. *Neuropsychologia, 40,* 401–410.

Corey, G. (1996). *Theory and practice of counseling and psychotherapy* (5th ed.). Pacific Grove, CA: Brooks/Cole.

Corey, G. R. (2001). *Theory and practice of counseling and psychotherapy* (6th ed.). Belmont, CA: Wadsworth.

Corey, G. R. (2004). *Theory and practice of group counseling* (6th ed.). Belmont, CA: Wadsworth.

Corey, G. R. & Corey, M. S. (2002). *I never knew I had a choice* (7th ed.). Belmont, CA: Wadsworth.

Cosgrave, E., McGorry, P., Allen, N., & Jackson, H. (2000). Depression in young people: A growing challenge for primary care. *Australian Family Physician, 29,* 123–127.

Cosmides, L., Tooby, J. Cronin, H., & Curry, O. (2003). *What is evolutionary psychology? Explaining the new science of the mind.* New Haven, CT: Yale University Press.

Costa, P. T., & McCrae, R. R. (1992). *Revised NEO personality inventory.* Odessa, FL: Psychological Assessment Resources.

Costa, P. T., & McCrae, R. R. (1995). Solid ground on the wetlands of personality: A reply to Block. *Psychological Bulletin, 117,* 216–220.

Costa, P. T., & McCrae, R. R. (1998). Personality assessment. In H. S. Friedman (Ed.), *Encyclopedia of mental health* (Vol. 3). San Diego: Academic Press.

Cotter, D., Mackay, D., Chana, G., Beasley, C., Landau, S., & Everall, I. P. (2002). Reduced neuronal size and glial density in area 9 of the dorsolat-eral prefrontal cortex in subjects with major depressive disorder. *Cerebral Cortex, 12,* 386–394.

Coupland, N. J. (2001). Social phobia: Etiology, neurobiology, and treatment. *Journal of Clinical Psychiatry, 62,* (Suppl. 1), 25–35.

Coupland, N. J. (2002). Worry WARTS have generalized anxiety attacks. *Canadian Journal of Psychiatry, 47,* 197.

Courtet, P. & Others. (2004). Serotonin transporter gene may be involved in short-term Risk of subsequent suicide attempts. *Biological Psychiatry, 55,* 46–51. (too many authors to list)

Cowan, P. A., & Cowan, C. P. (2001). What an intervention design reveals about how parents affect their children's academic achievement and social competence. In J. Borkowski, S. Landesman-Ramey, & M. Bristol (Eds.), *Parenting and the child's world: Multiple influences on intellectual and social-emotional development.* Mahwah, NJ: Erlbaum.

Cowley, M. A., Smart, J. L., Rubinstein, M., Cerdan, M. G., Diano, S., Horvath, T. L., Cone, R. D., & Low, M. J. (2001). Leptin activates anorexigenic POMC neurons through a neural network in the arcuate nucleus. *Nature, 411,* 480–484.

Coyne, J. C. (2000). Mood disorders. In A. Kazdin (Ed.), *Encyclopedia of psychology.* Washington, DC, & New York: American Psychological Association and Oxford University Press.

Cozby, P. C. (2004). *Methods in behavioral research* (8th ed.). New York: McGraw-Hill.

Crabbe, J. C. (2001). Use of genetic analysis to refine phenotypes related to alcohol tolerance and dependence. *Alcoholism: Clinical and Experimental Research, 25,* 288–292.

Crabbe, J. C. (2002). Genetic contributions to alcoholism. *Annual Review of Psychology, 53.*

Craighead, W. E., & Craighead, L. W. (2001). The role of psychotherapy in treating psychiatric disorders. *Medical Clinics of North America, 85,* 617–629.

Craik, F. I. M., & Lockhart, R. S. (1972). Levels of processing; A framework for memory research. *Journal of Verbal Learning and Verbal Behavior, 11,* 671–684.

Craik, F. I. M., & Salthouse, T. A. (Eds.). (2000). *The handbook of aging and cognition.* Mahwah, NJ: Erlbaum.

Craik, F. I. M., & Tulving, E. (1975). Depth of processing and retention of words in episodic memory. *Journal of Experimental Psychology: General, 104,* 268–294.

Cramer, P. (1999). Future directions for the Thematic Apperception Test. *Journal of Personality Assessment, 72,* 74–92.

Cramer, P., & Brilliant, M. A. (2001). Defense use and defense understanding in children. *Journal of Personality, 69,* 297–322.

Crano, W., & Brewer, M. (2002). *Principles and methods of social research* (2nd ed.). Mahwah, NJ: Erlbaum.

Crasilneck, H. B. (1995). The use of the Crasilneck bombardment technique in problems of intractible organic pain. *American Journal of Clinical Hypnosis, 37,* 255–266.

Crawford, C. B., & Salmon, C. A. (Eds.). (2004). *Evolutionary psychology, public policy, and private decisions.* Mahwah, NJ: Erlbaum.

Crawford, E. D. (2003). Use of algorithms as determinants for individual patient decision making, *Urology, 62, Supplement 1,* 13–19.

Crick, F., & Koch, C. (1998). Consciousness and neuroscience. *Cerebral Cortex, 8,* 97–107.

Crocker, J. (2001, August). *The costs of seeking self-esteem.* Paper presented at the meeting of the American Psychological Association, San Francisco.

Crocker, J., Major, B., & Steele, C. (1998). Social stigma. In D. T. Gilbert, S. T. Fiske, & G. Lindzey (Eds.), *Handbook of social psychology* (4th ed., Vol. 2). New York: McGraw-Hill.

Crooks, R., & Bauer, K. (2002). *Our sexuality* (8th ed.). Belmont, CA: Wadsworth.

Crosby, A. E., Cheltenham, M. P., & Sacks, J. J. (1999). Incidence of suicidal ideation and behavior in the United States, 1994. *Suicide and Life-Threatening Behavior, 29,* 131–140.

Crosby, F. J. (1991). *Juggling.* New York: Free Press.

Cross-National Collaborative Group. (1992). The changing rate of major depression. *Journal of the American Medical Association, 268,* 3098–3105.

Crowley, K., Callahan, M. A., Tenenbaum, H. R., & Allen, E. (2001). Parents explain more to boys than to girls during shared scientific thinking. *Psychological Science, 12,* 258–261.

Crowther, J. H., Sanftner, J., Bonifazi, D. Z., & Shepherd, K. L. (2001). The role of daily hassles in binge eating. *International Journal of Eating Disorders, 29,* 449–454.

Csikszentmihalyi, M. (1990). *Flow: The psychology of optimal experience.* New York: HarperPerennial.

Csikszentmihalyi, M. (1996). *Creativity.* New York: HarperCollins.

Cueller, I., & Paniagua, F. A. (Eds.). (2000). *Handbook of multicultural health.* San Diego: Academic Press.

Cummings, M. (2003). *Human heredity* (6th ed.). Belmont, CA: Wadsworth.

Curran, K., DuCette, J., Eisenstein, J., & Hyman, I. A. (2001, August). *Statistical analysis of the cross-cultural data: The third year.* Paper presented at the meeting of the American Psychological Association, San Francisco, CA.

Curtiss, S. (1977). *Genie.* New York: Academic Press.

Cushner, K., & Brislin, R. W. (1995). *Intercultural interactions* (2nd ed.). Newbury Park, CA: Sage.

Cutler, B. L., & Penrod, S. D. (1995). *Mistaken identities: The eyewitness, psychology, and the law.* New York: Cambridge University Press.

Czienskowski, U., & Giljohann, S. (2002). Intimacy, concreteness, and the "self-reference" effect. *Experimental Psychology, 49,* 73–79.

D

DaCosta, D., Larouche, J., Dritsa, M., & Brender, W. (2000). Psychosocial correlates of prepartum and postpartum depressed mood. *Journal of Affective Disorders, 59,* 31–40.

Dadds, M. R., Holland, D. E., Barrett, P. M., & Spence, S. H. (1999). Early intervention and prevention of anxiety disorders in children: Results at 2-year follow-up. *Journal of Consulting & Clinical Psychology, 67,* 145–150.

Dalfen, A. K., & Stewart, D. E. (2001). Who develops severe or fatal adverse drug reactions to selective serotonin reuptake inhibitors? *Canadian Journal of Psychology, 46,* 258–263.

Dalton, J. H., Elias, M. J., & Wandersman, A. (2001). *Community psychology.* Belmont, CA: Wadsworth.

Damasio, A. (Ed.). (2001). *The Scientific American book of the brain.* New York: Scientific American.

Damcott, C. M., Sack, P., & Shuldiner, A. R. (2003). The genetics of obesity. *Endocrinology and Metabolic Clinics of North America, 32,* 761–786.

D'Angelo, B., & Wierzbicki, M. (2003). Relations of daily hassles with both anxious and depressed mood in students. *Psychological Reports, 92,* 416–418.

Dannon, P. N., Dolberg, O. T., Schrieber, S., & Grunhaus, L. (2002). Three and six-month outcome following courses of either ECT or rTMS in a population of severely depressed individuals—preliminary report. *Biological Psychiatry, 51,* 687–690.

Dantzer, R. (2004). Innate immunity at the forefront of psychoneuroimmunology. *Brain, Behavior, & Immunity, 18,* 1–6.

Darley, J. M., & Latané, B. (1968). Bystander intervention in emergencies: Diffusion of responsibility. *Journal of Personality and Social Psychology, 8,* 377–383.

Darwin, C. (1965). *The expression of the emotions in man and animals.* Chicago: University of Chicago Press. (Original work published 1872)

Darwin, C. (1979). *The origin of species.* New York: Avenal Books. (Original work published 1859)

Das, J. P. (2000). Mental retardation. In A. Kazdin (Ed.), *Encyclopedia of psychology.* Washington, DC, & New York: American Psychological Association and Oxford University Press.

Dastzer, R. (2004). Innate immunity at the forefront of psychoneuroimmunology. *Brain, Behavior, & Immunity, 18,* 1–6.

Dattilio, F. M. (Ed.). (2001). *Case studies in couple and family therapy.* New York: Guilford.

Davidson, A. R., & Jacard, J. J. (1979). Variables that moderate the attitude-behavior relation: Results of a longitudinal survey. *Journal of Personality and Social Psychology, 37,* 1364–1376.

Davidson, J. E., & Callery, C. (2001). Care of the obesity surgery patient requiring immediate-level or intensive care. *Obesity Surgery, 11,* 93–97.

Davidson, P. S., & Glisky, E. L. (2002). Is flashbulb memory a special instance of source memory? Evidence from older adults. *Memory, 10,* 99–111.

Davidson, R. J. (1993). The neuropsychology of emotion and affective style. In M. Lewis & J. M. Haviland (Eds.), *Handbook of emotion.* New York: Guilford Press.

Davidson, R. J. (2000). Affective style, psychopathology, and resilience: Brain mechanisms and plasticity. *American Psychologist, 55,* 196–214.

Davidson, R. J., Shackman, A., & Pizzagalli, D. (2002). The functional neuroanatomy of emotion and affective style. In R. J. Davidson, K. R. Scherer, & H. H. Goldsmith (Eds.), *Handbook of affective sciences.* New York: Oxford University Press.

Davies, K. (2001). *Cracking the genome.* New York: Free Press.

Davison, G. C., & Neale, J. M. (1994). *Abnormal psychology* (6th ed.). New York: Wiley.

Davison, G. C., & Neale, J. M. (2001). *Abnormal psychology* (8th ed.). New York: Wiley.

Day. R. D. (2003). *Introduction to family processes* (4th ed.). Mahwah, NJ: Erlbaum.

De Benedittis, G., & Sironi, V. A. (1985). Deep cerebral electrical activity during the hypnotic state in man: Neurological considerations in hypnosis. *Review of Neurology, 55,* 1–16.

de Boysson-Bardies, B. (2001). *How language comes to children.* Cambridge, MA: MIT Press.

de Lacoste-Utamsing, C., & Holloway, R. L. (1982). Sexual dimorphism in the human corpus callosum. *Science, 216,* 1431–1432.

De Valois, K. K. (2000). *Seeing.* San Diego: Academic Press.

Deaux, K. (2001). Social identity. In J. Worell (Ed.), *Encyclopedia of gender and women.* San Diego: Academic Press.

DeBattista, C., Solvason, H. B., & Schatzberg, A. F. (1998). Mood disorders. In H.S. Friedman (Ed.), *Encyclopedia of mental health* (Vol. 2). San Diego: Academic Press.

deCharms, R. (1984). Motivation enhancement in educational settings. In R. Ames & C. Ames (Eds.), *Research on motivation in education* (Vol. 1). Orlando: Academic Press.

Deci, E., & Ryan, R. M. (1994). Promoting self-determined education. *Scandinavian Journal of Educational Research, 38,* 3–14.

Deci, E. L., & Ryan, R. M. (1995). Human autonomy: The basis for true self-esteem. In M. Kernis (Ed.), *Efficacy, agency, and self-esteem.* New York: Plenum.

Decruyenaere, M., Evers-Kiebooms, G., Welkenhuysen, M., Denayer, L., & Claes, E. (2000). Cognitive representations of breast cancer, emotional distress, and preventive health behavior: A theoretical perspective. *Psychooncology, 9,* 528–536.

Deeb, S. S., & Kohl, S. (2003). Genetics of color vision deficiencies. *Developments in Opthalmology, 37,* 170–187.

Dehaene, S., & Naccache, L. (2001). Towards a neuroscience of consciousness: Basic evidence and a workspace format. *Cognition, 79,* 1–37.

Dell, P. F. (2002). Dissociative phenomena of dissociative identity disorder. *Journal of Nervous and Mental Disorders, 190,* 10–15.

Dell, P. F., & Eisenhower, J. W. (1990). Adolescent multiple personality disorder: A preliminary study of eleven cases. *Journal of the American Academy of Child & Adolescent Psychiatry, 29,* 359–366.

Del-Moral-Hernandez, E. (2003). Neural networks with chaotic recursive nodes. *Neural Networks, 16,* 675–682.

Dement, W. C. (1978). *Some must watch while some must sleep.* New York: Norton.

Dement, W. C. (1999). *The promise of sleep.* New York: Delacorte Press.

Demerouti, E., Bakker, A. B., Nachreiner, F., & Schaufeli, W. B. (2001). The job demands-resources model of burnout. *Journal of Applied Psychology, 86,* 499–512.

Denmark, F. L., Russo, N. F., Frieze, I. H., & Eschuzur, J. (1988). Guidelines for avoiding sexism in psychological research: A report of the ad hoc committee on nonsexist research. *American Psychologist, 43,* 582–585.

Derrington, A.M., Allen, H., & Delicato, L. (2004). Visual mechanisms of motion analysis and motion perception. *Annual Review of Psychology, 54.* Palo Alto, CA: Annual Reviews.

Derryberry, D., & Reed, M. (2002). Information processing approaches to individual differences in emotional reactivity. In R. J. Davidson, K. R. Scherer, & H. H. Goldsmith (Eds.), *Handbook of affective sciences.* New York: Oxford University Press.

DeRubeis, R. J., & Crits-Cristoph, P. (1998). Empirically supported individual and group psychological treatments for adult mental disorders. *Journal of Consulting and Clinical Psychology, 66,* 37–52.

Deutsch, M., & Collins, M. (1951). *Interracial housing: A psychological evaluation of a social experiment.* Minneapolis: University of Minnesota Press.

Devine, P. G., Evett, S. R., & Vasquez-Suson, K. A. (1996). Exploring the interpersonal dynamics of intergroup contact. In R. M. Sorrentino & E. T. Higgins (Eds.), *Handbook of motivation and cognition: The interpersonal context* (Vol. 3). New York: Guilford Press.

Devlin, M. J., Golfein, J. A., Crino, J. S., & Wolk, S. L. (2000). Open treatment of overweight binge eaters with phentermine and fluoxetine as an adjunct to cognitive-behavioral therapy. *International Journal of Eating Disorders, 28,* 325–332.

Devries, L. K. (1998). *Insomnia.* New York: Harold Shaw.

Dick, F., Dronkers, N. F., Pizzamiglio, L., Saygin, A. P., Small, S. L., & Wilson, S. (2004). *Language and the brain.* Mahwah, NJ: Erlbaum.

Dickens, W. T., & Flynn, J. R. (2001). Heritability estimates versus large environmental effects: The IQ paradox resolved. *Psychological Review, 108,* 346–369.

Dickerson, F. B., Boronow, J. J., Stallings, C. R., Origoni, A. F., Cole, S., & Yelken, R. H. (2004). Association between cognitive functioning and employment status of persons with bipolar disorder. *Psychiatric Services, 55,* 54–58.

Dickson, G. L. (1990). A feminist post-structuralist analysis of the knowledge of menopause. *Advances in Nursing Science, 12,* 15–31.

Diener, E. (1999). Introduction to the special section on the structure of emotion. *Journal of Personality and Social Psychology, 76,* 803–804.

Diener, E. (2000). Subjective well-being: The science of happiness and a proposal for a national index. *American Psychologist, 55,* 34–43.

Diener, E., Lucas, R. E., & Oishi, S. (2001). The science of happiness and life satisfaction. In C. R. Snyder & S. J. Lopez (Eds.), *Handbook of positive psychology.* New York: Oxford University Press.

Diener, E., & Seligman, M. E. P. (2002). Very happy people. *Psychological Science, 13,* 81–84.

Diener, E., Suh, E. M., Lucas, R. E., & Smith, H. L. (1999). Subjective well-being: Three decades of progress. *Psychological Bulletin, 125,* 276–301.

DiGiacomo, M., & Adamson, B. (2001). Coping with stress in the workplace: Implications for new health professionals. *Journal of Allied Health, 30,* 106–111.

DiMatteo, M. R., & Martin, L. R. (2002). *Health psychology.* Boston: Allyn & Bacon.

Dinsmoor, J. A. (1998). Punishment. In W. O'Donohue (Ed.), *Learning and behavior therapy.* Boston: Allyn & Bacon.

Dion, K. L. (2003). Prejudice, racism, and discrimination. In I. B. Weiner (Ed.), *Handbook of psychology* (Vol. 5). New York: Wiley.

Dipboye, R. L., Wooten, K., & Halverson, S. K. (2004). Behavioral and situational interviews. In M. Hersen (Ed.), *Comprehensive handbook of psychological assessment* (Vol. 4). New York: Wiley.

Dobzhansky, T. G. (1977). *Evolution.* New York: Freeman.

Dodd, D. K. (1995). Robbers in the classroom: A deindividuation exercise. In M. E. Ware & D. E. Johnson (Eds.), *Demonstrations and activities in teaching of psychology* (Vol. 3). Mahwah, NJ: Erlbaum.

Dohm, F. A., Beattie, J. A., Aibel, C., & Striegel-Moore, R. H. (2001). Factors differentiating women and men who successfully maintain weight loss from women and men who do not. *Journal of Clinical Psychology, 57,* 105–117.

Dohrenwend, B. S., & Shrout, P. E. (1985). "Hassles" in the conceptualization and measurement of life event stress variables. *American Psychologist, 40,* 780–785.

Dollard, J., Doob, L. W., Miller, N. E., Mowrer, O. H., & Sears, R. R. (1939). *Frustration and aggression.* New Haven, CT: Yale University Press.

Dolphin, W. D. (2002). *Biological investigations* (6th ed.). New York: McGraw-Hill.

Domhoff, G. W. (1999). New directions in the study of dream content using the Hall/Van de Castle coding system. *Dreaming, 9,* 115–137.

Domhoff, G. W. (2001). A new neurocognitive theory of dreams. *Dreaming, 11,* 13–33.

Domhoff, G. W. (2003). *Senoi dream theory: Myth, scientific method, and the dreamwork movement.* Retrieved July 18, 2003 from the World Wide Web: http://dreamresearch.net/ Library/senoi.html

Domhoff, G. W., & Schneider, A. (1998). New rationales and methods for quantitative dream research outside the laboratory. *Sleep, 21,* 398–404.

Domino, G. (2000). *Psychological testing.* Upper Saddle River, NJ: Prentice-Hall.

Domjan, M. P. (1996). *Essentials of conditioning and learning.* Pacific Grove, CA: Brooks/Cole.

Dong, Y. T., & Church, A. T. (2003). Cross-cultural equivalence and validity of the Vietnamese MMPI-2. *Psychological Assessment, 15,* 370–377.

Donnerstein, E. (2001). Media violence. In J. Worell (Ed.), *Encyclopedia of gender and women.* San Diego: Academic Press.

Dooley, D. (2001). *Social science research methods* (4th ed.). Upper Saddle River, NJ: Prentice-Hall.

Doran, S. M., Van Dongen, H. P., & Dinges, D. F. (2001). Sustained attention performance during sleep deprivation. *Archives of Italian Biology, 139,* 253–267.

Doty, R. L. (2001). Olfaction. *Annual Review of Psychology* (Vol. 52). Palo Alto, CA: Annual Reviews.

Dougall, A. L., & Baum, A. (2001). Stress, health, and illness. In A. Baum, T.A. Revenson, & J.E. Singer (Eds.), *Handbook of health psychology.* Mahwah, NJ: Erlbaum.

Dougherty, D. M., Cherek, D. R., & Bennett, R. H. (1996). The effects of alcohol on the aggressive responding of women. *Journal of Alcohol Studies, 57,* 178–186.

Dovidio, J. E., & Penner, L. A. (2001). Helping and altruism. In M. Hewstone & M. Brewer (Eds.), *Handbook of social psychology.* London: Blackwell.

Dowd, E. T. (2002). Self-statement modification. In M. Hersen & W. H. Sledge (Eds.), *Encyclopedia of psychotherapy.* San Diego: Academic Press.

Doyle, T. F., Bellugi, U., Korenberg, J. R., & Graham, J. (2004). "Everybody in the world is my friend" hypersociability in young children with Williams syndrome. *American Journal of Medical Genetics, 214A,* 263–273.

Draguns, J. G. (1990). Applications of cross-cultural psychology in the field of mental health. In R. W. Brislin (Ed.), *Applied cross-cultural psychology.* Newbury Park, CA: Sage.

Drevets, W. C. (2001). Neuroimaging and neuropathological studies of depression: Implications for the cognitive-emotional features of mood disorders. *Current Opinions in Neurobiology, 11,* 240–249.

Drobes, D. J., Miller, E. J., Hillman, C. H., Bradley, M. M., Cuthbart, B. N., & Lang, P. J. (2001). Food deprivation and emotional reaction to food cues: Implications for eating disorders. *Biological Psychology, 57,* 153–177.

Druckman, D., & Bjork, R. A. (Eds.). (1994). *Learning, remembering, and believing.* Washington, DC: National Academy Press.

Duffy, K. (2003). *Community psychology* (3rd ed.). Boston: Allyn & Bacon.

Duffy, K., & Wong, F. K. (2003). *Community psychology* (3rd ed.). Boston: Allyn & Bacon.

Duka, T., Weissenborn, R., & Dienes, Z. (2001). State-dependent effects of alcohol on recollective experiences, familiarity, and awareness of memory. *Psychopharmacology, 153,* 293–306.

Duncombe, J., Harrison, K., Allan, G., & Marsden, D. (Eds.). (2004). *The state of affairs.* Mahwah, NJ: Erlbaum.

Dunifon, R., Duncan, G., & Brooks-Gunn, J. (2004). Long-term impact of parental organization and efficiency. In A. Kalil & T. DeLeiere (Eds.), *Family investments in children's potential.* Mahwah, NJ: Erlbaum.

Dunne, M. (2002). Sampling considerations. In M. W. Wiederman & B. E. Whitley (Eds.), *Handbook for conducting research on human sexuality.* Mahwah, NJ: Erlbaum.

Dunner, D. L. (2001). Acute and maintenance treatment of chronic depression. *Journal of Clinical Psychiatry, 62* (Suppl. 6), 10–16.

Dunner, D. L., Hendricksen, H. E., Bea, C., Budech, C. B., & Friedman, S. D. (2002). Dysthmic disorder: Treatment with citalopram. *Depression and Anxiety, 15,* 18–22.

Dunnett, S. B. (1989). Neural transplantation: Normal brain function and repair after damage. *Psychologist, 1,* 4–8.

Durgin, F. H. (2000). Sensory adaptation. In A. Kazdin (Ed.), *Encyclopedia of psychology.* Washington, DC, & New York: American Psychological Association and Oxford University Press.

Durrant, J. E. (2000). Trends in youth crime and well-being since the abolition of corporal punishment in Sweden. *Youth and Society, 31*(4), 437–455.

Dutton, D., & Aron, A. (1974). Some evidence for heightened sexual attraction under conditions of high anxiety. *Journal of Personality and Social Psychology, 30,* 510–517.

Dutton, R. C., Maurer, A. J., Sonner, J. M., Fanselow, M. S., Laster, M. J., & Eger, E. I. (2002). Isoflurane causes anterograde but not retrograde amnesia for Pavlovian fear conditioning. *Anesthesiology, 96,* 1223–1229.

Dweck, C. (1996). Social motivation: Goals and social-cognitive processes. In J. Juvonen & K. R. Wentzel (Eds.), *Social motivation.* New York: Cambridge University Press.

E

Eagly, A. H. (1997, August). *Social roles as an origin theory for sex-related differences.* Paper presented at the meeting of the American Psychological Association, Chicago.

Eagly, A. H. (2000). Gender roles. In A. Kazdin (Ed.), *Encyclopedia of psychology.* Washington, DC, and New York: American Psychological Association and Oxford University Press.

Eagly, A. H. (2001). Social role theory of sex differences and similarities. In J. Worell (Ed.), *Encyclopedia of women and gender.* San Diego: Academic Press.

Eagly, A. H. (2002). Social role theory of sex differences and similarities. In J. Worell (Ed.), *Encyclopedia of women and gender.* New York: Oxford University Press.

Eagly, A. H., & Chaiken, S. (1998). Attitude structure and function. In D. T. Gilbert, S. T. Fiske, & G. Lindzey (Eds.), *Handbook of social psychology* (4th ed., Vol. 2). New York: McGraw-Hill.

Eagly, A. H., & Crowley, M. (1986). Gender and helping behavior: A meta-analytic review of the social psychological literature. *Psychological Bulletin, 100,* 283–308.

Eagly, A. H., & Steffen, V. J. (1986). Gender and aggressive behavior: A meta-analytic review of the social psychological literature. *Psychological Bulletin, 111,* 3–22.

Eccles, J. S. (2004). Academic motivation and stage-environment fit. In R. Lerner and L. Steinberg (Eds.), *Handbook of adolescent psychology.* New York: Wiley.

Eccles, J. S., & Wiegfield, A. (2002). Motivational beliefs, values, and goals. *Annual Review of Psychology, 53,* 109–132.

Eccles, J. S., Wiegfield, A., & Schiefele, U. (1998). Motivation to succeed. In W. Damon (Ed.), *Handbook of child psychology* (Vol. 3). New York: Wiley.

Eckert, E. D., Heston, L. L., & Bouchard, T. J. (1981). MZ twins reared apart. In L. Gedda, P. Paris, & W. D. Nance (Eds.), *Twin research* (Vol. 1). New York: Alan Liss.

Edinger, J. D., Wohlgemuth, W. K., Radtke, R. A., Marsh, G. R., & Quillian, R. E. (2001). Cognitive behavioral therapy for treatment of chronic primary insomnia. *Journal of the American Medical Association, 285,* 1856–1864.

Educational Testing Service. (1992, February). *Cross-national comparisons of 9–13 year-olds' science and math achievement.* Princeton, NJ: Educational Testing Service.

Edwards, B. (1979). *Drawing on the right side of the brain.* Los Angeles: Tarcher.

Edwards, C. D. (1999). *How to handle a hard-to-handle kid.* Los Angeles: Free Spirit Pub.

Edwards, J. R., & Rothbard, N. P. (1999). Work and family stress and well-being: An examination of person-environment fit in the work and family domains. *Organizational Behavior and Human Decision Processes, 77,* 85–129.

Ehrhardt, A. A. (1987). A transactional perspective on the development of gender differences. In J. M. Reinisch, L. A. Rosenblum, & S. A. Sanders (Eds.), *Masculinity/femininity: Basic perspectives*. New York: Oxford University Press.

Eibl-Eibesfeldt, I. (1977). Evolution of destructive aggression. *Aggressive Behavior, 3*, 127–144.

Eimer, B. N. (2000). Clinical applications of hypnosis for brief and efficient pain management psychotherapy. *American Journal of Clinical Hypnosis, 43*, 17–40.

Einstein, G. O., McDaniel, M. A., Mazi, M., Cochran, B., & Baker, M. (2000). Prospective memory and aging: Forgetting intentions over short delays. *Psychology and Aging, 15*, 671–683.

Eisenberg, N., & Morris, A. S. (2004). Moral cognitions and prosocial responding in adolescence. In R. Lerner & L. Steinberg (Eds.), *Handbook of adolescent psychology*. New York: Wiley.

Eisenberg, N., & Murphy, B. (1995). Parenting and children's moral development. In M. H. Bornstein (Ed.), *Children and parenting* (Vol. 4). Hillsdale, NJ: Erlbaum.

Eisenberg, N., & Valiente, C. (2002). Parenting and children's prosocial and moral development. In M. H. Bornstein (Ed.), *Handbook of parenting* (2nd ed.). Mahwah, NJ: Erlbaum.

Eisenman, R. (2004). Cognitive-behavioral group therapy for social phobia: Basic mechanisms and clinical strategies. *American Journal of Psychiatry, 161*, 183.

Eissenberg, T., Stitzer, M. L., & Henningfield, J. E. (1999). Current issues in nicotine replacement. In D. F. Seidman & L. S. Covey (Eds.), *Helping the hard-core smoker*. Mahwah, NJ: Erlbaum.

Ekman, P. (1980). *The face of man*. New York: Garland.

Ekman, P. (1996). Lying and deception. In N. L. Stein, C. Brainerd, P. A. Ornstein, & B. Tversky (Eds.), *Memory for everyday emotional events*. Mahwah, NJ: Erlbaum.

Ekman, P., & Friesen, W. V. (1968). The repertoire of nonverbal behavior—Categories, origins, usage, and coding. *Semiotica, 1*, 49–98.

Ekman, P., & Friesen, W. V. (1971). Constants across cultures in the face and emotion. *Journal of Personality and Social Psychology, 17*, 124–129.

Ekman, P., Levenson, R. W., & Friesen, W. V. (1983). Autonomic nervous system activity distinguishes among emotions. *Science, 223*, 1208–1210.

Ekman, P., & O'Sullivan, M. (1991). Facial expressions: Methods, means, and moues. In R. S. Feldman & B. Rime (Eds.), *Fundamentals of nonverbal behavior*. Cambridge: Cambridge University Press.

Eliasson, A., Eliasson, A., King, J., Gould, B., & Eliasson, A. (2002). Association of sleep and academic performance. *Sleep and Breathing, 6*, 45–48.

Eliot, L. (2001). *What's going on in there? How the brain and mind develop in the first five years of life*. New York: Bantam Doubleday.

Elkind, D. (1978). Understanding the young adolescent. *Adolescence, 13*, 127–134.

Ellemers, N., Spears, R., & Doosje, B. (2002). Self and social identity. *Annual Review of Psychology* (Vol. 53). Palo Alto, CA: Annual Reviews.

Elliott, B. A., Beattie, M. K., & Kaitfors, S. E. (2001). Health needs of people living below the poverty level. *Family Medicine, 33*, 361–366.

Ellis, A. (1962). *Reason and emotion in psychotherapy*. New York: Lyle Stuart.

Ellis, A. (1996). A rational-emotive behavior therapist's perspective on Ruth. In G. Corey (Ed.), *Case approach to counseling and psychotherapy*. Pacific Grove, CA: Brooks/Cole.

Ellis, A. (2002). Rational emotive behavior therapy. In M. Hersen & W. H. Sledge (Eds.), *Encyclopedia of psychotherapy*. San Diego: Academic Press.

Ellis, H. C. (1987). Recent developments in human memory. In V. P. Makosky (Ed.), *The G. Stanley Hall Lecture Series*. Washington, DC: American Psychological Association.

Ellis, L., & Ames, M. A. (1987). Neurohormonal functioning and sexual orientation. *Psychological Bulletin, 101*, 233–258.

Ellsworth, P. C. (2002). Appraisal processes in emotion. In R. J. Davidson, K. R. Scherer, & H. H. Goldsmith (Eds.), *Handbook of affective sciences*. New York: Oxford University Press.

Elmes, D. G., Kantowitz, B. H., & Roediger, H. L. (2003). *Research methods in psychology* (7th ed.). Belmont, CA: Wadsworth.

Empson, J. A. C., & Clarke, P. R. F. (1970). Rapid eye movements and remembering. *Nature, 227*, 287–288.

Endler, N. S. (1995). *Personality theories* (4th ed.). Fort Worth: Harcourt Brace.

Eng, P. M., Fitzmaurice, G., Kubzansky, L. D., Rimm, E. B., & Kawachi, I. (2003). Anger expression and risk of stroke and coronary heart disease among male health professionals. *Psychosomatic Medicine, 65*, 100–110.

Engeland, A., Bjorge, T., Tverdal, A., & Sogaard, A. J. (2004). Obesity in adolescence and childhood and the risk of adult mortality. *Epidemiology, 15*, 79–85.

Engelman, H. S., & MacDermott, A. B. (2004). Presynaptic ionotropic receptors and control of transmitter release, *Nature Reviews: Neuroscience, 5*, 135–145.

Enger, E., & Ross, F. (2003). *Concepts in biology* (10th ed.). New York: McGraw-Hill.

Englander, E. K. (2003). *Understanding violence* (2nd ed.). Mahwah, NJ: Erlbaum.

Enoch, M. A., & Goldman, D. (2002). Problem drinking and alcoholism: diagnosis and treatment. *American Family Physician, 65*, 449–450.

Enstrom, J. E. (1999). Smoking cessation and mortality trends among two United States populations. *Journal of Clinical Epidemiology, 52*, 813–825.

Ephraim, D. (2000). Culturally relevant research and practice with the Rorschach comprehensive system in Iberoamerica. In R. H. Dana (Ed.), *Handbook of cross-cultural and multicultural personality assessment*. Mahwah, NJ: Erlbaum.

Eppley, K. R., Abrams, A. I., & Shear, J. (1989). Differential effects of relaxation effects on trait anxiety. *Journal of Clinical Psychology, 45*, 957–974.

Epstein, N. B., & Baucom, D. H. (2002). *Enhanced cognitive-behavioral therapy for couples*. Washington, DC: American Psychological Association.

Eriksen, T. H. (2001). Ethnic identity, national identity, and intergroup conflict: The significance of personal experiences. In R. D. Ashmore, L. Jussim, & D. Wilder (Eds.), *Social identity, intergroup conflict, and conflict resolution*. New York: Oxford University Press.

Erikson, E. H. (1968). *Identity: Youth and crisis*. New York: Norton.

Erikson, E. H. (1969). *Gandhi's truth*. New York: Norton.

Erwin, B. A., Heimberg, R. G., Juster, H., & Mindlin, M. (2002). Comorbid anxiety and mood disorders among persons with social anxiety disorder. *Behavior Therapy and Research, 40*, 19–35.

Etaugh, C., & Bridges, J. S. (2001). *Psychology of women: A life-span perspective*. Boston: Allyn & Bacon.

Etaugh, C., & Bridges, J. S. (2004). *Psychology of women: A life-span perspective* (2nd ed.). Boston: Allyn & Bacon.

European Agency for Safety and Health at Work. (2000). *Research on work-related stress*. Retrieved November 15, 2001, from http://agency.osha.eu.int/

Evans, D. L. (1999). Introduction: Assessing antidepressant effectiveness. *Journal of Clinical Psychology, 60* (Suppl. 4), 3.

Evans, D. L., Herbert, J. D., Nelson-Gray, R. O., & Gaudiano, B. A. (2002). Determinants of diagnostic prototypicality judgments of the personality disorders. *Journal of Personality Disorders, 16*, 95–106.

Evans, G. J., & Morgan, A. (2003). Regulation of the exocytotic machinery by cAMP-dependent protein kinase: Implications for presynaptic plasticity. *Biochemical Society Transactions, 31*, 824–827.

Evertson, C. M., Emmer, E. T., & Worsham, M. E. (2003). *Classroom management for elementary teachers*, (5th ed.). Boston: Allyn & Bacon.

Ewen, R. B. (2003). *An introduction to theories of personality* (6th ed.). Mahwah, NJ: Erlbaum.

Exner, J. E. (1974). *The Rorschach: A comprehensive system*. New York: Grune & Stratton.

Eysenck, H. J. (1952). The effects of psychotherapy: An evaluation. *Journal of Consulting Psychology, 16*, 319–324.

Eysenck, H. J. (1967). *The biological basis of personality*. Springfield, IL: Thomas.

Ezzo, J., Hadhazy, V., Birch, S., Lao, L., Kaplan, G., Hochberg, M., & Berman, B. (2001). *Acupuncture for osteoarthritis of the knee: A systematic review*. Unpublished manuscript, Project LEAD, Washington, DC.

F

Fals-Stewart, W., Golden, J., & Schumacher, J. A. (2003). Intimate partner violence and substance abuse: A longitudinal day-to-day examination. *Addictive Behavior, 28*, 1555–1574.

Faneslow, M. S., DeCola, J. P., & Young, S. L. (1993). Mechanisms responsible for reduced contextual conditioning with masses unsignaled unconditioned stimuli. *Journal of Experimental Psychology: Animal Processes, 19*, 121–127.

Fava, G. A., Rafanelli, C., Ottolini, F., Ruini, C., Cazzaro, M., & Grandi, S. (2001). Psychological well-being and residual symptoms in remitted patients with panic disorder and agoraphobia. *Journal of Affective Disorders, 65*, 185–190.

Fazio, R. H., Chen, J., McDonel, E. C., & Sherman, S. J. (1982). Attitude accessibility, attitude-behavior consistency, and the strength of the object-evaluation association. *Journal of Experimental Social Psychology, 18*, 339–357.

Fehr, B. (2004). A prototype model of intimacy interactions in same-sex friendships. In D. J. Mashek & A. P. Aron (Eds.), *Handbook of closeness and intimacy*. Mahwah, NJ: Erlbaum.

Fehr, B., & Broughton, R. (2001). Gender and personality differences in conceptions of love: An interpersonal theory analysis. *Personal Relationships, 8*, 115–136.

Feighner, J. P. (1999). Mechanisms of action of antidepressant medications. *Journal of Clinical Psychology, 60* (Suppl. 4), 4–13.

Fein, S., Goethals, G. R., Kassin, S. M., & Cross, J. (1993, August). *Social influence and presidential debates*. Paper presented at the meeting of the American Psychological Association, Toronto.

Feist, J., & Feist, G. J. (2002). *Theories of personality* (5th ed.). New York: McGraw-Hill.

Feldhusen, J. (1999). Giftedness and creativity. In M. A. Runco & S. Pritzker (Eds.), *Encyclopedia of creativity*. San Diego: Academic Press.

Feldman, D. H. (1997, August). *Hitting middle C: Toward a more comprehensive domain for creativity research*. Paper presented at the meeting of the American Psychological Association, Chicago.

Feldman, R. (1999, January). Commentary in Murray, B.: This architect builds a career in psychology. *APA Monitor*, p. 13.

Feng, A. S., & Ratnam, R. (2000). Neural basis of hearing in real world situations. *Annual Review of Psychology* (Vol. 51). Palo Alto, CA: Annual Reviews.

Fergusson, D. M., & Woodward, L. J. (2002). Mental health, educational, and social role outcomes of adolescents with depression. *Archives of General Psychiatry, 59,* 225–231.

Feshbach, S., & Weiner, B. (1996). *Personality* (4th ed.). Lexington, MA: Heath.

Festinger, L. (1954). A theory of social comparison processes. *Human Relations, 7,* 117–140.

Festinger, L. (1957). *A theory of cognitive dissonance.* Evanston, IL: Row Peterson.

Field, T. (2003). Stimulation of preterm infants. *Pediatric Review, 24,* 4–11.

Field, T. M., Scafidi, F., & Schanberg, S. (1987). Massage of preterm newborns to improve growth and development. *Pediatric Nursing, 13,* 386–388.

Fielder, F. E. (1978). Contingency model and the leadership process. In L. Berkowitz (Ed.), *Advances in experimental social psychology* (Vol. 11). New York: Academic Press.

Filley, C. M., Price, B. H., Nell, V., Morgan, A. S., Bresnahan, J. F., Pincus, J. H., Gelbort, M. M., Weissberg, M., & Kelly, J. P. (2001). Toward an understanding of violence: Neurobehavioral aspects of unwarranted physical aggression. *Neuropsychiatry, 14,* 1–14.

Fils-Aime, M.-L., Eckardt, M. J., George, D. T., Brown, G. L., Mefford, I., & Linnoila, M. (1996). Early-onset alcoholics have lower cerebrospinal fluid 5-hydroxyindoleacetic acid levels than late-onset alcoholics. *Archives of General Psychology.*

First, M. B., & Pincus, H. A. (2002). The *DSM-IV* text revision: Rationale and potential impact on clinical practice. *Psychiatric Services, 53,* 288–292.

Fisch, S. M., & Truglio, R. T. (Eds.). (2001). *"G" is for growing: Thirty years of research on children and Sesame Street.* Mahwah, NJ: Erlbaum.

Fischer, J., & Gochros, H. L. (1975). *Planned behavior change.* New York: Free Press.

Fisher, C. B. (2003). *Decoding the ethics code.* Thousand Oaks, CA: Sage.

Fiske, S. T. (1998). Stereotyping, prejudice, and discrimination. In D. T. Gilbert, S. T. Fiske, & G. Lindzey (Eds.), *The handbook of social psychology* (4th ed., Vol. 2). New York: McGraw-Hill.

Flavell, J. H., Miller, P. H., & Miller, S. A. (2002). *Cognitive development* (4th ed.). Upper Saddle River, NJ: Prentice-Hall.

Fleming, J. S., & Courtney, B. E. (1984). The dimensionality of self-esteem. *Journal of Personality and Social Psychology, 46,* 404–421.

Fleming, P. (2002, February). *AIDS and HIV prevalence in the United States.* Paper presented at the Conference on Retroviruses, Seattle.

Fleshner, N., Bagnell, P. S., Klotz, L., & Venkateswaran, V. (2004). Dietary fat and prostate cancer. *Journal of Urology, 171,* S19–S24.

Fletcher, J. S., & Banasik, J. L. (2001). Exercise self-efficacy. *Clinical Excellence in Nursing Practice, 5,* 134–143.

Floyd, M., McKendree-Smith, N. L., & Scogin, F. R. (2004). Remembering the 1978 and 1990 task forces on self-help therapies: A response to Gerald Rosen. *Journal of Clinical Psychology, 60,* 115–117.

Flynn, J. R. (1999). Searching for justice: The discovery of IQ gains over time. *American Psychologist, 54,* 5–20.

Foa, E. D., & Riggs, D. S. (1995). Posttraumatic stress disorder following assault: Theoretical considerations and empirical findings. *Current Directions in Psychological Science, 4,* 61–65.

Fodor, I., & Epstein, J. (2002). Agoraphobia, panic disorder, and gender. In J. Worell (Ed.), *Encyclopedia of women and gender.* San Diego: Academic Press.

Fogel, A. (2001). *Infancy* (4th ed.). Belmont, CA: Wadsworth.

Fogel, J. (2003). Health psychology: a new form of psychotherapy? *Medscape General Medicine, 16,* 29.

Fogoros, R.N. (2001). *Does stress really cause heart disease?* Retrieved October 10, 2001, from http://www.about.com

Folkman, S., & Moskowitz, J. T. (2004). Coping: Pitfalls and promises. *Annual Review of Psychology, 54.* Palo Alto, CA: Annual Reviews.

Ford, J. D. (1999). Disorders of extreme stress following war-zone military trauma: Associated features of posttraumatic stress disorder or comorbid but distinct syndromes? *Journal of Consulting and Clinical Psychology, 67,* 3–12.

Forgas, J. P. (Ed.). (2001). *Handbook of affect and social cognition.* Mahwah, NJ: Erlbaum.

Forshaw, M. (2002). *Essential health psychology.* New York: Oxford University Press.

Forsyth, J. P., & Savsevitz, J. (2002). Behavior therapy: Historical perspective and overview. In M. Hersen & W. H. Sledge (Eds.), *Encyclopedia of psychotherapy.* San Diego: Academic Press.

Fortin, N. J. Agster, K. L., & Eichenbaum, H. B. (2002). Critical role of the hippocampus in memory for sequence of events. *Nature Neuroscience, 5,* 458–462.

Foulkes, D. (1993). Cognitive dream theory. In M.A. Carskadon (Ed.), *Encyclopedia of sleep and dreams.* New York: Macmillan.

Foulkes, D. (1999). *Children's dreaming and the development of consciousness.* Cambridge, MA: Harvard University Press.

Foulks, E. (2002). Cultural issues. In M. Hersen & W. H. Sledge (Eds.), *Encyclopedia of psychotherapy.* San Diego: Academic Press.

Fowler, C. A., Wolford, G., Slade, R., & Tassinary, L. (1981). Lexical access without awareness. *Journal of Experimental Psychology: General, 110,* 341–362.

Fowles, D. (2003). Schizophrenia spectrum disorders. In I. B. Weiner (Ed.), *Handbook of psychology* (Vol. 8). New York: Wiley.

Fox, S. I. (1996). *Human physiology* (5th ed.). New York: McGraw-Hill.

Frank, J. D. (1982). Therapeutic components shared by all psychotherapies. In J. H. Harvey & M. M. Parks (Eds.), *Psychotherapy research and behavior change.* Washington, DC: American Psychological Association.

Frankl, V. (1984). *Man's search for meaning.* New York: Pocket Books.

Fraser, S. (Ed.). (1995). *The bell curve wars: Race, intelligence, and the future of America.* New York: Basic Books.

Frederich, R. C., Hamann, A., Anderson, S., & Others. (1995). Leptin levels reflect body lipid content in mice: Evidence for diet-induced resistance to leptin action. *Nature Medicine, 1,* 1311–1314.

Frederickson, B. L. (2001). The role of positive emotions in positive psychology. *American Psychologist, 56,* 218–226.

Frederickson, B . L., & Joiner, T. (2000). *Positive emotions trigger upward spirals toward emotional well-being.* Unpublished manuscript, University of Michigan, Ann Arbor, Department of Psychology.

Frederickson, B. L., & Joiner, T. (2002). Positive emotions trigger upward spirals of well being. *Psychological Science, 13,* 172–176.

Frederickson, B. L., & Levenson, R. W. (1998). Positive emotions speed recovery from the cardiovascular sequelae of negative emotions. *Cognition and Emotion, 12,* 191–220.

Frederikse, M., Lu, A., Aylward, E., Barta, P., Sharma, T., & Pearlson, G. (2000). Sex differences in inferior lobule volume in schizophrenia. *American Journal of Psychiatry, 157,* 422–427.

Freed, C. R., Greene, P. E., Breeze, R. E., Tsai, W. Y., DuMouchel, W., Kao, R., Dillon, S., Winfield, H., Culver, S., Trojanowksi, J. Q., Eidelberg, D., & Fahn, S. (2001). Transplantation of embryonic dopamine neurons for severe Parkinson's disease. *New England Journal of Medicine, 344,* 710–719.

Freedman, J. L. (1984). Effects of television violence on aggressiveness. *Psychological Bulletin, 96,* 227–246.

Freeman, A., & Reinecke, M. A. (1995). Cognitive therapy. In A. S. Gurman (Ed.), *Essential psychotherapies.* New York: Guilford Press.

Freeman, T. W., & Roca, V. (2001). Gun use, attitudes toward violence, and aggression among combat veterans with chronic post-traumatic stress disorder. *Journal of Nervous and Mental Disorders, 189,* 317–320.

Freud, S. (1917). *A general introduction to psychoanalysis.* New York: Washington Square Press.

Freud, S. (1953). The interpretation of dreams. In J. Strachey (Ed.), *The standard edition of the complete psychological works of Sigmund Freud.* New York: Washington Square Press. (Original work published 1900)

Friedman, H. S., & Schustack, M. W. (1999). *Personality: Classic theories and modern research.* Boston: Allyn & Bacon.

Friedman, J. I., Temporini, H., & Davis, K. L. (1999). Pharmacologic strategies for augmenting cognitive performance in schizophrenia. *Biological Psychiatry, 45,* 1–16.

Friedman, M., & Rosenman, R. (1974). *Type A behavior and your heart.* New York: Knopf.

Friedman, M. A., & Brownell, K. A. (1998). Obesity. In H. S. Friedman (Ed.), *Encyclopedia of mental health* (Vol. 3). San Diego: Academic Press.

Friedman, R., Myers, P., & Benson, H. (1998). Meditation and the relaxation response. In H.S. Friedman (Ed.), *Encyclopedia of mental health* (Vol. 2). San Diego: Academic Press.

Frieman, J. L. (2002). *Learning and adaptive behavior.* Belmont, CA: Wadsworth.

Fromm, E. (1947). *Man for himself.* New York: Holt, Rinehart & Winston.

Frost, R. O., & Steketee, G. (1998). Obsessive-compulsive disorder. In H. S. Friedman (Ed.), *Encyclopedia of mental health* (Vol. 3). San Diego: Academic Press.

Fu, Q., Heath, A. C., Bucholz, K. K., Nelson, E. C., Glowinski, A. L., Goldberg, J., Lyons, M. J., Tsuang, M. T., Jacob, T., True, M. R., & Eisen, M. A. (2002). A twin study of genetic and environmental influences on suicidality in men. *Psychological Medicine, 32,* 11–24.

Funder, D. C. (2001). Personality. *Annual Review of Psychology, 52.* Palo Alto, CA: Annual Reviews.

Fung, H. H., Carstensen, L. L., & Lang, F. R. (2001). Age-related patterns in social networks among European Americans and African Americans. *International Journal of Aging and Human Development, 52,* 185–206.

Furnham, A. (1988). Write and wrong: The validity of graphological analysis. *Skeptical Inquirer, 13,* 64–69.

Furth, H. (1971). Linguistic deficiency and thinking: Research with deaf subjects. *Psychological Bulletin, 75,* 52–58.

Furth, H. G., & Wachs, H. (1975). *Thinking goes to school.* New York: Oxford University Press.

Furumoto, L. (1991). "Paired associates" to a psychology of self: The intellectual odyssey of Mary Whiton Calkins. In G. A. Kimble, M. Wertheimer, & C. L. White, (1991). *Portraits of pioneers in psychology.* Washington, DC: American Psychological Association.

G

Gage, F. H. (2000). Mammalian neural stem cells. *Science, 287,* 1433–1438.

Gage, F. H., & Bjorklund, A. (1986). Cholinergic septal grafts into the hippocampal formation improve spatial learning and memory in aged rats by an atropine-sensitive mechanism. *Journal of Neuroscience, 6,* 2837–2847.

Galambos, N. L. (2004). Gender and gender-role development in adolescence. In R. M. Lerner & L. Steinberg (Eds.), *Handbook of adolescent psychology*. New York: Wiley.

Gallup Organization. (1999). *The 31st annual Phi Delta Kappa/Gallup Poll*. Princeton, NJ: Author.

Gana, K., Alaphilippe, D., & Bailly, N. (2004). Positive illusions and mental and physical health in later life. *Aging and Mental Health, 8*, 58–64.

Garb, H. N., Wood, J. M., Nezworksi, M. T., Grove, W. M., & Stejskal, W. J. (2001). Toward a resolution of the Rorschach controversy. *Psychological Assessment, 13*, 433–446.

Garbarino, S., Beelke, M., Costa, G., Violani, C., Lucidi, F., Ferrillo, F., & Sannita, G. (2002). Brain function and effects of shift work: implications for clinical neuropharmacology. *Neuropsychobiology, 45*, 50–56.

Garcia, J. (1989). Food for Tolman: Cognition and cathexis in concert. In T. Archer & L. Nilsson (Eds.), *Aversion, avoidance, and anxiety*. Mahwah, NJ: Erlbaum.

Garcia, J., Ervin, F. E., & Koelling, R. A. (1966). Learning with prolonged delay of reinforcement. *Psychonomic Science, 5*, 121–122.

Gardner, H. (1983). *Frames of mind*. New York: Basic Books.

Gardner, H. (1985). *The mind's new science*. New York: Basic Books.

Gardner, H. (1993). *Multiple intelligences*. New York: Basic Books.

Gardner, H. (1999). *The disciplined mind*. New York: Simon & Schuster.

Gardner, H. (2001, March 13). *An education for the future*. Paper presented to the Royal Symposium, Amsterdam.

Gardner, H. (2002). The pursuit of excellence through education. In M. Ferrari (Ed.), *Learning from extraordinary minds*. Mahwah, NJ: Erlbaum.

Garfield, S. L., & Kurtz, R. (1976). Clinical psychologists in the 70s. *American Psychologist, 31*, 1–9.

Garnets, L. D. (2002) Sexual orientation in perspective. *Cultural Diversity and Ethnic Minority Psychology, 8*, 115–129.

Garraghty, P. E. (1996, June). Neuroplasticity: From mechanisms to behavior. Paper presented at the meeting of the American Psychological Association, San Francisco.

Gartner, J., Larson, D. B., & Allen, G. D. (1991). Religious commitment and mental health: A review of the empirical literature. *Journal of Psychology and Theology, 19*, 6–25.

Garza, M. (1999). Review of Halonen/ Santrock. *Psychology* (3rd ed.). New York: McGraw-Hill.

Gast, U., Roodewald, F., Nickel, V., & Emrich, H. M. (2001). Prevalence of dissociative disorders among psychiatric patients in a German university clinic. *Journal of Nervous and Mental Disorders, 189*, 249–257.

Gaulin, S. J. C., & McBurney, D. H. (2004). *Evolutionary psychology* (2nd ed.). Upper Saddle River, NJ: Prentice-Hall.

Gazda, G. M., Horne, A., & Ginter, E. (2001). *Group counseling and psychotherapy*. Boston: Allyn & Bacon.

Gazzaniga, M. S., Ivry, R. B., & Mangun, G. R. (2001). *Cognitive neuroscience* (2nd ed.). New York: Norton.

Gedo, J. E. (2002). The enduring scientific contributions of Sigmund Freud. *Perspectives in Biology and Medicine, 45*, 200–211.

Gegenfurter, K. R., & Kiper, D. C. (2003). Color vision. *Annual Review of Neuroscience, 26*. Palo Alto, CA: Annual Reviews.

Gehring, W. J., & Knight, R. T. (2002). Lateral prefrontal damage affects processing selection but not attention switching. *Brain Research: Cognitive Brain Research, 2*, 267–279.

Gelder, M. G., Mayou, R., & Geddes, J. (1999). *Psychiatry* (2nd ed.). New York: Oxford University Press.

Gelfand, J.R., & Bookheimer, S. Y. (2003). Dissociating neural mechanisms of temporal sequencing and processing phonemes. *Neuron, 38*, 831–842.

Gentner, D., & Lowenstein, J. (2001). Relational thinking and relational language. In J. Byrnes & E. Amsel (Eds.), *Language, literacy, and cognitive development*. Mahwah, NJ: Erlbaum.

George, L. K. (2001). The social psychology of health. In R. H. Binstock & L. K. George (Eds.), *Handbook of the psychology of aging* (5th ed.). San Diego: Academic Press.

Gergen, K. J. (1994). *Realities and relationships: Soundings in social construction*. Cambridge, MA: Harvard University Press.

Gershoff, E. T. (2002). Corporal punishment by parents and associated child behaviors and experiences: A meta-analysis and theoretical review. *Psychological Bulletin, 128*, 539–579.

Gesell, A. (1934). *Infancy and human growth*. New York: MacMillan.

Gevins, A. S. (1999). What to do with your own personal brain scanner. In R. L. Solso (Ed.), *Mind and brain sciences in the 21st century*. Cambridge, MA: MIT Press.

Giannoni, M. (2003). Psychoanalysis and empirical research. *Journal of Analytical Psychology, 48*, 553–569.

Gibbons, F. X., & McCoy, S. B. (1991). Self-esteem, similarity, and reactions to active versus passive downward comparison. *Journal of Personality and Social Psychology, 60*, 414–424.

Gibbs, J. T., & Huang, L. N. (1989). A conceptual framework for assessing and treating minority youth. In J. T. Gibbs & L. N. Huang (Eds.), *Children of color*. San Francisco: Jossey-Bass.

Gibson, E. J. (2001). *Perceiving the affordances*. Mahwah, NJ: Erlbaum.

Gibson, R., & Mitchell, M. (2003). *Introduction to counseling and guidance* (6th Ed.). Upper Saddle River, NJ: Prentice-Hall.

Gigerenzer, G., & Selton, R. (Eds.). (2001). *Bounded rationality*. Cambridge, MA: MIT Press.

Gilbert, P. (2001). *Overcoming depression*. New York: Oxford University Press.

Gilbert, S. J., & Shallice, T. (2002). Task switching: A PDP model. *Cognitive Psychology, 44*, 297–337.

Giles, T. R., & Marafiote, R. A. (1998). Managed care and the practitioner. *Clinical Psychology and Practice, 5*, 41–50.

Gillani, N. B., & Smith, J. C. (2001). Zen meditation and ABC relaxation theory. *Journal of Clinical Psychology, 57*, 839–846.

Gilligan, C. (1982). *In a different voice*. Cambridge, MA: Harvard University Press.

Gilligan, C. (1996). The centrality of relationships in psychological development. In G. Noam & K. W. Fischer (Eds.), *Development and vulnerability in close relationships*. Mahwah, NJ: Erlbaum.

Gilligan, C. (1998). *Minding women: Reshaping the educational realm*. Cambridge, MA: Harvard University Press.

Gilman, S. L. (2001). Karen Horney, M.D., 1885–1952. *American Journal of Psychoanalysis, 15*, 1205.

Gjerde, P. F., Block, J., & Block, J. H. (1991). The preschool family context of 18-year-olds with depressive symptoms: A prospective study. *Journal of Research on Adolescence, 1*, 63–92.

Gladding, S. T. (1999). *Family therapy* (2nd ed.). Upper Saddle River, NJ: Prentice-Hall.

Gladue, B. A. (1994). The biopsychology of sexual orientation. *Current Directions in Psychological Science, 3*, 150–154.

Glaser, R., Robles, T. F., Shredian, J., Malarkey, W. B., & Kiecolt-Glaser, J. K. (2003). Mild depressive symptoms are associated with amplified and prolonged inflammatory responses after influenza virus vaccination in older adults. *Archives of General Psychiatry, 60*, 1009–1014.

Gleaves, D. H., May, M. C., & Cardena, E. (2001). An examination of the diagnostic validity of dissociative identity disorder. *Clinical Psychology Review, 21*, 577–608.

Goddard, L., Dritschel, B., & Burton, A. (2001). The effects of specific retrieval instruction on social problem-solving in depression. *British Journal of Clinical Psychology, 40*, 297–308.

Goenjian, A. K., Molina, L., Steinberg, A. M., Fairbanks, L. A., Alvarez, M. L., Goenjian, H. A., & Pynoos, R. S. (2001). Post-traumatic stress and depression reactions among Nicaraguan adolescents after Hurricane Mitch. *American Journal of Psychiatry, 158*, 788–794.

Goethals, G. R., & Demorest, A. P. (1995). The risky shift is a sure bet. In M. E. Ware & D. E. Johnson (Eds.), *Demonstrations and activities in teaching of psychology* (Vol. 3). Mahwah, NJ: Erlbaum.

Gold, B. (2002). Integrative approaches to psychotherapy. In M. Hersen & W. H. Sledge (Eds.), *Encyclopedia of psychotherapy*. San Diego: Academic Press.

Goldberg, R. (2003). *Clashing views on controversial issues in drugs and society* (5th ed.). New York: McGraw-Hill.

Golden, R. (2001, January 14). Personal communication. Richardson, TX: Program in Psychology, University of Texas at Dallas.

Goldman, S. L., Kraemer, D. T., & Salovey, P. (1996). Beliefs about mood moderate the relationship of stress to illness and symptom reporting. *Journal of Psychosomatic Research, 41*, 115–128.

Goldsmith, H. H. (2002). Genetics of emotional development. In R. J. Davidson, K. R. Scherer, & H. H. Goldsmith (Eds.), *Handbook of affective sciences*. New York: Oxford University Press.

Goldsmith, T. H., & Zimmerman, W. F. (2001). *Biology, evolution, and human nature*. New York: John Wiley.

Goldstein, E. B. (2002). *Sensation and perception* (6th ed.). Belmont, CA: Wadsworth.

Goldstein, I. L., & Ford, K. (2002). *Training in organizations*. Belmont, CA: Wadsworth.

Goldstein, J. M., Seidman, L. J., Horton, N. J., Makris, N., Kennedy, D. N., Caviness, V. S., Faraone, S. V., & Tsuang, M. T. (2001). Normal sexual dimorphism of the adult human brain assessed by in vivo magnetic resonance imaging. *Cerebral Cortex, 11*, 490–497.

Goldstein, R. B., Prescott, C. A., & Kendler, K. S. (2001). Genetic and environmental factors in conduct problems and adult antisocial behavior among adult female twins. *Journal of Nervous and Mental Disorders, 189*, 201–209.

Goldstein, R. B., Wickramaratne, P. J., Horwath, E., & Weissman, M. M. (1997). Familial aggregation and phenomenology of "early"-onset (at or before age 20 years) panic disorder. *Archives of General Psychiatry, 54*, 271–278.

Goleman, D. (1995). *Emotional intelligence*. New York: Basic Books.

Goleman, D., Kaufman, P., & Ray, M. (1993). *The creative spirit*. New York: Plume.

Golier, J. A., Yehuda, R., Lupien, S. J., & Harvey, P. D. (2003). Memory for trauma-related information in Holocaust survivors with PTSD. *Psychiatry Research, 121*, 133–143.

Gong-Guy, E. (1986). *Depression in students of Chinese and Japanese ancestry: An acculturation, vulnerability and stress model*. Unpublished dissertation, University of California, Los Angeles.

Gonzales, D. H., Nides, M. A., Ferry, L. H., Kustra, R. P., Jamerson, B. D., Segall, N., Herrero, L. A., Krishen, A., Sweeney, A., Buaron, K., & Metz, A. (2001). Bupropion SR as an aid to smoking cessation in smokers previously treated with bupropion: A randomized placebo-controlled study. *Clinical and Pharmacology Therapy, 69,* 438–444.

Goodstein, I. K., & Calhoun, J. F. (1982). *Understanding abnormal behavior.* Reading, MA: Addison-Wesley.

Gorell, J. M., Peterson, E. L., Rybicki, B. A., & Johnson, C. C. (2004). Multiple risk factors for Parkinson's disease. *Journal of Neurological Science, 217,* 169–174.

Gorenstein, E. E. (1997). *Case studies in abnormal psychology.* New York: Longman.

Gorman, J. M., & Kent, J. M. (1999). SSRIs and SNRIs: Broad spectrum of efficacy beyond major depression. *Journal of Clinical Psychology, 60* (Suppl. 4), 33–39.

Gotesdam, K. G., & Agras, W. S. (1995). General population-based epidemiological survey of eating disorders in Norway. *International Journal of Eating Disorders, 18,* 119–126.

Gottesman, I. I., & Goldsmith, H. H. (1994). Developmental psychopathology of antisocial behavior. In C. A. Nelson (Ed.), *Threats to optimal development.* Mahwah, NJ: Erlbaum.

Gottesman, I. I., & Shields, J. (1982). *The schizophrenic puzzle.* New York: Cambridge University Press.

Gottlieb, B. H. (1998). Support groups. In H. S. Friedman (Ed.), *Encyclopedia of mental health* (Vol. 3). San Diego: Academic Press.

Gottlieb, G. (2001). Origin of species: The potential significance of early experience for evolution. In W. W. Hartup, & R. A. Weinberg (Eds.), *Child psychology in retrospect and prospect.* Mahwah, NJ: Erlbaum.

Gottlieb, G. (2002). Nature and nurture theories. In A. Kazdin (Ed.), *Encyclopedia of psychology.* Washington, DC, & New York: American Psychological Association and Oxford University Press.

Gottlieb, G. (2004). Normally occurring environmental and behavioral influences on gene activity. In C. G. Coll, E. L. Bearer, & R. L. Lerner (Eds.), *Nature and nurture.* Mahwah, NJ: Erlbaum.

Gottman, J. M. (1994). *What predicts divorce?* Mahwah, NJ: Erlbaum.

Gottman, J. M., Coan, J., Carrere, S., & Swanson, C. (1998). Predicting marital happiness and stability from newlywed interactions. *Journal of Marriage and the Family, 60,* 5–22.

Gottman, J. M., Katz, L. F., & Hooven, C. (1997). *Meta-emotion: How families communicate.* Mahwah, NJ: Erlbaum.

Gottman, J. M., Ryan, K. D., Carrere, S., & Erley, A. M. (2002). Toward a scientifically based marital therapy. In H. A. Liddle & D. A. Santisteban (Eds.), *Family psychology.* Washington, DC: American Psychological Association.

Gottman, J. M., & Silver, N. (1999). *The seven principles for making marriages work.* New York: Crown.

Gottselig, J. M., Bassetti, C. L., & Achermann, P. (2002). Power and coherence of sleep spindle frequency activity following hemispheric stroke. *Brain, 125,* 373–383.

Gotz, M. E., Janetzky, B., Pohli, S., Gottschalk, S., Gsell, A., Tatshchner, T., Ransmyar, G., Leblhuber, F., Gerlach, M., Reichmann, H., Riederer, P., & Boning, J. (2001). Chronic alcohol consumption and cerebral indices of oxidative stress: Is there a link? *Alcoholism: Clinical and Experimental Research, 25,* 717–725.

Gould, E., Reeves, A. J., Graziano, M. S., & Gross, C. G. (1999). Neurogenesis in the neocortex of adult primates. *Science, 286*(1), 548–552.

Gould, S. J. (1981). *The mismeasure of man.* New York: Norton.

Graffin, N. F., Ray, W. J., & Lundy, R. (1995). EEG concomitants of hypnosis and hypnotic susceptibility. *Journal of Abnormal Psychology, 104,* 123–131.

Graf, P. (2004, August). *Prospective memory.* Paper presented at the 28th International Congress of Psychology, Beijing, China.

Graham, S. (1986, August). *Can attribution theory tell us something about motivation in Blacks?* Paper presented at the meeting of the American Psychological Association, Washington, DC.

Graham, S. (1992). Most of the subjects were white and middle class. *American Psychologist, 47,* 629–637.

Graham, S. (2001). Inferences about responsibility and values: Implication for academic motivation. In F. Salihi & C. Chiu (Eds.), *Student motivation: The culture and context of learning.* New York: Plenum.

Graham-Bermann, S., Eastin, J. A., & Bermann, E. A. (2002). Stress and coping. In J. Worell (Ed.), *Encyclopedia of women and gender.* New York: Oxford University Press.

Grau, C., Polo, M. D., Yago, E., Gual, A., & Escera, C. (2002). Auditory sensory memory as indicated by a mismatch negativity in chronic alcoholism. *Clinical Neurophysiology, 112,* 728–731.

Gray, C. (2002). Pediatricians taking a new look at corporal-punishment issue. *Canadian Medical Association Journal, 19,* 793.

Gray, C. R., & Gummerman, K. (1975). The enigmatic eidetic image: A critical examination of methods, data, and theories. *Psychological Bulletin, 82,* 383–407.

Gray, J. (1992). *Men are from Mars, women are from Venus.* New York: HarperCollins.

Graziano, W. J. (1995). Evolutionary psychology: Old music, but now on CDs? *Psychological Inquiry, 6,* 41–44.

Greco, M. (2004). The ambivalence of error: "scientific ideology" in the history of the life sciences and psychosomatic medicine, *Social Science & Medicine, 58,* 687–696.

Green, B. (2003). Focus on paroxetine. *Current Medical Research Opinions. 19,* 13–21.

Green, B. L., Lindy, J. D., Grace, M. C., & Leonard, A. C. (1992). Chronic posttraumatic stress disorder and diagnostic comorbidity in a disaster sample. *Journal of Nervous & Mental Disease, 180,* 760–766.

Greenberg, D. S. (2002). Polygraph fails scientific review in the USA. *Lancet, 360,* 1309.

Greenberg, M., Szmukler, G., & Tantam, D. (1986). *Making sense of psychiatric cases.* New York: Oxford University Press.

Greenglass, E. R. (1998). Gender differences in mental health. In H. S. Friedman (Ed.), *Encyclopedia of mental health* (Vol. 2). San Diego: Academic Press.

Greenough, W. T. (2000). Brain development. In A. Kazdin (Ed.), *Encyclopedia of psychology.* Washington, DC, & New York: American Psychological Association and Oxford University Press.

Greenough, W. T. (2001). Commentary. In J. W. Santrock, *Child Development* (9th ed.). Boston: McGraw-Hill.

Greenwald, A. G., & Banaji, M. R. (1995). Implicit social cognition: Attitudes, self-esteem, and stereotypes. *Psychological Review, 102,* 4–27.

Greenwald, A. G., Draine, S. C., & Abrams, R. L. (1996). Three cognitive markers of unconscious semantic activation. *Science, 273,* 1699–1702.

Gregory, R. J. (2004). *Psychological testing* (4th ed.). Boston: Allyn & Bacon.

Greven, P. (1991). *Spare the child: The religious roots of punishment and the psychological impact of physical abuse.* New York: Knopf.

Griffin, W. A. (2002). Family therapy. In M. Hersen & W. H. Sledge (Eds.), *Encyclopedia of psychotherapy.* San Diego: Academic Press.

Grigorenko, E. (2000). Heritability and intelligence. In R. J. Sternberg (Ed.), *Handbook of intelligence.* New York: Cambridge University Press.

Grodzinsky, Y. (2001). The neurology of syntax: Language use without Broca's area. *Behavior and Brain Sciences, 23,* 1–21.

Gronnerod, C. (2003). Temporal stability in the Rorschach method: a meta-analytic review. *Journal of Personality Assessment, 80,* 272–293.

Grunberg, N. E., Klein, L. C., & Brown, K. J. (1998). Psychopharmacology. In H. S. Friedman (Ed.), *Encyclopedia of mental health* (Vol. 3). San Diego: Academic Press.

Grush, J. E. (1980). Impact of candidate expenditures, regionality, and prior outcomes on the 1976 Democratic presidential primaries. *Journal of Personality and Social Psychology, 38,* 337–347.

Guilford, J. P. (1967). *The structure of intellect.* New York: McGraw-Hill.

Guimaraes, F. P. D. (2003). Recent theoretical convergences in psychoanalysis and their epistemological importance. *International Journal of Psychoanalysis, 84,* 1189–1202.

Gupta, P., & Dell, G. S. (1999). The emergence of language from serial order and procedural memory. In B. MacWhinney (Ed.), *The emergence of language.* Mahwah, NJ: Erlbaum.

Gutierrez-Lobos, K., Frohlich, S., Quiner, S., Haring, C., & Barnas, C. (2001). Prescription patterns and quality of information provided for consumers of benzodiazepines. *Acta Medica Austria, 28,* 56–59.

Guttman, N., & Kalish, H. I. (1956). Discriminability and stimulus generalization. *Journal of Experimental Psychology, 51,* 79–88.

H

Hakuta, K., Butler, Y. G., & Witt, D. (2000). *How long does it take English learners to attain proficiency?* (Linguistic Minority Institute Policy Report 2000–2001). Berkeley: University of California.

Haladyna, T. M. (2002). *Essentials of standardized testing.* Boston: Allyn & Bacon.

Halford, J. C., & Blundell, J. E. (2000). Pharmacology of appetite suppression. *Progress in drug research, 54,* 25–58.

Hall, R. V., & Hall, M. L. (1998). *How to select reinforcers* (2nd ed.). Austin: Pro-Ed.

Hallahan, D. P., & Kauffman, J. M. (2003). *Exceptional learners* (9th ed.). Boston: Allyn & Bacon.

Halpern, D. F. (2001). Sex difference research: Cognitive abilities. In J. Worell (Ed.), *Encyclopedia of women and gender.* New York: Oxford University Press.

Halpern, D. F. (2002). Teaching for critical thinking: A four-part model to enhance thinking skills. In S. Davis & W. Buskist (Eds.), *The Teaching of Psychology: Essays in Honor of Wilbert J. McKeachie and Charles L. Brewer.* Mahwah, NJ: Erlbaum.

Halpern, D. F. (2003). *Thought and Knowledge: An Introduction to Critical Thinking* (4th ed.). Mahwah, NJ: Erlbaum

Hambleton, R. K., Merenda, P. F., & Spielberger, C. D. (Eds.). (2004). *Adapting educational and psychological tests for cross-cultural assessment.* Mahwah, NJ: Erlbaum.

Hamilton, S., & Hamilton, M. (2004). Contexts for mentoring. In R. Lerner & L. Steinberg (Eds.), *Handbook of adolescence.* New York: Wiley.

Hammen, C. (2003). Mood disorders. In I. B. Weiner (Ed.), *Handbook of psychology* (Vol. 8). New York: Wiley.

Hammond, R. (2001, August). *Best practices for youth violence prevention.* Paper presented at the meeting of the American Psychological Association, San Francisco.

Handel, R. W., & Ben-Porath, Y. S. (2000). Multicultural assessment with the MMPI-2. In

R. H. Dana (Ed.), *Handbook of cross-cultural and multicultural personality assessment*. Mahwah, NJ: Erlbaum.

Handler, L. (1999). Introduction to the special series on personality assessment: Classics in contemporary perspective. *Journal of Personality Assessment, 72,* 144–146.

Hanna, A., & Remington, R. (2001). The representation of color and form in long-term memory. *Memory and Cognition, 24,* 322–330.

Hannigan, J. H., Spear, L. P., Spear, N. E., & Goodlet, C. R. (Eds.). (1999). *Alcohol and alcoholism.* Mahwah, NJ: Erlbaum.

Hannon, B., & Craik, F. I. (2001). Encoding specificity revisited: The role of semantics. *Canadian Journal of Experimental Psychology, 55,* 231–243.

Hanson, R. F., Saunders, B., Kilpatrick, D., Resnick, H., Crouch, J. A., & Duncan, R. (2001). Impact of childhood rape and aggravated assault on adult mental health. *American Journal of Orthopsychiatry, 71,* 108–119.

Harding, A. H., Day, N. E., Khaw, K. T., Binghma, S., Luben, R., Welsh, R., & Wareham, N. J. (2004). Dietary fat and the risk of clinical type 2 diabetes: the European prospective investigation of cancer-norfolk study. *Annals of Epidemiology, 159,* 73–82.

Harkness, S., & Super, C. M. (2002). Culture and parenting. In M. H. Bornstein (Ed.), *Handbook of parenting* (2nd ed., Vol. 2). Mahwah, NJ: Erlbaum.

Harley, C. W. (2003). Norepinephrine and serotonin axonal dynamics and clinical depression. *Experimental Neurology, 184,* 24–26.

Harlow, H. F. (1958). The nature of love. *American Psychologist, 13,* 673–685.

Harlow, H. F., & Zimmerman, R. R. (1959). Affectional responses in the infant monkey. *Science, 130,* 421–432.

Harmatz, M. (1997). Introduction to clinical psychology. In Santrock, J. W., *Psychology* (5th ed.). New York: McGraw-Hill.

Harris, D. M., & Kay, J. (1995). I recognize your face but I can't remember your name: Is it because names are unique? *British Journal of Psychology, 86,* 345–358.

Harris, J. R. (1998). *The nurture assumption.* New York: Free Press.

Harris, R. F., Wolf, N. M., & Baer, D. M. (1964). Effects of adult social reinforcement on child behavior. *Young Children, 20,* 8–17.

Harrison, Y., & Horne, J. A. (2000). The impact of sleep deprivation on decision making: A review. *Journal of Experimental Psychology: Applied, 6,* 236–249.

Harter, S. (1998). The development of self-representations. In W. Damon (Ed.), *Handbook of child psychology* (5th ed., Vol. 3). New York: Wiley.

Hartmann, D. P., Barrios, B. A., & Wood, D. D. (2004). Principles of behavioral observation. In M. Hersen (Ed.), *Comprehensive handbook of psychological assessment* (Vol. 3). New York: Wiley.

Hartmann, E. (1993). Nightmares. In M.A. Carskadon (Ed.), *Encyclopedia of sleep and dreams.* New York: Macmillan.

Hartocollis, P. (2003). Time and the psychoanalytic situation. *Psychoanalysis Quarterly, 72,* 939–957.

Hartvigsen, J., Lings, S., Lebouef, Y. C., & Bakketeig, L. (2004). Psychosocial factors at work in relation to low back pain and consequences of low back pain. *Occupational and Environmental Medicine, 61,* 2.

Harvey, A. G. (2001). Insomnia: Symptom or diagnosis? *Clinical Psychology Review, 21,* 1037–1059.

Harvey, J. H. (1995). *Odyssey of the heart.* New York: Freeman.

Harvey, J. H., & Fine, M. A. (2004). *Children of divorce.* Mahwah, NJ: Erlbaum.

Harvey, J. H., & Weber, A. L. (2002). *Odyssey of the heart* (2nd ed.). Mahwah, NJ: Erlbaum.

Hastie, R. (2001). Problems for judgment and decision making. *Annual Review of Psychology* (Vol. 52). Palo Alto, CA: Annual Reviews.

Hastie, R., Penrod, S. D., & Pennington, N. (1983). *Inside the jury.* Cambridge MA: Harvard University Press.

Hatcher, R., & Others. (1988). *Contraceptive technology, 1988–1989* (14th ed.). New York: Irvington.

Hauptmann, B., & Karni, A. (2002). From primed to learn: the saturation of repetition priming and the induction of long-term memory. *Brain Research: Cognitive Brain Research, 13,* 313–322.

Hawkins, G., & Zimring, F. E. (1988). *Pornography in a free society.* New York: Cambridge University Press.

Hayashi, Y, Tanaka, J., Morizumi, Y., Kitamura, Y., & Hattori, Y. (2004). Polymine levels in brain and plasma after acute restraint or water-immersion restraint stress in mice. *Neuroscience Letters, 355,* 57–60.

Hayes, N. (1997, July). The distinctive skills of a psychology graduate. *APA Monitor,* p. 33.

Hayflick, L. (1997). The cellular basis for biological aging. In C. E. Finch & L. Hayflick (Eds.), *Handbook of the biology of aging.* New York: Van Nostrand.

Haythronthwaite, J. A., Lawrence, J. W., & Fauerbach, J. A. (2001). Brief cognitive interventions for pain. *Annals of Behavioral Medicine, 23,* 42–49.

Heath, A. C., Todorov, A. A., Nelson, E. C., Madden, P. A., Bucholz, K. K., & Martin, N. G. (2002). Gene-environment interaction effects on behavioral variation and risk of complex disorders: the example of alcoholism and other psychiatric disorders. *Twin Research, 5,* 30–37.

Hebb, D. O. (1980). *Essay on mind.* Mahwah, NJ: Erlbaum.

Hebb, D. O. (2002). *The organization of behavior.* Mahwah, NJ: Erlbaum.

Hefferman, D. D., Harper, S. M., & McWilliam, D. (2002). Women's perceptions of the outcome of weight loss diets: A signal detection approach. *International Journal of Eating Disorders, 31,* 339–343.

Heiby, E. M., & Haynes, S. (2004). Introduction to behavioral assessment. In M. Hersen (Ed.), *Comprehensive handbook of psychological assessment* (Vol. 3). New York: Wiley.

Heider, F. (1958). Attitudes and cognitive organization. *Journal of Psychology, 21,* 107–122.

Heikkinen, M., Aro, H., & Loennqvist, J. (1992). Recent life events and their role in suicide as seen by the spouses. *Acta Psychiatrica Scandinavica, 86,* 489–494.

Heim, C., & Nemeroff, C. B. (2002). Neurobiology of early life stress: Clinical studies. *Seminars in Clinical Psychiatry, 7,* 147–159.

Heiman, G. W. (1995). *Research methods.* Boston: Houghton Mifflin.

Heinrichs, R. W. (2001). *In search of madness.* New York: Oxford University Press.

Heller, W., Nitschke, J. B., Etienne, M. A., & Miller, G. A. (1997). Patterns of regional brain activity differentiate types of anxiety. *Journal of Abnormal Psychology, 106,* 376–385.

Helmholtz, H. von. (1852). On the theory of compound colors. *Philosophical Magazine, 4,* 519–534.

Hendin, H. (1995). *Suicide in America.* New York: W. W. Norton.

Hendrick, C., & Hendrick, S. S. (2004). Sex and romantic love. In J. H. Harvey, A. Wentzel, & S. Sprecher (Eds.), *The handbook of sexuality in close relationships.* Mahwah, NJ: Erlbaum.

Hendrick, S. S. (2004). *Understanding close relationships.* Boston: Allyn & Bacon.

Heppner, P., & Lee, D. (2001). Problem-solving appraisal and psychological adjustment. In C.R. Snyder & S.J. Lopez (Eds.), *Handbook of positive psychology.* New York: Oxford University Press.

Herberman, R. B. (2002). Stress, natural killer cells, and cancer. In H. G. Koenig & H. J. Cohen (Eds.), *The link between religion and health.* New York: Oxford University Press.

Herbert, J. (1988). The physiology of aggression. In J. Groebel & R. Hinde (Eds.), *Aggression and war: The biological and social bases.* New York: Cambridge University Press.

Hergenhahn, B. R. (2001). *An introduction to the history of psychology* (4th ed.). Belmont, CA: Wadsworth.

Hergenhahn, B. R., & Olson, M. H. (2001). *An introduction to theories of learning* (6th ed.). Upper Saddle River, NJ: Prentice-Hall.

Herholtz, K. (2003). PET studies in dementia. *Annuals of Nuclear Medicine, 1,* 79–89.

Herrnstein, R. J., & Murray, C. (1994). *The bell curve: Intelligence and class structure in American life.* New York: Macmillan.

Herxheimer, A., & Petrie, K. J. (2001). *Melatonin for preventing and treating jet lag* [CD-ROM]. Retrieved from Cochrane Database System 1, CD No. 001520.

Herzberg, E. (2000). Use of TAT in multicultural societies: Brazil and the United States. In R. H. Dana (Ed.), *Handbook of cross-cultural and multicultural personality assessment.* Mahwah, NJ: Erlbaum.

Herzog, H. A. (1995). Discussing animal rights and animal research in the classroom. In M. E. Ware & D. E. Johnson (Eds.), *Demonstrations and activities in teaching of psychology* (Vol. 1). Mahwah, NJ: Erlbaum.

Hetherington, E. M. (2000). Divorce. In A. Kazdin (Ed.), *Encyclopedia of psychology.* Washington, DC, & New York: American Psychological Association and Oxford University Press.

Hetherington, E. M., & Kelly, J. (2002). *For better or for worse: Divorce reconsidered.* New York: Norton.

Hetherington, E. M., & Stanley-Hagan, M. (2002). Parenting in divorced and remarried families. In M. Bornstein (Ed.), *Handbook of parenting* (2nd ed.). Mahwah, NJ: Erlbaum.

Hewison, D. (2003). Searching for the facts in the clinical setting with couples. *Journal of Analytical Psychology, 48,* 341–354.

Hewitt, J. P. (2001). The social construction of self-esteem. In C. R. Synder & S. J. Lopez (Eds.), *Handbook of positive psychology.* New York: Oxford University Press.

Hewstone, M., Rubin, M., & Willis, H. (2002). Intergroup bias. *Annual Review of Psychology* (Vol. 53). Palo Alto, CA: Annual Reviews.

Hibbard, S. (2003). A critique of Lilienfeld et al. (2000). "The scientific status of projective techniques." *Journal of Personality Assessment, 80,* 260–271.

Hidalgo, R. B., & Davidson, J. R. (2001). Generalized anxiety disorder: An important clinical concern. *Medical Clinics of North America, 85,* 691–710.

Higgins, E. T., & Molden, D. C. (2004). How strategies for making judgments and decisions affect cognition. In G. V. Bodenhausen & A. J. Lambert (Eds.), *Foundations of social cognition.* Mahwah, NJ: Erlbaum.

Hilgard, E. R. (1965). *Hypnotic suggestibility.* Fort Worth, Harcourt Brace.

Hilgard, E. R. (1977). *Divided consciousness: Multiple controls in human thought and action.* New York: Wiley.

Hilgard, E. R. (1992). Dissociation and theories of hypnosis. In E. Fromm & M. R. Nash (Eds.), *Contemporary hypnosis research.* New York: Guilford Press.

Hill, C. E. (2000). Client-centered therapy. In A. Kazdin (Ed.), *Encyclopedia of psychology.* Washington,

DC, & New York: American Psychological Association and Oxford University Press.

Hill, C. E., & O'Brien, K. M. (1999). *Helping skills.* Washington, DC: American Psychological Association.

Hill, P. C., & Butter, E. M. (1995). The role of religion in promoting physical health. *Journal of Psychology and Christianity, 14,* 141–155.

Hill, P. C., & Pargament, K. I. (2003). Advances in conceptualization and measurement of religion and spirituality: Implications for physical and mental health research. *American Psychologist, 58,* 64–74.

Hilsenroth, M. J. (2004). Projective assessment of personality and psychopathology. In M. Hersen (Ed.), *Comprehensive handbook of psychological assessment* (Vol. 2). New York: Wiley.

Hirsch, B. J., Roffman, J. G., Pagano, M., & Deutsch, N. (2000, April). *Inner-city youth: Ties to youth development staff and adult kin.* Paper presented at the meeting of the Society for Research on Adolescence, Chicago.

Hobfoll, S. E. (1989). Conservation of resources: A new attempt at conceptualizing stress. *American Psychologist, 44,* 513–524.

Hobfoll, S. E., Johnson, R. J., Ennis, N., & Jackson, A. P. (2003). Resource loss, resource gain, and emotional outcomes among inner city women. *Journal of Personality and Social Psychology, 84,* 632–643.

Hobson, A. (2000). Dreams: Physiology. In A. Kazdin (Ed.), *Encyclopedia of psychology.* Washington, DC, & New York: American Psychological Association and Oxford University Press.

Hobson, J. A. (1999). Dreams. In R. Conlan (Ed.), *States of mind.* New York: Wiley.

Hobson, J. A., Pace-Schott, E. F., & Stickgold, R. (2000). Dreaming and the brain. *Behavior and Brain Sciences, 23,* 793–842.

Hochschild, T. L., Climbolic, G. K., Cohen, L. H., & O'Neill, S. C. (2004). Borderline personality features and instability of daily negative affect and self-esteem. *Journal of Personality, 72,* 111–138.

Hodges, J. R. (2000). Memory in the dementias. In E. Tulving & F. I. M. Craik (Eds.), *Oxford Handbook of Memory.* New York: Oxford University Press.

Hofferth, S. L. (1990). Trends in adolescent sexual activity, contraception, and pregnancy in the United States. In J. Bancroft & J.M. Reinisch (Eds.), *Adolescence and puberty.* New York: Oxford University Press.

Hogan, E. H. Nornick, B. A. & Bouchoux, A. (2002). Focus on communications: Communicating the message: Clarifying the controversies about caffeine, *Nutrition Today, 37,* 28–35.

Hogan, J. (1986). *Hogan Personality Inventory manual.* Minneapolis: National Computer Systems.

Hogan, R. T. (1987, August). *Conceptions of personality and the prediction of job performance.* Paper presented at the meeting of the American Psychological Association, New York City.

Hoge, M. A. (1998). Managed care. In H. S. Friedman (Ed.), *Encyclopedia of mental health* (Vol. 2). San Diego: Academic Press.

Holaday, M., Smith, D. A., & Sherry, A. (2000). Sentence completion tests: A review of the literature and results of a survey of members of the Society for Personality Assessment. *Journal of Personality Assessment, 74,* 371–383.

Holcomb, H. H., Cascella, N. G., Thaker, G. K., Medoff, D. R., Dannals, R. F., & Tamminga, C. A. (1996). Functional sites of neuroleptic drug action in the human brain. *American Journal of Psychiatry, 153,* 41–49.

Holland, P. C. (1996). The effects of intertrial and feature-target intervals on operant serial feature-positive discrimination learning. *Animal Learning & Behavior, 24,* 411–428.

Holmes, D. S. (1988). The influence of meditation versus rest on physiological considerations. In

M. West (Ed.), *The psychology of meditation.* New York: Oxford University Press.

Holmes, S. E., Slaughter, J. R., & Kashani, J. (2001). Risk factors in childhood that lead to the development of conduct disorder and antisocial personality disorder. *Child Psychiatry and Human Development, 31,* 183–193.

Holmes, T. H., & Rahe, R. H. (1967). The social readjustment rating scale. *Journal of Psychosomatic Research, 11,* 213–218.

Holm-Hadulla, R. M. (2003). Psychoanalysis as a creative shaping process. *International Journal of Psychoanalysis, 84,* 1203–1220.

Homma, K., Hashimoto, S., Nakao, M., & Homma, S. (2003). Period and phase adjustments of human circadian rhythms in the real world. *Journal of Biological Rhythms, 18,* 261–270.

Honts, C. (1998, June). Commentary. *APA Monitor,* p. 30.

Hood, A. S., & Morrison, J. D. (2002). The dependence of binocular contrast sensitivities on binocular single vision in normal and amblyopic human subjects. *Journal of Physiology, 540,* 607–622.

Hood, D. C., Frishman, L. J., Saszik, S., & Viswanathan, S. (2002). Retinal origins of the primate multifocal ERG: Implications for the human response. *Investigative Ophthalmology and Visual Science, 43,* 1673–1685.

Hoptf, M., David, A. S., Hull, L., Nkikalaou, V., Unwin, C., & Wessely, S. (2003). Gulf war illness—better, worse, or just the same? A cohort study. *British Medical Journal, 327,* 1370.

Hoptman, M. J., & Davidson, R. J. (1994). How and why do the two cerebral hemispheres interact? *Psychological Bulletin, 116,* 195–219.

Horn, J. L., & Donaldson, G. (1980). Cognitive development II: Adulthood development of human abilities. In O. G. Brim & J. Kagan (Eds.), *Constancy and change in human development.* Cambridge, MA: Harvard University Press.

Horney, K. (1945). *Our inner conflicts.* New York: Norton.

Horowitz, M. J. (1998). Psychoanalysis. In H. S. Friedman (Ed.), *Encyclopedia of mental health* (Vol. 3). San Diego: Academic Press.

Horton, D. M. (2001). The disappearing bell curve. *Journal of Secondary Gifted Education, 12,* 185–188.

Hotting, B., Kosler, F., & Roder, B. (2003). Crossmodal and intermodal attention modulate event-related brain potentials to tactile and auditory stimuli. *Experimental Brain Research, 148,* 26–37.

Hough, L. (2001). I/Owes its advances to personality. In B. W. Roberts & R. Hogan (Eds.), *Personality psychology in the workplace.* Washington, DC: American Psychological Association.

Hovey, J. D. (2000). Psychosocial predictors of acculturative stress in Mexican immigrants. *Journal of Psychology, 134,* 490–502.

Howard, K. I., Moras, K., Brill, P. L., Martinovich, Z., & Lutz, W. (1996). Evaluation of psychotherapy: Efficacy, effectiveness, and patient progress. *American Psychologist, 51,* 1059–1064.

Howard, M. W., & Kahana, M. J. (1999). Contextual variability and serial position effects in free recall. *Journal of Experimental Psychology: Learning, Memory, and Cognition, 25,* 923–941.

Howard, R. W. (2001). Searching the real world for signs of rising population intelligence. *Personality and Individual Differences, 30,* 1039–1058.

Howe, M. J. A., Davidson, J. W., Moore, D. G., & Sloboda, J. A. (1995). Are there early childhood signs of musical ability? *Psychology of Music, 23,* 162–176.

Howley, E. T. (2001). Type of activity: Resistance, aerobic and leisure versus occupational physical activity. *Medical Science and Sports Exercise, 33* (Suppl.), S364–369.

Hoyle, R. H., & Judd, C. M. (2002). *Research methods in social psychology* (7th ed.). Belmont, CA: Wadsworth.

Hsu, P., Yu, F., Feron, F., Pickles, J. O., Sneesby, K., & Mackay-Sim, A. (2001). Basic fibroblast growth factor and fibroblast growth factor receptors in adult olfactory epithelium. *Brain Research, 896,* 188–197.

Huber, D. E., Shiffrin, R. M., Lyle, K. B., & Ruys, K. I. (2001). Perception and preference in short-term word priming. *Psychological Review, 108,* 149–182.

Hublin, C., Kaprio, J., Partinen, M., & Koskenvu, M. (2001). Parasomnias: Co-occurrence and genetics. *Psychiatric Genetics, 11,* 65–70.

Huff, C. R. (2002). What can we learn from other nations about the problem of wrongful conviction? *Judicature, 86,* 91–97.

Humphreys, G. W. (2003). Conscious visual representations built from multiple binding processes: Evidence from neuropsychology. *Progress in Brain Research, 142,* 243–255.

Humphreys, M. S. (2001). Proactive interference and complexity. *Journal of Experimental Psychology: Learning, Memory, and Cognition, 27,* 872–888.

Humphreys, M. S., Tehan, G., O'Shea, A., & Bolland, S. W. (2000). Target similarity effects: Support for the parallel distributed processing assumptions. *Memory and Cognition, 28,* 798–811.

Hunsley, J., & Bailey, J. M. (1999). The clinical utility of the Rorschach: Unfulfilled promises and an uncertain future. *Psychological Assessment, 11,* 266–277.

Hunt, E. (1995). *Will we be smart enough? A cognitive analysis of the coming work force.* New York: Russell Sage.

Hunt, M. (1974). *Sexual behavior in the 1970s.* Chicago: Playboy.

Hunt, M. (1993). *The story of psychology.* New York: Anchor Books.

Hunt, R. R., & Ellis, H. C. (2004). *Fundamentals of cognitive psychology* (7th ed.). New York: McGraw-Hill.

Hunt, R. R., & Kelly, R. E. S. (1996). Accessing the particular from the general: The power of distinctiveness in the context of organization. *Memory and Cognition, 24,* 217–225.

Hurvich, L. M., & Jameson, D. (1969). Human color perception. *American Scientist, 57,* 143–166.

Huttenlocher, J., Haight, W., Bruk, A., Selzer, M., & Lyons, T. (1991). Early vocabulary growth: Relation to language input and gender. *Developmental Psychology, 27,* 236–248.

Huttenlocher, P. R., & Dabholkar, A. S. (1997). Regional differences in synaptogenesis in human cerebral cortex. *Journal of Comparative Neurology, 37* (2), 167–178.

Hy, L., & Loevinger, J. (1996). *Measuring ego development.* Mahwah, NJ: Erlbaum.

Hyde, J. S. (2004). *Half the human experience* (6th ed.). Boston: Houghton Mifflin.

Hyde, J. S., & DeLamater, J. D. (2003). *Understanding human sexuality* (8th ed.). New York: McGraw-Hill.

Hyde, J. S., & Mezulis, A. H. (2002). Gender difference research: Issues and critique. In J. Worell (Ed.), *Encyclopedia of women and gender.* San Diego: Academic Press.

Hyde, J. S., & Plant, E. A. (1995). Magnitude of psychological gender differences: Another side of the story. *American Psychologist, 50,* 159–161.

Hyman, S. (2001, October 23). *Basic and clinical neuroscience in the post-genomic era.* Paper presented at the centennial symposium on The Celebration of Excellence in Neuroscience, The Rockefeller University, New York City.

I

Iacono, W. G., & Lykken, D. T. (1997). The validity of the lie detector: Two surveys of scientific opinion. *Journal of Applied Psychology, 82,* 426–433.

Ickovics, J. (2001). *Identity and pregnant teens prospective study of HIV risk.* Unpublished manuscript, Center for Interdisciplinary Research on AIDS, Yale University, New Haven, CT.

Idson, L. C., & Mischel, W. (2001). The personality of familiar and significant people: The lay perceiver and the social-cognitive theorist. *Journal of Personality and Social Psychology, 80,* 585–596.

Impara, J. C., & Plake, B. S. (Eds.). (2001). *The fourteenth mental measurements yearbook.* Lincoln University of Nebraska Press.

Ironson, G., Solomon, G., Balbin, E., O'-Cleirigh, C., George, A., Schneiderman, N., & Woods, T. (2001, March). *Religious behavior, religious coping, and compassionate view of others is associated with long-term survival with AIDS.* Paper presented at the meeting of the American Psychosomatic Society, Monterey, CA.

Irwin, M. (2002). Psychoneuroimmunology of depression: clinical implications. *Brain, Behavior, and Immunity, 16,* 1–16.

Isotani, T., Tanaka, H., Lehmann, D., Pascual-Marqui, R.D., Kochi, K., Saito, N., Yagyu, T., Kinoshita, T., & Sasada, K. (2001). Source localization of EEG activity during hypnotically induced anxiety and relaxation. *International Journal of Psychophysiology, 41,* 143–153.

Iverson, G. L., & Barton, E. (1999). Interscorer reliability of the MMPI-2: Should TRIN and VRIN be computer scored? *Journal of Clinical Psychology, 55,* 65–70.

J

Jackson, L. C., & Greene, B. (2000). *Psychotherapy with African-American women.* New York: Guilford Press.

Jakicic, J. M. (2003). Exercise in the treatment of obesity. *Endocrinology and Metabolic Clinics of North American, 32,* 967–980.

James, R. K., & Gilliland, B. E. (2003). *Theories and strategies in counseling and psychotherapy* (5th ed.). Boston: Allyn & Bacon.

James, W. (1950). *Principles of psychology.* New York: Dover. (Original work published 1890)

Jameson, D., & Hurvich, L. M. (1989). Essay concerning color constancy. *Annual Review of Psychology* (Vol. 40). Palo Alto, CA: Annual Reviews.

Jamison, K. R. (1995). *An unquiet mind.* New York: Random House.

Jamurtas, A. Z., Goldfarb, A. H., Chung, S. C., Hegde, S., & Marino, C. (2000). Beta-endorphin infusion during exercise in rats. *Medical Science and Sports Exercise, 32,* 1570–1575.

Janicki, M. (2004). Beyond sociobiology: A kinder and gentler evolutionary view of human nature. In C. B. Crawford & C. A. Salmon (Eds.), *Evolutionary psychology, public policy, and private decisions.* Mahwah, NJ: Erlbaum.

Janis, I. (1972). *Victims of groupthink: A psychological study of foreign-policy decisions and fiascos.* Boston: Houghton Mifflin.

Janno, S., Holi, M., Tuisku, K., & Wahbeck, K. (2004). Prevalence of neuroleptic-induced movement disorders in chronic schizophrenia inpatients. *American Journal of Psychiatry, 16,* 160–163.

Jansen, N. W., van Amelsvoort, L. G., Kristensen, T. S., van den Brandt, P. A., & Kant, I. J. (2003). Work schedules and fatigue: A prospective cohort study. *Occupational and Environmental Medicine, 60,* Supplement 1, i47–i53.

Jarrett, R. B., Kraft, D., Doyle, J., Foster, B. M., Eaves, G. G., & Silver, P. C. (2001). Preventing recurrent depression using cognitive therapy with and without a continuation phase: A randomized clinical trial. *Archives of General Psychiatry, 58,* 381–388.

Jausovec, N., & Jausovec, K. (2001). Differences in EEG current density related to intelligence. *Brain Research: Cognitive Brain Research, 12,* 55–60.

Jay, T. M. (2003). Dopamine: A potential substrate for synaptic plasticity and memory mechanisms. *Progress in Neurobiology, 69,* 375–390.

Jenike, M. A. (2001). An update on obsessive-compulsive disorder. *Bulletin of the Menninger Clinic, 65,* 4–25.

Jenkins, S. (2002). Race and human diversity. In M. Hersen & W. H. Sledge (Eds.), *Encyclopedia of psychotherapy.* San Diego: Academic Press.

Jennings, L., & Skovholt, T. M. (1999). The cognitive, emotional, and relational characteristics of master therapists. *Journal of Counseling Psychology, 46,* 3–11.

Jensen, A. R. (1969). How much can we boost IQ and scholastic achievement? *Harvard Educational Review, 39,* 1–123.

Jensen, S. M., Barabasz, A., Barabasz, M., & Warner, D. (2001). EEG P300 event-related markers of hypnosis. *American Journal of Clinical Hypnosis, 44,* 127–139.

Jeong, J., Kim, D. J., Kim, S. Y., Chae, J. H., Go, H. J., & Kim, K. S. (2001). Effect of total sleep deprivation on the dimensional complexity of the waking EEG. *Sleep, 15,* 197–202.

Jernigan, T. L., Ostergaard, A. L., & Fennema-Notestine, C. (2001). Mesial temporal, diencephalic, and striatal contributions to single word reading, word priming, and recognition memory. *Journal of the International Neuropsychological Society, 7,* 67–78.

Johnson, A., & Proctor, R. W. (2004). *Attention: Theory and practice.* Thousand Oaks, CA: Sage.

Johnson, D. W., & Johnson, F. P. (2003). *Joining together: Group theory and group skills. (8th Ed.).* Boston: Allyn & Bacon.

Johnson, G. B. (2003). *The living world* (3rd ed.). New York: McGraw-Hill.

Johnson, M. H. (2002). Functional brain development during infancy. In G. Bremner & A. Fogel (Eds.), *Blackwell handbook of infant development.* Malden, MA: Blackwell.

Johnson, W., Bouchard, T. J., Krueger, R. F., McGue, M., & Gottesman, I. I. (2004). Just one g: consistent results from three test batteries. *Intelligence, 32,* 95–107.

Johnson-Laird, P. N. (2000). Thinking: Reasoning. In A. Kazdin (Ed.), *Encyclopedia of psychology.* Washington, DC, & New York: American Psychological Association and Oxford University Press.

Johnston, L. D., Bachman, J. G., & O'Malley, P. M. (1989, February 24). Teenage drug use continues decline [News release]. Ann Arbor: University of Michigan, Institute for Social Research.

Johnston, L. D., O'Malley, P. M., & Bachman, J. G. (2001, December). *Drug trends in U.S. adolescents.* Ann Arbor, MI: Institute for Social Research.

Johnston, L. D., O'Malley, P. M., & Bachman, J. G. (2003). *Monitoring the future national survey results on drug use, 1975–2002. Volume I: Secondary school students* (NIH Publication No. 03-5375). Bethesda, MD: National Institute on Drug Abuse.

Joiner, T. E., Steer, R. A., Abramson, L. Y., Mealsky, G. I., & Schmidt, N. B. (2001). Hopelessness depression as a distinct dimension of depressive symptoms among clinical and non-clinical samples. *Behavior Research and Therapy, 39,* 523–536.

Jones, D. L., Tanigawa, T., & Weiss, S. M. (2003). Stress management and workplace disability in the US, Europe, and Japan. *Journal of Occupational Health, 45,* 1–7.

Jones, E. E. (1998). Major developments in five decades of social psychology. In D. T. Gilbert, S. T. Fiske, & G. Lindzey (Eds.), *Handbook of social psychology* (4th ed., Vol. 1). New York: McGraw-Hill.

Jones, J. H. (1997). *Prejudice and racism* (2nd ed.). New York: McGraw-Hill.

Jones, M. (2002). *Social psychology of prejudice.* Upper Saddle River, NJ: Prentice-Hall.

Jones, M. C. (1924). A laboratory study of fear: The case of Peter. *Journal of Genetic Psychology, 31,* 308–315.

Jones, N., Kemenes, G., & Benjamin, P. R. (2001). Selective expression of electrical correlates of differential appetitive classical conditioning in a feedback network. *Journal of Neurophysiology, 85,* 89–97.

Jou, J., Shanteau, J., & Harris, R. J. (1996). An information processing view of framing effects: The role of causal schemas in decision making. *Memory and Cognition, 24,* 1–15.

Judge, T. A., & Bono, J. E. (2001). Relationship of core self-evaluation traits—self-esteem, generalized self-efficacy, locus of control, and emotional stability—with job satisfaction and job performance: A meta-analysis. *Journal of Applied Psychology, 86,* 80–92.

Jung, C. (1917). *Analytic psychology.* New York: Moffat, Yard.

Jussim, L., Ashmore, R., & Wilder, D. (2001). Introduction: Social identity and intergroup conflict. In R. D. Ashmore, L. Jussim, & D. Wilder (Eds.), *Social identity, intergroup conflict, and conflict resolution.* New York: Oxford University Press.

K

Kagan, J. (1992). Yesterday's premises, tomorrow's promises. *Developmental Psychology, 28,* 990–997.

Kagan, J. (1998). Biology and the child. In W. Damon (Ed.), *Handbook of child psychology* (5th ed., Vol. 3). New York: Wiley.

Kagan, J. (2000). Temperament. In A. Kazdin (Ed.), *Encyclopedia of psychology.* Washington, DC, & New York: American Psychological Association and Oxford University Press.

Kagan, J. (2003). Biology, context, and developmental inquiry. *Annual Review of Psychology, 53.* Palo Alto, CA: Annual Reviews.

Kahneman, D., & Tversky, A. (1995). Conflict resolution: A cognitive perspective. In K. Arrow, R. H. Mnookin, L. Ross, A. Tversky, & R. Wilson (Eds.), *Barriers to conflict resolution.* New York: Norton.

Kalichman, S. (1996). *Answering your questions about AIDS.* Washington, DC: American Psychological Association.

Kalick, S. M., & Hamilton, T. E. (1986). The matching hypothesis reexamined. *Journal of Personality and Social Psychology, 51,* 673–682.

Kalil, A., & DeLeire, T. (Eds.) (2004). *Family investments in children's potential.* Mahwah, NJ: Erlbaum.

Kamin, C. S., O'Sullivan, P. S., Younger, M., & Deterding, R. (2001). Measuring critical thinking in problem-based learning discourse. *Teaching and Learning in Medicine, 13,* 27–35.

Kamin, L. J. (1968). Attention-like processes in classical conditioning. In M. R. Jones (Ed.), *Miami symposium on the prediction of behavior: Aversive stimuli.* Coral Gables, FL: University of Miami Press.

Kamphaus, R. W., & Kroncke, A. P. (2004). "Back to the future" of the Stanford-Binet Intelligence Scales. In M. Hersen (Ed.), *Comprehensive handbook of psychological assessment* (Vol. 1). New York: Wiley.

Kandel, E. R., Schwartz, J. H., & Jessell, T. M. (2003). *Principles of neuroscience* (5th ed.). New York: McGraw-Hill.

Kanner, A. D., Coyne, J. C., Schaeter, C., & Lazarus, R. S. (1981). Comparisons of two modes of stress measurement: Daily hassles and uplifts versus major life events. *Journal of Behavioral Medicine. 4*, 1–39.

Kanner, A. M., & Balabanov, A. (2002). Depression and epilepsy: How closely related are they? *Neurology, 58*, S27–S39.

Karau, S. J., & Williams, K.D. (1993). Social loafing: A meta-analytic review and theoretical integration. *Journal of Personality and Social Psychology, 65*, 681–706.

Kassin, S. M., Tubb, V. A., Hosch, H. M., & Memon, A. (2001). On the "general acceptance" of eyewitness testimony research. *American Psychologist, 56*, 405–416.

Katchadourian, H. (1987). *Fifty: Midlife in perspective.* New York: Freeman.

Katz, L. F. (1999, April). *Toward a family-based hypervigilance model of childhood aggression: The role of the mother's and the father's meta-emotion philosophy.* Paper presented at the meeting of the Society for Research in Child Development, Albuquerque.

Kaufman, A. S., & Lichtenberger, E. O. (2002). *Assessing adolescent and adult intelligence* (2nd ed.). Boston: Allyn & Bacon.

Kaufmann, J. M., Mostert, M. P., Trent, S. C., & Hallahan, D. P. (2002). *Managing classroom behavior: A reflective, case-based approach* (3rd ed.). Boston: Allyn & Bacon.

Kavanaugh, D. J., & Wilson, P. H. (1989). Prediction of outcome with a group version of cognitive therapy for depression. *Behaviour Research and Therapy, 27*, 333–347.

Kawachi, I., & Kennedy, B. P. (2001). How income inequality affects health: Evidence from research in the United States. In J. A. Auerbach & B. K. Krimgold (Eds.), *Income, socioeconomic status, and health.* Washington, DC: National Policy Association.

Kay, J. (2002). Psychopharmacology: Combined treatment. In M. Hersen & W. H. Sledge (Eds.), *Encyclopedia of psychotherapy.* San Diego: Academic Press.

Kaye, W. H., Klump, K. L., Frank, G. K., & Strober, M. (2000). Anorexia and bulimia nervosa. *Annual Review of Medicine, 51*, 299–313.

Kazdin, A. E. (2000). *Essentials of conditioning and learning* (2nd ed.). Belmont, CA: Wadsworth.

Kazdin, A. E. (2001). *Behavior modification in applied settings* (6th ed.). Belmont, CA: Wadsworth.

Kazdin, A. E. (2002). Behavior analysis. In M. Hersen & W. H. Sledge (Eds.), *Encyclopedia of psychotherapy.* San Diego: Academic Press.

Kazdin, A. E., & Benjet, C. (2003). Spanking children: Evidence and issues. *Current Directions in Psychological Science, 12*, 99–103.

Kearney, C. A., & Vecchio, J. (2002). Contingency management. In M. Hersen & W. H. Sledge (Eds.), *Encyclopedia of psychotherapy.* San Diego: Academic Press.

Keating, D. P. (2004). Cognitive and brain development. In R. Lerner & L. Steinberg (Eds.), *Handbook of adolescent psychology.* New York: Wiley.

Keel, P. K., Mitchell, J. E., Miller, K. B., Davis, T. L., & Crowe, S. J. (1999). Long-term outcome of bulimia nervosa. *Archives of General Psychiatry, 56*, 63–69.

Keillor, J. M., Barrett, A. M., Crucian, G. P., Kortenkamp, S., & Heilman, K. M. (2002). Emotional experience and perception in the absence of facial feedback. *Journal of the International Neuropsychological Society, 8*, 130–135.

Kelai, S., Aissi, F., Lesch, K. P., Cohen-Salmon, C., Hamon, M., & Lanfumey, L. (2003). Alcohol intake after serotonin transporter inactivation in mice. *Alcohol and Alcoholism, 38*, 386–389.

Kelly, G. F. (2004). *Sexuality today* (updated 7th ed.). New York: McGraw-Hill.

Kelsoe, J. R., Spence, M. A., Loetscher, E., Foguet, M., Sadovinick, A. D., Remick, R. A., Khristich, J., Mroszkowski-Parker, Z., Brown, J. L., Masster, D., Ungerleider, S., Rapaport, M. H., Wishart, W. L., & Luebbert, H. (2001). A genome survey indicates a possible susceptibility locus for bipolar disorder on chromosome 22. *Proceedings of the National Academy of Science, 98*, 585–590.

Keltner, D., & Ekman, P. (2000). Emotion: An overview. In A. Kazdin (Ed.), *Encyclopedia of psychology.* Washington, DC, & New York: American Psychological Association and Oxford University Press.

Kempermann, G., & Gage, F. H. (1999, May). New nerve cells for the adult brain. *Scientific American, 48*–53.

Kendler, K. S., Myers, J., & Prescott, C.A. (2002). The etiology of phobias: An evaluation of the diathesis-stress model. *Archives of General Psychiatry, 59*, 242–248.

Kennaway, D. J., & Wright, H. (2002). Melatonin and circadian rhythms. *Current Topics in Medicinal Chemistry, 2*, 199–209.

Kennedy, P. G. E., & Folk-Seang, J. F. (1986). Studies on the development, antigenic phenotype and function of human glial cells in tissue culture. *Brain, 109*, 1261–1277.

Kesey, K. (1962). *One flew over the cuckoo's nest.* New York: Viking Press.

Kessler, R. C., Berglund, P., Demler, O., Jin, R., Koretz, D., Merikangas, K. R., Rush, J., Walters, E. E., & Wang, P. S. (2003). The epidemiology of major depressive disorder. *Journal of the American Medical Association, 289*, 3095–3105.

Kessler, R. C., McGonagle, K. A., Zhao, S., Nelson, C. B, Hughes, M., Eshleman, S., Wittchen, H., & Kendler, K. S. (1994). Lifetime and 12-month prevalence of *DSM-III-R* psychiatric disorders in the United States: Results from the National Comorbidity Study. *Archives of General Psychiatry, 51*, 8–19.

Kessler, R. C., Olfson, M., & Berglund, P. A. (1998). Patterns and predictors of treatment contact after first onset of psychiatric disorders. *American Journal of Psychiatry, 155*, 62–69.

Kessler, R. C., Stein, M. B., & Berglund, P. (1998). Social phobia subtypes in the National Comorbidity Survey. *American Journal of Psychiatry, 155*, 613–619.

Kiecolt-Glaser, J. K., Dura, J. R., Specher, C. E., Trask, O. J., & Glaser, R. (1991). Spousal caregivers of dementia victims. *Psychosomatic Medicine, 53*, 345–362.

Kiecolt-Glaser, J. K., McGuire, L., Robles, T. F., & Glaser, R. (2002a). Emotions, morbidity, and mortality: New perspectives from psychoneuroimmunology. *Annual Review of Psychology, 53*. Palo Alto, CA: Annual Reviews.

Kiecolt-Glaser, J. K., McGuire, L., Robles, T. F., & Glaser, R. (2002b). Psychoneuroimmunology and psychosomatic medicine: Back to the future. *Psychosomatic Medicine, 64*, 15–28.

Kikyo, H., Ohki, K., & Sekihara, K. (2001). Temporal characterization of memory retrieval process: An fMRI study of the "tip-of-the-tongue" phenomenon. *European Journal of Neuroscience, 14*, 887–892.

Kimble, G. A. (1961). *Hilgard and Marquis's conditioning and learning.* New York: Appleton-Century-Crofts.

Kimble, G. A. (1989). Psychology from the standpoint of a generalist. *American Psychologist, 44*, 491–499.

Kimbrough, S. K., Wright, D. L., & Shea, C. H. (2001). Reducing the saliency of intentional stimuli results in greater context-dependent performance. *Memory, 9*, 133–143.

Kimmel, A. (1996). *Ethical issues in behavioral research.* Cambridge, MA: Blackwell.

Kimmell, E., & Crawford, M. C. (2002). Methods of studying gender. In J. Worell (Ed.), *Encyclopedia of women and gender.* New York: Oxford University Press.

Kimoto, T., & Okada, M. (2004). Mixed states on neural network with structural learning. *Neural Networks, 17*, 103–112.

Kimura, D. (2000). *Sex and cognition.* Cambridge, MA: MIT Press.

King, R. N., & Koehler, D. J. (2000). Illusory correlations in graphological inference. *Journal of Experimental Psychology: Applied, 6*, 336–348.

Kinsey, A. C., Pomeroy, W. B., & Martin, E. E. (1948). *Sexual behavior in the human male.* Philadelphia: W. B. Saunders.

Kirsch, I. & Sapirstein, G. (1998). Listening to Prozac but hearing placebo: A meta-analysis of antidepressant medication. *Prevention and Treatment, 1*, Article 0002a, posted June 26, 1998. (Retrieved from http://www.journals.apa.org/prevention/volume1/pre0010002a.html).

Kitayama, S. (2002). Culture and basic psychological processes—Toward a system view of culture: Comment on Oyserman et al. (2002). *Psychological Bulletin, 128*, 89–96.

Kitchener, K. S., & King, P. M. (1981). Reflective judgment: Concepts of justification and their relationship to age and education. *Journal of Applied Developmental Psychology, 2*, 89–111.

Kite, M. (2001). Gender stereotypes. In J. Worell (Ed.), *Encyclopedia of women and gender.* San Diego: Academic Press.

Kitzmann, K., & Gaylord, N. K. (2002). Divorce and child custody. In J. Worell (Ed.), *Encyclopedia of women and gender.* New York: Oxford University Press.

Klein, K., & Boals, A. (2001). Expressive writing can increase working memory capacity. *Journal of Experimental Psychology: General, 130*, 520–533.

Klein, S. (2002). *Learning* (4th ed.). New York: McGraw-Hill.

Kliegel, M., Martin, M., McDaniel, M. A., & Einstein, G. O. (2001). Varying the importance of a prospective memory task: Differential effects across time- and event-based prospective memory. *Memory, 9*, 1–11.

Kline, W. B. (2003). *Interactive group work.* Upper Saddle River, NJ: Prentice-Hall.

Klinger, E. (2000). Daydreams. In A. Kazdin (Ed.), *Encyclopedia of psychology.* Washington, DC, & New York: American Psychological Association and Oxford University Press.

Klug, W. S., & Cummings, M. R. (2003). *Genetics: A molecular perspective.* Upper Saddle River, NJ: Prentice-Hall.

Kluznik, J. C., Walbek, N. H., Farnsworth, M. G., & Melstrom, K. (2001). Clinical effects of a randomized switch of patients from clozaril to generic clozapine. *Journal of Clinical Psychiatry, 62*, (Suppl. 5), 14–17.

Knox, J. M. (2002). Memories, fantasies, archetypes: An exploration of some connections between cognitive science and analytical psychology. *Journal of Analytical Psychology, 46*, 613–635.

Kobasa, S., Maddi, S., & Kahn, S. (1982). Hardiness and health: A prospective study. *Journal of Personality and Social Psychology, 42*, 168–177.

Kobasa, S. C., Maddi, S. R., Puccetti, M. C., & Zola, M. (1986). Relative effectiveness of hardiness, exercise, and social support as resources against illness. *Journal of Psychosomatic Research, 29*, 525–533.

Koenig, H. G. (2001). Religion and medicine: II. Religion, mental health, and related behaviors. *International Journal of Psychiatry, 31*, 97–109.

Koenig, H. G., & Cohen, H. J. (Eds.). (2002). *The link between religion and health.* New York: Oxford University Press.

Koenig, H. G., & Larson, D. B. (1998). Religion and mental health. In H. S. Friedman (Ed.), *Encyclopedia of mental health* (Vol. 3). San Diego: Academic Press.

Kohlberg, L. (1958). *The development of modes of moral thinking and choice in the years 10 to 16.* Unpublished doctoral dissertation, University of Chicago.

Kohlberg, L. (1969). Stage and sequence: The cognitive-developmental approach to socialization. In D. A. Goslin (Ed.), *Handbook of socialization theory and research.* Chicago: Rand McNally.

Kohlberg, L. (1976). Moral stages and moralization: The cognitive-developmental approach. In T. Lickona (Ed.), *Moral development and behavior.* New York: Holt, Rinehart, & Winston.

Kohlberg, L. (1986). A current statement on some theoretical issues. In S. Modgil & C. Modgil (Eds.), *Lawrence Kohlberg.* Philadelphia: Falmer.

Kohler, W. (1925). *The mentality of apes.* New York: Harcourt Brace Jovanovich.

Kohut, H. (1977). *Restoration of the self.* New York: International Universities Press.

Kok, G., Schaalman, H., Rutter, R. A., Van Empelen, P., & Brug, J. (2004). Intervention mapping: protocol for applying health psychology theory to prevention programs. *Journal of Health Psychology, 9,* 73–84.

Kolb, B. (1989). Brain development, plasticity, and behavior. *American Psychologist, 44,* 1203–1212.

Kolb, B., & Whishaw, I. Q. (2001). *Introduction to brain and behavior.* New York: Worth.

Kolb, B., & Whishaw, I. Q. (2003). *Fundamentals of human neurophysiology* (5th ed.). New York: Worth.

Kolb, L. (1973). *Modern clinical psychiatry* (8th ed.). Philadelphia: W.B. Saunders.

Kolchakian, M. R., & Hill, C. E. (2002). Dream interpretation with heterosexual dating couples. *Dreaming, 12,* 1–16.

Kondziolka D., Wechsler, L., Goldstein, S., Meltzer, C., Thulborn, K. R., Gebel, J., Jannetta, P., DeCesare, S., Elder, E. M., McGrogan, M., Reitman, M. A., & Bynum, L. (2000). Transplantation of cultured human neuronal cells for patients with stroke. *Journal of Neurology, 55,* 565–569.

Kopp, C. (1984). *Baby steps.* New York: Freeman.

Kornstein, S. G., & Clayton, A. H. (Eds.). (2002). *Women's mental health.* New York: Guilford.

Koss, M., & Boeschen, L. (1998). Rape. In H. S. Friedman (Ed.), *Encyclopedia of mental health* (Vol. 3). San Diego: Academic Press.

Kosslyn, S. M. (1994). *Image and brain: The resolution of the imagery debate.* Cambridge, MA: MIT Press.

Kosslyn, S. M. (2004, August). *Visual mental images in the brain.* Paper presented at the 28th International Congress of Psychology, Beijing, China.

Kotani, S., Kawahara, S., & Kirino, Y. (2002). Classical eyeblink conditioning in decerebrate guinea pigs. *European Journal of Neuroscience, 15,* 1267–1270.

Kraik, K. H. (2000). Personality: Methods of study. In A. Kazdin (Ed.), *Encyclopedia of psychology.* Washington, DC, & New York: American Psychological Association and Oxford University Press.

Kramer, P. D. (1993). *Listening to Prozac.* New York: Viking.

Krause, J. B., Taylor, J. G., Schmidt, D., Hautzel, H., Mottaghy, F. M., & Muller-Gartner, H. W. (2000). Imaging and neural modelling in episodic and working memory processes. *Neural Networks, 13,* 847–849.

Krauss, J. K., & Jankovic, J. (2002). Head injury and posttraumatic movement disorders. *Neurosurgery, 50,* 927–940.

Kris, A. O. (2002). Free association. In M. Hersen & W. H. Sledge (Eds.), *Encyclo-pedia of psychotherapy.* San Diego: Academic Press.

Krogh, D. (2000). *Biology.* Upper Saddle River, NJ: Prentice-Hall.

Krull, D. S. (2001). On partitioning the fundamental attribution error. In G. B. Moskowitz (Ed.), *Cognitive social psychology.* Mahwah, NJ: Erlbaum.

Krupa, D. J., Thompson, J. K., & Thompson, R. E. (1993). Localization of a memory trace in the mammalian brain. *Science, 260,* 989–991.

Kuch, K., & Cox, B. J. (1992). Symptoms of PTSD in 124 survivors of the Holocaust. *American Journal of Psychiatry, 149,* 337–340.

Kuenzler, A., & Beutler, L. E. (2003). Couple alcohol treatment benefits patients' partners. *Journal of Clinical Psychology, 59,* 791–806.

Kuhl, P. K. (1993). Infant speech perception: A window on psycholinguistic development. *International Journal of Psycholinguistics, 9,* 33–56.

Kuhl, P. K. (2000). A new view of language acquisition. *Proceedings of the National Academy of Science, USA, 97,* 11850–11857.

Kulik, J. A., Bangert-Drowns, R. L., & Kulik, C. C. (1984). The effectiveness of coaching for aptitude tests. *Psychological Bulletin, 95,* 179–188.

Kulik, J. A., Kulik, C. C., & Bangert-Drowns, R. L. (1985). Effectiveness of computer-based education in elementary schools. *Computers in Human Behavior, 1,* 59–74.

Kumpfer, K. L., Alvarado, R., & Whiteside, H. O. (2003). Family-based interventions for substance use and misuse prevention. *Substance Use and Misuse, 38,* 1759–1787.

Kutchinsky, B. (1991). Pornography and rape: Theory and practice? Evidence from crime data in four countries where pornography is easily available. *International Journal of Law and Psychiatry, 14,* 47–64.

L

La Greca, A., Silverman, W. K., Vernberg, E. M., & Prinstein, M. J. (1996). Symptoms of posttraumatic stress in children after Hurricane Andrew: A prospective study. *Journal of Consulting and Clinical Psychology, 64,* 712–723.

LaBar, K. S., Gitelman, D. R., Parrish, T. B., & Mesulam, M. M. (2002). Functional changes in temporal lobe activity during transient global amnesia. *Neurology, 58,* 638–641.

LaBar, K. S., & LeDoux, J. E. (2002). Emotional learning circuits in animals and man. In R. J. Davidson, K. R. Scherer, & H. H. Goldsmith (Eds.), *Handbook of affective sciences.* New York: Oxford University Press.

Labbe, E. E. (1998). Biofeedback. In H. S. Friedman (Ed.), *Encyclopedia of mental health* (Vol. 1). San Diego: Academic Press.

Labott, S. M., & Martin, R. B. (1990). Emotional coping, age, and physical disorder. *Behavioral Medicine, 16,* 53–61.

Laboure, H., Van Wymelbeke, V., Fantino, M., & Nicolaidis, S. (2002). Behavioral, plasma, and calorimetric changes related to food texture modification in men. *American Journal of Physiology: Regulatory, Integrative, and Comparative Physiology, 282,* R1501–R1511.

Labouvie-Vief, G. (1986, August). *Modes of knowing and life-span cognition.* Paper presented at the meeting of the American Psychological Association, Washington, DC.

Lachman, M. E. (2004). Development in midlife. *Annual Review of Psychology, 54.* Palo Alto, CA: Annual Reviews.

Lam, L. T., & Kirby, S. L. (2002). Is emotional intelligence an advantage? An exploration of the impact of emotional and general intelligence on individual performance. *Journal of Social Psychology, 142,* 133–142.

Lamb, M. E., Hwang, C. P., Ketterlinus, R. D., & Fracasso, M. P. (1999). Parent-child relationships: Development in the context of the family. In M. H. Bornstein & M. E. Lamb (Eds.), *Developmental psychology: An advanced textbook* (4th ed.). Mahwah, NJ: Erlbaum.

Lambert, A. J., Chasteen, A., & Payne, B. K. (2004). Finding prejudice in all the wrong places. In G. V. Bodenhausen & A. J. Lambert (Eds.), *Foundations of social cognition.* Mahwah, NJ: Erlbaum.

Lambert, M. J. (2001). The effectiveness of psychotherapy: What a century of research tells us about the effects of treatment. *Psychotherapeutically speaking—Updates from the Division of Psychotherapy (29).* Washington, DC: American Psychological Association.

Lambert, M. J., & Ogles, B. M. (2002). The efficacy and effectiveness of psychotherapy. In M. J. Lambert (Ed.), *Handbook of psychotherapy and behavior change* (5th ed.). New York: Wiley.

Lammers, H. B. (2000). Effects of deceptive packaging and product involvement on purchase intention: An elaboration likelihood model perspective. *Psychological Reports, 86,* 546–550.

Landrine, H., & Klonoff, E. A. (2001). Cultural diversity and health psychology. In A. Baum, T. A. Revenson, & J. E. Singer (Eds.), *Handbook of health psychology.* Mahwah, NJ: Erlbaum.

Lane, H. (1976). *The wild boy of Aveyron.* Cambridge, MA: Harvard University Press.

Lang, F. R., & Carstensen, L. L. (1994). Close emotional relationships in late life: Further support for proactive aging in the social domain. *Psychology and Aging, 9,* 315–324.

Lang, P. J., Davis, M., & Ohman, A. (2000). Fear and anxiety: Animal models and human cognitive psychophysiology. *Journal of Affective Disorders, 61,* 137–159.

Lange, C. G. (1922). *The emotions.* Baltimore: Williams & Wilkins.

Langenfeld, M. C., Cipani, E., & Borckardt, J. J. (2002). Hypnosis for the control of HIV/AIDS-related pain. *International Journal of Clinical and Experimental Hypnosis, 50,* 170–188.

Langer, L. L. (1991). *Holocaust testimonies: The ruins of memory.* New Haven: Yale University Press.

Langston, W. (2002). *Research methods manual for psychology.* Belmont, CA: Wadsworth.

Lapsley, D. K., & Narvaez, D. (Eds.) (2004). *Moral development, self, and identity.* Mahwah, NJ: Erlbaum.

Larcerda, F., von Hofsten, C., & Heimann, M. (Eds.). (2000). *Emerging cognitive abilities in early infancy.* Mahwah, NJ: Erlbaum.

Larsen, R. J., & Buss, D. M. (2002). *Personality psychology: Domains of knowledge about human nature.* New York: McGraw-Hill.

Larson, R. (2000). Toward a psychology of positive youth development. *American Psychologist, 55,* 170–183.

Larson, R., & Wilson, S. (2004). Adolescence across time and time: Globalization and the changing pathways to adulthood. In R. Lerner & L. Steinberg (Eds.), *Handbook of adolescent psychology.* New York: Wiley.

Lashley, K. (1950). In search of the engram. In *Symposium of the Society for Experimental Biology* (Vol. 4). New York: Cambridge University Press.

Latané, B. (1981). The psychology of social impact. *American Psychologist, 36,* 343–356.

Latané, B. (1996). Strength from weakness: The fate of opinion minorities in spatially distributed groups. In E. H. Witte & J. H. Davis (Eds.), *Understanding group behavior* (Vol. 1). Mahwah, NJ: Erlbaum.

Laurent, G., Stopfer, M., Friedrich, W., Rabinovich, M. I., Volkovski, A., & Abarbanel, H. D. (2001). Odor encoding as an active, dynamical process. *Annual Review of Neuroscience* (Vol. 25). Palo Alto, CA: Annual Reviews.

Lazar, S. W, Bush, G., Gollub, R. L., Fricchione, G. L., Khalsa, G., & Benson, H. (2000). Functional brain mapping of the relaxation response and meditation. *Neuroreport, 15,* 1581–1585.

Lazarus, A. A. (1996). A multimodal behavior therapist's perspective on the truth. In G. Corey (Ed.), *Case approach to counseling and psychotherapy* (4th ed.). Pacific Grove, CA: Brooks/Cole.

Lazarus, A. A., Beutler, L. E., & Norcross, J. C. (1992). The future of technical eclecticism. *Psychotherapy, 29,* 11–20.

Lazarus, R. S. (1991). On the primacy of cognition. *American Psychologist, 39,* 124–129.

Lazarus, R. S. (1993). Coping theory and research: Past, present, and future. *Psychosomatic Medicine, 55,* 234–247.

Lazarus, R. S. (2000). Toward better research on stress and coping. *American Psychologist 55,* 665–673.

Leadbeater, B. J., & Way, N. (2001). *Growing up fast.* Mahwah, NJ: Erlbaum.

Leahy, T. H., & Harris, R. J. (2001). *Learning and memory* (5th ed.). Upper Saddle River, NJ: Prentice-Hall.

Leary, M. R., Nezlek, J. B., Downs, D., Radford-Davenport, J., Martin, J., & McMullen, A. (1994). Self-presentation in everyday interactions. *Journal of Personality and Social Psychology, 67,* 664–673.

Leavitt, F. (2000). *Evaluating scientific research.* Upper Saddle River, NJ: Prentice Hall.

LeBoeuf, B. J., & Peterson, R. S. (1969). Social status and mating activity in elephant seals. *Science, 163,* 91–93.

LeDoux, J. E. (1996). *The emotional brain: The mysterious underpinnings of emotional life.* New York: Simon & Schuster.

LeDoux, J. E. (2000). Emotion circuits in the brain. *Annual Review of Neuroscience, 23,* 155–184.

LeDoux, J. E. (2001). *Emotion, memory, and the brain.* Retrieved October 15, 2001, from http://www.cns.nyu.edu/home/ledoux.html

LeDoux, J. E. (2002). *The synaptic self.* New York: Viking.

Lee, D. J., & Markides, K. S. (1990). Activity and mortality among aged persons over an eight-year period. *Journals of Gerontology: Social Sciences, 45,* S39–S42.

Lee, G., & Farhat, N. H. (2001). The bifurcating neuron network. *Neural Networks, 14,* 115–131.

Lee, I., Hsieh, C., & Paffenbarger, O. (1995). Exercise intensity and longevity in men. *Journal of the American Medical Association, 273,* 1179–1184.

Lee, Y. S., Cheung, Y. M., & Wurm, L. H. (2000). Levels-of-processing effects on Chinese character completion: The importance of lexical processing and test cue. *Memory and Cognition, 28,* 1398–1405.

Leganger, A., & Kraft, P. (2003). Control constructs: Do they mediate the relation between education and health behavior? *Journal of Health Psychology, 8,* 361–372.

Lehar, S. M. (2002). *The world in your head.* Mahwah, NJ: Erlbaum.

Leichtman, M. (2004). Projective tests. In M. Hersen (Ed.), *Comprehensive handbook of psychological assessment* (Vol. 2). New York: Wiley.

Leiter, M. P., & Maslach, C. (2001). Burnout and health. In A. Baum, T. A. Revenson, & J. E. Singer (Eds.), *Handbook of health psychology.* Mahwah, NJ: Erlbaum.

Leith, L. M. (1998). Exercise and mental health. In H. S. Friedman (Ed.), *Encyclopedia of mental health* (Vol. 2). San Diego: Academic Press.

Lemke, G. E. (2001). Glial control of neuronal development. *Annual Review of Neuroscience, 24.*

Lenneberg, E. (1967). *The biological foundations of language.* New York: Wiley.

Lenneberg, E. H., Rebelsky, F. G., & Nichols, I. A. (1965). The vocalization of infants born to deaf and hearing parents. *Human Development, 8,* 23–37.

Lepper, M., Greene, D., & Nisbett, R. (1973). Undermining children's intrinsic interest with intrinsic rewards: A test of the overjustification hypothesis. *Journal of Personality and Social Psychology, 28,* 129–137.

Lerner, R. M. (2000). Developmental psychology: Theories. In A. Kazdin (Ed.), *Encyclopedia of psychology.* Washington, DC, & New York: American Psychological Association and Oxford University Press.

Lerner, R. M. (2002). *Concepts and theories of human development* (3rd ed.). Mahwah, NJ: Erlbaum.

Lessard, N., Pare, M., Lepore, F., & Lassonde, M. (1998). Early-blind human subjects localize sound sources better than sighted subjects. *Nature, 395,* 278–280.

Lester, D. (1992). Cooperative/competitive strategies and locus of control. *Psychological Reports, 71(2),* 594.

Leunes, A., & Nation, J. (2002). *Sport psychology* (3rd ed.). Belmont, CA: Wadsworth.

Levanen, S., & Hamdorf, D. (2001). Feeling vibrations: Enhanced tactile sensitivity in congenitally deaf humans. *Neuroscience Letters, 301,* 75–77.

Levanen, S., Jousmak, V., & Hari, R. (1998). Vibration-induced auditory-cortex activation in a congenitally deaf adult. *Current Biology, 8,* 869–872.

LeVay, S. (1991). A difference in the hypothalamic structure between heterosexual and homosexual men. *Science, 253,* 1034–1037.

LeVay, S. (1994). *The sexual brain.* Cambridge, MA: MIT Press.

Leventhal, H., & Tomarken, A. J. (1986). Emotion: Today's problems. *Annual Review of Psychology, 37,* 565–610.

Leventhal, T., & Brooks-Gunn, J. (2004). Diversity in developmental trajectories across adolescence. In R. Lerner & L. Steinberg (Eds.), *Handbook of adolescent psychology.* New York: Wiley.

Levin, J. S., & Vanderpool, H. Y. (1989). Is religion therapeutically significant for hypertension? *Social Science and Medicine, 29,* 69–78.

Levine, D. S. (2000). *Introduction to neural and cognitive modeling* (2nd ed.). Mahwah, NJ: Erlbaum.

Levine, J. D., Gordon, N. C., & Fields, H. L. (1979). Naloxone dose dependently produces analgesia and hyperalgesia in postoperative pain. *Nature, 278,* 740–741.

Levine, J. M. (2000). Groups: Group processes. In A. Kazdin (Ed.), *Encyclopedia of psychology.* Washington, DC, & New York: American Psychological Association and Oxford University Press.

Levine, R. L. (2002). Endocrine aspects of eating disorders in adolescents. *Adolescent Medicine, 13,* 129–144.

Levy, L. (1979). Handwriting and hiring. *Dun's Review, 113,* 72–79.

Levy, T. M. (Ed.). (1999). *Handbook of attachment interventions.* San Diego: Academic Press.

Lewinsohn, P. (1987). The Coping with Depression course. In R. F. Munoz (Ed.), *Depression prevention.* New York: Hemisphere.

Lewinsohn, P. M., Antonuccio, D. O., Steinmetz, J., & Teri, L. (1984). *The coping with depression course: A psychoeducational intervention for unipolar depression.* Eugene, OR: Castalia.

Lewinsohn, P. M., & Gotlib, I. H. (1995). Behavioral therapy and treatment of depression. In E. E. Beckham & W. R. Leber (Eds.), *Handbook of depression* (2nd ed., pp. 352–375). New York: Guilford.

Lewinsohn, P. M., Joiner, T. E., & Rohde, P. (2001). Evaluation of cognitive diathesis-stress models in predicting major depressive disorder in adolescence. *Journal of Abnormal Psychology, 110,* 203–215.

Lewinsohn, P. M., Striegel-Moore, R. H., & Seeley, J. R. (2000). Epidemiology and natural course of eating disorders in young women from adolescence to young adulthood. *Journal of American Academy of Child and Adolescent Psychiatry, 39,* 1284–1292.

Lewis, M. (1997). *Altering fate: Why the past does not predict the future.* New York: Guilford Press.

Lewis, M., & Vitulano, L. A. (2003). Biopsychosocial issues and risk factors in the family when the child has a chronic illness. *Child and Adolescent Psychiatric Clinics of North America, 12,* 389–399.

Lewis, R. (2001). *Life* (4th ed.). New York: McGraw-Hill.

Lewis, R. (2003). *Human genetics* (5th ed.). New York: McGraw-Hill.

Lewis, R., Gaffin, D., Hoefnagels, M., & Parker, B. (2004). *Life* (5th ed.). New York: McGraw-Hill.

Lewis, R., Hoefnageis, M., Gaffi, D., & Parker, B. (2002). *Life* (4th ed.). New York: McGraw-Hill.

Li, D., Chokka, P., & Tibbo, P. (2001). Toward an integrative understanding of social phobia. *Journal of Psychiatry and Neuroscience, 26,* 190–202.

Lieber, C. S. (1997). Gender differences in alcohol metabolism and susceptibility. In S. C. Wilsnack & R. W. Wilsnack (Eds.), *Gender and alcohol.* New Brunswick, NJ: Rutgers Center of Alcohol Studies.

Light, L. L. (2000). Memory changes in adulthood. In S. H. Qualls & N. Abeles (Eds.), *Psychology and the aging revolution.* Washington, DC, & New York: American Psychological Association and Oxford University Press.

Lilienfield, S. O., Wood, J. M., & Garb, H. N. (2000). The scientific status of projective techniques. *Psychological Science in the Public Interest, 1(2),* 27–66.

Lilienfield, S. O., Wood, J. M., & Garb, H. N. (2001). *What's wrong with this picture?* Scientific American, May, 80–87.

Lindeman, M. (1998). Motivation, cognition, and pseudoscience. *Scandinavian Journal of Psychology, 39,* 257–265.

Linden, W., Lenz, J. W., & Con, A. H. (2001). Individualized stress management for primary hypertension: A randomized trial. *Archives of Internal Medicine, 161,* 1071–1080.

Lindqvist, R., & Aberg, H. (2002). Locus of control in relation to smoking cessation during pregnancy. *Scandinavian Journal of Public Health, 30,* 30–35.

Lindvall, O. (2001). Parkinson disease: Stem cell transplantation. *Lancet, 358* [Supplement], S48.

Lips, H. M. (2003). *A new psychology of women: Gender, culture, and ethnicity* (2nd ed.). New York: McGraw-Hill.

Lipsey, M. W., & Wilson, D. B. (1993). The efficacy of psychological, educational, and behavioral treatment: Confirmation from meta-analysis. *American Psychologist, 48,* 1181–1209.

Lister, P. (1992, July). A skeptic's guide to psychics. *Redbook,* pp. 103–105, 112–113.

Livanou, M., Basoglu, M., Marks, I. M., De, S. P., Noshirvani, H., & Lovell, K. (2002). Beliefs, sense of control, and treatment outcome in post-traumatic stress disorder. *Psychological Medicine, 32,* 157–165.

Lively, W. J. (2001). *Handbook of personality disorders.* New York: Guilford.

Lochman, J. J. (2000). A perception-action perspective on tool use development. *Child Development, 71,* 137–144.

Locke, E. A. (2002). Setting goals for life and happiness. In C. R. Snyder & S. J. Lopez (Eds.), *Handbook of positive psychology.* New York: Oxford University Press.

Locke, J. L. (1993). *The child's path to spoken language.* Cambridge, MA: Harvard University Press.

Locke, J. L. (1999). Towards a biological science of language development. In M. Barrett (Ed.), *The development of language*. Philadelphia: Psychology Press.

Loddenkemper, T., Dinner, D. S., Prayson, R., Bingaman, W., Dagirmanjian, A., & Wyllie, E. (2004). Aphasia after hemispherectomy in an adult with early onset epilepsy and hemiplegia. *Journal of Neurology, Neurosurgery, and Psychiatry, 75*, 149–151.

Loden, S. (2003). The fate of the dream in contemporary psychoanalysis. *Journal of American Psychoanalytical Association, 51*, 43–70.

Loehr, J. (1989, May). Personal communication. United States Tennis Association Training Camp, Saddlebrook, FL.

Loftus, E., & Ketcham, K. (1994). *The myth of repressed memory: False memories and allegations of abuse*. New York: St. Martin's Press.

Loftus, E. F. (2002). Memory faults and fixes. *Issues in Science and Technology, 18*, 4, 41–50.

Loftus, E. F. (2003). Our changeable memories: Legal and practical implications. *Nature Reviews: Neuroscience, 4*, 231–234.

Loftus, E. F., & Pickrell, J. (2001, June). *Creating false memories*. Paper presented at the meeting of the American Psychological Society, Toronto.

Logie, R. H. (1995). *Visuospatial working memory*. Hove, England: Erlbaum.

Longo, D. A., Lent, R. W., & Brown, S. D. (1992). Social cognitive variables in the prediction of client motivation and attribution. *Journal of Counseling Psychology, 39*, 447–452.

Lopez, S. R., & Guarnaccia, P. J. (2000). Cultural psychopathology: Uncovering the social world of mental illness. *Annual Review of Psychology, 51*. Palo Alto, CA: Annual Reviews.

Lord, R. G., & Brown, D. J. (2003). *Leadership processes and follower self-identity*. Mahwah, NJ: Erlbaum.

Lorenz, K. Z. (1965). *Evolution and the modification of behavior*. Chicago: University of Chicago Press.

Lott, B., & Maluso, D. (2002). Gender development: Social learning. In J. Worell (Ed.), *Encyclopedia of women and gender*. New York: Oxford University Press.

Louie, T. A., Curren, M. T., & Harich, K. R. (2000). "I knew we would win": Hindsight bias for favorable and unfavorable team decision outcomes. *Journal of Applied Psychology, 85*, 264–272.

Lowe, B., Spitzer, R. L., Grafe, K., Kroenke, K., Quneter, A., Zipfel, S., Buchholtz, C., Witte, S., & Herzog, W. (2004). Comparative validity of three screening questionnaires for DSM-IV depressive disorders and physicians' diagnoses. *Journal of Affective Disorders, 78*, 131–140.

Lubart, T. I. (2003). In search of creative intelligence. In R. J. Sternberg, J. Lautrey, & T. I. Lubert (Eds.), *Models of intelligence: International perspectives*. Washington, DC: American Psychological Association.

Lubinski, D. (2000). Measures of intelligence: Intelligence tests. In A. Kazdin (Ed.), *Encyclopedia of psychology*. Washington, DC, & New York: American Psychological Association and Oxford University Press.

Lucurto, C. (1990). The malleability of IQ as judged from adoption studies. *Intelligence, 14*, 275–292.

Luria, A., & Herzog, E. (1985, April). *Gender segregation across and within settings*. Paper presented at the biennial meeting of the Society for Research in Child Development, Toronto.

Luria, A. R. (1968). *The mind of a mnemonist*. New York: Basic Books.

Luria, A. R. (1973). *The working brain*. New York: Penguin.

Lutkin, C. A., & Curry, A. D. (2003). Stressful neighborhoods and depression: a prospective study of the impact of neighborhood disorder. *Journal of Health and Social Behavior, 44*, 34–44.

Lutz, D. J., & Sternberg, R. J. (1999). Cognitive development. In M. H. Bornstein & M. E. Lamb (Eds.), *Developmental psychology: An advanced textbook* (4th ed.). Mahwah, NJ: Erlbaum.

Lyall, V., Alam, R. I., Phan, D. Q., Heck, G. L., & DeSimone, J. A. (2002). Excitation and adaptation in the detection of hydrogen ions by taste receptor cells: a role for cAMP and CA 2+. *Journal of Neurophysiology, 87*, 399–408.

Lynch, G. (1990, June). *The many shapes of memory and the several forms of synaptic plasticity*. Paper presented at the meeting of the American Psychological Society, Dallas.

Lynn, R. (1996). Racial and ethnic differences in intelligence in the U.S. on the Differential Ability Scale. *Personality and Individual Differences, 26*, 271–273.

M

Maas, J. (1998). *Power sleep*. New York: Villard.

Maccoby, E. E. (1998). *The two sexes: Growing up apart, coming together*. Cambridge, MA: Harvard University Press.

Maccoby, E. E. (2000). Parenting and its effects on children: Reading and misreading behavior genetics. *Annual Review of Psychology, 51*. Palo Alto, CA: Annual Reviews.

Maccoby, E. E. (2002). Gender and group processes. *Current Directions in Psychological Science, 11*, 54–58.

Maccoby, E. E., & Jacklin, C. N. (1974). *The psychology of sex differences*. Palo Alto, CA: Stanford University Press.

MacKenzie, R. (2002). Group psychotherapy. In M. Hersen & W. H. Sledge (Eds.), *Encyclopedia of psychotherapy*. San Diego: Academic Press.

MacKinnon, D., Jamison, K. R., & DePaulo, J. R. (1997). Genetics of manic depressive illness. *Annual Review of Neuroscience, 20*, 355–373.

MacKinnon, D. F., Zandi, P. P., Cooper, J., Potash, J. B., Simpson, S. G., & Gershon, E. (2002). Comorbid bipolar disorder and panic disorder in families with a high prevalence of bipolar disorder. *American Journal of Psychiatry, 159*, 30–35.

MacLeod, C., Rutherford, E., Campbell, L., Ebsworthy, G., & Holker, L. (2002). Selective attention and emotional vulnerability: Assessing the casual basis of their association through the experimental manipulation of attentional bias. *Journal of Abnormal Psychology, 111*, 107–123.

MacWhinney, B. (Ed.). (1999). *The emergence of language*. Mahwah, NJ: Erlbaum.

Madden, D. J. (2001). Speed and timing of behavioral processes. In J. E. Birren & K. W. Schaie (Eds.), *Handbook of the psychology of aging* (5th ed.). San Diego: Academic Press.

Maddi, S. (1996). *Personality theories* (6th ed.). Pacific Grove, CA: Brooks/Cole.

Maddi, S. (1998). Hardiness. In H. S. Friedman (Ed.), *Encyclopedia of mental health* (Vol. 3). San Diego: Academic Press.

Maddux, J. (2001). Self-efficacy. In C. R. Snyder & S. J. Lopez (Eds.), *Handbook of positive psychology*. New York: Oxford University Press.

Mader, S. S. (2002). *Human biology* (7th ed.). New York: McGraw-Hill.

Mader, S. S. (2003). *Inquiry into life* (10th ed.). New York: McGraw-Hill.

Mader, S. S. (2004). *Biology* (8th ed.) New York: McGraw-Hill.

Mager, R. F. (1972). *Goals analysis*. Belmont, CA: Fearon.

Mahendran, R. (2001). Characteristics of patients referred to an insomnia clinic. *Singapore Medical Journal, 42*, 64–70.

Maier, K. J., Waldstein, S. R., & Synowski, S. J. (2003). Relation of cognitive appraisal to cardio-vascular activity, affect, and task engagement. *Annals of Behavior Medicine, 26*, 32–41.

Majeres, R. L. (1999). Sex differences in phonological processes: Speeded matching and word reading. *Memory and Cognition, 27*, 246–253.

Malakoff, D. (2003). Polygraph testing: DOE says fewer workers will face the machine. *Science, 301*, 1456.

Malapani, C., Deweer, B., & Gibbon, J. (2002). Separating storage from retrieval dysfunction of temporal memory in Parkinson's disease. *Journal of Cognitive Neuroscience, 114*, 311–322.

Mandler, G. (1980). Recognizing: The judgment of previous occurrence. *Psychological Review, 87*, 252–271.

Mandler, J. M. (1998). Representation. In W. Damon (Ed.), *Handbook of child psychology* (5th ed., Vol. 2). New York: Wiley.

Mandler, J. M. (2003). Conceptual categorization. In D. Rakison & M. Oakes (Eds.), *Early category and concept development*. New York: Oxford University Press.

Manes, Sahakain, B., Clark, L., Rogers, R., Antoun, N., Aitken, M., & Robbins, T. (2002). Decision-making processes following damage to the frontal lobe. *Brain, 125 (Pt. 3)*, 624–639.

Mangels, J. A., Picton, T. W., & Craik, F. I. (2001). Attention and successful episodic encoding: An event-related potential study. *Brain Research, 11*, 77–95.

Manji, H. K. (2001). Strategies for gene and protein expression studies in neuropsychopharmacology and biological psychiatry. *International Journal of Neuropsycho-pharmacology, 4*, 45.

Manji, H. K., Dreverts, W. C., & Charney, D. S. (2001). The cellular neurobiology of depression. *Nature Medicine, 7*, 541–547.

Mann, J. J., & Arango, V. (1999). The neurobiology of suicidal behavior. In D. G. Jacobs (Ed.), *The Harvard Medical School guide to suicide assessment and intervention*. San Francisco: Jossey-Bass.

Mann, S. (2003). Coping and social support. In I. B. Weiner (Ed.), *Handbook of psychology*, Vol. IX. New York: Wiley.

Manson, S. M., Ackerson, L. M., Dick, R. W., & Baron, A. E. (1990). Depressive symptoms among American Indian adolescents: Psychometric characteristics of the Center for Epidemiologic Studies Depression Scale (CES-D). *Psychological Assessment, 2*, 231–237.

Mantere, T., Tupala, E., Hall, H., Sarkoja, T., Rasanen, P., Bergstrom, K., Callaway, J., & Tihonen, J. (2002). Serotonin transporter distribution and density in the cerebral cortex of alcoholic and nonalcoholic comparison subjects: A whole-hemisphere autoradiograph study. *American Journal of Psychiatry, 159*, 599–606.

Maratsos, M. (1999). Some aspects of innateness and complexity in grammar acquisition. In M. Barrett (Ed.), *The development of language*. Philadelphia: Psychology Press.

Marcia, J. E. (1980). Ego identity development. In J. Adelson (Ed.), *Handbook of adolescent psychology*. New York: Wiley.

Marcia, J. E. (2001). Unpublished review of J. W. Santrock's *Adolescence* (9th ed.). New York: McGraw-Hill.

Marcus, E. (2002). Psychoanalytic psychotherapy and psychoanalysis: An overview. In M. Hersen & W. H. Sledge (Eds.), *Encyclopedia of psychotherapy*. San Diego: Academic Press.

Marcus, G. F. (2001). *The algebraic mind*. Cambridge, MA: MIT Books.

Marder, S. R., Davis, J. M., & Chouinard, G. (1997). The effects of risperidone on the five dimensions of schizophrenia derived by factor analysis: Combined results of the North American trials. *Journal of Clinical Psychiatry, 58*, 538–546.

Maril, A., Wagner, A. D., & Schacter, D. L. (2001). On the tip of the tongue: An event-related fMRI study of semantic retrieval failure and cognitive conflict. *Neuron, 31,* 653–660.

Maris, R. W. (1998). Suicide. In H. S. Friedman (Ed.), *Encyclopedia of mental health* (Vol. 3). San Diego: Academic Press.

Markman, A., & Gentner, D. (2001). Learning and reasoning. *Annual Review of Psychology* (Vol. 51). Palo Alto, CA: Annual Reviews.

Markovitz, J. H., Jonas, B. S., & Davidson, K. (2001). Psychological factors as precursors to hypertension. *Current Hypertension Reports, 3,* 25–32.

Marks, D. F., Sykes, C. M., & McKinley, J. M. (2003). Health psychology: Overview and professional issues. In I. B. Weiner (Ed.), *Handbook of psychology,* Vol. IX. New York: Wiley.

Marks, I. M. (1987). *Fears, phobias, and rituals.* New York: Oxford University Press.

Marlow, A. (1999). *How to stop time: Heroin from A to Z.* New York: Basic Books.

Marr, D. (1982). *Vision.* New York: Freeman.

Marra, M., Polito, A., De Fillippo, E., Cuzzolar, M., Ciarapica, D., Contaldo, F., & Scalfi, L. (2002). Are the general equations to predict BMR applicable to patients with anorexia nervosa? *Eating and Weight Disorders, 7,* 53–59.

Marsella, A. J. (2000). Culture and mental health. In A. Kazdin (Ed.), *Encyclopedia of psychology.* Washington, DC, & New York: American Psychological Association and Oxford University Press.

Marsland, A. L., Bachen, E. A., Cohen, S., & Manuck, S. B. (2001). Stress, immunity, and susceptibility to infectious disease. In A. Baum, T. A. Revenson, & J. E. Singer (Eds.), *Handbook of health psychology.* Mahwah, NJ: Erlbaum.

Martin, C. L., & Dinella, L. (2001). Gender development: Gender schema theory. In J. Worell (Ed.), *Encyclopedia of women and gender.* New York: Oxford University Press.

Martin, D. W. (2004). *Doing psychology experiments* (6th ed.). Belmont, CA: Wadsworth.

Martin, G., & Pear, J. (2003). *Behavior modification* (7th Ed.). Upper Saddle River, NJ: Prentice-Hall.

Martin, W. E., & Swartz-Kulstad, J. L. (Eds.). (2000). *Person-environment psychology and mental health.* Mahwah, NJ: Erlbaum.

Martinez, F., Oltra, S., Berges, M., Orellana, C., Prieto, F., Martinez-Garay, I., & Molto, M. D. (2004). Screening for microdeletions of the X-chromosome in non-specific mental retardation. *American Journal of Medical Genetics, 124,* 99–101.

Martini, F. (2001). *Fundamentals of anatomy and physiology* (5th ed.). Upper Saddle River, NJ: Prentice-Hall.

Masland, R. H., & Raviola, E. (2000). Confronting complexity: Strategies for understanding the microcircuitry of the retina. *Annual Review of Neuroscience,* Vol. 23. Palo Alto, CA: Annual Reviews.

Maslow, A. H. (1954). *Motivation and personality.* New York: Harper & Row.

Maslow, A. H. (1971). *The farther reaches of human nature.* New York: Viking.

Massimini, F., & Delie Fave, A. (2000). Individual development in bio-cultural perspective. *American Psychologist, 55,* 24–33.

Masson, J. M. (1988). *Against therapy.* New York: Atheneum.

Masten, A. S. (2001). Ordinary magic: Resilience processes in development. *American Psychologist, 56,* 227–238.

Masten, A. S., & Coatsworth, J. D. (1998). The development of competence in favorable and unfavorable environments: Lessons from successful children. *American Psychologist, 53,* 205–220.

Masters, W. H., & Johnson, V. E. (1966). *Human sexual response.* Boston: Little, Brown.

Matlin, M. W. (2004). *Cognition* (6th ed.). Belmont, CA: Wadsworth.

Matsumoto, D. (2000). *Culture and social behavior.* Belmont, CA: Wadsworth.

Matsumoto, D. (Ed.). (2001). *The handbook of culture and psychology.* New York: Oxford University Press.

Matsumoto, D., & Juang, L. (2004). *Culture and psychology* (3rd ed.). Belmont, CA: Wadsworth.

Matthews, G., & Dreary, I. J. (1998). *Personality traits.* Cambridge, England: Cambridge University Press.

Matthews, K. A., Gump, B. B., Harris, K. F., Haney, T. L., & Barefoot, J. C. (2004). Hostile behaviors predict cardiovascular mortality among men enrolled in the multiple risk factor intervention trial. *Circulation, 109,* 66–70.

Mattson, M. P. (2002). Neurogenetics: White matter matters. *Trends in Neuroscience, 25,* 135–136.

Mattys, S. L., & Jusczyk, P. W. (2001). Phonotactic cues for segmentation of fluent speech by infants. *Cognition, 78,* 91–121.

Maultsby, M. C., & Wirga, M. (1998). Behavior therapy. In H. S. Friedman (Ed.), *Encyclopedia of mental health* (Vol. 1). San Diego: Academic Press.

May, P. A., & Gossage, J. P. (2001). Estimating the prevalence of fetal alcohol syndrome: A summary. *Alcohol Research and Health, 25,* 159–167.

Mayer, E. L. (2002). Freud and Jung: the boundaried mind and the radically connected mind. *Journal of Analytical Psychology, 47,* 91–99.

Mayer, J. D., Salovey, P., & Caruso, D. R. (2002). *Mayer-Salovey-Caruso Emotional Intelligence Test (MSCEIT): User's Manual.* Toronto, Canada: Multi-Health Systems.

Mayer, R. (2000). Problem solving. In M. A. Runco & S. Pritzker (Eds.), *Encyclopedia of psychology.* San Diego: Academic Press.

McAllister, M. M. (2000). Dissociative identity disorder: A literature review. *Journal of Psychiatric and Mental Health Nursing, 7,* 25–33.

McAnulty, R. D., & Burnette, M. M. (2004). *Exploring human sexuality* (2nd ed.). Boston: Allyn & Bacon.

McBurney, D. H., & White, T. L. (2004). *Research methods.* Belmont, CA: Wadsworth.

McClelland, D. C. (1955). Some social consequences of achievement motivation. In M. R. Jones (Ed.), *Nebraska Symposium of Motivation.* Lincoln: University of Nebraska Press.

McClelland, D. C. (1978). Managing motivation to expand human freedom. *American Psychologist, 33,* 201–210.

McClelland, D. C., Atkinson, J. W., Clark, R., & Lowell, E. L. (1953). *The achievement motive.* New York: Appleton-Century-Crofts.

McClelland, J. L., & Rumelhart, D. E. (1986). *Parallel distributed processing: Explorations in the microstructure of cognition. Vol. 2: Psychological and biological models.* Cambridge, MA: MIT Press.

McConaghy, N. (1993). *Sexual behavior: Problems and management.* New York: Plenum Press.

McCrae, R. R., & Costa, P. T. (2001). A five-factor theory of personality. In L. A. Pervin & O. P. John (Eds.), *Handbook of personality.* New York: Guilford Press.

McCullough, M. E., Hoyt, W. T., Larson, D. B., Koenig, H. G., & Thoresen, C. (2000). Religious involvement and mortality: A meta-analytic review. *Health Psychology, 19,* 211–222.

McDade, T., Kuzawa, C., Adair, L., & Beck, M. (2004). Prenatal and early postnatal environments are significant predictors of total immunoglobulin E concentration in Filipino adolescents. *Clinical and Experimental Allegery, 34,* 44–50.

McDaniel, M. A., & Einstein, G. O. (2000). Strategic and automatic processes in memory retrieval: A multiprocess framework. *Applied Cognitive Psychology, 14,* S127–S144.

McDowell, M. J. (2001). Principle of organization: A dynamic-systems view of the archetype-as-such. *Journal of Analytical Psychology, 46,* 637–654.

McFarlane, T., Polivy, J., & Herman, C. P. (1998). Dieting. In H. S. Friedman (Ed.), *Encyclopedia of mental health* (Vol. 1). San Diego: Academic Press.

McGaugh, J. L. (2004). Function of learning and memory in the amygdala. *Annual Review of Neuroscience, 27.* Palo Alto, CA: Annual Reviews.

McGaugh, J. L., & Cahill, L. (2002). Emotion and memory. In R. J. Davidson, K. R. Scherer, & H. H. Goldsmith (Eds.), *Handbook of affective sciences.* New York: Oxford University Press.

McGrath, E., Strickland, B. R., Keita, G. P., & Russo, N. F. (Eds.). (1990). *Women and depression: Risk factors and treatment issues.* Washington, DC: American Psychological Association.

McGue, M., Bouchard, T. J., Iacono, W. G., & Lykken, D. T. (1993). Behavioral genetics of cognitive ability: A life-span perspective. In R. Plomin & G. E. McClearn (Eds.), *Nature, nurture, and psychology.* Washington, DC: American Psychological Association.

McGuire, P. A. (1999, May). Worker stress, health reaching critical point. *APA Monitor, 30,* 26–27.

McGuire, W. J. (2004). The morphing of attitude-change into social-cognition. In G. V. Bodenhausen & A. J. Lambert (Eds.), *Foundations of social cognition.* Mahwah, NJ: Erlbaum.

McIntosh, A. R. (2000). Towards a network theory of cognition. *Neural Networks, 13,* 861–870.

McIntyre, C. K., Pal, S. N., Marriott, L. K., & Gold, P. E. (2002). Competition between memory systems: acetylcholine release in the hippocampus correlates negatively with good performance on an amygdala-dependent task. *Journal of Neuroscience, 22,* 1171–1176.

McIver, T. (1988). Backward masking and other backward thoughts about music. *Skeptical Inquirer, 13,* 50–63.

McKay, D., & Tryon, W. W. (2002). Behavior therapy: Theoretical bases. In M. Hersen & W. H. Sledge (Eds.), *Encyclopedia of psychotherapy.* San Diego: Academic Press.

McKelvie, S. J., & Drumheller, A. (2001). The availability heuristic with famous names: A replication. *Perceptual and Motor Skills, 92,* 507–516.

McKendree-Smith, N., & Scogin, F. (2000). Depressive realism: Effects of depression severity and interpretation time. *Journal of Clinical Psychology, 56,* 1601–1608.

McKenna, M. C, Zevon, M. A., Corn, B., & Rounds, J. (1999). Psychosocial factors and the development of breast cancer: A meta-analysis. *Health Psychology, 18,* 520–531.

McKinlay, J. B. (1999, March). *Erectile dysfunction: The most overlooked biobehavioral marker of disease.* Paper presented at the meeting of the American Psychosomatic Association, Vancouver.

McKinlay, S.M., & McKinlay, J. B. (1984). *Health status and health care utilization by menopausal women.* Unpublished manuscript, Cambridge Research Center, American Institutes for Research, Cambridge, MA.

McLean, P. D., & Wood, S. R. (2001). *Anxiety disorders in adults.* New York: Oxford University Press.

McLoyd, V. C. (1999). Cultural influences in a multicultural society: Conceptual and methodological issues. In A. S. Masten (Ed.), *Cultural processes in child development.* Mahwah, NJ: Erlbaum.

McLoyd, V. C. (2000). Poverty. In A. Kazdin (Ed.), *Encyclopedia of psychology.* Washington, DC, & New York: American Psychological Association and Oxford University Press.

McLoyd, V. C., & Smith, J. (2002). Physical discipline and behavior problems in African American, European American, and Hispanic children:

Emotional support as a moderator. *Journal of Marriage and Family, 64,* 40–53.

McMillan, J. H. (2000). *Educational research* (3rd ed.). Upper Saddle River, NJ: Merrill.

McMillan, J. H. (2001). *Classroom assessment* (2nd ed.). Boston: Allyn & Bacon.

McMillan, J. H., & Wergin, J. F. (2002). *Understanding and evaluating educational research* (2nd ed.). Upper Saddle River, NJ: Prentice-Hall.

McNally, R. (1994). *Panic disorder: A critical analysis.* New York: Guilford.

McNulty, R. D., & Burnette, M. M. (2004). *Exploring human sexuality* (2nd ed.). Boston: Allyn & Bacon.

Meador, B. D., & Rogers, C. R. (1979). Person-centered therapy. In R. J. Corsini, *Current psychotherapies* (2nd ed.). Itasca, IL: Peacock.

Meador, K. J. (2002). Cognitive outcomes and predictive factors in epilepsy. *Neurology, 58,* S21–S26.

Mechler, F., & Ringach, D. L. (2002). On the classification of simple and complex cells. *Vision Research, 42,* 1017–1033.

Medin, D., Ross, R., & Markham, A. (2001). *Cognitive psychology* (3rd ed.). Fort Worth, TX: Harcourt.

Medin, D. L., Coley, J. D., Storms, G., & Hayes, B. (2003). A relevance theory for induction. *Psychonomic Bulletin Review, 10,* 517–532.

Medin, D. L., Proffitt, J. B., & Schwartz, H. C. (2000). Concepts: Structure. In A. Kazdin (Ed.), *Encyclopedia of psychology.* Washington, DC, & New York: American Psychological Association and Oxford University Press.

Meehl, P. E. (1962). Schizotonia, schizotypy, schizophrenia. *American Psychologist, 17,* 827–838.

Meehl, P. E. (1986). Diagnostic taxa as open concepts. In T. Millon & G. I. Klerman (Eds.), *Contemporary directions in psychopathology.* New York: Guilford.

Meichenbaum, D. (1977). *Cognitive-behavior modification: An integrative approach.* New York: Plenum Press.

Meichenbaum, D., Turk, D., & Burstein, S. (1975). The nature of coping with stress. In I. Sarason & C. Spielberger (Eds.), *Stress and anxiety.* Washington, DC: Hemisphere.

Melinder, K. A., & Andersson, R. (2001). The impact of structural factors on the injury rate in different European countries. *European Journal of Public Health, 11,* 301–308.

Melis, M., Camarin, R., Ungless, M. A., & Bonci, A. (2002). Long-lasting potentiation of GABAergic synapses in dopamine neurons after a single in vivo ethanol exposure. *Journal of Neuroscience, 22,* 2074–2982.

Meller, R., Harrison, P. J., Elliott, J. M., & Sharp, T. (2002). In vitro evidence that 5-hydroxytryptamine increases efflux of glial glutamate via 5-HT2a receptor activation. *Journal of Neuroscience Research, 67,* 399–405.

Melzack, R. (1973). *The puzzle of pain.* New York: Basic Books.

Memmler, R. L., Cohen, B. J., Wood, D. L., & Schwegler, J. (1995). *The human body in health and disease* (8th ed.). Philadelphia: Lippincott Williams & Wilkins.

Mendez, M. F., Chow, T., Ringman, J., Twitchell, G., & Hinkin, C. H. (2000). Pedophilia and temporal lobe disturbances. *Journal of Neuropsychiatry and Clinical Neurosciences, 12,* 71–76.

Merenda, P. F. Cross-cultural adaptation of educational and psychological testing. In R. K. Hambleton, P. F. Merenda, & C. D. Spielberger (Eds.), *Adapting educational tests for cross-cultural assessment.* Mahwah, NJ: Erlbaum.

Mervis, C. B. (2003). Williams syndrome: 15 years of psychological research. *Developmental Neuropsychology, 23,* 1–12.

Mesquita, B. (2002). Emotions as dynamic cultural phenomena. In R. J. Davidson, K. R. Scherer, & H. H. Goldsmith (Eds.), *Handbook of affective sciences.* New York: Oxford University Press.

Messer, W. S., & Griggs, R. A. (1989). Student belief and involvement in the paranormal and performance in introductory psychology. *Teaching of Psychology, 16,* 187–191.

Messinger, J. C. (1971). Sex and repression in an Irish folk community. In D. S. Marshall & R. C. Suggs (Eds.), *Human sexual behavior.* New York: Basic Books.

Metcalfe, J., & Mischel, W. (1999). A hot/cool system analysis of delay of gratification: Dynamics of will power. *Psychological Review, 106,* 3–19.

Metts, S. (2004). First sexual involvement in romantic relationships. In J. H. Harvey, A. Wentzel, & S. Sprecher (Eds.), *The handbook of sexuality in close relationships.* Mahwah, NJ: Erlbaum.

Metzel, J. M., & Angel, J. (2004). Assessing the impact of SSRI antidepressants on popular notions of women's depressive illness. *Social Science & Medicine, 58,* 577–584.

Meyer, G. J. (2001). Introduction to the special section in the special series on the utility of the Rorschach for clinical assessment. *Psychological Assessment, 13,* 419–422.

Meyer, R. G., & Osborne, Y. V. H. (1982). *Case studies in abnormal behavior.* Boston: Allyn & Bacon.

Meyer, R. G., Wolverton, D., & Deitsch, S. E. (1998). Antisocial personality disorder. In H. S. Friedman (Ed.), *Encyclopedia of mental health* (Vol. 2). San Diego: Academic Press.

Michael, R. T., Gagnon, J. H., Laumann, E. O., & Kolata, G. (1994). *Sex in America.* Boston: Little, Brown.

Michael, W. (1999). Guilford's view. In M. A. Runco & S. Pritzker (Eds.), *Encyclopedia of creativity.* San Diego: Academic Press.

Michinov, E., & Michinov, N. (2001). The similarity hypothesis: A test of the moderating role of social comparison orientation. *European Journal of Social Psychology, 31,* 549–556.

Middleton, F. A., & Strick, P. L. (2001). Cerebellar projections to the prefrontal cortex of the primate. *Journal of Neuroscience, 21,* 700–712.

Mignot, E. (2001). A hundred years of narcolepsy research. *Archives of Italian Biology, 139,* 207–220.

Mignot, E., & Thorsby, E. (2001). Narcolepsy and the HLA system. *New England Journal of Medicine, 344*(9), 692.

Miklowitz, D. J. (2002). *The bipolar disorder survival guide.* New York: Guilford.

Milgram, P., Vigehesa, H., & Weinstein, P. (1992). Adolescent dental fear and control. *Behavior Research and Therapy, 30,* 367–373.

Milgram, S. (1965). Some conditions of obedience and disobedience to authority. *Human Relations, 18,* 56–76.

Milgram, S. (1974). *Obedience to authority.* New York: Harper & Row.

Milgram, S., Liberty, H. J., Toledo, R., & Wackenhut, J. (1986). Response to intrusion in waiting lines. *Journal of Personality and Social Psychology, 51,* 683–689.

Miller, E. K., & Cohen, J. D. (2001). An integrative theory of prefrontal cortex function. *Annual Review of Neuroscience, 24.*

Miller, G. A. (1956). The magical number seven, plus or minus two: Some limits on our capacity for information processing. *Psychological Review, 48,* 337–442.

Miller, N. E. (1941). The frustration-aggression hypothesis. *Psychological Review, 48,* 337–442.

Miller, N. E. (1959). Liberalization of basic S-R concepts: Extension to conflict behavior, motivation, and social learning. In S. Koch (Ed.), *Psychology: A study of science.* New York: McGraw-Hill.

Miller, N. E. (1985). The value of behavioral research on animals. *American Psychologist, 40,* 432–440.

Miller, P. J. (2001, April). *Self-esteem as folk theory: A comparison of ethnographic interviews.* Paper presented at the meeting of the Society for Research in Child Development, Minneapolis.

Miller, R. R., & Grace, R. C. (2003). Conditioning and learning. In I. B. Weiner (Ed.), *Handbook of Psychology* (Vol. 4). New York: Wiley.

Miller-Jones, D. (1989). Culture and testing. *American Psychologist, 44,* 360–366.

Millis, R. M. (1998). Smoking. In H. S. Friedman (Ed.), *Encyclopedia of mental health* (Vol. 3). San Diego: Academic Press.

Milner, A. D., & Goodale, M. A. (1995). *The visual brain in action.* New York: Oxford University Press.

Miltenberger, R. G. (2001). *Behavior modification* (2nd ed.). Belmont, CA: Wadsworth.

Miltenberger, R. G. (2004). *Behavior modification.* (3rd ed.). Belmont, CA: Wadsworth.

Mineka, S., & Nugent, K. (1995). Mood-congruent memory biases in anxiety and depression. In D. L. Schacter, J. T. Coyle, G. D. Fischbach, M. M. Mesulam, & L. E. Sullivan (Eds.), *Memory distortion: How minds, brains, and societies reconstruct the past.* Cambridge, MA: Harvard University Press.

Mingolla, E. (2002). Neural models of motion integration and segmentation. *Neural Networks, 16,* 939–945.

Mingroni, M. A. (2004). The secular rise in IQ. *Intelligence, 32,* 65–83.

Mirksy, A. F., Bieliauskas, L. M., Van Kammen, D. P., Jonsson, E., & Sedvall, G. (2000). A 39-year followup of the Genain quadruplets. *Schizophrenia Bulletin, 3,* 5–18.

Mischel, W. (1968). *Personality and assessment.* New York: Wiley.

Mischel, W. (1973). Toward a cognitive social learning theory reformulation of personality. *Psychological Review, 80,* 252–283.

Mischel, W. (1995, August). *Cognitive-affective theory of person-environment psychology.* Paper presented at the meeting of the American Psychological Association, New York City.

Mischel, W. (2004). Toward an integrative science of the person. *Annual Review of Psychology,* Vol. 55. Palo Alto, CA: Annual Reviews.

Mischel, W., Cantor, N., & Feldman, S. (1996). Principles of self-regulation: The nature of will power and self-control. In E. T. Higgins & A. W. Kruglanski (Eds.), *Social psychology: Handbook of basic principles.* New York: Guilford Press.

Mischel, W., & Moore, B. S. (1980). The role of ideation in voluntary delay for symbolically presented rewards. *Cognitive Therapy and Research, 4,* 211–221.

Mischel, W., & Shoada, Y. (2001). Integrating dispositions and processing dynamics within a unified theory of personality: The cognitive affective personality system. In L. A. Pervin & O. P. John (Eds.), *Handbook of personality.* New York: Guilford Press.

Mischel, W., Shoada, Y., & Mendoza-Denton, R. (2002). Situation-behavior profiles as a locus of consistency in personality. *Current Directions in Psychological Science, 11,* 50–53.

Misra, A., Arora, N., Mondal, S., Pandey, R. M., Jailkhani, B., Peshin, S., Chaudhary, D., Saluja, T., Singh, P., Chandra, S., Luithra, K., & Vikram, N. K. (2001). Relation between plasma leptin and anthropometric and metabolic covariates in lean and obese diabetic and hyperlipidaemic Asian Northern Indian subjects. *Diabetes, Nutrition, and Metabolism, 14,* 18–26.

Mitisis, E. M., Halperin, J. M., & Newcorn, J. H. (2000). Serotonin and aggression in children. *Current Psychiatry Reports, 2,* 95–101.

Mito, N. J., Yoshino, H., Hosoda, T., & Sato, K. (2004). Analysis of the effect of leptin on immune function in vivo using diet-induced obese mice. *Journal of Endocrinology, 180,* 167–173.

Mittag, W., & Schwarzer, R. (1993). Interaction of employment status and self-efficacy on alcohol consumption: A two-wave study on stressful life transitions. *Psychology and Health, 8,* 77–87.

Miyake, A. (2001, September). Commentary on Carpenter, S., "A new reason for keeping a diary." *Monitor on Psychology, 32,* 68–70.

Mizes, J. S., & Miller, K. J. (2000). Eating disorders. In M. Herson & R. T. Ammerman (Eds.), *Advanced abnormal child psychology* (2nd ed.). Mahwah, NJ: Erlbaum.

Moffitt, T. E., Brammer, G. L., Caspi, A., Fawcet, J. P., Raleigh, M., Yuwiler, A., & Silva, P. A. (1998). Whole blood serotonin relates to violence in an epidemiological study. *Biological Psychiatry, 43,* 446–457.

Monahan, J. L., Murphy, S. T., & Zajonc, R. B. (2000). Subliminal mere exposure: Specific, general, and diffuse effects. *Psychological Science, 11,* 462–466.

Money, J. (1986). *Lovemaps: Clinical concepts of sexual/erotic health and pathology, paraphilia, and gender transposition in childhood, adolescence, and maturity.* New York: Irvington.

Monk, T. H. (1993). Shiftwork. In M. A. Carskadon (Ed.), *Encyclopedia of sleep and dreaming.* New York: Macmillan.

Monsell, S., & Driver, J. (Eds.). (2000). *Control of cognitive processes.* Cambridge, MA: MIT Press.

Montagnese, C. M., Szekely, A. D., Adam, A., & Csillag, A. (2004). Efferent connections of septal nuclei of the domestic chick. *Journal of Comparative Neurology, 469,* 437–456.

Monteith, M. J. (2000). Prejudice. In A. Kazdin (Ed.), *Encyclopedia of psychology.* Washington, DC, & New York: American Psychological Association and Oxford University Press.

Monteith, M. J., & Voils, C. I. (2001). Exerting control over prejudiced responses. In G. B. Moscowitz (Ed.), *Cognitive social psychology.* Mahwah, NJ: Erlbaum.

Moore, D. (2001). *The dependent gene.* New York: W. H. Freeman.

Moore, D. S. (2001). *Statistics* (5th ed.). New York: Worth.

Moore, T. E. (1995). Subliminal self-help auditory tapes: An empirical test of perceptual consequences. *Canadian Journal of Behavioural Science, 27,* 9–20.

Moore-Ede, M. C., Sulzman, F. M., & Fuller, C. A. (1982). *The clocks that time us.* Cambridge, MA: Harvard University Press.

Moretti, R. J., & Rossini, E. D. (2004). Thematic Apperception Technique (TAT). In M. Hersen (Ed.), *Comprehensive handbook of psychological assessment* (Vol. 2). New York: Wiley.

Morgan, D. L. (2002). *Essentials of learning and cognition.* New York: McGraw-Hill.

Morgan, T., & Cummings, A. L. (1999). Change experienced during group therapy of female survivors of childhood sexual abuse. *Journal of Consulting and Clinical Psychology, 67,* 28–36.

Moscovici, S. (1985). Social influence and conformity. In G. Lindzey & E. Aronson (Eds.), *Handbook of social psychology* (3rd ed., Vol. 2). New York: Random House.

Moses, J., Steptoe, A., Mathews, A., & Edwards, S. (1989). The effects of exercise training on mental well-being in a normal population: A controlled trial. *Journal of Psychosomatic Research, 33,* 47–61.

Moskowitz, G. B. (Ed.). (2001). *Cognitive social psychology.* Mahwah, NJ: Erlbaum.

Muchinsky, P. M. (2003). *Psychology applied to work* (7th ed.). Belmont, CA: Wadsworth.

Muhonen, T., & Torkelson, E. (2003). The demand-control-support model and health among women and men in similar occupations. *Journal of Behavioral Medicine, 26,* 601–613.

Muise, A. M., Stein, D. G., & Arbess, G. (2003). Eating disorders in adolescent boys. *Journal of Adolescent Health, 33,* 427–435.

Mulvihill, C. B., Davies, G. J., & Rogers, P. J. (2002). Dietary restraint in relation to nutrient intake, physical activity, and iron status in adolescent females. *Journal of Human Nutrition-Dietetics, 15,* 19–31.

Munoz, R. F. (1998). Depression—applied aspects. In H. S. Friedman (Ed.), *Encyclopedia of mental health* (Vol. 1). San Diego: Academic Press.

Murdock, B. B. (1999). The buffer 30 years later: Working memory in a theory of distributed associative model (TODAM). In C. Izawa (Ed.), *On human memory.* Mahwah, NJ: Erlbaum.

Murphy, R. A., Baker, A. G., & Fouquet, N. (2001). Relative validity effects with either one or two more valid cues in Pavlovian and instrumental conditioning. *Journal of Experimental Psychology: Animal Processes, 27,* 59–67.

Murphy, S., & Bennett, P. (2004). Health psychology and public health: Theoretical possibilities. *Journal of Health Psychology, 9,* 13–27.

Myers, A. (2003). *Experimental psychology* (5th ed.). Belmont, CA: Wadsworth.

Myers, A., & Hansen, C. (2002). *Experimental psychology* (5th ed.). Belmont, CA: Wadsworth.

Myers, D. G. (2000). *The American paradox.* New Haven, CT: Yale University Press.

Myerson, J., Rank, M. R., Raines, F. Q., & Schnitzler, M. A. (1998). Race and general cognitive ability: The myth of diminishing returns in education. *Psychological Science, 9,* 139–142.

N

Naidu, P. S., Singh, A., & Kulkarni, S. K. (2004). Reversal of reserpine-induced orofacial dyskinesia and cognitive dysfunction by quercetin. *Pharmacology, 70,* 59–67.

Nairn, R. C., & Merluzzi, T. V. (2003). The role of religious coping in adjustment to cancer. *Psycho-Oncology, 12,* 428–441.

Nakamura, J., & Csikszentmihalyi, M. (2002). The concept of flow. In C. R. Snyder & S. J. Lopez (Eds.), *Handbook of positive psychology.* New York: Oxford University Press.

Nakao, M., Fricchione, G., Myers, P., Zuttermeister, P. C., Barksky, A. J., & Benson, H. (2001). Depression and education as predicting factors for completion of a behavioral medicine intervention in a mind/body medicine clinic. *Behavioral Medicine, 26,* 177–184.

Nardi, A. E., Valenca, A. M., Nascimento, I., Mezzalama, M. A., & Zin, W. A. (2001). Hyperventilation in panic disorder and social phobia. *Psychopathology, 34,* 123–127.

Nardi, P. M. (2003). *Doing survey research.* Boston: Allyn & Bacon.

Nash, J. M. (1997, February 3). Fertile minds. *Time,* pp. 50–54.

Nash, M. R. (2001). The truth and the hype about hypnosis. *Scientific American, 285,* 46–49, 52–55.

Nash, M. R., & Nadon, R. (1997). The scientific status of research on hypnosis. In D. L. Faigman, D. H. Kaye, M. K. Saks, & J. Sanders (Eds.), *The West companion of scientific evidence.* St. Paul, MN: West Publishing.

Naslund, E., Hellstrom, P. M., & Krail, J. G. (2001). The gut and food intake: An update for surgeons. *Journal of Gastrointestinal Surgeons, 5,* 556–567.

Nathan, P. E. (1994). DSM-IV. *Journal of Clinical Psychology, 50,* 103–109.

Nathan, P. E., & Gorman, J. M. (Eds.). (2002). *A guide to treatments that work* (2nd Ed.). New York: Oxford University Press.

Nathan, P., E. & Langenbucher, J. (2003). Diagnosis and classification. In I. B. Weiner (Ed.), *Handbook of psychology* (Vol. 8). New York: Wiley.

Nathan, P. E., & Langenbucher, J. W. (1999). Psychopathology: Description and classification. *Annual Reviews of Psychology.* Palo Alto: Annual Reviews.

Nathan, P. E., Stuart, S. P., & Dolan, S. L. (2000). Research on psychotherapy efficacy and effectiveness: Between Scylla and Charybdis? *Psychological Bulletin, 126,* 964–981.

National Advisory Council on Economic Opportunity. (1980). *Critical choices for the 80s.* Washington, DC: U.S. Government Printing Office.

National Assessment of Educational Progress. (1997). *NAEP 1996 mathematics report card for the nation and the states.* Washington, DC: National Center for Education Statistics.

National Assessment of Educational Progress. (2001). *Reading gap widens between high- and low-performing fourth-grade students.* Washington, DC: National Center for Health Statistics.

National Center for Children Exposed to Violence. (2001). *Statistics.* New Haven, CT: Author.

National Center for Health Statistics. (1989, June). *Statistics on marriage and divorce.* Washington, DC: U.S. Government Printing Office.

National Center for Health Statistics. (1994). *Advance report of final mortality statistics, 1991. Monthly Vital Statistics Report, 42.*

National Center for Health Statistics. (2000a). *Births, deaths, marriages, and divorces.* Atlanta: Centers for Disease Control and Prevention.

National Center for Health Statistics. (2000b). *Prevalence of overweight among children and adolescents.* Hyattsville, MD: U.S. Department of Health and Human Services.

National Center for Health Statistics. (2000c). *Smoking.* Atlanta: Centers for Disease Control and Prevention.

National Center for Health Statistics. (2001a). *AIDS.* Atlanta: Centers for Disease Control and Prevention.

National Center for Health Statistics. (2001b). *Key health measures tracked in national survey.* Atlanta: Centers for Disease Control and Prevention.

National Center for Health Statistics. (2002). *Americas families and living arrangements.* Atlanta: Centers for Disease Control and Prevention.

National Center for PTSD. (2001). *What is post-traumatic stress disorder?* Washington, DC: Author.

National Commission on Sleep Disorders Research. (1993, January). *Report of the National Commission on Sleep Disorders Research.* Report submitted to the United States Congress and to the Secretary of the U.S. Department of Health and Human Services.

National Institute for Occupational Safety and Health. (2001). *Job stress in American workers.* Washington, DC: Centers for Disease Control and Prevention.

National Institute of Mental Health. (2000). *Suicide facts.* Washington, DC: Author. Retrieved January 26, 2000 from the World Wide Web: http://www.nimh.nih.gov/genpop/su_fact.htm

National Institute of Mental Health. (2001a). *Mental disorders in America.* Bethesda, MD: Author.

National Institute of Mental Health. (2001b). *The numbers count.* Bethesda, MD: Author.

National Institute of Mental Health. (2001c). *Post-traumatic stress disorder.* Washington, DC: Author.

National Institute of Neurological Disorders and Stroke. (2001). *Brain basics: Understanding*

sleep. Washington, DC: National Institutes of Health.

National Institute on Drug Abuse. (2001). *Common drugs of abuse.* Washington, DC: National Institutes of Health.

National Sleep Foundation. (2001). *2001 Sleep in America Poll.* Washington, DC: National Sleep Foundation.

Nehra, A., Blute, M. L., Barrent, D. M., & Moreland, R. B. (2002). Rationale for combination therapy of intraurethal prostaglandin E(1) and sildenafil in the salvage of erectile dysfunction patients during noninvasive therapy. *International Journal of Impotency Research, 14* (Suppl. 1), S38–S42.

Neisser, U., Boodoo, G., Bouchard, T. J., Boykin, A. W., Brody, N., Ceci, S. J., Halpern, D. F., Loehlin, J. C., Perloff, R., Sternberg, R. J., & Urbina, S. (1996). Intelligence: Knowns & unknowns. *American Psychologist, 51,* 77–101.

Neisser, U., & Hyman, I. E. (2000). *Memory observed* (2nd ed.). New York: Worth.

Nell, V. (2004). Translation and test administration techniques to meet the assessment needs of ethnic minorities, immigrants, and refugees. In M. Hersen (Ed.), *Comprehensive handbook of psychological assessment* (Vol. 1). New York: Wiley.

Nelson, C. (2003, April). *Gray matters: A neuroconstructivist approach to cognitive development.* Paper presented at the meeting of the Society for Research in Child Development, Tampa.

Nelson, D. L., Quick, J. C., & Simmons, B. L. (2001). Preventive management of work stress: Current themes and future challenges. In A. Baum, T.A. Revenson, & J.E. Singer (Eds.), *Handbook of health Psychology.* Mahwah, NJ: Erlbaum.

Nelson, M. E., Fiatarone, M. A., Moranti, C. M., Trice, I., Greenberg, R. A., & Evans, W. J. (1994). Effects of high-intensity strength training on multiple risk factors for osteoporotic fractures: A randomized controlled trial. *Journal of the American Medical Association, 272,* 1909–1914.

Nelson, T. D. (2002). *Psychology of prejudice.* Boston: Allyn & Bacon.

Nemeroff, C. B., & Schatzberg, A. F. (2002). Pharmacological treatments for unipolar depression. In P. Nathan & J. M. Gorman (Eds.), *A guide to treatments that work (2nd Ed.).* New York: Oxford University Press.

Nettelbeck, T., & Wilson, C. (2004). The Flynn effect: smarter, not faster. *Intelligence, 32,* 85–93.

Neverlien, P. O., & Johnsen, T. B. (1991). Optimism-pessimism dimension and dental anxiety in children aged 10–12. *Community Dentistry and Oral Epidemiology, 19,* 342–346.

Nevo, B. (1986). *Scientific aspects of graphology.* Springfield, IL: Thomas.

Newman, C. F., Leahy, R. L., Beck, A. T., Reilly-Harringont, N. A., & Gyulai, L. (2002). *Bipolar disorder: A cognitive behavior therapy approach.* Washington, DC: American Psychological Association.

Newstead, S., Handley, S., Harley, C., Wright, H., & Farrelly, D. (2004). Individual differences in deductive reasoning. *Quarterly Journal of Experimental Psychology, 57,* 33–60.

Niaura, R., Todaro, J. F., Strood, L., Spiro, A., Ward, K. D., & Weiss, S. (2002). Hostility, the metabolic syndrome, and incident coronary heart disease. *Health Psychology, 21,* 588–593.

Nichols, C. D., & Sanders-Bush, E. (2002). A single dose of lysergic acid diethyamide influences gene expression patterns with the mammalian brain. *Neuropsychopharmacology, 26k,* 634–642.

Nichols, M. P., & Schwartz, R. C. (2004). *Family Therapy* (6th ed.). Boston: Allyn & Bacon.

Nickerson, R. S., & Adams, M. J. (1979). Long-term memory for a common object. *Cognitive Psychology, 11,* 287–307.

Niehoff, D. (1999). *The biology of violence.* New York: The Free Press.

Nielson, S. L., Johnson, W. B., & Ellis, A. (2001). *Counseling and psychotherapy with religious persons.* Mahwah, NJ: Erlbaum.

Niki, K., & Luo, J. (2002). An fMRI study on the time-limited role of the medial temporal lobe in long-term topographical autobiographical memory. *Journal of Cognitive Neuroscience, 14,* 500–507.

Niles, B. L., Wolf, E. J., & Kutter, C. J. (2003). Posttraumatic stress disorder symptomatology in Vietnam veterans before and after September 11. *Journal of Nervous and Mental Disorders, 19,* 682–684.

Nishimura, M., Terao, T., Soeda, S., Nakamura, J., Iwata, N., & Sakamoto, K. (2004). Suicide and occupation: further supportive evidence for their relevance. *Progress in Neuropharmacology and Biological Psychiatry, 28,* 37–83.

Nobel, P. A., & Shiffrin, R. M. (2001). Retrieval processes in recognition and cued recall. *Journal of Experimental Psychology: Learning, Memory, and Cognition, 27,* 384–413.

Nolen-Hoeksema, S. (1995). Gender differences in coping with depression across the lifespan. *Depression, 3,* 81–90.

Nolen-Hoeksema, S. (2000). The role of rumination in depressive disorders and mixed anxiety/depressive symptoms. *Journal of Abnormal Psychology, 109,* 504–511.

Nolen-Hoeksema, S. (2004). *Abnormal psychology* (3rd ed.). New York: McGraw-Hill.

Nolen-Hoeksema, S., Larson, J., & Grayson, C. (1999). Explaining the gender difference in depressive symptoms. *Journal of Personality & Social Psychology, 77,* 1061–1072.

Nolen-Hoeksema, S., & Morrow, J. (1991). A prospective study of depression and distress following a natural disaster: The 1989 Loma Prieta earthquake. *Journal of Personality & Social Psychology, 61,* 105–121.

Nolen-Hoeksema, S., Parker, L. E., & Larson, J. (1994). Ruminative coping with depressed mood following loss. *Journal of Personality & Social Psychology, 67,* 92–104.

Norcross, J. C. (Ed.). (2002). *Psychotherapy relationships that work.* New York: Oxford University Press.

Norcross, J. C., & Kobayashi, M. (2000). Psychotherapy: Clinical practice. In A. Kazdin (Ed.), *Encyclopedia of psychology.* Washington, DC, & New York: American Psychological Association and Oxford University Press.

Norcross, J. C., & Newman, C. F. (1992). Psychotherapy integration: Setting the context. In J. C. Norcross & M. R. Gottfried (Eds.), *Handbook of psychotherapy integration.* New York: Basic Books.

Norcross, J. C., & Prochaska, J. O. (1983). Clinicians' theoretical orientations. *Professional Psychology: Research and Practice, 14,* 197–208.

Norcross, J. C., & Prochaska, J. O. (1988). A study of eclectic (and integrative) views revisited. *Professional Psychology: Research and Practice, 19,* 170–174.

Norem, J. K., & Cantor, N. (1986). Anticipatory and post-hoc cushioning strategies: Optimism and defensive pessimism in risk "situations." *Cognitive Therapy Research, 10,* 347–362.

Norris, F. N., Bryne, C. M., Diaz, E., & Kaniasty, K. (2001). *The range, magnitude, and duration of effects of natural and human-caused disasters: A review of the empirical literature.* Washington, DC: National Center for PTSD.

North, C. S., Tivis, L., McMillen, J. C., Pfefferbaum, B., Spitznagel, E. L., Cox, J. Nixon, S., Bunch, K. P., & Smith, E. M. (2002). Psychiatric disorders in rescue workers after the Oklahoma City bombing. *American Journal of Psychiatry, 159,* 857–859.

Notman, M. T., & Nadelson, C. C. (2002). Women's issues. In M. Hersen & W. H. Sledge (Eds.), *Encyclopedia of psychotherapy.* San Diego: Academic Press.

Nottelmann, E. D., Susman, E. J., Blue, J. H., Inoff-Germain, G., Dorn, L. D., Loriaux, D. L., Cutler, G. B., & Chrousos, G. P. (1987). Gonadal and adrenal hormone correlates of adjustment in early adolescence. In R. M. Lerner & T. T. Foch (Eds.), *Biological-psychological interactions in early adolescence.* Hillsdale, NJ: Erlbaum.

NOVA (2001, April 17). *Cracking the code of life.* Available on the World Wide Web at http://www.pbs.org/wgbh/nova/genome/ retrieved November 17, 2003.

Nucci, L. P. (2001). *Education in the moral domain.* New York: Cambridge University Press.

Nutt, D. J. (2001). Neurobiological mechanisms in generalized anxiety disorder. *Journal of Clinical Psychology, 62* (Suppl. 11), 22–27.

Nyberg, L. (2004, August). *Imaging cognition.* Paper presented at the 28th International Congress of Psychology, Beijing, China.

Nyberg, L., Forkstam, C., Petersson, K. M., Cabeza, R., & Ingvr, M. (2002). Brain imaging of human memory systems: between-systems similarities and within-system differences. *Brain Research: Cognitive Brain Research, 13,* 281–292.

Nystrand, A. (1996). New discoveries on sex differences in the brain. *Lakartidningen, 93,* 2071–2073.

Nystul, M. S. (1999). *Introduction to counseling.* Boston: Allyn & Bacon.

Oberbauer, A. M., Runstadler, J. A., Murray, A. D., & Havel, P. J. (2001). Obesity and elevated plasma leptin concentration in oMT1A-o growth hormone transgenic mice. *Obesity Research, 9,* 51–58.

O'Brien, G., & Opie, J. (1999). A connectionist theory of phenomenal experience. *Behavior and Brain Sciences, 1,* 127–148.

O'Callahan, M., Andrews, A. M., & Krantz, D. S. (2003). Coronary heart disease and hypertension. In I. B. Weiner (Ed.), *Handbook of psychology,* Vol. IX. New York: Wiley.

O'Connor, E. (2001, February). Marketing medications. *Monitor on Psychology, 32,* (2), 33.

O'Donnell, B. F. (2002). Forms of attention and attention disorders. *Seminars in Speech and Language, 23,* 99–106.

Offer, D., Ostrov, E., Howard, K. I., & Atkinson, R. (1988). *The teenage world: Adolescents' self-image in ten countries.* New York: Plenum.

Ogbu, J., & Stern, P. (2001). Caste status and intellectual development. In R. J. Sternberg & E. L. Grigorenko (Eds.), *Environmental effects on cognitive abilities.* Mahwah, NJ: Erlbaum.

Ogilvie, R. D., & Wilkinson, R. T. (1988). Behavioral versus EEG-based monitoring of all-night sleep/wake patterns. *Sleep, 11*(2), 139–155.

O'Hara, M., & Taylor, E. (2000). Humanistic psychology. In A. Kazdin (Ed.), *Encyclopedia of psychology.* Washington, DC, & New York: American Psychological Association and Oxford University Press.

Okagaki, L. (2000). Determinants of intelligence: Socialization of intelligence. In A. Kazdin (Ed.), *Encyclopedia of psychology.* Washington, DC, & New York: American Psychological Association and Oxford University Press.

Olds, J. M. (1958). Self-stimulation experiments and differential reward systems. In H. H. Jasper, L. D. Proctor, R. S. Knighton, W. C. Noshay, & R. T. Costello (Eds.), *Reticular formation of the brain.* Boston: Little, Brown.

Olds, J. M., & Milner, P. M. (1954). Positive reinforcement produced by electrical stimulation of the septal area and other areas of the rat brain. *Journal* *of Comparative and Physiological Psychology, 47,* 419–427.

O'Leary, C. (2004). Fetal alcohol syndrome. *Journal of Pediatric Child Health, 40,* 2–7.

O'Leary, V. E., & Flanagan, E. H. (2001). Leadership. In J.W. Worell (Ed.), *Encyclopedia of gender and women.* San Diego: Academic Press.

Oliner, S. P. (2001). Ordinary people: Faces of heroism and altruism. In S. G. Post, L. G. Underwood, J. P. Schloss, & W. B. Hurlbut (Eds.), *Altruism and altruistic love.* New York: Oxford University Press.

Olivardia, R., Pope, H. G., Mangweth, B., & Hudson, J. I. (1995). Eating disorders in college men. *American Journal of Psychiatry, 152,* 1279–1284.

Oliver, M. B., & Hyde, J. S. (1993). Gender differences in sexuality: A meta-analysis. *Psychological Bulletin, 114,* 29–51.

Oltmanns, T. F., & Emory, R. E. (2001). *Abnormal psychology* (3rd ed.). Upper Saddle River, NJ: Prentice-Hall.

Oltmanns, T. F., & Emory, R. E. (2004). *Abnormal Psychology* (4th ed.). Upper Saddle River, NJ: Prentice-Hall.

Onwuegbuzi, A. J., & Daley, C. E. (2001). Racial differences in IQ revisited: A synthesis of nearly a century of research. *Journal of Black Psychology, 27,* 209–220.

Oppenheimer, D. M. (2003). Not so fast! (and not so frugal!): rethinking the recognition heuristic. *Cognition, 90,* B1–B9.

Oren, D. A., & Terman, M. (1998). Tweaking the human circadian clock with light. *Science, 279,* 333–334.

Orfanos, S. D. (2002). Relational psychoanalysis. In M. Hersen & W. H. Sledge (Eds.), *Encyclopedia of psychotherapy.* San Diego: Academic Press.

Orlinsky, D. E., Grawe, K., & Parks, B. K. (1994). Process and outcome in psychotherapy. In A. E. Bergin & S. L. Garfield (Eds.), *Handbook of psychotherapy and behavior change* (4th ed.). New York: Wiley.

Orlinsky, D. E., & Howard, K. L. (2000). Psychotherapy: Research. In A. Kazdin (Ed.), *Encyclopedia of psychology.* Washington, DC, & New York: American Psychological Association and Oxford University Press.

Ormrod, J. E. (2004). *Human learning* (4th ed.). Upper Saddle River, NJ: Prentice-Hall.

Ortega, E. (2003). Neuroendocrine mediators in the modulation of phagocytosis by exercise: physiological implications. *Exercise and Immunology Review, 9,* 70–93.

Osborne, L., & Pober, B. (2001). Genetics of childhood disorders: XXVII. Genes and cognition in Williams syndrome. *Journal of the Academy of Child and Adolescent Psychiatry, 40,* 732–735.

Ost, L. (1991). Acquisition of blood and injection phobia and anxiety response patterns in clinical patients. *Behavior and Research Therapy, 23,* 263–282.

O'Toole, A. (2003, February). *Personal conversation.* Richardson, TX: Program in psychology, U. of Texas at Dallas.

Otte, C., Kellner, M., Arlt, J., Jahn, H., Holsboer, F., & Wiedemann, K. (2002). Prolactin but not ACTH increases sodium lactate-induced panic attacks. *Psychiatry Research, 2,* 201–205.

Otten, L. J., Henson, R. N., & Rugg, M. D. (2001). Depth of processing effects on neural correlates of memory encoding. *Brain, 124,* 399–412.

Ouelette, S. C., & DiPlacido, J. (2001). Personality's role in the protection and enhancement of health. In A. Baum, T. A. Revenson, & J. E. Singer (Eds.), *Handbook of health psychology.* Mahwah, NJ: Erlbaum.

Owen, A. M. (1997). Cognitive planning in humans: Neuropsychological, neuroanatomical, and neuropharmacological perspectives. *Progress in Neurobiology, 53* (4), 431–450.

Oyserman, D., Coon, H. M., & Kemmelmeir, M. (2002). Rethinking individualism and collectivism: Evaluation of theoretical assumptions and meta-analyses. *Psychological Bulletin, 128,* 3–72.

Ozer, D. (2001). Four principles for personality assessment. In L. A. Pervin & O. P. John (Eds.), *Handbook of personality.* New York: Guilford Press.

Ozer, D. J., & Riese, S. P. (1994). Personality assessment. *Annual Review of Psychology, 45,* 357–388.

P

Pacher, P., Kohegyi, E., Kecskemeti, V., & Furst, S. (2001). Current trends in the development of new antidepressants. *Current Medicine and Chemistry, 8,* 89–100.

Padma-Nathan, H. (1999, March). *Oral drug therapy for erectile dysfunction: What have we learned from the Viagra experience?* Paper presented at the meeting of the American Psychosomatic Association, Vancouver.

Paffenbarger, O., Hyde, R. T., Wing, A. L., & Hsieh, C. (1986). Physical activity, all-cause mortality, and longevity of college alumni. *New England Journal of Medicine, 324,* 605–612.

Page, A. C., & Hooke, G. R. (2003). Outcomes for depressed and anxious inpatients discharged before or after group cognitive therapy: A naturalistic comparison. *Journal of Nervous and Mental Disorders, 191,* 653–659.

Paivio, A. (1971). *Imagery and verbal processes.* New York: Holt, Rinehart & Winston.

Paivio, A. (1986). *Mental representations: A dual coding approach.* New York: Oxford University Press.

Paloutzian, R. (2000). *Invitation to the psychology of religion* (3rd ed.). Boston: Allyn & Bacon.

Paludi, M. A. (2002). *Psychology of women* (2nd ed.). Upper Saddle River, NJ: Prentice-Hall.

Pan, B. A., & Snow, C. E. (1999). The development of conversational and discourse skills. In M. Barrett (Ed.), *The development of language.* Philadelphia: Psychology Press.

Panskepp, J. (1993). Neurochemical control of moods and emotions: Amino acids to neuropeptides. In M. Lewis & J. M. Haviland (Eds.), *Handbook of emotion.* New York: Guilford Press.

Paquin, A. R. (2000). Dreams: Cross-cultured perspectives. In A. Katdin (Ed.) *Encyclopedia of psychology, vol. 3.* Washington DC and New York: American Psychological Association and Oxford University Press.

Park, C. L., & Adler, N. E. (2003). Coping style as a predictor of health and well-being across the first year of medical school. *Health Psychology, 22,* 627–631.

Park, D. C., Nisbett, R., & Hedden, T. (1999). Aging, culture, and cognition. *Journal of Gerontology, 54B,* P75–P84.

Parke, R. D. (2004). Development in the family. *Annual Review of Psychology, 54.* Palo Alto, CA: Annual Reviews.

Pascual-Leone, J., & Johnson, J. (1999). A dialectical constructivist view of representation. In I. E. Sigel (Ed.), *Development of mental representation.* Mahwah, NJ: Erlbaum.

Passchier, W., Knottnerus, A., Albering, H., & Walda, I. (2001). Public health impact of large airports. *Review of Environmental Health, 15,* 83–96.

Pate, R. H., & Bondi, A. M. (1992). Religious beliefs and practice: An integral aspect of multicultural awareness. *Counselor Education and Supervision, 32,* 108–115.

Patterson, C. J. (2000). Family relationships of lesbians and gay men. *Journal of Marriage and the Family, 62,* 1052–1069.

Patterson, C. J. (2002). Lesbian and gay parenthood. In M. H. Bornstein (Ed.), *Handbook of parenting* (2nd ed.). Mahwah, NJ: Erlbaum.

Patterson, D. R., & Jensen, M. P. (2003). Hypnosis and clinical pain. *Psychological Bulletin, 129,* 495–521.

Patterson, G. R., Debaryshe, B. D., & Ramsey, E. (1989). A developmental perspective on antisocial behavior. *American Psychologist, 44,* 329–335.

Paulus, P. B. (1989). An overview and evaluation of group influence. In P. B. Paulus (Ed.), *Psychology of group influence.* Mahwah, NJ: Erlbaum.

Paunonen, S., Jackson, D., Trzebinski, J., & Forserling, F. (1992). Personality structures across cultures: A multimethod evaluation. *Journal of Personality and Social Psychology, 62,* 447–456.

Paus, T., Collins, D. L., Evans, A. C., Leonard, G., Pike, B., & Zijdenbros, A. (2001). Maturation of white matter in the human brain: A review of magnetic resonance imaging. *Brain Research Bulletin, 54,* 255–266.

Pavlov, I. P. (1927). *Conditioned reflexes* (G. V. Anrep, Trans.). New York: Dover.

Payne, L. R., Smith, P. O., Sturges, L. V., & Holleran, S. A. (1996). Reactivity to smoking cues: Mediating roles of nicotine and duration of deprivation. *Addictive Behaviors, 21,* 139–154.

Pearce, J., & Bouton, M. E. (2001). Elementary associative learning. *Annual Review of Psychology.* Palo Alto, CA: Annual Reviews.

Pearson, S. (2003). Promoting sexual health services to young men: findings from focus group discussions. *Journal of Family Planning and Reproductive Health Care, 29,* 194–198.

Pedersen, P. B., & Carey, J. C. (2003). *Multicultural counseling in schools (*2nd Ed.*).* Boston: Allyn & Bacon.

Pegna, A. J., Caldara-Schnetzer, A. S., Perrig, S. H., Lazeyras, F., Khateb, A., Landis, T., & Seeck, M. (2002). Is the right amygydala involved in visuospatial memory? Evidence from MRI volumetric measures. *European Neurology, 47,* 148–155.

Pelak, V. S., & Liu, G. T. (2004). Visual hallucinations. *Current Treatment Options in Neurology, 6,* 75–83.

Penedo, F. J., & Others. (2004). Cognitive-behavioral stress management improves stress management skills and quality of life in men recovering from treatment of prostate caracinoma. *Cancer, 100,* 192–200.

Penfield, W. (1947). Some observations in the cerebral cortex of man. *Proceedings of the Royal Society, 134,* 349.

Peng, J., Qiao. H., & Xu, Z. B. (2002). A new approach to stability of neural networks with time-varying delays. *Neural Networks, 15,* 95–103.

Pengilly, J. W., & Dowd, E. T. (2000). Hardiness and social support as moderators of stress. *Journal of Clinical Psychology, 56,* 813–820.

Pennebaker, J. W. (1997). *Opening up: The healing power of expressing emotions* (Rev. ed.). New York: Guilford Press.

Pennebaker, J. W. (1997). Writing about emotional experiences as a therapeutic experience. *Psychological Science, 8,* 162–166.

Pennebaker, J. W. (2001). Dealing with a traumatic emotional experience immediately after it occurs. *Advances in Mind-Body Medicine, 17,* 160–162.

Pennebaker, J. W., & Beall, S. K. (1986). Confronting a traumatic event. Toward an understanding of inhibition and disease. *Journal of Abnormal Psychology, 95,* 274–281.

Pennebaker, J. W., & Graybeal, A. (2001). Patterns of natural language use: Disclosure, personality, and social integration. *Current Directions in Psychological Science, 32,* 90–93.

Pennebaker, J. W., Kiecolt-Glaser, J. D., & Glaser, G. (1988). Disclosure of traumas and immune function: Health implications for psychotherapy. *Journal of Consulting and Clinical Psychology, 56,* 239–245.

Pennix, B. W., Rejeski, W. J., Pandya, J., Miller, M. E., Di Bari, M., Applegate, W. B., & Pahor, M. (2002). Exercise and depressive symptoms: A comparison of aerobic and resistance exercise effects on emotional and physical function in older persons with high and low depressive symptomatology. *Journal of Gerontology: Psychological Sciences, 57,* P124–P132.

Peplau, L. A. (2002). *Current research on gender and sexuality.* Paper presented at the meeting of the American Psychological Association, Chicago.

Peplau, L. A. (2003). Human sexuality: How do men and women differ? *Current Directions in Psychological Science, 12,* 37–40.

Peplau, L. A., Fingerhut, A., & Beals, K. P. (2004). Sexuality in the relationships of lesbians and gay males. In J. H. Harvey & A. Wenzel (Eds.), *The handbook of sexuality in close relationships.* Mahwah, NJ: Erlbaum.

Perault, M. C., Favreliere, S., Minet, P., & Remblier, C. (2000). Benzodiazepines and pregnancy. *Therapy, 55,* 587–595.

Perkins, D. (1994, September). Creativity by design. *Educational Leadership,* pp. 18–25.

Perkins, K. A., Marcus, M. D., Levine, M. D., D'Amico, D., Miller, A., Broge, M., Ashcom, J., & Shiffman, S. (2001). Cognitive-behavioral therapy to reduce weight concerns improves smoking cessation outcome in weight-concerned women. *Journal of Consulting and Clinical Psychology, 69,* 604–613.

Perloff, R. M. (2001). *Persuading people to have safer sex.* Mahwah, NJ: Erlbaum.

Perls, F. (1969). *Gestalt therapy verbatim.* Lafayette, CA: Real People Press.

Perner, L. (2001). *The psychology of consumers.* Unpublished manuscript, George Washington University, Washington, DC.

Perse, E. M. (2001). *Media effects and society.* Mahwah, NJ: Erlbaum.

Person, L., & Taylor, E. J. (2002). Managing pain in outpatients: There are particular challenges to pain control in outpatient settings. *American Journal of Nursing, 102,* Supplement, 24–27.

Pert, A. B., & Snyder, S. H. (1973). Opiate receptor: Demonstration in a nervous tissue. *Science, 179,* 1011.

Pert, C. B. (1999). *Molecules of emotion.* New York: Simon & Schuster.

Pervin, L. A. (2000). Personality. In A. Kazdin (Ed.), *Encyclopedia of psychology.* Washington, DC, & New York: American Psychological Association and Oxford University Press.

Pervin, L. A., & John, O. P. (Eds.). (2001). *Handbook of personality.* New York: Guilford Press.

Peterson, C. (1988). *Personality.* Fort Worth: Harcourt Brace.

Peterson, C. (2000). The future of optimism. *American Psychologist, 55,* 44–55.

Peterson, C., Seligman, M. E. P., & Vaillant, G. E. (1988). Pessimistic explanatory style is a risk factor for physical illness: A thirty-five year longitudinal study. *Journal of Personality and Social Psychology, 55,* 23–27.

Petrill, S. A. (2003). The development of intelligence: Behavioral genetic approaches. In R. J. Sternberg, J. Lautrey, & T. I. Lubert (Eds.), *Models of intelligence: International perspectives.* Washington, DC: American Psychological Association.

Petry, N. M., Petrakis, I., Trevisan, L., Wiredu, G., Boutros, N. N., Martin, B., & Kosten, T. R. (2001). Contingency management interventions: From research to practice. *American Journal of Psychiatry, 158,* 694–702.

Pettigrew, T. F., & Tropp, L. R. (2000). Does intergroup contact reduce prejudice? Recent meta-analytic findings. In S. Oskamp (Ed.), *Reducing prejudice and discrimination.* Mahwah, NJ: Erlbaum.

Petty, R. E., & Cacioppo, J. T. (1986). The elaboration likelihood of persuasion. In L. Berkowitz (Ed.), *Advances in experimental social psychology* (Vol. 19). New York: Academic Press.

Petty, R. E., & Krosnick, J. A. (Eds.), (1995). *Attitude strength: Antecedents and consequents.* Mahwah, NJ: Erlbaum.

Petty, R. E., Wheeler, S. C., & Bizer, G. Y. (2000). Attitude functions and persuasion: An elaboration likelihood approach to matched versus mismatched messages. In G. R. Maio & J. M. Olson (Eds.), *Why we evaluate.* Mahwah, NJ: Erlbaum.

Pezdek, K., & Banks, K. W. (Eds.). (1996). *The recovered memory / false memory debate.* San Diego, CA: Academic Press.

Phaneuf, S., & Leeuwenburgh, C. (2001). Apoptosis and exercise. *Medical Science and Sports Exercise, 33,* 393–396.

Phares, E. J. (1984). *Personality.* Columbus, OH: Merrill.

Philips, H. C., & Rachman, S. (1996). *The psychological management of chronic pain* (2nd ed.). New York: Springer.

Phillips, W. T., Kiernan, R. M., & King, A. C. (2001). The effects of physical activity on physical and psychological health. In A. Baum, T. A. Revenson, & J. E. Singer (Eds.), *Handbook of health psychology.* Mahwah, NJ: Erlbaum.

Phinney, J. S. (1989). Stages of ethnic identity development in minority group adolescents. *Journal of Early Adolescence, 9,* 34–49.

Phinney, J. S. (2000). Ethnic identity. In A. Kazdin (Ed.), *Encyclopedia of psychology.* Washington, DC, and New York: American Psychological Association and Oxford University Press.

Phinney, J. S. (2003). Ethnic identity and acculturation. In K. M. Chun, P. B. Organista, & G. Marín (Eds.), *Acculturation.* Washington, DC: American Psychological Association.

Piaget, J. (1952). *The origins of intelligence in children.* New York: Oxford University Press.

Piaget, J., & Inhelder, B. (1969). *The child's conception of space* (F. J. Langdon & J. L. Lunzer, Trans.). New York: Norton.

Pickering, T. G. (2001). Mental stress as a causal factor in the development of hypertension and cardiovascular disease. *Current Hypertension Reports, 3,* 249–254.

Pikona-Sapir, A., Melamed, Y., & Elizur, A. (2001). The insanity defense: Examination of the extent of congruence between psychiatric recommendation and adjudication. *Medicine and Law, 20,* 93–100.

Pilkonis, P. A. (1999). Introduction: Paradigms for psychotherapy outcome research. *Journal of Clinical Psychology, 55,* 145–146.

Pilkonis, P. A., & Krause, M. S. (1999). Summary: Paradigms for psychotherapy outcome research. *Journal of Clinical Psychology, 55,* 201–206.

Pillow, D. R., Zautra, A. J., & Sandler, I. (1996). Major life events and minor stressors. *Journal of Personality and Social Psychology, 70,* 381–394.

Pinel, J. P. J. (2003). *Biopsychology* (5th ed.). Boston, Allyn & Bacon.

Pines, A. M., & Maslach, C. (2002). *Experiencing social psychology* (4th ed.). New York: McGraw-Hill.

Pines, M. (2001). *Seeing, hearing, and smelling the world.* Retrieved October 2001 from http://www.hhmi.org/senses.

Pinker, S. (1994). *The language instinct.* New York: William Morrow.

Pinker, S. (1999). *How the mind works.* New York: Norton.

Pintrich, P. R. (2000). The role of goal orientation in self-regulated learning. In M. Boekaerts, P. R. Pintrich, & M. Zeidner (Eds.), *Handbook of self-regulation.* San Diego: Academic Press.

Pintrich, P. R., & Schunk, D. H. (Eds.). (2002). *Motivation in education* (2nd ed.). Upper Saddle River, NJ: Prentice-Hall.

Piran, N. (2002). Eating disorders and disordered eating. In J. Worell (Ed.), *Encyclopedia of women and gender.* New York: Oxford University Press.

Pittenger, D. (2003). *Behavioral research design and analysis.* New York: McGraw-Hill.

Pittman, T. S. (1998). Motivation. In D. T. Gilbert, S. T. Fiske, & G. Lindzey (Eds.), *Handbook of social psychology* (4th ed., Vol. 1). New York: McGraw-Hill.

Plomin, R. (1999). Genetics and general cognitive ability. *Nature, 402* (Suppl.), C25–C29.

Plomin, R., & Craig, I. (2001). Genetics, environment, and cognitive abilities: Review and work in progress toward a genome scan for quantitative trait locus associations using DNA pooling. *British Journal of Psychiatry, 40,* 41–48.

Plutchik, R. (1980). *Emotion: A psychoevolutionary synthesis.* New York: Harper & Row.

Poling, A. & Carr, J. E. (2002). Operant conditioning. In M. Hersen & W. H. Sledge (Eds.), *Encyclopedia of psychotherapy.* San Diego: Academic Press.

Polsky, D., Onesirosan, P., Bauer, M. S., & Glick, H. A. (2002). Duration of therapy and health care costs of fluoxetine, paroxetine, and sertraline in 6 health plans. *Journal of Clinical Psychiatry, 63,* 156–164.

Pomplum, M., Reingold, E. M., & Shen, J. (2001). Investigating the visual span in comparative search: The effects of task difficulty and divided attention. *Cognition, 81,* B57–67.

Ponterotto, J. G., Casas, J. M., Suzuki, L. A., & Alexander, C. M. (Eds.). (2001). *Handbook of multicultural counseling.* Thousand Oaks, CA: Sage.

Popham, W. J. (2002). *Classroom assessment* (2nd ed.). Boston: Allyn & Bacon.

Posner, M. I., & Raichle, M. E. (1998). The neuroimaging of human brain function. *Proceedings of the National Academy of Science, USA, 95,* 763–764.

Post, S. G., Underwood, L. G., Scholls, J. P., & Hurlbut, W. B. (Eds.). (2002). *Altruism and altruistic love.* New York: Oxford University Press.

Powell, D. R. (2001). Early intervention and risk. In A. Fogel & G. Bremner (Eds.), *Blackwell handbook of infant development.* London: Blackwell.

Powell, L. (1992). The cognitive underpinnings of coronary-prone behaviors. *Cognitive Therapy & Research, 16*(2), 123–142.

Powell, R. A., & Symbaluk, D. G. (2002). *Introduction to learning and behavior.* Belmont, CA: Wadsworth.

Prager, K. J., & Roberts, L. J. (2004). Deep intimate connection: Self and intimacy in couple relationships. In D. J. Mashek & A. P. Aron (Eds.), *Handbook of closeness and intimacy.* Mahwah, NJ: Erlbaum.

Pratt, M. W., Danso, H. A., Arnold, M. L., Norris, J. E., & Filyer, R. (2001). Adult generativity and the socialization of adolescents. *Journal of Personality, 69,* 89–120.

Pressley, M. (1995). More about the development of self-regulation: Complex, long-term, and thoroughly social. *Educational Psychologist, 30,* 207–212.

Pressley, M. (2000). What should comprehension instruction be the instruction of? In M. Kamil (Ed.)., *Handbook of reading research.* Mahwah, NJ: Erlbaum.

Prieto, M., & Giralt, M. T. (2001). Effects of N-(2-chlorethyl)-N-ethyl-2-bromobenzylamine on alpha2-adrenoceptors which regulate the synthesis and release of noradrenaline in the rat brain. *Pharmacological Toxology, 88,* 152–158.

Prochaska, J. O., & Norcross, J.C. (2003). *Systems of psychotherapy: A transtheoretical analysis* (5th ed.). Belmont, CA: Wadsworth.

Proctor, R. W., & Wang, H. (2002). Influences of different combinations of conceptual, perceptual, and structural similarity on stimulus-response compatibility. Quarterly *Journal of Experimental Psychology, 55,* 59–74.

Provenzo, E. F. (2002). *Teaching, learning, and schooling in American culture: A critical perspective.* Boston: Allyn & Bacon.

Punamaki, R., & Joustie, M. (1998). The role of culture, violence, and personal factors affecting dream content. *Journal of Cross-Cultural Psychology, 29,* 320–343.

Purdy, J. E., Markham, M., Schwartz, B., & Gordon, W. M. (2001). *Learning and memory* (2nd ed.). Belmont, CA: Wadsworth.

Puri, B. K., Huttson, S. B., Saeed, N., Oatridge, A., Hajnal, J. V., Duncan, L., Chapman, M. J., Barnes, T. R., Bydder, G. M., & Joyce, E. M. (2001). A serial longitudinal quantitative MRI study of cerebral changes in first-episode schizophrenia using image segmentation and subvoxel registration. *Psychiatry Research, 106,* 141–150.

Puri, B. K., Richardson, A. J., Oatridge, A., Hajnal, J. V., & Saeed, N. (1999). Cerebral ventrical asymmetry in schizophrenia. *International Journal of Psychophysiology, 34,* 207–211.

Putnam, S. P., Sanson, A. V., & Rothbart, M. K. (2002). Child temperament and parenting. In M. Bornstein (Ed.), *Handbook of parenting* (2nd ed.). Mahwah, NJ: Erlbaum.

Q

Quality Assurance Project. (1990). Treatment outlines for paranoid, schizotypal, and schizoid personality disorders. *Australian & New Zealand Journal of Psychiatry, 24,* 339–350.

Qualls, P. J., & Sheehan, P. W. (1981). Electromyograph biofeedback as a relaxation technique: A critical appraisal and reassessment. *Psychological Bulletin, 90,* 21–42.

Quinlin, M., Mayhew, C., & Bohle, P. (2001). The global expansion of precarious employment. *International Journal of Health Services, 31,* 507–536.

R

Raabe, T. D., Deadwyler, G., Varga, J. W., & Devries, G. H. (2004). Localization of neurogulin isosoform and erbB receptors in myelinating glial cells. *Glia, 45,* 197–207.

Rabasca, L. (1999, May). Stress caused when jobs don't meet expectations. *APA Monitor, 30,* 24–25.

Rabasca, L. (2000, June) More psychologists in the trenches. *Monitor on Psychology, 31,* 50–51.

Radelet, M. L. (2002). Wrongful convictions of the innocent. *Judicature, 86,* 67–68.

Räikkönen, K., Matthews, K. A., Flory, J. D., Owens, J. F., & Gump, B. B. (1999). Effects of optimism, pessimism, and trait anxiety on ambulatory blood pressure and mood during everyday life. *Journal of Personality and Social Psychology, 76,* 104–113.

Rainer, G., & Miller, E. K. (2002). Timecourse of object-related neural activity in the primate prefrontal cortex during a short-term memory task. *European Journal of Neuroscience, 15,* 1244–1254.

Rains, G. D. (2002). *Principles of human neuropsychology.* New York: McGraw-Hill.

Rakic, P. (2002). Neurogenesis in adult primate neocortex: An evaluation of the evidence. *Nature Reviews: Neuroscience, 3,* 65–71.

Ramesch, M., & Roberts, G. (2002). Use of night-time benzodiazepines in an elderly inpatient population. *Journal of Clinical and Pharmacological Therapy, 27,* 93–97.

Ramey, C. T., Ramey, S. L., & Lanzi, R. G. (2001). Intelligence and experience. In R. J. Sternberg & E. L. Grigorenko (Eds.), *Environmental effects on cognitive abilities.* Mahwah, NJ: Erlbaum.

Ramey, S. L., & Ramey, S. T. (2000). Early childhood experiences and developmental competence. In S. Danzinger & J. Waldfogel (Eds.), *Securing the future: Investing in children from birth to college.* New York: Russell Sage Foundation.

Randi, J. (1997). *An encyclopedia of claims, frauds, and hoaxes of the occutt and supernatural.* New York: St. Martin's Press.

Rapaport, D. (1967). On the psychoanalytic theory of thinking. In M. M. Gill (Ed.), *The collected papers of David Rapaport.* New York: Basic Books.

Rapaport, S. (1994, November 28). Interview. *U.S. News and World Report,* p. 94.

Rappaport, J. L. (1989, March). The biology of obsessions and compulsions. *Scientific American,* 83–89.

Rasmussen, K. G. (1984). Nonverbal behavior, verbal behavior, resume credentials, and selection interview outcomes. *Journal of Applied Psychology, 69,* 551–556.

Ratner, N. B. (1993). Learning to speak. *Science, 262,* 260.

Raven, P. H., & Johnson, G. B. (2002). *Biology* (6th ed.). New York: McGraw-Hill.

Raz, N., Gunning-Dixon, F., Head, D., Williamson, A., & Acker, J. D. (2001). Age and sex differences in the cerebellum and the ventral pons. *American Journal of Neuroradiology, 22,* 1161–1167.

Razdin, U., & Sidhu, T. S. (2001). Need for research on health hazards due to noise pollution in metropolitan India. *Journal of the Indian Medical Association, 98,* 453–456.

Razmy, A., Lang, A. E., & Shapiro, C. M. (2004). Predictors of impaired daytime sleep and wakefulness in patients with Parkinson disease treated with older (Ergot) vs new (Nonergot) dopamine antagonists. *Archives of Neurology, 61,* 97–102.

Rebec, G. V. (1996, June). *Neurochemical and behavioral insights into mechanisms of action of stimulant drugs.* Paper presented at the meeting of the American Psychological Society, San Francisco.

Rector, N. A., & Beck, A. T. (2001). Cognitive behavioral therapy for schizophrenia: An empirical review. *Journal of Nervous and Mental Disorders, 189,* 278–287.

Reed, S. K. (2001). *Cognition* (5th ed.). Belmont, CA: Wadsworth.

Reed, S. K. (2004). *Cognition* (6th ed.). Belmont, CA: Wadsworth.

Rehm, L. P. (1998). Listening to Prozac and hearing noise: Commentary on Kirsch and Sapirstein's "Listening to Prozac but hearing placebo." *Prevention and Treatment, 1,* Article 0004c, posted June 26, 1998. (Retrieved from http://www.journals.apa.org/prevention/volume1/pre0010004c.html).

Reid, P. T., & Zalk, S. R. (2001). Academic environments: Gender and ethnicity in U.S. higher education. In J. Worrell (Ed.), *Encyclopedia of women and gender.* New York: Oxford University Press.

Reinder, A. A., Nijenhuis, E. R., Paans, A. M., Korf, J., Willemsen, A. T., & den Boer, J. A. (2003). One brain, two selves. *Neuroimage, 20,* 2119–2125.

Reinisch, J. M. (1990). *The Kinsey Institute new report on sex: What you must know to be sexually literate.* New York: St. Martin's Press.

Reinitz, M. T., Morrissey, J., & Demb, J. (1994). Role of attention in face encoding. *Journal of Experimental Psychology: Learning, Memory, and Cognition, 20,* 161–168.

Rescoria, R. A. (1966). Predictability and number of pairings in Pavlovian fear conditioning. *Psychonomic Science, 4,* 383–384.

Rescorla, R. A. (1988). Pavlovian conditioning: It's not what you think it is. *American Psychologist, 43,* 151–160.

Rescorla, R. A. (1996). Spontaneous recovery after training with multiple outcomes. *Animal Learning & Behavior, 24,* 11–18.

Rescorla, R. A. (2001). Experimental extinction. In R. R. Mowrer & S. B. Klein (Eds.), *Handbook of contemporary learning theories.* Mahwah, NJ: Erlbaum.

Restak, R. M. (1988). *The mind.* New York: Bantam.

Reuter-Lorenz, P., & Davidson, R. J. (1981). Differential contributions of the two cerebral hemispheres to the perception of happy and sad faces. *Neuropsychologia, 19,* 609–613.

Revelle, W. (2000). Individual differences. In A. Kazdin (Ed.), *Encyclopedia of psychology.* Washington, DC, and New York: American Psychological Association and Oxford University Press.

Revitch, E., & Schlesinger, L. B. (1978). Murder: Evaluation, classification, and prediction. In I. L. Kutash, S. B. Kutash, & O. B. Schlesinger (Eds.), *Violence.* San Francisco: Jossey-Bass.

Rex, T. S., Lewis, G. P., Geller, S. F., & Fisher, S. K. (2002). Differential expression of cone opsin mRNA levels following experimental retinal detachment and reattachment. *Molecular Vision, 8,* 114–118.

Reynolds, J., & Chelazzi, L. (2004). Neural mechanisms of attention. *Annual Review of Neuroscience, 27.* Palo Alto, CA: Annual Reviews.

Rezvani, A. H., & Levin, E. D. (2001). Cognitive effects of nicotine. *Biological Psychiatry, 49,* 258–267.

Rickels, K., & Rynn, M. A. (2001). What is generalized anxiety disorder? *Journal of Clinical Psychology, 62* (Suppl. 11), 46–50.

Ricther, M. A., Summerfeldt, L. J., Antony, M. M., & Swinson, R. P. (2003). Obsessive-compulsive spectrum conditions in obsessive-compulsive disorder and other anxiety disorders. *Depression and Anxiety, 18,* 118–127.

Riggio, R. E. (1986). Assessment of basic social skills. *Journal of Personality and Social Psychology, 51,* 649–660.

Riso, L. P., & Newman, C. F. (2003). Cognitive therapy for chronic depression. *Journal of Clinical Psychology, 59,* 817–831.

Roback, H. W., Barton, D., Castelnuovo-Tedesco, P., Gay, V., Havens, L., & Nash, J. (1999). A symposium on psychotherapy in the age of managed care. *American Journal of Psychotherapy, 53,* 1–16.

Robbins, T. W. (2000). From arousal to cognition: The integrative position of the prefrontal cortex. *Progress in Brain Research, 126,* 469–483.

Roberts, B. W., & Robins, R. W. (2004). Person-environment fit and its implications for personality development: a longitudinal study. *Journal of Personality, 72,* 89–110.

Roberts, D., Anderson, B. L., & Lubaroff, A. (1994). *Stress and immunity at cancer diagnosis.* Unpublished manuscript, Dept. of Psychology, Ohio State University, Columbus.

Roberts, J. E., Gotlib, I. H., & Kassel, J. D. (1996). Adult attachment security and symptoms of depression: The mediating roles of dysfunctional attitudes and low self-esteem. *Journal of Personality & Social Psychology, 60,* 310–320.

Robertson, L. C. (2003). Binding, spatial attention, and perceptual awareness. *Nature Reviews: Neuroscience, 4,* 93–102.

Robins, L., & Regier, D. (Eds.). (1991). *Psychiatric disorders in America.* New York: Free Press.

Robins, R. W., Trzesniewski, K. H., Tracey, J. L., Potter, J., & Gosling, S. D. (2002). Age differences in self-esteem from age 9 to 90. *Psychology and Aging, 17,* 423–434.

Rodin, J. (1984, December). Interview: A sense of control. *Psychology Today,* pp. 38–45.

Rodin, J. (1993). *Body traps.* New York: Morrow.

Rodin, J., & Langer, E. J. (1977). Long-term effects of a control-relevant intervention with the institutionalized aged. *Journal of Personality and Social Psychology, 35,* 397–402.

Rodrigues, M. S., & Cohen, S. (1998). Social support. In H. S. Friedman (Ed.), *Encyclopedia of mental health* (Vol. 3). San Diego: Academic Press.

Roediger, H. L., & Marsh, E. J. (2003). Episodic and autobiographical memory. In I. B. Weiner (Ed.), *Handbook of psychology* (Vol. 4). New York: Wiley.

Roehrs, T., & Roth, T. (1998). Reported in Maas, J. (1998). *Power sleep.* New York: Villard, p. 44.

Rogers, C. R. (1961). *On becoming a person.* Boston: Houghton Mifflin.

Rogers, C. R. (1974). In retrospect: Forty-six years. *American Psychologist, 29,* 115–123.

Rogers, C. R. (1980). *A way of being.* Boston: Houghton Mifflin.

Rogers, R. (2001). *Handbook of diagnostic and structured interviewing.* New York: Guilford.

Rogers, T. B., Kuiper, N. A., & Kirker, W. S. (1977). Self-reference and the encoding of personal information. *Journal of Personality and Social Psychology, 35,* 677–688.

Rogoff, B. (1990). *Apprenticeship in thinking.* New York: Oxford University Press.

Rogoff, B. (1998). Cognition as a collaborative process. In W. Damon (Ed.), *Handbook of child psychology* (5th ed., Vol. 2). New York: Wiley.

Rogoff, B. (2003). *The cultural nature of human development.* New York: Oxford University Press.

Rogosch, F. A., Cicchetti, D., Shields, A., & Toth, S. L. (1995). Parenting dysfunction in child maltreatment. In M. H. Bornstein (Ed.), *Handbook of parenting* (Vol. 4). Hillsdale, NJ: Erlbaum.

Rosch, E. (1973). On the internal structure of perceptual and semantic categories. In T. E. Moore (Ed.), *Cognition and the acquisition of language.* San Diego: Academic Press.

Rose, R. J., Koskenvuo, M., Kaprio, J., Sarna, S., & Langinvainio, H. (1988). Shared genes, shared experiences, and similarity of personality: Data from 14,228 adult Finnish co-twins. *Journal of Personality and Social Psychology, 54,* 161–171.

Rosen, K. S., & Burke, P. B. (1999). Multiple attachment relationships within families. *Developmental Psychology, 35,* 436–444.

Rosenbaum, M., Leibel, R. L., & Hirsch, J. (1997). Medical progress: Obesity. *New England Journal of Medicine, 337,* 396–407.

Rosenbloom, M. (2002). Chlorpromazine and the psychopharmacological revolution. *Journal of the American Medical Association, 287,* 1860–1861.

Rosenfeld, A. H. (1985, June). Depression: Dispelling despair. *Psychology Today,* pp. 28–34.

Rosenhan, D. L. (1973). On being sane in insane places. *Science, 179,* 250–258.

Rosenthal, D. L. (1963). *The Genain quadruplets.* New York: Basic Books.

Rosenthal, R. (1966). *Experimenter effects in behavioral research.* New York: Appleton-Century-Crofts.

Rosenthal, R. (1994). Interpersonal expectancy effects: A 30-year-perspective. *Current Dimensions in Psychological Science, 3,* 176–179.

Rosenthal, R., & DiMatteo, M. R. (2001). Meta-analysis: Recent developments in quantitative methods for literature reviews. *Annual Review of Psychology, 52,* 59–62.

Rosenzweig, M. R., Bennett, E. L., & Diamond, M. C. (1972, February). Brain changes in response to experience. *Scientific American,* 22–29.

Rosnow, R., & Rosenthal, R. (2002). *Beginning behavioral research* (4th ed.). Upper Saddle River, NJ: Prentice-Hall.

Rosnow, R. L. (1995). Teaching research ethics through role-playing and discussion. In M. E. Ware & D. E. Johnson (Eds.), *Demonstrations and activities in teaching psychology* (Vol. 1). Mahwah, NJ: Erlbaum.

Ross, C. A., & Norton, G. R. (1989). Differences between men and women with multiple personality disorder. *Hospital & Community Psychiatry, 40,* 186–188.

Rossi, F., Saggiorato, C., & Strata, P. (2002). Target-specific innervation of embryonic cerebellar transplants by regenerating olivocerebellar axons in the adult rat. *Experimental Neurology, 172,* 205–212.

Roth, D., Eng, W., & Heimberg, R. G. (2002). Cognitive behavior therapy. In M. Hersen & W. H. Sledge (Eds.), *Encyclopedia of psychotherapy.* San Diego: Academic Press.

Rothbart, M. K., & Bates, J. E. (1998). Temperament. In W. Damon (Ed.), *Handbook of child psychology* (5th ed., Vol. 3). New York: Wiley.

Rotter, J. B. (1966). Generalized expectancies for internal versus external control of reinforcement. *Psychological Monographs, 80,* (1, Whole No. 609).

Rowe, D. C. (1994). *The limits of family influence: Genes, experience, and behavior.* New York: Guilford Press.

Rowe, J. W., & Kahn, R. L. (1997). *Successful aging.* New York: Pantheon.

Rowe, S. M., & Wertsch, J. V. (2002). Vygotsky's model of cognitive development. In U. Goswami (Ed.), *Blackwell handbook of childhood cognitive development.* Malden, MA: Blackwell.

Roy, A. (1992). Genetics, biology, and suicide in the family. In R. W. Maris, A. L. Berman, J. T. Maltsberger, & R. I. Yufit (Eds.), *Assessment and prediction of suicide* (pp. 574–588). New York: Guilford.

Roy-Byrne, P. P. & Cowley, D. S. (2002). Pharmacological treatments for panic disorders, phobias, and generalized anxiety disorder. In P. Nathan & J. M. Gorman (Eds.), *A guide to treatments that work (*2nd ed.*).* New York: Oxford University Press.

Rozanski, A., Blumenthal, J. A., Kaplan, J. (1999). Impact of psychological factors on the pathogenesis of cardiovascular disease and implications for therapy. *Circulation, 99,* 2192–2217.

Rubel, E. W., & Fritzsch, B. (2002). Auditory system development: Primary auditory neurons and their targets. *Annual Review of Neuroscience* (Vol. 25). Palo Alto, CA: Annual Reviews.

Rubenzer, S., Ones, D. Z., & Faschingbauer, T. (2000, August). *Personality traits of U.S. presidents.* Paper presented at the meeting of the American Psychological Association, Washington, DC.

Rubin, D. C., & Kozin, M. (1984). Vivid memories. *Cognition, 16,* 81–95.

Rubin, Z., & Mitchell, C. (1976). Couples research as couples counseling. *American Psychologist, 31,* 17–25.

Ruby, N. F., Dark, J., Burns, D. E., Heller, H. C., & Zucker, I. (2002). The suprachiasmatic nucleus is essential for circadian body temperature rhythms in hibernating ground squirrels. *Journal of Neuroscience, 22,* 357–364.

Ruck, C. (2003). Psychosurgery. *Journal of Neurosurgery, 99,* 1113–1114.

Rudd, M. D., Joiner, T. E., & Rajab, M. H. (2001). *Treating suicidal behavior.* New York: Guilford.

Runco, M. (2004). Creativity. *Annual Review of Psychology, 54.* Palo Alto, CA: Annual Reviews.

Rusbult, C. E., Kumashiro, M., Coolsen, M. K., & Kirchner, J. L. (2004). Interdependence, closeness, and relationships. In D. J. Mashek & A. P. Aron (Eds.), *Handbook of closeness and intimacy.* Mahwah, NJ: Erlbaum.

Rusbult, C. E., Olsen, N., Davis, J. L., & Hannon, P. A. (2001). Commitment and relationship maintenance mechanisms. In J. H. Harvey & A. Wenzel (Eds.), *Close romantic relationships.* Mahwah, NJ: Erlbaum.

Ruse, M. (2002). A Darwinian naturalists's perspective on altruism. In S. G. Post, L. G. Underwood, J. P. Schloss, & W. B. Hurlbut (Eds.), *Altruism and altruistic love.* New York: Oxford University Press.

Rushton, J. P., Fulker, D. W., Neal, M. C., Nias, D. K. B., & Eysenck, H. J. (1986). Altruism and aggression: The heritability of individual differences. *Journal of Personality and Social Psychology, 50,* 1192–1198.

Russo, N. F. (1990). Overview: Forging research priorities for women's health. *American Psychologist, 45,* 373–386.

Ryan, J. D., & Cohen, N. J. (2004). Processing and short-term retention of relational information in amnesia. *Neuropsychologia, 42,* 497–511.

Ryan, J. M. (2001). Pharmacologic approach to aggression in neuropsychiatric disorders. *Seminars in Clinical Neuropsychiatry, 5,* 238–249.

Ryan, J. P., Atkinson, T. M., & Dunham, D. T. (2004). Sports-related and gender differences on neuropsychological measures of frontal lobe functioning. *Clinical Journal of Sports Medicine, 14,* 18–24.

Ryan, R. M., & Deci, E. L. (2000). Self-determination theory and the facilitation of intrinsic motivation, social development, and well-being. *American Psychologist, 55,* 68–78.

Ryan, R. M., & Deci, E. L. (2001). On happiness and human potentials: A review of research on hedonic and eudaimonic well-being. *Annual Review of Psychology* (Vol. 52). Palo Alto, CA: Annual Reviews.

Ryan-Finn, K. D., Cause, A. M., & Grove, K. (1995, March). *Children and adolescents of color: Where are you? Selection, recruitment, and retention in developmental research.* Paper presented at the meeting of the Society for Research in Child Development, Indianapolis.

Rymer, R. (1993). *Genie.* New York: HarperCollins.

S

Sachs, G. S. (2003). Unmet clinical needs in bipolar disorder. *Journal of Clinical Psychopharmacology, 23, 3,* Supplement 1, S2–S8.

Sacks, O. (1985). *The man who mistook his wife for a hat.* New York: Summit Books.

Salkind, N. J. (2003). *Exploring research* (5th ed.). Upper Saddle River, NJ: Prentice-Hall.

Salkovskis, P. M., Westbrook, D., Davis, J., Jeavons, A., & Gledhill, A. (1997). Effects of neutralizing on intrusive thoughts: An experiment investigating the etiology of obsessive-compulsive disorder. *Behaviour Research & Therapy, 35,* 211–219.

Salmon, C. (2004). The pornography debate: What sex differences in erotica can tell us about human sexuality. In C. B. Crawford & C. A. Salmon (Eds.), *Evolutionary psychology, public policy, and personal decisions.* Mahwah, NJ: Erlbaum.

Salmon, D. P. (2000). Alzheimer's disease. In A. Kazdin (Ed.), *Encyclopedia of psychology.* Washington, DC, & New York: American Psychological Association and Oxford University Press.

Salovey, P., & Birnbaum, D. (1989). Influence of mood on health-relevant cognitions. *Journal of Personality and Social Psychology, 57,* 539–551.

Salovey, P., & Mayer, J. D. (1990). Emotional intelligence. *Imagination, Cognition, and Personality, 9,* 185–211.

Salovey, P., & Pizarro, D. A. (2003). The value of emotional intelligence. In R. J. Sternberg, J. Lautrey, & T. I. Lubert (Eds.), *Models of intelligence: International perspectives.* Washington, DC: American Psychological Association.

Salovey, P., Rothman, A., Detweiler, J. B., & Steward, W. T. (2000). Emotional states and physical health. *American Psychologist, 55,* 110–121.

Salthouse, T. A. (1994a). The aging of working memory. *Neuropsychology, 8,* 535–543.

Salthouse, T. A. (1994b). The nature of the influence of speed on adult age differences in cognition. *Developmental Psychology, 30,* 240–259.

Salthouse, T. A. (2000). Adult development and aging: Cognitive processes and development. In A. Kazdin (Ed.), *Encyclopedia of psychology.* Washington, DC, & New York: American Psychological Association and Oxford University Press.

Sand, P. G., Godau, C., Riederer, P., Peters, C., Franke, P., Nothen, M. M., Stober, G., Fritze, J., Maier, W., Propping, P., Lesch, K. P., Riess, O., Sander, T., Bechmann, H., & Deckert, J. (2001). Exonic variants of the GABA (B) receptor gene and panic disorder. *Psychiatry and Genetics, 10,* 191–194.

Sanderson, W. C. (1995, March). Which therapies are proven effective? *APA Monitor,* p. 4.

Sangha, S., McComb, C., Scheibenstock, A., Johannes, C., & Lukowiak, K. (2002). The effects of continuous versus partial reinforcement schedules on associative learning, memory, and extinction in Lymnaea stagnalis. *Journal of Experimental Biology, 205,* 1171–1178.

Sanocki, T. (2001). *Student friendly statistics.* Upper Saddle River, NJ: Prentice-Hall.

Sanson, A., Smart, D., & Hemphill, S. (2002). Temperament and social development. In P. Smith & C. Hart (Eds.), *Blackwell handbook of childhood social development.* Malden, MA: Blackwell.

Santacruz, K. S., & Swagerty, D. (2001). Early diagnosis of dementia. *American Family Physician, 63,* 703–713.

Santrock, J. W. (2001). *Educational psychology.* New York: McGraw-Hill.

Santrock, J. W. (2003). *Child Development* (9th ed.). New York: McGraw-Hill.

Santrock, J. W. (2004). *Life-span development* (9th ed.). New York: McGraw-Hill.

Santrock, J. W., & Halonen, J. A. (2002). *Your guide to college success* (2nd ed.). Belmont, CA: Wadsworth.

Sarason, I. G., & Sarason, B. R. (2002). *Abnormal psychology* (10th ed.). Upper Saddle River, NJ: Prentice-Hall.

Sarbin, T. R., & Keen, E. (1998). Classifying mental disorders. In H. S. Friedman (Ed.), *Encyclopedia of mental health* (Vol. 1). San Diego: Academic Press.

Sarigiani, P. A., & Petersen, A. C. (2000). Adolescence: Puberty and biological maturation. In A. Kazdin (Ed.), *Encyclopedia of psychology.* Washington, DC, & New York: American Psychological Association and Oxford University Press.

Sasaki, S., Yoshimura, K., & Naito, K. (2004). The neural control of orienting: role of multiple-branching reticulospinal neurons, *Progress in Brain Research, 143,* 383–389.

Saucier, G. (2001, April). *Going beyond the big five.* Paper presented at the meeting of the Society for Research in Child Development, San Francisco.

Savage, I. M., Chang, Q., & Gold, P. E. (2003). Diencephalic damage increases hippocampal acetylcholine release during spontaneous alternation testing. *Learning and Memory, 10,* 242–246.

Savic, I. (2002). Sex differences in hypothalamic activation by putative pheromones. *Molecular Psychiatry, 7,* 335–336.

Savin-Williams, R., & Diamond, L. (2004). Sex. In R. Lerner & L. Steinberg (Eds.), *Handbook of adolescent psychology.* New York: Wiley.

Sax, L. J., Astin, A. W., Korn, W. S., & Manoney, K. M. (1995). *The American college freshman: National norms for fall, 1995.* Los Angeles: University of California at Los Angeles Higher Education Research Institute.

Saxe, L. (1998, June). Commentary. *APA Monitor,* p. 30.

Saxena, S., Brody, A. L., Schwartz, J. M., & Baxter, L. R. (1998). Neuroimaging and frontal-subcortical circuitry in obsessive-compulsive disorder. *British Journal of Psychiatry, 173* (Suppl. 35), 26–37.

Sayer, R., Law, E., Connelly, P. J., & Breen, K. C. (2004). Association of Acetylcholinesterase with Alzheimer's disease and response to cholinesterase inhibitors. *Clinical Biochemistry, 36,* 98–104.

Scarborough, E., & Furumoto, L. (1987). *Untold lives: The first generation of American women psychologists.* New York: Columbia University Press.

Scarr, S. (1984, May). Interview. *Psychology Today,* pp. 59–63.

Scarr, S., & Weinberg, R. A. (1983). The Minnesota adoption studies: Genetic differences and malleability. *Child Development, 54,* 182–259.

Schachter, S., & Singer, J. E. (1962). Cognitive, social, and physiological determinants of emotional state. *Psychological Review, 69,* 379–399.

Schacter, D. L. (1996). *Searching for memory.* New York: Basic Books.

Schacter, D. L. (1999). Consciousness. In M. S. Gazzaniga (Ed.), *The new cognitive neurosciences* (2nd ed.). Cambridge, MA: MIT Press.

Schacter, D. L. (2000). Memory: Memory systems. In A. Kazdin (Ed.), *Encyclopedia of psychology.* Washington, DC, & New York: American Psychological Association and Oxford University Press.

Schacter, D. L. (2001). *The seven sins of memory.* Boston: Houghton Mifflin.

Schafer, G. (1999). Early speech perception and word learning. In M. Barrett (Ed.), *The development of language.* Philadelphia: Psychology Press.

Schaffer, H. R., & Emerson, P. E. (1964). The development of social attachments in infancy. *Monographs of the Society for Research in Child Development, 29* (3, Serial No. 94).

Schaie, K. W. (1983). Consistency and changes in cognitive functioning of the young-old and old-old. In M. Bergner, U. Lehr, E. Lang, & R. Schmidt-Scherzer (Eds.), *Aging in the eighties and beyond.* New York: Springer.

Schaie, K. W. (1996). *Intellectual development in adulthood: The Seattle Longitudinal Study.* New York: Cambridge University Press.

Schaie, K. W., & Willis, S. L. (2001). *Adult development and aging* (5th ed.). Upper Saddle River, NJ: Prentice-Hall.

Schank, R., & Abelson, R. (1977). *Scripts, plans, goals, and understanding.* Mahwah, NJ: Erlbaum.

Scharff, L., Marcus, D. A., & Masek, B. J. (2002). A controlled study of minimal-contact thermal biofeedback treatment in children with migraine. *Journal of Pediatric Psychology, 27,* 109–119.

Schaubroeck, J., Jones, J. R., & Xie, J. L. (2001). Individual differences in utilizing control to cope with job demands: Effects on susceptibility to infectuous disease. *Journal of Applied Psychology, 86,* 114–120.

Scheier, M. F., & Carver, C. S. (1992). Effects of optimism on psychological and physical well-being: Theoretical overview and empirical update. *Cognitive Therapy and Research, 16,* 201–228.

Schiffman, J., & Walker, E. (1998). Schizophrenia. In H. S. Friedman (Ed.), *Encyclopedia of mental health* (Vol. 2). San Diego: Academic Press.

Schmolk, H., Buffalo, E. A., & Squire, L. R. (2000). Memory distortions develop over time: Recollections of the O. J. Simpson trial verdict after 15 and 32 months. *Psychological Science, 11,* 39–45.

Schneider, K. J. (2002). Humanistic psychotherapy. In M. Hersen & W. H. Sledge (Eds.), *Encyclopedia of psychotherapy.* San Diego: Academic Press.

Schneider, S. L. (2001). In search of realistic optimism: Meaning, knowledge, and warm fuzziness. *American Psychologist, 56,* 250–263.

Schneiderman, N., Antoni, M. H., Saab, P. G., & Ironson, G. (2001). Health psychology: Psycho-logical and biobehavioral aspects of chronic disease management. *Annual Review of Psychology* (Vol. 52). Palo Alto, CA: Annual Reviews.

Scholnick, E. K. (1999). Piaget's legacy: Heirs to the house that Jean built. In E. K. Scholnick, K. Nelson, S. A. Gelman, & P. H. Miller (Eds.), *Conceptual development: Piaget's legacy.* Mahwah, NJ: Erlbaum.

Scholnick, E. K., Nelson, K., Gelman, S. A., & Miller, P. H. (Eds.). (1999). *Conceptual development: Piaget's legacy.* Mahwah, NJ: Erlbaum.

Schredl, M., & Hofman, F. (2003). Continuity between waking activities and dream activities. *Conscious Cognition, 12,* 298–308.

Schulenberg, J. (1999, June). *Binge drinking trajectories before, during, and after college: More reasons to worry from a developmental perspective.* Paper presented at the meeting of the American Psychological Society, Denver, CO.

Schulenberg, J., O'Malley, P. M., Bachman, J. G., & Johnston, L. D. (2000). "Spread your wings and fly": The course of health and well-being during the transition to young adulthood. In L. Crockett & R. Silbereisen (Eds.), *Negotiating adolescence in times of social change.* New York: Cambridge University Press.

Schultz, A., Williams, D., Israel, B., Becker, A., Parker, E., James, S. A., & Jackson, J. (2000). Unfair treatment, neighborhood effects, and mental health in the Detroit metropolitan area. *Journal of Health and Social Behavior, 41,* 314–332.

Schultz, R., & Curnow, C. (1988). Peak performance and age among superathletes: Track and field, swimming, baseball, tennis, and golf. *Journal of Gerontology, 43,* 113–120.

Schunk, D. H. (2000). *Learning theories* (3rd ed.). Upper Saddle River, NJ: Prentice-Hall.

Schunk, D. H. (2004). *Learning theories* (4th ed.). Upper Saddle River, NJ: Prentice-Hall.

Schunk, D. H., & Ertmer, P. A. (2000). Self-regulation and academic learning: Self-efficacy enhancing interventions. In M. Boekaerts, P. R. Pintrich, & M. Zeidner (Eds.), *Handbook of self-regulation.* San Diego: Academic Press.

Schwartz, B. L. (2002). *Tip-of-the-tongue states.* Mahwah, NJ: Erlbaum.

Schwartz, T. (1999). *Kids and guns.* New York: Franklin Watts.

Scott, T. R. (2000). Taste. In A. Kazdin (Ed.), *Encyclopedia of psychology.* Washington, DC, & New York: American Psychological Association and Oxford University Press.

Sears, D. O., Peplau, L. A., & Taylor, S. E. (2000). *Social psychology* (10th Ed.). Upper Saddle River, NJ: Prentice-Hall.

Sechehaye, M. (1951). *Autobiography of a schizophrenic girl.* New York: Grune & Stratton.

Sedikides, C., Campbell, W. K., Reeder, G. D., & Elliot, A. J. (1998). The self-serving bias in relational context. *Journal of Personality and Social Psychology, 74,* 378–386.

Seffge-Krenke, I. (1995). *Stress, coping, and relationships in adolescence.* Mahwah, NJ: Erlbaum.

Segal, D. L., & Coolidge, F. L. (2000). Assessment. In A. Kazdin (Ed.), *Encyclopedia of psychology.* Washington, DC, & New York: American Psychological Association and Oxford University Press.

Segal, D. L., & Coolidge, F. L. (2004). Objective assessment of personality and psychopathology. In M. Hersen (Ed.), *Comprehensive handbook of psychological assessment* (Vol. 2). New York: Wiley.

Segrin, C. (2001). *Interpersonal processes in psychological disorders.* New York: Guilford.

Seidemann, E., Meilijson, I., Abeles, M., Bergman, H., & Vaadia, E. (1996). Simultaneously recorded single units in the frontal cortex go through sequences of discrete and stable states in monkeys performing a delayed localization task. *Journal of Neuroscience, 16,* 752–768.

Seidman, D. F., Rosecan, J., & Role, L. (1999). Biological and clinical perspectives on nicotine addiction. In D. F. Seidman & L. S. Covey (Eds.), *Helping the hard-core smoker.* Mahwah, NJ: Erlbaum.

Seidman, S. N. (2002). Exploring the relationship between depression and erectile dysfunction in aging men. *Journal of Clinical Psychiatry, 63, Supplement,* 5–12.

Seifer, R. (2001). Socioeconomic status, multiple risks, and development of intelligence. In R. J. Sternberg & E. L. Grigorenko (Eds.), *Environmental effects on cognitive abilities.* Mahwah, NJ: Erlbaum.

Sejnowski, T. (2001). *Seeing, hearing, and smelling the world* [Commentary]. Retrieved October 2001 from http://www.hhmi.org/ senses.

Sekular, R., & Blake, R. (2002). *Perception* (4th ed.). New York: McGraw-Hill.

Seligman, C., Olson, J. M., & Zanna, M. P. (Eds.). (1996). *The psychology of values.* Mahwah, NJ: Erlbaum.

Seligman, M. E. P. (1970). On the generality of the laws of learning. *Psychological Review, 77,* 406–418.

Seligman, M. E. P. (1975). *Helplessness: On depression, development and death.* San Francisco: W. H. Freeman.

Seligman, M. E. P. (1989). Why is there so much depression today? The waxing of the individual and the waning of the common. In *The G. Stanley Hall Lecture Series.* Washington, DC: American Psychological Association.

Seligman, M. E. P. (1990). *Learned optimism.* New York: Knopf.

Seligman, M. E. P. (1994). *What you can change and what you can't.* New York: Knopf.

Seligman, M. E. P. (2002). Positive psychology, prevention, and positive therapy. In C. R. Snyder & S. J. Lopez (Eds.), *Handbook of positive psychology.* New York: Oxford University Press.

Seligman, M. E. P., & Csikszentmihalyi, M. (2000). Positive psychology: An introduction. *American Psychologist, 55,* 5–14.

Seligman, M. E. P., & Pawelski, J. O. (2003). Positive psychology: FAQs. *Psychological Inquiry, 14,* 159–163.

Selye, H. (1974). *Stress without distress.* Philadelphia: W. B. Saunders.

Selye, H. (1983). The stress concept: Past, present, and future. In C. I. Cooper (Ed.), *Stress research.* New York: Wiley.

Serpell, R. (2000). Determinants of intelligence: Culture and intelligence. In A. Kazdin (Ed.), *Encyclopedia of psychology.* Washington, DC, & New York: American Psychological Association and Oxford University Press.

Seto, M. C., & Barbaree, H. E. (1995). The role of alcohol in sexual aggression. *Clinical Psychology Review, 15,* 545–566.

Shadubina, A., Agam, G., & Belmaker, R. H. (2001). The mechanism of lithium: State of the art, ten years later. *Progress in Neuropsychology and Biological Psychiatry, 25,* 855–866.

Shakesby, A. C., Anwyl, R., & Rowan, M. J. (2002). Overcoming the effects of stress on synaptic plasticity in the intact hippocampus: rapid actions of serotonergic and antidepressant agents. *Journal of Neuroscience, 22,* 3638–3644.

Shanks, D. R. (1991). Categorization by a connectionist network. *Journal of Experimental Psychology: Learning, Memory, and Cognition, 17,* 433–443.

Sharkey, K. M., & Eastman, C. I. (2002). Melatonin phase shifts human circadian rhythms in a placebo-controlled simulated night-work study. *American Journal of Physiology: Regulatory, Integrative, and Comparative Physiology, 282,* R454–R463.

Sharma, V. (2003). Atypical antipsychotics and suicide in mood and anxiety disorders. *Bipolar Disorder, 5, Supplement 2,* 48–52.

Shaughnessy, J. J., Zechmeister, E. B., & Zechmeister, J. S. (2003). *Research methods in psychology* (6th Ed.). New York: McGraw-Hill.

Shaver, P. (1986, August). *Being lonely, falling in love: Perspectives from attachment theory.* Paper presented at the meeting of the American Psychological Association, Washington, DC.

Shaywitz, B. A, Shaywitz, S. E., Pugh, K. R., & Others. (1995). Sex differences in the functional organization of the brain for language. *Nature, 373,* 607–609.

Sheldon, K. M., Ryan, R. M., Rawsthorne, L., & Ilardi, B. (1997). Trait self and true self: Cross-role variation in the Big Five traits and its relations with authenticity and subjective well-being. *Journal of Personality and Social Psychology, 73,* 1380–1393.

Shelton, R. C., & Hollon, S. D. (2000). Antidepressants. In A. Kazdin (Ed.), *Encyclopedia of psychology.* Washington, DC, & New York: American Psychological Association and Oxford University Press.

Shepard, R. N. (1967). Recognition memory for words, sentences, and pictures. *Journal of Verbal Learning and Verbal Behavior, 6,* 156–163.

Sher, K. J. (1993). Children of alcoholics and the intergenerational transmission of alcoholism: A biopsychological perspective. In J. S. Baer, G. A. Marlatt, & R. J. McMahon (Eds.), *Addictive behaviors across the life span.* Newbury Park, CA: Sage.

Sherif, M., Harvey, O. J., White, B. J., Hood, W. R., & Sherif, C. W. (1961). *Intergroup cooperation and competition: The Robbers Cave experiment.* Norman: University of Oklahoma Press.

Sherry, A., Dahlen, E., & Holaday, M. (2004). The use of sentence completion tests with adults. In M. Hersen (Ed.), *Comprehensive handbook of psychological assessment* (Vol. 2). New York: Wiley.

Sherwood, A., Light, K. C., & Blumenthal, J. A. (1989). Effects of aerobic exercise training on hemodynamic responses during psychosocial stress in normotensive and borderline hypertensive Type A men: A preliminary report. *Psychosomatic Medicine, 51,* 123–136.

Shevell, S. K. (2000). Color vision. In A. Kazdin (Ed.), *Encyclopedia of psychology.* Washington, DC, & New York: American Psychological Association and Oxford University Press.

Shewchuk, R. M., Johnson, M. O., & Elliott, T. R. (1999). Self-appraised social problem solving abilities, emotional reactions, and actual problem-solving performance. *Behavioral Research and Therapy, 38,* 727–740.

Shields, S., & Eyssell, K. M. (2002). History of the study of gender psychology. In J. Worell (Ed.), *Encyclopedia of women and gender.* New York: Oxford University Press.

Shields, S. A. (1991). Gender in the psychology of emotion. In K. T. Strongman (Ed.), *International Review of Studies of Emotion* (Vol. 1). New York: Wiley.

Shier, D., Butler, J., & Lewis, R. (1999). *Human anatomy and physiology* (8th ed.). New York: McGraw-Hill.

Shnek, Z. M., Irvine, J., Stewart, D., & Abbey, S. (2001). Psychological factors and depressive symptoms in ischemic heart disease. *Health Psychology, 20,* 141–145.

Shotland, R. L. (1985, June). When bystanders just stand by. *Psychology Today.* pp. 50–55.

Showers, C. (1986). *The motivational consequences of negative thinking.* Paper presented at the meeting of the American Psychological Association, Washington, DC.

Shultz, R. T., Grelotti, D. J., & Pober, B. (2001). Genetics of childhood disorders: XXVI. Williams syndrome and brain-behavior relationships. *Journal of the American Academy of Child and Adolescent Psychiatry, 40,* 606–609.

Siebner, H. R., Limmer, C., Peinemann, A., Drzezga, A., Bloem, B. R., Schwaiger, M., & Conrad, B. (2002). Long-term consequences of switching handedness: A positron emission tomography study on handwriting in "converted" left handers. *Journal of Neuroscience, 22,* 2816–2825.

Siegel, S. (1988). State dependent learning and morphine tolerance. *Behavioral Neuroscience, 102,* 228–232.

Siegle, G. J., Steinhauer, S. R., Thase, M. E., Stenger, V. A., & Carter, C. S. (2002). Can't shake that feeling: event-related fMRI assessment of sustained amygdala activity in response to emotional information in depressed individuals. *Biological Psychiatry, 51,* 693–707.

Siegler, R. S. (1998). *Children's thinking* (3rd ed.). Upper Saddle River, NJ: Erlbaum.

Silverman, N. N., & Corsini, R. J. (1984). Is it true what they say about Adler's individual psychology? *Teaching of Psychology, 11,* 188–189.

Silverstein, S. M., Menditto, A. A., & Stuve, P. (2001). Shaping attention span: An operant conditioning procedure to improve neurocognition and functioning in schizophrenia. *Schizophrenia Bulletin, 27,* 247–257.

Simeon, D., Guralnik, O., Knutelska, M., & Schmeidler, J. (2002). Personality factors associated with dissociation: Temperament, defenses, and cognitive schemata. *American Journal of Psychiatry, 159,* 489–491.

Simon, H. A. (1969). *The sciences of the artificial.* Cambridge, MA: MIT Press.

Simon, H. A. (1996). Putting the story together. *Contemporary Psychology, 41,* 12–14.

Simpson, H. B., Lombardo, I., Slifstein, M., Huang, H. Y., Hawang, D. R., Abi-Dargham, A., Liebowitz, M. R., & Laruelle, M. (2003). Serotonin transporters in obsessive-compulsive disorder. *Biological Psychiatry, 54,* 1414–1421.

Simpson, J. A. (1995). Self-monitoring and commitment to dating relationships: A classroom demonstration. In M. E. Ware & D. E. Johnson (Eds.), *Demonstrations and activities in teaching of introductory psychology.* Mahwah, NJ: Erlbaum.

Simpson, J. A., & Gangestad, S. W. (2001). Evolution and relationships: A call for integration. *Personal Relationships, 8,* 341–356.

Simpson, K. J. (2002). Anorexia nervosa and culture. *Journal of Psychiatric and Mental Health Nursing, 9,* 65–71,

Singer, D. G., & Singer, J. L. (1998). Television viewing. In H.S. Friedman (Ed.), *Encyclopedia of mental health* (Vol. 3). San Diego: Academic Press.

Singer, M., Gagnon, N., & Richards, E. (2002). Strategies of text retrieval: A criterion shift account. *Canadian Journal of Experimental Psychology, 56,* 41–57.

Singh, R. P. (1984, January). Experimental verification of locus of control as related to conformity behavior. *Psychological Studies, 29(1),* 64–67.

Sireci, S. G. (2004). Using bilinguals to evaluate the comparability of different language versions of a test. In R. K. Hambleton, P. F. Merenda, & C. D. Spielberger (Eds.), *Adapting educational tests for cross-cultural assessment.* Mahwah, NJ: Erlbaum.

Skinner, B. F. (1938). *The behavior of organisms: An experimental analysis.* New York: Appleton-Century-Crofts.

Skinner, B. F. (1948). *Walden Two.* New York: Macmillan.

Skinner, B. F. (1957). *Verbal behavior.* New York: Appleton-Century-Crofts.

Skinner, E. A., Wellborn, J. G., & Connell, J. P. (1990). What it takes to do well in school and whether I've got it. *Journal of Educational Psychology, 82,* 22–32.

Slaap, B. R., Nielsen, M. M., Boshuisen, M. L., van Roon, A. M., & den Boer, J. A. (2004). Five-minute recordings of heart rate variability in obsessive-compulsive disorder, panic disorder, and healthy volunteers. *Journal of Affective Disorders, 78,* 141–148.

Slavin, R. (1989). Cooperative learning and student achievement. In R. Slavin (Ed.), *School and classroom organization.* Mahwah, NJ: Erlbaum.

Slavin, R. E. (2000). *Educational psychology* (6th ed.). Boston: Allyn & Bacon.

Slife, B., & Yanchar, S. C. (2000). Unresolved issues in psychology. In B. Slife (Ed.), *Taking sides* (11th ed.). New York: Duskin McGraw-Hill.

Sloan, D. M., & Mizes, J. S. (1999). Foundations of behavior therapy in the contemporary health-care context. *Clinical Psychology Review, 19,* 255–274.

Sloan, P., Arsenault, L., Hilsenroth, M., & Harvill, L. (1996). Rorschach measures of post-traumatic stress in Persian Gulf War veterans: A three-year follow-up study. *Journal of Personality Assessment, 66,* 54–64.

Slobin, D. (1972, July). Children and language: They learn the same way around the world. *Psychology Today,* 71–76.

Smallwood, J., Obonsawin, M., & Heim, D. (2003). Task unrelated thought: The role of distributed processing. *Consciousness and Cognition, 12,* 169–189.

Smith, D. V., & Margolskee, R. F. (2001). Making sense of taste. *Scientific American, 284,* 32–39.

Smith, K. H., & Rogers, M. (1994). Effectiveness of subliminal messages in television commercials. *Journal of Applied Psychology, 79,* 866–874.

Smith, L. (2002). Piaget's model. In U. Goswami (Ed.), *Blackwell handbook of childhood cognitive development.* Malden, MA: Blackwell.

Smith, M. B. (2001). Humanistic psychology. In W. E. Craighead & C. B. Nemeroff (Eds.), *The Corsini encyclopedia of psychology and behavioral science* (3rd ed.). New York: Wiley.

Smith, M. L., Glass, G. N., & Miller, R. L. (1980). *The benefit of psychotherapy.* Baltimore: Johns Hopkins University Press.

Smith, S. M., & Fabrigar, L. R. (2000). Attitudes: An overview. In A. Kazdin (Ed.), *Encyclopedia of psychology.* Washington, DC, & New York: American Psychological Association and Oxford University Press.

Smith, S. M., & Vela, E. (2001). Environmental context-dependent memory: A review and meta-analysis. *Psychonomic Bulletin Review, 8,* 203–220.

Snow, C. (1999). Social perspectives on the emergence of language. In B. MacWhinney (Ed.), *The emergence of language.* Mahwah, NJ: Erlbaum.

Snowden, D. A. (1997). Aging and Alzheimer's disease: Lessons from the nun study. *Gerontologist, 37,* 150–156.

Snowden, D. A. (2001). *Aging with grace: What the nun study teaches us about longer, healthier, and more meaningful lives.* New York: Bantam.

Snowdon, D. A. (2003). Healthy aging and dementia: findings from the Nun study. *Annals of Internal Medicine, 139,* 450–454.

Snyder, M., & Stukas, A. A. (1999). Interpersonal processes: The interplay of cognitive, motivational, and behavioral activities in social interaction. *Annual Review of Psychology* (Vol. 49). Palo Alto, CA: Annual Reviews, Inc.

Sober, E. (2001). The ABC's of altruism. In S. G. Post, L. G. Underwood, J. P. Schloss, & W. B. Hurlbut (Eds.), *Altruism and altruistic love.* New York: Oxford University Press.

Soderstrom, M., Dolbier, C., Leiferman, J., & Stenhardt, M. (2000). The relationship of hardiness, coping strategies, and perceived stress to symptoms of illness. *Journal of Behavioral Medicine, 23,* 311–328.

Sofroniew, M. V., & Mobley, W. C. (2001). Nerve growth factor, neuroprotection, and neural repair. *Annual Review of Neuroscience, 24.* Palo Alto, CA: Annual Reviews.

Soja, P. J., Pang, W., Taepavarapruk, N., & McErlane, S. A. (2001). Spontaneous spike activity of spinoreticular tract neurons during sleep and waking. *Sleep, 24,* 18–25.

Solms, M. (1997). *The neuropsychology of dreams.* Mahwah, NJ: Erlbaum.

Solomon, H. M. (2003). Freud and Jung: An incomplete encounter. *Journal of Analytical Psychology, 48,* 553–569.

Sonnenberg, S. M., & Ursano, R. (2002). Psychoanalysis and psychoanalytic psychotherapy: Technique. In M. Hersen & W. H. Sledge (Eds.), *Encyclopedia of psychotherapy.* San Diego: Academic Press.

Sorensen, A., Adam, C. L., Findlay, P. A., Marie, M., Thomas, L., Travers, M. T., & Vernon, R. G. (2002). Leptin secretion and hypothalamic neuropeptide receptor gene expression in sheep. *American Journal of Physiology: Regulatory, Integrative, and Comparative Physiology, 282,* R1227–R1235.

Sorensen, B. K., Hojrup, P., Ostergard, E., Jorgensen, C. S., Enghild, J., Ryder, L. R. & Houen, G. (2002). Silver staining of proteins of electroblotting membrandes and intensification of silver staining of proteins separated by polyacrylamide gel. *Annals of Biochemistry, 304,* 33–41.

Sothern, M. S., Schumacher, H., von Almen, T. K., Carlisle, L. K., & Udall, J. N. (2002). Committed to kids: an integrated, 4-level team approach to weight management in adolescents. *Journal of the American Dietetic Association, 102,* S81–S85.

Spanos, N. P., & Chaves, J. F. (Eds.). (1989). *Hypnosis: The cognitive-behavior perspective.* Buffalo, NY: Prometheus.

Spearman, C. E. (1927). *The abilities of man.* New York: Macmillan.

Spector, A. C., & Kopka, S. L. (2002). Rats fail to discriminate quinine from denatonium: implications for the neural coding of bitter-tasting compounds. *Journal of Neuroscience, 22,* 1937–1941.

Spence, C., Kingstone, A., Shore, D. I., & Gazzaniga, M. S. (2002). Representation of visotactile space in the split brain. *Psychological Science,* 90–93.

Spencer, M. B. (2000). Ethnocentrism. In A. Kazdin (Ed.), *Encyclopedia of psychology.* Washington, DC, and New York: American Psychological Association and Oxford University Press.

Spera, S. P., Buhrfeind, E. D., & Pennebaker, J. W. (1994). Expressive writing and coping with job loss. *Academy of Management Journal, 37,* 722–733.

Speranza, M., Corcos, M., Atger, F., Paternitti, S., & Jeammet, P. (2003). Binge eating behaviors, depression, and weight control strategies. *Eating and Weight Disorders, 8,* 201–206.

Sperling, G. (1960). The information available in brief presentations. *Psychological Monographs, 74* (Whole No. 11).

Sperry, R. W. (1968). Hemisphere deconnection and unity in conscious awareness. *American Psychologist, 23,* 723–733.

Sperry, R. W. (1974). Lateral specialization in surgically separated hemispheres. In F. O. Schmitt & F. G. Worden (Eds.), *The neurosciences: Third study program.* Cambridge, MA: MIT Press.

Spetea, M., Rydelius, G., Nylander, I., Ahmed, M., Blieviciute-Ljungar, I., Lundeberg, T., Svensson, S., & Kreicergs, A. (2002). Alteration in endogenous opoid systems due to chronic inflammatory pain conditions. *European Journal of Pharmacology, 435,* 245–252.

Spiegler, M. D., & Guevremont, D. C. (2003). *Contemporary behavior therapy* (4th ed.). Belmont, CA: Wadsworth.

Springer, S. P., & Deutsch, G. (1998). *Left brain, right brain.* New York: Freeman.

Sprinthall, R. C. (2003). *Basic statistical analysis* (7th ed.). Boston: Allyn & Bacon.

Squire, L. (1990, June). *Memory and brain systems.* Paper presented at the meeting of the American Psychological Society, Dallas.

Squire, L. R. (1998). Interview. *Journal of Cognitive Neuroscience, 10,* 778–782.

Squire, L. R., & Kandel, E. R. (2000). *Memory: From mind to molecule.* New York: Worth.

Squire, L., Stark, C., & Clark, R. (2004). Analysis of memory. *Annual Review of Neuroscience, 27.* Palo Alto, CA: Annual Reviews.

Staddon, J. E., Chelaru, I. M., & Higa, J. J. (2002). A tune-trace theory of interval-timing dynamics. *Journal of the Experimental Analysis of Behavior, 77,* 105–124.

Stafford, J., & Lynn, S. J. (2002). Cultural scripts, memories of childhood abuse, and multiple identities: A study of role-played enactments. *International Journal of Experimental Hypnosis, 50,* 67–85.

Stahl, S. M. (2002). The psychopharmacology of energy and fatigue. *Journal of Clinical Psychiatry, 63,* 7–8.

Stangor, C. (2004). *Research methods for the behavioral sciences* (2nd ed.). Boston: Houghton Mifflin.

Stanley, M. A. (2000). Obsessive-compulsive disorder. In A. Kazdin (Ed.), *Encyclopedia of psychology.* Washington, DC, & New York: American Psychological Association and Oxford University Press.

Stanley, M. A., Diefenbach, G. J., & Hopko, D. R. (2004). Cognitive behavioral treatment for older adults with generalized anxiety disorder. *Behavior Modification, 28,* 73–117.

Stanley, M. A., & Turner, S. M. (1995). Current status of pharmacological and behavioral treatment of obsessive-compulsive disorder. *Behavior Therapy, 26,* 163–177.

Stanovich, K. E. (1999). *Who is rational? Individual differences in reasoning.* Mahwah, NJ: Erlbaum.

Stanovich, K. E. (2004). *How to think straight about psychology* (7th ed.). Boston: Allyn & Bacon.

Stanovich, K. E., & West, R. E. (2000). Individual differences in reasoning: Implications for the rationality debate? *Behavior and Brain Sciences, 23,* 645–665.

Steele, C. (2001). Zyban: An effective treatment for nicotine addiction. *Hospital Medicine, 61,* 785–788.

Steele, C. M. (1996, August). *A burden of suspicion: The role of stereotypes in shaping intellectual identity.* Paper presented at the meeting of the American Psychological Association, Toronto.

Steele, C. M., & Aronson, J. (1995). Stereotype threat and the intellectual test performance of African-Americans. *Journal of Personality and Social Psychology, 69,* 797–811.

Steers, W., Guay, A. T., Leriche, A., Gingell, C., Hargreave, T. B., Wright, P. J., Price, D. E., & Feldman, R. A. (2001). Assessment of the efficacy and safety of Viagra (sildenafil citrate) in men with erectile dysfunction during long-term treatment. *International Journal of Impotence Research, 13,* 261–267.

Stein, M. B., (2003). Attending to anxiety disorders in primary care. *Journal of Clinical Psychiatry, 64, Supplement 15,* 35–39.

Stein, M. T., & Ferber, R. (2001). Recent onset of sleepwalking in early adolescence. *Journal of Development, Behavior, and Pediatrics, 22,* S33–S35.

Steriade, M. (2004). Neocortical cell classes are flexible entities. *Nature Reviews: Neuroscience, 5,* 121–134.

Sternberg, E. M., & Gold, P. W. (1996). The mind-body interaction in disease. *Mysteries of the mind.* New York: Scientific American.

Sternberg, R. J. (1988). *The triangle of love.* New York: Basic Books.

Sternberg, R. J. (1997a). Educating intelligence: Infusing the triarchic theory into instruction. In R. J. Sternberg & E. Grigorenko (Eds.), *Intelligence, heredity, and environment.* New York: Cambridge University Press.

Sternberg, R. J. (1997b). *Successful intelligence.* New York: Simon & Schuster.

Sternberg, R. J. (2000). The holy grail of general intelligence. *Science, 289,* 399–401.

Sternberg, R. J. (2001). Is there a heredity-environment paradox? In R. J. Sternberg & E. L. Grigorenko (Eds.), *Environmental effects on cognitive abilities.* Mahwah, NJ: Erlbaum.

Sternberg, R. J. (2002). Intelligence: The triarchic theory of intelligence. In J. W. Gutherie (Ed.), *Encyclopedia of education* (2nd ed.). New York: Macmillan.

Sternberg, R. J. (2003a). *Cognitive psychology* (3rd ed.). Belmont, CA: Wadsworth.

Sternberg, R. J. (2003b). Contemporary theories of intelligence. In. I. B. Weiner (Ed.), *Handbook of psychology.* (Vol. 7). New York: Wiley.

Sternberg, R. J., & Grigorenko, E. L. (Eds.). (2001). *Environmental effects on cognitive abilities.* Mahwah, NJ: Erlbaum.

Sternberg, R. J., Lautrey, J., & Lubart, T. I. (Eds.). (2003). *Models of intelligence: International perspectives.* Washington, D.C: American Psychological Association.

Sternberg, R. J., & O'Hara, L. A. (2000). Intelligence and creativity. In R. J. Sternberg (Ed.), *Handbook of intelligence.* New York: Cambridge University Press.

Sternberg, R. J., & Spear-Swerling, P. (1996). *Teaching for thinking.* Washington, DC: American Psychological Association.

Steur, F. B., Applefield, J. M., & Smith, R. (1971). Televised aggression and the interpersonal aggression of preschool children. *Journal of Experimental Child Psychology, 11,* 442–447.

Stevenson, H. G. (1995, March). *Missing data: On the forgotten substance of race, ethnicity, and socioeconomic classifications.* Paper presented at the meeting of the Society for Research in Child Development, Indianapolis, IN.

Stevenson, H. W. (1992, December). Learning from Asian schools. *Scientific American,* pp. 6, 70–76.

Stevenson, H. W. (1995). Mathematics achievement of American students: First in the world by the year 2000? In C. A. Nelson (Ed.), *Basic and applied perspectives on learning, cognition, and development.* Minneapolis: University of Minnesota Press.

Stevenson, H. W. (1997, August), *Bronfenbrenner award address.* Paper presented at the meeting of the American Psychological Association, Chicago.

Stevenson, H. W. (2000). Middle childhood: Education and schooling. In A. Kazdin (Ed.), *Encyclopedia of psychology.* Washington, DC, & New York: American Psychological Association and Oxford University Press.

Stevenson, H. W., & Hofer, B. K. (1999). Education policy in the United States and abroad: What we can learn from each other. In G. J. Cizek (Ed.), *Handbook of educational policy.* San Diego: Academic Press.

Stevenson, H. W., Lee, S., Chen, C., Stigler, J. W., Hsu, C., & Kitamura, S. (1990). Contexts of achievement. *Monograph of the Society for Research in Child Development, 55* (Serial No. 221).

Stevenson, H. W., Lee, S., & Stigler, J. W. (1986). Mathematics achievement of Chinese, Japanese, and American children. *Science, 231,* 693–699.

Stewart, A., & McDermott, C. (2004). Gender in psychology. *Annual Review of Psychology, 54.* Palo Alto, CA: Annual Reviews.

Stewart, K. (1954). *Pygmies and dream giants.* New York: W.W. Norton.

Stickgold, R. (2001). Watching the sleeping brain watch us: Sensory processing during sleep. *Trends in Neuroscience, 24,* 307–309.

Stickgold, R., & Hobson, J. A. (2000). Visual discrimination learning requires sleep after training. *Nature Neuroscience, 3,* 1237–1238.

Stigler, J. W., & Hiebert, J. (1997, September). Understanding and improving classroom mathematics instruction. *Phi Delta Kappan, 79,* 14–21.

Stipek, D. (2001). *Motivation to learn* (4th ed.). Boston: Allyn & Bacon.

Stocchi, F., Vacca, L., Beradelli, A., Onofrj, M., Manfredi, M., & Ruggieri, S. (2003). Dual dopamine agonist treatment in Parkinson's disease. *Journal of Neurology, 250,* 822–826.

Stolley, K. S. (2001). *Groupthink.* Retrieved November 24, 2001, from http://www.about.com

Stone, A. A., Neale, J. M., Cox, D. S., Napoli, A., Valdimarsdottir, H., & Kennedy-Moore, E. (1994). Daily events are associated with secretory immune response to an oral antigen in men. *Health Psychology, 13,* 440–446.

Stoner, J. (1961). *A comparison of individual and group decisions, including risk.* Unpublished master's thesis, School of Industrial Management, MIT.

Stowell, J. R., McGuire, L., Glaser, R., & Kiecolt-Glaser, J. (2003). Psychoneuroimmunology. In I. B. Weiner (Ed.), *Handbook of psychology,* Vol. IX. New York: Wiley.

Straus, M. A. (1991). Discipline and deviance: Physical punishment of children and violence and other crimes in adulthood. *Social Problems, 38,* 133–154.

Straus, M. A., Sugarman, D. B., & Giles-Sims, J. (1997). Spanking by parents and subsequent antisocial behavior of children. *Archives of Pediatric and Adolescent Medicine, 151,* 761–767.

Strean, H. S. (1996). Resistance viewed from different perspectives. *American Journal of Psychotherapy, 50,* 29–31.

Strege, J. (1997). *Tiger: A biography of Tiger Woods.* New York: Broadway Books.

Streissguth, A. (1997). *Fetal alcohol syndrome: A guide for families and communities.* Baltimore: Brookes.

Striefel, S. (1998). *How to teach through modeling and imitation.* Austin, TX: Pro-Ed.

Striegel-Moore, R. H., Silberstein, L. R., & Rodin, J. (1993). The social self in bulimia nervosa: Public self-consciousness, social anxiety, and perceived fraudulence. *Journal of Abnormal Psychology, 102,* 297–303.

Strupp, H. H. (1995). The psychotherapist's skills revised. *Clinical Psychology: Science and Practice, 2,* 70–74.

Stuart, G. L., Treat, T. A., & Wade, W. A. (2000). Effectiveness of empirically based treatment for panic disorder delivered in a service clinic setting. *Journal of Consulting and Clinical Psychology, 68,* 506–512.

Sue, D. (2002). Culture specific psychotherapy. In M. Hersen & W. H. Sledge (Eds.), *Encyclopedia of psychotherapy.* San Diego: Academic Press.

Sue, S. (2000). Ethnocultural psychotherapy. In A. Kazdin (Ed.), *Encyclopedia of psychology.* Washington, DC, & New York: American Psychological Association and Oxford University Press.

Sue, S. (2003). In defense of cultural competence in psychotherapy and treatment. *American Psychologist, 58,* 964–970.

Sugarman, A., & DePottel, C. (2002). The unconscious. In M. Hersen & W. H. Sledge (Eds.), *Encyclopedia of psychotherapy.* San Diego: Academic Press.

Suhner, A., Schlagenhauf, P., Hofer, I., Johnson, R., Tschopp, A., & Steffen, R. (2001). Effectiveness and tolerability of melatonin and zopidem for the alleviation of jet lag. *Aviation, Space, and Environmental Medicine, 72,* 638–646.

Suinn, R. M. (1984). *Fundamentals of abnormal psychology.* Chicago: Nelson-Hall.

Sullivan, H. S. (1953). *The interpersonal theory of psychiatry.* New York: Norton.

Sullivan, K. T., & Christensen, A. (1998). In H. S. Friedman (Ed.), *Encyclopedia of mental health* (Vol. 1). San Diego: Academic Press.

Suls, J., & Swain, A. (1998). Type A–Type B personalities. In H. S. Friedman (Ed.), *Encyclopedia of mental health* (Vol. 3). San Diego: Academic Press.

Surprenant, A. M. (2001). Distinctiveness and serial position effects in tonal sequences. *Perception and Psychophysics, 63,* 737–745.

Susman, E. J., & Rogol, A. (2004). Puberty and psychological development. In R. Lerner & L. Steinberg (Eds.), *Handbook of adolescent psychology.* New York: Wiley.

Susman, E. J., Worrall, B. K., Murowchick, E., Frobose, C. A., & Schwab, J. E. (1996). Experience and neuroendocrine parameters of development: Aggressive behaviors and competencies. In D. M. Stoff & R. B. Cairns (Eds.), *Aggression and violence.* Mahwah, NJ: Erlbaum.

Sussman, S. (2001). School-based tobacco use prevention and cessation: Where are we going? *American Journal of Health Behavior, 25,* 191–199.

Sutker, P. B., & Allain, A. N. (1993). Behavior and personality assessment in men labeled adaptive sociopaths. *Journal of Behavioral Assessment, 5,* 65–79.

Swaab, D.F., Chung, W. C., Kruijver, F. P., Hofman, M. A., & Hestiantoro, A. (2003). Sex differences in the hyphothalamus in the different stages of life. *Neurobiology of Aging, 24,* Supplement 1, S1–S16.

Swaab, D. F., Chung, W. C., Kruijver, F. P., Hofman, M. A., & Ishunina, T. A. (2001). Structural and functional sex differences in the human hypothalamus. *Hormones and Behavior, 40,* 93–98.

Swann, W. B., De La Ronde, C., & Hixon, J. G. (1994). Authenticity and positive strivings in marriage and courtship. *Journal of Personality and Social Psychology, 66,* 857–869.

Swanson, J. (Ed.). (1999). *Sleep disorders sourcebook.* New York: Omnigraphics.

Swartz-Kulstad, J. L., & Martin, W. E. (2000). Culture as an essential aspect of person-environment fit. In W. E. Martin & J. L. Swartz-Kulstad (Eds.), *Person-environment psychology and mental health.* Mahwah, NJ: Erlbaum.

Szasz, T. S. (1961). *The myth of mental illness: Foundations of a theory of personal conduct.* New York: Hoeber-Harper.

T

Tager-Flusberg, H. (Ed.). (1994). *Constraints on language acquisition.* Mahwah, NJ: Erlbaum.

Tager-Flusberg, H. (1999). Language development in atypical children. In M. Barrett (Ed.), *The development of language.* Philadelphia: Psychology Press.

Tajfel, H. (1978). The achievement of group differentiation. In H. Tajfel (Ed.), *Differentiation between social groups.* London: Academic Press.

Takeuchi, T., Miyasa, A., Inugami, M., & Yamamoto, Y. (2001). Intrinsic dreams are not produced without REM sleep mechanisms. *Journal of Sleep Research, 10,* 43–52.

Tanaka-Matsumi, J. (2001). Abnormal psychology and culture. In D. Matsumoto (Ed.), *The handbook of culture and psychology.* New York: Oxford University Press.

Tang, M. P., Chon, H. C., Tsao, P. N., Tson, K. I., & Hsich, W. S. (2004). Outcome of very low birth weight infants with sonographic enlarged occipital horn. *Pediatric Neurology, 30,* 42–45.

Tannen, D. (1990). *You just don't understand!* New York: Ballantine.

Tapert, S. F., Brown, G. G., Kinderman, S. S., Cheung, E. H., Frank, L. R., & Brown, S. A. (2001). fMRI measurement of brain dysfunction in alcohol-dependent young women. *Alcohol: Clinical and Experimental Research, 25,* 236–245.

Tassi, P., & Muzet, A. (2001). Defining states of consciousness. *Neuroscience and Biobehavioral Review, 25,* 175–191.

Taub, E. (2001, April). *Adult brain plasticity.* Paper presented at the meeting of the Society for Research in Child Development, Minneapolis.

Tavris, C., & Wade, C. (1984). *The longest war: Sex differences in perspective* (2nd ed.). Fort Worth: Harcourt Brace.

Tavris, C. B. (in press). *Women and health psychology.* Mahwah, NJ: Erlbaum.

Taylor, S. (2002). Classical conditioning. In M. Hersen & W. H. Sledge (Eds.), *Encyclopedia of psychotherapy.* San Diego: Academic Press.

Taylor, S. E. (1998). Positive illusions. In H. S. Friedman (Ed.), *Encyclopedia of mental health* (Vol. 3). San Diego: Academic Press.

Taylor, S. E. (2001). Toward a biology of social support. In C. R. Snyder & S. J. Lopez (Eds.), *Handbook of positive psychology.* New York: Oxford University Press.

Taylor, S. E. (2003). *Health psychology* (5th ed.). New York: McGraw-Hill.

Taylor, S. E., & Brown, J. D. (1994). Positive illusions and well-being revisited: Separating fact from fiction. *Psychological Bulletin, 116,* 21–27.

Taylor, S. E., Klein, L. S., Lewis, B. P., Gurenewald, T. L., Gurun, R. A., & Updegraff, J. A. (2000). Biobehavioral responses in females: Tend-and-befriend, not fight-or-flight. *Psychological Review, 107,* 411–429.

Taylor, S. E., Peplau, L. A., & Sears, D. O. (2003). *Social psychology* (11th ed.). Upper Saddle River, NJ: Prentice-Hall.

Teasdale, J. D., Taylor, M. J., Cooper, Z., Hayhurst, H., & Paykel, E. S. (1995). Depressive thinking. *Journal of Abnormal Psychology, 104,* 500–507.

Temple, E. C., Hutchinson, I., Lang, D. G., & Jinks, A. L. (2002). Taste development: Differential growth rates of tongue regions in humans. *Brain Research: Developmental Brain Research, 135,* 65–70.

Tenenbaum, H. R., Callahan, M., AlbaSpeyer, C., & Sandoval, L. (2002). Parent-child science conversations in Mexican descent families: Educational background, activity, and past experience as moderators. *Hispanic Journal of Behavioral Sciences, 24,* 225–248.

Terao, A., Steininger, T. L., Morairty, S. R., & Kilduff, S. F. (2004). Age-related changes in histamine receptor mRNA levels in the mouse brain. *Neuroscience Letters, 13,* 18–84.

Terman, L. (1925). *Genetic studies of genius. Vol. 1: Mental and physical traits of a thousand gifted children.* Stanford, CA: Stanford University Press.

Terr, L. C. (1988). What happens to early memories of trauma? *Journal of the American Academy of Child and Adolescent Psychiatry, 27,* 96–104.

Tetreault, M. K. T. (1997). Classrooms for diversity: Rethinking curriculum and pedagogy. In J. A. Banks & C. A. Banks (Eds.), *Multicultural education* (3rd ed.). Boston: Allyn & Bacon.

Tharp, R. G. (1991). Cultural diversity and treatment of children. *Journal of Consulting & Clinical Psychology, 59,* 799–812.

Thayer, J. F., Rossy, I., Sollers, J., Friedman, B. H., & Allen, M. T. (1996, March). *Relationships among heart period variability and cardiodynamic measures vary as a function of fitness.* Paper presented at the meeting of the American Psychosomatic Society, Williamsburg, VA.

Thelen, E. (2000). Infancy: Perception and motor development. In A. Kazdin (Ed.), *Encyclopedia of psychology.* Washington, DC, & New York: Oxford University Press.

Thelen, E., & Smith, L. B. (1998). Dynamic systems theories. In W. Damon (Ed.), *Handbook of child psychology* (5th ed., Vol. 1). New York: Wiley.

Thiedke, C. C. (2001). Sleep disorders and sleep problems in childhood. *American Family Physician, 63,* 277–284.

Thigpen, C. H., & Cleckley, H. M. (1957). *Three faces of Eve.* New York. McGraw-Hill.

Thijssen, J. H. (2002). Relations of androgens and selected aspects of human behavior. *Maturitas, 41, Supplement,* 47–54.

Thomas, C. B. (1983). *Stress and coping.* Unpublished manuscript, Johns Hopkins University, Baltimore.

Thomas, M., Sing, H., Belenky, G., Holcomb, H., Mayberg, H., Dannals, R., Wagner, H., Thorne, D., Popp, K., Rowland, L., Welsh, A., Balwinksi, S., & Redmond, D. (2001). Neural basis of alertness and cognitive performance impairments during sleepiness: I. Effects of 24 hours of sleep deprivation on waking human regional brain activity. *Journal of Sleep Research, 9,* 335–352.

Thomas, R. M. (2001). *Recent human development theories.* Thousand Oaks, CA: Sage.

Thompson, M. J., Raynor, A., Cornah, D., Stevenson, J., & Sonuga-Barke, E. J. (2002). Parenting behavior described by mothers in a general population sample. *Child: Care, Health, and Development, 28,* 149–155.

Thompson, P. M., Giedd, J. N., MacDonald, D., Evans, A. C., & Toga, A. W. (2000). Growth patterns in the developing brain by using continuum sensor maps. *Nature, 404,* 190–193.

Thompson, R. (2000). Early experience and socialization. In A. Kazdin (Ed.), *Encyclopedia of psychology.* Washington, DC, & New York: American Psychological Association and Oxford University Press.

Thompson, R. A., Easterbrooks, M. A. & Walker, L. (2003). Social and emotional development in infancy. In I. B. Weiner (Ed.), *Handbook of psychology* (Vol. 6). New York: Wiley.

Thompson, S. C. (2001). The role of personal control in adaptive functioning. In C. R. Snyder & S. J. Lopez (Eds.), *Handbook of positive psychology.* New York: Oxford University Press.

Thompson, S. C., & Spacapan, S. (1991). Perceptions of control in vulnerable populations. *Journal of Social Issues, 47,* 1–22.

Thorne, B. M. (2001). Introversion-extraversion. In W. E. Craighead & C. B. Nemeroff (Eds.), *The Corsini encyclopedia of psychology and behavioral science* (3rd ed.). New York: Wiley.

Thrybom, T., Rooth, P., & Lindstrom, P. (2001). Effect of serotonin reuptake inhibitor on syndrome development in obese hyperglycemic mice. *Metabolism, 50,* 144–150.

Thurstone, L. L. (1938). *Primary mental abilities.* Chicago: University of Chicago Press.

Tinbergen, N. (1969). *The study of instinct.* New York: Oxford University Press.

Tissot, T. A. (2003). Probable meperidine-induced serotonin syndrome in a patient with a history of fluoxetine use. *Anesthesiology, 98,* 1511–1512.

Todd, G. S., & Gigerenzer, G. (2001). Precis of simple heuristics that make us smart. *Behavior and Brain Sciences, 23,* 727–741.

Tolan, P., Miller, L., & Thomas, P. (1988). Perception and experience of two types of social stress and self-image among adolescents. *Journal of Youth and Adolescence, 17,* 147–163.

Tolman, D. L., & Diamond, L. M. (2003). Desegregating sexuality research: Cultural and biological perspectives on gender and desire. *Annual Review of Sex Research, 12,* 33–74.

Tolman, E. C. (1932). *Purposive behavior in animals and man.* New York: Appleton-Century-Crofts.

Tolman, E. C. (1948). Cognitive maps in rats and men. *Psychological Review, 55,* 189–208.

Tolman, E. C., & Honzik, C. H. (1930). Degrees of hunger, reward and non-reward, and maze performance in rats. *University of California Publications in Psychology, 4,* 21–256.

Tomasello, M., & Slobin, D. I. (Eds.). (2004). *Beyond nature-nurture.* Mahwah, NJ: Erlbaum.

Torgersen, S. (1986). Genetic factors in moderately severe and mild affective disorders. *Archives of General Psychiatry, 43,* 222–226.

Tracey, T. J., Sherry, P., & Albright, J. M. (1999). The interpersonal process of cognitive-behavioral therapy. *Journal of Counseling Psychology, 46,* 80–91.

Trainor, L. J., McDonald, K. L., & Alain, C. (2002). Automatic and controlled processing of melodic contour and interval information measured by electrical brain activity. *Journal of Cognitive Neuroscience, 14,* 430–432.

Traub, R. D. (2004). Oscillations in the hippocampus. *Annual Review of Neuroscience, 27.* Palo Alto, CA: Annual Reviews.

Triandis, H. C. (1994). *Culture and social behavior.* New York: McGraw-Hill.

Triandis, H. C. (2001). Individualism and collectivism. In D. Matsumoto (Ed.), *The handbook of culture and psychology.* New York: Oxford University Press.

Trimble, J. E. (1989, August). *The enculturation of contemporary psychology.* Paper presented at the meeting of the American Psychological Association, New Orleans, LA.

Trimble, M. R., Mendez, M. F., & Cummings, J. L. (1997). Neuropsychiatric symptoms from the temporolimbic lobes. *Journal of Neuropsychiatry and Clinical Neuroscience, 9,* 429–438.

Trinidad, D. R., & Johnson, C. A. (2002). The association between emotional intelligence and early adolescent tobacco and alcohol use. *Personality and Individual Differences, 32,* 95–105.

Triplett, N. (1898). The dynamogenic factors in peacemaking and competition. *American Journal of Psychology, 9,* 507–533.

Trivers, R. (1971). The evolution of reciprocal altruism. *Quarterly Review of Biology, 46,* 35–57.

Trowell, J., Kolvin, I., Weeramanthri, T., Sadowski, H., Berelowitz, M., Glasser, D., & Leitch, I. (2002). Psychotherapy for abused girls. *British Journal of Psychiatry, 180,* 234–247.

Trull, T. J., & Widiger, T. A. (2003). Personality disorders. In I. B. Weiner (Ed.), *Handbook of psychology* (Vol. 8). New York: Wiley.

Tryon, R. C. (1940). Genetic differences in maze-learning ability in rats. In *39th Yearbook, National Society for the Study of Education.* Chicago: University of Chicago Press.

Tsuang, M. T., Stone, W. S., & Faraone, S. V. (2001). Genes, environment, and heredity. *British Journal of Psychiatry, 40,* (Suppl.), 18–24.

Tulving, E. (1972). Episodic and semantic memory. In E. Tulving & W. Donaldson (Eds.), *Origins of memory.* San Diego: Academic Press.

Tulving, E. (1983). *Elements of episodic memory.* New York: Oxford University Press.

Tulving, E. (1989). Remembering and knowing the past. *American Scientist, 77,* 361–367.

Tulving, E. (2000). Concepts of memory. In E. Tulving & F. I. M. Craik (Eds.), *The Oxford handbook of memory.* New York: Oxford University Press.

Tulving, E., & Thomson, D. M. (1973). Encoding specificity and retrieval processes in episodic memory. *Psychological Review, 80,* 352–373.

Turiel, E. (1983). *The development of social knowledge: Morality and convention.* New York: Cambridge University Press.

Turnbull, C. (1972). *The mountain people.* New York: Simon & Schuster.

Tversky, A., & Fox, C. R. (1995). Weighing risk and uncertainty. *Psychological Review, 102,* 269–283.

U

Ubell, C. (1992, December 6). We can age successfully. *Parade,* pp. 14–15.

UNDCP. (2001). *Global illicit drugs.* Geneva, Switzerland: United Nations.

United Nations. (1999). *Demographic yearbook.* Geneva, Switzerland: Author.

Uppaluri, C. R., Schumm, I. P., & Lauderdale, D. S. (2001). Self-reports of stress in Asian immigrants: Effects of ethnicity and acculturation. *Ethnic Distribution, 11,* 107–144.

U.S. Bureau of the Census. (2000). *Marriage statistics.* Washington, DC: Author.

U.S. Bureau of Justice Statistics. (2001). *Homicide rates.* Washington, DC: Author.

U.S. Department of Energy. (2001). *The human genome project.* Washington, DC: Author.

V

Vadum, A. E., & Rankin, N. O. (1998). *Psychological research.* New York: McGraw-Hill.

Vaillant, G. E. (1977). *Adaptation to life.* Boston: Little, Brown.

Vaillant, G. E. (1983). *The natural history of alcoholism.* Cambridge, MA: Harvard University Press.

Vaillant, G. E. (1992). Is there a natural history of addiction? In C. P. O'Brien & J. H. Jaffe (Eds.), *Addictive states.* Cambridge, MA: Harvard University Press.

Vaillant, G. E. (2002). *Aging well.* Boston: Little, Brown.

Vaillant, G. E. (2003). Mental health. *American Journal of Psychiatry, 160,* 1373–1384.

Valencia, R. R., & Suzuki, L. A. (2001). *Intelligence testing and minority students.* Thousand Oaks, CA: Sage.

Vallone, R. P., Griffin, D. W., Lin, S., & Ross, L. (1990). Overconfident prediction of future actions and outcomes by self and others. *Journal of Personality and Social Psychology, 58,* 582–592.

Van Ameringen, M., Lane, R. M., Walker, J. R., Rudaredo, C., Chooka, P. R., Goldner, E., Johnston, E., Lavallee, Y., Saibal, N., Pecknold, J. C., Hadrava, V., & Swinson, R. P. (2001). Sertaline treatment of generalized social phobia: 20-week, double-blind, placebo-controlled study. *American Journal of Psychiatry, 158,* 275–281.

Van Ameringen, M., Mancini, C., Farvolden, P., & Oakman, A. J. (2000). The neurobiology of social phobia: From pharmacology to brain imaging. *Current Psychiatry Reports, 2,* 358–366.

Van Ameringen, M., Oakman, J., Mancini, C., Pipe, B., & Chung, H. (2004). Predictors of response in generalized social phobia: Effect of age of onset. *Journal of Clinical Psychopharmacology, 24,* 42–48.

Van Buren, E., & Graham, S. (2003). *Redefining ethnic identity: Its relationship to positive and negative school adjustment out-comes for minority youth.* Paper presented at the meeting of the Society for Research in Child Development, Tampa, FL.

Van den Boom, D. C. (1994). The influence of temperament and mothering on attachment and exploration: An experimental manipulation of sensitive responsiveness among lower-class mothers with irritable infants. *Child Development, 65,* 1457–1477.

van Dielen, F. M., van 't Veer, C., Buurman, W. A., & Greve, J. W. (2002). Leptin and soluble leptin receptor levels in obese and weight-losing individuals. *Journal of Clinical Endocrinology and Metabolism, 87,* 1708–1716.

Van Elst, L. T., Ebert, D., & Trimble, M. R. (2001). Hippocampus and amygdala pathology in depression. *American Journal of Psychiatry, 158,* 652–653.

Van Gelder, R. N., Herzog, E. D., Scheartz, W. J., & Tagher, P. H. (2003). Circadian rhythms: In the loop at last. *Science, 300,* 1534–1535.

Van Goozen, S. H. M., Matthys, W., Cohen-Kettenis, P. T., Thisjssen, J. H., & van Engeland, H. (1998). Adrenal androgens and aggression in conduct disorder prepubertal boys and normal control. *Biological Psychiatry, 43,* 156–158.

van Praag, H. M. (2000). Serotonin disturbances and suicide risk: Is aggression or anxiety an interjacent link? *Crisis, 21,* 160–162.

Van Winkle, E. (2000). The toxic mind: The biology of mental illness and violence. *Medical Hypotheses, 55,* 356–368.

Vandell, D. L. (2000). Parents, peer groups, and other socializing influences. *Developmental Psychology, 36*(6), 699–710.

VandenBos, G. R. (2000). Schizophrenia. In A. Kazdin (Ed.), *Encyclopedia of psychology.* Washington, DC, & New York: American Psychological Association and Oxford University Press.

Vaughn, A. A., & Roesch, S. C. (2003). Psychological and physical health correlates of coping in minority adolescents. *Journal of Health Psychology, 8,* 671–683.

Vaughn, S., Bos, C. S., & Schumm, J. S. (2003). *Teaching exceptional, diverse, and at-risk students in the general education classroom* (3rd ed.). Boston: Allyn & Bacon.

Vernoy, M. W. (1995). Demonstrating classical conditioning in introductory psychology: Needles do not always make balloons pop! In M. E. Ware & D. E. Johnson (Eds.), *Demonstrations and activities in teaching psychology* (Vol. 2). Mahwah, NJ: Erlbaum.

Vernoy, M. W., & Kyle, D. (2003). *Behavioral statistics in action* (3rd ed.). New York: McGraw-Hill.

Versiani, M., Cassano, G., Perugi, G., Benedetti, A., Mastalli, L., Nadi, A., & Savino, M. (2002). Reboxetine, a selective norepinephrine reuptake inhibitor, is an effective and well-tolerated treatment for panic disorder. *Journal of Clinical Psychiatry, 63,* 31–37.

Viana de la Pena, E., & Belmonte, C. (2002). Specificity of cold thermotransduction is determined by differential ionic channel expression. *Nature Neuroscience, 5,* 254–260.

Vicari, S., Bellucci, S., & Carlesimo, G. A. (2001). Procedural learning deficits in children with Williams syndrome. *Neuropsychologia, 39,* 665–677.

Vigilione, D. J., & Taylor, N. (2003). Empirical support for interrater reliability of Rorschach comprehensive system scoring. *Journal of Clinical Psychology, 59,* 111–121.

Villani, S., & Sharfstein, S. S. (1999). Evaluating and treating violent adolescents in the managed care era. *The American Journal of Psychiatry, 156,* 458–464.

Viney, W., & King, D. B. (2003). *History of psychology* (3rd ed.). Boston: Allyn & Bacon.

Vogt, T. M., Mullooly, J. P., Ernst, D., Pople, C. R., & Hollis, J. F. (1992). Social networks as predictors of ischemic heart disease, cancer, stroke, and hypertension. *Journal of Clinical Epidemiology, 45,* 659–666.

Vokey, J. R., & Read, J. D. (1985). Subliminal messages: Between the devil and the media. *American Psychologist, 40,* 1231–1239.

Voudouris, N. J., Peck, C. L., & Coleman, G. (1985). Conditioned placebo responses. *Journal of Personality and Social Psychology, 48,* 7–53.

Vygotsky, L. S. (1962). *Thought and language.* Cambridge, MA: MIT Press.

W

Wachs, T. D., Bishry, Z., Sobhy, A., McCabe, G., Galal, O., & Shaeen, F. (1993). Relation of rearing environment to adaptive behavior of Egyptian toddlers. *Child Development, 54,* 396–407.

Wachs, T. D., & Kohnstamm, G. A. (Eds.). (2001). *Temperament in context.* Mahwah, NJ: Erlbaum.

Wadden, T. A., Foser, G. D., Stunkard, A. J., & Conill, A. M. (1996). Effects of weight cycling on the resting energy expenditure and body composition of obese women. *Eating Disorders, 19,* 5–12.

Wagner, K. D., & Ambrosini, P. J. (2001). Childhood depression: Pharmacological therapy. *Journal of Clinical Child Psychology, 30,* 88–97.

Wagner, R. K. (1997). Intelligence, training, and employment. *American Psychologist, 52,* 1059–1069.

Wagner, R. K., & Sternberg, R. J. (1986). Tacit knowledge and intelligence in the every-day world. In R. J. Sternberg & R. K. Wagner (Eds.), *Practical intelligence.* Cambridge, England: Cambridge University Press.

Wagner, U., Gais, S., & Born, J. (2001). Emotional memory formation is enhanced across sleep intervals with high amounts of rapid eye movement sleep. *Learning and Memory, 8,* 112–119.

Wahlsten, D. (2000). Behavioral genetics. In A. Kazdin (Ed.), *Encyclopedia of psychology.* Washington, DC, & New York: American Psychological Association and Oxford University Press.

Waldstein, S. R., Neumann, S. A., Drossman, D. A., & Novack, D. H. (2001). Teaching psychosomatic (biopsychosocial) medicine in United States medical schools: Survey findings. *Psychosomatic Medicine, 63,* 335–343.

Walker, E. F., Kestler, L., Bollini, A., & Hochman, K. (2004). Schizophrenia: Etiology and course. *Annual Review of Psychology, 54.* Palo Alto, CA: Annual Reviews.

Walker, L. E. (1999). Psychology and domestic violence around the world. *American Psychologist, 54,* 6–20.

Walker, L. J., & Pitts, R. C. (1998). Naturalistic conceptions of moral maturity. *Developmental Psychology, 34,* 403–419.

Wall, T. L., Shea, S. H., Chan, K. K., & Carr, L. G. (2001). A genetic association with the development of alcohol and other substance use in Asian Americans. *Journal of Abnormal Psychology, 110,* 173–178.

Wallace, B. E., Wagner, A. K., Wagner, E. P., & McDeavit, J. T. (2001). A history and review of quantitative electroencephalography in traumatic brain disorders. *Journal of Head and Trauma Rehabilitation, 16,* 165–190.

Wallace, R. K., & Benson, H. (1972). The physiology of meditation. *Scientific American, 226,* 83–90.

Wallerstein, R. S. (1989). The psychotherapy research project of the Menninger Foundation: An overview. *Journal of Consulting and Clinical Psychology, 57,* 195–205.

Wallston, K. A. (2001). Conceptualization and operationalization of perceived control. In A. Baum, T. A. Revenson, & J. E. Singer (Eds.), *Handbook of health psychology.* Mahwah, NJ: Erlbaum.

Walsh, W. B. (1995, August). *Person-environment psychology: Contemporary models and perspectives.* Paper presented at the meeting of the American Psychological Association, New York City.

Walsh, W. B., & Betz, N. E. (1995). *Tests and assessment* (3rd ed.). Upper Saddle River, NJ: Prentice-Hall.

Walsh, W. B., & Betz, N. E. (2001). *Tests and measurement* (4th ed.). Upper Saddle River, NJ: Prentice-Hall.

Walters, E., & Kendler, K. S. (1994). Anorexia nervosa and anorexia-like symptoms in a population based twin sample. *American Journal of Psychiatry, 152,* 62–71.

Wang, J., Zhao, C., Chen, B., & Liu, Z. L. (2004). Polymorphisms of dopamine receptor and transporter genes and hallucinations in Parkinson's disease. *Neuroscience Letters, 55,* 172–176.

Ward, N. S., & Franckowiak, R. S. (2004). Towards a new mapping of brain cortex functioning. *Cerebrovascular Disease, 17, Supplement 3,* 35–38.

Ward, R. A., & Grashial, A. F. (1995). Using astrology to teach research methods to introductory psychology students. In M. E. Ware & D. E. Johnson (Eds.), *Demonstrations and activities in teaching of psychology* (Vol. 1). Mahwah, NJ: Erlbaum.

Warnecke, R. B., Morera, O., Turner, L., Mermelstein, R., Johnson, T. P., Parsons, J., Crittenden, K., Freels, S., & Flay, B. (2001). Changes in self-efficacy and readiness for smoking cessation among women with high school or less education. *Journal of Health and Social Behavior, 42,* 97–110.

Waters, E., Merrick, S. K., Albersheim, L. J., & Treboux, E. (1995, March). *Attachment security from infancy to early adulthood.* Paper presented at the meeting of the Society for Research on Adolescence, Boston.

Watkins, C. E., Campbell, V. L., Nieberding, R., & Hallmark, R. (1995). Contemporary practice of psychological assessment by clinical psychologists. *Professional Psychology: Research and Practice, 26,* 54–60.

Watkins, C. E., & Guarnaccia, C. A. (1999). Introduction: The future of psychotherapy training: Psychodynamic, experimental, and eclectic perspectives. *Journal of Clinical Psychology, 55,* 381–383.

Watkins, E., & Subich, L. M. (1995). Career development, reciprocal work/nonwork interaction, and women's workforce participation. *Journal of Vocational Behavior, 47,* 109–163.

Watkins, L. R., & Maier, S. F. (2000). The pain of being sick. *Annual Review of Psychology* (Vol. 51). Palo Alto, CA: Annual Reviews.

Watras, J. (2002). *The foundations of educational curriculum and diversity: 1565 to the present.* Boston: McGraw-Hill.

Watson, D. (2001). Positive affectivity: The disposition to experience pleasurable emotional states. In C. R. Snyder & S. J. Lopez (Eds.), *Handbook of positive psychology.* New York: Oxford University Press.

Watson, D., Wiese, D., Vaidya, J., & Tellegen, A. (1999). The two general activation systems of affect: Structural findings, evolutionary considerations, and psychobiological evidence. *Journal of Personality and Social Psychology, 76,* 820–838.

Watson, D. L., & Tharp, R. G. (2002). *Self-directed behavior* (8th ed.). Belmont, CA: Wadsworth.

Watson, J. B. (1913). Psychology as the behaviorist views it. *Psychological Review, 20,* 158–177.

Watson, J. B. (1928). *Psychological care of the infant and child.* Philadelphia: Lippincott.

Watson, J. B., & Rayner, R. (1920). Conditioned emotional reactions. *Journal of Experimental Psychology, 3,* 1–14.

Wauters, M., Mertens, I. K., Chagnon, M., Rankinen, T., Considine, R. V., Chagnon, Y. C., Van Gaal, L. F., & Bouchard, C. (2001). Polymorphisms in the leptin receptor gene, body composition, and fat distribution in overweight and obese women. *International Journal of Obesity and Related Metabolic Disorders, 25,* 714–720.

Waysman, M., Schwarzwald, J., & Solomon, Z. (2001). Hardiness: An examination of its relationship with positive and negative long term changes following trauma. *Journal of Traumatic Stress, 14,* 531–548.

Webb, W. B. (2000). Sleep. In A. Kazdin (Ed.), *Encyclopedia of psychology.* Washington, DC, & New York: American Psychological Association and Oxford University Press.

Webster, J. M., Smith, R. H., Rhodes, A., & Whatley, M. A. (1999). The effect of a favor on public and private compliance: How internalized is the norm of reciprocity? *Basic and Applied Social Psychology, 21,* 251–260.

Wechsler, D. (1939). *The measurement of adult intelligence.* Baltimore: Williams & Wilkins.

Wechsler, H., Lee, J. E., Kuo, M., & Lee, H. (2000). College binge drinking in the 1990s—A continuing health problem: Results from the Harvard University School of Public Health 1999 College Alcohol Study. *Journal of American College Health, 48,* 199–210.

Weich, S., Lewis, G., & Jenkins, S. P. (2001). Income inequality and the prevalence of common mental disorders in Britain. *British Journal of Psychiatry, 178,* 222–227.

Weidemann, G., Georgilas, A., & Kehoe, E. J. (1999). Temporal specificity in patterning of the rabbit nictitating membrane response. *Animal Learning & Behavior, 27,* 99–109.

Weine, S. M., Becker, D. F., McGlashan, T. H., Laub, D., Lazrove, S., Vojvoda, D., & Hyman, L. (1995). Psychiatric consequences of "ethnic cleansing": Clinical assessments and trauma testimonies of newly resettled Bosnian refugees. *American Journal of Psychiatry, 152,* 536–542.

Weineke, J. K., Thurston, S. W., Kelsey, K. T., Varkonyi, A., Wain, J. C., Mark E. J., & Christiani, D. C. (1999). Early age at smoking initiation and tobacco carcinogen DNA damage in the lung. *Journal of the National Cancer Institute, 91,* 614–619.

Weiner, B. (1986). *An attributional theory of motivation and emotion.* New York: Springer-Verlag.

Weiner, I. B. (1997). Current status of the Rorschach Inkblot Method. *Journal of Personality Assessment, 68,* 5–19.

Weiner, I. B. (2001). Advancing the science of psychological assessment: The Rorschach inkblot test as exemplar. *Psychological Assessment, 13,* 423–432.

Weiner, I. B. (2004). Rorschach assessment: Current status. In M. Hersen (Ed.), *Comprehensive handbook of psychological assessment* (Vol. 2). New York: Wiley.

Weiner, I. B., Exner, J. E., & Sciara, A. (1996). Is the Rorschach welcome in the courtroom? *Journal of Personality Assessment, 67,* 422–424.

Weinraub, M., Hill, C., & Hirsh-Pasek, K. (2002). Child care: Options and outcomes. In J. Worell (Ed.), *Encyclopedia of women and gender.* New York: Oxford University Press.

Weisman, C. S., Maccannon, D. S., Henderson, J. T., Shortridge, E., & Orso, C. L. (2002). Contraceptive counseling in managed care. *Women's Health Issues, 12,* 79–95.

Weissberg, R. P., & Greenberg, M. T. (1998). School and community competence-enhancement and prevention programs. In W. Damon (Ed.), *Handbook of child psychology* (5th ed., Vol. 4). New York: Wiley.

Weissenborn, R., & Duka, T. (2000). State-dependent effects of alcohol on explicit memory: The role of semantic associations. *Psychopharmacology, 149,* 98–106.

Weissman, M., & Olfson, M. (1995). Depression in women: Implications for health care research. *Science, 269,* 799–801.

Weissman, M. M., & Others. (1999). Prevalence of suicide ideation and suicide attempts in nine countries. *Psychological Medicine, 29,* 9–18.

Wells, A., & Papageorgiou, C. (2001). Brief cognitive therapy for social phobia: A case series. *Behavior Research and Therapy, 39,* 713–720.

Wen, T. C., Rogido, M., Genetta, T., & Sola, A. (2004). Permanent focal cerebral isochemia activates erythropoietin receptor in the neonatal rat brain. *Neuroscience Letters, 355,* 165–168.

Whipple, B., Ogden, G., & Komisaruk, B. (1992). Analgesia produced in women by genital self-stimulation. *Archives of Sexual Behavior, 9,* 87–99.

Whitbourne, S. K. (2000). Adult development and aging: Biological processes and physical development. In A. Kazdin (Ed.), *Encyclopedia of psychology.* Washington, DC, & New York: American Psychological Association and Oxford University Press.

White, J. W. (2001). Aggression and gender. In J. Worell (Ed.), *Encyclopedia of gender and women.* San Diego: Academic Press.

Whitman, T. L., Borkowski, J. G., Keogh, D. A., & Weed, K. (2001). *Interwoven lives.* Mahwah, NJ: Erlbaum.

Whorf, B. L. (1956). *Language, thought, and creativity.* New York: Wiley.

Widiger, T. (2000). Diagnostic and statistical manual of disorders. In A. Kazdin (Ed.), *Encyclopedia of psychology.* Washington, DC, & New York: American Psychological Association and Oxford University Press.

Wiederman, M. W., & Whitley, B. E. (Eds.). (2002). *Handbook for conducting research on human sexuality.* Mahwah, NJ: Erlbaum.

Wielandt, H., Bolden, J., & Knudsen, L. B. (2002). The prevalent use of contraception among teenagers in Denmark and the corresponding low pregnancy rate. *Journal of Biosocial Science, 34,* 1–11.

Wierzbicki, M. (1999). *Introduction to clinical psychology.* Boston: Allyn & Bacon.

Wigfield, A., & Eccles, J. (Eds.). (2002). *Development of achievement motivation.* San Diego: Academic Press.

Wiggins, J. S., & Trapnell, P. D. (1997). Personality structure: The return of the big five. In R. Hogan, J. Johnson, & S. Briggs (Eds.), *Handbook of personality research.* San Diego: Academic Press.

Wilens, T. E., Spencer, T. J., Biederman, J., Girard, K., Doyle, R., Polisner, J., Solhkhah, D., Comeau, R., Monuteaux, M. C., & Parekh, A. (2001). A controlled clinical trial of bupropion for attention deficit hyperactivity disorder in adults. *American Journal of Psychiatry, 158,* 282–188.

Williams, C. C., & Zacks, R. T. (2001). Is retrieval-induced forgetting an inhibitory process? *American Journal of Psychology, 114,* 329–354.

Williams, J. D., & Gruzelier, J. H. (2001). Differentiation of hypnosis and relaxation by analysis of narrow band theta and alpha frequencies. *International Journal of Clinical and Experimental Hypnosis, 49,* 185–206.

Williams, P. T. (2001). Health effects resulting from exercise versus those from body fat. *Medical Science and Sports Exercise, 33* (Suppl.), S611–621.

Williams, R. B. (2002). Hostility, neuroendocrine changes, and health outcomes. In H. G. Koenig & H. J. Cohen (Eds.), *The link between religion and health.* New York: Oxford University Press.

Willingham, D. T. (2004). *Cognition: The thinking animal* (2nd ed.). Upper Saddle River, NJ: Prentice-Hall.

Willis, S. L., & Schaie, K. W. (1994). Assessing everyday competence in the elderly. In C. Fisher & R. Lerner (Eds.), *Applied developmental psychology.* Mahwah, NJ: Erlbaum.

Willis, S. L., & Schaie, K. W. (1999). Intellectual functioning in midlife. In S. L. Willis & J. D. Reid (Eds.), *Life in the middle: Psychological and social development in middle age.* San Diego: Academic Press.

Wilson, G. L. (2002). *Groups in context: Leadership and participation in small groups* (6th ed.). New York: McGraw-Hill.

Wilson, J. F. (2003). *Biological foundations of human behavior.* Belmont, CA: Wadsworth.

Wilson, J. P., Friedman, M. J., & Lindy, J. D. (Eds.). (2001). *Treating psychological trauma and PTSD*. New York: Guilford.

Wilson, M., & Daly, M. (2004). Marital cooperation and conflict. In C. B. Crawford & C. A. Salmon (Eds.), *Evolutionary psychology, public policy, and private decisions*. Mahwah, NJ: Erlbaum.

Winne, P. H., & Perry, N. E. (2000). Measuring self-regulated learning. In M. Boekaerts, P. R. Pintrich, & M. Zeidner (Eds.), *Handbook of self-regulation*. San Diego: Academic Press.

Winner, E. (1996). *Gifted children: Myths and realities*. New York: Basic Books.

Witelson, S. F., Kigar, D. L., & Harvey, T. (1999). The exceptional brain of Albert Einstein. *Lancet, 353*, 2149–2153.

Wolpe, J. (1963). Behavior therapy in complex neurotic states. *British Journal of Psychiatry, 110*, 28–34.

Wong, E. H., Sonder, M. S., Amara, S. G., Tinholt, P. M., Percey, M. F., Hoffman, W. P., Hyslop, D. K., Franklin, S., Porsolt, R. D., Bondignori, A., Carfagna, N., & McArthur, R. A. (2000). Reboxetine: A pharmacologically potent, selective, and specific norepinephrine inhibitor. *Biological Psychiatry, 47*, 818–829.

Wood, D. (2001). Established and emerging cardiovascular risk factors. *American Heart Journal, 141* (Suppl. 2), S49–57.

Wood, G. (1986). *Myth of neurosis: Overcoming the illness excuse*. New York: Perennial.

Wood, J. T. (2001). *Gendered lives* (4th ed.). Belmont, CA: Wadsworth.

Wood, W. (1987). Meta-analytic review of sex differences in group performance. *Psychological Bulletin, 102*, 53–71.

Woodruff-Pak, D. S. (1999). New directions for a classical paradigm: Human eyeblink conditioning. *Psychological Science, 10*, 1–3.

Worell, J., & Robinson, D. (1993). Feminist counseling therapy for the 21st century. *Counseling Psychologist, 21*, 92–96.

World Health Organization. (2000). *The World Health Report*. Geneva, Switzerland: Author.

Worrell, J. (Ed.). (2002). *Encyclopedia of women and gender*. New York: Oxford University Press.

Wright, J. C., Huston, A. C., Scantlin, R., & Kotler, J. (2001). The early window project: *Sesame Street* prepares children for school. In S. M. Fisch & R. T. Truglio (Eds.), *"G" is for growing*. Mahwah, NJ: Erlbaum.

Wrightsman, L., Greene, E., Nietzel, M. T., & Fortune, W. H. (2002). *Psychology and the legal system*. Belmont, CA: Wadsworth.

Wu, A. M., Tang, C. S., & Kwok, T. C. (2004). Self-efficacy, health locus of control, and psychological distress in elderly Chinese women with chronic illnesses. *Aging and Mental Health, 8*, 21–28.

Wyer, N. (2004). Value conflicts in intergroup perception: A social-cognitive perspective. In G. V. Bodenhausen & A. J. Lambert (Eds.), *Foundations of social cognition*. Mahwah, NJ: Erlbaum.

Yalom, I. D. (1995). *The theory and practice of group psychotherapy* (4th ed.). New York: Basic Books.

Yamamoto, J., Frequet, N., & Sandner, G. (2002). Conditioned taste aversion using four different means to deliver sucrose to rats. *Physiology and Behavior, 75*, 387–396.

Yanovski, S. Z., & Yanovski, J. A. (2002). Obesity. *New England Journal of Medicine, 346*, 591–602.

Yapko, M. (2001). Hypnosis in treating symptoms and risk factors of major depression. *American Journal of Clinical Hypnosis, 44*, 97–108.

Yardley, L., Owen, N., Nazareth, I., & Luxon, L. (2001). Panic disorder with agoraphobia associated with dizziness: Characteristic symptoms and psychosocial sequelae. *Journal of Nervous and Mental Disorders, 189*, 328–331.

Yarmey, A. D. (1973). I recognize your face but I can't remember your name: Further evidence for the tip-of-the-tongue phenomenon. *Memory and Cognition, 1*, 287–290.

Yasuno, F., Nishigawa, T., Tokunaga, H., Yoshiyama, K., Nakagawa, Y., Ikejiri, Y., Oku, N., Hashiawa, K., Tanabe, H., Shinozaki, K., Sugita, Y., Nishimura, T., & Takeda, M. (2000). The neural basis of perceptual and conceptual word priming: A PET study. *Cortex, 36*, 59–69.

Yau, K. (2002). Cellular and molecular mechanisms of olfaction. *Annual Review of Neuroscience* (Vol. 25). Palo Alto, CA: Annual Reviews.

Yidiz, A., Pauler, D. K., & Sachs, G. S. (2004). Rates of study completion with single versus split daily dosing of antidepressants: a meta-analysis. *Journal of Affective Disorders, 78*, 157–162.

Yonkers, K. A. (2003). Special issues in the treatment of depression in women. *Journal of Clinical Psychiatry, 64*, Supplement 18, 8–13.

Young, E., & Korzun, A. (1998). Psychoneuroendocrinology of depression: Hypothalamic-pituitary-gonadal axis. *Psychiatric Clinics of North America, 21*, 309–323.

Young, T. (1802). On the theory of light and colors. *Philosophical Transactions of the Royal Society of London, 92*, 12–48.

Zahm, S., & Gold, E. (2002). Gestalt therapy. In M. Hersen & W. H. Sledge (Eds.), *Encyclopedia of psychotherapy*. San Diego: Academic Press.

Zaimovic, G. G., Zambelli, U., Timpano, M., Reali, N., Bernasconi, S., & Brambilla, F. (2000). Neuroendocrine responses to psychological stress in adolescents with anxiety disorder. *Neuropsychobiology, 42*, 82–92.

Zajonc, R. B. (1965). Social facilitation. *Science, 149*, 269–274.

Zajonc, R. B. (1984). On the primacy of affect. *American Psychologist, 39*, 117–123.

Zakrzewski, R., & Hector, M. A. (2004). The lived experiences of alcohol addiction: men of alcoholics anonymous. *Issues in Mental Health Nursing, 25*, 61–77.

Zeki, S. (2001). Localization and globalization in conscious vision. *Annual Review of Neuroscience* (Vol. 24). Palo Alto, CA: Annual Reviews.

Zhu, J., Weiss, L. G., Prifitera, A., & Coalson, D. (2004). The Wechsler Intelligence Scales for children and adolescents. In M. Hersen (Ed.), *Comprehensive handbook of psychological assessment* (Vol. 1). New York: Wiley.

Ziegert, K. A. (1983). The Wedisih prohibition of corporal punishment: A preliminary report. *Journal of Marriage and the Family, 45*, 917–926.

Zilbergeld, B. (1992). *The new male sexuality*. New York: Bantam Books.

Zillmer, E. A., & Spiers, M. V. (2001). *Principles of neuropsychology*. Belmont, CA: Wadsworth.

Zimmerman, B. J. (2000). Attaining self-regulation: A social cognitive perspective. In M. Boekaerts, P. R. Pintrich, & M. Zeidner (Eds.), *Handbook of self-regulation*. San Diego: Academic Press.

Zimmerman, B. J., & Schunk, D. H. (Eds.). (2001). *Self-regulated learning and academic achievement*. Mahwah, NJ: Erlbaum.

Zimmerman, B. J., & Schunk, D. H. (2004). Self-regulating intellectual processes and outcomes. In D. Y. Dai & R. J. Sternberg (Eds.), *Motivation, emotion, and cognition*. Mahwah, NJ: Erlbaum.

Zisapel, N. (2001). Circadian rhythm sleep disorders. *CNS and Drugs, 15*, 311–328.

Zola, S. M., & Squire, L. R. (2001). Relationship between magnitude of damage to the hippocampus and impaired recognition in monkeys. *Hippocampus, 11*, 92–98.

Zuckerman, M. (1994). *Behavioral expressions and biosocial bases of sensation seeking*. New York: Cambridge University Press.

Zuckerman, M. (2000). Sensation seeking. In A. Kazdin (Ed.), *Encyclopedia of psychology*. Washington, DC, & New York: American Psychological Association and Oxford University Press.

Zuckerman, M., Kuhlman, D. M., Joireman, J., Teta, P., & Kraft, M. (1993). A comparison of three structural models for personality: The big three, the big five, and the alternate five. *Journal of Personality and Social Psychology, 657*, 757–768.

Zwislocki, J. J. (2002). *Auditory sound transmission*. Mahwah, NJ: Erlbaum.

Credits

Text and Line Art Credits

Chapter 1

p. 6 From Jane Halonen and John Santrock, *Psychology: Contexts and Applications, Third Edition*, McGraw-Hill, 1999. Copyright © 1999 The McGraw-Hill Companies. Reprinted with permission from The McGraw-Hill Companies. **Figure 1.3** From John Santrock, *Life-Span Development*, 9th Edition, Figure 2.8. Copyright © 2004 The McGraw-Hill Companies. Used with permission.

Chapter 2

Figure 2.6 From *Brain, Mind, and Behavior* by Floyd Bloom, Charles A. Nelson, Arlyne Lazerson. Copyright © 1985, 1988, 2001 by Educational Broadcasting Corporation. Used with the permission of W.H. Freeman and Company. **Figure 2.10** From *Brain, Mind, and Behavior* by Floyd Bloom, Charles A. Nelson, Arlyne Lazerson. Copyright © 1985, 1988, 2001 by Educational Broadcasting Corporation. Used with the permission of W. H. Freeman and Company. **Figure 2.15** From John Santrock, *Psychology, 6th Edition, Module On Evolution and Heredity.* **Figure 2.16** From J.T. Bonner, *The Evolution of Culture in Animals,* Princeton University Press, 1988. Copyright © 1988 Princeton University Press. Reprinted by permission of Princeton University Press.

Chapter 3

Figures 3.4, 3.16, 3.17, 3.19, 3.20 From John W. Santrock, *Life-Span Development, 8th Ed.,* Figures 9.5, 12.2, 13.1, 16.4, 16.5, 16.6. Copyright © 2002 The McGraw-Hill Companies, Inc. Reproduced with permission of The McGraw-Hill Companies. **Figure 3.15** From John Santrock, *Child Development,* 10th Edition, Figure 13.3. Copyright © The McGraw-Hill Companies. Reprinted with permission. **Figure 3.18** From John Santrock, *Educational Psychology,* 2nd Edition, Figure 3.7. Copyright © The McGraw-Hill Companies. Reprinted with permission. **Figure 3.21** From "The Nature of the Influence of Speed on Adult Age Differences in Cognition" from *Developmental Psychology,* 1994, 30, 240–259. Copyright © 1994 by the American Psychological Association. Adapted with permission. **Figure 3.22** From *Aging Well* by George Vaillant. Copyright © 2002 by George E. Vaillant, M.D. By permission of Little, Brown and Company, Inc.

Chapter 4

Figure 4.14 Reproduced with permission from *Ishihara's Tests for Colour Deficiency* published by Kanehara Trading Inc., located at Tokyo in Japan. Tests for color deficiency cannot be conducted with this material. For accurate testing, the original plates should be used. **Figure 4.15**

From *Introduction to Psychology, 7th edition,* by Hilgard, Atkinson and Atkinson. Copyright © 2003 Thomson Learning. Reprinted with permission of Wadsworth, an imprint of the Wadsworth Group, a division of Thomson Learning. Fax 800 730-2215. **Figure 4.22** From James J. Gibson, *The Perception of the Visual World.* Copyright © 1950 by Houghton Mifflin Company. Reprinted with permission. **Figure 4.23** From *Brain, Mind, and Behavior* by Floyd Bloom, Charles A. Nelson, Arlyne Lazerson. Copyright © 1985, 1988, 2001 by Educational Broadcasting Corporation. Used with the permission of W.H. Freeman and Company.

Chapter 5

p. 168 Quiz and Strategies: From *Power Sleep* by James B. Maas. Copyright © 1998 by James B. Maas, Ph.D. Used by permission of Villard Books, a division of Random House, Inc. **Figure 5.5** From *Brain, Mind, and Behavior* by Floyd Bloom, Charles A. Nelson, Arlyne Lazerson. Copyright © 1985, 1988, 2001 by Educational Broadcasting Corporation. Used with the permission of W.H. Freeman and Company. **Figure 5.6** Reprinted with permission from H. P. Roffwarg, J.N. Muzio, and W.C. Dement, "Ontogenetic Development of Human Dream-Sleep-Cycle," *Science,* 152, 604–609. Copyright © 1966 American Association for the Advancement of Science. **Figure 5.8** From John Santrock, *Adolescence,* 8th Edition. Copyright © The McGraw-Hill Companies. Reprinted with permission. **Figure 5.9** National Institute of Drug Abuse 2001, Teaching Packet for Psychoactive Drugs, Slide 9. **Figure 5.11** From *Journal of the American Medical Association,* 272, 1672–1677, 1994, data presented by H. Wechsler, Davenport, et al., *Journal of the American Medical Association,* 272, 1672–1677. With permission from the American Medical Association. **Figure 5.12** National Institute of Drug Abuse 2001, Teaching Packet for Psychoactive Drugs, Slides 12 and 13. **Figure 5.13** From L.D. Johnston, P.M. O'Malley, and J.G. Bachman, 2003, *Monitoring The Future National Survey Results on Drug Use, 1975–2002. Volume I: Secondary School Students* (NIH Publication No. 03-5375). Bethesda, MD: National Institute on Drug Abuse.

Chapter 6

Figure 6.13 From John Santrock, *Psychology,* 7th Edition. Copyright © 2003 The McGraw-Hill Companies. Reprinted with permission. **p. 213.** Data source: K. Curran, J. DuCette, J. Eisenstein and I.A. Hyman, August 2001, "Statistical Analysis of the Cross-Cultural Data: The Third Year." Paper presented at the meeting of the American Psychological Association, San Francisco, CA.

Chapter 7

Figure 7.10 From R. Halonen and J. Santrock, *Psychology: Contexts and Applications,* 3rd Edition, Figure 6.8. Copyright © The McGraw-Hill Companies. Reprinted with permission. **Figure 7.15** From Kassin, Tubb, Hosch, and Memon, *American Psychologist,* 56, 405–416. Copyright © 2001 by the American Psychological Association. Adapted with permission. **Figure 7.16** http://www.exploratorium.edu/exhibits/common_cents/index.html. Copyright © Exploratorium. With permission from the Exploratorium, San Francisco. **Figure 7.17** From Hermann Ebbinghaus, *Memory: A Contribution to Experimental Psychology,* 1885. Translated by Henry A. Ruger and Clara E. Bussenius, 1913.

Chapter 8

Figure 8.1 With permission from Dr. Ursula Bellugi. **Figure 8.6** From John Santrock, *Children, Seventh Edition.* Copyright © 2003 The McGraw-Hill Companies, Inc. Reprinted with permission from The McGraw-Hill Companies. **Figure 8.8** From John W. Santrock, *Educational Psychology.* Copyright © 2001 The McGraw-Hill Companies, Inc. Reprinted by permission of The McGraw-Hill Companies.

Chapter 9

Figure 9.5 Reprinted with the permission of Simon & Schuster Adult Publishing Group, from *Overweight: Causes, Cost and Control* by Jean Mayer. Copyright © 1968 by Prentice-Hall, Inc. **Figure 9.7** W. H. Masters and V. E. Johnson, *Human Sexual Response,* 1966, Little, Brown and Company. Reprinted by permission. **Figure 9.8** From John W. Santrock, *Life-Span Development, 8th Ed.* Copyright © 2002 The McGraw-Hill Companies, Inc. Reproduced with permission of The McGraw-Hill Companies. **Figure 9.18** From Diener and Seligman, "Very Happy People," *Psychological Science,* Vol. 13, pp. 81–84. Reprinted with permission from Blackwell Publishing, U.K.

Chapter 10

Figure 10.1 From *Psychology: A Scientific Study of Human Behavior,* by L.S. Wrightsman, C. K. Sigelman, and F. H. Sanford. Copyright © 1979, 1975, 1970, 1965, 1961 Brooks/Cole Publishing Company, a division of International Thomson Publishing Inc. By permission of the publisher. **Figure 10.8** Courtesy of Dr. Hans J. Eysenck. **Figure 10.14** From *MMPI-2 (Minnesota Multiphasic Personality Inventory-2) Manual for Administration, Scoring, and Interpretation, Revised Edition.* Copyright © 2001 by the Regents of the University of Minnesota. All rights reserved. Used by permission of the University of Minnesota Press. "MMPl-2" and "Minnesota Multiphasic Personality-2" are trademarks owned by the Regents of the University of

Photo Credits

Chapter 6

p. 192, © Marc Romanelli/Getty Images/The Image Bank; p. 194, © Sesame Workshop; p. 197, Courtesy of Animal Behavior Enterprises, Inc.; p. 199, © The Granger Collection, New York; p. 202, Courtesy of Professor Benjamin Harris; p. 203, © Marc Romanelli/Getty Images/The Image Bank; p. 206, © Nina Leen, Life Magazine/Timepix; p. 207, © Richard Cummins/Corbis; p. 209, © Bob Krist/Leo de Wys; p. 213, © Bob Daemmrich/The Image Works; p. 215L, © Kevin Mackintosh/Getty Images/Stone; p. 215M, © Image 100/Royalty-Free/Corbis; p. 215R, © Spencer Grant/PhotoEdit; p. 222, © Superstock

Chapter 7

p. 228, © Gary Conner/PhotoEdit; p. 232, © 2002 Exploratorium, www.exploratorium.edu; p. 233, © Michael Fredericks/The Image Works; p. 245L, © James L. Shaffer; p. 245M, © G. Aschendorf/Photo Researchers, Inc.; p. 245R, © Bob Krist/Getty Images/Stone; p. 250L, © AP/Wide World Photos; p. 250R, © Reuters/Rick Wilking/Archive Photos; p. 251, © AFP/Corbis; p. 252, © James L. Shaffer; p. 254, Courtesy of The Wellcome Institute Library, London; p. 258, © Joe McNally/Matrix

Chapter 8

p. 268, © Billy Hustace/Getty Images/The Image Bank; p. 270, Courtesy J.R. Verougstraete; p. 271T, Courtesy Mary Czerwinski; p. 271B, © Photodisc; p. 273, © Stock Montage; p. 274T, Palazzo de Mula, Venice, Chester Dale Collection, © 2002 National Gallery of Art, Washington, 1908. Oil on canvas, .620 x .811 (24 1/2 x 31 7/8), framed .863 x 1.054 x .107 (34 x 41 1/2 x 4 1/4); p. 274BL, © Scala/Art Resource, NY; p. 274BR, Paul Klee. *Dance You Monster To My Soft Song.* 1972. Gift, Solomon R. Guggenheim, 1938. Photograph by Lee B. Ewing © The Solomon R. Guggenheim Foundation, New York. (FN 38.508); p. 279T, © Diane L. Cohen/Getty Images; p. 279B, © Capital Features/Topham/The Image Works; p. 281L, © Holton/Superstock; p. 281R, © Superstock; p. 282, © James Balog; p. 283, © AFP/Corbis; p. 285T, From Curtiss, *Genie: A Psycholinguistic Study of a Modern Day "Wild Child,"* © 1977 Academic Press, Orlando, FL; p. 285, © 2003 University of Washington, Institute for Learning and Brain Sciences (I-LABS); p. 286, © Anthony Bannister/Animals Animals/Earth Scenes; p. 288, Courtesy National Library of Medicine; p. 291, Courtesy Francis Berger/Psychometrics, Inc.; p. 292, © Monkmeyer Press/Merrim; p. 294, © Shooting Star; p. 298, © Jill Cannefax/EKM Nepenthe; p. 299, © J.L. Bulcao/Getty Images; p. 300, © John Alcom/Zuma; p. 301L, © AP/Wide World Photos; p. 301M, Courtesy Nina Holton; p. 301R, Courtesy of Jim Cox/Salk Institute; p. 304L, © David Austin/Stock Boston; p. 304R, © Ben Simmons/The Stock Market; p. 306, Reprinted with permission of the Free Press, a division of Simon & Schuster, Inc., from

The Bell Curve by Richard J. Hernstein and Charles Murray. Jacket: © 1994 Simon & Schuster, Inc.

Chapter 9

p. 312, © Superstock; p. 314, © AP/Wide World Photos; p. 319, Dr. J. Sholtis, The Rockefeller University, New York, NY. ©1995 Amgen, Inc.; p. 322, Courtesy Office of the President, University of Pennsylvania; p. 323, © AFP/Corbis; p. 327TL, © Bob Coyle; p. 327TR, © Anthony Mercieca/Photo Researchers, Inc.; p. 327BL, © Seven-Olof Lindblad/Photo Researchers, Inc.; p. 327BR, © Jan Cannefax/EKM Nepenthe; p. 329, © Barry O'Rourke/The Stock Market; p. 331, © Deborah Davis/PhotoEdit; p. 334, Courtesy of Sandra Graham; p. 335, © Robert A. Isaacs/Photo Researchers, Inc.; p. 337, © Bernard Gotfryd/Woodfin Camp and Associates; p. 341, © Donald Dutton; p. 342TL, © Dale Durfee/Getty Images/Stone; p. 342TM, © Superstock; p. 342TR, © Richard Lord/The Image Works; p. 342BL, © Superstock; p. 342BM, © Superstock; p. 342BR, © Index Stock Imagery; p. 344L, © Photodisc; p. 344ML, © Photodisc; p. 344MR, © Paul Eckman; p. 344R, © Paul Eckman; p. 345, © Robert Harding Library

Chapter 10

p. 352, © Marty Loken/Getty Images/Stone; p. 354L, © National Portrait Gallery, Smithsonian Institution/Art Resource, NY; p. 354M, © AFP/Corbis; p. 354R, © Wally McNamee/Corbis; p. 356, © Bettmann/Corbis; p. 360T, © Bettmann/Corbis; p. 360B, © Bettmann/Corbis; p. 361T, © Lucas Film; p. 361B, © The Granger Collection, New York; p. 364, © Bettmann/Corbis; p. 366, Courtesy Martin Seligman; p. 368, Center for the Study of the Person; p. 369, © David Frazier PhotoLibrary, Inc.; p. 379, Reprinted by permission of the publishers from Henry A. Murray, "Thematic Apperception Test," Cambridge, MA: Harvard University Press. © 1943 by the President and Fellows of Harvard College. © 1971 by Henry A. Murray; p. 384, © Michael Newman/PhotoEdit

Chapter 11

p. 390, © Howard Berman/Getty Images/The Image Bank; p. 392, © Theo Westenberger/Getty Images; p. 393, © AP/Wide World Photos; p. 402, © Scala/Art Resource, NY; p. 403, © AP/Wide World Photos; p. 405, © Rex USA, Ltd.; p. 407TL, © Catherine Ursillo/Photo Researchers, Inc.; p. 407TM, © Monica Anderson/Stock Boston; p. 407TR, © AFP/Corbis; p. 407B, © Christopher Brown/Stock Boston; p. 409, © 1974 The Washington Post. Photo by Gerald Martineau; p. 411, © Erich Lessing/Art Resource, NY; p. 414, Courtesy Lewis Baxter and Michael Phelps/UCLA School of Medicine; p. 419T, © Bettmann/Corbis; p. 419B, © Alain Benainous/Getty Images; p. 421, *Landscape,* 1907. by August Neter. Reprinted by permission of Prinzhorn-Sammlung der Psychiatrischen Universitätsklinik Heidelberg; p. 422,

© Grunnitus/Monkmeyer Press; p. 423, © Monte S. Buchsbaum, M.D., Mt. Sinai School of Medicine, New York, NY; p. 424L, © Monte S. Buchsbaum, M.D., Mt. Sinai School of Medicine, New York; p. 424R, Courtesy of the Genain Quadruplets; p. 425, © Bob Daemmrich/The Image Works; p. 426, © AP/Wide World Photos

Chapter 12

p. 432, © Stacy Pickerell/Getty Images/Stone; p. 439, © W & O McIntyre/Photo Researchers, Inc.; p. 441, © Historical Pictures/Stock Montage; p. 442, © Scala/Art Resource, NY; p. 444, Courtesy Deke Simon; p. 445, © David Frazier PhotoLibrary, Inc.; p. 446, © Mary Levin/University of Washington; p. 453, © Michael Newman/PhotoEdit; p. 454, © Bob Daemmrich/Stock Boston; p. 459, Courtesy Stanley Sue

Chapter 13

p. 464, © Philip North-Coombes/Getty Images/Stone; p. 467T, George V. Mann, Sc. D.,M.D.; p. 467B, © David Stoecklein/The Stock Market; p. 473, © Superstock; p. 474, © Catherine Gehm; p. 475, Courtesy Vonnie McLoyd; p. 478, Photo by Todd Cheney. Courtesy Dr. Shelly Taylor; p. 489TL, © Don Smetzer/Getty Images/Stone; p. 489TR, © David Austen/Getty Images/Stone; p. 489M, © Nabeel Turner/Getty Images/Stone; p. 489BL, © Bob Daemmrich/Getty Images/Stone; p. 489BR, © David Austen/Getty Images/Stone; p. 490T, © Cary Wolkinsky/Stock Boston; p. 490B, © Peter Gregoire Photography; p. 493T, © John P. Kelly/Getty Images/The Image Bank; p. 493M, © Douglas Fischer/Getty Images/The Image Bank; p. 493B, © Bob Daemmrich/Getty Images/Stone; p. 494, © John Elk; p. 498, © Lloyd Wolf

Chapter 14

p. 504, © Gary Conner/PhotoEdit; p. 506, © AP/Wide World Photos; p. 508, © Romilly Lockyear/Getty Images/The Image Bank; p. 509, © John P. Kelly/Getty Images/The Image Bank; p. 517, © William Vandivert; p. 519T, © 1965 by Stanley Milgram, from the film *Obedience* distributed by Penn State Media Sales; p. 519B, © AP/Wide World Photos; p. 520T, © Scott T. Smith/Corbis; p. 520B, © Hughes Martin/Corbis; p. 521T, © Andrea Pistolesi/Getty Images/The Image Bank; p. 521B, © Jean-Marc Loubat/Photo Researchers, Inc.; p. 523T, © AP/Wide World Photos; p. 523B, © Alberto Garcia/Getty Images; p. 525L, © Reuters NewMedia Inc./Corbis; p. 525R, © Reuters NewMedia Inc./Corbis; p. 527TL, © Bob Daemmrich/The Image Works; p. 527TM, © Bill Gillette/Stock Boston; p. 527TR, © Spencer Grant/Index Stock Imagery; p. 527B, © Larry Kolvoord/The Image Works; p. 531T, © Bettmann/Corbis; p. 531B, © AP/Wide World Photos; p. 537L, © Kent Reno/Jeroboam; p. 537R, © David Young-Wolff/PhotoEdit; p. 543, © David Young-Wolff/PhotoEdit

Name Index

A

Abbey, A., 532
Abbie, A., 532
Abelson, J.L., 402
Abelson, R., 244
Abelson, R.P., 538
Aberg, H., 365
Abrams, A.I., 490
Abrams, D., 526
Abrams, R.L., 127
Abramson, L.Y., 416, 417
Acebo, C., 167
Achat, H., 366
Ackermann, P., 169
Adams, H.E., 398
Adams, M.J., 256
Adamson, B., 472
Adler, A., 358, 359, 361
Adler, N.E., 474, 483
Adler, T., 70
Adorno, T., 527
Agras, W.S., 324
Ahasan, R., 164
Aiken, L.R., 14, 291
Ainsworth, M., 95
Akert, K.M., 508
Alain, C., 161
Alan Guttmacher Institute, 106, 496
Alaphilippe, D., 365
Alberti, R., 487
Alberto, P, 216
Albrecht, T.L., 486
Albright, A., 282
Albright, J.M., 445
Alderman, M.K., 334, 507
Alexander, D.A., 472
Al-Issa, I., 395
Alkire, M.T., 163
Allain, A.N., 426
Allan, K., 249
Allen, D.N., 424
Allen, G.D., 488
Allen, H., 140
Allen, J., 127
Allen, J.E., 275
Allen, J.J., 410
Allen, J.J.B., 398
Alloy, L.B., 416, 417
Allport, G., 372, 528
Almagor, M., 375
Al-Mashaan, O.S., 385
Alpert, N.M., 242
Alterman, A.I., 217
Altmann, E.M., 256
Alvarado, R., 454
Amato, P.R., 97, 366
Ambrosini, P.J., 51
American Academy of Pediatrics, 270
American Association on Mental Retardation, 298
American Psychiatric Association, 392–393, 396, 398

American Psychological Association (APA), 255
American Sleep Apnea Association, 172
Ames, L.A., 331
Amsel, E., 281
Anastasi, A., 293
Anderson, B.L., 328, 476, 480
Anderson, C.A., 532
Anderson, D.R., 534
Anderson, E.M., 457
Anderson, M.C., 254
Anderson, N.B., 467
Anderson, N.H., 509
Anderson, R.A., 147
Andersson, R., 181
Andrade, C., 438
Andrews, A.M., 480
Angel, J., 435
Angold, A., 106
Antonucci, T.C., 115
Anwyl, R., 246
Apker, J., 486
Applefield, J.M., 533
Appleyard, S.M., 51
Arai, S., 51
Arana-Ward, M., 141
Arango, V., 419
Arbess, G., 323
Archer, D., 534
Archer, R.P., 380, 383
Archibald, A.B., 105
Arkowitz, H., 459
Arnkoff, D.B., 458
Aro, H., 419
Aron, A., 342
Aronson, E., 508, 513, 514, 523, 529
Aronson, J., 307
Asch, S.E., 509, 517, 518
Ashcraft, M.H., 239
Ashida, H., 70
Ashmore, R., 526
Astin, A.W., 493
Atkin, J.M., 336
Atkinson, D.R., 458
Atkinson, J.W., 333
Atkinson, R., 235, 236, 249
Attorney General's Commission on Pornography, 535
Auerbach, S.M., 490
Auger, C., 408
Auyang, S.Y., 271
Azar, S.T., 98
Azhar, M.Z., 448
Azuma, H., 25

B

Baars, B., 160
Bachman, G., 109

Bachman, J.G., 179, 181, 185
Bachnan, H.J., 305
Backman, L., 113
Bacon, M.K., 335
Baddeley, A., 24, 233, 237, 238, 254
Badgaiyan, R.D., 241
Baer, D.M., 216
Bailey, J.M., 380
Baillargeon, R., 90
Bailly, N., 365
Baker, A.G., 199
Baker, B., 480
Baker, N.L., 526
Baker, T.B., 496
Balabanov. A., 51
Baldo, M.V., 130
Baldwin, J.D., 23, 332
Baldwin, J.I., 23
Baldwin, J.L., 332
Ball, R., 411
Ball, S., 194
Baltes, P.B., 80, 113
Banaji, M.R., 528
Banasik, J.L., 364
Bandura, A., 11, 23, 70, 71, 219, 220, 283, 335, 364, 451, 485, 512, 533, 535, 536
Bangert-Drowns, R.L., 218
Banks, J., 26, 292
Banks, K.W., 255
Barbaree, H.E., 532
Barber, T.X., 176
Bard, P., 339
Barefoot, J.C., 534
Barker, L.M., 195
Barlow, D.H., 402, 448, 457
Barnes, M., 539
Baron, N., 284
Barrios, B.A., 384
Barron, K.E., 276
Barry, H., 335
Bartlett, F.C., 244
Bartlett, J.C., 237
Barton, E., 383
Bartoshuk, L.M., 149
Bassetti, C.L., 169
Basso, M.R., 346
Batson, C.D., 537
Battaglia, M., 401
Baucom, D.H., 451
Bauer, K., 110, 325, 326, 328
Baum, A., 467
Baumeister, R.F., 330, 370, 485, 532, 539
Baumrind, D., 96, 213
Baxter, L.R., 414
Bayles, K.A., 238
Baylor, D., 140
Beall, S., 17, 18
Bearer, E.L., 304
Beattie, M.K., 394
Beatty, J., 51, 148

Beauchamp, G.K., 149
Beauchamp, M.S., 135
Beck, A.T., 415, 448, 449, 450
Becker, A.J., 328
Beckham, E.E., 411
Beckman, M., 327
Bednar, R.L., 371
Behrman, B.W., 252
Beins, B., 17
Békésy, G. von, 144
Belk, A., 27
Bell, A.P., 331
Bellodi, L., 404
Bellucci, S., 270
Bellugi, U., 270
Belmonte, C., 123
Belsky, J.K., 113
Bem, D., 514
Benca, R.M., 414
Benes, F.M., 414
Benini, A.L., 319
Benjamin, L.T., 8
Benjamin, P.R., 199
Benjet, C., 213
Bennett, P., 467
Bennett, R.H., 532
Bennett, W.I., 322
Ben-Porath, Y.S., 383
Ben-Shakhar, G., 379
Benson, H., 490
Bereiter, C., 275
Berenbaum, S.A., 101
Berg, C., 112
Berger, F., 291
Berger, R.E., 186
Berglund, P.A., 403
Berkman, L.F., 486
Berko, J., 284, 285
Berkowitz, L., 532
Berkowitz, S.J., 406
Berlin, L., 80
Berman, S.M., 61
Bernstein, A.B., 418
Bernston, G.G., 536
Berridge, C.W., 341
Berry, J., 25, 473
Berscheid, E., 539, 540
Best, D., 102
Betch, T., 278
Bettman, J., 203
Betz, N.E., 14, 489
Beutler, L.E., 454, 459
Bhattacharjee, C., 495
Bhrolchain, M., 475
Bhugra, D., 328
Bi, G., 49
Billings, A.G., 486
Billman, G.E., 491
Billman, J., 11
Billmann, S.J., 172
Binet, A., 288

I-1

Subject Index